The Book of
World-Famous Music

CLASSICAL, POPULAR AND FOLK

James J. Fuld

THIRD EDITION
Revised and Enlarged

DOVER PUBLICATIONS, INC.
New York

Published in Canada by General Publishing Company, Ltd., 30 Lesmill Road, Don Mills, Toronto, Ontario.

Published in the United Kingdom by Constable and Company, Ltd., 10 Orange Street, London WC2H 7EG.

This Dover edition, first published in 1985, is the further revised and enlarged third edition of the work originally published by Crown Publishers, Inc., New York, in 1966, and revised and enlarged by Crown in 1971.

Manufactured in the United States of America
Dover Publications, Inc., 31 East 2nd Street, Mineola, N.Y. 11501

Library of Congress Cataloging in Publication Data

Fuld, James J., 1916–
    The book of world-famous music.

    Includes index.
    1. Music—Thematic catalogs.   2. Music, Popular (Songs, etc.)—Thematic catalogs.   3. Bibliography—First editions.
ML113.F8 1985   016.78   84-21232
ISBN 0-486-24857-7

CONTENTS

PREFACE TO THE DOVER EDITION   ix
FOREWORD BY WILLIAM LICHTENWANGER   xi
INTRODUCTION   1
   Determining When, and by Whom, a Musical Work
      Was First Published   3
   Determining the Date of a Particular Copy   5
     GENERAL   5
     ENGRAVED VERSUS FLAT PRINTING   10
     CURRENCIES AND PRICES   10
       UNITED STATES—GREAT BRITAIN—FRANCE—GERMANY—
       AUSTRIA—ITALY—U.S.S.R.—SPAIN
     WATERMARKS   14
     POSTAL DISTRICTS   15
       UNITED STATES—LONDON—PARIS—BERLIN—VIENNA
     NAMES OF CITIES   15
   Copyright Laws   16
     UNITED STATES—GREAT BRITAIN—FRANCE—GERMANY—
     AUSTRIA—ITALY—U.S.S.R.—SPAIN
     INTERNATIONAL PROVISIONS
   Research Procedure Used   25
   Relationship to Folk-Song Research and Phonograph Records   28
   Descriptions of First Appearances in Print   29
     GENERAL   29
     TERMINOLOGY   31
     ARRANGEMENTS CONSIDERED   33
     LIST OF ABBREVIATIONS   34
   Selection of Titles   60
   Well-Known Music by Women Composers   61
   Well-Known Music from Smaller Countries   61
   Wide Dispersal of Music Publishing in the United States   62
   Notes on Certain Composers and Publishers   63
   Note on the Musical Excerpts   71
   Special Message to Music Librarians   72
   General Note to the Reader   79
   Biographic and Other Information   79
   Acknowledgments   81
LIST OF COMPOSITIONS   84
SUPPLEMENT   669
INDEX   695

PLATES   following 338

To
The Librarians
Around the World
Who Have Made This Book Possible

"Women and music should never be dated."
—GOLDSMITH, *She Stoops to Conquer*, Act III, 1773

NOTE TO THE DOVER EDITION

For this Dover edition, a Supplement section has been prepared, adding new information and corrections that could not be accommodated, for reasons of space, within the main text of the book. The symbol † (dagger) in the text refers the reader to an entry in the Supplement, which begins on page 669. The reader must continue directly from that signal in the main text to the supplementary entry, and then return to the main text at the same point. The supplementary items are an integral part of the text and have been cross-referenced in this manner to preserve the sense of one unbroken reading.

When a text page includes references to more than one supplementary item, the following symbols are used, in the order shown: ‡ (double dagger), § (section mark), ‖ (parallels), # (number sign), ¶ (paragraph mark), and †† (two daggers). It should be noted, however, that the symbol * (asterisk) does *not* refer to the Supplement; see page 35.

PREFACE TO THE DOVER EDITION

Once again, in the 14 years since the first revision of *The Book of World-Famous Music*, new and significant information has been volunteered by readers and librarians, furnished by other musicologists or obtained by the author.

Thus, the composer of the melody of *The Star Spangled Banner* has finally been established from contemporary evidence. Particularly interesting discoveries relate to Bach's *Air for the G String*; Beethoven's *Symphony no. 7*; Brahms's *Wiegenlied*; Debussy's *Rêverie*; Gershwin's *Porgy and Bess*; Gilbert and Sullivan's *Iolanthe*; Massenet's *Manon*; several Verdi operas; Wagner's *Lohengrin* and *Tannhäuser*; and to *Apache Dance*; *God Rest You Merry, Gentlemen*; *Hail to the Chief*; *Happy Birthday to You*; *Irene (Goodnight, Irene)*; *Jingle Bells*; *Loch Lomond*; *Mexican Hat Dance—Jarabe Tapatio*; *Mulberry Bush*; *O Du Lieber Augustin*; *Polly-Wolly-Doodle*; *Pop Goes the Weasel*; *Russian Czarist National Anthem*; *The Sailor's Hornpipe*; *Shave and a Haircut, Bay Rum*; *The Skaters*; *St. Anthony Chorale*; *Tramp! Tramp! Tramp!*; *12th Street Rag*; *Twinkle, Twinkle, Little Star*; and *Yankee Doodle*.

Examination of eighteenth-century American secular musical manuscripts has led to important information about the melody of *The Star Spangled Banner* and other titles.

The Warehouse Delivery Book of B. Schott's Söhne publishing house in Mainz has provided new data about many of Wagner's most important operas, including the relationship of engraved to lithographed editions. The *Libroni* of the Ricordi publishing firm in Milan has led to new information about compositions by Verdi and other composers. The Delivery Book of the Spina publishing firm in Vienna has furnished new data about works by Johann Strauss.

The weekly *Illustrated London News* contains publication announcements of Gilbert and Sullivan and other English musical compositions. In addition, biographic information has been discovered about composers and authors about whom no such information was previously available. Helpful nineteenth-century international copyright procedures have been ascertained. New bibliographies have been published.

Thanks are gratefully given to the many readers, musicologists and librarians who helped in this revision.

J. J. F.

FOREWORD

*I*nto a world flooded (despite what unfulfilled authors may think) with books about music, flooded even with "bibliographies" to chart them and "reference books" to summarize and organize their content, Mr. Fuld has brought forth what a biologist of the book world could only call a "sport" —a magnificent sport. His book is at once a bibliography, a manual on the detection of first editions or first issues or first states, a guide to the primeval forms of some of the most widely loved music in Western culture, and—to me most interesting of all—a compendium of carefully winnowed data on the origins of the music and its creators. Do you wonder about the claims of the current campus minstrels that "Johnny I hardly knew ye" is an "old Irish folk song?" So does Mr. Fuld, and with very good grounds for doubt. Have you a set of Clementi orchestral parts for Beethoven's "Emperor" Concerto that you would like to date in comparison with the first German edition? Consider the story that watermarks have to tell. Are you aware of the public marriage between Bach's prelude and Gounod's superimposed melody that took place years before any words (let alone "Ave Maria") issued from the union? If you are old enough to remember the stirring days when Timoshenko moved ahead, you no doubt also remember "Meadowlands" and can identify the Soviet symphony of which it is a part; can you also determine which elements of "Two Guitars" are Russian, and why *Adeste Fideles* is sung to a "Portuguese Hymn"? One might guess that the Baby to whom one can't give anything but love would have a certain history, but to find that history neatly set down in one book alongside the histories of Central European folk songs, Anglican hymns, Italian operas, Latin-American dance tunes, and much, much else—that, I believe, is a new and refreshing experience in music book exploration.

Such few airy pickings can hardly suggest the extraordinary range of Mr. Fuld's interests. Even less can they indicate the care and extent of his research or the richness of the information he provides. As a collector of early editions, Mr. Fuld is concerned first of all with the processes by which such editions of music—notoriously more difficult to date than books—can be distinguished. Wisely, he does not allow his collector's zeal to push him beyond the bounds of evidence into wishful supposition. In search of evidence he has made use of those who have published before him, in fields as diverse as Beethoven research and the American civil rights movement. He has obtained help from librarians and from special researchers in many countries and many areas of investigation. Unlike most armchair bibliographers, he has himself pursued evidence from the United States to the Volga. Personal communications as well as printed sources, local currencies and postal zones as well as copyright practices, all have been studied—and both their principles and their specific testimony are herein disclosed. Some of his disclosures may seem superfluous or even naïve to a professional scholar of music; but then Mr. Fuld is writing for those who have few reference sources at hand as well as for those who have many. Even the most learned professionals will find in this book countless statements and findings of fact—or of inconclusive evidence—in a spectrum of learning so broad that no one dares call himself a professional.

So much learning, so many imponderables, so many more facts may mistakenly suggest a style no more "readable" than a telephone directory; and I suspect that the author's wit is so poker-faced that it may pass over the head of the casual or unsubtle reader. The wit is there, however, as when in discussing research procedures the author lays down Four Rules of Interlingual Correspondence (and very good rules they are), or when he turns, straight-faced, from a resounding account of "Glory Hallelujah" and "The Battle Hymn of the Republic" to consider evidence for the first appearance of "John Brown's baby has a cold upon its chest" (with gestures). I must confess, in that connection, that I feel a slight disappointment because Mr. Fuld did not see fit to give equal space to my own favorite parody on the "John Brown" song, a parody that begins "I wear my pink pajamas in the summer when it's hot."

It is curious that author and publisher studiously avoid the word "bibliography" in describing this book, since it is an excellent example of what the word meant when it first came into use over a century and a half ago: the detailed description of a select group of books (or, in this instance, publications in another form). Perhaps, as Mr. Cecil Hopkinson implies in his admirable discourse on bibliography (*The Journal of Documentation*, September 1955, pp. 119–129), the word has been debased by its more recent and eventually more common application to a mere list or catalog of publications. It is interesting, also, to judge the book by the criteria laid down by the late Richard S. Hill in his celebrated review of Mr. Hopkinson's Berlioz bibliography (*Journal of the American Musicological Society*, Spring 1953, pp. 177–184). Mr. Hill saw bibliographies as falling into three categories: the collector's bibliography, the musician's bibliography, and the historian's (or sociologist's) bibliography. Being first of all a collector, Mr. Fuld not surprisingly has emphasized the collector's interests. But he has by no means neglected the other two approaches. His book is filled with historical and other interesting data about the musical works themselves as well as about their early editions in print. If, in his descriptions, he seems to pay less attention to musical variants and musical content generally, it must not be overlooked that the descriptions are preceded by musical incipits and that the whole purpose of the book and the basis for selection of the works described in it are fundamentally musical. Unfettered by the traditional but often dubious lines of demarcation by which specialists try to separate "art" music from "popular" and "popular" from "folk," Mr. Fuld cuts across conventional boundaries and deals simply with music. He has selected hundreds of musical works in many categories, works that he feels have achieved a special status not because of "greatness" (and I for one deplore that nebulous term as applied to music) but because their melodies are "widely known today." He admits that the selection is to some extent bound to be subjective, and from his list of titles alone one can suspect that the author is particularly susceptible to Broadway show tunes of the past several decades. But subjectivity in such circumstances is inevitable, and I am happy to accept his selection because in general it seems to me both musically and sociologically justified.

There is one further criterion that, with bibliography as with scholarship in general, appears to me to be fading farther and farther from sight —certainly in the community of scholars with whom I have contact. Nowadays there is much discussion in musicological circles as to the "purpose" of scholarship, as though every scholarly endeavor has to justify itself by serving a "useful" function such as inventing a bomb or creating a better mousetrap or helping man understand himself or telling the public what music to listen to. Nonsense! "Pure science" is still revered by the natural scientists, and it should be even more revered by the humanists, envious though they are. Mr. Fuld's book certainly will be highly useful to everyone who has an interest in well-known music, and not only to librarians or collectors of musical first editions. That fact no doubt is what led a trade book publisher to publish it, but it is not really why Mr. Fuld has written it. Curiosity, the itch to enjoy a musical work even more by filling in its non-musical dimensions, the sport of mind that seeks to match receptivity to music with a complementary knowledge about it, the joy of finding out and sharing such secrets with others: it is in motives like these that this book had its origin, and in them it has its finest justification. I wish, in this day of music books jerry-built to "fill a need," that the same thing could be said more often.

William Lichtenwanger

Music Division, Library of Congress
July 1965

INTRODUCTION

SURPRISINGLY LITTLE BASIC HISTORICAL information is known about many of the melodies we hum or whistle—world-famous folk, classical or popular music—or about their composers and lyricists.

Virtually no historical information is available on such folk songs as *La Cucaracha, Frère Jacques, Goodnight Ladies, Mary Had a Little Lamb, Song of the Volga Boatmen,* or *When the Saints Go Marching In.*

There is hardly any satisfactory information about the first printings of Mendelssohn, Tchaikovsky, Wagner or most of the other classical masters.

Little or no reference information exists regarding such popular pieces as *Love's Old Sweet Song, 'O Sole Mio, Santa Lucia, Taps* or *Three Little Maids from School.*

And many composers, librettists and lyricists have almost as little biographic information written about them as about their works.

Such basic reference information as exists is often in little-known magazine articles or antiquarian music sellers' catalogues, or in the minds of music specialists around the world.

This book assembles this information for the first time. It is a comprehensive reference book of many hundreds of the world's best-known musical compositions, from over twenty-five countries and covering five hundred years of music.

An important source of this information is the first known printing of each of these compositions. Musically, a first printing frequently shows best the spontaneous musical intent of the composer. Historically, first printings mention important dedications, original singers and other interesting associations and contemporary information.

Finally, first printings of important music have an appeal similar to the first folio of Shakespeare. For it is through these rare editions, fresh from the printer, that one sees the newborn musical work as it hesitatingly came into the world.

Today we see attempts to re-create the past as vividly as possible—by reproducing the programs of first performances, by assembling contemporary music reviews, and by publishing the letters, documents and photographs relating to the masters. This is a retrospective period in history which seeks spiritual nourishment from the lasting artistic creations of earlier ages. First printings form part of the goal to learn more about enduring music.

A great amount of interesting historical information of all kinds has been discovered: The sources of *We Shall Overcome*, for example, were found. Gounod's *Ave Maria* was discovered to have been first composed and published as an instrumental composition for piano, violin and organ entitled *Méditation*, then with other words added to an orchestral arrangement having the same title, and finally with the present words for piano and voice as *Ave Maria*. Massenet's *Élégie* was discovered to have been initially composed and published as a piano work entitled *Mélodie*, then used as orchestral background to the tragedy *Les Érinnyes*, then arranged for violoncello and piano as *Mélodie*, and finally set to words as *Élégie-Mélodie*. The words of *Battle Hymn of the Republic* have been found in a printing earlier than the one previously considered the first printing.

The various historical data included in the book, it is hoped, will be of use to different readers according to their particular interests. For example, while changes in the music from one edition to another are at times noted in this book, the emphasis has been on the priority of printing. The task of the person desiring to compare the original musical text with its subsequent development will be facilitated by having a starting point, the first printing, which he can then use together with the original manuscript if available. First printings are commonly used as a basis for authentic editions of the masters, particularly if published during the composer's life and if the original manuscript is not available.

This book attempts to *trace each of the well-known melodies back to its original printed source*. The search for this and related historical reference information has been made systematically in the libraries and private collections in the leading countries of the world; and this book contains information accumulated by the author over a period of more than thirty years. In the case of a few composers and scattered compositions, such studies had already been made by others. But about 90 percent of the many hundreds of world-famous compositions in this book have never before been so studied.

The fascination of original printings has long attracted distinguished men. Aristotle is credited by Will Durant, in *The Life of Greece*, with having assembled the first extensive private collection of books. Aristotle is said to have paid the equivalent of $18,000 for only part of his library. Durant adds, "The ambition to possess old books became so widespread that men arose who specialized in dyeing and spoiling new manuscripts to sell them as antiquities to collectors of first editions." The systematic collecting of printed music began about 1600.

This book was conceived and developed as a basic reference book for all who are fascinated with well-known music and curious as to its origins.

DETERMINING WHEN, AND BY WHOM, A MUSICAL WORK WAS FIRST PUBLISHED

Ascertaining the first printing of a musical work is frequently a difficult challenge,[1] and the most logical place to begin is to determine when, and by whom, the work was first published. This date of first *publication* should be carefully distinguished from the date of the *particular copy* being examined. In the next section we shall consider how to establish the date of a particular copy, thereby enabling one to compare its date with the date of first publication.

We are now concerned, however, with determining when, and by whom, a work was first published, and this information is also necessary for other reasons: where several publishers issued the same composition at about the same time, perhaps in different countries, fixing the precise date of the first publication by each publisher is vital. Where only one publisher is involved, but he published a composition in different arrangements (e.g., for piano, two pianos, piano-vocal, orchestra), it is necessary to establish which arrangement he published first.

In a few instances, an "official" publication date is available. The entries at Stationers' Hall commencing July 1, 1842, include the date of first publication and the name of the publisher. These records are now at the Public Record Office, London.

In the United States since July 1, 1909, the date of first publication must be included in the application for copyright, and the applicant is ordinarily the publisher. This information is available at the Library of Congress, Washington, and has also been included in its published copyright catalogues.

These English and American entries also record many foreign publications. The date of publication is generally the date of first publication anywhere in the world, rather than the date of publication in the particular country.

In none of the other principal countries is the formal date of first publication available, and other techniques are necessary to determine the date of initial publication. The most common such technique is probably a contemporary listing, advertisement or review. Such a notice, however, cannot be relied upon blindly. Many times a work is noted in different publications at considerably different times; one of them may accurately indicate the first publication—the other or others must be wrong. In exceptional instances, all may be wrong! The notice may be of a forthcoming

---

[1] See, generally, Deutsch, *Music Bibliography*; Deutsch, *Brahms*; Hill, *Bibliography*; Hopkinson, *Bibliography*; and Oldman, *First Editions*.

publication, and actual publication may have been, and frequently was, delayed for a number of reasons. The notice may also appear weeks, months or more than a year after initial publication and still claim, tongue-in-cheek, "Just Published."

Much depends, of course, upon the particular periodical. It is this author's belief that the Hofmeister *Monatsbericht*, issued ordinarily monthly from 1829 to date, is generally reliable as to German and Austrian publications.[2] The *Allgemeine Musikalische Zeitung*, issued by Breitkopf & Härtel, should be accurate for its own publications, and the same should be true as to "house organs" issued by other publishing firms. *Le Ménestrel* is particularly eloquent as to its promised dates of Heugel's publications, the breaches of its promises accompanied by new promised dates (also sometimes subsequently broken), followed at last by a triumphant notice that the work has in fact been published. On the other hand, *La Bibliographie de la France* at times includes, in a particular weekly issue, items depending upon their category, their alphabetical order and available space in that weekly issue. The same is true of other periodicals during certain periods.

Since much depends upon what advertisement or advertisements one happens to find, it is believed that the safest bibliographic procedure is to identify the periodical or periodicals and give their dates. An advertisement is particularly helpful as it not only furnishes a date and the publisher, but also gives information as to price, arrangement and sometimes other facts.

Entries at Stationers' Hall before July 1, 1842, registration of titles in the United States before July 1, 1909, and the Dépôt Légal entries in France and similar entries in Italy were generally made soon after publication; these are considered at length below. The same is true as to the dates of receipt of copyright deposit copies in various libraries.

Another source of information regarding the date of original publication is the publisher, who must have in his files such data concerning works still covered by copyright. Some publishers will disclose this information; others seem afraid that the true purpose of the inquiry is to invalidate their copyrights, and they consequently claim that the information is not available. At times, information given by publishers is demonstrably wrong; at times, no doubt, it is intended to be self-serving. Unfortunately, wars have destroyed the records of many publishers—particularly those in Leipzig, Berlin, Milan and London.

Publishers' catalogues for particular years are useful in determining when a publisher issued a particular work, or a particular arrangement of the work. (A compilation of music publishers' catalogues in libraries around the world would be a most useful bibliographic project.)

Files of plate numbers of many music publishers have been compiled.

---

[2] Although criticized at times. See, e.g., Deutsch, *Brahms*, p. 126.

While one cannot rely blindly on these lists, they are extremely helpful in indicating when the work, or the particular arrangement, was first printed. It is hoped that over the years the plate numbers of more publishers in more countries will be analyzed, and the gaps in plate numbers narrowed.

A dated letter from a composer stating that he has this date received the first copy of his new work from the publisher would be ideal, particularly if accompanied by a confirming letter from the publisher. In a few cases, something close to this has been found. Some composers inscribe copies of their works, and their inscriptions, if dated, can be helpful. An owner sometimes indicates on his copy the date of its acquisition.†

Many Russian compositions during the Czarist period had to be approved by the censor, and the date of the censor's approval is stated on the music. Publication presumably followed shortly afterward. A similar approval appears in many Soviet Union publications since 1917. Soviet Union music published since 1931 is listed quarterly in *AML*.

A copy of the printed music itself, if its date can be determined, establishes that the work was at least published by that date; but, of course, another edition of the work may have been published earlier.

Biographies of composers sometimes contain information as to dates of publication. Also helpful, although not determinative, are the dates of composition and the dates and places of first performance. Both are therefore given in this book, where known; this information was obtained from standard reference works.

At times, one can establish with reasonable certainty that a particular copy is a first edition without determining the date of first publication, or even the date of the particular copy. However, it is natural that the more precise the information regarding both the date and details of first publication and the date of the particular copy, the more certain will be the conclusion.

DETERMINING THE DATE OF A PARTICULAR COPY

GENERAL

Determining the date of a particular copy is a many-sided study which requires two broad approaches, the one positive and the other negative. On the positive side, one examines the copy to see whether it conforms to the information obtained from a contemporary copyright entry, advertisement or other reliable source. On the negative side, one makes sure that there is no telltale evidence which indicates that the particular copy had to be printed at a later date. Sometimes the criterion may have a positive or negative implication. Both approaches vary according to country, period, type of music, publisher, and a great many other factors.

Ideally, a copy of the first printing of a particular work should be dated and identified as a first printing by the publisher before many worthy witnesses and placed in an accessible, bombproof vault; this does not happen.

There are on the positive side a number of helpful guides. As described below, American copyright procedure since 1790 generally calls for the claimant to deposit one or two copies of the work virtually at the time of publication. The Library of Congress (or prior recipient) has been noting the exact dates of receipt on the copyright deposit copies. The date of publication has been stated in catalogues since July 1, 1909, and the date of receipt of copies was so stated from July 6, 1891, to Feb. 29, 1932. In the many cases where the copyright deposit copies can be located, the first editions of American music since 1790 are the easiest group to date and identify as first printings. (Punctual filing is the general custom in this country; the few exceptions of a significant interval between the two dates as to compositions studied in this book are so indicated.)

English, French and Italian copyright laws, described below, also call for the deposit of copyright copies. The British Museum, from 1837 to date,[1] indicates the exact date of receipt, as does sometimes the Conservatoire in Paris and the S. Cecilia in Rome; in general, the Bibliothèque Nationale in Paris merely stamps the year of receipt. The German, Austrian and Russian copyright procedures do not provide for the deposit of copies, nor do most of the international copyright procedures.

Another positive identification in a few cases is a copy bearing a manually signed date, usually a presentation copy inscribed by the composer. Sometimes the date of the particular printing will appear. For example, for many years C. F. Peters editions have usually indicated the year of printing in the lower left-hand or right-hand corner of the back cover. Ricordi inserted an engraved date in many operatic arias about 1850. And

---

[1] In 1833 and 1834 the year, and sometimes the month, were noted; in 1835 and 1836 the month always appears; and from 1837 onward, the exact day. *English Plate Numbers*, p. 13.

The dates are noted in different colors: a blue stamp signifies a copyright deposit copy; a red stamp means that the copy was purchased; a green stamp signifies that the copy was donated; a black stamp is for colonial copyright deposit; and a yellow stamp was used for donations, but was frequently almost illegible and was replaced by the green stamp.

The year of receipt is usually shown by the last two numbers only, recently resulting in ambiguity as to the century; e.g., "37" may be either 1837 or 1937. If the date of receipt is handwritten, or is printed but without the words "British Museum" within the same oval, the year is 1870 or earlier. If the date of receipt is printed with the words "British Museum" within the same oval, and the month is given in two letters, the year is 1870 to 1912 (or in some cases, to 1925). Three letters in an oval were used from 1912 (or 1925) to 1929. The present round circle was used commencing in 1929. "MH" or "MR" is March. "MA" or "MY" is May. "JU" is June. "JY" is July.

Ricordi, Chappell and a few other publishers frequently impressed a date by a hand seal or "blind stamp" on music about the last quarter of the nineteenth century. Soviet Union publications state on the final page the date the work was set in type, and the date the printing was completed.

The exact names and addresses of many publishers have been studied from city directories, trade directories and advertisements, and the years of their use listed; this "imprint" of the publisher in the particular copy *must* be correct for the copy to be a first edition—that is, the name or address should not be a later name or address. Sometimes, a publisher had a specific trade name and address for only a few months. At other times, however, a publisher may have had the same name and address for too many years for its imprint to be helpful in determining the date of a particular copy. A number of music publishers had branches in Leipzig before World War II, but not afterward.

The price of the particular copy must be in the *then prevailing currency* for the copy to be a first edition, e.g., Thaler before 1874 and Marks thereafter. This is discussed at greater length below. If the exact price of the first printing is known from a contemporary notice, the particular copy should have that price.

Depending upon the type of music, the country and the publisher, music was generally published from engraved plates during the eighteenth and part of the nineteenth centuries. These copies are easily identified by the impression of the plate around the outer portion of the page, and also by its sharper and deeper printing appearance. Reprints were frequently made later by means of a transfer or lithographic or photographic process which gives a flatter appearance. This is also discussed further below at greater length.

If a copy is a first edition, it should not refer to anything occurring after the date of publication. If the work was published in 1825, a first edition should not refer to anything occurring after 1825.[2] This is the generality, and endless disqualifying examples could be mentioned. Obviously, the copy should not say that it is a revised, or new, or corrected, or second or simplified edition. Frequently the particular copy refers to arrangements of the same composition for other instruments, which arrangements were published at a later date. The first printing of a work originally composed for piano would not ordinarily list a dozen other arrangements including one for zither and Turkish band! In general, the fewer arrangements listed, the earlier the particular copy will be.

Many publishers, particularly during the past century, used the back cover or the verso of the front cover or the wrappers to advertise their other

---

[2] At times, however, a publisher may list forthcoming works as if they were already available.

publications. Obviously, the date of the particular copy cannot be earlier than the date of the latest other composition advertised. For example, most of Jurgenson's publications of Tchaikovsky's works list on the wrapper or elsewhere other Tchaikovsky works; thus, the first printing of op. 11 could not refer to op. 71. In the same way, separate printings of arias from operas, or songs from shows, usually list other arias or songs that have been printed. The fewer the number of arias or songs listed, the earlier the date a particular copy will usually be.

Watermarks, discussed further below, sometimes indicate the year in which the particular paper was manufactured. While the watermark does not indicate when the paper was subsequently used for printing, the watermark cannot be of a year later than the first publication of the composition.

The presence of postal districts, discussed later, may indicate a later printing. The type of paper used may be important. The particular punches and other engravers' tools used may be helpful in a few instances.[3] Fingering on piano compositions usually indicates a later edition, as may the presence of metronome numbers. In operatic and vocal works, the text being in more than one language usually, but not always, indicates a later printing.

French Royal Privileges, or Licenses ("Avec Privilège du Roi" or "A.P.D.R.") continued to 1790 when they were abolished with the advent of the Revolution. The Revolutionary government levied a tax or Timbre Fiscal in 1797 which continued until about 1840; the different stamps used during this period have been analyzed and their dates of use approximated.[4]

The presence or absence of copublishers or agents is difficult to assess, as it is logical for the principal publisher over the years both to add and to discontinue one or more copublishers and agents. However, the imprints of the copublishers and agents should be correct for the date involved. Equally difficult to judge is the presence of prices in more than one currency; it is not clear whether a Russian edition with prices in rubles is earlier than one with prices in rubles and francs, or whether the former is intended merely for the domestic market and the latter for the foreign market.[5] Nor is the comparative length of a composition a definite clue; sometimes a first printing is shortened in later editions, sometimes it is expanded. Nor is the presence of a misprint necessarily decisive: the first

[3] See Donald W. Krummel, "Graphic Analysis—Its Application to Early American Engraved Music," in *Notes*, March, 1959, p. 213.

[4] Hopkinson, *Parisian*, p. x. Élisabeth Lebeau, "Le Timbre Fiscal de la Musique en Feuilles de 1797 à 1840," in *Revue de Musicologie*, Paris, nos. 73–74, Nouvelle Série, XXVIIᵉ Année, 1ᵉʳ–2ᵉ Trimestre, 1945; NYPL.

[5] In general, the copies of Russian publications examined by the author in Soviet Union libraries have the same covers and title pages as copies in other parts of the world.

printing may be correct, but a plate may have worn out or be cracked, and the new plate may contain the misprint; or the demand for copies may be so great that two or more presses or printers may be necessary and the misprint may occur in the later printing.

The size of the copy is generally not significant except in the case of music printed during or shortly after World War I. Prior to that war, popular music in the Western world was usually printed in folio or large size, about 11″ by 14″. To conserve paper during the war, octavo or small-size paper was used, about 7″ by 10″. At the end of the war, the use of folio-size paper was resumed for about a year, after which the present quarto or medium-size paper, about 9″ by 12″, was used.

Internal study of the music, and in particular the comparison, bar by bar, of the music of one edition with that of another edition would no doubt aid in identifying the earlier edition. This has been done by others to the works of a few composers and, desirable as it would have been, it has seldom been undertaken by this author.

There is no doubt that an excellent, and perhaps the best, way to determine which of two copies is the earlier is to place them side by side and consider the differences, one by one. It will be rare (though it can happen) that one cannot thereby establish with reasonable certainty which is the earlier. Particularly where dates cannot be determined, this method is extremely important. Moreover, placing two copies next to each other reveals differences in kind, size and arrangement of type, etc., in such a way as one's own summaries would rarely disclose. For this reason, the author has assembled hundreds of photocopies of early printings of the compositions studied in this book; these copies are of the pages most sensitive to change, namely, the front and back covers, the title page and the first page of music.

The earlier of two engraved copies can frequently be determined by seeing which has the clearer or darker engraving.

A convenient way of determining which of two copies is earlier may be called the "A B C Rule." Assume that there are two copies, A and B, which are similar except that copy B has point X, but point X does not indicate which copy is the earlier. If a third copy, C, which is provably later, also has point X, it is likely that copy B is a transitional copy and that copy A is the earlier.

Lists of the plate numbers at the bottom of music pages are available for a number of publishers, and indicate the general numerical area in which the plate number of the first edition should ordinarily fall; however, as the same plate number is frequently used for up to a hundred years, a plate number cannot help fix the date of the particular copy being examined. †

Priority of edition can also sometimes be established by the publisher's numbering of copies from 1 up. Schott, for example, frequently gave consecutive numbers to the earliest printed orchestral scores of Wagner's operas, and the lower numbered copies are sometimes of a different edition than the higher numbered copies.

Over the years, differently worded legal and copyright claims and warnings have appeared on music printed in various countries. Presumably, these changes reflect, at least in part, new laws and court decisions. A study of the differently worded language should be of use in determining the date of a particular copy. †

ENGRAVED VERSUS FLAT PRINTING

Printing from engraved plates was the general practice in the musical world from about 1775 to about 1850. Other methods, such as typesetting, were used, but not as frequently as printing from engraved plates.[6]

In the second quarter of the nineteenth century, flatter processes began to be used, such as lithographic, offset, photographic or similar techniques. Printing from engraved plates, however, continued for more or less another half century, depending upon the country, the publisher, the kind of music, etc. Sometimes the title page would be printed by a flat process, perhaps to permit illustrations, and the music pages would be engraved.

Of particular interest is the fact that frequently, during the second and third quarters of the nineteenth century, the first edition, especially of classical music, was printed from engraved plates, whereas subsequent editions were printed from an offset or other flat process. The reason was commercial: engraved plates will yield only so many copies before the plates become worn or cracked; if a musical work became popular, justifying many copies, a flat process is more satisfactory since it permits mass printing. ‡

An engraved edition and an offset edition are frequently identical, the only difference being the method of printing. The two different methods are fortunately easy to distinguish: in the engraved edition, the printing is more sharply defined and appears "deeper," and one can actually see the ridges of the engraved plate as it was pressed into the outer margins of the page. By contrast, lithographic, offset or photographic printing is less sharp, gives a flatter appearance, and lacks the all-important ridges on the outer margins of the page.

Today, almost all printing, music or otherwise, including this book, is from one or another flat process.

CURRENCIES AND PRICES

One of the most helpful ways of determining whether a particular copy may be a first edition is its price. Price is important in several re-

---

[6] See, generally, A. Hyatt King, *Four Hundred Years of Music Printing* (London, rev. ed., 1968); BM.

spects: first, where the kind of currency has changed, the currency mentioned on the copy must be the kind used at the time of original publication (for example, if a work was published in 1870 in Germany when Thaler were the currency, a first edition would be priced in Thaler—not in Marks which were used commencing in 1874); and secondly, where the price is known from a contemporary advertisement, the copy should bear that price.

Finally, price is an important clue even where there is no contemporary advertisement, as inflation has been an established international fact for several centuries—particularly in Europe; while there are exceptions, the general rule is that the lower the price, the earlier the edition.[6A] In early nineteenth-century French music, there is a difference between "prix" and "prix net," the former usually being higher and earlier. In nineteenth- and early twentieth-century American sheet music, price is often shown by, for example, a 3 in a star or circle, meaning 30 cents. (It is interesting to note, in passing, that the cost of music has increased but little in comparison to the general inflation during the past 150 years. While general costs have risen many, many times during that period, a sheet of music costing a shilling or 25 cents about 1800 now costs only about two to three times this price.) Sometimes the original printed price on a particular copy has been erased; this is not helpful in determining the priority of the particular copy. The printed price may have been the earlier, lower price and the publisher may have erased it when he fixed a higher price. On the other hand, the printed price may have been the later, higher price but this harmful fact may have been erased by a mischievous collector or antiquarian music dealer. (For similar reasons, an imprint is sometimes erased.) An erasure followed by a pen and ink price is likewise inconclusive.

The price on a particular copy may also have been originally blank (as distinguished from originally printed and then erased). No conclusion can be inferred from this in establishing the priority of the particular copy. The publisher may have been uncertain as to price when he printed the first copies, in which case the particular copy would be a first edition. On the other hand, the first copies may have had a printed price, but then inflation set in and the publisher determined that in the next printing the price would be left blank to allow for greater flexibility in future pricing.

Following is a brief summary of currencies and prices in the principal countries as they affect this study.

[6A] One general exception resulted from the breaking in 1887 by Russia of an agreement of the publishers made in 1861 with France and Belgium; this led to Russian publishers reducing their prices after 1887. Letter from SSL. V. Bessel and Co.'s *Catalogue* published in 1888, at SSL, confirms these price reductions.

United States. Dollars and cents have been used in the United States since independence.[6B]

Great Britain. Pounds, shillings and pence have been used in Great Britain during all periods covered in this study. On Feb. 15, 1971, the pound was decimalized into 100 pence.

France. Before 1794, the unit of currency in France was a livre tournois, which equaled 20 sols.[7] After 1794, francs and centimes came into use (at the rate of 81 livres tournois to 80 francs) and have continued since.

Germany. Before the unification of Germany in 1871, the currency in the South German states followed that of Austria, described below.

In the North German states, before the unification of Germany, the unit of currency was the Thaler (Thlr.), at times known as the Reichsthaler (Rthlr.).[8] In Leipzig, then the center of the German music publishing world, a Thaler was equal to 30 Groschen (Gr.), a Groschen being equal to 10 Pfennig.[9] **Groschen changed to Neugroschen (Ngr.) on Jan. 1, 1841.**[10] This change, which affects Breitkopf & Härtel and the other publishers in Leipzig, is of the greatest help in this field.

In Prussia and the smaller states, the Thaler equaled 30 Silbergroschen (Sgr.), the latter being equal to 12 Pfennig.

The Mark was first authorized in Germany on Dec. 4, 1871, on the basis of three Marks being equal to one Thaler, but the continued use of the Thaler was expressly authorized. The adoption of Marks was encouraged (but not required) by a law dated July 9, 1873, and it seems quite clear that as to printed music **the Thaler changed to the Mark on Jan. 1, 1874.**[11]

The replacement of the Thaler by the Mark in the beginning of 1874 is of the greatest assistance in determining whether a particular copy was published before or after 1874. The Mark has continued in Germany to date, with one Mark being equal to 100 Pfennig. Tremendous inflation

---

[6B] An examination of Sonneck-Upton and Wolfe shows that shillings and pence were occasionally used on American sheet music to 1825. The agreement forming the Board of Music Trade in June, 1855, provided that prices of American music should thereafter be in "federal money"; letter from Dena J. Epstein, Chicago.

[7] Deferring to François Lesure in Krummel, p. 162. Hopkinson, *Parisian*, p. xi, says the change took place on April 9, 1795.

[8] There does not seem to be any period or periods in which the term "Reichsthaler" was consistently used.

[9] Deutsch, *Brahms*, p. 132.

[10] In the *AMZ* through Dec., 1840, prices are in Groschen; commencing Jan., 1841, they are in Neugroschen.†

[11] Letter from DS. In the Hofmeister *Monatsbericht*, all prices in Nov., 1873, are in the old currency; in Dec., 1873, most are in the old, a few in the new; in Jan., 1874, all are in the new, a few also indicating the equivalent old.

occurred in Germany after World War I, and about 1923 the term Renten Mark (R.M. or stabilized Mark) was used for a short period.

There are a number of cities which are near the borders of two countries which both countries have claimed as their own. As a result, the city sometimes "changed hands" from time to time. Or a city may have been occupied by a foreign power.

The only city of major importance from a music publishing standpoint affected by the foregoing is Bonn, where Simrock was located from about 1790 to about 1865. In this period, from 1795 to 1814, the French occupied Bonn, and as a result prices were given in francs during the time of the French military occupation.

Austria. Toward the end of the eighteenth century, the principal currency in Austria was the Gulden, also referred to as a Florin (Fl.); a Gulden was equal to 60 Kreuzer (Kr., x or xr.). Up to 1811, the only currency was the Conventions-Münze (Assimilated Currency established by treaties or conventions with other countries, e.g., the 1753 Convention between Austria and Bavaria). On March 15, 1811, a second currency was ordered into use, the Wiener Währung (Viennese currency), because of the inflation resulting in part from French occupation. Both currencies used Florins and Kreuzers, with 100 Florins C.M. being equal to 250 Florins W.W. Prior to 1811 it was not necessary to distinguish the particular currency, so that **the designation of either C.M. or W.W. indicates a date of 1811 or later.** The double currency arrangement continued informally for many years.[12]

The Kreuzer was replaced by the Neukreuzer (Nkr.) at the time the Österreichische Währung (Ö.W.) was introduced Jan. 24, 1857.[13] At the time of the replacement, 100 Neukreuzers equaled one Gulden. In the middle 1860's the Neukreuzers came to be known again merely as Kreuzers.[14] The Gulden and Kreuzer continued until 1892, when Austria adopted gold currency, and Kronenwährung replaced the Ö.W. The new currency was the Krone which was subdivided into 100 Heller. On Dec. 20, 1924, the present Schilling replaced the Krone, each Schilling being divided into 100 Groschen.

Italy. In the Papal States (central Italy until the last half of the nineteenth century), the scudo was used, which was equal to 100 bajocchi.

The lira was in circulation in several Italian states and duchies in

---

[12] See, generally, Dr. Josef Schey, *Allgemeines Bürgerliche Gesetzbuch*, 22nd ed. (Vienna, 1930), Appendix II A and D, at NYPL; and Deutsch, *Brahms*, p. 132.†

[13] The effect may have been slightly delayed. See *Meyers*, vol. 8, col. 1186; *GB*, vol. 13, p. 308; and Weinmann, *Strauss*, p. 85.

[14] 1864 (cf. Weinmann, *Strauss*, p. 91); 1862 or 1868 (*Meyers*, vol. 8, col. 1186).

the eighteenth century. During the Napoleonic period it was at par with the French franc, but with the end of the Napoleonic domination the equal valuation was discontinued.

Following the unification of Italy in 1861, the lira became the official currency of the Kingdom of Italy on Aug. 24, 1862. Par value with the French, Belgian and Swiss franc was established in 1866, and habit induced the general public in Italy to call the official lira the "franco."[15]

Ricordi, following custom and also with a view of simplifying its international transactions in Europe, in most instances indicated the price of its music publications in francs up to 1914 when the practice was discontinued.[16] Some publishers quoted prices in lire, others in francs.

U.S.S.R. The ruble and the kopeck have been in use in Russia and the Soviet Union throughout the period covered by this study.

Spain. The peseta, divided into 100 centimos, was introduced in its modern form in Spain by a law adopted Oct. 19, 1868,[17] and the peseta and the centimo have remained the units of currency to date. In the nineteenth and early twentieth centuries, the currency "reales" was used, four reales equaling one peseta.

WATERMARKS

Music printed before 1835 should be examined to see if there is a watermark in the paper indicating the year when the paper was manufactured. Of course, paper manufactured in one year may not have been used until a later year. However, such a watermark indicates a year before which the particular copy being examined could not have been printed.

From 1794–1811, there was a tax refund in England if exported English paper was watermarked as to date.[18] As a result, most English paper suitable for music printing was watermarked during this period. While the tax refund was eliminated in 1811, the practice continued in England for some years.

Watermarks in the form of distinctive designs or letters are probably more common and widespread than watermark dates. While research has been undertaken in this area by several persons in the musical field,[19] the

[15] Letter from Consulate General of Italy.

[16] Ricordi's 1875 *Catalogue*, Milan, states: "The prices are marked in Francs which correspond to the Italian Lire" (verso of title page); MIC.

[17] *Encyclopaedia Britannica* (London, 1957), vol. 17, p. 632.

[18] Oldman, *Watermark*, p. 70 (34 George III, chap. 20, 1794; and 51 George III, chap. 95, 1811; both at Bar Assn., New York, N.Y.).

[19] Robbins Landon, pp. 612–614; LaRue, *Watermarks* (summarizing in a general way the use of watermarks and including a bibliography of the subject).

author has not been able to utilize their research in this book. Much useful information should be derivable from watermarks after further studies are made and reported.

POSTAL DISTRICTS

One means of determining whether a particular copy was printed after a certain date is to notice whether a postal district appears as part of the address. As far as is known, no one has previously studied this approach. While the absence of a postal district is indicative, but not conclusive, that the particular copy was printed before postal districts were established for the particular city, it is certain that the indication of a postal district proves that the particular copy was printed after that date.

United States. Postal zone numbers (e.g., New York 22, N.Y.) came into use in the United States on May 1, 1943.[20] Zip code numbers (e.g., New York, N.Y. 10022) came into use on July 1, 1963.

London. London was divided into postal districts (e.g., W.C.) in 1856. In 1917 each postal district was further divided and the divisions given numbers (e.g., W.C.2).[21]

Paris. In an "Avis au Public" in 1900, the direction was first made to indicate the number of the arrondissement after the word "Paris" (e.g., Paris VIIIᵉ).[22]

Berlin. Postal districts in Berlin (e.g., Berlin C) were first established on Sept. 1, 1873.[23]

Vienna. Vienna was divided into six general postal districts (e.g., Wien I) on Aug. 18, 1830,[24] into nine districts in 1850, into 19 districts in 1892 and finally into 24 postal districts.

NAMES OF CITIES

There have been changes in name of a few cities in which music publishers or copublishers have been active.

Buda and *Pest* were separate cities until they joined in 1872 to become *Budapest.*

---

[20] Letter from United States Post Office.

[21] Letter from BM.

[22] Letter from Musée Postal, Paris, which also owns a specimen notice. A request to use numbers was probably made two years earlier but without success. *Id.*

[23] Letter from German Democratic Republic.

[24] Letters from Bibliothek der Österr. Post-u. Telegr. Verwaltung, Vienna, and the late Dr. Otto Erich Deutsch.

Christiania (or *Kristiania*) was the name of *Oslo* from 1624 to 1925.
St. Petersburg became *Petrograd* in 1914 and *Leningrad* in 1924.

COPYRIGHT LAWS

As explained above at page 3, the necessity or advisability of taking action under certain of the copyright laws has made it easier in many instances to determine who first published a work, the date first published, and also to find a first printing.

Following are summaries of the most important copyright laws of the principal countries and international copyright conventions as they relate to the dates and locations of first editions, namely: (a) the registration of titles; (b) the deposit of copies; and (c) as to American music, and foreign music protected by American copyright, the inclusion of the year of publication in the copyright notice in printed copies of the music.

UNITED STATES

Twelve of the thirteen original states passed copyright laws beginning in 1783, and on May 31, 1790, the first federal copyright law was enacted.[1] While "music" was not specifically mentioned until the Act of Feb. 3, 1831, musical compositions were copyrighted beginning in 1790.

One feature of American copyright laws, effective from Jan. 1, 1803, to date, which differs from the copyright laws of all other countries considered here, is the requirement that the copyright year be shown on printed works, an obvious aid.[2]

From 1790 to June 30, 1909, American copyright laws required, as a condition to copyright, that the title and a copy of the work be deposited; in actual practice, the legal requirements were usually, but far from always, observed. Under the 1790 law, the title had to be deposited before publication with the local District Court and a copy of the work delivered to the Secretary of State within six months after publication. Under the 1831 law, the copy was to be delivered within three months after publication to the District Court, and commencing 1846 copies had to be deposited with the Smithsonian Institution and the Library of Congress. In 1859 all deposits and records were transferred to the Department of

---

[1] Martin A. Roberts, *Records in the Copyright Office . . . 1790–1870* (Washington, 1939), p. 6; LC.

[2] Act of April 29, 1802, sec. 1; Act of Feb. 3, 1831, sec. 5; Act of July 8, 1870, sec. 97; and Act of March 4, 1909, sec. 18. All cited American legal authorities are at the Bar Assn., New York, N.Y.

the Interior (with additional deposits in the Library of Congress required commencing 1865). Deposits in the District Courts continued until 1870. In that year, almost all surviving copyright deposits and records were transferred to the Library of Congress.

In 1870, again a condition to copyright, the title had to be deposited with the Library of Congress "before publication," and two copies deposited with the Library of Congress "within ten days from the publication." By Act of March 3, 1891, the title had to be deposited "on or before the date of publication" and copies deposited "not later than the day of the publication."

The date of "copyright," as used herein for American music before July 1, 1909, means the earlier of the date of deposit of the title or the date of deposit of the work; the exact date of publication of the work is not determinable for American works of this period.

From July 1, 1909, to date, "After copyright has been secured by publication with the notice of copyright . . . , there shall be promptly deposited . . . (with) the Register of Copyrights, Washington, District of Columbia, two complete copies of the best edition thereof then published . . . ." Although it was finally held (after thirty years of uncertainty) that mere delay in depositing copies of the copyrighted work under the 1909 Act does not destroy the right to sue for copyright infringement, it is understood that publishers, to eliminate any doubt and for their own protection, generally had been and still are depositing copies promptly upon publication. This is generally borne out by copyright records, as mentioned on page 6.

Separate deposit of the title was eliminated in the 1909 Act.

GREAT BRITAIN

The 1710 copyright law (8 Anne, chap. 19) provided that nine copies of the copyrighted work "shall be" delivered to the warehouse keeper of the Company of Stationers, before publication, for the use of the Royal Library, Oxford University, Cambridge University, "the four Universities in Scotland,"[3] Sion College in London and the Faculty of Advocates in Edinburgh,[4] and forwarded by the warehouse keeper to the respective libraries on their demand.[5] It also provided for entry of the title, before publication, in the register book of the Company "in such manner as hath been usual." The 1801 copyright law (41 Geo. III, chap.

---

[3] The University Libraries at Edinburgh, Glasgow and St. Andrews, and the Library of the King's and Marischal Colleges, Aberdeen. Partridge, p. 34.

[4] Became the National Library of Scotland in 1925.

[5] All the English statutes mentioned are at the Bar Assn., New York, N. Y.

107) added copies for Trinity College and the Society of the King's Inns, both in Dublin.

In 1814 the copyright laws were amended (54 Geo. III, chap. 156) to provide: (a) one copy must be delivered to the British Museum within one month after publication in London; (b) the title must be entered at the Company of Stationers within one month after publication in London; and (c) eleven copies are to be delivered "on demand" of the warehouse keeper or the libraries indicated above (substituting the British Museum for the Royal Library) within twelve months after publication—the copies may be delivered to the Company of Stationers or to the respective libraries.[6] In 1836 the privilege was withdrawn from the four Universities in Scotland (6 and 7 Will. IV, chap. 110).

Under the comprehensive revision of the English copyright laws enacted July 1, 1842 (5 and 6 Vict., chap. 45): (a) one copy must be delivered to the British Museum within one month after publication in London; (b) the title is to be entered at the Company of Stationers, but no time period was specified within which the title must be entered; and (c) four copies are to be delivered "on demand" to the Bodleian Library, Oxford, the Public Library, Cambridge, the Library of the Faculty of Advocates, Edinburgh, and Trinity College, Dublin, under the procedure described above.

Compulsory entry of the title at Stationers' Hall, to obtain the benefits of copyright, was eliminated by the Copyright Act adopted Dec. 16, 1911, effective July 1, 1912;[7] voluntary registration of the title continued until Dec. 31, 1923.[8] However, a copy of each work had to be delivered to the British Museum within one month after publication, and upon demand to the Bodleian Library, Oxford, the University Library, Cambridge, the Library of the Faculty of Advocates, Edinburgh, Trinity College, Dublin, and, under certain conditions, to the National Library of Wales. The 1956 Copyright Act left these provisions unchanged.

Scottish and Irish publications were also generally subject to the above provisions.

Where, then, are all the lovely one to eleven copyright deposit copies mentioned in the English statutes? The answer is that many works were not copyrighted by the publishers under these Acts, that many of the copies which were deposited have since been lost or mislaid, and that copies of many works were not specifically requested by various libraries.

It is also clear that copies which were deposited in Great Britain were frequently not deposited promptly, as in the United States, and

---

[6] See, generally, Tyson, Appendix I.

[7] 1 & 2 Geo. 5, chap. 46, sec. 15.

[8] Letter from Public Record Office, London, which now has all the Stationers' Hall title entries from 1842–1923.

therefore may not be first printings. In many instances (for example, the Gilbert and Sullivan works), neither the scores nor the individual songs were deposited until months after the operetta was produced in London. In some cases, because of the different copyright consequences, a copy of an English work was deposited at the Library of Congress months before a later edition was deposited at the British Museum.

Stationers' Hall. A question is sometimes raised whether the entry at Stationers' Hall means that the work has been published or merely indicates an intention to publish. A. Hyatt King, the Keeper of the Music Room at the British Museum, and Alan Tyson, London, have stated the former.[9] It seems clear from the copyright laws and from the actual Stationers' Hall records, that, at least until 1841, an entry at the Company of Stationers meant that the work had actually been published. Every such entry until 1841 states "No. of Copies"; for example, the entry of the English edition of Beethoven's *Concerto no. 5* specifically refers to "11 copies."[10]

From 1814 to 1841 the entry of the title at Stationers' Hall was to be within one month after publication. After 1841, however, a substantial delay between first publication and entry at Stationers' Hall was not unusual, and a number of such delays are mentioned in this book. For example, Sir Arthur Sullivan's *The Lost Chord* was published on Feb. 1, 1877, but not entered at Stationers' Hall until seven years later.

Unlike American law, registration at Stationers' Hall was necessary, not to secure copyright, but as a condition precedent to the right to sue for infringement. Such registration at Stationers' Hall could be effected any time after publication.[11]

FRANCE

Under a law adopted July 19, 1793, two copies of every work had to be deposited at the Bibliothèque Nationale or at the Stamp Office of the Republic.[12] An ordinance of Oct. 24, 1814,[13] required five copies to be deposited: one for "notre bibliothèque"; one for the Chancellor of France; one for the Secretary of State at the Department of the Interior; one for the Director General of the Library; and one "pour le censeur."

[9] MacArdle, *First Editions*, p. 228. Tyson, p. 139.

[10] And these eleven copies were for the eleven libraries designated by statute. See p. 17, above.

[11] The propriety of delayed registration probably accounts for the large number of instances in which a work states that it was entered at Stationers' Hall, but there is no record of such an entry. Apparently the publisher planned to register the work later, or if necessary to enjoin an infringement, but never in fact did so.

[12] *Lois et Actes du Gouvernement* (Paris, 1807), vol. VII (1807), p. 211. All the French statutes mentioned are at the Bar Assn., New York, N.Y.

[13] *Bulletin des Lois* (Paris, 1814), no. 48, Ordinance no. 403.

By an ordinance adopted Jan. 9, 1828,[14] the five copies were reduced to two: one for "notre bibliothèque" and the other for "la bibliothèque du ministère de l'intérieur." Under a law adopted July 29, 1881, three copies of music must be deposited at the Minister of Interior in Paris or elsewhere.[15]

All that can be said about these requirements is that many copyright deposit copies of musical compositions are at the Bibliothèque Nationale and/or Conservatoire, Paris—and many are not.[16] There was no French requirement for separate registration of titles.

The number of copies in the first printing is stated in many of the Dépôt Légal entries commencing in the latter part of the nineteenth century.

As to the basic original records,[17] the Registers of the Royal Privileges from 1653 to 1790 are now in the Manuscript Department of the Bibliothèque Nationale, and show the exact date the privilege was granted (but not the date of publication).[18] It should be noted, however, that a large number of musical compositions appeared clandestinely without royal privilege; and, on the other hand, privileges were sought for works which in fact were not subsequently printed. Records during the Revolution and up to 1810 do not exist.

The underlying records from 1811–1828 and from 1842–1912 are at the Archives Nationales, Paris, and show the exact date of the "Dépôt Légal"; the records from 1829–1841 are lost. Since 1912, the records are at the Bibliothèque Nationale—to 1925 at the Département des Imprimés and since 1925 at the Département de la Musique.

The author is apparently the first musicologist to have examined the Dépôt Légal records for the purpose of determining publication dates of French works.†

---

[14] *Bulletin des Lois,* 1828, no. 209, Ordinance no. 7807. An unused receipt for deposit of music in 1852 refers to "trois exemplaires" (Archives, F 18 * VIII [15], p. 23). The Archives cannot explain this.

[15] *Bulletin des Lois de la République Française* (Paris, 1882), Ordinance no. 637.

[16] They are not at the Library of the Ministry of the Interior. With a twinkle, the latter wrote the author the Library was required to receive, but not to keep, copyright deposit copies!

A third copy was also delivered at times to the Beaux-Arts. At the beginning of the volume at the Archives, F 18 * VIII (59), Oct. 7, 1880–March 26, 1881, appear signed receipts for the three copies deposited, one signed by the Bibliothèque Nationale, one by the Conservatoire, and the third states "Reçu pour les Beaux-Arts." These third copies were later delivered to the Bibliothèque Nationale, Paris; Letter from Ministère d'État, Affaires Culturelles, Direction Générale des Arts et des Lettres.

[17] This paragraph was summarized from a letter from Mme Élisabeth Lebeau, BN.

[18] Michel Brenet, "La Librairie Musicale en France de 1653 à 1790," in *Sammelbände der Internationalen Musikgesellschaft,* Leipzig, 1906–7, p. 401; BN. See also Robert Estivals, *Le Dépôt Légal sous L'Ancien Régime de 1537 à 1791* (Paris, 1961); NYPL.

GERMANY

Until the unification of Germany in 1871, there was no central copyright law, and none of the separate German states is believed to have had any copyright laws requiring registration or deposit.

Because of the absence of copyright laws in Germany and also in Austria, and because of the high quality of the music published in those countries (much of which was pirated), a voluntary association of music publishers was formed May 23, 1829–May 12, 1830, called "Verein Deutscher Musikalienhändler."[18A] Austrian music publishers soon joined the association, and the association acquired increasing powers. Issues of Hofmeister *Monatsbericht* commencing Jan.–Feb., 1831, and continuing until April, 1838, showed the registration number of the "Grosse Inscriptionsbuch der Vereinigten Musikalienhändler," number 1 appearing in 1831, and number 5140 in 1838, an average of over 700 registrations a year. Thereafter, much central European music contained the notice: "Eingetragen in das Vereins-Archiv." The valuable records of this association, which continued until World War II, were maintained at Leipzig, but are said to have been destroyed during that war.[19]

Under the laws of June 11, 1870, and June 19, 1901, the Stadtrath in Leipzig was to keep a register of works copyrighted,[20] but these registers cannot now be located. No deposit of copies was required.

AUSTRIA

There was no law in Austria in the eighteenth or nineteenth centuries requiring either the registration of titles or deposit of copies. †

ITALY

Prior to the unification of Italy in 1861, some of the separate states had their own copyright laws;[21] however, from 1815 to 1859 the important music publishing city of Milan was part of Austria, which lacked

---

[18A] Max Schumann, *Zur Geschichte des Deutschen Musikalien-Handels* (Leipzig, 1929), pp. 16–18, and *Tradition und Gegenwart* (Leipzig, 1957), particularly, p. 14—both at NYPL. Dr. Heinrich M. Schuster, *Das Urheberrecht der Tonkunst* (Munich, 1891), p. 41, at BM, LC and YU; and Adolf Hüttl, "Die Geschichtliche Entwicklung des Musikalischen Urheberrechts" in *Archiv für Urheber-, Film- und Theaterrecht* (Baden-Baden, 1955), vol. 20, p. 305, at BSM, LC and UW.

[19] Letter, Börsenverein der Deutschen Buchhändler zu Leipzig.

[20] Statute in Copinger, *Copyright*, p. 683.

[21] Copinger, *Copyright*, p. 755. G. B. & G. Fumagalli, *Manuale del Bibliotecario* (Milan, 1894); BM and LC. It is said that in Italy in the first half of the nineteenth century it was the custom for a composer to sell an opera to a manager for two years, with exclusive right of representation, after which the opera became public property. *Grove's*, vol. 7, p. 249.

copyright laws. At least two works published by G. Ricordi in Milan about 1831–1832 mention on the title page "Edizione Privila. da Governa. Risole. N. 36347–4789;" the resolution was adopted on Dec. 18, 1830, but it has not been possible to locate its text.[21A]† And at least one other work published by Ricordi about 1844 states on the title page "Reg. nell' Arch. dell' Unione";[21B] it is not known what union is referred to—possibly the Verein Deutscher Musikalienhändler referred to under "Germany" above (Austrian publishers were also members of this union, and Milan was then part of Austria). Another work published by Ricordi about 1853 refers to section 8 of "Sovrana Patente 19 Ottobre 1846,"[21C] but this section of the sovereign patent, at UW, applying to the Austrian Empire, merely provides that a printed copy of a musical or dramatic work (distributed in place of a manuscript copy) does not destroy the author's right of public performance if the printed copy refers to this section.

The Papal States also granted privileges for the publication of musical compositions,[22] but the present location of the records is unknown. The records are not now at the Vatican Archives, the Italian copyright office mentioned two paragraphs below, or Biblioteca S. Cecilia (Conservatorio), Rome.

Under copyright laws adopted by the Italian government on June 25, 1865, Aug. 10, 1875, and May 18, 1882, up to three copies were to be deposited with the Prefect of the Province,[23] and many of these copyright deposit copies have been found at the Biblioteca S. Cecilia (Conservatorio), Rome, and Biblioteca Nazionale Centrale, Florence. Between 1865 and 1882 the deposits were to be made by the following June or December; after 1882 the deposits were to be made within three months after publication or performance.

The Italian copyright records from June 25, 1865, on are located at the Ufficio della Proprietà Letteraria Artistica e Scientifica, Presidenza del

[21A] The piano-vocal scores of Bellini's *Norma* (p.ns. 5900–5911) and Donizetti's *L'Elisire d'Amore* (p.ns. 6400–6427); both at JF. The resolution is dated and referred to in the *Gazzetta Privilegiate di Milano*, Feb. 4, 1832, no. 35, p. 140; Biblioteca Nazionale Braidense, Milan.

[21B] The piano-vocal score of Verdi's *Ernani* (p.ns. 16221–16241); JF.

[21C] The orchestral score of Verdi's *La Traviata* (p.ns. 21366–21376); see page 203, below.

[22] See, for example, *The Barber of Seville*—Overture, below, footnote 1B. ‡

[23] *Raccolta Ufficiale delle Leggi e dei Decreti del Regno d'Italia*, Law no. 2337, June 25, 1865; Law no. 2652, Series 2, Aug. 10, 1875; Law no. 756, Series 3, May 18, 1882 (and Royal Decree no. 1012, Series 3, Sept. 19, 1882); at Bar Assn., New York, N.Y.

Operatic scores were to be deposited with the Conservatory of Music in Naples and the Brera Library in Milan. *Id.*, Law no. 2587, Oct. 19, 1865. The latter library wrote this author that, according to ministerial decree, the scores were assigned to MIC.

Consiglio dei Ministri, 15 Via Boncompagni, Rome. These records have apparently not been examined before for the purpose of determining publication dates of Italian musical compositions.

U.S.S.R.

Under the Russian 1832 copyright law, registration was required as part of the copyright procedure, but deposit of copies was not provided for.[24] This procedure continued up to the Revolution. Soviet Union music librarians do not know the present whereabouts of these registration records.

Since the Revolution, Soviet Union music librarians say that copies of music compositions have been deposited with the principal music libraries;[24A] while this seems to be so, there are no identifying marks on the deposit copies. The systematic registration of musical works has been in effect since 1931 and reported quarterly in *AML*.

SPAIN

According to the copyright law dated June 10, 1847,[25] two copies of the work were to be deposited, one at the National Library and one at the Ministry of Public Instruction. The copyright law dated Jan. 10, 1879,[26] as amended, states that a general register is to be maintained at the Ministry of Fomento, and copies are to be deposited there and at the National Library.

A few of the copyright deposit copies are now at the National Library, Madrid. The copyright records are in the same building, care of Registro General de la Propiedad Intelectual, 20 Avenida de Calvo Sotelo, Madrid 1.[27]

[24] Statute in Copinger, *Copyright*, p. 786.

[24A] Twenty-two copies of musical works are to be deposited with libraries before the printer releases the printing. *Le Dépôt Légal—Son Organization et son Functionnement dans les Divers Pays* (Paris, 1938), pp. 27, 44 and 60; NYPL. It has not been possible to obtain from the Soviet Union or elsewhere copies of the following four laws cited in the above work: Ordonnance du Comité central exécutif et du Conseil des Commissaires du Peuple, concernant la remise de tous les imprimés parus sur le territoire de l'URSS, aux bibliothèques les plus importantes, du 13 septembre 1933; Ordonnance (numero 1156) du Conseil des Commissaires du Peuple, concernant les imprimés soumis au dépôt, du 20 novembre 1933; Règlement du Conseil de Commissaires du Peuple sur l'ordre d'édition des imprimés, du 10 août 1931; and Instruction du Commissaire du Peuple pour l'Instruction publique, du 7 janvier 1934.

[25] *Legislación de la Propiedad Literaria en España* (Madrid, 1863); NYPL (*IL).

[26] *Copyright Laws and Treaties of the World* (Washington, 1956), Spain, item 2, art. 34; Bar Assn., New York, N.Y.

[27] Dean Arthur Custer, Kingston, R.I., has been helpful in enabling the author to obtain this information.

INTERNATIONAL PROVISIONS

Before international copyright procedures were adopted, it was apparently the law in Europe and England that a work composed by a foreigner and previously published in a foreign country might thereafter become public property in other countries. To avoid such possible loss of copyright in other countries, there arose the practice of attempted simultaneous publication in important countries.

Great Britain made an early effort at international copyright. On July 31, 1838, an International Copyright Act was passed granting copyright protection in the British Empire to music first published in a foreign country where similar protection was afforded in the foreign country to music first published in the British Empire.[28]†

Many other countries have also had bilateral copyright treaties. For example, a relatively important Convention Littéraire was signed by France and Belgium on Aug. 22, 1852, providing for one copy of each work to be deposited for copyright.[29]

The Berne Convention of 1886, to which most Western nations (other than the United States and Russia) adhered, provided neither for registration nor copyright deposit copies. As pointed out below at p. 32, Russian publishers obtained the benefits of the Berne Convention by devious means.

Until 1891 no foreign composer or author could obtain copyright protection in the United States unless he was a resident of the United States. Commencing that year, in accordance with the Copyright Act of 1891, presidential proclamations extended copyright protection in the United States to the citizens of particular countries, for example, France (1891), Great Britain, Germany and Italy (1892), Austria (1907), Hungary (1912), Czechoslovakia (1927), and Finland (1928).[30] Russian citizens have never been included. Under this procedure, copies of the foreign publications are to be deposited at the Library of Congress, in the same manner as American publications, in order to obtain copyright protection in the United States.

As a result, the Library of Congress has a large number of copyright deposit copies of foreign music from 1891 to date, together with information as to the day, month and year of first publication. And to satisfy another American copyright requirement, copies of foreign music began to include the year of publication in the copyright notice.

---

[28] 1 & 2 Vict. c. 59; BM.

[29] The copies deposited in France under the British and Belgian Conventions are listed separately in BF. See, for example, Feb. 3, and June 16, 1855, pp. 95 and 426. A Beethoven work with the stamp of the French-Belgian Convention is at JF.

[30] Howell, Copyright, p. 290.

RESEARCH PROCEDURE USED

The main base of operations has been the New York Public Library. The center for the study of German and Austrian classical and popular music was Vienna, the principal work there being undertaken by Miss Louisa Cagwin, kindly recommended by Dr. Leopold Nowak. Miss Cagwin also visited the principal libraries at Munich, Salzburg, Bonn and elsewhere; her contribution to this work is most substantial. The copyright deposit copies and the broad holdings of the British Museum were examined initially by Mr. Ernest Warburton, recommended by Sir Jack A. Westrup. Some work was done at the Bibliothèque Nationale and the Conservatoire in Paris by Monsieur O. d'Estrade-Guerra.

In Europe, the author has himself done research in London, Paris, Vienna, Munich, Rome, Milan, Moscow, Leningrad and elsewhere. In the United States, the author examined the copyright deposit copies, broad holdings and copyright records at the Library of Congress and visited the principal music libraries in Boston, Cambridge, Philadelphia, New Haven, New York, Rochester and elsewhere. Miss Cagwin checked the principal libraries in Chicago, and Stanford, California.

The National Union Catalogue at the Library of Congress lists many of the principal holdings of many important libraries in the United States. The Catalog Collectif, Bibliothèque Nationale Suisse, Berne, the Union Catalogue, Openbare Muziekbibliotheek, 's-Gravenhage, and the Union Catalogue, National Library, Ottawa, are similar national catalogues for Swiss, Dutch and Canadian libraries. These central index files, apparently not duplicated in other countries,[1] led to the location of many items not otherwise found. The printed British Union Catalogue was, of course, helpful for works published prior to 1800. Printed catalogues of libraries, such as that of the Royal College of Music, were examined.

The entries at Stationers' Hall were searched for all English works, and for those continental works which state they were entered at Stationers' Hall, from 1787 to 1912 when compulsory entry was discontinued. The French Dépôt Légal records were also searched during the periods they are available, namely from 1811–1828 and 1842–1912.[2] The Italian and Spanish

---

[1] The Zentralkatalog der Wissenschaftlichen Bibliotheken des Landes Nordrhein-Westfalen, Cologne, does not contain music. Deutsche Staatsbibliothek, East Berlin, has a central index of music published before 1800 at libraries in East Germany.

[2] See p. 20, above.

copyright records were likewise examined for the period they have been in existence, namely, since 1865 and 1847, respectively.[3]

Musicologists in Europe and America furnished many helpful leads. Special libraries or institutes devoted exclusively to one composer were also contacted, e.g., Bach, Chopin, Foster, Grieg, Liszt, Mozart, Schumann, Tchaikovsky and Wagner. Bibliographic notes in collected editions were helpful in a few instances, e.g., Bach and Chopin.

Published letters of composers and publishers were studied. Phonograph records which were released considerably earlier than printed editions were important in several instances.

Correspondence was undertaken with publishers and successor publishers and also with a few living composers and lyricists. This approach proved fruitful in only a few instances.

Folk-song research was supplemented by studies at the folk-song centers of many countries (see *Relationship to Folk-Song Research and Phonograph Records* below).

Every private collection of printed music known to this author—both general and specialized—in Europe and in the United States was contacted. The former private collection of Dr. Werner Wolffheim was studied by means of the sale catalogue, annotated with names of purchasers; NYPL.

Libraries in Australia, Canada, Czechoslovakia, Denmark, Finland, Hungary, Ireland, Poland and Rumania have, by correspondence, been most helpful with regard to their respective music. On the other hand, correspondence to Mexico, Cuba (before and after Castro) and South American countries has been mostly unanswered.

When all of the foregoing was completed, and other special leads exhausted, a list of about a hundred unlocated first editions was compiled and sent to about six hundred libraries around the world which were listed in the *International Inventory of Musical Sources, Grove's,* or otherwise recommended and not previously searched. Every library mentioned in the *International Inventory of Musical Sources* in England, France, Germany, Switzerland and the United States was written to, plus a great many in Austria, Italy and other countries. Librarians in these countries kindly spent many hours checking the list of missing items, and in this way a great many were found.[4] Over 70 percent of the libraries replied that they had searched their holdings, and many favorably. There is also reason to believe that many others checked their holdings but, not finding any missing item, did not reply.

First editions of orchestral parts of symphonies, operas and ballets were particularly difficult to find (see *Special Message to Music Librarians,*

---

[3] See pp. 21 and 23, above.

[4] The Four Rules of Interlingual Correspondence: short sentences; simple words; no idioms; and try to use words with Latin roots.

below). In addition to searching at the above-mentioned sources, this author also examined the holdings of a number of the world's leading symphony orchestras and opera houses; however, it has not been practical to cover this possibly fertile, but difficult, source systematically. Finally, the author examined the holdings of Alfred J. Mapleson Music Library, New York City, the world's largest renter of orchestral parts and scores to performing societies around the world, which has been in existence for over 100 years. This important area of orchestral parts is sometimes overlooked in musicological research, particularly in the case of operas.

Perhaps, as to this pioneering book, the author should have taken the advice of the late Dr. Otto Erich Deutsch: "Never ... bring out a first edition at all, but ... circulate your book privately and wait for the corrections to come in."[5]

Location of Copies Described. No attempt has been made to compile a worldwide census of the copies described in this book. To the contrary—the attempt was to find anywhere one copy which seemed to be entirely satisfactory as a first edition, meeting all known positive requirements with no negative, disqualifying features. There is much to be said for examining every available copy throughout the world—unquestionably, variants and differences would be noted. However, such exhaustive examination was not realistic for this author any more than it has been for others.

As a practical matter, in the great majority of cases, a huge number of copies of a particular work had to be examined before a completely satisfactory one was located. In addition to examining copies in libraries and private collections, the author has for twenty years been cutting out of dealers' catalogues all listings of editions of the titles studied in this book. An attempt was made to receive every dealer's catalogue during this period as these catalogues contain a great amount of helpful bibliographic information.

Except as mentioned in this paragraph, no inference should be drawn that a particular library or collector does not have a particular edition because it or he is not shown as an owner. The British Museum was searched for copies, particularly copyright deposit copies, of all English works, as were the Bibliothèque Nationale for all French works, the Biblioteca S. Cecilia (Conservatorio) for all Italian works, and the Library of Congress for all American works. Thus, in the absence of human error, first editions of English, French, Italian and American works not shown as being at such respective library are probably not there.

At times more than one owner is indicated. While no systematic attempt was made to examine all known copies, curiosity inevitably led to examining and comparing additional available copies of a great many works

[5] *The New York Times*, Oct. 8, 1961, sec. 2, p. 13.

even after a satisfactory copy had been found. Where an additional correct copy was found, this is so indicated—since the new location may be geographically more convenient for someone who may want to examine it.

RELATIONSHIP TO FOLK-SONG RESEARCH AND
PHONOGRAPH RECORDS

FOLK-SONG RESEARCH

As many of the songs considered are folk songs, i.e., songs without any known author, usually of a simple nature and generally accepted, it is necessary to clarify the relationship of this study with folk-song research. Our present concern is with the earliest appearance in *print* of familiar melodies. Folk-song research is primarily confined to the *oral* tradition, particularly oral variants of the melody or words. Folk-song researchers and revivalists frequently do not seem to make the same effort to find early printed versions as they do to find later oral variants; this author believes that better coordination of the two lines of research would be mutually beneficial.

As to each folk song studied here, all known folk-song reference books have been examined. Reliable evidence is cited. However, a vague recollection of an aged person, without musical ability, that his grandfather, also without musical ability, had said he had heard the melody in *his* youth is not deemed worthy evidence. Nor is the too-frequent, general, unsubstantiated statement that the folk song is "extremely old, having been known for centuries."[1] As folk songs have been printed as such in so many countries since the sixteenth century, it may be meaningful that a well-known folk song did not appear in print until recently; in fact, it is believed by this author that some folk songs, e.g., *How Dry I Am* and *Old MacDonald Had a Farm* in their present forms, are recent in origin. Early field, special and commercial recordings of many folk songs have been made, and after considerable searching the author has been able to find several such recordings which preceded the printed versions mentioned in this book; these earlier recordings are noted. Player-piano rolls were also searched. In a few cases, a letter or diary entry containing a reference to the folk song has preceded the earliest known printed version. These have also been mentioned.

[1] It is not known why some folk-song writers attempt to vilify Stephen C. Foster. The most unfair—because completely unauthenticated—accusations are made about the originality of many of his songs. See, for example, (De) Camptown Races, Jeanie with the Light Brown Hair, Oh! Susanna, and Old Folks at Home, below. See, also in general, George Pullen Jackson, "Stephen Foster's Debt to American Folk-Song" in MQ, 1936, p. 54. That Foster (and Anton Dvořák and George Gershwin) was familiar with Negro and/or minstrel music is clear. But there is *not one single piece of evidence* that Foster's songs were not original with him.

The author has studied or had special studies made at the folk-song centers at: Library of Congress, Washington; Folklore Institute, Bloomington, Indiana; Cecil Sharp English Folk Song Society, London; School of Scottish Studies, and National Library, Edinburgh; Institute of Russian Literature, Leningrad; Deutsches Volksliedarchiv, Freiburg; Phonothèque Nationale, and Bibliothèque Nationale, Paris; Department of Irish Folk Music, University College, Dublin; and Svenskt Visarkiv, Stockholm. In each case, the information there known about the folk songs of the particular country has been incorporated into this book.

PHONOGRAPH RECORDS

While the focus of this book is on the original printing of each composition, there are several instances in which a phonograph record of a composition was released considerably before the publication of the music. For example, *Star Dust* was recorded by a small phonograph company in the Midwest more than a year before the sheet music edition was published. Similarly, the "Hold That Tiger" chorus in *Tiger Rag* was on phonograph records 15 years before it was included in the sheet music edition. *Rhapsody in Blue* was recorded six months before it was published. In the folk music field, *We Shall Overcome* and *When the Saints Go Marching In* were recorded before they were published.

These instances are mentioned in this book, as well as a number of others where the phonograph recording was historically particularly significant. For example, the original recording of *Lili Marleen* played a unique role in the success of the song.

In addition to field, special and commercial recordings, player-piano rolls were also searched for by the author for instances of special significance. More bibliographic information in these areas would be welcome.

DESCRIPTIONS OF FIRST APPEARANCES IN PRINT

GENERAL

Since it is impractical to reproduce the covers, title page, music pages and other pages of each work, it is necessary to select certain sensitive points which experience indicates are likely to change from edition to edition. These points differ depending upon the date and kind of music described.

In general, the following information is furnished as to the first print·ings: the title and opus number, composer, lyricist and name and address of publisher, ordinarily as shown on the title page or front cover; the year of publication; the colors and ornamentation of the covers or wrappers, if there are any, and of the title page; the price; the name of the opera or musical production; the arrangement of the edition, and whether the work is stated to be available in other arrangements or keys; usually, the names and addresses or number of copublishers or agents; the pages on which the music appears; miscellaneous other pages containing, for example, a list of subscribers, index, or cast; any dedication;[1] any dated watermark; the plate number at the bottom of the music page;[2] and any references to other musical compositions appearing on the particular copy. Additional special information is given where necessary.

If known, a "point of issue," distinguishing a first edition from later editions, has been set in boldface for rapid checking.

Pages printed from engraved plates are so indicated. The shape is upright, unless oblong is stated. Folio, quarto or octavo size is usually not mentioned except for music published during and at the end of World War I (see page 9) and in a few other cases. The copyright owner is the publisher unless otherwise stated. Geographical names have usually been Anglicized and addresses given in the American form. Legal notices are seldom mentioned unless they occupy an entire page (the absence or presence of legal and copyright warnings and claims, and their exact wording, would be a fertile area for study).

It may well develop in the future that two or more different editions of a particular work will meet the description contained in this book. Such information would be welcomed, and an attempt will be made with the informant to determine priority between the two editions.

Advertisements on a page are described as follows:

adv. *Nocturne.*	means that the one musical work advertised is *Nocturne.*
adv. *Conte..*	means that the one musical work advertised starts with the word *Conte.*
adv. *Conte..* and *Huit..*	means that *two* musical works are advertised, one starting with the word *Conte* and the other starting with the word *Huit.*
adv. *Conte..* - *Huit..*	means that *more than two* musical works are advertised, the first work starting with the word *Conte* and the last work starting with the word *Huit.*

---

[1] In some languages the dedicatee's name may unfortunately be given in the dative.

[2] If there is a different publisher's number on the title page, this is also indicated. The plate number has been omitted in the descriptions of many recent popular songs because experience indicates it is of little or no use in establishing first printings in this period.

In a few cases, the advertisement is described by mentioning its most prominent word, first prominent word, or general subject.

The owner of each described copy is also given. The library's shelf number is usually omitted unless the library is known to have two or more similar editions.

Where the words were printed before the music, the prior printing of the words is also described.[3]

TERMINOLOGY

In this book, the phrase "first edition" means the first regular printing prior to any change of any kind in any part of the work. To many, the phrase "first edition" means the first "general" printing, with minor changes in the covers or title page or text being referred to as the "second issue" or the "second state" of the first edition. To some, it is immaterial that there are changes in the wrappers or advertisements or imprint or price, or that an edition is engraved or offset, *if* the music pages remain unchanged.[4] To this author and in this book, the phrase "first edition" means the first state of the first issue of the first edition. Any change makes the next printing the "second edition." Where there are two or more editions, identical except as indicated, and it cannot be established which is the earlier, the word "variant" is used.[5]

A known change in the title page merely in, say, the price of the work or the address of the publisher is admittedly relatively minor, even if it occurred provably many years after the original printing, *provided one has checked all the music pages of the two printings, note for note, and found that the music pages of the later printing remain unchanged in every respect.*[5A] However, the important point is that, unless one is willing to make this painstaking musical check, is not an unnecessary risk being taken if one considers both printings as the first printing when at least the title page of one printing is known to be earlier than the title page of the second printing? Of course, changes are sometimes made in the music pages without any change in, say, the title page. But experience has shown that the title page is, for many reasons, frequently changed. It is unquestionably desirable, but usually not practical, to check every musical note of the two printings. But, *unless a note-by-note musical comparison has been made,* if

---

[3] Except original libretti of operas, which are described in Fuld, *Libretti.*

[4] This is a big "if" unless one has checked all the music, note for note.

[5] For many other views as to what is an "edition," see Unity Sherrington and Guy Oldham, *Music, Libraries and Instruments* (London, 1961), p. 147, at BM, and generally, John Carter, *ABC for Book-Collectors* (London, 1952), p. 85, at NYPL.

[5A] For example, by means of a Hinman Collator.

the title page of one printing is provably earlier than the title page of another printing, there is an unnecessary and increased risk of more important changes having been made in the musical text during the intervening time. For these reasons, to this author, the phrase "first edition" means the first printing prior to any change of any kind in any part of the work.

The first "regular" edition (i.e., the trade edition issued to the public) has been selected as the first edition rather than any professional edition (although a contrary argument can be made), because the regular edition is on public sale and is on paper intended to last, whereas the professional edition is a private printing issued free to persons in the music industry and is usually on cheap, brittle wood-pulp paper. Similarly, a song copyrighted in this country as an "unpublished" composition has not been considered as the first edition. "Vocal parts" (consisting only of the melody line and words) printed for the private use of singers and chorus of a musical composition are also considered "unpublished." In a few cases, the orchestral score of an opera has been called a first edition where copies were printed primarily for rental, and perhaps not sold.

The first known appearance of the melody in print has been described, whether it is in the form of sheet music, or included in a score, book or magazine. The first edition is not necessarily an authorized edition. It is immaterial in this book whether the first printing of a work occurs during the composer's lifetime or after his death.

The term "first edition" is reserved for an edition which not only meets any positive requirements and avoids all negative disqualifications, but also is confirmed by a contemporary dating, usually by reason of a copyright deposit stamp. "Probable first edition" means an edition which meets any positive requirements and avoids all negative factors, and, subjectively, has the "feel" of a first edition. "Possible first edition" means an edition which meets any positive requirements and avoids all negative factors, and could have been printed at the time the composition was first published. "Early edition" means an edition which has at least one negative or disqualifying factor.

Intended simultaneous publication of a composition in two or more countries is a most difficult problem since experience has shown that, while simultaneous publication may have been intended, it is frequently not achieved. If the evidence shows that a particular composition was published at or about the same time in two or more countries, both or all editions are described. If, however, in spite of the intent, one edition preceded the other or others by a substantial time, only the first to appear is considered the first edition, the others being mentioned briefly.

A special problem exists as to many Russian works published after 1886. Russia did not join the Berne International Copyright Convention.

Nonetheless, Russian publishers frequently obtained its benefits by having the work published in Germany a day or two before publication in Russia,[6] since compliance with the Berne Convention depended upon the place of first publication, rather than upon the nationality of the author. This "German" edition usually had all the music pages printed in Russia, plus a German title page. For the purpose of this book, the Russian edition is nonetheless considered the first edition, although the German edition is noted where located.

ARRANGEMENTS CONSIDERED

If a composer wrote a work for orchestra, but it was first printed in a piano arrangement, is the "first edition" the first printing of the earlier piano arrangement or the first printing of the later orchestral arrangement? It can be argued that the first printing of the melody in any form is the first edition of that melody; it is the melody that the man in the street hums. It can also be argued that where the work was first composed for orchestra, anything less[7] than a full orchestral arrangement is an "incomplete" edition, and that the first edition should be a complete edition of what the composer wrote.

The above example is typical of many different situations; these have been generally resolved in this book as set forth below. The basic principle is: the first arrangement to appear is described; and if originally composed for more instruments than are included in the first arrangement or as part of a larger work, the complete arrangement and larger work are also described.

Where the work was first published in the same arrangement as originally composed, this is the only arrangement considered.

Where the work was originally composed for orchestra, and publication of the orchestral score and parts took place at about the same time, both seem equally important and are considered. If the publication of one preceded the other by a substantial time, only the earlier is described.

If the work was originally composed for orchestra, and publication of the orchestral score (or parts) took place at about the same time as a piano arrangement, only the orchestral arrangement is considered.

If the work was originally composed for orchestra, and publication of a piano arrangement preceded the orchestral version by a substantial interval, both arrangements are described. However, where the interval is, say, twenty-five or more years—as is the case of some operas and light operas—the orchestral version is mentioned only briefly.

---

[6] H. W. Heinsheimer, *Fanfare for 2 Pigeons* (New York, N.Y., 1952), p. 96; NYPL. Letter from Anton J. Benjamin, G.m.b.H., Hamburg.

[7] Particularly if arranged by someone other than the composer.

Where operas, light operas or shows are concerned, and the single aria or song, or the overture, was published well before the piano-vocal or orchestral score, both the separate number and such score are considered. Where the separate number and the score were published at about the same time, only the more complete score is described. (Whereas today separate numbers usually precede the score by months, this was frequently not the case in the eighteenth and nineteenth centuries.)

Where operas or light operas are concerned, and a piano-vocal score appeared prior to, or at about the same time as, the piano solo arrangement (without words), only the more complete piano-vocal score is described. If the piano arrangement clearly preceded the piano-vocal score, both are considered.

LIST OF ABBREVIATIONS †

Following is a list of abbreviations and special terms used in this book. The list also serves as a bibliography of the principal works studied in connection with this book, and shows the libraries and private collectors who have cooperated in this project.

AAB	W. J. Burke and Will D. Howe, *American Authors and Books* (New York, N.Y., 1943); NYPL.
AAS	American Antiquarian Society, Worcester, Mass.
ABH	Arthur Billings Hunt, Wantagh, N.Y.
AH	Arthur Hedley, London.
AKM	Staatlich Genehmigte Gesellschaft der Autoren, Komponisten und Musikverleger, Vienna.
Allen, *Gilbert*	Reginald Allen, *The First Night Gilbert and Sullivan* (New York, N.Y., 1958); BM.
Allibone	S. Austin Allibone, *A Critical Dictionary of English Literature* (Philadelphia, 1871); NYPL.
Altmann	Wilhelm Altmann, *Richard Wagners Briefwechsel mit Seinen Verlegern* (Leipzig, 1911); NYPL.
American War Songs	*American War Songs* (Philadelphia, 1925); NYPL.
AML	(*Annals of Musical Literature*) Летопись музыкальной литературы (Moscow, 1931–); SSL (many issues at LC and NYPL). Apparently entitled *Notnaya Letopis'* (*Musical Annals*) from 1931 to 1938 and *Bibliografiya Myzykal'noi Literatury* about 1939–1940.
AMZ	*Allgemeine Musikalische Zeitung* (Leipzig, 1798–1848); NYPL.
AMZ *Int-Bl*	Same, *Intelligenz-Blatt* insert.
Anderson, *Beethoven*	Emily Anderson, *The Letters of Beethoven* (London, 1961); NYPL.

Archives	Archives Nationales, 60 Rue des Francs Bourgeois, Paris.
Arrangement	Adaptation for other instruments—for example, an arrangement of an orchestral work for piano or piano four hands. Generally, the more arrangements that are listed, the later the edition will be.
ASCAP	American Society of Composers, Authors and Publishers, New York, N.Y.
ASCAP	The *ASCAP Biographical Dictionary of Composers, Authors, and Publishers*, edited by Daniel I. McNamara (2nd ed., New York, N.Y., 1952); NYPL.
*(Asterisk)	Incomplete or defective.
AT	Alan Tyson, London.
AVH	Bibliothèque Anthony van Hoboken, Ascona, Switzerland, at ONB.
AW	Alexander Weinmann, Vienna.

BA	Beethoven-Archiv, Bonn.
Bach Gesellschaft	*Johann Sebastian Bach's Werke* (Bach Gesellschaft zu Leipzig) [Leipzig, 1851–1926]; NYPL.
Back cover	Outside of back cover.
Baker	*Baker's Biographical Dictionary of Musicians*, edited by Nicolas Slonimsky (5th ed., New York, N.Y., 1958); NYPL.
Bar Assn., New York, N.Y.	Association of the Bar of the City of New York, New York, N.Y.
B & H	Breitkopf & Härtel, Leipzig.
Baring-Gould	S. Baring-Gould, *English Minstrelsie* (Edinburgh, 1895–[1897]); NYPL.
BBC	British Broadcasting Company, London.
BCS	Biblioteca Centrală de Stat, Bucharest.
BE	Buffalo and Erie County Public Library, Grosvenor Reference Division, Buffalo, N.Y.
Beethoven Beiträge	*Beiträge zur Beethoven-Bibliographie*, edited by Kurt Dorfmüller (Munich, 1978).
Belden	Henry Marvin Belden, *Ballads and Songs Collected by the Missouri Folk-Lore Society* (Columbia, Mo., 1940); NYPL.
Bernstein	Leonard Bernstein, *The Joy of Music* (New York, N.Y., 1959); NYPL.

Bertensson-Leyda	Sergei Bertensson and Jay Leyda, *Sergei Rachmaninoff—a Lifetime in Music* (New York, N.Y., 1956); NYPL.
BF	*Bibliographie de la France* (Paris, 1811–); *ULS*, p. 444.
Bib. Mus.	*Bibliographie Musicale* (Paris, 1872–1874); *ULS*, p. 447.
BIM	Bibliothek der Internationalen Stiftung Mozarteum, Salzburg.
Bio. Dir. USSR	*Biographic Directory of the USSR* (New York, N.Y., 1958); NYPL.
Blanck	Jacob Blanck, *Bibliography of American Literature* (New Haven, 1955—); NYPL.
BM	British Library, British Museum, London.
BM Music Catalogue	W. Barclay Squire, *Catalogue of Printed Music Published between 1487 and 1800 Now in the British Museum* (London, 1912); BM.
BM Mus. Cat. Acc. 53	*Catalogue of Printed Music in the British Museum —Accessions—Part 53—Music in the Hirsch Library* (London, 1951); BM.
BMA	Musik-Akademie der Stadt Basel, Basel, Switzerland.
BMF	*Bibliographie Musicale Française* (Paris, 1875–1914); *ULS*, p. 447.
BMI	Broadcast Music, Inc., New York, N.Y.
BML	Bath Municipal Library, Bath, England.
BMM	Biblioteca Musical, Madrid.
BN	Bibliothèque Nationale, Paris.
BNA	Biblioteka Narodowa, Warsaw.
BNF	Biblioteca Nazionale Centrale, Florence.
BNM	Biblioteca Nacional, Madrid.
BOA	Boston Athenaeum, Boston.
BOB	Bergen Offentlige Bibliotek, Bergen, Norway.
BOD	Bodleian Library, Oxford.
Böhme	Franz Magnus Böhme, *Volksthümliche Lieder der Deutschen im 18. und 19. Jahrhundert* (Leipzig, 1895); NYPL.
BOL	Civico Museo Bibliografico Musicale, Bologna.
BOP	Bibliothèque de l'Opéra, Paris.

Bory	Robert Bory, *La Vie de Frédéric Chopin* (Paris [1951]); NYPL.
Botkin	B. A. Botkin, *A Treasury of American Folklore* (New York, N.Y., 1944); NYPL.
Botkin-Harlow	B. A. Botkin and Alvin F. Harlow, *A Treasury of Railroad Folklore* (New York, N.Y., 1953); NYPL.
BPL	Boston Public Library, Boston.
BR	Brown University, Providence, R.I.
[ ]	Brackets denote that information between the brackets does not appear in print, but has been obtained elsewhere.
Brahms Briefwechsel	Wilhelm Altmann, *Johannes Brahms im Briefwechsel mit Breitkopf & Härtel* et al. (Berlin, 1920); NYPL.
Brahms-Simrock	*Johannes Brahms und Fritz Simrock* (Hamburg, 1961); NYPL.
Brancour	René Brancour, *Massenet* (Paris, 1922); NYPL.
BRB	Bibliothèque Royale de Belgique, Brussels.
Brigham	Clarence S. Brigham, *History and Bibliography of American Newspapers 1690–1820* (Worcester, Mass., 1947); NYPL.
Brit. Mus. Biog.	James D. Brown and Stephen S. Stratton, *British Musical Biography* (Birmingham, 1897); NYPL.
Brown	Maurice J. E. Brown, *Chopin* (London, 1960); BM.
Brown, *Corrections*	Maurice J. E. Brown, "The Chopin Index—Corrections . . ." in *MT*, Jan. 1965, p. 28.
Browne	C. A. Browne, *The Story of Our National Ballads* (New York, N.Y., 1960); NYPL.
BS	Boyd Stutler, Charleston, W.Va. Collection now at State Archives, Charleston, W..Va.
BSM	Bayerische Staatsbibliothek, Munich.
BSS	Bibliothèque Saint-Sulpice, Montreal.
BUC	*The British Union-Catalogue of Early Music*, edited by Edith B. Schnapper (London, 1957); BM.
Bullen-Arnold	Frank T. Bullen and W. F. Arnold, *Songs of Sea Labour* (London, 1914); NYPL.
Burghauser	Jarmil Burghauser, *Antonín Dvořák, Thematic Catalog* (Prague, 1960); NYPL.
Burton	Jack Burton, *The Blue Book of Tin Pan Alley* (Watkins Glen, N.Y., 1950); NYPL.

BVM	La Bibliothèque de la Ville de Montréal, Montreal.
BY	Bryn Mawr College, Bryn Mawr, Pa.
©	Copyrighted.
CA	Public Library, Cardiff, Wales.
ca.	Circa.
Cambrian Minstrelsie	Cambrian Minstrelsie (Edinburgh, 1893); NYPL.
Canadian Copyright	Complete List of Canadian Copyright Musical Compositions, 1868–Jan. 19, 1889 (n.p., n.d.); TPL.
Casa Ricordi	Claudio Sartori, Casa Ricordi ([Milan], 1958); NYPL.
CB	Cary Bok, Camden, Me.
CBC	Canadian Broadcasting Corporation, Toronto.
CDC	Copyright deposit copy. The actual copy of a work deposited for copyright at the Library of Congress, the British Museum, the Bibliothèque Nationale, etc.
CG	Charles Gaynor, New York, N.Y.
CH	Cecil Hopkinson, London.
chap.	Chapter.
Chappell	W. Chappell, Popular Music of the Olden Time (London [1859]); BM.
Chappell, Copyright	F. P. Chappell and John Shoard, A Handy-Book of the Law of Copyright (London, 1863); NYPL.
Chávez Catalog	Herbert Weinstock, Carlos Chávez Catalog (Washington, 1944); NYPL.
Chinnéide	Veronica ní Chinnéide, "The Sources of Moore's Melodies" in The Journal of the Royal Society of Antiquaries of Ireland, Dublin, 1959, p. [109]; NLI.
Chopin Works	Fryderyk Chopin Complete Works (Warsaw, 1949–); NYPL.
Chusid	Martin Chusid; A Catalog of Verdi's Operas (Hackensack, N.J., 1974); LC and NYPL.
CI	The Curtis Institute of Music, Philadelphia.
Clark	Kenneth S. Clark, Stories of America's Songs (New York, n.d.); JF.
CLS	Charleston Library Society, Charleston, S.C.
CM	Conservatoire de Musique, Geneva.

CNL	Commonwealth National Library, Canberra, Australia.
CNO	Catalogue des Nouvelles Oeuvres Musicales Françaises (Paris, Jan.–March, 1875); ULS, p. 447.
Coirault, Chanson	Patrice Coirault, Notre Chanson Folklorique (Paris, 1941); NYPL.
Coirault, Recherches	P. Coirault, Recherches sur Notre Ancienne Chanson Populaire Traditionnelle (Paris, 1927–1933); BY.
COL	Columbia University, New York, N.Y.
col.	Column.
Colcord, Roll	Joanna C. Colcord, Roll and Go (Indianapolis, 1924); NYPL.
Colcord, Songs	Joanna C. Colcord, Songs of American Sailormen (New York, N.Y., 1938); LC.
Collective title front cover	A front cover not for one composition only, but for a collection of compositions.
COP	Bibliothèque du Conservatoire, Paris. Much of the music of this library has recently been transferred to the Bibliothèque Nationale, Paris.
Copinger, Copyright	Walter Arthur Copinger, The Law of Copyright (3rd ed., London, 1893); Bar Assn., New York, N.Y.
CP	Cole Porter Estate, New York, N.Y.
CPL	Chicago Public Library, Chicago.
CU	Cornell University, Ithaca, N.Y.
CUL	University Library, Cambridge.
DAR	David A. Randall, Bloomington, Ind.
Dave and Kathleen Thompson	Dave Thompson and Kathleen Thompson, Songs That Mother Used to Sing (Chicago, 1931); NYPL.
Dépôt Légal	French copyright deposit. The Dépôt Légal records are at the Archives Nationales, Paris.
Deutsch, Brahms	Otto Erich Deutsch, "The First Editions of Brahms" in The Music Review, Cambridge, May and Aug., 1940, pp. [123] and [255]; ULS, p. 1840.
Deutsch Festschrift	Festschrift Otto Erich Deutsch (Kassel, 1963); LC.
Deutsch, Music Bibliography	O. E. Deutsch, "Music Bibliography and Catalogues" in The Library, London, March, 1943, p. [151]; ULS, p. 1576.

Deutsch-Oldman, *Mozart-Drucke*   Otto Erich Deutsch and Cecil B. Oldman, "Mozart-Drucke" in *Zeitschrift für Musikwissenschaft*, Leipzig, Dec., 1931, p. 135; *ULS*, p. 3026.

Deutsch, *Plate Numbers*   Otto Erich Deutsch, *Musikverlags Nummern* (Berlin, 1961); LC.

Deutsch, *Schubert*   *Franz Schubert: Thematisches Verzeichnis Seiner Werke in chronologischer Folge von Otto Erich Deutsch*, revised and enlarged by W. Dürr, A. Feil, C. Landon, et al., in *Franz Schubert: Neue Ausgabe Sämtlicher Werke* (Kassel, 1978); NYPL.

DGB   Dezobry and Bachelet, *Dictionnaire Général de Biographie et d'Histoire* (Paris, 1895); NYPL.

DIB   Civico Instituto Musicale "Gaetano Donizetti," Bergamo, Italy.

Dichter-Shapiro   Harry Dichter and Elliott Shapiro, *Early American Sheet Music* (New York, N.Y., 1941); NYPL.

Dict. Am. Biog.   *Dictionary of American Biography* (New York, N.Y., 1928–); NYPL.

Dict. Nat. Biog.   *The Dictionary of National Biography* (London, [1921–1927]); NYPL.

DKB   Det Kongelige Bibliotek, Copenhagen.

DM   *Dizionario dei Musicisti* (Rome, 1922); NYPL.

DMP   Dvořák Museum, Prague.

Doerflinger   William Main Doerflinger, *Shantymen and Shantyboys* (New York, N.Y., 1951); NYPL.

Dombayev   Г. Домбаев, *Музыкальное Наследие П. И. Чайков ского — Справочник* (G. Dombayev, *Musical Heritage of P. I. Tchaikovsky—a Reference Book*) (Moscow, 1958); SSL and JF. (All dates in this work are Old Style.)

Dörffel   Alfred Dörffel, "Literarisches Verzeichnis" in *Musikalisches Wochenblatt*, Leipzig, 1870, Supplement; *ULS*, p. 1846.

Double pagination   The presence on each page of two sets of page numbers; usually, one for the entire piano-vocal score and one for the separate aria. In this way, the same plates could be used for both purposes.

Downes-Siegmeister   Olin Downes and Elie Siegmeister, *A Treasury of American Song* (New York, N.Y., 1943); NYPL.

DPL   Dundee Public Library, Dundee, Scotland.

DR   *Dizionario Ricordi* (Milan, 1959); LC.

DS	Deutsche Staatsbibliothek, East Berlin.
DTP	Detroit Public Library, Detroit, Mich.
DU	Landes- und Stadtbibliothek, Düsseldorf.
DUC	*Dictionnaire Universel des Contemporains* (5th ed., Paris, 1880); NYPL.
DUM	Carlo Schmidl, *Dizionario Universale dei Musicisti* (Milan, 1928–1929); LC.
Dwight's	*Dwight's Journal of Music* (Boston, 1852–1881); *ULS*, p. 895.
ed.	Edition.
EDM	*Enciclopedia della Musica* (Milan, 1963—); BN.
EDS	*Enciclopedia dello Spettacolo* (Rome, 1954–1962); NYPL.
EFDSS	The English Folk Dance and Song Society, London.
Eitner, *Buch*	Robert Eitner, *Buch- und Musikalien-Händler, Buch- und Musikaliendrucker* (Leipzig, 1904); NYPL.
Eitner, *Lexikon*	Robert Eitner, *Biographisch-bibliographisches Quellen-Lexikon der Musiker und Musikgelehrten* (Leipzig, 1900–1904); NYPL.
EL	Erlangen Library, Erlangen, Germany.
Elson, *Modern Music*	Louis C. Elson, *Modern Music and Musicians*, vol. 2 (New York, N.Y., 1912); NYPL.
EM	Eric Mandell, Philadelphia. This collection is now at Gratz College, Philadelphia.
Emurian, *Hymns*	Ernest K. Emurian, *Living Stories of Famous Hymns* (Boston, 1955); NYPL.
Emurian, *Songs*	Ernest K. Emurian, *Living Stories of Favorite Songs* (Boston, 1958); NYPL.
English Plate Numbers	Oliver W. Neighbour and Alan Tyson, *English Music Publishers' Plate Numbers in the First Half of the Nineteenth Century* (London, 1965); BM.
Engraved	Printed from engraved plates; see page 10, above.
Erk-Böhme	Ludwig Erk and F. M. Böhme, *Deutscher Liederhort* (Leipzig, 1893–1894); NYPL.
Erman	Wilhelm Erman and Ewald Horn, *Bibliographie der Deutschen Universitäten* (Leipzig and Berlin, 1904); NYPL.
ESM	Eastman School of Music, Sibley Music Library, Rochester, N.Y.

Etude	The Etude (Philadelphia, 1883–1957); *ULS*, p. 969.
EW	Dr. Edmund G. Wilson, Meyersdale, Pa.
Ewen, *Berlin*	David Ewen, *The Story of Irving Berlin* (New York, N.Y., 1950); NYPL.
Ewen, *Lighter Classics*	David Ewen, *The Lighter Classics in Music* (New York, N.Y., 1961); NYPL.
FDB	Frank V. De Bellis Collection, San Francisco State College, San Francisco, Cal.
FH	Foster Hall, Pittsburgh.
FHR	*Foster Hall Reproductions—Songs, Compositions and Arrangements by Stephen Collins Foster* (Indianapolis, 1933); NYPL.
Fitz-Gerald	S. J. Adair Fitz-Gerald, *Stories of Famous Songs* (London, 1898); NYPL.
Flood, *Bagpipe*	Wm. H. Grattan Flood, *The Story of the Bagpipe* (London, 1911); NYPL.
FLP	Free Library of Philadelphia, Philadelphia.
FM	*La France Musicale* (Paris, 1837–1869); *ULS*, p. 1053.
FO	The Folger Shakespeare Library, Washington.
Folk-Lore Record	The Folk-Lore Record (London, 1878–1882); *ULS*, p. 1032.
Ford	Robert Ford, *Song Histories* (Glasgow and Edinburgh, 1900); NYPL.
FR	Deutsches Volksliedarchiv, Freiburg, Germany.
Friedlaender	Max Friedlaender, *Das Deutsche Lied im 18. Jahrhundert* (Stuttgart and Berlin, 1902); NYPL.
Front cover	Outside of front cover.
Fuld, *American*	James J. Fuld, *American Popular Music (Reference Book) 1875–1950* (Philadelphia, 1955); NYPL.
Fuld, *Foster*	James J. Fuld, *A Pictorial Bibliography of the First Editions of Stephen C. Foster* (Philadelphia, 1957); NYPL.
Fuld, *Libretti*	James J. Fuld, *The Book of World-Famous Libretti* (New York, N.Y., 1984); LC.
Fuld-Davidson	James J. Fuld and Mary Wallace Davidson, *18th-Century American Secular Music Manuscripts: An Inventory* (Philadelphia, 1980); LC.
Gammond-Clayton	Peter Gammond and Peter Clayton, *A Guide to Popular Music* (London, 1960); NYPL.

GB	*Der Grosse Brockhaus* (Wiesbaden, 1952–1957); NYPL.
GBP	Bibliothèque Publique et Universitaire, Geneva.
GD	*Die Grossen Deutschen, Deutsche Biographie* (Berlin [1956–1957]); NYPL.
GE	*La Grande Encyclopédie* (Paris, n.d.); NYPL.
Geller	James J. Geller, *Famous Songs and Their Stories* (New York, N.Y., 1931); NYPL.
GEPB	*Grande Enciclopédia Portuguesa e Brasileira* (Lisbon, n.d.); NYPL.
Gerber	Ernst Ludwig Gerber, *Neues Historisch-Biographisches Lexikon der Tonkünstler* (Leipzig, 1813); NYPL.
Gershwin	Ira Gershwin, *Lyrics on Several Occasions* (New York, N.Y., 1959); LC.
GEU	Georgetown University Libraries, Washington.
GIT	Georgia Institute of Technology, Atlanta, Ga.
Gilbert	Douglas Gilbert, *Lost Chords* (Garden City, N.Y., 1942); NYPL.
GL	The State Central Museum of Musical Culture named for M. I. Glinka, Moscow.
Glen	John Glen, *Early Scottish Melodies* (Edinburgh, 1900); NYPL.
GM	Gesellschaft der Musikfreunde, Vienna.
GMM	*La Gazzetta Musicale di Milano* (Milan, generally 1842–1902); BN and MIC.
GMP	*Gazette Musicale de Paris* (Paris, 1834–1835); *ULS,* p. 2400.
Goldberg	Isaac Goldberg, *Tin Pan Alley* (New York, N.Y., 1930); NYPL.
Gomme †	Alice Bertha Gomme, *The Traditional Games of England, Scotland and Ireland* (London, 1894 and 1898); LC.
Graham	G. F. Graham, *The Songs of Scotland* (Edinburgh, 1848–1849); NYPL.
Green	Stanley Green, *The World of Musical Comedy* (New York, N.Y., 1960); LC.
Grial	Hugo de Grial, *Músicos Mexicanos* (Mexico City, 1965); photocopy at NYPL.
Grieg Catalogue	*Katalog over Griegutstillingen* (Bergen, 1962); BOB and JF.
Grieg, *Letters*	Edvard Grieg, *Briefe an die Verleger der Edition Peters* (Leipzig, 1932); NYPL.

Grieg, *Scots*	John Grieg, *Scots Minstrelsie* (Edinburgh, 1893–[1895]); NYPL.
Grove's	Grove's Dictionary of Music and Musicians, edited by Eric Blom (5th ed., London, 1954). Also, where so indicated, 3rd ed., edited by H. C. Colles, London, 1927.
Grun	Bernard Grun, *Prince of Vienna* (London, 1955); NYPL.
GU	Glasgow University, Glasgow.
HA	Hamilton College, Clinton, N.Y.
Halliwell	James Orchard Halliwell, *Popular Rhymes and Nursery Tales* (London, 1849); NYPL.
Handbuch Annual	Handbuch der Musikalischen Literatur, Erster-Zehnter Nachtrag, Anton Meysel, Friedrich Hofmeister or C. F. Whistling (Leipzig, 1818–1827); NYPL.
Harwell	Richard B. Harwell, *Confederate Music* (Chapel Hill, N.C., 1950); NYPL.
HC	Hobart College, Geneva, N.Y.
HD	Hessische Landes- und Hochschul-Bibliothek, Darmstadt, Germany.
HDB	Dr. Harry D. Bowman, Hagerstown, Md.
Heugel	Heugel & Cie., Paris.
Hill, *Bibliography*	Richard S. Hill, a review of "Cecil Hopkinson, a Bibliography of the Musical and Literary Works of Hector Berlioz," in *Journal of the American Musicological Society*, Richmond, Va., Spring, 1953, p. 77; NYPL.
Hirsch	Katalog der Musikbibliothek Paul Hirsch (Berlin, Frankfort and Cambridge, 1928–1947); NYPL.
HL	Henry E. Huntington Library, San Marino, Cal.
HMA	Harvard Music Association, Boston.
HOB	Öffentliche Bücherhallen, Hamburg.
Hoboken †	Anthony van Hoboken, *Joseph Haydn*, vol. 1 (Mainz, 1957); NYPL.
Hofer †	Mari Ruef Hofer, *Children's Singing Games, Old and New* (Chicago, 1901); LC.
Hofmeister Annual	(Initially) Kurzes Verzeichnis . . . in Deutschland und den Angrenzenden Ländern Gedruckter Musikalien . . . (Friedrich Hofmeister, Leipzig); *ULS*, p. 1220. Issued annually covering the years 1852–

Hofmeister *Handbuch*	(Initially) Adolph Hofmeister, *Handbuch der Musikalischen Literatur* (Leipzig, 1834–1943), covering the years 1829–1940; NYPL. Issued about every five years.
Hofmeister *Monatsbericht*	(Initially) *Musikalisch-Literarischer Monatsbericht Neuer Musikalien, Musikalischer Schriften und Abbildungen* (C.F. Whistling, Leipzig). Usually issued monthly from Jan., 1829– . UI has a virtually complete run. In addition, issues from 1829 to 1833 are at ZZ; issues from 1834 to date (except 1840) are at ONB; and 1840 is at BM.
Hopkinson, *Berlioz* †	Cecil Hopkinson, *A Bibliography of the Musical and Literary Works of Hector Berlioz* (Edinburgh, 1951); LC.
Hopkinson, *Bibliography*	Cecil Hopkinson, "The Fundamentals of Music Bibliography" in *The Journal of Documentation*, London, Sept., 1955, p. 119; NYPL.
Hopkinson, *Gluck*	Cecil Hopkinson, *A Bibliography of the Printed Works of C. W. von Gluck* (New York, N.Y., 1967), 2nd ed.; NYPL.
Hopkinson, *Parisian*	Cecil Hopkinson, *A Dictionary of Parisian Music Publishers 1700–1950* (London, 1954); NYPL.
Hopkinson, *Puccini*	Cecil Hopkinson, *A Bibliography of the Works of Giacomo Puccini* (New York, N.Y., 1968); LC.
Hopkinson, *Russian* †	Cecil Hopkinson, *Notes on Russian Music Publishers* (Cambridge, 1959); LC.
Howell, *Copyright*	Herbert A. Howell, *The Copyright Law* (Washington, 1952); NYPL.
HT	Howard-Tilton Memorial Library of Tulane University, New Orleans, La.
HU	Harvard University, Cambridge, Mass.
Hugill	Stan Hugill, *Shanties from the Seven Seas* (London, 1961); NYPL.
Humphries-Smith	Charles Humphries and William C. Smith, *Music Publishing in the British Isles* (London, 1954); NYPL.
HWM	Henry Watson Music Library, Manchester Public Libraries, Manchester.
† Imprint	Name and address (of the publisher); also, the date if shown.
IP	Max Arnim, *Internationale Personalbibliographie* (Leipzig, 1944); NYPL.

IU   Indiana University, Bloomington, Ind.

Jackson   George Pullen Jackson, *Spiritual Folk-Songs of Early America* (New York, N.Y., 1937); NYPL.

JAF   *Journal of American Folklore* (Boston, New York, N.Y., and Lancaster, Pa., 1888—); *ULS*, p. 1435.

JAF Index   Tristram P. Coffin, *An Analytical Index to the Journal of American Folklore* (Philadelphia, 1958); LC.

Jähns   Friedr. Wilh. Jähns, *Carl Maria von Weber in Seinen Werken* (Berlin, 1871); NYPL.

JB   Jacob Blanck, Chestnut Hill, Mass.

JF   James J. Fuld, New York, N.Y.

JFD   J. Francis Driscoll Estate, c/o J. Francis Driscoll, Jr., Flossmoor, Ill.

JFSS   *Journal of the Folk-Song Society* (London, 1899–1931); *ULS*, p. 1032.

JLH   Josephine L. Hughes, Charleston, S.C.

JM   Jacob Michael, New York, N.Y. Collection now at JNL.

JMM   Jean-Marie Martin, Hollogne-aux-Pierres, Belgium.

JNL   The Jewish National and University Library, Jerusalem.
†

Johansson   Cari Johansson, *French Music Publishers' Catalogues of the Second Half of the Eighteenth Century* (Stockholm, 1955); HU.

Jones, Handbook   F. O. Jones, *A Handbook of American Music and Musicians* (New ed., Buffalo, N.Y., 1887); NYPL.

JU   Juilliard School of Music, New York, N.Y.

Julian   John Julian, *A Dictionary of Hymnology* (London and New York, N.Y., 1892); NYPL.

KA   Badische Landesbibliothek, Karlsruhe, Germany.

Kane   Henry Kane, *How to Write a Song* (New York, N.Y., 1962); NYPL.

Kastner   Emerich Kastner, *Wagner-Catalog* (Offenbach a. M., 1878); NYPL.

KC   King's College, Cambridge.

KCPL   Kansas City Public Library, Kansas City, Mo.

KH   Konzerthausgesellschaft, Vienna.

Kidson, *Minstrelsy of England*	Alfred Moffat and Frank Kidson, *The Minstrelsy of England* (London, 1901); NYPL.
King, *Collectors*	A. Hyatt King, *Some British Collectors of Music* (Cambridge, 1963); BM.
Kinsky-Halm	Georg Kinsky and Hans Halm, *Das Werk Beethovens* (Munich, 1955); NYPL.
Kinsky, *Opern*	Georg Kinsky, "Berühmte Opern, Ihre Handschriften und Erstdrücke" in *Philobiblon*, Vienna, 1935, p. 363; *ULS*, p. 2196.
† Köchel	Dr. Ludwig Ritter von Köchel, *Chronologischthematisches Verzeichnis Sämtlicher Tonwerke Wolfgang Amadé Mozarts* (6th ed., edited by Franz Giegling, Alexander Weinmann and Gerd Sievers, Wiesbaden, 1964); LC.
KRS	Mrs. K. Ray Spencer Estate, c/o K. Ray Spencer, Helotes, Texas. Collection now at Baylor University Library, Waco, Texas.
† KSHS	Kansas State Historical Society, Topeka, Kansas.
KT	Kirov Theater, Leningrad.
KU	Universitäts- und Stadtbibliothek, Cologne.
Larousse XX	*Larousse du XXe Siècle* (Paris [1953–1955]); NYPL.
LaRue, *Watermarks*	Jan LaRue, "Watermarks and Musicology" in *Acta Musicologica*, Basel, 1961/II–IV, p. [120]; *ULS*, p. 35.
Laws	G. Malcolm Laws, Jr., *Native American Balladry* (Philadelphia, 1964); NYPL.
LBH	Bibliothek der Hansestadt, Lübeck, Germany.
LC	Library of Congress, Washington.
LCP	Library Company of Philadelphia, Philadelphia.
Legman	G. Legman, *The Horn Book* (New Hyde Park, N.Y., 1964); LC.
Lengfeld †	M. Lengfeld'sche Buchhandlung, *Catalogue 37* (Cologne, 1930); NYPL.
Liepmannssohn, *Katalog 233*	Leo Liepmannssohn, *Katalog 233* (Berlin, n.d.), 2. Teil; LC and JF.
LIHS	Long Island Historical Society, Brooklyn, N.Y.
Liszt Verzeichnis	*Thematisches Verzeichnis der Werke von F. Liszt* (Leipzig, 1855); NYPL.
LL	Lester S. Levy, Pikesville, Md. Collection now mostly at The Johns Hopkins University, Baltimore.

LLD	Lippische Landesbibliothek, Detmold, Germany.
LLM	Lenin Library, Moscow.
LML	Music Library, Central Library, Leeds, England.
LMU	Lincoln Memorial University, Harrogate, Tenn.
Loewenberg	Alfred Loewenberg, *Annals of Opera* (Geneva, 1955); NYPL.
Lomax, *North America*	Alan Lomax, *The Folk Songs of North America* (New York, N.Y., 1960); NYPL.
LPL	Leningrad Philharmonic Library, Leningrad.
LS	Landesbibliothek, Schwerin, Germany.
LTL	Lunacharsky Theatrical Library, Leningrad.
LUC	Library, Union of Soviet Composers, Moscow.
m.	Music.
MA	*Musical America* (New York, N.Y., 1898—); *ULS*, p. 1841.
MacArdle, *First Editions*	Donald W. MacArdle, "First Editions of Beethoven Published in England" in *The Monthly Musical Record*, London, Nov.–Dec. 1960, p. 228; *ULS*, p. 1806.
Macmillan Encyclopedia	Albert E. Weir, editor, *The Macmillan Encyclopedia of Music and Musicians* (New York, N.Y., 1938); NYPL.
MAP	Alfred Mapleson & Son, New York, N.Y.
Mattfeld	Julius Mattfeld, *Variety Music Cavalcade* (New York, N.Y., 1952); NYPL.
Mayer-Serra	Otto Mayer-Serra, *Música y Músicos de Latino-américa* (Mexico, 1947); NYPL.
MBC	Biblioteca del Conservatorio, Madrid.
MBM	Biblioteca Municipal, Madrid.
MC	Moscow Conservatory, Moscow.
MCNY	Museum of the City of New York.
MCO	*Musical Courier* (Philadelphia, New York, N.Y., and Evanston, 1880–1962); *ULS*, p. 1842.
MED	Morris E. Dry, New York, N.Y.
Le Ménestrel	*Le Ménestrel* (Paris, 1833–1940); *ULS*, p. 1709.
Mercure de France	*Mercure de France*—title varies (Paris, 1692–1820); *ULS*, p. 1713.

MET	Metropolitan Opera, New York, N.Y.
Metcalf	Frank Metcalf, *Stories of Hymn Tunes* (New York, N.Y., 1928); NYPL.
Meyers	*Meyers Lexikon* (8th ed., Leipzig 1936–1942); NYPL.
Meysel	[Karl Friedrich Whistling,] *Handbuch der Musikalischen Literatur* (Anton Meysel, Leipzig, 1817); NYPL.
MG	McGill University, Montreal.
MGG	*Die Musik in Geschichte und Gegenwart* (Kassel and Basel, 1949—); NYPL.
MHS	Maryland Historical Society, Baltimore.
MIC	Biblioteca del Conservatorio Giuseppe Verdi, Milan.
MIT	Massachusetts Institute of Technology, Cambridge, Mass.
ML	Mitchell Library, Glasgow.
MLS	Mitchell Library, Sydney, Australia.
MM	*Musica e Musicisti* (Milan, 1903–1905); *ULS*, p. 331.
MO	*Musical Opinion & Music Trade Review*—title varies (London, 1877—); *ULS*, p. 1843.
Moffat, *Minstrelsy of Ireland*	Alfred Moffat, *The Minstrelsy of Ireland* (London, 1897); NYPL.
Moffat, *Minstrelsy of Scotland*	Alfred Moffat, *The Minstrelsy of Scotland* (2nd ed., London, 1896); NYPL.
Mott	Margaret M. Mott, "A Bibliography of Song Sheets; Sports and Recreations in American Popular Songs," Part II, in *Notes*, Sept., 1950, p. 522.
MQ	*The Musical Quarterly* (New York, N.Y., 1915—); *ULS*, p. 1843.
MS	Museum Steyr, Steyr, Austria.
MSU	Musikwissenschaftliches Seminar der Universität, Heidelberg.
MT	*The Musical Times* (London, 1844—); *ULS*, p. 1844.
Mueller von Asow	Erich H. Mueller von Asow, *Richard Strauss, Thematisches Verzeichnis* (Vienna, 1959—); NYPL.
Muir	Percy H. Muir, "Thomas Moore's Irish Melodies 1808–1834" in *The Colophon*, Part XV (New York, N.Y., 1933), no page number; *ULS*, p. 726.
Müller-Reuter	Theodor Müller-Reuter, *Lexikon der Deutschen Konzertliteratur* (Leipzig, 1909); NYPL.

MW	*The Musical World* (London, 1836–1891); *ULS*, p. 1844.
mw.	Music and words.
NC	Newberry Library, Chicago.
NCL	National Central Library, London.
n.d.	No date.
NEC	New England Conservatory of Music, Boston.
NEDL	New England Deposit Library, Allston, Mass.
Nestyev	Israel V. Nestyev, *Prokofiev* (Stanford, Cal., 1960); NYPL.
Nettel	Reginald Nettel, *Seven Centuries of Popular Song* (London, 1956); NYPL.
Nettl, *National Anthems*	Paul Nettl, *National Anthems* (New York, N.Y., 1952); NYPL.
Newell	William Wells Newell, *Games and Songs of American Children* (New York, N.Y., 1883); LC.
New York Herald Tribune	*New York Herald Tribune* (New York, N.Y., 1924—); NYPL.
The New York Times	*The New York Times*—title varies (New York, N.Y., 1851—).
New York Tribune	*New York Tribune* (New York, 1841–1924); New York Herald Tribune, New York, N.Y.
Nicoll	Allardyce Nicoll, *A History of English Drama 1660–1900* (Cambridge, 1952–1959); NYPL.
NIE	*The New International Encyclopaedia* (2nd ed., New York, N.Y., 1925); NYPL.
Niecks	Frederick Niecks, *Frederick Chopin* (London, 3rd ed. [1902]); NYPL.
NLI	National Library of Ireland, Dublin.
NLO	National Library, Ottawa.
NLS	National Library of Scotland, Edinburgh.
NLW	National Library of Wales, Aberystwyth, Cardiganshire.
NMC	National Museum of Canada, Ottawa.
NML	Nanki Music Library, c/o Kyubei Oki, Odawara, Japan.
NMP	National Museum, Prague.

NOPL	New Orleans Public Library, New Orleans, La.
North Carolina F.	The Frank C. Brown Collection of North Carolina Folklore (Durham, N.C. [1952]–1962); NYPL.
Notes	(Music Library Association) Notes (Washington, 1934—); ULS, p. 1840.
n.p.	No place.
N.S.	New Style, as fixed by the Gregorian calendar. See O.S.
NU	Norwich University, Northfield, Vt.
NW	Northwestern University, Evanston, Ill.
NYDM	New York Dramatic Mirror (New York, N.Y., 1889–1917); ULS, p. 886.
NYHS	New-York Historical Society, New York, N.Y.
NYPL	New York Public Library, New York, N.Y.
NYPS	The New York Philharmonic-Symphony Society.
OBC	Oxford Book of Carols (London, 1928); NYPL.
ÖBL	Österreichisches Biographisches Lexikon 1815–1950 (Graz, 1957—); NYPL.
OCM	Percy A. Scholes, The Oxford Companion to Music (9th ed., London, 1955).
Odell	George C. D. Odell, Annals of the New York Stage (New York, N.Y., 1927–1949); NYPL.
Oldman, First Editions	Cecil B. Oldman, "Collecting Musical First Editions" in New Paths in Book Collecting, edited by John Carter (London, 1934), p. 95; YU.
Oldman, Watermark	Cecil B. Oldman, "Watermark Dates in English Paper" in The Library, London, June–Sept., 1944, p. 70; ULS, p. 1576.
OM	Openbare Muziekbibliotheek, 's-Gravenhage, Holland.
ONB	Österreichische Nationalbibliothek, Vienna.
O'Neill, Irish Dance	Capt. Francis O'Neill, The Dance Music of Ireland (Chicago, 1907); NYPL.
O'Neill, Irish Folk	Francis O'Neill, Irish Folk Music (Chicago, 1910); NYPL.
O'Neill, Waifs	Capt. Francis O'Neill, Waifs and Strays of Gaelic Melody (Chicago, 1922); HU.

O'Neill's Music	O'Neill's Music of Ireland, collected by Capt. Francis O'Neill (Chicago, 1903); NYPL.
op.	Opus.
Opera or operetta cover	See, Show cover.
Opie	Iona and Peter Opie, The Oxford Dictionary of Nursery Rhymes (Oxford, 1951); NYPL.
Orchestral parts	Orchesterstimmen—Parties d'Orchestre—Parti Staccate.
Orchestral score	Partitur—Partition d'Orchestre—Partitura.
O.S.	Old Style, before the adoption of the Gregorian calendar.*
OSK	Országos Széchényi Könyvtár, Budapest.
O'Sullivan, Songs of the Irish	Donal O'Sullivan, Songs of the Irish (Dublin, 1960); NYPL.
Ozark	Vance Randolph, Ozark Folksongs (Columbia, Mo., 1946–1950); NYPL.
p.	Page.
Parker	John Parker, Who's Who in the Theatre (6th and 13th eds., New York, N.Y., 1916 and 1961); NYPL.
Parry	K. L. Parry, Companion to Congregational Praise (London, 1953); NYPL.
Partridge	R. C. B. Partridge, The History of the Legal Deposit of Books Throughout the British Empire (London, 1938); ML.
PAU	Pan American Union, Washington.
Pazdírek	Franz Pazdírek, Universal-Handbuch der Musikliteratur Aller Zeiten und Völker (Vienna [1904–1910]); NYPL.
PBA	Prague Broadcasting Archives, Prague.
Perrow	E. C. Perrow, "Songs and Rhymes from the South" in JAF, April–June, 1915, p. 178.
PHS	Historical Society of Pennsylvania, Philadelphia.
Piano score	Klavierauszug—Partition piano—Spartito per pianoforte solo. Even in the case of an opera or musical play, words are not included.

* As Russia did not adopt the Gregorian calendar until 1918, nineteenth-century Russian dates by the old Julian calendar were twelve days behind the dates by the Gregorian calendar.

Piano score with underlying text	Klavierauszug mit unterlegtem (or beigefügtem) Text. A piano score in which the piano always plays the melody. Usually German or Austrian. Words are also included.
Piano-vocal score	Klavierauszug mit Text (frequently, Klavierauszug) —Partition chant et piano—Spartito per canto e pianoforte.
PM	Peabody Institute, Baltimore, Md.
PMI	Pierpont Morgan Library, New York, N.Y.
PMU	Percy Muir, Bishop's Stortford, Herts, England.
p.n.	Plate number (at the bottom of the music pages)— Plattennummer—Cotage (Nombre de planche)— Numero di lastra.
p.ns.	Plate numbers.
pp.	Pages.
Professional edition	A private edition usually issued on cheap paper free to persons in the music industry.
Prokofiev, *Autobiography*	S. Prokofiev, *Autobiography, Articles and Reminiscences* (Moscow [195—]); NYPL.
PRS	The Performing Right Society, Limited, London.
PUL	Princeton University, Princeton, N.J.
Pulling	Christopher Pulling, *They Were Singing* (London, 1952); NYPL.
PUS	Pushkin House, U.S.S.R. Academy of Sciences, Institute of Russian Literature. Leningrad.
RA	Reginald Allen, New York, N.Y. His collection is now largely at PML.
Raabe	Peter Raabe, *Franz Liszt* (Stuttgart and Berlin, 1931); NYPL.
Radiciotti	Giuseppe Radiciotti, *Gioacchino Rossini* (Tivoli, 1927–1929); NYPL.
RAM	Royal Academy of Music, London.
RBW	Emilie & Karl Riemenschneider Memorial Bach Library, Baldwin-Wallace College, Berea, Ohio.
RCM	Royal College of Music, London.
RCS	Mrs. Ruth C. Steinkraus Cohen, Westport, Conn.
RE	Rudolf Elvers, West Berlin.
Reddall	Henry Frederic Reddall, *Songs That Never Die* (Philadelphia, 1892); LC.
RG	Registro General de la Propiedad Intelectual, 20 Avenida de Calvo Sotelo, Madrid 1.

RGM	Revue et Gazette Musicale (Paris, 1835–1880); ULS, p. 2400.
RIA	Royal Irish Academy, Dublin.
Riemann	Riemann Musik Lexikon, edited by Wilibald Gurlitt (Mainz, 1959–1961); NYPL.
Riemenschneider	Sylvia W. Kenney, Catalog of the Emilie and Karl Riemenschneider Bach Library (New York, N.Y., 1960); NYPL.
Rimsky-Korsakov, My Musical Life	N. A. Rimsky-Korsakoff, My Musical Life (New York, N.Y., 1923); NYPL.
RISM	Répertoire International des Sources Musicales, vol. I (Munich, 1960); NYPL.
RM	Revue Musicale (Paris, 1827–1835); ULS, p. 2408.
RMG	(Russian Musical Gazette) Русская Музыкáльная Газета (St. Petersburg, 1894–1916); NYPL.
RML	Royal Music Library, British Museum, London.
Robbins Landon	H. C. Robbins Landon, The Symphonies of Joseph Haydn (London, 1955); NYPL.
Robbins Landon, Supplement	H. C. Robbins Landon, Supplement to the Symphonies of Joseph Haydn (New York, N.Y., 1961); NYPL.
Rogers	Charles Rogers, The Modern Scottish Minstrel (Edinburgh, 1855); NLS and LC.
ROH	Royal Opera House, London.
Rosenthal	Albi Rosenthal, "The 'Music Antiquarian'" in Fontes Artis Musicae, Paris, 1958, vol. 2, p. 80; NYPL.
Routley	Erik Routley, The English Carol (London, 1958); NYPL.
RU	Rutgers University, New Brunswick, N.J.
Rubinstein Catalogue	Catalog der im Druck Erschienenen Compositionen von Anton Rubinstein (Leipzig, 1868); NYPL.
Rudin	Cecilia Margaret Rudin, Stories of Hymns We Love (Chicago, 1934); NYPL.
s.	Musical show.
SA	Benedictine monastery, Seitenstetten, Lower Austria.
Saboly	Nicolas Saboly, Recueil de Noëls Provençaux (new ed., Avignon, 1824); NYPL.
SAC	Statní Archiv Český, Krumlov, Czechoslovakia.

SACEM	Société des Auteurs, Compositeurs et Éditeurs de Musique, Paris.
SADAIC	Sociedad Argentina de Autores y Compositores de Música, Buenos Aires.
Saint-Saëns Catalogue	Catalogue Générale et Thématique des Oeuvres de C. Saint-Saëns (Paris, 1897); NYPL.
Sandburg	Carl Sandburg, The American Songbag (New York, N.Y., 1927); NYPL.
Sandved	K. B. Sandved, The World of Music (London, 1954); NYPL.
Sartori	Claudio Sartori, Dizionario degli Editori Musicali Italiani (Florence, 1958); NYPL.
SB	Stadtbibliothek, Vienna.
SBB	Staatsbibliothek, Bremen.
SBW	Staatsbibliothek, West Berlin.
SC	Stanford University, Stanford, Cal.
Scarborough	Dorothy Scarborough, On the Trail of Negro Folk-Songs (Cambridge, Mass., 1925); LC.
SCH	Landesbibliothek, Schwerin, Germany.
Schmieder	Wolfgang Schmieder, Thematisch-Systematisches Verzeichnis der Musikalischen Werke von Johann Sebastian Bach (Leipzig, 1950); NYPL.
Schneider †	Max Schneider, Verzeichnis der bis zum Jahre 1851 Gedruckten . . . Werke von Johann Sebastian Bach in Bach-Jahrbuch (Berlin, 1906), p. [84]; NYPL.
SCR	Biblioteca S. Cecilia (Conservatorio), Rome.
Searle	Humphrey Searle, The Music of Liszt (London, 1954); NYPL.
sec.	Section.
SF	San Francisco Public Library, San Francisco.
SGAE	Sociedad General de Autores de España, Madrid.
SH	Robert-Schumann-Haus, Zwickau, Germany.
Sharp, English Folk-Carols	Cecil J. Sharp, English Folk-Carols (London, 1911); NYPL.
Sharp, English Folk-Chanteys	Cecil J. Sharp, English Folk-Chanteys (London, 1914); NYPL.
Sharp, Nursery Songs	Cecil J. Sharp, Nursery Songs from the Appalachian Mountains (London, 1921); NYPL.

Sharp, *Southern Appalachians*   Cecil J. Sharp, *English Folk Songs from the Southern Appalachians* (2nd ed., London, 1932); NYPL.

Show cover   A show cover has a uniform front cover for all titles from the musical show; it features the show and lists the individual titles from the show then published or to be published.

Sibelius Catalogue   Lauri Solanterä, *The Works of Jean Sibelius* (Helsinki, 1955); NYPL.

Signale   *Die Signale für die Musikalische Welt* (Leipzig, 1843–1941); *ULS*, p. 2545.

Silber   Irwin Silber, *Songs of the Civil War* (New York, N.Y., 1960); NYPL.

Simpson   Harold Simpson, *A Century of Ballads* (London, 1910); NYPL.

Simpson, *British Ballad*   Claude M. Simpson, *The British Broadside Ballad* (New Brunswick, N.J., 1966); NYPL.

SL   Schweizerische Landesbibliothek, Berne.

SLD   Sächsische Landesbibliothek, Dresden.

SLPL   St. Louis Public Library, St. Louis, Mo.

SM   St. Michael's College, Tenbury Wells, Worcestershire.

Smith, *Handel*   William C. Smith, *Handel, A Descriptive Catalogue of the Early Editions* (London, 1960); NYPL.

Smith, *Music of the Waters*   Laura Alexandrine Smith, *The Music of the Waters* (London, 1888); NYPL.

SMP   Smetana Museum, Prague.

SN   Státní Nakladatelství Krásné Literatury, Hudby a Umění, Prague.

SNM   Schiller-Nationalmuseum, Marbach am Neckar, Germany.

Songs of the Gilded Age   Margaret Bradford, *Songs of the Gilded Age* (New York, N.Y., 1960); NYPL.

Sonneck, *Dramatic Music*   Oscar George Theodore Sonneck, *Dramatic Music* (Washington, 1908); LC.

Sonneck, *Orchestral Music*   Oscar George Theodore Sonneck, *Orchestral Music Catalogue* (Washington, 1912); LC.

Sonneck, *Report*   Oscar George Theodore Sonneck, *Report on "The Star-Spangled Banner," "Hail Columbia," "America"* [and] *"Yankee Doodle"* (Washington, 1909); LC.

Sonneck-Upton   Oscar George Theodore Sonneck and William Treat Upton, *A Bibliography of Early Secular American Music* (Washington, 1945); LC.

Šourek	Otakar Šourek, *Dvořák's Werke* (Berlin, 1917); NYPL.
Spaeth	Sigmund Spaeth, *A History of Popular Music in America* (New York, N.Y., 1948); NYPL.
Sparling	H. Halliday Sparling, *Irish Minstrelsy* (3rd ed. revised, London [1893?]); NYPL.
SS	Saul Starr Estate, Eastchester, N.Y. Collection now at IU.
SSL	M. E. Saltykov-Shchedrin State Public Library, Leningrad.
Steger-Howe	Hellmuth Steger and Karl Howe, *Operettenführer* (Frankfurt, 1958); LC.
Stenhouse	William Stenhouse, *Illustrations of the Lyric Poetry and Music of Scotland* (Edinburgh, 1853); NYPL.
Stevenson	Robert Stevenson, *Music in Mexico* (New York, N.Y., 1952); NYPL.
STR	Bibliothèque Nationale et Universitaire, Strasbourg.
Strecker	Ludwig Strecker, *Richard Wagner als Verlagsgefährte* (Mainz, 1951); NYPL.
SU	Sutro Library, California State Library, San Francisco.
SUB	Stadt- und Universitätsbibliothek, Frankfurt.
SUH	Staats- und Universitätsbibliothek, Hamburg.
Sullivan-Flower	Herbert Sullivan and Newman Flower, *Sir Arthur Sullivan* (New York, N.Y., 1927); NYPL.
Supp.	Supplement.
SV	Svenskt Visarkiv, Stockholm.
SW	Stadtbibliothek, Winterthur, Switzerland.
SY	Syracuse University, Syracuse, N.Y.
Sydow	Bronislaw Edward Sydow, *Bibliografia F. F. Chopina* (Warsaw, 1949); NYPL.
TC	Trinity College, Dublin.
Tchaikovsky Catalogue	*Catalogue Thématique des Oeuvres de P. Tschaïkowsky*, edited by B. Jurgenson (Moscow, 1897); LC. The dates stated are the dates of composition (p. [2]).
Tchaikovsky Letters	Modeste Tchaikovsky, *The Life & Letters of Peter Ilich Tchaikovsky* (London, 1906); NYPL.
Teige	K. Teige, *Skladby Smetanovy* (Prague, 1893); LC.

Thompson	Oscar Thompson, *The International Cyclopedia of Music and Musicians*, edited by Nicolas Slonimsky (7th ed., New York, N.Y., 1956); NYPL.
TL	Tulane University, New Orleans, La.
TLW	Thüringische Landesbibliothek, Weimar.
TM	Tchaikovsky Museum, Klin, near Moscow.
Tozer	Ferris Tozer and Frederick J. Davis, *Sailors' Songs, or "Chanties"* (3rd ed., London, n.d.); LC.
TPL	Toronto Public Library, Toronto.
TU	Texas University, Austin, Tex.
TWS	Thomas W. Streeter, Morristown, N.J.
Tyson	Alan Tyson, *The Authentic English Editions of Beethoven* (London, 1963); BM.
UC	University of California, Berkeley, Cal.
UCH	University of Chicago, Chicago.
UDP	Ufficio della Proprietà Letteraria Artistica e Scientifica, Presidenza del Consiglio dei Ministri, 15 Via Boncompagni, Rome.
UEB	Universitätsbibliothek, East Berlin.
UI	University of Illinois, Urbana, Ill.
UIB	University of Illinois Bands, Urbana, Ill.
UL	University Library, Helsinki.
ULH	Universitäts- und Landesbibliothek Sachsen-Anhalt, Halle, Saale, Germany.
ULK	University of Louisville, Louisville, Ky.
ULO	University of London, London.
ULS	*Union List of Serials* (New York, N.Y., 1943).
UM	University of Michigan, Ann Arbor, Mich.
UMA	University of Maine, Orono, Me.
UMI	University of Minnesota, Minneapolis, Minn.
UNC	University of North Carolina, Chapel Hill, N.C.
UP	University of Pennsylvania, Philadelphia.
USMC	United States Marine Corps, Washington.
UT	University of Toronto, Toronto.
UTS	Union Theological Seminary, New York, N.Y.

UW	Universität Wien, Vienna.
Vallas	Léon Vallas, *Claude Debussy: His Life and Works* (London, 1933); NYPL.
Variety	*Variety* (New York, N.Y., 1905—); *ULS*, p. 2854.
vb.	Verso blank (i.e., the reverse of the previously mentioned page is blank).
vol.	Volume.
Wagner Letters	*Letters of Richard Wagner*, edited by Wilhelm Altmann (London, 1927); NYPL.
Waters, *Herbert*	Edward N. Waters, *Victor Herbert* (New York, N.Y., 1955); LC.
WCS	William C. Smith, Chislehurst, England.
WDBM	Westdeutsche Bibliothek (Staatsbibliothek), Marburg/Lahn, Germany.
Weil, *Copyright*	Arthur W. Weil, *American Copyright Law* (Chicago, 1917); NYPL.
Weinmann, *Strauss*	Alexander Weinmann, *Verzeichnis Sämtlicher Werke von Johann Strauss Vater und Sohn* (Vienna [1956]); NYPL.
Westrup-Harrison	J. A. Westrup and F. Ll. Harrison, *Collins Music Encyclopedia* (London and Glasgow, 1959); NYPL.
WH	The White House, Washington.
Whall	W. B. Whall, *Ships, Sea Songs and Shanties* (Glasgow, 1910); NYPL.
Whistling	C. F. Whistling, *Handbuch der Musikalischen Literatur* (Leipzig, 1828); NYPL.
Whistling, *Musikalischer Monatsanzeiger*	F. Whistling, *Musikalischer Monatsanzeiger*, Leipzig. The complete years of publication are not known, but 1840 is at ONB and 1841–1844 are at SBW.
White	William Carter White, *A History of Military Music in America* (New York, N.Y., 1944); NYPL.
White and Dean-Smith	Rev. E. A. White and Margaret Dean-Smith, *An Index of English Songs* . . . (London, 1951); NYPL.
Whittlesey-Sonneck	Walter R. Whittlesey and O. G. Sonneck, *Catalogue of First Editions of Stephen C. Foster* (Washington, 1915); LC.
WHS	Wisconsin Historical Society, Madison, Wis.
Wickes	E. M. Wickes, *True Stories of Famous Songs* (New York, N.Y. [1930]); BE.

WLS	Württembergische Landesbibliothek, Stuttgart.
WNH	W. N. H. Harding, Chicago, at BOD.
Wolfe	Richard J. Wolfe, *Secular Music in America 1801– 1825; A Bibliography* (New York, N.Y., 1964); NYPL.
Wolffheim	*Versteigerung der Musikbibliothek des Herrn Dr. Werner Wolffheim* (Berlin, 1928–1929); NYPL. This copy indicates the purchaser and price of each item.
WP	Wiener Philharmoniker Verein, Vienna.
WU	Wesleyan University, Middletown, Conn.
YU	Yale University, New Haven, Conn.
ZZ	Zentralbibliothek, Zurich.

SELECTION OF TITLES

Tremendous effort has been made to find out, as objectively as possible, what melodies are widely known today. Songbooks published throughout the world, record catalogues, concert and light concert programs and published lists were studied, and persons from many different countries were questioned.

However, one's background and personal preferences inevitably play an important role, and the final selection will, of course, be largely subjective.[1] No list will please everyone, and the omission of many titles will be regretted. It is easy to think of other well-known melodies. Nonetheless, it is hoped that the melodies which have been included will be generally recognized as *a fair sampling* of well-known melodies—melodies which are frequently hummed or whistled.

The list of titles should be balanced and representative—classical, popular and folk music of all kinds and from a great many countries should be included. Many different composers must be represented, and their relative importance substantially maintained; an attempt has been made to avoid favoritism toward American music. More old than recent compositions have been included—as Brahms said, "A piece of music that is still alive after fifty years is immortal."

---

[1] Every encyclopedia or reference book—from the *Britannica* to *Grove's*—must be subjective in large part as to what items to include.

WELL-KNOWN MUSIC BY WOMEN COMPOSERS

In the light of the Women's Liberation Movement, it is interesting to note that, although there has been no major feminine classical composer to date,[1] the following well-known lighter music in this book was composed by women:

Lady John Scott, *Annie Laurie*
Euphemia Allen, *Chopsticks*
Charlotte Barnard, *Come Back to Erin*
Mildred J. Hill, *Happy Birthday to You*
Carrie Jacobs-Bond, *I Love You Truly* and
     A Perfect Day
Annie Fortescue Harrison, *In the Gloaming*
Amy Woodforde-Finden, *Kashmiri Song*
Cecile Chaminade, *Scarf Dance*
Nora Bayes-Norworth, *Shine On, Harvest Moon*
Maude Nugent, *Sweet Rosie O'Grady*
Marie Cowan (maybe), *Waltzing Matilda*
Lady Caroline Nairne
 or Elizabeth Rainforth, *Wi' a Hundred Pipers*

WELL-KNOWN MUSIC FROM SMALLER COUNTRIES

Although most of the music included in this book is understandably from the "music-producing" countries, much well-known music is from other smaller countries, as the following list shows:

Argentina	Several, e.g., *El Choclo*
Australia	*Waltzing Matilda*
Canada	*Alouette*
China (Red)	*The East Is Red*
Cuba	Several, e.g., *Andalucia*
Czechoslovakia	Several, e.g., *The Bartered Bride-Overture*
Denmark	*Jealousy*
Finland	Several, e.g., *Finlandia*
Greece	*Never on Sunday*
Hawaii (before becoming part of the United States)	*Aloha Oe*

[1] Pauline Oliveros, "And Don't Call Them 'Lady' Composers," in *The New York Times*, Sept. 13, 1970, sec. 2, p. 23.

Holland	[We Gather Together]
Hungary	Several, e.g., Rakoczy March
Mexico	Several, e.g., La Cucaracha
Norway	Several, e.g., Peer Gynt
Portugal	April in Portugal
Rumania	Rumanian Rhapsody
Spain	Several, e.g., La Paloma
Sweden	[Good King Wenceslas]
Switzerland	Several, e.g., Yodel Call
West Indies	Rum and Coca-Cola

WIDE DISPERSAL OF MUSIC PUBLISHING IN THE UNITED STATES

In Great Britain, most music publishers have been in London.[1] In France, most music publishers have been in Paris. In Austria, most music publishers have been in Vienna. In Italy and Russia, music publishing was generally concentrated in a few cities. In Germany, which was not unified until 1871, important music publishing was distributed among a somewhat larger number of cities.[1]

By way of contrast, music publishing in the United States has been widely dispersed, a fact apparently not previously noted. Whatever may have been the reasons, the tendency was strong even before 1800 and has increased since then.[2] One would expect to find music publishers active in Baltimore, Boston, Chicago, New York City and Philadelphia. However, it is interesting to note that the following important American compositions studied in this book were first published in the following additional cities:

Albion, Mich.	The Sweetheart of Sigma Chi
Austin, Texas	The Eyes of Texas
Beverly Hills	Around the World
Buffalo	Arkansas Traveler
Cambridge, Mass.	The Dutch Company; My Bonnie Lies over the Ocean; Polly-Wolly-Doodle; There Is a Tavern in the Town.

---

[1] Humphries-Smith, p. 347. Hopkinson, Parisian, p. 129. Sartori, Hopkinson, Russian, and Deutsch, Plate Numbers, passim.

[2] Sonneck-Upton, p. 588; Wolfe, p. 1133; and Dichter-Shapiro, p. 165.

Charlestown, Mass.	*John Brown (Glory Hallelujah)*
Cincinnati	*Anchors Aweigh; Aura Lea (Love Me Tender); Say, Brothers, Will You Meet Us? (Glory Hallelujah); I'll Take You Home Again, Kathleen; Mighty Lak' a Rose; On the Road to Mandalay; When the Saints Go Marching In.*
Cleveland	*Nola; Oh, Bury Me Not on the Lone Prairie*
Detroit	*Oh, You Beautiful Doll; Till We Meet Again*
Fort Worth	*12th Street Rag*
Hollywood	*Deep in the Heart of Texas*
Honolulu	*Aloha Oe*
Indianapolis	*When You and I Were Young, Maggie*
Los Angeles	*Casey Jones; Trees*
Louisville	*Arkansas Traveller; Oh! Susanna* (authorized edition)
Memphis	*St. Louis Blues*
Milwaukee	*After the Ball; A Hot Time in the Old Town*
Nashville	*Swing Low, Sweet Chariot*
New Orleans	*Dixie; Three O'Clock in the Morning*
Newark	*I've Been Working on the Railroad*
Newburyport, Mass.	*Annie Lisle (Far Above Cayuga's Waters)*
Pittsburgh	*The Old Grey Mare*
St. Louis	*An Arizona Home (Home on the Range)*
San Francisco	*Sweet Betsey from Pike; Whispering*
Savannah	*Assembly; First Call*
Utica, N.Y.	*Rock of Ages*

NOTES ON CERTAIN COMPOSERS AND PUBLISHERS

The following bibliographic information has been obtained regarding a few composers and publishers which is believed not to be generally known and which may prove to be useful in other contexts.

V. BESSEL & CO.

This firm opened its Moscow branch in 1888.[1]

The firm's printing plant was at 26 Troitski Alley, St. Petersburg, until 1889. Thereafter, the plant was at 24 Troitski Street.[2]

[1] *Brief Sketches about the Activities of the Music Publishing Firm V. Bessel & Co.* (1894), p. 4; SSL.

[2] Letter from John H. Hind, Berkeley, Cal.

BOTE & BOCK

The address of this Berlin firm from 1838 to 1849 was 42 Jägerstr. From 1847 the firm had a branch at Breslau, since 1849 at Stettin, and since the 1850's at Posen. The main Berlin office from 1849 to Sept., 1873, was 27 Unter den Linden. From Oct., 1873, to 1943 its Berlin address was 37 Leipziger Str.[3]

CHOPIN

Maurice J. E. Brown's *Chopin* is a competent index of Chopin's French,[4] German and English editions. Although its descriptions of publications were not intended to describe first editions, they have led some dealers, and perhaps libraries and collectors, to describe their Chopin copies incorrectly. Brown mentions under "Publication" only the name of the publisher and the plate number (the year is also cited, but this does not appear on the printed music). Not mentioned are such critical information for the description of Chopin first editions as: distinguishing between the original music plates and changed music plates where both plates have the same plate number; stating whether the publication in that year was engraved or offset; stating the price in that year, the price frequently changing later; and, as to the English editions, stating the address of the publisher, and whether the publication in that year mentioned on the front cover only the particular work itself, or whether it had a collective title cover listing many works of Chopin, and if so, the latest work so listed.

GILBERT AND SULLIVAN

The dating of Gilbert and Sullivan piano-vocal scores is difficult solely on the basis of the imprint of their principal publisher, Chappell & Co., because it altered its name only once (adding "Ltd." on Dec. 7, 1896), and remained at one address, 50 New Bond Street, since 1856.[4A]Among other information useful in dating a particular copy is the fact that Chappell & Co. used a printer which conveniently changed its firm name and address frequently, and the following list is furnished primarily through the courtesy of William Reeves, London:

[3] Letter from Bote & Bock.

[4] Unfortunately, however, no examination was made by him of the basic Dépôt Légal records at the Archives in Paris, even in connection with Brown, *Corrections*. See also Brown's "Chopin and His English Publishers" in *Music & Letters* (London), Oct., 1958, p. 363; NYPL.

[4A]See also the date significance of the presence of London Postal Districts, p. 15 above.

Name	Address	Dates
Henderson, Rait & Fenton	23 Berners St.	1865–1872
Henderson, Rait & Fenton	69 Marylebone Lane	1874–July 1875
Henderson, Rait & Fenton	73, 74 Marylebone Lane	Aug. 1875–Aug. 14, 1880
Henderson, Rait & Fenton	3, 5 Marylebone Lane	Aug. 21–Nov. 20, 1880
Henderson & Rait	3, 5 Marylebone Lane	Nov. 27, 1880–Jan. 1881
Henderson, Rait & Fenton	3, 5 Marylebone Lane	Jan. 1881–June 1882
Henderson, Rait & Spalding	3, 5 Marylebone Lane	June 1882–1888
Henderson & Spalding	3, 5 Marylebone Lane	1888–1890
Henderson & Spalding, Ltd.	3, 5 Marylebone Lane	1893
Henderson & Spalding	3, 5 Marylebone Lane	1893–1894
Henderson & Spalding	1, 3, 5 Marylebone Lane	1894–1912

GRIEG—PETERS

Dan Fog of Copenhagen, who has made a study of Grieg first editions, advises that most of Grieg's early works from 1864–1880 were first published in Copenhagen by various publishers such as Chr. E. Horneman, C. C. Lose, and Horneman & Erslev; that these Copenhagen publishers were taken over by Wilhelm Hansen in 1875–1879; that later C. F. Peters began publishing Grieg's works; and that Hansen in 1889 sold Peters important rights to many of Grieg's works.

Determining the first edition of any Peters edition is an extremely difficult task as Peters uses to this day the same general format of front cover, title page, music pages and plate number as were used in the first printing. Even the publisher itself has been unable to advise how to distinguish early printings from later ones. The easiest case is when the copy being examined has its *original pink back cover*. Peters' back covers usually have, in the lower left-hand or right-hand corner, two numbers in very small type; these indicate the year the back cover was printed. Thus, "88" indicates 1888, "02" indicates 1902, etc., and the year of the copy being examined can then be compared with the year of original publication. New back covers were printed from time to time. These back covers also list other Peters Editions; the highest Peters Edition number so listed should not be much higher than the Peters Edition number of the particular work being examined, if the copy being examined is to be a first edition. (Incidentally, Peters Edition numbers should not be confused with plate numbers.) At times, the original pink back cover is blank; this is unfortunate.

Without the original pink back cover, the problem of dating a Peters Edition is more difficult. The following *internal* evidence has been discovered in copies that do have the original covers, and has been confirmed by the Bergen Offentlige Bibliotek, Bergen, Norway:

(a) C. F. Peters is shown at Berlin and Leipzig in the 1870's—at Leipzig only beginning March 31, 1880.[5]

(b) The colors of the title page were *brown*, black and white in the 1870's and 1880's; the brown changed to brownish-red in the 1890's, and to red in the 1900's.

(c) A footnote on the first music page to the engraver or lithographer, Röder, indicates the 1870's or 1880's. Footnote references on music pages to Peters Editions begin about 1890.

(d) Sometimes, examination of two different copies reveals other internal differences which may be helpful—fingering of piano pieces or metronome markings may have been added, for example.

JURGENSON

A bibliographic study of P. I. Jurgenson, Moscow, is needed. Hopkinson has written valuable notes on this publisher,[5A] and a brief history of the publisher is in *RMG*,[6] but it does not shed light on the problems considered here. Catalogues for a number of years have been found;[7] and no doubt others exist. Jurgenson began publishing in 1867.

The following information may be helpful in addition to that mentioned in Hopkinson: Jurgenson omitted his middle initial about 1871. From 1883–1894 his address was 10 Neglinnaya, Moscow; from 1898–1908 he was at 14 Neglinnaya. He usually did not show a street address before about 1900. He had a branch at 19 Thalstrasse, Leipzig, from 1898[8] to 1908. Sometime between 1895 and 1897 he began using the crown emblem, and the 1896 and 1900 prizes and dates are indicated on the title pages of many of his later printings. His most common French agent underwent a number of changes in the title of the firm which are helpful, namely, F. Mackar to 1889, F. Mackar & Noël from 1889–1895, and A. Noël after 1895. His Warsaw agent, G. Sennewald, was active to 1903, and his successor Warsaw agent, E. Wende & Co., was active 1905–1911; Idzikovski opened a branch office in Warsaw in 1911.[9] Jurgenson had two German agents, sometimes using one, sometimes the other: Rahter who was in Hamburg from 1879–1891 and who was in Leipzig commencing 1893[9A] and Robert Forberg who was active in Leipzig from 1862–1948;[8] when Forberg's address is 19 Thalstrasse, the printing is probably after 1900.

[5] Letter from VEB Edition Peters, Leipzig.
[5A] Hopkinson, *Russian*, p. 6.
[6] 1904, p. [385].
[7] 1883 and 1900 at MB; and 1889, 1897, 1902 and 1905 at NYPL.
[8] Letter, Deutsche Bucherei, Leipzig.
[9] Letters from BNA.
[9A] Rahter *Catalogues*; NYPL.

Following is plate number information regarding Jurgenson furnished for the first time. The information has been derived from Jurgenson catalogues, the Dombayev bibliography of Tchaikovsky (the exact title of which appears on page 40 above), a study from the Glinka Library, Moscow, plate number files at several libraries and other sources. It should be noted that the dates stated in the *Catalogue Thématique des Oeuvres de P. Tschaïkowsky* (Moscow, 1897), at LC, are the dates of composition, not the dates of publication (page [2]).

Jurgenson's plate numbers apparently were assigned on a reasonably regular ascending basis. In each case below, the highest plate number known for the year is given. The reason for the strange leap or gap in plate numbers in 1886 is not known.

Year	Highest Known Plate Number	Year	Highest Known Plate Number
1867	339	1892	17774
1868	602	1893	19010
1870	691	1894	19720
1871	1690	1896	20261
1872	1900	1897	20964
1873	2218	1898	22054
1874	2320	1899	24813
1875	2748	1900	25419
1876	2986	1901	26374
1878	3376	1902	27072
1879	3905	1903	28871
1880	4056	1904	30521
1881	4432	1905	31192
1882	5324	1906	31905
1883	5681	1907	32529
1884	6243	1908	33223
1885	6644	1910	34920
1886	6762 and 13379	1911	35911
1887	13639	1912	36586
1888	14128	1913	37289
1889	14676	1914	37949
1890	16054	1915	38840
1891	17437	1916	38911

PETERS—See GRIEG, above, at p. 65.

RICORDI

This firm commenced its publishing business in 1808 at 1108 Contrada S. Margherita; in 1809, it moved to 4068 Contrada di Pescaria Vecchia; in 1812, it moved to 1065 Contrada S. Margherita; in 1816, it moved to 1118

Contrada S. Margherita; in 1821, it moved to 1148 Contrada S. Margherita; in 1828, it moved to 1635 Via Ciovasso; from 1838 to at least 1860, it was at 1720 Contrada degli Omenoni; in 1867, it was at 1 Via Omenoni; in 1875, it was at 27, 29, 31 Galleria Vittorio Emanuele (and apparently also at 1 Via Omenoni) and was at the former address until Dec., 1888; it is also said that in 1884 it moved to 21 Viale di Porta Vittoria; in Jan., 1889, it moved to 9 S. Margherita; in 1910, it moved to Viale Campania; and in the same year it moved to 2 Via Berchet, its present address.[10]

The name of the firm changed over the years and was usually:

Gio. (or G. or Giovanni) Ricordi	1808—mid-1853[11]
Tito di Gio. Ricordi (rarely, Tito Ricordi)	mid-1853—1859
Apparently, either Tito di Gio. Ricordi, or	
R. Stabilimento Ricordi	1860—mid-1888[11A]
R. Stabilimento Tito di Gio. Ricordi	
e Francesco Lucca di G. Ricordi & C.	mid-1888—1897
G. Ricordi & C.	1898—

Its affiliates in Florence were in 1824, Ricordi e Grua, and the same year Ricordi, Pozzi e C.; in 1828, Ricordi e Compagno; 1840–1860, G. Ricordi e S. Jouhaud; and 1865–1871, Succursale Ricordi. In London, 1824–1828, were Grua e Ricordi, and in Naples, 1860, Ricordi e Clausetti.

Branch offices were opened in Naples in 1864, Rome in 1871, London in 1875,[10] Palermo and Paris in 1888, Lipsia (Leipzig) 1901, Buenos Aires 1904,[12] New York, N.Y., 1911, São Paulo 1927, Lörrach (a suburb of Basel) 1949, Genoa 1953, Toronto 1954, Sydney 1956 and Mexico City in 1958. †

Following is plate number information regarding Ricordi furnished for the first time. The information has been derived from dated Ricordi

---

[10] *Casa Ricordi*, pages 16 *et seq.* and a supplement therein without page number, augmented, and at times superseded, by information in Ricordi *Catalogues*, GMM, a Milan directory, and a letter from the Archivio di Stato, Milan (summarizing A.S.M. Atti di Governo-Commercio p.m. cart. 337).

From 1803–1808, Giovanni Ricordi was a music copyist and dealer in printed music and instruments; petition for License to Imperial Royal Government, dated Jan. 28, 1818, at Archivio di Stato, Milan.

[11] Giovanni Ricordi died March 15, 1853. The imprint is "Giovanni Ricordi" in the Ricordi *Supplement*, Milan, Jan.–April, 1853, and "Tito di Gio. Ricordi" in the May–July, 1853, issue; NYPL.

[11A] Ricordi bought the Lucca business on May 30, 1888; Sartori, p. 130. Tito Ricordi died on Sept. 7, 1888. See, generally, Hopkinson, *Puccini*.

[12] On title page of *Madama Butterfly* deposited at LC(CDC) on May 9, 1904, and thereafter. *Casa Ricordi*, supplement without page number, says that Ricordi had an agency in Buenos Aires until 1924, and opened a branch there only in that year, but this is incorrect. See, *e.g.*, the piano-vocal scores described in Hopkinson, *Puccini*, pp. 26 *et seq.*

Catalogues and *Supplements, La Gazzetta Musicale di Milano* (title changes in later years) published by Ricordi from 1842–1902, plate number files at Cecil Hopkinson, London, Richard Macnutt, Tunbridge Wells, Kent, and several libraries, data from the Frank V. de Bellis Collection at the San Francisco State College, and other sources. Heck has also suggested plate numbers for many years primarily on the basis of first performances of operas.† The Ricordi *Libroni*, described below, occasionally indicate an intended publication date, but usually show the date a work was assigned to the engraver. Although the highest plate number assigned for engraving in a year is, of course, higher than the highest plate number published during the year, the highest assigned plate number serves as a general confirmation of the highest published plate number.

Ricordi's plate numbers were assigned on a generally ascending basis, but the *Catalogues* and *Supplements* show many and wide exceptions. In each case below the *highest* known plate number published during the year is given. In 1890 there was a large jump in plate numbers.‡

Year	Highest Known Plate Number	Year	Highest Known Plate Number	Year	Highest Known Plate Number
1808	1	1840	12848	1870	42157
1811	100	1841	13375	1871	42477
1812	131	1842	14309	1872	42861
1813	150	1843	15902	1873	43628
1814	176	1844	16973	1874	44104
1815	200	1845	17957	1875	44359
1816	247	1846	19371	1876	44913
1817	300	1847	20235	1877	45640
1818	436	1848	21146	1878	46089
1819	652	1849	22271	1879	46755
1821	1116	1850	23053	1880	47140
1822	1418	1851	24012	1881	47816
1823	1802	1852	24880	1882	48477
1824	2138	1853	26131	1883	49036
1825	2347	1854	27780	1884	49554
1826	2777	1855	28568	1885	50361
1827	3310	1856	29234	1886	51072
1828	3987	1857	30180	1887	52297
1829	4235	1858	30833	1888	53376
1830	4835	1859	31287	1889	54178
1831	5288	1860	32826	1890	54989
1832	5911	1861	33822		and
1833	7331	1862	34843		94200
1834	7865	1864	36831	1891	94972
1835	9009	1865	39479	1892	95642
1836	9862	1866	40478	1893	96463
1837	10094	1867	40874	1894	97560
1838	10621	1868	41258	1895	98302
1839	11839	1869	41743	1896	100312

Year	Highest Known Plate Number	Year	Highest Known Plate Number	Year	Highest Known Plate Number
1897	100937	1904	110000	1911	114218
1898	102268	1905	111016	1912	114516
1899	103521	1906	111360	1913	114897
1900	103590	1907	112178	1914	115060
1901	104717	1908	112412	1915	115489
1902	107880	1909	113160	1916	116866
1903	108878	1910	113491		

The date of a Ricordi publication can thus be cross-checked in the five ways described above:

1. plate number;
2. name of firm;
3. address of firm;
4. cities in which branch offices were located; and
5. affiliates in other cities.

Ricordi has maintained from 1808 large manuscript books (or *Libroni*, as Ricordi refers to them) containing basic information about each composition published by the firm.†

RÖDER

C. G. Röder, Leipzig, changed its name to C. G. Röder G.m.b.H. in late 1904.[12A]

SIBELIUS

Sibelius' works seem to have been generally published in Finland and Germany without any consistent pattern as to simultaneous publication or priority. The copyright deposit copies in the Library of Congress and the British Museum are sometimes Finnish editions and sometimes German editions. The copyright deposit copies of different arrangements of the same work were occasionally published in different countries. The publishers themselves are not always clear on the point. The *Sibelius Catalogue* is useful, but in this respect not complete, and it did not concern itself with priority.

Sibelius' compositions had no opus numbers before 1904; and music published by Helsingfors Nya Musikhandel (Fazer & Westerlund) had no plate numbers before 1904.[13] The latter firm commenced publishing in 1898, became K. G. Fazer in 1904 and AB Fazers Musikhandel in 1919.[14]

[12A] Letter from present firm.
[13] Letter from UL.
[14] *Nordisk Leksikon for Bogvaesen* (Copenhagen, 1962), vol. 2, part 9, p. 109; UL.

SIMROCK

N. Simrock, Berlin, changed its name to N. Simrock, G.m.b.H., in 1901.[15]

TCHAIKOVSKY

The dates of Tchaikovsky's works stated in B. Jurgenson's *Tchaikovsky Catalogue* are the dates of composition, not the dates of publication (p. [2]).

MISCELLANEOUS

Limited imprint information regarding (a) Gade & Warny-Musikforlag, Copenhagen, appears below under *Jealousy,* (b) A. Iohansen, St. Petersburg, appears below under *Prelude in C Sharp Minor,* (c) G. Sennewald and E. Wende & Co., Warsaw, appears above under "Jurgenson," (d) Unión Musical Española, Madrid, appears below under *El Relicario,* and (e) A. Wagner y Levien, Mexico City, appears below under *Sobre las Olas.*

NOTE ON THE MUSICAL EXCERPTS

The music considered in this book is generally known, but the titles in many instances may not be familiar. This seems particularly true in the case of music by classical composers; persons who do not believe they know "any" classical music are constantly surprised when they learn that the music they immediately recognize is by Bach, Beethoven, Handel, Haydn, Liszt, Mendelssohn, Tchaikovsky, Wagner, etc.

The purpose of including the music is merely to suggest the main melody. It has been arranged as clearly as possible, on one staff. While the arrangements are believed sound, various slight liberties have been taken at times to make the arrangement as simple as possible to accomplish its limited objective.

It is not clear whether such a limited presentation of music, for this purpose, is subject to copyright laws. "Incipits" and excerpts of copyrighted music have been printed for years in this and other countries without copyright notice. Nonetheless, to avoid any question, permission has been requested from the copyright owners where the music is still protected by copyright in the United States. Appreciation is gratefully offered to the 65 publishers who granted permission; three did not consent.

[15] Letter from publisher.

SPECIAL MESSAGE TO MUSIC LIBRARIANS

The sad moral of this book is that it is frequently harder to locate first printings of important music from the eighteenth, nineteenth and twentieth centuries than of music from the sixteenth and seventeenth centuries.[1] The earlier material has been given special attention, carefully catalogued, listed in reference books, proudly exhibited, lovingly repaired and carefully placed on reserve shelves or in a rare book room. By way of contrast, first printings of the romantic masters, sometimes the only known copies, can frequently be borrowed from the library. The copies described in this book are scarce—they may well be the only existing copies. It is hoped that the libraries that own them, and other libraries discovering that they own copies of any of them, will take good care of them.

For example, the British Museum does not own a copy of the first printing of God Save the King. The Bibliothèque Nationale, Paris, does not own a copy of the first printing of La Marseillaise. The Library of Congress does not own a copy of the first printing of Dixie. And there is no known copy of the first edition of Beethoven's Symphony no.5 in Germany or Austria.

It seems astonishing, but it is believed true, that there is apparently nowhere in the world any known first printing of any of the major works listed below. This is indeed sad. If this book accomplishes nothing more, it will have been worth its effort if it helps persuade libraries to be on the alert for, and to preserve, first printings of the masters and the familiar music of the world.

Another unfortunate conclusion resulting from this search is that, as far as is known, there is no library anywhere in the world which has a large holding of first printings of orchestral parts of symphonies or operas since 1750 except, to some extent, the Royal Academy of Music, London, and the Library of The Musical Fund Society of Philadelphia at the Free Library of Philadelphia.

Until the early nineteenth century, orchestral parts of an instrumental work were published many years before the orchestral score. Until the early nineteenth century, there was no separate conductor of a symphony orchestra requiring an orchestral score;[2] the orchestra was led by the first violinist[2A] and/or the performer at the keyboard, one of whom was, for-

[1] See Hermann Baron, "The Music Antiquarian of Today" in Brio, London, Autumn, 1964, p. 4; BM.

[2] Harold C. Schonberg, The Great Conductors (New York, N.Y., 1967), p. 31; NYPL.

[2A] An example of a nineteenth-century operatic violin conductor's score, designated "Violino Principale," containing cues indicating when the other instruments begin to play, is discussed and illustrated in the author's "Nineteenth-Century Operatic Violin Conductors' Scores" in Notes, Dec., 1974, p. 278.

tunately, frequently the composer. As orchestras grew larger, and the music more complicated, a separate conductor became necessary and orchestral scores were required. Thus, after a period of uncertain pattern, commencing with about the middle of the nineteenth century, the orchestral parts and score of an instrumental work were generally published at about the same time.

The situation regarding the publication of orchestral scores and parts of operas and other choral music is different. Orchestral scores were generally published promptly. Occasionally, orchestral parts were published promptly. But in most cases manuscript orchestral parts were used for many decades; thus, no eighteenth-century printing of the orchestral parts of Handel's Messiah has been found although there were many early editions of the orchestral score.

As orchestral parts frequently either preceded the orchestral score, or were published at the same time as the score, the orchestral parts are of great musical interest and bibliographic value. Orchestral parts are understandably more difficult to handle and preserve than the orchestral score.[3] Nonetheless, to this outsider, the great musical libraries of the world should be willing to assume the responsibility of obtaining and preserving important editions of the orchestral parts of the classics of the masters.

Symphony orchestras, opera houses and ballet companies (and the Fleisher Collection at the Free Library of Philadelphia and commercial renters of orchestral parts to performing societies) have large holdings of orchestral parts. But, as far as is known, their attempt is mostly to have modern, frequently merely photocopied, editions; and these performing societies do not carefully preserve their holdings, or index them or make them generally available. It has also been a frequent practice for many years for performing societies illicitly to copy or photocopy orchestral parts. Orchestral parts of many works have apparently never been published and were available only in manuscript. Finally, the long-standing practice of publishers' renting, rather than selling, orchestral parts of many works has made it more difficult for libraries to acquire sets of orchestral parts.

Following are the principal works of which there is no known copy of the first printing. It would be appreciated if any music librarian, collector or dealer finding any of these would communicate with the author.

---

[3] Orchestral parts are also difficult to keep together before they are sold. About 1800, to keep the parts together, two small cuts seem to have been generally made near the left margin of each part, and string was inserted and tied. Most orchestral parts from this period reveal these two small cuts. A mint set of the first printing of the orchestral parts of Beethoven's Symphony no. 1 at the Library of Congress, Washington, D.C., apparently has the original string keeping the set together.

Composer	Title	Publisher

CLASSICAL MUSIC

J. S. Bach	*Sinfonie in D*	Sieber
Brahms	*Concerto for Piano no. 1*	Rieter-Biedermann
Chopin	*Nocturne, op. 9, no. 2*	Wessel, 6 Frith St.
Chopin	*Sonate, op. 35*	Troupenas
Debussy	*Rêverie*	Choudens
Dvořák	*Slavische Tänze, op. 46—Zweite Sammlung*	Simrock
Fučik	*Einzug der Gladiatoren*	Hoffmann's Wwe.
Mozart	*Le Nozze di Figaro, or Die Hochzeit des Figaro—K 492*	Imbault
Nicolai	*Die Lustigen Weiber von Windsor-Ouverture*	Bote & Bock
Rubinstein	*Deux Mélodies, op. 3*	Bernard, Cranz or Schreiber
Waldteufel	*Les Patineurs*	Durand Schoenewerk & Cie.
Weber	*Der Freischütz—Ouverture*	Schlesinger
Weber	*Oberon—Ouverture*	Schlesinger

POPULAR AND FOLK MUSIC, AND MISCELLANEOUS

Johann Brandl	*Du Alter Stefansturm*	Cranz
De Geyter	*L'Internationale*	Boldoduc
Thomas Dorsey	*When All the Saints Come Marching In*	Chicago Music Pub. Co.
(Ferdinand) Haas (Haase)	*Marsch aus Petersburg von Reg. Preobragensky*	Schlesinger
Léon Jessel	*Die Parade der Zinnsoldaten*	Heinrichshofen

Arrangement	Special	Title in This Book

CLASSICAL MUSIC

Arrangement	Special	Title in This Book
Orchestral Score		Air for the G String
Piano Part	No mention of orchestral parts	
Piano		
Piano	No reference to F. Benoit at bottom of p. 1	Funeral March
Piano		Rêverie
Piano Four Hands	Music pages engraved	
Orchestral Score		The Gladiators' Entry
Orchestral Score	p.n. 566	The Marriage of Figaro—Overture
Orchestral Score	No reference to Posen	The Merry Wives of Windsor—Overture
Piano		Mélodie in F
Orchestral Score		The Skaters
Piano	Price: 10 Gr.	
Orchestral Score	p.n. lower than 2944	

POPULAR AND FOLK MUSIC, AND MISCELLANEOUS

Arrangement	Special	Title in This Book
Orchestral Score or Parts		Viennese Popular Song
Sheet Music		
Sheet Music		When the Saints Go Marching In
Orchestral Score or Parts		Russian Czarist National Anthem
Piano or Orchestral Score	With less than 11 arrangements	The Parade of the Wooden Soldiers

Composer	Title	Publisher
C. W. K. (C. W. Kindleben)	*Studentenlieder*	
Alfred Margis	*Valse Bleue*	Salabert
Jean François Marmontel	*Quoi, Sans Vouloir Entendre*	
Manuel Ponce	*Dos Canciones Mexicanos*	Hofmeister
N. Serradell	*La Golondrina*	(Mexican)
Ferris Tozer and Frederick J. Davis	*Sailors' Songs, or "Chanties"*	
John Watlen	*Old Scots Songs,* 2nd Sett or 8th Number	
	Abdulla (or Abdallah) Bulbul Ameer	(Irish)
	The British Grenadiers	
	Brothers, Will You Meet Us	G. S. Scofield
	Cielito Lindo	(Mexican)
	Deutschlands Liederschatz	Michow
	Du, Du Liegst Mir im Herzen	Stock
	God Rest You Merry, Gentlemen	J. & C. Evans

Arrangement	Special	Title in this Book
Book		Gaudeamus Igitur
Piano	No reference to a later printing	
A Romance		For He's a Jolly Good Fellow
Piano		Estrellita
Sheet Music	Before 1883	
Book	2nd edition	Drunken Sailor
Booklet		Comin' Thro' the Rye
Sheet Music	Before 1900	
A "half sheet"	About 1750	
Leaf		Battle Hymn of the Republic
Sheet Music	Before 1919	
Booklet		Ta-Ra-Ra Boom-Der-É
Sheet Music		
Broadside		

In addition, the orchestral parts of the following instrumental works have not been located in first edition:

Composer	Title	Publisher	Title in This Book
Bach	Sinfonie in D	Sieber	Air for the G String
Berlioz	Symphonie Fantastique	Schlesinger	
Brahms	Symphonies 1–4	Simrock	

Composer	Title	Publisher	Title in This Book
Dvořák	Slavische Tänze, op. 46— Zweite Sammlung	Simrock	
Franck	Symphony in D Minor	Hamelle	
Grieg	Concerto for Piano	Fritzsch	
Rimsky-Korsakov	Capriccio Espagnol	Belaieff	
Sibelius	Finlandia	Helsingfors NYA Musikhandel	
J. Strauss	Du und Du	Schreiber	
J. Strauss	Geschichten aus dem Wienerwald	Spina	Tales from the Vienna Woods
J. Strauss	Tausend und Eine Nacht	Spina	A Thousand and One Nights
Suppé	Leichte Cavallerie— Ouverture	Siegel	Light Cavalry— Overture
Tchaikovsky	Concerto for Piano no. 1	Jurgenson	
Tchaikovsky	Marche Slave	Jurgenson	

Finally, as indicated above, the orchestral parts of so many operas and ballets have not been found in first edition, or in some cases the facts are sufficiently uncertain, that a list of unlocated first editions of orchestral parts of operas and ballets is not appropriate.

GENERAL NOTE TO THE READER

FOOTNOTES

The reader will note that the footnotes for each composition are numbered in order, starting with number 1. When more than one musical composition is discussed on a single page, the footnotes for the second work also start with number 1. Where there is more than one set of footnotes on a page, they are separated from each other by a thin rule.

INDEX

Every attempt has been made to have the index as complete as possible. Alternative titles have been included whenever known. Titles are listed both in the original language and in their English translation (except that titles in Russian have not been indexed as such).

There is one large index rather than a number of small ones.

The index, as well as the main contents, follow the order used by the Library of Congress, i.e., alphabetically by words, rather than by letters. Thus, *I Dreamt That I Dwelt in Marble Halls* precedes *Ich Liebe Dich*. Definite and indefinite articles in all languages, which are at the beginning of a title, are ignored, as are apostrophes, accents, cedillas, umlauts, and similar marks.

BIOGRAPHIC AND OTHER INFORMATION

It is surprising how many composers, librettists and lyricists of world-famous music are omitted from the standard biographic treatises, music and otherwise. As a result, an effort has been made to obtain basic biographic information regarding the composer, librettist and lyricist of every musical work considered in this book.

The following sources have been searched: musical biographies; general and national biographies and "Who's Who's"; individual biographies; obituary, biography and clipping files maintained at various libraries; newspaper indices; ASCAP files; theater-collection files; musical and theatrical magazines; libraries in various countries; university alumni associations; and other leads followed. Letters were also sent to the societies of authors and composers in other countries; to the publishers of the particular works and successor publishers; and to the composers and lyricists, if alive.

There are many composers and lyricists, however, for whom no biographic information has been found, or in some cases only incomplete information has been obtained. Any missing biographical facts would be appreciated regarding the following composers and authors:

NAME	TITLE IN THIS BOOK
Harry Birch	*Reuben and Rachel*
William Gooch	*Reuben and Rachel*
Ed. Haley or Healy	*While Strolling Through the Park One Day*
J. K.	*The Yellow Rose of Texas*
J. de Lau Lusignan	*Estudiantina*
Ferdinand (de) Lemaire	*Bacchanale—Samson and Delilah*
Percy Montrose	*Clementine*
Eddie Munson	*Ida*
Eddie Newton	*Casey Jones*
Michael Nolin	*Little Annie Rooney*
Meta Orred	*In the Gloaming*
John F. Palmer	*The Band Played On*
F. W. Riese (W. Friedrich)	*Ah! So Pure—Martha*
M. H. Rosenfeld (F. Belasco)	*Johnny Get Your Gun*
Giacomo Rossi	*Lascia Ch'io Pianga—Handel*
T. Lawrence Seibert	*Casey Jones*
H. S. Thompson	*Annie Lisle—(Far Above Cayuga's Waters)* and *Clementine*
Carlo Tiochet	*Ciribiribin*
G. Turco	*Funiculì—Funiculà*
J. Warner	*The Old Grey Mare—(Get Out of the Wilderness)*

Only the basic biographic data have been included, i.e., year and place of birth; principal occupation; and year and place of death, or, if the person is alive in mid-1971, his present place of residence. Reference is also made to the source of the information (as this frequently contains additional data), except in the case of the best-known composers and lyricists for whom there is, of course, abundant information. Where the source is not stated, information as to current place of residence has often been obtained informally, e.g., files at ASCAP.

No systematic attempt has been made in this book to mention the background and circumstances in which the particular musical work was written. For the major works, this information is readily available in the standard reference books. However, for the lesser works, where interesting information has been noted in widely scattered sources, it was thought worthwhile to assemble and briefly mention it.

ACKNOWLEDGMENTS

As stated in the Dedication, the librarians around the world have made this book possible. Librarians in hundreds of libraries have answered endless inquiries and helped find first printings, and the author is grateful to all of them for their tireless cooperation.

Among the music librarians and the "giants" in the musicological world who have been particularly helpful with information, advice or encouragement were: Madame Ekaterina Alekseeva, State Central Museum of Musical Culture named for M. I. Glinka, Moscow; C. W. Black, Mitchell Library, Glasgow; Prof. Dr. F. Blume, Schlüchtern, West Germany; Miss Carol Bridgman and Richard F. Frohlich, American Society of Composers, Authors and Publishers, New York, N.Y.; Maurice J. E. Brown, London; Jarmil Burghauser, Prague; Mary Chiesa, Biblioteca del Conservatorio Giuseppe Verdi, Milan; S. Foster Damon and Roger E. Stoddard, Brown University, Providence; Dr. Rudolf Elvers, West Berlin; O. d'Estrade-Guerra, Paris; Vladimir Fédorov, Bibliothèque du Conservatoire, Paris; Robert P. Giddings, then at Boston Public Library; the late Dr. H. Halm and Dr. Kurt Dorfmüller, Bayerische Staatsbibliothek, Munich; R. J. Hayes, National Library of Ireland, Dublin; Anthony van Hoboken, Ascona, Switzerland; the late Richard S. Hill, William Lichtenwanger (whose encouragement was particularly appreciated), Irving Lowens and James Boxley, Library of Congress, Washington; Miss Carolyn Jakeman, Houghton Library, Harvard University, Cambridge, Mass.; A. Hyatt King and Oliver W. Neighbour, British Museum, London; Dr. Karl-Heinz Köhler, Deutsche Staatsbibliothek, East Berlin; Dr. Donald W. Krummel, Newberry Library, Chicago; H. C. Robbins Landon, Vienna; Bernice B. Larrabee, formerly at the Free Library of Philadelphia; Mme Élisabeth Lebeau, Bibliothèque Nationale, Paris; Marion P. Linton, National Library of Scotland, Edinburgh, who has an uncanny ability to understand what information is desired and whose replies to questions are little articles by themselves; Dr. Hedwig Mitringer, Gesellschaft der Musikfreunde, Vienna; Kurtz Myers, Detroit Public Library; Dr. Leopold Nowak, Österreichische Nationalbibliothek, Vienna; Madame L. N. Pavlova-Sil'vansky, M. E. Saltykov-Shchedrin State Public Library, Leningrad, the most knowledgeable musicologist this author met in the Soviet Union; Dr. Fritz Raček, Stadtbibliothek, Vienna; Dr. Wolfgang Schmieder, Stadt- und Universitätsbibliothek, Frankfurt; Dr. Erich Seemann, Deutsches Volksliedarchiv, Freiburg; Brooks Shepard, Jr., Yale University, New Haven; Mrs. A. P. Vlasto, King's College, Cambridge, England; Alexander Weinmann, Vienna; and Prof. Emilia Zanetti, Biblioteca S. Cecilia (Conservatorio), Rome.

Dr. Otto Erich Deutsch, Vienna; Cecil Hopkinson, London; William Lichtenwanger, Washington; and Alan Tyson, London, kindly read portions of the manuscript and made many useful suggestions. Jean-Marie Martin, Hollogne-aux-Pierres, Belgium, did likewise with respect to portions of the manuscript relating to operas.

Perhaps the one person who has been most responsible for the completion of this book is Miss Louisa Cagwin, now at Mill Valley, Cal., but who was a student in Vienna recommended to the author by Dr. Nowak, and who, with the vast wealth of German and Austrian music available to her in Vienna, most ably studied the music from these important countries.

Thanks are given to the author's American friends and fellow collectors, Reginald Allen, Harry Dichter, Mrs. Josephine L. Hughes, W. Lloyd Keepers, Lester S. Levy, Eric Mandell, the late Elliott Shapiro, the late Sigmund Spaeth, the late Dr. Saul Starr and Dr. Edmund G. Wilson. Thanks are also offered to Harold Barlow, Josiah Q. Bennett, Dena J. Epstein, Dr. Alfred E. Fischer, W. N. H. Harding, Prof. Jan LaRue, Mrs. Ch. Pupko, Richard A. Reuss, Kenneth Roman, Jr., Eugene A. Sekulow, Nicolas Slonimsky, Julius J. Teller and Richard J. Wolfe.

Frederick Freedman also read portions of the manuscript and offered encouragement and numerous helpful suggestions. Irving Weill, of ASCAP, ably arranged most of the musical excerpts.

The author is particularly indebted to the staff at the New York Public Library where the bulk of the research was performed. Sydney Beck and Mrs. John Katchie. especially, were most encouraging and helpful, and the pages cheerfully responded to the seemingly endless number of call slips. As in the case of other libraries, there was a spirit of interest and cooperation that has helped to make this large task an ever-challenging and interesting one.

Special gratitude is given to my wife, not only for her understanding, tolerance and encouragement, but also for specific chores, of which there were many, and important contributions in the area of biographies. Even our three children were pressed into service at various times.

Needless to say, in spite of all the counsel and assistance from those mentioned above, all responsibility for errors of omission and commission is strictly the author's.

For the illustrations, thanks are offered to the following owners who granted permission to reproduce a few of their most valuable musical possessions: Bayerische Staatsbibliothek, Munich; Bibliothèque Nationale, Paris; the Trustees of the British Museum, London; Gesellschaft der Musikfreunde, Vienna; the State Central Museum of Musical Culture named for M. I. Glinka, Moscow; Harvard University, Cambridge, Mass.; Bibliothèque Anthony van Hoboken, Ascona, Switzerland; Lester S. Levy, Baltimore; Library of Congress, Washington; Pierpont Morgan Library (Reginald Allen Collection), New York, N.Y.; New York Public Library, New York, N.Y.; Österreichische Nationalbibliothek, Vienna; Biblioteca S. Cecilia (Conservatorio), Rome; M. E. Saltykov-Shchedrin State Public Library, Leningrad; Stadtbibliothek, Vienna; the late Dr. Saul Starr, Eastchester, N.Y., and Alan Tyson, London. *Alexander's Ragtime Band* was copyrighted 1911 by Irving Berlin, the copyright was renewed, and the reproduction of the front cover is used by permission of the Irving Berlin Music Corporation. Permission to reproduce several bars of *Lili Marleen* was granted by Edward B. Marks Music Corporation.

Last, but not least, thanks are gratefully given to the late Robert Simon of Crown Publishers for his confidence in this work.

LIST OF COMPOSITIONS

Abdulla Bulbul Ameer

The sons of the proph - et are brave men and bold

mw. Percy French. This song was composed for a smoking concert at Trinity College, Dublin, in 1877.[1] The song was first published by the author and Archie West, a college friend, in Dublin in 1877 under the above title, but no trace of this edition has been found. The song was not copyrighted by French. The earliest located edition was pirated and published by John Blockley, 3 Argyll Street, Regent Street, London W., on Feb. 18, 1886,[2] under the title *Abdul, the Bulbul Ameer,* "Composed and Arranged by Ali Baba," with no reference to French.[3] Another edition, perhaps earlier, without title, author, covers or imprint, and with slightly different music and words, spells the title *Abdallah Bulbul Ameer;* copy at Ethie Percy-French, Monks Eleigh, Ipswich, Suffolk, England, and JF. The song is at p. 162 of *The Scottish Students' Song Book* (Glasgow and London [1892]), beginning with the engraved "new and revised edition," "by special permission of Mr. John Blockley," also without reference to French;[4] ML. In a later song by French, he is described as the author of *Abdallah Bulbul Ameer.*[5]

There are other variants of the title, including "Ivan Skivitsky Skivar." "Bülbül Amîr" means in Turkish "nightingale chieftain." Because of the lack of an authorized, copyrighted edition, the music and words have changed somewhat over the years. No evidence is at hand supporting the suggestion[6] that the song dates back to the Crimean War (1854–56).

French was born in Clooneyquin, Ireland, in 1854, was an artist and entertainer, and died in 1920 in Formby, near Liverpool.[7]

[1] Information regarding this song and its author has been in part obtained from his daughter, Ethie Percy-French, Monks Eleigh, Ipswich, Suffolk, England, from a distant relative, R. B. D. French, Trinity College, Dublin, from an article by the latter "Percy French," in *Trinity*, Dublin, no. 6, Michaelmas, 1954, p. 22, at TC, and from James N. Healy, *Percy French and His Songs* (Cork, 1966), p. 5, at NYPL.

[2] This is the date of first publication in the entry at Stationers' Hall, the entry, however, being made almost two years later, on Jan. 6, 1888.

[3] Copy at Ascherberg, Hopwood & Crew, London, the present copyright owner and successor to John Blockley. The present copyright owner paid royalties to Percy French's widow.

[4] Not in the 1891 edition; NLS.

[5] *The Darlin' Girl from Clare* (London, 1906); LC (CDC).

[6] Spaeth, p. 471.

[7] John S. Crone, *A Concise Dictionary of Irish Biography* (Dublin, 1937), p. 73; NYPL.

Abide with Me

A - bide with me! Fast falls the e - ven - tide

The first printing of the words by Henry Francis Lyte is said to have been in a leaflet printed at Berry Head, Brixham, Devonshire, in Sept., 1847, but otherwise not described;[1] no copy has been found. An early printing of the words is in the *Remains of the Late Rev. H. F. Lyte, M.A.* (London, 1850), at p. 119; BM and JF. The poem is there said to be derived from "Abide with us" (St. Luke xxiv. 29) and at the foot reads: "Berry Head, September, 1847." Tradition has it that Lyte wrote the words after preaching his last sermon to his congregation at Brixham on Sept. 4, 1847. This is clearly wrong as a letter dated Aug. 25, 1847, includes the hymn, his "latest effusion," and it seems likely that it was written during his last visit to Berry Head a month or two earlier.[2]

The music by William Henry Monk was first printed in his *Hymns Ancient and Modern* (London, Preface dated Lent, 1861), as Hymn 14, together with the words, under the title "Evening." In this edition, published March 20, 1861, there are 273 hymns; the pages are not numbered.[3] It is not known which of the following two variants is the above edition: one, at BM, has a handwritten date of 1866 and the Contents page does not refer to a "larger edition"; the other, at JF, has a Contents page which does make such a reference. There are other minor differences in the two variants.

Lyte was born at Ednam, near Kelso, Scotland, in 1793, was ordained in 1815 and held a number of ecclesiastical posts, and died at Nice on Nov. 20, 1847.[4] Monk was born in Brompton in 1823, became an organist and Professor of Music, and died in 1889 in London.[5]

[1] Julian, p. 7.

[2] Parry, p. 272.

[3] *Grove's*, vol. 4, p. 433. MT, April 1, 1861, p. 28.

[4] *Dict. Nat. Biog.*, vol. XII, p. 365. Henry James Garland, *Henry Francis Lyte and The Story of "Abide with Me"* (Manchester, n.d.); NYPL. Garland says on p. 53 that the hymn was soon published in *The Torquay Times*; this is an error, as the newspaper did not begin publication until 1865; letter from the Borough Librarian, Torquay, Devonshire.

[5] *Dict. Nat. Biog.*, vol. XIII, p. 623.

Adeste Fideles

O   come   all   ye   faith - ful,   joy - ful   and   tri - um - phant
A - des - te   fi - de - les.   lae - ti   tri - um - phan - tes

An excellent recent pamphlet contains important new discoveries regarding this hymn.[1] The music and Latin words appear to have been written by John Francis Wade; at least, the three earliest known manuscripts dating from about 1750 are in his handwriting and signed by him.

The first printing of the words is in *The Evening Office of the Church, in Latin and English* ([London?] 1760); UTS. (Earlier editions of this work do not contain this hymn.) The words of *Adeste Fideles* in Latin and English are on the thirteenth unnumbered page in the "Proses" section, after p. 322. The English translation starts: "Draw near ye faithful Christians, With Joy to Bethlehem come." No indication of authorship.

The music first appeared in *An Essay on the Church Plain Chant* edited by Samuel Webbe (London, 1782) at p. xiii, together with the Latin words; BM. The standard English translation commencing "O come all ye faithful," was made by Frederick Oakeley in 1852 and first appeared in print in *A Hymnal for Use of the English Church* (London, 1852) on p. 26; BM. He had made a previous translation in 1841.

The hymn is frequently known as the "Portuguese Hymn," perhaps because Wade had made a copy for the use of the English College at Lisbon. The Latin words have sometimes been ascribed to St. Bonaventura in the thirteenth century or to an unnamed German or French poet in the seventeenth century. The music has also been ascribed to a Portuguese composer, Marcus Portogallo, and even to King John IV of Portugal. There is little evidence to support any of these claims. However, Vincent Novello said that John Reading, an Englishman, composed the melody in 1780 and this possibility cannot be ruled out.

Wade was born about 1710 and became a copier of plainchant and other music at Douay College, France, a great Catholic center; he died in 1786 at the age of seventy-five. Oakeley was born in London in 1802, was ordained priest in the Church of England and then received into the Roman Church and made Canon of Westminster where he remained until his death in 1880.[2]

---

[1] Dom John Stephan, *The "Adeste Fideles"* (South Devon, 1947); BM, HWMS and JF.

[2] Parry, p. 477.

After the Ball

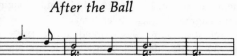

Af - ter   the   ball   is   o - ver

mw. Chas. K. Harris. Copyrighted Nov. 12, 1892,[1] by Chas. K. Harris &
Co., Milwaukee, Wis. First edition: Front cover has a drawing of sunbursts
and leaves and is purple, red and white. p. [2] adv. *Sleep.*. m. on pp. [3]–
[6]. p. [7] adv. *Only.*. Back cover adv. *Hello.*. - *School.*. LC(CDC). No
photograph on the front cover, which is completely different from subsequent covers; the front cover of the first edition is illustrated in Fuld,
American, p. [31].

Historical information regarding the song appears in Spaeth, p. 260,
and Charles K. Harris, *After the Ball* (New York, N.Y., 1926), p. 50, NYPL.
The melody was interpolated by Jerome Kern in *Show Boat* in 1927. Harris
was born in Poughkeepsie, N.Y., in 1867, became a banjo player, composer,
and lyricist, and died in New York City in 1930.[2]

Ah! So Pure—Martha

Ah!   So——   pure,   ah,——   so——   bright
Ach!   So——   fromm,   ach,——   so——   traut

m. F. von Flotow. w. W. Friedrich. The piano-vocal score of *Martha oder:
Der Markt zu Richmond*, was published about Jan. 4, 1848,[1] by H. F.
Müller, 1147 Kohlmarkt, Vienna. Three variants of a possible first edition have been found, with priority uncertain. In each, the title page lists
three copublishers and indicates the piano arrangement is by the composer.
vb. Index. vb. m. on pp. 1–266. p.n. 280. *Ach! So Fromm (Ah! So Pure)* is
on p. 192. Index and music pages engraved. In one variant at GM, the
price is blank and a 12-page libretto is included; in the second variant at JF,
the price is 15 Fl. as in the notices, and the libretto is not included; and in
the third variant at JMM, both the price and the libretto are present.

The separate sheet music of the song was published about April,
1848,[2] and a possible first edition is at SB: front cover lists 26 titles and

[1] Copyright records; LC.
[2] *ASCAP*, p. 217.

[1] *Wiener Zeitung*, Jan. 4, 1848, p. 12; UMI. Hofmeister *Monatsbericht*, March,
1848, p. 48. Both mention the price of 15 Fl.
[2] Hofmeister *Monatsbericht*, April, 1848, p. 63.

arrangements; m. on pp. 1–3 and 192–194 (double pagination); p.n. 280(15); music pages engraved; back cover blank.†

The orchestral score was printed about 1897[3] with French text by Choudens, 30 Bould. des Capucines, Paris; a "Nouvelle Edition," folio, without price, it has plate number A.C. 10,613 for the Overture on pages 1–35, and a lithographing of a manuscript score without plate number on pages 37–454. JMM and NYPL. The orchestral score with German text was not published until 1940 by Breitkopf & Härtel, Leipzig; BM.

Orchestral parts of the opera, published probably by August Cranz, with plate number 13007 for the Overture, the balance a different printing, of uncertain date but not earlier than 1876 (when Cranz commenced business), lithographed and without covers, are at CI. *Martha* was composed in 1847 and performed on Nov. 25, 1847, in Vienna.

The source of *Martha* was a ballet produced at Paris in 1844 entitled *Lady Harriette*, of which Flotow wrote the first act, and two others wrote the balance.[4] The music of the entire ballet has apparently not been published; two excerpts at BN and another at BM do not include the melody of this aria.

Flotow, a composer of light opera, was born in 1812 at Teutendorf, Mecklenburg; he died in 1883 at Darmstadt. W. Friedrich is believed to be a pseudonym for F. W. Riese, but no other biographic information has been located.

Ah! Sweet Mystery of Life

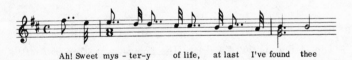

Ah! Sweet mys - ter-y   of life,   at last   I've found   thee

m. Victor Herbert. w. Rida Johnson Young. The music only of this song first appeared in print in the piano-vocal score of the show *Naughty Marietta*, in the Overture and Entr'acte, published Nov. 7, 1910,[1] by M. Witmark & Sons, New York, N.Y., and four other cities. In the first edition of the piano-vocal score, the front cover has a photograph of Emma Trentini and is brown, green and tan, and the score includes an *Entr'acte* which was eliminated in the second edition. LC(CDC) and JF. The music

---

[3] The cast page of the Choudens score mentions the 1897 Artistes. *Cf.* Kinsky, *Opern,* p. 379.

[4] Edward J. Dent, "A Best-Seller in Opera" in *Music & Letters*, London, April, 1941, p. 139; NYPL. *Friedrich von Flotow's Leben* by [Rose Rosine von Flotow] (Leipzig, 1892), p. [102]; NYPL. *Grove's* refers to the ballet as *Lady Henriette*; vol. 3, p. 162.

---

[1] Copyright records; LC.

only, separately printed as sheet music, was published on Nov. 21, 1910,[1] under the title *Dream Melody (Intermezzo)*; LC(CDC) and JF.

The song, with words, under the title *Ah! Sweet Mystery of Life (The Dream Melody)*, was also published on Nov. 21, 1910.[1] First edition: Front cover has a photograph of Emma Trentini and is green, brown and white. s. *Naughty Marietta*—16 titles listed. m. on pp. 2–4. p.ns. 5263; 11702–3. p. [5] blank. Back cover lists the shows *Ameer.. – Wonderland*. LC(CDC) and JF. The show opened in New York City on Nov. 7, 1910.

The composition at all times included words, and was sung from the very beginning of the operetta's career.[2] Herbert was born in Dublin, Ireland, in 1859, played the cello in Germany, and came to the United States in 1886 where he became a composer of operettas; one of the nine founders of ASCAP in 1914, he died in New York City in 1924. Young, an author, librettist and actress, was born in Baltimore in 1869 and died in Stamford, Conn., in 1926.[3]

Ain't Misbehavin'

No one to talk with, all by my-self, no one to walk with, but I'm hap-py on— the shelf

m. Thomas Waller and Harry Brooks. w. Andy Razaf. Published July 8, 1929,[1] by Mills Music Inc., 148–150 West 46th Street, New York, N.Y. First edition: Front cover refers to the revue *Connie's Hot Chocolates*, has a drawing of dancers and a musician, is red, pink and blue and lists 10 titles; no prices. p. [2] adv. *Sentimental..* and *I've..* m. on pp. 3–5. No plate number. Center fold adv. *Learn..* p. 3 mentions British and Australian agents. p. 4 adv. *Dizzy..* p. 5 adv. *Flapperette*. Back cover adv. *Let's..— Futuristic..* LC(CDC) and JF. *Connie's Hot Chocolates* opened in New York City on June 20, 1929.

Waller, a pianist and composer, was born in New York City in 1904 and died in Kansas City, Mo., in 1943.[2] Brooks, a pianist and composer, was born in Homestead, Pa., in 1895 and died in Teaneck, N.J. in 1970. Razaf, a lyricist, was born in Washington, D.C., in 1895 and died in North Hollywood, Cal., in 1973.[3]

2 Waters, *Herbert*, p. 360.
3 *ASCAP*, p. 551.

1 Copyright records; LC.
2 *ASCAP*, pp. 520 and 55, and ASCAP files.
3 *ASCAP*, p. 400. Obituary, *The New York Times*, Feb. 5, 1973.

Air for the G String—Bach

m. Johann Sebastian Bach. The first printing of this melody, Schmieder, no. 1068 (now commonly known as the *Orchestral Suite* no. 3, or *Overture*, in D), may have been published by Sieber, Paris, probably in parts at 4 Fr., 20 cent., in 1817 or earlier.[1] No copy has been located. It is listed in Meysel, 1817, p. 2, but not in *BF*, 1811–1817.

Dr. Alfred Dürr, Johann-Sebastian-Bach Institut, Göttingen, and Prof. F. Blume, Schlüchtern, West Germany, have written the author that they are not certain whether the above-mentioned Sieber edition ever was in fact published, and if it was, whether it was the *Overture* in D, Schmieder, no. 1068, or the *Overture* in D, Schmieder, no. 1069. If there was no Sieber edition, or there was one but it was Schmieder, no. 1069, then the first printing of this work was for piano four hands about March, 1843,[1A] by Au Bureau de Musique de C. F. Peters, Leipzig, under the title *Sinfonie ou Suite* with plate number 2827; JF. The work was then published for orchestra about Aug., 1854,[2] by Au Bureau de Musique de C. F. Peters, Leipzig, under the title *Ouverture ou Suite en Ré Majeur* for orchestral score (p.n. 3556) and orchestral parts (p.n. 3557) "publieé [sic] pour la première fois" by S. W. Dehn, no. 3; BSM and JF* (with prices and agents) and ZZ (without prices or agents)—priority not known.

The famous arrangement by A. Wilhelmj was published about May, 1871.[3] Probable first edition: *AIR von Joh. Seb. Bach für Violine mit Begleitung von Streichinstrumenten oder Pianoforte oder Orgel*, arranged by August Wilhelmj. Published by Gustav Lewy, Vienna. Price: **81 Kr./15 Sgr.** Front cover is black and white. vb. m. on pp. 3–5. p.n. 6(?). Back cover blank. Separate leaves or parts for violin solo, violin and viola, and cello and bass. PM. At the same time arrangements were also published by Lewy for violin and piano, and violin and organ. Other publishers' editions examined show the price in Marks, i.e., 1874 or later.

Wilhelmj placed Bach's melody a 9th lower than originally written,

---

[1] Schneider, p. 106. *MGG*, vol. I, p. 1038. See, also, Schmieder, no. 1068, and *Bach Gesellschaft* [vol. 31 (1)], p. xv.

[1A] Hofmeister *Monatsbericht*, March, 1843, p. 36. Schneider, p. 106. Nigel Simeone, London, called this printing to the attention of the author.

[2] Hofmeister *Monatsbericht*, Aug., 1854, p. [586].

[3] Hofmeister *Monatsbericht*, May, 1871, p. 82.

as above, and utilized the G string, the lowest string of a violin having a particularly rich tone. Bach was born at Eisenach in 1685 and died at Leipzig in 1750. Wilhelmj, a German violinist and composer, was born in Usingen, duchy of Nassau, in 1845; he died in London in 1908.

Alexander's Ragtime Band

Come on and hear,__ come on and hear__ Al-ex-an-der's rag-time band

mw. Irving Berlin. Published March 18, 1911,[1] by Ted Snyder & Co., 112 West 38 St., New York, N.Y. Probable first edition: Large photograph on the front cover of Emma Carus. Front cover has a drawing of a ragtime band and is red, pink, green and white. (See Plate I.) m. on pp. 2–5. Back cover adv. *When it Rains..* SS and JF (inscribed). Although the advertised song was published April 29, 1911,[1] the edition with Emma Carus' photograph is logically the first edition as she successfully introduced the song (so stated on each of the known 65 or more early editions, each with the name and small photograph of a different singer or "plugger"), and her photograph is the only one yet found on an early edition without an identifying name. The copyright of *That Peculiar Rag*, advertised in a variant edition, at JF, was assigned to Ted Snyder Co. on June 23, 1911.[1] There is also an edition with a small photograph and repeated name of Emma Carus on the front cover, advertising *Dear Mayme, I Love You!*, copyrighted in 1910; JF.

Berlin is also said to have introduced the song "without success" at the 1911 Annual Friars Club show,[2] and Eddie Miller and Helen Vincent are claimed to have been the first to sing the song in public.[3] The "Alexander" in the title is reportedly Jack Alexander, a cornet-playing bandleader who died in 1958.[4] It has been frequently pointed out that the song is not real ragtime. Berlin was born in Temun, Russia, in 1888, and now resides in New York City.

[1] Copyright records; LC. The first publication may have been in a professional edition.
[2] Ewen, *Berlin*, p. 50.
[3] Ray Walker, *Variety*, Oct. 20, 1954, p. 50.
[4] Obituary, *New York World-Telegram*, July 3, 1958; NYPL.

All the Things You Are

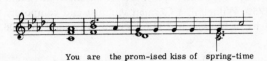

You are the prom-ised kiss of spring-time

© 1939 and 1940 by T. B. Harms Company. By consent.

m. Jerome Kern. w. Oscar Hammerstein, 2nd. Published by Chappell & Co., Inc., RKO Building, Rockefeller Center, New York City. The first copyright deposit copy, in professional edition, was published Oct. 11, 1939,[1] in a duet arrangement; it has not been published in a regular edition as a duet. The song was republished early in November for one voice (at a time) and piano, and the following is probably the first regular edition: Front cover is tan and black. s. *Very Warm for May*—6 titles listed. p. [2] adv. *I.*. m. on pp. 3–7. p.n. 981–5. Back cover adv. *Heaven.. - In..*[2] The show opened in New York City on Nov. 17, 1939. No piano-vocal score for the show has been published.

Kern was born in New York, N.Y., in 1885 and died there in 1945. Hammerstein was born in New York, N.Y., in 1895 and died in Doylestown, Pa., in 1960.

All Through the Night

Fain would some with vows per-suade me, all through the night

The authorship of the melody and words is unknown. The first known printing of the melody, with Welsh words and an English translation, was in 1784 in Edward Jones, *Musical and Poetical Relicks [sic] of the Welsh Bards:* "preserved by tradition and authentic manuscripts from remote antiquity; never before published . . ." (London, 1784); at BM and JF. This song appears on p. 56 under the title *Ar Hyd Y Nos.*

The English translation included by Jones does not mention the phrase

---

[1] Copyright records; LC.

[2] Copy at JF autographed by the composer in Boston during the tryout before New York City; this arrangement was not copyrighted at the time. After the show closed in New York City on Jan. 5, 1940, the arrangement for one voice and piano was copyrighted; the latter states near the top of p. 2, "Simplified edition by Albert Sirmay." LC (CDC) and JF. Albert Sirmay, New York City, states the procedure was adopted for copyright reasons.

"all through the night." There have been many subsequent translations of the poem into English; while none has become standard, most use this phrase and title. The 1794 edition of Jones's work[1] has the English subtitle *The Live-long Night* for this song.

Almost Like Being in Love

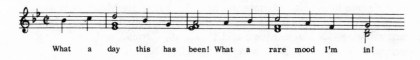

What a day this has been! What a rare mood I'm in!

m. Frederick Loewe. w. Alan Jay Lerner. Published March 13, 1947,[1] by Sam Fox Publishing Company, New York, N.Y., but copyrighted by the authors. First edition: Front cover has a drawing of two Scottish dancers and is green, red, brown and white. s. *Brigadoon*—11 titles listed. p. [2] adv. *Waitin'.. - I'll..* m. on pp. 3–5. Back cover adv. *The Heather.. - Down..* LC(CDC) and JF (autographed). The show opened in New York City on March 13, 1947. The piano-vocal score of *Brigadoon* was published June 25, 1948[1]; LC(CDC).

Loewe was born in Vienna in 1901, and resides in Palm Springs, Cal. Lerner was born in New York, N.Y., in 1918 and resides there.

Aloha Oe

Fare - well to thee, fare - well to thee
A - lo - ha oe! A - lo - ha oe!

mw. Liliuokalani, Princess Regent of Honolulu, Oahu, H.I. The song was probably first published in 1884 by J. M. Oat and Co., Honolulu, H.I., without mention of Liliuokalani. Possible first edition: The front cover is a collective title cover entitled "Mele Hawaii" ("Songs of Hawaii"), with

---

[1] See *Men of Harlech*, below.

[1] Copyright records; LC.

drawings of Hawaii; *Aloha Oe* is song no. 2 of nine songs listed, nos. 10–12 being blank. An 1884 Hawaiian copyright claim is blacked out.[1] m. on pp. 2–3. Hawaiian-English text. Back cover blank. Music pages engraved. Arrangement and copyright by H. Berger [director of Royal Hawaiian Band]. JF (only known copy). A later edition published by J. H. Soper, Honolulu, restores the 1884 Hawaiian copyright claim; JF.

The song was played by the Royal Hawaiian Band in San Francisco in August, 1883, and the song, referring to Liliuokalani, Princess Regent, was copyrighted in the United States on Nov. 14, 1884,[2] by Matthias Gray, 206 Post Street, San Francisco, Cal. Possible first edition: Front cover is black and white. p. [2] blank. Music and Hawaiian, German and English words on pp. 3–5, engraved. Back cover blank. LC(CDC).

I'm Saddest When I Sing contains virtually the same musical phrase as the above begining of the chorus of *Aloha Oe*, with instructions to play "Very slow." *I'm Saddest When I Sing* has music by Henry R. Bishop and words by Thomas H. Bayly and was published circa 1823–1834[2A] by Goulding & D'Almaine, 20 Soho Square, London. Possible first edition. Front cover has the price of 2/ and states that the publisher is a manufacturer of Piano Fortes. p. [2] blank. m. on pp. 1–4 (actually 3–6); additional words on p. 5 (actually 7). No plate number. Back cover blank. Engraved. JF. This musical phrase also appeared later in *There's Music in the Air* by Geo. F. Root, copyrighted March 11, 1847,[2] by Russell & Richardson, 291 Washington St., Boston; LC(CDC). The music of the verse of the song is derived from *The Rock Beside the Sea*, by Charlie C. Converse, copyrighted Aug. 6, 1852,[2] by Lee & Walker, Philadelphia; LC and JF (correcting Dichter-Shapiro, p. 150, as to year).

Aloha Oe was composed by Liliuokalani during her imprisonment in 1878 at Maunawili, Hawaii, by the Republican Government of Hawaii.[3] Lydia Kamekeha Liliuokalani was born in the Hawaiian Islands in 1838, was Queen of the Hawaiian Islands from 1891 to 1893 when she was deposed, and died in Honolulu in 1917.

---

[1] Hawaii's 1884 copyright records are missing. J. M. Oat, Jr., and Co. was listed in the 1884 Honolulu city directory. Soper succeeded Oat in 1886. Letter from Hawaii Public Archives, Honolulu.

[2] Copyright records; LC.

[2A] Humphries-Smith, p. 158. Harold Barlow, New York City, noted this similarity.

[3] Manuscript at Hawaii Public Archives, Honolulu; and a printed copy donated by Liliuokalani in 1897 to the Library of Congress. Emerson C. Smith, "Aloha 'Oe" in *Paradise of the Pacific*, Honolulu, Sept., 1954, p. 12; Hawaii Public Archives, Honolulu.

Alouette

A - lou-et - te gen-tille A - lou-et - te, A - lou-et - te je te plu - me-rai

According to Dr. Marius Barbeau, the recognized authority on French-Canadian folk songs, this song was born in France.[1] However, no French or other printing has been found[2] before its earliest known Canadian printing in 1879 in *A Pocket Song Book for the Use of the Students and Graduates of McGill College* (Montreal), p. 9, under the title, *Alouetté;*[3] MG. The song was then published about Nov. 30, 1885,[4] in the *McGill College Song Book* (Montreal), p. 14, under the title *Alouette;* the song is there described as an "old French-Canadian song."[5] MG and JF.

Although the gentle alouette is a favorite bird, it still is desired to "plumer la tête," i.e., pluck its head! The song is said to have been a work-song which was sung while women plucked fowls,[6] and also a voyageur boat song with a heavy beat for the paddlers.[7]

[1] Marius Barbeau, *Jongleur Songs of Old Quebec* (New Brunswick, N.J., 1962), p. 190; LC. Marius Barbeau, *Alouette!* (Montreal, 1946), p. 12; NMC and NYPL. See also *Encyclopedia of Music in Canada*, edited by Helmut Kallmann et al. (Toronto, 1981), p. 16; NYPL.

[2] The earliest known printing in France of *Alouette* is in *Revue des Traditions Populaires*, Paris, vol. VIII, 1893, by Julien Tiersot, p. 586; ULS, p. 2397. In (Prosper Tarbé) *Romancero de Champagne*, tome II (Reims, 1863), p. 246, at BN and NYPL, there is a poem entitled *L'Alouette;* its text, however, bears little resemblance to that of the folk song.

[3] A. D. Ridge, University Archivist at McGill University, informed the author of this printing. The book was apparently not copyrighted.

[4] The book was on this date "entered according to Act of Parliament of Canada . . . in the office of the Minister of Agriculture"; letter from NLO. A song entitled *L'Alouette* appears in *La Muse Populaire* (Montreal, 1880), vol. 2, p. 126, but the music and words are entirely different; BVM. The author is indebted to Helmut Kallmann, Toronto, for the last reference.

[5] This might mean either originally French, then Canadian—or from the French part of Canada.

[6] *Folk Songs of Old Vincennes* (Chicago, 1946), p. 68; BSS.

[7] Information from P. L. Forstall, Evanston, Ill.

Always

I'll be lov - ing you,   al - ways

mw. Irving Berlin. Published Sept. 16, 1925,[1] by Irving Berlin, Inc., 1607 Broadway, New York, N.Y. The copyright deposit copy at LC is a professional edition. Possible first regular edition: Front cover is orange, black and white. m. on pp. 2–5. Back cover adv. *Remember* (copyrighted as a published composition on July 27, 1925).[1] JF.

George S. Kaufman, tongue-in-cheek, suggested to Berlin that "always" was a long time for romance, and recommended that the opening line be more realistic, such as, "I'll be loving you Thursday." However, Berlin was an "incurable romanticist."[2]

Brief biographic information regarding Berlin appears under *Alexander's Ragtime Band*, above.

America the Beautiful

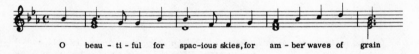

O   beau - ti - ful for   spac-ious skies, for   am - ber' waves of   grain

The poem, by Katharine Lee Bates, was first printed in the *Congregationalist*, Boston, July 4, 1895, p. 17; BPL. The musical setting to which the poem is sung today was originally known as *Materna* and was composed by Samuel A. Ward in 1882; the first known appearance of this music is to the poem *O Mother Dear, Jerusalem*, in *Parish Choir*, Boston, July 12, 1888; BPL.

The earliest known printing of the poem and this music together is in *Fellowship Hymns*, edited by Clarence A. Barbour, published Oct. 25, 1910,[1] by the Young Men's Christian Association Press, New York, N.Y., number 266; LC(CDC), NYPL and JF. It is not known who was responsible for first joining the poem and this music.

The song is also known by its opening words, *O Beautiful for Spacious*

---

[1] Copyright records; LC.

[2] *The New Yorker*, June 11, 1960, p. 39.

---

[1] Copyright records; LC. Ward probably died without hearing his music joined to the poem. Armin Haeussler, *The Story of Our Hymns* (St. Louis, 1952), at p. 451, at NYPL, states that the poem and Ward's music were printed together in an 1894 Protes-

Skies. An attempt was made in the 1920's to have it declared the national anthem. The story of Miss Bates's writing the poem after standing on the summit of Pikes Peak in Colorado and being impressed with the greatness of her country has been told many times; she subsequently revised the poem.

Miss Bates was born in 1859 at Falmouth, Mass., and was a poetess and Professor of English Literature at Wellesley College; she died at Wellesley, Mass., in 1929. Ward was born in Newark, N.J., in 1847, was an organist, choirmaster and music dealer, and died in Newark in 1903.[2]

American Patrol

m. F. W. Meacham. Copyrighted for piano March 30, 1885,[1] by Frank W. Meacham. First edition: Front cover has a drawing of an eagle and shield, and is black and white. No publisher or address stated on any page. m. on pp. 2–7. Back cover blank. LC(CDC). *We Must Be Vigilant*, with words by Edgar Leslie and music adapted by Joseph A. Burke, was sung to this melody in 1942 and during World War II.

Meacham was born in 1856 either in Buffalo or Brooklyn, became a composer and arranger, and died in Brooklyn in 1909.[2]

L'Amour-Toujours-L'Amour

L'a-mour- tou-jours-   l'a-- mour___   love, now at last, you've found me

© 1922 Harms, Inc. Copyright renewed. Used by permission.

tant Episcopal *Hymnal* but Mr. Haeussler has since written the author that this is a mistake.

[2] E. L. McFadden, "America's Great Peace Hymn" in *Etude*, Dec. 1947, p. 667.

[1] Copyright records; LC.

[2] New York City Death Records, Dec. 22, 1909; this and other information was discovered by Solomon Goodman, Long Island City, N.Y. Clipping file; NYPL Music Division.

m. Rudolf Friml. w. (English) Catherine Chisholm Cushing. Published May
31, 1922,[1] by Harms-Friml Corp., New York, N.Y. The copyright deposit
copies at LC and BM are professional editions. Possible first regular edition:
Subtitle is: *Love Everlasting*. Front cover is black and white and does not
mention other keys or arrangements. The publisher is Harms Incorporated,
New York, N.Y., with one copublisher. p. [2] blank. m. on pp. 3–5. p.n.
111–3. Back cover adv. *A Kiss* . . (copyrighted Sept. 12, 1922). JF (only
known copy). Although the title of the song is in French, the French lyric
(by Roger Casini) was not copyrighted until 1940.

Friml was born in Prague in 1879, made his home in the United States
after 1906, became a composer of operettas, and died in 1972 in Hollywood.[2] Cushing, an author, composer and librettist, was born at Mt.
Perry, Ohio, and died in New York City in 1952.[3]

An den Frühling—Grieg

m. Edvard Grieg. Published Oct. 5, 1886,[1] as no. 6 in *Lyrische Stückchen*,
op. 43, for piano, by C. F. Peters, Leipzig. First edition deposited at British
Museum Nov. 1, 1886: Front cover has a lyre in the middle of Edition
Peters no. 2154, says Heft III, mentions a French title and is pink, red and
black. vb. Title page has a dedication to Professor Isidor Seiss, an ornamental frame and is brown, black and white. p. [2] blank. m. on pp. 3–17.
p.n. 6954. *An den Frühling* is no. 6 on p. 14. p. [18] blank. Back cover is
unfortunately missing.[2] BM(CDC) and JF.

The title of the work was soon changed from *Lyrische Stückchen*
to *Lyrische Stücke*.[3] The work was being completed the end of July, 1886.[4]
Grieg was born in Bergen, Norway, in 1843 and died there in 1907.

---

[1] Copyright records; LC.
[2] Burton, p. 170. Obituary, *The New York Times*, Nov. 14, 1972.
[3] *ASCAP*, p. 105.

[1] The date stated in the entry at Stationers' Hall on Oct. 12, 1886. Not in Hofmeister *Monatsbericht*.
[2] The back cover of a Peters Edition is important; see p. 65 above. In the above
edition, there is no reference to Röder at the bottom of p. 3, nor to Peters Edition at
the bottom of music pages.
[3] The title had changed by 1889; dated copy at UP. *An den Frühling*, separately,
was first listed in Hofmeister *Monatsbericht*, Oct., 1889, p. 410.
[4] Grieg, *Letters*, letter dated July 25, 1886, p. 19.

Anchors Aweigh

An - chors a - weigh my boys

mw. Chas. A. Zimmerman (and Alfred H. Miles).

This is one of the few compositions in this book on which experts disagree as to first edition. The copyright copy deposited at the Library of Congress on April 24, 1907,[1] by The Rudolph Wurlitzer Co., Cincinnati, Ohio, mentions only Chas. A. Zimmerman, has the title on page 3 with an apostrophe, namely, "Anchor's," has no words, states copyrighted 1906, is a March and Two-Step, has a blue and white front cover with dedication to the Class of 1907, Midshipmen U.S. Naval Academy, and a photograph of Chas. A. Zimmerman as the composer, and says the price is 5. p. [2] adv. *The Winner.. - Salute..* m. on pp. 3–5. No p.n. Back cover adv. *Society..* Folio. LC(CDC). Richard S. Hill wrote this author he thought this the first printing. A similar edition with words on page 5 also credited to Zimmerman, possibly the first edition with words, has a different photograph of Zimmerman, p. [2] adv. *Salute.. - Megaphone..* (all copyrighted 1905) and back cover blank. NYPL and JF.

On the other hand, Elliott Shapiro advised this author he believed an edition published by Ida M. Zimmerman, Annapolis, Md., was the first printing. This edition was not deposited for copyright in 1906 or 1907, but also states that it was copyrighted in 1906. In this edition, the front cover is blue and white with a still different photograph of the composer, and also says the price is 5. p. [2] blank. m. on pp. 3–5. No p.n. Back cover blank. Has words on page 5. Music and words credited to Zimmerman only. Quarto. JF. Title on p. 3 has the apostrophe. JF.

Many persuasive arguments can be advanced on each side. Credit to Alfred H. Miles as a coauthor is given in current editions.[2] Zimmerman was born in Rhode Island in 1861, became Musical Director, U.S. Naval Academy, and died in Annapolis in 1916.[3] The song is said to have been written for, and sung at, the Army-Navy football game in 1906. Miles was born in Norfolk, Va., in 1883, was a Captain in the United States Navy and an author, and died in Norfolk, Va., in 1956.[4]

[1] Copyright records; LC.

[2] The factual basis for this is set forth in *Miles vs. Robbins Music Corporation,* 67 U.S. Patents Quarterly 78 (Southern District, New York, 1945); Bar Assn., New York, N.Y.

[3] Information from United States Navy.

[4] *ASCAP,* p. 348, and files at ASCAP.

Andalucía—Lecuona

m. Ernesto Lecuona. *Andalucía, Suite Española,* in which *Andaluza* appears
as the second composition, was published for piano Nov. 2, 1928,[1] by
Lecuona Music Co., 24-A Espada, Havana. Probable first edition, deposited
Jan. 8, 1929, at the Library of Congress: Front cover is tan and black
and lists six numbers of which no. 6 is *Malagueña,* another famous piece.
vb. The title page is the same as the front cover except black and white.
Music pages are unnumbered. *Andaluza,* the separate composition, is dedicated to Doris Niles who danced this piece in the Capitol Theater, New
York City, on June 21, 1923. No date, copyright claim or plate number.
Pages after the music pages and the back cover are blank. Music pages
are on glossy paper. LC(CDC).

Andalusia (as it is usually spelled) is a region in the southern part
of Spain. Ernesto Lecuona y Casado was born in Guanabacoa, Cuba, in
1896, became a composer and pianist, is credited with bringing the rumba
and conga rhythms to North America, and died in the Canary Islands in
1963.[2]

Andantino in D Flat—Lemare

m. Edwin H. Lemare. Published 1892 for organ by Robert Cocks & Co.,
New Burlington Street, London, W. Probable first edition deposited Dec. 22,
1892, at Library of Congress and Jan. 4, 1893, at the British Museum:
Oblong. Title page is plain, and black and white. Price: 1/6 net. p. [2]
blank. m. on pp. 1–5 (actually 3–7). p.n. 19500. There is an 1892 copyright
claim. Back cover adv. organ music by Westbrook. BM and LC (both CDC-
LC's copy has a front cover that is the same as the title page except salmon
and black; vb; and a back cover the inside of which adv. *A Collection of
Organ..,* and the outside of which adv. *Collection of the Choruses..*).
Novello & Company became the publisher later. In 1925 words were added
by Ben Black and Neil Moret (pseudonym for Charles N. Daniels) with the
title *Moonlight and Roses;* LC(CDC).

Lemare was born in Ventnor, Isle of Wight, England, in 1865, became

---

[1] Copyright records; LC.
[2] Obituary, *The New York Times,* Dec. 1, 1963.

an organist and a composer, held various posts in America[1] and died in 1934 in Los Angeles, Cal.

Annie Laurie

Max - well - ton braes   are   bon - nie,   where   ear - ly   fa's   the   dew

A vast amount of legend surrounds the poem telling the Romeo-and-Juliet romance about 1705 between William Douglas and Annie Laurie, members of two rival Scottish clans.[1] It has been claimed that the first appearance of the poem, allegedly by William Douglas, was in an Edinburgh newspaper; if so, it has not been found, and the claim has been questioned.[2] The first known printing of the poem is no. XXXVII, p. 107, in *A Ballad Book*, privately printed in [Edinburgh] by [Charles Kirkpatrick Sharpe] in [1823]; NLS.

The first known printing of the music, composed by Lady John Scott in 1835, appeared in vol. Third, New Edition of the *Vocal Melodies of Scotland*, arranged by Finlay Dun and John Thomson, and published at 15/ by Paterson & Roy, 27 George Street, Edinburgh; the preface of this volume is dated Oct., 1838; *Annie Laurie* is no. 27, on p. 89, with no mention of the composer. In the first edition of this collection, there is no indication on the title page that Thomson died.[3] NLS. The song was also printed by this publisher from this work in separate sheet music; JF. It was later said that the composer disliked publicity and "always thought the air and words had been stolen when she sent her music-book to be rebound."[4] The composer also edited parts of the poem and added a third stanza.

Little is known about William Douglas, the alleged author of the poem, except that he came from the Scottish lowlands, was a Jacobite cadet of the Queensberry family, and may have died in 1753 at Edinburgh. Alicia Anne Spottiswoode was born in Spottiswoode [*sic*], Scotland, and married Lord John Scott in 1836. She wrote many songs, and died at Spottiswoode in 1900.[4]

[1] Edwin H. Lemare, *Organs I Have Met* (Los Angeles, Cal., 1956); LC.

[1] Ford, p. 23; and Robert James Green, "The Romance of Annie Laurie" in *Etude*, March, 1939, p. 166.

[2] Ford, p. 25; questioned in a letter from NLS.

[3] 1841; *Grove's*, vol. VIII, p. 432. The words "New Edition" in the title apparently indicate that the collection is new, not that the edition is a later printing.

[4] The best history and analysis of the song, and biography of the composer, are in *Thirty Songs by Lady John Scott* (Edinburgh, 1910); LC and JF. See, also, Graham, vol. 3, p. 25.

Annie Lisle—(Far Above Cayuga's Waters)

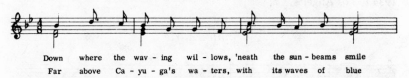

Down   where   the   wav - ing   wil - lows, 'neath   the sun - beams   smile
Far   above   Ca - yu - ga's   wa - ters, with   its waves of   blue

mw. H. S. Thompson. Published by Moulton & Clark, Newburyport, Mass. Probable first edition, deposited Jan. 9, 1858,[1] at LC: Front cover has a fancy border, mentions an 1857 copyright, and is black and white. p. [2] blank. m. on pp. 3–5. Back cover blank. No price or plate number. Not engraved. LC(CDC) and JF. Later published by Oliver Ditson & Co.

The "Alma Mater" of Cornell University, *Far Above Cayuga's Waters*, was later written to this melody. After much dispute, it now appears that Archibald C. Weeks and Wilmot M. Smith wrote the words in 1872.[2] The words appeared, probably for the first time, in *Carmina Collegensia*, edited by Henry Randall Waite (Boston, 1876) at p. 109, to the "Air-*Annie Lisle*"; LC, UM and JF.

The melody has also been used for the Alma Maters of other colleges. No biographic information has been found regarding Thompson, although the title page of *Annie Lisle* states that he was the author of other songs.[3] Weeks was born in Yaphank, N.Y., in 1850, graduated from Cornell in 1872, became a lawyer and died in Brooklyn, N.Y., in 1927.[4] Smith was born in Hauppauge, N.Y., in 1852, graduated from Cornell in 1874 and died in Patchogue, N.Y., in 1906.[4]

Anvil Chorus—Il Trovatore

Chi   del   gi - ta - no   i   gior - ni   ab - bel - la?

m. G. Verdi. w. Salvadore Cammarano. On April 23, 1853, a complete piano-vocal score of *Il Trovatore*, in which the *Coro di Zingari*, or *Anvil Chorus*, appears, was advertised by the Successori di B. Girard, Naples, but no copy with this imprint has been found. A piano-vocal score published by Stabilimento Musicale Partenopeo [Naples] has a title page refer-

---

[1] Copyright records; LC.

[2] "Who Wrote It?", *The Cornell Era*, Ithaca, N.Y., 1917, vol. 49, p. 450; CU.

[3] *Christian Science Monitor*, Boston, July 5, 1946, p. 16, lists some of his songs. See, also, *Clementine*, below.

[4] Information from CU.

ring to the performance of the opera in Rome on Jan. 19, 1853, a price of D. 6.00, and listing 21 separate pieces from the opera. vb. Cast-Index. vb. m. on pp. 1–195, oblong engraved. p.ns. intermittent between 10869–10987. Date of publication not known. Hopkinson, *Verdi*, 54A(a). BM, NLS and SCR. In a variant at the Naples Conservatory the title page refers to T. Cottrau.

A piano-vocal score was published Aug. 1–7, 1853,[1] by Tito di Gio. Ricordi, 1720 Contrada degli Omenoni, Milan. Oblong. The title page has a vignette, a dedication to Antonio Vasselli, the price as Fr. 40, and agents at Florence, Mendrisio [Switzerland], Paris (Blanchet) and London. vb. Index. Cast. m. on pp. 5–252, with double pagination. p.ns. 24842–24863. Engraved. The *Coro di Zingari* is no. 7, p. 58, p.n. 24847. There are nine corner dates up to June 9, 1853. Some arias have the earlier imprint of G. or Gio. Ricordi, and some were published after his death on March 15, 1853, and have the later imprint of Tito Ricordi. Hopkinson, *Verdi*, 54A(e). BM, Florence Conservatory, IU, MIC and JF. In the copies at BM, IU and JF, the engravers' initials are in accord with the engravers' names in the Ricordi *Libroni*, except that some pages with plate number 24859 have the initial K. The copy at NLS, stated by Hopkinson to have seven corner dates, has six, and more important the engravers' initials frequently are not in accord with the engravers' names in the Ricordi *Libroni*, e.g., pages with plate number 24843 should have only the initial H, for the engraver Pē, whereas the NLS copy has pages with this plate number with other initials.

As the Partenopeo, Naples, piano-vocal score cannot be dated, one cannot be certain whether it preceded or followed the Ricordi score. *Il Trovatore* was performed in Milan on Sept. 15, 1853, and in Naples on Oct. 4, 1853. The Boosey & Sons, London, score is dated by Hopkinson as 1853 (without substantiation) but also has English text and is presumably later than the Italian scores for that reason. The Escudier, Paris, score is 1854.

No early Ricordi printing of the separate sheet music of the *Anvil Chorus*, also probably published in Aug., 1853, has been found.† The Blanchet, Paris, printing of this separate piece was deposited for Dépôt Légal on Aug. 6, 1853, and is at BN; Archives. The Boosey & Sons, London, printing was received Aug. 9, 1853; BM. The date of the Naples printing is not known and no copy has been located.‡

---

[1] Announced "to be published in August," both in *GMM*, July 24, 1853, p. 133, and in *Ricordi Catalogue Supplement*, Milan, May–July, 1853, p. 23, NYPL. "Already published" in *GMM*, Aug. 7, 1853, and Aug. 14, 1853, p. 146. The engraving of the last number commenced June 14, 1853; and the "da pubblicarsi" date, and the date of receipt at the Office of Public Order, of the last numbers was August 6, 1853; Ricordi *Libroni*.

Apache Dance—Offenbach

m. J. Offenbach. The melody was first published for piano under the title *Valse des Rayons* from the ballet *Le Papillon*, which excerpt was entered for Dépôt Légal on Jan. 15, 1861,[1] by Heugel & Cie., Au Ménestrel, 2 bis Rue Vivienne [Paris]. First edition: Front cover states that the ballet is in two acts by Mme Marie Taglioni and Mr. de St. Georges, has a drawing of a dancer and two butterflies, lists eight numbers from the ballet, *Valse des Rayons* being number 4 at 6 francs, plus five others below, mentions a dedication to Madame La Comtesse de Morny and the dancer as Melle [sic] Emma Livry, refers to a Berlin agent and is brown and white. p. [2] blank. m. on pp. 1–9 (really 3–11). p.n. 3413(4). Back cover blank. There is also a separate leaf with a drawing of Emma Livry; vb. BN(CDC). This ballet was performed Nov. 26, 1860, in Paris. Apparently, no copy of the complete ballet was published.

Offenbach then used the melody again in his opéra-bouffe-féerie *Le Roi Carotte*, which was performed in Paris on Jan. 15, 1872. The melody appears in a ballet in the opera, entitled merely *Valse*, at p. 277 of the piano-vocal score which was entered for Dépôt Légal on Jan. 31, 1872,[2] by Choudens. BN(CDC), JMM and JF.

In neither *Le Papillon* nor *Le Roi Carotte* is the melody known as the *Apache Dance*. The melody became "The Apach's [sic] Dance" in 1908 when it was so danced by Mistinguett' [sic] and Max Dearly at the Moulin Rouge under the title *Valse Chaloupée*, arranged by Ch. Dubourg and published for piano by Choudens, Paris.[3] BN(CDC) and JF.

Jacques Offenbach was born as Jacques Levy at Offenbach-on-Main in 1819, but his early home was at Cologne and he used to refer to himself as "O de Cologne." He composed mostly at Paris and died there in 1880.

[1] Archives. The author is indebted to Harold Barlow, New York City, for this reference.

[2] *BF*, Feb. 17, 1872, p. 74.

[3] Anton Henseler, *Jakob Offenbach* (Berlin, 1930), p. 342, and George Grossmith, *"G.G."* (London, 1933), p. 48; both at NYPL. Richard Jackson, NYPL Music Division, and Andrew Lamb, Littlehampton, West Sussex, England, contributed this information.

April in Paris

A - pril in   Pa - ris,____   chest-nuts in blos - som

© 1932 Harms, Inc. Copyright renewed. Used by permission.

m. Vernon Duke. w. E. Y. Harburg. Published Dec. 5, 1932,[1] by Harms Incorporated, New York, N.Y. First edition: Front cover has a drawing of two fish, and is aqua, black and white. s. *Walk a Little Faster*—4 titles listed. m. on pp. 2–5. p.n. 8889-4. Back cover adv. *Let's.* . LC(CDC) and JF (inscribed by Duke and Harburg). The show opened in New York City on Dec. 7, 1932.

It is said that the title derives from a remark of Dorothy Parker during the rehearsal of the show that she wished she "were in April in Paris." Harburg had not been to Paris at the time he wrote the words of this song. The song was originally neglected and became appreciated only some years later.

Duke was born near Pskoff, Russia, in 1903. He was a composer of popular music under this, his assumed name, and of classical music under his original name, Vladimir Dukelsky, since abandoned. He died in Santa Monica, Cal., in 1969.[2] Harburg, an author, film producer and stage director, was born in New York City in 1898 and died in Los Angeles in 1981.[3]

April in Portugal

I   found my   A - pril dream   in   Port - u - gal with you
Co - im - bra é u-ma li - ção   de   so - nhoe tra - di - ção

© 1947 and 1953 by Chappell & Co. Inc. By consent.

m. Raúl Ferrão. w. José Galhardo. First published under the Portuguese title *Coimbra É uma Lição de Amor, Fado*, on Dec. 22, 1947,[1] by Sassetti & Ca., 54, Rua do Carmo, 58, Lisbon. First edition: Front cover has a photograph of Alberto Ribeiro, refers to the movie *Capas Negras*, and is brown and white. m. on pp. [2]–[3]. p.n. 922. The address of the publisher on p. [2] is 56, Rua do Carmo. Back cover adv. *És.. - Allō!..* LC (CDC).

[1] Copyright records; LC.
[2] Obituary, *The New York Times*, Jan. 18, 1969.
[3] Obituary, *The New York Times*, March 7, 1981.

[1] Copyright records; LC.

The Portuguese title means "Coimbra is a lesson of love," Coimbra being the former capital of Portugal which has a university famous for the lovemaking activities of its students. The American edition, with words by Jimmy Kennedy, was published in 1953. Ferrão, a composer of popular music, was born in Lisbon in 1890.[2] Galhardo, a lawyer and lyricist, was born in Lisbon in 1905.[2]

April Showers

Though A - pril show - ers_____ may come your way

m. Louis Silvers. w. B. G. de Sylva. Published Oct. 10, 1921,[1] by Harms Incorporated, New York, N.Y. (and Sunshine Music Co. Inc.). First edition: Front cover has a photograph of Al Jolson and is orange, gray and white. s. *Bombo*—6 titles listed. p. [2] blank. m. on pp. 3–5. p.n. 6390-3. Back cover adv. *Deep..* LC(CDC). The show opened in New York City on Oct. 6, 1921, and Al Jolson's singing of the song opening night drew 36 curtain calls. It has been said that de Sylva only shared in the composition of the melody.[2]

Silvers, a composer and conductor, was born in New York City in 1889 and died at Hollywood in 1954.[3] George Gard (Buddy) de Sylva, a composer, author and stage and screen producer, was born in New York City in 1895 and died in California in 1950.[4]

Aragonaise, Le Cid—Massenet

[2] *GEPB*, vol. XI, p. 146, and vol. XII, p. 71.

[1] Copyright records; LC.

[2] George P. Marshall, on the Oscar Levant television show, channel 13, New York, N.Y., Aug. 5, 1960.

[3] Obituary, *The New York Times*, March 28, 1954.

[4] *ASCAP*, p. 119.

m. J. Massenet. The piano-vocal score of *Le Cid* was published about Sept. 7, 1885,[1] by G. Hartmann, 20 rue Daunou, Paris. First edition: Front cover has only the title of the opera in many colors and designs. vb. Half-title page in brilliant colors. vb. Title page states that the [text] is by Ad. D'Ennery, L. Gallet and Ed. Blau, mentions the Académie Nationale de Musique, has a drawing of a scene from the opera, mentions the price of 20 francs and is in gold and other colors. vb. Dedication. vb. Cast. Index on two pages. vb. m. on pp. 1–355. p. [356] blank. p.n. G.H. 1571. Not engraved. BN(CDC) and JF. The *Aragonaise*, included in the Ballet, is at p. 157.

The full score of the opera was probably published by the same concern a few months later, about the date of the first performance, Nov. 30, 1885, in Paris. Probable first edition: Folio. Engraved. No title page or index page. m. on pp. 1–498. p.n. G.H. 1598. JMM. A proof of the full score, with corrections by Massenet, having 495 pages, had been at la Bibliothèque de l'Opéra, Paris (A. 645 b), but it is now missing. No early printing of orchestral parts of the opera has been found. The *Ballet* was published, probably a little later, as an engraved excerpt from the full score; BN and BPL. The *Ballet* was published as an extract from the piano-vocal score about Jan. 12, 1886,[2] at BN(CDC), and the *Aragonaise* was published for piano in 1887,[3] also at BN(CDC). Jules Massenet was born at Saint-Étienne in 1842 and died in Paris in 1912.

Arkansas Traveler

The first known printing of the melody was on Feb. 23, 1847,[1] by W. C. Peters (no city) under the title *The Arkansas Traveller and Rackinsac Waltz*. pp. [1] and [4] blank; m. on pp. [2]-[3]. No indication of composer; the arrangement is by William Cumming. Copublishers are Peters & Webster, Louisville, and Peters & Field, Cincinnati. p.n. 967. 1847 copyright claim on p. [2]. Engraved. No words. AAS and JF. In the Firth, Pond

---

[1] Deposited for Dépôt Légal on Sept. 7, 1885; Archives. *BMF*, Oct.–Dec., 1885, p. 128. *BF*, Jan. 2, 1886, p. 14.

[2] Deposited for Dépôt Légal on Jan. 12, 1886; Archives.

[3] Year of Dépôt Légal appears on copyright deposit copy at BN.

---

[1] Copyright records; LC.

& Co., New York, edition of 1851, the tune is called "A Western Refrain"; JF.

The famous dialogue story of the "Arkansas Traveler" probably first appeared in two variant uncopyrighted sheet music editions published by Blodgett & Bradford, Buffalo, N.Y., 1858–1863,[2] priority unknown—both by Mose Case;[2A] in one edition, F. F. Drigs, Dunkirk, is one of the copublishers, whereas in the other edition, Lints & Mathews, Erie, appears; both at JF. An almost identical uncopyrighted edition was published about Dec., 1863,[3] by Oliver Ditson & Co., Boston, with the credit to Mose Case and p.n. 22091; JF. The dialogue story is also said to have appeared in 1858–1860 in a version by Col. Faulkner;[4] the earliest edition found bearing his name has an 1859 copyright claim[4A] and is a large, colored lithograph entitled *The Arkansas Traveller*, "Designed by one of the natives and Dedicated to Col. S. C. Faulkner," containing the melody but without the dialogue story, printed by J. H. Bufford [Boston], at LC (Prints and Photographs Division). In an 1876 large cardboard printing by Col. S. C. Faulkner or B. S. Alford of the dialogue story and melody, the former claims to have been the original Arkansas Traveller in 1840; LC.

It has also been claimed that the melody of the *Arkansas Traveler* is derived from three different Irish tunes, *The Priest and His Boots, Johnny with the Queer Thing,* and *The Queen's Shilling*.[5] In this author's view, these three Irish tunes bear virtually no resemblance to the melody of the *Arkansas Traveler*.

In 1870 Currier and Ives lithographed two prints entitled *The Arkansas Traveller* and *The Turn of the Tune*, which illustrate and tell the traditional story—no music is included; MCNY.

---

[2] Dichter-Shapiro, p. 173. An advertisement in the Nov. 27, 1863, issue of the *Dunkirk Weekly Journal* refers to a musical store formerly occupied by F. F. Driggs (sic); Dunkirk Free Library, Dunkirk, N.Y. Lints & Mathews are listed in the *Financial Assessment of Erie County and General Business Directory* (1859), but not in the *Erie City Directory 1860–1861*, both at Erie Public Library, Erie, Pa. Both variants also refer to a D. J. Cook, Dunkirk, about whom no information has been found.

[2A] Case is listed as a guitarist in an 1859 Buffalo city directory. See Mary D. Hudgins, "Arkansas Traveler—A Multi-Parented Wayfarer," in *The Arkansas Historical Quarterly* (Fayetteville, Ark.), Summer, 1971, p. 145, at p. 149; NYPL.

[3] On the basis of the plate number.

[4] An excellent history of the *Arkansas Traveler* appears in James R. Masterson, *Tall Tales of Arkansaw* (sic) (Boston, 1943), pp. 186–254; NYPL.

[4A] But there is no record of such copyright at LC.

[5] Francis O'Neill, *Waifs*, p. 136. The melody of each of the three Irish tunes is set forth. No claim is made that any of them appeared in print prior to the *Arkansas Traveler*.

L'Arlésienne—(March of the Kings)

The first known printing of this Provençal air is under the title *Marcho dei Rèi* (*March of the Kings*), also said to be known as *Marche de Turenne*, in F. Vidal, *Lou Tambourin, Istori de l'Estrumen Prouvençau* (Avignon, n.d.), p. 258; BN (CDC, deposited 1864) and JF (with front cover stating 1864). The opening words of the song are "De matin, ai rescountra lou trin." The title of the book may be translated "The Tambourine, a History of the Provençal Instrument," and the opening words in French are: "Ce matin j'ai rencontré le train."

It has been said that this Provençal melody comes from the thirteenth century.[1] Georges Bizet used it in the opening bars of his music for Alphonse Daudet's drama *L'Arlésienne* (Arles being in Provence). In a footnote on the first music page of the piano-vocal score, Bizet stated that the melody was *Marcho dei Rèi* (*Air Provençal*). The piano-vocal score of *L'Arlésienne* was entered for Dépôt Légal on Nov. 13, 1872,[2] by Choudens, 265 Rue Saint Honoré, près l'Assomption, Paris. First edition: Front cover is buff and black with rustic drawings. vb. Title page reprints the front cover in brown and white, mentions that the play is by Alphonse Daudet, carries a dedication to Hippolyte Rodrigues, and indicates the price is 5 francs. vb. Index. m. on pp. 2–85. p.n. 2486. BN (CDC) and JF.

L'Arlésienne was performed Oct. 1, 1872, in Paris. The melody was included in the engraved orchestral first *Suite* from the music of the play, with p.n. 2542, in June, 1876 (COP [CDC]), and in the subsequent orchestral score of the incidental music of uncertain date, with p.n. 6647 (BM, BN, LC and NYPL).

Armide—Gluck

---

[1] Letter from BN. Saboly, p. 112. Thompson, p. 569.
[2] Archives. *BF*, Dec. 7, 1872, p. 582.

m. C. W. von Gluck. The above ballet music from Act IV, Scene II, was published in the orchestral score of *Armide* in Nov., 1777,[1] by Au Bureau du Journal de Musique, rue Montmartre, Paris. First edition: The title page mentions the first performance [in Paris] on Sept. 23, 1777, gives the price as 24 livres tournois, states that it was engraved by Mme Lobry and refers to the Royal Privilege. vb. m. on pp. 1–279. p. [280] blank. No plate number. Engraved. Folio. This ballet music is on p. 181. Copies at NYPL and JF and as stated as no. 45A in Hopkinson, *Gluck*, p. 57. No early printing of the orchestral parts of the opera has been noted.

Gluck was born in Weidenwang, in the Upper Palatinate, in 1714 and died in Vienna in 1787.

Around the World

A - round   the   world   I've   searched   for   you

m. Victor Young. w. Harold Adamson. Published Oct. 18, 1956,[1] by Victor Young Publications, Inc., 9538 Brighton Way, Beverly Hills, Cal. First edition: Front cover has a drawing of a large balloon on which appears (the name of the movie) *Around the World in 80 Days* and is purple and pink. Price .50¢ [sic]. m. on pp. [2]–[3]. No plate number. Back cover adv. *Around..* LC(CDC) and JF. While the melody was played in the movie, it was not sung there; and the words "in 80 days" do not appear in the song. The movie was copyrighted and released on Oct. 17, 1956.

Young, a composer and director, was born in Chicago in 1900 and died in Palm Springs, Cal., in 1956.[2] Adamson, an author, was born in Greenville, N.J., in 1906 and died in Beverly Hills, Cal., in 1980.[3]

Artist's Life

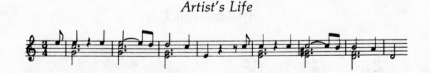

[1] *Mercure de France*, Nov., 1777, p. 170.

[1] Copyright records; LC.
[2] Obituary, *The New York Times*, Nov. 11, 1956.
[3] Obituary, *The New York Times*, Aug. 20, 1980.

m. Johann Strauss. Published about March 18, 1867,[1] for piano under the title *Künstler-Leben*, op. 316, C. A. Spina, Vienna. Probable first edition: Oblong. Front cover has a drawing of an artist with a lute, with four scenes depicting his life, a dedication to the Hesperusball-Comité, price of 80Nkr./15 Ngr., three agents and is black and white. Verso adv. works, including those by Johann Strauss up to op. 318, the latter also published for piano in Aug., 1867. m. on pp. 3–11. p.n. 19,229 (19,329 on front cover). Back cover blank. Verso of the front cover and music pages engraved. SB and JF.

The composition was performed Feb. 18, 1867. The orchestral parts were published about July 24, 1867.[2] In the probable first edition the collective title front cover reads, "Tänze für das Orchester," the highest op. no. listed is 319 (nos. 317–319 were published for orchestra Aug.–Oct., 1867[2]), the pages are engraved, the p.n. is 19,293, the publisher is as above, and the price is 5 Fl./3 Th., 5 Ngr.; ONB. Johann Strauss the younger was born in Vienna in 1825 and died there in 1899.

As Time Goes By

You must re-mem-ber this, a kiss is still a kiss, a sigh is just a sigh

mw. Herman Hupfeld. Published July 28, 1931,[1] by Harms Incorporated, 62 West 45th Street, New York, N.Y. First edition: Front cover has a photograph of Rudy Vallée, a drawing of an hourglass and is pink, aqua and white. No price. p. [2] adv. *Indian..* m. on pp. 3–7. p.n. 417–5. Back cover adv. *Two..* LC(CDC) and JF. No reference on front cover to the show *Everybody's Welcome*, which opened in New York City on Oct. 13, 1931.

The song was later sung by Dooley Wilson in the movie *Casablanca* starring Humphrey Bogart and Ingrid Bergman, which was released in 1942. Hupfeld, a composer and lyricist, was born in Montclair, N.J., in 1894 and died in the same city in 1951.[2]

---

[1] C. A. Spina, *Ablieferungsbuch*, SB. Hofmeister *Monatsbericht*, Aug., 1867, p. 316.
[2] C. A. Spina, *Ablieferungsbuch*, SB. Hofmeister *Monatsbericht*, Oct., 1867, p. [154].

[1] Copyright records; LC.
[2] *ASCAP*, p. 245.

Asleep in the Deep

Loud - ly the bell— in the old— tow-er rings

m. H. W. Petrie. w. A. J. Lamb. Copyrighted Dec. 7, 1897,[1] by Petrie Music Co., Chicago. Probable first edition of this favorite for bass singers: Front cover has a photograph of John Early, refers to Haverly's American-European Minstrels, lists three arrangements and is red, purple and white. pp. [2], [7] and back cover blank. m. on pp. [3]–[6]. p. [2] refers to the copyright in 1897 by Julie C. Petrie. p. [4] adv. *The Bell..* p. [5] adv. *The Tramp's..* p. [6] adv. *I Hear..* The first two advertised songs were copyrighted in 1895; no copyright record can be found of the third. JF. First sung at McVicker's Theater, Chicago.[2] Published by F. A. Mills commencing 1901.

Henry W. Petrie, a minstrel entertainer and composer, was born in Bloomington, Ill., in 1857 and died in 1925.[3] Arthur J. Lamb, a minstrel entertainer and author, was born in Somerset, England, in 1870 and died in Providence, R.I., in 1928.[3]

Assembly

The first known appearance of this American bugle call was in 1842 in George W. Behn, *Concise System of Instruction for the Volunteer Cavalry of the United States* (Savannah, Ga., 1842), p. 292; NYPL and JF.

Parody words commencing "There's a monkey in the grass" are frequently sung to this music.

At a Georgia Campmeeting

[1] Copyright records; LC.
[2] Geller, p. 111.
[3] *ASCAP*, pp. 388 and 289.

m. Kerry Mills (F. A. Mills). Copyrighted Aug. 9–14, 1897,[1] by F. A. Mills, 45 West 29th St., New York, N.Y. The copyright deposit copy at LC is a professional edition. Possible first regular edition: Front cover is red and white, has a rubber stamp signature of the publisher and refers to two co-publishers. p. [2] adv. *Rastus.. - Sweetheart..* m. on pp. 3–5. Back cover adv. *A Hot.. - Hickory..* All the songs advertised in this edition were copyrighted before Aug. 9, 1897.[1] No reference on the front cover to the song arrangement which was copyrighted later; JF.

This "cakewalk" march was popularized particularly by the stage team of Genaro & Bailey.[2] Frederick Allen Mills, a composer and publisher, was born in Philadelphia in 1869 and died in California in 1948.[3]

At Dawning

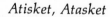

When the dawn flames in the sky I love you

Copyright 1906, Oliver Ditson Company. Used by permission.

m. Charles Wakefield Cadman. w. Nelle Richmond Eberhart (name does not appear on front cover). Copyrighted Nov. 8, 1906,[1] by Oliver Ditson Company, Boston. First edition: Front cover is a collective title page entitled *Songs by Charles Wakefield Cadman;* four songs are listed, of which this is the third, op. 29, no. 1. Front cover is red, yellow and white, and refers to three copublishers. Key is High Voice in A flat. p. [2] is blank. p. [3] has poem. m. on pp. 4–5, engraved. Back cover adv. *The Musicians..* LC (CDC). No drawing or arrangements on front cover.

John McCormack later popularized the song. Cadman, a composer, critic, pianist, lecturer and editor, was born at Johnstown, Pa., in 1881, and died at Los Angeles in 1946.[2] Eberhart, an author, was born in Detroit in 1871 and died at Kansas City in 1944.[2]

Atisket, Ataset

A - tis - ket a tas - ket,— a green and yel - low bas - ket

[1] Copyright records; LC.
[2] Geller, p. 170.
[3] ASCAP, p. 351.

[1] Copyright records; LC.
[2] ASCAP, pp. 70 and 137.

This children's song is apparently American, not English.[1] Its earliest known appearance in print is in A. H. Rosewig, *(Illustrated National) Nursery Songs and Games*, copyrighted Oct. 25, 1879[2] by W. F. Shaw [Philadelphia], p. [35], under the title *I Sent a Letter to My Love*. LC(CDC) and JF. There is no indication of authorship. The words "Atisket, Atasket" do not appear in the Rosewig book, but the title *Itisket, Itasket* is mentioned by Hofer, p. 15, 1901. The song was particularly revived in 1938 by Ella Fitzgerald.

Au Clair de la Lune

Au clair de la lu - ne, mon a - mi, Pier - rot

The first known printing of the melody is in the 1811 edition of *La Clé du Caveau* (Paris), p. 22; BN and JF. Adrien Boieldieu's *Les Voitures Versées*, performed in St. Petersburg on April 26, 1808, included this melody to other words; as far as is known, the opera was first published about 1820 by Boieldieu Jeune, Paris, the year of its performance in that city—copy at NYPL (melody at p. 185). Ignaz Moscheles' *Fantaisie et Variations* on the melody, op. 50, were published by Schlesinger, Berlin, in 1821–1822,[1] at LC; and Camille Pleyel's *Variations* on this air "*Chantée dans l'Opéra des Voitures Versées*" were published by Ignace Pleyel & Fils, Paris, probably about the same time,[2] at BN.

The first known printing of the words (and the melody) is in *Chants et Chansons Populaires de la France*, Deuxième Série ([Paris], 1843), on an unnumbered page, the 33rd of 42 songs; BN, BM, LC, NYPL and JF; the Introduction states that this is the first publication of *Au Clair de la Lune*. It is likely that this general collection was originally published in separate installments commencing about Feb. 26, 1842,[3] and *Au Clair de la Lune* may have therefore been first published in an earlier installment, but

---

[1] The song is not included in Opie. The Preface in the Rosewig book states that the book is the first collection containing any American nursery songs and children's plays. Hofer, p. 15, states that the song is American. The words, without music, are included as a British game in Gomme, vol. 1, p. 109, under the titles "Drop Handkerchief," "Wiskit-a-waskit" or "I wrote a letter to my love."

[2] Copyright records; LC.

---

[1] *MGG*, vol. 9, p. 618. *Handbuch Annual 1822* (Easter, 1821–Easter, 1822), p. 37.

[2] Hopkinson, *Parisian*, p. 100. Arrangements of the air were listed in BF commencing June 10, 1820, p. 317.

[3] *BF*, Feb. 26, 1842, p. 122.

no copy of any such earlier installment has been found. See the only
located separate issue at BN (Vmh 2640), particularly the back cover.

The song is sometimes said to have been composed by Lully, but no
confirmation of this has been found. Simone Wallon, at BN, wrote the
author that the melody is probably from the eighteenth century. Coirault
says that the song was called *(En) Roulant Ma Brouette* in the last quarter
of the eighteenth century, but the author has not been able to find a copy
of this song under this title printed at any time.[4]

Auld Lang Syne

Should   auld   ac–quain–tance   be   for – got, and   nev – er   brought   to   mind

The exact extent of Robert Burns's responsibility for the words and/or
music of *Auld Lang Syne* has always been a point of controversy.[1] However, it is generally agreed that he was not the author of the words of the
first verse—although it is not impossible that it underwent some revision
by him—and in most cases the first is the only verse people know.

The earliest version of the words with the title *Old-Long-Syne [sic]*,
and the opening line, "Should old Acquaintance be forgot," is in [James
Watson], *Scots Poems* (Edinburgh, 1711), part III, p. 71; NLS and YU.[2]
There were other printings of the words, including a version in 1787 in
vol. 1 of James Johnson's *The Scots Musical Museum* (Edinburgh),[3] p. 26,

---

[4] Coirault, *Chanson*, pp. 210 and 219. The words of *Roulant Ma Brouette* appear
in F. Bernard-Valville, *Le Petit Gagne-Petit* (Paris, An VIII [1800]), p. 13, BN, under the
title *Du Gagne-Petit*; the latter has also been searched in vain.

[1] The best history and analysis of the words and music of *Auld Lang Syne* are in
James C. Dick, *The Songs of Robert Burns* (London, 1903), pp. 400, 433 and 438; NYPL.
Glen, pp. 183 and 188, is also useful.

[2] The phrase alone, *auld lang syne*, appears in print at least as early as 1694. See
Dick, footnote 1, above, p. 435.

[3] There are four known editions of vol. 1, all having the price of 6/, all having a
vignette and none mentioning "In Six Volumes," but with different title pages: (a) publisher's name is not in the imprint and no frame around the vignette; (b) a frame
around the vignette and "Vol. I" in center of title page; (c) "Vol. I" to the left of title
page and "Johnson & Co." in imprint; and (d) "Vol. I" to the left of title page and
"James Johnson" in imprint. (a) is at BM, (d) is at LC and all four editions are at JF.
(a) is probably the earliest; the "Index" in (a) becomes "Index of Authors' names" in
the others. See J. W. Egerer, *A Bibliography of Robert Burns* (Edinburgh and London,
1964), p. 18; NYPL. When the entire work was republished, the price became 7/, and
each title page mentioned "In Six Volumes."

where it accompanied a melody which is not similar to the present melody. The first printing of Burns's—the present—words is in vol. 5 of this work (Edinburgh), in 1796–1797,[4] p. 426, to a still different melody that also bears no resemblance to the present melody. A manuscript by Burns of the words of *Auld Lang Syne* is at IU. Literally, the words "auld lang syne" mean "old long since."

The germ of the melody can be found under the title *The Duke of Bucclugh's Tune* in [Playford's] *Apollo's Banquet* (Fifth ed., London, 1687), no. 114; NLS and BUC, p. 789.[5] The melody developed under the titles *The Miller's Wedding* (in Bremner's *Scots Reels*, Edinburgh, ca. 1765, p. 41, BUC, p. 937, and JF, an important advance), *The Lasses of the Ferry*, *The Miller's Daughter*, *Sir Alexr. Don's Strathspey*, *Roger's Farewell*, and the *Overture* to William Shield's *Rosina* (London, 1783, p. 5, BUC, p. 947, and JF, another important advance). The melody later came to be known as *I Fee'd a Man at Martinmas*, these words by Burns appearing in vol. IV of *The Scots Musical Museum* (Edinburgh, [1792–1793]),[6] p. 407, under the title *O Can Ye Labor Lea, Young Man*; this is substantially the presently known melody.

The present words and present melody first appeared together about May 1, 1799,[7] in (George Thomson) *A Select Collection of Original Scotish* [sic] *Airs*, [Third] Set (London), p. 68; BUC, p. 1006 and JF. (**See Plate I.**) In the first edition of this Set, the preface is undated, and there are 25

---

[4] There are three known editions of vol. 5: (a) no mention of "In Six Volumes," and the volume number is shown as "V"; (b) no mention of "In Six Volumes," and the volume number is shown as "IIIII"; and (c) there is mention of "In Six Volumes." (a) is at BM and JF, (b) is at PMU, and (c) see BUC, p. 557. Priority between (a) and (b) is uncertain; (c) is later. See also the last sentence of the first paragraph of footnote 3, above.

Dick places the time of publication as the close of 1796; *Grove's*, in 1797 (vol. IV, p. 647). Nine copies of vol. 5 were entered at Stationers' Hall on May 13, 1797.

[5] Not in the edition ca. 1669; DPL.

[6] There are three known editions of vol. 4: (a) the imprint is James Johnson; (b) the imprint is Johnson & Co. and the vol. no. is shown as "IV"; and (c) the imprint is Johnson & Co., and the vol. no. is shown as "IIII." (a) see BUC, p. 557 (however, James Johnson became Johnson & Co. about 1790?—Humphries-Smith, p. 194); (b) is at BM; and (c) is at JF. Priority is uncertain although (a) is probably the earliest. Nine copies of vol. 4, published by James Johnson, were entered at Stationers' Hall on Feb. 2, 1793. See also the last sentence of the first paragraph of footnote 3, above.

[7] Nine copies were entered at Stationers' Hall on that date. J. Cuthbert Hadden, *George Thompson* (London, 1898), p. 118, says July, 1799, which is incorrect; NYPL. Advertised in *The Glasgow Courier*, Sept. 3, 1799, p. 3; ML.

The accompanying violin part for the [Third] Set is at JF.

settings by Kozeluch.[8] It is not clear whether Thomson or Burns brought the words and melody together. Beethoven later made a setting of *Auld Lang Syne*.[9]

Burns was born at Alloway, Scotland, in 1759, and died in Dumfries, Scotland, in 1796.

Aura Lea—(Love Me Tender)

When the black - bird in the spring, on the wil - low tree
Love me ten - der, love me sweet; nev - er let me go

m. Geo. R. Poulton. w. W. W. Fosdick. Copyrighted May 1, 1861,[1] by J. Church, Jr., 66 West 4th St., Cincinnati, Ohio. Probable first edition: Engraved. Front cover mentions a dedication to S. C. Campbell, Esq., of Hooley & Campbell's Minstrels and lists three copublishers. Price: 2½. p. [2] blank. m. on pp. 3–5. p.n. 231–4. Back cover blank. JF.

In 1956 a new lyric entitled *Love Me Tender* was written to the melody by Elvis Presley and Vera Matson. LC(CDC—back cover blank) and JF. Poulton died at Lansingburg, N.Y., in 1867; he was a composer and newspaper writer.† William Whiteman Fosdick was born in Cincinnati, Ohio, in 1825, became a poet and writer and died in 1862.[2]

Ave Maria—Bach-Gounod

A - ve Ma - ri - a, —— gra - ti-a ple - na

The Bach-Gounod *Ave Maria* has been nicely described as "a *cantabile* melody superimposed by Gounod on the first prelude, in C major, from Bach's *Das wohltemperirte Clavier*."[1]

The bibliographic history of Bach's *Well-Tempered Clavier* has been

---

[8] Cecil Hopkinson and C. B. Oldman, *Thomson's Collections of National Song*, in *Edinburgh Bibliographical Society Transactions* (Edinburgh, 1940) vol. II, part 1; NYPL. In this article, the [Third] Set is referred to as "Vol. II(a)." (Contrary to this article, the preface in the first edition of the [Second] Set is not dated.)

[9] Kinsky-Halm, p. 653.

---

[1] Copyright records; LC.

[2] *Dict. Am. Biog.*, vol. VI, p. 540.

---

[1] Westrup-Harrison, p. 42.

well reported,[2] three editions, each in two parts, having appeared at about the same time in 1801. One of the three editions was published by Hans Georg Nägeli, in Zurich, entitled *Das Wohltemperirte Clavier;*† BM, LC, ONB and JF. The second of the three editions was published by Hoffmeister & Comp., at Leipzig, at the Bureau de Musique, under the title *Le Clavecin Bien Tempéré;* RBW and BM.[3] The third publisher, N. Simrock, at Bonn, printed at least three early editions under the French title: (a) in what is said to be the earliest,[4] the words "Écrit par Sampier" appear on the title page (BM); (b) in another, Bach's name on the title page is given as "J. Seb. Bach" (RBW, although the catalogue states that the title page is not an integral part of this edition);[5] and (c) the title page has a background of circles together with a lyre in the center (RBW); this may be the ca. 1828 edition, as one part has prices in Thlr. and Sgr., as well as in Frs., and this may signify publication after the completion of the French occupation (1814).

While it has been said[6] that the Lavenu edition was the earliest printing of the Bach work in 1800, Lavenu was at the particular address only commencing 1805.[7] BUC, p. 78, refers to a Broderip and Wilkinson edition, ca. 1800; however, it has an 1808 watermark. Hirsch, vol. III, no. 56, refers to an edition published by Preston, London, said to be ca. 1800; it has, however, an 1815 watermark (pp. 61–62).

Prototypes of Bach's first *Prelude* were included in two *Notebooks* of Bach, but neither *Notebook* was published until well after 1801.[8]

The first printing of any portion of the *Well-Tempered Clavier* was in Friedrich Wilhelm Marpurg, *Abhandlung von der Fuge* (Berlin, 1753–4); BPL, LC and NYPL.[9] ‡

The melody of Gounod's *Ave Maria* first appeared in print about

---

[2] Edgar Refardt, *Briefe Hans Georg Nägelis an Breitkopf & Härtel,* in *Zeitschrift für Musikwissenschaft* (Leipzig, 1931), p. 389; NYPL. *Bach Gesellschaft* [vol. 14(3)], p. xx, and [vol. 45(1)], p. lxiv. Schneider, p. 100. *MGG,* vol. 1, p. 1039 (in a subsequent letter to the author, Prof. Blume agreed that the three editions appeared virtually simultaneously).

[3] *Riemenschneider,* no. 2471, p. 267, refers to an edition published by Hoffmeister & Kühnel. If there is such an edition, other than Hoffmeister & Comp., it has not been found, and would be later; Deutsch, *Plate Number,* p. 14.

[4] *Bach Gesellschaft,* footnote 2, above.

[5] *Riemenschneider,* no. 2443, p. 263 (but the catalogue does not state what edition it is part of, and the present Librarian at RBW does not know).

[6] By Kroll; see Schneider, footnote 2, above, p. 100.

[7] Letter from BM. An edition published by Lavenu is at RML, dated 1809(?).

[8] Johann Sebastian Bach, *Clavier-Büchlein vor Wilhelm Friedmann Bach*—Facsimile (New Haven, 1959), pp. 29 and 151; YU. *Das Notenbuch der Anna Magdalena aus dem Jahre 1725* in *Bach Gesellschaft* [vol. 43(1)], p. 39.

[9] Part of this work was also published by Kollmann in 1799, but not the entire work (*MGG,* footnote 2, above).

April 26, 1853,[10] under the title *Méditation sur le Ier Prélude de Piano de S. Bach*, for piano and violin solo with organ accompaniment, published by Heugel et Cie., au Ménestrel, Rue Vivienne 2 bis, Paris. Probable first edition: Front cover has a dedication to J. Zimmerman (Gounod's father-in-law), indicates the price is 7f.50 and mentions London and Mainz copublishers. vb. Next page blank. m. on pp. 2–9 (really 4–11). p.n. 1595. Back cover blank. Engraved. The part for piano also shows the music for the other instruments. COP (CDC) and BMI. The Peters edition of the foregoing, at NYPL, is listed in the Nov., 1853, issue of Hofmeister *Monatsbericht*, p. 439 (BM), and the Schott edition, at LBH, is listed in Hofmeister *Annual*, 1853, p. 13 (apparently not in the *Monatsbericht*). A piano solo arrangement, with p.n. 1618, was deposited on June 15, 1853, by Heugel for Dépôt Légal; BN and COP (both CDC). †

In 1856, words were added, but not the words of *Ave Maria*; the title remained *Méditation*, and the arrangement was for orchestra and chorus; BN(CDC).

It was not until about Aug. 1, 1859,[11] that *Ave Maria* was published. First edition: The title is *Ave Maria*; the publisher is Heugel et Cie. The front cover states that the song is sung by Mme Miolan-Carvalho,[12] mentions the French words are by Paul Bernard, and lists four arrangements of which the first is for soprano or tenor (and piano) at 3 f. p. [2] blank. m. on pp. 1–3 (really 3–5). p.n. 2437(1). Back cover blank. Music pages are engraved. BN(CDC). Arrangement no. 1 bis is for different voices; no. 2 En quatuor; and no. 3 for orchestra complete—all CDC at BN, and the last at JF.

Ave Maria, or "Hail, Mary," are the first words of the prayer of the Roman Catholic Church from the Angel Gabriel's address to Mary (Luke 1:28).

Gounod was born in Paris in 1818. It is interesting to note in connection with *Ave Maria* that he studied several years for the priesthood, but later renounced the plan, although composing much liturgical music. He died in Saint-Cloud in 1893. Brief biographic information regarding Bach appears above under *Air for the G String*.

[10] Dépôt Légal records at Archives. April 29, 1853, per letter from Heugel; Heugel has Gounod's signed sale of the composition dated April 6, 1853. *Le Ménestrel*, May 1, 1853, p. 4. BF, Sept. 24, 1853, p. 657. There are confusing and contradictory notes on *Ave Maria* in J.-G. Prod'homme and A. Dandelot, *Gounod* (Paris, 1911), vol. 2, p. [251] and p. [269], NYPL, in which it is also said that the first version of *Ave Maria* was originally published by L. Mayaud et Cie., Paris, on Dec. 24, 1852. Heugel denies this, and not the slightest trace can be found of this edition, or of any other reference to it.

[11] Letter from Heugel; Heugel has Gounod's sale of the composition dated July 5, 1859. *Le Ménestrel*, July 3, 1859 [sic], p. 247. BF, Aug. 13, 1859, p. 388. Aug. 18, 1859, per Dépôt Légal records at Archives. Deposited at BM on Oct. 11, 1859.

The Schlesinger, Berlin, edition of *Ave Maria* is in Hofmeister *Monatsbericht*, Jan., 1860, p. 17; NYPL. The Schott, Mainz, edition, at NYPL, is in *id.*, April, 1860, p. 78.

[12] First on May 24, 1859, per Prod'homme-Dandelot, fn. 10, above, vol. 2, p. 265.

Ave Maria—Schubert

A - ve Ma-ri - a!   mai - den— mild!
                        jung - frau—

m. Franz Schubert. English words by Walter Scott. Published April 5, 1826, in *Sieben Gesänge aus Walter Scott's Fräulein vom See*, op. 52, second part, by Math. Artaria, 258 Kohlmarkt, Vienna.[1] First edition: Title page has a dedication to Sophie, Gräfin v. Weissenwolf, and the price of the second part is Fl. 1. 15 x (Kr.) Conv. Mze. *Ave Maria* are the opening words of *Ellen's III. Gesang (Hymne an die Jungfrau)*, with English and German words, p. 11. p.n. 814. Oblong. Engraved. SB and JF. This song was composed in the spring or summer of 1825 and performed on Jan. 31, 1828, in Vienna.

The words bear no relation to the Roman Catholic prayer used by Gounod, and are taken from Sir Walter Scott's *The Lady of the Lake* (Printed for John Ballantyne & Co., Edinburgh, and Longman, Hurst, Rees and Orme and William Miller, London, by James Ballantyne & Co., Edinburgh, 1810), no. XXIX, *Hymn to the Virgin*, p. 136; BM. The German translation was by Adam Storck.

Schubert was born in Vienna in 1797 and died there in 1828. Scott was born in Edinburgh in 1771 and died at Abbotsford in 1832.

Away in a Manger

A - way in a   man-ger, no   crib for a   bed

Although the music and/or words of this Christmas carol are frequently attributed to Martin Luther, it has been conclusively shown by Richard S. Hill that he was the author of neither, and that this carol is not known in Europe and is entirely of American origin.[1]

The words were included in the *Little Children's Book: for Schools*

---

[1] Deutsch, *Schubert*, no. 839, p. 529. *Wiener Zeitung*, April 5, 1826, p. 339; UMI.

[1] Richard S. Hill, "Not So Far Away in a Manger" in *Notes*, Dec., 1945, p. 12.

and Families. By Authority of the General Council of the Evangelical Lutheran Church in North America (Philadelphia), copyrighted on June 16, 1885,[2] although the preface is dated "Christmas 1884." Two stanzas appear on p. 140 as a "Nursery" hymn, to music that is not the common music. No author of the words is stated. UTS. Subsequent research has not established who is the author of the words.

The common music (and words) were included in James R. Murray, *Dainty Songs for Little Lads and Lasses, for Use in the Kindergarten* (Cincinnati), copyrighted on May 7, 1887.[2] The song appears on p. 110 as "Luther's Cradle Hymn (Composed by Martin Luther for his children, and still sung by German mothers to their little ones)." NYPL. Hill believes that Murray was the composer of the music. He was born in Andover, Mass., in 1841–1842, and later went to Cincinnati to edit the *Musical Visitor* for The John Church Co.; it is believed that he died in 1904.

Ay—Ay—Ay

Si al - gu-na vez en   tu   pe-cho ay ya yay   mi   ca - ri - ño no lo a - bri - gas

mw. Osman Perez Freire. This song is said to have been published first in 1913 by Breyer Hermanos, 414 Florida, Buenos Aires.[1] In an edition so published, a possible first edition, after the title, are the words "Reminiscencias Cuyanas" (a region in northwest Argentina), there is a picture of a man singing to a lady, the price is B $0.60, and there is a no. 3664. The music and words appear on two unnumbered pages. Copy at Ricordi Americana, Buenos Aires. A similar edition lacks a street address for the publisher; JF (front cover is brown and tan, and back cover is blank). A Chilean edition of uncertain date, published by Casa Amarilla, Santiago, states that the song is a "Tonada Chilena" (Chilean song); JF. The first known dated edition is dated 1920 and was published by L. Maillochon, Paris, where the song is called a "Serenata Criolla";[2] JF. The autograph manuscript of the song is at PAU.

This song should not be confused with the Mexican *Cielito Lindo*, whose chorus begins, "Ay, ay, ay, ay." Freire was born in Santiago, Chile, in 1878, moved to Mendoza, Argentina, in 1886, went to Spain in the 1920's and died in Madrid in 1930.[3]

---

[2] Copyright records; LC.

[1] Letter from Ricordi Americana, Buenos Aires; and records at ASCAP.
[2] "Criolla" means Argentine.
[3] Letters from PAU and the Ministry of Foreign Relations, Republic of Chile.

Bacchanale—Samson and Delilah

m. Camille Saint-Saëns. The music was published, probably late in 1876,[1] by Durand, Schoenewerk & Cie., 4 Place de la Madeleine, Paris, in the piano-vocal score of *Samson et Dalila*. Possible first edition: Front cover is gray and black and states price as 15 f. vb. Title page has the imprint of the publisher to the right (not in the center) and a drawing of an Egyptian scene in many colors, and states that the piano arrangement of the opera is by the composer and that the French words are by Ferdinand Lemaire and the German translation by Richard Pohl. vb. Dedication to Madame Viardot-Garcia. vb. Index. vb. m. on pp. [1]–264, the *Bacchanale* on p. 198. The text is in French and German. p.n. 2186. Back cover blank. BN and JF (autographed by the composer). The opera was performed in Weimar in German on Dec. 2, 1877; it was not performed in French until 1890 in Rouen. The *Bacchanale* was printed separately in 1878 for piano, orchestral score and parts.[2]

The orchestral parts of the opera were entered for Dépôt Légal on April 18, 1878.[3] There are no covers. p.n. 2388. Engraved. BN(CDC). The orchestral score, probably published about the same time, has, in the probable first edition, a front cover in black and gray. vb. Dedication. vb. Title page is similar to that of the piano-vocal score, the name of the publisher continuing as Durand, Schoenewerk & Cie. vb. Cast and index. Instrumentation. m. on pp. 1–494. p.n. 2389. Music pages engraved. French and German text. BN (lacking back cover) and JMM (gray back cover).

Charles Camille Saint-Saëns was born in Paris in 1835 and died in Algiers in 1921. All that is known regarding Ferdinand (de) Lemaire is that he died in Bagnols-les-Bains (Lozère), France, in 1879.[4]

Il Bacio

Sul - le,   sul - le lab - bra,   sul - le lab - bra,   se po-tes

[1] *Bib. Mus.*, Aug.–Sept., 1876, p. 295. BF, Nov. 25, 1876, p. 670. The *Saint-Saëns Catalogue*, p. 103, however, says that the opera was composed from 1868 to 1877 and published in 1877.

[2] *Bib. Mus.*, Jan.–Feb., 1878, p. 10. BF, Feb. 23, 1878, p. 114.

[3] Archives. BF, May 18, 1878, p. 257.

[4] *EDM*, vol. II, p. 589.

m. L. Arditi. w. Aldighieri. *Il Bacio* was published March 27, 1860,[1] by Cramer, Beale & Chappell, 201 Regent Street and 67 Conduit Street, London. First edition: p. 1 has a dedication to Madlle. Piccolomini and the price is 3s. m. on pp. 1–10. p.n. 7351. Key of D. Italian text. Not engraved. BM (copyright copy deposited May 5, 1860). No front cover. The arrangement for piano with p.n. 7361 was deposited June 6, 1860; BM(CDC). †

Arditi has stated that the song was written while he was in England and sold in 1860 for fifty pounds to the Cramer firm.[2] Its title in English is *The Kiss*. Arditi was born in Crescentino, Piedmont, in 1822, became a composer and conductor and died in Hove, Brighton, in 1903.[3] Gottardo Aldighieri, an Italian baritone, was born in 1824 at Lazise, Lake of Garda, and died in 1906 in Verona.[4]

The Band Played On

Ca-sey would waltz with a straw-ber-ry blonde, and the band played on

m. John F. Palmer. w. Chas. B. Ward. This song was published in the *New York Sunday World*, June 30, 1895, p. 32, being stated there to have been "Written for the Sunday World." Palmer is credited with the music and Ward the words. LC and NYPL (both on microfilm). The regular sheet music edition was copyrighted July 12, 1895,[1] by The New-York Music Co., 57 West 28th St., New York, N.Y. First sheet music edition: Front cover is green and white, and has a dedication to the *New York Sunday World*. m. on pp. 2–5. Back cover adv. *The New.. - True..* LC(CDC). The sheet music edition omitting the name of John F. Palmer is apparently later; JF.

According to one writer, Palmer wrote almost all of the music as well as all of the words, but Ward, the owner of the publishing company, listed himself as the composer.[2] All that is known about Palmer is that he was an actor in New York City.[2] Ward, an actor, composer and publisher, was born in London in 1865 and died in New York City in 1917.[3]

[1] According to the entry at Stationers' Hall on May 5, 1860.

[2] Luigi Arditi, *My Reminiscences* (New York, N.Y., 1896), p. 61; NYPL.

[3] *Grove's*, vol. 1, p. 194.

[4] *EDS*, vol. 1, p. 254.

[1] Copyright records; LC.

[2] Geller, p. 75. He may have been too young to have been the John Palmer who was born in 1877 in Albany, N.Y., became a pianist and entertainer, and later an employee at Steinway & Sons, and died in Albany in 1943; obituary, *MA*, Sept., 1943.

[3] *ASCAP*, p. 521.

The Barber of Seville-Overture—Rossini

m. G. Rossini. Rossini used essentially the same *Overture* for his *Aureliano in Palmira*, performed in Milan on Dec. 26, 1813, *Elisabetta*, performed in Naples on Oct. 4, 1815, and *Il Barbiere di Siviglia*, performed in Rome on Feb. 20, 1816.[1]

The first printing of the *Overture* was probably in 1814[1A] for piano under the title Gran Sinfonia nell' opera, *Aureliano in Palmira*, by Gio. Ricordi, 1065 Conta. di Sa. Margherita, Milan.[1B] m. on pp. 1–7. p.n. 164. Oblong. Engraved. No reference on page 1 to *Il Barbiere di Siviglia*. MIC. Later printings refer to *Il Barbiere di Siviglia* on page 1;[1C] Biblioteca Palatina, Parma, and NYPL. The later printing, with the same plate number 164, also served as the *Overture* to Rossini's piano-vocal score of *Il Barbiere di Siviglia* published by the same concern in 1824–1827 with a title page showing the publisher without a street address and a Florence agent, Gio. Ricordi, Pozzi e Co.; JF.

The *Overture* to *Der Barbier von Sevilla* was published for piano in 1819–1820[2] by S. A. Steiner und Comp., Graben no. 572, Vienna, at 30 xr., on pp. 2–9, with p.n. 2877, engraved and oblong; ONB (MS-28046). During 1820–1821, the orchestral score of the *Overture* of this opera was published by Carli, Paris, at 9 fr.; no copy has been found.[3] †

Between Sept. 29, 1820, and Feb., 1821,[4] a piano-vocal score of *Il Barbiere di Siviglia* was published by Breitkopf & Härtel, Leipzig, with

---

[1] The author is grateful to Prof. Philip Gossett, Chicago, for information regarding this title. See Gossett, *passim*, and dissertation on the *Operas of Rossini* at PUL.

None of the operas is listed in Meysel or in the *Handbuch Annual* through 1818.‡

[1A] On the basis of the plate number and imprint. The Ricordi *Libroni* list this publication, but without a date.

[1B] Ricordi was the copyist for the La Scala Opera House, where *Aureliano in Palmira* had its first performance, and had control over the music. Lucherini, Florence, published a piano arrangement of this *Overture* on uncertain date; BM. Lorenzi, Florence, did also; MIC. Ratti e Cencetti, Rome, received a privilege from the Papal States in 1821 to do likewise; letter from SCR, and copy of *Overture* at SCM.

[1C] This may be the edition listed in *Handbuch Annual* 1819 (Easter, 1818–Easter, 1819), p. 47; NYPL.

[2] *Handbuch Annual* 1820 (Easter, 1819–Easter, 1820), p. 30; ONB. The opera was performed in Vienna in German on Sept. 28, 1819. Excerpts from the opera began to be freely published from this time forward.

[3] *Handbuch Annual* 1821 (Easter, 1820–Easter, 1821), p. 3, ONB.

[4] *AMZ Int-Bl*, Feb., 1821.

Italian and German text at 5 Thlr.; there are at least two editions that may have been so published: one, lithographed with 174 pages and plate number 3671, at ONB and JF, and the other, typeset, with 144 pages and without plate number, at BM. Another contemporary edition with 158 pages, other information lacking, was listed in H. Baron *Catalogue* no. 64 (London, [1863]), no. 273; *Catalogue* at H. Baron, London, and JF. Between Easter, 1820, and Easter, 1821,[4A] a piano-vocal score of this opera was published by Mechetti, Vienna, without plate number, at ONB.

Philip Gossett, Chicago, believes the first piano-vocal score of *Il Barbiere* was probably published in 1820–1821 by Boieldieu Jeune, Paris; a copy of this edition, with Italian text and plate number 994, at 36 francs, is at LC.[4B] Mr. Gossett also believes Carli, Paris, published a piano-vocal score after Boieldieu, but in 1820–1821; copies of this printing with a partially Italian title page are at LC, UNC and JMM, and with an entirely French title page, at JMM.

The first printing of the orchestral score of the entire *The Barber of Seville* was by A La Lyre Moderne, 6 Rue Vivienne, Paris. There are two editions, the earlier evidently having been published before Sept. 19, 1821, as the title page states "Représenté pour la première fois le [blank]", without indication of place of performance; the later edition (and the reprint of April, 1827, or thereafter by the successor publisher, A. Petit) refer to the presentation of the opera at Lyons on Sept. 19, 1821.[5] In both editions, the title is *Le Barbier de Séville*, the price is 60 f., the verso of the title page is blank, there is a cast page, the music is on pages 2–393, the text is in Italian and French (the latter translation by Castil-Blaze), p. [394] is blank, the p.n. is 346, and the pages are engraved. The earlier edition is at LC (with an appendix of nine pages) and JF (in old binding without appendix); the later edition is at BM (price changed in ink to the later price of 100 fr.), BPL, COP and JMM. The opera was first performed in French in Lyons on Sept. 19, 1821. On the cast page, in the earlier edition, there is one column

---

[4A] *Handbuch Annual* 1821, p. 74; ONB.

[4B] On the basis of plate number and other external and internal evidence. Letter from Mr. Gossett. The opera was performed in Paris on Oct. 26, 1819. The reference in *BF*, Nov. 2, 1822, is to the Boieldieu piano score at 15 francs; BN.

The date of the earliest Italian piano-vocal score of this opera by Sonzogno, Milan, is not known; see Radiciotti, vol. III, p. 208. A piano-vocal score was published by Ricordi Milan, without street address and with plate numbers up to 3310 (copy at JF); the engraving of the pieces commenced up to June 29, 1827, according to the Ricordi *Libroni*.

[5] Kinsky, *Opern*, p. 374, says 1821. Wolffheim, p. 312, says 1821. Sonneck, *Dramatic Music*, p. 142, says before 1824. Radiciotti, vol. III, p. 208, says 1824. Only in the case of Sonneck do we know which of the two editions was being dated.

The orchestral score published at 100 fr. by the successor publisher, A. Petit, Paris, at BN and NYPL, is April, 1827, or later; Hopkinson, *Parisian*, p. 67.

of cast; in the later edition and in the Petit reprint, there are two columns of cast, one for Lyon and one for Paris. (Curiously, the one column in the earlier edition lists, without indication of city, the cast which is designated in the later edition for Paris; also, the reference on the cast page in each case is to the Théâtre Royal de l'Opéra-Comique which coincides with neither the place of the 1821 performance at Lyons, le Grand Théâtre, nor the place of the May 6, 1824, performance in French at Paris, l'Odéon.)

The orchestral score published under the title *Almaviva o sia il Barbiere di Siviglia* by Leopoldo Ratti, Gio. Batta Cencetti e Comp., Rome (SCR, BM and JMM), could not have been published until at least 1829 as the title page refers to the composer as "Cav^e." which decoration of the Legion of Honor he received in that year.[6] An orchestral score was also published by G. G. Guidi, Florence; Jean-Marie Martin, Hollogne-aux-Pierres, Belgium, believes the year of publication was 1864. A probable reprint, with presumably the original plate number 2342, is at NYPL.

No early piano-vocal score of *Aureliano in Palmira* has been found or known to have been published.[7] Piano-vocal scores of *Elisabetta* were published in 1819–1820[8] by N. Simrock, Bonn and Cologne (NC, NYPL, UC, UI and JF, and by Breitkopf & Härtel, Leipzig (BPL and LC). Orchestral parts of the *Overture* to *Elisabetta* were published in 1820–1821 by Simrock (p.n. 1796, price 6 frs., engraved—at BSM) and Breitkopf & Härtel, no copy found.[9] No orchestral score or parts of either opera has been published.

The engraving of the orchestral parts of the opera for the strings commenced on Oct. 2, 1862, with plate numbers 34537–34540, according to the Ricordi *Libroni*, but the earliest discovered parts, oblong engraved, have the imprint of G. Ricordi & C., necessitating a year not earlier than 1898;

---

[6] Radiciotti, vol. III, p. 299. The p.n. is 234. The publisher began business in 1822; Sartori, p. 127. (In 1821 the publisher had received a privilege to publish certain music; see footnote 1B, above.) Kinsky, *Opern*, p. 374, gives the date of the Ratti orchestral score as "about 1830." Radiciotti, vol. III, p. 208, gives no date. *BM Mus. Cat. Acc. 53*, p. 352, states "1816?". Sonneck, *Dramatic Music*, p. 142, says "182–".

The original title of the opera was *Almaviva o sia l'Inutile Precauzione*. The title *Il Barbiere di Siviglia* was first used in Bologna on Aug. 10, 1816.

[7] Piano-vocal scores of *Aureliano* published by G. Ricordi, Milan, with p.ns. 26463–26491 (1855–1856, according to the Ricordi *Libroni*) are at BOL, LC, SCR and UC. Another published by Schonenberger, Paris, in 1855 is at BN, BPL and UC. Radiciotti, vol. III, p. 202. A piano score published by Sauer & Leidesdorf, Vienna, about 1825 has a different overture; BM and BSM.

[8] *Handbuch Annual* 1820 (Easter, 1819–Easter, 1820), p. 45; NYPL. Other early piano-vocal scores of *Elisabetta* were published by Boieldieu, Paris (BN, COP, HU and UNC), Carli, Paris (BSM and JMM) and Pacini, Paris (COP, LC, NW, TL, FDB and UI). The earliest Ricordi edition that has been found has p.ns. 26602–26625 (about 1856, according to the Ricordi *Libroni*); BOL, COP, SCR and UC. Radiciotti, vol. III, p. 205.

[9] *Handbuch Annual* 1821 (Easter, 1820–Easter, 1821), p. 3; NYPL.

at MET, ROH and JF*. The orchestral parts of the opera for other instruments commenced on July 9, 1881, with plate number 47569; such parts, folio engraved, without imprint or covers, are also at MET and JF*.

Gioacchino Rossini was born in Pesaro in 1792 and died in Paris in 1868. Cesare Sterbini, the librettist, was born in Rome in 1784 and died there in 1831.[10]

Barcarolle—The Tales of Hoffmann

Bel - le nuit, ô   nuit_ d'a-mour, sou - ris _   à nos   i - vres - ses!

The melody of the *Barcarolle*, by J. Offenbach, was first used in his opera *Die Rhein Nixen*, produced in Vienna on Feb. 4, 1864.[1] The manuscript of the opera is at ONB, and the melody is in the opening bars of the *Overture* and on p. 4 of the second act to the words "Komm' zu uns." Neither the opera, the *Overture* nor this aria was apparently printed, but a *Potpourri* from the opera was published about May, 1864,[2] by C. A. Spina, Vienna, which includes the melody. The *Potpourri* is no. 83 of *Anthologie Musicale* for piano, p.n. 18066, the particular melody appearing on p. 16; ONB. The opera was originally written in French and entitled *Les Fées du Rhin*; it apparently was not so produced or published.

As the *Barcarolle* from the opera *Les Contes d'Hoffmann* (*The Tales of Hoffmann*), it was published in Feb. or March, 1881, by Choudens, Père & Fils, 265 Rue St. Honoré, Paris, in the piano-vocal score of the opera. First edition: On the title page, the words of the opera are attributed to J. Barbier and M. Carré. (In subsequent editions, the name M. Carré has either been blacked out, as at BM, or is omitted.[3]) Verso of title page has legal notices. Dedication by Offenbach to his son. vb. Cast and index. vb. m. on pp. 1–242; the *Barcarolle et Choeur* on p. 151. p.n. 5100. BN(CDC), JMM and JF. The separate sheet music of the *Barcarolle*, in three arrangements, 13, 13 bis and 13 ter, p.ns. 5172, 5147 and 5158, seems to have

---

[10] *DR*, p. 1010.

[1] The author is indebted to Harold Barlow, New York City, for this information. A printed libretto of the opera, dated 1864, is at NYPL and JF, the particular words at p. 31.

[2] Hofmeister *Monatsbericht*, May, 1864, p. 91.

[3] Carré had been the coauthor with Barbier of the play of the same name which had been produced in Paris in 1851; he died in 1872, nine years before the opera was performed.

been published about the same time as the piano-vocal score;[4] BN(CDC) and first two at JF. The piano score has p.n. 5163; BN(CDC). The first performance of the opera (which had been left incomplete at Offenbach's death) was on Feb. 10, 1881, in Paris.

The orchestral score of *Les Contes d'Hoffmann* was printed in 188—[5] by Choudens Père et fils, 30 Boulevard des Capucines, Près la Rue Caumartin, Paris. Title page has a drawing of three women. vb. Cast and index page with p.n. 5100. vb. The copy at LC is partly a lithographing of a manuscript score, is numbered 77 and has music on pages 5–366 and plate number 5303; pages up to 87 are in great confusion, with both repeated and unused page numbers. The copy at BM is numbered 43 and has regular printed music on pages 1–354. In each, the *Barcarolle* is on page 181. Jean-Marie Martin, Hollogne-aux-Pierres, Belgium, considers the LC copy earlier. Later orchestral scores, with 374 and 395 pages, are at JMM.

Orchestral parts of the opera, with plate number 5285, lithographed, published by Choudens, 30 Boulevard des Capucines, Paris, possibly their first printing, with covers, are at CI.

Brief biographic information regarding Offenbach appears under *Apache Dance*. Jules Paul Barbier, the lyricist, was born in Paris in 1822 and died in Paris in 1901.[6]

Barnacle Bill the Sailor

It's on-ly me from o-ver the sea said Bar-na-cle Bill the sail - or

In its present form, this is apparently a relatively "recent" folk song. While the words are probably somewhat older, their first known appearance in print was in a privately printed book of bawdy songs, *Immortalia* (n.p., probably American, 1927), edited by "A Gentleman about Town" (not

---

[4] The piano-vocal score is listed in *BF*, Mar. 12, 1881, p. 159 (with words by J. Barbier only) and *Bib. Mus.*, Jan.–Mar., 1881, p. 8. The sheet music was entered for Dépôt Légal on Feb. 28 and Mar. 19, 1881, Archives, and is in *BF*, Mar. 26, 1881, p. 191. The BM copy of the piano-vocal score, with Carré's name blacked out, was deposited Mar. 17, 1881.

[5] Sonneck, *Dramatic Music*, p. 120. BM dates its copy "1881?"

[6] Baker, p. 85.

identified), p. 109, under the title *Ballochy Bill the Sailor;*[1] IU and JF. One stanza of the words was then published on Sept. 14, 1928,[2] in Frank Shay, *More Pious Friends and Drunken Companions* (New York, N.Y., 1928), without a reference that it is a later edition, at p. 102, under the title *Rollicking Bill the Sailor.* LC(CDC) and JF. In other versions, Bill is sometimes known as *Bollocky Bill.*[3]

The Carson Robison and Frank Luther sheet music edition, the first known printing of the music, and with the words "cleaned up" for public consumption (omitting "But we have only one bed!" etc.), was published on April 3, 1929,[2] by Southern Music Pub. Co. Inc., 145 W. 45th St., New York, N.Y. Possible first edition: Front cover has a drawing of Barnacle Bill, refers to Victor Record 40043,[3A] and is blue, black and white. p. [2] adv. *Just..* m. on pp. 3–5. Extra stanzas on p. 5. Back cover adv. *Broken..* (The two advertised songs were published on or before May 2, 1929.)[2] JF.

It has been said that the song was previously known under the title *Abram Brown,*[4] but no printing of it has been found under this title.

While the music and words of this particular song are apparently of recent origin, the tradition of the "night-visitor" is an old one in folk ballads, having been traced back to 1578.[5] See, for example, the three songs collected by Robert Burns, *Wha Is That at My Bower Door* (in James Johnson, *The Scots Musical Museum* [Edinburgh, 1792], vol. IIII, p. 347, at BM and JF); *Oh, Open the Door* (in [George Thompson], *A Select Collection of Original Scotish [sic] Airs* [First] Set, London, 1793, p. 21, BUC, p. 1006 and JF); and *O Let Me in This Ae Night* (in *The Poetry of Robert Burns*, edited by William Ernest Henley and Thomas P. Henderson [Edinburgh, 1897], vol. 3, p. 274, at NYPL).

The Bartered Bride-Overture—Smetana

m. B. Smetana. The first printing of the *Overture* to *The Bartered Bride* in any form was in the piano-vocal score of *Prodaná Nevěsta* published in

---

[1] This information was furnished by Richard A. Reuss, Bloomington, Ind.

[2] Copyright records; LC.

[3] Legman, pp. 201 and 225.

[3A] Recorded Dec. 28, 1928; letter from RCA Record Division, New York, N.Y.

[4] Colcord, *Songs*, p. 182. The song is not in the 1924 edition of her book; LC. Hugill, p. 440.

[5] *The Poetry of Robert Burns*, referred to in text above, vol. 3, p. 375. The author is indebted to Gershon Legman, La Jolla, Cal., for the information in this paragraph.

Sept., 1872,[1] by Matice Hudebni, Prague. Possible first edition: Title page in Czech has drawings of country scenes, the librettist is referred to as K. S. (Karel Sabina), the piano arrangement is by the composer, the prices are 8 zl. - 20 franků - 6 rublů, and the colors are tan, black and white. vb. Dedication to Konstantine Nikolajevic. vb. Cast in Czech and German, also stating that the first performance was in Prague on May 2, 1866. m. on pp. 4–181, the *Overture* for piano four hands. No plate number. Text in Czech and German. p. [182] blank. Correction leaf. HU and JF. AT's title page is green, not tan. Umělecká Beseda was a later publisher in Prague; BPL.

The orchestral score of the *Overture* was published separately in 1887[1] by Ed. Bote & G. Bock, 37 Leipziger Str., Berlin, and 23 Wilhelm Str., Posen, under the title *Lustspiel-Ouverture: Ouvertura . . . "Prodaná Nevěsta."* A possible first printing lists four arrangements, the Partitur, at M. 8.00, indicates the publisher has branches at four other cities and mentions E. F. Steinacker, Leipzig, and Joh. Hoffmann's Witwe, Prague. m. on pp. 3–37. p.n. 13142. Folio. BPL. Similar editions are at LC and NYPL except that each of the latter has an "opera front cover" under the German title *Die Verkaufte Braut*, lists from the opera the piano-vocal score, piano score, nine arias, the overture in seven arrangements and many other arrangements, and consequently is probably later.

The orchestral score of the opera was published about 1893[2] by Bote & Bock, Berlin. In a possible first printing, the front cover is red, white and blue, with the German title *Die Verkaufte Braut*. The *Overture* is printed with p.n. 13142 on pp. 3–37. The remainder is a lithographing of a manuscript sometimes with p.n. 13726. Act I, m. on pp. 38–248; Act II, m. on pp. 1–196; and Act III, m. on pp. 1–212. Text in Czech and German. LC(stamped Sept. 29, 1903), BM, CI and ONB.

Orchestral parts of the opera, with plate numbers 13143 for the *Overture* and 13727 for the balance, lithographed, possibly their first printing, with covers, are at CI.

Smetana was born in Litomyšl, S.E. Bohemia, in 1824 and died in Prague in 1884. Sabina, a Czech librettist and journalist, was born in Prague in 1813 and died in 1877.[3]

---

[1] Teige, p. 60.
[2] Letter from publisher.
[3] *GB*, vol. 16, p. 277.

Basin Street Blues

Ba-sin Street,— is the street,— where dark e - lite,— al-ways meet

Copyright © 1928 by Mayfair Music Corp. © Copyright 1933 by Mayfair Music Corp. Copyright renewed and assigned to Mayfair Music Corp., 31 West 54th Street, New York, N.Y. 10019. By permission.

mw. Spencer Williams. Published Feb. 18, 1929,[1] as parts for small orchestra, by Triangle Music Publishing Co., Inc., New York, N.Y. No set of
these orchestral parts has been located; the copyright entry at LC makes
no reference to words being included in the orchestral parts.

The sheet music edition of the music and words was published Feb. 13,
1933,[1] by Joe Davis Inc., 1658 Broadway, New York, N.Y. First edition:
Front cover has a photograph of The Rollickers and is brown and white.
m. on pp. 2–3. p.n. 1109–2. Back cover adv. *A $1,000,000..* LC(CDC).

Williams was born in New Orleans (naturally!) in 1889, worked as a
Pullman porter on railroad trains, was a pianist and composer and died in
Flushing, N.Y., in 1965.[2]

Battle Hymn of the Republic—
(Say, Brothers, Will You Meet Us?—John Brown—
Glory Hallelujah—
John Brown's Baby Has a Cold upon His Chest)

Glo - ry glo - ry Hal - le - lu - jah!   Glo - ry glo - ry Hal - le - lu - jah!

The fascinating written story of *Battle Hymn of the Republic*, its predecessors, *Say, Brothers, Will You Meet Us?*, *John Brown* and *Glory Hallelujah*,
and its successor, *John Brown's Baby Has a Cold upon His Chest*, has
never been told.[1]

[1] Copyright records; LC.
[2] Obituary, *The New York Times*, July 17, 1965.

---

[1] The author is indebted to Boyd B. Stutler, Charleston, W. Va., for much valuable
help in connection with *Glory Hallelujah* and its related titles, and to William Lichtenwanger, Washington, D.C., in connection with *Say, Brothers Will You Meet Us?* Some
of Stutler's information on the subject, the best study that has been made, is in his
Glory, Glory Hallelujah! (Cincinnati, 1960); NYPL.

The written record begins in 1857–1858. On Dec. 19, 1857,[2] there was a copyright entry by Charles Dunbar, *Camp Meeting Harp and Revival Chorister*. Though no copy of a book with this title has been found, a book entitled *The Union Harp and Revival Chorister*, with the collection selected and arranged by Charles Dunbar, and a statement that it was published in Cincinnati in 1858, has been found; and it contains at page 264 the music and words of "My Brother Will You Meet Me."[2A] BR and Cincinnati Public Library. The opening words are "Say my brother will you meet me." The music of the *Glory Hallelujah* chorus is present, but not the words. No copyright entry was made for this book in 1858, although Dunbar copyrighted several other books during that year and copyrighted the second edition of *The Union Harp and Revival Chorister* on April 30, 1859;[2] LC(CDC) and UTS.

On Nov. 27, 1858,[2] *Brothers, Will You Meet Us?* was copyrighted as a separate hymn by G. S. Scofield, New York, N.Y. No copy of this separate publication has been located, but it was soon reproduced in the Dec., 1858, issue of *Our Monthly Casket*, published by the Lee Avenue Sunday School, Brooklyn, vol. 1, no. 8, p. 152; LIHS. On p. 143 it is stated that the song "has just [been] issued on cards." The music and words of the *Glory Hallelujah* Chorus are present. The opening words of the song are *"Say, brothers, will you meet us,"* and the song became known as a Methodist hymn by this title. The words also appear in Part Second of *Lee Avenue Collection*, New York, N.Y., 1859, p. 182, and refer to the above music; UTS. The words and music were also copyrighted on Jan. 27, 1859,[2] in *Devotional Melodies*, compiled by A. S. Jenks (Philadelphia, 1859), p. 59, at UTS; in the first printing of this book there are only 198 pages.

Fort Sumter was fired on in April, 1861, and on Sunday, May 12, 1861, *John Brown* was played publicly, perhaps for the first time, at a flag-raising ceremony for the training of Northern recruits at Fort Warren, near Boston. Contemporary newspapers reported troops playing and singing the song as they marched in Boston on July 18, 1861,[2B] and a rash of printings suddenly reflected the popularity of the new song.

John Brown was copyrighted on July 16, 1861,[2] as a broadside with music and words by C. S. Hall, 256 Main Street, Charlestown, Mass. In

---

[2] Copyright records; LC.

[2A] This textual pattern appeared as early as 1810 as "O Brethren Do You Know Him" (repeated twice) in Elias Smith and Abner Jones, *Hymns, Original & Selected* (4th ed., Portland, Me., 1810), p. 316 (without music), at BR and LC; not in the three earlier editions, at BR. †

[2B] E.g., *Boston Daily Advertiser*, July 19, 1861, p. 4, and *Boston Evening Transcript*, same date, p. 1; both at BPL. ‡

addition to the *Glory Hallelujah* Chorus, this song has the familiar opening line, "John Brown's body lies a mouldering in the grave." Under the title appear the words "Origin, Fort Warren"—whether this refers to the music, the words or to the fort where it was played is not known—probably the latter; no printing under this title has been found. The broadside is at BPL, BR, BS and BMI. Also at the BPL is another broadside, with words only, entitled *John Brown Song!* This has the same words as above. While no publisher is mentioned, the address is the same as above, and it was probably printed by the same publisher either shortly before or shortly after the broadside with music. The song was copyrighted in sheet music form on July 19, 1861,[2] by J. W. Turner, Boston, under the title *The Popular John Brown Song* and the next day by Russell & Pattee, Boston, under the title *John Brown's Song;* both at JFD.

(It should be mentioned that the John Brown in the song was a Sergeant at Fort Warren, not the antislavery crusader famous for his raid on Harpers Ferry in 1859; however, the latter's celebrity led to the parody.)

A few days later, on July 24, 1861,[2] the song with substantially the same words was first copyrighted under the title *Glory, Hallelujah,* by Oliver Ditson & Co., 277 Washington St., Boston; in the first printing of this edition, the pages are engraved, and there is no reference on the front cover to "Piano. Guitar."[3] JF. *Dwight's,* July 27, 1861, states that *Glory! Hallelujah,* "a Popular refrain, as sung by the Federal Volunteers . . . [is a] people's tune said to have originated with the Massachusetts' Volunteers at Fortress Munroe. . . . At this time one can hardly walk on the streets for five minutes without hearing it whistled or hummed." (Advertisement of Oliver Ditson & Co., p. 136.) A great many other editions of *John Brown* and *Glory, Hallelujah* followed in 1861, 1862 and succeeding years.[4]

It has long been believed[5] that the first printing of the words of *Battle Hymn of the Republic* by Julia Ward Howe was in the Feb., 1862, issue of *The Atlantic Monthly* (Boston), p. 10; ULS, p. 370, and JF. This issue was copyrighted on Jan. 16, 1862,[2] and announced as "Ready Today" in the Jan. 18, 1862, issue of the *Boston Daily Evening Transcript,* p. 3, col. 5, at BPL, and as "Ready Today" in the Jan. 20, 1862, issue of the *New-York Daily Tribune,* p. [1], col. 2, at NYPL.

It has not been realized that the entire poem was contained in the Jan. 14, 1862, issue of the *New-York Daily Tribune,* p. 4, col. 6;[6] NYPL and

---

[3] This edition should be earlier than the one described in Dichter-Shapiro, p. 111.

[4] Some of the other editions are listed in Dichter-Shapiro, pp. 111–112.

[5] See, e.g., Blanck, vol. 4, p. 364.

[6] No attempt has been made to determine whether there was more than one edition of this newspaper on the particular day.

JF. Strangely, the poem is here stated to be "From The February Atlantic Monthly," and the only logical explanation is that the magazine sent out advance proofs or excerpts for newspaper release.

The poem had been written at Willard's Hotel, Washington, D.C. (or, alternatively, in a nearby Union Army tent), in the early dawn of Nov. 19, 1861, and the first printings do not contain the "Glory Hallelujah" Chorus or indicate that the poem was intended to be sung to that melody. A puzzling publication of the poem is in William C. Whitcomb, *Praising God in Troublous Times, a Thanksgiving Discourse delivered in Lynnfield Centre and Stoneham, November 21, 1861.* "Published . . . Salem, Mass. . . . 1861." The verso of the title page has a dedication dated Jan., 1862. On the inside of the back cover are the words of the *Battle Hymn*. BOA and LCP. It has not been possible to date this publication.

The first printing of the poem of the *Battle Hymn of the Republic* set to music was copyrighted on April 9, 1862,[2] by Oliver Ditson & Co., 277 Washington St., Boston. Probable first edition: The words are attributed to "Mrs. Dr. S. G. Howe," and "adapted to the favorite Melody of Glory Hallelujah." Front cover indicates the price is "2½"[7] and lists five agents. p. [2] and back cover blank. p.n. 21454. m. on pp. 3–5. Engraved. BOA, NYPL, LL and JF. Mrs. Howe, famous as a reformer and sociological writer as well as poetess, was born in New York City in 1819, moved to Boston, and died in Middletown, R.I., in 1910.

No printing of the version *John Brown's Baby Has a Cold upon His Chest* has been found prior to Nov. 14, 1923,[2] when this parody to the tune *The Battle Hymn of the Republic* was included in Annetta Eldridge and Ruth E. Richardson, *Stunt Songs for Social Sings* (Denver,·Col., and Franklin, Ohio), p. 14; LC(CDC—48 pages).[8]

Boyd Stutler has suggested the possibility that the melody and/or words of *Glory Hallelujah* may have been derived from the Swedish *Bröder Viljen I Gå Med Oss* or from a lyric by Charles Wesley. The Kungl. Biblioteket, Stockholm, has written this author that the Swedish song is known "only since the latter part of the nineteenth century," and the Svenskt Visarkiv, Stockholm, has written this author that this Swedish song dates "from about 1875." No lyric by Charles Wesley has been traced that is similar to *Glory Hallelujah*.

On the basis of a lifetime study of this song, Boyd S. Stutler has concluded that none of the claims to the composition of the *Glory Hallelujah*

---

[7] *Dwight's* advertised this sheet of music at 25 cents in the March 1, 1862, issue and in the four April issues.

[8] Leah Rachel Clara Yoffie, "Three Generations of Children's Singing Games in St. Louis" in *JAF*, Jan.–March, 1947, p. 45.

song can be sustained. The most persistent claims have been made on behalf of William Steffe of Philadelphia, Thomas Brigham Bishop of New York City, and Frank E. Jerome of Russell, Kansas.

Beautiful Dreamer

Beau - ti - ful dream-er,   wake un - to   me, ___   star-light and dew-drops are

mw. Stephen C. Foster. Copyrighted March 10, 1864,[1] by Wm. A. Pond & Co., 547 Broadway, New York, N.Y. First edition: Front cover states "the last song ever written," the price is 3, and there are four copublishers.[2] **vb.** m. on pp. 3–6. p.n. 5922. Back cover blank. Engraved. LC(CDC) and FH. Front cover says the song was "composed but a few days previous to his death"; yet the front cover of another of his songs, copyrighted July 1, 1863, states that Foster was the "Author of Beautiful Dreamer."[3] In any event, no trace of an edition of *Beautiful Dreamer* earlier than the copyright deposit copy has been found.

Foster was born near Pittsburgh, Pa., in 1826 and died in New York City on Jan. 13, 1864.

Beautiful Ohio

m. Mary Earl, a pseudonym for Robert A. (Keiser) King. Published Jan. 18, 1918,[1] by Shapiro, Bernstein & Co., 224 West 47th Street, New York, N.Y. First edition: Front cover has a drawing of the Ohio River and is red, brown, blue and white. p. [2] adv. *Boogie..* m. on pp. 3–5. Back cover adv.

---

[1] Copyright records; LC.
[2] Front cover is illustrated in Fuld, *Foster*, no page number.
[3] *Willie Has Gone to the War*; FH and JF.

---

[1] Copyright records; LC.

Long.. - Liberty.. Folio. LC(CDC) and JF. No arrangements are listed on the front cover, which is entirely different from that of later editions. A revised edition in which the 9th to 16th bars were changed, and a vocal edition with words by Ballard MacDonald, were published on Oct. 4, 1918.[1]

Robert A. King, a composer, was born in New York City in 1862 and died there in 1932.[2]

Beer Barrel Polka

Roll   out   the   bar - rel
Ŝko - da____   lás - ky

Ŝkoda Lásky: Copyright MCMXXXIV by Shapiro, Bernstein & Co. Inc., New York. Copyright renewed. By permission.
Beer Barrel Polka: Copyright MCMXXXIX by Shapiro, Bernstein & Co. Inc.. New York. By permission.

m. Jaromír Vejvoda. w. Vašek Zeman. Published May 16, 1934,[1] under the title *Ŝkoda Lásky* (Modřanská polka) by Jana Hoffmanna Vva, Karlova 29n, Prague. The Czech title means *Lost Love.* Possible first edition: Front cover has a drawing of a girl apparently dancing. Pages [2]–[3] have the music and words, treble staff only; p.n. 5339; to the left is a photograph of the composer and to the right a list of his works. 1934 copyright claim. Octavo. Oblong. No agents for other cities are listed. Front cover does not say 1935, refer to phonograph records or mention "Národni správa," the National administration after the Nazi annexation in 1938. Other details not known. SN. *Beer Barrel Polka (Roll Out the Barrel),* with additional credits to Lew Brown and Wladimir A. Timm, was published in 1939 by Shapiro, Bernstein & Co., New York, N.Y.

Because the National Broadcasting Corporation prohibited a reference to an alcoholic drink in the title of a song, this song was introduced on NBC stations as "The Barrel Polka," to the amusement of the entertainment industry.[1A]

Vejvoda, a composer, was born in 1902 in Zbraslav, Czechoslovakia, and now resides in Prague.[2] Zeman, a writer, was born in 1909 in Prague and now resides in Canada.[2]

---

[1] Copyright records; LC.
[2] Obituary, *The New York Times*, April 14, 1932.

---

[1] Copyright records; LC.
[1A] Gilbert, p. 300.
[2] Letter from SN.

Begin the Beguine

When they be - gin ——————————— the be - guine

© 1935 Harms, Inc. Copyright renewed. Used by permission.

mw. Cole Porter. Published Oct. 16, 1935,[1] by Harms Incorporated, New York, N.Y. Probable first edition: Front cover has a drawing of a crown and is silver, blue and white. s. *Jubilee*—7 titles listed. m. on pp. 2–7. p.n. 676-6. Back cover adv. *You're.. - Buddie..* All the songs advertised in this edition were published on or before Oct. 16, 1935. JF (autographed). The above edition is the same, to the extent possible, as the other contemporary, regular edition, copyright deposit copies at LC from the same show. *Jubilee* opened in New York City on Oct. 12, 1935.

Cole Porter has said that *Begin the Beguine* was his favorite song.[2] Porter was born in Peru, Indiana, on June 9, 1891.[3] His first song, *The Bobolink Waltz*, was published Oct. 6, 1902, when he was eleven years old; LC, CP and JF. He died in Santa Monica, Cal., in 1964.

Bei Mir Bist Du Schön

"Bei   mir   bist Du   schön,"__   please   let   me ex - plain

© 1933 by Samuel Secunda. © 1937 by Harms, Inc. Copyrights renewed. Used by permission.

m. Sholom Secunda. w. J. Jacobs. First published under the title *Bei Mir Bistu Shein*, on Sept. 25, 1933,[1] by the composer. Probable first edition: Front cover, in blue and white, has the title and other text in English and Hebrew letters, shows three photographs and refers to the Yiddish musical comedy *I Would If I Could*. m. on pp. 2–5. Back cover in Hebrew letters. EM. The song had been written for and sung in this show in the Public Theater, Second Avenue at Fourth Street, New York, N.Y., since Oct., 1932, by its star, Aaron Lebedeff. The copyright was assigned in 1937 to

[1] Copyright records; LC.

[2] *The New York Times*, June 8, 1962, p. 36.

[3] Porter was born two years earlier than had been previously reported; *The New York Times*, June 9, 1981, p. B4.

[1] Copyright records; LC. The front cover of the copyright deposit copy is illustrated in *Life*, Chicago, Jan. 31, 1938, p. 39.

J. & J. Kammen Music Co., and in the same year English words were added by Sammy Cahn and Saul Chaplin, the title changing to its present title.

At a Long Island beach, Jacobs, an actor, was recognized by some girls; to reassure his wife, he said "Bei mir bist du schön." The song, initially popularized by the Andrews Sisters, has also been referred to as "Buy a Beer, Mr. Shane" and "My Mere Bits of Shame." Secunda was born in Alexandria, Russia, in 1895, was a musical conductor and director in New York City and died there in 1974.[2] Jacob Jacobs was born in 1890 near Humana, Austria, became an actor and theater manager in New York City and died in 1977.[3]

Believe Me If All Those Endearing Young Charms— (Fair Harvard)

My— lodg - ing is on— the cold————— ground
Be - lieve me if all those en - dear-ing young charms
Fair— Har - vard! Thy sons to thy ju - bi - lee throng

There is controversy as to whether the melody of this song is English, Irish or Scottish, Chappell claiming the former, Moore, Baring-Gould and O'Neill claiming the second, and Robert Burns claiming the last.[1] The melody was first printed in *Vocal Music: or the Songster's Companion* (London, 1775), p. 18, to the words of *My Lodging Is on the Cold Ground*, a favorite "mad" song;[2] *BUC*, p. 1048, and JF. The composer of the melody is not known.

The words of *Believe Me If All Those Endearing Young Charms* are incontrovertibly Irish, having been written by Thomas Moore. The words, and the music, first appeared in Thomas Moore's *A Selection of Irish Melodies*, Second Number of the First Volume, p. 99, in 1807–1808.[3] In the first printing of this work, any watermark should be not later than

2 Obituary, *The New York Times*, June 14, 1974.

3 Information from author and ASCAP files.

1 Chappell, pp. 529 and 785; Baring-Gould, p. vi; and O'Neill, *Irish Folk*, p. 184. Burns's setting of the melody is in (George Thomson) *A Select Collection of Original Scotish* [*sic*] *Airs*, 4th Set (London [1798]), p. 76, at *BUC*, p. 1006, and JF.

2 "Mad" describes a song of an extravagant nature sung by someone who has become insane through love. *My Lodging* was also published in sheet music form with and without a publisher's imprint at about the same time as in *Vocal Music*; *BUC*, p. 721, BPL and JF. The words of *My Lodging* had previously been sung to a since discarded melody; Chappell, p. 529.

3 Muir, 13th unnumbered page, fixes the year of publication at 1808. Chinnéide, p. 119, however, fixes the year as 1807, in which case any watermark of the first printing could not be later than 1807.

1807 or 1808, the imprint should be J. Power, London, and W. Power, Dublin, in that order, and there should be a thin cromlech, not a ruined tower, in the vignette on the title page.[4] In the first printing, the last word on the last line of the advertisement page opposite the title page is "Strand." Footnotes on pp. 75, 84 and 91 were reset in later editions; for example, in the first edition, on p. 75, in the second footnote, last line, the first word is "our." No copy meeting these requirements with a dated watermark has been found. A copy with an 1808 watermark, possibly meeting these requirements, was listed in Scribner's *Catalogue 139* (New York, N.Y., n.d.) under "Moore," *Catalogue* at JF, but the present location of the copy is not known. Otherwise satisfactory copies, with no dated watermark in the text, possible first editions, are at HU, KC and JF (latter copy has 1804 watermark in end paper); HU and JF copies have blue hard covers without a drawing of a seated woman. Some later editions have p.n. 50.

On the occasion of Harvard University's 200th anniversary on Sept. 8, 1836, Rev. Samuel Gilman wrote an ode to the melody which has become known as *Fair Harvard*, and which subsequently became Harvard's Alma Mater. The words were first printed under the title *Ode* in an *Order of Services at the Centennial Celebration of Harvard University* [Cambridge, Mass.], Sept. 8, 1836, HU, and the music and words were first printed together in 1836–1842 under the title *Ode Sung at the Second Centennial Celebration* (Boston, Parker & Ditson, n.d.), HU and JF.[5]

Moore was born in Dublin in 1779 and died in Bromham, near Devizes, in 1852. Rev. Samuel Gilman was born in Gloucester, Mass., in 1790–1791, became a Pastor in Charleston, S.C., and died in Kingston, Mass., in 1858.[5]

Bell Bottom Trousers

From *Bottoms Up!* Copyright MCMXXXIII, Shawnee Press, Inc., Delaware Water Gap, Pa. Copyright renewed. Used by permission.

While no doubt somewhat older, no printing of this song has been found earlier than in the book *Bottoms Up!* edited by Clifford Leach and pub-

---

[4] Muir, 12th and 13th unnumbered pages.

[5] Hamilton Vaughan Bail, "Fair Harvard and its Author, Samuel Gilman" in *Harvard Alumni Bulletin*, Boston, June 5, 1936, p. [1107], and June 12, 1936, p. [1157]; *ULS*, p. 1174. Dichter-Shapiro, p. 220.

lished July 10, 1933,[1] by Paull-Pioneer Music Corporation, 119 Fifth Avenue, New York, N.Y. The music and words are on p. 113, where it is described as a Navy Song, by courtesy of R. E. Sumner. LC(CDC). In the first printing of the book, the songs on pp. 44 and 114 have copyright dates of 1907 and 1933.

The song is said to have been previously sung to the melody of *Home, Dearie, Home,* and the melody of this title in a 1948 book is similar.[2] However, the four earlier printings of this title that have been found have an entirely different melody.[3] It has also been said that the predecessor of *Bell Bottom Trousers* is *Rosemary Lane* or *Home Boys Home.*[4] Three versions of the former are published in *JFSS,* Nov., 1918, p. 1, but neither the music nor words are similar in this author's opinion. An alternative title of *Rosemary Lane* is *The Oak and the Ash,* a version of which is in Chappell, p. 457.[5] No printing has been found of *Home Boys Home,* which may have been intended to be *Home, Dearie, Home.*

<h2 style="text-align:center">*Bell Song—Lakmé*</h2>

Ah! Ah! Ah!   Ah! Ah! Ah!__   Ah! Ah! Ah! Ah!   Ah! Ah! Ah!__   Ah!

m. Léo Delibes. w. Edmond Gondinet and Philippe Gille. First published in the piano-vocal score of *Lakmé* the middle of April, 1883,[1] by Heugel & Fils, au Ménestrel, 2 bis Rue Vivienne, Paris. First edition: Front cover is blue, red, white and gold, with drawings of flowers. vb. Indian motifs in red. vb. Cast page states "Ouvrage représenté sur la scène de l'Opéra-Comique en avril 1883" without indication yet of the exact date. vb. Index. vb. m. on pp. 1–272, the *Bell Song* on p. 145. p.n. 5683. There are no annexes on pp. 273 and 275, or reference thereto on p. 39. BN(CDC), JMM and JF. The

---

[1] Copyright records; LC.

[2] Frank Shay, *American Sea Songs and Chanteys* (New York, N.Y., 1948), p. 144; NYPL. This book previously appeared under the title *Iron Men and Wooden Ships* in 1921 (NYPL) and in an enlarged edition in 1924 (NYPL); however, the melody did not appear in either of these earlier editions.

[3] Smith, *Music of the Waters,* p. 25; Tozer, p. 26; Colcord, *Roll,* p. 87; and Colcord, *Songs,* p. 167.

[4] Legman, p. 412.

[5] Mrs. Ruth Noyes at EFDSS kindly located many of the printings in this paragraph.

[1] "Paraîtra demain lundi," April 16, 1883, in *Le Ménestrel,* April 15, 1883, p. 160. April 11–12, 1883, according to a letter from the publisher. The listing in the Jan.–

separate sheet music of the *Légende* or *Bell Song*, p.n. 5701, was entered for Dépôt Légal on May 8, 1883;[2] BN(CDC). *Lakmé* was performed on April 14, 1883, in Paris.

Orchestral scores of *Lakmé* without a title page are at COP, LC and JMM. Probable first edition: The p.n. is 7675 and the name of the publisher is still Heugel et Fils. m. on pp. 1–467. p. [468] blank. Lithographed. The *Bell Song* is at p. 261. The publisher advises the orchestral score was published Oct. 16, 1883; this seems unlikely.

Delibes was born in St. Germain du Val, Sarthe, in 1836 and died in Paris in 1891. Gondinet, a dramatic author, was born in Laurière, Haute-Vienne, in 1829 and died in Neuilly, Seine, in 1888.[3] Gille, also a dramatist, was born in Paris in 1831 and died in 1901.[4]

The Bells of St. Mary's

The bells of St. Ma - ry's Ah! Hear they are call - ing

m. A. Emmett Adams. w. Douglas Furber. Published March 2, 1917,[1] by Ascherberg, Hopwood & Crew, Ltd., 16 Mortimer Street, Regent Street, London, W. First edition deposited the next day at BM: Front cover is black and white, indicates price is 1/6 (U.S.A. 60¢, France 2-50) and mentions a New York publisher. m. on pp. 2–7. p.n. 9634. Back cover adv. *Laddie.. - Mate..* Folio. BM(CDC). The song has been adopted as the Alma Mater of St. Mary's College, St. Mary's, Cal.

March, 1883, issue of *BMF*, p. 15, seems premature. A copy dated April 14, 1883, and inscribed by the composer was listed in Baron, *Catalogue 71* (London [1965]), no. 195; JF. The listing in *BF*, May 12, 1883, p. 302, is late. Other issues of *Le Ménestrel* from March, 1883, on confirm the mid-April publication date.

[2] Archives.

[3] *GE*, vol. 18, p. 1193.

[4] *NIE*, vol. IX, p. 764.

[1] Copyright records; LC.

Adams, a composer, was born in Australia in 1890 and died in London in 1938.[2] Furber, an actor, playright and lyricist, died in London in 1961 at the age of seventy-five.[3] The two met when Adams arrived in London during World War I.

Berceuse—The Firebird

m. Igor Stravinsky. Published 1910–1911[1] by P. Jurgenson, Moscow and Leipzig, for piano and orchestral score, priority uncertain. Possible first edition of the piano arrangement: Title page is in Russian and French, the Russian title being Жаръ-Птица, and the French title, L'Oiseau de Feu, there is reference to M. Fokine, there are three agents in St. Petersburg, Warsaw and Kiev (in Russian), there is a crown, there are no street addresses, and the colors are red, black and white. vb. Dedication in Russian and French to André Rimsky-Korsakow. vb. Cast in Russian and verso in French. m. on pp. 5–70. p.ns. 34903-19. The Berceuse is at p. 63. The year 1910 appears on p. 70—the date of completion of the composition. The Warsaw agent is E. Bende i Ko. (E. Wende & Co.); BM, HU, AT, JMM and JF (inscribed)—front cover in tan, red and black; back cover has price of 4 Rb. 50k. A later edition shows L. Idzikovski as the agent in both Warsaw and Kiev; BPL, PML and JMM.

Possible first edition of the orchestral score: Front cover is red, yellow and black and in Russian and French. vb. Title page is the same as in the possible first edition described above except the arrangement is for orchestra, the colors are black and white, and L. Idzikovski is the agent in both Warsaw and Kiev. Verso has instructions. Dedication to André Rimsky-Korsakow. vb. Cast in Russian. vb. Cast in French. Orchestral instruments. m. on pp. 9–180. p.n. 34920. The year 1910 appears on p. 180. Back cover reads: Edition P. Jurgenson, Moscou, Leipzig. Partition 50 Rb. Parties d'Orchestre—. The Berceuse is at p. 163. LC and ONB. As L. Idzikovski did not open a branch office in Warsaw until 1911 (see, above, p. 142), the first edition may show E. Bende (Wende) i. Ko. as the Warsaw agent, as in the case of the piano arrangement described above.

---

[2] Obituary, New York Tribune, Oct. 31, 1938.

[3] Obituary, The New York Times, Feb. 21, 1961.

---

[1] The piano arrangement is listed in Hofmeister Monatsbericht, June, 1911, p. 142. The orchestral score does not seem to be listed.

A possible first printing, incomplete, of the orchestral parts of the ballet by Jurgenson, with plate number 36022, is at PML. A *Suite* was arranged for orchestral score and published later[2] with p.n. 35965 (BPL) and for orchestral parts with p.n. 35966 (FLP).

The Firebird was performed on June 25, 1910, in Paris by Diaghilev's Russian Ballet. Stravinsky was born near St. Petersburg in 1882 and died in New York City in 1971.

Berceuse—Jocelyn

Oh! Ne t'é - veille-pas en - cor_____pour qu'un bel an-ge de ton rê - ve

m. Benjamin Godard. w. Armand Silvestre and Victor Capoul. The *Berceuse* is not in the first printing of the piano-vocal score of the opera *Jocelyn*, deposited late 1887 at BN.[1] Probably its first printing was in sheet music, entered for Dépôt Légal on Oct. 29, 1888,[2] where it was added as no. 27 for soprano or tenor at the end of the arias. Front cover in black and white states that the opera was derived from the poem by Lamartine, the price of this aria (in two arrangements) is 5F, there are three piano arrangements of the piano scores, and the publisher is Choudens Père et Fils, 30 Boulevard des Capucines (près la Rue Caumartin), Paris. p. [2] blank. m. on pp. 1–5 (actually 3–7). p.n. 8095 for no. 27. Back cover adv. works by Andran.. - Villebichot. BN(CDC). An arrangement for mezzo-soprano or bass, no. 27 bis, with p.n. 8078 was entered for Dépôt Légal the same day; BN(CDC).

The second printing of the piano-vocal score[3] includes *Berceuse* at p. 105. No edition has been found published by Choudens Père et Fils, but only by Choudens Fils (at the address given above), the name adopted in 1888.[4] Possible first edition: Front cover (but not title page) says "2me Edition," and there is a price on the front cover of 15 fr. The piano arrange-

[2] An orchestral arrangement of the *Suite* is listed in Hofmeister *Monatsbericht*, April, 1912, p. 81.

[1] BMf, Oct.–Dec., 1887, p. 56.

[2] Archives. The *Berceuse* sheet music is listed in BMF, Oct.–Dec., 1888, p. 56.

[3] No reference has been found in BF or BMF to the second printing of the piano-vocal score so that its date is unknown. No copyright deposit copy is now at BN or COP.

[4] Hopkinson, *Parisian*, p. 27.

ment was made by the composer. op. 100. There is a dedication page to Daniel Barton. m. on pp. [4]–265. p.n. 7045 (same as in first printing of the piano-vocal score). HU, JMM and JF.* The opera was performed at Brussels on Feb. 25, 1888, but not in Paris until Oct. 13, 1888.

While the plate number of the orchestral score of the opera is slightly lower than that of the piano-vocal score, the earliest known orchestral score includes the *Berceuse* and has the later imprint, so that it appeared after at least the first printing of the piano-vocal score. Possible first edition of the orchestral score of *Jocelyn:* Folio. Title page has a drawing of three women and elaborate frames. The publisher is Choudens Fils, 30 Bould. des Capucines (près la Rue Caumartin), Paris. vb. Index (without page numbers). vb. m. on pp. 1–409, engraved. p.n. 7909. *Berceuse* is on p. 140. p. [410] blank. LC;[5] also JMM with music pages not engraved.

Lithographed orchestral parts of the opera, with plate number 7124, folio, without covers, are at Choudens, Paris.

Godard was born in Paris in 1849 and died at Cannes in 1895. Silvestre, an author, financial inspector and publisher, was born in Paris in 1837 and died in Toulouse in 1901.[6] Capoul, known mostly as an opera tenor, was born in Toulouse in 1839; he sang the part of the hero in *Jocelyn* in Paris in 1888, and died in Pujaudran du Gers in 1924.[7]

The Best Things in Life Are Free

The   moon   be - longs   to   ev - 'ry - one

mw. B. G. de Sylva, Lew Brown and Ray Henderson. Published Aug. 15, 1927,[1] by de Sylva, Brown and Henderson, Inc., 745 Seventh Ave., New York, N.Y. First edition: Front cover has a drawing of a flapper reading a newspaper, mentions the Collegiate Musical Comedy *Good News* with George Olsen, lists eight titles and is red, black and white. m. on pp. 2–5. Back cover adv. *Good.. - A Girl..* No price or plate number. LC(CDC) and JF.

Good News opened in New York City on Sept. 6, 1927, but the piano-vocal score was not published until Dec. 9, 1932,[1] by Samuel French, New

---

[5] Sonneck, *Dramatic Music*, p. 58.
[6] *Larousse XX*, vol. 6, p. 358.
[7] *Grove's*, vol. 2, p. 54.

[1] Copyright records; LC.

York, N.Y.; DTP. Brief biographic information regarding de Sylva appears above under *April Showers*. Brown, a lyricist, publisher and producer, was born in Odessa, Russia, in 1893, and died in New York City in 1958.[2] Henderson, a composer, pianist and publisher, was born in Buffalo in 1896 and died in Greenwich, Conn., in 1971.[3]

Bill Bailey, Won't You Please Come Home?

Won't you   come   home, Bill Bai - ley,   won't you   come   home?

mw. Hughie Cannon. Copyrighted April 5, 1902,[1] by Howley, Haviland & Dresser, 1260–1266 Broadway, New York, N.Y. First edition: Front cover has drawings of a crying woman and a man, and a picture of Miller & Kresko, mentions two other songs by Cannon, gives the price as 5, mentions a Chicago branch and a London agent and is black, red and white. p. [2] adv. *Way.. - My..* m. on pp. [3]–[6]. p. [3] adv. *Appearances..* p. [4] adv. *Starlight.* p. [5] adv. *Tell..* p. [6] adv. *Come..* p. [7] adv. *Dance..* Back cover adv. *Fare.. - Oh..* LC(CDC).

The story of the song may have actually happened to a Bill Bailey, but it is not clear who was the real Bill Bailey. The most likely candidate appears to have been Willard Godfrey Bailey, known as "Bill," a trombonist and music teacher from 1894–1907 in Jackson, Mich., where the song is said to have been written.[2] There were a number of songs referring to Bill Bailey; *Ain't Dat a Shame*, at JF, preceded this song in 1901, and there were several songs after 1902.

---

[2] Obituary, *The New York Times*, Feb. 6, 1958.
[3] Obituary, *The New York Times*, Jan. 2, 1971.

---

[1] Copyright records; LC. On March 14, 1902, two other titles had been registered for copyright: "Dear Billy, Won't You Please Come Home?" and "Won't You Please Come Home, Bill Bailey?" However, no copy was subsequently deposited for copyright, or otherwise seen or heard of, under either of these titles. Thornton Hagert, Arlington, Va., advised the author of these earlier title registrations.

[2] George Swetnam, "How 'Bill Bailey' Came Home" in *The Pittsburgh Press*, July 25, 1965, p. 4; Don Durst, "Bill Bailey Really Did Come Home," 10 articles in *Jackson Citizen Patriot*, Jackson, Mich., Jan. 30–Feb. 19, 1966; and Roger Hankins, "Those Bill Bailey Songs" in *The Ragtimer*, Weston, Ontario, Canada, a series of articles commencing Sept.–Oct., 1970. Articles or photocopies are at Michael Montgomery, Detroit, Mich., and Solomon Goodman, Long Island City, N.Y., who advised the author thereof; photocopies also at JF.

See *Frankie and Johnny*, below, for the curious connection that exists between *Bill Bailey, Won't You Please Come Home?* and *Frankie and Johnny*.

Cannon was born in Detroit, Mich., in 1877, became a variety player, pianist, composer and lyricist, went to the poorhouse of Wayne County, Mich., in 1910 from drinks and drugs, and died in Toledo, Ohio, in 1912.[3]

The Birth of the Blues

They heard the breeze in the trees,— sing-ing weird— mel - o - dies

© 1926 Harms, Inc. Copyright renewed. Pub. by arr. with Ross Jungnickel Inc. Used by permission.

m. Ray Henderson. w. B. G. de Sylva and Lew Brown. Published June 23, 1926,[1] by Harms, Incorporated, New York, N.Y. First edition: Front cover has a drawing of a lady dancer and is orange, black and white. s. *George White's Scandals—Eighth Annual Edition*—3 titles listed. p. [2] adv. *My..* m. on pp. 2–5 (really 3–6). p.n. 7748-4. p. [7] adv. *Oh..* Back cover adv. *Play.. - Here..* LC(CDC). The show opened in New York City on June 14, 1926.

Leonard Bernstein points out that this song is not a true "Blues," i.e., it is not a rhymed couplet, with the first line repeated, in iambic pentameter.[2] Brief biographic information regarding Henderson and Brown appears above under *The Best Things in Life Are Free*.

Blow the Man Down

As I was a walk - ing down Par - a - dise Street, way! Hey!

The first known printing of this song is in Robert C. Adams, *On Board the "Rocket"* (Boston, 1879), p. 319, where the music and words appear under

---

[3] Birth and death certificates at Michael Montgomery, Detroit, Mich., and Solomon Goodman, Long Island City, N.Y., who furnished this biographic information. Geller, p. 205. *The Presto* (magazine), Chicago, Feb. 10, 1910, p. 26; NYPL. Cannon's tombstone at Hill Grove Cemetery, Connellsville, Pa., mentions *Bill Bailey*.

[1] Copyright records; LC.

[2] Bernstein, p. 109.

the title *Knock a Man Down*, a "popular song"; LC (copyright copy deposited June 26, 1880[1]) and LCP. The words "knock" and "blow" were equivalents in the days of the old Atlantic sailing packet ships. This is a halliard (halyard) or hauling chanty.[2] It has been said that the song was taken from an old Negro song *Knock a Man Down*,[3] but no evidence of any Negro song of this name has been found. *Blow the Man Down* has also been assumed to be of British origin.[4]

Blue Danube

m. Johann Strauss. This most famous of all waltzes was first published about Feb. 15, 1867, by C. A. Spina, Vienna, for piano, under the title *An der Schönen, Blauen Donau*.[1] Possible first edition: Front cover has an attractive drawing of the Danube River and a dedication to the Wiener Männergesang-Verein, mentions that it is op. 314, the year 1867, three copublishers, and the price of 80 Nkr./15 Ngr. and is tan and white. (See **Plate VII**.) Verso adv. works by the three Strausses. m. on pp. 3-11. p.n. 19,216. Back cover blank. Oblong. Verso of front cover and music pages are engraved.

There are two variants which fulfill the above description, each having a different verso of the title page: in one, Johann Strauss's works stop at op. 310 but Joseph Strauss's op. 209, 211 and 213 are included (SB); in the other, Johann's op. 311 is included but Joseph's op. 209, 211 and 213 are not (BM—K 5 b 17—and JF). Johann's op. 310 and Joseph's op. 209, 211 and 213 were all published before Feb. 15, 1867,[1] so that priority between the two variants is uncertain. The paradox may result from the fact that the publisher was so deluged for orders, he had to have a hundred new copper plates made to print over a million copies.[2]

The waltz was originally accompanied by words by Josef Weyl and so

---

[1] Copyright records; LC.

[2] Smith, *Music of the Waters*, p. 18; Whall, p. 90; and Doerflinger, p. 17.

[3] Hugill, p. 199. He also says that others believe the melody resembles *Stille Nacht*, which is absurd. Mr. Hugill, Aberdovey, Wales, was helpful with this song.

[4] Laws, p. 279.

---

[1] C. A. Spina, *Ablieferungsbuch*, SB. See, also, Hofmeister *Monatsbericht*, May, 1867; p. 80.

[2] Ewen, *Lighter Classics*, p. 294.

first performed in Vienna on Feb. 15, 1867. It was not printed in a piano-vocal arrangement, however, until about Sept., 1867;[3] ONB.†

The orchestral parts were published about May 11, 1867.[4] In the probable first edition, there is a collective title front cover entitled "Tänze für das Orchestra," the highest op. no. listed is 319 (no prices for 316 or 318; 315, 317 and 319 were also published for orchestra about May 11, 1867[4]), the pages are engraved, the p.n. is 19,242, the publisher is as above, and the price is 5 Fl./3 Th., 5 Ngr; ONB.

When Brahms was asked to autograph the fan of Strauss's wife, after the first bars of the waltz he added: "Unfortunately not by Brahms."‡ Brief biographic information regarding Strauss appears under *Artist's Life*.

Body and Soul

My heart is sad and lone - ly,   for you I cry; for you, dear, on - ly

© 1930 Chappell & Co. Ltd. Copyright renewed and assigned to Harms, Inc. Used by permission.

m. John W. Green. w. Robert Sour and Edward Heyman. The song was published Feb. 18, 1930,[1] by Chappell & Co., Ltd., 50 New Bond Street, London, W.1. The copies deposited at the British Museum the next day and at the Library of Congress the next week are English professional editions. Probable first regular edition: Printed in England. Front cover has a drawing of Medusa, is green, brown, black and white, the price is 2/, and there are references to the publisher's branch in Sydney and to Harms, Incorporated. m. on pp. 2–7. p.n. 30370. Back cover adv. *A Little..* and *I'll..* (both copyrighted in 1929). CG. Frank Eyton's name also appears as a co-lyricist in English editions. (The song with different lyrics was printed from the show *Three's a Crowd*, which opened in New York City on Oct. 15, 1930, and published in the United States the previous day;[1] however, this version was not sung in the show or since.) While Gertrude Lawrence herself did not feature the song, she was largely responsible for its success.

Green, a composer, conductor, pianist and movie executive, was born in New York City in 1908 and resides in Beverly Hills, Cal.[2] Sour, a lyricist

---

[3] Hofmeister *Monatsbericht*, Sept., 1867, p. 152.

[4] C. A. Spina, *Ablieferungsbuch*, SB. See, also, Hofmeister *Monatsbericht*, Sept., 1867, p. 152.

---

[1] Copyright records; LC.

[2] *ASCAP*, pp. 196 and 230.

and Vice-President of Broadcast Music, Inc., was born in New York City in 1905 and resides there. Heyman, a lyricist, was born in New York City in 1907 and resides in Los Angeles.[2] Eyton, a lyric writer and dramatic author, was born in London in 1894 and resides there.[3]

Bolero—Ravel

© 1929. Permission for reprinting by Durand & Cie., Paris, France, copyright owner, and Elkan-Vogel Company, Inc., Philadelphia, Pa., Agent.

m. Maurice Ravel. Published about March 28, 1929,[1] for piano by A. Durand & Fils, Editeurs, Durand & Cie., 4 Place de la Madeleine, Paris. First edition: Front cover in red and white, lists five arrangements only two of which have prices, the price of this arrangement being 12.50. vb. m. on pp. 1–8 (really 3–10). p.n. 11,671. p. [11] and back cover blank. BN and LC (both CDC). The arrangement for four hands, one piano, by the composer, p.n. 11,659, was published about the same day;[1] BN and LC (both CDC).

The orchestral score was published about Nov. 6, 1929.[2] First edition: Front cover and title page are the same, listing five arrangements, four with prices, the price of this arrangement 100 (the prices are "Maj. comprise"), the colors of both pages being **red** and white. The order of the imprint is reversed from that of the piano arrangement, Durand & Cie. preceding A. Durand & Fils. Verso of each page blank. Composition of orchestra. Noticès. m. on pp. 1–66. p.n. 11,779 (on p. 66). Dedication to Ida Rubinstein (on p. 1). BN and LC (both CDC) and JF. No early printing of the orchestral parts, with plate number 11,780, has been found.

It has been said that although the title is Spanish, and Ravel knew Spain, this work bears only the slightest resemblance to the authentic Spanish dance of that name. *Bolero* was composed in 1928 and performed as a ballet on Nov. 22, 1928, in Paris.[3] Ravel was born in Ciboure, in the Pyrenees, France, in 1875 and died in Paris in 1937.

---

[3] Parker, 13th ed., p. 461.

[1] Copy deposited that day at BN; published April 5, 1929, per copyright records at LC.

[2] Copy deposited that day at BN; published Oct. 10, 1929, per copyright records at LC.

[3] Rollo H. Myers, *Ravel* (New York, N.Y., 1960), p. 80; YU. *Catalogue de l'Oeuvre de Maurice Ravel* (Paris, n.d.), pp. 20 and 27; YU.

Boola

Boo - la boo - la,_____ Boo - la boo - la

The first printing of this melody, virtually note for note in the important bars, is in the song *La Hoola Boola*, where the words "Hoola Boola" are also frequently used. *La Hoola Boola* was copyrighted Feb. 24, 1898, by Howley Haviland & Co., 4 East 20th St., New York, N.Y.,[1] although the year in the copyright notice on the music is the previous year. The song is called a "Hawaiian Ditty . . . Up To Dated," with words and music by Bob Cole and Billy Johnson. First edition: Front cover has a drawing of two Hawaiians and is orange, black and white. p. [2] adv. *Sweet.. - The Old..* m. on pp. 3–5. Back cover adv. *She's.. - Say..* LC(CDC) and JF.

One writer claims that the melody derives from an even older Hawaiian song entitled "Moanalua."[2] The only song by that name located so far bears little resemblance to the melody under consideration.[3]

Yale Boola was copyrighted March 9, 1901, by Chas. H. Loomis, 833 Chapel Street, New Haven, Conn.[1] In the first edition for piano, there is the notice on p. 2: "Adapted by permission of Howley, Haviland & Dresser" (the successor publisher of *La Hoola Boola*). Front cover is black and white, five arrangements (for other instruments) are listed, there is a drawing of a lady holding a pennant, the authorship is credited to A. M. Hirsh and the song is called a March & Two-Step. m. on pp. 2–5. Back cover blank. The music pages are engraved. LC(CDC).[4]

Cole and Johnson were Negro entertainers who broke away from the minstrel tradition; in the first month of their association in the late 1890's they played at Poli's Theater in New Haven with great success.[5] Allan M. Hirsh graduated from Yale in 1901, became the head of a pipe company and died in New York City in 1951 at the age of seventy-three.[6]

---

[1] Copyright records; LC.

[2] Gurre Ploner Noble, *Hula Blues* (Honolulu, 1948?), p. 43; NYPL. The author is indebted to Harold Barlow, New York City, for this reference.

[3] In *Aloha Collection of Hawaiian Songs* (Boston, 1901), p. 94; LC(CDC).

[4] The illustration in Mott, p. 541, is not that of the first edition.

[5] Geller, p. 195; and Goldberg, p. 157.

[6] Obituary, *The New York Times*, Dec. 22, 1951.

Bourrée (Gavotte)—Bach

m. Johann Sebastian Bach. This melody for violin solo was first published
about Dec., 1802,[1] by N. Simrock, Bonn, as *Tempo di Bourrée*, in B minor,
in [*Partita I*] *Sonata I* in G minor, under the general title, *Tre Sonate per
il Violino solo senza Basso*, p. 13. Engraved. p.n. 169. Verso of title page
blank. m. on pp. 3–43. Back cover blank. Price blank. No reference to
"Nuova Editione." ONB. This is the title given in *AMZ*. In a variant, additional words "Studio o sia" precede "Tre Sonate"; the additional words
and the price "6 Francs" are in different and heavier type. JF; *Hoboken
Bach*, no. 117. The variant may have been issued at the same time for the
French market during the French occupation of Bonn in 1802. The work
had been composed about 1720 in Cöthen. Schmieder, no. 1002. The
famous *Chaconne*, and the *Gavotte and Rondo* that was selected as one of
six classical works to be carried by the spacecraft *Voyager*, are in the same
work, pp. 26 and 40.

Saint-Saëns arranged this piece for piano in 1861 under the title
Gavotte en si Mineur de la 2ᵉ Sonate de Violon.[2] Brief biographic information regarding Bach appears above under *Air for the G String*.

Bow, Bow, Ye Lower Middle Classes—Iolanthe

Bow, bow, ye   low-er mid-dle clas-ses!

m. Arthur Sullivan. w. W. S. Gilbert. Although *Iolanthe* was performed in
London on Nov. 25, 1882, nothing from this opera was deposited at the
British Museum until July 14, 1883, when 20 editions of the whole or parts
of *Iolanthe* were deposited by Chappell & Co., 50 New Bond Street, London
W. In the first printing of the words in the libretto, which had been issued
by opening night,[1] the words of the song mentioning De Belville are on

---

[1] *AMZ Int-Bl*, Dec., 1802, p. 44. The price is indicated here as 1 Thlr. 14 Gr. *Bach
Gesellschaft* [vol. 27(1)], p. xvi. Schneider, p. 104, had given 1809 as the earliest date.
Schmieder, 1002.

[2] *Saint-Saëns Catalogue*, p. 90.

[1] Allen, *Gilbert*, pp. xviii and 203. Fuld, *Libretti*, p. 147. The facts relating to American
performances of the opera are set forth in *The "Iolanthe" Case*, 15 Fed. 439 (Circuit Court,
District Md., Feb. 21, 1883); NYPL.

p. 29; RA and JF. According to a letter from the publisher, the *March of the Peers*, containing the music only, was issued in a piano arrangement by Berthold Tours about Nov., 1882.[1A] In the copyright deposit copy of this arrangement, possibly a first edition, the front cover is black and white, the price is 4/, page [2] is blank, the music is on pages 1–7 (really 3–9), the p.n. is 17641 and the back cover blank; BM(CDC).

The first printing of the music and words together was in the piano-vocal score, published on Nov. 25, 1882.[2] First edition: Title page mentions five operas by the authors but no plate number. Cast and index. m. on pp. [I]-X, and [3]-134, with this song at p. 21. p.n. 17,614 at bottom of p. [I]. The printer on p. 134 is Henderson, Rait & Spalding, 3 & 5 Marylebone Lane, Oxford Street, London W. Four-page advertisement of 1882 Christmas Number (No. 125) and other music. RA (blue and gray paper covers) and JF (blue, gold and black cloth covers). In the July 14, 1883, copyright deposit copy, the plate number has been moved to the title page; BM(CDC); also at RA and JF.

Sir Arthur Sullivan was born in London in 1842 and died there in 1900. Sir William Schwenck Gilbert was born in London in 1836 and died in Harrow Weald, Middlesex, in 1911.

The Bowery

The   Bow - 'ry,   the   Bow - 'ry!

m. Percy Gaunt. w. Chas. H. Hoyt. The first printing of this song is as one of a group of *Songs from Hoyt's A Trip to Chinatown*, p. [3]. This booklet was copyrighted May 21, 1892,[1] by T. B. Harms & Co., 18 East 22nd St., New York, N.Y.; p. [3] states the copyright is also by Hoyt & Thomas. First edition: front cover of the 15-page booklet has a drawing of a girl and a man and is orange, blue and white. No advertisements on inside pages. Lyrics are in large type. Pages are numbered at the top center. The word "Said" appears in the 5th verse at the end of the first page of *The Bowery*. Back cover blank. LC(CDC) and JF. The separate green and white sheet music edition, with six titles listed from the show, was not deposited for copyright and was apparently printed later; JF.

[1A] *ILN*, Dec. 30, 1882, p. 692 ("Now Ready").

[2] The date of publication stated in the entry at Stationers' Hall on Jan. 15, 1883. *ILN*, Dec. 30, 1882, p. 692 ("Now Ready").

[1] Copyright records; LC.

A *Trip to Chinatown* first played in Decatur, Ill., on Sept. 18, 1890, and in New York City on Dec. 8, 1890. The "Bowery" was the center of fast life in New York City in the 1890's. Gaunt, Hoyt's musical director, was born in England and died in New York City in 1896 at the age of 44.[2] Hoyt was born in Concord, N.H., in 1859 and died in Charlestown, N.H., in 1900.[3]

The British Grenadiers

With a   tow, row, row, row, row, row, to the Brit - ish Gren - a - diers

The British Grenadiers appeared in print in a number of editions, beginning about 1750,[1] the exact chronological order of which has not been established: (a) A single sheet, without imprint, under the title *The British* (with old style "s") *Granadiers* [*sic*], at ML and JF; (b) Same as (a) except that under the title appears "Within Compass of the German Flute," at RCM; (c) A single sheet, without imprint, under the same title (with modern style "s"), at HU (Julian Marshall collection, Houghton Library); (d) A single sheet, with the imprint "Sk:" (illern), under the correct title, "Sung by Mr. Reinhold in Harlequin every where," at ML and JF; (e) Same as (d) except that it is one of three songs, the other two being *Hunting the Hare* and *Shinkin*, at JF; and (f) in (A. Smith) *The Musical Miscellany* (Perth, 1786), p. 231, *BUC*, p. 958. HU also has a broadside, about 1776, entitled "*A New Song to the Tune of 'British Grenadiers,'*" containing different words, but no music.

The origin of this song has been ably studied, the authors mentioning

---

[2] *MT*, vol. 37, p. 686.

[3] Douglas L. Hunt, *The Life and Work of Charles H. Hoyt* (Nashville, Tenn., 1945), NYPL.

[1] Kidson, in *Moffat's Minstrelsy*, p. 315, refers to a "half sheet" of about 1750, and Flood, below, mentions a similar printing about 1760; they are not otherwise described, nor can they presently be located. If their dating is accurate, only (a), (b) and (c) above could qualify, as Skillern did not commence to publish alone until 1777–1778 (Humphries-Smith, p. 295); each of (a), (b) and (c) above is, however, a "full sheet," although blank on the reverse side. Skillern's 1782 *Catalogue*, at BM, does not list this song.

BUC, p. 963, also lists a copy under the title *Some Talk of Alexander*, at SM, but the copy cannot be presently located.

possible sources of the melody in Dutch, English, Scottish or Irish tunes.[2] It can hardly have all these antecedents; several are remote indeed.

The earliest known reference to the song is in [George] Farquhar, *The Recruiting Officer* (London [1706]), in the Epilogue, where it is referred to as "the Granadeer March—Row, row, tow"; BM. The *Boston Chronicle*, June 26/29, 1769, refers to the song having been included in a Boston concert on June 26, 1769; BPL. †

One of the possible antecedents of *The British Grenadiers*, *All Those That Be Good Fellows*, served as the melody for the first published verse in the English language written on the mainland of North America, "Good Newes from Virginia." A copy of this broadside (words only, but stated to be to the tune of *All Those That Be Good Fellows*) published in March, 1623, in London is at the Gilcrease Institute of American History and Art, Tulsa, Okla.

By the Beautiful Sea

By   the   sea,   by   the   sea,   by   the   beau - ti - ful   sea

m. Harry Carroll. w. Harold R. Atteridge. Published May 20, 1914,[1] by Shapiro, Bernstein & Co. Inc., Broadway and 39th St., New York, N.Y. Possible first edition: Front cover has a drawing of a scene by the sea, a photograph of The Du For Trio and is blue, purple, red and white. m. on pp. 2–5. Back cover is red and white, and adv. *Off.. - Heart..* All the songs advertised in this edition were published before May 20, 1914. JF. A variant with the back cover in blue and white is at JB. The front cover of a different edition is illustrated in Mott, p. 549.

Carroll, a composer, pianist and vaudeville artist, was born in Atlantic City, N.J., in 1892, and died in Santa Barbara, Cal., in 1962.[2] Atteridge, a playwright and lyricist, was born in Lake Forest, Ill., in 1886 and died in 1938.[2]

---

[2] Kidson, footnote 1, above. Chappell, pp. 152 and 772. W. H. Grattan Flood, "Fresh Light on Old English Airs—'The British Grenadiers'" in *MT*, Dec. 1, 1913, p. 802. Captain H. Oakes-Jones, "The Old March of the English Army" in *The Journal of the Society of Army Historical Research*, London, Jan., 1927, p. 5; NYPL. Simpson, *British Ballad*, p. 15.

[1] Copyright records; LC.
[2] *ASCAP*, pp. 78 and 16, and ASCAP files.

By the Light of the Silvery Moon

By the light———— of the sil - ver - y moon'

© 1909 Jerome H. Remick & Co. Copyright renewed and assigned to Remick Music Corp. Used by permission.

m. Gus Edwards. w. Ed Madden. Published Aug. 13, 1909,[1] by Gus Edwards Music Pub. Co., 1331 Broadway, New York, N.Y. The copyright deposit copy is a professional edition. Possible first regular edition: Front cover has a drawing of a couple in a canoe, refers to F. Ziegfeld Jr.'s *Follies of 1909* and to a selling agent, and is green, black and white. p. [2] adv. *This..* m. on pp. 3–5. Back cover adv. *Sunbonnet..* The two songs advertised in this edition were published before Aug. 13, 1909. JF.

The title and song were inspired by a moonlight trip in a gondola in Venice in 1905.[2] Edwards, a composer, producer and developer of young stars, was born in 1879 in Hohensallza, Germany, and died in 1945 in Los Angeles.[2] Edward Madden, a lyricist, was born in 1878 in New York City and died in Hollywood in 1952.[3]

By the Waters of Minnetonka

Moon ———— dear, ———— how———— near—

Copyright 1914, Theodore Presser Company. Used by permission.

m. Thurlow Lieurance. w. J. M. Cavanass. Published Dec. 14, 1914,[1] by Theo. Presser Co., 1712 Chestnut Street, Philadelphia. First edition: Front cover is a collective title page, entitled "Indian Songs" by the composer, and is brown, orange and white. 12 titles listed. p. [2] blank. m. on pp. 3–7. p.n. 12125-6. Dedication to Mr. Alfred Williams. Back cover adv. *My..* - *When..* Separate leaf for violin or flute; vb. LC(CDC).

"Minnetonka" in Sioux Indian language means "large round water." Lieurance, an authority on Indian music lore who recorded and harmonized hundreds of Indian songs, was born in 1878 in Oskaloosa, Iowa, and died

---

[1] Copyright records; LC.

[2] Mrs. Gus Edwards writing in "Voice of Broadway," *New York Journal American*, Aug., 18, 1949, p. 13; NYPL.

[3] *ASCAP*, pp. 139 and 329.

---

[1] Copyright records; LC.

in Boulder, Col., in 1963.[2] Cavanass was born in Monrovia, Ind., in 1842, was a newspaper editor and active in church work, and died in Chanute, Kansas, in 1919.† Lieurance wrote the author that he furnished the material for the words of the song, and that Cavanass merely arranged the rhymes for a fee.

The Caissons Go Rolling Along

O - ver hill,   o - ver dale,   we have hit the dust - y   trail

This song first appeared in print, without authorization from, or credit to, its composer, Edmund L. Gruber, in *U.S. Field Artillery March*. The credit was entirely to John Philip Sousa. The arrangement for orchestra was published on Jan. 22, 1918, for military band on Feb. 26, 1918, and for piano on Feb. 27, 1918.[1] No early printings of the first two arrangements have been found. Possible first printing of the piano arrangement: Folio size, with the common words, published by Carl Fischer, Cooper Square, New York, N.Y. Front cover has a photograph of a metal relief of the 306th Field Artillery, is dedicated to it, and is brown, green and white. p. [2] blank. m. on pp. 3–7. p.n. 20784-5. Back cover adv. *Celebrated..* JF. On p. 3 is the claim that the song was copyrighted in 1917 by John Philip Sousa, but no record of such copyright has been found. ‡

The words and music of the song were written by Gruber for the 5th Artillery, in the Philippine Islands, in 1907, on the occasion of the reunion of two portions of his regiment which had long been separated.[2] *Songs of the United States Military Academy*, edited by Lieutenant Philip Egner and Frederick C. Mayer (West Point, N.Y., 1921), p. 26, at LC and NYPL, contains the first printing authorized by Gruber. The words in this edition are also attributed to R. M. Danford and Wm. Bryden, but they later acknowledged in affidavits that they merely made suggestions in the verses and claimed no authorship.[3] Beginning in 1936, an edition under the title *The Caissons Go Rolling Along (Artillery Song)*, and giving sole credit to Gruber, has been published by Shapiro, Bernstein & Co., Inc., New York, N.Y.

[2] *ASCAP*, p. 307, and ASCAP files.

[1] Copyright records; LC.

[2] The facts are told in the decision of *Egner et al.* vs. *E. C. Schirmer Music Co.*, 48 Fed. Supp. 187 (Dist. Court, Mass., 1942), NYPL; and *The New York Times*, Magazine section, p. 62, April 21, 1957.

[3] Affidavits formerly in the possession of the late Elliott Shapiro, New York, N.Y., and examined by this author; their present whereabouts is unknown.

The song has subsequently been adapted (both music and words) by H. W. Arberg, and designated the official song of the United States Army under the title *The Army Goes Rolling Along*. Gruber was born in Cincinnati in 1879; the army was his career, and he died in 1941 where he had been in command, at Fort Leavenworth, Kan.[4]

California Here I Come

Cal - i - for - nia, here I come!

© 1924 M. Witmark & Sons. Copyright renewed. Pub. by arr. with Ross Jungnickel Inc. Used by permission.

mw. Al Jolson, Bud de Sylva and Joseph Meyer. Published Jan. 7, 1924,[1] by M. Witmark & Sons, New York, N.Y. First edition: Front cover has a drawing of five California oranges, refers to the show *Bombo* (but not a show cover), has a photograph of Al Jolson and is orange, green and white. p. [2] adv. *In..* and *Just..* m. on pp. 3–5. p.n. 8302; 16924-3. Back cover adv. *That..* LC(CDC) and JF. *Bombo* opened in New York City on Oct. 6, 1921 [*sic*].

Jolson, known mainly as a stage, screen and radio singer, was born in Washington, D.C., in 1886, and died in California in 1950.[2] Brief biographic information regarding de Sylva appears above under *April Showers*. Meyer, a composer, was born in 1894 at Modesto, Cal., and resides in New York City.[2]

The Campbells Are Coming

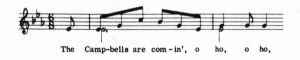

The Camp-bells are com-in', o ho, o ho,

The first known appearance in print of this song is either in *The Caledonian Pocket Companion*, "containing Fifty of the most favourite Scotch Tunes," by Mr. Oswald, printed about 1745 for J. Simpson, London, vol. 3, p. 12, under the above title (*BUC*, p. 747), or in *Caledonian Country Dances*,

---

[4] Letter from General Services Administration, St. Louis, Mo.

[1] Copyright records; LC.
[2] *ASCAP*, pp. 258 and 347.

printed about 1745 for I. Walsh, London, 4th book, p. 89 or 389, under the title *Hob or Nob* (*BUC*, p. 228, and JF). Only the second edition of the latter has been located. The first dated printing is in 1748 in *A Choice Collection of 200 Favourite Country Dances*, printed for Jno. Johnson, London, vol. 4, p. 78, under the title *Hob or Nob* (*BUC*, p. 228).

There has been considerable controversy as to the origin and nationality of the song. *The Scots Musical Museum* reported in 1790 that the song was said to have been composed on the imprisonment of Mary Queen of Scots in Lochleven Castle in 1567.[1] W. H. Grattan Flood claimed it was an Irish tune, *An Seanduine*, first printed in 1745.[2] No copy of such a printing has been located, and the eminent Irish folk-song authority, Donal O'Sullivan, wrote this author that *An Seanduine*, or as it is sometimes known, *Seandhuine Dhota* (meaning, Burnt Old Man), was not known to him in print prior to the printings mentioned above, and that the Irish tune was probably derived from *The Campbells Are Coming*.[3] Scholes maintains it was originally a country dance, *Hob or Nob*.[4] Kidson and Grieg-Stenhouse believe the song was written about 1715 when a rebellion broke out against George I and was suppressed by John Campbell.[5]

Both the melody and the words are referred to in a letter dated April 11, 1716, under the title *The Campbells Are Coming, Oho, Oho!*[6]

(De) Camptown Races—(Sacramento)

mw. Stephen C. Foster. Copyrighted Feb. 19, 1850,[1] by F. D. Benteen, Baltimore, under the title *Gwine To Run All Night*. First edition: Front cover refers to Foster's Plantation Melodies as sung by the Christy &

[1] Edinburgh, vol. III, p. vi; *BUC*, p. 557, and JF. (Nine copies of this volume were entered at Stationers' Hall on Mar. 20, 1790.) There are two known early editions of vol. 3: (a) the imprint is James Johnson, and (b) the imprint is Johnson & Co., both at JF; priority unknown. When the entire work was republished, the price became 7/, and each title page mentioned "In Six Volumes."

[2] Flood, *Bagpipe*, p. 140. O'Neill, *Irish Dance*, p. 7.

[3] See, also, O'Sullivan, *Songs of the Irish*, p. 75.

[4] *OCM*, p. 148. Moffat, *Minstrelsy of Scotland*, p. 209, says that *Hob and Nob* was the name in England.

[5] In *JFSS*, vol. VI, 1922, p. 104. Grieg, *Scots*, vol. 3, p. xxiii, quoting Stenhouse.

[6] In *The Correspondence of The Rev. Robert Wodrow* (Edinburgh, 1843), vol. II, p. 146; NYPL. See, also, Graham, vol. 3, p. 151.

[1] Copyright records; LC.

Campbell Minstrels and New Orleans Serenaders, and lists three titles, the third being *Gwine To Run All Night*.[2] Price: 25 Cts. Copublisher: W. T. Mayo, New Orleans. p. [2] and back cover blank. m. on pp. 3–5. p.n. 1657. Engraved. LC(CDC) and FH. Brief biographic information regarding Foster appears above under *Beautiful Dreamer*.

No printing of the melodically similar folk song *Sacramento* has been found which precedes the above, and it is generally agreed that this windlass or capstan shanty, also known as *Doodah* and *Hoodah*, was derived from *De Camptown Races*.[3]

Can Can—Offenbach

This "immoral" dance first appeared in Jacques Offenbach's *Orphée aux Enfers* (*Orpheus in the Underworld*) which was performed in Paris on Oct. 21, 1858. The piano-vocal score of the "opéra bouffon" was published about the same month[1] by Heugel et Cie., au Ménestrel, 2 bis Rue Vivienne, Paris. First edition: On the title page there is a dedication to Ludovic Halévy, there is a reference to the Bouffes Parisiens, the opera is in two

[2] Front cover is illustrated in Fuld, *Foster*, no page number.

[3] Hugill, p. 114, claims that both Foster's song and *Sacramento* derive from a Negro song, *The Sailor Fireman*, said to have appeared in a book entitled *Nigger Melodies* (New York, N.Y., 1850); no copy of such a book containing this song has been found. Hugill has not replied to an inquiry as to the location of a copy.

Legman, p. 294, states that Foster cribbed a Negro folk song for Foster's song, but furnishes no substantiation. This author has never seen any evidence of a prior folk song similar to Foster's and does not believe there was one.

The opening major triad of L. M. Gottschalk's *The Banjo* (New York, N.Y., 1855), at LC and JF, uses the same rhythmic and melodic pattern, but the resemblance ceases thereafter. (The Escudier, Paris, edition of *Le Banjo* was published in 1856; BN(CDC)—*BF*, Dec. 6, 1856.) The same is true as to the opening major triad of *Roll, Jordan Roll* published in 1862 as no. 2 of "Songs of the Freedmen of Port Royal" by Miss Lucy McKim, Philadelphia; copy at Thornton Hagert, Arlington, Va.

There is a greater similiarity to *De Camptown Races* in the last eight bars of *Lord, Remember Me* in *Slave Songs of the United States* (New York, N.Y., 1867), p. 12; LC.

Dena J. Epstein, Chicago, Harold Barlow, New York City, and Thornton Hagert, Arlington, Va., furnished the information included in the preceding two paragraphs of this footnote.

[1] Oct. 8, 1858, per letter from the publisher. Oct. 15, 1858, according to Dépôt Légal records; Archives. "Sous Presse" in *Le Ménestrel*, Nov. 7, 1858, p. 4. Not listed in *BF* until Dec. 25, 1858. The opera was revised into four acts in 1874.

acts, the words are by Hector Crémieux and the price is 8F. vb. Cast and index. vb. m. on pp. 1–147, the music of the *Can Can* (though not so named) on p. 134. p.n. 2372. Engraved. BN(CDC) and JF. The sheet music edition of the dance, the *Grand Galop*, appeared the following month with the composer's name misspelled on the front cover![2] At Heugel and JF. The piano score has p.n. 3781; BN. The orchestral score and parts of the opera do not seem to have been published. In 1938 the *Can Can* was inserted in *La Gaîté Parisienne*, a ballet from several of Offenbach's works.

In the opera, the *Can Can* immediately follows a minuet for contrast.[3] Tongue-in-cheek, Saint-Saëns used a slow version of the *Can Can* melody for the "Tortoises" in his *Le Carnaval des Animaux*. Premier Khrushchev, on a visit from the Soviet Union to the United States in 1959, saw the filming of the movie *Can Can* in Hollywood and termed the dance "immoral." Brief biographic information regarding Offenbach appears above under *The Apache Dance*. Crémieux, a librettist for many operas, was born in Paris in 1828 and died there in 1892.[4]

El Capitan

Most of this march by John Philip Sousa, including the portion quoted above, was included in solos and choruses entitled *You See in Me* and *Behold El Capitan* in the comic opera *El Capitan*. The first printing of the piano-vocal score, deposited Feb. 4, 1896, at LC, states "Property of John Philip Sousa . . . Not For Sale" and is engraved. The first regular printing of the piano-vocal score, copyrighted April 27, 1896,[1] has this melody in the solos and choruses mentioned above, no. 5b and no. 7 bis, pp. 67 and 95. Front cover has a drawing of a knight and is in many colors. vb. Title page mentions that the book is by Charles Klein, there is **no** price, and the publisher is The John Church Company, Cincinnati, New York and Chi-

---

[2] Nov. 11, 1858, per letter from the publisher. Not in *Le Ménestrel* or *BF*. A few other separate numbers from the opera were first published by E. Bertin, Paris (BN [CDC]), but the *Menuet et Galop* was apparently first published by Heugel.

[3] The *Can Can* was a dance of Parisian origin and came into vogue about 1830. Anatole Chujoy, *The Dance Encyclopedia* (New York, N.Y., 1949), p. 85. Pierre Mariel, *Paris Cancan* (Bonn, 1959). Both at NYPL.

[4] *Larousse XX*, vol. 2, p. 569.

[1] Copyright records; LC.

cago. Copyright notice. Cast. vb. Contents. vb. m. on pp. 7–199. No p.n.
LC(CDC) and JF. No march, as such, is included. The comic opera opened
in New York City on April 20, 1896.

The above melody was soon enlarged into a march, and the latter was
copyrighted in its now familiar form on May 18, 1896,[1] for piano. First
edition: Front cover has a photograph of the composer (without medals),
lists 18 arrangements and is black and white. m. on pp. 2–5. p.n. 11840-4.
Back cover adv. *King..* LC(CDC) and JF. The band parts arrangement of
the march was deposited three days later[1]—with p.n. 11878-5; LC(CDC).
The *El Capitan* song, with p.n. 11918, was deposited June 29–July 3,
1896;[1] BR.

No orchestral arrangement of the comic opera has apparently been
published.[2]

Sousa, the "March King," was born in Washington, D.C., in 1854,
and died in Reading, Pa., in 1932.

Capriccio Espagnol—Rimsky-Korsakov

m. N. Rimsky-Korsakov. Published about July, 1888, by M. P. Belaieff,
Leipzig.[1] No undisputed first edition of the orchestral score has been located, and any of the following four printings could be the first edition. One
printing has a front cover in blue and black, with the title, *К а п р и ч ч и о,*
in Russian only, and no reference to the year 1888. vb. Title page,
in many colors, lists the orchestral score, parts, supplementary parts and
arrangement for piano four hands, the price of the score being M9/R4.50.
vb. m. on pp. 1–93. p.n. 97. p. [94] blank. Inside and outside of back cover
blank. SSL and JF. Another edition is the same except that the front cover
is red and black and the back cover is missing; COL. In the third variant,
the otherwise same front cover is green and black, there is a blank leaf following the title page, and the inside and outside of the back cover are
blank; the paper has shredded in places, and the prices on the title page
are missing; NYPL. The preceding three editions seem to have been for sale
in Russia. In the fourth variant, the front cover is black and gray, with

----

[2] *The New York Times,* Jan. 2, 1965, p. 9 (the manuscript orchestral score is in the
Sousa family home in Long Island).

----

[1] Hofmeister *Monatsbericht,* July, 1888, p. 259, listing the orchestral score, the
orchestral parts and the reduction for piano four hands, the orchestral score in octavo
at 9 marks net.

text in Russian and French and the year 1888 printed, the verso is blank, and the inside and outside of the back cover are blank; JF.

Possible first editions of the orchestral parts, with plate number 98, but without covers, are at CI, FLP and RAM. The arrangement for piano four hands has plate number 99; BM.

The work was composed in 1887 and performed Oct. 31, 1887, in St. Petersburg. Rimsky-Korsakov was born in Tikhvin, Novgorod, in 1844 and died in St. Petersburg in 1908.

Caprice Viennois—Kreisler

© 1910. By permission of copyright owner, Charles Foley Inc., New York, N.Y.

m. Fritz Kreisler. Published for violin and piano on Sept. 15, 1910,[1] by B. Schott's Söhne, Mainz. First edition: Front cover is entitled *Kompositionen für Violine u. Klavier*, lists three titles of which *Caprice Viennois* is no. 2 at 2 M, and is purple and light and dark green. vb. Title page lists 15 violin works by Kreisler (no reference to Röder at the bottom of the page). vb. m. on pp. [3]–7. p.n. 29033. op. 2. p. [8] and inside of back cover blank. Outside of back cover adv. *Alfred..* Separate violin part: m. on pp. [2]–3; pp. [1] and [4] blank; same p.n. LC and BM* (both CDC), and JF.

Tambourin Chinois, another well-known Kreisler work for violin and piano, was published the same day[1] as no. 3 of the above compositions; LC(CDC). Kreisler was born in Vienna in 1875 and died in New York City in 1962.

Careless Love

Love,   oh   love, oh   care - less   love

---

[1] Copyright records; LC. Hofmeister *Monatsbericht*, Oct., 1910, p. 249; NYPL.

Words of this song, one of the earliest blues, appeared in Howard W. Odum, "Folk-Song and Folk-Poetry as Found in the Secular Songs of the Southern Negroes" in *Journal of American Folklore*, Lancaster, Pa., and New York, N.Y., July–Sept., 1911, p. 286, under the title *Kelly's Love; ULS*, p. 1435. Words also appeared in 1915 under the title *Careless Love* in Perrow, p. 147, with a notation "From Mississippi; country whites; MS of R. J. Slay; 1909." As "Kelly's" and "Careless" have similar sounds, one is probably a corruption of the other; but which came first is not known.

The music (and words) were published on Jan. 1, 1921,[1] under the title *Loveless Love*, a "Blues Ballad," with music and words attributed to W. C. Handy. First edition: Front cover has a drawing of a girl's face in a heart and is orange, black and white. The publisher is Pace & Handy Music Co. Inc., 232 West 46th Street, New York, N.Y. m. on pp. 2–5. Back cover adv. Pace.. No price or plate number. LC(CDC), NYPL and JF.

Carioca

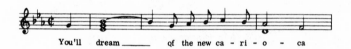

You'll   dream _____   of the new ca - ri - o - ca

© 1933 by Max Dreyfus. Copyright renewed and assigned to T. B. Harms Company. By consent.

m. Vincent Youmans. w. Gus Kahn and Edward Eliscu. Published Dec. 27, 1933,[1] by T. B. Harms Company, 1619 Broadway, New York, N.Y. First edition: Front cover has a photograph of Fred Astaire and Dolores Del Rio and is yellow, black and white. Movie, *Flying Down to Rio*—4 titles listed. m. on pp. 2–11. Notice on p. 2 that the copyright was by Max Dreyfus and the composer. p.n. 387-10. Back cover adv. *I've.. - One..* The type of the titles at the top of the front cover, and in the box at the bottom of the front cover, is lighter than in later editions. LC(CDC). *Flying Down to Rio* was released Dec. 20, 1933, and copyrighted Dec. 29, 1933.[1]

Youmans, a composer, was born in New York City in 1898 and died in Colorado in 1946.[2] Kahn, a lyricist, was born in Coblenz, Germany, in 1886, and died in California in 1941.[2] Eliscu, a lyricist, actor and director, was born in New York City in 1902 and lives there.[2]

[1] Copyright records; LC.

[1] Copyright records; LC.

[2] *ASCAP*, pp. 550, 263 and 142.

Carnaval—Schumann

m. Robert Schumann. Published about Sept.–Oct., 1837,[1] for piano, by Breitkopf & Härtel, Leipzig. Probable first edition: Front cover has a dedication to Mons. Charles Lipiński, mentions that it is oeuv. 9, states that the price is 1 Thlr. 12 **Gr.**, and refers to a Paris agent. vb. m. on pp. 3–31; the above *Marche des "Davidsbündler" contre les Philistins* appears on p. 26. p. [32] blank. p.n. 5813. Engraved. Folio. HU and JF.

With a magnifying glass, one can see that a humorous face has been engraved in each of the letters of "Carnaval" on the title page! The work had been composed in 1834–1835. Schumann was born in Zwickau, Saxony, in 1810 and died near Bonn in 1856.

Carry Me Back to Old Virginny

Car - ry   me back   to   old   Vir-gin - ny

mw. James A. Bland. Copyrighted Aug. 5, 1878,[1] by John F. Perry & Co., **538 Washington St.,** Boston. Probable first edition: Front cover lists six songs by James Bland of Callender's Georgia Minstrels, of which this is the last at 3½, and is black and white; five agents are listed. p. [2] adv. *Prices..* m. on pp. 3–5. p.n. 1403-3. Back cover adv. *Contents..* No drawing of an old Negro on the front cover. SS.

It should be no surprise that *Carry Me Back to Old Virginny* is the official state song of the Commonwealth of Virginia; yet, it has recently been attacked as abhorrent to the Black race.[2] Bland, America's pioneer

---

[1] "Unter der Presse," *AMZ Int-Bl*, Aug., 1837, col. [21]. Hofmeister *Monatsbericht*, Sept.–Oct., 1837, p. 119. Dörffel, p. 3, gives the price as "15" Gr., but this is not in accord with the printed music or the two above-mentioned contemporary notices. Hofmann, *Schumann*, p. 23.

---

[1] Copyright records; LC.

[2] *The New York Times*, March 2, 1970, p. 28.

Negro songwriter, was born of free Negro parents in Flushing, N.Y., in 1854, and died in Philadelphia in 1911.[3]

Casey Jones

Ca - sey___ Jones! Mount - ed to the cab - in___

m. Eddie Newton. w. T. Lawrence Seibert. Copyrighted April 7, 1909,[1] by Southern California Music Co., 332–334 So. Broadway, Los Angeles, Cal. First edition: Front cover has a drawing of a railroad engine, photographs of, presumably, the authors, mentions Edward Barnes and is in red, black and white. m. is on pp. [3]–5. The song was copyrighted by the authors. p. [2] and back cover are blank. No other publisher is listed on the front cover. LC(CDC).

While the above is the first printing of the complete song, there has been much discussion of its origin.[2] John Luther "Casey" Jones was an engineer on Illinois Central Railroad's best railroad train, the "Cannon Ball Express," from Chicago to New Orleans. On April 29, 1900, as the train was about to smash into a stalled freight train, he told everyone else to jump, and he was the only one killed. Jones's friend Wallace Saunders, from Mississippi, a Negro engine-wiper, is said to have adapted or written a ballad regarding the heroic tale, which was sung by Negro railroad men and then allegedly adapted by two white vaudevillians, Newton and Seibert, of whom no other biographic information has been found.

Most of the words of the ballad, other than of the chorus, were printed in May, 1908, i.e., before the sheet music edition described in the first paragraph. This prior printing was in the May, 1908, issue of *The Railroad Man's Magazine* (New York, N.Y.), p. 764; NU. No music was included. An introductory note states that the words are from a "song . . . supposed to have been sung by [Casey Jones's] Negro fireman."

---

[3] John Jay Daly, *A Song in His Heart* (Philadelphia, 1951), p. 48; NYPL.

[1] Copyright records; LC. The originality of at least part of the song is indicated by the fact that the copyright was conceded and upheld in *Shapiro, Bernstein & Co., Inc.* vs. *E. C. Schirmer Music Co.* (U.S. Dist. Ct., Boston, Mass., 1942, Civil Action no. 1349).

[2] *JAF*, 1909, p. 362. *JAF*, 1913, p. 165. Botkin-Harlow, p. 40. Botkin, p. 241. *New York Tribune*, July 15, 1957, p. 6. Lomax, *North America*, p. 553. Scarborough, p. 249. Jack Styles, "The Man at the Throttle Was Casey Jones," in *Sing Out!*, New York, N.Y., Fall, 1957, p. 28; NYPL. Fred J. Lee, *Casey Jones* (Kingsport, Tenn., 1939); NYPL.

In the obituary of Bert Leighton, *The New York Times*, Feb. 12, 1964, it is said that *Casey Jones* is sometimes attributed to him and his brother.

Caucasian Sketches—Ippolitov-Ivanov

m. M. Ippolitov-Ivanov. Published about Dec., 1895,[1] for orchestral score under the Russian title Кавказскіе Эскизы, and the French title *Esquisses Caucasiennes*, Suite for orchestra, op. 10, by P. Jurgenson, Moscow. Possible first edition: Front cover and title page are identical except that the former is in Russian and the latter in French, and the former is blue and gray while the latter is black and white.[2] There is a dedication to I. Pitoéff; four arrangements are listed, three with prices, the Russian price of the orchestral score being 3 Rbl. There is no crown or street address in the imprint, which lists three agents (G. Sennewald in Warsaw). Verso of front cover and verso of title page blank. Composition of orchestra. m. on pp. 4–77; the above *Procession of the Sardar* at p. 55. p.n. 20148. p. [78] and inside of back cover blank. Outside of back cover adv. *Ars*—Schubert (all of which appear to have been published prior to 1895). MC, NYPL and SSL.

A possible first edition of the orchestral parts, with the front cover the same as that of the orchestral score, and with plate number 20149, was also published about Dec., 1895.[1] RAM. A later edition of the arrangement for piano four hands, with plate number 20150, is at NYPL. The subsequent arrangement for piano, with plate number 28520, is at JF. The work was composed in 1894–1895 and performed on Feb. 5, 1895, in Moscow.

Ippolitov-Ivanov was born in Gatchina in 1859; although a composer of the old Czarist order, he was highly considered by the Soviet Union and died in Moscow in 1934.

Chanson

Chan - son-ette, Chan - son-ette, love was born when we met, for ev - er and a
There's a song in the air, but the fair se - ño - ri - ta does-n't seem to

[1] Hofmeister *Monatsbericht*, Dec., 1895, p. 514.

[2] There is a printing notice at the bottom of the front cover that does not appear on the title page.

m. Rudolf Friml. Published Aug. 30, 1920,[1] for piano by G. Schirmer, Inc., New York, N.Y. First edition: Front cover is purple, green and white and mentions three other arrangements. Quarto. p. [2] blank. m. on pp. 3–5. p.n. 28196-c. Back cover adv. *Mourning.. - Love..* LC(CDC).

Lyrics by Dailey Paskman, Sigmund Spaeth and Irving Caesar were added in 1923 and the title changed to *Chansonette*. In 1937, a different lyric was written by Bob Wright and Chet Forrest and additional music was added, Herbert Stothart being credited as a cocomposer, and the song, with the title changed to *The Donkey Serenade*, was inserted the same year in the movie *The Firefly*. Brief biographic information regarding Friml appears above under *L'Amour-Toujours-L'Amour*.

Chant sans Paroles—Tchaikovsky

m. P. Tchaikovsky. Published about May, 1868,[1] for piano as no. 3 in *Souvenir de Hapsal—Trois Morceaux*, op. 2, by P. I. Jurgenson, Moscow. Probable first edition: Front cover, in French, has a drawing of the ruins of a castle, a dedication to V. V. Davidoff, the price of 1.50 for the complete work and separate prices for the three individual numbers (*Chant sans Paroles* being 50 c.), refers to two agents, mentions "Impr" P. Jurgenson and is black and white. p. [2] blank. m. on pp. 3–17. p.n. 430–2. Engraved. Back cover blank. No arrangements on front cover and no reference to "Nouvelle édition." JF (only known copy).

On a late variant Tchaikovsky wrote (in Russian): "Leave me alone . . . I don't know how to write witty inscriptions." GL. (**See Plate I.**) In this variant, the front cover is not engraved and says "Lith" de P. Jurgenson, and a third agent in Milan has been added. No early copy has been found of *Chant sans Paroles*, separately. The work was composed in June–July, 1867 (O.S.). Peter Ilich Tchaikovsky was born at Kamsko-Votinsk, Viatka, in 1840, and died at St. Petersburg in 1893.

---

[1] Copyright records; LC.

---

[1] The complete work and the individual numbers were listed in Hofmeister *Monatsbericht*, May, 1868, p. 74. Dombayev, p. 64, says merely 1868.

Charleston

Charles - ton!   Charles - ton!   Made   in   Car - o - lin - a

© 1923 Harms, Inc. Copyright renewed. Used by permission.

mw. Cecil Mack and Jimmy Johnson. Published Sept. 5, 1923,[1] by Harms, Incorporated, New York, N.Y., with quotation marks around the title. First edition: Front cover is black, orange and white. s. *Runnin' Wild*—4 titles listed. m. on pp. 2–5. p.n. 6870-4. Back cover adv. *Love..* LC(CDC) and JF. The show opened in New York City on Oct. 29, 1923.

Cecil Mack is a pseudonym of Richard C. McPherson, a composer, lyricist and publisher, who was born in Norfolk, Va., in 1883 and died in New York City in 1944.[2] Johnson was a composer and pianist who was born in New Brunswick, N.J., in 1894 and died in New York City in 1955.[2]

Che Farò Senza Euridice—Orfeo ed Euridice

Che fa - rò sen-za Eu-ri - di - ce   do-vean - drò sen-za il mio   ben!

m. C. W. von Gluck. w. Raniero de Calzabigi. The orchestral score of the first or Italian version of *Orfeo ed Euridice* was published in 1764 by Duchesne, Libraro, nell' a strada di San Giacomo, al dissotto della Fontana di San Benedetto, al Templo del Gusto, Paris. First edition: Frontispiece. The title page mentions that the opera was performed in Vienna in 1764 [*sic*], that the engraving was by Chambon and the year 1764. vb. Argomento. Personaggi. m. on pp. 1–158. No plate number. Engraved. Folio. This aria is at p. 129. Copies at NYPL and JF and as stated as 30A in Hopkinson, *Gluck*, p. 23.†

No early printing of the orchestral parts of the opera has been noted. The opera was performed in Vienna on Oct. 5, 1762. Brief biographic information regarding Gluck appears above under *Armide*. Calzabigi, a librettist, was born in Leghorn in 1714 and died in Naples in 1795.[1]

---

[1] Copyright records; LC.
[2] *ASCAP*, pp. 328 and 256, and ASCAP files.

---

[1] *Grove's*, vol. 2, p. 25.

Chicken Reel

The first known printing of the *Chicken Reel* was on June 25, 1910,[1] when it was published for piano by its claimed composer, Jos. M. Daly, in Boston. First edition: Front cover mentions after the title, "or Performer's Buck" and is gray, green and white. m. on pp. 2–5. Subtitle on p. 2: "Buck Dance." Back cover adv. *Scented.*. LC(CDC) and JF. Four months later this composition was republished as a "Two-Step and Buck Dance."[1] Daly was born in Boston in 1891, became a composer and director and lives in New York City.[2]

It is not clear whether the *Chicken Reel* was wholly or partially an original composition by Daly or whether he merely recorded a folk melody.

El Choclo

m. A. G. Villoldo. Probably first published by L. F. Rivarola, Buenos Aires, Argentina, for piano, no later than the first few months of 1911.[1] Possible incomplete first edition: Front cover describes the composition as a "Tango Criollo,"[2] has a dedication to José L. Roncallo, a drawing of an ear of corn and a man, says no. 2460, and is tan, black and white. The music commences on p. 2. The balance of the sheet music, probably p. 3 and back cover, is missing. JF. "El Choclo" means, roughly, "Corn." Words were added at an undetermined later date. Further information regarding the original Argentine publication has not been obtainable.

It is believed that this piece introduced the modern tango to Europe as a ballroom dance.[3] It was published early in 1911 by Édouard Salabert, Paris, for piano and for orchestra, as "Le Vrai Tango Argentin." On p. 2

---

[1] Copyright records; LC.

[2] *ASCAP*, p. 106.

[1] The priority and dating of the Argentine publication are inferred from the above reference to it in the Salabert edition. The Salabert editions were mentioned in *BMF*, April–June, 1911, pp. 10 and 14. The composition is not listed in Pazdírek (1904–1910).

[2] "Criollo" means Argentine.

[3] *Grove's*, vol. 8, p. 305.

of the piano edition is "Publié par arrangement avec F. Rivarola de Buenos Aires." This edition contains a full-page description of the tango as a dance. BN* (CDC—date stamped "1911"), ONB and JF (also at JF a copy not referring to Rivarola but with a 1911 copyright notice). There is also a Brazilian edition published by A. Marquez da Silva, S. Paulo, of uncertain date—*El Choclo* is still described as a "Tango Argentino"; BNM. The current Argentine edition refers to this tango as a "Tango-Milonga."

Angel G. Villoldo, a composer, lyricist, singer and poet, was born in Buenos Aires in 1864 and died there in 1921.[4]

Chopsticks

(Two Hands)

This composition was deposited Feb. 3, 1877, at the British Museum under the title *The Celebrated Chop Waltz*, arranged as a Duet & Solo for the Pianoforte by Arthur de Lulli and published by Howard & Co., 28 Great Marlborough Street, London, and Mozart Allen, 130 South Portland Street, Glasgow. First edition: Front cover indicates the price is 3/ and is black and white. m. on pp. 2–7. No p.n. Back cover blank. BM (CDC). On p. 3 appears: "This part (primo part of the duet) must be played with both hands turned sideways, the little fingers the lowest, so that the movements of the hands imitate the chopping; from which the waltz gets its name." Both the usual opening notes, and the subsequent descending thirds, are included in this edition. Arthur de Lulli was the pseudonym of Mozart Allen's sister, Euphemia, who was sixteen years old in 1877 and who died in 1949.[1] It is understood that in England the descending thirds are claimed to be an original work of Euphemia Allen.

Curiously, also in 1877, Alexander Borodin's daughter played four bars of music similar to the first part of *Chopsticks*, which Borodin called *The Coteletten Polka* ("Coteletten" being derived from the French "*côtelette*" meaning "cutlet," i.e., a chop). Borodin wrote variations on the theme, as did Rimsky-Korsakov, and Cui and Liadov assisted. The collection was published for piano in 1878–1879[2] under the title *Paraphrases*,

[4] Letter from SADAIC.

[1] See, generally, the article by Alfred V. Frankenstein, " 'Chopsticks'; a Musicological Mystery," in *The American Mercury*, New York, N.Y., March, 1932, p. 372; *ULS*, p. 188.

[2] The title page says 1878. Hofmeister *Monatsbericht*, Sept., 1879, p. 268; HU. The BM copy was deposited Dec. 23, 1879.

by Rahter, Hamburg, and Büttner, St. Petersburg; BM and JF. An additional paraphrase was later added by Liszt. In the Borodin version, the four bars are similar, but far from identical, to the usual opening notes of *Chopsticks;* the descending thirds are not included.

There may be a common source to both de Lulli's *Chop Waltz* and to Borodin's *Coteletten Polka,* but if it had previously appeared in print, it has not yet been found. Whether there is any connection between the "movement of two forefingers picking at the keys of a piano" and "the movement of a pair of Chinese eating utensils" is also unknown.

Chorale, Erkenne Mich, Mein Hüter— St. Matthew Passion, Bach

Er - ken - ne mich, mein   Hü - ter, mein   Hir - te nimm mich an.

The above *Chorale* is based on *Mein G'müt ist mir verwirret* composed by Hans Leo Hassler in 1601, and first published to the words *Herzlich thut mich verlangen* in *Harmoniae Sacrae* (Görlitz, 1613), p. 455; Niedersächsische Staats- und Universitätsbibliothek, Göttingen, West Germany.†

The orchestral score of Johann Sebastian Bach's *Grosse Passionsmusik nach dem Evangelium Matthaei* was published about Feb. 20, 1830,[1] in der Schlesinger'schen Buch- und Musikhandlung, Berlin. Probable first edition: Title page has a dedication to the Crown Prince of Prussia, and mentions the price of 18 Rth. for the orchestral score, the piano-vocal score without price and the plate number 1570. vb. Subscribers' list on four pages, including Mendelssohn. Text on eight pages. m. on pp. 5–324, this *Chorale* on p. 65. Engraved. Folio. ONB and JF. *Hoboken Bach,* no. 26.

The piano-vocal score was published at about the same time or shortly thereafter[2] by the same firm in an oblong edition with plate number 1571, subscribers' list and index page. The index is printed on a separate leaf and there is no reference to "Sion . . ." on pp. 25, 112 and 136. BM and JF. Incomplete choral parts, with plate number 1687, probably published in 1831, are at RBW. No printing of the orchestral parts of the *Passion* is known until after 1894.[3] The *Passion* was performed on April 15, 1729, in

---

[1] *Berliner Allgemeine Musikalische Zeitung,* Feb. 20, 1830, p. [57]; NYPL. Hofmeister *Monatsbericht,* Jan.–Feb., 1830, p. 10.

[2] *Berliner Allgemeine Musikalische Zeitung,* May 15, 1830, p. [153]; NYPL. Hofmeister *Monatsbericht,* Jan.–Feb., 1830, p. 11.

[3] Schmieder, p. 342. Deutsch, *Plate Numbers,* p. 10. Letter from Alfred Dürr, Göttingen, Germany.

Leipzig. Brief biographic information regarding Bach appears above under *Air for the G String*.

Cielito Lindo

Ay!   Ay!   Ay!   Ay!_____   Cie - li - to lin - do

The earliest known printing of this song was in 1919[1] by Enrique Munguia, 30 Ave. Francisco I. Madero, Mexico, D.F. In this folio-size edition, the song is described as a "popular song," no composer or lyricist is mentioned, it was arranged by L. Nuño, and it was published together with *La Pajarera*. Front cover is brown, blue and tan. *Cielito Lindo* is on pp. 2–3. p.n. 282. The second song is on the next two pages. Back cover adv. *Concha—Clementina*. JF. "Cielito Lindo" means "Beautiful Heaven."

Otto Mayer-Serra, the distinguished authority on Latin American music, has written the author that it has been established that Quirino Mendoza y Cortez is the composer of this song, that a copyright was granted to Mendoza in Mexico in 1929 when he presented proof that this song was an original work,[2] and that since then he has been collecting the usual composer's royalties from Promotora Hispano Americana de Música, S.A., Mexico, D.F.

The chorus of the song which begins with the words "Ay, ay, ay, ay" should not be confused with Freire's song with a similar name.[3]

La Cinquantaine

m. Gabriel-Marie. Entered for Dépôt Légal on Dec. 23, 1887,[1] for piano by Richault & Cie., 4 Bd. des Italiens, Paris 1ᵉʳ. First edition: Front cover

---

[1] The sheet music bears a claim of copyright in this year. It was not deposited that year in the Library of Congress.

[2] *Grove's*, vol. 3, p. 316, states that this song became popular in Mexico about 1830. Nicolas Slonimsky, Boston, believes that Mendoza merely arranged an old song. Grial, p. 263.

[3] See page 121, above.

---

[1] Archives.

has a dedication to Ernest Binon, the piece is referred to as an "Air dans le Style ancien," the price is 5f, reference is made to an arrangement for violin or violoncello and to two other pieces by the composer. vb. m. on pp. 1–5 (really 3–7). p.n. 17494. Next two pages and back cover blank. BN(CDC).

"La Cinquantaine" means "Golden Wedding Anniversary." Gabriel-Marie, a conductor, critic and composer, was born in Paris in 1852 and died in 1928 while traveling in Spain.[2]

Ciribiribin

Ci-ri-bi-ri-bin, che bel fac-cin, che sguar-do dol-ce ed as-sas-sin!

m. A. Pestalozza. w. Carlo Tiochet. Published 1898–1899,[1] by Carisch & Jänichen, Milan, or by Carlo Schmidl, Trieste (then part of Austria). The Carisch & Jänichen copy of this "Duetto Umoristico" was deposited with the Prefect of Milan on Sept. 21, 1899,[2] and a copy so dated is now at SCR. Possible first edition: Front cover has a drawing of a couple kissing, a dedication to Cesare Gravina and is green and white. No price is printed (stamped L2.50), and there are no arrangements. m. on pp. 2–3. p.n. C. 40 J. Words are reprinted on a separate leaf; verso adv. *Danze..* Back cover adv. *Ballabili.. no. 6.* SCR (CDC).

The earliest known Schmidl copy is identical to the Carisch & Jänichen copy except for the change in publisher, no price is stamped and the back cover adv. *Marenco.. no. 11;* JF. Albert Pestalozza, a composer of operettas and songs, was born in 1851 and died in 1934 at Turin.[3] No biographical information has been found regarding Tiochet.

---

[2] Baker, p. 1029.

[1] April 5, 1898, according to a letter from Carisch S.A., and both copies described above have an 1898 copyright claim by Carisch & Jänichen. However, the copyright copy was deposited by Carisch & Jänichen on Sept. 21, 1899, and present copies of the song mention an 1899 copyright date. The earliest mention in Hofmeister *Monatsbericht* is Dec., 1899, p. 588, where the publisher is Schmidl. The first Carisch & Jänichen edition in Hofmeister *Monatsbericht* is in Feb., 1900, p. 88; NYPL.

[2] Copyright records; UDP.

[3] *Musica d'Oggi* (Milan, 1934) p. 235; NYPL.

Clair de Lune—Debussy

m. Claude Debussy. Published May or June, 1905,[1] by Eugène Fromont, Boulevard Malesherbes, 40 Rue d'Anjou, Paris, as no. 3 of a suite for piano entitled *Suite Bergamasque*. First edition of this Suite: Front cover is red and tan, mentions the year 1890, the price of 5 fr. and a London agent. m. on pp. 1–27, *Clair de Lune* commencing on p. 14. p.n. 1404. pp. [28] and [29] blank. p. [30] adv. 16 titles. Inside and outside of back cover blank. BN and LC* (both CDC).

This work may have been composed as early as 1890, but it was not published until 1905.[1] Debussy was born at St. Germain-en-Laye in 1862 and died in Paris in 1918.

Clementine

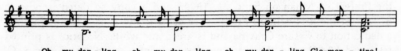

Oh my dar - ling, oh my dar - ling, oh my dar - ling Cle-men - tine!

The words, set to since discarded music, first appeared in print in *Down by the River Lived a Maiden*,[1] with "Song and Chorus" by H. S. Thompson, and copyrighted Dec. 28, 1863,[2] by Oliver Ditson & Co., 277 Washington St., Boston. First edition: m. on pp. 3–5. p.n. 22089. p. [2] and back cover blank. Engraved. LC(CDC) and LL.

The traditional music, together with the words, was copyrighted under the title *Oh My Darling Clementine* on Oct. 13, 1884,[2] by the same publisher, 451 Washington St., Boston, with "Words & Music" by Percy

[1] Debussy wrote Fromont on April 21, 1905, that it was not yet ready and "je viendrai donc mardi pour signer et vous remettrai la *Suite Bergamasque*" (letter at Jean Jobert, the successor publisher). *Suite Bergamasque* was entered for Dépôt Légal June 24, 1905; Archives. Two copies were deposited at the Library of Congress on June 26, 1905 (copyright records; LC). Vallas, pp. 74 and XXXI. *MGG*, vol. 3, p. 66, mentions that the work was published 1890–1905 by Durand et Fils, but Durand has written the author that it was first published in 1905. Lesure, p. 74 (June 1905).

In 1882–1884, Debussy had composed his first version of *Clair de Lune*, with words by Paul Verlaine, but this first version was not published until May, 1926, in a musical Supplement to *La Revue Musicale*, Paris, p. 8; BM, BN, LC, NYPL and JF. Vallas, p. LXXIV.

[1] The author is indebted to Lester S. Levy, Baltimore, for this information.

[2] Copyright records; LC.

Montrose. First edition: m. on pp. 3–5. p.n. 50674. p. [2] and back cover blank. Engraved.[3] LC(CDC) and JF. In 1885 the song, varying in part from the traditional setting, was published under the title *Clementine* by Willis Woodward & Co., New York, N.Y., with Song and Chorus credited to Barker Bradford; JF.

The song is probably American—e.g., the references to "canyon" and "a miner, forty-niner"; although it may be English. An English edition of unknown date was published by W. Paxton, 19 Oxford St., London W., similar to the Woodward edition above, with p.n. 734; SS. It lacks any notice of entry at Stationers' Hall, which further decreases the likelihood that it is of English origin. No biographic information has been found regarding any of the possible authors mentioned above.[4]

The melody of *Clementine* is, curiously, quite similar to the melodies of (a) *Ovio* in Lowell Mason, *The Song Garden*, Second Book (New York, N.Y., 1864), p. 202, at NYPL, (b) *Come to Jesus* in Joseph Hillman, *The Revivalist* (Troy, N.Y., 1868), p. 80, at LC(CDC) and BR, and (c) *Es Sangen Drei Engel*, quoted in Erk-Böhme, vol. III, p. 735, Third Melody.[5]

Colonel Bogey—(included in The Bridge on the River Kwai)

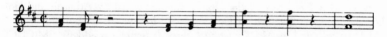

m. Kenneth J. Alford (F. J. Ricketts). Deposited Feb. 19, 1914, at BM for military band by Hawkes & Son, Denman Street, Piccadilly Circus, London W. First edition: Nine folio single-sided sheets, each containing four instrumental parts, and one quarter-sheet, all enclosed in a red-brown folder. Front cover of the folder adv. *Melodious.. - The Red..* Verso adv. *The H.S..* The sheets have p.n. 5074. Outside of back cover of the folder adv. *Method..*, and inside of back cover adv. *Tutors..* BM(CDC). The piano arrangement, with p.n. 5399, was deposited March 23, 1916; BM(CDC).

---

[3] Front cover is illustrated in Fuld, *American*, p. [33].

[4] See also *Annie Lisle*, above.

[5] Harold Barlow, New York City, advised the author of the first named similarity. George Pullen Jackson, *Spiritual Folk-Songs of Early America* (New York, N.Y., 1937), p. 175; NYPL.

The reference in Erk-Böhme, vol. III, p. 735, Third Melody, to Julius Maier, *Deutsche Volkslieder* (Leipzig, n.d.), vol. II, no. 9 (copy at Universitätsbibliothek, Tübingen, Germany) is incorrect.

The march was revived in 1958 by its inclusion in the music in the movie *The Bridge on the River Kwai*.[1] The title apparently derives from the word used in golf. Alford, whose real name was Frederick J. Ricketts, was a composer of many marches who was born in 1881 and died in 1945.[2]

Columbia, the Gem of the Ocean

Oh {Co - lum - bia the/ gem of the o - cean
{Bri - tan - nia {pride

There has been considerable controversy whether this song was American under the above title, or English under the title *Britannia, the Pride of the Ocean* or similar title. There is no purpose served in repeating the previous various arguments here, and only new material will, in general, be mentioned.[1]

The earliest English edition was deposited at the British Museum on July 18, 1852, by T. E. Purday, 50 St. Paul's Churchyard, London, under the title *Britannia the Gem of the Ocean*. The front cover states that the song was "Written and Composed by D. T. Shaw" (the singer in America mentioned in the 1843 American edition). BM(CDC) and JF. The next edition, entitled *The Pride of the Ocean*, was deposited by Addison and Hollier, London, at the BM on Dec. 2, 1852. It says at the bottom of p. 1: *"Melody collected by Mr. Davenport abroad"* (emphasis added). BM(CDC).

The English version is said to have had the words written by Stephen Joseph Meany, an Irish journalist (died 1890), and the melody by Thomas E. Williams of London (died 1854). However, no substantiation at all has been given to support this claim, and there is no reference in the English editions mentioned above or below to either of the alleged authors. The poem is not in a volume of poems by Stephen Joseph Meany, his only known published work, *Shreds of Fancy* (Ennis [Ireland], 1841); BM. Also note the statement in the above English edition that the "Melody [was] collected . . . abroad."

Other early editions published in London, none of which refers to the alleged authors, or to any other authors, are: (c) *The Red, White & Blue*, published by Maine and deposited in 1855, at BM(CDC); (d) *The Red, White & Blue*, H. White, also deposited in 1855, at BM(CDC); (e) *The Pride of the Ocean*, B. Williams, deposited in 1858, at BM(CDC); (f)

---

[1] See report of a lawsuit in the *Daily Telegraph and Morning Post*, London, July 30, 1964, p. 17; JF.

[2] Gammond-Clayton, p. 7.

[1] The English claim is set forth in *MT*, March 1, 1915, p. 159, and *OCM*, p. 117. More temperate statements are in Spaeth, p. 98, and Browne, p. 96.

Britannia, the Pride of the Ocean, B. Williams, ca. 1847–1859,[2] at BR; (g) *The Red, White & Blue,* Davidson's Musical Treasury, ca. 1847–1860, at BR and JF; (h) *Britannia, the Pride of the Ocean,* Harry May, n.d., at JF; (i) *Britannia, the Pride of the Ocean!,* Musical Bouquet, n.d., at JF; and (j) *The Red, White & Blue,* D'Almaine & Co., ca. 1852–1858, at JF.

It is significant that no English edition was entered at Stationers' Hall from 1828 to 1884.

Columbia, the Gem of the Ocean was copyrighted in the United States on April 24, 1843,[3] by George Willig, 171 Chesnut [*sic*] St., Philadelphia, under the title *Columbia the Land of the Brave.* This edition probably contains the first printing of the melody: p. [1] has a drawing of an American flag with 26 stars and 25 [*sic*] stripes. "Written & Composed by David T. Shaw . . . Arranged by T. A. Beckett." Sung by W. G. Plumer and D. T. Shaw. m. on pp. [1]–[3]. p. [4] blank. Engraved. LC and JF. Interestingly, the words, "Columbia the Land of the Brave," do not appear in the song. The title was changed to the present American title in 1844 in the edition published by Osbourn; JF. Thomas à Beckett, an English musician and actor, who had long been a resident of Philadelphia, later claimed to be the sole author of the song, but no early edition so states.[4]

The song is also known in both England and America by its final words, *The Red, White and Blue,* unfortunately the colors of the flags of both countries. †

Come Back to Erin

Come back to E - rin, Ma-vour-neen, Ma-vour-neen

m. Claribel. Published Jan. 2, 1866,[1] by Boosey & Co., 28 Holles Street, London. Possible first edition: Front cover has a dedication to Miss Florence Knowlys, states that it was written and composed for Madame Sherrington and that the price is 4/, lists two keys of which this edition is no. 2 in C, refers to an arrangement as a Valse and is black and white. vb. m. on pp. 1–9 (really 3–11). No p.n. Back cover adv. *Somebody - My..* JF.

---

[2] Dates are either per Humphries-Smith or *English Plate Numbers.*

[3] Copyright records; LC.

[4] Browne, p. 100, is incorrect in this respect; the Osbourn edition merely states: "Adapted & Arranged by T. à Beckett"; JF.

[1] Information from the publisher.

Claribel was a pseudonym for Charlotte Alington Barnard, an English poetess and amateur composer who was born in 1830 and who died in Dover in 1869.[2] She has been credited with being the first composer to receive royalties from the publisher on the sale of the composer's songs.[3]

Come to the Fair

The sun is a - shin - ing to wel - come the day

© 1917 by Enoch & Sons; renewed 1944. Copyright and renewal assigned to Boosey & Hawkes Inc. Reprinted by permission.

m. Easthope Martin. w. Helen Taylor. Frequently mistaken for a folk song, *Come to the Fair* was one of three songs included in a booklet entitled *Three More Songs of the Fair*, which was published June 14, 1917,[1] and a copy of which was deposited at BM on July 20, 1917, by Enoch & Sons, 58 Great Marlborough Street, London W. Possible first edition: Front cover has drawings of a drummer and a fair, is red, white and black and shows three keys (this being Medium). vb. Title page has prices of 3/ and $1, and New York, Paris and Toronto agents. Words on pp. 2–3. m. on pp. 4–20, this song on p. 4 with p.n. 4962. p. [21] adv. *Fairings.* Back cover adv. *Songs..* BM(CDC). A similar edition in low key, has p.n. 4961 for this song; p. [21] adv. *Speed..* (copyrighted in 1916); and back cover adv. *Three..* JF.* The title of the booklet was later changed to *Three More Songs from the Fair.*

Martin was born in Stourport, Worcestershire, in 1882, became a composer and died in London in 1925.[2] All that is known about Helen Taylor is that she was a lyric writer and translator and died in London in 1943.[2]

Comin' Thro' the Rye

Gin a bod - y meet a bod - y com - in' thro' the rye

[2] *Grove's,* vol. 1, p. 440.
[3] Simpson, p. 145.

---

[1] Copyright records; LC.
[2] Information from PRS.

It has been frequently observed that the melodies of this song and *Auld Lang Syne* have a considerable similarity, and the melodic antecedents of *Auld Lang Syne* are thus to some extent also those of *Comin' Thro' the Rye*.[1] The extent of Burns's actual contribution to the latter song is similarly uncertain.

At first, the separate existence of *Comin' Thro' the Rye* was a bawdy one. Burns collected a version which was printed privately after his death about 1800 in *The Merry Muses of Caledonia*[2] and which fully justifies the privacy of its publication.

The first appearance in print of *Comin' Thro' the Rye* is said to be in John Watlen's *Old Scots Songs* [Edinburgh?], 2nd Sett or 8th Number, about Aug., 1794;[3] however, no copy has been located, or in fact even claimed ever to have been seen, so this claim awaits proof. Nine copies of the first known printing were entered at Stationers' Hall on June 29, 1796, by Longman and Broderip, 26 Cheapside and 13 Haymarket, London, under the title *If a Body Meet a Body*. p. [1] blank. p. [2] states that the song was sung by Mrs. Henly at the Royal Circus in the new Pantomime called *Harlequin Mariner*, the music adapted by J. Sanderson, the words by Mr. Cross. Price 1s. m. on pp. [2]–[3]. p. [4] has an arrangement for the German flute or guitar. Engraved. No plate number. BM. It is unlikely that Cross did any more than clean up the text for public consumption. Within a year the song was printed in vol. V of *The Scots Musical Museum*.[4] The opening words are frequently "Gin a Body" rather than "If a Body," although the meaning is the same.

Concerto for Orchestra—Bartók

[1] See *Auld Lang Syne*, above, p. 115. It has also been suggested that a specific melodic source for *Comin' Thro' the Rye* is *I've Been Courting at a Lass*, in vol. IV of *The Scots Musical Museum*, p. 316.

[2] The original is at Lord Rosebery. It was privately reprinted in 1959 at Edinburgh; Burns's version is at p. 112. JF.

[3] Glen, pp. 57 and 192. See also Davidson Cook, "Watlen's 'Scotch Songs'" in *The Scots Magazine*, Glasgow, Oct., 1933, pp. 56 and 150; *ULS*, p. 2518. There is a sheet-music edition of *If a Body Meet a Body*, "The words written by a Lady, and the Music composed at her request by John Watlen"; this edition was printed both for the Author and for G. Walker and has an 1813 watermark. JF.

[4] See *Auld Lang Syne*, above, p. 115.

m. Béla Bartók. Published for orchestral score on March 20, 1946,[1] by
Boosey & Hawkes, London. First edition: Front cover is tan and black. vb.
Title page is black and white, says Full Score and mentions branches of
Boosey & Hawkes in New York City, Sydney, Toronto and Cape Town
only, and without mention of a selling agent. Instrumentation. m. on pp.
[1]–[147]. p. [1] mentions that the work was written for the Koussevitzky
Music Foundation in memory of Mrs. Natalie Koussevitzky, a 1946 copyright by Hawkes & Son (London), Ltd. and plate number 9009. p. [148]
adv. Concertos.. Inside back cover is blank. Outside back cover adv. works
by the composer. Folio. BM and LC (both copies deposited March 21,
1946), NYPL and JF. The orchestral parts with plate number 8730 are for
rental by Boosey & Hawkes, New York City.

The Concerto was completed Oct. 8, 1943, and performed by the
Boston Symphony Orchestra under Serge Koussevitzky in New York City
on Dec. 1, 1944. Bartók was born in Nagyszentmiklós, Hungary, in 1881 and
died in New York City in 1945.

Concerto for Piano—Grieg

m. Edvard Grieg. Published about May, 1873,[1] by E. W. Fritzsch, Leipzig,
for orchestral score, piano part and orchestral parts. Probable first edition
of the orchestral score: Title page states Concert für Pianoforte mit Begleitung des Orchesters, op. 16; there is a dedication to Edmund Neupert;
the three arrangements mentioned above are listed (and the parts in four
groups), with prices in Thlr. and Ngr., the price of the orchestral score
being 4 Thlr. 15 Ngr.; and there are four lines of agents, the year 1872,
and p.ns. 205.206.207. vb. m. on pp. 1–104, a lithographic reproduction of
a manuscript score. p.n. 207. Upright. BM (copy purchased Oct. 3, 1874),
RAM (with yellow and black front cover) and JF.

A probable first engraved printing of the orchestral parts with the
same listed prices and plate numbers is at William Reeves, London.

The Concerto was composed in 1868 and performed on April 3,
1869, in Copenhagen. Brief biographic information regarding Grieg appears
under An den Frühling.

---

[1] Copyright records; LC.

[1] Musikalisches Wochenblatt, Leipzig, May 2, 1873, p. 279; NYPL. From the date
on the title page, this work may have been published in 1872. It was not listed in
Hofmeister until 1875.

Concerto for Piano no. 1—Brahms

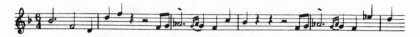

m. Johannes Brahms. The piano part only was published April 6, 1861,[1] by J. Rieter-Biedermann, Winterthur. As the orchestral parts were not published until March 11, 1862,[1] it is possible that the first printing of the piano part did not refer to the orchestral parts; however, no copy has yet been found of the piano part which does not refer to the orchestral parts. Possible first edition of the piano part: Front cover states *Concert für das Pianoforte* mit Begleitung des Orchesters, op. 15; the publisher is as above followed by Leipzig, bei Fr. Hofmeister; the price with Orchester is 7 Thlr. and für Pianoforte allein 2 Thlr. 10 Ngr; and the colors are green, lavender, black and white. vb. m. on pp. 3–53. p.n. 170. Back cover blank. Music pages engraved. GM(Aus dem Nachlass von Johannes Brahms) and JF.

Probable first edition of the orchestral parts: Front cover refers only to the arrangements for orchestral parts and for piano alone, without prices, and is brown, black and tan. vb. There are 20 parts; engraved; p.n. 170. Back cover missing. JF. The orchestral score was not published until Jan. 30, 1875;[1] in what is probably the earliest edition the publisher is shown at both Leipzig and Winterthur—GM(Aus dem Nachlass von Johannes Brahms), BM and JF.

The *Concerto* was composed in 1858 and performed Jan. 27, 1859, in Leipzig. Brahms was born in Hamburg in 1833 and died in Vienna in 1897.

Concerto for Piano no. 1—Liszt

m. F. Liszt. Published early 1857[1] for orchestral score and for solo part with accompaniment for second piano by Carl Haslinger, Vienna. Probable first edition of the orchestral score: Front cover is tan, red and black. Title page states *1tes Concert für Pianoforte und Orchester*; there is a dedication

---

[1] Deutsch, *Brahms*, p. 135. Hofmann, *Brahms*, p. 33. The piano part is mentioned in Hofmeister *Monatsbericht*, May, 1861, p. 82. The orchestral parts are mentioned in the June, 1862, issue of this work, p. 100, at the price of 6 Rthlr. 20 Ngr. The orchestral score is mentioned in the Oct., 1875, issue, p. 208.

---

[1] Hofmeister *Monatsbericht*, Jan., 1857, p. 18. Müller-Reuter, p. 346, says May, 1857. According to the latter, the orchestral parts (p.n. 14,509) were not published until June, 1872.

to Henry Litolff and reference to the two arrangements mentioned above, the price of the orchestral score being Fl. 4.30 xr.C.M.; and the colors of the title page are gray, tan and black. Verso and following page blank. m. on pp. 3–82, engraved. p.n. 11,933. LC, GM* and JF. The solo part with accompaniment for second piano has plate number 11,934; JF.

The *Concerto* was sketched about 1830, completed in 1849, and revised in 1853 and 1856. It was performed on Feb. 17, 1855, in Weimar, with Liszt at the piano and Berlioz conducting. Franz Liszt was born in Raiding, Hungary, in 1811 and died at Bayreuth in 1886.

Concerto for Piano no. 1—Tchaikovsky

m. P. Tchaikovsky. The year of publication by P. Jurgenson, Moscow, cannot be established and may range from 1875–1880.[1] Nor is the relative priority of the arrangements clear; if the orchestral parts (p.n. 2591)[2] were the first to appear, a satisfactory first printing has not been located. A set of parts without covers or imprint, but with some of the parts engraved, is at SSL.

Possible first printing of the orchestral score: Title page says: *Concerto pour le Piano*, op. 23; there is a dedication to Hans von Bülow; four arrangements are listed—orchestral score at 6 Rb., piano with orchestra at 9 Rb., one piano at 4 Rb. and two pianos at 8 Rb; Edition Jurgenson appears at the top; and Brandus & Co., Paris, is a coagent. vb. m. on pp. 1–154. p.n. 2590. Not engraved. No covers. GL, COP and JU. A similar edition, with a front cover which says: "2de Edition Revue et Corrigée," [sic] is at SSL. The first edition may have had engraved music pages. The arrangement for two pianos has p.n. 2592.[2]

The *Concerto* was completed Feb. 21, 1875, and performed in Boston on Oct. 25, 1875. It was first dedicated to Nicholas Rubinstein, who pronounced it unplayable, then to Hans von Bülow. The recording of this *Concerto* by Harvey Lavan (Van) Cliburn, Jr., was the first classical long playing recording to sell a million copies. Brief biographic information regarding Tchaikovsky appears above under *Chant sans Paroles*.

---

[1] The orchestral parts are listed in Hofmeister *Monatsbericht*, March/April, 1876, p. 45; the orchestral score Oct., 1880, p. 279. Dombayev, p. 46, gives 1879 as the year of publication.

[2] *Jurgenson Catalogue*, Moscow, 1889, p. 192; NYPL.

Concerto for Piano no. 2—Rachmaninoff

m. S. Rachmaninoff. Published about Oct., 1901,[1] for orchestral score, orchestral parts and two pianos by A. Gutheil, Moscow. Probable first edition of the orchestral score: Front cover in gray and black has title in Russian, 2-й Концертъ, and in French, 2d Concerto pour Piano. vb. A multicolored title page, in French only, has the title Second Concerto pour le Piano, op. 18; a dedication to N. Dahl; the three arrangements mentioned above, the prices of the Partition being R.7, M.15, and Fr. 19; Edition Gutheil at the top; four agents; and p.ns. 8102/4. vb. m. on pp. 3–116. p.n. 8102. Inside and outside of back cover blank. NYPL, BM* and JF.

Possible first editions of the orchestral parts, with plate number 8103, but without covers, are at CI and RAM. An early printing of the two-piano arrangement, with plate number 8104, is at ONB.

The Concerto was completed April 21, 1901, and received its first complete performance on Oct. 27, 1901, in Moscow. Sergei Rachmaninoff was born in Novgorod in 1873 and died in 1943 in California.

Concerto for Piano no. 5—Beethoven

m. L. van Beethoven. On Nov. 1, 1810, eleven copies of this Concerto were received at Stationers' Hall[1] from Clementi & Compy., 26 Cheapside, London, under the title Grand Concerto for the Pianoforte, op. 64, by Lewis

---

[1] Bertensson-Leyda, p. 410. Hofmeister Monatsbericht, Oct., 1901, p. 533. Breitkopf & Härtel, Musik-Verlagsbericht (Leipzig, 1901), p. 16; NYPL.

[1] The entry at Stationers' Hall on this date says: "Received eleven copies." The number eleven was required by the then English copyright law for eleven specific libraries—see, above, p. 18.

A letter from Beethoven to Breitkopf & Härtel said that this Concerto should "appear on November 1, 1810" (Letter 262, dated July 2, 1810, in Anderson, Beethoven, p. 276).

[sic] van Beethoven.[2] The entry at Stationers' Hall does not indicate whether the piano part, the orchestral parts or both were entered at the time (probably only the piano part); in any event, only the piano part has been found in a copyright deposit copy. In the copyright deposit copy of the piano part, there is only one price on the front cover of this copy, 10/6d; the watermark is "D.G.," without year, and the plate mark at the bottom of each music page is "Beethoven's Con. Op.————," without the opus number. m. on pp. 1–37 (lacking pp. 7–8 and 15–16). p. [38] blank. BOD (also at BM, h 376 [7], but not CDC). Another copy of the piano part at the British Museum has one price on the front cover, no watermark, and the opus number "64" included at the bottom of the music pages (h 383 a [2]). A copy at the Royal College of Music has an 1810 watermark, a second price, clumsily added, "without Accts. 8s," and the opus number included; also at JF.[3]

Only one possible first edition of fifteen orchestral parts published by Clementi & Comp. has been found; it has an 1810 watermark, there are two prices on the front cover and the opus number is included; JF (BM's set has an 1819 watermark, h 383 a [2]).[3]

The first German edition of the orchestral parts (with its proper op. no. 73) was published in Feb., 1811, by Breitkopf & Härtel, Leipzig;[4] BA. The *Emperor Concerto* was composed in 1809 and performed on Nov. 28, 1811, in Leipzig. Beethoven was born in Bonn in 1770 and died in Vienna in 1827.

Concerto for Violin—Beethoven

---

[2] Cecil Hopkinson was the first to mention the priority of this edition in First Edition Bookshop *Catalogue 62*, London, n.d., no. 384; JF. See, generally, Tyson, p. 79.

[3] The foregoing record is confusing. Most English music up to 1811 or a little later had watermarks as to year (see, above, p. 13). If the piano part was published first, it may have been necessary to have hastily added a second price without accompaniments, which addition was eliminated later when the orchestral parts were available. On the other hand, the orchestral parts may have been ready only when the piano part was reprinted. Finally, there are textual differences in the various editions.

[4] Kinsky-Halm, p. 196.

m. Ludwig van Beethoven. Published Aug. 1808,[1] for violin and seventeen orchestral parts by Bureau des Arts et d'Industrie, Vienna and Pest. First edition: Title is *Concerto pour le Violon* avec accompagnement de deux Violons . . . Composed and dedicated to Monsieur de Breuning. Oeuvre 61. p.n. 583. Engraved. In the first issue the price is f (blank), at AVH (presentation copy to dedicatee), GM, NYPL and JF. Later issues have the price f [7], at Staatliche Hochschule für Musik und Darstellende Kunst, Berlin-Charlottenburg, and f [4], at BSM.†

Concerto for Violin—Mendelssohn

m. Felix Mendelssohn Bartholdy. The *Concert für die Violine* was published for orchestral parts about June 18, 1845,[1] by Breitkopf & Härtel, Leipzig. First edition: Front cover of Violino Principale part states op. 64, the publisher has London and Milan agents, there is a legal claim, the price with orchestra is 4 Thlr. and with piano 2 Thlr., the plate number is 7210 and the work was registered at the Vereinsarchiv. Engraved. JF (mostly August Wilhelmj' set).

The orchestral score was published about April, 1862,[2] by the same concern in engraved octavo at 4 Thlr. 20 Ngr., with p.n. 10334 and m. on pp. 1–180; BM, HU and JF (August Wilhelmj' copy). The work was completed in Frankfurt on Sept. 16, 1844, and performed in Leipzig on March 13, 1845. Mendelssohn was born in Hamburg in 1809 and died in Leipzig in 1847.

---

[1] Kinsky-Halm, p. 146. The Clementi & Co., London, edition of the orchestral parts was published in the late summer or autumn of 1810; Tyson, pp. 55–56. The work was published as a piano concerto by Bureau des Arts et d'Industrie in Aug., 1808, and by Clementi & Co. about two years later.

---

[1] *AMZ*, June 18, 1845, p. 431. Müller-Reuter, p. 89, states June, 1845. Hofmeister *Monatsbericht*, July, 1845, p. [98]. ‡

[2] Müller-Reuter, p. 89, states April, 1862. Hofmeister *Monatsbericht*, June, 1862, p. 99.

Coronation March—Meyerbeer

m. G. Meyerbeer. The piano-vocal score of the opera *Le Prophète*, in which *La Marche du Sacre* or *Coronation March* appeared, was published July 25, 1849,[1] by Brandus et Cie., 87 Rue Richelieu, and Troupenas & Cie., 40 Rue Vivienne, Paris. Probable first edition: Half-title page. vb. Next page blank. A portrait of the composer faces the title page. Title page has drawings of scenes from the opera, mentions M. E. Scribe as the librettist, is dated 1849, has no price, and mentions three agents. vb. Cast and index. vb. m. on pp. 1–380, *La Marche du Sacre* commencing on p. 262. p.ns. 5103, 5104(1–25) and 5109(5). French text only. Engraved. BM(R.M. 12. c. 6.) and JF. Proof sheets with Meyerbeer's corrections are at JF. *La Marche du Sacre* was probably published separately for piano a few weeks before the piano-vocal score;[2] no copy has been found. The Breitkopf & Härtel, Leipzig, piano-vocal score, with German and French texts, was published later in 1849;[3] ONB. The opera was performed in Paris on April 16, 1849.

The orchestral score of the opera was deposited March 31, 1851,[4] by Brandus et Cie., 87 Rue Richelieu, Paris. The copyright deposit copy lacks a title page. m. on pp. [1]–794. Supplements—no. 1, 3 pp.; no. 2, 10 pp.; and no. 1(B)—18 pp. p.n. 5101. Engraved. *La Marche du Sacre* commences on p. 556. BN(CDC). Similar copies at BM (H. 612. n.) and JMM with a title page including Troupenas et Cie. as copublisher, and a cast and index page. JMM's copy has corrections by Meyerbeer himself. As the business of Troupenas et Cie. was sold in July, 1850,[5] to Brandus et Cie., Jean-Marie Martin, Hollogne-aux-Pierres, Belgium, considers the edition mentioning Troupenas et Cie. as a copublisher earlier.

A probable first edition of the orchestral parts of the opera, engraved, with plate number 5102, without covers, is at MAP.

Giacomo Meyerbeer was born in Berlin in 1791 and died in Paris in 1864.

---

[1] *RGM*, July 22 and 29, 1849, pp. 232 and 240. Copies were deposited Aug. 2, 1849; Dépôt Légal records at Archives. *BF*, Aug. 25, 1849, p. 424.

[2] *RGM*, July 8, 1849, p. 216.

[3] Hofmeister *Monatsbericht*, Nov., 1849, p. 133.

[4] Dépôt Légal records; Archives. *BF*, May 3, 1851, p. 229, without price.

[5] Hopkinson, *Parisian*, p. 116.

Country Gardens

This melody first appeared in 1728 under this title in *The Quaker's Opera* printed in London for J.W., at p. 37; *BUC*, p. 866. The melody also came to be known as *The Vicar of Bray*.[1] Chappell included two versions in *A Collection of National English Airs* (London, 1838–1840)[2] which provide an interesting link between the 1728 version and the "Handkerchief Dance" tune collected by Cecil J. Sharp and Herbert C. MacIlwaine in 1907[3] and popularized by Percy Grainger in 1919.

Credo, Missa Solemnis—Beethoven

m. Ludwig van Beethoven. The *Missa* was published in March–April, 1827,[1] in orchestral score and for orchestral and vocal parts by B. Schott Sons, Mainz. First edition of orchestral score: Front cover with title as *Messe Solennelle* is gray and black, without price. vb. Decorated title page has a dedication to Archduke Rudolph and mentions op. 123, Paris and Antwerp branches of the publisher and the year 1827. vb. Two-page subscription list headed by five Kings. Next page blank. m. on pp. 2–299, the *Credo* on p. 115. p. [300] blank. p.n. 2346. Folio. Engraved. BM, ONB and JF. Copies for sale have a price on the front cover and lack the subscription list.

The first edition of the 25 orchestral parts and 8 vocal parts has the same title page as that of the orchestral score. p.n. 2534. Engraved. BM*, GM* and JF*. The piano-vocal score, with p.n. 2582, was also published at about the same time.

The *Credo* was one of the three sections performed in Vienna on May 7, 1824. Brief biographic information regarding Beethoven appears above under *Concerto for Piano no. 5*.

---

[1] Chappell, p. 652.
[2] Vol. I, p. 45, and vol. II, p. 13 and nos. 25 and 26; NYPL.
[3] *Morris Dance Tunes*, London, Set 1, no. 3; BM (CDC).

---

[1] Kinsky-Halm, p. 359.

La Cucaracha

La cu-ca - ra - cha,_ la cu-ca - ra - cha,_

The earliest known appearance of this song in print is as one of two songs in *Canciones Mexicanas*, published April 27, 1916,[1] by Enrique Munguia, 30 Ave. Francisco I. Madero, Mexico City, and 136 San Francisco, Guadalajara. Front cover is red and white with a few designs and mentions that the arrangements are by José de J. Martinez. p. [2] blank. The other song, *La Valentina*, is on pp. 3–5. p.n. 270. The music and words of *La Cucaracha* are on pp. 6–7. Back cover adv. compositions of Manuel M. Ponce. LC(CDC).

Carlos Chávez included the song, for piano only, in 1914 in his *Cantos Mexicanos*, op. 16, published in 1921 by Wagner y Levien Sucs., Mexico City, the song being described as a "Song of the Revolution 1914/5." LC and NYPL.[2] The Mexican Revolution of 1910 overthrew Díaz; thereafter, there was much fighting between different leaders, including Pancho Villa. Wallace Beery played the role of Villa in the movie *Viva Villa*, which popularized the song in 1934. *La Cucaracha* literally means "The Cockroach," and was the name of the girl in the song![3]

A minor version of *La Cucaracha* appears as *Las Tristas Horas* in Eleanor Hague, "Mexican Folk-Songs" in *Journal of American Folklore*, Lancaster, Pa., and New York, N.Y., July–Sept., 1912, p. 263; *ULS*, p. 1435.

A Mexican has recalled the generally similar music and words of *La Cucaracha* that he had heard in 1885 in Mexico at the age of 5; see Vicente T. and Virginia R. R. de Mendoza, *Folklore de San Pedro Piedra Gorda* (Mexico, D.F., 1952), p. 128; NYPL.

Daisy Bell—(A Bicycle Built for Two)

Dai - sy,   Dai - sy,   give me your an - swer, do!

mw. Harry Dacre. Although the author of the song was an Englishman, this song was written while he was visiting the United States, and copyright deposit copies at both the British Museum and the Library of Congress are

---

[1] Copyright records; LC.

[2] *Chávez Catalog*, p. 3. No United States copyright entry can be found for *Cantos Mexicanos*.

[3] Nicolas Slonimsky, *Music of Latin America* (New York, N.Y., 1945), pp. 222 and 230; NYPL. Sandburg, p. 289. Grial, p. 259.

American editions. The song was published Aug. 29, 1892,[1] or Nov. 30, 1892,[2] and deposited on Dec. 1, 1892, at Washington and on Dec. 13, 1892, in London. First edition: Title is *Daisy Bell*. Published by T. B. Harms & Co., 18 East 22nd St., New York, N.Y. Front cover mentions Francis, Day & Hunter, 195 Oxford Street, London, and is red, green and white. p. [2] blank. m. on pp. 3–5. Back cover adv. *Hear.. - True..* BM and LC (both CDC). The English edition was published by Francis, Day & Hunter and has a photograph of the person who made the song famous, Katie Lawrence; JF.

The song is frequently known today as *A Bicycle Built for Two*. When Dacre came to the United States he brought a bicycle on which he had to pay customs duty; a friend joked that it was fortunate that the bicycle had not been built for two as the duty would have been double.[3] Harry Dacre's real name has been said to have been Frank Dean or Henry Decker; a professional songwriter, he was born in 1860 in Lancashire, England, and died in 1922 in London.†

Dance of the Corregidor—The Three-Cornered Hat

© 1921. Reproduced by permission of J. & W. Chester Ltd., London.

m. Manuel de Falla. The ballet *El Sombrero de Tres Picos* was published for piano on March 29, 1921,[1] by J. & W. Chester, Ltd., 11 Great Marlborough Street, London W. 1. First edition: Front cover is red, yellow and black with a drawing of a man in a three-cornered hat. vb. On the title page, the title is also given in French (*Le Tricorne*) and in English; the ballet is by G. Martínez Sierra, after the novel by P. A. de Alarcón; the publisher is shown also at Geneva, and there is a Belgian affiliate. Verso names designer of front cover. Dedication: A Leopoldo Matos. Next page states, among other things, that the choreography was by Leonide Massine, the Curtain and Scenery, and (the design of) the Costumes were by Pablo Picasso, and the first performance was on July 22, 1919, in London. Cast. Synopsis of story on pp. vi–xv in French and English. vb. m. on pp. [1]–78, the *Danse du Corregidor* on p. 49. p.n. 9710. No back cover.[2] BM (copyright copy deposited April 5, 1921), JMM and JF (with back cover stating price is 20/ (Fr. 30)).

---

[1] Date in entry at Stationers' Hall on June 1, 1893.

[2] Copyright records; LC.

[3] Geller, p. 100.

---

[1] Copyright records; LC. "Just Published," according to the May, 1921, issue of MO, p. 671.

[2] The outside of the back cover of an otherwise similar edition has the price of 20/ (Fr. 30); inside of back cover blank. NYPL.

The orchestral score of the *Danse du Corregidor* was not published until Dec., 1952,[3] when it was included in an octavo orchestral score of the entire ballet. The following copy purchased Feb. 4, 1953, by LC may be the first edition: Front cover is red, yellow and black. vb. Title page gives the title in three languages and has the same London imprint as described above. Verso has printing information. Index and instrumentation. Cast. Synopsis of story in English and French on pp. v–xiv. m. on pp. 1–254, the *Danse [sic] of the Corregidor* on p. 158. p. 1 has 1921 and 1949 copyright claims. p.n. 43C. p. [255] adv. *Selected..* (Falla). p. [256] adv. *Selected..* (Stravinsky). p. [257] adv. *Symphonic..* p. [258] blank. LC. The folio or-

Orchestral parts of the entire ballet exist only in manuscript, and this *Danse* has not been published separately or otherwise.[3A]

The *Danse du Corregidor* was not included in the earlier version of the mime, *El Corregidor y la Molinera*,[4] performed in Madrid April 7, 1917, but apparently not published under that name. The ballet *El Sombrero de Tres Picos* was apparently not published in Spain, as copies in leading Spanish libraries are the Chester edition. Falla was born in Cadiz in 1876; he lived alternately in Spain and France until he finally settled in Argentina where he died in 1947. Martínez Sierra was born in Spain in 1880 and became a poet and critic.[5]

Dance of the Hours—La Gioconda

m. Amilcare Ponchielli. A piano-vocal score of *La Gioconda* (in which *Danza delle Ore* or the *Dance of the Hours* appears) was deposited May 1, 1876,[1] with the Prefect of Milan by Ricordi, Milan. Curiously, two completely different piano-vocal scores were then deposited Nov. 7, 1876, at S. Cecilia, Rome, and the next day at the British Museum by Ricordi,[2] and it is not known which, if either, is the same as that deposited earlier with

[3] Information from the publisher.

[3A] Information from publisher.

[4] Jaime Pahissa, *Manuel de Falla, His Life and Works* (London, 1954), pp. 96 and 185; NYPL.

[5] *Larousse XX*, vol. 4, p. 719.

[1] Copyright records; UDP.

[2] A piano-vocal score was entered at Stationers' Hall on Oct. 27, 1876, with date of publication given as Oct. 14, 1876. A piano-vocal score was also announced in the Oct. 22, 1876, issue of *GMM*, p. 357. It is not known which of the two piano-vocal scores is referred to in either case.

the Prefect of Milan. In the British Museum copy, the title page is red, black and white, mentions that the words are by Tobia Gorrio (a pseudonym of Arrigo Boito) and the price Fr. 15, and shows R. Stabilimento Ricordi additionally only at Naples, Rome, Florence and London (including street address). Verso has the Ricordi "Ars et Labor" emblem. Cast. vb. Text on pp. [5]–27. Index. m. on pp. 1–370, the *Dance* commencing on p. 255. p.n. 44864. Inside of back cover blank. Outside of back cover is green and gold, and has "Ars et Labor" emblem. Front cover is missing. The S. Cecilia copy also has a dedication page to Maddalena Mariano-Masi preceding the title page; the verso has a drawing of the composer; the text ends at p. 25, followed by an index; the music ends at p. 345; and the *Dance* commences at p. 242. There are no covers. SCR (105.A.21).† Another copy at S. Cecilia (7.F.32), although incomplete, is similar to the British Museum's. It seems likely that the British Museum copy is earlier, as later copies (e.g., SCR 7.C.1.) are similar to SCR 105.A.21.

The engraving of the orchestral parts of the opera for the strings commenced in May, 1880, with plate numbers 46963–46966, according to the Ricordi *Libroni*. A probable first edition of these parts, folio engraved, without covers, published by Tito di Gio. Ricordi, is at MET.

The earliest known orchestral score of the opera was deposited at the Library of Congress on Jan. 25, 1904, by G. Ricordi & C., Milan, and five other cities. Possible first edition: Four folio volumes, with simple front covers, no title page, price or plate number,‡ the music being lithographed from a manuscript. The *Dance* commences in vol. 3, p. 726. LC(CDC). Also at JMM.

The orchestral score of the *Danza delle Ore* was published with p.n. 98,656 on pp. 718–791 by G. Ricordi & C., Milan, an excerpt from an orchestral score of the opera. NYPL.§

The opera was performed on April 8, 1876, in Milan. Ponchielli was born near Cremona in 1834 and died in Milan in 1886.

Dancing in the Dark

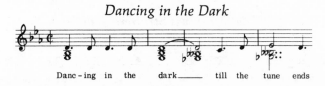

Danc - ing in the dark___ till the tune ends

m. Arthur Schwartz. w. Howard Dietz. Published May 26, 1931,[1] by Harms, Incorporated, New York, N.Y. First edition: Front cover has a photograph of Fred Astaire and others holding instruments and is red, white and black. s. *The Band Wagon*—4 titles listed. p. [2] adv. *Indian.*. m. on pp. 3–7. p.n.

[1] Copyright records; LC.

398–5. Back cover adv. *Body.. - Practising..* LC(CDC) and JF(inscribed by the composer). The show opened in New York City on June 3, 1931.

Schwartz, a composer and producer, was born in Brooklyn, N.Y., in 1900 and died in New York City in 1984.[2] Dietz, a lyricist and motion picture executive, was born in New York City in 1896 and died there in 1983.[2]

Danse Macabre—Saint-Saëns

m. Camille Saint-Saëns. The above principal melody of this work was first composed and published under the title *Danse Macabre* as a song, with words by Henri Cazalis, for piano, by Enoch Père et Fils, 23 Boulevard St. Martin, Paris, a copy being deposited at BM on June 11, 1872.[1] Probable first edition: Front cover is black, gray and white and has a drawing of hundreds of skeletons dancing to the music of a skeleton violinist. Dedication to Gustave Jacquet. Price 6 fr. pp. [2] and [3] blank. m. on pp. 2–7 (really 4–9). p.n. E. P. & F. Back cover blank. BM(CDC). The rights to this work were transferred by Enoch to Durand, Schoenewerk et Cie. on Jan. 27, 1875.[2]

Saint-Saëns's arrangement of this work for orchestra was sold to Durand, Schoenewerk et Cie. on Jan. 28, 1875,[2] and published that year by the firm, 4 Place de la Madeleine, Paris. First edition: Front cover is gray and black, has a dedication to Madame C. Montigny Remaury, refers to the piece as a "Poëme Symphonique," op. 40, and lists six arrangements, the orchestral score at 8 f. vb. Title page is the same as the front cover, except in black and white. vb. Poem by Henri Cazalis, and Note. vb. m. on pp. 1–54. p.n. 2140. BN*(CDC) and JF. Brief biographic information regarding Saint-Saëns appears above under *Bacchanale.*

The Darktown Strutters' Ball

I'll be down to   get you in a   tax - i   hon - ey, you   bet - ter be   read - y

---

[2] *ASCAP,* pp. 444 and 122. Obituaries, *The New York Times,* Sept. 5, 1984, and July 31, 1983.

---

[1] The *Saint-Saëns Catalogue,* p. 61, mistakenly gives the year as 1873.
[2] Letter from Durand & Cie., Paris.

mw. Shelton Brooks. Published Jan. 18, 1917,[1] by Will Rossiter, 71 W. Randolph St., Chicago. First edition: Front cover has a drawing of couples dancing, a photograph of Sophie Tucker, is blue, orange and white and mentions that it is published for Band & Orchestra. m. on pp. 2–3. Back cover adv. *Summer's..* LC(CDC).

The Darktown Strutters' Ball is believed to be the earliest jazz record made; with *Indiana*, it was recorded for Columbia (no. A2297) in New York City on or about Jan. 30, 1917, by the Original Dixieland Jass [sic] Band, led by Dominick James (Nick) La Rocca, and released on May 31, 1917.[2] Record at JF. Brooks, a composer, lyricist and entertainer, was born in Amesburg, Ontario, in 1886 and lives in Fontana, Cal.[3]

Deck the Hall with Boughs of Holly

Deck the hall with boughs of hol - ly, fa, la, la, la, la, la, la, la, la

The music was first printed in *Musical and Poetical Relicks* [sic] *of the Welsh Bards:* "preserved by tradition and authentic manuscripts from remote antiquity; never before published . . ." by Edward Jones, London, 1784. The music appears on p. 64 under the title *Nôs Galan*. The title and words are in Welsh only, the title meaning "New Year's Night." *BUC*, p. 559, and JF. One authority boldly claims that the melody may date from the days of the Druids, 2,000–3,000 years ago, on the basis of a statement in Caesar's *Commentaries* that "The Druids always commenced their celebrations from the preceding night."[1]

The words of *Deck the Hall with Boughs of Holly* are apparently American, and no publication of them has been found anywhere before *The Franklin Square Song Collection*, selected by J. P. McCaskey, and published in New York in 1881. The words and music appear at p. 120 without any credit as to words; the music is acknowledged to be a "Welsh Air." In the first edition of this work, deposited at LC on Aug. 27, 1881,[2] vol. 1 is not mentioned on the covers or title page, and there is no reference to 1884 on the verso of the title page. LC(CDC-M1619. M151) and JF.

---

[1] Copyright records; LC.
[2] *Guiness Book of World Records* (New York, N.Y., 1966), p. 181. *Columbia Records,* New York, N.Y., Sept., 1917, p. 11; NYPL.
[3] *ASCAP*, p. 56.

[1] *Cambrian Minstrelsie*, vol. III, p. x.
[2] Copyright records; LC.

Margaret Dean-Smith, Fernhurst, Haslemere, Surrey, believes that the words are of American origin—in the wake of the "Old English" conception of Christmas popularized by Washington Irving.[3]

Deep in My Heart, Dear

Deep   in   my   heart,   dear

m. Sigmund Romberg. w. Dorothy Donnelly. Published Nov. 11, 1924,[1] by Harms Incorporated, New York, N.Y. First edition: Front cover has a drawing of leaves and is red, white and blue. s. *In Heidelberg*—4 titles listed.[2] m. on pp. 2–9. p.n. 7192-8. Back cover adv. *Memory.*. LC(CDC) and JF. The name of the show was first changed to *The Student Prince in Heidelberg*, and finally to *The Student Prince*. The show opened in New York City on Dec. 2, 1924. The piano-vocal score of the show was not published until June 24, 1932;[1] LC(CDC).

Romberg, a composer, conductor and music collector, was born in Hungary in 1887 and died in New York City in 1951.[3] Donnelly, a lyricist and librettist, was born in New York City in 1880 and died in 1928.[3]

Deep in the Heart of Texas

The   stars   at   night   are   big   and   bright

m. Don Swander. w. June Hershey. Published Dec. 3, 1941,[1] by Melody Lane Publications, Inc., 1549 North Vine St., Hollywood, Cal., and 1619 Broadway, New York, N.Y. The copyright deposit copy is a professional edition. Possible first regular edition: Front cover has a drawing of music notes, a photograph of Jimmy Blair, and is blue and white. m. on pp. 3–5 (actually 2–4). Quartette arrangement on p. [6]. Back cover adv. *Lazybones*

---

[3] Letter from Margaret Dean-Smith.

[1] Copyright records; LC.

[2] Front cover is illustrated in Fuld, *American*, p. [34].

[3] *ASCAP*, pp. 419 and 125.

[1] Copyright records; LC.

—*Moon..* All the songs advertised in this edition were published on or before Dec. 3, 1941. JF.

The authors are husband and wife, now living in Manhattan Beach, Cal. Don Swander, a musician, was born in 1905 in Marshalltown, Iowa, and his wife was born four years later in Los Angeles. She had never been to Texas at the time she wrote the words.[2]

Deep River

Deep————— riv - er,   my home   is   o - ver   Jor - dan

The first known printing of this Negro spiritual was in late 1875[1] in *The Story of the Jubilee Singers* (London, 1875), p. 196. There is no reference on the title page to "second edition." BM(CDC) and JF.

This spiritual became known largely as the result of the efforts of eleven young colored singers, formerly slave children, who toured the United States, England and Europe on behalf of Fisk University, Nashville, Tenn.

Deep River is one of many Negro spirituals that have to do with "crossing the Jordan," a metaphor signifying the longing for a better life both in this world and after death.

The Desert Song

Blue   heav - en and   you   and   I

m. Sigmund Romberg. w. Otto Harbach and Oscar Hammerstein 2nd. Published Dec. 15, 1926,[1] by Harms, Incorporated, New York, N.Y. First edition: Front cover has a drawing of a couple in the desert and is yellow, blue and white. s. *The Desert Song*—7 titles listed, including *The Desert Song.* p. [2] adv. *My.. - Little..* m. on pp. 3–5. p.n. 7897-3. p. [6] adv. *What.. - I..* p. [7] adv. *Serenade - Deep..* Back cover adv. *Riff.. - "It."* LC(CDC). The name of the show was originally *Lady Fair*, and *One Alone* and other

[2] Letters from the authors.

[1] There is a Note following the title page dated Aug. 31, 1875. The BM copy was deposited Nov. 1, 1875.

[1] Copyright records; LC.

songs were published under the show's earlier name; LC(CDC) and JF. The show opened in New York City on Nov. 30, 1926. The piano-vocal score of the show was published by Chappell & Co., Ltd., London, at 8/, on May 20, 1927[1]; LC(CDC) and JF.

Romberg was once playing a bridge hand and mumbled that he did not know how many trumps were out. George W. Meyer, his partner, whistled *One Alone* to give him a hint. Romberg did not catch the hint, miscounted the trumps and went down. When Meyer explained his attempted hint, Romberg replied: "Of course I immediately recognized the music as mine—but who pays attention to the words?" Harbach (originally, Hauerbach), a lyricist and playwright, was born in Salt Lake City, Utah, in 1873, and died in New York City in 1963.[2] Brief biographical information regarding Romberg and Hammerstein appears above under *Deep in My Heart, Dear,* and *All the Things You Are.*

Dinah

Din - ah_____   is there an-y-one   fin - er

m. Harry Akst. w. Sam M. Lewis and Joe Young. Published Aug. 12, 1925,[1] by Henry Waterson, Inc., 1571 Broadway, New York, N.Y. First edition: Front cover has a drawing of an owl and dancers and is red, black and white. s. *The New Plantation* (show cover). p. [2] adv. *Colorado.. - Oh!..* m. on pp. 3–5. p.n. 1675-3. Back cover adv. *Laughin'.. - Reason..* LC(CDC).†

Akst, a composer, was born in New York City in 1894 and died in Hollywood in 1963.[2] Lewis, a lyricist, was born in New York City in 1885 and died there in 1959.[3] Young, a lyricist and singer, was also born in New York City, in 1889, and died in 1939.[3]

Dixie

I__   wish I   was__ in the land of   cot - ton

[2] *ASCAP,* p. 214, and ASCAP files.

---

[1] Copyright records; LC.

[2] *ASCAP,* p. 6; and obituary, *The New York Times,* April 3, 1963.

[3] *ASCAP,* pp. 306 and 551, and ASCAP files.

m. Daniel Decatur Emmett. The printed history of *Dixie*[1] is most interesting, and commences with the complete run of programs of Bryant's Minstrels for 1859–1861.[2] The first time that *Dixie* is mentioned is in no. 9, vol. II, which announces "Mr. Dan Emmett's original Plantation Song and Dance, *Dixie's Land*." There is no date on the program, but it coincides with the playbill for April 4, 1859, at New York City, the date of its first performance; HU.

From these programs, it appears that *Dixie* was played only intermittently for a year and a half by the Bryant's Minstrels and only in New York City.[2A] It seems clear that it was the sudden popularity of the song in New Orleans, La., commencing April 9, 1860, described below, that was responsible for the success of the song. Only commencing Oct. 29, 1860, was *Dixie* included by the Bryant's Minstrels in each performance, and as the final number.

Dixie's words were probably first published Sept. 23, 1859,[3] in *Bryant's Power of Music* (New York, N.Y.) at p. 36 under the title *Dixie's Land;* YU, BPL and George Bird Evans, Bruceton Farms, West Virginia. The first line is traditional and reads "I wish I was in de land of cotton." The words of many of the songs were included in the Bryant's Minstrels' programs mentioned above, but the words of *Dixie* were not so printed until the program for the week commencing Aug. 27, 1860.

The first known performance of *Dixie* in New Orleans, La., was on April 9, 1860, when it was included in the extravaganza *Pocahontas;* the song was such a hit that it was sung in 13 additional performances in that month.[3A] It is thus probable that the undated broadside of *Dixie's Land* by Hopkins, printer, 823 Tchoupitoula Street, New Orleans, La., followed this first New Orleans performance. No original of this broadside has been found, but photocopies are at HT and JF. The same printer, at the above

---

[1] The best history of *Dixie* is by Hans Nathan, *Dan Emmett* (Norman, Okla., 1962), chap. 16, at NYPL, a revision of his article entitled "Dixie", in MQ, Jan. 1949, p. 60.

Emmett had previously used the phrase "Dixie's Land" in his song, *Jonny Roach* (sometimes, *Johnny Roach*), performed by the Bryant's Minstrels in March, 1859. Nathan, *Dan Emmett*, this fn. 1, pp. 244 and 294. The words were published in *Bryant's Power of Music*, referred to in the text, at p. 23.

[2] *Bryant's Songs and Programme* [sic], n.p., for 1859–1860 is at HU, and for 1860–1861 at JF.

[2A] The date of the *New York Herald* article, mentioning *Dixie's* popularity, referred to in Nathan, *Dan Emmett*, fn. 1 above, p. 271, is Jan. 11, 1862, not Jan. 11, 1860; NYPL.

[3] Copyright records; LC.

[3A] Miss Dorothy Blackmar, New Orleans, La., advised the author of this information. *The New Orleans Daily Crescent*, April 10, 1860, p. 1; HT. *Memories of the Professional and Social Life of John E. Owens by His Wife* (Baltimore, 1892), p. 110; NYPL.

address, issued two versions of *Hopkins' New-Orleans 5 Cent Song-Book*
each containing the words of *Dixie;* one is dated 1861 and the other was
issued after the commencement of the Civil War (April 12, 1861). Both
versions at LC. †

Another undated broadside, entitled *Dixie's Land*, without mention of
publisher, is at LMU.⁴ H. De Marsan, 38 and 60 Chatham St., New York,
N.Y., published two broadsides, one entitled *Dixie's Land*, with the traditional words, at JF, and the other entitled *Dixey's Land*, with words commencing "Away down south," and an 1860 copyright claim (but no such
copyright was, in fact, filed), at NYPL. These two broadsides could have
been printed, according to the imprint shown in New York City *Directories*
at NYHS, from May, 1859, to May, 1861.‡

The music of *Dixie* was first printed by a New Orleans publisher without authorization about April 29, 1860, ⁴ᴬ soon after the above-mentioned
first known performance in New Orleans on April 9, 1860. The publisher
was P. P. Werlein, 5 Camp St., New Orleans, and the plate number was
547; words were also included. Although the edition stated that it was
entered for copyright, the copyright records for Louisiana for that year are
not at the Library of Congress and could not be found in Louisiana. In this
first edition, there is no mention of Emmett or Bryant's Minstrels, and the
title is "I Wish I Was in Dixie." The "song" is credited to W. H. Peters
and the music to J. C. Viereck, the front cover refers to "Piano" and
"Guitar," the price is 3½, and there are four copublishers. (**See Plate I.**) In
the piano edition, the music is on pages 2–5. Engraved. Back cover blank.
The music bears a crude resemblance to the original, but the words are
quite different, commencing "Come along, boys."⁴ᴮ HMA, NYPL and JF.
No copy of the edition for guitar has been located.

A few days later the second printing of the music and words was
published by P. P. Werlein, this time with plate number 549 and with the
words credited to J. Newcomb. The title on the front cover is the same; on
p. 2 the title is "Dixey's Land." The music and words are closer to the
traditional. LC (not CDC) and JF.⁴ᴬ Werlein's third printing within another
10 days had plate number 550 and was a reversion to the Peters-Viereck
edition but marked "Corrected Edition"; JF.⁴ᴬ

⁴ The broadside, at LMU, illustrated in Richard Harwell, "Lincoln and Dixie," in *Lincoln
Herald*, Harrogate, Tenn., no. 487a.

⁴ᴬ Receipt of copies was acknowledged in *The New Orleans Daily Crescent*,
April 30, 1860, p. 6; HT. Miss Dorothy Blackmar, New Orleans, La., discovered this
important information.

The second printing was noted in the May 5, 1860, issue of *The Daily Picayune*,
New Orleans, and the third printing in the May 13, 1860, issue of the same newspaper;
HT.

⁴ᴮ Many of the early printings of *Dixie*, showing the varying texts and music, have
been assembled on microfilm at NYPL.

The first authorized, and also the first Northern, printing of *Dixie* was on June 21, 1860,[3] by Firth, Pond & Co., 547 Broadway, New York, N.Y., under the title "I Wish I Was in Dixie's Land," engraved, no reference on front cover to "Guitar" and back cover blank; LC(CDC), NYPL, LL, SS and JF. Dan D. Emmett is credited as sole author, and Bryant's Minstrels are mentioned. Emmett later stated: "I did not publish it . . . until it was issued by Mr. P. P. Werling [Werlein], of New Orleans. He published it in Mr. Peters' name. . . ."[5] The words are the traditional words.

Dixie has been banned in a number of schools where militant Black students have demonstrated against it as a "racist" song.[6]

While Emmett wrote many manuscript copies of *Dixie* in his later years, it is likely that the manuscript of the music and words inherited by George Bird Evans, Bruceton Farms, W. Va., a descendant by marriage, is the original manuscript.

An authorized contemporary explanation of "Dixie" appears in the *Programme* of the Bryant's Minstrels for the week commencing February 18, 1861, at JF:

"As many inquiries have been made in regard to the meaning of 'Dixie Land,' and as to its location, it may be well to remark that, with the Southern Negroes, Dixie Land is but another name for home."

The word "Dixie" may be of English origin, Dixie being an honored English family name dating back to the fourteenth century or earlier.[7] Members of the family emigrated to the Massachusetts and Carolina colonies commencing in 1629.[8]

Daniel Decatur Emmett, an early "Negro minstrel," was born in Mount Vernon, Ohio, in 1815 and died there in 1904.

[5] *New York Clipper*, April 6, 1872, p. 5; SU.

[6] See the discussions, pro and con, on this question in Chauncey Durden, "On Playing of 'Dixie,'" in the [Richmond] *Times-Dispatch*, Jan. 25, 1969, sec. B, p. 5, at Richmond Public Library, Richmond, Va.; and *The New York Times*, Feb. 25, 1969, p. 28.

[7] The Rev. William Betham, *The Baronetage of England* (London, 1802), vol. II, p. 127; NYPL. The Dixie family continues to this day in England—Sir Wolstan Dixie, Market Bosworth, Leicestershire, being the current head.

[8] Walter Goodwin Davis, *The Ancestry of Sarah Stone* (Portland, Me., 1930), p. 27; The New York Genealogical and Bibliographical Society, New York, N.Y. *The South Carolina Historical and Genealogical Magazine* (Charleston, S.C.), vol. 15, p. 111; vol. 19, p. 178; vol. 23, p. 56; and vol. 38, p. 28. *ULS*, p. 2641. The name was sometimes spelled in the colonies as "Dixey," "Dixsey" or in some other variant.

Don Juan—Richard Strauss

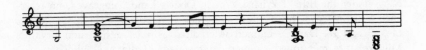

m. Richard Strauss. Published in orchestral parts in Jan., 1890,[1] by Jos. Aibl, Munich. A possible first edition, but lacking the front cover, is at NYPS, with plate number 2641.

Possible first edition of the orchestral score published in June, 1890:[1] Front cover is yellow and black. vb. Title page has a dedication to Ludwig Thuille, states that the work is a tone poem after Nicolaus Lenau, says op. 20, lists the orchestral score and parts at 20 Mk. each, with prices for separate parts and the arrangement for piano four hands without price. Verso has poem by Lenau. m. on pp. 3–96. p.n. 2640. Inside back cover blank. Back cover adv. works by Strauss up to op. 21 (also published in 1890).[2] Folio. BM.

The tone poem was composed in 1887–1889 in Munich and performed on Nov. 11, 1889, in Weimar. Strauss was born in Munich in 1864 and died in Garmisch-Partenkirchen, Bavaria, in 1949.

Down by the Old Mill Stream

Down   by   the   old   mill   stream

mw. Tell Taylor. Published Aug. 12, 1910,[1] by Tell Taylor, Chicago. First edition: Front cover has a drawing of the old mill stream, a photograph of Tell Taylor and is green and white. m. on pp. 2–4. Male quartette on p. 5.

---

[1] Mueller von Asow, p. 83. Müller-Reuter, p. 603. Hofmeister *Monatsbericht*, Nov., 1890, p. 467 (orchestral score and parts).

[2] Hofmeister *Monatsbericht*, Nov., 1890, p. 511.

---

[1] Copyright records; LC.

Back cover adv. *Honey*. LC(CDC). The copyright deposit copy has Earl Smith's name printed as coauthor on p. 2, but his name does not appear in the original copyright records or in later editions, and a court has held that he was not a coauthor entitled to renewal rights.[2]

Taylor was born in Vanlue, near Findlay, Ohio, in 1876, became a songwriter and died in 1937 in Chicago. He was buried in Findlay.[3]

Down in the Valley

Down in the   val - ley,   the val - ley so   low

The words appeared in July–Sept., 1917, in G. L. Kittredge, "Ballads and Songs" in *Journal of American Folklore*, Lancaster, Pa., and New York, N.Y., p. 346, with a note that the words were communicated by Prof. Belden, and sent to him by Miss Goldy M. Hamilton, who had them from Frank Jones, West Plains High School, Mo., 1909–1910; *ULS*, p. 1435.

Variants of both the words and music were included in *Tommy's Tunes*, collected by F. T. Nettleingham (London, 1917), p. 82; BM, LC, NYPL and JF.

The common melody and words appear in an unpublished manuscript deposited on April 11, 1922, at the Library of Congress, as a Kentucky mountain folk song arranged by Eliot H. Robinson, Boston. The words also appear in *JAFL*, 1926, p. 83, and 1927, p. 22.

The common melody and words were published in *Ozark Life*, July, 1927, Kingston, Ark., p. 7, at University of Arkansas, Fayetteville, Ark., and in Sandburg (1927), pp. 148 and 213.

The song is also known as *Bird in a Cage*, *Birmingham Jail* and *Down on the Levee*, but no printing of the words or music under any of these titles is known to precede the printings above described.

Based in large part on this song, Kurt Weill and Arnold Sundgaard

---

[2] *Jerry Vogel Music Co.* vs. *Foster Music Publisher*, 147 F. 2d 614 (Circuit Court of Appeals, Second Circuit, 1945); NYPL.

[3] Obituary, *New York Herald Tribune*, Nov. 24, 1937, and information from present publisher.

wrote a short folk opera entitled *Down in the Valley* to be performed by small amateur or school groups. It was produced on July 15, 1948, at Bloomington, Ind. The piano-vocal score, with the front cover a reproduction of a painting by Grandma Moses, was copyrighted on April 16, 1948,[1] and published by G. Schirmer, Inc., 3 East 43rd Street, New York, N.Y. LC(CDC) and JF (inscribed by the composer).

Drink to Me Only with Thine Eyes

Drink to me on - ly with__ thine eyes__ and   I__   will pledge with   mine

m. Unknown. w. Ben Jonson. The words were first published after March, 1616, in the poem *To Celia* in a collection of poems by Jonson called *The Forrest*, included in *The Workes of Benjamin Jonson*, at p. 829. There are three variant editions: in one the title page reads "Imprinted at London by Will Stansby" (BM), in the second "London printed by W. Stansby and are to be sould by Rich. Meighen" (BM and LC), and in the third "London Printed by William Stansby (LC and NYPL). Priority is unknown.[1] Commencing about 1750 the poem was sung to several other musical settings all of which have been forgotten.[2]

The present well-known melody was first published about 1780 in a number of editions with priority uncertain, none of them claiming entry at Stationers' Hall. Interestingly, all of the early printings, except (g) below, are in the form of a glee for three voices. Following is the group of early printings: (a) John Lee, at the Corner of Eustace Street in Dame Street (no. 70), Dublin, dated ca. 1780 by BM; (b) T. Straight, 138 St. Martin's Lane near Charing Cross [London], 1777/8—ca. 1783[3], at LC; (c) Babb's Musical Circulating Library, 132 Oxford Street facing Hanover Square [London], ca. 1780, at CA; (d) Dale [London], 1783–1821, is mentioned by one authority[4] but no copy has been located; (e) and (f) Major and Barford,

---

[1] Copyright records; LC.

[1] H. L. Ford, *Collation of the Ben Jonson Folios 1616–31—1640* (Oxford, 1932), p. 4; NYPL. The *Workes* was entered at Stationers' Hall on Jan. 20, 1615 (O.S.).

[2] *BM Music Catalogue*, vol. I, pp. 403–404.

[3] All dates are per Humphries-Smith.

[4] Kidson, *Minstrelsy of England*, p. 316.

dated ca. 1790 in *BM Music Catalogue,* are later according to Humphries-Smith; (g) in *Elegant Extracts for the Guittar* [sic], vol. I, p. 20, originally printed in London by J. Preston, 97 Strand, 1778–1787, the only known copy, however, having a 1795 watermark, at BM; (h) E. Rhames, Dublin, ca. 1790, at NLI; (i) A. Bland, 23 Oxford Street, London, 1784–1792, at JF; (j) in J. W. Callcott, *A Select Collection of Catches, Canons and Glees* [London?], p. 16 (watermarked "79"—at JF—however, the composer's name is followed by "B.M.," meaning presumably "Bachelor of Music" which title he acquired in 1785,[5] and the British Museum dates its copy as ca. 1790); (k) there may be other contemporary British editions, and (l) there are several American editions in the late 1780's.[6]

All attempts to discover the composer of this beautiful melody have proved unavailing.[7] There is no foundation for the claim that the composer was Mozart or Col. R. Mellish. A new possible contender is J. W. Callcott since his collection mentioned above states "the whole Composed, Selected & Arranged" by him—about as broad a claim as could be made. The collection could have been published after 1785 even though individual songs had been composed by him and performed and published by others before then; although born in 1766, he began writing music for a play in 1780 and glees for the Catch Club in 1784.[8] *Drink to Me Only with Thine Eyes* is generally described as a glee in the early editions, and none of the editions listed in the preceding paragraph is proved to have been published before this time. All the other songs in the collection appear original.

Ben Jonson was born probably at Westminster in 1573 and died in 1637.

Drinking Song—La Traviata

Li - bia   mo li - bia-mo né   lie - ti   ca - li - ci

[5] *Dict. Nat. Biog.,* vol. 3, p. 708.
[6] Sonneck-Upton, p. 113.
[7] Chappell, p. 707.
[8] *Dict. Nat. Biog.,* vol. 3, p. 708.

m. G. Verdi. w. F. M. Piave. The aria of the *Drinking Song* or *Libiamo ne' lieti calici* was published as a separate piece for piano and voice about March 28, 1853,[1] by Tito di Gio. Ricordi, Milan, as No. 3, with p.n. 25093; GM. The Blanchet, Paris, separate printing was deposited for Dépôt Légal on April 18, 1853, and is at BN; Archives. The Boosey & Sons, London, separate printing was received on June 2, 1853, at BM.

The only printing of the piano-vocal score of the original version of *La Traviata* was by Clausetti e Co., rimpetto al R. Teatro S. Carlo no. 18, Naples. Oblong. The title page states that the work was deposited at the Conservatory, mentions the price as Dti. 6, and refers to a piano arrangement at Dti. 4. vb. m. on pp. 5–189, engraved. p.ns. 1631–1646 and 1651. p. [190] blank. Naples Conservatory, NLS and Ricordi Archives. Hopkinson, *Verdi*, 55A(c), dating publication as "?1853," but in any event before May, 1854.

Portions of the original version of the opera are also in the piano-vocal score published in mid-1854 or later by Stabilimento Musicale Partenopeo, Naples, but the balance of the score reflects the changes made by Verdi for the second version. Copy at Istituto di Studi Verdiani, Parma; an excerpt is illustrated in Chusid, p. 159. Hopkinson, Verdi, 55B(g).

The first printing of the piano-vocal score of the second version of the opera was about Jan. 7, 1855,[2] by Tito di Gio. Ricordi, Milan. In the first printing, on the title page, the piano arrangement is stated to be by Luigi Truzzi (only) and the Paris agent is Blanchet. Some arias have the earlier imprint of Giovanni Ricordi, some the later imprint of Tito di Gio. Ricordi; and some arias mention Truzzi only, and some Truzzi and Muzio. There are 11 corner dates up to June 16, 1854. The engravers of no. 6 on plate number 25096 are known from the Ricordi *Libroni* to have been Milanesi and Brioschi, whose initials were K and S, and only these initials appear on the pages with these plate numbers. Similarly, only the initial S appears on the pages with plate number 25099. BM, NLS and Museo Teatrale alla Scala, Milan. The Escudier, Paris, edition of the piano-vocal score was not published until Sept., 1855.

The date of the first printing of the orchestral score of *La Traviata* is uncertain, Chusid, p. 156, suggesting about 1855, which may be a little early, and Hopkinson, *Verdi*, 55D, suggesting about 1880. The score is engraved folio, with music on pages 1–298, the above aria on page 28. The plate numbers 21366–21376 would ordinarily indicate a date about 1849,

---

[1] *GMM*, March 28, 1853, p. 58. *Ricordi Catalogue Supplement*, Milan, Jan.–Apri, 1853, p. 2; NYPL. The corner date on the separate aria is March 7, 1853. The engraving commenced March 8, 1853, and the "da pubblicarsi" date and the date of receipt at the Office of Public Order was April 16, 1853; Ricordi *Libroni*.

[2] *GMM*, Jan. 7, 1855, p. 6. *Ricordi Catalogue Supplement*, Milan, Jan.–March, 1855, p. 3; NYPL. The engraving of the last number commenced June 14, 1854, the "da pubblicarsi" date of the last numbers was Feb. 3, 1855, and the date of receipt at the Office of Public Order of the last numbers was Jan. 25, 1855; Ricordi *Libroni*.

but such year is not possible; the Ricordi *Libroni* unfortunately are not helpful as to date. The bottom of page 1 refers to Tito di Gio. Ricordi[3] and to a Sovereign Patent dated Oct. 19, 1846 (which has not been traced). A copy with a title page with the above imprint is at the Bologna Conservatory; other copies without a title page are at BM, BN, LC, NYPL, RAM, JMM and JF. While no date can thus be established, the *La Traviata* orchestral score was published "early," and it was the only orchestral score of a Verdi opera to be published contemporaneously or almost contemporaneously with early performances, until the latest Verdi operas.

Oblong engraved orchestral parts of the opera, with plate numbers 21337 et al., folio, without covers, are at MET and JF*. The plate numbers again would ordinarily indicate a date of about 1849, but such year is not possible and the date of publication of these orchestral parts is not known. However, the imprint Tito di Gio. Ricordi is early, there is the reference to an 1846 Sovereign Patent, and this is probably the first edition.

The opera was performed March 6, 1853, in Venice. Brief biographic information regarding Verdi appears above under *Anvil Chorus*. Piave, a librettist, was born in Murano in 1810 and died in Milan in 1876.[4]

Drunken Sailor—(Monkey's Wedding—
John Brown Had a Little Injun—Ten Little Injuns)

The music and words of *The Monkey's Wedding* appear in an American music manuscript about 1800. The melody is in the major. NC. Fuld-Davidson, p. 49.

The printed story of *Drunken Sailor* probably begins in 1824–1825 with the inclusion of the melody under the strange title *Columbus*, without words but with dance instructions, in *Cole's Selection of Favourite Cotillions*, no. 2, published by John Cole, 123 Market St., Baltimore, with p.n. 106, at p. 4; Wolfe, no. 1988, p. 204, and JF. In the first edition of this *Selection*, page 4 has music but has no parentheses around the plate number at the bottom of the page. The melody, in the major, is substantially as given above. *Drunken Sailor or Columbus* was included without words

---

[3] A style discontinued no later than 1888.
[4] *EDS*, vol. 8, p. 95.

in *Divertimento for the Pianoforte* stated to be copyrighted April 25, 1825, by Willig's Music Store, 74 Market St., Baltimore (Wolfe, no. 5770, p. 560), and published later by Geo. Willig, Baltimore, on one page together with two other dances, with p.n. 1671; JF. The latter may be a reprint of an edition originally published in the late 1820's.[1]

No printing of the words of *Drunken Sailor* has been found before Ferris Tozer and Frederick J. Davis, *Sailors' Songs, or "Chanties"* (3rd ed., London, n.d.), p. 46, under the title *What to Do with a Drunken Sailor*, published in 1891;[2] LC and NYPL. The song is not in the first printing of this book deposited in the BM on Aug. 4, 1887, and no copy of the second edition, published Feb. 17, 1890,[2] has been located.

To the same melody is *Monkeys [sic] Wedding* published, with words, 1832–1847[3] by Firth & Hall, 1 Franklin Square, New York, N.Y. Possible first edition: pp. [1] and [4] blank. p. [2] has a drawing of a monkey in wedding clothes. m. on pp. [2]–[3]. Engraved. JF. The last verse mentions the tune *The Drunken Sailor*.

The words of *John Brown Had a Little Injun* and *Ten Little Injuns*, to the same melody, were included in *Old John Brown*, arranged by J. Gibson of the Gibson Troupe, published by Oliver Ditson, 115 Washington St., Boston, and copyrighted by Chas. C. Clapp on April 17, 1849.[4] JF and LL. In England, the song became known as *Ten Little Negroes* (or *Niggers*).[5]

The above versions of the melody are in the major. *Drunken Sailor* also may be in the minor, but the melody is changed slightly in addition to the change from major to minor. No earlier printing of the melody in the minor has been found than in Sharp, *English Folk-Chanteys*, London, in 1914, p. 8; NYPL and JF. A Ukrainian folk song, entitled *The Cossack*, published about 1800,[6] is in the minor and rather similar to the minor version of *Drunken Sailor*.

The *Drunken Sailor* is sometimes known by its longer title, *What Shall We Do with a Drunken Sailor?* The song is a halyard shanty.[7]

---

[1] Information from Richard J. Wolfe, Bloomington, Ind.

[2] Letter from Boosey & Hawkes, Inc., a successor publisher. The second edition was withdrawn Feb. 28, 1890, for a reason not now known. The first edition contained 24 songs, the second edition 40 songs, and the third edition 50 songs.

[3] Dichter-Shapiro, p. 192.

[4] Copyright records; LC.

[5] Opie, p. 328. Sheet music editions under these titles are at JF. The latter title is now considered passé; *The New York Times*, May 30, 1964, p. 19.

[6] In *A Collection of Melodies, Chiefly Russian*, published by Rt. Birchall, London, p. 30, and so dated by BM (H. 2170).

[7] Tozer, p. 46. Bullen-Arnold, p. 16. Colcord, *Roll*, p. 30.

Du, Du Liegst Mir im Herzen

Du, du liegst mir im Her - zen, du, du, liegst mir im Sinn

This folk song is said to have originated around 1820 in the northern part of Germany. The melody is stated to have been set to four-part harmony by Pax in 1820 but not to have been composed by him.[1] The earliest known written reference to it is in the 1826 *Handbuch Annual*, p. 57, where it is listed for voice with piano, published by Stock, in Bremen, at 2 Gr; no copy has been located.

The first available dated printing of the words is in F. H. Schulze, *Neuer Liederkranz* (Tübingen, Germany, 1827) no. 116, p. 106; FR. The words also appeared in four undated "Flugblätter" or pamphlets about the same time: (a) *Sechs Schöne Neue Lieder*, no imprint, at TLW; (b) *Fünf Neue Lieder*, Frankfurt, at DS; (c) *Drei Neue Lieder*, Halle, at DS; and (d) *Schöne Neue Lieder*, no imprint, at DS. Photostats of the foregoing are at FR.

The first available printing of the music, together with the words, is in *Das Taschen-Liederbuch* (Passau, 1828) no. 69, p. 113; FR.

Du und Du—Die Fledermaus

m. Johann Strauss. On the basis of both plate number and the Hofmeister *Monatsbericht*, it would appear that the first printing of this melody was in *Potpourri I* from the operetta *Die Fledermaus*, arranged for piano four hands and published about June, 1874,[1] by Friedrich Schreiber, Vienna; no copy published by Schreiber has been located. The arrangement for piano two hands does not seem to be listed in the *Monatsbericht*, but one authority dates it the same month;[2] a copy published by Schreiber, no. 150 of Anthologie Musicale, listing 159 titles, with p.n. 23393, engraved, but referring to Marks (rather than Thaler), is at JF.

---

[1] Erk-Böhme, vol. II, no. 578, p. 404.

[1] P. 117.

[2] Weinmann, *Strauss*, p. 130.

Again, on the basis of the Hofmeister *Monatsbericht*,[3] there were published about Nov., 1874, a piano-vocal score of the operetta, a separate printing of *Du und Du* for orchestra, and separate printings for piano four hands and piano. Probable first edition of the piano-vocal score: The price is Fl.6.30 Nkr./**Th.4** and the publisher is **Friedrich Schreiber**, Vienna. Front cover is brown and black. vb. Title page indicates the words and the piano arrangement are by Richard Genée. m. on pp. 2–168. p.n. 23422. The *Du und Du* waltzes are scattered throughout the piano-vocal score, but the phrase "du und du" does not seem to be in the operetta. No back cover. GM, NC and JF.[4] The price in Thalers was changed almost immediately by Schreiber to a price in Marks.

No first printing of the orchestral arrangement of *Du und Du*, op. 367, has been located. In the earliest edition discovered, there are 22 engraved parts published by Aug. Cranz, Hamburg, and C. A. Spina, Vienna (Cranz succeeding Schreiber in 1879), and the works of Strauss are listed to op. 408 (1883). p.n. F.S. 23543. SB. The arrangement of *Du und Du* for piano four hands published by Friedrich Schreiber, with music pages engraved, p.n. 23544, prices of Fl. 1.35 Nkr. and 22-½ Ngr. and no other Strauss works listed, is at SB.

In the piano arrangement of *Du und Du*, published by Friedrich Schreiber, Vienna, the front cover has a drawing of a clown, is turquoise, black and white, lists the arrangements for piano and piano four hands and has the price for piano of 90 Nkr./15 Ngr. p. [2] and back cover blank. m. on pp. 3–11. p.n. 23536. Music pages engraved. There are two variants of the foregoing with priority unknown: in one, the words at the bottom of the front cover, "Eigenthum des Verlegers," are on a straight line (at ONB and BM)—in the other, the words are curved (at JF).

The orchestral score of *Die Fledermaus* was published by Gustav Lewy [Vienna] in 1874–1875, a lithographing of a manuscript score with 367 and 95 pages. Bibliothek der Städtischen Bühnen, Mainz (lacking title page).[5] No early printing of the orchestral parts of the opera has been found.

The operetta was performed April 5, 1874, in Vienna. Brief biographic information regarding Strauss appears above under *Artist's Life*.

---

[3] Pp. 225, 243, 248 and 233.

[4] *Johann Strauss Gesamtausgabe*, Ser. II, vol. 3 (Vienna, 1974), p. 507, Vorlage E.

[5] *Id.*, p. 505, Vorlage B. The orchestral score published by Cranz, Leipzig, was published later as he came to Vienna in 1876; *id.*, p. 507, Vorlage D.

The Dutch Company

The Dutch Com-pa-ny   is   the best   com - pa-ny

The words were first published under the title *Die Deutsche Companie* in *Selected Songs Sung at Harvard College from 1862 to 1866*, edited by William Allen Hayes (Cambridge, 1866), p. 70; LC and JF (presentation copy dated July 5, 1866).

The music, together with the words, was first included in the 1873 edition of *Carmina Yalensia* (New York, N.Y.), copyrighted on July 21st of that year,[1] p. 52; LC(CDC) and JF.

The East Is Red (Tung Fang Hung)

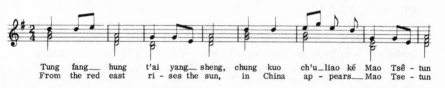

Tung fang__ hung   t'ai yang__ sheng, chung kuo   ch'u__liao ké Mao Tsê - tun
From the red east   ri - ses the sun,   in   China   ap - pears__Mao Tse - tun

The East Is Red is a folk song from Northern Shensi Province that has been virtually adopted as the national anthem of Red China. The song was apparently originally known both in Chinese and in English as *The East in Red Glow*. An early publication of the song is in *Songs of New China*, published in Peking in June, 1953, p. 2, under the earlier title; NYPL and JF.

Although described in Communist Chinese publications as a "folk song," the song is also said to have been written in 1944 with words by Li Yu-yuan.[1] Perhaps the melody is of folk origin, and new words were added.

The melody has Western-style harmony and is published, even in Red Chinese publications, in Western-style notation.

---

[1] Copyright records; LC.

[1] *Songs of New China*, referred to in text above. *Unity Is Strength* (Peking, 1964), Contents page; JF.

No other information is known regarding the song or its lyricist, inquiry to Red China being so far unanswered.

When Communist China orbited a satellite on April 25, 1970, the satellite broadcast a record of *The East Is Red* for the world to hear.[2]

Easter Parade

In   your East - er   bon - net   with   all   the frills   up - on   it

mw. Irving Berlin. Published Sept. 22, 1933,[1] by Irving Berlin, Inc., 1607 Broadway, New York, N.Y. First edition: Front cover has a drawing of people cheering a parade and is red, black and white. s. *As Thousands Cheer*—6 titles listed, the last of which is *The Funnies*. m. on pp. 2–5. Back cover adv. *When..* LC(CDC) and JF. The show opened in New York City on Sept. 30, 1933.

The melody is adapted from Irving Berlin's *Smile and Show Your Dimple* (1917), whose introduction also furnished part of the principal melody of his *Cheek to Cheek* (1934); both at JF. Brief biographic information regarding Berlin appears above under *Alexander's Ragtime Band*.

1812 Overture—Tchaikovsky

m. P. Tchaikovsky. Published about July, 1882,[1] for orchestral score, orchestral parts, piano and piano four hands by P. Jurgenson, Moscow, under the Russian title *1812—Торжественная Увертюра*, and the French title *1812 Ouverture Solennelle*, op. 49. Possible first edition of the orchestral score: Front cover in French mentions Edition Jurgenson, two agents, J. Jurgenson, St. Petersburg, and G. Sennewald, Warsaw, and the four arrangements mentioned above, the price of the orchestral score being 3 Rub./Mk. 9. vb. Title page in Russian is brilliantly colored with a photograph of a domed building, lists **no arrangements** and has no street ad-

---

[2] *The New York Times*, April 26, 1970, p. 1.

---

[1] Copyright records; LC.

[1] Hofmeister *Monatsbericht*, July, 1882, p. 188. Dombayev, p. 40, says merely 1882.

dresses or crown. vb. m. on pp. 3–75, including the scoring for "Canon" (!).
p.n. 4592. p. [76] and the inside of back cover blank. Outside of back cover
adv. Tchaikovsky's works only to op. 48. There are two variants of the
foregoing edition, with priority unknown: one with green and black covers
is at HU, and the other with tan and black covers is at JF.

The "Canon" orchestral part has 406 bars of rests and 16 bars in
which the cannon is sounded in quarter and half notes, in C, D or E in the
bass, in loudness ranging from "ff" to "ffff"! Possible first printing of the
orchestral parts, with plate number 4593, but without covers, are at FLP
and RAM. The piano arrangement has plate number 4594, and the
arrangement for piano four hands has plate number 4595;[2] both at LLM.
The German edition of D. Rahter, Hamburg, of the orchestral score was
printed by Jurgenson; BM and BPL.

The work was completed Nov. 19, 1880, and performed Aug. 20, 1882,
in Moscow. Brief biographic information regarding Tchaikovsky appears
above under *Chant sans Paroles.*

Eili, Eili

Ei - li ei - li!

m. probably by Jacob Sandler. First published in late 1906 under the full
title *Eli, Eli, Lomo Ozavtoni,* without mention of the composer's name, by
S. Goldberg, 398 Grand St., New York, N.Y.[1] First edition: Front cover
has a photograph of the late Sophia Karp, refers to "Piano" and "Violin"
arrangements (this edition being the piano arrangement), mentions that it
was arranged by J. Rumshisky, repeats the title in Hebrew letters, and is
blue and white. p. [2] blank. m. on pp. 3–5, the title on p. 3 being *Eili Eili.*
Back cover adv. *My.. - Russian..* EM and JF.

The full title means, "My God, my God, why has thou forsaken me?"
and is taken from the second verse of the Twenty-second Psalm of David.
This song had been widely believed to be a folk song, one music critic
believing that the melody was the "echo of some tribal chant sung in the

---

[2] *Jurgenson Catalog,* Moscow, 1889, p. 195; NYPL.

[1] A large part of the information regarding *Eili, Eili,* came from Eric Mandell,
Philadelphia. Copyright records at LC show two copies were deposited Jan. 2, 1907; the
sheet music bears a 1906 copyright claim.

days of the Babylonian captivity."[2] However, in 1925 Sandler sued to enjoin a music publisher from publishing the song. Sandler stated that he had written the song in 1896 for a play, *Brocha,* in which Sophia Karp was playing and which was produced in the Bowery in March of that year. Sandler was refused an injunction on the ground that he had permitted the song to enter the public domain by waiting until 1919 to copyright it in his name while it was being published widely in this country and other countries, including Russia.[3]

The judge in that case, John C. Knox, later wrote that he believed that Sandler was the author of the song and that Sandler sued primarily to obtain the credit of authorship, not royalties—Sandler had said he felt like a father who was told he could not have his own child.[4] Sandler was born in Russia and died at the age of seventy-four in Brooklyn, N.Y., in 1931.[5]

Élégie—Massenet

m. J. Massenet. This melody, with its varied and interesting history, was originally entitled *Mélodie, no. 5,* in *Étude du Style et du Rythme, 10 Pièces de Genre pour le Piano, op.* 10, and entered for Dépôt Légal on Dec. 27, 1866,[1] by E. & A. Girod, 16 Boulevart [*sic*] Montmartre, Paris. First edition: Title page has a dedication to Elvire & Edwige Remaury and the price of 15 francs. vb. m. on pp. 1–37, with double pagination for the separate pieces. p.n. 5065 (1–10). *Mélodie* on p. 16. p. [38] blank. Engraved. COP(CDC). LC also has the above edition with a black and white front cover; vb; and inside and outside of back cover blank.

The melody was then used by Massenet as part of his orchestral music for *Les Érinnyes,* a "Tragédie antique" by Leconte de Lisle, which was performed in Paris on Jan. 6, 1873, where it served as background music to Elektra's *Invocation,* Act II, no. 8. The *Invocation* was included in *Musique pour une Pièce Antique, Les Érinnyes, 3ᵐᵉ Suite d'Orchestre,* for piano,

[2] Quoted in John C. Knox, *A Judge Comes of Age* (New York, N.Y., 1940), p. 183; NYPL.

[3] The facts are set forth in the court decision of *Sandler et al.* vs. *Katz,* United States District Court, Southern District of New York, E 26/349, June 8, 1925.

[4] Knox, footnote 2, above, p. 183.

[5] Obituary, *New York Herald Tribune,* March 1, 1931.

[1] Archives. *BF,* Feb. 16, 1867, p. 78.

which was entered for Dépôt Légal on July 22, 1873,[2] by G. Hartmann, 19 Boulevard de la Madeleine, Paris. Copies were deposited at BM on Nov. 14, 1873, and at COP in 1873, having p.n. 676. BM and COP (both CDC). No orchestral arrangement of this Suite has been found. (Massenet composed another 3me Suite d'Orchestre entitled Scènes Dramatiques, not related to the above; FLP).

The piano-vocal score of the entire Les Érinnyes, published by G. Hartmann at the same address, has no p.n.; the copy at BN is marked 1878 (also at JF). The orchestral score of the entire Les Érinnyes, similarly published, with p.ns. 918–919, dates no later than 1879 since the publisher moved to a different address that year;[3] COP and NYPL.

Meanwhile, the Mélodie was published, still under that title, for violoncello and piano about July, 1873,[4] by E. & A. Girod. An early edition has p.n. 5499; RCM.

The title Élégie—Mélodie first appeared about Feb. 20, 1875,[5] when words by Louis Gallet were added for mezzo-soprano to the piano arrangement. First edition: The publisher is E. & A. Girod, 16 Boulevard Montmartre, Paris, the dedication is to Marie Brousse and the price 3 francs. m. on pp. 2–3. p.n. M. 1. Back cover blank. COP(CDC).

Brief biographic information regarding Massenet appears above under Aragonaise. Leconte de Lisle, the celebrated French poet, was born at Saint-Paul on the Île de Bourbon in 1818 and died at Louveciennes in 1894. Louis Gallet, a writer and dramatist, was born in Valence in 1835 and died in Paris in 1898.[6]

Emperor's Hymn—Haydn

Gott er-hal-te Franz den Kai-ser, un-sern gu-ten Kai-ser__Franz!

m. Joseph Haydn. This national anthem, the only one composed by a major composer, was first published under the title on the front cover, Gott,

[2] Archives. BF, Aug. 9, 1873, p. 405.

[3] Hopkinson, Parisian, p. 56.

[4] BF, July 26, 1873, p. 381.

[5] Dépôt Légal records, Archives. BF, March 20, 1875, p. 157, lists Élégie for piano at 3 francs—it is not known whether this is the same as the piano-vocal arrangement described above; if different, a copy has not been located.

[6] Larousse XX, vol. 3, p. 693.

Erhalte den Kaiser! in 1797 with words by Lorenz Leopold Haschka.[1] First edition: Oblong. Front cover states that the song was first sung on Feb. 12, 1797 (Francis I's birthday), and this particular copy has a manuscript dedication dated Feb. 21, 1797. p. [2] contains the music, arranged for piano, and the words. p. [3] contains four verses of words. Back cover blank. No publisher. No plate number. Typeset. ONB.

The melody, slightly revised, was included in the second movement of Haydn's "*Emperor*" *Quartet no. 3*, op. 76. The Quartet was published in 1799 in parts by Artaria et Comp., Vienna, with a vignette of Haydn[2] (BM—Hirsch III, 299), and by Longman, Clementi & Compy., London (*BUC*, p. 466, and AT)—virtually simultaneously.[3]

On Aug. 26, 1841, Hoffmann von Fallersleben wrote *Das Lied der Deutschen*, commencing *Deutschland, Deutschland über Alles*, to this music. The song was published Sept. 1, 1841, by Hoffmann und Campe, Hamburg, under the above title. Probable first edition: Front cover mentions the Sept. 1, 1841, date, a Stuttgart copublisher, Paul Neff, and the price, 2 gGr. p. [2] blank. m. on pp. [3]–[4] for guitar and piano, with the words of three verses. LC and JF. (The latter copy was one of a "remainder" of the first printing and distributed as the first edition, with an accompanying history of the song, to the members of the Maximilian Society in 1917.) This edition agrees with the description of the first edition by Liepmannssohn.[4] It also agrees with the description given by Böhme except that the latter also mentions a portrait of Hoffmann.[5] Perhaps this was on a wrapper; in view of there being less than a week between composition and publication, perhaps also the portrait was not in the first edition but in a later edition. It also agrees with a description by Gerstenberg,[6] except that the latter gives the printer as Fabricius, which does not appear in the copy described above. No copy has been found of this song either with Hoffmann's portrait or with the printer's name. †

Haydn was born in Rohrau, Lower Austria, in 1732 and died in Vienna

---

[1] Otto Erich Deutsch, "Erstdrucke der Musik in Periodischer Literatur" in *Die Musikforschung*, Kassel, Jan.–March, 1963, p. 51; NYPL. Hoboken, vol. 2, no. XXVI a: 43.

[2] Illustrated in Hirsch, vol. III, Plate VII.

[3] The *Quartet* was also published by other publishers at about the same time. See, generally, Hoboken, p. 429. Nine copies of the English edition were deposited at Stationers' Hall on June 13, 1799. The Artaria edition was advertised in *Wiener Zeitung*, July 20, 1799, p. 2450, UMI and an erroneous missing 21st bar (a rest) on p. 16 of the Viola part of *Quartet no. 3* was soon corrected. The above copy at BM is the first edition.

[4] Liepmannssohn, *Katalog 233*, 2. Teil, no. 1667.

[5] P. 1.

[6] Heinrich Gerstenberg, *Deutschland über Alles* (Munich, 1933), p. 46; NYPL.

in 1809. Haschka, an Austrian poet, was born in Vienna in 1749 and died in 1827. August Heinrich Hoffmann, a German poet, was born in 1798 at Fallersleben and died in 1874 at Korvei.

Entr'acte-Gavotte—Mignon

m. Ambroise Thomas. The *Entr'acte-Gavotte* was published for piano about Dec. 16, 1866,[1] by Heugel & Cie., au Ménestrel, 2 bis Rue Vivienne, Paris, but no first printing has been found. It probably has a price of 4.50 Fr., a p.n. about 3410, and the front cover will list about 21 separate numbers from the opera *Mignon*.[2]

The piano-vocal score of *Mignon* was published about Jan. 14, 1867,[3] by the same publisher. First edition: Front cover is green-gray with blue and red printing. vb. Half-title. vb. Title page has a miniature drawing of Mignon, and states that the words are by Michel Carré & Jules Barbier; price—15f. vb. Cast and index. Two pages of advertisements. Notice. Blank page. m. on pp. 2–311, the *Entr'acte* on p. 145. p.n. 3445. p. [312] blank. Not engraved. BN(CDC) and JF (inscribed by the composer). The piano score was published about Jan. 30, 1867.[4] *Mignon* was performed in Paris on Nov. 17, 1866.

The orchestral score of *Mignon* was entered for Dépôt Légal by the same publisher on June 14, 1867.[5] First edition: Front cover is black and white and the copies are numbered. vb. Title page. vb. Cast and index. Next three pages are blank. m. on pp. 1–556, engraved; the *Entr'acte* is at p. 249. p.ns. 4682 and 4681 [*sic*]. BN(CDC) and JMM.

Lithographed orchestral parts of the opera, with plate number 4682, folio, without covers, are at Heugel et Cie., Paris. Thomas was born in Metz in 1811 and died in Paris in 1896. Carré, a dramatist, was born in Paris in 1819 and died in Argenteuil in 1872.[6] A brief biography of Barbier appears above under *Barcarolle*.

[1] *Le Ménestrel*, Dec. 16, 1866, p. 24.

[2] On the basis of other separate numbers from the opera deposited at BN.

[3] It was originally scheduled to appear Jan. 1–5, 1867 (*Le Ménestrel*, Dec. 16, 1866, p. 24), but the date was postponed to Jan. 14, 1867 (*Id.*, Jan. 13, 1867, p. 56). It was entered for Dépôt Légal on Feb. 1, 1867; Archives.

[4] *Le Ménestrel*, Jan. 13, 1867, p. 56.

[5] Archives. *BF*, July 6, 1867, p. 304.

[6] *Larousse XX*, vol. 2, p. 12.

Erlkönig—Schubert

Wer   rei - tet   so   spät   durch   Nacht   und   Wind?
Who   ri - deth   so   late   thro'   night   and   wind?

m. Franz Schubert. w. Johann Wolfgang von Goethe. Published March 31, 1821,[1] "in Comission bey Cappi und Diabelli, " 1133 Graben, Vienna, as Schubert's "1tes Werk." First edition:[2] Oblong. Engraved. Title page refers to Goethe's ballad, has a dedication to Moritz Graf Dietrichstein and has the prices of 2 Fl. W.W./1 Fl. C.M. Verso of title page and next page blank. m. on pp. 4–15. No publisher's number, plate number or metronome indication. Back cover blank but has Schubert's autographed initials and control number. PML (copy number 13) and JF (copy number 11).

Erlkönig was first heard in concerts at the home of a friend of Schubert's in Vienna commencing in December, 1820, and then publicly performed in Vienna on Jan. 25, 1821. A group of Schubert's friends joined together to publish Erlkönig and other early songs by subscription at their expense. Brief biographic information regarding Schubert appears above under his Ave Maria. Goethe was born in Frankfurt in 1749 and died in Weimar in 1832.

España—Chabrier

m. Emmanuel Chabrier. The orchestral score was published Jan. 9, 1884,[1] by Enoch Frères & Costallat, 27 Boulevd. des Italiens, Paris. Possible first edition: Front cover is brown and tan, has a dedication to Charles Lamour-

---

[1] Sammler, Vienna, March 31, 1821, p. 156; SC.

[2] Deutsch, Schubert, no. 328, p. 198. Dr. Georg Kinsky, "Signierte Schubert-Erstdrucke" in Philobiblon, Vienna, 1931, vol. 1, p. 183; NYPL.

---

[1] Letter from publisher. Dec. 1883, per Grove's, vol. II, p. 148, without indicating the arrangement.

eux, is described as a "Rapsodie pour Orchestre" and has six arrangements, of which this is the first at 10 f. vb. Title page is the same as the front cover except in brown and white. vb. m. on pp. 1–61. p.n. 891. p. [62] and inside and outside of back cover blank. COP, SC (inscribed by the composer) and JF. The orchestral parts were issued Jan. 16, 1884.[1] No possible first printing has been located; early printings with p.n. 892 are at COP, SY and JF. *España* was performed in Paris on Nov. 4, 1883.

Emile Waldteufel made an arrangement of *España* for piano which was published in 1886[2] and Waldteufel has consequently sometimes been credited as its composer. BM(CDC). Chabrier was born at Ambert, Puy-de-Dôme, in 1841 and died in Paris in 1894.

Estrellita

Es - tre - lli - ta del le - ja no cie - lo

© 1914, renewed 1941 by Associated Music Publishers, Inc. Used by permission.

m. M. M. Ponce. *Estrellita* is the second composition in Ponce's *Dos Canciones Mexicanas*, which was listed in Hofmeister *Monatsbericht*, Oct., 1913, p. 218, at NYPL, for piano at 1.50 Mk. published by Friedrich Hofmeister, Leipzig. No copy has been found which had been published by Friedrich Hofmeister.

However, a copy of *Dos Canciones Mexicanas* was deposited at the Library of Congress on March 16, 1914, with a claim of publication on Feb. 24, 1914;[1] this copy has a 1914 copyright claim by Friedrich Hofmeister, but was published by A. Wagner y Levien Sucs. S. en C., 1A Capuchinas 21, Mexico City, and Av. San Francisco 35, Apartado Núm. 353, Puebla, Guadalajara, Monterrey. This may be the first printing. Front cover has a drawing of ancient Mexicana in many colors. m. on pp. 2–5. p.n. 368. *Estrellita* is no. XIV on pp. 4–5. Back cover adv. *Últimas..* No price. LC(CDC). A French edition published by W. Bessel & Cie., Paris, in 1928 states that the 1914 copyright is by the composer; JF. A current edition published by Josef Weinberger, Vienna, states that the 1914 copyright is by F. Hofmeister, Leipzig; JF.

<hr />

[2] *Bib. Mus.*, April–June, 1886, p. 21. BM's copy was deposited Oct. 1, 1886.

[1] Copyright records; LC.

"Estrellita" means "little star."[2] Manuel M. Ponce, a Mexican composer, was born in Fresnillo, Mexico, in 1882, studied and taught for a while in Germany and elsewhere, and died in Mexico City in 1948.[3]

Estudiantina

m. P. Lacome. w. J. de Lau Lusignan. Entered for Dépôt Légal on Dec. 22, 1881,[1] for duet and piano by Enoch Frères et Costallat, 27 Bould. des Italiens, Paris. First edition: Front cover is a collective title front cover entitled "Duos à Deux Voix Égales," listing six titles, of which *Estudiantina* is no. 4, has a drawing of leaves and flowers, a dedication to M. & Mme Simon-Girard, gives the price as 6 fr., mentions a London agent, and is green and white. p. [2] blank. m. on pp. 1–9 (really 3–11). p.n. 586. Back cover adv. *Chanson.. - Noël.* COP and BM (both CDC).

Emile Waldteufel's arrangement of this song for piano four hands was entered for Dépôt Légal on April 14, 1883,[2] and as a consequence he is frequently stated as its composer. BM(CDC—piano two hands). Paul Lacome, a composer of operettas and other musical works (not to be confused with Paul Lacombe), was born in 1838 in Houga, Gers, and died there in 1920.[3] No biographic information is available regarding de Lau Lusignan other than that he died in 1895.[4]

---

[2] See, generally, Stevenson, p. 231; and David López Alonso, "Historia de una Canción," in *Orientación Musical*, Mexico City, April, 1953, p. 9, at NYPL. The latter author, in *Manuel M. Ponce* (Mexico City, 1950), p. 53, at NYPL, mentions a report that *Estrellita* was merely an arrangement, and not an original work, by Ponce. However, Miss Carmen Sordo Sordi, Chief of Musical Investigations, Instituto Nacional de Bellas Artes, Mexico City, advised this author that *Estrellita* is now considered in Mexico to be an original work by Ponce.

[3] Westrup-Harrison, p. 508.

---

[1] Archives. The copyright deposit copy at COP is stamped "1881." In *Bib. Mus.*, Jan.–March, 1882, p. 7. BM's copy was received April 27, 1882.

[2] Archives. *BF*, April 7, 1883, p. 217, "pour piano," i.e., perhaps piano two hands. BM's copy was received May 1, 1883.

[3] Baker, p. 894.

[4] Letter from SACEM.

Etude, op. 10, no. 3—Chopin

m. Fréd. Chopin. Published almost at the same time in Paris, Leipzig and London, but the French publication was probably the first.[1] Probable first French edition published about June 8, 1833, by Maurice Schlesinger, 97 Rue Richelieu, Paris, under the title *Etudes*, op. 10, the above being no. 3: Front cover has a dedication to J. [*sic*] Liszt, the price is 18f, and there is a reference to Kistner, Leipzig. vb. m. on pp. 1–54. p.n. 1399. In no. 1, bar 27, the fingering in the first group of semiquavers is 1 2 3 5—later corrected to 1 2 4 5.[2] No. 3 commences on p. 11. Engraved. COP and JF.

Probable first German edition published about July–Aug., 1833, by Fr. Kistner,[3] Leipzig, under the title *Douze Grandes Études* [*sic*]: The front cover of Book I has a correct dedication, the price is 1 1/6 Rthlr., and there is a reference to Schlesinger, Paris. m. on pp. 2–27. p.n. 1018. p. [28] blank. Engraved. ONB and AT.

The earliest English edition, first published about Aug., 1833, that has been found is a "New & Revised Edition" by Wessel & Co., 6 Frith Street, Soho Square, London. The title is *Douze Grandes Etudes*; there is a dedication to J. [*sic*] Liszt and Ferd. Hiller and the price of each book is 6/. p.n. of Book I is 960. m. on pp. 2–23. p. [24] blank. Engraved. Not a collective title front cover. BM. Alan Tyson, London, believes this the first English edition and that the words "New & Revised" merely refer to the "additional fingering by [Chopin's] Pupil, I. Fontana"—the quoted phrase appearing on the front cover.

The above *Etude* was composed Aug. 25, 1832. Chopin was born near Warsaw in 1810 and died in Paris in 1849.

---

[1] The French edition is listed in *BF*, June 8, 1833, p. 360, and in *RM*, July 6, 1833, p. 184. The German edition is in Hofmeister *Monatsbericht*, July–Aug., 1833, p. 54. Brown, p. 42, gives the French edition as July, and the German and English editions as Aug. See, also, Brown, *Corrections*, p. 29.

[2] *Chopin Works*, vol. II, p. 143. See also Arthur Hedley, "Chopiniana," in *MT*, Jan., 1965, p. 31.

[3] Brown, p. 42, gives the original German publisher as Probst-Kistner, but this is probably an error since Kistner purchased Probst's business on May 28, 1831; while the name "Probst-Kistner" was used at first, it is not believed that this work was published under this imprint. Richard Linnemann, *Fr. Kistner 1823/1923* (Leipzig, 1923), pp. 1 and 43; NYPL. See, also, Brown, *Corrections*, p. 29. Kistner is shown as the publisher in the Hofmeister *Monatsbericht* mentioned in footnote 1.

Eugen Onegin Waltz—Tchaikovsky

m. P. Tchaikovsky. The piano-vocal score of Евгеній Онѣгинъ was published about May, 1879,[1] by P. Jurgenson, Moscow. Probable first edition: Front cover is yellow and black, in Russian. vb. Title page, also in Russian, mentions that the text is adapted from Pushkin, there is no street address or crown emblem for the publisher, the agents—both on one line—are I. Jurgenson, St. Petersburg, and G. Sennewald, Warsaw, and the price is 6 rub. vb. Cast and index. m. on pp. 4–249, the text in **Russian only**, and the *Waltz* at p. 120. p.n. 3302-23. The date of approval by the censor, Sept. 30, 1878(O.S.), appears at the bottom of p. 249. p. [250] blank. p. [251] contains Russian words and music translating the French words on pp. 141–142. p. [252] blank. Inside and outside of back cover blank. No reference to "Edition Jurgenson" at the top of the title page, and no arrangements listed on the title page. HU (purchased June 15, 1899) and LLM. A similar edition, but adding German words and mentioning "Edition Jurgenson" at the top of the title page, and lacking covers, is at GM and JMM. An edition similar to GM's, but showing the St. Petersburg and Warsaw agents on two lines, is at GL. The D. Rahter, Hamburg, edition of the piano-vocal score was published about Nov., 1889.[2]

The Jurgenson edition of the piano score of the opera has p.n. 3303, and the Jurgenson edition of the piano edition of the *Entracte & Valse* has p.n. 3314.[3] No copy of either has been found; they were presumably published about the same time as the piano-vocal score.

The orchestral score of *Eugen Onegin* was published shortly after Sept. 30, 1888 (O.S.),[4] this date of the censor's approval appearing on the title page. Possible first edition: title page is in Russian, is brown, tan and black against a drawing of leaves, the imprint is P. Jurgenson, Moscow, without street address or crown emblem, lists the orchestral score at 150 rub., the orchestral parts without price and four other arrangements, mentions Mackar & Noël, Paris, G. Sennewald, Warsaw, and two other agents and

---

[1] Hofmeister *Monatsbericht*, May, 1879, p. 158. On Feb. 6, 1879, Tchaikovsky wrote N. F. von Meck that he would "write Jurgenson to send a copy of *Eugen Onegin* to Bülow." *Tchaikovsky Letters*, p. 334.

[2] Hofmeister *Monatsbericht*, Nov., 1889, p. 501.

[3] *Jurgenson Catalog*, Moscow, 1889, p. 197; NYPL.

[4] Dombayev, p. 7, says 1880, but this seems unlikely.

the date mentioned above. vb. Cast and index. vb. m. on pp. 5–365. p.n. 3901. Text in Russian and German. The *Waltz* is on p. 156. MC and COP. A similar edition, with a front cover in Russian, and in two shades of green, but stating that it is the 2nd edition, is at SSL. The D. Rahter, Hamburg, edition of the orchestral score, using the above Jurgenson plates, was published about Nov., 1890;[5] NEC. Jurgenson's orchestral score of the *Waltz* with p.n. 17154 is at COL; Rahter's edition,[6] using Jurgenson's earlier plates with p.n. 14263, is at BPL.

A possible first printing of the orchestral parts of the opera, published by Jurgenson, has plate number 17601 (1891–1892); covers lacking. MET.

Eugene Onegin was completed Feb. 1, 1878 (N.S.) and performed March 29, 1879, in Moscow. Brief biographic information regarding Tchaikovsky appears above under *Chant sans Paroles*.

Evening Prayer—Hansel and Gretel

A - bends, will ich schla - fen gehn, vier - zehn En - gel um mich_ stehn

m. Engelbert Humperdinck. w. Adelheid Wette. The piano-vocal score of *Hänsel und Gretel*, in which the *Evening Prayer*, or *Abendsegen* duet appears, was received by LC on Feb. 7, 1894,[1] from B. Schott's Söhne, 5 Weihergarten, Mainz. Possible first edition: Front cover is gray and black. vb. Title page states no. 25618, the price as 8 Marks, and the publisher's affiliates in London, Brussels and Paris, the latter's address being 70 Rue du Faubourg St. Honoré. No reference on title page to piano arrangements for two and four hands. m. on pp. [1]–136, engraved, the *Evening Prayer* on p. 62. There are two variants of the above, with priority unknown: the copy at SB has no copyright notice at the bottom of the title page; the copyright deposit copy at LC does.† The sheet music edition of the *Abendsegen* was also probably published by Feb., 1894, but no early edition has been found.

The first printing of the orchestral score still shows the address of the Paris affiliate as 70 Rue du Faubourg St. Honoré and was probably published about April, 1894.[2] The title page is the same as that of the piano-

---

[5] Hofmeister *Monatsbericht*, Nov., 1890, p. 503.
[6] *Id.*, Aug., 1892, p. 275.

[1] Hofmeister *Monatsbericht*, April, 1894, p. 173, at 8 MK.
[2] *Id.*, also April, 1894, p. 173, but without price. ‡

vocal score except that there is no arrangement, price or copyright notice.
vb. Dedication to parents. Cast. Separate title page in blue and white for
Overture, listing the orchestral score and parts of the opera (without prices)
and of the Overture (with prices), and with the same Paris address. vb.
Overture on pp. 1–28, engraved, with p.n. 25617. p. [29] blank. p. [30] adv.
Die Meistersinger.. m. on pp. 1–353, a lithographing of a manuscript score.
The *Evening Song* is at p. 158. No plate number. p. [354] blank. JF (only
known copy). This edition is earlier than the orchestral score deposited
for copyright at LC on Dec. 21, 1894, with the title page listing the additional arrangement for piano four hands, with price, and having the later
Paris address of 40 Rue d'Anjou, and with engraved printed score and
plate number 25617. LC(CDC).

A possible first edition of the orchestral parts of the opera, with plate
number 25617 for the Vorspiel and plate number 25751 for the balance,
with covers, but lithographed, may also have been published about Dec.,
1894; CI and MET.*

The opera was performed in Weimar on Dec. 23, 1893. Humperdinck
was born in Siegburg, Rhine provinces, in 1854 and died in Berlin in 1921.
Adelheide Wette, Humperdinck's sister, was born in Siegburg in 1858 and
died in Eberstadt, Germany, in 1916.[3]

Fantaisie-Impromptu—Chopin

m. Fréd. Chopin. Published May 21, 1855,[1] by Ad. Mt. Schlesinger, 34
Linden, Berlin, for piano. It is not clear whether it was first printed
separately or included in the complete collection of *Oeuvres Posthumes*.
Possible first edition of the separate publication: Front cover is entitled
Oeuvres Posthumes, listing eight titles of which *Fantaisie-Impromptu*, op.
66, is the first at 2/3 Thlr., the complete collection being listed also at 5
Thlr., refers to Jules Fontana and mentions foreign agents and p.ns. 4392-

---

[3] *Meyers*, vol. 12, p. 1326.

[1] Date of publication stated in the entry made on May 23, 1855, at Stationers' Hall.
Signale, May 16, 1855, p. 182, mentions the complete collection, without price. The
separate publication and the complete collection (at 5 Thaler) are advertised in *Berliner
Musik-Zeitung Echo*, July 16, 1855, p. 224; NYPL. The separate publication is listed in
Hofmeister *Monatsbericht*, Aug., 1855, p. 807, and the complete collection at 5 Thaler
the following month, p. 823. Brown, p. 85, gives the German date as in the above text.

4401. vb. m. on pp. 3–11, engraved. p.n. 4392. Bars 10 and 22 have no accents.[2] p. [12] blank. Two pages of comments in German and French by Jules Fontana, dated Paris, May, 1855, regarding publication. There are three variants of the foregoing: one at ONB has the printer at the bottom of the front cover as L. Burkhardt and no reference to a Petersburg agent; another at JF was printed by Nietack and refers to Dufour & Co. as the Petersburg agent; in the third variant, the printer is L. Burkhardt and there is a reference to Dufour & Co., copy at Burnett & Simeone, London—priority of the variants is uncertain. A copy at LC is the same as ONB and has the original wrappers in yellow and black; verso adv. Neue.. Inside of back cover continues verso of front cover. Outside of back cover blank.

La Collection Complète, published by Schlesinger, Berlin, has a portrait of Chopin facing the title page. The title page is the same as the first variant described above (with the price of the complete collection at 5 Thlr.) vb. Two pages of comments, as above. m. on pp. 3–97, engraved, with Fantaisie-Impromptu at p. 3. p. [98] blank. Copy at H. Kyburz, Basel.

The French edition of La Collection Complète was deposited July 28, 1855,[3] by J. Meissonnier Fils, 18 Rue Dauphine, Paris. Front cover is similar in appearance to that of the German edition except that the price is 20 francs unbound and 30 francs bound. There is reference to A. M. Schlesinger, Berlin. There are three portraits of Chopin on one page and the same preface dated Paris, May, 1855. p.ns. 3523-3532. All music pages are engraved. BN and COP (latter stamped 1855—both CDC); also LC. COP also has the separate Fantaisie Impromptu, with music pages engraved, published by J. Meissonnier Fils (not CDC).

An English edition of Fantaisie Impromptu of uncertain date, but generally contemporary, was published by Ewer & Co., London. Possible first edition: Front cover has the price of 3/ and there are references to the Berlin and Paris agents. vb. m. on pp. 3–11, engraved. Back cover blank. No p.n. AT.

The work had been composed in 1834 and performed in Paris in March, 1855. Its Moderato Cantabile theme became the basis in 1918 of the song I'm Always Chasing Rainbows.[4] Brief biographic information regarding Chopin appears above under his Etude.

---

[2] Chopin Works, vol. IV, p. [54].

[3] Dépôt Légal records; Archives. BF, Sept. 1, 1855, p. 640. RGM, Feb. 10, 1856, p. 48. Brown, p. 85, gives the Feb., 1856, date apparently on the basis of the last reference; see also Brown, Corrections, p. 29.

As the preface is dated Paris, May, 1855, it is just possible that the work was also published in Paris that month.

[4] Fuld, American, p. 27.

The Farmer in the Dell

The farm - er in the dell,——— the farm - er in the dell

The first known printing of the music and words was April 30, 1883,[1] in William Wells Newell, *Games and Songs of American Children* (New York, N.Y., 1883), p. 129, where it is said that the game is sung and played on "New York streets." LC(CDC) and JF. The game is known in England under the name *Farmer's Den,*[2] but no prior English printing has been found.

The game must have derived from Germany, as the following are the directions printed in 1847 for a German children's game known as *Der Kirmessbauer:*

> "Es fuhr ein Bauer ins Holz . . .
> Der Bau'r nahm sich ein Weib . . .
> Das Weib nahm sich ein Kind . . .
> Das Kind nahm sich eine Magd . . . ," etc.

Eduard Fiedler, *Volksreime und Volkslieder in Anhalt-Dessau* (Dessau, 1847), p. 61, no. 89; HU.

"The Bride Cuts the Cake" is sung to this melody.

Fiddler on the Roof

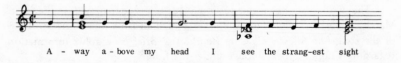

A - way a - bove my   head   I   see the strang-est   sight

m. Jerry Bock. w. Sheldon Harnick. The song *Fiddler on the Roof* was published Nov. 9, 1964,[1] by Sunbeam Music Corp., 22 West 48th Street,

---

[1] Copyright records; LC.
[2] Gomme, vol. II, p. 420, without music. See, also, *JAF Index*, p. 193.

---

[1] Copyright records; LC.

New York, N.Y. 10036. First edition: Front cover has a drawing of a fiddler on a roof, mentions Zero Mostel and others, refers to the musical of the same name, shows a selling agent and is in many colors against a yellow background; no other titles listed and no price. m. on pp. 2–3. No plate number. Back cover adv. Vocal.. LC(CDC) and JF.

The piano-vocal score of the show Fiddler on the Roof was published July 26, 1965,[1] at $12.50, the back cover stating "First Printing." LC(CDC) and JF. The musical opened in New York City on Sept. 22, 1964. Bock, a composer, was born in 1928 in New Haven.[2] Harnick, a lyricist, was born in 1924 in Chicago.[2]

Finlandia—Sibelius

m. Jean Sibelius. First published for piano in Nov., 1900,[1] by Helsingfors Nya Musikhandel, Fazer & Westerlund, Helsinki. Probable first edition: Front cover states that Finlandia is a tone-poem for orchestra but mentions only the piano arrangement, has a drawing of a tree, refers to Breitkopf & Härtel, Leipzig, and is yellow, brown and green. m. on pp. 3–13. Back cover adv. Album.. - Guitarr.. No price, opus number or plate number. UL.

The orchestral score was published in March, 1901,[2] by the same concern. Possible first edition: Front cover is similar to that described above but now lists orchestral score, orchestral parts and piano arrangement. m. on pp. 2–25. Back cover is same as that described above. Still no prices, opus number or plate number; UL. A variant, priority unknown, is the same except the back cover is blank; GM. No first edition of the orchestral parts has been found; early editions, with Breitkopf & Härtel plate number Orch. B. 1618, without covers, are at CI and RAM.

The Breitkopf & Härtel piano and orchestral editions of Finlandia were apparently not published until 1905.[3]

The first two bars above are almost identical with the first two bars of the second part of Emil Genetz, Herää Suomi! ("Arise, Finland!"), com-

[2] The Biographical Encyclopaedia & Who's Who of the American Theatre (New York, N.Y., 1966), pp. 305 and 517; NYPL.

[1] Letter from UL based upon information from the Finnish publisher.

[2] Id. In Hofmeister Monatsbericht, April, 1901, p. 163.

[3] Breitkopf & Härtel Musik-Verlagsbericht, Leipzig, 1905, pp. 1 and 4; NYPL.

mencing with the words "Vasta kun leijona," published in 1882 for male chorus in Helsinki; in Suomen Ylioppilaskunnan *Albumi Elias Lönnrotin Kunniaksi* ("Federation of Finnish Student Unions, *Album to Honor Elias Lönnrot*") (Helsinki, 1882), Supplement, p. IV; UL and JF.

Finlandia was composed in 1899 as part of an orchestral suite entitled *Finland Awakes* which was performed in Helsinki on Nov. 4, 1899, but not then published; *Finlandia* was revised as a separate work in 1900. Sibelius was born in Hameenlinna (formerly known as Tavastehus), Finland, in 1865 and died near Helsinki in 1957.

First Call

The earliest known printing of this American bugle call was in 1842 in George W. Behn, *A Concise System of Instruction for the Volunteer Cavalry of the United States* (Savannah, 1842), p. 296; NYPL and JF. One authority on military music says that *First Call* is similar to *Le Garde à Vous*, but no piece with this title has been found which is similar to *First Call*.[1] Another commentator states that *First Call* derives from the French cavalry,[2] but no such precedent has been found.

The call is now frequently used at horse-racing tracks. In the same connection, it was effectively introduced by Frank Loesser in the *Fugue for Tinhorns*, in the musical show *Guys and Dolls* (1950), piano-vocal score, p. 10. JF.

The First Noel

The____ first____ No - el the____an - gel did say

---

[1] White, p. 265. NYPL has an entirely dissimilar *Le Garde à Vous*. Another dissimilar *Garde à Vous* is in Georges Kastner, *Manuel Général de Musique Militaire* (Paris, 1848), music p. 28; COP, NYPL and JF.

[2] Gustav Kobbé, "The Trumpet in Camp and Battle" in *The Century Magazine*, New York, N.Y., Aug., 1898, p. 537; ULS, p. 635.

The words of this old carol[1] were first printed in 1823 in Davies Gilbert, *Some Ancient Christmas Carols with the Tunes to Which They Were Formerly Sung in the West of England* (2nd ed., London, 1823), no. IX, pp. 28–29; BM, NYPL and JF. There is no title for the carol, but the opening words are "The first Nowel" [sic]. Contrary to the title of the book, there is no music to this carol. This carol is not in the first edition of this book (1822), which had only eight carols; LC.

The music, together with the words, first appeared in 1833 in William Sandys, *Christmas Carols, Ancient and Modern; Including the Most Popular in the West of England* (London, 1833), on the fourth page of the music supplement at the end of the book under the title *The First Nowell;* BM and JF. The melody, while differing in detail, is basically the same as that now in use.

The Flight of the Bumble Bee—Rimsky-Korsakov

m. N. Rimsky-Korsakov. *The Flight of the Bumble Bee* was first printed in the piano-vocal score of *The Tale of Tsar Saltan (Сказка о Царь Салтанъ)*, about Sept. 28, 1900 (N.S.), by Bessel & Co. Possible first edition of the piano-vocal score: Front cover is black and gray, in Russian, and the imprint is V. Bessel & Co., 54 Nevsky, St. Petersburg, and 12 Petrovka, Moscow. Verso and next two pages blank. Title page is multicolored, in Russian, has a facsimile of six bars of music in the composer's handwriting, a scene from the opera, mentions that the libretto is by V. I. Bielsky after Pushkin, lists the piano-vocal score at 10 rubles and the piano score at 6 rubles, and mentions the publisher's first name, Vasili, and the date Sept. 16, 1900 (O.S.). vb. Index. Cast. m. on pp. 5–281. Censor's approval date of July 13, 1900 (O.S.), is on p. 281. p.n. 4849. Text in Russian. *The Flight of the Bumble Bee* is on pp. 159–162. p. [282] and inside of back cover blank. Back cover adv. 22 numbers and arrangements from the opera, including the orchestral score of the opera at 150 rubles and the orchestral parts without price, but not *The Flight of the Bumble Bee.* ONB and JF(autographed by the composer). The English translation of the opera is sometimes given as *The Fairy Tale of Tsar Saltan.*

The orchestral score of the opera was also apparently published about Sept. 28, 1900 (N.S.), and a copy dated by hand Sept. 25, 1901 (O.S.), is at

[1] Routley, p. 96.

SSL. First edition: Front cover is red and gray, in Russian, and the imprint is as above. Title page is also similar to that of the piano-vocal score and includes the Sept. 16, 1900 (O.S.), date. **(See Plate II.)** vb. Cast. vb. Index. Composition of orchestra. m. on pp. 5–462. p.n. 4882. Back cover blank. (Similar copy, with March 5, 1903 (O.S.), handwritten date, at LPL.) No early printing of the orchestral parts of the opera has been found.

The Flight of the Bumble Bee was apparently first published separately in 1927 for piano and for orchestra.[1] It is not included in the *Suite* published about July, 1901,[2] with p.n. 4880; BM. The opera was composed in 1899–1900 and performed Nov. 3, 1900 (N.S.), in Moscow. Brief biographic information regarding Rimsky-Korsakov appears above under *Capriccio Espagnol*. Vladimir Ivanovich Bielsky, a Russian librettist, was born in 1866 and died in 1946.[3]

Flow Gently Sweet Afton

Flow   gent - ly   sweet_   Af - ton   a - mong   thy   green   braes

m. J. E. Spilman. w. Robert Burns. The words, together with an older version of the music, were first printed in the fourth volume of *The Scots Musical Museum* (Edinburgh, 1792–1793), p. 400.[1]

The modern version of the music, known particularly in America, was copyrighted June 18, 1838,[2] by George Willig, 171 Chesnut [*sic*] Street, Philadelphia. pp. [1] and [4] blank. m. on pp. 2–3. No p.n. Engraved. No reference to a second or later edition. JF.

Brief biographic information regarding Burns appears above under *Auld Lang Syne*. Jonathan Edwards Spilman was born in 1812 in Greenville, Ky., became a lawyer, then a minister, and died in 1896 in Flora, Ill.[3]

---

[1] Letter from W. Bessel & Cie., Paris.

[2] The copy at BM was received July 24, 1901.

[3] Information from LTL. See, also, Rimsky-Korsakov, *My Musical Life, passim.*

---

[1] For a discussion of the different editions of this volume, and their locations, see *Auld Lang Syne,* footnote 6.

[2] Copyright records; LC.

[3] Earl R. Hoover, "J. E. Spilman," in *The Register of the Kentucky Historical Society,* Frankfort, Ky., July, 1968, p. 222; NYPL.

The Flying Dutchman-Overture—Wagner

m. Richard Wagner. The piano-vocal score of *Der Fliegende Holländer* was published about Sept.–Dec., 1844,[1] by C. F. Meser, Dresden. Possible first edition: The title page makes legal claims, states the price is 8 Thlr., mentions the year 1844 and has an emblem and plate number 275. vb. Dedication. vb. Half-title page. Cast and index. m. on pp. 3–274, engraved. Folio. BM (CDC deposited Jan. 5, 1861), LC and JF (copy with green and black covers). A variant edition, mentioning Stationers' Hall on the title page, probably a little later, was offered in Hans Schneider *Catalog 276* (Tutzing, West Germany, 1984), no. 36; *Catalog* at JF. No reference on title page to Hermann Müller.

Twenty-five copies of the orchestral score of the opera were published in 1844–1845[2] "Als Manuscript authographirt." First edition: On the title page, the name of the publisher (C. F. Meser, Dresden) is not printed but is rubber-stamped. Vol. I has music on pages 1–150. Vol. II has music on pages [150 bis]–413. Folio. ONB (S.M. 2353A). No printing of the orchestral parts by Meser has been found; a printing by Adolf Fürstner, Berlin, with plate number 2761 [1880's], lithographed and with covers, is at CI and MET*.

Wagner himself paid for publishing the piano-vocal and orchestral scores of *The Flying Dutchman*. The opera was completed in Oct., 1841, and performed in Dresden on Jan. 2, 1843. Wagner was born in Leipzig in 1813 and died in Venice in 1883.

---

[1] *Signale*, Sept., 1844, first undated week, p. 295, says the piano-vocal score of the opera will be published in a few weeks. *Id.*, Oct., 1844, first undated week, p. 315, lists the *Overture* for piano. Hofmeister *Monatsbericht*, Oct., 1844, p. 153, lists the piano-vocal score without price and other selections, including the *Overture* for piano, with prices. Whistling, *Musikalischer Monatsanzeiger*, Oct., 1844, p. 163, lists the *Overture* for piano and Dec., 1844, p. 206, lists the piano-vocal score, all with prices; SBW. Klein, pp. 18–19.

[2] Ernest Newman, *The Life of Richard Wagner* (New York, N.Y., 1933), vol. I, p. 413; NYPL. *Grove's*, 3rd ed., vol. 5, p. 607, says 1844. The title page of the copy described above has a notation which suggests 1845. A later edition of the orchestral score published by C. F. Meser, Berlin and Dresden, has a title page referring to a law dated June 11, 1870; BPL, BM and LC. Klein, pp. 16–17.

The Flying Trapeze

He'd fly thro' the   air with the   great - est of   ease

In what is probably the first printing of this song, the credits are: "Written and Sung by George Leybourne. Arranged by Alfred Lee." Front cover, in many colors, has a drawing of a man in vest and shorts standing on a mattress in the center of a music hall, a large photograph of his face (Leybourne's?), and a drawing of three trapezes with a girl flying between two of them. p. [2] and back cover blank. m. on pp. 3-7. The date of publication was about Jan. 19, 1867.[1] No plate number. The publisher is Charles Sheard, London. Copy at B. Feldman & Co., Ltd., London, successor to Charles Sheard. A similar copy advertising on the back cover *Blind Man's Buff* could not have been published before 1880; JF.

The earliest American editions bear 1868 copyright dates.

The song was apparently based on a real-life acrobat of the time, Léotard, who first introduced the flying trapeze act in London in the 1860's.[2] The arrangement by Alfred Lee may have been of a theme from Offenbach's *Le Papillon* (1860), in Act 2, Scene 1, in the key of B flat. Johann Strauss included the melody of *The Flying Trapeze* as one of a group of English popular melodies during his visit to London in Aug.–Oct., 1867, in his *Festival Valse Comique* (English title) or *Erinnerung an Covent-Garden* (German title). The song is also sometimes known as *The Man on the Flying Trapeze*. The melody was slightly revised in an arrangement under the latter title by Walter O'Keefe, published by Robbins Music Corporation, New York City, in 1933.

Joe Saunders was a pseudonym of George Leybourne, who was born in 1842 in the Midlands of England, became a comic singer in London and provincial music halls under the name of the "Lion Comique," and who died in London in 1884. Alfred Lee was probably born in London in 1839 and died there in 1906.

---

[1] *ILN*, Jan. 19, 1867, p. 67. The author is indebted to Andrew Lamb, Littlehampton, West Sussex, England, for information regarding this title.

[2] Pulling, p. 192.

For He's a Jolly Good Fellow—(Malbrouk—
We Won't Go Home till Morning!—
The Bear Went over the Mountain)

Mal-brouk s'en	va -	t'en guer	- re,	Mi-ron-ton, ton, ton, Mi-ron-tai	-	ne
We won't go	home	till morn	- ing,	we won't go home till morn	-	ing
For he's	a	jol-ly good fel	- low,	for he's a jol-ly good fel	-	low
The bear went	o-ver	the moun	- tain,	the bear went o-ver the moun	-	tain

It is said that the melody was used in 1781 by the well-known French dramatist Jean-François Marmontel, in his romance *Quoi, sans Vouloir Entendre*,[1] but no copy has been located.

The melody was originally associated with the *Malbrouk* song, the words of which appear in a collection of street songs, *Chansons, Vaudevilles et Ariettes Choisis par Duchemin*, published by Valleyre, on p. 10 under the title *La Mort de M. de Marlb'roug*; BN. The collection is not dated but is believed to be between 1762 and 1778.[2] The song is also said to have been referred to in a play by Charles Simon Favart, *Les Rêveries Renouvellées des Grecs* performed and printed in 1779 in Paris, p. 26;[2] however, there is an error in the citation, and the reference cannot be confirmed in the copy at BN.

Commencing early in 1783, there was a rash of printings of the *Malbrouk* melody under that title or the title *Marlbourouck*, or other variation, apparently brought about when a nurse sang it to one of Marie Antoinette's infants as a lullaby about 1781. *Mercure de France* lists at least 10 printings by different publishers in 1783–1784, not all with words, the earliest of which in May 31, 1783, p. 240, is entitled *Air de Marlbourouck*, with nine variations for piano, published by Levasseur, Paris; no copy has been located. Other French editions were printed without name of publisher, and there were many early foreign printings. Various contemporary French and other editions are at BN, COP, BM and JF.

The melody *Calino Casturame*, included in the English seventeenth-

[1] Max Friedlaender, "Das Lied vom Marlborough" in *Zeitschrift für Musikwissenschaft* (Leipzig, 1924), pp. 302–328; NYPL. The romance does not seem to be in *Oeuvres Complètes de Marmontel* (Paris, 1819), 18 vols.; NYPL.

[2] Coirault, *Recherches*, p. 223. Coirault, *Chanson*, p. 35. BN has a manuscript arrangement of the melody for violin dated 1769–1789 (Vm⁷ 4865).

century manuscript *Fitzwilliam Virginal Book*, at CUL, is quite similar to the melody quoted above. [2A] The song became known in England and America as *We Won't Go Home till Morning!* The earliest known English printing is a song version by Charles Blondel, published ca. 1841-1846[3] by C. W. Manby, 85 Fleet Street, London, at 2/, with engraved music pages; LC and JF.* The earliest known American printing was copyrighted March 16 and April 7, 1842,[4] by Thomas Birch [New York, N.Y.], arranged by William Clifton and with engraved music pages; LC(CDC).

In its best known form, *For He's a Jolly Good Fellow*, surprisingly, no early printing has been found; this may mean that these words were not sung until well into the nineteenth century. The word "jolly" gives away its English origin. Yet, the earliest printing that could be found is in an American songster, *The Old Clown's "W-H-O-A January" Songster* (New York, N.Y.), copyrighted Nov. 19, 1870,[4] the words of *For He's a Jolly Good Fellow* appearing on p. 39, without music but stated to be to the "Air: 'We Won't Go Home till Morning' "; LC. It is classed as an English folk song in Louis C. Elson, *Folk Songs of Many Nations* (Cincinnati, Ohio, 1905), p. 52; LC.

The Bear Went over the Mountain seems to be of even more recent origin. Its earliest known appearance in print is in *Twice 55 Community Songs*, published Feb. 6, 1920,[5] by Birchard & Company, Boston, no. 61; in the earliest version of this book to contain this song, there is a 1919 copyright claim, and there is no pagination. LC (CDC). This version is probably American (there are no bears in England!)

There have been many attempts to trace the simple melody of this song to older sources. One writer believes the melody derives from an ancient Arabic or Spanish melody;[6] the resemblance seems remote. Cha-

[2A] See William Chappell, *Old English Popular Music* (London, 1893), p. 84; BM. The melody is referred to by Shakespeare in *Henry V*, act IV, scene 4. Harold Barlow, New York City, advised the author of this similarity.

[3] Humphries-Smith, p. 225.

[4] Copyright records; LC.

[5] Copyright records; LC. In the April–June, 1920, issue of *JAF* appear the words of *The Bear Went over the Mountain* with a reference to the common melody; Emelyn E. Gardner, "Some Play-Party Games in Michigan," p. 91.

[6] Nettl, p. 22. Paul Nettl, "First of the Song Hits," in *American German Review*, Philadelphia, April, 1948, p. 17; *ULS*, p. 147. Paul Nettl, "Marlborough" in the *Musical Digest*, New York, N.Y., Aug., 1947, p. [42]; *ULS*, p. 1842. See, also, Wilhelm Tappert, *Musikalische Studien* (Berlin, 1868), p. 60; NYPL. The allegedly similar Arabic or Spanish melody, *A Cazar Va don Rodrigo*, is quoted in Felipe Pedrell, *Cancionero Musical Popular Español* (Cataluña, [1919-1920]), vol. 1, musical section in the rear, no. 26, p. 22, at NYPL, where it is said to be from Francesco de Salinas, *De Musica* (Salamanca, 1577), libri VII; NYPL.

teaubriand was responsible for the completely unauthenticated statement
that the song derives from a melody sung by a French soldier during the
crusades in Jerusalem.[7] It has also been suggested that the song was first
known as the *Duke de Guise*,[8] but no printing of the melody under that
title has been located, and any prior similarity may be confined to the
words only. Coirault believes the melody to be a hunting song of the
eighteenth century.[9]

For Me and My Gal

The bells, are ring - ing____ for me and my gal

m. Geo. W. Meyer. w. Edgar Leslie and E. Ray Goetz. Published Jan. 24,
1917,[1] by Waterson Berlin & Snyder Co., Strand Theatre Bldg., Broadway
at 47th St., New York, N.Y. First edition: Front cover has a drawing of
Cupid watching a marriage, and is brown, orange and white. m. on pp.
2–3. p.n. 681-2. Back cover adv. *When..* Folio. LC(CDC) and JF.

Meyer, a composer, was born in Boston in 1884 and died in New York
City in 1959.[2] Leslie, a lyricist and publisher, was born in Stamford, Conn.,
in 1885 and died in New York City in 1976.[2A] Goetz, a lyricist and producer, was born in Buffalo, N.Y., in 1886 and died in Conn. in 1954.[3]

Frankie and Johnny

Frank-ie and John - ny were lov - ers,___ oh, Lord - y how_ they could love

The devil's advocate, this writer believes that, on the basis of the written
record, *Frankie and Johnny* is not so ancient as some of the folk-song writers

[7] *Grove's*, vol. 5, p. 527.
[8] Elson, *Modern Music*, p. 441.
[9] Coirault, *Recherches*, p. 228.

[1] Copyright records; LC.
[2] Obituary, *The New York Times*, Aug. 29, 1959.
[2A] Obituary, *The New York Times*, Jan. 24, 1976.
[3] *ASCAP*, p. 185.

would have one believe. Some of the folk-song writers date the song back to the 1840's, others to the 1850's, 1860's, or 1880's.[1] The St. Louis version is said to derive from a shooting by Frankie Baker of Albert Britt on Oct. 15, 1899.[2] As far as this writer has been able to find, there is no written substantiation of any of the foregoing; if there is, it is not referred to in any of the many articles on the song; nor has it been found by this writer.

The first known appearance in print of the music, a variation of the familiar melody, is under the title *He Done Me Wrong*,[3] with the subtitle *Death of Bill Bailey*. mw. Hughie Cannon. Copyrighted April 7, 1904,[4] by Howley, Dresser Company, 1440 Broadway, New York, N.Y. First edition: Front cover has a photograph of the author and is blue, green, gray and white. p. [2] adv. *Your..* m. on pp. [3]–[6]. p. [7] adv. *I'll..* Back cover adv. *You're.. - Mary..* LC(CDC) and JF. The next known appearance of the music, also a variant of the familiar melody, is in *Bill You Done Me Wrong*, copyrighted on April 9, 1908, by The Star Music Publishers, with the copyright by Tell Taylor.[4] The music and words are credited to Leighton and Leighton;[5] LC(CDC) and JF.

The song was published under the title *Frankie and Johnny* on April 10, 1912,[4] by Tell Taylor with music and words credited to Leighton Bros. and Ren Shields; LC(CDC) and JF. This version varies the traditional words and music and contains an original chorus.

The first known traditional setting of the music appears in the verse of *You're My Baby*, published on May 28, 1912,[4] with the music credited to Nat. D. Ayer and the words to A. Seymour Brown and published by Jerome H. Remick & Co., New York and Detroit. First edition: Front cover

---

[1] Belden, p. 330. Spaeth, p. 206. Thomas Beer, *The Mauve Decade* (London, 1926), p. 120, at NYPL, speaks mysteriously of a manuscript copy of 12 stanzas made by an officer in 1863; the alleged manuscript is not illustrated, quoted or located, and Beer is now dead.

[2] See, generally, Bruce Redfern Buckley's unpublished doctoral dissertation entitled *Frankie and Johnny (Frankie and Her Men: A Study of the Inter-relationships of Popular and Folk Traditions)*, 1962; IU. John Huston, *Frankie and Johnny* (New York, N.Y., 1930), p. 104; LC. *Ozark*, vol. II, p. 125. Scarborough, p. 84. Sandburg, p. 75. Perrow, p. 178. *Missouri Historical Review*, Columbia, Mo., vol. 34, Jan., 1940, p. 292; *ULS*, p. 1775. Legman, p. 507.

[3] A song with the interesting title *Honey You've Done Me Wrong*, by Harold M. Vernon, was copyrighted March 7, 1898, by T. B. Harms & Co., New York, N.Y., according to copyright records at LC. It has entirely different music and words. The copyright deposit copy at LC is a professional edition. A possible first regular edition is at JF.

[4] Copyright records; LC.

[5] The obituary of Bert Leighton, *The New York Times*, Feb. 12, 1964, states that he was credited with the authorship of the song, or alternatively that the Leighton brothers popularized the song shortly before the turn of the century.

has a photograph of an unnamed girl. m. on pp. 2–5. No p.n. Back cover adv. *When.*. LC(CDC).

No printing of the familiar words commencing "Frankie and Johnny were lovers" has been found before the 1920's.[6] This seems strange indeed for such an allegedly old and well-known song. The most exhaustive study of the words only is by Bruce Redfern Buckley who analyzed the different folk and popular versions of the words in a 289-page unpublished doctoral dissertation cited in footnote 2. Probably his most interesting finding is that the name "Johnny" occurs for the first time in the 1912 *Frankie and Johnny* sheet music edition referred to above. Was the new name to help avoid possible copyright infringment of previous words? To help justify a new copyright?

There is a curious connection between *Bill Bailey, Won't You Please Come Home?* and *Frankie and Johnny*.[7] Thus, the earliest printing of the music of *Frankie and Johnny* refers to Bill Bailey in the subtitle, and the song was by the same person who wrote the *Bill Bailey* song. Even the above-mentioned Leighton brothers' song, with "Bill" in the title, refers to Bill Bailey in the text of the song. No explanation for this connection has been given.

The song is also said to have been known as *Franky* or *Frankie and Albert* or other variant. Some of the melody also appears as *My Baby in a Guinea-Blue Gown*, in R. Emmet Kennedy, *Mellows* (New York, N.Y., 1925), p. 166; NYPL. But no printing of the familiar music or words has been found under any of these other titles prior to those described above.

Der Freischütz-Overture—Weber

[6] Scarborough, 1925, p. 84, (Frankie and "Albert") and Sandburg, 1929, p. 78. Bruce Redfern Buckley, Bloomington, Ind., referred to in footnote 2 above, wrote the author that the first known printing of the familiar words was in the *Whizz Bang Annual of 1922*, but no copy of this publication has been located. Predecessors of the familiar words can perhaps be found as far back as 1908: Buckley, footnote 2, above, pp. 110–111, citing the Copeland MS 1908; Perrow, p. 129, citing a 1909 source; Howard W. Odum, "Folk-Poetry as Found in the Secular Songs of the Southern Negroes" in *JAF*, 1911, p. 351; the 1912 *Frankie and Johnny* sheet music edition mentioned in the text above; and W. H. Thomas, "Some Current Folk-Songs of the Negro" in *Texas Folk-Lore Society Publications*, Austin, Texas, 1912, p. 12, at TU.

[7] Albert Brouse, Glendale, Cal., has been helpful regarding this paragraph.

m. Carl Maria von Weber. The first printing of the *Overture* from *Der Freischütz* was an arrangement for piano published in 1820 by Schlesinger, Berlin, at 10 Gr. No copy with this price has been found; perhaps this edition was merely listed in *Handbuch Annual*, 1821, for the year 1820, p. 59, and never published, as it was listed again in the following year's *Handbuch*, p. 40, at 8 Gr. The latter edition is oblong and entitled *Ouverture* . . . *Der Freyschuetz* [sic], arranged for piano by the composer. Price: 8 Gr. Publisher: In der Schlesingerschen Buch- und Musikhandlung. m. on pp. 4–9. p.n. 1078. Back cover blank. Engraved. ONB, RE and JF. The 1821 *Handbuch* also lists piano arrangements of the *Overture* published by Spehr, Braunschweig; Berra, Prague; Steiner et Co., Vienna; Schott, Mainz; and Weigl, Vienna. The Schlesinger arrangement of the *Overture* for piano four hands has p.n. 1115; LLD, SLD and ULH.

An orchestral arrangement of the *Overture* was listed in the *Handbuch Annual*, 1823, for the year 1822, p. 2, published by Schlesinger, Berlin. It is not stated there whether this refers to orchestral parts or orchestral score;[1] a set of the orchestral parts with p.n. 1176 (1822–1823)[2] is at LLD. An orchestral score of the *Overture* by this publisher with a collective-title title-page and p.n. 2913 (1843)[2] is at COL.

The Schlesinger edition of the piano-vocal score of the opera is believed to be the first[3] and was listed in the *Handbuch Annual*, 1822, for the year 1821, p. 56. Probable first edition: The front cover is tan and black, the title *Der Freischütz*, and the publisher In der Schlesingerschen Buch- und Musikhandlung, Berlin. vb. Title page mentions the Dichtung is by Friedrich Kind, the p.n. is 1088 and the price 6 Rtth. 12 Gr. vb. Personen. m. on pp. 4–177. p.n. 1078. p. [178] and inside and outside of back cover blank. Oblong. Engraved. JMM and JF. In a later edition, the Personen page also includes an index. ONB. The same *Handbuch* also lists piano-vocal scores published by Schott, Mainz; Cappi, Vienna; and Weigl, Vienna.

The first printing of the orchestral score of the opera is believed to have been published 1824–1831[4] under the title *Robin des Bois, ou Les Trois Balles* . . . *imité de Der Freyschütz* by Castil-Blaze, 9 Rue du Faubourg Montmartre, près du Boulevard, Paris. Possible first edition: Title page states that the opera was presented for the first time in Paris on Dec.

---

[1] Jähns, no. 277, p. 303, indicates it is the orchestral parts.
[2] Deutsch, *Plate Numbers*, p. 21.
[3] Jähns, p. 303.
[4] Hopkinson, *Parisian*, p. 23.

7, 1824, and lists the orchestral score at 80 francs, the orchestral parts at the same price and three other arrangements. vb. Cast. vb. Thematic index. m. on pp. 2–39 and 2–302. p.n. 20. Engraved. French text only. BM and JMM.* Three lines of advertisements do not appear at the bottom of the thematic index page.

A possible first printing of the orchestral score of the opera with the original German text was about Aug., 1849,[5] under the title *Der Freischütz* by Schlesinger'sche Buch u. Musikhandlung, Berlin. Possible first edition: Front cover is gray and black, contains legal notices and shows the price as blank Thlr. Verso and next three pages blank. Portrait of Weber. Title page same as front cover except in black and white. vb. Cast and index page, dated Berlin, 1849. vb. m. on pp. 3–262. p.n. 3512. Engraved. No reference on title page to revised edition. BN, LC and JF.

An early lithographed printing of the orchestral parts of the opera by Schlesinger'sche Buch—u. Musikhandlung (Rob. Lienau), Berlin, and Carl Haslinger qdm Tobias, Vienna, with plate number S. 1176 (1822–1823)[2] for at least part of the opera, is at ROH. The Castil-Blaze orchestral score described above also refers to orchestral parts but no copy of the orchestral parts has been found.

The *Overture* to this opera was one of the first to include the principal music from the opera itself; the excerpt quoted above appears in the opera in the aria, *Leise, leise.*

The opera was completed May 13, 1820, in Dresden, the *Overture* performed in Copenhagen on Oct. 8, 1820, and the opera performed in Berlin on June 18, 1821. Weber was born in Eutin, Germany, in 1786 and died in London in 1826. Johann Friedrich Kind, a librettist and author, was born in Leipzig in 1768 and died in Dresden in 1843.[6]

Frère Jacques

Frè - re   Jac - ques, frè - re   Jac - ques, dor - mez - vous? Dor - mez - vous?

The melody of *Frère Jacques* was apparently first printed in the 1811 edition of *La Clé du Caveau, à l'usage de tous les Chansonniers français, des*

---

[5] Hofmeister *Monatsbericht,* Aug., 1849, p. 90. The year 1849 appears on the cast and index page. Deutsch, *Plate Numbers,* p. 21. Kinsky, *Opern,* p. 372. Jähns, p. 303, says 1843; Anthony van Hoboken, Ascona, Switzerland, has a note mentioning a plate number 2913, but no such printing has been yet found or mentioned elsewhere.

[6] *Grove's,* 3rd ed., vol. III, p. 22.

Amateurs, Auteurs, Acteurs du Vaudeville . . . (Paris), p. 309, no. 726 (title on index p. 17); BN and JF.

The first known printing of the words, together with the music, is in Charles Lebouc, *Recueil de Rondes avec Jeux et de Petites Chansons* (Paris, [1860]), p. 24; BN(CDC).

The Bibliothèque Nationale has this melody in a manuscript collection about 1775–1785 entitled *Recueil de Timbres de Vaudevilles*,[1] no. 300, under the title *Frère Blaise (canon)*. No printing of this canon under this title and with this melody has been found.

One writer tries, it is believed without success, to trace this song to Frescobaldi's *Fra Jacopino* in 1637.[2]

Funeral March—Chopin

m. Fréd. Chopin. The *Funeral March*, or *Marche Funèbre*, was published in May, 1840, as the slow movement of Chopin's *Sonate*, op. 35, for piano, in Paris and in Leipzig. No complete copy of the first French edition has been found. The copy deposited at the Conservatoire in May, 1840, lacks a front cover. m. on pp. 1–19. p.n. 891. Engraved. Back cover blank. The *March* is on pp. 14–16. COP(CDC). The first Troupenas edition differs from later Troupenas editions in many respects, although they all have the same plate number.[1] In the first edition, the name of the engraver, F. Benoit, does not appear at the bottom of p. 1, and there are many differences in the text of the music; for example, the lower note of the first beat of the bass in measure 5, p. 12, of the first edition is G, whereas in later editions it is E flat. It is possible that the edition deposited at the Conservatoire was never commercially issued with a front cover, as the later Troupenas editions are similar in the above respects to the Breitkopf & Härtel edition.

Probable first German edition: Publisher is Breitkopf & Härtel, Leipzig.[2] There are references on the front cover to Troupenas & Co. and

[1] Weck. C. 196.
[2] Nettl, *National Anthems*, p. 24. *Fra Jacopino* is quoted in Wilhelm Tappert, *Sang und Klang aus Alter Zeit* (Berlin, 1906), p. 81; NYPL.

[1] Later Troupenas editions are at COP, AH and JF.
[2] *AMZ*, May 20, 1840, p. 456. Whistling, *Musikalischer Monatsanzeiger*, May, 1840, p. 97; ONB. Hofmeister *Monatsbericht*, May, 1840, p. 70; UI.

Wessel & Co., and the price is 1 Thlr. 4 Gr. vb. m. engraved on pp. 3–23. In bar 68, the last note in the upper stave is a C with octave, instead of E flat.[3] p.n. 6329. Back cover blank. SB and JF.

The English edition was not published by Wessel & Co., London, until about July, 1840.[4] Probable first English edition: Front cover states title as *Grande Sonate . . . Les Agrémens* [*sic*] *au Salon. No. 39.*†

Although the *Funeral March* had been composed in 1837, it was not published until 1840 with the complete Sonata. It was published separately on Nov. 17, 1849, after Chopin died.[5] Brief biographic information regarding Chopin appears above under his *Etude.*

Funeral March of a Marionette—Gounod

m. Ch. Gounod. This composition for piano was apparently first published in London on July 13, 1872,[1] while Gounod was living in England. The copy deposited at the Bibliothèque Nationale in 1872 under the English title above was published by Goddard & Co., 4 Argyll Place, Regent Street, London W.[2] Probable first edition: Front cover has a dedication to Madame Viguier, the price is 4 s., there is a Washington agent, and the colors are lavender and black. Verso adv. *Musical..* Title page duplicates the front cover in black and white. m. on pp. 2–7. p.n. 122. p. [8] adv. *The Worker..* - *La Siesta.* Inside of back cover adv. *The Roses..* - *The Pianist's..* Outside of back cover adv. *Maid..* - *Love..* No reference to other arrangements. BN and BM (both CDC).

The earliest French edition was published for piano on Nov. 1, 1873,[3] under the title *Marche Funèbre d'une Marionnette* by H. Lemoine, 256 Rue St. Honoré and 17 Rue Pigalle, Paris, with p.n. 7523; copies of this edition

---

[3] *Chopin Works*, vol. VI, p. 128.

[4] *MW*, July 9, 1840, p. 30. The dates mentioned above are in accordance with Brown, p. 123.

[5] Brown, pp. 111 and 123.

---

[1] The date of publication stated in the entry at Stationers' Hall on Aug. 14, 1872.

[2] The copy at the Bibliothèque Nationale states that it was deposited in accordance with the "Convention Franco-Anglaise." The copy at the British Museum was deposited Jan. 31, 1873.

[3] Date was furnished by the publisher. Entered for Dépôt Légal Nov. 8, 1873; Archives. *BF*, Nov. 22, 1873, p. 623. This French edition also lists an arrangement for piano four hands.

were deposited at the Bibliothèque Nationale and Conservatoire, Paris, in 1873. The publisher states that an attractive edition, with text and many drawings, and without a p.n., was published by it in 1873, but it was deposited only in 1882; at BN and COP (both CDC), SC and JF.

The orchestral score was published late in 1879[4] by H. Lemoine, 17 Rue Pigalle, Paris. First edition: Apparently no front cover or title page. p. [1] blank. m. on pp. 2–19. p. [20] blank. p.n. 8148. Engraved. BN(CDC) and JF. Brief biographic information regarding Gounod appears above under his *Ave Maria*.

Funiculì—Funiculà

Jam - mo   jam - mo   ncop - pa, jam - mo,   jà

m. L. Denza. w. G. Turco. The copy deposited on Nov. 12, 1880, at the British Museum is probably the same as that deposited Oct. 2, 1880,[1] with the Prefect of Milan by Ricordi, Milan, and is likely to be the first edition. Front cover is **olive-green,** black and white; on the **left** is a drawing of a funicular to volcanic Mt. Vesuvius; the title is written in a **semicircle;** there are **two** keys (this copy being no. 1 in F major); the year 1880 is mentioned and the price is Fr. 5 No other translations or arrangements. The publisher is Ricordi, Milan and three other cities, and there are references to Moscow, London and Paris offices. vb. Poem on p. 1. m. on pp. 2–14, with the p.n. 47126. Verso of back cover blank. The back cover has the Ars et Labor symbol. Later editions have a completely different front cover.

This song was composed in 1880 to celebrate the funicular which was built that year to the summit of Mt. Vesuvius. It was later mistaken as a folk song by Rimsky-Korsakov and Richard Strauss. Luigi Denza was born at Castellammare di Stabia in 1846, held important musical positions in London commencing 1876 and died there in 1922.[2] No biographic information is available regarding G. Turco.

---

[4] The copyright copy was deposited in 1879. *BMF*, Jan.–Mar., 1880, p. 6.

[1] Copyright records; UDP. The Ricordi *Libroni* state the engraving commenced Aug. 29, 1880.

[2] Thompson, pp. 440 and 580.

Für Elise—Beethoven

m. Ludwig van Beethoven. This composition for piano was first published in 1867 in a book entitled *Neue Briefe Beethovens. Nebst einigen ungedruckten Gelegenheitscompositionen . . .* by Ludwig Nohl, published by J. G. Cotta'schen Buchhandlung (Stuttgart, 1867). The music of *Für Elise* is on pp. 28–33. ONB and JF.

This work was composed on April 27, 1810, as a leaf in an album.[1] Nohl, who discovered the manuscript, gave the title *Für Elise;* however, he most likely misread Beethoven's writing of the name "Therese." Brief biographic information regarding Beethoven appears above under *Concerto for Piano no. 5.*

Gaudeamus Igitur

Gau - de - a - mus   i - gi - tur,   ju - ve - nes   dum   su - mus

Gaudeamus Igitur is regarded as the oldest student song and as the embodiment of the free and easy student life. Its alleged stemming from the thirteenth century is apparently based solely on a Latin manuscript dated 1287 at the Bibliothèque Nationale, Paris,[1] which Erk-Böhme[2] and evidently others have not looked at. The words of two of the verses of the poem commencing "Scribere proposui" are nearly identical to the words of two of the later verses in *Gaudeamus Igitur*, but (a) the words "Gaudeamus Igitur" nowhere appear; (b) the words of the all-important first *Gaudeamus Igitur* verse are absent; and (c) most important, there is music in the manuscript, but it bears no resemblance whatsoever to the well-known melody.

---

[1] Kinsky-Halm, WoO 59, p. 505.

[1] Notre-Dame 273 bis, feuillet 120, recto; coté Français 25408. All the verses are reprinted in Edélstand du Méril, *Poésies Populaires Latines du Moyen Age* (Paris, 1847), p. 125; NYPL. The music is not reproduced. The same verses, and still other music, are in *Piae Cantiones Ecclesiasticae et Scholasticae* (Greisswald, 1582), p. 60; UL. The development of the words is traced in Dr. A. Rutgers van der Loeff, *Drie Studentenliederen* (Leiden, 1953), p. 43; NYPL.

[2] Erk-Böhme so state at vol. III, p. 490.

A German translation of all the verses was made about 1717 by Johann Christian Günther commencing "Brüder, lasst uns lustig sein,"[3] and this German text, without music, was printed in *Sammlung von Johann Christian Günthers* (Frankfurt and Leipzig, 1730) at p. 298 (at BM).

Apart from the 1267 Latin manuscript of the second and third verses mentioned above, the oldest known version of the Latin words is in a handwritten student songbook between 1723 and 1750 now at the Westdeutsche Bibliothek, Marburg;[4] it differs considerably from the present version. The first known appearance of the modern version of the Latin words is in *Studentenlieder* by C. W. K. [indleben], published in Halle in 1781, p. 52; a German translation is also given. Kindleben states at p. 56 that he made important changes in the Latin text. No copy of this work has been located,[5] but an 1894 facsimile reprint is at DS and HU.

By 1782 the melody was so well known that, in August Niemann's *Akademisches Liederbuch* (Dessau and Leipzig), at YU, three poems are designated to be sung to it (under the German title). The first known[6] printing of the present melody is in *Lieder für Freunde der Geselligen Freude*, published in Leipzig in 1788, at p. 24; BSM. Here, the music accompanies the German translation mentioned above.

Perhaps the first known appearance of the Latin words and the melody together was in Ignaz Walter's operatic setting of *Doktor Faust*, performed in 1797 in Bremen; in this opera, the students in Auerbach's cellar sing *Gaudeamus Igitur*. No printing of the music of this opera has been found. An undated contemporary libretto published by Friedrich Meiers Erben, Bremen, is at LC; the words of *Gaudeamus Igitur*, mostly indicated as "Gaudeamus etc.," are at p. 21. The melody is particularly well known because of its inclusion in Brahms, *Akademische Fest-Ouverture* for orchestra published in 1881.

The Girl I Left Behind Me

I'm___ lone-some since I crossed the hills, and o'er the moor___ that's___ sedg - y

---

[3] Erk-Böhme, vol. III, pp. 488–492. Friedlaender, vol. II, p. 6.

[4] Handschrift Ms. germ 4° 722, p. 470 (formerly Meusebach Samml. 8028 at DS).

[5] A copy had been at DS; Erman, no. 15642. It is no longer there and it is not at WDBM.

[6] See, also, a puzzling reference to a Greek translation of the song, dated 1788, in Erman, no. 16003. No copy is located, and there is no indication whether music was included.

The earliest known version of the melody was printed about 1810 in Hime's *Pocket Book for the German Flute or Violin* (Dublin, n.d.), vol. III, p. 67, under the title *The Girl I Left Behind Me*; NLI. Manuscripts containing the melody, dating back to about 1770, mentioned in Chappell, p. 708, have not been located.

The earliest known printing of the words is in a booklet "printed in the Year 1808" entitled *The Girl I Left Behind Me, with the Answer. To which is added Ellen O'Moore, Erin Go Bragh, The Galley Slave.* Neither the name nor the city of the printer is stated; the booklet may have been printed in Ireland. The words of *The Girl I Left Behind Me* are on p. 2, without music. Octavo. Copy offered by a New York City bookseller— present whereabouts unknown; photocopy at JF. The next known printing of the words is in *Rhymes of Northern Bards*, edited by John Bell, Jr. (Newcastle-upon-Tyne, 1812), p. 84, without music, under the title *Blyth Camps, or, the Girl I Left Behind Me*; BPL and JF.

Thomas Moore considerably revised the melody to its present version in the 7th Number of his *A Selection of Irish Melodies*, at p. 7, published Oct. 1, 1818,[1] when he ventured a new and unsuccessful text, *As Slow Our Ship*, to the melody. In what is probably the first printing of the 7th Number, there is an 1815 watermark, and the publisher is J. Power, 34 Strand, London, with no reference to Dublin; HU and JF.[2]

A new version of the words by Samuel Lover was deposited Jan. 1, 1855, at BM by Duff & Hodgson, 65 Oxford Strt., London. Probable first edition: Front cover is black and white, mentions that it is sung by E. L. Hime, and the price is 2/. p. [2] blank. m. on pp. 1–5 (really 3–7). p.n. 1835. Engraved. Back cover blank. BM(CDC). Lover was born in Dublin in 1797, lived in London for considerable periods and died in Dublin in 1868.[3]

There is considerable controversy as to whether the melody of this

---

[1] Publication date appears on the title page. One copy was entered at Stationers' Hall on Oct. 14, 1818.

[2] Muir, on the 12th unnumbered page, says the first printing of the 7th Number should have the imprint of both J. Power (London) and W. Power (Dublin), but on the next page says that it should have the imprint of the former only. The copy entered at Stationers' Hall on Oct. 14, 1818, had as the publisher "J. Power, Strand, London." The edition published by W. Power, Dublin, also with an 1815 watermark, is at NLI.

[3] *Dict. Nat. Biog.*, vol. 12, p. 176.

song was originally English or Irish.[4] The melody is also said to have been known as *Brighton Camp;* however, no earlier printing of it has been found under this title, and the *Brighton Camp Quick March,* entered in Stationers' Hall on Nov. 12, 1792, has a completely different melody; BM.

Git Along Little Dogies (Whoopee Ti Yi Yo)

Whoop-ee, ti-yi-yo, git a-long, lit-tle do-gies, it's your mis-for-tune, and none of my own

On Feb. 21, 1893, at Brownwood, Texas, Owen Wister recorded in his journal that he heard a "unique song . . . Only a cowboy could have produced such an effusion."[1] The words of the song were written in his journal, which was later published as *Owen Wister Out West; His Journals and Letters,* edited by Fanny Kemble Wister (Chicago, 1958), p. 153; NYPL. The words also appeared in Andy Adams, *The Log of a Cowboy* (Boston and New York, 1903), p. 313, and in Sharlot M. Hall, "Old Range Days and New in Arizona" in *Out West,* Los Angeles, March, 1908, p. [181], where the song is described as an "Old trail-song of the 'Eighties' "; both at NYPL.

The music (and words) were included in John A. Lomax, *Cowboy Songs* (New York, N.Y., 1910), p. 89; LC, NYPL and JF. Wister's recording of the music is included in John A. Lomax and Alan Lomax, *American Ballads and Folk Songs* (New York, N.Y., 1934), p. 386; NYPL. Two writers claim, without presenting any earlier publication, that this cowboy song was modeled on an old Irish ballad *The Old Man's Lament.*[2]

A "dogie" is a cowboy's term for a motherless calf that is poor and undersized.

---

[4] Chappell, p. 708. O'Neill, *Irish Folk,* p. 177. O'Neill, *Waifs,* p. 44, gives *The Spalpeen Fanach* as the Irish title of the song.

[1] The author is deeply indebted to John I. White, Westfield, N.J., and Joseph C. Hickerson, Library of Congress, for information regarding this title.

[2] Alan Lomax, *The Folksongs of North America* (New York, N.Y., 1960), p. 357, and Oscar Brand, *The Ballad Mongers* (New York, N.Y., 1962), p. 44, both at NYPL.

Give My Regards to Broadway

Give my   re - gards   to   Broad   -   way

mw. Geo. M. Cohan. Copyrighted Oct. 20, 1904,[1] by F. A. Mills, 48 West 29th St., New York, N.Y. First edition: Front cover has a drawing of a man speaking on a telephone and is green, gray and white. s. *Little Johnny Jones.* m. on pp. [3]–[6]. pp. [2], [7] and back cover blank. LC(CDC) and JF. The show opened in New York City on Nov. 7, 1904; after it lasted only two months, Cohan took it on the road and brought it back to New York in 1905 when it became a hit.

Cohan was a versatile composer, lyricist, actor, playwright and producer. He was born in Providence in 1878 and died in New York City in 1942.[2]

The Gladiators' Entry

m. Julius Fučik. The composition appears to have been originally published in orchestral parts for large orchestra about July, 1900,[1] under the title *Einzug der Gladiatoren,* op. 68, by Joh. Hoffmann's Wwe., Prague, at K 2.50 - Mk 2.50; no copy of this edition has been located. The piano arrangement, with p.n. 4617, was published about Jan., 1901,[1] but early copies at SB and JF were probably published after Nov., 1901 as they refer to the arrangement for zither.

This march is used, among other purposes, in circuses and to introduce wrestling matches around the world. Fučik was born in Prague in 1872 and died in Berlin in 1916. He was a pupil of Dvořák, and became Bandmaster of the Austrian 86th and 92nd Regiments.[2]

---

[1] Copyright records; LC.

[2] *ASCAP*, p. 90.

[1] The orchestral parts are listed in Hofmeister *Monatsbericht,* July, 1900, p. 327; the piano arrangement in Jan., 1901, p. 3; and the zither arrangement in Nov., 1901, p. 612.

[2] Thompson, p. 634.

Glow-Worm

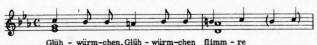

Glüh - würm-chen, Glüh - würm-chen flimm - re

m. Paul Lincke. w. Bolten-Bäckers. A copy of *Glühwürmchen Idyll*, or *Glow-Worm*, arranged for piano, was deposited at LC on April 30, 1902,[1] by Apollo-Verlag, Berlin. Probable first edition of this arrangement: Front cover is green and tan, the show *Lysistrata* is mentioned, and there are references to vocal and piano arrangements. Verso adv. *Paul..* in black and tan. Title page in green and white lists 15 titles from the show and the libretto, the price of this piece being 1.50 M. m. on pp. 2–7. p.n. 308. p. [8] adv. *Operetten..* Back cover missing. There is no reference to Otto Linde-mann as the arranger. LC(CDC).

The piano-vocal arrangement of *Glühwürmchen* was deposited on May 3, 1902,[1] at LC. A possible first edition, lacking covers, but with the same title page described above, has p.n. 313; p. [2] blank. m. on pp. 3–7. p. [8] adv. *Salon-Musik..* no. 16. A show title page with no arrangements of the song; JF. The covers of the copyright deposit copy, but not the inside pages, are at LC: The front cover, and the verso, are the same as those of the piano arrangement, described above. The inside back cover adv. *Kon-zert..* The outside back cover adv. *Humoristische..* no. 10.

The piano-vocal score of *Lysistrata* deposited on July 9, 1902,[1] at LC is probably a first edition. Front cover is purple and orange and mentions arrangements with and without words. vb. Title page is similar to the front cover but in black and white, and lists 15 titles and the libretto, the price of the piano-vocal score being 10 M, and mentions Bolten-Bäckers. vb. Dedica-tion to Dr. Leo Leipziger. vb. Cast. vb. Index. m. on pp. 2–91. p.ns. 320. 325. The words and music of *Glühwürmchen* are at p. 62. p. [92] adv. *Frau.. - Lysistrata.* Back cover missing. LC(CDC).

Lysistrata was performed in Berlin on March 31, 1902. Lincke, a com-poser of operettas and a music publisher (Apollo-Verlag), was born in Berlin in 1866 and died in Hahnenkee, Germany, in 1946.[2] Heinz Bolten-Bäckers was born in 1871 in Chemnitz, Germany, became a theater and movie director and died in 1938, probably in Berlin.[3]

[1] Copyright records; LC.

[2] Edmund Nick, *Paul Lincke* (Hamburg, 1953); NYPL.

[3] *Id.*, p. 30. Friedrich Pruss von Zglinicki, *Der Weg des Films* (Berlin, 1956), p. 347; NYPL.

Go Down, Moses

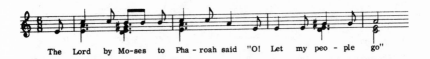

The Lord by Mo-ses to Pha-roah said "O! Let my peo-ple go"

This spiritual was referred to in a letter from the Rev. Mr. Lockwood to the American Missionary Association dated Sept. 4, 1861, the letter being printed, at least in part, in the *National Anti-Slavery Standard* (New York City), Oct. 12, 1861, third unnumbered page, third column.[1] The letter tells of a prayer meeting on Sept. 4, 1861, at Fortress Monroe where Negroes were singing this melody, with the accent on the last syllable. Some words are included, but no music. *ULS*, p. 1913.

The music and words of the spiritual were clearly foreshadowed in the song copyrighted Dec. 5, 1861,[2] under the title *The Song of the "Contra-bands"—O! Let My People Go*. Possible first edition: Front cover states that the words and music were obtained through the Rev. L. C. Lockwood, Chaplain of the "Contrabands" at Fortress Monroe, has four drawings of patriotic shields, the price is 2½, the publisher is Horace Waters, 481 Broadway, New York, N.Y., and there is a Boston copublisher. m. on pp. 2–5, engraved. Back cover adv. *New Music.*. JF. The sheet music states "This Song has been sung for about nine years by the Slaves of Virginia." The present version of the song is in *Jubilee Songs*, as sung by the Jubilee Singers of Fisk University (Nashville, Tenn.), copyrighted March 11, 1872,[2] and published in New York, N.Y., at p. 22. There is no mention of "Complete" or "New Edition." LC(CDC), NYPL and JF.

Go Down, Moses is the first still well-known Negro spiritual to have appeared in print.[3] A "Contraband" was a Negro slave who escaped to the Union lines during the Civil War. Fortress Monroe, also known as Fort Monroe, is at Old Point Comfort, Va.; for two years after the close of the Civil War, Jefferson Davis was imprisoned there.

[1] Dena J. Epstein, Chicago, informed the author of this letter.

[2] Copyright records; LC.

[3] "One writer claims that *Go Down, Moses* resembles an old Jewish chant, *Cain and Abel*"; Laurence B. Ellert, *Music—Art, Music and Literature Keep Memory Alive* (Cincinnati, 1940), p. 19, at NYPL. The writer has not been identified, and no chant of that name has been found.

God Bless America

God   bless   A - mer - i - ca

mw. Irving Berlin. Published Feb. 20, 1939,[1] by Irving Berlin, Inc., 799 Seventh Ave., New York, N.Y. First edition: Front cover states: "First Performance by Kate Smith Armistice Day, 1938," mentions three keys at the top, Medium in F being the copyrighted key, and is pink, purple and white. p. [2] has poem. m. on pp. 3–5. The top of p. 3 repeats the references to Kate Smith and the key. Back cover mentions arrangements of the song for Voice and Piano in 3 keys, Concert Orchestra, Women's Voices, Group Singing, Mixed Voices, Men's Voices, Band, Children's edition—1st and 2nd Grades, followed by a three-line imprint. LC(CDC) and JF (two copies inscribed, one by Irving Berlin and the other by Kate Smith).

Although the chorus of the song had been written in 1918,[2] it was not copyrighted or published until an unpublished copy was deposited on Oct. 27, 1938.[1]

The phrase "God Bless America" has been used frequently as the title of a song, the earliest known being before 1800. A broadside of the words (only) of a song *General Washington's Birth-Day* "to be sung to the tune of *God Bless America*" was printed before his death in 1799. No printing of the music or words of this *God Bless America* has been found, nor has the music of *General Washington's Birth-Day*; but the meter of the words of *General Washington's Birth-Day* exactly fits the music of *God Save the King*, as do the opening words "God Bless America." The author has seen this broadside (n.p., n.d.), and it is described in Charles Hamilton's *Auction Catalogue*, New York, N.Y., Dec. 12, 1968, no. 284 (extract from *Catalogue* at JF), but the present owner of the broadside is not known. Another song entitled *God Bless America*, with music and words by Robert M. Bird, was copyrighted May 17, 1834,[1] by Fiot, Philadelphia; LC(CDC). In 1917, the year before Berlin wrote his song, there were two songs copyrighted under this title,[1] one by E. Manning and the other with music by Reginald De Koven (the latter at UTS).

Manuscripts of the words of Berlin's song are at LC and JF.† Brief biographic information regarding Berlin appears above under *Alexander's Ragtime Band*.

---

[1] Copyright records; LC.

[2] *The New York World-Telegram and Sun*, Magazine Section, Nov. 6, 1954, p. 10; copy at that newspaper. The introduction—rarely heard—was written for Kate Smith's broadcast; letter from the composer, at JF.

God Rest You Merry, Gentlemen

God   rest you   mer - ry   gen - tle - men let   noth - ing you dis - may

The words of this carol are first to be found in the *Roxburghe Collection,* III, 452, about 1770; BM.[1] The first printing of the present melody is said to have been in a broadside printed by J. & C. Evans, Long-lane, London, about 1796, but no copy of this broadside has been found.

The earliest known printing of the present melody, and words, is in a satirical pamphlet, *The Man in the Moon,* by William Hone (London, 1820), without page numbers. No reference on title page to a later edition. BM—09525 1. 33 (7).

The title has two separate meanings, depending upon where there is a pause or comma. The word "rest" means "keep." One thought is, "God rest you, merry gentlemen"; the other, perhaps a solecism, is, "God rest you merry, gentlemen"! †

God Save the King

God   save   our   Lord   the King,   long live our   no - ble King
My   coun - try   'tis   of thee, sweet land of   lib - er - ty

One of the most fascinating aspects of *God Save the King* is the difference between the first known two printings and the next group of printings. In the first printings in 1744, the opening words are "God save our Lord the King." Then, the Young Pretender, Bonnie Prince Charlie, landed in Scotland in mid-July, 1745, and the word "King" became ambiguous. In the next group of printings, in late 1745, the opening words are "God save great George our King"—and the word "George" is in larger type for emphasis.

Chappell, p. 704, stated that the anthem was first printed in *Harmonia*

---

[1] See, generally, *JFSS,* 1915, p. 212; Routley, p. 89; *OBC,* p. 25; Chappell, p. 752; and Sharp, *English Folk-Carols,* p. 63.

The words of the Roxburghe Ballad are reproduced in *The Roxburghe Ballads,* ed. by J. Woodfall Ebsworth, vol. VII (Hertford, 1893), p. 775; BM. The ballad is *To Its Own Tune of, Tidings of Comfort and Joy* (no music is included, however). The ballad is one of "Four Choice Carols for Christmas Holidays," this being for Christmas Day.

A since-discarded melody was once sung to these words. This old melody is in William Sandys, *Christmas Carols Ancient and Modern* (London, 1833), in the un-numbered musical appendix; BM and JF.

Anglicana; inasmuch as no copy of such work had been found containing the anthem, it had generally been agreed that Chappell erred. However, a unique copy of *Harmonia Anglicana* has recently been found at the Library of Congress, and there is no question but that this volume precedes the volume retitled *Thesaurus Musicus,* previously believed to contain the first printing of the anthem.[1] *Harmonia Anglicana,* "A Collection of . . . Songs, Several of them never before Printed" (London), was apparently published in one volume, the anthem appearing on p. 22 in two stanzas only. A publication date between April 20 and Nov. 16, 1744, is probable.[2] **(See Plate II.)**

The collection was then retitled *Thesaurus Musicus,* and expanded into two volumes, the first printing under this title containing only the two stanzas of the anthem; *BUC,* p. 1004, HL and JF. The anthem was publicly performed and sung at the Drury Lane Theatre on Sept. 28, 1745, as a patriotic response to the threat from the Young Pretender. Thereafter, there were a number of editions, all with the changed opening words, three or more verses and of uncertain relative priority. Among these are: A reprint of *Thesaurus Musicus*[3] with identical title page, at *BUC,* p. 1004, NYPL, NC and JF; in *The Gentleman's Magazine,* London, Oct., 1745, p. 552 (in the Contents on p. [506], the song is described as "a new song" and the title is the original opening phrase), *ULS,* p. 1097, and JF; a single sheet[4] without imprint with three stanzas, this being the first known separate printing of the anthem, at *BUC,* p. 1004, and JF; and another single sheet without imprint with four stanzas,[5] at *BUC,* p. 1004.

The history of *God Save the King* has been studied by many authorities and an entire book was written recently on the anthem by Percy A.

---

[1] Donald W. Krummel, "God Save the King," in *MT,* March, 1962, p. 159. Precedence is shown by: (a) the absence of signs of alteration on the title page of *Harmonia Anglicana,* while there are such signs in *Thesaurus Musicus;* (b) the A B C principle, described above at page 9, *Thesaurus Musicus* appearing in two editions; and (c) other changes in the text—for example, the progressive addition of fingering in the bass of the last bar on p. 70 in (i) *Harmonia Anglicana,* (ii) the first printing of *Thesaurus Musicus,* and (iii) the second printing of *Thesaurus Musicus.*

[2] These are the dates suggested by Percy A. Scholes, *God Save the Queen!* (London, 1954), p. 13, at NYPL, for the first printing of *Thesaurus Musicus,* and the dates also seem valid for *Harmonia Anglicana.* The earlier date of April 20, 1744, derives from a composition listed on the title page of *Thesaurus Musicus,* which is also on the title page of *Harmonia Anglicana.* Neither *Harmonia Anglicana* nor *Thesaurus Musicus* was entered at Stationers' Hall.

[3] Probably published in Dec., 1745; Scholes, footnote 2, above, p. 13.

[4] Hogarth's picture *The March to Finchley* (1745) shows a street hawker selling *God Save the King* as a single sheet; BM.

[5] As the fourth verse relates to Marshal Wade's leaving for Scotland, which occurred on Oct. 6, 1745, this edition was published sometime after that date.

Scholes.[6] The phrase "God Save the King" is to be found many times in the Old Testament[7] (the first printing of which is slightly beyond the scope of this work!). It has been conjectured that the anthem was originally in Latin.[8] Perhaps the first printing of the English words only of the anthem appear etched on a Jacobite drinking glass dated perhaps as early as 1725. The glass is illustrated in Scholes's book,[9] and is now at the Philadelphia Museum of Art; while the glass has been dated at about 1725, it is impossible to determine when the words were etched.

The music, with its Gaillard style, has some possible antecedents, including one by John Bull, but the similarity with any of them is far from complete. Nor is there convincing proof as to the authorship of either the original music, the original words, the adaptation of either into its present form, or the combining of the music and words, although there have been many claimants. It seems likely that the song was originally an obscure and unpopular ballad—and someone made an important transformation of this ballad into an anthem no later than 1744.

The music was printed in the American colonies in 1761 in James Lyon, *Urania* (Philadelphia), p. 190, as *Whitefield's* hymn (copies at LC, NYPL, PHS and JF), and soon used for various American patriotic verses.

The words of *America*, by Samuel Francis Smith, were written for, performed at, and published in a broadside, without music, under the title *Celebration of American Independence* by the Boston Sabbath School Union, at Park Street Church [Boston], July 4, 1831.[10] BR, HU and AAS. There were originally five stanzas. The first printing of the words (five stanzas) with the music was on Nov. 5, 1832,[11] under the title *America* in Lowell Mason, *The Choir* (Boston, 1832), p. 273.† The first sheet music edition was published sometime later, with four stanzas, by C. Bradlee, Boston, under the title *My Country! 'Tis of Thee* (at LC, NYPL, LL, SS and JF), and other subsequent printings were also confined to four verses. Smith, an American clergyman and hymn writer was born in Boston in 1808 and died there in 1895.[12] Authors in many other countries have also written words to this melody.

---

[6] See footnote 2, above. The book was unfortunately written before the discovery of *Harmonia Anglicana*. See also, Frank Kidson, *MT*, Dec., 1916, p. 537; and Percy H. Muir in a heated exchange of views with Mr. Scholes in *The Music Review*, Cambridge, Feb., 1943, p. 63; May, 1943, p. 141; and Aug., 1943, p. [210]. *ULS*, p. 1840.

[7] See e.g., I Samuel iv. 24.

[8] Scholes, footnote 2, above, chap. IX.

[9] Opposite p 57.

[10] Illustrated in Charles E. Goodspeed, *A Yankee Bookseller* (Boston, 1937), opposite p. 292; NYPL.

[11] Copyright records; LC. See, generally, Sonneck, *Report*, p. 73. Mason was the organist at the Park St. Church.

[12] *Dict. Am. Biog.*, vol. XVII, p. 342.

Gold and Silver Waltz

m. Franz Lehár. This waltz was published about Dec., 1903,[1] for piano by
Julius Chmel, 86 Mariahilferstrasse, Vienna VII, and Leipzig. Probable first
edition: Front cover has a dedication to Princess Pauline Metternich-Sándor,
the title is *Gold und Silber Walzer (L'Or et l'Argent)*, the melody is printed
on the front cover, two arrangements are listed, orchestral parts at 4 Mk
and piano at 2 Mk, and there is reference to an agent in Riga. Front cover
is dark green and white. p. [2] blank. m. on pp. 3–9. p.n. 771. Back cover
adv. *Das Gewisse.. - Gold..* Copy at Bosworth & Co., Cologne, the successor
publisher.

A Chmel printing of the orchestral parts, with p.n. 772 on some of the
parts, a lithographing of a manuscript, is at SB (Aus dem Archiv Franz
Lehárs) and at Bosworth & Co., Cologne.[2] (In a variant edition, probably
later, the front cover refers prominently to an "International copyright";
EW.)

The *Gold and Silver Waltz* was composed for an elaborate ball given
by Princess Metternich on Jan. 27, 1902.[3] Lehár was born in Komorn,
Hungary, in 1870, the son of a Viennese bandmaster, and died in Bad Ischl,
Austria, in 1948.

Goldberg Variations—Bach

m. Johann Sebastian Bach. The most famous of the less than 20 works by
Bach published during his lifetime, the *Clavier Ubung bestehend in einer*

---

[1] Hofmeister *Monatsbericht*, Dec., 1903, p. 660.

[2] The orchestral parts are not listed in Hofmeister *Annual*, 1899–1904.

[3] Details regarding the "Redoute" are in the *Österreichische Volkszeitung*, Vienna,
Jan. 28, 1902, p. 8; ONB. Apparently, von Peteani is in error in suggesting that the ball
was during the winter of 1899; Maria von Peteani, *Franz Lehár* (Vienna, 1950), p. 53,
at NYPL.

Aria mit verschiedenen Veraenderungen vors Clavicimbal mit 2 Manualen
was published in 1742 by Balthasar Schmid, Nuremberg. First edition:
Title page states, in translation, that this "Keyboard Practice consisting of
an Aria with 30 variations for the harpsichord with two manuals [was]
prepared for the enjoyment of music-lovers," lists Bach's musical titles
and has plate number 16. m. on pp. 1–32. Engraved. Owners shown in
Georg Kinsky, *Die Originalausgaben der Werke Johann Sebastian Bach*
(Vienna et al., 1937), p. 124 (Alfred Cortot's copy now belonging to JF);
NYPL. *Hoboken Bach*, no. 112.†

Golliwogg's Cake Walk-Children's Corner—Debussy

m. Claude Debussy. Published for piano about July, 1908,[1] in *Children's
Corner* suite, or *Coin des Enfants*, by A. Durand & Fils, 4 Place de la
Madeleine, Paris. First edition: Front cover has a drawing of an elephant
holding the string of a balloon or golliwogg, is gray, white, green, brown
and red, says "Juillet 1908" and has a stamped autograph of the composer.
vb. The title page lists the entire suite at 5 fr. and the six pieces separately.
vb. m. on pp. 1–28, engraved,[2] *Golliwogg's Cake Walk* on pp. 24–28. p.n.
7188(I-VI). The printer is Chaimbaud et Cie. There is a dedication to the
composer's daughter, Claude-Emma—"Chouchou." pp. [29] and [30] and
inside and outside of back cover blank. CDC at BN*, COP and LC*. The
work was composed in 1906–July, 1908, and performed in Paris on Dec.
18, 1908. Brief biographic information regarding Debussy appears above
under *Clair de Lune.*

La Golondrina

A - don - de i - rá____   ve - loz   y   fa - ti - ga   -   da

[1] This month appears on the front cover. Listed in *BMF*, July–Sept., 1908, pp. 4
and 15. Copies were deposited for copyright on Sept. 30, 1908, at the Archives, Paris,
and the Library of Congress. Lesure, p. 118.

[2] It is probable that the copies on sale were not engraved.

m. Narciso Serradell. The earliest known printing of this Mexican song is in the form of a sheet of music "Presented with the compliments of the Mexican National Railway" in Sept. 1883. The front cover has colored drawings of the Mexican and American flags, mentions the above date and states that it was copyrighted that month[1] by L. W. Stevenson and printed by Poole Bros., Chicago. The composer's name is nowhere mentioned. m. on pp. [2]–3, the words in English and Spanish. The back cover has a map of the Mexican National and Texas Mexican Railways and Connections. JF.

Serradell was born in Alvarado, Vera Cruz, Mexico, in 1843. The song was composed in 1862, in a competition with friends, when the composer was nineteen years old. The words were originally French, having been translated into Spanish by Francisco Martínez de la Rosa. The date of first publication has not been established, the composer after 1862 spending time in prison for revolutionary activity and in France, before returning to Mexico as a teacher. Serradell died in 1910, presumably in Mexico.[2]

Good King Wenceslas

Good King Wen - ces - las looked out   on   the feast of   Ste - phen

m. Unknown. w. The Rev. J. M. Neale. The music was first printed in *Piae Cantiones Ecclesiasticae et Scholasticae,* a Collection of Church and School Song, chiefly Ancient Swedish, published at Greisswald, near Rostock, Germany, in 1582, by Theodoric Petri of Nyland, Finland (then part of Sweden). The music appears on p. 94 as a Spring Song with a Latin text commencing "Tempus adest floridum" ("Spring has unwrapped her flowers"). UL.

In 1853 the Rev. Neale received a copy of this book from the English Minister in Stockholm, G. J. R. Gordon, and wrote the words of *Good King Wenceslas* specifically to this music. The new song was published in *Carols for Christmas-Tide* by J. Alfred Novello, London & New York, with a

---

[1] Copyrighted July 6, 1883, according to copyright records at LC, L. W. Stevenson being from Laredo, Texas; the words (presumably the English translation) are ascribed to the Rev. Thos. M. Westrup. LC has a reissue of this edition, dated Jan., 1885.

[2] Manuel M. Ponce, *Nuevos Escritos Musicales* (Mexico City, 1948), p. [97]; NYPL. Grial, p. 273.

Preface dated SS. Simon & Jude, 1853. The dedication is to The Lord Bishop
of Oxford, and the Rev. T. Helmore did the musical settings and harmonies.
This edition contained the music for piano and vocal harmony, and a copy
was deposited at BM on Jan. 10, 1854, with the price of 4s. 6d. The Preface
mentions "Piae Cantiones" and says that *Tempus adest floridum* is of the
thirteenth century and that the music is assumed to be of the same date as
the earlier words. *Good King Wenceslas* is on pp. 28–29. Copy also at NC.
The Preface also mentions that a cheap edition wtihout harmonies (i.e.,
words and melody line only) was being published simultaneously; copies
(at 0/6) are at HU and NYPL. A still cheaper edition (at three halfpence),
with words only, was deposited at BM on May 2, 1855.

Wenceslas was a legendary King of Bohemia in the tenth century,
famous for his generosity.[1] John Mason Neale was born in London in 1818,
was ordained, and died in 1866 in East Grinstead, Sussex.[2]

Goodnight Ladies

Good - night   la - dies___   good - night   la - dies

Both the melody and words of the first part of this song were clearly
indicated in 1847 in *Farewell Ladies*, written, composed and sung by E. P.
Christy, and copyrighted Nov. 19, 1847,[1] by Jaques and Brother, 385 Broadway, New York, N.Y. Probable first edition: Front cover is a collective title
cover in blue, black and white, with drawings of Christy, six minstrels,
dancers and children, and lists 12 titles of which this is the third ("Farewell" being misspelt "Farwell"); the price is 37 Cts or 50 Colored. p. [2]
and back cover blank. m. on pp. 2–4 (really 3–5). JF.

The first known printing of the complete song as we now know it was
on May 16, 1867,[1] in *Carmina Yalensia*, compiled and arranged by Ferd.

---

[1] *OBC*, p. 136. Anne G. Gilchrist claims, it is submitted unconvincingly, that *Good
King Wenceslas* is derived from the Dutch *Het Patertje* (*The Little Friar*) in "A Note
on the Dutch 'Patertje' and 'Good King Wenceslas' " in *Journal of the English Folk
Dance and Song Society*, London, Dec., 1936, p. 72; NYPL.

[2] *Dict. Nat. Biog.*, vol. XIV, p. 143.

[1] Copyright records; LC. The copyright copy deposited Nov. 19, 1847, at LC has a
blank front cover and is obviously a proof. However, eight days before, another song
with a collective title front cover was deposited by the publisher; the front cover was
tan, black and white, 12 titles were listed and *Farewell Ladies* was no. 3.

V. D. Garretson, and published by Taintor Brothers & Co., 229 Broadway, New York, N.Y. The song appears on p. 47 under the title, *Good Night.* LC(CDC) and JF.

The second part of the song, beginning with the words "Merrily We Roll Along," has the same melody as *Mary Had a Little Lamb,* which see.

The melody of the first part of the song, as embellished, is the melody of *Someone's in the Kitchen with Dinah,* which see.

Goodnight Sweetheart

Good - night   sweet-heart,   till   we   meet   to - mor - row

mw. Ray Noble, Jimmy Campbell and Reg Connelly. Published March 23, 1931,[1] by Campbell, Connelly & Co., Ltd., 10–11 Denmark Street, London, W.C.2. The copy deposited on March 18, 1931, at LC is an English professional edition with p.n. CCS 84 and the music on pp. 1–3. A possible first regular edition, consistent with the foregoing, has a front cover in blue, black and white, a drawing of a moon and stars and of a couple in embraces, a photograph of Philip Ridgeway and the price 1/. The verso of the front cover adv. *We..* and the back cover adv. *Good..* JF. The advertised songs were published on or before March 12, 1931.[1] A professional copy of the American version by Rudy Vallee was published[1] and received by BM on Oct. 3, 1931.

Noble, a bandleader and composer, was born in 1903 in Brighton.[2] Campbell, a songwriter, was born in 1903 at Newcastle-on-Tyne and died in 1967 in London.[3] Connelly, a music publisher and songwriter, was born in 1898 at Buckhurst Hill, England, and died in 1963 in Bournemouth.[4]

---

[1] Copyright records; LC.

[2] Paul Eduard Miller, *Miller's Yearbook of Popular Music* (Chicago, 1943), p. 83; NYPL. The 1903 year of birth appears in records of the Registrar General, London; information from Andrew Lamb, Littlehampton, West Sussex, England.

[3] Obituary, *The New York Times,* Aug. 20, 1967.

[4] Obituary, *New York Herald Tribune,* Sept. 24, 1963.

Grand Canyon Suite—Grofé

m. Ferde Grofé. Published Aug. 24, 1932,[1] for piano by Robbins Music Corporation, 799 Seventh Avenue, New York, N.Y. First edition: Front cover is brown and gray. vb. Title page has a dedication to Paul Whiteman, lists five movements (of which *On the Trail*, excerpted above, is no. 3), and the price is $2.00. m. on pp. 2–44, *On the Trail* at p. 15. No plate number. Inside back cover blank. Outside back cover has emblem of Robbins Music Corp. and Metro Goldwyn Mayer. LC(CDC) and NYPL.

The orchestral score of the *Suite* was published in octavo on Jan. 22, 1943,[1] the publisher having the same imprint as above. First edition: Front cover is brown and black. Verso has a foreword. Title page has the price of $3.50. Two pages of program notes. m. on pp. 4–170, a lithographing of a manuscript. pp. [171] and [172] blank. Inside back cover has publisher's note. Outside back cover has publisher's emblem. LC(CDC) and BPL.

The *Grand Canyon Suite* was performed in Chicago on Nov. 22, 1931. Grofé, a composer and arranger, was born in New York City in 1892.[2]

Grande Valse Brillante—Chopin

m. Fréd. Chopin. Published for piano as op. 18 about June, 1834,[1] by Maurice Schlesinger, 97 Rue Richelieu, Paris; about July–Aug., 1834,[2] by

---

[1] Copyright records; LC.
[2] *ASCAP*, p. 202.

---

[1] *BF*, June 28, 1834, p. 424. See, in general, *Chopin Works*, vol. IX, p. 121.
[2] Hofmeister *Monatsbericht*, July–Aug., 1834, p. 60. *AMZ Int-Bl*, Sept., 1834, p. 36.

Breitkopf & Härtel, Leipzig; and about July–Aug., 1834,[3] by Wessel & Co., 6 Frith Street, Soho Square, London. Probable first French edition: Front cover has a dedication to Mademoiselle Laura Horsford, the price is 6f and there are references to the other two publishers. Verso and following page blank. m. on pp. 2–9. p.n. 1599. Back cover blank. Engraved. COP, BM, AT and JF.

Probable first German edition: Front cover has Horsford's last name spelled "Harsford," the price is 16 Gr. and there are references to the other two publishers. The next two pages and the back cover are blank. m. on pp. 4–11. p.n. 5545. Engraved. JF.

A copy of the probable first English edition was deposited at BM in March, 1835. Front cover is not a collective title front cover and shows the publisher's address as stated above. There is an alternate title to the composition, *Invitation pour la Danse*, the dedicatee's name is spelled "Horsford," the price is 3/, and there are references to the other two publishers. Next two pages blank. m. on pp. 2–9. p.n. 1157. Back cover blank. Engraved. BM(CDC).

This waltz was composed in 1831. Brief biographic information regarding Chopin appears above under his *Etude*.

Great Day!

When   you're   down____   and   out,   lift   up   your   head____   and   shout

m. Vincent Youmans. w. William Rose and Edward Eliscu. Published June 22, 1929,[1] by Vincent Youmans, Inc., 67 West 44th St., New York, N.Y. First edition: Front cover has a drawing of the sun over a country scene and is yellow, blue, green, brown and white. s. *Great Day!*—4 titles listed. m. on pp. 2–5. Back cover adv. *Vincent..* LC(CDC) and JF.

The show opened in New York City on Oct. 17, 1929, but, in spite of

---

[3] Entered at Stationers' Hall on Aug. 30, 1834. Brown, in a letter, explains his July date as follows: "The copy of op. 13 in the British Museum has the acquisition date 'July 1834'; it advertises op. 17. Since the publisher's number of op. 18 is so close to that of op. 17, I assumed . . . that it was published at the same time as op. 17."

Brown, p. 64, gives the date of the French edition as June, 1834, and the German and English editions as July, 1834. The French edition cannot be later than July 18, 1834, as Chopin inscribed and dated a copy on that date (Brown, p. 64; Bory, p. 104).

[1] Copyright records; LC.

its containing two other important songs by Youmans, *More Than You Know* and *Without a Song*, it closed after only 36 performances. Brief biographic information regarding Youmans and Eliscu appears above under *Carioca*. William ("Billy") Rose was born in New York City in 1899 and has had a varied career as a songwriter, showman, columnist and art collector; he died in Montego Bay, Jamaica, in 1966.[2]

Greensleeves

A - las, my love,— you do me wrong,— to cast me off — dis-court - eous-ly

There are many references to *Greensleeves* commencing in the late sixteenth century, perhaps the most famous being Falstaff's: "Let the sky . . . thunder to the tune of *Green Sleeves*."[1]

The well-known words were probably first published in Sept., 1580, as a separate ballad by Richard Jones, as there appears in the Registers of the Stationers' Company in that month a license to him of "A new Northern Dittye of the *Lady Greene Sleeves*." No copy has been found. The words appear in *A Handefull of Pleasant Delites* (London, 1584), p. B ii, by Clement Robinson and divers others, published by Richard Ihones [sic]; the words are there described as "A New Courtly Sonet [sic] of the Lady Greensleeves. To the new Tune of—'Greensleeves' ". BM and BOD.

No printing of the melody has been found prior to its inclusion in 1652[2] in *A Booke of New Lessons for the Cithern & Gittern* (London), p. 31, under the title *Greene-Sleeves*, without words; *BUC*, p. 790. Although today the ballad is sung slowly and soulfully, the Shakespearean reference and its inclusion in *The Dancing Master* commencing with the 7th edition in 1686, London, at BM indicate that it was originally a vigorous dance tune.

---

[2] Obituary, *The New York Times*, Feb. 11, 1966.

---

[1] *The Merry Wives of Windsor*, act V, scene 5 (1597). See also *Old Hundred*, below. The history of *Greensleeves* has been well treated in Chappell, vol. 1, p. 227.

[2] W. Chappell, *A Collection of National English Airs* (London, 1840), vol. II, frontispiece and p. 118, shows the melody in William Ballet's *Lute Book* (at NYPL); the manuscript of the *Lute Book* is dated 1594 according to Routley, p. 127. John M. Ward, "Apropos *The British Broadside Ballad and its Music*" in *Journal of the American Musicological Society*, Richmond, Va., Spring, 1967, p. 44; LC.

Guys and Dolls

When you see a guy____ reach for stars in the sky____
When you see a dame____ change the shape of her frame____

"Guys and Dolls" by Frank Loesser. © 1950 Frank Loesser. Used by permission.

mw. Frank Loesser. The song *Guys and Dolls* was published Sept. 15, 1950,[1] by Susan Publications, Inc. The copyright copy deposited at the Library of Congress is a professional edition. Probable first regular edition: Front cover has a drawing of guys and dolls and is red, white and black. s. *Guys & Dolls*—15 titles listed, the last of which is *It*.. (same as on professional edition). No price. Edwin H. Morris and Company, Inc., 1619 Broadway, New York 19, N.Y., is the sole selling agent. vb. m. on pp. 3–5. No plate number. Back cover adv. *Guys*..—*I've*.. LC and JF. (The first song from the show in regular edition deposited as a copyright copy at the Library of Congress has the same front cover as that described above; later songs either list 14 titles, or the 15th title is different, or front cover is red and white.)

The piano-vocal score of the show *Guys & Dolls* was published Sept. 3, 1953,[1] by Edwin H. Morris & Co., Ltd., London; BM (copyright copy deposited that day) and JF (autographed by Loesser). The show opened in New York City on Nov. 24, 1950. Loesser, a composer and lyricist, was born in New York City in 1910 and died there in 1969.[2]

Gypsy Love Song

Slum - ber   on,   my   lit - tle gyp - sy sweet-heart

m. Victor Herbert. w. Harry B. Smith. The copy deposited at LC for copyright on Oct. 7, 1898,[1] by M. Witmark & Sons, New York, N.Y., and

---

[1] Copyright records; LC.
[2] Obituary, *The New York Times*, July 29, 1969.

---

[1] Copyright records; LC.

Chicago, with the title *Gipsy* [*sic*] *Love Song* on the front cover, is a professional edition. Probable first regular edition, deposited for copyright on Oct. 24, 1898[1]: Front cover has the same title, is purple, yellow and white, refers to the comic opera *The Fortune Teller*, and does not mention any arrangement of this song in various keys or other songs from the comic opera.[2] p. [2] adv. *Successful..* m. on pp. 3–5. p.n. 1417-3. pp. [6], [7] and back cover blank. LC (CDC) and JF.

The piano-vocal score of *The Fortune Teller* was deposited at LC on Nov. 26, 1898.[1] First edition: Front cover is blue, green and white with five photographs. vb. Title page has a price of $2.00. vb. Cast. Contents. m. on pp. 1–181. p.n. 1445. The *Gypsy Love Song* starts at p. 121. LC (CDC) and JF.

The Fortune Teller opened in New York City on Sept. 26, 1898. Brief biographic information regarding Herbert appears above under *Ah! Sweet Mystery of Life*. Smith, a librettist, lyricist and actor, was born in Buffalo in 1860 and died in New Jersey in 1936.[3]

Hail! Hail! The Gang's All Here—(The Pirates of Penzance)

Hail! Hail! The gang's all here, what the heck do we care, what the heck do we care
Come, friends, who plough the sea, truce to nav-i-ga-tion, take an-oth-er sta-tion

The first known printing of *Hail! Hail! The Gang's All Here* is a march arranged for band under this title by Herman Bellstedt and published April 17, 1908,[1] by The Fillmore Bros. Co., Cincinnati, Ohio. The earliest copy that has been located has a copyright renewal notice, but it does contain the well-known words and music; JF. The song was subsequently reprinted under this title by a number of publishers.

The origin of these words has been the subject of considerable speculation. One writer has suggested that they were composed during the Spanish-American War by a young naval reserve officer in Southern waters.[2] There is also a puzzling note in the United States Copyright Office that Theodora Morse wrote the words in 1904, but there is no confirmation of

---

[2] Front cover is illustrated in Fuld, *American*, p. [36].
[3] *ASCAP*, p. 467.

---

[1] Copyright records; LC.
[2] Letter from H. A. Smith in *The New York Times*, Feb. 20, 1927, quoted in Isaac Goldberg, *The Story of Gilbert and Sullivan* (New York, N.Y., 1935), p. 242; NYPL.

this, and she is no longer alive; in 1917, a sheet music edition of the song under this title was published by Leo. Feist, Inc., New York, N.Y., with the music credited to Theodore Morse (the husband of Theodora Morse) and Arthur Sullivan, and the words credited to D. A. Esrom (Dolly or Theodora Morse). JF. It has also been suggested that Theodore Morse wrote the words.[3] It seems generally agreed that the words are American.

The melody originally was known as *Come, Friends, Who Plough the Sea*, from Gilbert and Sullivan's *The Pirates of Penzance*. This comic opera was produced first in Paignton, England, on Dec. 30, 1879, a single performance for English copyright purposes. It was produced in New York City on Dec. 31, 1879, but not in London until April 3, 1880. No entry was made at Stationers' Hall until Aug. 18, 1880, and instead of the usual date of publication being stated in the entry, there appeared the time of first performance. No deposits were made at BM from the comic opera until Dec. 17, 1880.[4] To protect the copyright, Gilbert wrote that there would be no early publication, and in June, 1880, *The New York Times* said no copies of the piano-vocal score were available.[5]† According to the publisher, the English piano-vocal score was published about Sept., 1880;[6] however, the first English edition of this score refers to *The Martyr of Antioch*, which was not produced until Oct. 15, 1880.

The title *The Pirates of Penzance* was entered for copyright in Washington by John Stetson on Feb. 2, 1880,[1] and by Lee & Walker on March 13, 1880.[1] There is no record of copies having been received, no copies have been located, and it is possible that publication never took place. The authorized American piano-vocal score, published by J. M. Stoddart & Co., Philadelphia, was deposited Nov. 27, 1880; LC(CDC).

Reginald Allen, New York City, the Gilbert and Sullivan authority, told this author he believes the English piano-vocal score preceded the American piano-vocal score—for example, the American score prints the English finale, which differed from the American finale. Probable first edition of the English piano-vocal score: Front cover is blue and gray, mentions the Vocal Score at 5/ and the Pianoforte Score at 3/, and the publisher is Chappell & Co., 50 New Bond Street, W., City Branch—15 Poultry, E.C., London. Verso adv. *Rimbault's.*. Title page is similar to the front cover and has Sullivan's stamped signature. Cast and index. m. on pp. [3]–135, the *Chorus of Pirates*, "Come, Friends, Who Plough the Sea," commencing on p. 116. p. [136] adv. *Olivette*. Inside of back cover adv. *Old.*. Outside of

---

[3] Spaeth, p. 337.

[4] The piano-vocal score was entered for copyright in Ottawa on Dec. 23, 1880, by Gilbert and Sullivan; *Canadian Copyright*, p. 23.

[5] Information from Reginald Allen, New York City.

[6] Letter from publisher.

back cover adv. *The Martyr..* and *Trial..* No plate number. The printer is Henderson, Rait, & Fenton, 3 & 5 Marylebone Lane, Oxford St., London W. BM*(CDC), RA and JF.

The *Chorus of Pirates* without words, and the pianoforte score, were also deposited at BM on Dec. 17, 1880. Neither the first English nor the first American libretto contains the words of this *Chorus;* RA. Actually, the first English libretto was printed by Henderson & Rait (1881), not Henderson, Rait & Fenton (1880) as in the case of the piano-vocal score, piano score and separate sheet music. Brief biographic information regarding Gilbert and Sullivan appears above under *Bow, Bow, Ye Lower Middle Classes.*

Hail to the Chief

Hail   to the Chief who in   tri - umph ad - van - ces!

There is something strange about the history of this song. While there are many early American printings with the music usually ascribed to "Mr. Sanderson," apparently the prolific English songwriter, James Sanderson, not one English printing has been found, after tremendous search, either in England or America. And it is understood that the melody is not known in England. Perhaps an English edition will be found later; otherwise, it may be that the Sanderson referred to is not the English James Sanderson or is a pseudonym. †

The words are by Walter Scott and first appeared in his *The Lady of the Lake* (Printed for John Ballantyne & Co., Edinburgh, and Longman, Hurst, Rees and Orme and William Miller, London, by James Ballantyne & Co., Edinburgh, 1810), no. XIX, *Boat Song*, p. 69; BM. The poem is an imitation of the "sorrains" or boat songs of the Highlanders of Scotland composed in honor of a favorite chief.

The earliest printings of the music—all American and usually with words—were published commencing about 1812: (a) *Hail to the Chief,* published by John Paff, New York, N.Y., 1812?, without the numeral "3" added to lower margin, Wolfe, p. 772, no. 7769; (b) same title, published by Carr's Music Store, Baltimore, 1812–1814, Wolfe, p. 772, no. 7770; (c) *March & Chorus in the Dramatic Romance of The Lady of the Lake,* published by G. E. Blake, Philadelphia, 1812–1814, Wolfe, p. 773, no. 7779, and JF; and (d) same title, published by G. Willig, Philadelphia, 1812–1815, Wolfe, p. 773, no. 7780. (a), (c) and (d) give the author as "Mr. Sander-

son"; (b) mentions no author. The music is later sometimes known as
Roderick Dhu's March, Wreaths for the Chieftain and *Erie and Champlain.*†

Dramatic adaptations of Scott's *The Lady of the Lake* are mentioned
frequently in Nicoll as to England, and in Odell as to America. While Rossini, Henry Bishop and others wrote music for some of these dramatic
versions, Sanderson does not seem to be mentioned anywhere except in the
sheet music of this one song! A letter to Scott dated Aug. 31, 1811, requests
"a copy of the music of the *Boat-Song, Hail to the Chief,* as performed at
Covent Garden"; unfortunately, there is no indication of the composer.[1]

This march has been played in this country for many years to announce the arrival or recognize the presence of the President of the United
States; it is not known exactly when this custom began. The first Presidential inaugural at which the march was played was President Van
Buren's, on March 4, 1837.[2] The accompanying words are now all but
forgotten. Brief biographic information regarding Scott appears above
under *Ave Maria* (Schubert). James Sanderson, the English songwriter, was
born in Washington, Durham, England, in 1769 and died in London about
1841.[3]

Hallelujah!

Sing "Hal - le - lu - jah!___ Hal - le - lu - jah!"

m. Vincent Youmans. w. Leo Robin and Clifford Grey. Published April 22,
1927,[1] by Harms, Incorporated, New York, N.Y. First edition: Front cover
is red, white and blue. s. *Hit the Deck*—4 titles listed. p. [2] adv. *I..* and
Like.. m. on pp. [2]–5 (actually 3–6). p.n. 7988-4. p. [7] adv. *Adelai.* Back
cover adv. *Chérie..* LC(CDC) and JF. The show opened in New York City
on April 25, 1927.

Hallelujah! was Youmans's first published song, composed during

---

[1] Letter from Adam Ferguson from Lisbon in John Gibson Lockhart, *Memoirs of
the Life of Sir Walter Scott* (Boston and New York, 1901), vol. 2, p. 224; NYPL. An
examination of a great many programs of the Covent Garden, London, in 1810 and
1811, at NYPL Theater Division, fails to mention either *The Lady of the Lake* or the
Boat Song, Hail to the Chief.

[2] Ben: [sic] Perley Poore, *Perley's Reminiscences of Sixty Years in the National Metropo-
lis* (Philadelphia, 1886), vol. I, p. 201; NYPL.‡.

[3] *Grove's,* vol. VII, p. 400.

[1] Copyright records; LC.

World War I at Great Lakes, but was not used until 1927.[2] Brief biographic information regarding Youmans appears above under *Carioca*. Robin, a lyricist, was born in Pittsburgh in 1900 and resides in Beverly Hills, Cal.[3] Grey, a lyricist and scenarist, was born in Birmingham, England, in 1887 and died in Ipswich, England, in 1941.[3]

Hallelujah Chorus—Messiah

Hal - le - lu - jah!   Hal - le - lu - jah!

m. G. F. Handel. Words compiled and adapted by Charles Jennens. The *Hallelujah Chorus* was not included in the *Songs in Messiah* engraved about 1749 during Handel's lifetime,[1] but was first published July 7–23, 1767,[2] after Handel's death, in the complete *Messiah an Oratorio in Score*. The bibliographic history of the *Messiah* has been ably recorded by William C. Smith.[3]

What is the first edition of the complete *Messiah an Oratorio in Score* is not clear to this author. According to William C. Smith, *Handel, A Descriptive Catalogue of the Early Editions* (London, 1960), p. 124, there is only one copy that is "No. 1" in all respects. This copy was issued complete in one volume. On the title page, the letters "add" in "additional" are thick, and the crossbars of the "t" in "Alterations" project further to the left of the stems; and, in the text, the rest sign is omitted from the Bass vocal part on p. 180, stave 2, bars 2 and 3, and there are no natural marks under, for example, the first and fourth notes of the sixth bar of the Organo part on p. 19 of the Appendix. Copy owned by Mr. Smith.[3A]

Mr. Smith was not aware that the Royal Academy of Music, London, had a copy of the complete *Messiah* issued in three separate parts, each part with its own title page and index page, and with a blank page at the

[2] Green, p. 133.

[3] *ASCAP*, pp. 412 and 199.

[1] Nor, of course, was the melody in the *Overture* published in 1743. The words were published in the libretto or word-book of the *Messiah* printed by George Faulkner in Dublin in 1742; BM.

[2] *Public Advertiser*, London, July 4, 1767, p. [3] ("ready ... 7th inst.") and July 23, 1767, p. [3] ("now ready"); BM.

[3] William C. Smith, "The Earliest Editions of Messiah," in *Concerning Handel* (London, 1948), p. 67, at NYPL; and Smith, *Handel*, p. 116.

[3A] The title page of Mr. Smith's copy is illustrated in his "The Earliest Editions of Messiah," in *Concerning Handel* (London, 1948), plate no. 5; NYPL.

end or at the front of each part as necessary. It is thus possible that the first edition of the *Messiah* was this edition issued in parts (similar to the manner in which many of Charles Dickens' and others' works were first published). A copy at the British Museum (RM. 7.g.6) had been issued in three separate parts, but has only one title page and one index. Gerald Coke, Jenkyn Place, Bentley, Hants, England, also owns a copy of the second separate part. These copies have the two textual "No. 1" points noted above, but are "No. 2" as to the two title page points. Possibly the title page in Mr. Smith's copy was a lingering proof page or had irregular inking?

It is clear that in the first edition there is no portrait opposite the title page. The publisher is Randall & Abell, successors to the late M. J. Walsh in Catharine Street in the Strand, London. (**See Plate II;** according to Mr. Smith, this title page is "No. 2.") vb. Two page list of subscribers. Index. vb. m. on pp. 1–188 and Appendix, pp. 1–35. Appendix, p. [36] blank. No plate number. The *Hallelujah Chorus* is at p. 144.

Five other copies of the one-volume edition, with the text as Smith "No. 1," but with the title page as Smith "No. 2," are at COL, BMI, PML, Cambria County Library, Johnstown, Pa., and JF. A similar one-volume copy was listed as no. 63 in *Catalogue 22* of the Leamington Book Shop, Washington, D.C., n.d. (*Catalogue* at JF); name of present owner not known. These six copies are partly "No. 2" to Smith because of the title page, and these copies might be second edition to this author because they were not issued in separate parts. A three-volume copy, with one index and no blank pages, was sold at Sotheby & Co., London, May 8, 1972, no. 103, to D. M. Jones (address unknown). Another one-volume copy was listed as Smith "No. 1" in the *Catalogue* of Sotheby & Co., London, for March 15, 1971, no. 133, but on further examination it was a combination of Smith text "No. 1," title page "No. 2" and other text partly "No. 3"; e.g., the figuring 7 appears on p. 9, stave 3, bar 2.†

The *Messiah* was performed in Dublin on April 13, 1742. George Frederic Handel was born in Halle, Lower Saxony, in 1685, came to live in London and died there in 1759.

Happy Birthday to You

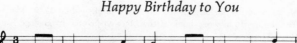

The melody was originally published as *Good Morning to All* in Mildred J. Hill and Patty S. Hill, *Song Stories for the Kindergarten* (Chicago, 1893), p. 3. On the title page, the music in the book is credited to Mildred J. Hill. The copyright copy was deposited at the Library of Congress on Oct. 16, 1893; copies also at BPL, BR, NYPL, SS and JF.

Apparently without authorization, the words and music of *Happy Birthday to You* were included in *Harvest Hymns*, compiled and edited by Robert H. Coleman, and published by him in Dallas, Texas, on March 4, 1924.[1,1A] Number 218, entitled *Good Morning to You!*, has *Happy Birthday to You* as the second stanza. There is no credit for authorship of words or music or special copyright notice. LC(CDC) and JF. Coleman included this song in at least three other collections published by him in 1930–1933; LC and NYPL.

Happy Birthday to You was sung without authorization in the musical show *As Thousands Cheer*, and a lawsuit relating thereto was reported in *The New York Times*, Aug. 15, 1934, p. 19, col. 6. (*Jessica M. Hill* vs. *Sam H. Harris et al.*, United States District Court, Southern District of New York, New York, N.Y., File no. E78–350).

The first authorized publication of *Happy Birthday*, with credit to Mildred J. Hill and Patty S. Hill, was as a march without words, by Clayton F. Summy Co., Chicago, on Dec. 27, 1934;[1] no first edition has been found, but a microfilm at the publisher shows this arrangement has p.n. 3022. After three other piano arrangements of the march, also without words, two arrangements, with words by the same persons, retitled *Happy Birthday to You*, were published by the same concern on Dec. 6, 1935.[1] One is octavo and has a collective title front cover, entitled *Union School Chorus Music*. This song is no. 96, the last of 16 titles on the front cover. The price is 8 cents. p. [2] is blank. m. on p. [3]. p.n. 3076. Back cover adv. *Glad.. - Cuckoo..* LC(CDC). No first edition of the other has been found; it was probably a piano-vocal arangement with p.n. 3075 (early edition at JF).

Happy Birthday to You is probably the most frequently sung music, at least in this country. Mildred J. Hill, a church organist, concert pianist, composer and authority on Negro spirituals, was born in Louisville, Ky., in 1859 and died in Chicago in 1916.[2] Dr. Patty Smith Hill was born in Louisville, Ky., in 1868, wrote the words for the 1893 book while she was Principal of the Louisville Kindergarten Training School, became Professor

---

[1] Copyright records; LC.

[1A] Harold Barlow, New York City, was responsible for finding this publication.

[2] *ASCAP*, p. 233.

Emeritus of Education at Columbia University and died in New York City in 1946.[3] †

The song, both as *Good Morning to All* and as *Happy Birthday to You*, bears a similarity to *A Happy New Year* included in *The Story of the Jubilee Singers* (London, 1875), p. 213, at BM(CDC) and JF, and a considerable similarity to *Happy Greeting to All* included in *The Anniversary & Sunday School Music Book No. 1* (New York, N.Y., 1858), p. 17, at BR. *Happy Birthday* also bears a similarity to *Good Night to You All* in Asa Fitz, *The Exercise Song Book* (Boston, 1858), p. 28, at BPL and JF.[4]

Happy Days Are Here Again

'Cause hap - py days___ are here a - gain!

© 1929 Advanced Music Corp. Copyright renewed. Used by permission.

m. Milton Ager. w. Jack Yellen. Published Nov. 7, 1929,[1] by Ager, Yellen & Bornstein, Inc., 745 7th Ave., New York, N.Y. Possible first edition: Front cover has a drawing of a pianist and three dancers and is purple, orange and white. Movie, *Chasing Rainbows*—3 titles listed. m. on pp. 2–5. Back cover adv. *Lucky.. - Everybody..* All the songs advertised in this edition were published on or before Nov. 7, 1929. JF. The movie was copyrighted Jan. 6, 1930,[1] but apparently not released until Feb. 21, 1930.

This song became the theme song of Franklin D. Roosevelt's New Deal in 1933. Ager, a composer and publisher, was born in Chicago in 1893 and died in Los Angeles in 1979.[2] Yellen, a lyricist and publisher, was born in Poland in 1892 and resides in Springville, N.Y.[2]

Happy Farmer—Schumann

---

[3] *The New Yorker,* March 8, 1941, p. 12; *ULS*, p. 2006. This article also contains additional general material on the song, as does Sigmund Spaeth, "The 3 Top Songs of All Time," in *Variety*, Jan. 10, 1962, p. 184. Information from COL. ‡

[4] Harold Barlow, New York City, advised the author of these similarities.

[1] Copyright records; LC.

[2] *ASCAP*, pp. 5 and 549, and ASCAP files. Obituary of Ager, *The New York Times*, May 8, 1979, p. B15.

m. Robert Schumann. *Album für die Jugend*, op. 68, containing *Fröhlicher Landmann*, or *Happy Farmer*, was published Jan., 1849,[1] for piano by Schuberth & Comp., Hamburg and New York. The first edition contains 40 Clavierstücke (later increased to 43), and there is no supplement, *Musikalische Haus- und Lebensregeln*. Title page is tan and white, shows the price as 2 Thlr., refers to Milan, London and Paris copublishers and makes a mistaken claim of an 1846[2] copyright in the United States. vb. Index, engraved. vb. m. on pp. 1–62, engraved, this composition at p. 10. p.n. 1232. AVH, DU, LC and SH.

This work was composed in 1848. The Deutsches Volksliedarchiv, Freiburg, has confirmed that *Fröhlicher Landmann* is not a folk song. Brief biographic information regarding Schumann appears above under *Carnaval*.

Hark! The Herald Angels Sing

Hark! The her-ald an-gels sing,__ glo-ry to the new-born King!

m. Felix Mendelssohn Bartholdy. w. mostly Charles Wesley. The words of this hymn first appeared in John Wesley and Charles Wesley, *Hymns and Sacred Poems* (London, 1739), p. 206, as a "Hymn For Christmas-Day." The opening lines are "Hark how all the Welkin rings—Glory to the Kings of Kings." The first edition of this collection was published by William Strahan, with 16 preliminary pages and 223 pages of hymns;[1] JF.

The opening lines were changed by George Whitefield in 1753 to "Hark! The Herald Angels sing—Glory to the new-born King!"; and other changes were also made. George Whitefield, *A Collection of Hymns for*

---

[1] Dörffel, p. 15. Hofmeister *Monatsbericht*, Jan., 1849, p. 7. Hofmann, *Schumann*, p. 151.

[2] Corrected to 1849 in later editions. There is no record of a copyright now at LC either for 1846 or 1849. The title page is illustrated in, and there is an interesting discussion of this work in, Rudolf Steglich, "Zwei Titelzeichnungen zu Robert Schumanns Jugendalbum als Interpretationsdokumente" in *Deutsches Jahrbuch der Musikwissenschaft für 1959* (Leipzig, 1960), p. 38; NYPL.

---

[1] Rev. Richard Green, *The Works of John and Charles Wesley* (London, 1896), p. 15; NYPL. The difference between the first and third editions is not indicated, and other editions have not been located for comparison. See, also, Julian, pp. 487 and 1259.

Social Worship (London, 1753), p. 24; LC. Further changes were made in *A Collection of Psalm and Hymn Tunes Never Published Before* (London), p. 88, where the hymn is entitled *The Nativity*; the dedication pages are dated August 18, 1769; and the editor's preface is signed M. Madan.[2] NYPL.

The music and other words were first published about June, 1840,[3] as *Fest-Gesang für Männerchor* by Breitkopf & Härtel, Leipzig, for piano and male chorus. Probable first edition: Price is 1 Thlr. vb. m. on pp. 3–23, engraved. p.n. 6418. Back cover blank. This music accompanies the second song commencing "Vaterland" on p. 6. No opus number. GM. The music was composed for a festival commemorating the invention of printing, which festival took place at Leipzig on June 24–25, 1840, and the *Festgesang* was performed the first day.

Dr. W. H. Cummings, principal of the Guildhall School of Music and Organist of Waltham Abbey, England, regretted that Wesley's fine hymn had never been associated with one particular melody. When he found that Mendelssohn's *Festgesang* fitted the hymn, he brought the two together,[4] and the combined song was published Dec. 24, 1855.[5] On Dec. 2, 1856, a possible first edition was deposited at the British Museum: *Hark the Herald Angels Sing*, Christmas Hymn, adapted and arranged by William H. Cummings, and published by J. J. Ewer & Co., 390 Oxford Street, London. Front cover is red, black and white. Price 1/. vb. m. on pp. 3–7. p.n. Mendelssohn Christmas Hymn. Back cover blank. Engraved. Verses 1 and 3 are arranged for unison singing, verse 2 for mixed voices. BM(CDC). As almost a year passed between the date of publication and the date of deposit of the above copy at the British Museum, a variant edition identical to the above edition, but with a back cover advertising "Newest Compositions," is also a possible first edition. JF.

Brief biographic information regarding Mendelssohn appears above under his *Concerto for Violin*. Charles Wesley, the younger brother of John Wesley, was born at Epworth, Lincolnshire, England, in 1707, was a preacher and wrote over 6,000 hymns before he died in London in 1788.

---

[2] *The Nativity* is not in the circa 1765 edition of this work; BM.

[3] Hofmeister *Monatsbericht*, June, 1840, p. 119. The work was not published in England until 1869 according to a letter from the present publisher.

[4] Mendelssohn, also, wrote in a letter dated April 30, 1843, that there ought to be other words to no. 2, and that if the right ones were hit upon, he was sure the piece would be liked very much; quoted in MT, Dec. 1, 1897, p. 810. It is not known whether Cummings knew of this letter in 1855.

[5] According to the entry at Stationers' Hall on Jan. 21, 1856.

The Heavens Are Telling the Glory of God—
The Creation—Haydn

Die　Him - mel　er - zäh - len die　Eh - re - Got - tes
The　heav - ens are　tell - ing the　glo - ry　of　God____

m. Joseph Haydn. The orchestral score of *Die Schoepfung—The Creation* was published by Haydn himself in Vienna about Feb. 26, 1800.[1] First edition: The title page is in German and English, states that the work is an oratorio, lists Haydn's positions, says "Vienna, 1800," and has Haydn's stamped initials; no price given. vb. Subscribers' list on seven pages. vb. m. on pp. 1–301; continuation of other pages on pp. 302–3. p. [304] blank. Text in German and English. The above *Chorus* is at p. 99. No plate number. Folio. Engraved. *BUC*, p. 456, LC and JF. The authorship of the text is not entirely clear.

Haydn published the work himself because he rightly believed that he would make more money from it than if he gave it to a regular publisher.[2] Orchestral parts of *Die Schöpfung* were published in 1801-2 by Simrock, Bonn, with plate number 188; Musikvereinsarchiv, Vienna. An unauthorized piano-vocal score of *Die Schöpfung* was published in 1799 by F. Mollo u. Comp., Vienna, with plate number 120; AVH and Landesbibliothek, Weimar. An authorized piano-vocal score was published on March 8, 1800,[3] by Artaria und Compagnie, Vienna; *BUC*, p. 456, and JF. *The Creation* was performed privately on April 29 and 30, 1798, in Vienna, and in public on March 19, 1799, also in Vienna. Brief biographic information regarding Haydn appears above under *Emperor's Hymn*.

[1] Hoboken, vol. 2, no. XXI: 2, p. 30. *Wiener Zeitung*, Feb. 26, 1800; ONB. *AMZ*, March 19, 1800, p. 441. Franz Artaria and Hugo Botstiber, *Josef Haydn und das Verlagshaus Artaria* (Vienna, 1909), p. 76; NYPL.

[2] Letters from Dr. Karl Geiringer, Santa Barbara, Cal., and H. C. Robbins Landon, Pistoia, Italy.

[3] *Wiener Zeitung*, March 8, 1800; ONB. The Breitkopf & Härtel, Leipzig, pianovocal edition was announced in April, 1800, to appear in several weeks; *AMZ Int-Bl*, April, 1800, p. 53. The André, Offenbach, edition was also published in 1800.

Hello, Ma Baby

Hel-lo! Ma ba - by, hel-lo! Ma hon - ey, hel-lo! Ma rag - time gal

mw. [Joseph E.] Howard & [Ida] Emerson. On Jan. 25, 1899,[1] T. B. Harms & Co., 18 East 22nd St., New York, N.Y., deposited a professional edition at LC. Possible first regular edition: Front cover has a drawing of a Negro couple talking on a telephone and is orange, black and white. p. [2] adv. *In..* m. on pp. [3]–[6]. p. [7] adv. *Don't.. - At..* The number 4 does not appear in the lower left-hand corner of the first page of music of either the professional edition or the above regular edition. Back cover adv. *I Want.. - Since..* All the songs advertised in this edition were copyrighted before Jan. 25, 1899.[1] JF. *Sweet Suzanne*, advertised in another edition, was copyrighted on Feb. 23, 1899.[1]

This was the first well-known song to refer to the telephone. Howard was a versatile composer, lyricist and performer who was born in New York, N.Y., in 1878 and died in Illinois in 1961.[2] No biographic information is available regarding Emerson.

Here's to————and————(Drink It Down, Drink It Down)

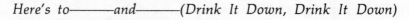

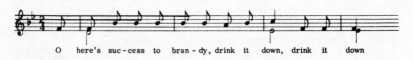

O here's suc - cess to bran - dy, drink it down, drink it down

This song first appeared under the title *Brandy and Water*,[1] a "Spirited Ballad," by Julien Carle, copyrighted on Oct. 1, 1853,[2] at LC by Winner & Shuster, 110 Nh. Eighth St., Philadelphia. First edition: Front cover as above. Oblong. p. [2] and back cover blank. m. on pp. 3–5. No plate number. Engraved. LC(CDC) and JF.

The song also became known later as *Balm of Gilead* and *Bingo*. It is not known whether Julien Carle actually composed the song or merely arranged it; in either event, no biographic information is available regarding him.

[1] Copyright records; LC.
[2] *ASCAP*, p. 241, and ASCAP files.

---

[1] Lester S. Levy, Baltimore, advised the author of this printing.
[2] Copyright records; LC.

He's Got the Whole World in His Hand

He's got the whole world— in His hand,— He's got the whole world in His hand—

The words of this spiritual were published in Arthur Huff Fauset, "Negro Folk Tales from the South" in the *Journal of American Folklore*, New York, N.Y., July–Sept., 1927, p. 294, with a note that the spiritual was heard near Tuskegee, Ala.; *ULS*, p. 1435.

The music (and words) were included in Edward Boatner, *Spirituals Triumphant—Old and New* (Nashville, Tenn., 1927), no. 68. LC (copyright copy deposited Dec. 27, 1927). The title page mentions A. M. Townsend, D.D., Secretary. The front cover also states "(Revised and Enlarged)," but these words are believed to refer to the spirituals, and not to the edition, as no earlier edition of this collection has been found or is believed to have been published.

Hoch Soll Er Leben

Hoch soll er le - ben, hoch soll er le - ben, drei - mal hoch!

The first known printing of the music and words of this convivial toasting song is in *Pan—Ein Lustiges Liederbuch für Gymnasiasten*, arranged by Dr. Friedrich Polle (Dresden, 1877), no. 257, p. 189; FR.[1]

Home on the Range

Oh, give me a home where the buf - fa - lo roam, where the deer and the an - te-lope play

m. Daniel E. Kelley. w. Dr. Brewster M. Higley. The words were probably first published in the Dec., 1873, issue of *The Smith County* (Kansas)

---

[1] Deutsches Volksliedarchiv, Freiburg, advised the author of this printing.

Pioneer under the title, *Oh, Give Me a Home Where the Buffalo Roam,*
according to the Feb. 19, 1914, issue of the same newspaper (which reprinted the poem). KSHS. The words were next probably printed under the
title *Western Home,* in the March 21, 1874, issue of the *Kirwin* (Kansas)
Chief, according to the Feb. 26, 1876, issue of the newspaper (which reprinted the poem). KSHS. This 1876 newspaper disproves the claim that
the song was first composed in 1885 under the title *Colorado Home.*[1]

The music (and words) were first published under the title *An Arizona
Home,* the music ascribed to Mrs. W. M. Goodwin and the words to Wm.
Goodwin. The copyright deposit copy at LC states that it was copyrighted
1904, but in a later lawsuit it appeared that it was copyrighted Feb. 27,
1905,[2] and the copyright copy was deposited on the later date. First edition:
The publisher is Balmer & Weber Music House Co., St. Louis. Front cover
has a drawing of a cowboy and girl, and is green, blue and white. p. [2]
blank. m. on pp. 3–5, engraved. p.n. 5401–4. pp. [6], [7] and back cover
blank. LC(CDC), JF and Complainants' Exhibit "A" in lawsuit referred to
in footnote 2 below (court records at Federal District Court, Southern District, New York, N.Y.). The words of *Home on the Range* were in G. F.
Will, "Songs of the Western Cowboys," in *Journal of American Folklore,*
Boston and New York, N.Y., April–June, 1909, p. 257; *ULS,* p. 1435. The
words and music were then included in John A. Lomax, *Cowboy Songs*
(New York, N.Y., 1910), p. 41; NYPL and JF.

The fascinating story of how a supposed folk song was tracked down
to its lyricist, composer, date of composition and date of first publication
is best described in Kirke Mechem, "Home on the Range."[3] The words and
music were written in 1872 or early 1873 in Smith County, Kansas, and
the song is now the official Kansas State Song. Kelley was a musician and
entertainer who was born in North Kingston, R.I., in 1843 and who died in
Waterloo, Iowa, in 1905. Higley was a pioneer doctor who was born in
Rutland, Ohio, in 1823 and who died in Shawnee; Okla., in 1911.

Home! Sweet Home!

Be it ev - er so hum - ble, there's no___ place like home

[1] This claim is best set forth in a sheet music edition of *Colorado Home,* published
by Paull-Pioneer Music Corp., New York, N.Y., in 1934; JF.

[2] The facts are set forth in the court decision *Southern Mus. Pub. Co. Inc.* vs.
Bibo-Lang, Inc., 10 Fed. Supp. 972 (Southern District, N.Y., 1935); NYPL.

[3] In *The Kansas Historical Quarterly,* Topeka, Nov., 1949, p. 313; *ULS,* p. 1485.
See also, Margaret Arvilla Nelson, *Home on the Range* (Boston, 1947); NYPL.

m. Henry R. Bishop. w. John Howard Payne. The music at first accompanied other words in *Melodies of Various Nations,* one copy of which was entered at Stationers' Hall on Dec. 29, 1821. The title of the song was then *To the Home of My Childhood,* a Sicilian air, with words by Thomas Bayly. The publisher was Goulding, D'Almaine, Potter & Co., 20 Soho Square, London; it was to be had at 7 Westmorland Street, Dublin; the price is 15/; the pages are engraved; and this song is at p. 69. BM and JF. The story is that a Sicilian air was needed to complete an international group so Bishop obliged by composing one.[1]

The song with its present words appeared in the opera *Clari or The Maid of Milan,* produced May 8, 1823, in London.[2] The separate sheet music edition of the song was not entered at Stationers' Hall, but one copy of the piano-vocal score of the opera was entered on Sept. 8, 1823. Priority as between the two is uncertain; however, the song was an immediate success, and one or both of the sheet music edition and piano-vocal score must have been published soon after the opera was performed.

Probable first edition of the sheet music: The publisher is as given above; the song is sung by Miss M. Tree; the price is 1/6; the music is on pp. 1–4; the pages are engraved; no p.n.; and any watermark should not be later than 1823. JF (copy watermarked 1820). Payne's name nowhere appears!

Probable first edition of the piano-vocal score of the opera: The publisher is as given above; the price is 18/; the music of *Home! Sweet Home!* commences at p. 27; and the pages are engraved. BM and LSL. The first printing of the libretto was by John Miller, 69 Fleet Street, London, and is dated 1823; BM, NYPL and JF. Whether the libretto preceded or followed the sheet music and piano-vocal score is not known; it was not separately entered at Stationers' Hall.

Bishop, a composer and conductor, was born in London in 1786 and died there in 1855. Payne was born in New York City in 1791, went to London in 1820 where he wrote several plays and subsequently died in Tunis in 1852.

---

[1] There is no substantiation to the statement made in Scribner, *Rare Book Catalogue 139,* New York, n.d., at JF, that Bishop remembered the melody as a *Ranz des Vaches,* and merely rearranged it.

Francis Scott Key wrote new words to Bishop's music about 1832 entitled *The Home of the Soul;* LC, LSL, NYPL and JF.

[2] The opera played each year from 1823–1833 and at times thereafter; Nicoll, vol. IV, p. 377, and actual programs at NYPL. The opera was first performed in New York on Nov. 12, 1823; Odell, vol. III, p. 96.

Hootchy Kootchy Dance

Curiously, Congressman Sol Bloom from New York claims credit for this rhythmic dance melody. In his *Autobiography* he wrote that he was the press agent for the Chicago World's Columbian Exposition in 1893.[1] At a press showing of one of the Midway dancers, "Little Egypt," some music was needed; he composed it on the spot and played it on the piano, but failed later to copyright the piece.

The music has many exotic titles as indicated by the various sheet music editions: (a) *Hoolah! Hoolah!*, the *Dance of the Midway* and the *Coochi-Coochi Polka*, its first printing, was deposited March 5, 1895,[2] at LC by Richter & Hopf, 1612 Third Ave., New York City, for piano solo. First edition: No mention of any other arrangement. p. [2] and back cover blank. m. on pp. [3]–5. Credit is given to Adam Ferry (Fery on p. [3]); LC(CDC). (b) *Danse du Ventre* (literally, *Dance of the Belly*) deposited April 8, 1895;[2] LC(CDC). (c) *Kutchi Kutchi*, deposited about May 22, 1895[2] —no copy located. (d) *The Streets of Cairo*, deposited July 24, 1895;[2] LC(CDC). And (e) *Kutchy Kutchy*, deposited Aug. 20, 1895;[2] LC(CDC).

Parody words commencing "Oh they don't wear pants in the Southern part of France" are frequently sung to this music. The words "Hoochee Koochee Koochee" appeared in the 1863 song *The Ham Fat Man;* BR. *American Heritage* (New York, N.Y.) carried an interesting article on the Chicago Fair and the *Hoolah! Hoolah!* dance in Oct., 1960, p. [18]; NYPL.

The opening five notes, including harmony and meter, are identical to the opening five notes of the song *Colin Prend Sa Hotte* in J. B. Cristophe Ballard, *Brunettes ou Petits Airs Tendres* (Paris, 1719), vol. 2, p. 280; LC.[3] In J. B. Wekerlin, *Échos du Temps Passé* (Paris [1857]), vol. 2, p. 119, at BN, the song is reprinted as a "Chanson à danser" with the comment that the first phrase of the melody resembles almost note for note an Algerian or Arabic melody known as *Kradoutja*, and that the melody has been popular in France since 1600. No printing of *Kradoutja* has been found.

[1] *The Autobiography of Sol Bloom* (New York, N.Y., 1948), p. 135; LC.
[2] Copyright records; LC.
[3] Harold Barlow, New York City, was helpful in connection with this earlier printing.

Bloom was a representative from New York in Congress from 1923 to 1949. He had been born in Illinois in 1870, was in the theatrical and music publishing business before entering politics and died in Washington, D.C., in 1949.[4]

Hora Staccato

m. Grigoras Dinicu. This work for violin and piano was composed in 1906 by Dinicu,[1] but it is believed that it was not published until July 16, 1930,[2] when it was published as transcribed by Jascha Heifetz, the publisher being Carl Fischer, Inc., Cooper Square, New York City. Possible first edition: The piano part has a yellow and red front cover which says B 2224 and has a price of 80 cents. vb. Title page lists many Heifetz arrangements and transcriptions and shows the publisher at three additional cities. m. on pp. 2–7. p.n. 25685–9. Page 7 says "New York, Dec. 1929." Page 8 has a photograph of Heifetz. Inside of back cover blank. Outside of back cover has publisher's emblem. Violin part on pp. 1–3; p. [4] blank. BPL.

The earliest known Rumanian printing of the work, also for violin and piano, and giving sole credit to Dinicu, was in 1951, by Editură de Stat Pentru Literatură și Artă, Bucharest; BCS. The original Dinicu manuscript and agreement between Dinicu and Heifetz are at the Library of Congress. Dinicu, a violinist and composer, was born in 1889 in Bucharest and died there in 1948.[1]

[4] *Biographical Directory of the American Congress 1774–1961* (Washington, 1961), p. 566; NYPL.

[1] Viorel Cosma, *Compozitŏri și Muzicologi Români* (Bucharest, 1965), p. 119; NYPL. Letter from BCS.

[2] Copyright records; LC.

A Hot Time in the Old Town

When   you   hear   dem   a   bells   go   ding,   ling   ling

The melody of the chorus was first printed under the title *In Old Town To-night*, copyrighted Feb. 6, 1896,[1] by Joseph Flanner, 211, 213 and 215 Grand Avenue, Milwaukee, Wis., with the words and music credited to Cad. L. Mays of Hunter & Mays. First edition: Front cover is red and white and says that the song is "An Up to Date Hot Stuff Coon Song." p. [2] blank. m. on pp. [3]–[6]. p. [7] blank. Back cover adv. *A Few..* LC(CDC) and JF.

A Hot Time in the Old Town was copyrighted July 2, 1896,[1] by Willis Woodward & Co., 842–844 Broadway, New York, N.Y., with the words and music credited to Theo. A. Metz. Front cover has a drawing of a cotton plantation, a photograph of Josephine Sabel and is orange, blue and white. m. on pp. 2–5. Back cover adv. *Dance.. - Battle..* LC(CDC). No co-publisher on the front cover, and no reference to Joe Hayden either on the front cover or on inside pages. The words, and the arrangement of the music, are different from those in the Flanner printing.

The two publishers later combined their editions under the presently familiar title, with sole credit to Theo. A. Metz for the music and Joe Hayden for the words. The music and words are those in the Woodward printing.

Interestingly, the words and title of the earlier Flanner printing are *not* "in the old town," but rather "in Old town." This supports the belief that a specific town, Old Town, was referred to, and it is further believed that this Old Town was in Louisiana.[1A] The Louisiana State Library, Baton Rouge, has confirmed to the author that there was an Old Town in that state in the 1890's (also known as Marion, about 25 miles up the Calcasieu River from Lake Charles), although the town does not exist today. In the Woodward printing, and in the combined and current editions, the words and title are "in the old town."

It is said that the song was written for the McIntyre & Heath minstrels by their bandmaster, Theodore A. Metz, and that words were added later

---

[1] Copyright records; LC.

[1A] Geller, p. 138. Geller adds that the McIntyre and Heath Minstrels played in Old Town in 1896; the author has not been able to confirm this. There is an Old Town today in Maine.

by Joe Hayden, a singer in the minstrel troupe.[2] A poster allegedly inspired the idea that there would be a hot time tonight for those who came to the minstrel show. Metz was a composer, musician and publisher who was born in Hanover, Germany, in 1848 and died in New York City in 1936.[3] No further biographic information has been found regarding Mays or Hayden.

How Dry I Am

The melody is from the hymn *(O) Happy Day*, the earliest known printing of which was in *The Wesleyan Sacred Harp*, compiled by the Rev. W. McDonald and S. Hubbard (Boston, 1855), p. 14; LC(CDC). The copyright claim is 1854, but the copyright copy was deposited Jan. 8, 1855.[1] There is no reference to any composer (the L. M. mentioned meaning Long Metre). It is not clear from the Preface whether this is the first printing of the contents.

The melody is frequently attributed to Edward F. Rimbault, the English composer and scholar, but without designation of the title.[2] The composition with the closest melody is believed to be *Happy Land*, published by J. Duff & Co., London, on April 28, 1837.[3] BM(CDC). The words of *O Happy Day* are by the Rev. Philip Doddridge and were printed in his *Hymns* (London, 1755), p. 20; BM.

The words *How Dry I Am* seem to be of more recent origin. Although no doubt older, the earliest known printing of any part of them to this melody is in a song of this name with music by Tom A. Johnstone and

---

[2] *Songs of the Gilded Age*, p. 36. It has been claimed that James A. Bland wrote *Hot Time in Our Town* and *In the Old Town Tonight* (John Jay Daly, *A Song in His Heart* [Philadelphia, 1951], p. 62; NYPL). Mr. Daly has written this author that Bland's songs bear no relation to the well-known song, and no copies of Bland's songs have been found. See, also, Gilbert, p. 212 .

The Jamaican song commencing *When I Go Home* bears an extraordinary similarity to *A Hot Time in the Old Town* and must have been derived from the latter song. The Jamaican song was included in Walter Jekyll, *Jamaican Song and Story* (London, 1907), p. 254; LC. Harold Barlow, New York City, noted this similarity.

[3] *ASCAP*, p. 346.

[1] Copyright records; LC.

[2] Rimbault was born in London in 1816 and died there in 1876. Homer A. Rodeheaver, *Hymnal Handbook for Standard Hymns and Gospel Songs* (Chicago and Philadelphia, 1931), p. 148; NYPL. Spaeth, p. 198.

[3] Copy entered at Stationers' Hall on that day.

words by Will B. Johnstone from the musical comedy *Up in the Clouds,*
which was published April 26, 1921;[1] LC(CDC) and JF. The words and
music of the first repeated phrase are present; thereafter, the words and
music are completely different from the current version. The complete
current version apparently first appeared on June 20, 1933,[1] in *Good Fellow
Songs,* p. 5, edited by Clarence Gaskill and L. C. Ernest, and published by
Luz Bros. Music Publishers, New York, N.Y.; LC(CDC).

The music of the complete *How Dry I Am,* without words, was included in Vocalion record A 14315, *Old Timers,* played by The Bar Harbor
Society Orchestra and probably released in 1922;[3] JF.

Prohibition and repeal unquestionably accounted for the popularity of
the song.

Humoreske—Dvořák

m. Ant. Dvořák. Published for piano as no. 7 of *Humoresken,* op. 101, in
the autumn of 1894[1] by N. Simrock, Berlin. Probable first edition: Front
cover is black and gray, mentions the price of Mk 4 and the 1894 copyright
claim. vb. Title page is the same as the front cover except in green, brown
and white. m. on pp. 2–14, no. 7 on pp. 10–11. p.n. of the Erstes Heft (nos.
1–4) 10278, and of the Zweites Heft (nos. 5–8) 10279. Back cover adv.
piano works of Brahms up to op. 119 (1893). GM.

This piece was composed Aug. 7–27, 1894. Antonín Dvořák was born
near Prague in 1841 and died in Prague in 1904.

Hungarian Dance no. 5—Brahms (Kéler)

[3] *Vocalion Records Catalogue for 1923* (to Aug., 1922), New York, N.Y., p. 42;
NYPL.

[1] Burghauser, p. 318. Šourek, p. x. Hofmeister *Monatsbericht,* Feb., 1895, p. 46.

This Hungarian dance was first published for piano with Béla Kéler as the composer about May, 1859.[1] Probable first edition: The title is *Bártfay Emlék* (*A Memory of Bártfa*—a town, now in Czechoslovakia)—Czárdás (a dance). There is a drawing of the town on the front cover which has a dedication to Albert Dessewffy,[2] and mentions that the op. no. is 31; the price is 65 új (new) kr.; and the publisher is Rózsavölgyi és társa (and Co.), Pesten (i.e., Pest, before the joining of Buda and Pest in 1872). p.n. 512. The music covers at least two pages. Further details not known. OSK.

Brahms included virtually the identical dance as no. 5 of the *Ungarische Tänze* "arranged" by him for piano four hands, which were published in March, 1869,[3] by Simrock, 18 Jägerstrasse, Berlin. First edition: Front cover lists two books, each at 1 Thlr. 15 Sgr., the second book being incorrectly shown as "No. 2-10." Wood-pulp paper. m. on pp. 2-29, no. 5 on the last four pages. p.n. 336. Back cover blank. No opus number (to emphasize that the music was not original with Brahms). BM (CDC received June 18, 1869).

Kéler was born in Bártfa, Hungary, in 1820, became a composer and bandmaster and died in Wiesbaden in 1882. Brief biographic information regarding Brahms appears above under his *Concerto for Piano no. 1*.

Hungarian Rhapsody no. 2—Liszt

m. F. Liszt. Published for piano about Nov., 1851,[1] under the title *Rhapsodie Hongroise II* by Bartholf Senff, Leipzig. Probable first edition: Front cover is green and black, has the title in the plural and p.ns. 23 and 26. vb. Title page has the title in the singular, a dedication to Count Ladislas Teleky, mentions a Petersburg agent and the price of 25 Ngr. vb. m. on pp. 3-19. p.n. 26. Music pages engraved. p. [20] and inside and outside of back cover blank. JF.

Raabe and *Grove's* report that this work was also published in 1851

[1] Hofmeister *Monatsbericht*, May, 1859, p. 79.

[2] Consistent with Hungarian custom, the last name appears first—thus, on the front cover, Kéler's name appears as Kéler Béla, and Dessewffy's name appears as Dessewffy Albert.

[3] According to Deutsch, *Brahms*, p. 265. On May 4, 1869, the work was entered at Stationers' Hall, and the date of publication was there given as May 1, 1869. Hofmeister *Monatsbericht*, June, 1869, p. 101. Hofmann, *Brahms*, p. 271.

[1] Hofmeister *Monatsbericht*, Nov., 1851, p. 215.

by Ricordi, Milan,[2] and the 1855 *Liszt Verzeichnis,* p. 15, states that the work was published without authority by another (undesignated) publisher. However, no Ricordi edition from that year has been found, and Ricordi catalogues from 1848–1852 and for 1855 do not include it; NYPL. The earliest Ricordi edition that has been found has p.n. 42433 indicating a year about 1872; SCR and TLW.

This work was composed in 1847. Brief biographic information regarding Liszt appears above under his *Concerto for Piano no. 1.*

Hunt Theme

It is not known whether the above hunting call is in the folk tradition or was part of an original work by Procida Bucalossi.[1] Its earliest discovered printing is in an otherwise apparently original work, *A Hunting Scene,* "composed" by him and arranged for piano, a copy of which was deposited at BM on July 4, 1884, by Chappell & Co., London, with p.n. 17,942 and the price of 4/-; BM(CDC). A set of band parts published by Riviere & Hawkes, London, also at BM, is dated [1885] in BM's catalogue.

In its earliest known appearances in print, mentioned above, the melody is accompanied by the words: "Tantivy! Tantivy! Tantivy! A-hunting we will go!" Music quite similar to the above appears without emphasis or repetition in the 4th–8th bars on p. 3 of *Tantivy, My Boys, Tantivy,* "A favorite Hunting Song," with music by Thos. Costellow and words by Mr. Upton, published 1782–1792[2] by Longman and Broderip, 26 Cheapside and 13 Hay Market [London]; JF. Bucalossi, a composer of light music, was born in Italy and died in 1918 at the age of eighty.†

Hymn to the Sun—Rimsky-Korsakov

2 Raabe, p. 262. *Grove's,* vol. 5, p. 285.

1 Mrs. Margaret M. Mott, at BE, and Alan Tyson, London, have been helpful in connection with this title.

2 Humphries-Smith, p. 216.

m. N. Rimsky-Korsakov. w. V. Bielsky. The *Hymn to the Sun* was included in a piano-vocal score of *Coq d'Or* with Russian text only,[1] which was published about Aug., 1908, by P. Jurgenson, Neglinny pr. 14, Moscow, and Thalstrasse 19, Leipzig, under the Russian title of the opera, Золотой Пѣтушокъ. Probable first edition: Front cover, in Russian, has five vignettes from the opera, mentions the year 1908 and is multicolored. vb. Title page, in Russian, lists three arrangements, but only two have prices, the orchestral score 150 p. (i.e., rubles) and the piano-vocal score 8 p.; mentions V. Bielsky as the librettist (after Pushkin), and the imprint has a crown and St. Petersburg, Warsaw and Kiev agents. Verso of title page has a printed reproduction of a manuscript. Dedication by the composer dated April 10, 1908 (O.S.). Statement by Bielsky. vb. Statement by the composer. Cast. m. on pp. 7–206; the *Hymn to the Sun* at p. 101. p.n. 32404-8. Back cover has a small emblem. CM and GL*. About three months later the piano-vocal score was reissued with Russian and French texts, the same page and plate numbers, but with the price of 5 rubles for the third arrangement, the piano score; BM and JF.

The orchestral score of *Coq d'Or* was probably published at about the same time as the piano-vocal score as it is listed with price in the latter and its p.n. is a little lower than that of the piano-vocal score; however, it does not appear to be in Hofmeister *Monatsbericht* or *Annual* 1908–1911. Probable first edition: Front cover and title page of the orchestral score are substantially the same as those of the piano-vocal score except that on the title page a fourth arrangement has been added, the orchestral parts at 75 rubles, A. Rouart et Co., Paris (1908–1910)[2] has been substituted for the Kiev agent, and there are separate title pages in French and Russian, verso of each blank. Preface. Remarks. Cast. Composition of orchestra. m. on pp. 7–366, with Russian and French texts. p.n. 32402. Next two pages and inside and outside of back cover blank. MC and SSL.

A possible first printing of the orchestral parts of the opera has plate number 32412, was also probably published at about the same time, and is lithographed; without covers. CI and MET*.

No information is known regarding the publication of the separate sheet music of the *Hymn to the Sun*, and no early printing has been found.

The melody of the *Hymn to the Sun* is also in the *Introduction et Cortège de Noces* published separately for orchestra with p.n. 32402; there is no reason to believe its publication preceded that of the orchestral score;

---

[1] Hofmeister *Monatsbericht*, Aug., 1908, p. 207. The edition with Russian and French texts is in the Nov., 1908, issue, p. 318.

[2] Hopkinson, *Parisian*, p. 106.

LC. The *Suite* from the opera for orchestra has p.n. 33585 and was apparently published about a year later; LC.

Le Coq d'Or, or *The Golden Cockerel*, was at first suppressed by the government. As the opera was not performed until Oct. 20, 1909, in St. Petersburg, the publication of the piano-vocal and orchestral scores preceded the performance by about a year. Brief biographic information regarding Rimsky-Korsakov and Bielsky appears above under *Capriccio Espagnol* and *The Flight of the Bumble Bee.*

I Ain't Got Nobody

On April 8, 1914,[1] this song, as an unpublished composition, was copyrighted by David Young, with words by him and music by Charles Warfield; LC(CDC). On Jan. 28, 1915,[1] the song, with the word "Much" added at the end of the title, was copyrighted as an unpublished composition by Peyton & Williams, with words and music credited to them. On Feb. 7, 1916,[1] the song, with the shorter title, was copyrighted as a published composition by Craig & Co., with music by Spencer Williams & Dave Peyton and words by Roger Graham, but the copyright deposit copies are professional editions.

Two regular editions were published by Craig and Company, Roger Graham, Mgr., 145 North Clark Street, Chicago, Ill., and it has not been possible to establish priority. One edition has the shorter title, the words are credited to Roger Graham and the music to Spencer Williams & Dave Peyton, there is a drawing on the front cover of a lady crying, the colors of the front cover are sepia and white, and the price is 5. m. on pp. 2–5. No plate number. Back cover adv. *A Little.*. The other edition has the longer title, with the word "Much" added at the end, the words are credited to Roger Graham (only) and the music to Spencer Williams, there is a drawing on the front cover of five men and a lady, the front cover has many colors, and there is no price. m. on pp. 2–5. No plate number. Back

[1] Copyright records; LC.

cover adv. *Lake.. - Saskatoon.* Advertised songs in both editions were published in 1915. Both copies at JF.

On April 3, 1916, Frank K. Root & Co. began to publish the song with different titles and credits. Copies at JF.

All the foregoing relates to the same song. Spencer Williams and Roger Graham are now recognized as the authors of the song, and it is not known who the others were, nor what role they played. Brief biographic information regarding Williams appears above under *Basin Street Blues.* Graham, a songwriter, was born in 1885 and died in Chicago in 1938.[2]

I Can't Give You Anything but Love (Baby)

I   can't give you   an - y - thing but   love,   ba - by

Copyright 1928 by Mills Music, Inc.; renewed 1956. By permission.

m. Jimmy McHugh. w. Dorothy Fields. According to the copyright records at LC, this song, without "(Baby)" in its title, was published from *Harry Delmar's Revels* on March 6, 1928, by Jack Mills, Inc., New York, N.Y. No copy has been found from this show, which opened in New York City on Nov. 28, 1927. Possibly the copyright deposit copy was a professional edition, and perhaps the song was never published in regular edition from this show as the song was included only during rehearsals and was then removed.[1]

Probably the first regular edition of the song states that it is from *Blackbirds of 1928,* which opened in New York City on May 9, 1928. Probable first edition: "(Baby)" does not appear in the title either on the front cover or on p. 3. Nine titles are listed on the front cover, which has a drawing of four blackbirds and is orange, black and white. The publisher is Jack Mills, Inc., 148–150 W. 46th Street, New York, N.Y., p. [2] *Out..* (published 1923). m. on pp. 3–5. Back cover adv. *I.. - Jack..* JF. The number of titles and the advertisements are the same as in the songs which were first published from the show on May 25, 1928.[2] Later editions add "(Baby)" in the title either on the front cover, p. 3 or both.

[2] Obituary, *The New York Times,* Oct. 27, 1938.

[1] Kane, p. 163.

[2] Two other songs from the show published June 9, 1928, list eight titles on the front cover. This group omitted *Baby* and *Porgy* and added *I Must Have That Man.*

McHugh, a composer, was born in Boston in 1894 and died in Beverly Hills, Cal. in 1969.[3] Fields, a lyricist, was born in Allenhurst, N.J., in 1905 and died in New York City in 1974.[4]

I Could Have Danced All Night—My Fair Lady

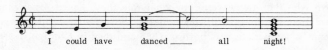

© 1956 by Alan Jay Lerner and Frederick Loewe. Chappell & Co. Inc., Publisher. By consent.

m. Frederick Loewe. w. Alan Jay Lerner. Copyrighted March 23, 1956, by the authors;[1] the copyright deposit copy is a professional edition. Probable first regular edition: Front cover has drawings of Bernard Shaw, Rex Harrison and Julie Andrews and is pink, black and white. Price: 50¢. s. *My Fair Lady*—7 titles listed. Published by Chappell & Co., RKO Bldg., Rockefeller Center, New York, N.Y. p. [2] blank. m. on pp. 3–7. p.n. 4065-5. Back cover has the letters "C Co" with a small scroll. JF. *My Fair Lady* opened in New York City on March 15, 1956.

The piano-vocal score of *My Fair Lady* was published Oct. 25, 1956,[1] and a few paperbound copies were sold with the footnote "1st repro-OCT-2" at the bottom of the title page, and the footnote "1st repro-OCT-1" at the bottom of the two succeeding pages; JF (autographed by the composer and lyricist). On Nov. 9, 1956, a clothbound copyright copy was deposited at LC with these footnotes deleted; LC(CDC) and JF. Five million copies of the long-playing record from the show were sold through March, 1964. Brief biographic information regarding the authors appears above under *Almost Like Being in Love.*

I Dreamt That I Dwelt in Marble Halls—The Bohemian Girl

m. M. W. Balfe. w. Alfred Bunn. Published about Dec. 7, 1843,[1] as sheet music from the opera *The Bohemian Girl*, by Chappell, 50 New Bond Street,

---

[3] Obituary, *The New York Times*, May 25, 1969.
[4] Obituary, *The New York Times*, March 29, 1974.

---

[1] Copyright records; LC.

[1] MW, Dec. 7, 1843, p. 408.

London. Probable first edition: Engraved. Front cover lists no arrangements in other keys, mentions Miss Rainforth as the singer, the price 2s, and refers to a Paris agent. p. [2] blank. m. on pp. 1–5 (actually 3–7). The title on p. 1 is *The Dream*. p.n. 6742. Back cover blank. JF.

The piano-vocal score of the opera was published Feb. 9, 1844.[2] In the copyright deposit copy, the imprint on the title page is as above, and the price is £2.2.0. vb. m. on pp. 1–271, *The Dream* on p. 106. p.ns. 6742–6814, scattered. p. [272] blank. Engraved BM(CDC) and JF (copy also contains index page, verso blank, before music pages).

The orchestral score and parts of the opera do not seem to have been published. The opera was performed in London on Nov. 27, 1843. Michael William Balfe was born in Dublin in 1808 and died there in 1870.[3] Alfred Bunn was born in 1796/7 and died in Boulogne in 1860.[3]

I Get a Kick out of You

I   get   no   kick from cham – pagne

mw. Cole Porter. Published Nov. 23, 1934,[1] by Harms, Incorporated, New York, N.Y. First edition: Front cover has photographs of stars and scenes from the show *Anything Goes*, and is red, green, black and white. 7 titles listed. m. on pp. 2–7. p.n. 546-6. Back cover adv. *My.. - Adelai.* LC(CDC) and JF.

The show *Anything Goes* opened in New York City on Nov. 21, 1934. The piano-vocal score of the show was published by Chappell & Co., Ltd., London, without a price on the title page, on July 14, 1936;[1] LC(CDC). Brief biographic information regarding Porter appears above under *Begin the Beguine*.

I Got Rhythm

I___   got   rhy – thm,___   I ___   got   mu – sic

[2] According to the entry at Stationers' Hall the same date. *MW*, Feb. 22, 1844, p. 69.

[3] *Grove's*, vol. I, pp. 370 and 1014.

[1] Copyright records; LC.

m. George Gershwin. w. Ira Gershwin. Published Oct. 14, 1930,[1] by New
World Music Corporation, New York, N.Y. First edition: Front cover has
a drawing of a cowgirl and is pink, black and white. s. *Girl Crazy*—6
titles listed. m. on pp. 2–5. p.n. 354-4. Back cover adv. *Strike.. - I've..*
LC(CDC) and JF. The show opened the same day in New York City.

The song, sometimes mistakenly sung "I've Got Rhythm," was originally introduced in the show by Ethel Merman.[2] A famous piano arrangement of the song by the composer was included at p. 144 in *George Gershwin's Song Book* published July 20, 1932,[1] by the same publisher and
signed by the composer; LC(CDC) and JF. *"I Got Rhythm" Variations for
Orchestra and Piano Solo* was published for two pianos on June 22, 1934,[1]
by the same publisher without other arrangements on the title page;
LC(CDC) and JF.

The piano-vocal score of *Girl Crazy* was published May 20, 1954,[1] by
the same publisher; LC(CDC) and JF. George Gershwin was born in New
York City in 1898 and died in Beverly Hills, Cal., in 1937. Ira Gershwin
was born two years earlier in New York City and died in 1983 in Beverly
Hills.

I Love Coffee, I Love Tea

I love cof - fee, I love tea, I like the boys and the boys like me

The words of this song seem foreshadowed by a little poem included in
James Orchard Halliwell, *The Nursery Rhymes of England* (London, 1842),
p. 86, at NYPL: "One, two, three—I love coffee,—And Billy loves tea."
No music is included. The complete words in their presently known form
appeared in 1915 in Perrow, p. 186, where it is stated that the words were
collected "From Mississippi; country whites; MS. of Miss Reedy; 1909."[1]
No music is included. The opening words are sometimes *I Like Coffee, I
Like Tea. I Love Coffee* was also a rope-skipping rhyme.[2]

The melody has been played for decades, frequently on the black
notes of the piano, followed by crossed-hand variations, but no early print-

---

[1] Copyright records; LC.
[2] See Gershwin, p. 341.

[1] The words are also in verse 15 of *Paper of Pins*, or *The Keys of Heaven*, in
Sharp, *Southern Appalachians*, vol. II, p. 46. Cf. *North Carolina F.*, vol. III, p. 128.
[2] Botkin, pp. 791, 795 and 799. See, also, *JAF Index*, p. 200. Michael Stoner, New
York City, has been helpful in connection with this title.

ing has been found.[3] Two bars of a similar melody, to the common words, are included in *Java Jive*, with music credited to Ben Oakland and words to Milton Drake, published by Advanced Music Corporation, New York, N.Y., in 1940; JF. Two bars of the common music and words are also included in a patriotic version of *I Love Coffee (I Love Tea)* by Vick Knight published in 1943 by Carmichael Music Publications, Hollywood, Cal.; JF.

I Love You Truly

I love you tru - ly, tru - ly, dear

mw. Carrie Jacobs-Bond. This song was first printed in a book entitled *Seven Songs* copyrighted by her on Jan. 7, 1901.[1] Probable first edition: Carrie Jacobs-Bond's address is **42 31st Street,** Chicago (her address from 1899 to 1904).[2] Front cover is gray and black and has a drawing of wild roses. vb. Photograph of the composer. vb. Titles of the seven songs. vb. m. on pp. 3–15. Testimonial. *Compositions.* Three pages of poems. Three blank pages. Back cover lists *Compositions.. I Love You Truly* is on p. 11, and is dedicated to A.B.H. The 1901 copyright appears throughout. NYPL (inscribed) and JF. *I Love You Truly* was not separately deposited for copyright at the time.

Jacobs-Bond, a composer and poetess, was born in Janesville, Wis., in 1862 and died in Hollywood in 1946.[3]

I Want a Girl (Just like the Girl That Married Dear Old Dad)

I want a girl just like the girl

© 1911. Permission granted by Harry von Tilzer Music Pub. Co. (a division of Teleklew Productions, Inc.)

[3] A different melody, with the opening words "Some love coffee," appears in Sharp, *Nursery Songs,* no page number, and also in Sharp, *Southern Appalachians,* vol. II, p. 383 (not in the 1917 edition, at NYPL).

[1] Copyright records; LC.
[2] According to the Chicago city directories; CPL.
[3] *ASCAP,* p. 45.

m. Harry von Tilzer. w. Will Dillon. Published May 1, 1911,[1] by Harry
von Tilzer Music Publishing Co. The copyright deposit copy is a professional edition. Possible first regular edition: Front cover has a drawing of
a girl in a bonnet and is blue, orange and white. The publisher is Harry
von Tilzer Music. [sic] Publishing Co., 125 W. 43rd St., New York, and
four other cities. p. [2] Male Quartette. m. on pp. 3–5. Back cover adv. All..
(copyrighted in 1910). JF.

The title is "merely the living out neurotically of an unresolved Oedi-
pus complex."[2] Von Tilzer was born in Detroit, Mich., in 1872, was active
in many phases of the theatrical business and died in New York City in
1946.[3] Dillon, a lyricist, was born in Cortland, N.Y., in 1877 and died in
Ithaca, N.Y., in 1966.[3]

I Wonder Who's Kissing Her Now

m. Jos. E. Howard [and Harold Orlob]. w. Will M. Hough and Frank R.
Adams. The sheet-music edition and the copyright renewal state that the
song was copyrighted in 1909 but no record of a 1909 copyright can be
found in the Copyright Office.[1] From copyright renewal records, the song
was published Feb. 1, 1909. Possible first edition: Front cover has a drawing
of a prince outdoors at nighttime, has photographs of Howard, Hough and
Adams and is pink, orange, purple and white. The publisher is Chas. K.
Harris, New York and Chicago. There is no mention of Harold Orlob. s.
The Prince of To-Night—15 titles listed. m. on pp. 3–5. pp. [2], [6] and
[7] blank. Back cover adv. six shows, Prince.. - Time.. (all produced in 1909
or earlier). JF (inscribed by Howard). The Prince of To-Night opened in
Chicago on Feb. 8, 1909.[2]

In settlement of a litigation in 1948, Howard, the publisher and others
agreed to show Harold Orlob under Howard's name as co-composer of this
song in future printings.[3] Apparently, Orlob claimed to have been the sole

---

[1] Copyright records; LC.

[2] Dr. Nathaniel S. Lehrman, "Intermarriage: Abnormal or Normal" in The
Psychological Implications of Intermarriage (New York, N.Y., 1966), p. 45; Federation
of Jewish Philanthropies of New York, New York, N.Y.

[3] ASCAP, pp. 516 and 123, and ASCAP files.

---

[1] Copyright records; LC.

[2] The song was subsequently introduced in, and published from, Goddess of
Liberty, which opened in New York City, on Dec. 22, 1909, and Miss Nobody from
Starland, which opened in Milwaukee on Jan. 30, 1910.

[3] Copy of stipulation of settlement at JF.

composer of the melody when he was working for Howard.[4] Howard has stated that the idea for the song came when he heard a college student wistfully ask the question of a friend.[5] Adams, however, claimed that the question was asked about a girl who did not appear at one of his parties.[6]

Brief biographic information regarding Howard appears above under *Hello, Ma Baby.* Orlob, a composer and producer, was born in Logan, Utah, in 1885 and resides in New York City.[7] Hough, a lyricist and librettist, was born in Chicago in 1882 and died in Carmel, Cal., in 1962.[7] Adams, a lyricist and playwright, was born in Morrison, Ill., in 1883 and died in Whitehall, Mich., in 1963.[7]

Ich Liebe Dich—Grieg

Du mein Ge - dan - ke, du mein Sein   und   Wer - den!
Min Tan - kes Tan - ke e - ne   Du   er   vor - den

m. Edvard H. Grieg. Danish words: H. C. Andersen. This song was published at Grieg's expense about April 5, 1865[1] on p. 7 of *Hjertets Melodier (Melodies of the Heart)* for piano and voice by Chr. E. Hornemans Forlag og Eiendom (publisher and owner), Copenhagen. Probable first edition: Engraved. Front cover has a dedication to the lyricist, the op. no. is 5, the price is 60 (pfennig), and there is a reference to an agent, C. Warmuth, at Christiania (the name of Oslo 1624–1925). Danish text. Probably: vb; m. on pp. 3–9; p.n. 91; and p. [10] blank. BOB has two copies: the above engraved first printing, and the other not engraved but inscribed and dated Feb., 1869.

The title of the song in Norwegian is *Jeg Elsker Dig.* The song was inspired by the love of Grieg for his cousin, Nina Hagerup, which love her parents unsuccessfully tried to oppose because he was a musician. In the manuscript of the work, also at BOB, appears its date of composition, Dec., 1864. Brief biographic information regarding Grieg appears above under *An den Frühling.* Hans Christian Andersen, the well-known writer of children's stories, was born in Odense, Denmark, in 1805 and died in Copenhagen in 1875.

[4] *The New York Times,* June 4, 1961, sec. I, p. 85. *Variety,* June 14, 1961, p. 47.
[5] *The New York Times,* May 21, 1961, sec. I, p. 87.
[6] Geller, p. 211.
[7] *ASCAP,* pp. 241, 378, 240 and 3, and ASCAP files.

[1] *Faedrelandet,* Copenhagen, April 5, 1865, p. 2; DKB. *Grieg Catalogue,* p. 5. Dag Schjeldrupebbe, *Edvard Grieg 1858–1867* (Oslo and London, 1964), p. 210; NYPL.

Ida Sweet as Apple Cider

m. Eddie Munson. w. Eddie Leonard. Copyrighted Aug. 26, 1903,[1] by Jos. W. Stern & Co., New York, N.Y. The copyright deposit copy is a professional edition. Possible first regular edition: Front cover has a photograph of Eddie Leonard and is blue and white. Publisher is at 34 East 21st St.[2] p. [2] blank. m. on pp. 3–7. p.n. 3733-5. p. [8] adv. *You're.. - The Picture..* p. [9] blank. Back cover adv. *When..* Nine of the songs advertised in this edition were copyrighted on or before Aug. 19, 1903;[1] the copyright date of the tenth song, if published, has not been found. JF.

No biographic information has been found regarding Eddie Munson. Leonard, a composer, lyricist and actor, was born in Richmond, Va., in 1875 and died in New York City in 1941.[3]

If I Loved You—Carousel

m. Richard Rodgers. w. Oscar Hammerstein 2nd. Published March 23, 1945,[1] by Williamson Music, Inc., RKO Bldg., Radio City, New York, N.Y. First edition: Front cover has a drawing of a carousel and is pink, green and white. s. *Carousel*—5 titles listed. **(See Plate II.)** m. on pp. 2–5. p.n. 587–4. Back cover adv. *Oklahoma - People..* LC(CDC), LL and JF. The show opened in New York City on April 19, 1945.

Rodgers has stated that, of all his shows, the music of *Carousel* was

---

[1] Copyright records; LC.

[2] The address coincides with that in the *Telephone Directory of the New York Telephone Company*, March 1, 1903, p. 612; NYPL.

[3] *ASCAP*, p. 301.

---

[1] Copyright records; LC.

the most significant and his favorite.[2]† The piano-vocal score of the show was published Dec. 17, 1945,[1] and in the first printing the address of the publisher is the same as that given above, the score is paperbound and there is no price on the title page; LC(CDC) and JF. Rodgers was born in New York City in 1902 and died there in 1979. Brief biographic information regarding Hammerstein appears above under *All the Things You Are.*

If You Knew Susie like I Know Susie

Copyright MCMXXV by Shapiro, Bernstein & Co. Inc. New York. Copyright renewed MCMLII and assigned to Shapiro, Bernstein & Co. Inc. Published by joint arrangement between Shapiro, Bernstein & Co. Inc., and Ross Jungnickel, Inc., New York. Used by permission of both publishers.

mw. B. G. de Sylva. Published March 18, 1925,[1] by Shapiro, Bernstein & Co. Inc., Cor. Broadway & 47th Street, New York, N.Y. First edition; Front cover has a photograph of Al Jolson, refers to only the show, *Big Boy* (but not a show cover), and is red, black, gray and white. p. [2] adv. *At..* m. on pp. 3–5. Back cover adv. *At.. - The Vale.* LC(CDC).

Joseph Meyer was later added as a coauthor of the song. The show, *Big Boy,* opened in New York City on Jan. 7, 1925. Brief biographic information regarding de Sylva and Meyer appears above under *April Showers* and *California Here I Come.*

I'll Follow My Secret Heart

© 1934 by Chappell & Co., Ltd. Copyright renewed. Published by Chappell & Co. Inc. By consent.

mw. Noël Coward. Published Feb. 16, 1934,[1] by Chappell & Co., Ltd., 50 New Bond Street, London W. 1. First edition: Front cover has a drawing

---

[2] *The New York Times,* June 27, 1962, p. 41. Transcript of television show *Youth Wants to Know,* April 1, 1956, p. 9; JF.

---

[1] Copyright records; LC.

[1] Copyright records; LC. A story regarding the composing of the song is in Kane, p. 62.

of a sophisticated woman and is yellow, blue and white. Price: 2/. s. *Conversation Piece*—6 titles listed. m. on pp. 2–7. p.n. 31968. Back cover adv. seven shows by the author. BM (copyright copy deposited Feb. 21, 1934). The *Valse* arrangement for piano solo was deposited at BM the same day.

   Conversation Piece opened in London on Feb. 16, 1934. The piano-vocal score of the show was published March 22, 1934;[1] BM(CDC). Coward, a composer, lyricist, actor and director, was born in Teddington, England, in 1899 and died in Jamaica, British West Indies, in 1973.[2]

I'll Give to You a Paper of Pins

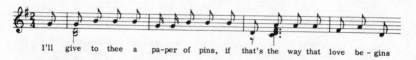

I'll   give   to   thee   a   pa-per of pins, if   that's the   way that   love   be - gins

The first known printing of this song was Dec. 31, 1869,[1] under the title *Paper of Pins*, composed and arranged by E. Mack and with words by "A Lady." Probable first edition: Publisher is Lee & Walker, 922 Chestnut St., Philadelphia, and there are two agents. The price is 3. p. [2] blank. m. on pp. 3–5. p.n. 10784. Back cover blank. Engraved. JF. (The copyright renewal copy at LC is the same except that the price has been increased to 3½, and the renewal claimant is Mrs. E. Mack.) One authority gives the name of this song as *The Keys of Heaven*,[2] but no earlier printing has been found under this name. The song has been said to have had its origins in Scotland, England, Jamaica and elsewhere,[3] but the above printing is the earliest known proof of the song.

I'll See You Again

I'll   see   you   a - gain

[2] Obituary, *The New York Times*, March 27, 1973.

---

[1] Copyright records; LC. Newell, pp. 51–55, says that the song is in James O. Halliwell, *The Nursery Rhymes of England* (London), no. 479. This is an error as it is not in the 1st or 1842 edition at NYPL, or the 2nd, 3rd or 4th editions in 1843, 1844 or 1846 at BM. Opie does not mention this song.

[2] Sharp, *Southern Appalachians*, vol. II, p. 45.

[3] Belden, p. 507.

mw. Noël Coward. This song was first published as a duet on July 3, 1929,[1] and deposited as such eight days later at BM in what is probably a professional edition. Publisher is Chappell & Co., Ltd., 50 New Bond Street, London W.1. Front cover is blue and white and lists seven titles from the show *Bitter Sweet*. m. on pp. 2–7. p.n. 30122. Back cover lists *Popular..* BM(CDC). The song version was deposited in a regular edition on Aug. 5, 1929, at BM. First edition: Front cover is red, blue, black and white. 10 titles are listed, this title listed both as a Song Version and as a Duet. m. on pp. 2–7. p.n. 30149. Same back cover as above. BM(CDC) and JF.

Bitter Sweet opened in London on July 18, 1929. The piano-vocal score, published Aug. 19, 1929,[1] was deposited the next day at LC and the following day at BM; LC and BM (both CDC) and JF. Brief biographic information regarding Coward appears above under *I'll Follow My Secret Heart*.

I'll See You in My Dreams

I'll see you in my dreams

© Copyright 1924 (renewed) Leo Feist, Inc., New York, N.Y. Used by permission.

m. Isham Jones. w. Gus Kahn. Published Dec. 19, 1924,[1] by Leo Feist, Inc. The copyright deposit copy is a professional edition. Possible first regular edition: Front cover has a drawing of a Spanish girl, a photograph of Paul Whiteman and is red, white and blue. The publisher's address is Feist Building, New York City. p. [2] adv. *Southern..* and *Doo..* m. on pp. 3–5. p.n. 5533-3. p. 4 adv. *Good..* Back cover adv. *Dear..* and *Eliza.* All the songs advertised in this edition were published on or before Dec. 19, 1924. JF.

Jones, a composer, musician and conductor, was born in Coalton, Ohio, in 1894 and died in Florida in 1956.[2] Brief biographic information regarding Kahn appears above under *Carioca*.

---

[1] Copyright records; LC. A story about the composing of the song is in Kane, p. 62.

[1] Copyright records; LC.

[2] *ASCAP*, p. 260; and obituary, *The New York Times*, Oct. 20, 1956.

I'll Take You Home Again, Kathleen

I'll   take you home a–gain, Kath–leen,   a – cross the o – cean wild and   wide

mw. Thomas P. Westendorf. The first printing of this song was in Church's *Musical Visitor* (Supplement), Cincinnati, March, 1876. LC(CDC) and *ULS*, p. 1844. This printing preceded the sheet music edition; JF.

The history of this song has been ably written by Richard S. Hill in "Getting Kathleen Home Again."[1] The song is at times mistaken as an Irish ballad. That it was written in Kentucky to cheer up a homesick wife who wanted to return East[2] is shown by Hill to be unlikely. Westendorf, a musician and composer, was born in Bowling Green, Caroline County, Va., in 1848 and died in Chicago in 1923.[1]

I'm Called Little Buttercup—H.M.S. Pinafore

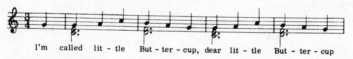

I'm   called lit – tle   But – ter – cup, dear lit – tle   But – ter – cup

m. Arthur Sullivan. w. W. S. Gilbert. *H.M.S. Pinafore*, the comic opera in which this song appeared, was performed in London on May 25, 1878, and a copy of the piano-vocal score was deposited at BM on June 20, 1878,[1] by Metzler & Co., 37 Great Marlborough Street, London W. First edition: Front cover is gray, black and red; price is 4/. verso adv. *New..* Title page in black and white is similar to the front cover. Cast. Index. m. on pp. [4]–106, the printer on the last page being Henderson, Rait, and Fenton, 73 & 74 Marylebone Lane, Oxford St., London W. No plate number. p. [107] adv. **Shortly to be produced . . . Carmen."** p. [108] adv. *The Sorcerer* and *The Dance..* p. [109] adv. *Metzler..* Back cover adv. *The Sorcerer.* No Overture.[2] This song is on p. 8. BM*, RA and JF. The pianoforte score was deposited at BM on Sept. 26, 1878.

---

[1] *Notes*, June, 1948, p. 338. See also *Richmond Times Dispatch*, May 17, 1936, Section V, p. 1; photocopy at LC Music Division.

[2] Geller, p. 5.

---

[1] Although the piano-vocal score was promptly deposited at BM, it was not entered at Stationers' Hall until May 30, 1879. *ILN*, June 15, 1878, p. 560.

[2] Sullivan wrote only a small portion of the Overture. George Baker, "Gilbert and Sullivan Operas—Who Wrote the Overtures?", *MO*, Feb., 1955, p. 273. John Wolfson, New York, N.Y., called the author's attention to this point.

No contemporary printing of *I'm Called Little Buttercup* in separate sheet music has been found or referred to,[2A] and it is not known whether one was published.

An orchestral score of the comic opera, under the German title *Amor an Bord (Love on Shipboard)*, was printed by Henry Litolff, Braunschweig, about 1885.[3] First edition: Front cover is black and gray. vb. Title page is black and white, without price. vb. m. on pp. 1–228, a lithographing of a manuscript. German text only. No plate number. BM, LC, RA and JF. No orchestral parts of the comic opera have been published. Brief biographic information regarding Gilbert and Sullivan appears above under *Bow, Bow, Ye Lower Middle Classes.*

I'm Just Wild About Harry

I'm   just wild ___ a-bout   Har - ry

© 1921 M. Witmark & Sons. Copyright renewed. Used by permission.

mw. Noble Sissle and Eubie Blake. Published June 23, 1921,[1] by M. Witmark & Sons, New York, N.Y. First edition: Front cover has a drawing of feet shuffling along and is orange, black and white. s. *Shuffle Along*—20 titles listed. The producer of the show is The Nikko Producing Co., Inc. m. on pp. 2–4. p.ns. 7773; 16482-3. p. [5] adv. *One..* and *Night..* Back cover adv. *Gypsy..* LC(CDC). The show opened in New York City on May 23, 1921.

The song became Harry Truman's presidential campaign theme song in 1948, and the manuscript of the song was later donated to the Truman Memorial Library, Independence, Mo.[1A] Sissle was born in Indianapolis, Ind., in 1889, became a lyricist, musician and conductor and died in Tampa, Fla., in 1975.[2] Blake was born in Baltimore in 1883, became a composer, actor and musician and died in Brooklyn, N.Y., in 1983.[3]

[2A] Not, for example, entered at Stationers' Hall, advertised in *MW*, listed in the piano-vocal score, listed in other sheet music from the comic opera, or deposited at BM; and the publisher is uncertain. *ILN*, Sept. 28, 1878, p. 304, merely refers to "separate songs," without identifying them.

[3] Per Reginald Allen, New York City. The orchestral score is not in Hofmeister *Annual 1881–1900*, nor in *Litolff Catalogues*, Braunschweig, ca. 1895–1900; LC and NYPL. The German piano-vocal score is in Hofmeister *Monatsbericht*, Aug., 1882, p. 240.

---

[1] Copyright records; LC.
[1A] *The New York Times*, Sept. 27, 1967, p. 43.
[2] Obituary, *The New York Times*, Dec. 18, 1975.
[3] Obituary, *The New York Times*, Feb. 13, 1983.

I'm Looking Over a Four Leaf Clover

I'm look - ing   o - ver   a   four   leaf   clo - ver

© 1927 Jerome H. Remick & Co. Copyright renewed and assigned to Remick Music Corp. Used by permission.

m. Harry Woods. w. Mort Dixon. Published Jan. 17, 1927,[1] by Jerome H. Remick & Co., New York and Detroit. The copyright deposit copy has handwritten music notes and a black and white front cover, and may be a professional edition: m. on pp. [1]–3 (actually 2–4). p.n. 341-3. LC(CDC) and JF. Possible first regular edition: Front cover has a drawing of four-leaf clovers, a photograph of Earl and Bell, and is green, brown and white. m. on pp. 2–5. p.n. 304-4. Back cover adv. *Don't..* (published 1926[1]). JF. *All..* and *No..*, advertised on the back covers of other editions were published Jan. 17, 1927, and June 27, 1927.[1]

Woods, a composer and lyricist, was born in North Chelmsford, Mass., in 1896 and died in Phoenix, Ariz., in 1970.[2] Dixon, a lyricist, was born in New York City in 1892 and died in Bronxville, N.Y., in 1956.[3]

In a Persian Market

Back - sheesh, back - sheesh,_   Al   -   lah

Copyright 1920 by Bosworth & Co., Ltd. By permission.

m. Albert W. Ketèlbey. On Nov. 9, 1920,[1] a copy published for piano by Bosworth & Co., Ltd., 8 Hedden Street, Regent Street, London W.1, was deposited at BM. First edition: Folio. Front cover is yellow, black and white and has a drawing of a Persian market scene. p. [2] blank. m. on pp. 1–11 (really 3–13); a few words are included. p.n. 16240. p. [14] adv. *Valse..* p. [15] adv. *At..* Back cover adv. *100..* Four arrangements are listed on the front cover, piano solo at 2/6; it is not known when the other arrangements (full orchestra, small orchestra and military band) were published. BM(CDC). The song version was published in 1925; BM(CDC).

[1] Copyright records; LC.
[2] Obituary, *The New York Times*, Jan. 15, 1970.
[3] Obituary, *The New York Times*, March 24, 1956.

[1] Not in MO until July, 1921, p. 815.

Ketèlbey was born Albert William Ketelbey on Aug. 9, 1875, in Aston Manor, Aston, Erdington, Warwick, England,[2] and died on the Isle of Wight in 1959.

In My Merry Oldsmobile

Come   a - long with   me   Lu - cile

m. Gus Edwards. w. Vincent Bryan. Copyrighted June 12, 1905,[1] by M. Witmark & Sons, New York, London and Chicago. The copyright deposit copy at LC is a professional edition. Possible first regular edition: Front cover has a drawing of a couple in an Oldsmobile, a photograph of Thos. J. Quigley and is aqua, black and white. p. [2] blank. m. on pp. 3–5. p.n. 7193-3. Back cover adv. *Good-Bye.. - If..* All songs advertised in this edition were copyrighted on or before June 12, 1905. JF.

This, probably the best known automobile song, did not originate in Detroit. Brief biographic information regarding Edwards appears above under *By the Light of the Silvery Moon*. Bryan had been a screen director with Charlie Chaplin and Harold Lloyd and died in Hollywood, Cal., in 1937, at fifty-four.[2]

In the Gloaming

In   the gloam - ing   oh,   my   dar - ling

m. Annie Fortescue Harrison (Lady Arthur Hill). w. Meta Orred. The words were first printed in Meta Orred's *Poems* (London, 1874), p. 134, the copyright copy of which was deposited at BM on Jan. 19, 1875. BM(CDC).

A sheet music edition of the song was deposited Dec. 12, 1877, at BM by Hutchings & Romer, 9 Conduit Street, Regent Street, London. First edi-

[2] On the basis of a birth certificate obtained by Nicolas Slonimsky, Los Angeles. See, generally, Gammond-Clayton, p. 123, and Sandved, p. 1088.

[1] Copyright records; LC.

[2] Obituary, *The New York Times*, April 28, 1937.

tion: The authorship of the song is as given above. Front cover is black
and white, has a dedication to and says it is sung by Signor Campobello,
the price is 4/ and the publisher has a wholesale warehouse at 10 & 11
Little Marlborough Street, Regent Street [London] W. p. [2] blank. m. on
pp. 1–5 (really 3–7). p.n. 9718. Back cover adv. *Abbey.. - Yes..* No keys or
other songs mentioned on front cover. BM(CDC).

Annie Fortescue Harrison composed the song in 1877 shortly before
she married Lord Arthur Hill, the comptroller in Queen Victoria's house-
hold.† She died in England in 1944 at the age of ninety-three.[1] Orred was
a poetess and writer of literary works published in the 1870's and died in
1953.[2]

In the Good Old Summertime

In the good old sum - mer time

m. George Evans. w. Ren Shields. Copyrighted May 24, 1902,[1] by Howley,
Haviland & Dresser, 1260–1266 Broadway, New York, N.Y. First edition:
Front cover has a drawing of a couple in a rowboat, lists 13 arrangements
and is red, green and white.[2] p. [2] adv. *Just..* m. on pp. 3–5. No p.n. Back
cover adv. *A Little..* LC(CDC) and JF. The song was soon introduced by
Blanche Ring in *The Defender*,[3] and the edition with a drawing of roses
and referring to the show, *The Defender* (which opened in New York City
on July 3, 1902), appeared later.

Evans, the "Honey Boy," was born in Wales in 1870, came to the
United States at the age of seven and became a black-faced comedian and
minstrel; he died in Baltimore in 1915.[4] Shields, a composer, lyricist and
vaudeville actor, was born in Chicago in 1868 and died in New York City
in 1913.[5]

[1] Obituaries: *New York Herald Tribune*, Feb. 4, 1944; *Variety*, Feb. 16, 1944; and
MO, March, 1944. The latter reports her age at death as ninety-five. See, also, Simpson,
p. 168.
[2] Allibone, vol. II, p. 1197; and letter from publisher.

[1] Copyright records; LC.
[2] Front cover is illustrated in Fuld, *American*, p. [37].
[3] Geller, p. 191.
[4] Obituary, *The New York Times*, March 6, 1915.
[5] *ASCAP*, p. 454.

Indian Love Call

When I'm call - ing   you, ____   oo - oo   -   oo - oo - oo!

m. Rudolf Friml. w. Otto Harbach and Oscar Hammerstein 2nd. Published under the title *The Call*, on Sept. 2, 1924,[1] by Harms, Incorporated, New York, N.Y. First edition: Title on the front cover is **The Call.** Front cover is blue, red, purple and white. s. *Rose-Marie*—5 titles listed. Title on page 2 is *Indian Love Call*. m. on pp. 2–7. p.n. 7117-6. Back cover adv. *Memory..* LC(CDC) and JF. The show opened in New York City on Sept. 2, 1924.

The song is said to be President Eisenhower's favorite.[2] The piano-vocal score of *Rose-Marie* was published Feb. 18, 1925;[1] the title page of the first edition shows the copyright years as MCMXXIV (inked out) and MCMXXV. LC(CDC). Brief biographic information regarding Friml, Harbach and Hammerstein appears above under *L'Amour-Toujours-L'Amour*, *The Desert Song* and *All the Things You Are*.

Intermezzo—Cavalleria Rusticana

m. Pietro Mascagni. A copy of the piano-vocal score of *Cavalleria Rusticana* was deposited with the Prefect of Milan on June 10, 1890.[1] A copy was also deposited at the S. Cecilia Library in Rome on July 8, 1890, and a similar copy was purchased by the British Museum on Aug. 22, 1890. Probable first edition of the piano-vocal score: Publisher is Edoardo Sonzogno, 14 Via Pasquirolo, Milan. Front cover is red and many shades of brown, green,

[1] Copyright records; LC.
[2] *The New York Times*, Jan. 23, 1957, p. 31.

[1] Copyright records; UDP.

white and gray and has a drawing of blossoms against a wooden background. vb. Half-title page. vb. Title page mentions the librettists, G. Targioni-Tozzetti and G. Menasci, and the year 1890. Copyright notice. Dedication to Conte Florestano de Larderel. vb. Index. vb. Cast. vb. Text on pp. [XI]–XVI. m. on pp. 1–168, the *Intermezzo* on p. 125. p.n. 492. Inside of back cover blank. Price of L.10 on outside of back cover. SCR*(CDC), BM and JF. The earliest discovered piano edition of the *Intermezzo* has p.n. 509; ONB. The opera was performed May 17, 1890, in Rome.

A possible first edition of the orchestral parts of the opera, with plate number 496, lithographed, without a copyright claim on each part, with covers, may also have been published in 1890; CI and MET*. Some engraved folio parts with plate number 586, with covers, are also at CI.

E. Sonzogno published the orchestral score of the opera with an 1890 copyright claim; whether it was published that year is not known. Because of the plate number and the presence of a copyright claim (see page 24 above), it was probably published later. This possible first edition is folio, lacks a title page, has music on pp. 1–272, the *Intermezzo* on p. 204, the music pages are engraved, the p.n. is E 1478 S and there is the 1890 copyright claim by E. Sonzogno, Milan. CI and JF. A lithographed copy of a manuscript score which states "3a Edizione," without copyright claim, without title page, without text (to make it possible to write in the text in the language of the country where the opera was performed), with 335 pages, of uncertain date and folio, is at Jean-Marie Martin, Hollogne-aux-Pierres, Belgium. He believes the first printing of the orchestral score was a lithographed copy of a manuscript score. Sonzogno has written this author that it did not sell the orchestral score to Ed. Bote & G. Bock, Berlin, until 1911, and the latter firm has confirmed that its orchestral score was published after the Sonzogno orchestral score. Copies of the Bote & Bock orchestral score, without plate number or title page, are at BM and NC. Kinsky also mentions a Bote & Bock orchestral score with p.n. 18720, indicating a date well after 1900;[2] LC.

The *Intermezzo*, separately, was published for orchestral score and parts about 1891 by Ed. Bote & G. Bock, Berlin, with p.ns. 13540 and 13541; NYPL and SB.

Mascagni was born in Leghorn in 1863 and died in Rome in 1945. Targioni-Tozzetti, one of the two librettists, was born in Leghorn in 1863 and died there in 1934.[3] Menasci, the other librettist, was born in Leghorn in 1867 and died there in 1925.[3]

---

[2] Kinsky, *Opern*, p. 390. Deutsch, *Plate Numbers*, p. 9.
[3] *DM*, pp. 475 and 320. Letter from the publisher.

L'Internationale

De - bout, les dam - nés de la terre!_____

m. Pierre Degeyter. w. Eugène Pottier. The words were first published, without music, in Eugène Pottier, *Chants Revolutionnaires* (Paris, 1887), p. [17], with a dedication to "citoyen Lefrançais, membre de la Commune." LC. The words had been written in Paris in June, 1871, during the uprising following the French defeat by the Germans a few months before.[1]

The music (and words) are said to have been first printed by M. Boldoduc, apparently in Lille, in 1888,[1] but no copy has been found. The song was sung there for the first time in July, 1888. The song was said to have been then printed by Delory in 1894 and Lagrange in 1898,[1] but no copies of these editions have been found.

Inciting political strife, the song was itself the subject of an 18-year lawsuit between Pierre Degeyter and his brother, Adolphe, as to the authorship of the melody.[2] During this period, the music was frequently ascribed merely to "Degeyter." Pierre finally prevailed. *L'Internationale* was the official anthem of the Soviet Union from 1917 to 1944. Pierre Chrétien Degeyter was born in 1848 in Ghent, Belgium, became a woodcarver in Lille and died in Paris in 1932.[1] Eugène Ediné Pottier was born in Paris in 1816; a transport worker there, he became a member of the Commune in 1871 and died in 1887.[1]

Introduction et Rondo Capriccioso—Saint-Saëns

m. Camille Saint-Saëns. This work for violin and orchestra was published

---

[1] Alexandre Zevaès, *Eugène Pottier et "L'Internationale"* (Paris, 1936); NYPL. *Eugène Pottier—L'Internationale* (Moscow, 1939); NYPL.

[2] Nettl, *National Anthems*, p. 129.

for violin and piano on Jan. 15, 1870,[1] by G. Hartmann, 19 Boulevard de la Madeleine, Paris. Possible first edition: Folio. The title page has a dedication to Monsieur Sarasate, the price is 10 f., there are English and German prices and agents, the piano arrangement is by Georges Bizet, and the printer is Arouy, Paris. No opus number. vb. m. on pp. 1–17. p.n. 377. p. [18] blank. Violin part on pp. 1–8. JF.

The orchestral parts were published in Feb., 1875,[1,2] by Durand, Schoenewerk et Cie., 4 Place de la Madeleine, Paris. Possible first editions, folio, with plate number 2068 are at CI and JF but lack front covers. The orchestral score was published in Aug., 1879,[1] by the same firm. Possible first edition: the price is 8 f., the opus number is 28, and the printer is Michelet, Paris. vb. m. on pp. 1–46, engraved. p.n. 2591. Quarto. P. 46 states that the engraver is L. Parent. BN and BPL.

The work was composed in 1863. Brief biographic information regarding Saint-Saëns appears above under *Danse Macabre.*

Invitation to the Dance—Weber

m. Carl Maria von Weber. Weber sent the corrected proof of *Aufforderung zum Tanze (Invitation to the Dance)* to the printer on July 16, 1821, receiving the first printed copies on July 31, 1821.[1] He had just played the piano in a famous concert in Berlin on June 25, 1821.[2] There are six different known early Berlin editions of this composition, all for piano, engraved, oblong, dedicated to "seiner Caroline," op. 65, price 18 gr., p. [2] blank, music on pp. 3–14 and p.n. 1096: (a) The publisher is "In der Schlesinger-schen Buch-und Musikhandlung," and the title page says "Gespielt vom Componisten in seinem Concerte zu Berlin," AT and JF (see Plate VII); (b) Same as (a) except that there is no reference to the concert in Berlin,[3]

[1] Letter from present publisher. *Saint-Saëns Catalogue*, p. 16.
[2] *CNO*, Jan., 1875, p. 7. *RGM*, March 21, 1875, p. 96.

[1] Jähns, no. 260, p. 284. In *Handbuch Annual* 1822 (from Easter, 1821, to Easter, 1822), p. 33.
[2] *Grove's*, vol. 9, p. 208.
[3] (b) seems later than (a), as (b) has two horizontal lines below the composer's name with blank space between them., i.e., where the reference to the Berlin concert had been. Both are excellent engraved impressions.

copy at Albi Rosenthal, London; (c) A completely restyled title page in which the publisher is "In Ad: Mt: Schlesinger's Buch-und Musikhandlung," the heading on p. 3 is the German title only and there are no other words at the top or bottom of the page, BSM; (d) Same as (c) except that on p. 3 there is also an English subtitle, C. M. v. Weber . . . is in the upper left-hand corner, and Berlin . . . is in the bottom right-hand corner, JF; (e) Same as (d) except the words "Einzig rechtmässige Original-ausgabe" have been added to the bottom left-hand corner of p. 3, ONB; and (f) The publisher is "Bei Ad. Mt. Schlesinger, Verleger," and there are references to Paris and Vienna publishers, JF.[4]

Priority as among the six early printings is not known. Perhaps unaware of all the alternatives, Jähns considered the general type of (c), (d) or (e) the earliest;[4] Hirschberg (f);[5] and Alan Tyson, London, and this author (a) as it alone has a contemporary quality since it refers to the Berlin concert where the work was apparently played, and the music was published shortly after the concert.

The composition is also frequently known as *L'Invitation pour la Valse*; the first printing under this popular mistranslation may have been by Maurice Schlesinger, Paris, announced on Oct. 26, 1821.[6] The work was composed in the summer of 1819. Brief biographic information regarding Weber appears above under *Der Freischütz—Overture.*

Irene (Goodnight, Irene)

I - rene good - ni - ght

A possible source of this melody is *Irene, Good Night*, with music and words by Gussie L. Davis, sung by Edwin Harley of Haverly's Mastodon Minstrels and published by Geo. Propheter, Jr., 20 W. 14th St., New

---

[4] Leopold Hirschberg, *Reliquienschrein des Meisters Carl Maria von Weber* (Berlin, 1927), p. xii, no. 73(b); NYPL.

[5] See Hirschberg, preceding footnote.

[6] See Alan Tyson, "Maurice Schlesinger as a Publisher of Beethoven, 1822–1827," in *Acta Musicologica* (Basel, Oct.–Dec., 1963), Fasc. IV, vol. XXXV, p. 183; NYPL.

York, N.Y., and 640 Race St., Cincinnati, Ohio, with copyright claims by the publisher of 1886 and 1887; JF. The melody line and words of the first two bars are the same as those set forth above, and the song is in ¾ time, but the harmony is different throughout and the melody line and words do not resemble those of the well-known melody after the first two bars. As the "feel" of the song is similar to the well-known melody, this song may either have been an adaptation of an existing folk song or have been the source for its later adaptation into a folk song. The melody is also known as *Goodnight, Irene.*

Though there is no known other early printing of either the music or the words of the chorus of *Irene*, the words of a number of the accompanying stanzas were published in the *Journal of American Folklore*, Boston, New York, N.Y., and Lancaster, Pa., 1909, p. 245; 1911, pp. 286, 380 and 387; 1913, p. 168; and 1915, p. 141.[1] *ULS*, p. 1435. The word "Irene" does not appear in the title or words of any of these stanzas.

An unpublished field recording was made of the chorus and accompanying stanzas of *Irene* in July, 1933, sung by Leadbelly with guitar and recorded in State Prison Farm, Angola, La., by John A. Lomax. LC (Archive of Folk Song—AFS 120 B 1).

The music and words of the chorus and accompanying stanzas of *Irene* were included in *Negro Folk Songs as Sung by Lead Belly*, edited by John A. Lomax and Alan Lomax (New York, N.Y., 1936), p. 235; LC(CDC), NYPL and JF. It is there said that Leadbelly learned the chorus of the song from his Uncle Terrell. Huddie "Leadbelly" Ledbetter, a Louisiana Negro long-time convict and king of the twelve-string guitar players, popularized the song.

Irish Washerwoman

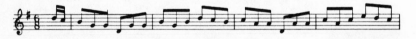

The first known printing of this dance is in Neil Gow's *A Third Collection of Strathspey Reels &c for the Piano-forte, Violin and Violoncello* (Printed for the Author, Edinburgh), p. 31, under the title *The Irish Washerwoman.* Nine copies were entered at Stationers' Hall on March 6, 1792. *BUC*, p. 392, and JF. The dance appeared in 1794 in vol. IV of James Aird's *A Selection of Scotch, English, Irish and Foreign Airs* (Glasgow), p. 8; *BUC*, p. 13. The dance apparently developed independently of the melodically similar *Scotch Bagpipe Melody*, which see below.

---

[1] Harold Barlow, New York City, noted most of these printings.

It Ain't Gonna Rain No Mo'

Oh! It ain't gon-na rain no mo' no mo', it ain't gon-na rain no mo'

mw. Wendell W. Hall. Published Dec. 4, 1923,[1] by Forster Music Publisher, Inc., 235 South Wabash Ave., Chicago. The copyright entry, and the following probable first edition at the top of p. 3, state that the song is a "modern version of the old southern melody." Front cover has a drawing of a Negro standing under a holey umbrella and is orange, black and white. p. [2] adv. Sad.. and Lonely.. m. on pp. 3–4. The copyright is in the name of the composer. 24 extra verses on p. 5. p. 4 adv. Chinky. p. 5 adv. Where.. Back cover adv. When.. and Rose.. All the songs advertised in this edition were published on or before Dec. 11, 1923. JF. Wendell Woods Hall, a composer, lyricist, singer and guitarist, was born in St. George, Kans., in 1896 and died in Mobile, Ala., in 1969.[2]

As is stated above, the song is based on an old folk song.[3] While no prior printing under this title has been found, printings of the folk song beginning in 1927 under the title Ain't Gonna Rain show the melody of the last four bars of the eight-bar chorus almost identical to that in the last four bars of the Hall version. E.g., Sandburg, p. 141. Sandburg reports that the folk song came from Kentucky and other Southern states and is at least as old as the 1870's.

Certainly, there is a similar melody in the last four bars of Satan's Camp A-Fire in Slave Songs of the United States (New York, N.Y., 1867), p. 27; LC. A similar melody also appears as Twenty-Five Miles to London in Journal of American Folklore, New York, N.Y., and Lancaster, Pa., July–Sept., 1911, p. 315. Curiously, the words of a refrain "Ain't goin' to rain no mo'" under the title I Ain't Bother Yet appear in the same issue at page 277. ULS, p. 1435.[4]

[1] Copyright records; LC.

[2] ASCAP, p. 210, and ASCAP files.

[3] Satis N. Coleman and Adolph Bregman, Songs of American Folks (New York, N.Y., 1942), p. 102; NYPL. North Carolina F., vol. III, p. 517.

[4] Harold Barlow, New York City, furnished all the information in this paragraph.

It Came upon the Midnight Clear

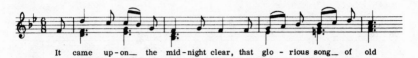

It came up-on— the mid-night clear, that glo - rious song— of old

m. Richard Storrs Willis. w. Edmund H. Sears. The words of this hymn were first printed in the *Christian Register*, Boston, Dec. 29, 1849, p. 206; *ULS*, p. 681. The music first appeared on Dec. 6, 1850,[1] in R. Storrs Willis, *Church Chorals and Choir Studies* (New York, N.Y., 1850), p. 93, to the poem, *See Israel's Gentle Shepherd Stand;* LC, NYPL and JF (Lowell Mason's copy).

No printing of the words and music together has been found before Oct. 6, 1910,[1] when they were included in Hollis Dann, *Christmas Carols and Hymns for School and Choir* (New York, N.Y.), p. 71; LC and NYPL. Willis was born in Boston in 1819, became a composer and writer on music and died in Detroit in 1900.[2] Sears was born in 1810 in Massachusetts, became an American Unitarian clergyman and poet and died in 1876.[3]

It's a Long, Long Way to Tipperary

It's a long way——— to Tip-per - ar - y

mw. Jack Judge and Harry Williams. A professional edition was deposited Oct. 15, 1912, at BM by B. Feldman & Co., London. Possible first regular edition: Folio. Front cover says the song is sung by Miss Minnie Muir and Jack Judge, the price is 6d, the address of the publisher is 2 & 3 Arthur Street, New Oxford Street, W.C., the publisher's no. is 549 and the colors are black and white. p. [2] adv. *Take.. - The Month..* m. on pp. 2–5 (actually 3–6). No p.n. Back cover advertises Feldman's Sixpenny Editions up to no. 531. Copy at publisher. There are, of course, no references in this edition to the 1914–1918 war.

This song was written and published before World War I but became

---

[1] Copyright records; LC.

[2] Metcalf, p. 43.

[3] *NIE*, vol. 20, p. 649.

popular only during that war. According to one story, the song was the sole work of Judge, but Williams had lent money to Judge, and Judge repaid the loan in this way.[1] Judge was an English vaudeville actor who was born in 1878 and who died in 1938.[2] Williams was a fellow townsman and vaudeville trouper who died in 1930.[3]

I've Been Working on the Railroad—(The Eyes of Texas)

I've been work-ing on the rail - road, all the live long day
(The) eyes of Tex - as are up - on you,

The first known appearance in print of *I've Been Working on the Railroad* is under the title *Levee Song*, in *Carmina Princetonia* (8th ed., Martin R. Dennis & Co., Newark, N.J., 1894), p. 24; LC(CDC), PUL and JF. The book was copyrighted on May 16, 1894.[1] There was also copyrighted the same day, *Levee Song*, "As Sung at Princeton," issued by the same publisher, and a copy was deposited at the same time,[1] but no copy of this separate publication has been found.

The words of *The Eyes of Texas* were written to the above melody by John Lang Sinclair for a minstrel show presented by students of the University of Texas on May 12, 1903.[2] The song, however, was not published until 1918 when it was included in *The University of Texas Community Song Book* (published in Austin, Texas, and dated Dec. 25, 1918; LC(CDC received Feb. 11, 1919) and TU. The song appears on page [1]. The opening words, "The eyes of Texas are upon you," were taken from the similar admonishment of the then University President, William L. Prather, who had adapted them from the similar advice the latter had heard as a student from General Robert E. Lee, as President of Washington College, "Young gentlemen, the eyes of the South are upon you." Sinclair was born in 1880 in Boerne, Texas, graduated from The University of Texas in 1904, became a farmer, writer and tax advisor, and died in New York City in 1947.[2]

[1] *The New York Times*, Oct. 1, 1933, Magazine sec., p. 21. See, also, Browne, p. 252.

[2] Obituary, *The New York Times*, July 29, 1938.

[3] Clipping files concerning Jack Judge and Harry Williams; NYPL Music Division. The Harry Williams mentioned above should not be confused with the American lyricist of the same name.

[1] Copyright records; LC.

[2] Bluford Hester, "Copyrighting 'The Eyes of Texas'" in *Alcade* (Austin, Tex.), Feb., 1949, p. 109, and other magazine and newspaper clippings; TU.

I've Got You Under My Skin

I've   got   you_____   un - der   my   skin

© 1936 by Chappell & Co. Inc. Copyright renewed. By consent.

mw. Cole Porter. Published Sept. 11, 1936,[1] by Chappell & Co., Inc., RKO
Building, Rockefeller Center, New York, N.Y. First edition: Front cover has
a photograph of Eleanor Powell and a drawing of a dancer and is red, white
and blue. Movie, *Born to Dance*—7 titles listed. No price. m. on pp. 2–5.
p.n. 655-4. Back cover adv. *Easy.. - Rolling..* LC(CDC) and JF. *Born To
Dance* was released Nov. 17, 1936, and copyrighted Nov. 23, 1936. Brief
biographic information regarding Porter appears above under *Begin the
Beguine.*

I've Told Ev'ry Little Star

I've   told   ev-'ry lit - tle star,   just how sweet I think you are

© 1932 by T. B. Harms Company. Copyright renewed. By consent.

m. Jerome Kern. w. Oscar Hammerstein 2nd. Copyrighted Oct. 28, 1932,[1]
by the composer. First edition: Published by T. B. Harms Company, New
York, N.Y. Front cover is blue, black and white and has drawings of
flowers. s. *Music in the Air*—4 titles listed. No price. m. on pp. 2–5. p.n.
338-4. Back cover adv. *Try.. - I..* LC(CDC) and JF. The show opened in
New York City on Nov. 8, 1932.

The piano-vocal score of *Music in the Air* was issued by the same
publisher at $5.00 on Feb. 14, 1933.[1] LC(CDC) and JF. Brief biographic
information regarding Kern and Hammerstein appears above under *All the
Things You Are.*

---

[1] Copyright records; LC.

[1] Copyright records; LC.

Jealousy

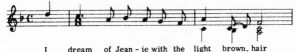

m. Jacob Gade. Published under the title *Jalousie*, a "Tango Tzigane" (Gypsy Tango), by **Gade & Warny-Musikforlag**, Copenhagen, on Sept. 15, 1925, for piano and orchestral parts.[1] Possible first edition of the piano arrangement: Front cover has title and publisher as above, a drawing of a monocled gentleman, a lady and two hearts, and is orange, black and white. No price. m. on pp. 2–5. p.n. 1. Back cover is blank. DKB (copyright copy deposited Feb. 13, 1926). In a variant, the back cover advertises *Valentino..* - *Maggidudi* (all compositions by Gade published 1900-1923[2]); JF.

The Det Kongelige Bibliotek, Copenhagen, also has the copyright copy of the orchestral parts for salonorkester, likewise deposited Feb. 13, 1926. The parts are octavo, have p.n. 2 and indicate the street address of the publisher as Østergade 8. DKB(CDC).

The publishing firm of Gade & Warny–Musikforlag was formed in 1925 and *Jalousie* was its first publication. In Oct., 1930, Gade withdrew, and the firm became Warny & Co. and later Warnys Musikforlag.[3] Gade was born in 1879 in Vejle, Denmark, became a violinist and composer[4] and died in Assens, Denmark, in 1962.

Jeanie with the Light Brown Hair

I   dream   of Jean - ie with the light brown. hair

mw. Stephen C. Foster. Copyrighted June 5, 1854,[1] by Firth, Pond & Co., 1 Franklin Square, New York, N.Y. First edition: Front cover has a drawing of "Jeanie," is lithographed, refers to three agents and is tan, black and white. There is no price "4" [40 cents] in the lower right-hand corner of the

---

[1] Copyright records; LC.
[2] Letter from the composer.
[3] *Musik og Handel*, Copenhagen, Dec. 15, 1931, p. 4; DKB.
[4] *Kraks Bla Bog* (Copenhagen, 1962), p. 447; NYPL.

---

[1] Copyright records; LC.

front cover.[2] p. [2] blank. m. on pp. 3–5. p.n. 2796. Back cover blank.[3] FH, LC(CDC) and JF.

"Jeanie" was, of course, Foster's wife, the former Jane McDowell. "Jeanie's light brown hair" has been the central theme of an advertising company for a hair-coloring formula![4] Brief biographic information regarding Foster appears above under *Beautiful Dreamer*.

Jim Crack Corn

Jim crack corn I don't care,   Jim crack corn I don't care,

The first known printing of this song was on Jan. 20, 1846,[1] under the title *Jim Crack Corn, or The Blue Tail Fly* by F. D. Benteen, Baltimore. First edition: p. [1] is blank. m. on pp. [2] and [3], p. [2] indicating that this is song no. 5 of The Virginia Minstrels. p.n. 771. p. [4] blank. Engraved. LC(CDC) and JF.

When Lincoln went to speak at Gettysburg, he is said to have asked for this song.[2] Dan Emmett is sometimes claimed to be the author of *Jim Crack Corn*,[3] but there is no substantiation of this claim.

The opening notes of the song are similar to those in *Miss Lucy Long*, copyrighted in 1842 by George Willig, Philadelphia, LC and JF; A. Fiot, Philadelphia, LC; Millets Music Saloon, New York, N.Y., LC; and Atwill, New York, N.Y., LC.

---

[2] Front cover is illustrated in Fuld, *Foster*, no page number.

[3] Legman, pp. 294 and 511, says Foster "plagiarized" and "pirated" *Jeanie with the Light Brown Hair* from *To Daunton Me*, in James Johnson, *The Scots Musical Museum* (Edinburgh, 1788), vol. II, no. 182, p. 190; at *BUC*, p. 557, and JF. There is no similarity between the two songs.

[4] E.g., *The New York Times*, June 21, 1964, Magazine sec., p. 26.

---

[1] Copyright records; LC. It has been erroneously said that this song first appeared in the *Ethiopian Glee Book* in 1844; *The People's Song Book* (New York, N.Y., 1948), p. 26, at NYPL, and quoted in Laws, p. 256. The first volume of the *Ethiopian Glee Book* was not published until 1847; this song did not appear in the first volume (at LC and NYPL), but did appear in the second volume published in 1848, at p. 64 (also at LC and NYPL).

[2] Oscar Brand, *Singing Holidays* (New York, N.Y., 1957), p. 10; NYPL.

[3] Notes in Copyright Office, LC. Emmett arranged a *De Blue Tail Fly*, but (a) he merely arranged it, he did not compose it, and (b) the *De Blue Tail Fly* he arranged has completely different melody and words. Hans Nathan, *Dan Emmett* (Norman, Okla., 1962), pp. 302, 310 and 429; NYPL.

Jingle Bells

Jin - gle bells, jin - gle bells, jin - gle all the way

mw. J. Pierpont. Copyrighted under the title *One Horse Open Sleigh* on Sept. 16, 1857,[1] by Oliver Ditson & Co., 277 Washington St., Boston. Probable first edition: Front cover mentions a dedication to John P. Ordway and lists four agents. The price is 2½. p. [2] blank. m. on pp. 3–5. p.n. 18200. Back cover blank. Engraved. JF.

The song was republished in 1859 under the revised title *Jingle Bells, or the One Horse Open Sleigh;* JF. The song is said to have been originally written for a local Sunday-school entertainment.[2]† The word "jingle" in the title and opening phrase is apparently an imperative verb. James Pierpont was born in Boston in 1822, became a composer and died in Winter Haven, Fla., in 1893.[3] James Pierpont was a son of John Pierpont, the grandfather of John Pierpont Morgan, the banker and founder of The Pierpont Morgan Library.

Johnny Get Your Gun

mw. F. Belasco (M. H. Rosenfeld). Copyrighted May 1, 1886,[1] by T. B. Harms & Co., 819 Broadway, New York, N.Y. First edition: Front cover says that the song is an "Ethiopian Song" written for and sung by Sheffer and Blakely, and is blue, green and white. m. on pp. [2]–5. Back cover adv. *Go.. - Poor..* LC(CDC).

The famous "Dance" in this piece comes after the song portion. Monroe H. Rosenfeld was born in 1861 in Richmond, Va., became a newspaper reporter in New York City, wrote this song under the name F. Belasco and died in 1918 in New York City.[2]

[1] Copyright records; LC.
[2] Burton, p. 9.
[3] Gladys N. Hoover, " 'I Have a Song in My Head,' " in *The Boston Sunday Globe*, Dec. 22, 1946, p. A–3; BPL. Frank W. Lovering, "Jingle Bells," in *MCO*, Dec., 1959, p. [39]; Frank W. Lovering, "The First 'Jingle Bells,' " in *Yankee*, Dublin, N.H., Dec., 1962, p. 62; NYPL. The author is indebted to Everett V. Ballard, San Francisco, for the first two references.

[1] Copyright records; LC.
[2] Obituary, *The New York Times*, Dec. 13, 1918.

Joy to the World

Joy   to   the world, the   Lord   is   come!

m. Lowell Mason. w. Isaac Watts. The words first appeared in I. Watts, *The Psalms of David* (London, 1719), p. 253, as a translation of the last five verses of Psalm 98; BM.

The music (and the words) were first printed in Lowell Mason, *The Modern Psalmist* (Boston, 1839), under the title *Antioch* on p. 144; LC(CDC) and JF. The latter work was deposited on Aug. 20, 1839,[1] and the 1839 date appears on the copyright deposit copy both on the title page and in the copyright claim.

Mason stated in *The Modern Psalmist* that *Antioch* was "From Handel." Two brief excerpts from Handel's *Messiah* are probably the bases for the credit: the four opening notes of the chorus *Lift up Your Heads,* and the introduction to the recitative *Comfort Ye My People.* However, the credit seems overly generous, as most of the music is believed original.

Mason was born in Medfield, Mass., in 1792, became a music teacher and composer of hymn tunes and died in Orange, N.J., in 1872.[2] Watts was born in Southampton, England, in 1674, became an Independent minister and hymn writer and died at Theobalds, England, in 1748.[3]

Kaiser-Walzer

m. Johann Strauss. Published probably late Oct., 1889,[1] for piano as op. 437 by N. Simrock, Berlin. First edition: Front cover has a drawing of a crown, lists five arrangements, but only the piano arrangement has a price, 2 Mk. m. on pp. 2–11. p.n. 9266. Back cover blank. SB and LC (copyright copy deposited Nov. 11, 1889). Unlike most Strauss waltzes, this edition is upright, not oblong.

The orchestral parts were probably published late Jan., 1890.[2] First

[1] Copyright records; LC.
[2] *Dict. Am. Biog.*, vol. XX, p. 371.
[3] *Dict. Nat. Biog.*, vol. 20, p. 978.

[1] Hofmeister *Monatsbericht*, Nov., 1889, p. 486.
[2] Violin part deposited at LC Feb. 17, 1890. Hofmeister *Monatsbericht*, June, 1890; p. 235.

edition: Front cover of 1st violin part is similar to that described above, large size, upright and lists 10 arrangements, nine with prices, this for gr. Orchester at 12 Mk. p.n. 9274. First music page refers to 24 orchestra parts. LC*(copyright copy deposited Feb. 17, 1890—violin part only). Brief biographic information regarding Strauss appears above under *Artist's Life*.

Kamennoi-Ostrow—Rubinstein

m. A. Rubinstein. This piece is no. 22 in *Kamennoi-Ostrow*, "Album de Portraits pour Piano," op. 10, which was published about April 28, 1855,[1] by les fils de B. Schott, Mainz. Possible first edition of the entire Album, 1re Série, nos. 1–24: Title page has publisher's no. 13530, the price is blank and there are five agents. m. on pp. 1–165, engraved. p.ns. 13530–13553.[2] The music of no. 22 is on pp. 146–153 (also, pp. 2–9, double pagination); the title *Kamennoi-Ostrow* is repeated; there is no reference to "Rêve Angélique"; the heading mentions Mademoiselle Anna de Friedebourg; p.n. 13551. ONB. There are no printed prices in Marks. A similar copy at the Leningrad Philharmonic Library has a second title page for nos. 17–24 which refers to three Suites each at 4 fl. 48 kr. and lists the 24 nos. separately, no. 22 at 54 kr. A similar copy at the Saltykov Library in Leningrad has its original yellow and black front and back covers.

Kamennoi-Ostrow was also published in Russia by Jurgenson (p.n. 162, at MC) and by Bessel (p.n. 2225, at SSL), but these editions are later as Jurgenson began publishing in 1861 and Bessel in 1869.

Kamennoi-Ostrow ("Rock Island") was an island resort in the Neva. The work was composed in 1853–1854. Anton Rubinstein was born in Volhynia, Russia, in 1830, traveled to Germany about 1856 and died in Peterhof in 1894.

Kashmiri Song

Pale hands I loved   be - side the Sha - li - mar——

---

[1] The printing or publication date in the Schott *Auslieferungslager* is April 28, 1855; 50 copies of the entire Album were printed. *Kamennoi-Ostrow* is listed in Hofmeister *Monatsbericht*, July, 1855, p. 794—the entire Album, 1re Série, nos. 1–24, at 12 fl.; three Suites at 4 fl. 48 xr. each; and the numbers singly, no. 22 at 54 xr. Compare *Rubinstein Catalogue*, p. 4.

[2] These p.ns. would be 1858 according to Deutsch, *Plate Numbers*, p. 23.

m. Amy Woodforde-Finden. w. Laurence Hope. The words were first printed on p. 93 of *The Garden of Kama and Other Love Lyrics from India,* arranged in verse by Laurence Hope (London, 1902). BM (copyright copy deposited Dec. 9, 1901).

The music was first published, together with the words, in *Four Indian Love Lyrics* by Weekes & Co., 14 Hanover Street, London W., the copyright copy being deposited at BM on July 9, 1902. First edition: Two keys are mentioned, this copy being no. 1 for contralto or baritone. The price is three shillings, and there is reference to a Chicago agent. The *Kashmiri Song* commences on p. 10. p.n. 4655. There is no reference to "New Edition." BM(CDC).

The poem tells the allegedly true story of the doomed love of a married English lady for a son of an Indian Rajah in Kashmir, presently a disputed area between India and Pakistan. The lady, Adela Florence Cory, was born in Stoke Bishop, Gloucestershire, England, in 1865 and was married to General Malcolm Nicholson, stationed in India; when she returned to England, she published the poems under the pen name of Laurence Hope. She died in Madras in 1904.[1] Mrs. Amy Ward was born in Valparaiso, Chile, in 1860, married Col. Woodforde-Finden in Bombay, India, in 1893, lived in India for many years and died in London in 1919.[2]

Keep the Home Fires Burning

Keep the home fires   burn - ing,   while your hearts are   yearn - ing

m. Ivor Novello. w. Lena Guilbert Ford. This song was first published under tne title *'Till the Boys Come Home* on Oct. 8, 1914,[1] by Ascherberg, Hopwood and Crew, Ltd., 16 Mortimer Street, Regent Street, London W. First edition, deposited the same day at BM: Title: *'Till The Boys Come Home.* Folio. Front cover mentions two keys, this copy being in the key of F; the price is 1/6; and there is reference to a New York agent. p. 2 prints the words. m. on pp. 3–7. p.n. 9551a. Back cover adv. *A Jovial.. - Wrap..* BM(CDC). The copyright copy at LC, deposited Oct. 15, 1914, is in the key of G and has p.n. 9551b. A new edition was published in 1915.

---

[1] Emurian, *Songs,* p. 101. *Dict. Nat. Biog.,* Supp. 1901–1911, vol. III, p. 14.

[2] Sandved, p. 1006.

[1] Copyright records; LC.

Novello, a pseudonym adopted for David Ivor Davies, was born in Cardiff in 1893, became a composer, lyricist and actor, and died in London in 1951.[2] This song was allegedly written at the urging of his mother.[3] Ford was born in Elmira, N.Y., about 1866, moved to London, where she became a journalist, and was killed during a German dirigible raid on London in 1918.†

Kentucky Babe

'Skeet - ers am a hum-min' on de hon - ey suck - le vine, sleep, Ken-tuck - y   babe!

m. Adam Geibel. w. Richard Henry Buck. Copyrighted Sept. 21, 1896,[1] by White-Smith Music Publishing Co., Boston, New York and Chicago. First edition: Front cover has a photograph of Isadore Rush in full length and is black and white. p. [2] adv. *May..* and *Coons..* m. on pp. 3–5. p.n. 10083–3. Back cover blank. LC(CDC). Front cover is entirely different from the cover on which Bessie Davis's picture appears, and does not refer to the Schottische arrangement.

Geibel was born near Frankfurt, Germany, in 1855 and became blind at an early age; he was a composer, organist and conductor and died in Philadelphia in 1933.[2] Buck, a lyricist, was born in Philadelphia in 1870 and died in Pennsylvania in 1956.[2]

The Kerry Dance

O   the days of the Ker - ry danc - ing, O   the ring of the   pi - per's tune!

While this song is usually attributed to J. L. Molloy, the music of the first eight bars is virtually identical, note for note, to that in *The Cuckoo*, written and composed by Miss Margaret Casson and published about 1790 by G. Goulding, 6 James Street, Covt. Garden, London. Probable first edition: Price 1 sh. m. on pp. 1–4. Engraved. *BUC*, p. 170, and JF.

Molloy added the music of a new middle portion, and a different set of

[2] Gammond-Clayton, p. 154.
[3] Peter Noble, *Ivor Novello* (London, 1951), p. 53; NYPL.

[1] Copyright records; LC.
[2] *ASCAP*, pp. 176 and 64.

words, in his *The Kerry Dance*. On April 21, 1879, a copy of the following probable first edition was deposited at BM by Boosey & Co., 295 Regent Street, London W.: Front cover is black and white, has two keys at the top (this copy being in the key of F), says that the song is sung by Madame Lemmens Sherrington, and the price is 2/. p. [2] blank. m. on pp. 1–9 (really 3–11). No plate number. Back cover adv. *If.. - Choice..* BM(CDC).

No biographic information is available regarding Margaret Casson. Brief biographic information regarding Molloy appears below under *Love's Old Sweet Song*.

A Kiss in the Dark

Oh, that kiss · in ___ the dark

m. Victor Herbert. w. B. G. de Sylva. Published Sept. 12, 1922,[1] by Harms, Incorporated, New York, N.Y. First edition: Front cover has a drawing of a lady dancing and is orange, black and white. s. *Orange Blossoms—6* titles listed. m. on pp. 2–5. p.n. 6524-4. Back cover adv. *Indian..* and *Devotion.* LC(CDC) and JF.

Orange Blossoms opened in New York City on Sept. 19, 1922, and the piano-vocal score was published the following day.[1] First edition: Same general front cover as that described above; the price is $2.50; and the music is on pp. 4–128; LC(CDC). Brief biographic information regarding Herbert and de Sylva appears above under *Ah! Sweet Mystery of Life* and *April Showers*.

Kiss Me Again

Sweet sum - mer breeze,   whis - per - ing   trees

m. Victor Herbert. w. Henry Blossom. First copyrighted as part of *If I Were on the Stage. Character Song* on Oct. 13, 1905,[1] by M. Witmark & Sons, New York, N.Y., and three other cities. First edition: Subtitle *Kiss Me*

---

[1] Copyright records; LC.

[1] Copyright records; LC.

Again does not appear on the front cover, but only on p. "1." Front cover has a photograph of Fritzi Scheff and is brown, tan and white. s. *Mlle. Modiste*—16 titles listed. m. on pp. 1–8 (actually 3–10). p.n. 7295 x. pp. [2] and [11] blank. Back cover adv. *Latest..* LC(CDC).[2] *Kiss Me Again*, as a separate song under that title, was published on April 16, 1915,[1] with a new verse, words and music.

Mlle. Modiste opened in Trenton, N.J., on Oct. 7, 1905, and in New York City on Christmas of that year. The piano-vocal score was copyrighted Oct. 30, 1905.[3] Possible first edition: Front cover is generally the same as that described above; the price is $2.00; and the music is on pp. 5–152; JF. Brief biographic information regarding Herbert appears above under *Ah! Sweet Mystery of Life.* Blossom, a lyricist and playwright, was born in St. Louis, Mo., in 1866 and died in New York City in 1919.[4]

K-K-K-Katy

K-K-K - Ka-ty, beau-ti-ful Ka-ty, you're the   on-ly g-g-g-girl that I a-dore

© Copyright 1918 (renewed) Leo Feist, Inc., New York, N.Y. Used by permission.

mw. Geoffrey O'Hara. This stuttering song was published March 16, 1918,[1] by Leo. Feist, Inc., New York, N.Y. The copyright deposit copy at LC is a professional edition. Possible first regular edition: Folio. Front cover has a drawing of a soldier and a girl and is purple, red, brown and white. m. on pp. 2–3. p.n. 3815-2 (also on professional CDC). The address of the publisher is Feist Building. Three arrangements mentioned on p. 2 (also on professional CDC). Back cover adv. *Songs the Soldiers . . .*, an "80-page" booklet (published May 25, 1918[2]). JF. Another edition is identical to the above except that the ad on the back cover starts with the words "Music Will Help . . ."; however, this ad also refers to the same 80-page booklet. JF. At least one issue of the octavo "War Edition" of *K-K-K-Katy* has the p.n. 3911-2. JF. †

O'Hara was born in Chatham, Ontario, Canada, in 1882, became a composer, lyricist and lecturer and lives in Pawling, N.Y.[3]

---

[2] See, generally, Waters, *Herbert*, p. 293.
[3] Information from publisher.
[4] *ASCAP*, p. 44.

---

[1] Copyright records; LC.
[2] The earlier edition of this booklet, having 72 pages was published Jan. 28, 1918.
[3] *ASCAP*, p. 375.

Eine Kleine Nachtmusik (K 525)—Mozart

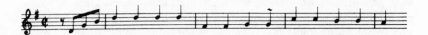

m. W. A. Mozart. Three editions of the parts of this *Serenade*, published about 1827,[1] have been found with priority unknown. In each case, the title is *Serenade* for two violins, alto, violoncello and contrabasse, the p.n. is 4964, the price is f. 2, and the publisher is J. André, Offenbach on the Main. The first variant, "Aus Koechel's Mozart Sammlung," has the title page in German and the music pages are engraved;[2] GM. The second variant has the title page in French except that it states in German "No. 2 der nachgelassenen Werke" and the music pages are offset; BSM. The third variant is the same as the second except that it lacks the one line in German; JF.

The title "Eine Kleine Nachtmusik" does not appear in any of the above editions although Mozart used this title in his own Verzeichnis. The work was completed Aug. 10, 1787. Mozart was born in Salzburg in 1756 and died in Vienna in 1791.

Kol Nidre

Kol   ni - dre v'e - so - re ush' vu - e va - ch'ro - me

Reference to the words of *Kol Nidre*, כל נדרי, dates back to the ninth century, but the melody is believed to have been composed between the middle of the fifteenth and the middle of the sixteenth centuries, reflecting the *Minnesang* influence of southern Germany during the preceding several centuries.[1] The song is in a manuscript collection of synagogue

[1] Köchel, p. 588. Deutsch, *Plate Numbers*, p. 6. Hofmeister *Monatsbericht*, Aug., 1839, p. 98.

[2] Curiously, Köchel misdescribed his own set, now at GM: instead of the French words he gives on p. 589, "Edit. faite d'après la partition originale," there appears in his copy "Ausgabe nach dem Original Manuscript." The right-hand portion of the title page of one of the parts (including the price) is missing in his copy; another part is complete but the price is blank. Another set, otherwise identical to GM's, including being engraved, has the later price of Mk. 3.60; JF.

[1] A. Z. Idelsohn, "The Kol Nidre Tune" in *Hebrew Union College Annual* (Cincinnati, 1932), p. 493; NYPL. See, also, Eric Mandell, "Kol Nidre" in *Jewish Digest*, Houston, Tex., Oct., 1959, p. 13; NYPL.

songs dating from about 1765 by Ahron Beer, a cantor in Berlin.† The manuscript is in the Birnbaum collection, Hebrew Union College, Cincinnati.

The earliest known printing of the song was either in 1839 in Maier Kohn, *Vollständiger Jahrgang von Terzett- und Chorgesängen der Synagoge in München* (Munich), in vol. III, p. 85,[2] at EM; or about that year in S. Sulzer, *Schir Zion* (*The Song of Zion*) (Vienna), vol. I, p. 156, at BM.

The *Kol Nidre* is sung by the Ashkenazim, Jews of Germany and other countries, to express their deep religious feelings on the eve of Yom Kippur, the Day of Atonement. "Kol Nidre" means "All of My Vows." Max Bruch based his *Kol Nidrei* for violoncello and orchestra on this melody in 1881.

Komm, Komm! Held Meiner Träume—Der Tapfere Soldat

© 1908 Ludwig Doblinger (Bernhard Herzmansky). Copyright renewed. Used by permission M. Witmark & Sons.

m. Oscar Straus. w. Rudolf Bernauer and Leopold Jacobson. The pianovocal score of *Der Tapfere Soldat* (*The Chocolate Soldier*), in which the song *Komm, Komm! Held Meiner Träume* (known in America as *My Hero*) appears, was copyrighted on Sept. 28, 1908,[1] by Ludwig Doblinger, 10 Dorotheergasse, Vienna, and 21 Täubchenweg, Leipzig. First edition: Front cover is black and light green. vb. Title page has a drawing of a soldier and girl and is red, white and blue. Price is K 12, M 10, and of piano score, K 6 M 5. The libretto is said to be an adaptation of Bernard Shaw's *Helden* (*Arms and the Man*). Cast and index. m. on pp. 3–139. p.n. 4015. This song is at p. 18. p. [140] blank. Back cover missing. LC(CDC), ONB and JF.

The publication of the piano-vocal score preceded the first performance of the operetta on Nov. 14, 1908, in Vienna. Early sheet music editions, probably published at about the same time as the piano-vocal score,[2] listing five arrangements of the song, have p.n. 4026 and the above imprint;[3] ONB and JF. The piano score, with p.n. 4076, was published Dec. 18, 1908;[1] ONB.

[2] The author is indebted to Eric Mandell, Philadelphia, for this information. The Kohn work is referred to in Alfred Sendrey, *Bibliography of Jewish Music* (New York, N.Y., 1951), no. 6226; NYPL.

[1] Copyright records; LC.

[2] The sheet music edition and piano-vocal score are in Hofmeister *Monatsbericht*, Nov., 1908, p. 310. The publisher advises that the sheet music edition was published Nov. 12, 1908, and the piano-vocal score four days later.

[3] In later sheet music editions, Doblinger's Leipzig address is 10 Karlstrasse.

Straus was born in Vienna in 1870 and died in Bad Ischl, Austria, in 1954.[4] Bernauer was born in Hungary in 1880, produced many plays in Europe (gave Marlene Dietrich her first part when she was a sixteen-year-old drama student), became a librettist and British citizen and died in London in 1953.[5] Jacobson, a librettist, was born in Czernowitz, Austria, in 1873 and died in a gas chamber in Poland in 1945.[6]

Kyrie-B Minor Mass—Bach

Ky - ri - e e-le   i - son, Ky - ri - e e - le - i - son

m. Johann Sebastian Bach. The history of the printings of *Die Hohe Messe in H-Moll*, or *B Minor Mass*, in which the above *Kyrie* is the opening chorus, is interesting. The piano-vocal score was published about Easter, 1833,[1] by N. Simrock, Bonn, with a front cover reading "Kirchen-Musik von Joh. Seb. Bach. Herausgegeben von Adolph Bernhard Marx. Clavierauszug. IIIter Band. Preis Francs (blank). Bonn bei N. Simrock. 2890. 2891. 2892. 2893. 2894. 2895. 3038." Contemporary announcements[1] list the *Kirchen-Musik* Dritter Band as "enthaltend" (containing) the *B Minor Mass*.

In the probable first edition of the piano-vocal score (in addition to the above-described front cover), the title page is engraved, gives the prices of this piano-vocal score as 20 Fr. and of the five choral parts as 11.75 Fr. (both in accord with contemporary announcements), states that the Partitur is available at 48 Francs, and has a reference to H. G. Nägeli, Zurich.[2] Oblong. m. on pp. 2–126, also engraved. p.n. 3038. The front cover does not mention the *Mass*, and the title page does not mention *Kirchen-Musik*. HU (complete copy, including front cover); copies without front cover at LC, NYPL and JF.

---

[4] Obituary, *The New York Times*, Jan. 13, 1954. See, generally, Grun, chap. VII.

[5] NYPL Music Division Clipping File.

[6] Information from AKM.

[1] *AMZ Int-Bl*, May, 1833, first page, announcing publication of this new music at Easter. Hofmeister *Handbuch*, 1834, p. 267. Hofmeister *Monatsbericht*, Jan.–Feb., 1834, p. 9. Simrock *Catalogue*, ca. 1834, p. 64; NC.

[2] It is clear from Smend, footnote (6) below, that both Simrock's and Nägeli's names should appear. Nägeli died in 1836.

In a later edition of the piano-vocal score, the title page has a blue lithographed sun-blaze similar to that of the 1845 orchestral score, gives the price of the choral parts as 12 Fr. (and 50, added in ink)—as stated in the 1845 orchestral score and in accord with a later announcement[3]— and does not refer to H. G. Nägeli. The edition is otherwise the same as the earlier edition. RBW (complete); without front cover at BM (purchased 1853), BSM and CB. No first printing of the choral parts has been found; a set was included in L. Liepmannssohn *Catalogue No. 35* (Paris, ca. 1868), no. 54—*Catalogue* at JF.

The first half of the orchestral score is listed in the Nov.–Dec., 1833, issue of the Hofmeister *Monatsbericht*,[4] entitled "Messe." First edition: Published with Nägeli's name above Simrock's. Front cover is gray and black. **(See Plate III.)** No title page. m. on pp. 1–95. p.n. 6.[5] Engraved. BM, LC, RBW, AVH and JF. *Hoboken Bach*, no. 17. Smend says the second printing of the first half of the orchestral score was entitled "Die Hohe Messe" and Simrock's name came first;[6] GM and RBW. Another edition of the first half of the orchestral score was published by Nägeli and described as "3te Band, Kirchen-Musik."[7]

The second half of the orchestral score, although promised for publication for Easter, 1834,[8] was not in fact published until about March, 1845.[9] The title is *Die Hohe Messe,* and Simrock's name precedes Nägeli's. Price: 60 Fr. There is the blue sun-blaze background on the title page, and the price of the choral parts is 12 Fr. vb. m. on pp. 3–95, engraved. p. [96] blank. p.n. 4377. BM, GM, LC, RBW, AVH and JF (with blue and black covers). *Hoboken Bach*, no. 18.

No printing of the orchestral parts of the *Mass* is known until after 1894.[10]

Bach presented the *Kyrie* and *Gloria* portions of the *Mass* to the Elector of Saxony in July, 1733, and completed the balance of the *Mass* by about 1738. Eight parts of the *Mass* were borrowed from church cantatas and one secular work; however, the above *Kyrie* opening chorus was com-

---

[3] Simrock *Catalogue,* dated 1851, p. 64; NC.

[4] P. 95; HD and ONB. Hofmeister *Handbuch,* 1834, p. 252.

[5] A strange plate number.

[6] Friedrich Smend, *Johann Sebastian Bach, Kritischer Bericht,* Serie II, Band 1 (Kassel, 1956), pp. 59–61 and 404–405; SC. Simrock and Nägeli had a dispute as to who should properly publish the *Mass,* and compromised, using both names.

[7] First Edition Bookshop *Catalogue 61,* London, n.d., no. 3; *Catalogue* at JF.

[8] The title page of the first printing of the first half of the orchestral score so promises.

[9] Hofmeister *Monatsbericht,* March, 1845, p. 42. AMZ *Int-Bl,* April 2, 1845, p. 248. Simrock *Catalogue,* 2nd Supp., 1846, p. 26; NC.

[10] Schmieder, p. 315. Deutsch, *Plate Numbers,* p. 10. Letter from Alfred Dürr, Göttingen, Germany.

posed for this *Mass*. "Kyrie eleison" is Greek and means "Lord, have mercy upon us." While all parts of the *Mass* had been rehearsed privately with a piano as early as Sept. 30, 1813, in Berlin, the earliest known public performance of substantial portions of the *Mass* with an orchestra was on Feb. 20, 1834, in Frankfurt.†

The first four introductory bars of the *Kyrie*, preceding the above music excerpt, were printed in Christoph Nichelmann, *Die Melodie nach Ihrem Wesen* (Danzig, 1755), music no. 95; NYPL and JF. Brief biographic information regarding Bach appears above under *Air for the G String*.

Largo—Handel

m. G. F. Handel. w. [Nicola Minatò]. Handel's *Largo* was originally an aria in the now forgotten opera *Xerxes;* the scene is a desert, and the tenor describes the cool shade of a tree. *Xerxes* was published in orchestral score on May 30, 1738,[1] for I. Walsh, at the Harp & Hoboy in Catherine Street in the Strand, London. Publisher's no. 633. vb. Table of Songs. Verso adv. *Musick..* m. on pp. 1–107. Engraved. p. [108] blank. The aria *Ombra Mai Fu (The Shade Never Was)*, with the directions "Larghetto e Piano," is on p. 7. The composer's name is printed on the title page as "Mr. Handel." Folio. BM and JF. No early printing of the orchestral parts of *Xerxes* has been noted.

Xerxes (known as *Serse* in Italian), was performed in London on April 15, 1738. Brief biographic information regarding Handel appears above under *Hallelujah Chorus*. Minatò, a native of Bergamo and a Count, was a poet and librettist.[2]

Lascia Ch'io Pianga—Handel

| Las - cia | ch'io pian - ga | mia cru - da sor - te |
| Ni - ta! | Jua - ni - ta! | Ask thy soul if we should part |

m. G. F. Handel. w. [Giacomo Rossi]. The music was first composed by Handel as a *Sarabande*, without words, for his first opera *Almira*, per-

---

[1] Smith, *Handel*, p. 68, no. 1. "This Day is Publish'd"; *The London Daily Post, and General Advertiser*, May 30, 1738, p. [2], at BM.

[2] *DUM*, vol. 2, p. 105. *EDS*, vol. VII, p. 613.

formed in Hamburg on Jan. 8, 1705; however, no publication is known of either *Almira* or the *Sarabande* until the Ausgabe der Deutschen Händelgesellschaft, Leipzig, 1873. NYPL. The *Sarabande* is on p. 81 of this edition.

The opera *Rinaldo*, in which the aria *Lascia Ch'io Pianga* (*Let Me Cry*) appears, was published in orchestral score about April 24, 1711,[1] under the English title *Song's in the Opera of Rinaldo*, for J. Walsh, Harp & Hoboy, in Katherine Street, near Somerset House in ye Strand, London, and J. Hare . . . First edition: Verso of title page blank. A Table of Songs. m. on pp. 1–65, this aria on p. 40. Engraved. p. [66] blank. The composer's name is printed on the title page as "Mr. Hendel" [*sic*]. BM and HWMS. *Rinaldo* was performed on Feb. 24, 1711, in London. No early printing of the complete orchestral parts of *Rinaldo* has been noted.

Handel's aria later served as the basis for *Juanita*, a song by the Honble [*sic*] Mrs. Norton and included in her six *Songs of Affection*, a copy of which was deposited in BM on Dec. 24, 1853, by Chappell, 50 New Bond Street, London. Brief biographic information regarding Handel appears above under *Hallelujah Chorus*. No biographic information is available regarding Rossi. Caroline Elizabeth Sarah Norton, the granddaughter of Richard Sheridan, was born in London in 1808 and died there in 1877.[2]

The Last Time I Saw Paris

The   last time I   saw   Par - is her   heart was warm and   gay

m. Jerome Kern. w. Oscar Hammerstein 2nd. Published Sept. 16, 1940,[1] by Chappell & Co. Inc., RKO Building, Rockefeller Center, New York, N.Y. The copyright copy deposited at the Library of Congress is a professional edition. Possible first edition: Front cover is red, white and blue and has a photograph of Kate Smith with a statement that she successfully introduced the song. A London agent is also mentioned. m. on pp. 2–5. Page 2 has a dedication to Noel Coward. p.n. 1053–4. Back cover adv. *Chappell's*.. (published in 1934). JF. In this edition, as in the professional

[1] Smith, *Handel*, p. 56, no. 1. (London) *Daily Courant*, April 24, 1711, p. [2]; BM.
[2] *Dict. Nat. Biog.*, vol. 14, p. 651.

[1] Copyright records; LC.

copyright deposit copy, the copyright year is stated as MCMXL (not 1940), no chords are indicated in letters, and in the first repeat bar "a tempo" appears twice.

The tragic fall of Paris to the Nazis inspired Hammerstein to write the words, and he asked Kern to write the music. Brief biographic information regarding Kern and Hammerstein appears above under *All the Things You Are*.

Leonore Overture no. 3—Beethoven

m. L. v. Beethoven. The first printing of the *Leonore Overture no. 3* was of the orchestral parts in July, 1810,[1] under the title *Ouverture à grand Orchestre de l'Opéra Leonora* and published by Breitkopf & Härtel, Leipzig. First edition: Price is 2 Rthlr. There are 23 parts. p.n. 1603. Engraved. GM and JF.* The orchestral score was not published until June, 1828[1]—by the same publisher. This *Overture* was composed in 1806 and performed March 29, 1806, in Vienna. Brief biographic information regarding Beethoven appears above under his *Concerto for Piano no. 5*.

While the above melody was included in *Leonore Overture no. 2*, which had been performed on Nov. 20, 1805, in Vienna as part of the first production of *Fidelio*, *Leonore Overture no. 2* was not published until Oct., 1842.[2]

It has been customary for about 100 years to perform the *"Fidelio"* Overture (the last to be written) as the curtain-raiser for the opera *Fidelio*; the well-known *Leonore Overture no. 3* is performed as the bridge to Act II, Scene 2, of the opera. It is not known whether Wagner, Balfe, Seidl, Mahler or someone else began this tradition.[3]

---

[1] Kinsky-Halm, p. 192.

[2] *Id.*, p. 190.

[3] See *Programs*, Metropolitan Opera (New York, N.Y.), Jan. 12, 1966, p. 8, and Dec. 29, 1970, p. 19; NYPL.

Let Me Call You Sweetheart

Let   me   call   you "Sweet-heart"

m. Leo Friedman. w. Beth Slater Whitson. Published April 8, 1910,[1] by Leo Friedman, 59 Dearborn St., Chicago, Ill. First edition: Front cover has a drawing of a lady **full-face** (not profile) in the country, a photograph of an undesignated man (Leo Friedman?) and is brown and white. m. on pp. 2–4. p. [5] adv. *The Passion..* Back cover adv. *My!..* and *Kisses..* LC(CDC).

Friedman was born in Elgin, Ill., in 1869, became a composer and publisher and died in Chicago in 1927.[2] Whitson, a lyricist, was born in Goodrich, Tenn., in 1879 and died in Tenn. in 1930.[2]

Liebesfreud and *Liebesleid—Kreisler*

m. Fritz Kreisler. *Liebesfreud* was published for violin and piano on Sept. 15, 1910,[1] by B. Schott's Söhne, Mainz and four other cities. First edition: Front cover states "Klassische Manuskripte" and lists 12 compositions of which this is "Alt-Wiener Tanzweisen: no. 1"; the price is 1.50 M; there are references to New York and Moscow agents; and the colors are brown,

[1] Copyright records; LC.
[2] *ASCAP*, pp. 168 and 537.

[1] Copyright records; LC. Hofmeister *Monatsbericht*, Oct., 1910, p. 249.

orange and tan. Notice. List of Kreisler's works, including three original compositions. m. on pp. 2–7. p.n. 29028. pp. [8] and [9] blank. Back cover adv. *Alfred.*. No reference on front cover to 1911 Russian copyright. LC(CDC).

Liebesleid was published the same day as *Liebesfreud*. The first edition of *Liebesleid* is the same as above except that it is "no. 2," p. [2] is blank, the music is on pp. 3–7, and the p.n. is 29029. LC(CDC).

Liebesfreud and *Liebesleid* were among a group of compositions composed by Kreisler, but for a long time as a "hoax" attributed by him to others or, as in these cases, to folk sources.[2] The titles may be translated *Love's Joy* and *Love's Sorrow*. *Schön Rosmarin*, another well-known Kreisler work for violin and piano, was published the same day[1] as no. 3 of the above set; LC(CDC). Brief biographic information regarding Kreisler appears above under *Caprice Viennois*.

Liebestod—Tristan und Isolde

Mild und lei - se   wie er lä-chelt,   wie das Au - ge hold er öff - net

mw. Richard Wagner. Both the orchestral score and piano-vocal score of *Tristan und Isolde*, in which the *Liebestod* is the concluding scene, were published about five years before the opera was produced. The orchestral score was completed by Wagner on Aug. 7, 1859,[1] and on Feb. 3, 1860, he acknowledged receipt of printed copies.[2] Copies of the piano-vocal score were sent to Wagner on Oct. 22, 1860.[3] The opera's first performance, however, was not until about five years later, June 10, 1865, in Munich.

Probable first edition of the orchestral score: Publisher is Breitkopf & Härtel, Leipzig, and the price is 36 Thlr. Verso of title page blank. Cast and contents. Vocal parts and orchestration. m. on pp. 3–441, engraved. *Liebestod* on p. 425. p.n. 10000. BM, ONB and JF. Klein, pp. 28–29.

[2] Louis P. Lochner, *Fritz Kreisler* (New York, N.Y., 1950), chap. 25; NYPL.

[1] *Wagner Letters*, vol. 2, p. 60.
[2] Letter from Wagner to B & H; Altmann, vol. 1, p. 187. Kinsky, *Opern*, p. 385, gives the date of receipt as Jan. 13, 1860. Hofmeister *Monatsbericht*, April, 1860, p. 77. Müller-Reuter, p. 458, gives the date of publication as June, 1860, and Kastner, p. 47, says "Mitte 1860." The first act was in proof sheets by Oct. 19, 1858; *Wagner Letters*, vol. 2, p. 12.
[3] Letter from B & H to Wagner of that date; Altmann, vol. 1, p. 202. Hofmeister *Monatsbericht*, Dec., 1860, p. 217.

The earliest orchestral parts of the opera that have been found, possibly their first printing, have plate number 19563 (1892) and are lithographed; covers lacking. MET.

Probable first edition of the piano-vocal score: Same imprint. The price is 10 Thlr. Verso of title page blank. Cast and index. vb. m. on pp. 3–250, engraved. *Liebestod* on p. 244. p.n. 9942. BM (H. 637. f., purchased May 1873), GM (Aus dem Nachlass Johannes Brahms) and JF. Klein, p. 31, states that the cast and index are on both the recto and verso; he does not locate such a copy nor state why such a copy is earlier than the copy described above. Brief biographic information regarding Wagner appears above under *The Flying Dutchman—Overture.*

Liebestraum—Liszt

m. Franz Liszt. The melody of *Liebestraum* first appeared as a song entitled *O Lieb* with words by F. Freiligrath about Nov., 1847.[1] Probable first edition: Publisher is Fr. Kistner, Leipzig, the price is 10 Ngr., the only plate number is 1559 and there are six pages of music. Other details not known. TLW. In 1850[2] *O Lieb* was reprinted as one of *Drei Lieder* with p.n. 1755; BM.

Liebestraum, arranged as a piano composition, was first published about Dec., 1850,[3] by the same concern under the title *Liebesträume, 3 Notturnos,* no. 3. Probable first edition: Front cover states that the price is 1 Thlr. and mentions a Paris agent. vb. m. on pp. 4–22, engraved. p.n. 1751. The poem is on p. 16, and no. 3 is on p. 17. JF. Brief biographic information regarding Liszt appears above under *Hungarian Rhapsody No. 2.*

Light Cavalry-Overture—Suppé

[1] Hofmeister *Monatsbericht*, Nov., 1847, p. 180. Raabe, vol. 2, pp. 278 and 346. Searle, pp. 53, 171 and 183.

[2] *Id.*, Dec., 1850, p. 196; and Raabe and Searle, footnote 1.

[3] *Id.*, Dec., 1850, p. 185; and Raabe and Searle, footnote 1.

m. Franz von Suppé. The first printing of the *Overture* to *Leichte Cavallerie* was an arrangement for piano published about Feb., 1868,[1] by F. Glöggl, 6 Herrngasse, Vienna. In the composer's own copy, probably a first edition, the front cover has a drawing of cavalry soldiers, there is a dedication to Director Carl Treumann, the words are by Carl Costa, the price is 12½ Ngr. and 63 Nkr., 16 other excerpts from the opera and the piano-vocal score lack prices, and there is a Leipzig agent. m. on pp. 2–9. p.n. 2078. Back cover blank. Engraved. SB.

The piano-vocal score of the opera was published probably before Sept., 1868,[2] by F. Glöggl, 6 Herrngasse, Vienna. The title page of the composer's own copy, probably a first edition, is similar to that described above, still without a price for the piano-vocal score or excerpts. m. on pp. 2–89 with double pagination. p.n. 2078-2078(14). p. [90] blank. Engraved. SB. An edition published by C. A. Spina, Vienna, about Sept., 1868,[2] with prices for the piano-vocal score (6 Fl. Ö.W.—4 Thlr.) and excerpts is at BM (purchased Oct. 3, 1874).

The *Overture* was published for orchestral score and orchestral parts about Sept., 1869,[3] by C. F. W. Siegel, 1 Dörrienstr., Leipzig. There are two variants of a possible first edition of the orchestral score, priority unknown. One has a yellow and black front cover. vb. Title page states that the arrangement is for grosses Orchester at 1 Thlr., lists the orchestral parts at 2¼ Thlr. and an arrangement for small orchestra, and mentions p.ns. 3843-3845. m. on pp. 2–40. p.n. 3843. BM. An identical copy is at BPL but with a gray and black front cover. No early printing of the orchestral parts has been found.

An orchestral score of the entire opera, of uncertain date but early, was published by F. Glöggl with the same front cover as for the piano arrangement of the *Overture* except there is no price for the *Overture*. A lithographing of a manuscript score on pp. 1–101. No plate number. Back cover blank. ONB. No early printing of the orchestral parts has been found.

The opera was performed March 21, 1866, in Vienna. Suppé was born in Split (Spalato) (now Yugoslavia), in 1819 and died in Vienna in 1895. Costa, a librettist, was born in Vienna in 1832 and died there in 1907.[4]

---

[1] Hofmeister *Monatsbericht*, Feb., 1868, p. 22.
[2] *Id.*, Sept., 1868, p. 158; the publisher shown is C. A. Spina, Vienna.
[3] *Id.*, Sept., 1869, p. 150.
[4] *ÖBL*, vol. 1, p. 155.

Lili Marleen

| Vor | der | Ka-ser – ne | vor dem gros-sen Tor | stand | ei – ne | La-ter-ne, und | steht | sie noch | da-vor |
| Under-neath the | lan – tern | by the | bar-rack gate, | dar-ling | I | re-mem-ber the | way | you used | to wait |

m. Norbert Schultze. w. Hans Leip. The words were written in 1915 by Leip, a German soldier, on his way to the Russian front, as a parting from his sweetheart. His "Lili Marleen" was really a combination of two girls, his own, Lili, and his buddy's, Marleen. The poem to the composite girl was published in 1937 in a book of Leip's poems entitled *Die Kleine Hafenorgel* (meaning *The Little Harbor Organ*) (Hamburg), p. 32; BSM.[1]

Lale Andersen, a singer in late-evening literary cabarets in Munich and Berlin for students and young people, liked the poem, and in the late 1930's had it unsuccessfully set to other music by a friend. Meanwhile, in 1938 in Berlin, Schultze had also set 10 of Leip's poems to music, and in Sept.–Nov., 1939, Andersen's record, with Schultze's music, was issued on Electrola EG 6993;[2] record at Deutsche Staatsbibliothek Rundfunkarchiv, East Berlin.

A booklet of five of the songs, entitled *Lili Marleen*, was published about May 8, 1940,[3] by Apollo-Verlag, Paul Lincke, Berlin SW 68. Possible first edition: Front cover has a drawing of a girl waiting by a street lantern in front of a barrack gate and is in many colors. No price. m. on pp. [2]–11, *Lili Marleen*, the first song, on p. [2]. p.n. 435a–d. Back cover adv. *Paul..* BM and JF.

The song was not initially a success, but on Aug. 18, 1941, a German shortwave radio station in Belgrade happened to include Andersen's record-

---

[1] Letter from Leip. See, generally, Col. Barney Oldfield, "Saga of 'Lili Marlene'" in *Variety*, March 31, 1965, p. 2; and Derek Jewell, "When Lilli Went to War—for Both Sides" in *The New York Times*, magazine section, Nov. 19, 1967, p. 52.

[2] Sept.–Nov., 1939, *Supplement to Electrola Columbia Hauptkatalog 1939/40* (Berlin), pp. 501 and 503; NYPL. Not in the *Hauptkatalog* through Aug. 1939, at NYPL, which contains phonograph records up to EG 6902. On the record EG 6993, "Lili Marleen" has a co-title "Lied eines Jungen Wachtpostens." Curt Riess, *Knaurs Weltgeschichte der Schallplatte* (Zurich, 1966), p. 300, at LC, says this recording of *Lili Marleen* was originally released on Electrola 4198, but this seems incorrect.

[3] Copyright records; LC.

ing[4] in its program directed to Rommel's troops in North Africa. The program was heard by both German and British troops in Africa, and the song then became an immediate hit. Marlene Dietrich, among others, subsequently sang it. In the United States, the title is spelled "Lilli Marlene."

Schultze, born in 1911,[5] was a prominent Nazi propaganda composer of such titles as *Bombs on England* and *The Panzers Are Rolling in Africa*; after the war, he returned to his home town—Brunswick, Germany—and is now living in West Berlin, where he has been writing music for television and movies. Leip was born in 1893 in Hamburg, became a poet and novelist, and died in 1983[6] in Fruthwilen/Thurgau, Switzerland. Andersen fell out of favor early in the war because of her dislike for the war and because she attempted unsuccessfully to escape to Switzerland during the war; she died in Vienna in 1972.[7]

Limehouse Blues

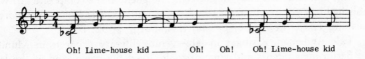

Oh! Lime-house kid ——— Oh! Oh! Oh! Lime-house kid

© 1922 Ascherberg, Hopwood & Crew, Ltd. Copyright renewed. Used by permission of Harms, Inc.

m. Philip Braham. w. Douglas Furber. Published May 10, 1922,[1] by Ascherberg, Hopwood & Crew, Ltd., 16 Mortimer Street, London W.1. First edition deposited May 25, 1922, at LC: Folio. Front cover indicates the song is from the revue *A to Z*, lists six titles, is yellow, red, black and white and refers to Teddie Gerrard. p. [2] blank. m. on pp. 1–5 (really 3–7). p.n. 10,640–13. Back cover adv. numbers from the revue. LC(CDC). The copy at BM was not deposited until March 30, 1925. *A to Z* opened in London, Oct. 11, 1921.

"Limehouse" is London's East End. Braham was a composer who was born in 1881 and died in London in 1934.† Brief biographic information regarding Furber appears above under *The Bells of St. Mary's*.

---

[4] It is not known whether the Belgrade radio played the Lale Andersen recording on a German Electrola EG 6993 record (two record label variants at JF—in one, probably the earlier, "Lili Marien" [sic] is on the same line as the composer and lyricist; in the other, "Lili Marlen" [sic] is on the line by itself), a Hungarian His Master's Voice HU 337—ORA 4198 repressing (at JF), an English His Master's Voice EG 6993 repressing (at JF), or other repressing.

[5] Information furnished by Andrew Lamb, Littlehampton, West Sussex, England, who obtained it from Schultze.

[6] Obituary, *The New York Times*, June 8, 1983.

[7] Obituary, *The New York Times*, Aug. 30, 1972.

---

[1] Copyright records; LC.

Listen to the Mocking Bird

Lis-ten   to the   mock - ing   bird,   lis-ten   to the   mock - ing   bird

m. Richard Milburn. w. Alice Hawthorne. Copyrighted April 17, 1855,[1] by Winner & Shuster, 110 North Eighth St., Philadelphia. First edition: Engraved. Front cover mentions that the song is a "Sentimental Ethiopian Ballad," has a drawing of a mocking bird facing to the left, a dedication to Aaron R. Dutcher, refers to Piano and Guitar and lists three agents. Price: 25 Cts. m. on pp. 2–5. No p.n. Back cover blank. LC(CDC) and JF.

President Lincoln is said to have likened this song to the "laughter of a little girl at play."[2] The melody was composed by a Negro barber and beggar in Philadelphia, Dick Milburn. His imitation of the warbles of the mocking bird was overheard by Septimus Winner; "Alice Hawthorne" was a pseudonym, Winner's mother's maiden name. Winner was born in Philadelphia in 1827, became a composer and publisher and died in 1902.

Winner is the only known composer to have been tried for treason because of a song. The song was *Give Us Back Our Old Commander* (General McClellan, who had been dismissed by President Lincoln), published in 1862 by the composer; LC(CDC) and JF. Winner was ultimately acquitted.[2]

Little Annie Rooney

She's   my   sweet - heart,   I'm   her   beau

mw. Michael Nolan. A copy was deposited on April 4, 1889, at BM by Francis Bros. and Day, Blenheim House, 195 Oxford St., London W. Probable first edition: Front cover is brown, red, green, blue and white, has drawings of a young man (Michael Nolan?) and a pair of lovers and says the song was also sung by Miss Alice Maydue. Price: 4/. p. [2] blank. m. on pp. 1–4 (actually 3–6). p. "5" prints the words. Back cover adv. *I'm.. - The Belles.* BM(CDC). All that is known regarding Michael Nolan is

---

[1] Copyright records; LC.

[2] Charles Eugene Claghorn, *The Mocking Bird—The Life & Diary of Its Author* (Philadelphia, 1937), p. 30; NYPL.

that he was an Irishman who sang in English music halls and composed a few songs.[1]

Annie Rooney was a three-year-old cousin of the composer when the song was written.[2]

A Little Bit of Heaven, Shure They Call It Ireland

Shure, a   lit - tle bit   of heav - en fell from   out the sky one day

© 1914 M. Witmark & Sons. Copyright renewed. Pub. by arr. with Ross Jungnickel Inc. Used by permission.

m. Ernest R. Ball. w. J. Keirn Brennan. Published June 29, 1914,[1] by M. Witmark & Sons, New York, Chicago and London. The copyright deposit copy at LC is a professional edition. Possible first regular edition: Front cover has a drawing of a lassie, a photograph of Chauncey Olcott and is green, brown and white. s. *The Heart of Paddy Whack*—4 titles listed. m. on pp. 2–4. p.n. 6277; 13315-3 (only the latter in the professional CDC). p. [5] adv. *Mother.. - I..* (the songs advertised on this page were published 1910–1912). Back cover adv. *The Artistic..* JF. The above edition is the same, to the extent possible, as the other contemporary, regular edition, copyright deposit copies from the same show; LC. *The Heart of Paddy Whack* opened in New York City on Nov. 23, 1914.

Ball, a composer, was born in Cleveland in 1878 and died in California in 1927.[2] Brennan, a lyricist and singer, was born in San Francisco in 1873 and died in California in 1948.[2]

Little Brown Jug

Ha, ha, ha,   you and me, "Lit - tle Brown Jug" don't   I   love thee

mw. ("Put into shape and filled up by") Eastburn. Copyrighted Feb. 18, 1869,[1] by Jos. E. Winner, 545 N. Eighth St., Philadelphia. First edition:

---

[1] Geller, p. 45.
[2] *New York Herald Tribune*, Sept. 22, 1955, p. 21.

---

[1] Copyright records; LC.
[2] *ASCAP*, pp. 19 and 52.

---

[1] Copyright records; LC.

Collective title front cover entitled "Universal Favorites," of which this is no. 8 and last. p. [2] blank. m. on pp. 3–5. No p.n. Back cover adv. music published by J. E. Winner. Engraved. LC(CDC). The song was published by others in 1869—C. H. Ditson & Co., New York, N.Y., on Nov. 11, 1869[1] (LC, CDC), Hamilton S. Gordon, New York, N.Y., "1869" but no record of copyright (JF), and W. H. Boner & Co., Philadelphia, "1869" but also no record of copyright (JF). However, in view of the believed identity of the composer and the publisher, it is reasonable to assume that Winner was the first publisher.

Eastburn is a pseudonym for Joseph Eastburn Winner,[2] the publisher of the first printing. He was a younger brother of the composer and publisher Septimus Winner, was born in Philadelphia in 1837, lived, composed and published in Philadelphia and died there in 1918.[3]

Little Grey Home in the West

When the gold-en sun sinks in the hills,—and the toil of a long day is o'er

m. Hermann Löhr. w. D. Eardley-Wilmot. Published Oct. 30, 1911,[1] by Chappell & Co. Ltd., 50 New Bond Street, London W. First edition, deposited the next day at LC: Front cover lists no keys at the top and is black and white. Price: 1/6 (60¢). m. on pp. 2–5. p.n. 24963. p. [6] repeats the words. p. [7] and back cover adv. *Chappell.*. LC(CDC). Two copies deposited at BM on Dec. 20, 1911, list two and three keys, respectively, at the top of the front cover.

The song was played in Paris on the occasion of Queen Elizabeth's visit when engaged to the Duke of Edinburgh.[2] Löhr was born in 1871 in Plymouth, England, worked with Chappell & Co., Ltd., London, for over thirty years and died in 1943 at Tunbridge Wells.[3] Miss D. Eardley-Wilmot was born in 1883 in London, was engaged in writing and voice training and resides in London.[2]

---

[2] Dichter-Shapiro, p. 146.
[3] Letter from the composer's grandnephew, C. E. Claghorn, Riverside, Conn.

[1] Copyright records; LC.
[2] Letter from family of Miss Eardley-Wilmot.
[3] Obituary, *Etude*, Feb., 1944.

Loch Lomond

Oh!   Ye'll   tak' the high   road and   I'll   tak' the low   road

The earliest printing of this song was probably about 1840-1841,[1] when it was published in sheet-music form under the title *Bonnie Loch Loman*. The front cover states that the song is from the *Vocal Melodies of Scotland*, and is arranged with symphonies and accompaniments for the piano forte by Finlay Dun and John Thomson; the volume number and price are blank and there is a reference to Stationers' Hall; there is a decorative border; and the publisher is Paterson & Roy, 27 George Street, Edinburgh. vb. p. 1 (actually p. 2) states "Written by a Lady. Arranged by Finlay Dun." m. on pp. 1-2 (actually 2-3) and on p. [4], engraved. No plate number. Back cover advertises contents of the four volumes of the *Vocal Melodies of Scotland*. BM—H. 1248. ff. (1). The song was not in fact included in any of the four volumes of *Vocal Melodies of Scotland*, at NLS, nor entered at Stationers' Hall.†

There are melodic phrases in *Loch Lomond* which are similar to phrases in *The Bonniest Lass in A' the World* (in Thomson, *Orpheus Caledonius*, London, 1733, vol. II, p. 57, *BUC*, p. 1006); and *Robin Cushie* (in MacGibbon, *A Collection of Scots Tunes*, Edinburgh, 1742, vol. I, p. 22, *BUC*, p. 639), which song later became *Kind Robin Loes Me* (in James Johnson's *The Scots Musical Museum*, London 1796-1797, vol. V, p. 492, *BUC*, p. 557, and JF). However, in this writer's opinion, *Loch Lomond* is sufficiently different to be considered a distinct song.

There is a legend that *Loch Lomond* had its origin in 1746 when Bonnie Prince Charlie was retreating from England to Scotland.[2] One of his followers, about to be executed, allegedly said to his sweetheart who had come from Scotland to say good-bye to him: "Ye'll take the high road, and I'll take the low road [i.e., the grave], and I'll be in Scotland afore ye." Another story is that Lady John Scott and her husband heard a boy singing the song on the street and Lady John Scott then popularized the song about 1845.[3] On the other hand, William Black, the novelist, thought that the song was wholly of recent origin.[4]

---

[1] The preface of the 4th volume of *Vocal Melodies of Scotland* is dated Oct., 1840; letter from NLS. John Thomson died on May 6, 1841; *Grove's*, vol. VIII, p. 432.

[2] Grieg, *Scots*, vol. 3, p. xxv.

[3] Moffat, *Minstrelsy of Scotland*, p. 34.

[4] Ford, p. 279.

Loch Lomond, a substantially different melody, and without words, was included in *A Favorite Collection of Popular Country Dances* [no.] 14, published by Skillern & Challoner, 25 Greek Street, Soho, London, ca. 1806-1810;[5] JF.

London Bridge

Lon - don Bridge is   fall - ing down,   fall - ing down,   fall - ing down

The words of this children's game first appeared in print about 1744 in *Tommy Thumb's Pretty Song Book* (London?), vol. 2, p. 52;[1] BM.

The melody, although common in Great Britain[2] as well as in the United States, does not seem to have been printed until Oct. 25, 1879,[3] when it was included in A. H. Rosewig, (*Illustrated National*) *Nursery Songs and Games* by W. F. Shaw [Philadelphia], p. [30] under the title *London Bridge Is Falling Down*. Words are included. LC(CDC) and JF.†

Londonderry Air

The first known printing of this melody was in 1855 in *The Petrie Collection of the Ancient Music of Ireland*, edited by George Petrie (Dublin, 1855), vol. I, p. 57; BM and JF. The melody appears without a title. A note indicates it was collected by Miss J. Ross of the county of Londonderry, Ireland, from the unpublished melodies of that county, and the melody thereby acquired its present title.[1] Many lyrics have been set to this music, perhaps the best known being *Danny Boy* in 1913 with words by Fred. E. Weatherly.

---

[5] Humphries-Smith, p. 239.

---

[1] Opie, p. 272.
[2] Gomme, vol. I, p. 333, and vol. II, p. 441.
[3] Copyright records; LC.

[1] An interesting analysis of the melody was made by Anne G. Gilchrist in "A New Light upon the Londonderry Air" in *JFSS*, Dec., 1934, p. 115.

Long, Long Ago!

Tell me the tales that to me were so dear, long, long a-go,   long, long a-go

mw. Thomas Haynes Bayly. Possible first edition: Published by Cramer, Addison & Beale, 201 Regent Street and 67 Conduit Street, London. Engraved. Price: 2/. p. [2] blank. m. on pp. 1–5 (actually 3–7). p.n. 2538. Back cover blank. BM (copy purchased in 1874) and JF. The British Museum dates this copy 1835, i.e., before Bayly died in 1839, but Humphries-Smith dates the additional premises at 67 Conduit Street as ca. 1841–1844.[1] Perhaps the song was first published without reference to the additional premises. Although the front cover says that the song was entered at Stationers' Hall, there is no record there of such entry from 1833–1884. The song was soon printed by a number of American publishers, one of them, Hewitt & Jaques, 239 Broadway, New York, N.Y., in 1837–1841,[2] JF.

The words of the song are in the author's collected *Songs, Ballads, and Other Poems* (London, 1844), vol. II, p. 219; BM(CDC). In 1942 a new lyric was written to the melody entitled *Don't Sit Under the Apple Tree with Anyone Else but Me* by Lew Brown, Charlie Tobias and Sammy Slept. Bayly was born at Bath, England, in 1797, lived virtually his whole life in England as a songwriter, novelist and dramatist, and died in 1839.[3]

Look for the Silver Lining

Look   for _____   the sil - ver lin - ing

m. Jerome Kern. w. B. G. de Sylva. Published Jan. 24, 1920,[1] by T. B. Harms Company, New York, N.Y.† The first copyright copy is a folio professional edition deposited about ten months before the production of the show *Sally*, and the next copyright copy deposited Dec. 14, 1920,[1] also probably a professional edition, is quarto, black and white, and refers to the

---

[1] P. 120.
[2] Dichter-Shapiro, p. 205. Six other early American editions are at JF.
[3] *Dict. Nat. Biog.*, vol. I, p. 1371.

[1] Copyright records; LC.

Plate I

Alexander's Ragtime Band
Saul Starr Estate, Eastchester, N. Y.

Used by permission of Irving Berlin Music Corp.

Dixie
New York Public Library

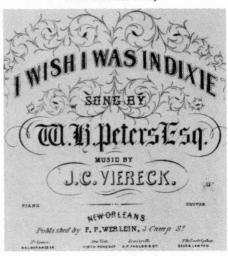

Auld Lang Syne
James J. Fuld, New York

Chant sans Paroles
Glinka Museum, Moscow

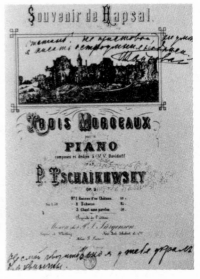

Plate II

If I Loved You
Lester S. Levy, Baltimore

God Save the King
Library of Congress, Washington, D.C.

The Flight of the Bumble Bee, Rimsky-Korsakov
Saltykov-Shchedrin Library, Leningrad

Hallelujah Chorus
British Museum, London

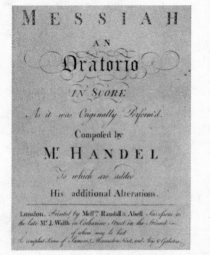

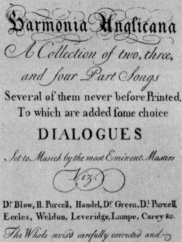

Plate III

Ol' Man River
James J. Fuld, New York

Kyrie, B Minor Mass
Anthony van Hoboken, Ascona, Switz.

Polonaise, op. 53
Harvard University, Cambridge, Mass.

Rhapsody in Blue
James J. Fuld, New York
Used by permission of New World Music Corp.

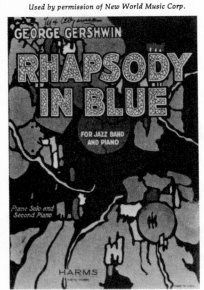

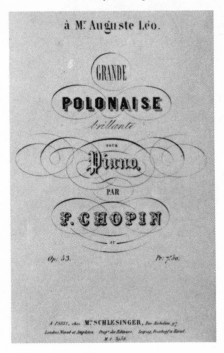

Plate IV

The Star Spangled Banner
Library of Congress, Washington, D.C.

Soldiers' Chorus
Bibliothèque Nationale, Paris

Symphony no. 1, Brahms
James J. Fuld, New York

Symphony no. 5, Beethoven
British Museum, London

Plate V

Symphony (Unfinished), Schubert
Österreichische Nationalbibliothek, Vienna

Three Little Maids from School
Pierpont Morgan Library
(Reginald Allen Collection), New York

Toreador Song
Bibliothèque Nationale, Paris

Symphony no. 101 (Clock), Haydn
Anthony van Hoboken, Ascona, Switz.

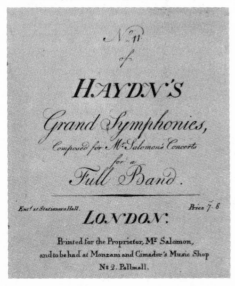

Plate VI

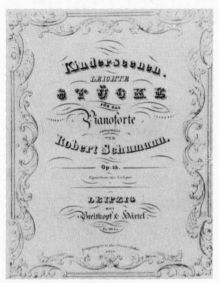

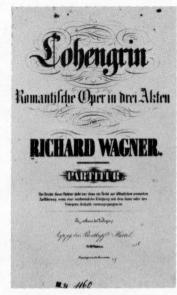

Wedding March, Lohengrin
Österreichische Nationalbibliothek, Vienna

Träumerei
Bayerische Staatsbibliothek, München

Wedding March, A Midsummer Night's Dream
Gesellschaft der Musikfreunde, Vienna

Triumphal March
S. Cecilia, Rome

Plate VII

Invitation to the Dance
Alan Tyson, London

Blue Danube
Stadtbibliothek, Vienna

La Marseillaise
British Museum, London

Plate VIII

Silent Night
James J. Fuld, New York

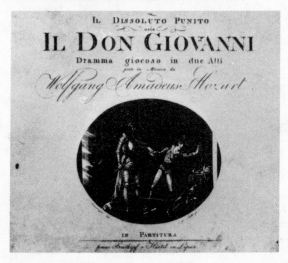

**Minuet,
Don Giovanni**

*Österreichische
Nationalbibliothek,
Vienna*

Three Blind Mice (1609)
James J. Fuld, New York

show. Both at LC(CDC). Probable first regular edition: Quarto. Front cover has photographs of Marilyn Miller and Leon Errol and is red, yellow, white and blue. s. *Sally*—7 titles listed. m. on pp. 2–5. p.n. 171-4. Back cover adv. *Left.. - A Heart..* JF. The above described regular edition is the same, to the extent possible, as the other contemporary, regular edition, copyright deposit copies from the same show; LC.

 Sally opened in New York City on Dec. 21, 1920. The piano-vocal score of *Sally* was published by Chappell & Co., Ltd., 50 New Bond Street, London, W.2, on Sept. 15, 1921,[1] with a gray and black front cover without photographs and a price of 8/. LC(CDC). Brief biographic information regarding Kern and de Sylva appears above under *All the Things You Are* and *April Showers*.

The Lord's Prayer

Copyright 1935 by G. Schirmer, Inc. By permission.

m. Albert Hay Malotte. Published Oct. 2, 1935,[1] by G. Schirmer, Inc., New York, N.Y. First edition: Front cover has a drawing of a biblical scene, two keys and price of 50 cents, and is tan, black and white. p. [2] blank. m. on pp. 3–7. Dedication on p. 3 to John Charles Thomas. p.n. 36829c. Back cover adv. *O Lord.. - The Lord..* This edition is for medium or high voice. LC(CDC). The text is from St. Matthew, chap. 6, verses 9 *et seq.*

 Malotte was born in Philadelphia in 1895, was a composer of religious and choral works and died in Los Angeles in 1964.[2]

The Lost Chord

<hr>

[1] Copyright records; LC.
[2] Obituary, *The New York Times*, Nov. 18, 1964.

m. Arthur Sullivan. w. Adelaide A. Proctor. Published Feb. 1, 1877,[1] by
Boosey & Co., 295 Regent Street, London W. Possible first edition: Front
cover lists three keys (this copy being no. 3 in A flat), mentions that the
song is sung by Madame Antoinette Sterling and refers to two arrangements, Pianoforte at 2/ and Pianoforte & Harmonium accompaniment at
2/6. m. on pp. 2–7. The word "Music" on p. 2 is misspelled "Msik." No
plate number. Back cover adv. *New Songs.*. No reference on the front cover
to an orchestral arrangement. RA. Another copy, no. 2 in G, also lists three
keys, "Music" is spelled correctly and is otherwise the same as above; AT.
These editions seem earlier than two editions with four keys, even though
the editions with four keys have the lower price of 2/ for the Pianoforte
& Harmonium arrangement; JF.

The circumstance of Sullivan's composing of this music on the occasion of the fatal illness of his brother, Frederick, is well known.[2] Brief biographic information regarding Sullivan appears above under *Bow, Bow,
Ye Lower Middle Classes.* Proctor was an English poetess who was born in
London in 1825 and died in Malvern in 1864.[3]

The Love of Three Oranges-March—Prokofiev

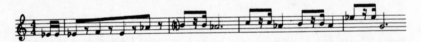

m. Sergei Prokofiev. A piano-vocal score of *L'Amour des Trois Oranges,*
"Printed for the Private use of the Chicago Opera Association," was deposited at LC on Nov. 10, 1919, by the composer, New York City. The
edition is a lithographing of a manuscript copy, the work is described as
op. 35 [*sic*] and the music is on pp. 2–272 with French text only. LC(CDC).
The opera was performed in Chicago on Dec. 30, 1921.

The first regular edition of the piano-vocal score of the opera was
published Sept. 15, 1922,[1] by A. Gutheil, Moscow, and Breitkopf & Härtel,
Leipzig (actually printed by the latter). First edition: Front cover has the
title in Russian, *Любовь къ Тремъ Апельсинамъ,* and French, gives the correct op. no., 33, mentions that the words are also by the composer (after
Carlo Gozzi), refers to British and French agents and is yellow, green and
black. vb. Title page is similar to the front cover but in black and white.

---

[1] According to the entry at Stationers' Hall on March 7, 1884, seven years later.
ILN, Feb. 3, 1877, p. 112 ("This day").

[2] See, e.g., Sullivan-Flower, p. 113.

[3] *Dict. Nat. Biog.,* vol. XVI, p. 416.

[1] Copyright records; LC. Hofmeister *Monatsbericht,* Oct., 1922, p. 158. Nestyev,
p. 507. Prokofiev, *Autobiography,* p. 287.

No price indicated. Cast. m. on pp. 1–252, poor quality paper, the text in Russian and French. The *March* is on p. 85. p.n. 10321. p. [253] and back cover blank. LC(CDC), NYPL and JF.

The *March*, arranged for the piano by the composer, was deposited Aug. 5, 1922, at BM, published and printed as in the case of the piano-vocal score. First edition: Folio. Front cover is in Russian and French and blue and white. No price. p. [2] blank. m. on pp. 3–5. p.n. 10317. Back cover blank. BM(CDC).

No early printing of the orchestral score or parts has been noted.

The *Suite Symphonique de l'Opéra L'Amour des Trois Oranges* for orchestral score was published about Dec., 1926,[2] by Édition Russe de Musique (Russischer-Musikverlag, G.m.b.H.), Berlin, as op. 33 bis. First edition: Front cover is tan and black, in Russian and French and says 1919. vb. Title page is black and white, in Russian and French and mentions depots in seven cities. vb. Index. Instrumentation. m. on pp. 1–107. p.n. R.M.V. 429. p. [1] mentions the 1926 copyright date. p. [108] blank. Back cover missing. LC (copyright copy deposited March 3, 1927). Prokofiev was born in Sontsovka, Russia, in 1891, lived outside the Soviet Union for a while after the Revolution, returned there in 1935, and died in Moscow in 1953.

Lover

Lov - er,___ when I'm near you___ and I

m. Richard Rodgers. w. Lorenz Hart. Published Feb. 15, 1933,[1] by Famous Music Corporation, 719 Seventh Ave., New York, N.Y., First edition: Front cover is blue and black. p. [2] adv. *We..* and *While..* m. on pp. 3–7. Back cover adv. *Jazz..* LC(CDC) and JF (inscribed by the composer).

This song was originally written for the movie *Love Me Tonight*,[2] and was so first copyrighted as an unpublished composition on May 4, 1932,[1] the movie being released Aug, 13, 1932, and copyrighted Aug. 25, 1932. Brief biographic information regarding Rodgers appears above under *If I Loved You*. Hart, his first collaborator, was born in New York City in 1895 and died there in 1943.[3]

---

[2] Hofmeister *Monatsbericht*, Dec., 1926, p. 271; NYPL.

---

[1] Copyright records; LC.
[2] *The Rodgers and Hart Song Book* (New York, N.Y., 1951), p. 91; NYPL.
[3] *ASCAP*, p. 220.

Lover, Come Back to Me!

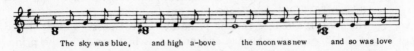

The sky was blue,   and high a-bove   the moon was new   and so was love

m. Sigmund Romberg. w. Oscar Hammerstein 2nd. Published Sept. 12, 1928,[1] by Harms Incorporated, New York City. First edition: Front cover has a drawing of a lady pirate and is red, white and blue. s. *The New Moon* —9 titles listed, but this song is not included. p. [2] adv. *Serenade - Deep..* m. on pp. [2]–5 (actually 3–6). p.n. 8208-4. p. [7] adv. *The Rigg.. - "It."* Back cover adv. *Your.. - Mother.* LC(CDC) and JF. The punctuation in the title is changed in some later editions. One bar in the middle portion of the refrain is the same as a bar in the first theme in Tchaikovsky's *June Barcarolle, The Seasons,* op. 37, no. 6.

The New Moon opened in New York City on Sept. 19, 1928, and the piano-vocal score of the show was published on Dec. 27, 1928.[1] LC(CDC). Brief biographic information regarding Romberg and Hammerstein appears above under *Deep in My Heart, Dear* and *All the Things You Are.*

Love's Old Sweet Song

Just a song at   twi - light,   when the lights are   low

m. J. L. Molloy. w. C. Clifton Bingham. Published Oct. 13, 1884,[1] by Boosey & Co., 295 Regent Street, London W. Probable first edition deposited Nov. 5, 1884, at BM: Front cover has three keys at the top (this copy being in the key of E flat), mentions that the song is sung by Mdme. Antoinette Sterling and gives the price as 2/. p. [2] adv. *The Diamond..* m. on pp. 1–5 (actually 3–7). No plate number. Back cover adv. *Maid.. - Uncle..* There is no mention on the front cover of a pianoforte solo arrangement. BM(CDC). Antoinette Sterling received a royalty for a number of years for introducing *Love's Old Sweet Song.*[2]

---

[1] Copyright records; LC.

[1] According to the entry at Stationers' Hall on Sept. 7, 1892, almost eight years later.

[2] William Boosey, *Fifty Years of Music* (London, 1931), p. 26; NYPL.

Sir Arthur Sullivan denied he used the first two bars of this song for the opening bars of his *When a Merry Maiden Marries* from *The Gondoliers* (1889); his classic reply was: "We had only eight notes between us." James Lyman Molloy was born in King's (now Offaly) County, Ireland, in 1837, was called to the English bar, became a composer and died in Henley-on-Thames, England, in 1909.[3] Bingham was born in Bristol, England, in 1859, was a prolific lyricist and died in London in 1913.[4]

Mack the Knife—The Threepenny Opera

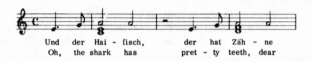

Und der Hai - fisch,   der hat Zäh - ne
Oh, the shark has   pret - ty teeth, dear

Moritat: © 1928 Universal Editions. Copyright renewed and assigned to Weill-Brecht-Harms Co. Inc. Used by permission.
Mack the Knife: © 1955 Weill-Brecht-Harms Co. Inc. Used by permission.

m. Kurt Weill. w. Bert Brecht. *Moritat von Mackie Messer* (in English, known as *Mack the Knife*) was included in the opera *Die Dreigroschenoper* (*The Threepenny Opera*), the piano-vocal score of which was published Nov. 2, 1928,[1] by Universal-Edition A.G., Vienna and **Leipzig.** Possible first editions deposited at the Library of Congress on Dec. 5, 1928, and purchased by the British Museum on Nov. 29, 1929, have a modernistic front cover with white script on light and dark green. vb. Simple title page. Performance rights. Cast and index of acts. Index of music. m. on pp. 5–73. p.n. 8851. This song is on pp. 7–9. Back cover missing. BM and LC(CDC). A similar copy at JF has a back cover listing, among other works, seven excerpts from the opera up to no. 9652, and in the lower left-hand corner appears "No. 131 I. 1929." Another similar copy with a blank cover has been offered by Hans Schneider, Tutzing, West Germany. This edition may have been intended for the foreign market. A variant possible first edition has the "standard" Universal-Edition plain front cover in light and dark green, and the back cover lists, among other works, two excerpts from the opera up to no. 8848, the highest number is 8965, and in the lower left-hand corner appears "No. 131 XII. 1928." ONB and JF. All the above copies include "Nr. 11a" and "Nr. 19a."

Die Dreigroschenoper was performed on Aug. 31, 1928, in Berlin. The separate sheet music edition of the song, with p.n. 9772, was not published

[3] *Dict. Nat. Biog.,* Supp. 1901–1911, vol. II, p. 629.
[4] Obituary, *MA,* April 5, 1913, p. 37.

[1] Copyright records; LC. The publisher confirms the date. Hofmeister *Monatsbericht,* Nov., 1928, p. 279.

until May 31, 1929;[2] a probable first edition, with "V. 1929." at the bottom of the back cover, is at JF. The opera was performed over 10,000 times throughout Central Europe from 1928–1933 and translated into 18 languages; it showed well the moral decadence of the period.[3] *Mack the Knife*, with English words by Marc Blitzstein, was published in 1955.† Weill was born in Dessau in 1900, became an American citizen in 1943 and died in New York City in 1950.[4] Brecht, a German dramatist, was born in 1898 and died in 1956.[5]

Die Dreigroschenoper was written as a modern version of the enduring *The Beggar's Opera*, by John Gay and Dr. Christopher Pepusch and performed on Jan. 29, 1728, in London. The first edition of *The Beggar's Opera*, by majority consensus, was published by John Watts, London, in 1728, octavo, with no music on page 53 and the text of the play ending on page 58, followed by 16 pages of music.[6] *BUC*, p. 96, NYPL and JF. A slightly later edition has music on page 53 and the text ends on page 59. *BUC*, p. 96.

Mademoiselle from Armentières

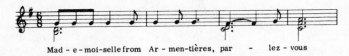

Mad - e - moi-selle from Ar - men-tières, par - lez - vous

The first known printing of this World War I song, also known as *Hinky Dinky Parlez-Vous*, is probably in *Ye A.E.F. Hymnal*, published by Berger-Levrault, 18 Rue des Glacis, Nancy (France); LC. This book cannot be dated exactly but the 4th edition was published Oct. 1, 1919,[1] by Henry Mayers, Brooklyn, N.Y., and it is likely that the first edition was published in France late 1917 or 1918. The Berger-Levrault copy mentioned in the first sentence was donated to LC on Nov. 8, 1919, and it is not known whether it is the 1st, 2nd or 3rd French edition. The music pages are unnumbered, the next to last containing *Hinkey-Dinkey Parlez-Voo*, with correct melody and parody words; LC. Copies of the 4th edition are at LC (CDC) and NYPL.

[2] Information from publisher.
[3] Green, p. 227.
[4] *ASCAP*, p. 528.
[5] *GD*, vol. 5, p. 510.

[6] *The Rothschild Library; A Catalogue of the Collection of Eighteenth-Century Printed Books and Manuscripts Formed by Lord Rothschild* (Cambridge, England, 1954), no. 928; NYPL.

[1] Copyright records; LC.

There were other early printings of the song. *Inky-Pinky-Parley-Vous* was deposited on Jan. 28, 1919, at BM with music and words credited to Will Hythe and published by E. Marks & Son, London. The melody varies considerably from the common melody, and the words differ also. On Sept. 10, 1919, *Mademoiselle from Armentières* was deposited at BM, written and composed by Harry Carlton and J. A. Tunbridge and published by B. Feldman & Co., London. The melody is closer—but not the words. Copies at publisher and JF.

It has been stated[2] that the melody of this song derives from (a) the American *Snapoo*, (b) the English *Skiboo*, allegedly sung by the British Army in the 1880's,[3] or (c) the German *Die Drei Reiter* (*The Three Horsemen*), an old German student song, in Erk-Böhme, p. 560. The precedents have also been given as *Snappoo Snappoo* and *Snipoo*. It is even claimed that the melody, in the major, derives from (d) *When Johnny Comes Marching Home*, in the minor, and also (e) *Mademoiselle de Bar-le-Duc*. Several of the claimed precedents have not been found in an early printing. None is at all clearly the source, and the alleged derivation from any of these melodies, to this author, is unlikely. The song has also been stated to be a parody of (f) a verse ballad by the poet Ludwig Uhland, *Der Wirtin Töchterlein* (included in *The Oxford Book of German Verse*, 3rd ed., Oxford, 1967, at p. 263).[3A] The melody of *Armentières* is a simple one, and some similarity with other simple melodies is inevitable.

It has also been said that the original words of *Armentières* were written in a café in Armentières, France, in March, 1915, by Edward C. H. Rowland.[4] Also, that his friend, Lt. Gitz Rice, a Canadian composer, set the words to music, allegedly to an adaptation of *Mademoiselle de Bar-le-Duc*; the latter melody has not been found either here or in Paris.[5, 6] Authorship of the song has also been claimed by Alfred J. Walden (using the pseudonym of Harry Wincott).[6] These claims remain unsubstantiated.

[2] Melbert B. Cary, *Mademoiselle from Armentières* (New York, N.Y., 1930 and 1935), vol. 2, Introduction; LC and BR. Edward Arthur Dolph, *"Sound Off!"* (New York, N.Y., 1929), p. 82; LC. John T. Winterich, *Mademoiselle from Armentieres* [sic] (Mount Vernon, N.Y., 1953); NYPL. *JAF*, Oct., 1921, p. 386. *JAF*, July–Sept., 1923, p. 300. *JAF*, Oct., 1934, p. 369. Sandburg, p. 440.

[3] An authentic version appears in *Tommy's Tunes*, collected by F. T. Nettleingham (London, 1917), p. 22; BM, LC, NYPL and JF.

[3A] John Brophy and Eric Partridge, *The Long Trail* (London, 1965), p. 52; NYPL.

[4] Obituary, *New York Herald Tribune*, March 14, 1955. Rowland died at Belmont Sutton, England, at the age of seventy-two, having spent a half century in show business.

[5] Mentioned in the obituary in the preceding footnote. Rice was born in New Glasgow, Nova Scotia, in 1891, was a composer and lyricist and died in New York City in 1947; *ASCAP*, p. 406 (also making the claim of authorship).

[6] Spaeth, p. 409.

Maine Stein Song

Fill _____ the steins to dear old Maine!

m. E. A. Fenstad. w. Lincoln Colcord. The melody only was copyrighted for band parts on March 28, 1901,[1] under the title *"Opie" Two-Step*, p.n. 634, by Carl Fischer, New York, N.Y. LC(CDC). The words only were first published in The University of Maine magazine, *The Maine Campus*, Orono, Me., Feb. 15, 1905, p. 124; UMA.

The melody and words together were first published, as sheet music, under the title *"Opie"—The University of Maine Stein Song* on June 23, 1910,[1] by Carl Fischer, Cooper Square, New York, N.Y. First edition: Front cover has a photograph of the University of Maine campus, misspells Colcord's name as "Colord," mentions the publisher's Boston and Chicago addresses, and is green, black and white. m. on pp. 2–7. p.n. 13696-6. Back cover adv. *Canoeing - Whistler.*. LC(CDC).

Rudy Vallee later popularized this song. Prof. Adelbert W. Sprague subsequently received credit for having arranged the music to his roommate's words.[2] The song is not to be confused with *A Stein Song* by Frederic Field Bullard and Richard Hovey. Fenstad was born in 1870 in Trondheim, Norway, came to the United States at the age of eighteen, became a bandmaster of the United States Army and died in Washington in 1941.[3] Colcord was born in 1883 at sea off Cape Horn, graduated from the University of Maine in 1906, became a novelist, poet and editor and died in 1947 at Belfast, Maine.[4] †

The Man I Love

Some-day he'll come a-long,   the man I love;   And he'll be big and strong,

[1] Copyright records; LC.
[2] Clipping from *Bangor Commercial*, date not stated; UMA.
[3] Obituary, *MA*, Oct. 10, 1941.
[4] *AAB*, p. 148. Obituary, *Bangor Daily News*, Nov. 16, 1947; UMA.

m. George Gershwin. w. Ira Gershwin. First published from the show *Lady, Be Good!* on Dec. 1, 1924,[1] by Harms, Incorporated, New York, N.Y. First edition: Front cover is blue, purple and white, with the misprint of the title at the top "The Man I Loved" [*sic*]. Three titles from the show *Lady, Be Good!* are listed. m. on pp. 2–5. p.n. 7276-4. Back cover adv. June.. LC (copy donated by Ira Gershwin in 1980) and JF. This edition was probably a small advance first edition.† The song was subsequently inserted in, and published from, the show *Strike Up the Band* in 1927 and 1929.

"The best popular song ever written" is the description of this song by perhaps the leading authority of popular songs.[2] Yet, the song was dropped from *Lady, Be Good!* before it reached New York City on Dec. 1, 1924, was subsequently considered for another show but rejected, and Ziegfeld wanted it for Marilyn Miller in *Rosalie* but this plan also was dropped before the show reached New York City. It was finally included in the two versions of *Strike Up the Band* in 1927 and 1929.[3] Brief biographic information regarding George and Ira Gershwin appears above under *I Got Rhythm.*

March of the Dwarfs—Grieg

m. Edvard Grieg. Grieg's *Lyrische Stücke*, vol. V, for piano, op. 54, in which the *March of the Dwarfs* appears, was published probably late 1891[1] by C. F. Peters, Leipzig. Probable first edition: Front cover has the name Grieg in an extremely ornate design, is red, tan and black and mentions Edition Peters no. 2651. vb. Title page has a dedication to Julius Röntgen and is brownish-red, black and white. m. on pp. 2–23, with Edition Peters at the bottom of music pages. p.n. 7637. No. 3 on p. 8 is entitled *Troldtog. Zug der Zwerge. Marche des Nains. March of the Dwarfs.* pp. [24] and [25] blank. Back cover adv. Grieg's Works up to op. 53 and Edition Peters up to no. 2539 and states in lower right-hand corner "91," i.e., 1891. LC. The work was sent to Peters on Sept. 17, 1891.[2] Brief biographic information regarding Grieg appears above under *An den Frühling.*

[1] Copyright records; LC.

[2] Sigmund Spaeth, in *The New York Times*, April 2, 1950, Magazine sec., p. 41.

[3] See Gershwin, p. 3; and Ira Gershwin's Foreword in *The George and Ira Gershwin Song Book* (New York, N.Y., 1960), p. xi, at NYPL.

[1] The copy described above is dated 1891. Hofmeister *Monatsbericht*, Jan., 1892, p. 8.

[2] Grieg, *Letters*, p. 39.

Marche Militaire—Schubert

m. Franz Schubert. Published for piano four hands as no. 1 in *3 Marches Militaires* on Aug. 7, 1826,[1] by Ant. Diabelli et Comp., 1133 Graben, Vienna. First edition: Oblong. Engraved. Title page states "Oeuv. 51," p.n. 2236, and price Fl. 1. 15 x C.M. The composer's first name is given in French. pp. [2] and [3] blank. m. on pp. 4–19. p. [20] blank. SB and JF. This work was composed about 1822. Brief biographic information regarding Schubert appears above under his *Ave Maria.*

Marche Slave—Tchaikovsky

This melody, popularized by Tchaikovsky and Cui, was originally a Serbian folk song the opening words of which were "Sunce žarko ne" ("The sun does not shine"). The earliest known printing of the melody and words is in 1879 in *Južno-Slovjenske Narodne Popievke*[1] (*Jugo-Slav Folk Songs*) collected by Fr. Š. Kuhač, published in Zagreb, vol. 2, p. 159; SSL and JF.

Tchaikovsky completed his Славянскій Маршъ or *Marche Slave*, op. 31, on Oct. 7, 1876. It was performed in Moscow on Nov. 17, 1876, but it was not published for several years. The arrangement for piano four hands seems to have been published about May, 1879.[2] Possible first edition: Front cover is gray and black and in French, and lists four arrangements, for orchestral score and parts without prices and for piano four hands and piano two hands with prices. vb. Title page is in Russian (except that the French title *Marche Slave* also is given) and is red, black and white. Listed are arrangements only for piano four hands at 1 p. (ruble) 50 k. and piano at 1 p. Publisher is P. Jurgenson, Moscow, with St. Petersburg and Warsaw agents. m. on pp. 2–27. p.n. 3040. p. [28] and inside of back cover blank. Outside of back cover adv. Brasseur—Donizetti. BN* and JF. A

---

[1] Deutsch, *Schubert*, no. 733, no. 440. *Wiener Zeitung*, Aug. 7, 1826, p. 754; UMI.

[1] In this book, an editor's note to this song refers to Kor. Stanković, *Srbske Narodne Pesme* (Bečku, 1862), but neither the music nor words of this song are in the earlier book; BM.

[2] Hofmeister *Monatsbericht*, May, 1879, p. 149.

similar edition of an arrangement for piano has p.n. 3041 and music on pp. 2–17 and mentions censor's approval on Feb. 3, 1879, at the bottom of p. [18]; GL and JF.

The orchestral score of *Marche Slave* seems to have been published about March, 1880.[3] Possible first edition: Front cover in French only is brown and black; while it lists four arrangements (score, parts, piano four hands and piano), the parts are not priced. The score is 3 Rb., 9 Mk., and D. Rahter, Hamburg, is listed as the German agent. vb. Title page is in Russian, does not refer to Rahter, lists only the two piano arrangements and is red, black and white. m. on pp. 2–65. p.n. 3038. Back cover adv., among others, four Tchaikovsky works, two with prices and two without, 1879 or earlier. BPL*, MC and SSL. No first printing of the orchestral parts has been found; it is known to have p.n. 3039.[4] Brief biographic information regarding Tchaikovsky appears above under *Chant sans Paroles.*

César Cui used the same melody in his *Orientale*, the ninth piece in *Kaléidoscope*, 24 pieces for violin, op. 50, published about 1894.[5]

Marching Through Georgia

Hur - rah! Hur-rah! We bring the Ju - bi - lee!

mw. Henry Clay Work. Copyrighted Jan. 9, 1865,[1] by Root & Cady, 95 Clark Street, Chicago. First edition: Front cover has a drawing of an American flag, a dedication to Cousin Mary Lizzie Work and a reference to Maj. Gen. Sherman's famous march "from Atlanta to the Sea." Price: 3. p. [2] adv. *Cabinet..* and *Late..* m. on pp. [3]–5. p.n. 424-3. Back cover adv. *The Musical..* Not engraved. LC(CDC) and JF.

Work, the composer of the most hated song in the South, was born in Middletown, Conn., in 1832. A composer of Civil War and temperance songs, he was also an inventor of different kinds of machines and toys, and died in Hartford, Conn., in 1884.[2]

---

[3] Hofmeister *Monatsbericht*, March, 1880, p. 50. Dombayev, p. 40.

[4] *Jurgenson Catalog*, Moscow, 1889, p. 193; NYPL. A "Nouvelle édition" of the orchestral parts with the same p.n. is at FLP.

[5] Hofmeister *Annual*, 1894, p. 62.

---

[1] Copyright records; LC.

[2] *American War Songs*, p. 90.

Margie

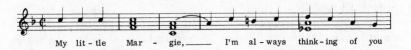

My lit - tle Mar - gie, _____ I'm al - ways think - ing of you

m. Con Conrad and J. Russel Robinson. w. Benny Davis. Published Nov. 3, 1920,[1] by Waterson, Berlin & Snyder Co., Strand Theatre Building, New York, N.Y. First edition: Front cover has a blue, black and white design by Barbelle and mentions that it is an operatic edition. p. [2] adv. *When..* m. on pp. 3–5. Back cover adv. *Sudan.* LC(CDC) and JF.

Con Conrad, a pseudonym for Conrad K. Dober, was born in New York City in 1891, became a composer, pianist, producer and actor, and died in Van Nuys, Cal., in 1938.[2] Robinson was born in Indianapolis in 1892, was a pianist for piano rolls and in various phases of the music business and died in Palmsdale, Cal., in 1963.[3] Davis was born in New York City in 1893, became a lyricist, actor and producer and died in North Miami, Fla., in 1979.[4]

The Marines' Hymn

From the halls of Mon - te - zu - ma, to the shores of Trip - o - li

The music of this song was composed by Jacques Offenbach for an "opéra bouffe," *Geneviève de Brabant*—the three-act version—in particular, for a song in the opera called *Couplets des Deux Hommes d'Armes.* This song was entered for Dépôt Légal as sheet music on Jan. 17, 1868,[1] by Heugel et Cie., au Ménestrel, 2 bis Rue Vivienne, Paris, as no. 11 from the opera. First edition: Price is 3 fr. m. on pp. 2–3. p.n. 3595(11). Back cover blank. BN(CDC).

The piano-vocal score of *Geneviève de Brabant* was published about Feb. 16, 1868.[2] First edition: Half-title page. vb. Title page refers to the Théâtre des Menus Plaisirs, the librettists Hector Crémieux and Etienne

[1] Copyright records; LC.
[2] *ASCAP*, p. 94.
[3] *ASCAP*, p. 414, and obituary, *The New York Times*, Oct. 2, 1963.
[4] *ASCAP*, p. 111, and obituary, *The New York Times*, Dec. 21, 1979.

[1] Archives. *Le Ménestrel*, Jan. 19, 1868, p. 64.
[2] *Le Ménestrel*, Feb. 16, 1868, p. 96. Entered for Dépôt Légal on Feb. 19, 1868; Archives.

Tréfeu, the piano arrangement at 8 fr. and this arrangement at 12 fr., and A. Hammond et Cie., London. vb. Cast. Notice. Index. Verso adv. *Partitions..* m. on pp. 1–225, the *Couplets* on p. 128. p.n. 3610. The printer at the bottom of p. 1 is Moucelot (not Michelet). p. [226] blank. COP(CDC), JMM and JF. The opera was produced in two acts in 1859 (without the *Couplets*), in three acts in Paris on Dec. 26, 1867, and in five acts in 1875. The piano score has p.n. 4976; BN(CDC). Brief biographic information regarding Offenbach appears above under *Apache Dance*.

Geneviève de Brabant was produced in New York City on Oct. 22, 1868, a libretto of the English version was published by Gray & Green, New York, N.Y., in 1868,[3] and *The Geneviève de Brabant Songster* was published in New York City in the following year.[4]

The words of *The Marines' Hymn* were said to have been written by (a) an unknown Marine in 1847[5] (this is too early if the words were written to accompany the above music); (b) Col. Henry C. Davis, United States Marine Corps;[6] (c) L. Z. Phillips;[7] and/or (d) Gen. Chas. Doyen.[8] The earliest known appearance in print of the words, four stanzas, without music, was in *The National Police Gazette*, New York, N.Y., June 16, 1917, p. 3.† Then, the first stanza of the words, without music, was in an article in the June 23, 1918, issue of the *Kansas City Journal* (at KC), which article was reprinted in its entirety in the July 10, 1918, issue of *The Quantico Leatherneck*, the Marines' newspaper (at LC).

The earliest known appearance in print of all the words (and the music) is in an uncopyrighted sheet music edition marked "Printed but not Published by U.S.M.C. Publicity Bureau 117–19 E. 24th St. New York, N.Y. August 1, 1918." USMC and JF. *The Marines' Hymn* was first copyrighted on Aug. 18, 1919,[9] by the United States Marine Corps. The song was also published by *The Quantico Leatherneck* [Washington], without date, but almost certainly after the July 10, 1918, newspaper article mentioned above; LC, SS and JF*. Copies of the folio edition printed by the United States Marine Corps Publicity Bureau seen by the author have a date in the 1940's at the bottom of p. [3]. Major General B. H. Fuller, whose picture as Commandant of the United States Marine Corps appears on an edition printed by L. Z. Phillips, became the Commandant on July 9, 1930.

---

[3] Copy at JF.

[4] *Cantabrigia Bookshop Catalogue 6*, Cambridge, Mass., n.d., no. 271; JF.

[5] According to the sheet music edition issued by the United States Marine Corps Publicity Bureau; JF.

[6] *The Book of Navy Songs* (New York, N.Y., 1926), p. 127; NYPL.

[7] According to the first copyright entry on Aug. 18, 1919; LC.

[8] According to *The Quantico Leatherneck* sheet music edition mentioned in the text.

[9] Copyright records; LC.

In a cartoon,[10] there was a drawing of atomic scientists marching and singing: "From the cyclotron of Berkeley to the labs of M.I.T., We're the lads that you can trust to keep our country strong and free."

The Marriage of Figaro-Overture—Mozart

m. W. A. Mozart. It is possible that the first printing of the *Overture* to *Le Nozze di Figaro*, or *Die Hochzeit des Figaro*, was the edition advertised in June, 1787, by Balzer of the piano score of the opera by J. B. Kucharcz, mentioned by Deutsch-Oldman;[1] but no printed copy has been found. The *Overture* was published in June, 1790, for piano in *Bibliothek der Grazien*, Jahrg. 2, Heft 6, by Rath. Bossler, Speier, p. 52; BM. In 1791–1792[2] Rellstab, Berlin, issued excerpts from the opera for piano and voice, including the *Overture*; an incomplete set is at RE, lacking the *Overture*. Other incomplete sets but including the *Overture* were listed in dealers' catalogues,[3] but their present locations are unknown. A set of the *Ouverture du Mariage de Figaro* and 25 arias was published by Imbault, 627 Rue S. Honoré près l'Hôtel d'Aligre au Mont d'Or, Paris, for piano and voice with p.n. 430 presumably after the first performance of the opera in Paris on March 20, 1793;[4] BN. Manuscript copies of the piano-vocal score of the opera were advertised in the *Wiener Zeitung*, July 1, 1786; ONB.

The piano-vocal score of the opera, published in 1796[5] by Nicolaus Simrock, Bonn, has been noted with three different title pages, one with a price of 11 florins (BM—Hirsch IV, no. 99, ONB—MS 10220, and JF); the second with a price of 20 francs (BM—Hirsch IV, no. 100); and the third with a price of 24 francs (ONB—MS 48356). Whether the edition with the price in florins was published before the French occupation of Bonn in 1796 required prices in francs or after the French left in 1814 is uncertain. The problem of establishing priority is further complicated by the presence of

---

[10] *The New Yorker*, Jan. 18, 1958, p. 36.

[1] Deutsch-Oldman, *Mozart-Drucke*, p. 146. Manuscript copies are at NMP and ONB; printed copies may never have been made. Köchel 492, p. 544, no. 10.

[2] Rudolf Elvers, *Die bei J.F.K. Rellstab in Berlin bis 1800 Erschienenen Mozart-Drucke*, in *Mozart-Jahrbuch*, Salzburg, 1957, p. 158; NYPL. See, generally, Köchel, p. 536.

[3] Schneider, *Catalogue 51*, Tutzing, West Germany, n.d., no. 334; JF. Baron, *Catalogue 68*, London, n.d., no. 73; JF.

[4] Imbault was at this address from ca. 1788–1794; Hopkinson, *Parisian*, p. 61.

[5] Deutsch, *Plate Numbers*, p. 26.

advertisements in the two editions at ONB: MS 10220 advertises up to Haydn's *Creation* (1800) and MS 48356 advertises up to Paer's *Elonora* (1804). An edition at BSM advertises only to Steibelt's *Roméo et Juliet* (1793), but the price has been erased. In all variants the music is on pp. 2–228 with the text in Italian and German, the p.n. is 28 and the music pages are engraved.

The first printing of the *Overture* for orchestra was in 1795[6] by Jean André, Offenbach sur le Mein, for orchestral parts under the title *Ouverture de l'Opéra Le Nozze di Figaro* à grand Orchestre, Oeuvre 48. The p.n. is 790 and the price Fl. 1.30 xr. Engraved. LLD.

The first printing of the orchestral score of the entire opera is said, in the 6th edition of Köchel, p. 545, to be about 1795 by Imbault, Paris, with p.n. 566. No copy has been found by Alexander Weinmann, Vienna, or this author. The author believes that such an edition was not published, and, in that case, the earliest edition of the orchestral score of the opera was published 1806—Sept., 1809[6A] under the title *Le Nozze di Figaro* by Au Magasin de Musique, 76 Rue de Richelieu, Paris. Probable first edition: The title page has a price of 48 f.[6B] and a publisher's number 366. vb. Index. vb. Cast. m. on pp. 2–129 and vb.; 1–186; 1–116; and recto blank, 2–127 and vb. p.n. 566–1—566–4. Text in Italian and French. Engraved. BN (D 8786), LC and JF (latter copy has a blank leaf at end of second and third acts).

Orchestral parts of the opera were published in 1807 by Simrock, Bonn, with plate number 550;[6C] no copy has been found.

The opera was completed by Mozart on April 29, 1786, in Vienna, and performed May 1, 1786, in Vienna. Brief biographic information regarding Mozart appears above under *Eine Kleine Nachtmusik*. Lorenzo Da Ponte, the librettist, was born in Ceneda, Republic of Venice, in 1749 and died in New York City in 1838.[7]

---

[6] *Id.*, p. 6.

[6A] Copy with label stating "Ier. Prix de Composition 1809" awarded to Félix Cazot by Conservatoire Impérial de Musique, Paris; at JF. The awarding of the prize was announced in *Gazette Nationale ou le Moniteur Universel*, Paris, Sept. 6, 1809, p. 986, col. 2; Archives and NYPL. Köchel (3rd ed. with supplement, Ann Arbor, Mich., 1947), p. 1,022. Hopkinson, *Parisian*, p. 84. The opera had been performed in Paris in French in 1793 and then again in Paris in Italian on Dec. 23, 1807.

[6B] The author has seen another copy at a dealer with the price of 60 f. This should be a later edition since the reissue by Frey, Paris, who acquired the business of Au Magasin de Musique in 1811, also has the price of 60 f. NYPL. Hopkinson, *Parisian*, p. 84. In the copy at BM, the price appears to have been erased.

[6C] Köchel (6th ed.), p. 545.

[7] *Grove's* (3rd ed.), vol. IV, p. 227.

La Marseillaise

Al-lons, en-fants de la pa - tri - e! Le jour de gloire est ar - ri - vé

mw. Claude Rouget de Lisle. The French national anthem was composed the night of April 24/25, 1792, in Strasbourg, and was first published shortly thereafter under the title *Chant de Guerre pour l'Armée du Rhin* by Ph. J. Dannbach, Strasbourg.[1] First edition: There is a dedication to Maréchal Lukner. Oblong. m. on p. [2]. Three additional stanzas on p. [3]. p. [4] blank. (See Plate VII.) STR and BM. The composer's name does not appear. The title *La Marseillaise* had not yet been attached to the song— nor is there yet any reference to the volunteers from Marseilles.

Although the *Marseillaise* is now known as a song of revolution, it was originally written by a royalist officer as a patriotic song in support of the then French royal government which had declared war on April 20, 1792, against the Emperor Francis of Austria and King Frederick William II of Prussia. Subsequently, volunteers from Marseilles heard the song and joined in the storming of the Tuileries on Aug. 10, 1792. The song was thereafter quickly reprinted a great many times, usually under the title *Marches des Marseillais* or variant thereof.[2]

Rouget de Lisle was born in Lons-le-Saunier, Montaigu, France, in 1760. The son of royalist parents, he was an officer in the army and belonged to the constitutional party. When he refused to support the abolition of the crown, he was imprisoned. He subsequently lived in poverty and died in Choisy-le-Roi, France, in 1836.

Mary Had a Little Lamb

Mar - y had a lit - tle lamb, lit - tle lamb, lit - tle lamb
Mer - ri - ly we roll a - long, roll a - long, roll a - long

---

[1] A. Rouget de Lisle, *La Vérité sur la Paternité de la Marseillaise* (Paris, 1865). Constant Pierre, *La Marseillaise* (Paris, 1887). Julien Tiersot, *Histoire de la Marseillaise* (Paris, 1915). All at NYPL.

[2] An excellent catalogue of most of the early French editions is in Constant Pierre, *Les Hymnes et Chansons de la Révolution* (Paris, 1904), pp. 224–225; NYPL and JF.

The words of *Mary Had a Little Lamb*, by Sarah J. Hale, were first printed in *Juvenile Miscellany*, a magazine, New Series, Boston, vol. V. no. 1 for Sept. (and Oct.), 1830, p. 64. In what is generally believed to be the first edition of this issue, the initials "S.J.H." do not appear under the poem. NYPL; see also *ULS*, p. 1479. The poem was printed in book form later that year in Mrs. Sarah J. Hale, *Poems for Our Children* (Boston, 1830), p. 6, at BOA, HU, IU and NYPL, and first set to music (but not the presently known melody) in *Juvenile Lyre* (Boston, 1831), p. 61, at BPL.

The melody which presently accompanies the words was first published as the second part of *Goodnight (Ladies)* to the words "Merrily We Roll Along" in 1867. See *Goodnight Ladies*, above. *Mary Had a Little Lamb* was first set to this melody, as far as is known, in H. R. Waite, *Carmina Collegensia* (Boston), copyrighted May 9, 1868,[1] p. 153, where the song is included among "Songs of Hobart," a college at Geneva, N.Y. HC, NYPL and JF.

Described by one authority as "the best known four-line verses in the English language,"[2] the poem tells of an incident that actually happened.[3] A piece of wool from the first fleece of the lamb that inspired the poem, and a manuscript of the poem, were auctioned at Sotheby Parke-Bernet, New York, N.Y., April 11, 1972, no. 43. Hale was born in Newport, N.H., in 1788, was an author and editor and died in 1879.

Maryland, My Maryland—
(O Tannenbaum, O Tannenbaum!; Lauriger Horatius)

	O	Tan - nen - baum, O	Tan - nen - baum, wie	treu sind dei - ne	Blät - ter!
	Thou	wilt not cow - er	in the dust,	Ma - ry - land, my	Ma - ry - land
	Lau - ri - ger	Ho - ra - ti - us,	quam dix - is - ti	ve - rum!

The written story of *Maryland, My Maryland* commences in 1799 when the essential part of the melody was first published in *Melodien zum Mild-*

---

[1] Copyright records; LC.

[2] E. V. Lucas, cited in Opie, p. 300.

[3] Richard Walden Hale, "'Mary Had a Little Lamb' and Its Author" in *The Century Illustrated Monthly Magazine*, New York, N.Y., March, 1904, p. 738; *ULS*, p. 635.

heimischen Liederbuche (Gotha, 1799), no. 464, p. 526, to the opening words, "Es lebe hoch."[1] KA.

The "Zweyte Violine" accompaniment to the foregoing is at JF; the first violin part has not been located; the words, separately, are at LC.

The poem *O Tannenbaum, O Tannenbaum!* was first published in 1820 in Berlin in two forms. The more significant was its setting to the melody in the preceding paragraph in August Zarnack, *Weisenbuch zu den Volksliedern für Volkschulen*, vol. II, no. 51, p. 53. COP and HU. The poem also appeared without music the same year in probably a companion volume, August Zarnack, *Deutsche Volkslieder*, vol. II, no. 51, p. 29. FR and HU.

The poem *Lauriger Horatius* also came to be sung to this melody, its first known appearance in print, without music, being in a *Commersbuch* published in "Germania." The name of the author and the year of publication do not appear in the work but are known from later editions to be Gustave Schwab and 1815. Strangely, there seem to be two different versions of the 1815 edition: in one, the poem is no. 101, p. 171 (at KU); in the other, the poem is no. 138, p. 229 (at SNM). The opening words mean: "Poet of the laurel wreath, Horace, true thy saying."

James Ryder Randall, a native of Baltimore, wrote the poem *Maryland, My Maryland* on April 26, 1861,[2] while a Professor of English Literature at Poydras College, Pointe-Coupée, La., and the poem, without music, was first published in the New Orleans *Sunday Delta*, May 5, 1861,[3] on the first page. NOPL. The poem was reprinted in the *Charleston* (S.C.) *Mercury*, May 11, 1861, p. 4 (at CLS), and later in the year in Frank Moore, *The Rebellion Record* (New York, N.Y.), vol. I, p. 93 (at NYPL). The first printing of the poem in Baltimore was in the Baltimore *South*, May 31, 1861, p. 1; Enoch Pratt Free Library, Baltimore, Md. Broadsides of the poem, of

---

[1] See, in general, Erk-Böhme, no. 176, p. 548. The melody is also said in Spaeth, p. 144, to fit *Mihi Est Propositum* and perhaps originally belonged to this text which has been ascribed to Walter de Mapes, a deacon at Oxford in the twelfth century. However, the melody of *Mihi Est Propositum* as given in *The University Song Book* (London, 1901), p. 172, at NYPL, bears no relationship to that of *Maryland, My Maryland*. A study of the words of *Mihi Est Propositum* appears in Dr. A. Rutgers van der Loeff, *Drie Studentenliederen* (Leiden, 1953), p. 5; NYPL. The common melody may also have been used with another student song, *Gott Grüss Dich, Bruder Straubinger*.

[2] The date established by the state of Louisiana and shown on a historical marker now located at the site of the former Poydras College, near New Roads, Pointe-Coupée Parish, La. The poem was written the night of April 23/24, 1861, according to *The Poems of James Ryder Randall*, edited by Matthew Page Andrews (New York, N.Y., 1910), p. 11; NYPL.

[3] Andrews, footnote 2, above, says it was published in the April 26, 1861, issue, but the New Orleans Public Library advises this is an error.

uncertain dates, also appeared; Scribner *Catalogue 139* (New York, N.Y., n.d.), no page or item number, and Middle Atlantic Chapter of the Antiquarian Booksellers' Association of America, Inc. *Catalogue 10* (n.p., n.d.), no. 136 (both *Catalogues* at JF). See, also, Edwin Wolf 2nd, *American Song Sheets, Slip Ballads and Poetical Broadsides 1850–1870* (Philadelphia, 1963), nos. 1397 *et seq.*; NYPL.

Maryland, My Maryland, as a song, was copyrighted Oct. 11, 1861,[4] by Miller & Beacham, Baltimore. First edition: The only credit as to authorship is "Written by a Baltimorean in Louisianna. Music Adapted & Arranged by C.E." Engraved. Front cover has a drawing of a shield and says "Crescite et Multiplicamini." Price: 2½. p. [2] blank. m. on pp. 3–5. p.n. 3364. The back cover of the copyright copy deposited on Oct. 11, 1861, advertises *New and Popular Music..* LC(CDC); also at JF. However, another copy at the Library of Congress, otherwise identical to the above, has a blank back cover, and this copy bears a note in Rebecca Lloyd Nicholson's hand:[5] "One of the first copies struck off . . ." LC; also at JF.

The first Confederate publication of the song, on Jan. 22, 1862, was by A. E. Blackmar & Bro., 74 Camp St., New Orleans, the words are credited to Randall, the music to "a Lady of Baltimore," there is a copyright claim of 1862, and there is no statement on the front cover by Randall as to the disposition of the copyright of his poem.[6] JF. Randall was born in Baltimore in 1839, was a poet, teacher and editor of several Southern newspapers and died in 1908.

Mary's a Grand Old Name

For it is Ma - ry,   Ma - ry, plain as an - y name can   be

mw. Geo. M. Cohan. Copyrighted Oct. 3, 1905,[1] by F. A. Mills, 48 West 29th St., New York, N.Y. First edition: Front cover has a photograph of Fay Templeton and is green, orange, brown and white. s. *Forty-Five*

---

[4] Copyright records; LC.

[5] Rebecca Lloyd Nicholson was probably responsible for the publication of the song. See Andrews, footnote 2, above, and Harwell, p. 53.

[6] Harwell, p. 129; and Dichter-Shapiro, p. 122. "Forthcoming" (*The New Orleans Daily Crescent,* Jan. 21, 1862); "Received yesterday" (*The Daily Picayune,* New Orleans, Jan. 23, 1862); both at HT. Miss Dorothy Blackmar, New Orleans, La., the granddaughter of the publisher, advised the author of these newspaper notices.

---

[1] Copyright records; LC.

Minutes from Broadway—6 titles listed. p. [2] blank. m. on pp. 3–5. p. [6]
adv. *Give.. - If..* p. [7] blank. Back cover adv. *Josie.. - Fare..* LC(CDC).
Forty-Five Minutes from Broadway opened in New York City on Jan. 1,
1906. Brief biographic information regarding Cohan appears above under
Give My Regards to Broadway.

Massa's in de Cold Ground

All de dark-eys am a - weep - ing   Mas-sa's in de cold, cold ground

mw. Stephen C. Foster. Copyrighted July 7, 1852,[1] by Firth Pond & Co.,
1 Franklin Sq., New York, N.Y. First edition: Engraved. Front cover has a
delicate design, refers to one other song by Foster and lists two agents.[2]
Price: 25¢. p. [2] blank. m. on pp. 3–5. p.n. 1620. Back cover adv. two
columns of the latest music, the first piece being *Byerly's.* LC(CDC), FH
and JF. Brief biographic information regarding Foster appears above under
Beautiful Dreamer.

La Mattchiche

m. Ch. Borel-Clerc. Copies of *La Mattchiche* for piano were deposited for
Dépôt Légal on Aug. 19, 1905,[1] by Librairie Hachette & Cie., 79 Boulevard
Saint-Germain, Paris. Possible first edition: Front cover states that the song
is the grand Parisian success of 1905, that it is the celebrated popular
march on Spanish motives, has a photograph of Mmes Derminy and Paule
Morly who are said to dance the composition at the Alcazar d'Été in the
revue *Ça Mousse*, states that the composition is sung by Mayol and that
it is published with the authorization of Casa Dotésio, Spain, and lists six
arrangements, this one for piano at 2 (francs). vb. m. on pp. 1–4 (actually
3–6). Dedicated to MM. de Gorsse, G. Nanteuil and Febvre. p.n. 2481. p.
[7] blank. Back cover adv. *Le Jeune.. - Bill Bayley* [sic]. No foreign agents
listed on front cover, and no dance instructions on an inner page. BN(CDC).

[1] Copyright records; LC.
[2] Front cover is illustrated in Fuld, *Foster*, no page number.

[1] Archives. *BMF*, July–Sept. 1905, p. 8, strangely lists Salabert as the publisher.
The Anton J. Benjamin, Hamburg, edition is listed in Hofmeister *Monatsbericht*, March,
1906, pp. 108–109; a copy of this edition is at ONB.

The fact that the statement appears on the front cover, and also on p. 1, that the song is published with the authorization of Casa Dotésio, Spain, makes it likely that it was first published in Spain, but no such edition has been found in leading libraries in Madrid or Bilbao, Casa Dotésio being located in the latter city. On the other hand, the composer was born in Pau, France, in 1879, and was known as a French composer of popular songs for Maurice Chevalier and others before he died in 1959.[2]

To complicate the matter further, an American edition deposited at the Library of Congress on Feb. 5, 1906,[3] states that this "Latest Parisian March Craze" is a true Brazilian dance, *La Tortille*, based on the motives of the celebrated song *Ma Peau d'Espagne*. Neither of these titles has been traced.

The music seems to be known in the United States as *La Sorella*, and it is also known as *La Maxixe* or *Polo*. The parody words to the music are well known in this country: "My ma gave me a nickel, to buy a pickle; I didn't buy a pickle, I bought some chewing-gum."

Mazel Tov

Cho - son   ka - le   ma - zel tov

m. Sigmund Mogulesco. w. Sigmund Mogulesco and/or Joseph Lateiner. This melody is partly original and partly based upon the melody of the Serbian folk song used by Tchaikovsky in his *Marche Slave*, which see. The song was written for *Blihmele* (*Little Flower*), a Jewish operetta, performed in Oct., 1894, in New York City. The words of *Choson Kale Mazel Tov*, which are original, were included on an unnumbered page in *Die Harfe*, in Hebrew (*The Harp*), a collection of songs from the Yiddish theater, stated to be copyrighted in 1895 by J. Katzenelenbogen, 35 Ludlow Street, New York, N.Y.[1] BCS and EM. It is not clear in this collection whether Lateiner or Mogulesco wrote the words.

---

[2] Baker, p. 182. He was also a member of SACEM, the French ASCAP.

[3] *Sorella*, published by Conservatory Publication Society, New York, N.Y.; LC (CDC).

---

[1] Part of the information regarding *Mazel Tov* was obtained from Biblioteca Centrală de Stat, Bucharest, and Eric Mandell, Philadelphia. The publisher was at this address in 1895; *New York City Directories* at NYPL.

The Harp (*Hebrew Songs*) was copyrighted by Jacob Katzenelenbogen on Oct. 8, 1892, according to the copyright records at LC; however, no copy of this work has been found so it is impossible to know whether it contained the words and/or music of *Mazel Tov*.

No printing of the melody has been found prior to the inclusion of the music and words in a collection of songs from *Blihmele*, published Dec. 21, 1909,[2] by Hebrew Publishing Co., 83-87 Canal Street, New York, N.Y., with both music and words credited to Mogulesco. Possible first edition: Front cover claims that *Blihmele* has been performed over one thousand times in America and Europe, is blue and white, lists the piano arrangement at $2 and the violin arrangement at $1 (this arrangement is for piano), and 14 numbers, the second number listed being *Choson Kale Mazl Tov* [*sic*]. vb. m. on pp. 3–33. The title on p. 4 is *Chusen Kale Masel Tow*. pp. [34] and [35] blank. Back cover adv. *Catalogue*.. LC(CDC) and JF*. This song was also published the same day in separate sheet music for violin with identical front cover in red and white; JF.

The title *"Choson Kale Mazel Tov"* means "Bridegroom, Bride—Congratulations." Mogulesco, a composer, was born in Slatopoli, Bessarabia, Russia, in 1858, came to the United States and died in New York City in 1914.[3] Lateiner, a playwright, was born in Jassy, Rumania, in 1853, also came to this country and died in New York City in 1935.[4]

Meadowlands—Symphony no. 4, Knipper

Ekh, Po - lysh - ko   po - le (dy),   po-lysh-ko shi-ro-ko   po - le!

m. Lev Knipper. w. Victor Gusyev. This stirring song is included in Knipper's *Symphony no. 4*, a *Poem of a Young Communist Warrior*, op. 41, which employs a tenor solo, a bass solo and two choruses. The orchestral score of the *Symphony* was published sometime between March 29, 1936 (the later of two dates relating to Soviet publication procedure, mentioned on p. 145 of the score), and July 17, 1936, the date of receipt of a copy of the score by the Glinka Conservatory, Moscow.[1] Probable first edition: Front cover is tan and black, with a red star, hammer and sickle, the title in Russian only, Четвертая Симфония, Music Publisher, Moscow, 1936. Title page contains similar information in different arrangement, in Russian only, mentions the years 1933–1934 and p.n. 14746. Orchestra composition.

[2] Copyright records; LC. The publisher moved to 50 Eldridge Street, New York, N.Y., about 1915; *New York City Directories* at NYPL.

[3] Zalmen Zylbercwajg, *Lexicon of the Yiddish Theater* (New York, N.Y., 1931), vol. 2, column 1180, in Hebrew; NYPL.

[4] *The Universal Jewish Encyclopedia* (New York, N.Y., 1948), vol. 6, p. 547; NYPL.

[1] *AML*, April–June, 1936, p. 19.

m. on pp. 3–145. p. 145 contains much information relating to Soviet publishing procedure and the price of 18 p. (rubles) 25 k. (kopecs) for the music and 1 p. 50 k. for the binding. Russian text only. The *Meadowlands* song is at p. 14. GL and LPL.

An edition of the song for chorus a cappella at 5 kopecs was listed in *AML*, Oct.–Dec., 1934, p. 2;[2] the title is Степная Кавалерийская *(Field Cavalry Song)*. No early printing has been found. The *Symphony* was performed in Moscow in March, 1933. Knipper was born in Tiflis in 1898, studied for a while in Germany and resides in the Soviet Union.[3] Gusyev was born in Moscow in 1909 and died in 1944.[4]

Méditation—Thaïs

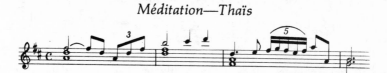

m. J. Massenet. The piano-vocal score of *Thaïs*, in which the *Méditation* appears, was published in Jan.–Feb., 1894,[1] by Heugel & Cie., au Ménestrel, 2 bis Rue Vivienne, Paris. First edition:[2] Front cover is highly ornamental and colored. Inside of cover blank. Title page has a drawing of two heads, says that the libretto is by Louis Gallet after Anatole France's novel, and is also in many colors. Price: 20 frs. vb. Cast. Table of two index pages; at the bottom of the second page are the numbers, 934-1-94. vb. Acte II has **three** tableaux. m. on pp. 1–250, *Méditation* on p. 127. p.n. 7644. Inside of back cover blank. Back cover has a drawing of a lyre in many colors. BM (purchased June 13, 1894), JMM and JF. The second edition has numbers 5406-3-94 at the bottom of second index page and Acte II has two tableaux; BN(CDC), JMM and JF (inscribed by the composer in March, 1894). *Thaïs* was performed in Paris on March 16, 1894. *Méditation* was published separately for piano at 5 francs at about the same time,[1] but no early printing has been located. *Thaïs* was later revised with the tableau *L'Oasis* added, the tableau *La Tentation* deleted, and other changes made.

---

[2] *AML*, April–June, 1935, p. 6, mentions a 1934 edition for piano and chorus; a later edition, with probably the original p. n. 14554, is at JF.

[3] Baker, p. 843.

[4] Information from LTL.

---

[1] January, 1894, appears at the bottom of the second page of the Table of index pages. The second edition was entered for Dépôt Légal on March 1, 1894; Archives. The piano-vocal score (first or second edition?), piano score and separate sheet music are listed in *Le Ménestrel*, March 11, 1894, p. 80, and in *BMF*, Jan.–Mar., 1894, p. 8. JF's copy of the second edition of the piano-vocal score was inscribed March, 1894.

[2] Jean-Marie Martin, Hollogne-aux-Pierres, Belgium, aided in this title.

The orchestral score of *Thaïs* was copyrighted Sept. 21, 1894.[3] First edition: Front cover is black and tan. vb. There is no title page or other page before the music which appears on pp. 1–560. Acte II has three tableaux. p.n. 9434. Music pages engraved. *Méditation* at p. 277. Both sides of back cover blank. BN and COP(both CDC) and LC.

Lithographed orchestral parts of the opera, with plate number 9346, folio, without covers, are at Heugel et Cie., Paris.

Brief biographic information regarding Massenet appears above under *Aragonaise*.

Mélodie in F—Rubinstein

m. Anton Rubinstein. It is not presently possible to state the year of composition, the year of publication, or the first publisher of Rubinstein's *Deux Mélodies* for piano, op. 3, in which *Mélodie in F* is the first of the two compositions.

On the basis of plate numbers, Ad. Mt. Schlesinger, 34 Linden, Berlin, may have been the first publisher. Possible first edition: Front cover has the title, *2 Mélodies* pour le Piano, there is a dedication to S.A.I. Madame la Grande Duchesse, Hélène Pawlona, the price is ½ Thlr., the copublishers are Bernard, St. Petersburg, and Lehnhold, Moscow, and there is reference to Rubinstein's *Ondine*. p. [2] blank. m. on pp. 3–7. Back cover blank. Engraved. p.n. 3783, suggesting an original publication in 1850-1851, but the earliest announcement of such publication is 1854.[1] No opus number stated. JF. The earliest Hofmeister reference is in Oct., 1852,[2] to an edition by Bernard, St. Petersburg (Hamburg, Cranz). A later Bernard edition (referring to Rubinstein's op. 50) is at the Glinka Conservatory, Moscow, with p.n. 2828. No Cranz edition has been found. *Grove's* indicates Schreiber, Vienna, was the publisher,[3] but no date is indicated, and no copy has been found. The Bote & Bock, Berlin, edition at GM, the Lewy, Vienna, edition at ONB, and the Siegel, Leipzig, and Spina, Vienna, editions were apparently published in 1858.[4] The *Rubinstein Catalogue* also lists an edi-

[3] This statement appears in the copy at LC. Entered for Dépôt Légal on Sept. 20, 1894; Archives. BF, Dec. 1, 1894, p. 766, without price.

[1] Deutsch, *Plate Numbers*, p. 21. Hofmeister *Annual*, 1854, p. 57. Rubinstein's *Ondine* was published during his childhood; *Rubinstein Catalogue*, p. 14.

[2] Hofmeister *Monatsbericht*, p. 180.

[3] 3rd ed., vol. IV, p. 468.

[4] Hofmeister *Annual*, 1858, p. 72.

tion by Rózsavölgyi, Pest,[5] and there is an edition by F. Lucca, Milan, with p.n. 22197, at JF. An edition by Brandus & Dufour, Paris, with p.n. B et Cie. 9943, is about 1858;[6] AT. Jurgenson's edition at LPL is 1861 or later since he began publishing in Moscow that year.

The *Mélodie in F* was composed in the home of the dedicatee mentioned above, his hostess, on Kamennoi Island in the Neva. It is said that Rubinstein did not play it with a slow, sugary *rubato*, but rather quite fast.[7] Brief biographic information regarding Rubinstein appears above under *Kamennoi-Ostrow*.

Men of Harlech

We - le goel - certh wen yn ffla - mio a thaf - o - dau tân yn bloedd - io
Men of Har - lech! Day is break - ing; Sax - on tramp the earth is shak - ing

The music was first published without words under the Welsh and English titles *Gorhoffedd Gwŷr Harlech—The March of the Men of Harlech*, in the 1794 edition of Edward Jones, *Musical and Poetical Relicks [sic] of the Welsh Bards*, London, p. 124. A copy was entered at Stationers' Hall on July 15, 1794, this copy now at BM: address is 122 in Mount Street, near Berkeley Square; BM(CDC), also at JF. A later edition has the address no. 3 in Green Street, Grosvenor Square; NLW.

The Welsh words usually associated with the above melody were composed by the nineteenth-century poet John Ceiriog Hughes, and published in his *Cant O Ganeuon (One Hundred Songs)* (Wrexham, Wales, 1890), at NLW.[1] The English words were first published in *Cambrian Minstrelsie* (Edinburgh, 1893), vol. III, p. 184; NLW and NYPL.

It has been said that the *March* was probably composed during the Wars of the Roses, when Harlech Castle was besieged on behalf of King Edward IV (1468–1469).[2] The Castle was a celebrated fortress in Wales, built about A.D. 530, and is perhaps the oldest British fort whose remains are still standing.

---

[5] P. [3].

[6] Hopkinson, *Berlioz*, p. 196, and Hopkinson, *Parisian*, p. 17.

[7] Catherine Drinker Bowen, *"Free Artist" The Story of Anton and Nicholas Rubinstein* (New York, N.Y., 1939), p. 107; NYPL.

---

[1] The author is indebted for the information in this paragraph to David Jenkins, Keeper of Printed Books, The National Library of Wales.

[2] *Cambrian Minstrelsie*, referred to in the text, vol. III, p. x.

Merry Widow Waltz

m. Franz Lehár. w. Victor Léon and Leo Stein. *Die Lustige Witwe,* or *The Merry Widow,* was performed on Dec. 28, 1905, in Vienna, and the first printings of music from this operetta (including all those described below) show a **1905 copyright.** The publisher was Ludwig Doblinger, 10 Dorotheergasse, Vienna I.[1] The *Waltz* probably appeared first in Dec., 1905, or Jan., 1906, in *Ballsirenen Walzer* which is listed for piano and for small and salon orchestra on the front cover of other music from the operetta with an "operetta cover" (at JF), whereas the *Walzer-Intermezzo* is not yet listed.[2] No copy of *Ballsirenen Walzer* for piano has been found with an "operetta cover"; a copy listing 11 arrangements of the *Waltz,* has p.n. 3354; JF. An early printing of the arrangement of *Ballsirenen Walzer* for "grosses orchester," "Aus dem Archiv Franz Lehárs," lists five arrangements and has p.n. 3362; SB.

Possible first printing of the *Walzer-Intermezzo* for piano: "Operetta cover" in green and white, listing 33 titles and arrangements from the operetta, this title at 1.80 K. and 1.50 Mk., K. F. Köhler is the Leipzig agent, Shapiro, Bernstein & Co. is the New York City agent and there is reference to a Riga agent. p. [2] blank. m. on pp. 3–5. p.n. 3370. Back cover adv. no. 25, *Cupido.. - Muss..* EW. A piano-vocal arrangement, *Walzer-Intermezzo: Lippen Schweigen,* first published about June, 1906,[3] not an "operetta cover," with 12 arrangements of the song and p.n. 3464 is at the publisher.

The piano-vocal score of *Die Lustige Witwe* was published Jan. 30, 1906.[4] Possible first edition: Front cover is purple and green. vb. Title page has a photograph of two stars, is blue and white, lists this score at K 12/ M 10 and the piano arrangement at half such prices, K. F. Köhler is the

---

[1] The publisher made a number of changes in its imprint and agents at the time. It is clear that a copy with K. F. Köhler as the Leipzig agent is earlier than a copy showing the publisher itself at Leipzig. It is not clear whether Shapiro, Bernstein & Co. or Chappell & Co., Ltd., is the earlier agent in New York City. Some early editions show an agent in Rumania, some do not; some show a Riga agent, some do not—the implications as to priority are not known.

[2] However, both the *Ballsirenen Walzer* and *Walzer-Intermezzo* for piano are listed in Hofmeister *Monatsbericht,* Jan., 1906, p. 23. The publisher wrote the author that *Walzer-Intermezzo* for piano was published Jan. 11, 1906.

[3] Hofmeister *Monatsbericht,* June, 1906, p. 316.

[4] Information from publisher. Hofmeister *Monatsbericht,* Feb., 1906, p. 67.

Leipzig agent, there is a Rumanian agent and Chappell & Co., Ltd., is also
an agent. vb. Cast and index. m. on pp. 4–142. p.n. 3366. ONB and JF.
A possible first printing of the piano score, similar to the foregoing except
Shapiro, Bernstein & Co. is the New York agent, and there is a Riga agent,
with p.n. 3367, is at JF.

Brief biographic information regarding Lehár appears above under
Gold and Silver Waltz. Léon, a lyricist, was born in Vienna in 1860 and
died there in 1940.[5] Leo Stein (a pseudonym for Leo Rosenstein), also a
lyricist, was born in 1862 and died in 1921.[6]

The Merry Wives of Windsor-Overture—Nicolai

m. Otto Nicolai. The *Overture* to *Die Lustigen Weiber von Windsor* was
published about April, 1850,[1] for orchestral score, piano and piano four
hands by Ed. Bote & G. Bock, Berlin. Early edition of the orchestral score
of the *Overture:* Title page also mentions the French title of the opera, *Les
Joyeuses Commères de Windsor*, the price in Thlr. is erased, and Leipzig,
Paris, London and Barcelona agents. The publisher is at 27 Unter den
Linden, and 33e Französische Strasse, Berlin, and 21 Wilhelm Strasse,
Mylius Hotel, Posen, and in four other cities. No other arrangement or
title is mentioned. vb. m. on pp. 3–81. p.n. 1847. p. [82] blank. Engraved.
JF. It is believed that the first edition does not mention Posen.

A first printing of the piano arrangement of the *Overture* was deposited at BM on Aug. 7, 1850. Possible first edition: Title page lists four
arrangements of the entire opera without prices and the three arrangements
of the *Overture* mentioned above with prices, this for piano at 20 Sgr., the
publisher is shown at Berlin, Breslau and Stettin without street addresses,
and there are three foreign agents. m. on pp. 2–15, engraved. p.n. 1601(A).
Back cover blank. BM(CDC).

About Dec., 1850,[2] the piano-vocal score of the opera was published
without finales. Probable first edition: Title page mentions the German
title only, refers to Shakespeare, states that the words are by H. S. Mosenthal, lists seven arrangements and titles, the first three without prices,

[5] Information from AKM.
[6] NYPL Music Division Biographical File.

---

[1] Hofmeister *Monatsbericht*, April, 1850, pp. 54, 57 and 61.
[2] *Id.*, Dec., 1850, p. 193.

this arrangement being 4½ Thlr., the publisher is given at Berlin, Breslau and Stettin without street addresses and there are agents at Paris, New York and St. Petersburg. vb. Next page has incipits, the Partitur of the *Overture* being priced at 2 Thlr. and the p.ns. being 1720-1732. m. on pp. 2–111. The *Overture* has p.n. 1601(A) and the balance p.ns. 1720-1728. p. [112] blank. Engraved. BM. The complete piano-vocal score was published about Oct., 1851,[3] at 10 Thlr., with two blank prices on the otherwise similar title page, with music up to p. 226 and with the p.ns. as in the previously described arrangement. Engraved. BM (deposited Feb. 9, 1852).

A copy of the orchestral score of the entire opera was deposited at BM on July 5, 1856, by the same publisher. Possible first edition: Although oblong, the title page is the same as that of the piano-vocal score without finales. vb. m. on pp. 1–837, a lithographing of a manuscript score. p. [838] blank. BM(CDC). No early printing of the orchestral parts of the opera has been found.

The opera was completed Dec. 11, 1847, and performed March 9, 1849, in Berlin. Nicolai was born in Königsberg in 1810 and died in Berlin two months after the first performance of the opera. Hermann Salomon von Mosenthal, a German dramatist, was born in Kassel in 1821 and died in 1877.[4]

Mexican Hat Dance—Jarabe Tapatío

The earliest known printing[1] of the above melody is in sheet music entitled *Jarabe Tapatío*, arreglo para piano por A. Macías C., and published Nov. 2, 1916,[2] by Edmundo C. Argüelles, El Paso, Texas. Front cover is gray and black. m. on pp. 1–3. p.n. 32. LC (copyright copy deposited Nov. 25, 1916). The copyright records also state that the arranger, Antonio Macías, is a citizen of Mexico, domiciled in El Paso.

---

[3] *Id.*, Oct., 1851, p. 200.

[4] *NIE*, vol. 16, p. 317.

[1] Joseph C. Hickerson, Head, Archive of Folk Culture, Library of Congress, Washington, D.C., called the author's attention to this printing.

[2] Copyright records; LC.

The earliest known Mexican written reference to the above melody is the issuance of a Mexican copyright on July 8, 1919, for *Jarabe Tapatío*, arranged for F. A. Partichela, and published by Wagner y Levien, Sucrs., Mexico City. The original receipt no. 667 for the copyright has been seen by the author at Promotora Hispano Americana de Música, S.A., Mexico City. No copy of this printing of *Jarabe Tapatío* has been found, but it is believed to be the same as the Partichela arrangement published as *Mexican Hat Dance—Popular Jarabe Tapatío* in 1933 by Edward B. Marks Music Corporation, New York, N.Y.; JF.

The Jarabe Tapatío is the national dance of Mexico, and is said to have been first danced in its present form at the Coliseo in Mexico City on July 9, 1790.[3] The Jarabe is a Spanish dance, and the dance became popular with the people of Guadalajara, who are called Tapatíos. There are also a number of other melodies that accompany, and are known as, *Jarabe Tapatío*, some having been printed in the nineteenth century.

Michelle

mw. John Lennon and Paul McCartney. Published Dec. 16, 1965,[1] by Northern Songs Ltd., James House, 71–75 New Oxford Street, London W.C. 1. First edition: Front cover has a photograph of the four Beatles holding brooms and a basket, and is black and white; the price is 3/. m. on pp. [2]–4. The bottom of page 2 has legal claims and the telephone number, TEM 4864. The bottom of page 4 states that the sole selling agents are Campbell Connelly & Co. Ltd., 10 Denmark Street, London W.C. 2. LC (copyright copy deposited Dec. 22, 1965) and JF.

Lennon was born in Liverpool, England, in 1940[2] and died in New York City in 1980. McCartney was born in Allerton, a suburb of Liverpool, in 1942.[3] The other two of the Beatles playing and singing quartet were George Harrison and Ringo Starr.

[3] Guillermina Dickins, *Dances of Mexico* (London, [1954]), p. 30; NYPL.

[1] Copyright records; LC.
[2] *Current Biography* (New York, N.Y., Nov., 1966), p. 32; NYPL.
[3] *Current Biography Yearbook—1965* (New York, N. Y., 1966), p. 255; NYPL.

Midsommarvaka—Alfvén

m. Hugo Alfvén. The orchestral score and parts of *Midsommarvaka* (meaning *Midsummer Vigil*), op. 19, were published about Oct., 1908,[1] by Wilhelm Hansen, Copenhagen and Leipzig. Possible first edition: Front cover in gray and black says Wilhelm Hansen Edition no. 1209. vb. Title page states that the work is a Swedish rhapsody, is blue, green, black and white, has a dedication to the composer's brother Gösta, and lists four arrangements without prices. Text in Swedish. vb. Instrumentation. vb. m. on pp. 3–66. No copyright notice. p.n. 13974. p. [67] blank. Back cover adv. Anderson—Svendsen. FLP and NYPL. No reference to Oslo or Stockholm agents.

Possible first printing of the orchestral parts: Front cover in gray and black says Wilhelm Hansen Edition no. 1209a. vb. p.n. 13974. Inside of back cover blank. Outside of back cover adv. Bendix—Svendsen. NYPS* and FLP* (cover at JF). The arrangement for piano four hands was published at about the same time.[1]

Midsommarvaka was performed in Stockholm on May 10, 1904. Alfvén was born in Stockholm in 1872 and died in Faluns, Sweden, in 1960.

Mighty Lak' a Rose

Sweet-est li' - 'l fel - ler,   ev - 'ry-bod - y knows;   dun - no what to call him

m. Ethelbert Nevin. w. Frank L. Stanton. Copyrighted Sept. 6, 1901,[1] by The John Church Company. Possible first edition: Front cover has a design in the center, is red and white and refers to two voices (this copy being for

---

[1] Sven E. Svensson, *Hugo Alfvén* (Uppsala, 1946), p. 195; NYPL. Hofmeister *Monatsbericht*, Oct., 1908, pp. [261] and 268.

[1] Copyright records; LC.

low voice). The publisher is shown at Cincinnati, Chicago, New York, Leipzig and London. m. on pp. 2–3. p.n. 14032-2. Dedication on p. 2 to Mrs. Adele Laeïs Baldwin. Back cover blank. JF.

Nevin, a composer, was born in Edgeworth, Pa., in 1862, and died in New Haven, Conn., on Feb. 17, 1901, the year in which he composed *Mighty Lak' a Rose*, and before its publication.[2] Stanton was born in Charleston, S.C., in 1857, became a poet and journalist with the *Atlanta Constitution* and died in 1927.[3] Mrs. Frank L. Stanton has advised that the poem *Mighty Lak' a Rose* appeared in this newspaper about 1895–1896,[4] but an examination of this newspaper for part of this period has not been successful.

The Minstrel-Boy

The min-strel-boy— to the war is gone, in the ranks of death— you'll find— him

This song was first published about Dec., 1813,[1] in the 5th Number (the first number of the third volume) of *A Selection of Irish Melodies* with symphonies and accompaniments by Sir John Stevenson and characteristic words by Thomas Moore. First edition: Imprint is J. Power, . . . 34 Strand (London) and . . . W. Power, 4 Westmoreland Street, Dublin, in that order. An erratum note appears on the Advertisement opposite the title page, there is an engraved footnote on p. 3, and there are two printed footnotes on p. 5.[2] *The Minstrel-Boy* appears on p. 23. JF.

The words were original with Moore. The melody is said, in the Index and on p. 22, to be *Moreen*, but no earlier printing of the melody has been found. The first bar is similar to the opening theme in W. A. Mozart, *Flute Quartet in A* (K 298), first movement. Brief biographic information regarding Moore appears above under *Believe Me If All Those Endearing Young Charms*.

---

[2] *ASCAP*, p. 369.
[3] *ASCAP*, p. 478; and Dave and Kathleen Thompson, p. 100.
[4] Information from Atlanta Public Library which has a run of this newspaper.

[1] 1813 is given as the year of publication in Muir, 13th unnumbered page, and Chinnéide, p. 122, but the Advertisement opposite the title page is dated Dec., 1813, which allows little time for printing.

[2] Muir, 12th and 13th unnumbered pages.

Minuet in G—Beethoven

m. Ludwig van Beethoven. This *Minuet* was published about March 30, 1796,[1] as *Menuett no. II* in *VI Menuetten für das Clavier* by Artaria et Comp., Vienna. First edition: Oblong. Engraved. Front cover mentions this is the 2ten Theil, p.n. 641 and the price 30xr. m. on pp. 2–7, this *Minuet* in G on p. 3. Back cover blank. There is no opus number. ONB and JF.

While perhaps written for orchestra, this work was first published for piano. Brief biographic information regarding Beethoven appears above under *Concerto for Piano no. 5.*

Minuet—Boccherini

m. Luigi Boccherini. This *Minuet* is no. 5 in *Sei Quintetti*, per due Violini Alto et due Violoncelli Concertanti, opera XIII, which was published about Jan., 1775,[1] by G. B. Venier, Rue St. Thomas du Louvre vis-à-vis le Château d'eau, Paris. Probable first edition: Front cover mentions that this is Libro secondo di Quintetti, and the price is 12 (livres tournois). In the first violin part, the verso of the front cover is blank; next page has a Catalogue, with Boccherini's works listed only to op. 13; m. on pp. 2–25, this *Minuet* on p. 20; and back cover is blank. All five parts have the identical front cover. Engraved. No plate number. BN and JF*.

This work was composed in 1771. Although the front cover states "A.P.D.R.," the Société des Amis de la Bibliothèque Nationale could find no "Privilège du Roi" granted for this work. Boccherini was born in Lucca in 1743 and died in Madrid in 1805.

[1] Kinsky-Halm, WoO 10, p. 442. *Wiener Zeitung*, March 30, 1796, p. 882; UMI.

[1] *Mercure de France*, Jan., 1775, vol. 1, p. 205. Yves Gérard, *Thematic, Bibliographical and Critical Catalogue of Luigi Boccherini* (London, 1969), no. 275, pp. 299 and 304–7; BM. Gérard refers to this work as opus 11, no. 5. Johansson, p. 167, refers to *Annonces, Affiches et Avis Divers*, Paris, March 2, 1775, but this date seems erroneous (apparently complete set at BN).

Minuet, Don Giovanni—Mozart

This *Minuet*, used merely as incidental background music to sung recitatives, was probably first published in the piano-vocal score of *Il Dissoluto Punito osia il D. Giovanni* by Wolffgango Mozard [*sic*] in late 1792–early 1793[1] by B. Schott, Mainz, at pp. 87 and 98. There are five variants of this piano-vocal score. In all, the music is on pp. 3–207, the p.n. is 138, the text is in Italian and German, the shape is oblong and all pages are engraved. In one variant, there are two blank pages after the title page followed by a page of Personen, and the price on the title page is Fl. 10. This variant seems earliest, as it was apparently issued before the subscribers' list was closed and before the list of arias was completed. This particular copy has the signature of Zulehner, the arranger of this piano edition, on pages 113 and 161, and the printed ink is particularly dark. JF.† The second variant is the same except that the two blank pages are filled with a page of Subscribenten‡ and a page of Verzeichnis der Stücke, without page numbers; (Hirsch IV, 134), BSM and JF; this seems the earliest regular edition. The third variant omits the subscribers' page, and the verso of the title page combines Personaggi with an index of arias with page numbers; BM. The fourth variant is the same as the third with an additional price on the title page of Fr. 21; JF.§ In the first, second, fourth and fifth variants, p. [208] is blank; in the third variant, this page has an advertisement. While some excerpts from the opera were published prior to the piano-vocal score,[2] the *Minuet*—in view of its relative unimportance in the opera—does not seem to have been among them.‖

The first printing of the orchestral score of the opera was about July 1801# by Breitkopf & Härtel, Leipzig, under the title *Il Dissoluto Punito osia il Don Giovanni* by Wolfgang Amadeus Mozart on the first title page in Italian which has an oval vignette. (**See Plate VIII.**) vb. Title page in German. Cast. Index. m. on pp. 6–590 in two volumes. Text in Italian and German. German title page at beginning of second volume. No p.n. Typeset. Oblong. While there is a reference on the verso of the German title page that the German text is by Friedrich Rochlitz, the first printing probably does not contain Rochlitz's separate German text as a supplement.[3] The *Minuet* is at pp. 237 and 259. BM, ONB, JMM and JF.¶

---

[1] Köchel 527, p. 597. Gerber, vol. 3, p. 485. Deutsch, *Plate Numbers*, p. 23.

[2] Köchel, p. 598.

[3] *Ibid.*, p. 597. Rochlitz's supplement was probably needed later to correct the many errors in the German translation on the music pages.

Orchestral parts of the opera were apparently not published until after 1894.[4] The opera was completed Oct. 28, 1787, and performed the next day in Prague. Brief biographic information regarding Mozart and the librettist Lorenzo Da Ponte appears above under *Eine Kleine Nachtmusik* and *The Marriage of Figaro—Overture.*

Minuet—Paderewski

This *Minuet* was published about Aug. 1887,[1] as no. 1 *Menuet* in *Humoresques de Concert,* I. Cahier, for piano in the complete Cahier and as no. 1 *Menuet* separately, by J. [*sic*] J. Paderewski, op. 14, by Ed. Bote & G. Bock, 37 Lepiziger Strasse, Berlin, and 23 Wilhelm Strasse, Posen, and four other cities. Possible first edition of the complete Cahier: There is a dedication to Madame Annette Essipoff-Leschetizky, the price is M 2.50 for the Cahier and M 1.50 for the *Menuet,* there is a Leipzig agent and the front cover is brown and white. m. on pp. 3–15. p.n. 13268. Back cover adv. works for piano by composers from Bargiel to Zarzycki. GM.

One variant of the *Menuet,* separately, is the same as the foregoing except that the music is on pp. 3–7; ONB. In a second variant, the back cover adv. works by Paderewski from op. 1 to op. 14; GM. The third and fourth variants are the same as the second except that the third adds a London agent on the front cover and the fourth adds a New York agent; both at JF. Priority of the variants is unknown.

The story of Paderewski's writing this *Minuet* in imitation of Mozart is well known. Paderewski was born in Podolia, Poland, in 1860 and died in New York City in 1941.

Mississippi—Grofé

[4] Köchel, p. 598. Deutsch, *Plate Numbers,* p. 10.

[1] Hofmeister *Monatsbericht,* Aug., 1887, p. 346.

m. Ferde Grofé. Published in orchestral parts on July 9, 1926,[1] by Leo Feist, Inc., 231–35 W. 40th Street, New York, N.Y. First edition: Front cover describes the work as a Tone Journey, a Descriptive Suite in four movements (of which *Mardi Gras*, excerpted above, is no. 4), has a drawing of the Mississippi River, is black and white, gives the price as $3.00, states that it is also published for piano solo and arranged for orchestra by the composer and refers to four foreign affiliates of the publisher. No plate number. Octavo. LC(CDC) and NYPL.

The piano arrangement was published on Aug. 26, 1926,[1] by the same concern. First edition: Front cover has a drawing of the Mississippi River, is red, gray and white, gives the price as $1.00 and refers to two foreign affiliates. p. [2] adv. *Barcelona*. m. on pp. 3–15. p.n. 5864–13. Back cover adv. *You.. - Lantern..* LC(CDC) and JF. Brief biographic information regarding Grofé appears above under *Grand Canyon Suite*.

The Missouri Waltz

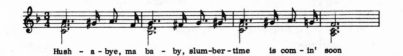

Hush - a - bye, ma ba - by, slum-ber - time   is com - in' soon

This melody was originally published for piano only, on Oct. 10, 1914,[1] "From an Original Melody Procured by John Valentine Eppel, Arranged for Piano by Frederic Knight Logan." The copyright is by Frederic Knight Logan, but the publisher is The Knight-Logan Comp., 4031 West Monroe St., Chicago, Ill. First edition: Front cover refers to Eppels' [*sic*] Orchestra and is black and white. Price: 60¢. p. [2] blank. m. on pp. 3–7. No p.n. Back cover adv. *New..* LC(CDC) and JF. A revised edition was published on Nov. 4, 1914, and an edition with words by J. R. Shannon on Jan. 28, 1916.[1]

The Missouri Waltz has come to be associated with President Harry S Truman, a Missourian, and is the official song of the state. The word "procured" in the first printing, described above, has helped to give rise to unsubstantiated rumors as to the authorship of the melody; the melody has

---

[1] Copyright records; LC.

---

[1] Copyright records; LC.

also been said to have had a Negro or Indian source.[2] Eppel was born in
Iowa City, Iowa, in 1871, was a railroad man and then a musician and
died in California in 1931.[3] Logan was born in Oskaloosa, Iowa, in 1871,
became a composer and musical director and died in 1928.[4]

Moldau—(Hatikva)

(Kol___ od ba - lei - vav   pe - ni - ma)

The *Moldau* with music by B. Smetana appears in the symphonic poem
Má Vlast (in German, *Mein Vaterland*), no. II, *Vltava*, which was published in Dec., 1879,[1] for piano four hands by Fr. A. Urbánek, Prague.
Probable first edition: Title page in Czech and German has a drawing of a
lovely lady almost floating in air and other scenes along the Moldau River
in Bohemia, is green, black and white, and refers to agents in Vienna and
Leipzig. m. on pp. 2–31. p.n. 5. Back cover blank. SMP.

The orchestral score of *Vltava* was issued by the same publisher in
Feb., 1880.[1] Possible first edition: Title page is in Czech and German with a
border design. Price: 7 fl. - 14 Mk. vb. m. on pp. 3–62. p.n. 16. Back cover
blank. In one variant, the front cover, without price, is gray, black and tan;
GM*. In another variant purchased by BM April 19, 1898, the front cover,
with a price of 5 zl. - 10 Mk. changed in ink to 7 and 14, is blue and black;
BM (h.3913.a.)—also at BPL (with the higher prices on a sticker on the
front cover) and JF (without covers). The orchestral parts were published
in May, 1880, and the piano arrangement in Dec., 1884.[1] The work was
completed Dec. 8, 1874, and performed on April 4, 1875, at Zofin. The old
Latin form of "Moldau" is "Multava."[2] Brief biographic information regarding Smetana appears above under *The Bartered Bride—Overture.*

An extremely similar melody, consistently in the minor, serves as the
music for the Israeli national anthem, *Hatikva*, התקוה, meaning *Hope.*[3]

---

[2] "Note," in *Missouri Historical Review*, Columbia, Mo., April, 1946, p. 443; *ULS*,
p. 1775. According to another story, Logan heard an old Negro playing the melody on
his guitar in Oskaloosa; the Negro said his grandfather had said "he heard the Indians
play it when he was a boy"(!). Wickes, p. 13.

[3] Information from present publisher.

[4] *ASCAP*, p. 312.

[1] Teige, p. 78.

[2] *Grove's*, vol. 7, p. 847.

[3] Peter Gradenwitz, *The Music of Israel* (New York, N.Y., 1949), p. 301; NYPL.
Hatikva is sometimes spelled slightly differently.

The words of *Hatikva* by Naphtali Herz Imber were first published in his בַּרְקָאִי, *Barkai* (*Break of Dawn*) in Jerusalem in 1886 under the title תִּקְוָתֵינוּ *Tikvatenu* (*Our Hope*) p. 10; JNL. Imber, born in 1856 in Kloczow, came to Palestine as private secretary to a British diplomat and journalist, became a poet and died in New York City in 1909.

The music of *Hatikva*, together with the words, were first published in *Vier Lieder* using "Syrischer Melodien" arranged by S. T. Friedland and printed by C. G. Röder, Leipzig, with two forewords dated July 11 and Aug., 1895, under the title *Sehnsucht* on p. 10; JNL, JM and EM. There is no recognized composer of the melody. *Hatikva* was adopted in 1897 as the Zionist anthem at the first International Zionist Congress at Basel,[4] but has not been adopted as the national anthem of the State of Israel.

Both the *Moldau* and *Hatikva* melodies are similar to *Ack, Värmeland, du Sköna* (*Oh, You Beautiful Wermland* [a province in Western Sweden]), a song with words written in 1822 by the Swedish historian Anders Fryxell. The melody was widely known in Sweden but is probably of Dutch origin.[5] And the basic melody is also said to be similar to Basque, Bohemian, German, Polish, Rumanian and Spanish folk songs.[6] The *Hatikva* melody may also derive from the Sephardic Jewish melody for *Hallel.*†

Moment Musicale—Schubert

m. Franz Schubert. This piano composition was first published in *Album Musicale*, vol. 1, under the title *Air Russe* on Dec. 19, 1823,[1] by Sauer & Leidesdorf, Vienna, with p.n. 490. AVH. It was included in the spring of 1828 as no. 3 in *Momens Musicals* [*sic*], oeuvre 94, published by M. J. Leidesdorf, Vienna, who probably invented the title. The composer's first name is in French. AT and SB. Brief biographic information regarding Schubert appears above under his *Ave Maria*.

---

[4] Part of the above information regarding *Hatikva* came from Eric Mandell, Philadelphia.

[5] Letter from SV. Smetana lived in Sweden from 1856 to 1861.

[6] Gradenwitz, *op. cit; Encyclopedia Judaica* (Jerusalem, 1971), vol. 7, pp. 1470–1471.

[1] Deutsch, *Schubert*, no. 780, p. 471. *Wiener Zeitung*, Dec. 19, 1823, p. 1184; UMI.

Mon Homme

Je l'ai tell'-ment dans la peau qu'j'en d'viens mar - teau

m. Maurice Yvain. w. Albert Willemetz and Jacques-Charles. Published Oct. 16, 1920,[1] by Francis Salabert, 35 Bd. des Capucines, Paris, and three other cities. Possible first edition: Folio. Front cover has a photograph of Mistinguett and Harry Pilcer, refers to the revue *Paris Qui Jazz*, mentions arrangements for piano solo and Schottisch Espagnole and is blue, green and white. m. on pp. 2–3. p.n. 1655. p. 3 adv. *T'Auras..* (published the same day[1]). Back cover adv. numbers from *Paris Qui Jazz*.[2] JF.

This "tear-jerker" is known in the United States as *My Man* and was popularized by Fanny Brice in the *Ziegfeld Follies of 1921*. Yvain was born in Paris in 1891 and composed French musical comedies and other musical works.[3] Willemetz was born in Paris in 1887, became a librettist and Honorary President of SACEM, the French society of authors, composers, etc., and resides in Paris.[4] Jacques-Charles was born in Paris in 1882, produced many revues in Paris, was a librettist and wrote the French lyrics for many Berlin and Gershwin songs and lives in Paris.[5]

Moonlight Sonata—Beethoven

m. Ludwig van Beethoven. Perhaps the most famous piano composition in the world, the *Moonlight Sonata* was published about March 3, 1802,[1]

---

[1] Copyright records; LC. These records also mention an American arrangement for band published May 24, 1920, copy received May 25, 1921; it is believed the first year should read 1921.

[2] The first edition might have a "show cover" as LC has a copy of the Schottisch Espagnole of this song, deposited Jan. 12, 1921, with a show cover.

[3] *Grove's*, vol. 9, p. 389.

[4] *Who's Who in France* (5th ed., Paris, 1961), p. 2928; HU.

[5] Information from SACEM.

---

[1] Kinsky-Halm, p. 67. *Wiener Zeitung*, March 3, 1802, p. 765; UMI.

as *Sonata Quasi una Fantasia*, opera 27, no. 2, by Gio. Cappi, Sulla Piazza di St. Michele N. 5, Vienna. First edition: The address of the publisher is "5" (changed to "4" in the second edition). Oblong. Engraved. Front cover has a dedication to Damigella Contessa Giulietta Guicciardi, has the composer's first name in Italian, indicates the p.n. is 879 and gives the price as f. 1.30. m. on pp. 2-15. Back cover blank. BSM, LC, AVH and JF (only located copies). Composed 1801. The nickname *Moonlight Sonata* is said to have been given about 1850 by the music critic Ludwig Rellstab, and refers to the moonlight on the Lake of Lucerne. Brief biographic information regarding Beethoven appears above under his *Concerto for Piano no. 5*.

Mother Machree

Sure I love the dear sil - ver that shines in your hair

m. Chauncey Olcott and Ernest R. Ball. w. Rida Johnson Young. Published Aug. 18, 1910,[1] by M. Witmark & Sons, New York, N.Y. Possible first edition: Front cover has a photograph of Chauncey Olcott and is green, purple and white. No other arrangements are mentioned. s. *Barry of Ballymore*—6 titles listed (a "show cover"). The publisher is shown at New York and four other cities. p. [2] adv. *Teach..* (published May 11, 1910). m. on pp. 3-5. p.ns. 5142 and 11439-3. Back cover lists other Olcott productions, all produced before 1910. The other titles on the front cover were published on or before Sept. 12, 1910, and the above edition is the same, to the extent possible, as the other contemporary, regular edition, copyright deposit copies at LC from the show.[2] A variant edition is the same as the foregoing except p. [2] is blank. Both copies at JF.

Barry of Ballymore played in Kansas City, Mo., on Oct. 9, 1910, reaching New York City on Jan. 30, 1911. The song, however, became popular only when it was featured some years later by the Irish tenor John McCormack. Olcott, a composer and singer, was born in Buffalo, N.Y., in 1858 and died in Monte Carlo in 1932.[3] Brief biographic information regarding Ball and Young appears above under *A Little Bit of Heaven—Shure They Call It Ireland* and *Ah! Sweet Mystery of Life*.

[1] Copyright records; LC.
[2] See, also, Fuld, *American*, p. 55.
[3] *ASCAP*, p. 376.

Mulberry Bush

Here we go 'round the mul-ber-ry bush, the mul-ber-ry bush, the mul-ber-ry bush

The first four bars of this children's song are clearly foreshadowed in the extraordinarily entitled dance *Piss Upon the Grass* in *Caledonian Country Dances*, Book the Third (London, ca. 1740), pp. 36 and 120 (double pagination); *BUC, p. 228, and JF**.

The complete melody of the children's song was known as *Nancy Dawson* and was published in the Oct., 1760, issue of *The Universal Magazine*, London, p. 208, as "A New Song," with other words (BM, *ULS*, p. 2838, and JF), and about the same time in a music sheet entitled *Nancy Dawson* without imprint (BM). Nancy Dawson was a famous dancer of the time.[1]

The first known appearance in print of the words of *Mulberry Bush* was in *Popular Rhymes, Fireside Stories, and Amusements of Scotland* [by Robert Chambers] published without music in Edinburgh, 1842. The words appear at p. 65 under the title *Here We Go Round the Mulberry Bush*.[2] NYPL. (The words are not in the 1826 edition of this book; ML).

The music and many of the common words of *Mulberry Bush* are printed together in Asa Fitz, *The Exercise Song Book* (Boston, 1858), under the title *Morning Song*, p. 15; BPL and JF. The opening words, "This is the way...," and the closing words, "So early in the morning," are present, but the words "mulberry bush" are not. In 1859 Chappell wrote that the melody was sung in children's games as "Here we go round the mulberry-bush."[3]†

Musetta's Waltz—La Bohème

Quan - do me'n vo'_____quan-do me'n vo' so - let - ta per la   via

[1] Chappell, p. 718. Baring-Gould, vol. VIII, p. vii. The latter also mentions that the song was included in 1760 in *The Apollo, or the Songster's Universal Library*, but this work has not been located.

[2] Subsequently, however, there was no loyalty to the name of the bush. Sometimes it was a "Bramble Bush" (Halliwell, p. 224), or "Gooseberry Bush" (*Folk-Lore Record*, 1881, p. 174), or "Barberry Bush" (Newell, in text, p. 87), or "Strawberry Bush" (Newell, in text, p. 224).

[3] Chappell, p. 719.

m. Giacomo Puccini. w. Giuseppe Giacosa and Luigi Illica. Copyright copies of the piano-vocal score *La Bohème*, in which *Musetta's Waltz, Quando Me'n Vo'*, appears, were deposited on Jan. 25, 1896, with the Prefect of Milan[1] (this copy so dated now at S. Cecilia Library, Rome), and on Jan. 27, 1896, at the Library of Congress, Washington, by G. Ricordi & C., Milan, Rome, Naples, Palermo, Paris and London. Possible first edition: Front cover is in brown and gold. Half-title page. The title page indicates the price of Fr. 15, but does **not** refer to the first performance of the opera in Turin on Feb. 1, 1896. Copyright notices. Personaggi. vb. Index. vb. Extract from Murger. vb. Quadro Primo. vb. m. on pp. 1–269, engraved, with dividers for the other three acts. p. 269 is **entirely** in C time, and not at all in ¾ time. p.n. 99000. p. [270] blank. The above aria is at p. 126. Back cover at LC has Ars et Labor. LC and SCR (both CDC).

Both of the above copyright deposit copies have engraved music pages. It is almost certain that commercial copies in 1896 did not have engraved pages, and a copy inscribed by Puccini on Mar. 19, 1896, was not engraved.[2] A possible first printing of the first regular commercial edition is the same as that described above except that: the music pages are not engraved; there is the half-title page; the next two pages are blank; a photograph and a dedication to Marchese Carlo Ginori-Lisci are included; and the following page is blank. Title page and p. 269 are as indicated above. JMM and JF. An early printing of the sheet music of this aria, entitled *Valzer di Musetta*, has p.n. 99345; JF.

The engraving of the orchestral score of *La Bohème* commenced, according to the Ricordi *Libroni*, on Oct. 9, 1895, with plate number 99010, but the earliest orchestral score of *La Bohème* that has been found has an 1898 copyright claim on the title page, and an 1896 and a Nuova Edizione 1898 claim on the first music page. Folio. Four volumes. Ricordi is shown at the cities mentioned above, and also at Leipzig and Buenos-Aires. m. on pp. [1]–274. Music pages engraved. p.n. 99010. The above aria is in vol. 2, p. 132. BBC*, SCR, JMM and JF.[3] Similarly, the engraving of the orchestral and choral parts of the opera commenced, according to the Ricordi *Libroni*, on Oct. 9, 1895, with plate numbers 99002–99011. †

Puccini was born in Lucca in 1858 and died in Brussels in 1924. Giacosa was born in Turin in 1847 and died there in 1906.[4] Illica was born in Castell' Arguato, Piacenza, in 1857, was a journalist and librettist and died in the city of his birth in 1919.[5]

---

[1] Copyright records; UDP. *GMM*, Feb. 7, 1896. See, generally, Hopkinson, *Puccini*, p. 14. The Ricordi *Libroni* state the engraving commenced June 28, 1895.

[2] Copy sold at Parke-Bernet Galleries, New York, N.Y., Dec. 4, 1962, no. 174.

[3] The orchestral score was published in octavo in 1920 with p.n. 115561.

[4] *EDS*, vol. 5, p. 1212.

[5] Baker, p. 756.

My Beautiful Lady

To   you,   beau-ti-ful   la-dy

m. Ivan Caryll. w. C. M. S. McLellan. Published Feb. 14, 1911,[1] by Chappel & Co. Ltd., 41 East 34th St., New York, N.Y., London and Melbourne. First edition: Front cover has a drawing of two ladies in pink, a 1910 copyright claim and is pink, brown and white. s. *The Pink Lady*—12 titles listed. p. [2] adv. *Phryne*. m. on pp. [3]–[6]. p.n. 6297–4. p. [7] adv. *Lazyland*. Back cover adv. *Valse*. LC(CDC) and JF. An orchestral arrangement was published the same day[1] as the above sheet music edition. *My Beautiful Lady* is also known as *The Kiss Waltz*.

The *Pink Lady* opened in New York City on March 13, 1911, but not in London until April 11, 1912. The piano-vocal score was published March 29, 1911,[1] by the same publisher at the same address. First edition: There is a 1910 copyright claim on p. 1. m. on pp. 1–169. p.n. 24621. LC(CDC). Ivan Caryll, a pseudonym for Félix Tilken, was born in Liège, Belgium, composed for the London stage, then came to America and died in New York City in 1921.[2] McLellan was born in Bath, Me., lived in London commencing in 1897 as a playwright and satirical writer and died in London in 1916 at the age of fifty-one.[3]

My Blue Heaven

When   whip-poor-wills   call_____   and   ev'-ning is   nigh

m. Walter Donaldson. w. George Whiting. No record can be found of this song having been copyrighted in sheet music in the 1920's;[1] the publisher advises the song was published on Sept. 2, 1927. Possible first edition: Front cover has a drawing of a blue heaven, a photograph of Walter Donaldson and is blue, orange, black and white. The publisher is Leo. Feist, Inc., Feist Building, New York, N.Y. p. [2] adv. *Baby..* m. on pp. 3–5. p.n.

[1] Copyright records; LC.
[2] Gammond-Clayton, p. 41.
[3] NYPL Theater Division Clipping File.

[1] The earliest copyrighted arrangement was for orchestra on Oct. 10, 1927. Copyright records; LC.

5997-3. p. 4 adv. *Good..* Back cover adv. *You..* - *Cheerie..* The advertised songs in this edition were published on or before July 25, 1927. JF.

The release of the song was delayed in part because of a believed conflict with Irving Berlin's *Blue Skies* which had been published on Jan. 14, 1927.[2] Donaldson, a composer and lyricist, was born in Brooklyn, N.Y., in 1893 and died in California in 1947.[3] Whiting, a lyricist, singer and actor, was born in Chicago in 1884 and died in 1943.[3]

My Bonnie Lies over the Ocean

My   bon - nie lies   o - ver   the   o - cean

The first known printing of this song was on Jan. 15, 1881,[1] in the 2nd edition of William H. Hills's *Students' Songs* (Cambridge, Mass.) under the title *My Bonnie*, p. 9; LC(CDC). The song is not in the 1st edition of this collection (1880, at HU), and a publisher's notice in the 2nd edition says that it contains entirely new songs, most of them appearing in print for the first time. No composer or lyricist is given for *My Bonnie*, and none is known.[2]

The chorus of this song bears some similarity to *That Beautiful Land,* included in *Bradbury's Golden Chain* (New York, N.Y., 1861), p. 124;[3] NYPL.

My Buddy

Nights   are   long   since   you   went   a - way

© 1922 Jerome H. Remick & Co. Copyright renewed and assigned to Remick Music Corp. Used by permission.

[2] Wickes, p. 15.

[3] *ASCAP*, pp. 124 and 536.

[1] Copyright records; LC.

[2] In a sheet music edition published in 1882 under the title *Bring Back My Bonnie to Me* by T. B. Harms & Co., New York, N.Y., the words and music are credited to H. J. Fulmer, a pseudonym for Charles E. Pratt; JF. This edition makes substantial changes from the traditional song and it is likely that the authorship claim relates to the changes, not to the traditional song. Spaeth, p. 224.

[3] Harold Barlow, New York City, advised the author of this similarity.

m. Walter Donaldson. w. Gus Kahn. Published Sept. 6, 1922,[1] by Jerome
H. Remick & Co., New York and Detroit. First edition: Front cover has a
drawing of a girl looking at flowers, is yellow, black and white and says
"Operatic Edition." p. [2] blank. m. on pp. 3–5. No plate number. Back
cover adv. *Down.*. LC(CDC) and JF. Brief biographic information regarding Donaldson and Kahn appears above under *My Blue Heaven* and
Carioca.

My Dream Girl

My   dream   girl,_____   oh, my one on - ly dream   girl

m. Victor Herbert. w. Rida Johnson Young. Published May 3, 1924,[1] by
Harms, Incorporated, New York, N.Y. First edition: Front cover has a
drawing of a dream girl and is aqua, red and white. s. *The Dream Girl*—2
titles listed. m. on pp. 2–5. p.n. 7054-4. Back cover blank. LC(CDC) and
JF. The show opened in New Haven, Conn., on April 22, 1924, reaching
New York City on Aug. 20, 1924. No piano-vocal score has been published. Brief biographic information regarding Herbert and Rida Young
appears above under *Ah! Sweet Mystery of Life.*

My Gal Sal

They called   her   friv - o - lous   Sal

mw. Paul Dresser. Copyrighted March 6, 1905,[1] by The Paul Dresser Pub.
Co., 51 West 28th St., New York, N.Y. First edition: Front cover sets forth

---

[1] Copyright records; LC. Buddy Shays, an orchestra leader who used this song as
his signature on the radio, unsuccessfully sought to prevent Buddy Rogers, another radio
orchestra leader, from doing likewise. Alfred M. Shafter, *Musical Copyright* (2nd ed.,
Chicago, 1939), p. 434; NYPL.

---

[1] Copyright records; LC.

---

[1] Copyright records; LC.

the words of the chorus and is green, gold and white. p. [2] adv. *Mary..* m. on pp. 3–5. Inscribed to Miss Nan Baker. No p.n. Back cover adv. *She..* - *Mary..* LC(CDC) and JF. There is no photograph of Louise Dresser on the front cover, nor any reference to Jos. W. Stern & Co.

Both the original and current sheet music show the melody as above, with the last note of the second bar as B flat. It is frequently played, however, as C.

Dresser was born in Terre Haute, Ind., in 1858, became a composer, lyricist, publisher, actor, playwright and producer, and died in New York City in 1906.[2] He was born Paul Dreiser and was the older brother of the novelist Theodore Dreiser.

My Heart Stood Still

I took one look at you, that's all I meant to do

© 1927 Harms, Inc. Copyright renewed. Used by permission.

m. Richard Rodgers. w. Lorenz Hart. Published May 17, 1927,[1] by Chappell & Co. Ltd., 50 New Bond Street, London W.1. First edition deposited May 27, 1927, at BM: Front cover is green, orange, blue and white. s. *London Pavilion Revue—One Dam [sic] Thing After Another*—4 titles listed. m. on pp. 2–5. p.n. 29280. p. 5 adv. *The Melba..* p. [6] adv. *Whistle..* p. [7] adv. *Cherie..* Back cover adv. *Pianoforte..* BM(CDC). The song was originally written for, and introduced in, the above show which opened in London on May 20, 1927.

The song was subsequently bought back[2] and inserted in the show *A Connecticut Yankee*, which opened in New York City on Nov. 3, 1927 (the song from this show published on Oct. 14, 1927).[1] The title phrase is said to have been derived from a remark made by a female friend of the authors when scared by a taxi in Paris.[3] Brief biographic information regarding Rodgers and Hart appears above under *If I Loved You* and *Lover*.

---

[2] *ASCAP*, p. 129.

---

[1] Copyright records; LC.
[2] *The Rodgers and Hart Song Book* (New York, N.Y., 1951), p. 15; NYPL.
[3] Deems Taylor, *Some Enchanted Evenings* (New York, N.Y., 1953), p. 41; NYPL.

My Melancholy Baby

m. Ernie Burnett. w. Geo. A. Norton. On Oct. 31, 1911,[1] a manuscript with words by Maybelle E. Watson and music by Ernie Burnett, entitled *Melancholy*, was copyrighted as an unpublished composition.[2] The same melody, but with a different lyric by Geo. A. Norton, was published under the title *Melancholy* on Oct. 25, 1912, by Theron C. Bennett Co., but the copyright deposit of *Melancholy* was not made until Jan. 10, 1939.[1] Possible first edition: Title, *Melancholy*. Front cover has a drawing of two plants, a photograph of Jas. E. Maloney, shows the publisher at Memphis, Omaha, New York and Denver and is green, black and white. m. on pp. 2–5. p.n. 6193. P. 5 states the printer was Walton Process, Chicago.[3] Back cover adv. *Only..* and lists 15 titles. JF (inscribed by the composer).

The title was changed to *My Melancholy Baby* on Nov. 5, 1914, and the deposit for copyright under this new title was made on Sept. 29, 1938.[1] The song was first sung at Denver's Dutch Mill, a showplace of the West. Burnett was born in Cincinnati in 1884, became a composer and was active in vaudeville and died in Saranac Lake, N.Y., in 1959.[4] Norton, a librettist, was born in St. Louis in 1880 and died in Tucson, Ariz., in 1923.[5]

Ben Light also has claimed to have composed the music of *My Melancholy Baby* in 1909 at the age of sixteen when he was a piano player at Maynard's, a Denver nightclub, but he never copyrighted the song or brought suit to enforce his claim.[6]

My Old Kentucky Home

The sun shines bright in the old Ken-tuck-y home

mw. Stephen C. Foster. Copyrighted Jan. 31, 1853,[1] by Firth, Pond & Co., 1 Franklin Square, New York, N.Y. First edition: Title is, *My Old Kentucky*

---

[1] Copyright records; LC.

[2] The best histories of the song are in the court decisions in *Shapiro, Bernstein & Co. Inc.* vs. *Jerry Vogel Music Co., Inc.*, 161 Fed. (2nd) 406 (2nd Circuit Court of Appeals, 1947) and 73 Fed. Supp. 165 (Dist. Ct., Southern District, N.Y., 1947); NYPL.

[3] Burnett advised this author that Walton was the original printer.

[4] Obituary, *The New York Times*, Sept. 12, 1959.

[5] *ASCAP*, p. 373.

[6] Obituary, *The New York Times*, Jan. 6, 1965. He died at Pacific Palisades, Cal., at the age of seventy-two.

---

[1] Copyright records; LC.

Home, Good Night. Front cover states that this is no. 20 of Foster's Plantation Melodies, refers to Christy's Minstrels and to two other songs and lists
three agents. Price: 25¢.² Title on p. 2 is in two lines, **the first line curved.**
m. on pp. 2–5. p.n. 1892. Back cover blank. Engraved. LC(CDC), FH, SS
and JF. Brief biographic information regarding Foster appears above under
Beautiful Dreamer.

My Wild Irish Rose

My   wild   I - rish   rose

mw. Chauncey Olcott. Copyrighted Jan. 7, 1899,¹ by M. Witmark & Sons,
Witmark Building, New York, Schiller Building, Chicago, and three other
cities. First edition: Front cover has a drawing of a girl with a lyre and
is green, red and white. s. *A Romance of Athlone*—6 titles listed.² p. [2]
adv. three shows, *A Romance.. - Minstrel..* m. on pp. [3]–[5]. p.n. 2164.
p. [3] adv. *Because.* p. [4] adv. *Fortune..* p. [5] adv. *American..* Back cover
adv. *Down.. - Darktown..* LC(CDC). *A Romance of Athlone* opened in
New York City on Jan. 9, 1899. Brief biographic information regarding
Olcott appears above under *Mother Machree.*

Mysterioso Pizzicato

© 1914 Jerome H. Remick & Co. Copyright renewed and assigned to Remick Music Corp. Used by
permission.

The first known appearance of this music is in the *Remick Folio of Moving
Picture Music,* vol. I, published March 24, 1914,¹ by Jerome H. Remick &
Co., New York and Detroit. First edition: Front cover is orange and red,
the price is $1.00 (orchestral parts are also listed at 50 cents each) and there
is no reference to "Revised Edition." The title page does not state "Made in
U.S.A." The music, compiled and edited by J. Bodewalt Lampe, appears
on pp. 3–48. *Mysterioso Pizzicato* is no. 89 on p. 38. LC(CDC) and JF*.

The music was played as a background to scary scenes in the old silent
movies.

---

² Front cover is illustrated in Fuld, *Foster,* no page number.

¹ Copyright records; LC.

² Front cover is illustrated in Fuld, *American,* p. [38].

¹ Copyright records; LC.

Nancy Lee

The   sail - or's wife, the sail - or's star___ shall be

m. Stephen Adams. w. Frederick E. Weatherly. Published March 11, 1876,[1] by Boosey & Co., 295 Regent Street, London W. Probable first edition deposited May 7, 1876, at the British Museum: Front cover says that the song is sung by Mr. Maybrick, has a dedication to Miss Ethel Santley, a price of 4s and is black and white. m. on pp. 2–11. No plate number. Back cover adv. *Let.. - The Island..* Not engraved. No reference to other keys or arrangements. BM(CDC).

This song was originally submitted with sentimental words but William Boosey, the publisher, said it must be a sea song.[2] Stephen Adams is a pseudonym adopted by Michael Maybrick, a baritone and composer who was born in Liverpool in 1844 and died in Buxton in 1913.[3] Weatherley, a lawyer, lyricist and radio broadcaster, was born in Portishead, Somerset, England, in 1848, and died in London in 1929.[4]

Narcissus

m. Ethelbert Nevin. *Water Scenes*, op. 13, of which *Narcissus* is no. 4, was copyrighted May 28, 1891,[1] by G. Schirmer, Jr. [New York, N.Y.], for piano. First edition: Quarto. The front cover is green and gray. vb. Title page is illustrated, indicates that *Water Scenes* contains five pieces for the pianoforte and states that the publisher is The Boston Music Co., Boston, Mass. Price: $1.25. vb. m. on pp. 2–27, *Narcissus* appearing on p. 15 and having p.n. 161. Next four pages blank. Back cover missing. LC(CDC). No arrangements of any song are mentioned. Another, undeposited, copy at LC is identical to the foregoing and also has a back cover the inside of which is blank and the outside of which has merely a small design of water scenes; also at JF. Brief biographic information regarding Nevin appears above under *Mighty Lak' a Rose.*

---

[1] According to the entry at Stationers' Hall on Feb. 12, 1877.

[2] William Boosey, *Fifty Years of Music* (London, 1931), p. 18; NYPL. Simpson, p. 193.

[3] Baker, p. 1052.

[4] Obituary, *New York Herald Tribune*, Sept. 8, 1929.

---

[1] Copyright records; LC.

National Emblem March

(And the mon - key wrapped its tail a - round the flag - pole)

m. E. E. Bagley. This march was copyrighted June 30, 1906,[1] for band by Ernest S. Williams, Boston; the earliest copy discovered advertises a 1914 song, at LC. A piano arrangement was copyrighted by the same publisher on May 27, 1907.[1] First edition of the piano arrangement: Front cover has a drawing of an American flag, the address of the publisher is Music Hall Bld., and the colors are red, white and blue. p. [2] blank. m. on pp. 3–5. p.n. 91-3. Back cover adv. *All..* and *Dancing..* LC(CDC) and JF. A vocal arrangement with words by M. F. Sexton was copyrighted on March 23, 1908.[1]

The above melody is frequently known by its parody words, *And the Monkey Wrapped Its Tail Around the Flagpole.* The march obtains its title from the inclusion of a few bars of *The Star Spangled Banner.* Edwin E. Bagley, a bandmaster, was born in 1857 and died in 1922.[2]

Nearer, My God, to Thee

Near - er, my God, to Thee, near - er to Thee

m. Lowell Mason. w. Sarah F. Adams. The first printing of the words was in 1841[1] in *Hymns and Anthems,* compiled by W. J. Fox (London), Book Second, no. LXXXV, the pages being unnumbered. BM(CDC).

The music (and the words) were copyrighted on April 5, 1859,[2] in *The Sabbath Hymn and Tune Book,* edited by Lowell Mason, Edwards A. Park and Austin Phelps (New York, N.Y.), p. 244.[3] LC(CDC) and JF.

Sarah Flower Adams, an English poetess and hymn writer, was born in Great Harlow, Essex, in 1805, married William Bridges Adams in 1834

---

[1] Copyright records; LC.

[2] *Band Encyclopedia,* edited by Kenneth Berger (Evansville, Ind., 1960), p. 53; LC.

[1] Only the year of first publication is stated in the entry at Stationers' Hall 12 years later, on Dec. 13, 1853.

[2] Copyright records; LC.

[3] See, generally, Emurian, *Hymns,* p. 91.

and died in London in 1848.[4] Brief biographic information regarding Mason appears above under *Joy to the World*.

Never on Sunday

Ap' to pa - ra - thy-ro mou stel-no e-na dhi - o ke tri - a ke 'tes-se-ra fi - li a
Oh, you can kiss me on a Mon-day, a Mon-day, a Mon-day is ver-y, ver-y good

Music and Greek words, Manos Hadjidakis. The first printing of this song is uncertain. An early Greek edition is entitled, in Greek letters, *Ta Pedhia Tou Pirea* (meainng *The Children of Piraeus*), the front cover refers to the motion picture *Illya [Jamais le Dimanche]* by J. Dassin (the husband of Melina Mercouri), has a large photograph of Melina Mercouri, refers to a Fidelity phonograph record made by her, is in black and white and is published by Gaetanos, 10 Arsakeou Street, Athens. m. on pp. 2–3. Greek text only. Page 2 has a 1960 copyright claim by Michel Gaetanos. p.n. M. 2946 G. Back cover adv. a catalogue of works published by Gaetanos, but states at the bottom, October, 1961. JF.

As *Les Enfants du Pirée*, the song was published on June 15, 1960,[1] with French words; LC(CDC). As *Never on Sunday*, the song was published on Aug. 8, 1960,[1] with English words; BM(CDC) and LC(CDC). The movie *Never on Sunday* was released in the United States on Oct. 27, 1960; the release date of the movie in Europe is not known. Hadjidakis was born in Xanthe, Greece, in 1925.[2]

Night and Day

Night and day_____ you are the one

[4] *NIE*, vol. 1, p. 127.

---

[1] Copyright records; LC.
[2] Information from Greek Consulate, New York City.

mw. Cole Porter. Published Nov. 18, 1932,[1] by Harms, Incorporated, New York, N.Y. First edition: Front cover is yellow, black and white. s. *Gay Divorce* [*sic*]—3 titles listed.[2] p. [2] adv. *Indian..* m. on pp. 3–7. p.n. 8879-5. Back cover adv. *You're..* LC(CDC, deposited Nov. 23, 1932) and JF(autographed). *Gay Divorce* opened in New York City on Nov. 29, 1932; when the show was made into a movie in 1934, the last word of the title became "Divorcee."

The song was specially written to fit the limited voice range of Fred Astaire, the star of the musical show—most of the song stays within a few notes. Brief biographic information regarding Porter appears above under *Begin the Beguine*.

A Night on the Bald Mountain—Mussorgsky

m. Modeste Mussorgsky. Published late 1886–1888[1] for orchestral score and parts by V. Bessel & Cie., St. Petersburg. Possible first edition of the orchestral score: Front cover in French has a dedication to Vladimir Stassov, the work is described as a Fantaisie, published posthumously, and completed and scored by Rimsky-Korsakov, the price of the orchestral score is 3 r. and of the parts is 6 r., there is a property claim for all countries, and Leipzig and Paris agents are listed; the colors are gray and black. vb. Title page is same as front cover except in black and white. Verso has notices in Russian and French and the censor's approval dated July 25, 1886. m. on pp. 3–65. Address on page 65 is 26 Troitski Alley.[2] No plate number on any page.

---

[1] Copyright records; LC.

[2] Front cover is illustrated in Fuld, *American*, p. [39].

---

[1] Yury Keldysh and Vas. Yakovlev, *M. P. Mussorgsky, Statji i Materialy* (Moscow, 1932), p. [301], say 1886; LC. The date of the censor's approval is July 25, 1886. Hofmeister *Monatsbericht*, Dec., 1888, p. 523.

[2] Bessel was at this address until 1889; thereafter at 24 Troitski Street. Letter from SSL to John H. Hind, Berkeley, Cal.

p. [66] blank. BPL. A later edition shows the publisher also at Moscow,[3] and has plate number 1538 and other changes; BM and HU.

No possible first printing of the orchestral parts has been found; a Bessel, Petrograd[4] and Moscow, printing with plate number 1539 is at NYPS. An arrangement for piano four hands is said to have been published at about the same time.[5] *A Night on the Bald Mountain* was performed in St. Petersburg on Oct. 27, 1886. Mussorgsky was born in Karevo, Pskov, in 1839 and died in St. Petersburg in 1881.

No Other Love—(Victory at Sea)

No oth - er love have I_____   on - ly my love for you

© 1953 by Richard Rodgers & Oscar Hammerstein II. Williamson Music, Inc., Publisher. By consent.

m. Richard Rodgers. w. Oscar Hammerstein 2nd. Published April 17, 1953,[1] by Williamson Music, Inc., RKO Bldg., Radio City, New York, N.Y., but copyrighted by the authors. The copyright deposit copy at LC is a professional edition. Probable first regular edition: Front cover has a drawing of a backstage scene and is yellow, purple and white. s. *Me and Juliet*—5 titles listed. m. on pp. 2–5. p.n. 878-4. Back cover adv. *Oklahoma! - South..* JF.

Me and Juliet opened in New York City on May 28, 1953. The piano-vocal score of the show was published Nov. 31, 1953,[1] in cloth at $8.00; LC(CDC) and JF.

The melody was originally composed for a television series entitled *Victory at Sea*, beginning Oct. 26, 1952,[2] in which this melody was designated *Beneath the Southern Cross*, a tango. More than $1 million of record albums of *Victory at Sea* have been sold. *Victory at Sea*, for piano, was published, however, only on July 5, 1954,[1] arranged as a Symphonic Scenario by Robert Russell Bennett, and published by the above publisher at $1.00. *Beneath the Southern Cross* appears on p. 6. LC(CDC) and JF.

---

[3] The Moscow branch was opened in 1888. *Brief Sketches about the Activities of the Music Publishing Firm V. Bessel & Co.* (1894), p. 4; SSL. The prices of this edition were reduced to 2.50 and 4.50 rubles confirming that this edition is later; see p. 11, above.

[4] 1914 or later.

[5] Keldysh and Yakovlev, footnote 1 above.

---

[1] Copyright records; LC.

[2] *Rodgers and Hammerstein Fact Book* (New York, N.Y., 1955), p. 196; NYPL and JF.

Victory at Sea was published for band on Nov. 14, 1955;[1] LC(CDC). One excerpt from *Victory at Sea* entitled *Guadalcanal March* had been published for piano on Sept. 19, 1952;[1] LC(CDC) and JF. Brief biographic information regarding Rodgers and Hammerstein appears above under *If I Loved You* and *All the Things You Are.*

Nobody Knows de Trouble I've Seen

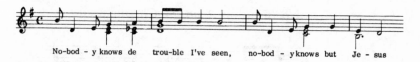

No-bod - y knows de   trou-ble I've seen,   no-bod - y knows but   Je - sus

The diary of William Francis Allen, still in manuscript, has an entry from Charleston, S.C., dated May 27, 1865, giving the melody line and the words of the Negro spiritual *Nobody Knows the Trouble I See*, and commenting: "This song is sung considerably in our schools," p. 32; WHS.[1] The melody is in the major but somewhat different from the presently familiar melody. Mary Ames refers to the song *Nobody Knows but Jesus*, in an entry for June 20, 1865, in her *From a New England Woman's Diary in Dixie in 1865* (Springfield, Mass., 1906), p. 64; UMI. And the spiritual was reported sung on Oct. 17, 1865, by a Negro woman and audience in Charleston, S.C., and also as being sung spontaneously by the Negroes on Edisto Island, S.C., when they were told that the land on which they had settled was to be returned to their former owners, in the *Autobiography of Oliver Otis Howard* (New York, N.Y., 1902), vol. 2, p. 238; NYPL.

The spiritual first appeared in print on Nov. 13, 1867,[2] in *Slave Songs of the United States* (New York, N.Y.) under the title *Nobody Knows the Trouble I've Had*, p. 55. In the copyright deposit copy at the Library of Congress the name of the publisher appears as "A. Simpson [& [Co., [sic]]" on the title page. In this book, the melody, similar to the Allen version mentioned above, is somewhat different from the common melody and is in the major. A footnote states that the song was a favorite in the colored schools of Charleston, S.C., in 1865.

The melody appears in the minor and still different from its usual form in *Jubilee Songs*, as sung by the Jubilee Singers, of Fisk University (Nashville, Tenn.), copyrighted March 11, 1872,[2] and published in New

---

[1] The author is indebted to Dena J. Epstein, Chicago, for all the references in this paragraph. †

[2] Copyright records; LC.

York, N.Y., under the title *Nobody Knows the Trouble I See, Lord!*, at p.
[5]. There is no mention of "Complete" or "New Edition." LC(CDC), NYPL
and JF.

The melody appears in its presently familiar major form in *Hampton
and Its Students*, copyrighted March 18, 1874,[2] and published in New
York City, under the title *Nobody Knows de Trouble I've Seen*, p. 181.
LC and JF.

Nocturne, op. 9, no. 2—Chopin

m. Fréd. Chopin. The *Trois Nocturnes*, oeuvre 9, of which the above is
no. 2, were probably first published about Dec., 1832,[1] for piano by Fr.
Kistner, Leipzig. Probable first edition: Front cover has a dedication to
Madame Camille Pleyel, the price is **14 Gr.**, there is a reference to M.
Schlesinger, Paris, and the p.n. is 995. m. on pp. 2–13, engraved. Back
cover blank. No reference on the front cover to no. 2 being available separately. LBH, AVH and JF.

The earliest French printing, possibly contemporary with or even
earlier than the above, may have been in Maurice Schlesinger's *Album
des Pianistes*, 6me année, Paris; AT. These *Albums* were generally published around Christmas or New Year, and this particular *Album* was
claimed to be of "Morceaux inédits" (in France?); Brown, *Corrections*, p.
29. The printing is the same as that of the separate sheet music edition
described below. The French sheet music edition published by M. Schlesinger, Paris, was probably issued early in 1833.[2] The front cover has the

---

[1] This date, as well as the French and English dates, are those suggested by Brown,
p. 55. See Zofia Lissa, "Chopin im Lichte des Briefwechsels von Verlegern Seiner Zeit
Gesehen" in *Fontes Artis Musicae* (Paris, 1960), p. 46; NYPL. The German edition is
listed in Hofmeister *Monatsbericht*, Jan.–Feb., 1833, p. 7; HD. Niecks, vol. II, p. 350,
says Jan., 1833, for the German edition. See, in general, *Chopin Works*, vol. VII, p. 124.

Brown gives the original German publisher as Probst-Kistner, but this is probably
an error; see footnote 2 under *Etude, op. 10, no. 3—Chopin*, above, and Brown, *Corrections*, p. 28. Kistner is shown as the publisher in the Hofmeister *Monatsbericht*
mentioned in the preceding paragraph. However, Probst-Kistner is shown as the publisher in a review in *Iris im Gebiete der Tonkunst*, Berlin, Aug. 2, 1833, p. 121; *ULS*,
p. 1374.

[2] See footnote 1, above. The earliest reference to the French edition in a French
periodical is in the Nov. 23, 1834, issue of *GMP*, p. 380.

same dedication, a price of 6f, a street address of 97 Rue Richelieu, refers to Fr. Kistner and has p.n. 1287. m. on pp. 2–13. Back cover blank. Engraved. COP, AT and JF.

The English edition by Wessel & Co., London, is said to have been published in June, 1833;[3] the earliest located edition shows the publisher at 67 Frith Street (after ca. 1839) and has a collective front cover listing Chopin to op. 43; JF. The *Nocturnes* were composed in the spring 1830–1831. Brief biographic information regarding Chopin appears above under his *Etude*.

Nola

m. Felix Arndt. This piano composition was deposited for copyright on March 24, 1915, by Felix Arndt as an unpublished composition. It was published on Nov. 20, 1916,[1] by Sam Fox Pub. Co., Cleveland. First edition: Front cover has a silhouette of a lady's head and is black, tan, gray and white. m. on pp. 3–7. pp. [2], [9] and back cover blank. p. [8] adv. *Simplicity.* Folio. LC(CDC). Words were added in 1924 by James F. Burns.

Arndt, a composer, pianist, recording and piano roll artist, was born in New York City in 1889 and died in 1918.[2]

Norwegian Dance—Grieg

m. Edvard Grieg. The *Norwegische Tänze,* op. 35, of which the above is no. 2, was published for piano, four hands about Oct., 1881,[1] by C. F.

---

[3] See footnote 1, above. The English edition was not entered at Stationers' Hall from 1832 to 1835.

---

[1] Copyright records; LC.

[2] *ASCAP,* p. 14.

[1] Hofmeister *Monatsbericht,* Oct., 1881, p. 252.

Peters, Leipzig. Probable first edition: Oblong. Front cover says only: Edition Peters no. 2056. Grieg *Norwegische Tänze* zu 4 Händen. Opus 35. The title page is **brown**, black and white[2] with a classical background. m. on pp. 2–35. p.n. 6507. Page 2 states: "Stich und Druck der Röder'schen Officin in Leipzig." Back cover states "81" (i.e., 1881) and lists Peters Editions to no. 1848. RCM. An identical copy lacking front and back covers was deposited at the British Museum on Nov. 18, 1881. A variant edition, possibly a first edition, also has a brown, black and white title page and is otherwise the same as the foregoing edition except that it has hard covers, there is no reference to Röder on page 2 and its back cover is blank; JF (Christmas greetings—1881?—inscribed by the composer). The work was completed by Aug. 22, 1881, and was to be sent to Peters "in the next days."[3] Brief biographic information regarding Grieg appears above under *An den Frühling*.

Nur Wer die Sehnsucht Kennt—Tchaikovsky

Nur wer die	Sehn–sucht kennt,	weiss was ich	lei - de!
Nyet! Tawl- ko	tawt ktaw znahl	svee–dahn–yah	zhahzh–doo
On - ly the	sad of heart,	can tell my	an - guish

m. P. Tchaikovsky. Шесть Романсовъ (*Six Romances*), op. 6, of which the above, originally entitled Нѣтъ, Только Тотъ Кто Зналъ, is no. 6, was composed Nov. 15–Dec. 17, 1869 (O.S.), approved by the censor on Dec. 17, 1869 (O.S.),[1] and published in 1870[2] by P. I. Jurgenson, Moscow, for piano with Russian text only. There are three early printings of the complete work, all in Russian only, with p. [2] blank, music on pp. 3–23, engraved music pages, double pagination, p.ns. 644–649, no. 6 is dedicated to Mme Khvostova, and the back cover is blank. In one printing, believed the earliest, the front cover is also engraved and black and white, and does not list the six pieces or indicate prices; SSL. In the second, the front cover is lithographed in green and white and lists the six pieces separately, no. 6 at 60 (kop.); LLM. The third is the same as the second except the colors of the front cover are orange and white; LLM. As later editions, at GL and LPL, have lithographed music pages and front covers generally similar to

---

[2] See page 66 above.
[3] Grieg, *Letters*, p. 8.

---

[1] This date of the censor's approval is printed on each of the six numbers.
[2] Dombayev, p. 28.

the second and third printings described above, it is believed that the edition at SSL is the earliest.

The words were adapted by Mey from Goethe's poem *Nur Wer die Sehnsucht Kennt*, which had been first published in Goethe's *Wilhelm Meisters Lehrjahre* (Berlin, 1795), vol. 2, p. 265; BM and YU. In the printings of the song described above, the poem is incorrectly ascribed to Heine. The song is known in English as *None but the Lonely Heart*. Brief biographic information regarding Tchaikovsky appears above under his *Chant sans Paroles*.

Oberon-Overture—Weber

m. Carl Maria von Weber. The first printing of the *Overture* to *Oberon* was published by Welsh & Hawes, 246 Regent Street, London, in the piano-vocal score of the opera, ten copies of Part 1 of which, including the *Overture*, were deposited at Stationers' Hall on April 24, 1826. The title page has a subtitle, the *Elf King's Oath*, mentions that the Poetry is by R. J. ([*sic*]—corrected later) Planche (without an accent on the last letter) and that the piano arrangement is by the composer, and the price is blank. vb. m. on pp. 1–64. p.ns. 3106-3111. Parts 2 and 3 were deposited May 6 and 22, 1826, and have p.ns. 3112-3121 and 3126. Engraved. BM(CDC-H 690).

The first regular edition has three title pages and no additional plate number in Part 3, but with the librettist's initials corrected to "J.R." and the accent added. BM (Hirsch IV, 1297a), AT, NYPL and JF.

While p.n. 1376 of the piano-vocal score, published by Ad. Mt. Schlesinger, Berlin, would ordinarily indicate an 1825 publication date,[1] this does not appear to be so in fact. The piano arrangement of the *Overture* was not completed until after April 9, 1826,[2] and the Schlesinger piano-vocal score was not listed in *Handbuch Annual* until the 1827 edi-

---

[1] Deutsch, *Plate Numbers*, p. 21.

[2] The greater part of the orchestral score was completed when Weber came to England in March, 1826, but among other things the *Overture* had still to be composed. The orchestral score of the *Overture* was finished on April 9, 1826, and the piano arrangement shortly thereafter. Sotheby & Co. *Catalogue*, London, June 11, 1963, item no. 167; JF. Jähns, no. 306, p. 392.

tion, from Easter, 1826, to Easter, 1827.[3] As *Oberon* was first performed in London on April 12, 1826, and as the Welsh & Hawes edition was deposited 12 days later, it is almost certain that the English edition was published first.

Schlesinger published the orchestral parts and orchestral score of the *Overture* in middle or late 1826.[4] The orchestral parts are entitled *Ouverture zu der Oper: Oberon*, the p.n. is 1383, the price 2 Rth. 12 Gr. or 15 Sgr., and the imprint is In Ad. Mt. Schlesinger's Buch-und Musikhandlung, 34 Unter den Linden, Berlin. Engraved. LS. No copy of the 1826 orchestral score of the *Overture* has been found; copies with a collective title page and with p.ns. to 2913A (1843)[1] are at COL and LC. An orchestral score of the entire opera for Türkische Musik[5] with p.n. 1384 is at LLD.

The orchestral score of the entire opera was published May 15, 1874,[6] by Schlesinger. Probable first edition: Price is 30 Rmk. and the imprint is Schlesinger'schen Buch-u. Musikhandlung, Rob. Lienau, Berlin. vb. m. on pp. 1–240, engraved. p.n. 6823. English and German text. BM, BSM, NYPL,[3] JMM and JF. No early printing of the orchestral parts of the opera has been found.

Brief biographic information regarding Weber appears above under *Der Freischütz—Overture*. James Robinson Planché, a dramatist, was born in London in 1796 and died there in 1880.[7]

Oh, Bury Me Not on the Lone Prairie

Oh, bur - y me not_____ on the lone prai - rie

This song has had a rather strange history. It begins with a poem by Rev. E. H. Chapin entitled "The Ocean-Buried" (*sic*) in the *Southern Literary Messenger*, Richmond, Va., Sept., 1839, p. 615; NYPL. The opening words

---

[3] P. 28. Copies of the Schlesinger edition are at GM, LLD, LS and JF. The *Overture* for piano, with the same p.n. was published by Schlesinger about the same time; LBH—*Handbuch Annual, ibid.*

[4] *Handbuch Annual* 1827 (Easter, 1826–Easter, 1827), pp. 2 and 3.

[5] Turkish music at this period meant a band of specific wind and percussion instruments that had developed under the influence of the Turkish Janissary bands.

[6] Letter from Robert Lienau, Berlin. Kinsky, *Opern*, p. 374, says 1872, but this is not consistent with the p.n. If 1872 is the correct year, the price of the first printing would have to be in Thalers.

[7] *Grove's* (3rd ed.), vol. 4, p. 204.

are "Bury me not in the deep, deep sea!" This printing appears to make unlikely the claimed authorship of the words by Capt. William H. Saunders of the U.S. Army in the 1840's.[1]

The next known step is a song entitled *Bury Me Not on the Lone Prairie*, with words and music by William Jossey and copyrighted Nov. 9, 1907,[2] by Clarence E. Sinn & Bros., Criterion Theatre Bldg., Chicago, Ill. Familiar words are present, but the music is not the well-known music. Probable first printing: Front cover has a drawing of a cowboy on the ground next to a horse, refers to "The End of the Trail" and is brown, tan and green. p. [2] blank. m. on pp. 3–5. No plate number. Back cover adv. *Long.. - Rabbit..* LC(CDC) and JF.

The song next appeared as *The Dying Cowboy* in John A. Lomax, *Cowboy Songs* (New York, N.Y., 1910), p. 3. The words are basically a paraphrase of the words in *The Ocean Burial*, and the eight bars of music end in the minor and are not the familiar music. LC, NYPL and JF.

The well-known music, together with the words, appears in Mellinger E. Henry, "Still More Ballads and Folk-Songs from Southern Highlands," in *Journal of American Folklore*, New York, N.Y., Jan.–March, 1932 (*ULS*, p. 1435), p. 152, under the title *The Lone Prairie (The Dying Cowboy)*. It is there stated that the song is a "fragment from western North Carolina." In this text, the third word is "out," rather than "not." In 1934 Carson S. Robison popularized a generally similar melody under the title, *Carry Me Back to the Lone Prairie;* LC(CDC) and JF.

Perhaps a reply to the above is *The Sailor Boy's Grave*, with music and words by J. Martin, copyrighted June 3, 1841,[2] by F. D. Benteen, Baltimore, and "A correct edition" copyrighted July 9, 1841,[2] by Saml. Carusi, Baltimore. The opening words are "Oh bury me not in the dark cold grave." Copies of both are at LC(CDC) and JF. Neither edition has the well-known music.

Rev. Chapin's poem, with minor changes, was set to music in *The Ocean Burial*, with both music and words credited to Geo. N. Allen and stated to have been copyrighted in 1849[3] by S. Brainard, Cleveland. The opening words are "O! bury me not in the deep, deep sea." The music again is not the well-known music. This version of the music and words was also printed, perhaps earlier, on one side of a folio broadside by O. B. Powers, without indication of city and without a copyright claim; JF.

A musical setting of *Oh, Bury Me Not on the Lone Prairie* appears without background discussion in *Journal of American Folklore*, Boston,

---

[1] Belden, p. 387. Laws, p. 134.
[2] Copyright records; LC.
[3] But there is no record of such copyright in the copyright records; LC.

Mass., and New York, N.Y., July–Sept., 1901, p. 186; the music, however, is not the familiar music; *ULS*, p. 1435. The next printing was in 1905 as one of the *Folk Songs of the West and South* (Newton Center, Mass.), harmonized by Arthur Farwell, vol. IV, no. 27, p. 4, under the title *The Lone Prairie*; NYPL. The opening words are "O bury me out on the lone prairie," with a footnote saying that in some versions the word "out" is "not." The music is not the familiar music.

It has been said that this song was authored by H. Clemons of Deadwood, Dakota Territory, in 1872[4]—whether this refers to the music or words or both, and which music or words, is not known.[5]

Oh! Dear, What Can the Matter Be?

Oh! Dear,   what can the mat-ter be? Dear, dear! What can the mat-ter be?

The first printing of the music and words of this song may have been in *Elegant Extracts for the Guittar* [*sic*], vol. II, p. 17. The difficulty in fixing the date of vol. II is that the title page of vol. II is printed as "Vol. I" but has another "I" added in manuscript so as to read "Vol. II." The imprint for vol. I is J. Preston, 97 Strand, London, indicating a date of ca. 1778 to 1787.[1] A copy of vol. II without watermark is at ML—a copy with watermarks of 1795 and 1796 is at BM. (Vol. III, with the same title page and "II" added in manuscript, contains the *Marseillaise* and could not have been published before 1792.)

The words of the song were included in the Mansfield MS., a manuscript collection of Scots songs compiled probably by Elizabeth St. Clair between 1770 and 1780, under the title *O What Can the Matter Be*, p. 41.[2]

A sheet music edition of the song was entered at Stationers' Hall on July 26, 1792, by Rt. Birchall, 133 New Bond Street, London, under the title *O! Dear What Can the Matter Be*, "Now first Published." Probable first edition: p. [1] blank. m. on pp. 2–3, arranged as a duet. No p.n. Price 1s. "To her Royal Highness the Duchess of York." P. 4 has an arrangement for two German flutes. Engraved. BM and JF.

[4] N. Howard Thorp, *Songs of the Cowboys* (Boston, 1921), p. 62; LC.

[5] See, also, *Ozark*, vol. II, p. 184; *North Carolina F.*, vol. 2, p. 611; and *JAFL*, 1957, p. 240.

[1] All dates are per Humphries-Smith.

[2] Frank Miller, *The Mansfield Manuscript* (Dumfries, 1935), p. 13; BM and NYPL. Opie, p. 249. The present location of the manuscript is not known.

On Sept. 17, 1792, another sheet music edition was entered at Stationers' Hall "Engraved from the Original Manuscript" for 1, 2, 3, 4 or 5 voices by J. Dale, 19 Cornhill and 132 Oxford Street facing Hanover Square, London. BM and JF. Other possibly first printings[1] are by: (a) Preston & Son, 97 Strand, London (ca. 1789–1798), JF; (b) Stewart & Co., Edinburgh[3] (ca. 1795), KC; (c) Longman and Broderip, 26 Cheapside and 13 Haymarket, London (1782–1798), JF; and (d) E. Rhames, 16 Exchange St., Dublin (ca. 1776–1778 or ca. 1778–1806), seen by the author at Sotheran's Book Store, London.

Oh dem Golden Slippers

mw. James Bland. Copyrighted Feb. 10, 1879,[1] by John F. Perry & Co. (no street address), Boston. First edition: Front cover has a drawing of a Negro couple, lists three titles and is black and white. p. [2] adv. *Perry's.*. m. on pp. 3–5.) The title on p. 3 is *Oh, dem Golden Slippers!* p.n. 1413-3. Back cover adv. *Little.. - Dot..* The top of the front cover does not refer to Lotta and Ed. Marble. LC(CDC). Brief biographic information regarding Bland appears above under *Carry Me Back to Old Virginny.*

O Du Lieber Augustin—(Polly Put the Kettle On— Did You Ever See a Lassie?)

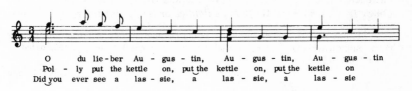

The first known printing of the music was in 1788–1789[1] in *Sechs Variationen über das Volkslied: Ei du Mein Lieber Augustin* arranged for piano

[3] This is the edition said to have been used by Johnson when he included the song in *The Scots Musical Museum*, Edinburgh, vol. 5, p. 510, in 1797. Stenhouse, p. 434.

[1] Copyright records; LC.

[1] Deutsch, *Plate Numbers*, p. 23.

by [Jos. Friedr.] Kirmair and published by B. Schott, Mainz. Possible first edition: Front cover mentions p.n. 77 and the price of 24 kr. DS (library number: DMS 31059). The only other known pre-1800 printing[2] is in *Deux Airs Favoris* arranged for piano by Kirmair, published in 1799 by J. André, Offenbach, with p.n. 1355;[2] BSM.

The first known printing of the words of *O Du Lieber Augustin* was probably in *Augustin*, "Favorit-Walzer, nach dem Böhmischen" published by Breitkopf und Härtel, Leipzig, about 1800. Oblong. Typeset. m. on p. [2]. w. on p. [3]. p. [4] blank. JF. There is no plate number, but the type used was from about this period.† The words were also published in two "Flugblätter" or pamphlets, one entitled *Drey* [sic] *Schöne Neue Lieder*, published in Steyr, Austria, in 1815, at MS, and the other entitled *Fünf Schöne Neue Lieder* (n.p., n.d.), at TLW (photocopies of each at FR). The first word is sometimes sung "Ach," and the second word is sometimes sung "Mein."

It seems clear that this song was not known as such before the end of the eighteenth century.[3] The legend is that, in 1679, Augustin, a wandering and begging Viennese minstrel, was found drunk and thrown into the plague pit; however, he regained consciousness and survived, cheating the Black Plague. Largely by piecing together unrelated excerpts, it has been suggested that the melody is older than the end of the eighteenth century;[4] the efforts are not persuasive to this author. The melody became particularly popular in England and America about 1830 in connection with the song entitled *Buy a Broom;*[5] copies at BM, LC, NYPL and JF.

The melody is frequently associated with the song *Molly* (or *Polly*) *Put the Kettle On*, the opening notes of early printings of which are identical with those of *O Du Lieber Augustin*. Chappell, p. 795, says that *Polly* was arranged for piano by Dale about 1794, but no publication by Dale has been located before ca. 1809–1810 under the title *Molly Put the Kettle On or Jenny's Baubie;*[6] JF. *Jenny's Baubee or Jenny Put the Kettle On* was

---

[2] *Id.*, p. 6. The melody also appears as the German melody in *Friendship, Love & Wine* published by G. Willig, Philadelphia, which Sonneck-Upton, p. 150, dated as about 1800, but which Wolfe, p. 286, no. 2881, redated as "1818?"

[3] Leopold Schmidt, *Das Volkslied im Alten Wien* (Vienna, 1947), p. 41, NYPL; and Erk-Böhme, vol. II, p. 750.

[4] Erich Schenk, "Die Melodie des Liedes 'O, Du Liaber [sic] Augustin'" in *Volkslied Volkstanz-Volksmusik* (Vienna, July–Dec., 1948), p. [49]; FR. Hellmut Federhofer, "Zur 'Augustin' Melodie" in *Jahrbuch des Österreichischen Volksliedwerks* (Vienna, 1952), vol. I, p. 53; FR. Wilhelm Tappert, *Musikalische Studien* (Berlin, 1868), p. 29; NYPL. Paul Nettl, *Forgotten Musicians* (New York, N.Y., 1951), p. 5, NYPL, refers to *Kuhreigen* in J. J. Rousseau's *Dictionnaire de Musique* (Paris, 1768), NYPL, as an antecedent, but the reference cannot be located in the work cited.

[5] A. Hyatt King, "English Pictorial Music Title-Pages, 1820–1885," in *The Library*, London, March, 1950, p. 264; NYPL.

[6] Humphries-Smith, p. 125.

published by McDonnell, Dublin, ca. 1790–1810,[7] and *Molly Put the Kettle On* was published by Paff, New York City, 1803–7[8, 9]—both at JF.

The melody is also used in connection with *Did You Ever See a Lassie?* the earliest known printing of which is in Jessie H. Bancroft, *Games for the Playground, Home, School and Gymnasium* (New York, N.Y., 1909), p. 261, published Dec. 8, 1909;[10] LC.

Oh! How I Hate to Get Up in the Morning

Oh! How I hate to get up in the morn - ing

mw. Irving Berlin. Published July 23, 1918,[1] by Waterson, Berlin & Snyder Co., Strand Theatre Bldg., Broadway at 47th St., New York, N.Y. First edition: Front cover has a drawing of an Army bugler, a photograph of Rae Samuels and is blue, pink, orange, black and white. m. on pp. 2–3. Dedication on p. 2 to Private Howard Friend "who occupies the cot next to mine and feels as I do about the 'bugler.'" p.n. 801. Back cover adv. *At..* Folio. No reference to any show. LC(CDC) and JF. Brief biographic information regarding Berlin appears above under *Alexander's Ragtime Band.*

Oh Johnny, Oh Johnny, Oh

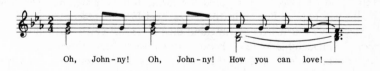

Oh,   John - ny!   Oh,   John - ny!   How   you   can   love!____

[7] *Id.*, p. 222.

[8] Wolfe, p. 229, no. 2252.

[9] *Jenny's Baubee* is a controversial subject outside the scope of this discussion. Chappell, p. 795; Opie, p. 353; and Glen, p. 213.

[10] Copyright records; LC.

[1] Copyright records; LC.

m. Abe Olman. w. Ed. Rose. Published Feb. 5, 1917,[1] by Forster Music Publisher Inc., 509 So. Wabash Ave., Chicago. First edition: Front cover has a drawing of "Johnny" in a country scene with many ladies and a photograph of Abe Olman, is red, green, yellow, blue and white, and refers to an Australian agent; no price. m. on pp. 2–3. No plate number. Back cover adv. *Dancing..* Folio. LC(CDC). The "Patriotic Version" was published later.

Olman, a composer, pianist and publisher, was born in Cincinnati in 1888 and died in Rancho Mirage, Cal., in 1984.[2] Rose, a lyricist, was born in Chicago in 1875 and died in Evanston, Ill., in 1935.[2]

O Little Town of Bethlehem!

O   lit - tle town of   Beth - le - hem, how still   we — see thee   lie

m. L. H. Redner. w. [Rev. Dr. Phillips Brooks]. Both the music and words were published for the first time in *The Church Porch*, edited by William R. Huntington (New York, N.Y., 1874), hymn no. 43. NYPL. The hymn is entitled *St. Louis*, said to be merely a different spelling of the composer's first name, Lewis.[1] The author of the words is not mentioned in this collection.

Inspired by his visit to Bethlehem on Christmas Eve, 1865, the Rev. Brooks wrote the words for the Christmas, 1868, Sunday school program in the Church of the Holy Trinity, Philadelphia, of which he was then the rector, and Mr. Redner composed the music for the program.[2] The Rev. Brooks was born in Boston in 1835, was a celebrated preacher, was elected Bishop of Massachusetts in 1891 and died in 1893.[3] Lewis H. Redner was born in Philadelphia in 1831, became a real estate broker, was organist in the Rev. Brooks's Church of the Holy Trinity at the time the hymn was written and died in Atlantic City, N.J., in 1908.[4]

---

[1] Copyright records; LC.

[2] *ASCAP*, pp. 377 and 421. Obituary, *The New York Times*, Jan. 10, 1984.

[1] Emurian, *Hymns*, p. 97.

[2] Charles Bancroft, *O Little Town of Bethlehem* (Philadelphia, 1968); FLP. Rudin, p. 38.

[3] *NIE*, vol. 4, p. 22.

[4] NYPL Music Division Biographic File.

O Mein Papa

O   mein Pa - pa   war   ei - ne wun - der - ba - re Clown

O *Mein Papa:* Copyright MCMXLVIII, MCML by Musikverlag und Bühnenvertrieb Zürich A.G.,
Zurich, Switzerland.
Oh! My Pa-Pa: Copyright MCMLIII by Shapiro, Bernstein & Co. Inc., New York. By permission.

mw. Paul Burkhard. Published Nov. 17, 1948,[1] by Musikverlag und Bühnenvertrieb Zürich A.G., Zurich. Possible first edition: Front cover has a
drawing of a master of ceremonies and is black and white. s. *Der Schwarze
Hecht.* p. [2] adv. *von..* m. on pp. 3–5. Back cover blank. LC (copyright
copy deposited Dec. 18, 1953), BM and JF. Published on the same day
was a booklet of four songs from the show, including *O Mein Papa;* LC
(copyright copy deposited March 24, 1954).[1] The musical show was retitled
Feuerwerk about Dec., 1950. *Oh! My Pa-Pa,* with English words by John
Turner and Geoffrey Parsons, was published in 1953.

Burkhard was born in Zurich in 1911 and is a conductor and composer
in Switzerland.[2]

Oh, Promise Me!

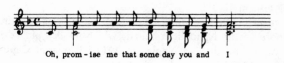

Oh, prom - ise me that some day you and   I

m. Reginald De Koven. w. Clement Scott. Copyrighted Sept. 26, 1889,[1]
by G. Schirmer, 35 Union Square, New York, N.Y. First edition: Front
cover refers to Chas. E. Knorr, mentions two keys (the copyright deposit
copy is in A flat), op. 50, the price as 35¢ and is blue and white. m. on pp.
2–5. p.n. 7550. Back cover adv. *Music..* (not, *New Music..*) LC(CDC).
Front cover does not refer to the operetta *Robin Hood* or to an arrangement for any instrument other than piano.

The song was inserted in the operetta *Robin Hood,* which opened in
Chicago on June 9, 1890, in its second performance to satisfy Jessie Bart-
lett Davis, one of the singers in the operetta, who had been dissatisfied with
her material in the operetta.[2] The first edition of the piano-vocal score of

[1] Copyright records; LC.
[2] *Grove's,* vol. I, p. 1025.

[1] Copyright records; LC.
[2] Geller, p. 107. Mrs. Reginald De Koven, *A Musician and His Wife* (New York,
N.Y., 1926), p. 135; NYPL.

the operetta, copyrighted March 16, 1891,[1] did not include *Oh, Promise Me!* LC(CDC). De Koven was born in Middletown, Conn., in 1859, became a composer, director and music critic and died in Chicago in 1920.[3] Scott was born in England in 1841, was a drama critic in both London and New York and died in London in 1904.[4]

'O Sole Mio!

('O so - le mi - o!_____ 'O so - le mi - o!)

m. E. di Capua. w. G. Capurro. The following copy, a probable first edition, was deposited March 17, 1899, with the Prefect of Naples[1] (this copy so dated now at S. Cecilia, Rome), by Libreria Editrice Bideri, **84 Constantinopoli**, Naples. Front cover is blue and white, has a drawing of a man serenading a seated girl, a dedication to Tomasino Rebolla, references to La Tavola Rotonda and an 1894 Exposition in Milan, the price of Cent. 50 and the no. M. 356. m. on pp. [2] and [3]. Back cover adv. songs published by Bideri up to no. 291. SCR(CDC). On Nov. 2, 1899, an edition was deposited at the same library published by G. Ricordi & C., Milan, with p.n. 102935;† also at JF.‡

The title means "Oh, My Sun!" Edoardo di Capua was born in Naples in 1864, composed many Neapolitan ballads which he also played in small theaters and cafés, and died in Naples in 1917.[2] Giovanni Capurro was born in Naples in 1859 and died there in 1920.[3]

Oh! Susanna

I ___ came from Al - a - bam - a wid my ban - jo on my knee

mw. [Stephen C. Foster]. An unauthorized printing, the first edition, was

[3] Mrs. De Koven, *ibid.*
[4] Obituary, *NYDM*, July 2, 1904.

[1] Copyright records; UDP. The publisher, however, advises that the song was first published (composed? sung?) in 1898.
[2] Baker, p. 1029.
[3] *EDS*, vol. 2, p. 1741.

copyrighted Feb. 25, 1848,[1] by C. Holt Jr., 156 Fulton St., New York, N.Y. Front cover mentions the Christy Minstrels and lists 16 titles, only **three** of which are followed by prices, *Oh! Susanna* being no. 8 at 25¢.[2] p. [2] blank. m. on pp. [3]–[5]. No plate number. Back cover blank. Engraved. There is no mention of Stephen C. Foster. LC(CDC), FH and KRS. The publication by W. C. Peters & Co., Louisville, Ky., authorized by Foster, was copyrighted Dec. 31, 1848;[1] LC.

The song had been sung in public as early as Sept. 11, 1847,[3] and was parodied before the end of 1848 in connection with the Gold Rush.[4] Brief biographic information regarding Foster appears above under *Beautiful Dreamer*.

Oh, What a Beautiful Mornin'—Oklahoma!

Oh, what a beau - ti - ful morn - in'

© 1943 by Williamson Music, Inc. By consent.

m. Richard Rodgers. w. Oscar Hammerstein 2d. Published March 12, 1943,[1] by Marlo Music Corporation without address [New York, N.Y.] First edition: Front cover refers to the musical show *Away We Go!*, has a drawing of a cowboy and cowgirl, lists five titles and is brown, yellow and white.[2] p. [2] adv. *Songs.*. m. on pp. 3–5. p.n. 516-3. The copyright owner is Williamson Music, Inc., New York, N.Y., and the sole selling agent Crawford Music Corporation, New York, N.Y. Back cover adv. *Boys.*. - *People.*. LC(CDC) and JF.

The name of the show was soon changed from *Away We Go!* to *Oklahoma!* and the show opened in New York City on March 31, 1943, under the new name. The piano-vocal score of *Oklahoma!* was published Dec. 1, 1943,[1] by Williamson Music Inc. (printed "Corp." on the title page and p. 5), sole selling agent Crawford Music Corporation, RKO Bldg., Radio City, N.Y., with a blue and gray cardboard front cover. LC(CDC) and JF. Brief biographic information regarding Rodgers and Hammerstein appears above under *If I Loved You* and *All the Things You Are*.

---

[1] Copyright records; LC.

[2] Front cover is illustrated in Fuld, *Foster*, no page number.

[3] FHR, p. 11. Hugill, p. 116, reports that Sigurd Sternvall wrote that the text and melody of a Swedish song, *Susannavisan*, with similar melody, can be traced back to the 1750's. This is absurd. The Svenskt Visarkiv, Stockholm, wrote this author that *Susannavisan* is "known only since about 1880."

[4] JAF, 1943, p. 104, footnote 19.

---

[1] Copyright records; LC.

[2] Front cover is illustrated in Fuld, *American*, p. [40].

Oh Where, Oh Where Has My Little Dog Gone—
(Zu Lauterbach)

Oh   where,   oh   where has my   lit - tle dog   gone
Zu   Lau - ter bach hab' ich mein Strumpf   ver - loren

The melody of this song was originally known as *Zu Lauterbach Hab' Ich Mein Strumpf Verloren* (*At Lauterbach I Lost My Sock*), the first known printing of the music (and words) of which were in *Alte und Neue Volks-Lieder*, arranged by L. Richter *et al.* (Leipzig, [1846]), p. 46; HU and JF. The words had previously appeared in two "Flugblätter" or pamphlets: one, entitled *Vier Schöne Neue Lieder* (1831, no imprint), at FR; and the other, entitled *Neue Gesellschafts-Lieder* (no date or imprint) at ER, with a photostat at FR. There are four towns in Germany with the name of Lauterbach, and it is not known which one is meant![1]

A similar melody had been included by Beethoven in his *Sinfonie Pastorale* in the third movement, Lustiges Zusammensein der Landleute, published in May, 1809, for orchestral parts by Breitkopf & Härtel, Leipzig; see *Symphony no. 6—Beethoven*, below.

An even older but similar melody is an unnamed dance tune in a manuscript from about 1260 at the Bodleian Library, Oxford.[1A]

It seems clear that Sep. Winner is the author of the American words. On Sept. 9, 1864,[2] there was deposited at the Library of Congress *Der Deitcher's Dog* with sole authorship credited to him and with himself as the publisher at 933 Sp. Garden St., Philadelphia. The opening words are as given in the heading above.[3] First edition: Front cover has a dedication to E. F. Dixey, the price is 3, and there is no "& Co." in the imprint. p. [2] blank. m. on pp. 3–5. No plate number. Back cover blank. Engraved. LC(CDC). Of three known English editions (two entitled *The Dutchman's Lee-tle Dog* and the third *The Little Wee Dog*), at JF, credit as to authorship is given Sep. Winner. Brief biographic information regarding Winner appears above under *Listen to the Mocking Bird*.

[1] Erk-Böhme, vol. II, pp. 768–769, nos. 1009 and 1010.

[1A] Manuscript Douce, 139, quoted in William Chappell, *Old English Popular Music* (London, 1893), p. [215], 4th line; BM. Harold Barlow, New York City, advised the author of this similarity.

[2] Copyright records; LC.

[3] Compare the opening words of the well-known Scottish song *The Blue Bells of Scotland*: "Oh where and oh where is your Highland laddie gone?"

Oh, You Beautiful Doll

Oh, you beau - ti - ful doll, — you great, big beau - ti - ful doll!

© 1911 Jerome H. Remick & Co. Copyright renewed and assigned to Remick Music Corp. Used by permission.

m. Nat. D. Ayer. w. Seymour Brown. Published Sept. 13, 1911,[1] by Jerome H. Remick & Co., New York and Detroit. Possible first edition: Front cover has a drawing of a "doll" in a bonnet, states "Popular Edition" and is blue, pink, white, yellow and green. m. on pp. 2–5. Back cover adv. *Love.. - Twilight..*, with a musical excerpt from *The Oceana..* LC (CDC) and JF.

Nathaniel Davis Ayer was born in Boston in 1887, went to England where he composed mostly for the stage and died in Bath, England, in 1952.[2] Brown, a lyricist, librettist and actor, was born in Philadelphia in 1885 and died there in 1947.[3]

Old Black Joe

I'm com-ing, I'm com-ing, for my head is bend-ing low

mw. Stephen C. Foster. Copyrighted Nov. 8, 1860,[1] by Firth, Pond & Co., 547 Broadway, New York, N.Y. First edition: Front cover says that the song is no. 49 of Foster's Melodies, mentions two other songs by him, the price as 2½ and three agents.[2] p. [2] blank. m. on pp. 3–5. p.n. 5011. Back cover blank. Engraved. LC(CDC), FH, NYPL and JF. Brief biographic information regarding Foster appears above under *Beautiful Dreamer.*

Old Folks at Home

Way down up - on the Swa - nee Riv - er, far, far a - way

[1] Copyright records; LC.
[2] Obituary, *New York Herald Tribune*, Sept. 21, 1952. Gammond-Clayton, p. 14.
[3] *ASCAP*, p. 57.

[1] Copyright records; LC.
[2] Front cover is illustrated in Fuld, *Foster*, no page number.

mw. [Stephen C. Foster]. Copyrighted Oct. 1, 1851,[1] by Firth, Pond & Co.,
1 Franklin Sq., New York, N.Y. First edition: Front cover has a **clear leaf**
design in between the letters of "Ethiopian Melody," refers to Christy's
Minstrels, says that the song was written and composed by E. P. Christy,
gives the price as 25¢ and mentions one agent.[2] p. [2] blank. m. on pp. 3–5.
p.n. 1332. Back cover blank. Engraved. LC(CDC), FH, NYPL, SS and JF.
There is no mention of Stephen C. Foster—he had sold the song to
Christy.

The song is frequently known by its opening words, *Way down upon*
de Swanee ribber, and also as *Swanee River*. It is the official song of the
State of Florida. One commentator has stated that *Old Folks at Home* was
"very likely borrowed" from *Annie Laurie*,[3] which is absurd. Brief biographic information regarding Foster appears above under *Beautiful*
Dreamer.

The Old Grey Mare—(Get Out of the Wilderness)

Oh! The old   grey mare, she   ain't what   she used to be

The above melody was originally known as *Down in Alabam*, with music
and words credited to J. Warner, and copyrighted Feb. 17, 1858,[1] by Wm.
Hall & Son, 239 Broadway, New York, N.Y. First edition: Front cover
mentions the subtitle, *Ain't I Glad I Got Out de Wilderness*, refers to
Bryant's Minstrels, gives the price as 2½ and lists three agents (one of
which, at Marysville, Cal., was then the third largest city in the state as a
result of the gold rush). p. [2] blank. m. on pp. 3–5. p.n. 4178. Back cover
blank. Engraved. LC(CDC) and JF. No biographic information has been
found regarding J. Warner. The song also came to be known by a variant of
the subtitle mentioned above, *Get Out of the Wilderness*; John Church, Jr.,
Cincinnati, copyrighted such an edition in 1860; JF. Another early variant,
entitled *Go in the Wilderness*, was included in *Slave Songs of the United*
States (New York, N.Y., 1867), p. 14; LC(CDC).

There has been a gradual progression from *Down in Alabam* to *The*
Old Grey Mare. The second stanza of the former commences: "Old blind
horse come from Jerusalem." In 1911 the words are given as: "Old grey
hoss come a-tearin' out o' the wilderness . . . Down in Alabam"; Mrs. L. D.

---

[1] Copyright records; LC.
[2] Front cover is illustrated in Fuld, *Foster*, no page number.
[3] Phillips Barry, "The Origin of Folk-Melodies" in *JAF*, 1910, p. 440.

---

[1] Copyright records; LC.

Ames, "The Missouri Play-Party," in *JAF*, July–Sept., 1911, p. 311, words only but referring to the correct melody. The phrase "ain't what she used to be" is not included in the words.

Persistent claims have been made that the words of *The Old Grey Mare* were written by Gus Bailey after such an animal "loaded with kettles, tin cups and frying pans, dashed up the hill . . . with a rattling noise" at the Second Battle of Bull Run (Manassas), Va., about 2:00 A.M. on Aug. 29, 1862.[2] The State of Texas Historical Survey Committee erected a marker at Blum, Texas, Bailey's home town. Gus Bailey was a soldier in Gen. Hood's Texas Brigade who later became a circus showman and musician, and died in Houston in 1896.

The *Old Grey Mare*, "arranged" by Frank Panella, was published April 5, 1915,[1] by Panella Music Co., Pittsburgh, as a Fox-Trot or Schottische for orchestra. Although words were included, the phrase "ain't what she used to be" is not. LC(CDC). On Oct. 6, 1915,[1] an arrangement for One Step, Two Step or March for piano, without words, was published by the same publisher: Front cover has a drawing of an old grey mare, mentions that the song is arranged by Frank Panella and is black, grey and white. p. [2] adv. *That..* m. on pp. 3–5. Back cover adv. *My..* LC(CDC). The first printing of the common phrase mentioned above, together with the music, is in a slightly later sheet music edition identical with the foregoing, and by the same publisher, except that p. [2] contains the words of four verses and two choruses, and the back cover advertises *That..* MED and JF. The "Song" version was not published until Oct. 4, 1917, by Joe Morris Music Co. Panella was born in 1878, became a composer particularly of marches, played in bands and died in 1953 in Pittsburgh.[3]

Old Hundred

All peo - ple that on earth do dwell

The music is said to have been composed by Louis Bourgeois for Psalm 134 of the 1551 edition of the Genevan Psalter.[1] The only located copy of this

---

[2] J. B. Hood, *Advance and Retreat* (New Orleans, La., 1880) p. 32; Olga Bailey, *Mollie Bailey* (Dallas, Texas, 1943), p. 38; and *The Handbook of Texas*, edited by Walter Prescott Webb (Austin, Texas, 1952), vol. 1, p. 96. All at NYPL. See also Col. Harold B. Simpson, *Hood's Texas Brigade* (Waco, Texas, 1968), p. 257; LC.

[3] Simpson, footnote 2 above, p. 217.

---

[1] Julian, p. 43. *Grove's*, vol. 1, p. 846. Waldo Selden Pratt, *The Music of the French Psalter of 1562* (New York, N.Y., 1939), p. 134; NYPL.

edition is said to have been in what was then known as the State Library, Dresden,[2] but the copy was destroyed during the war in 1945; according to surviving records at the library, its title was *Pseaumes de David, mis en rime Françoise par Clement Marot et Theodore le Besze* (Geneva, 1551), octavo size.[3] The only located copy of the 1552 edition of the Genevan Psalter, at SUB, was also destroyed during the war. No microfilm exists at either library. Curiously, the 1553 edition, at GBP, has no music for Psalm 134 (and no words or music for Psalm 100). The 1554 edition of the Genevan Psalter, Louys Bourgeois, *Pseaulmes LXXXIII de David* (Lyon, 1554), bass part, p. 84, contains the bass harmony for Psalm 134, which fits the music in question. BM (K. 8. i. 4. [16]).

In England, in 1560–1561, in three works, the music accompanied Psalm 100: Thomas Sterneholde and others, *Psalmes of David in English* (Jhon Day, London, 1560), p. 163, at Society of Antiquaries of London, Burlington House, London; and Thomas Sterneholde and others, *Fovre Score and Seven Psalmes of David in English Mitre* (n.p., 1561), no page number, at St. Paul's Cathedral Library, London.[4] In both the above printings, Sterneholde is stated to be the author. In another printing of the latter work with the same title, but with "Foure" rather than "Fovre" in the title and other minor variations in the title page, W. Ke. [William Kethe] is stated to be the author; BM (C. 36. bb. 4—the "Britwell" copy). The music may have even older antecedents.[5]

Shakespeare's *The Merry Wives of Windsor* (1597) stated, "They do no more adhere and keep place together than the *Hundredth Psalm* to the tune of *Green Sleeves*" (act II, scene 1). Little is known about Bourgeois; he was born in Paris about 1510 and was still living in 1561. Sterneholde was from Hampshire or Gloucestershire, became a groom of the robes to Henry VIII and Edward VI and died in 1549.[6] Kethe was a Scotsman who died about 1593.[7]

Old MacDonald Had a Farm

Old Mac-Don-ald had a farm,   E - I - E - I - O

---

[2] *Grove's*, vol. 1, p. 848, fn. 1.

[3] Letter from the present library, Sächsische Landesbibliothek, Dresden.

[4] The music is also said to accompany Psalm 100 in John Day, *Hondert Psalmen David's* (London, 1561), at BM (1220. c. 39. l.). Rev. W. H. Havergal, *A History of the Old Hundredth Psalm Tune* (New York, N.Y., 1854) p. 2; NYPL. However, this statement is incorrect.

[5] *OCM*, p. 708; *Grove's*, vol. 6, p. 184.

[6] Julian, pp. 857 and 860.

[7] *Id.*, p. 623.

The words of *Old MacDonald Had a Farm* may well have derived from a song by Mr. [Thomas] D'Urfey published in 1706, the opening words of which are "In the Fields in Frost and Snow." The song, without a title, tells of country life and states at intervals:

> Here a Boo, there a Boo, everywhere a Boo...
> Here a Whoo, there a Whoo, everywhere a Whoo...
> Here a Bae, there a Bae, everywhere a Bae...

These words without music were published in a libretto of *Wonders in the Sun or, The Kingdom of the Birds*, a comic opera (London, 1706), p. 50, and the words with since-discarded music were published about Aug. 7, 1706,[1] in *Songs in the New Opera, Call'd Wonders in the Sun or, The Kingdom of the Birds* (London), p. 2, and probably in the same year in a separate sheet without name or city of publisher; all at BM.[2] The comic opera opened in London on April 5, 1706.

Additional stanzas, perhaps in the original singing, appeared in print the next year, stating at intervals:

> Here a Cou, there a Cou, everywhere a Cou...
> [Here a Goble, there a Goble, everywhere a Goble...]
> Here a Cackle, there a Cackle, everywhere a Cackle...
> Here a Quack, there a Quack, everywhere a Quack...
> Here a Grunt, there a Grunt, everywhere a Grunt...

Wit and Mirth: or, Pills to Purge Melancholy (London, 1707), 2nd edition, p. 237; BM. The song was known as "In Praise of a Country Life" in *A New Academy of Compliments: or, the Lover's Secretary* (London, ca. 1750), 16th edition, p. 136;[3] BM and HL. D'Urfey, a composer and singer, was born in Exeter in 1653 and died in 1723.[4]

The words developed and became known in this country as *The Gobble Family* in *Bob Hart's Plantation Songster* (New York, N.Y., 1862), p. 34, at LC; as *The Three Contrabands* in *Christy's Bones and Banjo Melodist* (New York, N.Y., 1867), p. 30, at LC; as *The Gibble Gobble Family* in *Dick Martz's Sensational Songster* (New York, N.Y., 1871), p. 17, at LC; and as *In the Merry Green Fields of Oland* in *George Christy's Essence of Old Kentucky* (New York, N.Y., [ca. 1865]), p. 31, at LC.[5] No music is included in any of the above songsters; nor is the name Mac-Donald mentioned.

---

[1] *Daily Courant*, London, Aug. 7, 1706, p. [2]; BM.
[2] Oliver Neighbour, at the British Museum, advised the author of these printings.
[3] Ed Cray, Los Angeles, noted this printing.
[4] *Grove's*, 3rd ed., vol. 5, p. 425.
[5] See also *North Carolina F.*, vol. 3, p. 174.

The music of *Old MacDonald Had a Farm* may have derived from the music of *Litoria! Litoria!*, copyrighted Aug. 19, 1859, as Students' Songs No. 8 as sung by the Students of Yale College by Firth Pond & Co., 547 Broadway, New York, N.Y.[6] First edition. The front cover refers to a New Haven agent and has no price. p. [2] blank. m. on pp. [3]–5. No plate number. Back cover blank. Not engraved. LC(CDC), NYPL and JF.

The first known printing of the familiar music (and words) of this folk song was in Oct., 1917,[7] in *Tommy's Tunes*, collected by F. T. Nettleingham and published by (curiously) Erskine MacDonald, London. On page 84, the title is given as "Ohio," and it is "Old MacDougal" who has the farm.[8] BM, LC, NYPL and JF.

Ol' Man River—Showboat

Ol' man riv-er, dat ol' man riv-er, he must know sump-in', but don't say noth-in'

© 1927 by T. B. Harms Company. Copyright renewed. By consent.

m. Jerome Kern. w. Oscar Hammerstein 2nd. Published Nov. 30, 1927,[1] by T. B. Harms Company, New York, N.Y. First edition: Front cover has a drawing of a **lyre** and is orange, blue and white. s. *Show Boat*—3 titles listed. (**See Plate III.**) p. [2] adv. *Sunny*. m. on pp. 3–7. p.n. 308-5. p. [8] blank. p. [9] adv. *Who?* Back cover adv. *Cinderella.*. JF (only known copy†). The three advertised songs were published in 1925–1926. The above edition is the same, to the extent possible, as the other contemporary, regular edition, copyright deposit copies from the same show; LC(CDC).

Show Boat opened in New York City Dec. 27, 1927, and the piano-vocal score was published April 5, 1928,[1] by the same American concern with a red, yellow, black and gray front cover showing people boarding a gangplank. LC(CDC), BR* (Kern's copy) and JF.

The words of *Ol' Man River* have subsequently been modified to eliminate certain references deemed by some to be offensive.

It is interesting to note that *Bill*, subsequently included in *Show Boat*, had been originally published from the show *Oh, Lady! Lady!!*, on Feb. 2, 1918;[1] LC(CDC), SS and JF. An excerpt of the song is also included at p. 56 in the piano-vocal score of *Oh, Lady! Lady!!* published on April 9, 1918;[1] LC(CDC), BR and JF (latter two copies previously owned by

[6] Saul Starr, New York City, advised the author of this possibility.

[7] This date appears on the verso of the title page.

[8] Joseph C. Hickerson, Library of Congress, informed the author of this printing.

[1] Copyright records; LC.

Jerome Kern). Brief biographic information regarding Kern and Hammerstein appears above under *All the Things You Are.*

The Old Oaken Bucket

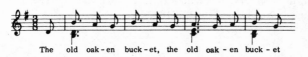

The old oak-en buck-et, the old oak-en buck-et

m. G. Kiallmark. w. Samuel Woodworth. The melody was originally known as *Araby's Daughter* and was composed by G. Kiallmark. One copy of the song was entered at Stationers' Hall on Feb. 19, 1822, by J. Power, London. Probable first edition: The front cover states that *Araby's Daughter* is a ballad from Moore's celebrated poem *Lalla Rookh*, the price is 2/0, and the street address of the publisher is 34 Strand. p. [2] blank. m. on pp. 3–7. p.n. 620. Back cover blank. Engraved. BM and JF. Thomas Moore's *Lalla Rookh* was published in England in the spring of 1817, and the poem *Farewell to Araby's Daughter* appears in the third episode, *The Fire Worshippers;* BM.

Samuel Woodworth composed the poem *The Old Oaken Bucket* during the summer of 1817 in New York City, and the poem was published in the *Republican Chronicle,* New York, N.Y., June 3, 1818, under the title *The Bucket* signed with his pseudonym "Selim."[1] RU. *The Bucket* was soon thereafter set to music other than the above well-known melody.

The first known printing of *The Old Oaken Bucket* to the tune of *Araby's Daughter* may have been in *The Amateur's Song Book,* "by an Amateur" (Boston, 1843), the music and words at p. 157; Josephine L. Hughes,[2] LC, BR and JF. This book is known in two editions, both with the same title page and 1843 copyright notice. One consists of 108 pages, at LC and NYPL, and lacks *The Old Oaken Bucket.* The other, expanded to 216 pages, includes the song; it is possible, however, that the expanded edition was published in a later year. The common music and words of *The Old Oaken Bucket* were included in *The Boston Melodeon,* arranged by E. L. White (Boston, 1846), p. 80, this book having been copyrighted June 13, 1846;[3] BPL.

In 1864 Currier and Ives created a large colored lithograph entitled

---

[1] See, generally, the article by Josephine L. Hughes and Richard J. Wolfe, "The Tunes of 'The Bucket'" in *Bulletin of the New York Public Library,* Nov., 1961, p. 555; NYPL.

[2] Mrs. Hughes, Charleston, S.C., discovered this printing.

[3] Copyright records; LC.

The Old Oaken Bucket. The well, in which the original Old Oaken Bucket hung, is at the edge of Old Oaken Bucket Road, Scituate, Mass., and the Bucket's original bail is at the town's Historical Society.[4]

George Kiallmark (the father) was born at King's Lynn, England, in 1781, became a composer, violinist and teacher and died at Islington, England, in 1835.[5] Woodworth was born at Scituate, Mass., in 1785, was a poet and journalist and died in 1842.[6]

The Old Refrain (Viennese Popular Song)—Brandl-Kreisler

m. Johann Brandl. The music of this song was composed by Johann Brandl under the title *Du Alter Stefansthurm* for his operetta *Der Liebe Augustin,* and was published about March, 1887,[1] for piano and voice by Aug. Cranz, Hamburg. Probable first edition: Front cover mentions the operetta, with words by Hugo Klein, lists two titles, *Du Alter Stefansthurm* at Mk. 1. 20 Pf., and refers to Vienna and Brussels affiliates. p. [2] blank. m. on pp. 3–7. p.n. C. 27258. Back cover adv. *Beliebte..* ONB and SB. The song was also published for orchestra about the same month;[2] no early printing has been found.

Curiously, when Fritz Kreisler transcribed the song for violin, the American edition did not acknowledge Brandl's authorship of the melody or its original title,[3] whereas the later German edition acknowledged both. Kreisler's transcription was published April 19, 1915,[4] under the title *Viennese Popular Song,* by Carl Fischer, Cooper Square, New York, N.Y. First edition: Front cover is entitled *Austrian Folk Songs* transcribed for violin with piano accompaniment, lists three titles of which this is the second at 50 Cents, mentions a Boston address for the publisher and a Chicago

---

[4] *The New York Times,* July 15, 1962, sec. 10, p. 9.

[5] *Grove's,* 3rd ed., vol. III, p. 20.

[6] *NIE,* vol. 23, p. 716.

---

[1] Hofmeister *Monatsbericht,* March, 1887, p. 159; NYPL. *Cranz Catalogue,* Hamburg, 1887 (to the end of 1886), p. 410; LC.

[2] Hofmeister *Monatsbericht,* March, 1887, p. [138]; NYPL.

[3] However, Kreisler's first manuscript copyright deposit at LC on April 4, 1914, under the title *Vienna Popular Song,* refers to Brandl.

[4] Copyright records; LC.

agent and is yellow, black and gray. There is no reference to "The Old Refrain." vb. Title page is the same as the front cover except black and white. m. on pp. 2–5. p.n. 18710-6. Dedicated to Felix Winternitz. p. [6] adv. *Serenade - Legende.* p. [7] blank. Back cover adv. *Indian.. - Slavonic..* Separate violin part: pp. [1] and [4] blank. m. on pp. 2–3. Same p.n. LC(CDC) and BM* (copyright copy deposited April 19, 1915). Kreisler lived chiefly in New York City at the time, and the edition by B. Schott's Söhne, Mainz, under the title *Wiener Volkslied, Du Alter Stefansturm von J. Brandl,* was apparently not published until about March, 1916[5] (with a 1915 copyright claim by Carl Fischer, New York); BMA and JF (variants).

The composition is now generally known as *The Old Refrain.* Brandl was born in 1835 at Kirchenberk, Bohemia, was a composer of many operettas and other compositions, and died in Vienna in 1913.[6] Brief biographic information regarding Kreisler appears above under *Caprice Viennois.*

On the Road to Mandalay

Come you back to Man - da - lay, where the old flo - til - la lay

Copyright 1907 by G. Schirmer, Inc. By permission.

m. Oley Speaks. w. Rudyard Kipling. The poem was first published[1] in *The Scots Observer,* Edinburgh, June 21, 1890, p. 124, under the title *Mandalay; ULS,* p. 1901.

The music, and the words, were copyrighted on Nov. 18, 1907,[2] by The John Church Company, Cincinnati and four other cities. First edition: Front cover has a drawing of a Mandalayan palace and is green, red and white. p. [2] blank. m. on pp. 3–11. p.n. 15732-9. Back cover blank. LC(CDC). No reference to high and low voices on front cover or p. 3.

Speaks was born in Canal Winchester, Ohio, in 1874, became a composer and singer and died in New York City in 1948.[3] Kipling was born in Bombay, India, in 1865 and died in London in 1936.

---

[5] Hofmeister *Monatsbericht,* March, 1916, p. 35.

[6] *Riemann,* p. 217.

[1] James McG. Stewart, *Rudyard Kipling, A Bibliographical Catalogue* (Toronto, 1959), p. 80; NYPL.

[2] Copyright records; LC.

[3] *ASCAP,* p. 473.

On Top of Old Smoky

On   top   of   old   Smo - ky,_____   all   cov - e red with   snow

The words appeared in E. C. Perrow, "Songs and Rhymes from the South" in *Journal of American Folklore*, Lancaster, Pa., and New York, N.Y., April–June, 1915, p. 159, with the notation "From North Carolina; mountain whites; MS. written for E. N. Caldwell; 1913"; *ULS*, p. 1435.

The music appeared under the title *The Little Mohee* in Loraine Wyman and Howard Brockway, *Lonesome Tunes* (New York, N.Y., 1916), p. 52, with the notation "from Harlan County, Ky." LC. The accompanying words tell a story about Mohee, an Indian girl.[1] In other versions of this song, "Mohee" is sometimes spelled "Mohea," and the title is *Pretty Mohea*.

The music and words of *On Top of Old Smoky* are included under the title *The Wagoner's Lad* in Olive Dame Campbell and Cecil J. Sharp, *English Folk Songs from the Southern Appalachians* (New York, N.Y., and London, 1917), p. 215, with the notation "sung by Miss Memory Shelton at Alleghany, N.C., July 29, 1916." NYPL.

Onward, Christian Soldiers

On - ward, Chris - tian   sol - diers,   march-ing as   to   war

m. Arthur S. Sullivan. w. Rev. Sabine Baring-Gould. The words of this hymn were written in 1864 for a Children's Festival at Hornury Bridge, England, and were published in *Church Times*, London, Oct. 15, 1864, p. 331; *ULS*, p. 690.

The music, and the words, were published in *The Musical Times*, London, Dec. 1, 1871, p. [311]; BM, *ULS*, p. 1844, RA and JF. The hymn

---

[1] Laws, p. 233, analyzes whether *The Little Mohea* may be an American remaking of the English *The Indian Lass*.

is there said to be one of four popular hymns set to music expressly for *The Hymnary* published by Novello, Ewer and Co., London. This concern published a number of editions of *The Hymnary*. While one, with words only, was published about Dec. 1, 1871, the editions containing music were not published until about Oct. 1, 1872.[1]

Brief biographic information regarding Sullivan appears above under *Bow, Bow, Ye Lower Middle Classes*. Baring-Gould was born in Exeter in 1834, became a Rector, author and collector of folk songs, and died in Lew-Trenchard in 1924.[2]

Otchi Tchorniya

O - tchi chorn - i - ya——— o - tchi strass - ni - ya

A Soviet Union musicologist has written this author that *Otchi Tchorniya* or *Dark Eyes* is not a Russian folk song, but rather a cabaret song from the repertoire of Moscow gypsies which was popular among the middle classes until the Revolution. He further wrote that at the present time it does not appear in the repertoire and is not known to the younger generation.†

The first known printing of *Otchi Tchorniya* was shortly after March 7, 1884, the date of the censor's approval (which appears on the sheet music), by A. Büttner, probably in Moscow, according to a Soviet Union musicologist. No copy of an edition published by Büttner has been found, but Büttner's edition was republished before 1897[1] by A. Gutheil, 10 Kuznetsky Bridge, Moscow, with a new front cover but with it is said Büttner's original music pages. In Gutheil's reprint, entirely in Russian, there is a collective front cover entitled Любимыя Пѣсни Московскихъ Цыганъ (*Favorite Songs of Moscow Gypsies*), listing 157 titles of which this is no. 131, Очи Черныя, Очи Страстныя, "a Gypsy Romance to the melody of the 'Hommage-Valse' by Hermann." m. on pp. 2-3. p.n. K. 1817 G. (perhaps,

---

[1] The dates of publication of the various editions are easily traced in successive advertisements in *MT*, from Nov. 1, 1871, to Nov. 1, 1872, at pp. [257], [297], 582 and 630. BM, *ULS*, p. 1844, RA and JF. Several editions of *The Hymnary* are at UTS and JF.

[2] *Grove's*, vol. 1, p. 436.

[1] Gutheil's St. Petersburg agent was A. Iohansen, 44 Perspective de Nevsky. See *Prelude in C Sharp Minor—Rachmaninoff*.

Gutheil's son, Karl, who carried on the business after his father's death in 1883).†

Over the Rainbow

Some - where   o - ver the rain - bow way   up   high

m. Harold Arlen. w. E. Y. Harburg. Published Jan. 18, 1939,[1] by Leo Feist inc. [sic], 1629 Broadway, New York, N.Y. The copy deposited at LC is a professional edition. Possible first regular edition: Front cover has photographs of scenes from the movie *The Wizard of Oz* (five titles listed), and is red, blue, brown and white. m. on pp. 2–5. p.n. 7067-4. p. 5 adv. *Wayne..* Centerfold adv. *Legion..* Back cover adv. *Over.. - We're..* JF (inscribed by the composer and the lyricist). All the songs advertised and listed in this edition were published on or before July 7, 1939. The regular edition was probably not printed until about this date as *The Wizard of Oz* was not copyrighted until Aug. 7, 1939,[1] or released until Aug. 10, 1939, and all the deposited songs from the movie are professional copies except *We're Off to See the Wizard*, which was published and deposited in a regular edition on July 7, 1939.

Judy Garland was seventeen years old when she sang the song in *The Wizard of Oz*. The song, with an octave leap in the melody, had been deleted three times from the print of the film, only to be restored each time.[2] *Over the Rainbow* was awarded the "Oscar" for the best movie song in 1939 by the Academy of Motion Picture Arts and Sciences. Arlen, a composer, was born in Buffalo in 1905 and lives in New York City. Brief biographic information regarding Harburg appears above under *April in Paris*.

Over There

O - ver there_____   o - ver there

[1] Copyright records; LC.
[2] Edward Jablonski, *Harold Arlen, Happy with the Blues* (New York, N.Y., 1961), p. 120; NYPL. *The New York Times*, Aug. 10, 1961, p. 17.

mw. George M. Cohan. Published June 1, 1917,[1] by William Jerome Publishing Corporation, Strand Theatre Bldg., 47th St. & Broadway, New York, N.Y. Probable first edition: Front cover has a photograph of Nora Bayes and is red, white and blue.[2] m. on pp. [2]–[3]. Back cover adv. *If..* LC(CDC) and JF (autographed). Another, unattractive, edition by William Jerome Publishing Corporation may have preceded the foregoing. It has a brown, black and tan front cover with a photograph of Harry Ellis, and says "The Master Patriotic Song." m. on pp. 2–3. Back cover adv. *Cotton..* (copyright transferred April 12, 1917.[1]) JF.

"There is the whole arrogance of the strength of the New World in its lines."[3] The United States had entered World War I on April 6, 1917, and the song was first professionally sung by Nora Bayes.[4] The verse of the song is adapted from *Johnny Get Your Gun*, which see. Brief biographic information regarding Cohan appears above under *Give My Regards to Broadway*.

Pack Up Your Troubles in Your Old Kit-Bag

m. Felix Powell. w. George Asaf. Published Nov. 23, 1915,[1] by Francis, Day & Hunter, 138–140 Charing Cross Road, London, W. C. First edition: Front cover states that it is a Prize Marching Song, no. 1401, Sixpenny Popular Edition and mentions a New York affiliate. p. [2] blank. m. on pp. [1]–5 (actually 3–7). p.n. 14009. Back cover adv. *Still.. - The Rest..* The words "Smile, Smile, Smile" do not appear in the title. BM (copyright copy deposited Dec. 6, 1915).

This song was written by two Welsh brothers, Felix Powell, who died in Brighton, England, in 1942, and George Henry Powell, who wrote under the pseudonym George Asaf and lived from 1880 to 1951.[2]

---

[1] Copyright records; LC.
[2] Front cover is illustrated in Fuld, *American*, p. [41].
[3] Colonel Walter Elliott, quoted in Pulling, p. 82.
[4] Ward Morehouse, *George M. Cohan* (Philadelphia, 1943), p. 127; NYPL.

[1] Copyright records; LC.
[2] *OCM*, p. 760. Obituary, *Etude*, April, 1942.

La Paloma

Cuan - do ———— sa - li de la Ha - ba - na val - ga - me   Dios

mw. Sebastian Yradier. In 1859 "*La Paloma* (Cancion Americana con acompañamiento de Piano" by "Sebastian Iradier" was registered at the copyright office in Madrid[1] as no. 6,341 by Calcografía de E. A. Gil. The copyright deposit copy cannot be found, and no copy by this publisher has been located at a Spanish or other library; and it has not been possible to ascertain in what city Gil was located.

However, a possible first edition has been found, although E. A. Gil's name does not appear; he may merely have been the engraver or printer. The title is *La Paloma*, "Cancion Americana con acompañamiento de Piano" (same as the copyright registration). The front cover has a dedication to Da. Sarolta Bujanovics, prima donna assoluta del Real Teatro de Madrid, and the price of 12 Rs (Reales); no publisher is named, merely a store for music and pianos at 16 Calle del Principe. m. on pp. 3–7; Spanish text only. Engraved. (Incomplete description). BMM. The Librarian at Biblioteca Musical, Madrid, has written this author that he believes this edition was published about 1859.†

An interesting aspect of the above Spanish copyright record and Spanish printing is its reference to the song as a "Cancion Americana." An exhaustive search in the United States has so far failed to unearth a North American, Central American or South American printing in or before 1859. The song is called a "Mexikanisches Lied" in an early edition published by J. Hoffmann, Prague; JF.

It is also said that it was the habanera form that was "American," and that Yradier was in Havana in the 1850's and reintroduced the habanera to Spain upon his return.

La Paloma was published in 1864 in France under the title *La Colombe* by Heugel & Cie., au Ménestrel, 2 bis Rue Vivienne, Paris. It is likely that the song was published in this sheet music form on Sept. 29, 1864,[2] at 5 francs, but no early copy has been found. The song was also included about this date or up to a few months later[3] in a book of 25 songs by

---

[1] Copyright records; RG.

[2] Information from the publisher. *BF*, Dec. 17, 1864, p. 598.

[3] *Fleurs d'Espagne* was mentioned in the Sept. 25, 1864, issue of *Le Ménestrel* as to be issued to subscribers, p. 344, and then advertised in the Dec. 11, 1864, issue, p. 16. W. N. H. Harding, Chicago, advised the author of this printing.

Yradier entitled *Fleurs d'Espagne—Chansons Espagnoles*[4] by the same publisher as no. 14, *La Paloma (Colombe)*. The song has p.n. 3105(2). French words by Tagliafico are also included. WNH and JF.

The song is known in English as *The Dove*. Yradier was born in Sauciego in 1809 and died in Vitoria in 1865.[5]

Papillons d'Amour—À la Bien-Aimée

m. Edouard Schütt. Copyrighted March 7, 1900,[1] "Chez" N. Simrock, Berlin. First edition: Front cover and title page show title as *Papillons d'Amour, Souvenirs Viennois, Cinq Morceaux pour Piano*, op. 59, of which *À la Bien-Aimée* is no. 2, have a drawing of butterflies and a sleeping girl, mention a London agent, and are black and white. Price of no. 2 is Mk. 2. Both versos blank. m. on pp. 3–10. p.n. 11396. p. [11] adv. compositions of Schütt up to op. 59. pp. [12], [13] and back cover blank. LC(CDC). The orchestral arrangement was published in 1908; LC(CDC).

Schütt was born in St. Petersburg in 1856, became a pianist, conductor and composer in Germany and Austria, and died in Obermais, near Meran, Austria, in 1933.[2]

The Parade of the Wooden Soldiers

m. Léon Jessel. Published probably late 1905[1] under the title *Die Parade der Zinnsoldaten* ("Tin" Soldiers) for piano at 1.20 Mk. and for orchestra at

---

[4] See also *Toreador Song*.
[5] Westrup-Harrison, p. 734.

---

[1] Copyright records; LC. Hofmeister *Monatsbericht*, July, 1900, p. 344; NYPL.
[2] *Grove's*, vol. 7, p. 642.

---

[1] The piano arrangement bears a 1905 copyright claim. Hofmeister *Monatsbericht*, April, 1906, p. 166.

2 Mk., op. 123, by Heinrichshofen's Verlag, Magdeburg. No first printing
has been found of either arrangement. The earliest located edition for piano
lists 11 arrangements and has a drawing of tin soldiers in many colors; m.
on pp. 2–5; p.n. 9249; and back cover adv. *Ach.. - Das Weihnachtsglöck-
chen*, no. 7. JF.

Jessel was born in Stettin in 1871, was a composer of operettas and
died in Berlin in 1942.[2]

Parlez-Moi d'Amour

Par - lez - moi   d'a - mour, re - di - tes moi

mw. Jean Lenoir. The song was published Dec. 31, 1930,[1] and the following,
possible first, edition was deposited June 20, 1931, at BN by Smyth, 17
Faubourg Montmartre, Paris: Folio. Front cover in blue and white has a
photograph of Lucienne Boyer, mentions five recordings and lists two
arrangements, this for piano and voice at 6 fr. and voice alone at 1 fr. 50.
No agent or copublisher is mentioned. m. on pp. [2] and [3]. p.[2] states
"Copyright 1930." p.n. 1056. Back cover adv. *Ritorna.. - Le Hop..* BN
(CDC).

The song is also known in English-speaking countries as *Speak to Me
of Love*.[2] Lenoir, a composer and lyricist, was born in Paris in 1891 and
resides there.[3]

The Peanut Vendor

Music and Spanish words by Moisés Simons. On Feb. 11, 1928,[1] a manuscript copy of *El Manisero* was deposited at LC by Moisés Simons Rodríguez, Havana; LC(CDC).

The first known printing of the song was on Dec. 28, 1929,[1] when it
was included in a booklet of songs from the revue *Cubanola*, all by Moisés

[2] *Riemann*, vol. I, p. 878.

[1] Copyright records; LC. The Amercan copyright copy was not deposited at the
Library of Congress until June 3, 1931.

[2] See, generally, Sandved, pp. 307 and 1561.

[3] Information from composer.

[1] Copyright records; LC.

Simons, almost certainly published in Havana. Probable first edition: Front cover in red and white says that the revue was presented for the first time on May 15, 1929, on the Roof-Garden, Hotel Plaza, Havana, with the orchestra of the composer. Verso has a Cuban copyright notice and the year 1929. m. on pp. 1–83. No. 4 on p. 11 is *Manisero*, with music and Spanish words only. p. [84] has Index. Inside back cover blank. Back cover says: December 1929, Molina y Ca., Casa Editora. NYPL.

Herbert Marks had heard the song while on a honeymoon in Cuba in 1928,[2] and on June 9, 1930,[1] an edition entitled *The Peanut Vendor (El Manisero)* was published, with English words by Louis Rittenberg, by Marks's firm, Edward B. Marks Music Co., New York, N.Y. On Aug. 20, 1930,[1] another edition was published with additional English words by Marion Sunshine. Moisés Simons (Rodríguez) was born in Havana in 1888[3] or 1890,[4] was a composer, lyricist and orchestra leader in Cuba and died in Madrid in 1945.

Peer Gynt—Grieg

m. Edvard Grieg. Excerpts from *Peer Gynt*, op. 23, were first published in March, 1876,[1] by C. C. Lose, Copenhagen: *Solveigs og Peer Gynts Sange*, for piano and voice, and *Dandse af Anitra og Pigerne* for piano. In May, 1876, *Mellemaktsmusik* and *Dandse hos Dovregubben*, and in June, 1876, *Dandse af Anitra og Pigerne*, were published for piano four hands. In the first edition of the first four titles, only these four titles were listed on the front cover; in a slightly later edition of the first four titles, and in the first edition of the fifth title, all five titles were listed. The text is in Norwegian. BOB* and JF*. The arrangements were by the composer, and there are references to Kristiania (the name of Oslo 1624–1925) and Stockholm agents. *Morgenstimmung* or *Morning Mood*, quoted above, is not included in any of the foregoing. *Peer Gynt* was composed to H. Ibsen's play in 1875 and performed Feb. 24, 1876, at Kristiania (Oslo).

[2] Information from Mr. Marks.
[3] Letter from PAU.
[4] Letter from SACEM.

[1] Dan Fog *Catalogue no. 197* (Copenhagen, 1969), no. 856; JF. Letter from Wilhelm Hansen, the successor publisher to C. C. Lose. See, generally, p. 65, above, and *Grieg Catalogue*, p. 6.

On Oct. 8, 1877,[2] *Peer Gynt*, still op. 23, arranged for piano four hands by the composer, was published by C. F. Peters, **Leipzig & Berlin,** and the following probable first edition was deposited at BM on Nov. 20, 1877: Oblong. Title page is brown, black and white, mentions H. Ibsen and has a baroque ornament. m. on pp. 2–37. p.n. 5956. p. 2 refers to Röder . . . Leipzig. p. [38] blank. Covers missing. *Morgenstimmung* is on p. 13. Also at BOB.

The first *Suite* from *Peer Gynt*, op. 46, for orchestra, which includes *Morgenstimmung*, was published about Oct., 1888,[3] by C. F. Peters, Leipzig—the orchestral score at 6 Mk. and the orchestral parts at 12 Mk. The orchestral score has plate number 7188; a possible first edition, but without covers, is at NYPL and JF (inscribed). The orchestral parts have plate number 7189; a possible first edition, also without covers, is at RAM.

The orchestral score of the complete *Peer Gynt* was published in 1908[4] by C. F. Peters, Leipzig. Probable first edition: Front cover states Edition Peters no. 3224 and is red, pink and black. vb. Title page refers to H. Ibsen, is black and white and the printer is C. G. Röder G.m.b.H., Leipzig. Text. Index. vb. m. on pp. 5–259. pp. [260] and [261] blank. Back cover advertises Edition Peters nos. to 3120. NYPL. Brief biographic information regarding Grieg appears above under *An den Frühling*.

Peg o' My Heart

Peg o' my heart, ———— I love you, we'll nev - er part, ———— I love you

m. Fred Fisher. w. Alfred Bryan. Published March 15, 1913,[1] by Leo. Feist, Inc., Feist Building, New York, N.Y. First edition: Front cover has a photograph of Laurette Taylor standing, refers to the comedy of the same name, mentions that it is the Prize Song and is light green, dark green and white. m. on pp. 2–5. p.n. 2997-4. p. 3 adv. *Old..* p. 4 adv. *Love..* Back cover adv. *I'll.. - You..* LC(CDC). "Inc." was added later on the front cover after Leo. Feist.

---

[2] According to the entry at Stationers' Hall on Oct. 31, 1877. Hofmeister *Monatsbericht,* Oct., 1877, p. 285.

[3] Hofmeister *Monatsbericht,* Oct., 1888, p. 394.

[4] Hofmeister *Annual,* 1908, p. 61.

---

[1] Copyright records; LC.

Fisher, a composer, lyricist and publisher, was born in Cologne, Germany, in 1875 and died in New York City in 1942.[2] Bryan, a lyricist, was born in Brantford, Ontario, in 1871 and died in Gladstone, N.J., in 1958.[3]

A Perfect Day

When you   come   to the end   of   a   per - fect day

© 1910. Used by permission of copyright owner, Boston Music Co., Boston.

mw. Carrie Jacobs-Bond. A large part of the words were first set to a different melody entitled *A Memory* and included in a tall, narrow booklet of songs by this composer entitled *The Smile Songs* which was published Feb. 10, 1910,[1] by P. F. Volland & Co., Chicago. LC(CDC) and JF.

The song in its present form was published April 29, 1910,[1] by Carrie Jacobs-Bond & Son, Incorporated, Fine Arts Building, Chicago, under the title *A Perfect Day*. First edition: Front cover has the words of the first stanza, a drawing of flowers and is brown, tan, pink and green. p. [2] blank. m. on pp. 3–6. P. 3 states "Sung by Mr. David Bispham" and indicates that the copyright was by the author. p. [7] and back cover blank. The Cello Obbligato is on a leaf; vb. LC(CDC) and JF. No keys on the front cover, and no reference to "Low" on inside pages.

A Perfect Day was composed at the Mission Inn, Riverside, Cal., in 1909. Brief biographic information regarding the author appears above under *I Love You Truly*.

Peter and the Wolf-March—Prokofiev

mw. Sergei Prokofiev. This work was published as a piano score about July–Sept., 1937,[1] under the Russian title Петя и Волк, and the French title

<hr />

[2] *ASCAP*, p. 158.

[3] *The New York Times*, Aug. 24, 1952, p. 34. *ASCAP*, p. 61. Obituary, *The New York Times*, April 2, 1958.

<hr />

[1] Copyright records; LC.

<hr />

[1] *AML*, July–Sept., 1937, p. 28. Nestyev, p. 509. Prokofiev, *Autobiography*, p. 300.

Pierre et le Loup, op. 67, by the State Music Publishers, Moscow. Probable
first edition: Front cover is in Russian and French, and blue and tan. vb.
Title page is also in Russian and French mentioning Moscow 1937. vb. m.
on pp. 3–44, the *March* on p. 41. p.n. 15277. The text is in Russian, French
and English. Back cover has price of 5 rub. 40 kop. and a number of dates
relating to the Soviet printing procedure, the last of which is in June 20,
1937. LUC, SSL and JF.

The orchestral score of this "Conte Symphonique pour Enfants" was
probably published in Dec., 1940,[2] by the same concern. Probable first
edition: Front cover is in Russian and French, and is blue and white. vb.
Title page is also in Russian and French, mentioning Moscow and Leningrad 1940. Story and orchestra composition. m. on pp. 3–79. p.n. 16066.
p. [80] lists a number of dates relating to Soviet printing procedure, the last
of which is Nov. 12, 1940. Back cover has price of 15 rub. 75 kop. LPL,
LUC and JL. No early printing of the orchestral parts has been noted.

The work was composed in 1936 and performed May 2, 1936, in Moscow. Brief biographic information regarding Prokofiev appears above under
The Love of Three Oranges—March.

Petite Tonkinoise

Je suis go-bé d'un' pe-ti-te   c'est une An - na, c'est une An-na, une An-na-mi - te

m. Vincent Scotto. w. Villard and Christiné. The following copy, a possible
first edition, was deposited July 30, 1906,[1] at LC by Christiné, 14 Passage
de l'Industrie, Paris. Front cover in blue and white has a photograph of
presumably Polin, the creator of the song, at the Ambassadeurs, mentions
Esther Lekain at the Folies-Bergère, has a dedication to Mlle Lucienne
Muguet and the price is 1f. 75. No agents in other countries listed. pp. [2]
and [3] blank. m. on pp. [4] and (5). p.n. 495. pp. [6] and [7] and back
cover blank. Folio. Included is a separate insert with melody line and words
only. LC(CDC). Christiné later published at 33 Faubourg St. Martin, Paris.

Scotto was born in Marseilles in 1874, became a composer and died in
Paris in 1952.[2] Villard is a pseudonym of Georges Lascombe, a lyricist, who

---

[2] *AML*, Oct.–Dec., 1940, p. 42. See, also, footnote 1.

[1] Copyright records; LC.
[2] Letter from representative.

was born in Marseilles in 1879 and who died in France in 1927.[3] Henri
Christiné, a composer of songs and operettas, was born in Geneva in 1867
and died in Nice in 1941.[4]

Pictures at an Exhibition—Mussorgsky

m. Modeste Mussorgsky. This work[1] was published for piano in late 1886–
early 1887,[2] under the combined Russian title, Картинки съ выставки,
and the French title, Tableaux d'une Exposition, by B. (sic) Bessel & Cie.,
St. Petersburg. Probable first edition: Front cover in Russian and French,
in gray and black, has a dedication to Vladimir Stassov, states that the
work is a series of 10 pieces, the price is three rubles, there is a border
design and there are references to Breitkopf & Härtel, Leipzig, and I.
Hamelle, Paris. vb. Title page same as front cover except in white, blue and
black. Page [2] has the story of the 10 pieces in Russian and French and
the censor's approval on Sept. 11, 1886. m. on pp. 3–34. p.n. 1560. The date
of composition, 1874, appears on page 3. The address of the Bessel printing plant on page 34 is 26 Troitski Alley. Inside of back cover has a catalogue of the publisher dated Jan. 19, 1887. Outside of back cover is blank.
BN and SSL. Later editions show one or more of the following changes,
among others: the publisher is shown at St. Petersburg and Moscow, the
music is on pages 3–33, the plate number is 1560* and the address of the
Bessel printing plant is 24[3] Troitski Street; copies at LC, John H. Hind,
Berkeley, Cal., and JF. Vladimir Stassov, the dedicatee, was the critic who
arranged a posthumous exhibition in 1873 of the paintings of Victor Alexander Hartmann, the subject of this musical composition.

---

[3] Letter from widow.
[4] Larousse XX, vol. 2, p. 247.

---

[1] The author is indebted to John H. Hind, Berkeley, Cal., for almost all the
information given regarding this work.
[2] The date of the censor's approval on page 2 is Sept. 11, 1886. The date of the
catalogue on the inside of the back cover is Jan. 19, 1887. Yury Keldysh and Vas.
Yakovlev, M. P. Mussorgsky, Stat'i i Materialy (Moscow, 1932), p. 297, say 1886; L.C.
Not in Hofmeister Annual, 1886–90.
[3] See above, A Night on the Bald Mountain, footnote 2.

There have been several transcriptions of this work for orchestra. Probably the most famous transcription, by Maurice Ravel, was performed in Paris under Sergei Koussevitzky's direction on May 3, 1923, and published on Nov. 16, 1929,[4] by Édition Russe de Musique, Paris, and five other cities; LC(CDC). Brief biographic information regarding Mussorgsky appears above under *A Night on the Bald Mountain.*

Pilgrims' Chorus—Tannhäuser

Be - glückt darf nun   dich,—o Hei - math, ich schau - en

mw. Richard Wagner. The first printing of the *Gesang der Älteren Pilger bei Ihrer Heimkehr* was in the orchestral score of *Tannhäuser* published about the end of Nov., 1845, by [C. F. Meser, Dresden].[1] First edition: The title is *Tannhäuser und der Sängerkrieg auf Wartburg,* the Partitur is "Als Manuscript von der Handschrift des Componisten auf Stein gedruckt" and mentions Dresden and the year 1845; no publisher or price. vb. Cast and index. vb. m. on pp. 1–450. The last page is signed and dated in lithography "Richard Wagner, Dresden, 13 April, 1845." Folio. *The Pilgrims' Chorus* is at p. 385. The first edition was limited to 100 copies. BM (Hirsch II, 955), BOP, HU, ONB, YU and JF. A similar orchestral score inscribed by Wagner to Schumann is at Richard Wagner-Gedenkstätte, Bayreuth, and one to Liszt is at Wahnfried, Bayreuth. Another copy at ONB has many additions in contemporary manuscript and bears Wagner's handwritten note that on Feb. 7, 1847, he conducted the thirteenth performance of this opera from this score.[1A]†

The piano-vocal score of the opera was not published until about Nov., 1846.[2] Probable first edition: Title page gives the price as 8 Thlr., and publisher is stated to be C. F. Meser, Dresden. vb. Half-title page. Cast and index. m. on pp. 3–263. p.n. 325. p. [264] blank. Music pages engraved. The *Pilgrims' Chorus* is at p. 226. Folio. This piano-vocal score also sets forth the first version of the opera. There are two variants of this edition: in the earlier, there is no mention on the Cast and index page of

---

[4] Copyright records; LC.

[1] *Signale,* fourth of five undated weeks in Nov., 1845, p. 380. Title page says 1845. Hofmeister *Monatsbericht,* Jan., 1846, p. 9. The publisher is not named in the orchestral score but is named in Hofmeister. The latter also gives the price as 12 Thlr.

[1A] Cecil Hopkinson, *Tannhäuser* (Tutzing, West Germany, 1973), p. 8; BM and JF. Klein, pp. 20–21.

[2] Hofmeister *Monatsbericht,* Nov., 1846, p. 178. Klein, pp. 22–23.

"Typendruck von G. B. Teubner in Leipzig"; copies at SC and JF. In the later variant, there is such mention; copy at BOD. There is such mention in the printing of the second version of the opera, with 273 pages. The three noted copies of the first version show a slightly different plate number on certain pages, e.g., plate number 325.9 on page 86. It is possible that the first printing has plate number 325 throughout, but no such copy has yet been located. The sheet music excerpt of the *Pilgrims' Chorus* was probably published at about the same time;[3] no copy has been found. There is no reason to believe that the *Overture*, which contains this melody, was published separately for orchestra or piano prior to the scores described above.

No printing of the orchestral parts by Meser has been found, but some pages of some of the parts at CI and MET* have plate number M (Meser?) 3500; most of these pages, however, have Adolf Fürstner, Berlin, plate numbers 2946, 4001 and/or 4301. All are lithographed and have covers.

Wagner himself paid for publishing the orchestral and piano-vocal scores of *Tannhäuser*. The opera was completed April 13, 1845, in Dresden, and performed there on Oct. 19, 1845.

The Paris version was written there in Jan., 1861, and performed there on March 13, 1861. The first edition of the piano-vocal score of the revised version was published by G. Flaxland, 4 Place de la Madeleine, Paris, about July 22, 1861,[4] at 15 francs with engraved music on pp. 2–344 and p.n. 435; BM, BN(CDC), Brandeis University, Waltham, Mass., JMM and JF (inscribed by the composer).

The orchestral parts of this revised version were published by Durand & Schoenewerk, 4 Place de la Madeleine, Paris, about 1885,[5] with plate number D.S. 4063; a lithographed set without covers, a possible first edition, is at RAM.

The orchestral score of this revised version was published in Dec., 1891,[6] by A. Durand et Fils, 4 Place de la Madeleine, Paris, in folio size, with plate number D.S. 4332. Possible first editions are at BM, RAM, UM, JMM and JF. No copy has been found with the publisher shown as Durand & Schoenewerk. Brief biographic information regarding Wagner appears above under *The Flying Dutchman—Overture*.

---

[3] Hofmeister, preceding footnote, p. 179.

[4] Entered for Dépôt Légal on July 22, 1861; Archives. *BF*, Aug. 10, 1861, p. 386.

[5] Hopkinson, *Parisian*, p. 40.

[6] Information from Jean-Marie Martin, Hollogne-aux-Pierres, Belgium.

Pizzicati—Sylvia

m. Léo Delibes. The ballet *Sylvia*, in which the *Pizzicati* appears, was published for piano about July 2, 1876,[1] by Heugel & Cie., au Ménestrel, 2 bis Rue Vivienne, Paris. First edition: Front cover is silver and light and dark ·green. vb. Half-title page. vb. Title page has the subtitle *La Nymphe de Diane*, mentions the first performance was in Paris on June 14, 1876, the price 10 francs and the year 1876. vb. Cast. vb. Drawing of Rita Sangalli as Sylvia. vb. Catalogue Thématique followed by two pages of themes. (All preceding pages in blue ink.) m. on pp. 1–147, *Divertissement—Pizzicati* on p. 116. p.n. 6041. p. [148] blank. BN(CDC), JMM (inscribed by the composer) and JF. The separate printing of *Pizzicati* for piano was published about the same time;[1] no first printing has been found.

The *Suite d'Orchestre* from *Sylvia* was entered for Dépôt Légal on May 8, 1879,[2] for orchestral parts and score by Heugel et Fils at the same address, *Pizzicati* being the third piece. The first edition of the orchestral parts has p.n. 6577; BN(CDC)*. Probable first edition of the orchestral score, probably published about the same time: Front cover is light and dark blue and lists three arrangements, the orchestral score and orchestral parts at 25 f. and supplementary parts at 2 f. vb. Title page is the same as front cover but in blue and white. vb. Half-title page. vb. Index. m. on pp. 1–105. p.n. 6577. p. [106] blank. Index and music pages engraved. Back cover lacking. BM*, BPL and JF.

Apparently the orchestral score of the entire ballet has not been published. Orchestral parts of the ballet, a lithographing of a manuscript, without plate number, folio, without covers, are at Heugel et Cie., Paris. Brief biographic information regarding Delibes appears above under *Bell Song*.

[1] *Le Ménestrel*, July 2, 1876, p. 256, lists the piano score, and also the *Pizzicati* at 4.50 fr. *Bib. Mus.*, Aug.–Sept., 1876, p. 299. The piano score was entered for Dépôt Légal on July 15, 1876; Archives.

[2] Archives. *BF*, June 7, 1879, p. 353. *Bib. Mus.*, July–Sept., 1880, p. 53, orchestral parts and score.

Play Gypsies-Dance Gypsies—Countess Maritza

Komm   Zi - gány, komm   Zi - gány, spiel   mir ins   Ohr_____
Play   gyp-sies, dance   gyp-sies,   play   while you   may_____

© 1924 and 1926 Harms, Inc. Copyright renewed. Used by permission.

m. Emmerich Kálmán. w. Julius Brammer and Alfred Grünwald. The first printing of *Gräfin Mariza* (*Countess Maritza*, as it is known in the United States), in which *Komm Zigány!* appears, was probably in the piano-vocal score of the operetta published about March, 1924, by W. Karczag, 36/38 Nürnbergerstrasse, Leipzig, and 6 Linke Wienzeile, Vienna. Possible first edition: Front cover has a drawing of a Countess in many colors and the publisher is shown also at New York. vb. Title page lists the piano score for two hands with accompanying text and the piano-vocal score, without prices, and mentions a 1924 copyright. Cast and index. m. on pp. 3–132, this song at p. 41. p.n. 1641. Back cover missing. JF.

The piano score for two hands with accompanying text, with p.n. 1656, was published March 14, 1924;[1] ONB, LC and JF. No first printing of the sheet music of *Komm Zigány!* with p.n. 1652, has been found.[2] *Gräfin Mariza* was performed on Feb. 28, 1924, in Vienna.

Play Gypsies—Dance Gypsies, with English words by Harry B. Smith, was published in 1926. Kálmán was born in Siofok, Hungary, in 1882 and died in Paris in 1953.[3] Brammer, a librettist, was born in 1877 in Schradice, Moravia (now part of Czechoslovakia), and died in 1943 in Juan-les-Pins, France.[4] Grünwald, a librettist and playwright, was born in Vienna, came to the United States in 1940 and died at the age of sixty-seven in Forest Hills, L.I., N.Y., in 1951.[5]

---

[1] Copyright records; LC. Hofmeister *Monatsbericht*, June, 1924, p. 84. It is possible that the piano score was published prior to the piano-vocal score, as the former contains only the Vorspiel and 16 numbers, whereas the latter adds nos. 7a, 10a, 10b, 13a, 13½, 13¾ and 14½.

[2] Also in Hofmeister, preceding footnote.

[3] Steger-Howe, p. 59.

[4] Information from AKM.

[5] Obituary, *The New York Times*, Feb. 25, 1951.

Poëm—Fibich

m. Zdenko Fibich. This melody was published about March, 1895,[1] for piano in Part IV, no. 14, of *Nálady, Dojmy a Upomínky, Stimmungen, Eindrücke und Erinnerungen* (meaning "Moods, Impressions and Reminiscences"), "Little Pieces," op. 41, by Fr. A. Urbánek, Prague. Probable first edition: Title page of part IV (*Upomínky-Erinnerungen*) is blue, black and white, says number 13,313 and has no price. vb. m. on pp. 3–46; this piece, without special title, is no. 14 of part IV, and no. 139 of the entire set, on p. 16, with its own date (presumably, of composition) April 13, 1893. NYPL.

The melody was then included in the symphonic poem *V Podvečer, Am Abend*, published in orchestral score, op. 39, about March, 1896,[2] by the same concern. Probable first edition: Front cover is red, gray and black, with the prices of 8 K. and 8 Mk. vb. Title page is brown, gray and white. vb. m. on pp. 3–47, this melody at p. 22. p.n. 933; p. 47 says 13989. p. [48] blank. Inside and outside of back cover blank. BM, NYPL and JF.

The *Poëm*, an arrangement of the melody for violin and piano, was published about Oct.–Nov., 1909,[3] by the same concern. First edition: Front cover, in English, has a photograph (presumably of the composer), states that the arrangement is by Jan Kubelík, refers to a Kiev agent, has the prices of 1 K 80 h and 1 Mk 50 Pf., gives the publisher's Prague address as next to the National Theater, and is green, gray and black. vb. Title page is the same as the front cover except in green, tan and black. m. on pp. 2–3. p.n. 1551. p. [4] blank. Inside of back cover blank. Outside of back cover adv. Dvorak–Wittich. Violin part on p. 1; p. [2] blank. LC(CDC) and JF.

Fibich, a composer, was born in Šebořice in 1850 and died in Prague in 1900.[4]

---

[1] Hofmeister *Monatsbericht*, March, 1895, p. 92.

[2] *Id.*, March, 1896, p. 91.

[3] Copyright copy deposited Nov. 18, 1909, at LC. Hofmeister *Monatsbericht*, Jan., 1910, p. 4.

[4] *Grove's*, vol. 3, p. 79.

Poet and Peasant-Overture—Suppé

m. Fr. v. Suppé. The *Overture* to *Dichter und Bauer* was published about May, 1854,[1] for piano four hands and for piano by Jos. Aibl, Munich. Possible first edition of the arrangement for piano four hands: Oblong. Title page mentions the arranger is C. T. Brunner and lists the two arrangements, the price of this arrangement being Fl. 1. 21 Kr./ 22½ Ngr., and there is a Leipzig agent under which there is a one-line notice. m. on pp. 2–17. p. [18] blank. p.n. 1227. Not engraved. SCH and JF.

Possible first edition of the arrangement of the *Overture* for piano: Upright. Title page is the same as that described above, the price of this arrangement being 54 Kr./ 15 Ngr. m. on pp. 3–11. p.n. 1228. Not engraved. SB. A variant edition with a two-line notice under the Leipzig agent is at NYPL.

About June, 1854,[2] the *Overture* was published for 8-, 12- and 15-part orchestras by the same concern. A probable first edition with a collective title front cover (of which this is no. 25), prices of Fl. 4.30 Kr. and Thlr. 2.15 Ngr., engraved pages and p.n. 1033 is at BSM. About Jan., 1865,[3] the *Overture* was published by the same concern for large orchestra—both orchestral parts and orchestral score. A probable first edition of the 23 orchestral parts, with prices of Fl. 6.18 Kr. and Thlr. 3.15 Ngr., engraved pages and p.n. 1033 or 1702 is at BSM. A "Neue Ausgabe" of the orchestral score, with p.n. 1766, is at LLD.

Dichter und Bauer, a "Posse" or comical play with incidental music, was performed Aug. 24, 1846, in Vienna. Neither a piano-vocal score nor orchestral score or parts of the play have been published (but the *Overture* has been published by Aibl for at least 59 different combinations of instruments!). Brief biographic information regarding Suppé appears above under *Light Cavalry—Overture*.

---

[1] Hofmeister *Monatsbericht*, May, 1854, p. 544. A later edition of the *Overture* for piano, at SCH, lists many arrangements of the *Overture* with their p.ns. One such arrangement is said to have p.n. 788 and is for piano four hands, violin, flute and cello; it has not been possible to date this arrangement (which may be earlier than the two piano arrangements mentioned above), and no copy has been found.

[2] *Id.*, June, 1854, p. 558.

[3] *Id.*, Jan., 1865, p. 2.

Polka, Schwanda—Weinberger

m. Jaromír Weinberger. The *Polka* was included in the piano-vocal score of *Švanda Dudák—Schwanda, der Dudelsackpfeifer* published March 31, 1928,[1] by Universal-Edition A.G., Vienna and Leipzig. First edition: Front cover has the usual Universal-Edition format in light and dark green with no. 8967. vb. Title page is plain, states that the text is by Miloš Kareš and the translation by Max Brod, has legal and copyright claims and says printed in Austria. Cast and other information. m. on pp. 3–288, the *Polka* at p. 112. p.n. 8967. Czech and German text throughout. Inside back cover blank. Outside back cover adv. *Opern.*. Nr. 48, II. 1928 (probably, Feb., 1928). LC(CDC), BM, ONB and JF*. The *Polka*, separately, for piano, with plate number 9693, was probably published later; early edition at JF.

The orchestral score of the opera claims a 1929 copyright by the same publisher. Probable first edition: Front cover and title page are similar to those of the piano-vocal title page except the Universal-Edition no. is 8824. Verso of each blank. No intermediate page. Vol. 1 has music on pp. [1]–454; vol. 2 has music on pp. [1]–295, with p. [296] blank. The *Polka* is in vol. 1, p. 226. p.n. 8824. Folio. BM, JMM and ONB. An early set of the orchestral parts of the opera, with plate number 9331, is for rental at G. Schirmer, New York City.

The title of the opera means "Schwanda, the Bagpiper." The opera was performed in Prague on April 27, 1927. Weinberger was born in Prague in 1896, left Czechoslovakia in 1939, settled permanently in the United States and died in St. Petersburg, Fla., in 1967.[2]

Polly-Wolly-Doodle

Oh, I went down south for to see my gal, sing_ Pol-ly Wol-ly Doo-dle all the day

[1] Copyrights records; LC. Hofmeister *Monatsbericht*, May, 1928, p. 129.
[2] Obituary, *The New York Times*, Aug. 11, 1967.

This song with its references to the South and Louisiana is believed to be American in origin, perhaps Negro and minstrel.[1] The first known appearance of the music and words is in *Students' Songs*, published and arranged by Harvard Students, and copyrighted June 9, 1880,[2] by S. P. Clarke [Boston], p. 10; HU.

Polonaise, op. 53—Chopin

m. F. Chopin. This piano composition was probably first published by Breitkopf & Härtel, Leipzig, under the title *Polonoise* [sic], Nov. 14–20, 1843.[1] Possible first edition: Front cover has a dedication to Monsieur Auguste Leo, the price is 1 Thlr. and there are references to Paris and London copublishers. vb. m. on pp. 3–19, engraved. p.n. 7002. Back cover blank. ONB, AT and JF. A similar copy is at LC with wrappers in blue and black, the outside back cover of which advertises Chopin's works up to op. 65.

The French edition was published about Dec. 14, 1843,[2] by Mce. Schlesinger, 97 Rue Richelieu, Paris, under the title *Grande Polonaise Brillante*. Possible first edition: Front cover has the same dedication (Léo with

---

[1] *North Carolina F.*, vol. III, p. 538. Compare the first eight bars of *Lord, Remember Me* in *Slave Songs of the United States* (New York, N.Y., 1867), p. 12, at LC; Harold Barlow, New York City, furnished this information. *Polly-Wolly-Doodle* is similar to *Needle's Eye* as set forth in William A. Owens, *Swing and Turn* (Dallas, Texas, 1936), p. 9, at NYPL. No earlier American printing of this version of *Needle's Eye* is known. No early English printing of any version of *Needle's Eye* is known; letter from The English Folk Dance and Song Society, London.

[2] Copyright records; LC.

---

[1] *AMZ*, Nov. 22, 1843, pp. 783 and 855, so state. Whistling, *Musikalischer Monatsanzeiger*, Dec., 1843, p. 229; SBW. Hofmeister *Monatsbericht*, Dec., 1843, p. 182. The German, French and English dates given above generally coincide with those given in Brown, p. 142. See, in general, *Chopin Works*, vol. VIII, p. 146.

[2] Copies were deposited Dec. 14, 1843, for Dépôt Légal; Archives. *RGM*, Dec. 24, 1843, p. 438. *BF*, March 23, 1844, p. 148.

an accent), the price is 7f. 50 and there are references to London and Leipzig copublishers. **(See Plate III.)** Next two pages blank. m. on pp. 2–11. p.n. 3958. p. [12] blank. Engraved. HU and JF. This edition is believed earlier than the otherwise identical edition entitled *8ᵉ Polonaise;*[2A] BMI.

The English edition does not appear to have been published until about April 16, 1845,[3] by Wessel & Co., 67 Frith Street, Corner of Soho Square, London, as no. 57 in its Complete Collection of the Compositions of Frederic Chopin, *Eighth Polonoise* [sic]. Probable first edition: Front cover is a collective title front cover listing up to op. 56 (op. nos. 54–56 also being advertised in April, 1845) and gives the price as 3/6. vb. m. on pp. 1–11. p.n. 5306. Previous pages engraved. Back cover adv. *Page A.*. BM (copyright copy deposited April 16, 1845) and JF*. The *Polonaise* was composed in 1842. It was used in 1945 for the song *Till the End of Time.* Brief biographic information regarding Chopin appears above under his *Etude.*

Polonaise Militaire, op. 40—Chopin

m. Fréd. Chopin. The *Polonaise Militaire* was probably first published by Breitkopf & Härtel, Leipzig, as no. 1 of *Deux Polonoises* [sic] for piano about Nov. 11, 1840.[1] Probable first edition: Front cover has a dedication to Jules Fontana, the price is 16 **Gr.**, and there are references to Paris and

---

[2A] The title of the copy deposited for Dépôt Légal is *Grande Polonaise Brillante;* the title advertised in *RGM* is *Huitième Polonaise Brillante,* which includes elements of the titles of both French editions; the BMI copy, not presently available for further comparison, has the rubber stamp of Brandus et Cie, which commenced business in 1846, whereas the HU and JF copies have the earlier rubber stamp of Maurice Schlesinger; and Maurice J. E. Brown, London, believes the BMI edition is a later collected edition.

[3] Copyright copy deposited that day at BM. *MW,* April 24, 1845, p. 193.

[1] *AMZ,* Nov. 11, 1840, p. 959. Whistling, *Musikalischer Monatsanzeiger,* Nov., 1840, p. 191; ONB. Hofmeister *Monatsbericht,* Dec., 1840, p. 165; BM. Owing to the latter, Brown, p. 116, gives the date of German publication as Dec., 1840; his French and English dates generally coincide with those given above. Niecks, vol. II, p. 348, gives Nov., 1840, as the German date. See, in general, *Chopin Works,* vol. VIII, p. 142.

Grove's, vol. 2, p. 265, says that this composition was first published separately by an unspecified publisher with a dedication to Titus Woyciehowski; this seems an error.

London copublishers. vb. m. on pp. 3–11, engraved. "Polonaise No. 1" is on p. 3. p.n. 6331. Back cover blank. ONB and JF.

The French edition was published about Dec., 1840, by E. Troupenas & Cie, 40 Rue Neuve Vivienne, Paris, under the title *Deux Polonaises*. First edition: Front cover has the same dedication, abbreviates Chopin's first name without an accent, the price is 6f. and there are references to London and Leipzig copublishers. Next two pages blank. m. on pp. 2–9. p.n. 977. Back cover blank. Engraved. COP(copyright copy deposited Dec., 1840)[2] and BM.

The English edition does not appear to have been published until about Nov. 18, 1841,[3] when Wessel & Co., 67 Frith Street, Corner of Soho Square, London, printed it as no. 43 in its Complete Collection of the Compositions of Frederic Chopin, *Les Favorites*. Possible first edition: Front cover is a collective title front cover listing up to op. 42 (op. nos. 40 and 41 having been previously published) and gives the price as 4/. vb. m. on pp. 1–13. p.n. 3557. Previous pages engraved. Back cover adv. *Page E.*. JF. A copy at BM, purchased Feb. 26, 1853, lacks the front cover, has the same music pages as described and has a back cover advertising *Page A.*. with an (earlier) address, 6 Frith Street. The *Polonaise* was composed Oct., 1838. Brief biographic information regarding Chopin appears above under his *Etude*.

Polovtsian Dances—Prince Igor

Oo–lyeh-tahee.nah.krihl-yakh vyeht–rah..tih vkrahee rawd–noy rawd-nah-yah pyess-nyah   nah-shał

mw. A. Borodin. A copy of the orchestral score of Князь Игорь (*Prince Igor*), inscribed by M. P. Belaieff, Leipzig, the publisher, and dated by him Dec. 3, 1888, establishes the publication of that score by that date.[1] Probable first edition: Title page is in Russian only and has a drawing of military objects in many colors. vb. Dedication to Ubanobura. vb. Portrait of the composer with a few bars of music. vb. Notices in Russian and French. Index and cast in Russian, French and German. m. on pp. 1–667.

---

[2] According to Niecks, vol. II, p. 348, but no such copyright deposit copy has been found.

[3] *MW*, Nov. 18, 1841, p. 335.

[1] The orchestral score, orchestral parts and piano-vocal score of the opera (at M.30), and the orchestral score and orchestral parts of the *Polovtsian Dances* are listed in Hofmeister *Monatsbericht*, Feb., 1889, pp. 50 and 79. The *Polovtsian Dances and Chorus* for piano is in the April, 1889, issue, p. 161; copy at JF. See, also, Belaieff *Catalogue*, Leipzig, 1895, p. 26; NYPL.

Text in Russian only. No. 17, *Половецкая Пляска съ Хоромъ* (*Polovtsian Dances and Chorus*) on p. 351. p.n. 115. p. [668] blank. SSL. Another copy of this edition also has a front cover in many colors, in Russian, French and German, listing seven arrangements (only six with prices), the orchestral score priced at M. 240/R. 120, changed in ink to 180/63, and adding A. Büttner, St. Petersburg, to the imprint; vb. COP.

The orchestral parts of the opera, with plate number 116, were published at about the same time at M. 180/R. 90;[1] an early set, with plate numbers 116–142, without covers, is at MAP.

The piano-vocal score of the opera was published at about the same time.[1] Probable first edition: Many-colored title page in Russian. vb. Dedication to Ubanobura. vb. Portrait of the composer with a few bars of music. vb. Four notes from the publisher in Russian and French. Index and cast in Russian, French and German. m. on pp. I–XVI and 1–372. Text in Russian, French and German.†

. The music of the *Polovtsian Dances* was performed in concert version on March 11, 1879, in St. Petersburg, but the opera was not completed by Borodin before his death and had to be completed after his death by Rimsky-Korsakov and Glazunov. The opera was performed on Nov. 4, 1890, in St. Petersburg. Alexander Borodin was born in St. Petersburg in 1834 and died there on Feb. 28, 1887. The above melody of the *Polovtsian Dances* was used in 1953 for a popular song entitled *Stranger in Paradise*.

Pomp and Circumstance—Elgar

(Land of   Hope_ and   Glo - ry,   Mother   of__ the   Free _____)

m. Edward Elgar. *Pomp and Circumstance*, Military Marches for Full Orchestra, op. 39, no. 1, Quick March in D Major, was copyrighted in the United States on Oct. 25, 1901,[1] and an arrangement for orchestral parts deposited that day at LC by Boosey & Co., 295 Regent Street, London W., and 9 East Seventeenth Street, New York. First edition: Folio. Front cover in gray and black lists the two *Quick Marches*, no price or other arrangements, and there is a 1901 copyright notice followed by four lines of other notices. vb. p.n. 3354 (and a separate letter for each instrument). Inside and outside of back cover blank. Not engraved and appears to be a regular

[1] Copyright records; LC.

trade edition. LC(CDC). The *March* was composed at Birchwood in July, 1901, and performed in Liverpool on Oct. 19, 1901.

The orchestral score of this March was deposited Jan. 21, 1902,[1] at LC. Folio. Front cover has a dedication to Alfred E. Rodewald and the members of the Liverpool Orchestral Society, lists the two *Quick Marches*, the price is five shillings, the only other arrangements listed are band parts at 12/6 and pianoforte arrangement at 2/, and there is a 1902 copyright notice. vb. m. on pp. 1–26. p.n. 3413. Back cover missing. Engraved and almost certainly a proof copy.† On the same day[1] there was deposited at LC an arrangement for pianoforte; no price or other arrangements listed; engraved and also presumably a proof copy.

The phrase "Pride, pomp and circumstance" occurs in *Othello*, act III, scene iii.

On May 22, 1902,[1] the *Coronation Ode* was deposited at LC with words by Arthur Christopher Benson, and arranged for piano and chorus. First edition: Octavo. Gray and black front cover. vb. Title page says that the work was "Composed for the **Grand Opera Syndicate, Covent Garden, for the State Performance, July 1st, 1902,**"[2] gives the op. no. as 44 and the price as 2/6, and there is a 1902 copyright notice. vb. Words on five unnumbered pages. m. on pp. 2–80 (engraved, probably an advance copy). p.n. 3608. Back cover missing. LC(CDC). The orchestral score was deposited at LC July 17, 1902.[1] First edition: Folio; price. 15/; there is a handsome dedication page to King Edward VII; m. on pp. 1–65; no p.n. or arrangements. A regular trade edition. LC(CDC). The *Coronation Ode* was performed at Sheffield on Oct. 2, 1902.

Land of Hope and Glory, the same music arranged for piano to considerably different words by Arthur C. Benson, was deposited at LC on June 26, 1902.[1,3] Folio. No arrangements or keys. Price is 2/. p. [2] blank. m. on pp. 1–9 (actually 3–11). p.n. 3670. pp. [10], [11] and back cover blank. Engraved and almost certainly a proof copy. LC(CDC).

The same publisher's imprint appears on all the above editions. No copy of any of the foregoing compositions or arrangements was deposited at BM until July 15, 1902. Elgar was born in Broadheath, near Worcester, in 1857 and died in Worcester in 1934.[4] Benson, a man of letters, was born in Crowthorne, Berkshire, England, in 1862 and died in Cambridge in 1925.[5]

---

[2] Edward VII's coronation was set for June 26, 1902, but was postponed because of his illness until Aug. 9, 1902.

[3] The date of publication was June 25, 1902, according to the entry at Stationers' Hall on March 13, 1906 [sic].

[4] Percy M. Young, *Elgar O. M.* (London, 1955), p. 99; NYPL.

[5] *Dict. Nat. Biog.*, 1922–1930 (London, 1937), p. 76.

Pop Goes the Weasel

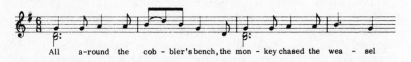

All   a-round the   cob - bler's bench, the mon - key chased the wea - sel

The melody, probably originally used to accompany an old English dance, was possibly first published under the title *Pop Goes the Weasel* by Boosey & Sons, 28 Holles Street, Oxford Street, London, and a copy of this edition was deposited at BM on March 14, 1853. Possible first edition: Engraved. Front cover states that *Pop Goes the Weasel* is an old English dance, the price is 1s and two other titles are mentioned. m. on p. 2, the only words being the words of the title. p. 3 has instructions for doing the dance. Back cover blank. BM(CDC). The melody is slightly different from the one presently known.

Pop Goes the Weasel could also have been first printed in the United States, as Berry & Gordon, 297 Broadway, New York, N.Y., published a song version with this name with an 1853 copyright claim; however, there is no copyright record at LC showing the exact date of copyright. The melody is the common melody, but the words are not familiar. Possible first edition, engraved, at JF. Another edition of *Pop Goes the Weasel* was published with an 1853 copyright claim by T. C. Andrews, 66 Spring Garden St., Philadelphia, but there is no copyright record at LC showing the exact date of copyright. The sheet music states that "This is an old and very animated English dance that has lately been revived among the higher classes of Society" and "Lately introduced at Her Majesty's . . . Balls." This piece is listed as the first of "Gems of the Ball Room," contains instructions for doing the dance and has the common melody without words. Possible first editions, engraved, at LC and JF. Other American editions, at LC and JF, followed shortly.

The common words apparently are American. In L. O. Emerson, *The Golden Wreath* (Boston, 1856), p. 196, appear to the second part of the common music: "All around the Cobbler's house, The monkey chased the people, And after them in double haste, Pop, went the Weasel." BPL, LC(CDC) and Diana R. Tillson, New Canaan, Conn.†

In *Old Songs for Young America*, harmonized by Clarence Forsythe (New York, N.Y., 1901), p. 13, appear to the common music: "All around the chicken coop, The possum chased the weasel, That's the way the money went, Pop, goes the Weasel! A penny etc." LC(CDC). In *The Family Music Book* (New York, N.Y., 1914), p. 619, appear the music and the words as they are commonly known today; LC and NYPL.

The "weasel" was originally a metal tool used by hatmakers in England which was popped (i.e., pawned).[1] In the American words, however, the weasel is unmistakably an animal.†

Poupée Valsante—Poldini

m. Ed. Poldini. The following edition of *Marionettes* for piano, in which *Poupée Valsante* is the second number, was deposited Aug. 13, 1895, by G. Ricordi & C. with the Prefect of Milan[1] (which copy so dated is now at S. Cecilia, Rome), and is probably a first edition: Front cover is in many colors. vb. Title page in blue and white has a dedication to Arthur Nikisch (corrected in later editions to Nikisc), the price is 5 Fr. and the publisher is shown at Milan, Rome, Naples, Palermo, London and Paris, 12 Rue de Lisbonne. Ars et labor. Index. vb. m. on pp. 1–36. p.n. 98302. *Poupée Valsante* is on p. 6 with a drawing of a dancing doll in yellow and black. pp. [37]–[39] blank. Back cover: Ars et labor in gray and white. SCR (CDC).

Poldini was born in Budapest in 1869, lived in Switzerland most of his life as a composer, and died in Vevey, Switzerland, in 1957.[2]

Praise the Lord and Pass the Ammunition!!

Praise the Lord, and pass the am - mu - ni-tion! Praise the Lord

mw. Frank Loesser. Published Aug. 21, 1942,[1] by Famous Music Corp., 1619 Broadway, New York, N.Y., the copyright deposit copy at LC being a professional edition. Possible first regular edition: Front cover has a drawing of troops passing ammunition, there is an exhortation to "Buy war bonds and stamps for victory" and the colors are red, white and black. p. [2] describes the story behind this song. m. on pp. [3]–5. No plate number. Back cover tells about Kay Kyser. JF (autographed).

---

[1] Gomme, vol. II, p. 63. *Ozark*, vol. III, p. 368.

[1] Copyright records; UDP. Breitkopf & Härtel *Musik-Verlagsbericht*, Leipzig, 1895, p. 18; NYPL.

[2] *Riemann*, vol. II, p. 424.

[1] Copyright records; LC.

Chaplain William Maguire's famous words spoken on a U.S. Navy warship during the Japanese sneak attack on Pearl Harbor inspired the title of this World War II song. Brief biographic information regarding Loesser appears above under *Guys and Dolls*.

Prayer of Thanksgiving (We Gather Together)

As a thanksgiving song for the victory in 1597 of Prince Maurice of Orange, a founder of the Dutch Republic, in the Spanish War, Adrianus Valerius wrote new words to a melody that was well known at the time. The new words commenced "Wilt heden Nu treden Voor God den Heere" (meaning, "We will today now step before God the Lord"), and the then well-known melody was *Hey Wilder dan Wild* (meaning, *Wilder than Wild*).[1] The words and melody were included in Adrianus Valerius, *Nederlandtsche Gedenck-Clanck* (meaning, *Netherlands' Remembered Sounds*) (Haarlem, 1626), p. 170. *RISM*, p. 494. No earlier printing of the melody under any title is known.

After six of the Dutch songs had been arranged by Eduard Kremser for men's chorus about Feb., 1878,[2] with German words, an English tranlation by Dr. Theodore Baker was copyrighted on Dec. 29, 1894[3] for mixed voices by G. Schirmer, New York, N.Y. The latter version by Dr. Baker is the version now sung in the United States. Possible first edition of the English version: Front cover is a collective title front cover of Octavo Choruses for mixed voices, in green and white, this being no. 632, at 35[¢], designated "Six Ancient Folksongs of the Netherlands (A.D. 1626)." vb. m. on pp. 3–30. p.n. 16090. No. 6, *Prayer of Thanksgiving* is on p. 26. Inside of back cover blank. Back cover adv. up to no. 600. NYPL.

The song has been very popular in Holland over the centuries as a religious battle song, and was sung particularly during World War II until

---

[1] Fl. van Duyse, *Het Oude Nederlandsche Lied* (Antwerp, 1903), vol. 1, p. [550]; NYPL.

[2] Hofmeister *Monatsbericht*, Feb., 1878, p. 64, with German words by Joseph Weyl and published by Schrottenbach & Co., Vienna. An early edition published by F. E. C. Leuckart, Leipzig, is at GM and NYPL.

[3] Copyright records; LC.

the Nazis forbade it. Valerius was born in Middelburg in 1575, became a lawyer, poet, musician and historian, and died in Veere in 1625.[4] Baker was born in New York City in 1851, became a literary editor with G. Schirmer and died in Dresden in 1934.[4]

Prelude, op. 28, no. 7—Chopin

m. Fréd. Chopin. The *Preludes*, op. 28, seem to have been published about the same time in Paris, Leipzig and London. A copy of the French edition was deposited in Aug.–Sept., 1839,[1] at the Conservatoire, Paris; by Ad. Catelin et Cie., 26 Rue Grange Batelière, Paris, under the title *24 Préludes*. First edition: Front cover mentions no opus number, has a dedication to Camille Pleyel, the price is 7 f. 50 and there are references to the London and Leipzig copublishers. Next two pages blank. m. on pp. 2–17, no. 7 on p. 9, of vol. I. p.n. 560. Vol. II has same front cover and p.n. m. on pp. 2–25. Engraved. COP(CDC); also at BN (not copyright deposit copy) and AT.

The German edition was published about Sept. 11, 1839,[2] by Breitkopf & Härtel, Leipzig, under the title *Vingt-quatre Préludes*. There are two variants, priority unknown. In each, the front cover is in blue and black. vb. Title page has a dedication to J. C. Kessler, mentions that it is oeuvre 28, and there is a strange reference to Pleyel & Co., Paris, as a copublisher. Next two pages blank. m. on pp. 4–39, engraved, no. 7 on p. 10. p.n. 6088. p. [40] and inside of back cover blank. In one variant, the price is 2 Rthlr., the price mentioned in Hofmeister; ONB (outside of back cover adv. various works, including Chopin up to op. 34 [1838]) and JF. In the other variant, with a restyled title page, the price is 2 Thlr., the price mentioned in *AMZ*;[2] BM (copy purchased Sept. 18, 1857) and NYPL.

The English edition was entered Aug. 30, 1839,[3] at Stationers' Hall by

---

[4] *Grove's*, vol. 8, p. 655, and vol. 1, p. 360.

[1] The copy states September, but the handwritten list of Dépôt Légal music received at BN states August. Brown, p. 102, gives June, 1839, for the French edition on the basis of an announcement in a Polish journal, *Gazeta Lwówska*, Lwów, on June 22, 1839 (Sydow, p. 68, no. 748), which Brown believes refers to the French edition. Niecks, vol. II, p. 352, also gives Sept., 1839. See, in general, *Chopin Works*, vol. I, p. 71.

[2] *AMZ*, Sept., 11, 1839, p. 731. Hofmeister *Monatsbericht*, Sept., 1839, p. 117.

[3] Brown gives Jan., 1840, on the basis of the advertisement in *MW*, Jan. 23, 1840, p. 62. See, also, Brown, *Corrections*, p. 30.

Wessel & Co., 67 Frith Street, Corner of Soho Square, London, under the
title *Twenty Four Grand Preludes*. Possible first edition: Front cover has a
dedication to Camille Pleyel, the op. no. is blank in the first book, the price
is 6/- ea., and there are references to Catelin & Co., Paris, and Breitkopf &
Co. [sic], Leipzig. Next two pages blank. m. on pp. 2–20, no. 7 on p. 9.
p.n. 3098. Front cover of the second book states op. 28. vb. Next page
advertises *Page A.*. with the (earlier) address of 6 Frith Street. m. on pp. 2–
24. p.n. 3099. p. [25] blank. Engraved except for the advertisement page.
JF. The *Preludes* were composed from 1836 to Nov., 1838. Brief biographic
information regarding Chopin appears above under his *Etude*.

Prelude in C Sharp Minor—Rachmaninoff

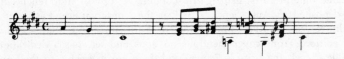

m. S. Rachmaninoff. This *Prelude* was included as no. 2 *Prélude* in *Morceaux de Fantaisie* for piano, op. 3, published in 1893[1] by A. Gutheil, 10
au Pont des Maréchaux Maison Junker, Moscow. Probable first edition:
Front cover in blue, black and white says Édition Gutheil, has a dedication
to Monsieur A. Arensky, five numbers are listed from op. 3, the *Prélude* at
40 c., and there are references to the agents, A. Iohansen, 44 Perspective
de Nevsky,[2] St. Petersburg, and L. Idzikowski, Kiev. m. on pp. 2–5. p.n.
6516. Back cover blank. In French throughout. No additional arrangements
of the *Prelude* on the front cover. CUL.

The *Prelude* was composed by Rachmaninoff in 1892 at the age of
nineteen, and performed Sept. 26, 1892, in Moscow. Brief biographic information regarding Rachmaninoff appears above under his *Concerto for
Piano no. 2*.

Prélude à l'Après-Midi d'un Faune—Debussy

[1] Bertensson-Leyda, p. 405.
[2] A later edition shows Iohansen's at 50 Perspective de Nevsky; GL and JF. SSL
has written the author that A. Iohansen was at 44 Perspective de Nevsky until 1895;
in the 1896 St. Petersburg directory he is shown at both 44 and 50 Perspective de
Nevsky; and commencing in 1897 he is shown at 50 Perspective de Nevsky. This super-
sedes Hopkinson, *Russian*, p. 5.

m. Claude Debussy. Published for orchestral score and orchestral parts not later than Oct., 1895,† by Eugène Fromont, Boulevard Malesherbes, 40 Rue d'Anjou, Paris. Possible first edition of the orchestral score: Front cover is red and green. vb. Title page in red, black and white has a dedication to Raymond Bonheur, states Églogue de S. Mallarmé, lists the orchestral score at 10 fr., the orchestral parts at 15 fr., supplementary parts at 1.50 fr. and piano four hands at 6 fr. vb. m. on pp. 1–31. p.n. 1091. pp. [32]–[34] blank. No page listing Debussy's compositions, particularly *Suite Bergamasque* (1905), included. Inside and outside of back cover blank. BPL. HMA, JMM and JF.

No complete first edition of the orchestral parts has been found. Possible first editions with plate number 1119, but without covers, are at CI and RAM. A probable first edition for piano four hands arranged by the composer, with plate number 1094, is at SC. The work was composed in 1892–1894 and performed in Paris on Dec. 22, 1894. Brief biographic information regarding Debussy appears above under *Clair de Lune*.

Prelude, Parsifal—Wagner

m. Richard Wagner. The piano-vocal score of *Parsifal* was published April 25–May 1, 1882,[1] by B. Schott's Söhne, Mainz. First edition: The title page refers to *Parsifal* as "Ein Bühnenweihfestspiel," mentions that the piano arrangement is by Joseph Rubinstein, has legal notices, refers to affiliates of the publisher in three other cities and a Leipzig agent, states that the work was entered in Stationers' Hall and has plate number 23406; no price. vb. Cast. m. on pp. 2–261. p. [262] blank. Folio. Lithographed.[2]

The Schott *Auslieferungslager* states that on April 25, 1882, 1,000 lithographed copies and 20 "Kupferdr." (copperplate, i.e., engraved) copies were published; the lithographed copies were listed before the engraved copies. Schott also published a "Verzeichniss der Druckfehler" (list of errata) in the first printing, some of which printing errors were corrected in the "2nd edition"; for example, on page 5, 6th stave, 1st bar, left hand, the

---

[1] Letter from successor publisher. Vallas, p. lviii.

[1] Letter from Schott to Wagner dated May 1, 1882; Strecker, p. 233. The same date is stated in the entry at Stationers' Hall on May 9, 1882. Hofmeister *Monatsbericht*, Sept. 1882, p. 282.

[2] The copy stated in *The Mary Flagler Cary Music Collection* (New York, N.Y., 1970), p. 14, at PML, to be "engraved throughout" is incorrectly described. It is lithographed throughout.

first note is erroneously E flat—corrected in the 2nd edition to B flat. Verzeichniss at Ulrich Drüner, Stuttgart; copy at JF.†

The orchestral score of *Parsifal* was published Oct. 6, 1882–1884[3] by the same concern. First edition: The title page is similar to that of the piano-vocal score, omitting the reference to Rubinstein, substituting the plate number 23571 and having additional legal notices. vb. Cast. vb. m. on pp. 1–377. p. [378] blank. Folio. Engraved, except for the title page. BM (Hirsch II 941), NYPL (copy no. 43 dated July 16, 1885, and received by NYPL Oct. 15, 1885) and JF (copy no. 16).‡ Copy no. 52 is lithographed; BM (636 i). The *Vorspiel* or *Prelude*, separately, was published in orchestral score and parts about Oct., 1882;[4] a posssible first printing, engraved, incomplete, of the orchestral parts, is at JF.

The earliest orchestral parts of the opera that have been found, possibly their first printing, have plate number 23703 and covers, and are lithographed (1882–6);[5] CI and MET. *Parsifal* was performed in Bayreuth on July 26, 1882. Brief biographic information regarding Wagner appears above under *The Flying Dutchman—Overture*.

Les Préludes—Liszt

m. F. Liszt. Published in orchestral score about April–May, 1856,[1] as no. 3, *Les Préludes* (nach Lamartine) in *Symphonische Dichtungen* für grosses Orchester by Breitkopf & Härtel, Leipzig. Probable first edition: Title page

---

[3] Oct. 6, 1882, according to a letter from Schott to the author. Müller-Reuter, p. 465, says Oct., 1882. But Wagner was in a dispute with Lucca, the Milan music publisher, regarding the Italian rights to *Parsifal*, and a letter from Schott to Wagner, dated Sept. 30, 1882, acknowledges that Schott will delay publication of the orchestral score until solution of the Lucca matter, particularly since the orchestral score will not be ready until spring; Strecker, p. 239. Scribner Book Store *Catalogue 112* (New York, N.Y., n.d.), no. 186 says Nov., 1883; *Catalogue* at JF. Deutsch, *Plate Numbers*, p. 23, says specifically 1883. *Grove's*, 3rd ed., vol. 5, p. 607, 1884.§

[4] The orchestral score was published Oct. 7, 1882, according to the entry at Stationers' Hall on Nov. 9, 1882. Hofmeister *Monatsbericht*, Dec., 1882, p. 377 (orchestral score and parts).

[5] Müller-Reuter, p. 465, says Oct., 1882. 1884–6, on the basis of the plate number; Deutsch, *Plate Numbers*, p. 23.‖

---

[1] April, 1856, per Müller-Reuter, p. 266, but May, 1856, at p. 293. Hofmeister *Monatsbericht*, June, 1856, p. 993. To be published "soon"; *Liszt Verzeichnis*, 1855, p. 93.

lists nine numbers but there are prices for only six, namely, nos. 2–7,[2] the price of no. 3 being 2 Thlr. 15 Ngr. vb. Statement in German dated Weimar, March, 1856. Same statement in French. Foreword in German. Same foreword in French. m. on pp. 1–97. p.n. 9056. p. [98] blank. Music pages engraved. BRB, RCM and JF. The orchestral parts were not published until about Jan., 1865.[3]

Les Préludes were composed about 1848, revised in the early 1850's and performed Feb. 28, 1854, in Weimar. Brief biographic information regarding Liszt appears above under his Concerto for Piano no. 1.

A Pretty Girl Is Like a Melody

A pret - ty girl____ is like a mel - o - dy____

mw. Irving Berlin. Published June 26, 1919,[1] by Irving Berlin Inc., 1587 Broadway, New York, N.Y. First edition: Front cover has a drawing of a girl in a costume and is blue, white, blonde and red. s. Ziegfeld Follies of 1919—eight titles listed, all without prices. m. on pp. 2–5. No plate number. Back cover adv. Mandy. Quarto. LC(CDC) and JF.

The Ziegfeld Follies of 1919 opened in New York City on June 16, 1919. Brief biographic information regarding Berlin appears above under Alexander's Ragtime Band.

Priests' March—Mendelssohn

m. Felix Mendelssohn Bartholdy. Athalia, in which the Kriegsmarsch der Priester appears, was published in a piano-vocal score by Ewer & Co., New-

---

[2] Whereas all of nos. 2–7 are in Hofmeister Annual, 1856, p. 1, nos. 1, 8 and 9 are in Hofmeister Annual, 1857, p. 1.

[3] Jan., 1865, per Müller-Reuter. Hofmeister Monatsbericht, June, 1865, p. 90.

---

[1] Copyright records; LC.

gate St., London, a copy of which was deposited Aug. 12, 1848, at BM. First
edition: Title page in red, black and white gives the title as *The Music to
Racine's Athalie*, the English lyrics are by W. Bartholomew, the price is
21/, op. 74, Posth: Work, no. 2, and there is reference to Breitkopf &
Haertel, Leipzig. vb. Words on next three pages. vb. m. on pp. 2–125, the
March on p. 100 for piano four hands. No plate number. Title page and
music pages engraved. BM(CDC). On Jan. 2, 1849, the *Overture and March*
was deposited by the same publisher in separate arrangements for piano
and piano four hands; BM(CDC). The Breitkopf & Härtel, Leipzig, piano-
vocal edition of *Athalia* was published about Dec. 27, 1848[1] (copy at JF
with price of 5 Thlr., engraved, and p.n. 7899), and the *Kriegsmarsch der
Priester* was published by them about the same time for piano and piano
four hands.[2]

The orchestral score of *Athalia* was also published about Dec. 27,
1848,[3] by Breitkopf & Härtel, Leipzig. Possible first edition: Green and
black front cover. vb. Next two pages blank. The title page refers to
Racine, mentions op. 74, no. 2 der nachgelassenen Werke, indicates J.
Maho, Paris, and Ewer & Co., London, are co-agents, and the price is 10
Thlr. vb. m. on pp. 3–185, the *Kriegsmarsch der Priester* on p. 147. p.n.
7914. Next three pages and inside and outside of back cover blank. Music
pages engraved. ONB, BM and JF. No copy of the orchestral parts published about the same time by this concern[3] has been found. The orchestral
score was not published in London until May, 1883, when Novello, Ewer
and Company issued it;[4] copy at Novello & Company Ltd., London. Engraved orchestral parts of the *War March of the Priests*, without imprint
or plate number but apparently published by Novello, Ewer and Company,
London, are at RAM.

The music to *Athalia* was composed in 1843, and the entire work was
performed Dec. 1, 1845, in Berlin. Brief biographic information regarding
Mendelssohn appears above under his *Concerto for Violin*.

Prize Song—Wagner

Mor - gen - lich leuch-tend___ in___ ro - si - gem Schein, von Blüth und Duft___

[1] *AMZ*, Dec. 27, 1848, p. 864. Müller-Reuter, p. 115. Hofmeister *Monatsbericht*,
Jan., 1849, p. 12.

[2] *AMZ*, Dec. 27, 1848, p. 864. Hofmeister *Monatsbericht*, Jan., 1849, pp. 5 and 9.

[3] *AMZ*, Dec. 27, 1848, p. 864. Müller-Reuter, p. 115. Hofmeister *Monatsbericht*,
March–April, 1849, p. 43. The piano score of *Athalia* was published by Breitkopf &
Härtel about July, 1849; Hofmeister *Monatsbericht*, July, 1849, p. 71.

[4] Letter from Novello & Company Ltd.

mw. Richard Wagner. *Die Meistersinger von Nürnberg,* in which Walther's *Preislied* appears, was published in a piano-vocal score on May 9, 1868,[1] by B. Schott's Söhne, Mainz. The following first edition was deposited July 29, 1868, at BM: Title page states that the piano arrangement is by Karl Tausig and there are references to four concerns in Brussels, London, Paris (1 Rue Auber [Mon. du Gd. Hôtel]) and Leipzig; no price. vb. Dedication to King Ludwig II. vb. Cast. vb. m. on pp. 1–402, "Morgenlich leuchtend" on p. 264. p.n. 18975. Music pages engraved. The arranger of the Vorspiel is H. v. Bülow. BM(CDC); copy also at JF. An identical copy at LC has a front cover in black and tan. vb. Inside and outside of back cover blank. An identical copy at JMM has a black and blue front cover. Klein, pp. 34–35. The proof copy of the second and third acts, with corrections by Wagner, is at JF.

The orchestral score of *Die Meistersinger von Nürnberg* was published by the same concern on July 6, 1868.[2] Possible first edition: Title page has a legal notice, and the same imprint as in the piano-vocal score; no price. vb. Dedication to King Ludwig II. vb. p. (A) cast. p. (B) vocal parts and orchestral instruments. m. on pp. 1–570. p.n. 18469. pp. (A) and (B) and music pages engraved. †

Engraved orchestral parts of the opera, having the same plate number 18469, without covers, probably their first printing, are at ROH. A sheet music arrangement of Walther's *Preislied* was published at 36 xr. about March, 1869.[3]

Die Meistersinger von Nürnberg was completed Oct. 10, 1867, and produced June 21, 1868, in Munich. Brief biographic information regarding Wagner appears above under *The Flying Dutchman—Overture.*

Put on Your Old Grey Bonnet

Put   on your   old   grey   bon-net with the   blue rib - bon   on   it

---

[1] According to the entry at Stationers' Hall on June 26, 1868. Wagner, in a letter to Franz Schott on April 24, 1868, requested copies of the piano-vocal score, which he wrote were then ready; Altmann, vol. II, p. 67. Kastner, p. 67, says "Ausgegeben am 25. April 1868." Hofmeister *Monatsbericht,* July, 1868, p. 121, at 18 Fl.‡

[2] According to the entry at Stationers' Hall on Nov. 24, 1868. In Wagner's letter, referred to in the preceding footnote, he recognized that the orchestral score was not yet ready. Wagner wrote Franz Schott on July 15, 1868, acknowledging the receipt of a copy of the orchestral score; Strecker, p. 198.

[3] Hofmeister *Monatsbericht,* March, 1869, p. 58.

m. Percy Wenrich. w. Stanley Murphy. Published Nov. 5, 1909,[1] by Jerome
H. Remick & Co., New York and Detroit. First edition: Front cover has a
drawing of a lady in a grey bonnet and is purple, brown, blue and grey.[2]
p. [2] blank. m. on pp. 3–5. Back cover adv. My.. No plate number.
LC(CDC) and JF.

Wenrich, a composer and pianist, was born in Joplin, Mo., in 1880 and
died in New York City in 1952.[3] Murphy, a lyricist, was born in Dublin,
Ireland, in 1875, and died in the United States in 1919.[3]

Put Your Arms Around Me, Honey

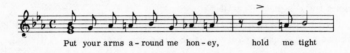

Put your arms a - round me hon - ey,   hold   me tight

© MCMX York Music Co. © MCMXXXVII renewed Broadway Music Corp.

m. Albert von Tilzer. w. Junie McCree. Published Sept. 15, 1910,[1] by The
York Music Co., Albert Von Tilzer, M'g'r., 1367–9 Broadway, N.Y. The
copyright deposit copy at the Library of Congress is a professional edition.
Possible first regular edition: Front cover has a drawing of a country scene,
a photograph of Elizabeth Murray, refers to the production *Madame
Sherry* and is red, green and white. m. on pp. 2–5. Back cover adv. *Dinah—
Nora..* (all advertised songs copyrighted in 1909). No reference at bottom
of p. 5 to Teller, Sons & Dorner (nor in professional CDC). JF. *Madame
Sherry* opened in New York City on Aug. 30, 1910.

Von Tilzer was born in Indianapolis in 1878, became a composer and
died in Los Angeles in 1956.[2] McCree was born in Toledo, Ohio, in 1865,
became a lyricist and actor, and died in New York City in 1918.[2]

Quartet, op. 59—Beethoven

[1] Copyright records; LC.
[2] Front cover is illustrated in Fuld, *American*, p. [42].
[3] *ASCAP*, pp. 531 and 364.

[1] Copyright records; LC.
[2] *ASCAP*, pp. 515 and 320.

m. Ludwig van Beethoven. Published in parts in Jan., 1808,[1] by Au Bureau des arts et d'industrie, Vienna. First edition: Front cover states "Trois Quatours pour deux Violons, Alto et Violoncello." p.ns. 580, 584 and 585. Price is f 8. Reference is made to a Pesth agent. vb. Dedication to le Comte de Rasoumoffsky. The above musical excerpt is from the first movement of the first *Quartet*, with plate number 580. Engraved. Folio. BM, CI and SB. Brief biographic information regarding Beethoven appears above under *Concerto for Piano no. 5.*

Quartet, op. 11—Tchaikovsky

m. P. Tchaikovsky. *Quatuor,* op. 11, was published in 1872[1] in separate parts and as a score by P. Jurgenson, Moscow. Possible first printing of the parts: The title page is in many colors, in Russian, and refers to an affiliate in St. Petersburg. The music pages are engraved and have French text. p.n. 1900. Though the front cover in yellow and black, with the price of 3 rubles, in French, says "2de Édition," this may relate solely to the front cover. SUB and JF.

Possible first printing of the score: Music engraved on pages 1–8; there is a dedication to Mr. S. Ratschinsky. p.n. 1900a. The *Andante Cantabile* appears on page 4. All words on music pages are in French. Front cover lacking. In one variant, there is a reference at the bottom of page 8 to P. Jurgenson; in the other variant, priority unknown, there is no such reference. Both variants at JF; first variant also at GM. No mention of Nouvelle or Nouv. Édition.

The above first theme of the *Andante Cantabile* is a great Russian folk song, *Vanya Sat Drinking,*[2] which Tchaikovsky allegedly heard a plasterer[3] or a baker[3] or a carpenter[4] (!) sing. The folk song, also known as *Vanya Sat on the Divan,* apparently had never before appeared in print; whether Tchaikovsky altered the folk song is not known. The second theme, beginning in the 56th bar of this second movement, was original with Tchaikovsky[2] and is perhaps as well known as the above first theme.

[1] Kinsky-Halm, p. 139. *Wiener Zeitung,* Jan. 9, 1808. *AMZ,* Jan. 27, 1808, p. 288.

[1] Dombayev, p. 58. Hofmeister *Annual,* 1873, p. 334. It is possible that the parts were published first, and the score later.

[2] Gerald Abraham, *The Music of Tchaikovsky* (New York, N.Y., 1946), p. 105; NYPL.

[3] John Gee and Elliott Selby, *The Triumph of Tchaikovsky* (London, 1959), p. 59; NYPL.

[4] Thompson, p. 580.

Tchaikovsky's first *Quartet* was completed Feb., 1871 (O.S.), and performed March 28, 1871 (N.S.), in Moscow. Brief biographic information regarding Tchaikovsky appears above under *Chant sans Paroles*.

Quartet—Rigoletto

Bel-la fi-glia del-l'a mo - re, schia-vo son de' vez-zi tuo - i

m. G. Verdi. w. F. M. Piave. The *Quartetto*, no. 16, was first to be published as a separate piece for piano and voices about May 1, 1851,[1] by Giovanni Ricordi, Milan, with plate number 23086, at Fr. 4.50. A first printing without double pagination is in the piano-vocal score described below at MIC. The Blanchet, Paris, separate publication of the *Quartet* was deposited for Dépôt Légal on May 1, 1851, and two copies are at BN; Archives.

The piano-vocal score of *Rigoletto* was announced by Ricordi to be published on May 25, 1852.[2] A so-called "Advance Complete Edition" is described in Hopkinson, *Verdi*, 53A, although his indicated date of "? 1850–1851" is seriously erroneous as five corner dates are from March 25, 1852–May 25, 1852. The score is oblong. The title page has a red border, without vignette, and refers only to the piano-vocal score at Fr. 40; the opera is dedicated to Antonio Vasselli. The publisher is Giovanni Ricordi, Contrada degli Omenoni N. 1720, Milan, and lists Florence, Mendrisio [Switzerland], London and Paris (F. Blanchet) agents. vb. p.ns. 23070–23090, but not complete. Music pages engraved. Italian text. The *Quartet*, *Un Dì, Se Ben Rammentomi (One Day, If I Remember Rightly)*, as indicated above, is no. 16, with p.n. 23086. This score is largely a collection of separate pieces, although a few arias have double pagination;

---

[1] *Ricordi Catalogue Supplement*, Milan, Jan.–March, 1851, p. 3; NYPL. GMM, Index 1850. As published, *GMM*, June 8, 1851, p. 110. Hofmeister *Monatsbericht*, July, 1851, p. 143. The engraving commenced March 17, 1851, and the "da pubblicarsi" (for publication) date was May 1, 1851; Ricordi *Libroni*. Curiously, Hopkinson, *Verdi*, does not consider Ricordi's separate pieces from this opera.

[2] *GMM*, May 23, 1852, p. 96, to be published two days later. *Ricordi Catalogue Supplement*, Milan, Jan.–April, 1852, p. 3; NYPL. As published, *GMM*, June 13, 1852, p. 110. Hofmeister *Monatsbericht*, Sept., 1852, pp. 160 and 153. The engraving of the last number commenced March 23, 1852, and the "da pubblicarsi" date of the last numbers was May 25, 1862; Ricordi *Libroni*. The Bureau Central de Musique, Paris, piano-vocal score was apparently not published until Dec., 1852.

contrary to Hopkinson, there is thus no continuous pagination. This is the only collection to include *Parmi veder le lagrime* on plate number 23070. Not every aria is included. The publication dates indicated by Hopkinson are for the 1851 separate pieces, not for the 1852 separate pieces or the piano-vocal score. The engraver of no. 9 with plate number 23079 is known from the Ricordi *Libroni* to have been Grassi, whose initial was N, and this initial appears on all pages with this plate number. MIC.

This collection may not be "Advance" since its latest corner date, May 25, 1852, is later than the latest corner date, April 4, 1852, mentioned in the first regular edition below. The collection is also not "complete," and, without an index or continuous pagination, it is hardly an "edition."†

Quintet, op. 163—Schubert

m. Franz Schubert. Published in parts about Jan. 20, 1853,[1] by C. A. Spina, Vienna. Probable first edition: Front cover has the title *Grand Quintuor (en Ut) pour Deux Violons, Alto et 2 Violoncelles*, Oeuvre 163; publisher's number 9101; legal claim; prices of Rth. 3, 15 Ngr. and f. 5, 15 x.C.M.; the publisher is stated to be the successor to A. Diabelli & Co., 1133 Graben; and there are Paris and London agents. The plate number is that of the predecessor company, D. & C. no. 9101. Engraved. Folio. BM, GM, SB and JF.

The *Quintet* was composed probably in Aug.–Sept., 1828, but not performed publicly until Nov. 17, 1850, in Vienna, i.e., after Schubert's death. Brief biographic information regarding Schubert appears above under his *Ave Maria*.

---

[1] Deutsch, *Schubert*, no. 956, p. 613. *Signale*, Jan. 20, 1853, p. 40. Hofmeister *Monatsbericht*, Feb., 1853, p. 263.

Quintet, op. 44—Schumann

m. Robert Schumann. Published in parts about Sept. 20, 1843,[1] by Breitkopf & Härtel, Leipzig. Probable first edition: Front cover has the title *Quintett für Pianoforte, 2 Violinen, Viola und Violoncello;* dedication to Clara Schumann; op. 44; publisher's claim; price of 3 Thlr.; publisher's number 6899; claim of deposit in the Vereinsarchiv; and a green border. p.n. 6899. Music pages engraved. Folio. BM (h. 88 j. [3]), LC (including slightly later blue and black covers) and JF.

The *Quintet* was composed in 1842. Brief biographic information regarding Schumann appears above under *Happy Farmer.*

Rakoczy March

The first known printing of the *Rakoczy March* was in 1820[1] in the *Auswahl der Beliebtesten Märsche für das Löbl. K. K. 32te Linien Infanterie Regiment Fürst Esterhazy* for piano published by Pietro Mechetti qm Carlo, im Michaelerhaus der k.k. Reitschule gegenüber no. 1221, Vienna. Probable first edition: Front cover states that the collection was "composed" by Nic. Scholl, the head of the Musical Chapel of Prince Esterhazy, and arranged for piano by Hieronymus Payer and that the price is 30 x. C.M. vb. m. on pp. 1–7, the *Rakotzy Marsch* is no. 1 on p. 1. p.n. 825. Back cover blank. Engraved. Oblong. BSM. The *Rakoczy Marsch* alone was shortly thereafter

---

[1] *AMZ,* Sept. 20, 1843, p. 687. Hofmeister *Monatsbericht,* Oct., 1843, p. 147. Dörffel, p. 10. Hofmann, *Schumann,* p. 103.

---

[1] *Handbuch Annual* 1821 (Easter, 1820–Easter, 1821), p. 66.

published for piano four hands under the title *Beliebter Marsch* by the same publisher with p.n. 848; OSK.

This Hungarian *March* by an unknown composer was popularized by the army of Prince Ferencz Rakoczy, the leader of the Hungarian revolt against Austria in 1703–1711, was his favorite march and named after him, and was sung as a song in the eighteenth century;[2] however, no printing has been found earlier than those described above. The *March* became more widely known in the middle of the nineteenth century as a result of Berlioz's insertion of it in his *Damnation of Faust* and Liszt's use of it in his *Hungarian Rhapsody no. 15.*

Not mentioned by Hopkinson in his *Berlioz* are the first publications of Berlioz' arrangement of the *March* by J. Treichlinger, Pest, probably in 1846, found and researched by H. Baron, London. These publications are of the original shorter version that Berlioz had with him in Hungary in that year; all other known editions are the revised longer version. Treichlinger began to publish in 1842. One edition, probably the earlier, has a title page in French, entitled *Rákoczy Marche Hongrois,* and lists two arrangements, this copy for piano, and another for piano four hands. The other edition has a title page in Hungarian, entitled *Rákóczy Induló (March)* and lists a third arrangement for piano six hands. In each case, the plate number is 138 and the music is on pages 3–7, engraved. Copies at JF.

Rapsodie on a Theme of Paganini

Nicolo Paganini's *Caprice* no. 24 was published in 1820[1] in his *24 Capricci per Violino solo,* op. la, by Gio. Ricordi, 1118 Conta. di sa. Margherita, Milan. Probable first edition: Front cover has a dedication to "Artists" and gives the price of Lir. 9. Itale. m. on pp. 2–46, no. 24 on p. 44. p.n. 403. Engraved. ONB, Manoug Parikian, London, and JF. The *24 Capricci* were com-

---

[2] The best histories of the *Rakoczy March* are in Bence Szabolcsi and Tóth Aladár, *Zenei Lexikon* (Budapest, 1935), p. 379, at OSK and NYPL, and in Émile Haraszti, *Berlioz et la Marche Hongroise* (Paris, 1946), p. 33 and plate no. 11, at NYPL.

[1] G. I. de Courcy, *Paganini, the Genoese* (Norman, Okla., 1957), vol. II, p. 373; NYPL. *Handbuch Annual* 1821 (Easter, 1820–Easter, 1821), p. 13.†

posed 1801–1807. Paganini was born in Genoa in 1782 and died in Nice in 1840.

S. Rachmaninoff's *Rapsodie sur un Thème de Paganini*, op. 43, was published Dec. 31, 1934,[2] in orchestral score for piano and orchestra by Carl Fischer, Inc., New York, N.Y., the copyright being in the name of Charles Foley, New York, N.Y. Two editions were published that day. One (copyright no. E pub. 45959) is said to have been an octavo score,[3] and an octavo score, the same as that described below, except with black and gray covers, is at LC (not CDC). The other (copyright no. E pub. 46479) is quarto. First edition of the quarto printing: Front cover is gold and black. vb. Title page given composer, title and imprint as above, and adds Partition d'Orchestre, Édition Tair; no price. vb. m. on pp. 1–119. Variation XVIII, an inversion of *Caprice no. 24*, is on p. 70. p.n. R 1. p. [120] and inside and outside of back cover blank. No street address for either the publisher or copyright owner. LC (CDC received Jan. 4, 1935) and JF (inscribed). The arrangement for piano four hands was published March 14, 1935.[2] Rachmaninoff's *Rapsodie* was composed July 3–Aug. 18, 1934, and performed in Baltimore Nov. 7, 1934. Brief biographic information regarding Rachmaninoff appears above under his *Concerto for Piano no. 2*.

Raymond-Overture—Thomas

m. Ambroise Thomas. The piano-vocal score of *Raymond* was entered for Dépôt Légal on Oct. 3, 1851,[1] by the Bureau Central de Musique, 8 Rue Favart, Paris. First edition: Title page has a subtitle, *Ou Le Secret de la Reine*, the librettists are Rosier and de Leuven, the price is 15 f., and there are references to London and Mainz agents. vb. Cast and index. m. on pp. 2–288, the *Ouverture* on p. 2. p.n. 1224. Engraved. BN(CDC), JMM and JF.

The orchestral score of *Raymond* was entered for Dépôt Légal on Jan. 24, 1852, by the same publisher. First edition: Title page is the same as above, except that it is larger and lists the orchestral score at 400 f., the

---

[2] Copyright records; LC.

[3] Information from copyright owner.

[1] Archives. Year of deposit appears on copyright copy at BN. *BF*, Dec. 20, 1851, p. 696.

orchestral parts at the same price,[2] the Partition in 8° (octavo) at 15 f. and
the Mise en scène at 9 f. vb. m. on pp. 1–605. p.n. 1225. p. [606] blank.
Engraved. BN(CDC). The orchestral score and parts of the Overture are
not listed on the title page. A possible first printing of the orchestral parts
of the opera, engraved, with plate number BC 1226, folio, without covers,
are at Heugel et Cie., Paris.

Raymond was produced in Paris on June 5, 1851. Brief biographic
information regarding Thomas appears under Entr'acte-Gavotte—Mignon.
Joseph Bernard Rosier, a dramatic author, was born in Paris in 1804 and
died in Marseilles in 1880.[3] Adolphe de Leuven, Count Ribbing, also a
dramatic author, was born in 1800 and died in 1884.[4]

The Red River Valley

From this val-ley they say you are go-ing,_I shall miss your sweet face and your smile

A pencil manuscript of the words of The Red River Valley bears the nota-
tion at the bottom "Nemaha 1879, Harlan 1885" and sets forth five stanzas.
The University of Iowa, Iowa City, Iowa (Edwin Ford Piper Collection).
Nemaha and Harlan are towns in western Iowa.

The first printing of the music and words was in sheet music entitled
In the Bright Mohawk Valley, with music and words credited to James J.
Kerrigan, and copyrighted June 4, 1896[1] by Howley, Haviland & Co., 4
East 20th Street, New York, N.Y. First edition: Front cover is light and
dark green and white, states that the song was sung by John W. Rice and
the price is 4. p. [2] adv. I'll.. - I.. m. on pp. 3–5. No plate number. Back
cover adv. The Arrival.. - Belfry.. Folio. LC(CDC).

Recent research indicates that this folk song did not originally refer
to the Mohawk Valley in New York State, or to the Red River Valley in
Texas, but rather to the Red River that flows into Lake Winnipeg, Mani-
toba, Canada.[2] It is believed that the song was sung in the Northwest Ter-
ritories in Canada during the Rebellion of 1869.

---

[2] The orchestral parts are mentioned in BF, March 6, 1852, p. 141.
[3] GE, vol. 28, p. 950.
[4] DUC, pp. 1157 and 1890. IP, vol. 2, p. 50.

[1] Copyright records; LC.
[2] Edith Fowke, " 'The Red River Valley' Re-Examined" in Western Folklore,
Berkeley and Los Angeles, Cal., July, 1964, p. 163; NYPL.

El Relicario

Pi - sa mo - re - na,   pi - sa con   gar - bo

m. José Padilla. w. Oliveros and Castellvi. Published 1918 by Unión Musical Española (Antes Casa Dotesio), 34 Carrera de San Jerónimo, Madrid.[1] Possible first edition: Folio. Front cover in green, red and white, says the song is the creation of Mari-Focela with a photograph presumably of her, there is a drawing of a bullfight ring, the publisher has branches at Bilbao, Barcelona, Santander and Valladolid, and the price is Ptas. 2. p. [2] blank. m. on pp. 1–4 (actually 3–6). p. 1 has a dedication to D. José Pérez de Rozas, a 1918 copyright claim and p.n. 20399. p. [5] has words. Back cover adv. *On Rigole*. JF. This edition is believed earlier than a similar edition with a tan, gold and brown front cover which mentions a 1919 copyright and adds a Paris branch; JF.

José Padilla Sánchez, one of Spain's most popular composers, was born in 1889 in Almería, near Granada, Spain, and died in 1960 in Madrid.[2] Armando Oliveros Millán, a Spanish lyricist, was born in 1884 and is believed to be living in Barcelona.[3] José Na. Castellvi García, also a Spanish lyricist, was born in 1887 and died in 1961.[3]

Remember

Re - mem - ber the night, —— the night —— you said

mw. Irving Berlin. This song was deposited for American copyright in a quarto professional edition on July 27, 1925,[1] under the unusual title *You Forgot to Remember*; LC(CDC) and JF. It is believed that the song was never printed in a regular edition in this country under the title *You Forgot to Remember*, even though the song is so listed in *Irving Berlin Songs* (an

---

[1] Union Musical Española was at 34 Carrera Jerónimo, Madrid, from 1916–1925, and at 26 Carrera de San Jerónimo from 1925 to the present time, according to a letter from this firm.

[2] Obituary, *The New York Times*, Oct. 26, 1960.

[3] Information from SGAE.

[1] Copyright records; LC. An American octavo "Artist Copy" of *You Forgot to Remember* was also published; JF.

undated booklet published by Irving Berlin Music Corporation, New York, N.Y.; JF). A regular edition of *You Forgot to Remember* was published by Francis, Day & Hunter, Ltd., London; JF.

Possible first regular edition: Title, *Remember*. Front cover has a photograph of Irving Berlin, is red, white and blue, and the publisher is Irving Berlin, Inc., 1607 Broadway, New York, N.Y. m. on pp. 2–5. Back cover adv. *Alone at Last* (published June 25, 1925[1]). JF. Brief biographic information regarding Berlin appears above under *Alexander's Ragtime Band*.

Requiem—Fauré

Ky - ri - e,   Ky - ri - e,   Ky - ri - e   e - le - i - son

m. Gabriel Fauré. Published Feb. 21, 1900,[1] in piano-vocal score by J. Hamelle, 22 Boulevard Malesherbes, Paris. First edition: Front cover is blue, gray and black, states that the *Requiem* is for "Soli, Choeurs & Orchestre," lists the piano-vocal score at 10f., the choral parts at 2f.50 and the orchestral score and parts without prices, refers to the predecessor firm, J. Maho, claims a 1900 American copyright and states that the printer is Bigeard & Fils, Paris. Next three pages blank. Title page is similar to the front cover except in blue, black and white. vb. Index. vb. m. on pp. 1–78. Latin words. Page 1 mentions opus number 48. p.n. 4531. Page 78 refers again to Bigeard, and also to the engraver, J. Guidez, Paris. pp. [79]–[80] blank. Inside and outside of back cover blank. BM*, BN(CDC), LC* (copyright copy received April 11, 1900[2]) and HU. Octavo choral parts also have plate number 4531; CI.

The *Requiem* was published for "orchestra" on Sept. 16, 1901,[1] but it is not known whether this is the orchestral score, orchestral parts or both. Possible first edition of the orchestral score: Folio. Front cover is same as that of the piano-vocal score except that it lists six lines of arrangements, the orchestral score at 25 f., and no printer is stated. Next three pages blank. Title page is similar to the front cover except in blue, black and white. vb. m. on pp. 1–128. p.n. 4650. Page 128 refers to the engraver,

[1] Letter from publisher.
[2] Copyright records; LC.

J. Guidez, and to the printer, A. Chaimbaud et Cie., 18 Rue de la Tour-d'Auvergne, Paris. Inside and outside of back cover blank. BPL and LC. A possible first edition of the orchestral parts, but lacking a front cover, is at CI with plate number 4651.

The *Requiem* was composed in 1887 and performed in Jan., 1888, in Paris. Fauré was born in Pamiers, France, in 1845 and died in Paris in 1924.

Reuben and Rachel

Reu-ben, I have long been think-ing, what a good world this might be

m. William Gooch. w. Harry Birch. Possible first edition: Engraved. Front cover has a drawing of a couple, the song is described as a "Comic Duett" [*sic*], the price is 3½, the publisher is White, Smith & Perry, 298, 300 [*sic*] Washington St., Boston, with three agents, and there is an 1871 copyright claim.[1] p. [2] blank. m. on pp. 3–5. p.n. 470. Back cover blank. JF. No biographic information has been found concerning either author.

Le Rêve, Manon—Massenet

En-fer-mant les yeux je vois là   bas

m. Jules Massenet. w. Henri Meilhac and Philippe Gille. The piano-vocal score of *Manon* was published about Jan. 22, 1884,[1] by G. Hartmann, 20 Rue Daunou, Paris. First edition: Half-title page in rust and white. vb. Dedication to Madame C. Miolan-Carvalho. Two blank pages. Engraving. Title page in dark and light tan says "Direction Léon Carvalho," states the opera is in five acts and six scenes, has the price of 20f. and mentions that

---

[1] There is no record of such a copyright in the copyright records at LC. The earliest copyright deposit copy, deposited March 2, 1878, at LC, has a later imprint.

[1] Jean-Marie Martin, Hollogne-aux-Pierres, Belgium, has been helpful in connection with this title. Entered for Dépôt Légal on Jan. 22, 1884; Archives. *BF*, Feb. 9, 1884, p. 95. *BMF*, Jan.–Mar., 1884, p. 9.

the printer is Fouquet, Paris. vb. Cast. Index on two pages. vb. m. on pp. 1–387, *Le Rêve* on p. 171. p.n. 1356 on Cast page only. p. [388] blank. The "Duo Final" is not included in this first edition. Lithographed. BN(CDC) and JF. The separate sheet music of *Le Rêve* was published about April 7, 1884;[2] BN(CDC).

A possible first edition of the orchestral parts of the opera, with plate number G. H. [G. Hartmann, Paris] 1415, lithographed, without covers, folio, is at ROH.

Probable first edition of the orchestral score of the opera: Folio. No title page or other preliminary pages. p.n. 1446. m. on pp. 1–183 (end of second act). p. 184 (beginning of third act) pasted over. *Menuet*, a separate octavo publication, with a title page listing five arrangements, the price of the orchestral score probably erased and rubber-stamped "6" and showing the publisher at 20 rue Daunou, Ancne., rue Nve. St. Augustin, Paris; m. on pp. 2–7; p.n. 1457; p. [8] blank; lithographed. The folio score resumes at p. 193 (partially pasted over) to p. 422. JF (copy no. 13—only known copy).[3]†

Manon was performed in Paris on Jan. 19, 1884. Brief biographic information regarding Massenet and Gille appears above under *Élégie* and *Bell Song*. Meilhac, a dramatist, was born in Paris in 1831 and died there in 1897.[4]

Reveille

The first known printing of this bugle call *Reveille* was in 1836 in Brevet Captain S. Cooper, *A Concise System of Instructions and Regulations for the Militia and Volunteers of the United States, Comprehending the Exercises and Movements of the Infantry, Light Infantry, and Riflemen; Cavalry and Artillery* (Philadelphia), p. 235; LC, NYPL and JF.

This bugle call may have been composed in 1831 by a Frenchman. Thus, this *Le Réveil* appears in Georges Kastner, *Manuel Général de*

---

2 Entered for Dépôt Légal on April 7, 1884. *BF*, May 3, 1884, p. 283. *BMF*, April–June, 1884, p. 24.

3 Kinsky, *Opern*, p. 386. When the orchestral score was republished about 1930, the original G. Hartmann plate number, G. H. 1446, was included, together with a reference on page 1 to Röder. After the printer's name and new address on page 422 is "XXX"—probably meaning 1930. JMM.

4 *NIL*, vol. 15, p. 356.

Musique Militaire à l'Usage des Armées Françaises (Paris, 1848), on music page 25, no. 8. COP, NYPL and JF. A great many drumbeats and trumpet calls are set forth, all "Par Melchior, Chef de Musique, 1831." Whether they were composed or arranged by Melchior is not clear—nor whether 1831 is the year of authorship, the year Melchior was Chef de Musique, or the year of promulgation. Earlier music pages in this book set out trumpet calls (including other calls entitled "Le Réveil") previously in use, so that *Le Réveil* on music page 25 may have been an original composition.[1] This is the only well-known American bugle call studied in this book that may well have had a foreign origin and which is still in use today in a foreign country (France).

Rêverie—Debussy

m. C. Debussy. The first printing of *Rêverie*, for piano, is said to have been in 1890–1891 by Choudens, Paris,[1] and François Lesure, Bibliothèque Nationale, Paris, has written the author that he saw a copy in a private collection that has since been dispersed. No copy has been found.†

Debussy composed the work in 1890, sold it to Choudens who sold it to Hartmann who again transferred it to Fromont.[1] Hartmann did not publish it, and on April 21, 1904, Debussy wrote Fromont protesting the latter's publication of it.[1] Brief biographic information regarding Debussy appears above under *Clair de Lune*.

Rhapsody in Blue

---

[1] White, p. 264, says, without any explanation or substantiation, that *Reveille* "dates from the Crusades."

[1] Vallas, pp. 70 and XXX, and Lesure, p. 69. Choudens wrote the author that it did not publish *Rêverie*; and *Rêverie* is not listed in Choudens *Catalogues*, Paris, issued in 1893, at BN, or in 1900, at LC.

m. George Gershwin. Published Dec. 31, 1924,[1,2] for Piano Solo and Second Piano by Harms, Incorporated, New York, N.Y. Probable first edition: Front cover states "For Jazz Band and Piano," has an extremely modernistic design and is red, purple, white and blue. (**See Plate III.**) vb. The title page has a dedication to Paul Whiteman and is black and white. m. on pp. 2–42 (arranged for piano four hands). p. 2 has a 1924 copyright claim. p.n. 7206-41. Inside and outside of back cover blank. Estate of Ira Gershwin, Beverly Hills, Cal., and JF (inscribed by the composer). The copyright deposit copy at LC is the same as the above except that the outside of the back cover adv. *Somebody.. - So..* The arrangement for Piano Solo was published Aug. 24, 1927;[2] LC(CDC).

A set of the orchestral or band parts, with a 1925 copyright claim, was received or bound May 2, 1927,[3] by the New York Public Library, although no record at the Copyright Office, Library of Congress, of the copyright of such arrangement has been found. The earliest known copyright of an instrumental arrangement was on May 27, 1938,[2] a score for symphonic band, with p.n. 19902-70; LC(CDC) and NYPL.

Rhapsody in Blue was composed for a famous jazz concert at Aeolian Hall, New York City, on Feb. 12, 1924, with the composer at the piano and Paul Whiteman conducting. A recording was made by the same performers on June 10, 1924,[4] Victor record no. 55225; NYPL and JF.† Brief biographic information regarding Gershwin appears above under *I Got Rhythm.*

The Ride of the Valkyries—Wagner— (Die Walküre, Das Rheingold, Siegfried and Götterdämmerung)

m. Richard Wagner. *Der Ritt der Walküren* was probably first published

[1] Part of *Rhapsody in Blue* was copyrighted as an unpublished composition on June 12, 1924. While the printed copyright catalogue does not show it, the copyright index at LC states that the copyright was of an unpublished composition, and the actual deposit consists merely of a few pages of excerpts for piano in manuscript; LC.

[2] Copyright records; LC.

[3] According to NYPL card index. The incomplete parts still at NYPL lack a copyright notice. Nor is there an imprint or plate number.

[4] Brian Rust, "Paul Whiteman: A Discography," in *Recorded Sound*, London, July, 1967, p. 221; BM and NYPL.

in a separate piano arrangement in mid-1863[1] by B. Schott's Söhne, Mainz. The following possible first edition was deposited at BM on June 26, 1863: Front cover has a dedication to Prince Rudolph Liechtenstein, the piano arrangement is by C. Tausig, the price is 1 Fl. 21 kr., and the publisher has three affiliates at Brussels, London and Paris (the address of the latter being 30 Rue Neuve St. Augustin) and agents at Leipzig and Rotterdam. vb. m. on pp. 1–13. p.n. 17279. Back cover blank. Not engraved. No other arrangements on front cover. BM(CDC); also at BSM.

The piano-vocal score of *Die Walküre* was published by the same concern on July 29, 1865.[2] Probable first edition: Title page states the piano arrangement is by Karl Klindworth, the imprint is as above except that the French address is now 6 Rue Auber, Maison du Grand Hôtel.[3] vb. Dedicatory poem on two pages "Dem Königlichen Freunde" (King Ludwig II of Bavaria) dated Starnberg, Summer 1864.[4] Cast and index. Next two pages blank. m. on pp. 2–274, *Der Ritt der Walküren* on p. 169. p.n. 17995. All pages engraved except title and dedication pages.†

The orchestral score of *Die Walküre* was published on Sept. 1, 1874,[5] by the same concern. Possible first edition: Title page states *Der Ring des Nibelungen, Ein Bühnenfestspiel*, there is a dedication to King Ludwig II of Bavaria and the imprint is as above except that the French street address is now **6 Rue du Hasard Richelieu** and the Rotterdam agent is omitted, and there is a publisher's number 20800; *Die Walküre* is not mentioned on the title page. Legal notice. Next page reads: Erster Tag: *Die Walküre*. vb. Cast and index. vb. Orchestration. vb. m. on pp. 1–457, *Der Ritt der Walküren* on p. 273. p. [458] blank. p.n. 21170. Music pages and two preceding pages engraved. Such copies, with a legal notice on the verso of the title page, are at BM (CDC, entered at Stationers' Hall on Sept. 25, 1874, and deposited in the British Museum on Oct. 8, 1874—no number), ONB (copy no. 81) and JF (probably two numbers, trimmed). Klein, p. 41, states the verso of the title page is blank; such a copy, no. 53, is at BMI.‡ (In some higher-numbered copies, the French street address is sometimes

---

[1] On the basis of the p.n. (Deutsch, *Plate Numbers*, p. 23) and the French address (Hopkinson, *Parisian*, p. 111). The copy described above may not be the edition in Hofmeister *Monatsbericht*, March, 1871, p. 44, priced at 17½ Ngr. §

[2] According to the entry at Stationers' Hall on Sept. 21, 1865. ‖ Wagner wrote Franz Schott on July 15, 1865, that he had not received copies; Altmann, vol. II, p. 87. On July 31, 1865, Wagner wrote that he is "today" sending Wesendonk a copy; Strecker, p. 174. Hofmeister *Monatsbericht*, Oct., 1865, p. 176.

[3] The London address also changed from 95 to 159 Regent Street.

[4] Kastner, p. 42.

[5] According to the entry at Stationers' Hall on Sept. 25, 1874. Wagner's letter of Sept. 9, 1874, to A. L. Mazière indicates that the orchestral score had not yet been published; Altmann, vol. II, p. 178. Hofmeister *Monatsbericht*, Sept., 1874, p. 179. Kinsky, *Opern*, p. 385, accord. #

blank.) The first known separate orchestral score of *Der Ritt der Walküren* has p.n. 22139; NYPL.

Lithographed orchestral parts of the opera, with plate number 24051 (ca. 1887),† possibly their first printing, with covers, are at CI and MET*.

The poem of the entire *Der Ring des Nibelungen* was written before the music, and privately printed in 50 copies at Wagner's expense by E. Kiesling, Zurich, in Feb., 1853;[6] PML (Wagner's copy) and JF.

With respect to the music in the balance of *Der Ring des Nibelungen*, the piano-vocal score of *Das Rheingold* was published by the same concern about March, 1861.[7] Klein, pp. 38–39. The first edition may have a black and white title page, engraved music pages and plate number 16152; BM (copyright copy deposited April 11, 1861), YU and JF. However, there is also another edition, which Wagner complained of[7] and which may be earlier, with an illustrated tan, black and white title page, engraved music pages and the same plate number; JF. Curiously, both an edition with a black and white title page and an edition with a green, black and white title page (with illustration Wagner complained of) were published later with lithographed music pages.

The piano-vocal score of *Siegfried* was published Aug. 10, 1871.[8] The first regular edition has lithographed pages, the plate number is 20326 and the address of the French affiliate is 1 Rue Auber, Mn. du Gd. Hôtel, but there are two variant editions with priority unknown: in one, a copyright copy of which was deposited at the British Museum on Oct. 10, 1871, the verso of the title page is blank (H 637j)—also at JF with Hermann Levi bookplate; in the other, the verso of the title page has a legal notice, at BM (Hirsch M 1255), NYPL and JF. (The address of the French affiliate changed in Jan., 1872; Hopkinson, *Parisian*, p. 111. A slightly later edition, with the address of the French affiliate blank, also has the verso of the title page blank. JF.) ‡

The piano-vocal score of *Götterdämmerung* was published on March 19 or April 19, 1875.[9] The first edition has lithographed pages, the plate number is 21500 and the address of the French affiliate is 6 Rue du Hasard Richelieu. BM (copyright copy deposited July 18, 1875), NYPL and JF. §

The orchestral scores of *Das Rheingold*, *Siegfried* and *Götterdämmerung* were published in March, 1873, Jan., 1876, and June, 1876.‖ First

---

[6] Strecker, p. 36.

[7] Hofmeister *Monatsbericht*, April, 1861, p. 74; NYPL. #

[8] The first date mentioned in the Schott *Auslieferungslager* is Aug. 10, 1871, on which date 400 copies were printed or published. ¶

[9] There were two entries at Stationers' Hall: on May 6, 1875, stating the March 19, 1875, publication date; and on May 24, 1875, stating the April 19, 1875, publication date. Hofmeister *Monatsbericht*, June, 1875, p. 130. ††

editions, copies numbered 11, 15 and 26, were deposited at BM on Aug. 19, 1873, May 23, 1876, and Aug. 11, 1876, with p.ns. 20800, 21544 and 21953, with engraved music pages; the address of the French affiliate in each case is **6 Rue du Hasard Richelieu**, and the verso of the title page is blank; all at BM (CDC). Also at BMI and JF (*Siegfried* with blue and black covers). Klein, pp. 36–37 (but not all 100 copies of *Das Rheingold* are first edition), 44–45 and 48–49.

The earliest orchestral parts that have been found of *Das Rheingold*, *Siegfried* and *Götterdämmerung*, possibly their first printings, have plate numbers 25090, 25091 and 25092 (ca. 1891)† and covers, and are lithographed; CI and MET*.

Siegfried Idyll was published in orchestral score on Feb. 1, 1878,‡ and in orchestral parts about the same time. Strangely, the edition of the orchestral score with lithographed music pages may precede the edition with engraved music pages. The title page of the lithographed edition shows the address of the Paris publisher as 6 Rue du Hasard Richelieu (Feb., 1877–March, 1879[10]); BM (copyright copy received May 8, 1878—h 1582 [6]). The edition with engraved music pages has the Paris address blank, perhaps indicating a printing after March, 1879; BM (Hirsch M 1260) and JF. The plate number in each edition is 22430. Engraved orchestral parts, also with plate number 22430, and with covers showing the later Paris address of 19 Boulevard Montmartre, are at RAM.

The music of *Die Walküre* was completed the end of April, 1856, and the opera performed June 25, 1870, in Munich. Brief biographic information regarding Wagner appears above under *The Flying Dutchman—Overture*.

Ritual Fire Dance—El Amor Brujo

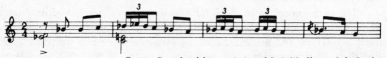

m. Manuel de Falla. w. G. Martinez Sierra. The first printing of the *Ritual Fire Dance*, under the title *Danza del Fin del Día*, was deposited May 26, 1920, at BM in a piano-vocal arrangement. The copyright deposit copy lacks the back cover, the publisher's name has been cut off the bottom of the front cover, and there is no p.n.; there is no indication of the publisher or his address except that the bottom of p. 8 mentions: "A. Rodríguez." In this excerpt, the front cover is yellow, pink, black and white, and has a drawing of the head of a Spanish woman. p. [2] blank. m. on pp. 1–8 (really 3–10). BM(CDC).

J. & W. Chester, Ltd., London, wrote the author that it was not the publisher of this excerpt and that it was probably printed privately for the composer in Spain. However, Chester did publish the separate *Danse Rituelle du Feu* for piano in April, 1921, and owns the following copy with a dedication from the composer dated June 1, 1921. First edition: Front cover is gray and black, refers to Chester Library and the price is 2/6 (Fr. 3.75). vb. The title page gives the address of the publisher, 11 Great Marlborough Street, London W.1, plus a Geneva address and a Belgian agent and has a 1921 copyright claim. vb. m. on pp. [1]–[8]. p.n. 9713. Next three pages blank. Back cover adv. *Two.. - The Curse..* Copy at publisher.

The piano-vocal score of the entire ballet *El Amor Brujo* was deposited at BM on Nov. 16, 1921, by J. & W. Chester, Ltd., 11 Great Marlborough Street, London W.1. First edition: Front cover has a drawing of a Spanish couple, the additional French title *L'Amour Sorcier*, and is black and white. vb. Title page also has the English title, *Love the Magician*, gives the price as 15 shillings (Fr. 22.50), additional addresses in Geneva and Brussels, and a 1921 copyright notice. vb. Cast. Argument. Synopsis. vb. m. on pp. 1–40. p.n. 9713. pp. [41] and [43] blank. p. [42] adv. *Les Grands..* Back cover has a drawing of a guitar. The *Danse Rituelle du Feu* is on p. 16. BM(CDC) and JF. The French piano-vocal edition by Eschig was published in Oct., 1925, and regular Spanish printings are believed to be even later.[1]

The orchestral score of the entire ballet was published by J. & W. Chester, Ltd., in May, 1924, according to the publisher, but no copy was deposited at BM until Nov. 20, 1929. Possible first edition: Front cover is gray and black, refers to Chester Library, and the price is 40/ (Fr. 60.00). vb. Title page also has a French title, four arrangements, the address as above and Paris and Brussels places. Printed in Austria. Verso has legal notices. m. on pp. 3–108. p.n. 41. There is a 1924 copyright claim on p. 3. *Danse Rituelle du Feu* is on p. 41. Inside and outside of back cover blank (missing in BM copy). BM(CDC), publisher, JMM and JF.

Orchestral parts of the entire ballet were published by J. & W. Chester, Ltd., London, with plate number 41a; early printing at publisher.

The ballet was performed in Madrid in 1915; the copyright for all

---

[1] Letter from Éditions Max Eschig, Paris. Copies of *El Amor Brujo* at the following important Spanish libraries are the Chester edition: BNM, MBC and MBM.

countries of the ballet was assigned to J. & W. Chester, Ltd., in 1919, Falla's contract with Eschig having expired.[2] Brief biographic information regarding Falla and Sierra appears above under *Dance of the Corregidor*.

Robin Adair

What's this dull town   to me? Rob - in's not   near

The melody of *Robin Adair* was first known with other words under the title *Ellen A Roon*, which was sung in the opera *The Beggar's Wedding*, two different piano-vocal scores of which were published in 1729. One piano-vocal score indicates the opera is by Mr. Char. Coffey and was printed for N. Rich, London, the words and music of *Ellen A Roon* being on separate pages as Air LII; CUL. The other piano-vocal score gives no author of the opera, states that this is the 2d Edition and was printed for I: Walsh, I: Hare and I: Young, London, *Ellen A Roon* being on p. 48; BM (not in first edition by these printers, BM). A broadside with different words was published without imprint about 1740 under the title *Ailen Aroon*, an Irish Ballad, at BM, and the title is also spelled *Eileen Aroon*, *Aileen Aroon* and in other variants. This old melody has been claimed by various authorities to be of Irish, Scottish and English origin.[1]

The words of *Robin Adair* were written by Lady Caroline Keppell in the early 1750's about her lover, a surgeon, Robert Adair, whom she was permitted to marry only in a later year.[1] The earliest known printing of the song *Robin Adair* is in 1793 in vol. II of *The Edinburgh Musical Miscellany* (Edinburgh), p. 304, with words slightly different than those now known; NYPL, *BUC*, p. 953, and JF. The song was featured by Mr. Braham early in the nineteenth century. After her marriage to Robert Adair in 1758, Lady Caroline died in 1769 at the age of thirty-two.

Rock-a-Bye Baby

Rock - a - bye ba - by   on   the tree top

[2] Letter from J. & W. Chester, Ltd. Jaime Pahissa, *Manuel de Falla, His Life and Works* (London, 1954), p. 84; NYPL.

[1] Fitz-Gerald, p. 12. Moffat, *Minstrelsy of Scotland*, p. 261.

The words of this lullaby were first published about 1765[1] in *Mother Goose's Melody* (John Newbery, London), p. 39, with the opening words as "Hush-a-bye, Baby, on the tree top."

About 1872, Effie I. Crockett, then about fifteen years old and baby-sitting for a restless baby, composed the above music and changed the opening words.[2] The song was published probably in 1884 under the title *Rock-a-Bye Baby*, the pseudonym Effie I. Canning being adopted by the composer. Probable first edition: Collective title front cover is headed "Beautiful Songs Sung by Mlle. Patti Rosa," there are drawings of the singer and a lake, 11 songs are listed, no. 5, *Rock-a-Bye Baby* at 40 (cents), the publisher is Charles D. Blake & Co., 488 Washington St., Boston, there are five agents and a copyright claim of 1884[3] that appears originally to have been printed as 1883.[3] p. [2] blank. m. on pp. 3–5, **engraved.** P. 3 credits the words and music to Effie I. Canning, has a dedication to John P. Curran and the copyright is 1886.[3] p.n. 130–3. p. 3 adv. *Our.*. p. 4 adv. *Bye.*. p. 5 adv. *The Old.*. Back cover adv. *Baby's.. - She's.*. BR. The above edition seems earlier than a similar edition with a single title front cover, with music pages not engraved and p.n. 144-3; JF. In neither of the two editions is there a reference to or drawing of *The Old Homestead* which was produced in Boston in 1886.

Effie I. Crockett, a relative of Davy Crockett, was born in Rockland, Me., in 1857, became an actress, married Harry J. Carlton and died in Boston in 1940.[4]

Rock of Ages

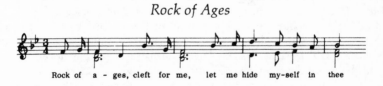

Rock of a - ges, cleft for me, let me hide my-self in thee

The first four lines of the words of *Rock of Ages* by Augustus Toplady were published in the Oct., 1775, issue of *The Gospel Magazine*, London, of which he was then Editor, p. 474, and the entire poem was published

---

[1] Opie, p. 61. No copy of the Newbery edition is known. The earliest located edition was a reprint published about 1785 by Isaiah Thomas, Worcester, Mass.; AAS.

[2] Frances Turgeon Wiggin, *Maine Composers and Their Music* ([Rockland, Me.?] 1959), p. 14; NYPL.

[3] There is no entry of any such copyright in the copyright records at LC, the earliest copyright being April 28, 1887, of the Waltz arrangement "From Canning's beautiful song of same name"; LC (CDC).

[4] Obituary, *The New York Times*, Jan. 9, 1940.

in the Feb., 1776, issue of the magazine, p. 131;[1] *ULS*, p. 1138. The poem also appeared in 1776 in *Psalms and Hymns for Public and Private Worship*, collected (for the most part) and published by Augustus Toplady (London), p. 308; BM. Augustus Montague Toplady, a clergyman, was born at Farnham, Surrey, in 1740 and died in London in 1778.[2]

The music, and the words, were first published in Thomas Hastings and Lowell Mason, *Spiritual Songs for Social Worship* (Utica, N.Y.), p. 84. The copyright notice on the verso of the title page says "Entered" (presumably, the title) on April 16, 1831, but all copies seen state 1832 on the title page and have a Preface dated Jan., 1832. There are two variants: in one, the Index to the Music is on p. 154 and the Table of First Lines on pp. 155–156 (at UTS and JF); in the other, the Table of First Lines is on pp. 155–160, and the Index to the Music on pp. 161–162 (at UTS and JF). The former with extremely small type on pp. 154–156 is probably earlier. Although this book does not make the claim, Thomas Hastings was the composer of the music.[3] He was born in Connecticut in 1787, was a composer of many hymns and a pioneer in church music and died in 1872.

Romance, op. 44, no. 1—Rubinstein

m. Anton Rubinstein. The first book of *Soirées à St. Petersbourg*, Six Morceaux pour le Piano, op. 44, in which the *Romance* in E flat major appears, was probably first published about Dec., 1859,[1] by C. F. Kahnt, Leipzig. Possible first edition of the first book: Front cover has a dedication to Countess Gisella de Stadion-Than-Warthausen and the prices of the three books on the front cover are 10 Ngr., 15 Ngr. and 25 Ngr. m. on pp. 2–7, no. 1, *Romance*, on p. 2. p.n. 658. It is not known whether the pages are engraved nor whether the back cover is blank. GL and WLS.

M. Bernard, St. Petersburg, published the *Romance* separately on unknown date with p.n. N 21 A no. 11; later editions at LLM, LPL and JF. Jurgenson, Moscow, and Bessel, St. Petersburg, also published the *Romance*

[1] Julian, pp. 970 and 1693.

[2] *NIL*, vol. 22, p. 346.

[3] Mary Browning Scanlon, "Thomas Hastings" in MQ, April, 1946, p. 265, at p. 273. Lewis C. Granniss, *Connecticut Composers* (New Haven, 1935), p. 46; YU.

[1] Hofmeister *Monatsbericht*, Dec., 1859, p. 202.

separately but they commenced publishing in 1861 and 1869, respectively.[2]
Brief biographic information regarding Rubinstein appears above under
Kamennoi-Ostrow.

Romance, op. 24, no. 9—Sibelius

m. Jean Sibelius. This *Romance* in D flat was published about March,
1902,[1] for piano by Helsingfors Nya Musikhandel, Fazer & Westerlund,
Helsinki. Probable first edition: Front cover says *Romance* for piano
solo, and Breitkopf & Härtel, Leipzig, is shown as an agent and lithographer. p. [2] blank. m. on pp. 3-7. Back cover adv. Cassl.. - Sibelius.. As
stated on page 70, Sibelius' compositions published before 1904 had no
opus number, and music published by this concern before 1904 had no
plate number; as a result, the above edition has neither opus number nor
plate number. No price stated. UL and JF.

Breitkopf & Härtel, Leipzig, did not publish this *Romance* until about
1905,[2] and published the entire op. 24, *Zehn Stücke* für Pianoforte zu 2
Händen, about Oct., 1908.[3] Brief biographic information regarding Sibelius
appears above under *Finlandia.*

Romeo and Juliette—Tchaikovsky

m. P. Tchaikovsky. The *Ouverture* à la tragédie de Shakespeare *Roméo
et Juliette* was published for orchestral score about May, 1871,[1] by Ed.
Bote & G. Bock, 33 Französische Str. and 27 Unter den Linden, Berlin, and
21 Wilhelm Strasse, Mylius Hotel, Posen. Probable first edition: Front
cover, mostly in French, is yellow and black. vb. Title page, also mostly in
French, shows the publisher also at Breslau, Lichtenberg, Stettin, Simon,

---

[2] Hopkinson, *Russian,* pp. 6 and 2.

[1] Hofmeister *Monatsbericht,* March, 1902, p. 119.
[2] Not in the Breitkopf & Härtel *Verzeichnis,* Leipzig, "bis ende 1902"; NYPL. In
Breitkopf & Härtel *Musikverlags-Bericht,* Leipzig, 1905, p. 4; NYPL.
[3] Hofmeister *Monatsbericht,* Oct., 1908, p. 273.

---

[1] Hofmeister *Monatsbericht,* May, 1871, p. 82.

Leipzig and Leede, contains legal notices, gives the price as **3 Thlr.**, and is
tan, black and white. vb. m. on pp. 3–201. p.n. 9325. p. [202] blank. Back
cover missing. No other arrangements listed on front cover or on title
page. SSL, MC, HMA* and JF. Some copies contain a page of errors after
page [202]. There is no dedication to M. Balakirev. An early Bote & Bock
edition of the orchestral parts, with p.n. 10297, is at CI. Early Bote &
Bock editions for piano four hands, with p.n. 10676, and for piano, with
p.n. 11545, are at YU.

A Russian orchestral score with Bote & Bock plates was published by
W. Bessel et Cie., St. Petersburg, before ca. 1875;[2] COP. The first version
of this work was completed Nov. 27, 1869, and performed March 16, 1870,
in Moscow; it was revised in 1870 and again in 1880. Brief biographic information regarding Tchaikovsky appears above under *Chant sans Paroles.*

A Room with a View

A room— with a   view,   and   you,   and   no   one to wor - ry us

mw. Noël Coward. Published[1] and a copy deposited at BM on Feb. 28,
1928, by Chappell & Co., Ltd., 50 New Bond Street, London W. 1. First
edition: Front cover is blue and white; while *Charles B. Cochran's 1928
Revue* is mentioned, *This Year of Grace* is not—7 titles are listed, this
song at 2s. p. [2] blank. m. on pp. 1–5 (actually 3–7). p.n. 29567. Back
cover adv. *Just..* BM(CDC).

The musical show opened in London on March 22, 1928, under the
name *This Year of Grace*, and on April 28, 1928, another song from the
show, *Teach Me to Dance like Grandma,* was deposited at BM with a green,
orange and white front cover mentioning *This Year of Grace.* The piano-
vocal score of *This Year of Grace; Charles B. Cochran's 1928 Revue* was
published on May 14, 1928,[1] at 10/ by the same concern; BM(CDC),
LC(CDC) and EW. Brief biographic information regarding Coward appears
above under *I'll Follow My Secret Heart.*

---

[2] Bessel is shown without a Moscow branch; Hopkinson, *Russian*, p. 2. Dombayev,
p. 39, and the *Tchaikovsky Catalogue*, p. 89, confirm that the work was originally published
by Bote & Bock.

---

[1] Copyright records; LC.

Rosamunde Ballet—Schubert

m. Franz Schubert. Published in 1867[1] in orchestral score as no. 6, *Ballet-Musik aus Rosamunde no. 1 u 2*, in *Ouverturen und Entr'actes* für das Orchester componirt von Franz Schubert, by C. A. Spina, Vienna. Probable first edition: Front cover is yellow and black. vb. Title page has title as above, lists six numbers, the price of this being Fl. 2.70 Nkr./ Rthlr. 2.10 Ngr., and the year 1867. The music of the *Ballet no. 1* in G major is on pp. 2–23, followed by two blank pages and the music of *Ballet no. 2* on pp. 24–53. p.n. 19,404. p. [54] and inside and outside of back cover blank. Engraved. Octavo. GM(Aus dem Nachlass von Johannes Brahms) and JF. While the piano arrangement of the *Balletmusik* from *Rosamunde* has a slightly lower p.n., 19401, the title page states "1868"; SB.

Although the music to *Rosamunde* was composed in the autumn of 1823 and the play was performed Dec. 20, 1823, in Vienna, the Ballet music was first published posthumously 44 years later. Brief biographic information regarding Schubert appears above under his *Ave Maria*.

The Rosary

The hours I spent with thee, dear heart

m. Ethelbert Nevin. w. Robert Cameron Rogers. The poem was included at p. 92 in Robert Cameron Rogers, *The Wind in the Clearing, and Other Poems* (New York, N.Y.), copyrighted Nov. 19, 1894.[1] LC (CDC) and NYPL.

The music and the words were copyrighted Aug. 29, 1898,[1] by G. Schirmer, Jr. [New York, N.Y.] First edition: Front cover is tan, black and white, lists *A Life Lesson*, the publisher is Boston Music Co., Boston, Mass., and states at the bottom: "Design copyright 1898." p. [2] blank. m. on pp. 3–5. p.n. 434. p. [6] adv. *Herbstgefühl*. p. [7] adv. *Modern.*. Back cover blank. LC(CDC). Brief biographic information regarding Nevin appears

---

[1] Deutsch, *Schubert*, no. 797, p. 497. The year 1867 appears on the title page. Not in Hofmeister *Monatsbericht* until Oct., 1868, p. 164.

---

[1] Copyright records; LC.

above under *Mighty Lak' a Rose*.[2] Rogers, a poet and journalist, was born in Buffalo in 1862 and died in Santa Barbara, Cal., in 1912.[3]

Roses from the South

m. Johann Strauss. Published for piano Oct. 2, 1880,[1] under the title *Rosen aus dem Süden*, op. 388, by Aug. Cranz, Hamburg. Probable first edition: Front cover has a drawing of roses and Mount Vesuvius, states that the composition is a *Walzer nach Motiven der Operette, Das Spitzentuch der Königin* (*The Queen's Lace Handkerchief*), is dedicated to King Humbert I of Italy (with a drawing of his coat of arms), the price is Fl. 1, Mk. 1.80, and there are references to Vienna and St. Petersburg agents. m. on pp. 2–11. p.n. 25206. Back cover adv. works by Johann, Joseph and Edward Strauss—the works by Johann up to op. 390 which had been published about April, 1880.[2] No arrangements listed on front cover. SB and JF.

The orchestral parts of *Rosen aus dem Süden*, with p.n. 25270, were published about June, 1881,[3] by the same concern; possible first printings are at KH* and WP*. The piano-vocal score of *Das Spitzentuch der Königin*, with p.n. 25221, was also published about June, 1881;[4] ONB. An orchestral score of the operetta, a lithographing of a manuscript, without p.n. or indication of publisher, and of uncertain date, is at BM and SB. The operetta was produced Oct. 1, 1880, in Vienna. The word "South" in the title refers to Spain, the locale of the operetta. Brief biographic information regarding Strauss appears above under *Artist's Life*.

[2] See, also, Vance Thompson, *The Life of Ethelbert Nevin* (Boston, 1913), p. 191; NYPL.

[3] W. Stewart Wallace, *A Dictionary of North American Authors* (Toronto, 1951), p. 388; NYPL.

[1] According to the entry at Stationers' Hall on Jan. 6, 1881. Hofmeister *Monatsbericht*, Nov., 1880, p. 337. Weinmann, *Strauss*, p. 105.

[2] Weinmann, *Strauss*, p. 106.

[3] Hofmeister *Monatsbericht*, June, 1881, p. 135; LC.

[4] *Id.*, p. 151. Weinmann, *Strauss*, p. 136.

Roses of Picardy

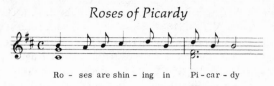

Ro - ses are shin - ing in   Pi - car - dy

© 1916 by Chappell & Co. Ltd. Copyright renewed. Published by Chappell & Co. Inc. By consent.

m. Haydn Wood. w. Fred. E. Weatherly. Published Dec. 4, 1916,[1] by Chappell & Co., Ltd., 50 New Bond Street, London W. First edition: Folio. Front cover is plain, in black and white, mentions branch offices at New York, Melbourne and Toronto, and the price is 1/6 (60¢). m. on pp. 2–7, in the key of D. p.n. 26429. Back cover adv. *Dame.. - Red..* No keys on the front cover.[2] LC (copyright copy deposited Dec. 6, 1916).

The song became a World War I favorite, Picardy being a region in northern France. Wood was born in Slaithwaite, England, in 1882, became a composer of light and serious music and a violinist, and died in London in 1959.[3] Brief biographic information regarding Weatherly appears above under *Nancy Lee.*

Row, Row, Row Your Boat

Row, row,   row your boat   gent - ly down the   stream

This song is apparently American, and perhaps of minstrel origin. Almost the common words, but to a different melody, appear in *Row, Row Your Boat, or The Old Log Hut,* copyrighted Oct. 4, 1852,[1] by Firth, Pond & Co., 1 Franklin Square, New York, N.Y. First edition: Engraved. Front cover states that the song was sung by Master Adams of Kunkels Nightingale Opera Troupe, ascribes the music to R. Sinclair, the price is 25¢ and there are two agents. m. on pp. 2–5. p.n. 1768. Back cover blank. LC(CDC— deposited Oct. 12, 1852, at the Clerk's Office, Southern District, New York, and Dec. 3, 1852, at Smithsonian Institution, Washington, D.C.) and JF. The same words to a different but unfamiliar melody were copyrighted Dec. 13, 1854,[1] under the title *Gently down the Stream* by Berry & Gordon, New York, N.Y., referring to Geo. Christy and Wood's Minstrels; LC(CDC) and JF.

The common music, and the common words, appear for the first time

---

[1] Copyright records; LC.

[2] The copyright copy deposited at BM on Jan. 11, 1917, has three keys on the front cover.

[3] Gammond-Clayton, p. 246. Obituary, *The New York Times,* March 13, 1959.

[1] Copyright records; LC.

in *The Franklin Square Song Collection*, selected by J. P. McCaskey, published in New York, N.Y., in 1881. The music and words are at p. 69; E. O. Lyte's name is given as the composer or adapter of the music and words. In the first edition of this work,[2] deposited at LC on Aug. 27, 1881,[1] vol. I is not mentioned on the covers or title page, and there is no reference to 1884 on the verso of the title page. Also at JF.

The song is a round or canon.

Rudolph the Red-Nosed Reindeer

Ru-dolph, the   red - nosed rein - deer   had a ver - y shin - y   nose

Copyright 1949—St. Nicholas Music Inc. By permission.

mw. Johnny Marks. Published May 9, 1949,[1] by St. Nicholas Music Publishing Co. (no address given) [New York, N.Y.] First edition: Front cover has a drawing of Santa Claus and reindeer led by Rudolph, is red, green, black and white, and refers to Keys Music, Inc., 146 West 54th Street, New York 19, N.Y., as sole selling agents; no price or arrangements. m. on pp. 2–3. No plate number. No copyright warning at top of p. 2. Back cover adv. *Happy..* Both the front cover and page 2 state that the song is based on the book of the same name. LC(CDC).

Rudolph the Red-Nosed Reindeer was originally a story written in 1939 by Robert L. May for Montgomery Ward, & Co., Inc., Chicago, several million copies of which were published in pamphlet form on Nov. 1, 1939,[1] and given away by that concern to its customers at Christmas that year.[2] Copy at Robert L. May, Evanston, Ill. The author was then and still is employed by that concern in Chicago. More than 79,000,000 records of the song have been sold, and the original Gene Autry record is said to rank second in sales only to Bing Crosby's *White Christmas*. John D. Marks, a composer, lyricist and writer, was born in Mount Vernon, N.Y., in 1909, and lives in New York City.[3]

---

[2] M 1619. M 151.

[1] Copyright records; LC.

[2] Barbara Bundschu, "Rudolph's Bright Nose Changes Santa Legend" in *Musigram*, Covina, Cal., Dec., 1962, p. 10; NYPL. *The New York Times*, Dec. 25, 1969, p. 39.

[3] *ASCAP*, p. 337.

Rule Britannia

Rule Bri-tan-nia! Bri-tan-nia rule the waves; Bri-tons nev - er will be slaves

m. Thomas Augustine Arne. w. Either David Mallet or James Thomson. The words of *Rule Britannia* were published Aug. 19, 1740,[1] in the libretto of *Alfred: A Masque,* printed for A. Millar, over-against St. Clement's Church in the Strand, London, p. 42. There are two variants of this edition, priority unknown: in one, there is a price of one shilling on the half-title page, BM and JF; the other lacks a price and half-title page, BM. As stated on the title page of the libretto, *Alfred* was presented at Cliffden on Aug. 1, 1740.

The music and words of *Rule Britannia,* the "celebrated Ode, in Honour of Great-Britain," were published in early 1741[2] as an addition to *The Music in the Judgment of Paris,* composed by Thomas Augustine Arne and printed for Henry Waylett, at the Black Lyon in Exeter Change in ye Strand, London, p. 62. The music is printed in orchestral score. *BUC,* p. 41, and JF. The earliest score of *Alfred,* lacking *Rule Britannia,* was published in 1751, and with the song in 1757; *BUC,* p. 41. The earliest separate printing of the song was about 1755; *BUC,* p. 41.

The Ode was written in commemoration of the accession of the House of Hanover. In the original 1740 and 1741 versions, the text reads "rule" the waves; later, "rule" was sometimes changed to "rules"—with a different meaning. The authorship of the words is in dispute as between Mallet and Thomson.[3] Arne was born in London in 1710 and died there in 1778.[4]

Rum and Coca-Cola

Drink - in' rum and Co - ca —— Co - la, go down "Point Koo - mah - nah"

© Copyright 1944, 1956 Leo Feist, Inc., New York, N.Y. Used by permission.

[1] William Hayman Cummings, *Dr. Arne and Rule, Britannia* (London, 1912), p. 116; NYPL. The year 1740 appears on the title page, as does the statement that the masque was presented Aug. 1, 1740.

[2] The verso of the title page sets forth a grant of Royal Privilege and License from George the Second to Arne to publish certain works, dated Jan. 29, "1740–1 [*sic*], in the Fourteenth Year of Our Reign," i.e., 1741.

[3] Kidson, *Minstrelsy of England,* pp. 306 and 318.

[4] *Grove's,* vol. 1, p. 208.

Much of the origin of this song is known as a result of the information set forth in two copyright infringement actions, one relating to the music[1] and the other relating to the words.[2] It appears that in 1906 Lionel Belasco in Port of Spain, Trinidad, British West Indies, composed much of the above melody and other words under the title *L'Année Passée* (*Last Year*) which was included in a collection entitled *Calypso Songs of the West Indies* by Massie Patterson and Lionel Belasco, published Dec. 31, 1943,[3] by M. Baron Co., 8 West 45th St., New York 19, N.Y., at p. 22. First edition: Front cover is tan and black. vb. Title page mentions Free Transcription by Maurice Baron and the price is $1.50. Foreword (including a reference to television in the last paragraph). Contents. m. on pp. 2–25. p. [26] adv. *Ah.. - Where..* Inside of back cover blank. Outside of back cover: M B Co. LC(CDC) and JF*. No biographical data about Belasco is known.

Meanwhile, in Feb., 1943, Rupert Grant, a singer in a Calypso tent in Port of Spain, whose platform title in the tent was "Lord Invader," composed and sang much of the new words of *Rum and Coca-Cola* to Belasco's music. These words of *Rum and Coca-Cola* were included in a booklet entitled *Victory Calypsoes, 1943 Souvenir Collection*, published and copyrighted in Trinidad on March 1, 1943, by Lion and Atilla. Probable first edition: A small booklet of words. Front cover is yellow and black. Price 50¢. Unpaged. Near the end are the words of "Rum and Coca-Cola (By Invader)." LC. Grant died in 1961 in New York City at the age of forty-seven.[4]

The sheet music edition of *Rum and Coca-Cola*, with words credited to Morey Amsterdam and the music credited to Jeri Sullavan and Paul Baron, was copyrighted as an unpublished composition on Sept. 27, 1944, and published Dec. 11, 1944, by Leo Feist, Inc., New York, N.Y.[3] This sheet music edition was held to infringe the music of Lionel Belasco and the words of the "Lord Invader."[5] However, all court injunctions against Leo Feist, Inc., were subsequently dissolved and all adverse claims disposed of, and Feist became free to exercise and license all rights in this composition as copyright proprietor, and continues to credit the first three persons mentioned in this paragraph for the words and music of *Rum and Coca-Cola*.

---

[1] *Maurice Baron* vs. *Leo Feist, Inc.*, 78 Fed. Supp. 686 (Southern District, N.Y. 1948), affirmed, 173 Fed. (2nd) 288 (2nd Circuit Court of Appeals, 1949); NYPL.

[2] *Khan* vs. *Leo Feist, Inc.*, 70 Fed. Supp. 450 (Southern District, N.Y. 1947), affirmed, 165 Fed. (2nd) 188 (2nd Circuit Court of Appeals, 1947); NYPL.

[3] Copyright records; LC.

[4] *Sing Out!*, New York, N.Y., Dec., 1961–Jan., 1962, p. 53; NYPL.

[5] See, also, Louis Nizer, *My Life in Court* (New York, N.Y., 1961), p. 233, at NYPL, and Spaeth, p. 558. Nizer also refers to an untraced song *King Ja-Ja*.

Rumanian Rhapsody, op. 11, no. 1—Enesco

m. Georges Enesco. Published in orchestral score on Oct. 15, 1909,[1] by
Enoch & Cie., 27 Bd. des Italiens, Paris. Possible first edition: Title page is
in lavender, green and white with a drawing of leaves, lists the three
Rhapsodies, each for orchestral score, parts and separate parts, the price
of *no. 1* orchestral score being 10 [francs]; *no. 2* has prices, but not *no. 3;*
and there is a reference to London and Brunswick agents. vb. m. on pp. 1–
89. Page 1 has a dedication to B. Crocé-Spinelli. p.n. 6058. p. [90] blank.
Folio. NYPL. A variant, priority not known, has a blue and white title page
which refers only to the London agent and has other differences; LC.

The orchestral parts were published on Oct. 23, 1909.[1] Possible first
editions, but without a front cover, with plate number 6059, are at CI and
NYPS. NYPS has a front cover of *Rhapsody no. 2*, similar to the title
pages described above, showing the price of the orchestral parts of *no. 1*
as 25 [francs]. The *Rhapsody no. 1* was performed in Paris on Feb. 7, 1908.
Enesco was born in Dorohoiù, Rumania in 1881, and died in Paris in 1955.

Ruslan and Ludmila-Overture—Glinka

m. M. I. Glinka. The piano-vocal score of Русланъ и Людмила was published in 1856[1] by F. Stellovsky, 27 Grande Morskaia, Maison de Laufert,
St. Petersburg. Possible first edition: Front cover in Russian is gray and
black, lists six agents and the price of 20 Rub. vb. Next page blank. Portrait of composer. Title page in Russian. vb. Cast and index in German and
Russian. vb. m. on pp. 1–396, engraved, the music of the *Overture* on p. 1.
p.n. 301.(1)–301.(26). Text in German and Russian. p. 396 has censor's
approval dated Feb. 9, 1856. Inside of back cover blank. Outside of back
cover adv. various Russian works and two German works, *Dudelsack..* and
Das Raaben.. BN, ONB* and JF (not all preliminary pages in all copies).

---

[1] Letter from publisher.

[1] Based on the date of the censor's approval, Feb. 9, 1856.

The first known printing of the orchestral score of the *Overture* to
Rouslane et Ludmila was published about Feb. 1858,[2] by C. F. W. Siegel,
Leipzig. Possible first edition: Front cover is pink and black. vb. Title page
has a dedication to Mr. H. Berlioz, the price is 1½ Rth., and five publishers
are listed headed by C. F. W. Siegel, Leipzig. vb. m. on pp. 3–66. p.n. 1.
Engraved. Octavo. BPL. A variant edition omits M. M. Bernard et Stellovsky, St. Petersburg, and substitutes the Schott concerns at Mainz, Brussels
and London; LLD. Priority between the variants is unknown.

The orchestral score of the opera was published probably in late 1878[3]
by Mrs. Golubeff. Possible first edition: Front cover in Russian is gray and
black. vb. Title page in Russian is green, black and white, mentioning that
the text is based on a poem by A. S. Pushkin. vb. Title page in German. vb.
Dedication in Russian to the composer's brother. vb. Notice dated Sept. 16,
1878, in Russian and German that this orchestral score is to be sold at 25
Rub. by Mrs. Golubeff, sister of the above-mentioned publisher, Stellovsky.
Cast in Russian and German. Index in Russian. Index in German. m. on pp.
1–723. p.ns. 7000-9. All pages after dedication page engraved. p. [724]
blank. Back cover blank. Folio. SSL, BM and LC. There is also a De Luxe
edition of the above orchestral score with wider margins bound in full
leather; LC. Priority between the variants is unknown. No early printing
of the orchestral parts of the opera has been found.

Ruslan and Ludmila was composed in 1838–1841 and performed Nov.
27, 1842, in St. Petersburg. Michael Ivanovitch Glinka was born in Novos-
passkoi, Govt. of Smolensk, in 1803 and died in Berlin in 1857.

Russian Czarist National Anthem

Baw - zheh Tsah - ryah hrah - nee!   Seel - nih dyehr - zhahv - nih

m. Alexei Lvov. w. W. A. Zhukovsky. In 1833 Czar Nicholas I commanded
Alexei Lvov, director of the Imperial court choir, to compose a Russian
national anthem. Possible first edition: Front cover, in Russian, gives the
title as *Боже Царя Храни!* (*God Save the Czar!*) for one voice and piano,
states "Song of the Russians," the price is 2 rubles and the engraver and
printer is Andrei Shteding, St. Petersburg. vb. m. on p. 2 (actually 3). p.n.
6. Back cover blank. Engraved. No mention of Lvov or Zhukovsky
although this particular copy is signed by A. Lvov on the front cover.
BM.[1] Shteding was publishing as early as 1829, and a Widow Shteding

[2] Hofmeister *Monatsbericht*, Feb., 1858, p. 18.
[3] Based on the date in the Notice in the score, Sept. 16, 1878. Wolffheim, p. 277.

[1] Oliver W. Neighbour, BM, discovered and researched this item.

published a *Musical Album* for 1835 with a censorship date of Dec. 12, 1834, in which the first item is "God Save the Czar!"[2]

Another possible first edition, and a probable first edition in the form in which it was composed, namely, for choir, was published by K. Petz, St. Petersburg. The price is 150 kopecks. m. on pp. 2–3. p.n. 39. Back cover blank. Engraved. No mention of Lvov or Zhukovsky. As Petz started to publish about 1810,[3] p.n. 39 may indicate a date about 1833. JF. A "New Edition," also in Russian, published by Karl Petz, states prominently on the front cover "Property of the Publisher"; this edition is an arrangement for piano and one voice and has p.n. 38. BSM.†

About July, 1839,[4] Ad. Mt. Schlesinger, Berlin, published an arrangement for orchestral score and chorus, with p.n. 2324, mentioning Lvov. JF. About June 1840,[5] the same publisher issued an arrangement for piano and voice, also mentioning that the poem was by "Joukowsky," with p.n. 2551; early edition at JF.

Lvov composed the music in the autumn of 1833, and soon thereafter Zhukovsky wrote the words.[6] The hymn made such a good impression on the Czar and Czarina when it was performed in the Court Chapel in Nov., 1833, by a choir and orchestra that it was formally decreed on Dec. 4, 1833, to be the official anthem.[6] Lvov was born in Reval in 1798 and died near Kovno in 1870.[7] Zhukovsky was born in Tula in 1783, became a poet and tutor of Czar Alexander II and died in 1852 in Baden-Baden.[8] A manuscript of the anthem, signed by Lvov and dated March 2, 1834, is at SC.

A controversy once existed as to whether Lvov actually composed the *Russian Czarist National Anthem*.[9] An article in *RMG*, 1903, p. 1313, signed "Tenor," pointed to *Marsch aus Petersburg von Reg. Preobragensky*, by Haas, no. 99, published by Ad. Mt. Schlesinger, Berlin, orchestral score, with allegedly p.n. 1620. The trio of the march, set forth in the article, is

[2] B. Vol'man, *Russkie Notnye Izdaniia XIX – Nachala XX Veka* (Leningrad, 1970), p. 194; BM and NYPL.

[3] Hopkinson, *Russian*, p. 8.

[4] AMZ, July 17, 1839, p. 558.

[5] Hofmeister *Monatsbericht*, June, 1840, p. 118.

[6] "Lvov's Memoirs" in *Russkii Arkhiv* (Moscow, 1884), vol. 22, part II, p. 225, and part III, p. 65; LC and NYPL. MT, Feb. 1, 1915, p. 82. Letter from SSL.

Zhukovsky had written another patriotic poem in 1814 entitled *The Prayer of the Russian People*. (*Polnoe Sobranie Sochinenii—Complete Works of V. A. Zhukovsky*, edited by A. S. Arkhangel'sky, St. Petersburg, 1902, vol. 2, p. 77, at SSL, NYPL and LC.) This poem became the third stanza, and the poem of the *Russian Czarist National Anthem* became the first stanza of a further poem by Zhukovsky entitled *Folk Songs* (*Id.*, vol. 4, p. 23). Contrary to Nettl, *National Anthems*, p. 128, no printing has been found in the Soviet Union or elsewhere of Lvov's music set to Zhukovsky's 1814 poem.

[7] *Grove's*, vol. 5, p. 451.

[8] *NIE*, vol. 23, p. 855. Böhme, p. 563.

[9] Nicolas Slonimsky, New York City, called this controversy to the attention of the author.

identical with that of the anthem. Heirs of Schlesinger wrote the author
of the article that the march was published 1820–1822. The plate number suggests an 1830–1831 date.[10] It is, however, listed for the first time in Hofmeister in the 1839 *Handbuch* covering the period Jan., 1834–Dec., 1838, p.
10. An excellent article in *RMG*, 1904, p. 198, sets forth arguments on both
sides but comes to no conclusion. Unfortunately, no copy of the march has
been found. Ferdinand Haas (Haase?) was born in 1787 and died in 1851 and
for some time was Kapellmeister of the Preobragensky Regiment; he apparently never openly protested against Lvov's "borrowing" of his march,
if that was, in fact, the case.

Subsequent research is said to have confirmed Lvov's composition, and
this continues as the view of Soviet Union musicologists.[11]

Saber Dance—Khatchaturian

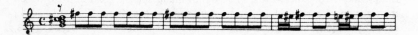

m. A. Khatchaturian. The ballet *Гаянэ* (*Gayaneh*), in which *Танец с Саблями*
(*Saber Dance* or *Sword Dance*) appears, was first published in an arrangement for piano four hands in the middle of 1945 by the State Music Publishers, Moscow and Leningrad. The following copy was deposited Aug. 29,
1945, at the Lenin Library, Moscow, and is probably the first printing: Front
cover is hard and in light and dark blue and gold. Title page, in Russian,
is in light and dark tan and black and mentions the year 1945. Two pages
in Russian. vb. m. on pp. 5–537. p.n. 18144. The *Saber Dance* is on p. 503.
P. [538] has index and mentions the date April 23, 1945, as part of the
Soviet publishing procedure.[1] Back cover has the price 100 rubles. LLM,
BM, JMM and JF.

An orchestral arrangement of the *Saber Dance* is included in the

---

[10] Deutsch, *Plate Numbers*, p. 21.

[11] Н. Соловьёв, *Алексей Федорович Львов. Его Гимн и Деятельность* (N. So-
lov'yev, *Alexei Feodorovich Lvov, His Anthem and Activities*) (St. Petersburg, 1908), p.
3; and Б. С. Штейнпресс and И. М. Ямпольский, *Энциклопедический Музыкальный
Словарь* (B. S. Shteinpress and I. M. Yampol'sky, *Encyclopedic Musical Dictionary*)
(Moscow, 1959), p. 13. Both at SSL; latter also at LC. Madame L. N. Pavlova-Sil'vansky,
at SSL, kindly called these two authorities to the author's attention.

[1] Not in *AML* until July–Dec., 1946, p. 55.

Gayaneh Third Suite published in 1947 by the same concern. Possible first edition: Front cover in Russian and English is light and dark green and black. vb. Title page is the same as the front cover and mentions the year 1947. Instrumentation. m. on pp. 3–178. No plate number. The *Saber Dance* is no. 5 on p. 126. p. [179] has index. p. [180] mentions the date July 4, 1946, as part of the Soviet publishing procedure.[2] Inside of back cover blank. Outside of back cover has price 68 rub. SSL, BM, NYPL, JMM and JF.

The orchestral score of the entire ballet has not yet been published.[3] Nor has any early printing of the orchestral parts of the entire ballet been found. The *Saber Dance* was not published separately for piano or for orchestra prior to the dates mentioned above. *Gayaneh* was performed Dec. 9, 1942, in Molotov, U.S.S.R. Aram Khatchaturian was born in Tiflis in 1903 of Armenian extraction, lived in Moscow and died in 1978.[4]

Sailing

Sail - ing,   sail - ing   o - ver the bound-ing main

mw. Godfrey Marks. Published in 1880[1] by Reid Brothers, 436 Oxford Street, London W. Possible first edition: Front cover refers to three keys, of which this is no. 3 in D, mentions that the song is sung by Egbert Roberts, the price is 4/ and the New York agent is Williams & Sons. p. [2] blank. m. on pp. 1–9 (actually 3–11). No plate number. Back cover adv. *Only.. - Full..* No other song mentioned on front cover. JF.

James Frederick Swift, who wrote under the pseudonym of Godfrey Marks, was born in Manchester in 1847, became an organist and composer and died in Wallasey, Cheshire, in 1931.[1]

---

[2] Not in *AML* until Oct.–Dec., 1948, p. 28.
[3] Letter from SSL.
[4] Obituary, *The New York Times*, May 3, 1978.

---

[1] Obituary, *The Liverpool Echo*, Jan. 9, 1931; copy with composer's daughter, Ruby G. Swift, Wallasey, Cheshire.

The Sailor's Hornpipe

The earliest known printing of this melody is about 1775 under the title *The Colledge* [sic] *Hornpipe* in *The Compleat Tutor for the Violin* by Geminiani, published by C. & S. Thompson, London, at page 20.[1] *BUC*, p. 368.[2]

Chappell, p. 740, says that the tune was an old sailors' song called *Jack's the Lad*, but no printing under this title has been found. If the dance is of Irish origin,[3] no Irish printing has been found prior to the one described above.

Salut d'Amour—Elgar

m. Edward Elgar. *Salut d'Amour*, op. 12, was apparently first published for orchestral score and orchestral parts about Oct., 1889,[1] by B. Schott's Söhne, Mainz. Possible first edition of the orchestral score, deposited Jan. 3, 1901, at BM: The title page lists eight titles under the heading Repertoire des Orchestres et Harmonies, of which *Salut d'Amour* is the last at 2 M; after the title appears the subtitle *Liebesgruss*, Morceau Mignon; and the publisher has affiliates in London, Paris, Brussels and Sydney. vb. m. on pp. 1–11. p.n. 24787. p. [12] adv. Arditi.. - Wagner.. Octavo. Covers lacking. This edition does not refer to Humperdinck's *Hänsel und Gretel* (1894).

[1] Nigel Simeone, London, has been helpful in connection with this title.

[2] *BUC*, p. 368, also states that the above *Tutor* is the same as Geminiani's *New and Compleat Instructions for the Violin*, of the same approximate date, at RCM, but a letter from RCM states otherwise.

[3] O'Neill, *Irish Folk*, p. 301.

[1] Hofmeister *Monatsbericht*, Oct., 1889, p. 394. The publisher has confirmed that the orchestral score was published in 1889. However, the price in Hofmeister and in the Schott *Catalogue*, Mainz, 1894, p. 336, LC, is shown as 1 M, not 2 M as in the BM copy.

BM. A possible first printing of the orchestral parts, with the same plate number 24787, is at BM. Subsequent arrangements indicate that the work was dedicated to Carice. *Salut d' Amour* was composed in 1889 and performed in London on Nov. 11, 1889.

The arrangements for piano, and for violin and piano, were published about Jan., 1890;[2] copies with the same p.n. as that of the orchestral score, 24787, were also deposited BM on Jan. 3, 1901. Brief biographic information regarding Elgar appears above under *Pomp and Circumstance*.

Santa Lucia

Ve-ni-te all   a-gi-le   bar-chet-ta mi - a   San - ta— Lu - ci - a!

mw. T. Cottrau. Published probably late 1850 or 1851 by Stabilimento Musicale Partenopeo Successore di B. Girard e Co., 35 S. Pietro a Majello, Naples, of which Cottrau was then the manager.[1] Probable first edition: Front cover is entitled *Collezione Completa delle Canzoncine Nazionali Napoletane*, listing numbers for piano and for guitar, but neither *Santa Lucia* nor the composer is mentioned on the front cover. m. on pp. 2–3. p. 2 has a dedication to Mlle. Adolphine Deutz, followed by the place and date (composition, dedication, performance, publication?) of Naples, Oct. 28, 1850, T. Cottrau F. Price 15 Gr. p.n. 9640 C. Back cover blank. Engraved. JF (possibly a Kingdom of Naples copyright deposit copy). After Italy was unified and the first national copyright law was enacted on June 25, 1865, a second edition was deposited Oct. 30, 1865, with the Prefect of Naples[2] which mentions that the first edition had p.n. 9640; the second edition had p.n. 13649 and the publisher was then known as T. Cottrau, 49 Largo di Palazzo, Naples.[3] SCR(CDC—103.G.1[38]).

Teodoro Cottrau, a composer, lyricist, publisher, journalist and politician, was born in Naples in 1827 and died there in 1879.[1]

---

[2] Hofmeister *Monatsbericht*, Jan., 1890, pp. 9 and 11. Schott *Catalogue*, Mainz, 1893, p. 48; LC.

[1] Sartori, pp. 53 and 77. *DM*, p. 164, gives 1849 as the year, but the Oct. 28, 1850, date appears in both of the editions mentioned in the text.

[2] Copyright records; UDP.

[3] A still later edition published by T. Cottrau, Piazza Municipio, Naples, has plate number 8061, but publisher's number 17838; SS. Piazza Municipio was Cottrau's address at the time of his death in 1879; Sartori, p. 53.

Say It with Music

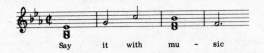

Say   it   with   mu - sic

mw. Irving Berlin. Published March 21, 1921,[1] by Irving Berlin, Inc., 1607 Broadway, New York, N.Y. The copyright deposit copy is a professional edition; LC. Probable first regular edition: Front cover states "Hazzard" Short (in later editions, corrected to read "Hassard" Short), has a photograph of a music box and is purple, orange and white. s. *Music Box Revue* —10 titles listed. p. [2] adv. *In..* m. on pp. 3–5. Back cover adv. *In.. - Behind..* All the other songs listed from this show were published in Oct. and Nov., 1921. JF. The above edition is the same, to the extent possible, as other, regular edition, copyright deposit copies at LC from the same show.

The first *Music Box Revue* opened in New York City on Sept. 22, 1921. A special lyric for the song was written by the composer on the occasion of ASCAP's 50th anniversary. *The New York Times*, Feb. 16, 1964, sec. 11, p. 9. Brief biographic information regarding Berlin appears above under *Alexander's Ragtime Band.*

Scarf Dance—Chaminade

m. C. Chaminade. The *Pas des Echarpes*, 3ᵉ Air de Ballet was published for piano about July–Sept., 1888,[1] by Enoch Frères & Costallat, 27 Bould. des Italiens, Paris. First edition: Front cover in brown and white has a drawing of a branch and three butterflies, the price is 6f.—4/, and there is reference to a London affiliate. p. [2] blank. m. on pp. 1–7 (actually 3–9). p.n. 1512. Back cover blank. BN(CDC).

[1] Copyright records; LC.

[1] *BMF*, July–Sept., 1888, p. 35. It was not entered for Dépôt Légal until Oct. 25, 1888; Archives. *BF*, Nov. 17, 1888, p. 733. *Pas des Echarpes* and *Callirhoë* were later assigned op. no. 37.

The "Dance of the Scarves" was originally in the ballet *Callirhoë*, produced in 1888 at Marseilles. A piano score of *Callirhoë* was published Sept. 20, 1888.[2] First edition: Front cover is red and gray. vb. Title page mentions that *Callirhoë* is a Ballet Symphonique by Elzéard Rougier, there is a dedication to Édouard Brunel, the price is 10 fr. and the imprint is as given above. vb. Distribution. vb. m. on pp. 1–99 (engraved—advance copy?). p.n. 1505. COP (CDC). A lithographed copy at JMM (inscribed by the composer).

A *Suite d'Orchestre* from *Callirhoë* was published June 20, 1890,[3] by the same concern, no. 2 being *Pas du Voile* (*Dance of the Veil*). Possible first edition of the orchestral score: Front cover is red and gray. vb. Next two pages blank. Title page in red and white lists the orchestral score at 10 fr., orchestral parts at 25 fr., and supplementary parts at 2 fr. vb. m. on pp. 1–83, no. 2 at p. 22. p.n. 1733. p. [84] and inside of back cover blank. Outside of back cover adv. *España—Capricante*. LC and NYPL. Cécile Chaminade, a pianist and composer, was born in Paris in 1861 and died in Monte Carlo in 1944.[4]

Scheherazade—Rimsky-Korsakov

m. N. Rimsky-Korsakov. Published about Jan., 1890,[1] as a symphonic suite for orchestral score and orchestral parts by M. P. Belaieff, Leipzig. Possible first edition of the orchestral score: Front cover in Russian, has the title Шехеразада, a drawing of minarettes and is gray, black and red. vb. Title page in French is framed by an oriental design and is in many brilliant colors; there is a dedication to Vladimir Stassoff; after the title appears "d'après 'Mille et une Nuits' "; op. no. 35; four arrangements are listed, the orchestral score at M 24/R 12; p.ns. 178–180. Synopsis in Russian and French. m. on pp. 3–227. p.n. 178. Inside and outside of back cover blank. BSM; also at JF without covers. The same edition, except adding A. Büttner, St. Petersburg, as the agent on the title page, is at SSL. A copy at

---

[2] Letter from the publisher. *BMF*, July–Sept., 1888, p. 35. It was not entered for Dépôt Légal until Nov. 7, 1888; Archives. *BF*, Dec. 1, 1888, p. 762.

[3] Letter from the publisher. Sonneck, *Orchestral Music*, p. 76.

[4] *Grove's*, vol. 2, p. 156.

[1] Hofmeister *Monatsbericht*, Jan., 1890, p. 2, mentioning the German price as M 24.

BM, probably intended for the European market, is the same as the BSM copy except the front cover is in Russian and French, in gray and black, and states 1889.

Early printings of the orchestral parts with p.n. 179 are at CI and FPL. An early edition of the arrangement for piano four hands, with p.n. 180, published about Feb., 1890,[2] is at JF. *Scheherazade* was composed in 1888 and performed in 1889 in St. Petersburg. Brief biographic information regarding Rimsky-Korsakov appears above under *Capriccio Espagnol.*

School-Days

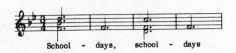

School - days, school - days

Copyright MCMVI and MCMVII by Gus Edwards Pub. Co., New York. Copyright renewed MCMXXXIV and assigned to Shapiro, Bernstein & Co. Inc., New York, and Mills Music Inc., New York. By permission of both publishers.

mw. [Will D.] Cobb and [Gus] Edwards. Copyrighted Nov. 16, 1906,[1] by Gus Edwards Music Pub. Co., 1512 Broadway, New York, N.Y. Possible first regular edition[2] deposited March 2, 1907, at LC: Front cover has a drawing of school children and is black, tan and white. p. [2] adv. *If..* m. on pp. 3–5. The copyright claim on p. 3 is 1907. Back cover adv. *I'll..* LC(CDC).

Cobb, a lyricist, was born in Philadelphia in 1876 and died in New York City in 1930.[3] Brief biographic information regarding Edwards appears above under *By the Light of the Silvery Moon.*

---

[2] *Id.*, Feb., 1890, p. 49.

---

[1] Copyright records; LC.

[2] It is possible that there was an earlier printing of the song. Correspondence between the Library of Congress and the publisher, on file in the Copyright Office, indicates that the first copies of the song were deposited Jan. 24, 1907, entry of which was made in the Copyright Office under date of Nov. 16, 1906; the publisher later requested the cancellation of this copyright. Thereafter, a professional edition was published and deposited on Feb. 1, 1907; the 8th–12th bars of the second stanza of the Introduction in this professional edition mention "level hills," the copyright claim being 1907; LC(CDC). However, the regular edition described in the text above refers to "forty stories." A professional edition of the latter version states that it was copyrighted in 1906; JF.

[3] *ASCAP*, p. 89.

Scotch Bagpipe Melody

This melody first appeared in print in 1609 to the words "Oft have I ridden upon my gray nag" in *Pammelia*, published in London, p. 30. *RISM*, p. 425. Although it is not so stated, this work was collected by Thomas Ravenscroft. The melody then was included in 1651 under the title *Sedanny, or Dargason* in *The English Dancing Master*, London, p. 71. *BUC*, p. 317. As *The Melody of Cynwyd*, the music appears in the 1794 edition of Edward Jones, *Musical and Poetical Relicks of the Welsh Bards*, London, p. 129.[1]

There are also earlier manuscript and ballad references to *Dargason* and *Sedanny*, but without music; the song is said to date from the second half of the sixteenth century.[2] The song apparently developed independently of the melodically similar *Irish Washerwoman*, which see above.

Semper Fidelis

m. John Philip Sousa. The above part of the march was included in Sousa's *A Book of Instruction for the Field-Trumpet and Drum* (New York, N.Y., 1886), no. 6, p. 112 at p. 115, copyrighted Dec. 27, 1886;[1] LC(CDC).

The entire march was copyrighted Dec. 29, 1888,[1] for band parts by Harry Coleman, 228 North 9th St., Philadelphia, Pa.; there is no p.n. in the copyright deposit copy at LC.

It is not known whether the piano edition of the entire march preceded or followed the band parts. Possible first printing of the piano edition: Front cover has a dedication to the Officers and Men of the United States Marine Corps, there is a drawing of flags, rifles and a bugle, the colors are black and white, the composer is described as Band Master,

---

[1] For the two different editions of this work, see *Men of Harlech*, above.
[2] Chappell, p. 64.

---

[1] Copyright records; LC. The earliest copyrighted piano edition is a simplified edition in 1894; LC(CDC).

United States Marine Corps,[2] and the price is 4; same imprint as above. p. [2] blank. m. on pp. 3–5. No plate number. Back cover adv. *Gladiator.. - Odaliska..*; the three advertised pieces that could be checked (all by Sousa) were copyrighted in 1885–1886. No reference on the front cover to "Solo. Duet." JF. Brief biographic information regarding Sousa appears above under *El Capitan.*

September Song

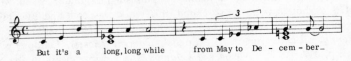

But it's a   long, long while   from May to De - cem - ber—

m. Kurt Weill. w. Maxwell Anderson. Published Sept. 24, 1938,[1] by Crawford Music Corporation, 1619 Broadway, New York. First edition: Front cover is red, gray and white. s. *Knickerbocker Holiday*—3 titles listed. m. on pp. 2–5. Back cover adv. *I..* and *By..* LC(CDC). †

Knickerbocker Holiday opened in New York City on Oct. 19, 1938. Brief biographic information regarding Weill appears under *Mack the Knife.* Anderson, a dramatist and lyricist, was born in Atlantic, Pa., in 1888 and died in Stamford, Conn., in 1959.[2]

Serenade—Drigo

m. Richard Drigo. *Les Millions d'Arlequin,* a ballet, in which *Serenade* appears, was published for piano about Feb., 1901,[1] by Jul. Heinr. Zimmermann, Leipzig, and the following probable first edition was deposited at LC on March 19, 1901: Front cover is red, black and white, has a drawing of a Harlequin, mentions that the ballet is by Marius Petipa and was

---

[2] Sousa was Band Master of the United States Marine Corps from 1880 to 1892; *ASCAP*, p. 471. Front cover is illustrated in Fuld, *American,* p. [45].

---

[1] Copyright records; LC.
[2] *ASCAP*, p. 10.

---

[1] Copyright records; LC. Hofmeister *Monatsbericht*, March, 1901, p. 117.

presented for the first time in St. Petersburg on Feb. 10, 1900, the price is M. 10 and the publisher is shown at three other cities. vb. Title page is brown and white. vb. Dedication to the Empress of Russia. vb. Cast. vb. m. on pp. 3–135, no. 4 on p. 25 is *Sérénade* (without a reference to a 1909 assignment). p.ns. 3247-3369. 1901 copyright notice. p. [136], inside back cover and back cover blank. LC(CDC) and JF. The *Sérénade* separately was published for piano about July, 1901.[2]

Drigo was born in Padua in 1846, composed and conducted in Italy and St. Petersburg and died in Padua in 1930.[3]

Serenade—Moszkowski

m. Moritz Moszkowski. *Sechs Stücke* for piano, op. 15, vol. I, of which *Serenata* was no. 1, was published about Oct., 1877,[1] by Julius Hainauer, Breslau. First edition: Title page is magenta, tan, black and white, there is a dedication to Frau Gräfin Flora Matuschka v. Toppolczau, the price of the first volume is 2 Mk. 25 Pf. and that of the second volume 2 Mk. 75 Pf., four other agents are shown and the six pieces are priced separately, *Serenata* at 1 Mk. m. on pp. 2–13, *Serenata* on p. 2. p.n. 1902. p. [14] blank. BM(CDC received Nov. 20, 1877) and JF.

Moszkowski was born in Breslau in 1854, became a pianist and composer and died in Paris in 1925.[2]

Serenade-Schwanengesang—Schubert

Lei - se flie - hen mei - ne Lie - der   durch die Nacht_ zu Dir

m. Franz Schubert. w. Rellstab. The song cycle *Schwanengesang*, of which the 4th no. of the first book is *Ständchen*, or *Serenade*, was published

[2] Hofmeister *Monatsbericht*, July, 1901, p. 353.
[3] *Grove's*, vol. 2, p. 768.

[1] Hofmeister *Monatsbericht*, Oct., 1877, p. 291.
[2] *Grove's*, vol. 5, p. 911.

Easter, 1829,[1] by Tobias Haslinger, 572 Sparkasse am Graben, Vienna. Probable first edition: Oblong. Engraved. Title page mentions that this is Schubert's last work, the publisher's number 5370 and the prices f. 3 C.M., F. 2. vb. Vignette of a swan above which reads "Praenumerations Exemplar" (subscription copy). vb. List of contents. vb. m. on pp. 1–89, including title page of the second book. The name "Rellstab" appears on p. 1. *Ständchen* is on p. 28. p.ns. 5371–5384. SB (copy formerly belonging to Otto Erich Deutsch), BM(F.409.cc.), Dr. Mario Valente, Los Angeles, and JF. The British Library copy has a subscribers' list. In the next edition, there is no page with vignette for subscribers and the list of contents is on the verso of the title page; BM.

Rellstab's poem had previously been included in his *Gedichte* (Berlin, 1827), booklet 1, p. 101; SW. Schubert might have used the manuscripts which Rellstab gave to Beethoven and which, after the latter's death, are said to have been delivered to Schubert.[2]

Schubert's song cycle was finished Aug.–Oct., 1828. Brief biographic information regarding Schubert appears above under his *Ave Maria*. Ludwig Rellstab, a poet, was born in Berlin in 1799 and died there in 1860.[3]

Serenade—Toselli

m. Enrico Toselli. The *Serenata* for violin and piano, op. 6, was deposited Jan. 5, 1901,[1] with the Prefect of Florence by Edizioni Al Mondo Musicale, Florence. First edition: Front cover in blue and white has a dedication to the composer's friend, Giuseppe Bellesi, a photograph presumably of the composer, the price Fr. 4, and a claim of "Copyright 1900 by C. Graziani— Walter." vb. m. on pp. 3–5, engraved. p.n. 615. pp. [6] and [7] blank. Back cover adv. Compositions of Toselli from op. 2 to op. 7. No other arrangement mentioned. SCR(CDC). In a slightly later edition, p. [7] has the melody for violin; SCR and BNF. A number of lyricists later added words to the melody, which is sometimes known as *Rimpianto*.

Toselli was born in Florence in 1883, was seventeen years old at the time of the publication of his *Serenata*, became a pianist and composer and died in Florence in 1926.[2]

[1] Deutsch, *Schubert*, no. 957, p. 614.† *Wiener Zeitung*, March 23, 1829, p. 304; UMI.
[2] *Grove's*, 3rd ed., vol. 5, p. 614.
[3] *GB*, vol. 9, p. 671.

[1] So stated on the copyright deposit copy at SCR. Two copies of the violin and piano edition were also deposited Jan. 7, 1901, at LC; copyright records at LC.
[2] *Grove's*, vol. 8, p. 519.

Sextet—Lucia di Lammermoor

Chi mi fre-na in tal mo-men-to? Chi tron - cò del-l'i - re il cor - so

m. G. Donizetti. w. Salvatore Cammarano. Eight pieces from the opera *Lucia di Lammermoor*, p.ns. 8987-8996, were published separately for piano about Jan., 1836, but the *Sextet*, *Chi mi frena*, was not among them.[1] The first printing of the *Sextet* was apparently in the piano-vocal score of the opera published about Feb., 1838,[2] by Gio. Ricordi, Milan. Probable first edition of the piano-vocal score, more an assemblage of separate pieces: Oblong. Engraved. Title page has a dedication to Il Signor Marchese del Carretto, the prices are 30 Fr. and 11.30 Fl. cm., and there are references to G. Ricordi e Co., Florence, and B. Girard e Co., Naples. vb. Index showing p.ns. 10076-10094. Cast. Music pages have only separate pagination for each piece—no continuous pagination for the entire piano-vocal score. In many cases the plate numbers in the index are higher than the plate numbers at the bottom of the music pages, and the higher plate numbers shown in the index are not printed on the music pages. The *Sextet* is in the Finale to the 2nd act with plate number 10086. Verso of last music page blank. MIC. The next edition, probably the first regular edition, is identical except there is continuous pagination for the entire piano-vocal score, and the higher plate numbers are also shown on the music pages; NYPL and JF.

A piano-vocal score was published at perhaps about the same time by B. Girard e Ci., Naples, the city in which the opera was first performed on Sept. 26, 1835; copy at SCR. The edition published by Latte, Paris, was presumably issued at the time of the production of the opera in Paris on Aug. 10, 1839; JMM. Probably the first separate sheet music edition of the *Sextet* was published by Gio. Ricordi, Milan, at 3 Fr. and 1.9 Fl., with p.n. 10086, oblong, engraved; ONB*. An early oblong, engraved piano score of the opera by this publisher has p.ns. 8865 *et seq.* and 10151 *et seq.*; SCR.

The engraving of the orchestral parts of the opera for the strings commenced in Aug., 1864, with plate numbers 36262-36265, according to the Ricordi *Libroni*, but the earliest discovered parts, oblong engraved, have the imprint G. Ricordi & C., necessitating a year not earlier than 1898; at MET and JF*. The orchestral parts of the opera for other instruments com-

---

[1] Hofmeister *Monatsbericht*, Jan., 1836, p. 6. Several of the separate pieces are at SCR. The engraving of the separate pieces with p.ns. 10076-10094 commenced April 28-May 16, 1837, with the engraving of the *Sextet* commencing May 1, 1837, according to the Ricordi *Libroni*.

[2] Hofmeister *Monatsbericht*, Feb., 1838, p. 27.

menced on Jan. 21, 1884, with plate number 49079; such parts, folio engraved, without covers, are also at MET and have an imprint of that time, R. Stabilimento Musicale Ricordi.

The preparation of the orchestral score of the opera commenced on Nov. 11, 1893, according to the Ricordi *Libroni*, with plate number 96838; an orchestral score of the opera published by G. Ricordi & C., Milan, Rome, Naples, Palermo and London, in three folio volumes, a lithographing of a manuscript copy, with p.n. 96838, was deposited at LC on Jan. 26, 1904. Also at JMM. Perhaps at about the same time an orchestral score of the opera was published by E. Sonzogno, Milan, also a lithographing of a manuscript copy, but without p.n.; DIB. Gaetano Donizetti was born in Bergamo in 1797 and died there in 1848. Brief biographic information regarding Cammarano appears above under *Anvil Chorus*.

Shall We Dance?—The King and I

Shall we dance? On a bright cloud of mu-sic shall we

Copyright © 1951 by Richard Rodgers and Oscar Hammerstein, II. Used by permission of Williamson Music, Inc.

m. Richard Rodgers. w. Oscar Hammerstein 2nd. Published March 19, 1951,[1] by Williamson Music, Inc., RKO Bldg., Radio City, New York, N.Y. The copyright copy deposited at the Library of Congress is a professional edition. Probable first regular edition: Front cover is purple, red and white with Thai designs. s. *The King and I*. Four titles listed, but not *Shall We Dance?* m. on pp. 2–5. p.n. 814–4. The copyright is in the names of the authors. Back cover adv. *Oklahoma! - State..* JF. The other titles listed or advertised were published on or before Feb. 16, 1951.[1]

The King and I opened in New York City on March 29, 1951. The piano-vocal score of the show was published on Dec. 14, 1951,[1] with a red and blue paper binding at $6 (cloth binding also listed at $8) and without building or street address. LC(CDC). Brief biographic information appears above regarding Rodgers under *If I Loved You*, and regarding Hammerstein under *All the Things You Are*.

[1] Copyright records; LC.

Shave and a Haircut, Bay Rum

Shave   and___a hair - cut,   bay   rum

This musical phrase may have been first suggested in Chas. Hale, *At a Darktown Cakewalk*, published Feb. 28, 1899,[1] by Belmont Music Co., 1006 N. 43d St., Philadelphia, Pa.; the phrase appears throughout the piece. First edition: Green and white front cover. p. [2] blank. m. on pp. 3-5. Back cover blank. LC(CDC). The phrase is next suggested in H. A. Fischler, *Hot Scotch Rag*, published Jan. 7, 1911,[1] by Vandersloot Music Pub. Co., Williamsport, Pa. LC(CDC). The similar musical phrase (without words) occurs in the third and fourth bars of the Trio on p. 4. The next printing is in the song *Bum Diddle-de-um Bum, That's It!,*[1A] published Dec. 5, 1914,[2] by Leo. Feist, Inc., 231 West 40th St., New York, N.Y., with music by Jimmie V. Monaco and words by Joe McCarthy. SS and JF. The similar musical phrase (without the common words) occurs in the last two bars of the song.

Shave and a Haircut was recorded as a folk melody in 1939 by Rosalind Rosenthal and Herbert Halpert; LC (Music Division—Recording Laboratory, 3646 B4).[3] Unfortunately, the condition of the record does not presently permit verification of the music and words.

Music and words similar to the common music and words appear in the song *Shave and a Haircut—Shampoo*, published Aug. 3, 1939,[2] by Larry Spier, Inc., 1619 Broadway, New York, N.Y., with music and words by Dan Shapiro, Lester Lee and Milton Berle; JF. The musical phrase also appears in the last three bars of *Gee, Officer Krupke* in the piano-vocal score of Leonard Bernstein's *West Side Story* (1959), p. 178;[4] LC(CDC) and JF.

The musical phrase is also known by other titles and words, and the rhythm alone is frequently tapped or otherwise sounded.

---

[1] Harold Barlow, New York City, advised the author of this printing.

[1A] The late Dr. Saul Starr, Eastchester, N.Y., called the author's attention to this song.

[2] Copyright records; LC.

[3] The Library of Congress, Music Division, *Check-list of Recorded Songs in the English Language . . . to July 1940* (Washington, 1942), p. 360; LC.

[4] See the title *Tonight*, below.

She Didn't Say "Yes"

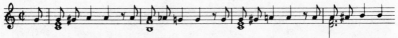

She did-n't say "yes," she did-n't say "no," she did-n't say "stay," she did-n't say "go"

© 1931 by T. B. Harms Company. Copyright renewed. By consent.

m. Jerome Kern. w. Otto Harbach. Copyrighted Oct. 26, 1931,[1] by Jerome Kern. Probable first edition: Front cover is brown and blue-purple, has a drawing of dancers and lists eight titles from the show *The Cat and the Fiddle*, the second title of which is *Misunderstood;*[2] the publisher is T. B. Harms Company, New York, N.Y. m. on pp. 2–5. p.n. 444-4. Back cover adv. *Try.. - I..* There is a subtitle "Ballad of Indecision" on the front cover and p. 2, which is omitted in later editions. YU (American Theater collection).

The Cat and the Fiddle opened in New York City on Oct. 15, 1931, and the piano-vocal score of the show was published by the same concern on Feb. 2, 1932,[1] with a similar front cover at $5.00. LC(CDC) and JF. Brief biographic information regarding Kern and Harbach appears above under *All the Things You Are* and *The Desert Song.*

She'll Be Comin' Round the Mountain

She'll be com - in' round the moun - tain when she comes

Substantially this melody under the title *When the Chariot Comes* was copyrighted Feb. 6, 1899,[1] in William E. Barton, *Old Plantation Hymns* (Boston), p. 44, where it is described as a "recent" Negro melody. LC(CDC) and JF.

---

[1] Copyright records; LC.
[2] *Misunderstood* was never copyrighted or published, and the title was eliminated from subsequent editions.

---

[1] Copyright records; LC. It has been suggested that the song is a secular reworking of the folk hymn *Old Ship of Zion;* Lomax, *North America,* p. 414. To this author, the connection, if any, is remote.

The words must be even more "recent"; in any event, no printing of the words has been found prior to 1927 when the music and words were included in Carl Sandburg, *The American Songbag* (New York, N.Y.), p. 372. A note states that mountaineers adapted *When the Chariot Comes* into this song which was then spread by railroad work gangs in the Midwest in the 1890's. NYPL. *She'll Be Comin' Round the Mountain (When She Comes)* was later popularized by the Mustang Band of Southern Methodist University, Dallas, Texas.

Shine On, Harvest Moon

m. Nora Bayes-Norworth. w. Jack Norworth. Copyrighted Nov. 7, 1908,[1] by Jerome H. Remick & Co., New York and Detroit. First edition: Front cover has a drawing of a moon over a harvest, photographs of Nora Bayes and Jack Norworth and is orange, blue, green and brown. p. [2] adv. principally *Sweetheart..* m. on pp. 3–5. No p.n. Back cover adv. principally *There..* The upper right-hand corner of the front cover is blank. LC(CDC) and JF (inscribed by the composer).

Nora Bayes was born in Los Angeles in 1880 as Dora Goldberg, became a musical comedy star, was married for a time to Jack Norworth and died in Brooklyn, N.Y., in 1928.[2] Jack Norworth, a composer, lyricist and actor, was born in Philadelphia in 1879 and died in California in 1959.[3]

Short'nin' Bread

Mam-my's li'l   ba - by loves short' - nin', short' - nin'

The first known appearance in print of substantially the music of this song was in an article by E. C. Perrow, "Songs and Rhymes from the South" in *Journal of American Folklore*, Lancaster, Pa., and New York, N.Y., April–June, 1915, p. 142, under the title *Shortened Bread*. ULS, p. 1435. A note states succinctly that the music is an adaption of *Run, Nigger, Run!*; from East Tennessee; mountain whites; from memory; 1912. The words are different from the present common words. Different words are also in

---

[1] Copyright records; LC.
[2] Obituary, *The New York Times*, March 20, 1928.
[3] *ASCAP*, p. 373. Obituary, *The New York Times*, Sept. 2, 1959.

Thomas W. Talley, *Negro Folk Rhymes* (New York, N.Y., 1922), pp. 173 and 187; NYPL.

The first known printing of the common words and music is under the title *Short'nin' Bread* in Dorothy Scarborough, *On the Trail of Negro Folk-Songs*, published Sept. 21, 1925,[1] in Cambridge, Mass., p. 150 (without reference to a second printing); LC(CDC), NYPL and JF. An unpublished version, with music and words credited to Reese Dupree, was copyrighted Feb. 12, 1925,[1] by Clarence Williams Pub. Co., Inc., New York, N.Y.; it was published by this concern in 1938. Jacques Wolfe added to the popularity of the song, his sheet music edition (with Clement Wood) being published June 20, 1928,[1] by Harold Flammer, Inc. [New York, N.Y.].[2]

Show Me the Way to Go Home

Show me the way to go home, I'm tired and I want to go to bed

mw. Irving King. A professional edition was deposited Feb. 23, 1925, at BM by Campbell, Connelly & Co., 16 Tottenham Court Road, London W. 1. The following regular edition was deposited March 18, 1925, at LC and is probably the first regular edition: Front cover has a photograph of (presumably) the Hal Swain Princess Toronto Orchestra, is black and white, and the price is 6d. m. on pp. 2–3. p.n. 1. Back cover adv. *Do..* LC(CDC).

In 1901 a somewhat similar thought, but to different music, was copyrighted by M. Witmark & Sons, New York, N.Y., with words by Archie Morrow and music by Wilford Herbert, under the title *Show Me the Way to Go Home, Babe;*[1] BM(CDC).

The entire melody of the chorus of *Show Me the Way to Go Home* stays within a four-note range. Irving King is a combined pseudonym of Reg. Connelly and Jimmy Campbell,[2] brief biographic information regarding whom appears above under *Goodnight Sweetheart*.

[1] Copyright records; LC.

[2] See, also, *JAF*, April–June, 1913, p. 171, and *North Carolina F.*, vol. III, p. 535.

[1] Information from the late Elliott Shapiro. The song mentioned in Spaeth, p. 450, has not been traced, and was disputed by Elliott Shapiro.

[2] Copyright records; LC.

Siboney

Si - bo - ney_____ de mi sue -ño__ si no̲o̲-yes la

© Copyright 1929 (renewed) Leo Feist, Inc., New York, N.Y. Used by permission.

mw. Ernesto Lecuona. It is probable that this song was first published in Cuba as the American copyright copy deposited May 29, 1929,[1] states on the front cover, "The Tune That All Havana Dances to"; LC (a professional edition, with American words by Dolly Morse, published the same day by Leo. Feist, Inc., New York, N.Y.)

Possible first edition, published in Cuba early in 1929: Front cover has the title *Canto Siboney—Cancion*, is blue, black and white, and shows the publisher as Agencia Internacional de Propiedad Intelectual, Candido G. Galdo, P. O. Box 2013, Havana, Cuba. m. on pp. [2]–[5]. P. [2] states that the song was registered in Cuba conforming to law and was Copyright by E. Lecuona, 1929. Back cover has copyright and performance notices. JF. This Cuban edition seems earlier than another Cuban edition published by Lecuona Music Corporation, Apartado no. 143, Havana, Cuba; JF.

Another early edition published in Cuba has a green, red and white front cover stating above the title, "Obras de Exito" ("Successful Works"), the imprint is the same as the other possible first edition except there is no mention of Candido G. Galdo, the copyright owner is Ernesto Lecuona, and the balance of the edition is the same as the possible first edition described above. JF (copy states "11A Edicion").

Brief biographic information regarding Lecuona appears above under *Andalucía.*

The Sidewalks of New York

East   side,   West   side,   all   a - round   the   town

mw. Chas. B. Lawlor and James W. Blake. Copyrighted Aug. 27, 1894,[1] by Howley, Haviland & Co., 4 East 20th Street, New York, N.Y. First edition: Front cover is blue and white and refers to an English agent; while

---

[1] Copyright records; LC. The publisher's files also indicate that *Siboney* was first published in Cuba.

[1] Copyright records; LC.

the price "4" is printed,[2] the words "March 4" and "Waltz 4" are not. p. [2] adv. *Marine..* and *Senator..* m. on pp. 3–5. Dedicated to Little Dollie Golding. Back cover adv. *The Watermelon.. - Egyptian..* LC(CDC).

The song is also known by the opening words of its Chorus: *East side, West side,* and became Al Smith's official campaign song for President in 1928.[3] Lawlor, a composer, singer and actor, was born in Dublin in 1852 and died in New York City in 1925.[4] Blake, a lyricist, was born in New York City in 1862 and died there in 1935.[4]

Silent Night

Stil - le Nacht,   hei - li - ge Nacht!   All - es schläft,   ein - sam wacht
Si - lent night,   ho - ly night!   All is calm,   all is bright

m. Franz Gruber. w. Joseph Mohr. *Stille Nacht, Heilige Nacht!* was published about Sept.–Oct., 1832,[1] as the fourth song in *Vier Ächte Tyroler-Lieder* for soprano solo or four voices with piano accompaniment by A. R. Friese, Dresden, without mention of the composer or the lyricist. Probable first edition: Oblong. Front cover has a colored drawing of the Strasser sisters and brother from the Zillerthal, the p.n. 81 and the price 12 Gr. **(See Plate VIII.)** pp. [2] and [3] blank. m. on pp. 2–5 (actually 4–7), *Stille Nacht, Heilige Nacht!* on p. 5, the last page. Back cover blank. BM (Hirsch M 1291 [18]), PML and JF.

The history of this song, once believed to have been a folk song, is now well known.[2] Mohr, then assistant priest in Oberndorf near Salzburg, wrote the words in 1818. His friend, Gruber, then an organist and teacher in nearby Arnsdorf, composed the music on Dec. 24, 1818. On that Christmas Eve the song was first performed in the church of Oberndorf. The song became widely known and was particularly popularized by the Strasser sisters and brother.

[2] Front cover is illustrated in Fuld, *American,* p. [46].
[3] See, also, *The American Weekly,* New York, N.Y., Dec. 12, 1950, p. 21; LC.
[4] *ASCAP,* pp. 295 and 41.

[1] Hofmeister *Monatsbericht,* Sept.–Oct., 1832, p. 81; ZZ. A. R. Friese published in Dresden from the middle of 1828 to Sept. 2, 1834, then moving to Leipzig; *Neuer Nekrolog der Deutschen, 1848* (Weimar, 1850), vol. 1, p. 699; SLD and NYPL.
[2] Erk-Böhme, p. 576. Otto Erich Deutsch, *Stille Nacht, Heilige Nacht!* (Vienna, 1937); NYPL. Luis Grundner, *Stille Nacht, Heilige Nacht* (Salzburg [1951?]); NYPL. Charles Cudworth, "The True 'Stille Nacht,'" MT, Dec., 1964, p. 892.

Gruber was born in 1787 in Inn, Austria, and died in Hallein in 1863. Mohr was born in 1792 in Salzburg and died in Wagrain, near Salzburg, in 1848.

Silver Threads Among the Gold

Dar - ling, I am grow-ing old,_____   sil - ver threads a-mong the gold

m. H. P. Danks. w. Eben E. Rexford. Copyrighted Feb. 17, 1873,[1] by Charles W. Harris, 750 Broadway, New York, N.Y. First edition: Front cover lists seven other songs, *Don't.. - Bring..*; the price of *Silver Threads Among the Gold* is 3½; and the publisher is shown also at a Troy address. p. [2] blank. m. on pp. [3]–5. Back cover adv. *Select..* No p.n. LC(CDC).

Hart Pease Danks was born in New Haven in 1834, became a singer and composer and died in Philadelphia in 1903.[2] Rexford was born in Wisconsin in 1848, became an authority on gardening and floriculture and died in Wisconsin in 1916.[3]

Simple Aveu—Thomé

m. Francis Thomé. Published under the title *L'Aveu* on March 18, 1878,[1] for piano by Durand, Schoenewerk & Cie., 4 Place de la Madeleine, Paris. First edition: Front cover is gray and black, states that *L'Aveu* is a song

---

[1] Copyright records; LC.

[2] NYPL Music Division Biographical and Clipping Files. Geller, p. 1.

[3] Wisconsin Federation of Music Clubs, *Wisconsin Composers* (n.p., 1948), p. 64; NYPL. Dave and Kathleen Thompson, p. 89.

---

[1] Letter from publisher. Deposited for Dépôt Légal on May 11, 1878; Archives. *BMF*, March–April, 1878, p. 22. *BF*, June 8, 1878, p. 305.

without words and gives the opus number as 25 and the price as 5 f.
Verso adv. Extrait du Catalogue. Title page is same as front cover except
in black and white. m. on pp. 2–5. p.n. 2459. p. [6] blank. Inside and outside of back cover continues the Catalogue. Folio. Music pages engraved.
BN(CDC).

Thomé, a composer, was born in Port Louis, Mauritius, in 1850 and
died in Paris in 1909.[2]

Sing a Song of Sixpence

Sing   a song of six-pence, a   pock-et full of rye,   four-and-twen-ty black-birds

The first printing of the words was about 1744 in *Tommy Thumb's Pretty
Song Book* (London?), vol. 2, p. 8.[1] BM.

The words have been set to music many times, the most familiar
setting at least in the United States being that of J. W. Elliott whose
National Nursery Rhymes and Nursery Songs was published about Nov.
1, 1870,[2] and a copy deposited at BM on Jan. 5, 1871, by George Routledge
and Sons, London. Possible first edition: Front cover is orange-red, brown
and gold. Half-title page. Two blank pages. Drawings of subjects relating
to nursery rhymes and songs. Title page. Seal of the engraver. Two-page
preface. Contents. Half-title page. vb. m. on pp. 1–[111], *Sing a Song of
Sixpence* on p. 32. Seal of the engraver. Four pages of advertisements, the
first advertisement on the first page being *Griset's*.. BM(CDC). Another
copy, dated by the original owner Jan. 3, 1871, is identical except for the
first two pages of advertisements, the first advertisement on the first page
being *Little*..; JF.

It is not generally known that J. W. Elliott is the composer of the
music generally associated in the United States with the following nursery
songs, all of which appeared for the first time in his *National Nursery
Rhymes and Nursery Songs: Hey, Diddle Diddle; Humpty Dumpty; I Love
Little Pussy; Jack and Jill; Little Bo-Peep; Little Jack Horner; Pussy-Cat,
Pussy-Cat*; and *See-Saw, Margery Daw*. As there was no copyright protection in the United States at the time for English compositions, they were
freely republishable. James William Elliott was born in Warwick in 1833,
became an organist and composer, and died in 1915.[2]

---

[2] *Grove's*, vol. 8, p. 428.

---

[1] Opie, p. 394, which also has interesting background information about the poem.
[2] MT, Nov. 1, 1870, p. 672. *Brit. Mus. Biog.*, p. 138.

The Skaters

m. Emile Waldteufel. *Les Patineurs* was published by Hopwood & Crew, 42 New Bond St., London W., for piano on Oct. 31, 1882, while Waldteufel was under contract to this London publisher.[1] Possible first edition: Front cover is red, brown and white, has a drawing of two women skaters, refers to Paris and Madrid publishers, gives the price as 4/ and mentions Duet, Septett, Full Orchestra and Military Band parts. vb. m. on pp. 1–10, lithographed. p. 1 contains dedication to Coquelin Cadet. p.n. H&C 2369. p. [11] blank. Back cover adv. *Souviens.. - Toujours..* BM (deposited Jan. 25, 1884). The orchestral parts, with plate number H&C 2388, were published in Dec., 1882; Chappell International Music Publishers Ltd., Ilford, Essex, England.

Publication rights for France were assigned to Durand Schoenewerk & Cie. on Nov. 3, 1882, and the piano publication by this firm was deposited for Dépôt Légal on Dec. 28, 1882; BN(CDC).

Waldteufel, whose family name was Lévy, was born in Strasbourg in 1837, became a composer of light pieces and arranger of others' works and died in Paris in 1915.

Slaughter on Tenth Avenue

m. Richard Rodgers. Published Oct. 24, 1936,[1] by Chappell & Co., Inc., RKO Building, Rockefeller Center, New York, N.Y. First edition: Front cover has a drawing of a "Modern Ballet," states "Piano Solo" and is blue, black and white. m. on pp. 2–13. p.n. 657-12. Reference on p. 2 to the show *On Your Toes.* Back cover adv. *It's.. - The Heart..* LC(CDC) and JF (inscribed by the composer).

---

[1] Andrew Lamb, Littlehampton, West Sussex, England, is an authority on Waldteufel and has provided most of the information about this title.

Les Patineurs was entered at Stationers' Hall on Nov. 4, 1882.

---

[1] Copyright records; LC.

On Your Toes opened in New York City on April 11, 1936; no piano-vocal score of the show has been published. Brief biographic information regarding Rodgers appears above under *If I Loved You*.

Slavonic Dance, op. 46, no. 8—Dvořák

m. Anton Dvořák. The *Slavische Tänze*, op. 46, were originally composed for piano four hands from March 18–May 7, 1878, but the orchestration was completed by Aug. 22, 1878, and it is likely that publication of the two arrangements occurred at about the same time[1] by N. Simrock, Berlin. According to the entry at Stationers' Hall,[2] the orchestral score was published on Nov. 1, 1878.

As the orchestral score has been found with music pages engraved, it seems likely that the arrangement for piano four hands was similarly printed, but no engraved edition of the latter arrangement has been found. Three early variants of the second book of the arrangement for piano four hands have been located, with priority unknown. In all, the title page is red, black and white and states that there are two books and the year 1878. m. on pp. 2–37. p.n. 8041 (the p.n. of the first book is 8040). Dance no. 8 is in the second book at p. 28. p. [38] blank. In one variant, no agent is shown on the title page; JF. In the second variant, a London and three other agents are shown; DMP (autographed by the composer March 3, 1880) and ONB. In the third variant, there is no London agent, but three other agents are shown; BPL.

Probable first edition of the second book of the orchestral score: Front cover is gray and black. vb. Title page is red, black and white, states that there are two books, the price of the orchestral score is 9 Mk. and that of the orchestral parts 25 Mk., three agents are shown (but no London agent) and the year 1878 is stated. m. on pp. 2–136, **engraved.** p.n. 8051 (the p.n. of the first book is 8050). p. [137] blank. Back cover missing. BPL.

An engraved edition of the first book of the orchestral parts is at CI, but its second book, with p.n. 8054, is offset printed (similar second book at FPL). Brief biographic information regarding Dvořák appears above under *Humoreske*.

---

[1] Hofmeister *Monatsbericht*, Dec., 1878, lists the orchestral score and parts at p. 374, and the arrangement for piano four hands at p. 378. See, generally, Burghauser, pp. 182 and 188, and *Antonín Dvořák Complete Edition* (Prague, 1955), Series III, vol. 19, p. x, and Series V, vol. 5, p. viii, NYPL.

[2] On Jan. 20, 1879.

Slavonic Dance, op. 72, no. 2—Dvořák

m. Anton Dvořák. The third and fourth books of *Slavische Tänze*, op. 72, were composed from June 9–July 9, 1886, for piano four hands, and they were published in this arrangement on Oct. 15, 1886,[1] by N. Simrock, Berlin. Possible first edition of the third book: Title page is red, black and white and refers to the four books of op. 46 and op. 72. m. on pp. 2–31, Dance no. 2 on p. 12. p.n. 8697. p. [32] blank. GM "aus dem Nachlass von Johannes Brahms." The p.n. of the fourth book is 8698.

The orchestration of the third and fourth books of *Slavische Tänze* was completed Jan. 5, 1887, but the publication of the orchestral score did not take place until about Nov., 1887.[2] Possible first edition: Front cover has the title in German and Czech, in black and gray, the price of the orchestral score is 9 Mk. and of the orchestral parts 25 Mk.; the publisher is N. Simrock, Berlin; no agents are listed; and the year 1887 is shown. vb. Title page is in German and lists no agents. Legal notice in German and English. m. on pp. 3–114. p.n. 8786. The printer is Röder'schen Officin in Leipzig. LC. The p.n. of the fourth book is 8788.

Possible first printings of the orchestral parts of the third book, with p.n. 8787, are at CI and FPL. The above Dance no. 2 was performed on Jan. 6, 1887, in Prague. Brief biographic information regarding Dvořák appears above under *Humoreske*.

Sleeping Beauty Waltz—Tchaikovsky

m. P. Tchaikovsky. The *Sleeping Beauty Ballet*, op. 66, was completed by Tchaikovsky Sept. 1, 1889, and performed Jan. 15, 1890, in St. Petersburg.

---

[1] According to the entry at Stationers' Hall on Nov. 12, 1886. Simrock wrote Dvořák on Oct. 21, 1886, that op. 72 has "just been published" and asked for an orchestral arrangement. Hofmeister *Monatsbericht*, Nov., 1886, p. 412. See, generally, Burghauser, pp. 260 and 263, and *Antonín Dvořák Complete Edition* (Prague, 1955), Series III, vol. 20, p. xi, and Series V, vol. 5, p. ix, NYPL.

[2] Hofmeister *Monatsbericht*, Nov., 1887, p. [522].

The relative order of publication of various arrangements of the *Ballet*, the *Suite* from the *Ballet*, and the *Waltz* is not certain, publication probably commencing about Nov. or Dec., 1889.[1]

A. Ziloti's piano arrangement of the *Ballet*, was probably the first to be published by P. Jurgenson, Moscow. Possible first edition: Title page is in French in many colors, has a dedication to Jean Wsewolojsky, has the title *La Belle au Bois Dormant*, there are two arrangements, this for piano at 6 Rbl. and a simplified edition without price, there is no crown, the Paris agent is Mackar & Noël (March, 1889–1896)[2] and there are three other agents. vb. m. on pp. 3–207, the *Waltz* on p. 58. p.n. 15895. SSL.

A probable first German printing of the piano arrangement of the *Ballet*, about June, 1890,[3] is at HU. The title is *Dornröschen*, the publisher is D. Rahter, Hamburg, no other arrangement is listed, the Paris agent is somehow F. Mackar (until March, 1889),[4] and the plate number is the Jurgenson plate number of 15895.

A copy of the orchestral score of *Sleeping Beauty* printed by P. Jurgenson, Moscow, was received by LC on Aug. 23, 1905. Probable first edition: Front cover is green, black and white is in Russian only, with the title Спящая Красавица, lists three other arrangements, the price of the orchestral score is 150 rubles, there is no crown, and there are two agents, J. Jurgenson, St. Petersburg, and G. Sennewald, Warsaw. vb. Title page in black and white is in German with the title *Dornröschen*. vb. m. on pp. 1–705, a lithographing of a manuscript. The *Waltz* commences at p. 220. No plate number. p. [706] and inside of back cover blank. Outside of back cover has one line in Russian.[5] No early printing of the orchestral parts of the *Ballet* has been found.

A possible first edition of the orchestral score of the *Suite* from the *Ballet*, published by P. Jurgenson, has a blue and white front cover in Russian. vb. Title page in many colors is in French, is also op. 66 (front cover has the op. no. as 66a), six arrangements are listed, the orchestral score at 5 Rbl./11 Mk., the orchestral parts, supplementary parts and three piano arrangements, there is a crown, the publisher is shown at 14 Neg-

---

[1] "My ballet will be published in November or December (O.S.). Siloti is making the pianoforte arrangement." Tchaikovsky to N. F. von Meck, Aug. 6, 1889 (O.S.). *Tchaikovsky Letters*, p. 586.

[2] Hopkinson, *Parisian*, pp. 83 and 94.

[3] Hofmeister *Monatsbericht*, June, 1890, p. 243.

[4] Hopkinson, *Parisian*, p. 83.

[5] There is a puzzling reference in the *Tchaikovsky Catalogue*, p. 68, to an orchestral score of the *Ballet* with p.n. 15896 and pp. 1–701; Soviet music librarians believe this an error.

linny pr., Moscow, and 19 Thalstrasse, Leipzig, and there are two agents, J. Jurgenson, St. Petersburg, and G. Sennewald, Warsaw. vb. m. on pp. 3–91, the *Waltz* on p. 65. p.n. 15896. p. [92] and inside of back cover blank. Outside of back cover adv. *Compositions..* including Tchaikovsky up to op. 71 (1892). BM (purchased April 19, 1898), FPL and HU. A possible first edition of the orchestral parts of the *Suite*, with plate number 25238, but without covers, is at RAM.

A possible first German printing of the orchestral score of the *Suite*, about Aug., 1900,[6] is at BPL. The same arrangements are present as in the Jurgenson edition, the publisher is D. Rahter, Hamburg and Leipzig, the only agent shown is P. Jurgenson, Moscow, and there is neither a p.n. nor an indication where the score was printed.

The earliest discovered separate printing of the *Valse*, op. 66, no. 6, has p.n. 14375 [*sic*] and is for two pianos, eight hands, the publisher being P. Jurgenson; NYPL (early edition). The Jurgenson edition for piano has p.n. 15895; NYPL*. The Jurgenson edition for piano simplified by E. Langer has p.n. 16044, and Rachmaninoff's arrangement for piano four hands has p.n. 17016; both at SSL. The Jurgenson orchestral score of the *Waltz* has p.n. 17154 (at ESM and NC), and the Jurgenson orchestral parts have p.n. 17155 (at UI). A Rahter orchestral score of the *Walzer* has p.n. 22; BPL. Brief biographic information regarding Tchaikovsky appears above under *Chant sans Paroles*.

Smiles

There are   smiles ____   that make us   hap - py

m. Lee S. Roberts. w. J. Will Callahan. Published Aug. 25, 1917,[1] by Lee S. Roberts, Fine Arts Bldg., Chicago, Ill. First edition: Front cover has a drawing of a girl smiling and is orange, green and black. m. on pp. 2–3. Back cover adv. *The Ragtime..* LC(CDC) and JF. The copyright was assigned on July 19, 1918,[1] to Jerome H. Remick & Co.

---

[6] Hofmeister *Monatsbericht*, Aug., 1900, p. 376. Other arrangements are listed on pp. 385 and 389.

---

[1] Copyright records; LC.

The song was written as a cheerful song for soldiers and civilians which did not mention the war.[2] Roberts, a composer, was born in Oakland, Cal., in 1884, and died in California in 1949.[3] Callahan, a lyricist, was born in Columbus, Ind., in 1874, and died in New Smyrna Beach, Fla., in 1946.[4]

Smoke Gets in Your Eyes

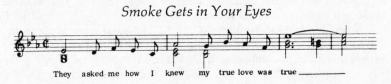

They asked me how I knew my true love was true_____

m. Jerome Kern. w. Otto Harbach. Published Nov. 3, 1933,[1] by T. B. Harms Company, 1619 Broadway, New York, N.Y. Probable first edition: Front cover refers to the original title of the musical show *Gowns by Roberta*, has a drawing of a lady holding cloth, is green, black and white, lists six titles and has an introductory phrase to the title of this song, "When Your Heart's on Fire." p. [2] blank. m. on pp. 3–5. The copyright is in the name of the composer. p.n. 362-3. Back cover adv. *I've.. - One..* JF. All the songs advertised or listed were published on or before Nov. 3, 1933. The above edition is the same, to the extent possible, as the other contemporary, regular edition, copyright deposit copies at LC from the same show.

The name of the show was soon shortened to *Roberta*, and under the latter name it opened in New York City on Nov. 18, 1933, with Bob Hope, among others, in its cast. The piano-vocal score of *Roberta* was published May 25, 1950,[1] by Chappell & Co., Ltd., London, at 10/; LC(CDC) and JF.

It is said that *Smoke Gets in Your Eyes* was Kern's favorite among his songs.[2] Brief biographic information regarding Kern and Harbach appears above under *All the Things You Are* and *The Desert Song*.

---

[2] Wickes, p. 1.

[3] *ASCAP*, p. 411.

[4] *American War Songs*, p. 165; and *ASCAP*, p. 72.

[1] Copyright records; LC.

[2] Sigmund Spaeth, *The New York Times*, April 2, 1950, Magazine sec., p. 41.

Sobre las Olas (Over the Waves)

m. Juventino Rosas. Published about Aug., 1888,[1] for piano by A. Wagner y Levien, 15 Coliseo Viejo, Mexico City. Possible first edition: Front cover in Spanish has the title *Sobre las Olas*, a dedication to Señora Calista G. de Alfaro, a drawing of a woman standing over water, mentions that the publisher is also a manufacturer of pianos at 14 Zuleta, refers to the agent, Friedrich Hofmeister, Leipzig, and is green, brown and white; no price. p. [2] blank. m. on pp. 3–11. p.n. W. y. L. 76. Printer: Oscar Brandstetter, Leipzig. Back cover adv. *Aguirre.. - Araujo.*. JF.

The Waltz form became popular in Mexico after Napoleon III named Maximilian, Archduke of Austria, Emperor of Mexico in 1863.

Rosas, a pure-blooded Otomi Indian, was born in Santa Cruz de Galeana, Guanajuato, Mexico, in 1868, became a violinist and composer, fell in love (unsuccessfully) with the dedicatee Calista Gutiérrez, and died at Batabano, Cuba, in 1894.[2]

Soldiers' Chorus—Faust

Gloire   im - mor - tel-le de nos   a - ïeux___   sois   nous

m. Ch. Gounod. w. Jules Barbier and Michel Carré. The *Choeur des Soldats* from the opera *Faust* was published in separate sheet music about May 1, 1859,[1] by Choudens, 265 Rue St. Honoré, Paris. No first edition has been found. On the basis of other copyright deposit copies of separate sheet

---

[1] Hofmeister *Monatsbericht*, Aug., 1888, p. 314. Coliseo Viejo no. 15 is the address of the publisher in a directory of Mexico City for 1893–1894; LC. The publisher was at IIa Calle de San Francisco no. 11 in 1899–1907, and at Avenida de San Francisco no. 35 in 1913–1919; directories at LC and NYPL. No directory for 1888 has been found in the United States or in Mexico.

[2] *Grove's*, vol. 7, p. 231; *Macmillan Encyclopedia*, p. 1576; Mayer-Serra, p. 857; and Grial, p. 38.

---

[1] *Le Ménestrel*, May 1, 1859, p. 176. Deposited for Dépôt Légal on June 3, 1859; Archives. BF, July 16, 1859, p. 341.

music from the opera at BN, the front cover lists 16 morceaux détachés (some in additional keys) and works by other composers and the plate number is A.C. 652 (12). The opera was produced in Paris on March 19, 1859.

The piano-vocal score of *Faust* was published about May 20, 1859,[2] by Choudens, 265 Rue St. Honoré, près l'Assomption, Paris. First edition: Title page is black and white, has miniatures of Marguerite, Mephistopheles and Faust, mentions that the piano arrangement is by Léo Delibes, the price is 15 F., and four agents are listed. (See Plate IV.) vb. Cast and index. vb. m. on pp. 1–224, the *Choeur des Soldats* on p. 142. p.n. A. C. 664. Not engraved. BN(CDC) and JF (inscribed by Gounod to his sister).

The orchestral score of *Faust* was deposited for Dépôt Légal on Aug. 29, 1860,[3] by Choudens, 265 Rue St. Honoré, près l'Assomption, Paris. First edition: Title page is black and white, lists four agents; no illustration or price. Next two pages blank. Legal notice. Cast and index. vb. m. on pp. 1–531. No double pagination in Act V or elsewhere. p.n. A. C. 675. p. [532] blank. Music pages engraved. BN(CDC–Exemplaire N. 17) and BPL. The *Choeur des Soldats* is at p. 342.

Orchestral parts of the opera published by Choudens, 265 Rue St. Honoré, with plate number 2, lithographed, possibly their first printing, with covers, are at CI. Photocopies of parts published by Bote & Bock, Berlin, with plate number 8292 (1869), folio, are at MAP.

The Soldiers' Chorus was originally composed by Gounod for his *Ivan le Terrible,* but this opera is believed not to have been performed or published. Brief biographic information regarding Gounod appears above under his *Ave Maria.* Brief biographic information regarding Barbier and Carré appears above under *Barcarolle* and *Entr'acte—Gavotte.*

Some Enchanted Evening—South Pacific

Some en-chant-ed eve - ning ____ you may see a stran - ger

[2] "To appear between May 15 and 20"; per *Le Ménestrel,* May 1, 1859, p. 176. Deposited for Dépôt Légal on June 16, 1859; Archives. *BF,* July 30, 1859, p. 366. The various dates in J.-G. Prod'homme and A. Dandelot, *Gounod* (Paris, 1911), vol. 2, p. 257, are erroneous; NYPL. Cecil Hopkinson, "Notes on the Earliest Editions of Gounod's *Faust*" in *Deutsch Festschrift,* p. [245].

[3] Archives. *BF,* Sept. 15, 1860, p. 438.

m. Richard Rodgers. w. Oscar Hammerstein 2nd. Published Feb. 23, 1949,[1] by Williamson Music, Inc., RKO Bldg., Radio City, New York, N.Y. First edition: Front cover has a drawing of an island in the South Pacific and is purple, blue and white. s. *South Pacific*—3 titles listed. p. [2] adv. *Oklahoma - People..* m. on pp. 3–7. The copyright is in the name of the authors. p.n. 731–5. Back cover adv. Rodgers.. LC(CDC) and JF (autographed by the composer).

South Pacific opened in New York City on April 7, 1949, and the piano-vocal score of the musical play was published Oct. 25, 1949.[1] First edition: Front cover is paper or cardboard in light and dark blue, and has the above imprint. vb. Title page gives the price of the paper-bound edition at $6.00 and the cloth-bound at $8.00. LC(CDC) and JF. The cloth-bound edition was deposited at LC on Dec. 5, 1949. Brief biographic information regarding Rodgers and Hammerstein appears above under *If I Loved You* and *All the Things You Are.*

Some of These Days (Some o' Dese Days)

A song entitled *Some o' Dese Days*, with music and words credited to Frank Williams, was copyrighted Jan. 12, 1905,[1] by The Attucks Music Publishing Company, 1255–1257 Broadway, New York, N.Y. Following are the words and music of the beginning of the Chorus of the 1905 *Some o' Dese Days:*

'Cause some o' dese   days _____ you'll call me   hon - ey,—

First edition: Front cover has a drawing of a Negro, a photograph of Louise Langdon and is red, blue, and white. m. on pp. 2–5. Back cover adv. *Why..* LC(CDC) and JF. No biographical information has been found regarding Frank Williams.[2]

---

[1] Copyright records; LC.

[1] Copyright records; LC.

[2] He may have been the Frank B. Williams, a blind lyricist, who died Feb. 6, 1942, at the age of seventy-three in Harlem Hospital, New York City. *Variety*, Feb. 11, 1942, p. 46. The publisher was founded by Richard C. McPherson (Cecil Mack) to promote the compositions of Negroes; Spaeth, p. 346.

On July 6, 1910,[1] *Some of These Days*, with music and words credited to Shelton Brooks, was published by The Wm. Foster Music Co., Chicago, Ill.; this is the well-known song. First edition: Front cover has a drawing of a man and a girl, and is yellow, blue and white. m. on pp. 2–5. Back cover adv. J. J. J.. LC(CDC). The song was assigned to Will Rossiter 19 days later. No excerpt from this song is included in this book as permission has not been received. Brief biographic information regarding Brooks appears under *The Darktown Strutters' Ball*.

Some of These Days was popularized by Sophie Tucker.[3] It bears no resemblance to the Negro spiritual having the same name.[4]

Someday I'll Find You

Some-day   I'll   find   you,   moon-light   be - hind   you

© 1930 by Chappell & Co. Ltd. Copyright renewed. Published by Chappell & Co. Inc. By consent.

mw. Noël Coward. Published Aug. 20, 1930,[1] by Chappell & Co., Ltd., 50 New Bond St., London, W. 1. First edition: Front cover has photographs of Gertrude Lawrence and the composer, refers to the comedy *Private Lives*, the price is 2/ and the publisher is shown also at New York and Sydney. m. on pp. 2–5. p.n. 30594. Back cover adv. seven titles and two arrangements from *Bitter Sweet*. BM (copyright copy deposited Sept. 2, 1930) and JF.

Private Lives opened in London on Sept. 24, 1930. Brief biographic information regarding Coward appears above under *I'll See You Again*.

---

[3] See, generally, Sophie Tucker, *Some of These Days* (n.p., 1945), p. 114; NYPL.

[4] See, e.g., Hall Johnson, *The Green Pastures Spirituals* (New York, N.Y., 1930), p. 17; NYPL.

[1] Copyright records; LC.

Someone to Watch over Me

There's a some-bod-y I'm long-ing to see,   I hope that he   turns out to be

m. George Gershwin. w. Ira Gershwin. Published Nov. 3, 1926,[1] by Harms, Incorporated, New York, N.Y. First edition: Front cover is red, black and white. s. *Oh, Kay!*—4 titles listed. p. [2] adv. *My..* m. on pp. 3–7. p.n. 7851-5. p. [8] adv. *Just..* p. [9] adv. *Oh..* Back cover adv. *That..* - *So..* LC(CDC) and JF.

Someone to Watch over Me was originally a fast dance and rhythm number. One day George Gershwin happened to play it very slowly and it was recognized as a warm and charming melody, which was later introduced by Gertrude Lawrence.[2] *Oh, Kay!* opened in New York City on Nov. 8, 1926. Brief biographic information regarding George and Ira Gershwin appear above under *I Got Rhythm.*

Someone's in the Kitchen with Dinah

Some-one's in the house with Di - nah,   some-one's in the house I   know_____
Fee,_____ fie,____ fiddly-i-o,   fee, _____ fie,____ fiddly-i - o - o

The words and a different melody appear under the title *Old Joe, or Somebody in the House with Dinah* published by Duncombe, 10 Middle Row, Holborn, London, ca. 1835–1848,[1] the "music composed" by J. H. Cave. Possible first edition: Front cover has a drawing of two Negroes and Dinah, the price is 1/6, the publisher's number is 190 and the colors are black and white. m. on pp. 2–4. No plate number. Engraved. WNH and JF. (James H. Cave is described on the sheet music of the song *Sweet Lucy Neal*, also published by Duncombe, as "The celebrated American banjo player"; whether this means he was American or played the American banjo is not

---

[1] Copyright records; LC.

[2] Gershwin, p. 111, and *The George and Ira Gershwin Song Book*, foreword by Ira Gershwin (New York, N.Y., 1960), p. xi; NYPL.

---

[1] Humphries-Smith, p. 137. *Old Joe*, published by John Mitchell, London, was entered at Stationers' Hall on Jan. 12, 1847; no copy has been found.

clear—copy at WNH.) This version of the song also appears in Davidson's *Universal Melodist* (London, 1848), vol. I, p. 321, under the title *Dere's Some One in de House wid Dinah*, As Sung by the Ethiopian Serenaders, without mention of authorship; NYPL, WNH and JF.

The words appear without music and without credit as to authorship under the title *Somebody's in de House wid Susey*, in *White's New Ethiopian Song Book* (H. Long & Brother, 43 Ann Street, New York, N.Y. [1849–1854]), p. 23. HU. The song *Some Body in de House wid Dinah* is listed as title no. 6 on the front cover of the sheet music of *Negro Melodies* Sung by The Ethiopian Serenaders, The American Banjo Players, published by D'Almaine & Co., 20 Soho Square, London (ca. 1834–1858[2]). Copy formerly belonging to Elliott Shapiro—present location unknown; photocopy of title page at JF. The song *Old Joe or Some One in the House wid Dinah* is listed as title 15 on the front cover of the sheet music of *A Selection of Ethiopian Songs* published by B. Williams, 11 Paternoster Row and 170 Great Dover Rd., London (ca. 1846–1859[3]); JF. *Dere's Some One in de House wid Dinah* was included in a broadside, with words only, by Forth, Pocklington [Yorkshire, England], with the number 147, but without date; photocopy at JF. Forth's firm was started in 1835, according to the present owner, and continues today. It has not been possible to date this broadside.†

No early printing of the melody of this song has been found, either alone or with the words of *Someone's in the Kitchen with Dinah*. As the late Sigmund Spaeth pointed out to the author, the melody is basically an embellishment of the melody of *Goodnight Ladies*, which see.

Sometimes I Feel like a Motherless Child

Some-times   I   feel   like   a   moth - er - less child

The first known appearance in print of *Sometimes I Feel like a Motherless Child* is in William E. Barton, *Old Plantation Hymns*, copyrighted Feb. 6, 1899,[1] by Lamson, Wolffe and Company, Boston, New York and London, p. 18, under the title *Motherless Child*. LC(CDC) and JF.

[2] *Id.*, p. 126.
[3] *Id.*, p. 335.

[1] Copyright records; LC.

Sometimes I'm Happy

Some-times I'm hap-py, some-times I'm blue,____

© 1927 Harms, Inc. Copyright renewed. Used by permission.

m. Vincent Youmans. w. Irving Caesar and Clifford Grey. Published in a slightly different form Sept. 23, 1925,[1] by Harms, Incorporated, New York, N.Y. First edition: Front cover has a drawing of a couple on a night out and is blue, black and white. s. *A Night Out*—4 titles listed.[2] m. on pp. 2–5. p.n. 7524-4. Back cover adv. *June..* LC(CDC) and JF. The musical play, *A Night Out*, never opened in New York City.[3]

The melody of *Sometimes I'm Happy* had previously been used with another title and lyrics, *Come on and Pet Me*, which was published Nov. 10, 1923,[1] from the musical comedy *Mary Jane McKane*, by the same concern. First edition: Front cover is red, black and white, states that the lyrics are by Wm. Carey Duncan and Oscar Hammerstein II and lists four titles from the musical comedy. p. [2] blank. m. on pp. 3–5. p.n. 6925-3. Back cover adv. *Love..* LC(CDC) and JF. *Come on and Pet Me* was cut from the show before it reached New York City on Dec. 25, 1923.[3]

As *Sometimes I'm Happy*, the song was reintroduced (but without the original extended ending) into the show *Hit the Deck*, which opened in New York City on April 25, 1927. In the slightly revised version of the song, Clifford Grey was omitted as co-lyricist. Brief biographic information regarding Youmans appears above under *Carioca*. Caesar, a lyricist, was born in New York City in 1895 and resides there.[4] Brief biographic information regarding Grey appears above under *Hallelujah!*

Son of a Gun—(Son of a Gambolier; Dunderbeck; and Rambling Wreck from Georgia Tech)

I'm a son of a, son of a, son of a, son of a, son of a Gam-bo-lier
Oh Dun-der-beck, oh Dun-der-beck, how could you be so mean?
I'm a ram-bling wreck from Geor-gia Tech and a heck of an en-gi-neer

---

[1] Copyright records; LC.
[2] Front cover is illustrated in Fuld, *American*, p. [47].
[3] Green, p. 133.
[4] *ASCAP*, p. 71.

This melody is used with many titles and words, the earliest of which is probably *Son of a Gambolier*, the music and words of which were included in the 1873 edition of *Carmina Yalensia* (New York, N.Y.), copyrighted July 21, 1873,[1] p. 63; LC(CDC) and JF.

The melody is also known as *Dunderbeck*,[2] the words of which appeared in *"Our Own Boys"* Songster (New York, N.Y., 1876), p. 6, under the title *Dunderbeck's Machine*, to the "Air—*Thomas's Machine*." *Dunderbeck's Machine* is there said to be "By Ed. Harrigan," but this might also mean "sung by" Ed. Harrigan. JF. The music and words of *Dunderbeck* appear in *Carmina Princetonia* (8th ed., Martin R. Dennis, Newark, N.J.), p. 32; the book was copyrighted May 16, 1894.[1, 3] LC(CDC) and JF.

The music and words of *Son of a Gun* appear in *Dartmouth Songs* (Hanover, N.H.), p. 60; this collection was copyrighted June 24, 1898.[1] JF.

As *Rambling Wreck from Georgia Tech*,[4] the melody was published in a sheet music edition having this name, stated to be copyrighted in 1919 by Frank Roman, but no record of such copyright can be found. Probable first edition: Front cover has a drawing of a football player, credits music and words to Frank Roman, and is yellow, brown and white. m. on pp. 2–3. Back cover blank. No publisher is indicated. Folio. NYPL. The words "I'm a rambling rake of poverty" appear in the 1873 song mentioned above.

The national source of the melody is not known. The author has been advised by members of the British Museum Music Room and by Donal O'Sullivan, the Irish folk song authority, that the melody is not English or Irish.

Sonata in A Major (Rondo alla Turca-K 331)—Mozart

m. W. A. Mozart. Published between June 9, and Aug. 25, 1784,[1] under the

---

[1] Copyright records; LC.

[2] See Sigmund Spaeth, *Read 'Em and Weep* (New York, N.Y., 1926), p. 88; NYPL.

[3] The copyright records also show a separate copyright entry for *Dunderbeck*, music and words, the same day by the same publisher; no copy of the separate publication has been found.

[4] See, Marion Luther Brittain, *The Story of Georgia Tech* (Chapel Hill, N.C., 1948), p. 254; NYPL. Frank Roman was band leader at the Georgia Institute of Technology from 1913 to 1928; letter from GIT. It is probable that Roman merely arranged the song and was not the author of the words.

---

[1] Mozart wrote his father June 9–12, 1784, that he had given the three *Sonatas* to Artaria to engrave. Emily Anderson, *The Letters of Mozart & His Family* (London, 1938), vol. 3, p. 1312; NYPL.

The three *Sonatas* were announced in the *Wiener Zeitung*, Aug. 25, 1784, p. 1949, at f. 2.30 xr; ONB.

title *Trois Sonates* pour le Clavecin ou Pianoforte by Artaria Comp., Vienna. Probable first edition: Oblong. Engraved. Front cover has the title framed by a garland of flowers, states Oeuvre VI, mentions the letters, C.P.S.C.M. and the price, f. 2.30 xr. m. on pp. 4 (the verso of the front cover)–41, *Sonata II* on p. 15, *Alla Turca* on p. 22. p.n. 47. Back cover blank. In the first edition, the sharp used on *all* the plates is ✳, not ♯. AT and JF.[2] Later editions at BM and ONB. The work was composed in mid-1778 in Paris. Brief biographic information regarding Mozart appears above under *Eine Kleine Nachtmusik*.

This *Turkish March* was not composed for, nor included in, the first performances or printed scores of Mozart's *Die Entführung aus dem Serail*; however, it is common today to perform the *Turkish March* in the third act of this opera.

Sonata in C Major (K 545)—Mozart

m. W. A. Mozart. Published for piano Feb. 16, 1805,[1] by Bureau d'Arts et d'Industrie, Vienna, under the title *Sonate Facile*. Oeuvre Posth. Price is 54x. m. on pp. 2–11. p.n. 416. Probably engraved. Incomplete description. SAC. The work had been composed June 26, 1788, in Vienna. In a popular arrangement, it is known as *In an Eighteenth Century Drawing Room*. Brief biographic information regarding Mozart appears above under *Eine Kleine Nachtmusik*.

Sonate Pathétique—Beethoven

m. Ludwig van Beethoven. Published about Dec. 18, 1799,[1] for piano by Hoffmeister, Vienna. Probable first edition: Oblong. Engraved. Front cover has the title *Grande Sonate Pathétique* pour le Clavecin ou Piano-Forte, a dedi-

---

[2] Köchel, p. 325. Deutsch—Oldman, *Mozart-Drucke*, p. 142 (the three text editions referred to were the result of replaced plates—information from Deutsch). Deutsch, *Music Bibliography*, p. 152. Information from Alan Tyson, London.

[1] Köchel, p. 617. *Wiener Zeitung*, Feb. 13 [sic], 1805, p. 638; UMI.

[1] *Wiener Zeitung*, Dec. 18, 1799, p. 4313; UMI.

cation to Prince Charles de Lichnowsky, states Oeuvre 13, and has a drawing of two cherubs and an angel. m. on pp. 1–19. No plate number. Back cover blank. BSM, GM and ULO. This publisher subsequently reengraved the work with various changes, including the addition of p.n. 92; AT.

Kinsky-Halm believes the first printing to have been published by Joseph Eder, am Graven (Vienna), with p.n. 128, in the spring of 1799,[2] but Richard S. Hill and Alan Tyson have shown well that the Eder edition followed Hoffmeister's earlier edition.[3] The work was composed 1798–1799. Brief biographic information regarding Beethoven appears above under his *Concerto for Piano no. 5.*

<h2 style="text-align:center">Song of India—Sadko</h2>

Nyeh schyest al - mah–zov vkah–men–nikh pyeh–shchyeh–rakh

mw. N. Rimsky-Korsakov. *Sadko* was first composed in 1867 as a tone-poem by Rimsky-Korsakov as op. no. 7, performed Dec. 9, 1867, in St. Petersburg and shortly thereafter published for orchestral score and piano four hands by Jurgenson, Moscow.[1] However, the earlier version of *Sadko* does not contain the *Song of India. Sadko* was reorchestrated in 1892 as op. no. 5, still a tone-poem, but the revision also lacks the *Song of India.*[2]

Sadko was composed as an opera in 1894–1896, using some of the thematic material from the previous symphonic poem,[3] and the opera was performed Jan. 7, 1898, in Moscow. The orchestral score, orchestral parts and piano-vocal score of the opera were published about Aug., 1897,[4] by M. P. Belaïeff, Leipzig. Possible first edition of the orchestral score of the opera: Title page is decorated in many colors, in Russian only, with the title Садко. vb. Statement by the composer dated 1896 with p.ns. 1430 and

---

[2] P. 29; the authors admit that the date of Eder's publication cannot be ascertained.

[3] Hill, in his book review of Alexander Weinmann, *Wiener Musikverleger und Musikalienhändler,* in *Notes,* June, 1958, p. 396. Tyson in "Beethoven's 'Pathétique' Sonata and Its Publisher" in *MT,* May, 1963, p. 333.

[1] Rimsky-Korsakov, pp. 71, 95 and 263. Copies of the orchestral score, with p.n. 601, are at GM and UM. A copy of the arrangement for piano four hands, with p.n. 602, is at HOB. Hofmeister *Handbuch 1868–1873,* p. II.

[2] The revised tone-poem also published by Jurgenson, Moscow, has p.n. 14646 for the orchestral score and 14647 for the orchestral parts; both at FPL.

[3] M. Montagu-Nathan, *Rimsky-Korsakof* (London, 1921), p. 57; NYPL.

[4] Hofmeister *Monatsbericht,* Aug., 1897, p. 349. The prices shown are orchestral score 240 Mk., orchestral parts 180 Mk., and piano-vocal score 20 Mk.

1434. Cast. Composition of orchestra. vb. m. on pp. 1–570, the *Song of India* at p. 322. p.n. 1430. No price. No arrangements listed. Text in **Russian only.** No date. LC. A variant omits the pages between the title page and the music pages; MC.

A possible first edition of the orchestral parts of the opera, with plate number 1431, without covers, is at MAP. A possible first printing of the piano-vocal score with Russian text only, p.n. 1434 (and no additional p.ns.), and a front cover listing six arrangements, is at JMM; *Пѣсня Индійскаго Гостя*, or *Song of India*, appears at p. 232. *Song of India* (literally, *Song of Indian Guest*) is also known as the *Hindu Song* or *Chanson Indoue*. No early printing of the sheet music has been found. Brief biographic information regarding Rimsky-Korsakov appears above under *Capriccio Espagnol*.

The Song of Songs

Song of songs, song of mem-o-ry and bro-ken mel - o - dy of love and life

© 1914 by Chappell & Co. Ltd. Copyright renewed. Published by Chappell & Co. Inc. by consent.

m. Moya. w. Maurice Vaucaire. Published July 28, 1914,[1] under the title *Chanson du Coeur Brisé*[2] (*The Song of Songs*) by Chappell & Co., Ltd., 41 East 34th Street, New York, N.Y. First edition: Front cover has the title in the order indicated in the previous sentence, says the song was created by M. Henri Leoni aux Ambassadeurs, is purple and white, lists four arrangements with French and American prices (the Piano et Chant at 2.50 frs. (60¢)), and the publisher is shown to have branches in four other cities. m. on pp. 2–7. French and English words; p. 2 states that the English words are by Clarence Lucas. p.n. 6606. Back cover adv. *J'Aime.*. Front cover has no drawing of a lady, no keys and no reference to a new edition. LC(CDC). As far as can be determined, the song was not published first in France or England.

Moya is a pseudonym of Harold Vicars, who was born in London, became a conductor and composer in England and the United States and died in Providence, R.I., in 1922.[3] Vaucaire, a French dramatic author, was born in Versailles in 1865 and died in 1918.[4]

---

[1] Copyright records; LC.
[2] Literally, *The Song of the Broken Heart*.
[3] *ASCAP*, p. 514.
[4] Parker, 3rd ed., p. 770, and 13th ed., p. 1528.

Song of the Vagabonds

Sons of toil____ and dan-ger, will you serve____ a stran-ger

m. Rudolf Friml. w. Brian Hooker. Published Oct. 7, 1925,[1] by Henry Waterson Inc., 1571 Broadway, New York, N.Y. First edition: Front cover has a photograph of Dennis King and is yellow, black and white. s. *The Vagabond King*—2 titles listed. m. on pp. 2–5. p.n. 1698-4. Back cover *If.. - Fallin'..* LC(CDC).

The Vagabond King opened in New York City on Sept. 21, 1925, and the piano-vocal score of the musical play was published Aug. 17, 1926.[1] LC(CDC). Brief biographic information regarding Friml appears above under *L'Amour-Toujours-L'Amour*. Hooker, a lyricist and educator, was born in New York, N.Y., in 1880 and died in New London, Conn., in 1946.[2]

Song of the Volga Boatmen

Yo__ heave ho! Yo__ heave ho! Let us give a__pull, give an-oth-er pull!
Yay-ee ooh - nyem! Yay-ee ooh-nyem! Yehsh-cheeaw rah - zeek, yehsh-cheeaw rahz!

Бурлацкая, the *Song of the Volga Boatmen*, was first published in 1866[1] in Сборникъ Русскихъ Народныхъ Пѣсенъ (*A Collection of Russian Folksongs*), assembled by M. Balakirev and published by A. Johansen, 44 Nevsky Prospect, St. Petersburg, p. 78. The title of the song means, literally, *Song of the Barge Haulers*. The entire book is in Russian only, with m. on pp. 4–79 and p.ns. 216-255, this song being the last, no. 40, with p.n. 255.

There are two variants of the book, with priority unknown: in one, there is no price, no Leipzig agent and no statement under the title on p. 78; PUS. In the other, the prices are 3 Rub/ 3 Thlr, A. Whistling is the Leipzig agent, and under the title on p. 78 it is stated that the song was

[1] Copyright records; LC.
[2] *ASCAP*, p. 239.

[1] According to a letter from the Academy of Science of U.S.S.R., Institute of Russian Literature (Pushkin House), Leningrad, which states that the date has been established by Ye. V. Gippius (Hippius), and confirmed on the basis of Balakirev's autograph.

written down in lower Novgorod; ONB. The latter has a handwritten date, May 23, 1869, and the German price in Thalers confirms a pre-1874 date. The song was issued in sheet music by P. Jurgenson, Moscow, under the title *Эй Ухнемъ!*, about 1886,[2] with p.n. 11065; JF.

This work chantey was sung by *burlaks*, men who made their living by pulling big boats laden with grain upstream on the Volga River. It is said that the song begins with a strong down beat, indicating the gigantic effort of strength made by the *burlaks* to set the boat in motion; and the strong accentuation thereafter is based on their need to walk in step.[3]

Songs My Mother Taught Me—Dvořák

Als   die   al - te   Mut - ter
Songs my   Moth - er taught me

m. Anton Dvořák. w. Adolf Heyduk. Published Aug. 20, 1880,[1] as *Als die Alte Mutter*, no. 4, in *Zigeunermelodien* op. 55, or *Gypsy Songs*, for piano and voice, by N. Simrock, Berlin. Probable first edition: Front cover is gray and black and has a price of Mk. 4. vb. Title page has a dedication to the K. K. Kammersänger, Gustav Walter, refers to an edition for tenor or soprano and another edition for baritone or alto and mentions the year 1880. m. on pp. 2–23. p.n. 8170 Original-Ausgabe. *Als die Alte Mutter* is on p. 12. The heading on p. 2 reads: *Zigeunermelodien. (Gypsy Songs.)* The words are in German and English.[2] This edition is for baritone or alto. BM (copy deposited Dec. 8, 1880) and GM. The edition for higher voice may have the preceding plate number.

This edition precedes the edition mentioned by Burghauser and Šourek, which has p.n. 8219 and German, English and Czech words;[3] JF. The *Zigeunermelodien* were composed in Jan. and Feb., 1880. Brief biographic information regarding Dvořák appears above under *Humoreske*. Heyduk, a Czech poet, was born in Reichenburg, Bohemia, in 1835 and died in Pisek, Bohemia, in 1923.[4]

---

[2] On the basis of the p.n.
[3] Program note, about 1903, of concert by Nadina Slaviansky; JF.

[1] According to the entry at Stationers' Hall on Nov. 23, 1880.
[2] Hofmeister *Monatsbericht*, Oct., 1880, p. 307, confirms that the first printing had German and English words.
[3] Burghauser, p. 211; and Šourek, pp. xxv and 34. In a letter, Burghauser agreed that the edition with p.n. 8170 is earlier.
[4] *Meyers*, vol. 5, p. 1527.

Sophisticated Lady

© 1933 by Gotham Music Service, Inc. © renewed 1961. By permission of Mills Music, Inc.

m. Duke Ellington. Published May 31, 1933,[1] by Gotham Music Service Inc., 1619 Broadway, New York, N.Y. First edition: Front cover has a drawing of a sophisticated lady and is aqua and white. p. [2] adv. *Dizzy..* and *Flapperette.* m. on pp. 3–5. p. 4 adv. *Soliloquy.* p. 5 adv. *Kitten..* Center fold advertisement. Back cover adv. *Zez..* No reference on p. 3. to Song edition. LC(CDC) and JF (autographed by the composer). The vocal edition with words by Irving Mills and Mitchell Parish was published Oct. 10, 1933.

Edward Kennedy ("Duke") Ellington, a composer and orchestra leader, was born in Washington, D.C., in 1899 and died in New York City in 1974. [2]

The Sorcerer's Apprentice—Dukas

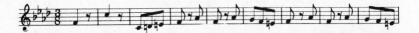

m. Paul Dukas. *L'Apprenti Sorcier*, Scherzo d'après une ballade de Goethe, was published about the fall of 1897 for orchestral score, orchestral parts and piano four hands[1] by A. Durand & Fils, 4 Place de la Madeleine, Paris. Probable first edition of the orchestral score: Front cover is tan, brown and green. vb. Two blank pages. Title page is the same as the front cover except in white, brown and green, and lists only the **three** arrangements mentioned above, the orchestral score at 15 f. vb. Story. Editorial note. m. on pp. 1–74. p.n. 5302. Two blank pages. Inside of back cover blank. Outside of back cover has a drawing of a lyre. NEC.

Possible first printings of the orchestral parts, with p.n. 5292, but all without front covers, are at CI, COP, FLP and HU. The copyright deposit copy of the arrangement for piano four hands, with three arrangements listed on the title page and p.n. 5314, is at BN, and a copy inscribed by the composer is at JF. The work was composed in 1897 and performed May 18, 1897, in Paris. Dukas was born in Paris in 1865 and died there in 1935.

[1] Copyright records; LC.

[2] Obituary, *The New York Times*, May 25, 1974.

[1] Only these three arrangements are listed in *BMF*, Oct.–Dec., 1897, pp. 8 and 21. The arrangement for piano four hands is in *BF*, Dec. 25, 1897, p. 877.

The Sound of Music

The   hills are a-live   with the sound of   mu - sic

m. Richard Rodgers. w. Oscar Hammerstein 2nd. The song *The Sound of Music* was published Sept. 25, 1959,[1] by Williamson Music, Inc., RKO Building—Rockefeller Center, New York 20, N.Y. The copy deposited for copyright is a professional edition. Probable first regular edition: Front cover is in blue, gold and white, and features Mary Martin. s. *The Sound of Music*—no other titles listed. Price is 60 cents. p. [2] blank. m. on pp. 3–7. p.n. 1077–5. Back cover blank. JF.

The show *The Sound of Music* opened in New York City on Nov. 16, 1959. The piano-vocal score of the show was published Nov. 23, 1960,[1] with tan and red paper covers at $7.50 by Williamson Music, Inc., 609 Fifth Ave., New York 17, N.Y.; LC(CDC).

Brief biographic information regarding Rodgers and Hammerstein appears above under *If I Loved You* and *All the Things You Are.*

Souvenir—Drdla

m. Franz Drdla. Published about Oct., 1904,[1] for violin and piano by Josef Weinberger, Leipzig. Probable first edition: Front cover is black and gray and otherwise the same as the title page. vb. Title page is in red and white, has a dedication to Franz Naval and the price of 2 Mk. vb. m. on pp. 3–7. p.n. 1367. pp. [8], [9], and back cover blank. No arrangements on front cover

---

[1] Copyright records; LC.

[1] Hofmeister *Monatsbericht*, Aug., 1888, p. 314.

or title page, no Paris agent, the lithographer is C. G. Röder, G.m.b.H., Leipzig, and there is no copyright notice on p. 3. Insert for violin: pp. [1] and [4] blank; m. on pp. 2–3; same plate number. ESM.

Drdla, Czech violinist and composer, was born in Žďár, Moravia, in 1868 and died in Bad Gastein, Austria, in 1944.[2]

Soviet Union National Anthem

Sah–yooz nye–roo-shee-mwih ress-poob-leek svaw-bawd-nihkh splaw-tee-lah nah-vyeh-kee

m. A. V. Alexandrov. w. Sergei Mihalkov and Gabriel El-Registan. *Гимн Советского Союза* (*Hymn of the Soviet Union*) was published in the Jan. 1, 1944, issue of *Литература и Искусство*[1] (*Literature and Art*), an organ of the Board of the Union of Soviet Writers, apparently on the first page. GL (photocopy at JF).

Shortly thereafter,[1A] the *Anthem* was published separately by the State Musical Publishers, Moscow. Front cover has a drawing of a hammer and sickle, a star and the year 1944. m. on pp. [2]–[3]. Back cover has the words, and information regarding Soviet music publishing procedure, including the fact that the work was submitted for publication Dec. 24, 1943, that 1,000,000 copies were printed, and the price was 50 k. GL (photocopy at JF). †

The *Anthem* was performed by the Soviet Army Chorus on the radio on New Year's Eve, Dec. 31, 1943. Alexander Vasilyvich Alexandrov was born in 1883 in Blakhenoe, State of Ryazan, of a peasant family, became a composer, conductor of choruses and professor, and died in 1946 near Berlin.[2] Sergei Vladimirovich Mikhalkov was born in 1913 in Moscow, became a poet, playwright and author of children's works and is a member of the Board of the Union of Soviet Writers.[3] El-Registan was born in Samarkand in 1899, became a poet and died in 1945.[1]

Spring Song—Mendelssohn

---

[2] *Grove's*, vol. 2, p. 764.

[1] Information furnished by the Ministry of Culture, USSR.
[1A] *AML*, Jan.–March, 1944, p. 4.
[2] Information furnished by LTL.
[3] *Bio. Dir. USSR*, p. 405.

m. Felix Mendelssohn Bartholdy. *6 Lieder ohne Worte*, The Fifth Book of Original Melodies, op. 62, was probably first published for piano by J. J. Ewer & Co., 72 Newgate St., London, a copy of this edition being deposited at BM on Feb. 4, 1844. First edition of the Ewer publication: Front cover is black and white with a brown ornamental border, has price of 5/ and as agents, N. Simrock, Bonn, H. Lemoine, Paris, and Lucca, Milan. vb. m. on pp. 1–17, no. 6, Allegretto Grazioso *(Spring Song)*, on p. 14. p.n. Mendelssohn, Op: 62 [*sic*]. p. [18] blank. Engraved. BM(CDC), AT and JF*.

Sechs Lieder ohne Worte, Vtes Heft, was published for piano by N. Simrock, Bonn, about May, 1844,[1] with a dedication to Frau Dr. Clara Schumann geb. Wieck, at 3 Frs. 50c., with p.n. 4343, Milan, London and Lyons agents, and engraved. There are three variants, priority unknown: in one, at GM, the Milan agent is to the left; in the second, at JF, it is the London agent; and in the third, at JF, it is the Lyons agent.

A likely contemporaneous French edition, impossible to date precisely, was published as *Six Romances*, Cinquième Recueil, by Benacci et Peschier, 2 Rue St. Côme, Lyons.[2] A possible first edition is at JF. The work was composed June 1, 1842, in Denmark Hill, London. Brief biographic information regarding Mendelssohn appears above under his *Concerto for Violin*.

St. Anthony Chorale

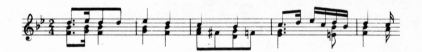

Frequently attributed to Joseph Haydn, it is now believed that this *Chorale* is probably an old Burgenland pilgrims' chant and not an original composition by Haydn.[1] The *Chorale* is included in an eighteenth-century manuscript in orchestral parts, not in Haydn's hand, but with the contemporary notation that the overall work was by Haydn; the manuscript is at the Gymnasialbibliothek, Zittau, East Germany. Haydn had composed

---

[1] Hofmeister *Monatsbericht*, May, 1844, p. 71.

[2] Hopkinson, *Parisian*, p. 8. Mendelssohn wrote his German publisher on Sept. 11, 1844, as to one of the later books of *Songs without Words*:
"I ask you to determine yourself the day of publication, with the gentlemen from London and Lyons ..." Charles Hamilton, *Auction Catalogue no. 12* (New York, N.Y., 1966), no. 126; catalogue at JF.

---

[1] Hoboken, II, 46. Letters from Dr. Karl Geiringer, Santa Barbara, Cal., and H. C. Robbins Landon, Pistoia, Italy. Karl Geiringer, *Brahms, His Life and Work* (New York, N.Y., 2nd ed., 1947), p. 251; NYPL.

the overall work in 1780–1789 for the military band of Prince Esterházy for eight instruments; the second movement was entitled "Chorale St. Antoni." C. F. Pohl, the biographer of Haydn and then the Librarian at the Gesellschaft der Musikfreunde, Vienna, made an orchestral score from these parts, and in Nov., 1870, had a copy of the score made for Brahms.

Brahms composed his *Variationen über ein Thema von Jos. Haydn* in the summer of 1873 in an arrangement for two pianos and in another arrangement for orchestra, but it was always intended for orchestra. The arrangement for two pianos was published by N. Simrock, Berlin, on Nov. 2, 1873.[2] First edition of the arrangement for two pianos: The front cover is a collective-title front cover listing 25 "Original-Compositionen und Arrangements für Zwei Pianoforte," the last of which is this work, has the opus no. 56b, the price is 4½ [Mark], and there are references to Stationers' Hall and to C. G. Röder, Leipzig. m. on pp. 2–15, vb; and pp. 1–14. p.n. 7386. Folio. Not engraved. BM (copyright copy deposited Feb. 24, 1874). Brahms and Clara Schumann played the arrangement for two pianos in Bonn in Aug., 1873.†

The arrangements for orchestral score and parts were published by the same concern on Feb. 1, 1874.[3] First edition of the orchestral score: The title page has the opus no. 56a, the price is 9 Marks, there is a reference to Stationers' Hall and the lithographer is C. G. Röder, Leipzig. m. on pp. 2–83. p.n. 7395. p. [84] blank. Octavo. Not engraved. BM (copyright copy deposited March 27, 1874), BPL and JF. The orchestral arrangement was performed in Vienna on Nov. 2, 1873.

No copy of the orchestral parts in first edition has been found with a front cover. Copies of the possible first edition, lacking a front cover, with plate number 7396, not engraved, are at CI and HU.

Haydn's work was not published until April 4, 1932[4] [sic], when it was published as *Divertimento (Feldpartita) für 8 Stimmigen Bläserchor*, for orchestral score and parts, by Fritz Schuberth Jr., Leipzig, edited by Dr. Karl Geiringer. A copy of the orchestral score is at NYPL. A set of the orchestral parts is at BM.

No printing of the *Chorale* is known before Brahms' *Variations* mentioned above. If there were words to the *Chorale*, they are not known.

[2] According to the entry at Stationers' Hall on Jan. 12, 1874. Deutsch, *Brahms*, p. 143, refers to a later edition with p.n. 7397. Not in Hofmeister *Monatsbericht*, 1873–74.‡

[3] According to the entry at Stationers' Hall on Feb. 20, 1874. Deutsch *op. cit.*, says Nov., 1874. The orchestral score is listed in Hofmeister *Monatsbericht*, Sept., 1874, p. [168], but not the orchestral parts. §

[4] Copyright records; LC.

St. Louis Blues

St. Lou-is wo-man____   wid her dia - mon' rings

© Copyright MCMXIV by W. C. Handy. © Copyright renewed MCMXLII by W. C. Handy. Published by Handy Brothers Music Co. Inc. With permission.

mw. W. C. Handy. Published under the title *The Saint Louis Blues*, Sept. 11, 1914, by Pace & Handy Music Co., Memphis, Tenn.[1] First edition: Front cover is blue and white, states that it is "The First Successful 'Blues' Published. The Most Widely Known Ragtime Composition," mentions that W. C. Handy is the composer of *The Memphis Blues* and has the price of 5 (50¢).[2] m. on pp. 2–5. The copyright is in the name of the composer. Back cover adv. *Your..* LC(CDC) and JF (autographed by the composer).

The chorus of the *St. Louis Blues* was taken directly from an earlier piece without words by W. C. Handy entitled *The Jogo Blues*,[3] published July 26, 1913,[1] by Pace & Handy Music Co., Memphis, Tenn. First edition: Front cover is red, white and blue, has a drawing of a piano player, a dedication to Mr. John Ross, Memphis, Tenn., states that the piece was played by Handy and His Bands as The Memphis Itch and mentions that Handy was the author of *The Girl You Never Have Met.* m. on pp. 2–5. p. 2 and back cover adv. *The Girl..* LC(CDC) and JF.

"I hate to see de ev'nin' sun go down"—the opening words of *St. Louis Blues*—were said by Handy in a later year to refer to his hungry and cold days in St. Louis when he was unemployed and, as the sun went down, he had to find a cobblestoned Mississippi levee on which to sleep.[4] *St. Louis Blues* has been recorded between 800 and 900 times in the United States alone. Handy was born in a Florence, Ala., log cabin in 1873, and died in New York City in 1958.

[1] Copyright records; LC. Wickes, p. 17, states that 10,000 copies were published and sold by Handy alone, before he moved to Memphis; this seems doubtful and no such copy has been found.

[2] Front cover is illustrated in Fuld, *American*, p. [44].

[3] Front cover is illustrated in W. C. Handy, *Father of the Blues*, Foreword by Abbe Niles (New York, N.Y., 1941), opposite p. 124. NYPL.

[4] Obituary, *The New York Times*, March 29, 1958.

Star Dust

Some-times I   won-der why I   spend the   lone-ly   night dream-ing of a   song?

Copyright 1929 by Mills Music, Inc.; renewed 1957. By permission.

m. Hoagy Carmichael. On Oct. 31, 1927, more than a year before it was published, *Star Dust* was recorded as a "Stomp," a medium fast and jazzy tempo, without words, in Richmond, Ind., on Gennett record no. 6311 by Hoagy Carmichael & His Pals;[1] record at IU and JF.

Star Dust was then published as a piano composition without words on Jan. 29, 1929,[1A] by Mills Music Inc., 148–150 West 46th St., New York, N.Y. The copyright records at LC show that both copyright deposit copies were returned to the publisher. They were probably professional editions as the copyright copy deposited at BM on Jan. 26, 1929 [*sic*], is a professional edition.

Possible first regular edition of the piano composition without words: Front cover has a drawing of Japanese lanterns and a silhouette of an orchestra, and is green, black and white. p. [2] adv. *Estelle*. m. on pp. 3–7. p. 4 adv. *Dizzy*.. p. 5 adv. *Flapperette*. p. 6 adv. *Jack*.. p. 7 adv. *Popular*.. Back cover adv. *A Treat*.. *Estelle* was published Nov. 15, 1930; the other advertised compositions were published in 1927 or earlier. The above edition does not state, near the top of p. 3, "Also Published As A Song." JF (autographed).

Hoagy Carmichael is said to have composed and whistled this song while walking across the Indiana University campus in 1927. Stuart Gorrell, a schoolmate, named it *Star Dust*.[2] The original manuscript, deposited Jan. 5, 1928, is at LC, in the key of D major, for piano, a very plain arrangement, without words and with no indication of tempo. On May 10, 1929, a vocal edition was published, with words by Mitchell Parish, copies being deposited on Aug. 17, 1933, at LC. Carmichael always wrote "Stardust," the publishers "Star Dust," and the dictionaries "Star-dust."

Star Dust earned about $50,000 a year in gross royalties from 1958–

---

[1] Brian Rust, *Jazz Records A–Z 1897–1931* (Hatch End, Middlesex, England, 1961), p. 134; BM and LC. *The Jazzfinder*, New Orleans, La., March, 1948, p. 18, and Dec. 1948, p. 25; NYPL.

[1A] Copyright records; LC.

[2] See, generally, Hoagy Carmichael, *The Stardust Road* (New York, N.Y., 1946), p. 124, NYPL; and George Marek, "Silver Anniversary of 'Star Dust,'" in *Good Housekeeping Magazine*, New York, N.Y., Sept., 1955, p. 17, NYPL.

1963,[3] and has been recorded between 800 and 900 times in the United States alone. Carmichael was born in Bloomington, Ind., in 1899, became a composer, actor and performing artist and died in Palm Springs, Cal., in 1981.[3A] Parish was born in Shreveport, La., in 1900, became a staff lyricist for music publishers and lives in New York City.[4]

The Star Spangled Banner

O___ say can you see by the dawn's ear - ly light

The melody of *The Star Spangled Banner*[1] was originally known as *The Anacreontic Song*, which was published probably 1779–1780[2] by Longman & Broderip, 26 Cheapside, London. First edition: p. [1] blank. m. on pp. 2–4. Page 2 states that the song is Sung at the Crown and Anchor Tavern in the Strand—the Words by Ralph Tomlinson Esq. late President of that Society,[3] and the price is 6d. Engraved. BM, BPL, HL, IU, LC, MHS, NYPL, RAM, LL and JF. In the second printing by this publisher, it has a second address at 13 Haymarket. The first printing of the words of *The Anacreontic Song*, without music, was in Aug., 1778, in no. IV of *The Vocal Magazine, or British Songster's Miscellany* (London), Song 566, p. 147, without title, the opening words of which are *To Anacreon, in Heav'n, where he sat in full glee.* FO, LC and JF.

It has recently been established that John Stafford Smith was the composer of the music. In a ten-volume manuscript of "Recollections" by

---

[3] Prospectus of Mills Music Trust, n.p., 1965, pp. 9 and 15; Securities and Exchange Commission, Washington, D.C.

[3A] *ASCAP*, p. 75. Obituary, *The New York Times*, Dec. 28, 1981.

[4] *ASCAP*, p. 382.

---

[1] See, generally, Oscar George Theodore Sonneck, *The Star Spangled Banner* (Washington, 1914); Joseph Muller, *The Star Spangled Banner* (New York, N.Y., 1935); and P. W. Filby and Edward G. Howard, *Star-Spangled Books* (Baltimore, 1972); LC and NYPL. Also, William Lichtenwanger, "Star-Spangled Bibliography," in *College Music Symposium* (Binghamton, N.Y., 1972), vol. 12, p. [94].

[2] Muller, *op. cit.*, p. 15. The publisher had this address only until Dec., 1782; Humphries-Smith, p. 216. There was no entry of *The Anacreontic Song* in Stationers' Hall between 1774 and 1786.

[3] The Anacreontic Society, a convivial society in London in which concerts were given and songs were sung by the members.

Richard Stevens for 1777 he referred to "the Anacreontic Song... which Stafford Smith set to Music..." (manuscript at Pendlebury Music Library, Cambridge University).[4] In addition, John Stafford Smith's *A Fifth Book of Canzonets, Catches, Canons and Glees* (London), entered at Stationers' Hall on May 8, 1799, states on the title page that he is the "Author of...the Anacreontic," and on p. 33, where *The Anacreontic Song* appears, "harmonized by the Author."†

The Anacreontic Song soon became well known both in England and America, and its melody was also used as the setting for about 85 different printed American poems, almost all of a patriotic nature, from 1790 to 1820.[5] Key himself wrote a poem in 1805, commencing *When the Warrior Returns*, commemorating Stephen Decatur's triumph in the war with Tripoli, to the melody of *The Anacreontic Song*, in which the phrase "By the light of the star-spangled flag of our nation" appeared.[6]

The occasion of Francis Scott Key's writing of the poem of *The Star Spangled Banner* was patriotic and exciting.[7] Securing the release of a friend under a flag of truce, Key was aboard a ship the night of Sept. 13–14, 1814, watching the English bombardment of Fort McHenry preparatory to an attack on Baltimore. While the bombardment continued, it was proof that the fort had not surrendered. But suddenly the bombardment ceased, and it was not known whether the fort had surrendered or the attack upon it had been abandoned. Key paced the deck during the entire night. As soon as dawn came, he turned his glass to the fort and saw that "our flag was still there." On his way to shore Key finished the poem, arriving in Baltimore from the ship Sept. 14–17, 1814.[8]

A broadside of the poem was published Sept. 17–19, 1814, under the title *Defence of Fort M'Henry*, to the "Tune—Anacreon in Heaven." No printer is indicated and there is no border on the broadside. Found with

---

[4] William Lichtenwanger, District Heights, Md., found this reference in vol. 1, pp. 63–73, of "Recollections." and reported it in "The Music of 'The Star-Spangled Banner' From Ludgate Hill to Capitol Hill," in *The Quarterly Journal of the Library of Congress*, July, 1977, p. 136, at pp. 148–149, and "The Music of 'The Star-Spangled Banner,'" in *College Music Symposium* (Boulder, Col., 1978), vol. 18, no. 2, p. [35], at p. 54.

[5] Richard S. Hill, "The Melody of 'The Star Spangled Banner' in the United States Before 1820" in *Essays Honoring Lawrence C. Wroth* (Portland, Me., 1951); NYPL.

[6] *Id.*, pp. 18–19. The poem, to the "Tune—Anacreon," was published in the [Boston] *Independent Chronicle*, Dec. 30, 1805, last page, without mention of Key; BPL.

[7] See, generally, Introductory Letter of Chief Justice R. B. Taney in *Poems of the Late Francis S. Key, Esq.* (New York, N.Y., 1857), p. [13]; NYPL and JF.

[8] For new information as to the date of Key's return, the author is indebted to Dr. Harry D. Bowman, Hagerstown, Md., who noted a letter in the *New York Gazette and General Advertiser*, Sept. 20, 1814, p. 2, at NYHS, that Key returned to Baltimore on Sept. 17, 1814.

the earliest of Key's manuscripts (see below), this broadside is generally considered the earliest printing of the words of *The Star Spangled Banner*, and, of course, the earliest broadside.[9] MHS (Walters Art Gallery copy); also at LC. Then, another broadside, also entitled *Defence of Fort M'Henry*, was published; no printer is indicated; and there is a border on the broadside—IU and NYHS. An early broadside, similarly entitled, stating at the bottom "[For sale at the office of the Chronicle]," is now owned by a dealer —photocopies at LC and JF.[10] A broadside entitled *General Hull and the Defence of Fort M'Henry* refers to the Battle of New Orleans and would have to have been published after Jan. 8, 1815; LL. A broadside entitled *Bombardment of Fort M'Henry* printed by John H. Toy, St. Paul's Lane and Market Street, [Baltimore] was published 1823—as the printer did not occupy the premises until that year; MHS.

The poem was printed in the *Baltimore Patriot*, an evening newspaper, Sept. 20, 1814, p. 2, at MHS, and in the [Baltimore] *American & Commercial Daily Advertiser*, the following morning, p. 2, at LC.

Probably not later than about Oct. 19, 1814, and certainly before Nov. 18, 1814, Key's poem and the accompanying music were published in sheet music form by Thomas Carr.[11] It is frequently believed, although

[9] The Sept. 20, 1814, issue of the *Baltimore Patriot*, referred to in the text, states that the song "has already been extensively circulated."

A letter from Severn Teackle to Phillip Wallis, dated Sept. 23, 1814, states: "We have a song composed by Mr. Key of G.Town which was presented to every individual in the Fort in a Separate sheet—you may have seen it as it has been published." Letter owned by Mrs. Irving Berlin, New York, N.Y. Which of the broadsides is referred to, or whether the reference is to the song in sheet music, is not clear.

[10] According to the dealer, the original owner was a member of the Pennsylvania Legislature in Harrisburg in 1814–1815; there was a *Harrisburg Chronicle* in 1814–1815; and the poem was not printed in this newspaper in these years. There was no "Chronicle" newspaper in these years in Maryland, New York City, Philadelphia or Washington.

[11] The *Baltimore American and Commercial Advertiser*, Oct. 19, 1814, p. [3], at MHS, and *Baltimore Federal Gazette*, same date, p. [3], at PM, state that "After the play [*Count Benyowski*] Mr. Hardinge will sing a much admired *New Song*, written by a gentleman of Maryland, in commemoration of the *Gallant Defense of Fort M'Henry*, called, *The Star-Spangled Banner*."

Baltimore Federal Gazette, Nov. 18, 1814, p. [2], at PM, states: "*The Star-Spangled Banner* . . . Mr. T. Carr has it for sale, at his music store, in this city." The purpose of this statement was not to announce Carr's publication, but rather to prove that "The bards of our nation will soon vie with those in Britain in spirited and appropriate national songs." *The Star Spangled Banner* is shown as one successful, published example, and the newspaper proceeds to print another patriotic song.

The music was arranged by Thomas Carr at "Mr. Key's request, in his presence and from his manuscript;" letter from the publisher's daughter, quoted in Muller, footnote 1, above, p. 46. See, also, Muller, p. 28. The Maryland Historical Society, Baltimore, has been unable to advise as to Key's "presence" in Baltimore in Sept.– Dec., 1814. The prominent misprint indicates a hasty publication—possibly as early

there is no proof, that Carr suggested the glamorous title, *The Star Spangled Banner*, from his sense of salesmanship. First edition: p. [1] blank. p. [2] states: The Star Spangled Banner, A **Pariotic** [*sic*] Song; and the publisher is shown as Carrs Music Store, 36 Baltimore Street, Baltimore. **(See Plate IV)**. m. on pp. [2]–[3]. p. [4] blank. Engraved. No mention of Key. Ten copies are known: LC, IU (Townsend-Dichter-Scribner-Lilly copy), MHS, Johns Hopkins University, Baltimore (LL copy), Moravian Music Foundation, Winston-Salem, N.C., NYPL, UM, WH (Elliott Shapiro—BMI copy), The Dietrich Brothers Americana Corporation, Wilmington, Del. (W. Ward Beam—TWS copy), and JF. The TWS or Streeter copy was auctioned at $23,000 to a dealer for The Dietrich Brothers Americana Corporation on April 20, 1967, at Parke-Bernet Galleries, New York, N.Y., item no. 1068; this is believed to be the highest price ever paid for a piece of printed music. Other printings followed shortly in magazines,[12] songsters,[13] newspapers (more than 20 before Dec. 31, 1814),[14] at least one almanac[14] and sheet music.[15]†

as Sept. 19, 1814. The Carr family published *Hail Columbia*, the country's original national anthem, five days after its first advertised performance on April 26, 1798; Sonneck-Upton, p. 171.

It is difficult to say whether Carr's publication preceded or followed the singing at the Baltimore Theatre.

[12] The *Analectic Magazine* for Nov., 1814, the first magazine in which the words of *Defence of Fort M'Henry* appeared, is common (*ULS*, p. 239), but not with the original wrappers for that issue, of which the only known copies are at AAS, HU, IU, MHS and Boston Athenaeum. It was published in Philadelphia and advertised as available on Nov. 1, 1814; *The Star Spangled Banner*, a catalogue to be published in 1971 by the Maryland Historical Society, Baltimore.

[13] Four songsters in which the words appear were published in 1814: *The American Muse: or, Songster's Companion* (New York, N.Y.), at BPL and BR; *American Patriotic and Comic Modern Songs* (Newburyport, Mass.), at BPL, BR and IU; *The Columbian Harmonist, or Songster's Repository* (New York, N.Y.), at HU; and *National Songster* (Hagers-Town, Md.), at LC, IU, MHS and NYHS. While the order of priority is uncertain, Hill doubted that the Hagers-Town songster, which could not have been published until Nov. 19, 1814, was the first; Hill, footnote 5, above, p. 25.

[14] Dr. George J. Svejda, *History of the Star Spangled Banner from 1814 to the Present* (Baltimore, 1969), p. 83; LC and MHS.

[15] Two Philadelphia sheet music editions which may have been published as early as 1814 could not have been published until after Oct. 12–19, 1814, as both mention that the song was sung by Mr. Hardinge. One sheet music edition is *The Battle of the Wabash* with the words of *Fort McHenry* added; in one variant, p. [4] is blank—Wolfe, p. 819, no. 8329A; in the other variant, which Wolfe considers the second edition, p. [1] is blank. The other sheet music edition is *Washington Guards*, also with the words added; however, Wolfe, p. 822, no. 8356, considers this "1816?"—because of the "music store" imprint, and style (letter from Wolfe).

Perhaps the first mechanical rendition of *The Star Spangled Banner* was made about 1890 on a Regina (N.J.) 18½" revolving perforated metal disc no. 104; NYPL

This author believes that insufficient credit for the popularity of *The Star Spangled Banner* song, the popularity of that title, and possibly the originality of the title itself, has been given to the traveling Warren & Wood Chestnut Street Company from the Old Drury Theatre, Philadelphia. This company played in Washington from June 16 to Aug. 13, 1814, was inactive because of the hostilities from Aug. 14 to Oct. 11, 1814, resumed in Baltimore from Oct. 12 to Nov. 21, 1814, and played in Philadelphia from Nov. 28, 1814, to April 17, 1815, and then again in Baltimore, Washington and Alexandria.[16] On at least four occasions, commencing Oct. 19, 1814, with a singing by Mr. Hardinge, advance notice appeared in the local press that *The Star Spangled Banner* (under that title) was to be sung at the Theatre. And that it was sung, without advance newspaper notice, on many other occasions during the troubled period is shown by the Nov. 18, 1814, issue of the *Baltimore Federal Gazette*, which reports that *The Star Spangled Banner* (under that title) is "repeatedly sung at the Theatre" with "continued applause" and is "fully appreciated"; (p. [2], at PM). It is even possible that Mr. Hardinge suggested the title. Certainly the "exposure" of the song by reason of its frequent singing under its new title before hundreds of persons, with perhaps the audience joining in the singing,[17] would be greater than by reason of its availability in sheet music at Carrs Music Store.

Whereas the earliest broadside, newspaper printing and sheet music do not refer to Key, his authorship was publicly acknowledged as early as Sept. 24, 1814, when the *Defence of Fort M'Henry*, by "F. S. Key," was published in the *Frederick-Town Herald* of that date, p. [3]; Enoch Pratt Free Library, Baltimore, Md.

(Record Division; uncatalogued). A similar Regina 27" disc no. 4028, probably a little later, is at JF. An early (the first ?) recording was made in 1896 on a cylinder by the Edison Concert Band; Edison National Historic Site, West Orange, N.J. Sousa's Band under the direction of Arthur Pryor recorded the anthem on one of the earliest Victor records, no. 336, in Oct., 1900.

[16] Reese D. James, *Old Drury of Philadelphia* (Philadelphia, 1932); NYPL. The four advance newspaper notices are at p. 158, *The Baltimore Patriot* (and two other Baltimore newspapers), Oct. 19, 1814 (Mr. Hardinge is singer), and, p. 170, May 31, 1815 (Mr. Steward is singer); p. 174, *The Daily National Intelligencer*, Washington, July 4, 1815 (Mr. Steward); and p. 177, *The Alexandria Daily Gazette*, Sept. 12, 1815 (Mr. Steward).

Original Baltimore playbills, including that of Oct. 19, 1814, are at MHS. The playbill for Nov. 12, 1814, announced the singing of *The Star Spangled Banner* "(2nd time here);" Mr. Hardinge is singer.

[17] The cast and/or the audience had sung *God Save the King* in London under similar patriotic conditions commencing Sept. 28, 1745 (the Pretender marching on London from Scotland). Percy A. Scholes, *God Save the Queen!* (London, 1954), pp. 1 and 30; NYPL.

The earliest of Key's manuscripts, the Walters of 1814, is at MHS; it was sold at auction at $24,000 on Jan. 5, 1934, at American Art Association, New York, N.Y., item 264. The Cist of 1840 is at LC. The Gen. Keim of 1842 is at PHS. The Espie of 1842 is at GEU. The Mahar of 1842 appears to be lost. The Howard of about 1840 may be mythical and, in any event, has not been located. The only known contemporary manuscript of the words under the title *Fort Mc Henry*, is in Miss Susan Assheton's Book [Philadelphia], Jan. 20, 1789—); JF.

Unlike the *Marseillaise* which was published in England the same year it was published in France, and in the United States a year later, and in both countries frequently thereafter,[18] *The Star Spangled Banner* does not seem to have been published soon abroad. The earliest known foreign publication of *The Star Spangled Banner* was about 1842 by D'Almaine & Co., 20 Soho Square, London; BM (copy received Nov. 1, 1842). It was published for piano in 1859 by John André, Offenbach o/M; slightly later edition with English words at JF. No early French printing is known; in 1856–1859 when Ledentu, 6 Boulevart des Italiens, Paris, published two series of national songs, the only American national song included was *Hail Columbia*; JF.[18]

One of the principal attractions at the Smithsonian Institution, Washington, D.C., is the gigantic shell-holed Star Spangled Banner that Francis Scott Key saw flying over Fort McHenry. Key was born at Pipe's Creek, Frederick County, Md., in 1780 and died in Baltimore in 1843.[19]

"The Star-bespangled Genius of America . . ." was a marvelous phrase used in the American colonies in 1780.[20] "Star-spangled," or variant, has been traced back to 1591 and was used, among others, by Marlowe, Shakespeare, Milton and Coleridge. As mentioned above, Key had used the phrase "star-spangled flag" in 1805 for another poem to the melody of *The Anacreontic Song*.

---

[18] *BUC*, p. 904. Sonneck-Upton, p. 251. The D'Almaine & Co. edition at the British Museum is earlier than the one described in Muller, footnote 1 above, no. 26, p. 119. Hofmeister *Annual* 1859, p. 80. The John André edition was arranged by Charles Voss; G. Andre, Philadelphia, also published the Voss arrangements—see Muller, *supra*, no. 42, p. 173, and no. 53, p. 210. Hopkinson, *Parisian*, p. 73.

[19] There was an Anacreontic Society in Baltimore from at least 1807 to 1826. Key was not a member in the 1820's. The Maryland Historical Society, Baltimore, is unable to say whether he was a member in an earlier year. Letters from MHS.

[20] Roger Butterfield, New York City, advised the author of these earlier references. Timothy Matlack, *An Oration Delivered March 16, 1780 before . . . the American Philosophical Society . . . Philadelphia* (Philadelphia, 1780), p. 25; NYPL. In 1591, Joshua Sylvester in his translation of *Du Bartas*, I, ii. 1172, stated: "Above the Heavn's Star-spangled Canopy." Shakespeare's *The Taming of the Shrew*, IV, v, 31 (1596) reads: "What stars do spangle heaven with such beautie?" See, generally, *The Oxford English Dictionary* (Oxford, 1933), vol. X, p. 506, col. 1, and p. 840, col. 1.

The Stars and Stripes Forever!

m. John Philip Sousa. Copyrighted for piano May 14, 1897,[1] by The John Church Company, Cincinnati, New York and Chicago. First edition: Front cover has a drawing of "the stars and stripes," a photograph of the composer (without medals), lists 18 arrangements of which the piano arrangement is 50 (cents) and is black and white. m. on pp. 2–5. p.n. 121287-4. Back cover adv. *The Marvelously..*, and only five titles are listed in large type after "The March King" near the top of the back cover. Leipsic [*sic*] is not listed at the bottom of the front cover. LC(CDC).

The arrangement for instrumental parts was copyrighted June 5, 1897.[1] A number of variants, priority unknown, all with publisher's number 358 and plate number 12376-9, are at BBC, CBC, DTP, NCL, ULK and JF. The "Song" version was copyrighted in 1898, with words also by Sousa.

Sousa composed the march while on a ship from England to the United States in the fall of 1896 and "paced the deck with a mental brass band playing the march fully a hundred times during the week I was on the steamer."[2] Brief biographic information regarding Sousa appears above under *El Capitan*.

Steamboat Bill

m. Leighton Bros. w. Ren Shields. Published Nov. 17, 1910,[1] by F. A. Mills, Incorporated, 122 West 36th St., New York, N.Y. First edition: Front cover has a drawing of a steamboat and "Bill" and is red, pink, blue and black. p. [2] adv. *Valley.. - That..* m. on pp. 3–5. Back cover blank. LC(CDC).

---

[1] Copyright records; LC.
[2] From a letter by Sousa quoted in *American War Songs*, p. 151.

---

[1] Copyright records; LC.

Bert Leighton, one of the Leighton Brothers, was born in Beecher, Ill., in 1877, became a vaudeville performer, composer, lyricist and real estate dealer and died in San Francisco in 1964.[2] No biographic information is available about his brother. Brief biographic information regarding Shields appears above under *In the Good Old Summer Time*.

A Stein Song

For it's al-ways fair weath-er when good fel-lows get to-geth-er

m. Frederic Field Bullard. w. Richard Hovey. Copyrighted June 16, 1898,[1] by Oliver Ditson Company, Boston. First edition: Front cover has a red, black and white collective title: "Songs by Frederic Field Bullard"—9 titles listed; only one key is mentioned for this song; and agents are indicated in New York, Philadelphia and Chicago. pp. [2] and [3] blank. m. on pp. 2–5 (actually 4–7), engraved. p.n. 4-31-61037-4. pp. [8] and [9] blank. Back cover adv. *Selected.*. LC(CDC).

The song is frequently known as *It's Always Fair Weather When Good Fellows Get Together*. The poem had previously appeared in Bliss Carman and Richard Hovey, *More Songs from Vagabondia* (Boston, 1896),[2] p. 27; LC(CDC deposited Nov. 27, 1896). A later edition at LC states that the first edition was published in Oct., 1896. The song is not to be confused with the *Maine Stein Song*.

Bullard was born in Boston in 1864, became a music teacher and composer and died in Boston in 1904.[3] Richard Hovey was born in Normal, Ill., in 1864, became a poet and died in New York City in 1900.[4]

Stephanie-Gavotte

[2] *ASCAP*, p. 300. Obituary, *The New York Times*, Feb. 12, 1964.

[1] Copyright records; LC. The song is said to have been composed in Feb., 1898, and published the next month; Clark, p. 21.

[2] Blanck, vol. II, p. 53.

[3] Baker, p. 226.

[4] *Dict. Am. Biog.*, vol. 9, p. 273.

m. Alphons Czibulka. Published about Oct., 1880,[1] for piano by E. M. Wetzler, 36 Ferdinandstrasse, Prague. Possible first printing with a single title front cover: There is a dedication to Princess Stephanie of Belgium, the op. no. is 312, the prices are M. 1. 50 and fr. -.90 Ö.W., six arrangements are listed, and the publisher is also shown at Vienna. m. on pp. 2–7. p.n. 586. Back cover adv. *Verzeichniss..* BSM.

An edition with a collective title front cover is entitled "Alphons Czibulka's Salon-Compositionen für das Pianoforte," and lists eight titles, the last of which is *Stephanie-Gavotte* at 90 kr., 1 Mk. 50; no other arrangements of any composition are listed; there is no Vienna address and no dedication. The pages after the front cover are the same as those described in the preceding paragraph. ONB. Although this edition lists no arrangements, it seems unlikely that the first printing of a composition with the partial name of a royal dedicatee in its title would omit the full name of the royal dedicatee on the front cover.

Czibulka was born in Szepes-Varallya, Hungary, in 1842, became a pianist, bandmaster and composer, and died in Vienna in 1894.[2]

Stormy Weather

Don't know why___ there's no sun up in the sky, storm-y weath-er

m. Harold Arlen. w. Ted Koehler. Published April 13, 1933,[1] by Mills Music, Inc., 1619 Broadway, New York, N.Y. First edition: Front cover has a drawing of three profiles, mentions Ethel Waters, George Dewey Washington and Duke Ellington and is red, pink, white and black. s. *Cotton Club Parade-22nd Edition*—6 titles listed. p. [2] adv. *The Bells.. - Take..* m. on pp. 3–5. p. 4 adv. *Dizzy..* p. 5 adv. *Popular..* Center fold adv. *Learn..* Back cover adv. *The Most..*; the address of the publisher on the back cover is 148–150 West 46th St., New York, N.Y. LC (CDC) and JF (inscribed by the composer).

[1] Hofmeister *Monatsbericht*, Oct., 1880, p. 284.
[2] Thompson, p. 399.

[1] Copyright records; LC.

This song was originally written for Cab Calloway, but as he was not in this edition of the *Cotton Club Parade*, it was introduced by Ethel Waters.[2] George Gershwin pointed out that no musical phrase is repeated during the first eight bars.[2] Brief biographic information regarding Arlen appears above under *Over the Rainbow*. Koehler, a lyricist, was born in Washington, D.C., in 1894 and died in Santa Monica, Cal., in 1973.[3]

Strike Up the Band!

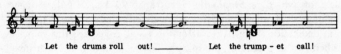

Let the drums roll out!_____ Let the trump-et call!

© 1927 New World Music Corp. Copyright renewed. Used by permission.

m. George Gershwin. w. Ira Gershwin. Published Sept. 14, 1927,[1] by New World Music Corporation, New York, N.Y. First edition: Front cover has a drawing of a girl hitting a drum and is red, white and blue. s. *Strike Up the Band*—5 titles listed. m. on pp. 2–5 (actually 3–6). p.n. 51-4. p. [2] adv. *Chérie..* p. [7] adv. *Just..* Back cover adv. *That.. - So..* The words "Edgar Selwyn" on the front cover are in red. LC(CDC) and JF.

The show tried out in Philadelphia in Sept., 1927, but did not reach New York City.[2] When the show was revived in 1929, reaching New York City this time, the front cover of the reissued sheet music was slightly changed; for example, the words "Edgar Selwyn" on the front cover are in blue. JF. The piano-vocal score of the revised show was published May 9, 1930,[1] with a red, white and blue front cover, at $5.00; LC(CDC) and JF.

Ira Gershwin wrote additional lyrics in 1936 for the University of California at Los Angeles, and the song under the name *Strike Up the Band for U.C.L.A.* is the official song of the University; JF. Brief biographic information regarding George and Ira Gershwin appears above under *I Got Rhythm*.

Summertime—Porgy and Bess

Sum-mer - time_____ an' the liv - in' is eas - y

© 1935 by Gershwin Publishing Corporation. Copyright renewed. By consent.

---

[2] Edward Jablonski, *Harold Arlen, Happy with the Blues* (New York, N.Y., 1961), pp. 61–67; NYPL.

[3] *ASCAP*, p. 281, and obituary, *The New York Times*, Jan. 22, 1973.

---

[1] Copyright records; LC.

[2] Gershwin, p. 224, and Green, p. 113.

m. George Gershwin. w. DuBose Heyward. Both the separate sheet music edition of this song, and the piano-vocal score of the opera, *Porgy and Bess*, in which the song was included, were published Sept. 28, 1935,[1] by Gershwin Publishing Corp., RKO Bldg., New York, N.Y. First edition of the separate sheet music: Front cover has a drawing of a plantation scene and is black and white; no price, key or other title is mentioned. p. [2] blank. m. on pp. 3–5. The copyright is in the name of the composer. p.n. **G-1-3.** Back cover adv. *Summertime - My..* LC(CDC) and JF. *Porgy and Bess* opened in Boston on Sept. 30, 1935, and in New York City on Oct. 10, 1935.

First edition of the piano-vocal score of *Porgy and Bess:* Front cover is black and gray and adds Rockefeller Center to the address of the publisher. vb. Next three pages blank. Photograph of the composer. Title page in black and white, without price. Drawing of a Negro and a mule. Index of Scenes. Cast. Story; in the 4th line of the first column, the word "Negro" is incorrectly printed with a lower-case "n" (upper-cased in pen and ink). Dedication to "My Parents." m. on pp. 1–559, *Summertime* on p. 15. No plate number. p. [560] and inside and outside of back cover blank. No index of songs. LC(CDC received Sept. 30, 1935) and JF.

The piano-vocal score of *Porgy and Bess*, which is signed by the composer and lyricist on p. [561], states that it is the "limited first edition" and has a colored title page, is not, however, the first edition as it states on p. [561] that it was "printed in October, 1935"; and the word "Negro" has the corrected upper-case "N" on the 4th line in the 1st column on the page headed "Story." NYPL and JF.†

Brief biographic information regarding George Gershwin appears above under *I Got Rhythm*. Heyward, a playwright, poet and lyricist, was born in Charleston, S.C., in 1885 and died in Tryon, N.C., in 1940.[2]

Sur le Pont d'Avignon

Sur le pont d'A - vi - gnon l'on y dan - se, l'on y dan - se

The first known appearance of this French children's round is in 1845–1846 in Du Mersan, *Chansons et Rondes Enfantines* (Paris, n.d.), the music and words being on p. [128], under the title *Le Pont d'Avignon*. While no date is printed in the book, the copyright deposit copy at BN was deposited in 1845, but is also marked 1846 and the binding says 1846. Copy also at UP.

[1] Copyright records; LC.
[2] *ASCAP*, p. 231.

The song was included in Adolphe Adam's *Le Sourd*, an opéra comique, performed in Paris on Feb. 2, 1853, and appeared in the piano-vocal score of the opera published in the same year by Boieldieu, Paris, at p. 58; BN, BM(CDC), and NYPL.

The bridge over the Rhone river, Pont St.-Bénézet, was originally completed in 1185 and part of the bridge is still standing, but is not used. According to the Michelin *Guide* for Provence (Paris, 1969), p. 63, the bridge was originally intended for pedestrians and cavaliers and was too narrow for the dancing of a round. It was under the bridge that people used to dance, and the song is said to have originated in a tavern on the island of Barthelesse, in the middle of the Rhone river, the tavern standing under one of the arches of the famous bridge.

The Swan—Saint-Saëns

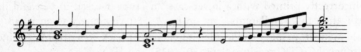

m. C. Saint-Saëns. *Le Cygne* for violoncello and piano was entered for Dépôt Légal on May 23, 1887,[1] by Durand & Schoenewerk, 4 Place de la Madeleine, Paris. First edition: Front cover is the same as the title page except in gray and black. vb. Title page is in black and white, states that *Le Cygne* is an extract from *Le Carnaval des Animaux* and the price is 5 f. vb. m. on pp. 1–3. p.n. 3767. p. [4] and inside of back cover blank. Outside of back cover adv. Accursi - Schumann. The separate violoncello part has the same p.n. BN(CDC).

Saint-Saëns composed *Le Carnaval des Animaux* for two pianos, two violins and seven other instruments in Feb., 1886, for a Mardi-Gras concert that year, organized by the violoncellist Lebouc, who played *Le Cygne* at the première. After this performance and several others, the composer forbade its further performance, a decree revoked only by his will. Thus, the orchestral score and parts of *Le Carnaval des Animaux* were not published until May 10, 1922,[2] i.e., after his death on Dec. 16, 1921. First edition of the score: Front cover is black and white. vb. Title page is the same as the front cover, refers to the composition as a Grande Fantaisie Zoologique, indicates the instrumentation, the publisher is A. Durand & Fils, Durand & Cie., at the address mentioned above, and lists five arrange-

---

[1] Archives. *BMF*, April–June, 1887, p. 29. The arrangement for piano is in the Oct.–Dec., 1887, issue, p. 51. The arrangement for violin has p.n. 3891; JF.

[2] Copyright records; LC.

ments, four with prices, the orchestral score at 30 fr. vb. Notice. vb. Index. vb. m. on pp. 1–61, *Le Cygne* at p. 45. p.n. 10,154. p. [62] blank. Back cover lacking. BN(CDC). Also at JF (with three blank leaves after both the front cover and before the blank inside and outside back cover).

The first edition of the parts of *Le Carnaval des Animaux* has the same front cover as indicated above, the price of the parts also being 30 fr. vb. p.n. 10,155, with inside and outside of back cover blank. BN(CDC).

Le Carnaval des Animaux also amusingly includes the melodies of the *Can Can* (for the "Tortoises") and *Sylphs' Ballet* (for the "Elephant"). The parody use of these copyrighted melodies may have created legal problems. And Saint-Saëns may not have wanted to encourage others to take liberties with *his* music. Either or both of these factors may possibly have contributed to the suspended performance and delayed publication of *Le Carnaval des Animaux*. Brief biographic information regarding Saint-Saëns appears above under *Danse Macabre*.

Swanee

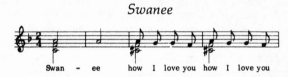

Swan - ee   how I love you how I love you

m. George Gershwin. w. I. Caesar. Published Oct. 31, 1919,[1] by T. B. Harms and Francis, Day & Hunter, New York, N.Y. First edition: Front cover has a drawing of a couple, says Staged by Ned Wayburn at the Capitol Theatre, N.Y., and is green, black and white. m. on pp. 2–5. p.n. 5935-4. Back cover adv. *Yearning*. Folio. LC(CDC) and JF.

Swanee was later successfully introduced by Al Jolson in the show *Sinbad*. Brief biographic information regarding Gershwin and Caesar appears above under *I Got Rhythm* and *Sometimes I'm Happy*.

Sweet Adeline

Sweet A - del - ine,_____ my A - del - ine,_____

m. Henry W. Armstrong. w. Richard H. Gerard. Copyrighted Nov. 18,

---

[1] Copyright records; LC.

1903,[1] by M. Witmark & Sons, New York, N.Y. Probable first edition: Front cover has an introductory title, *You're the Flower of My Heart*, a drawing of a girl in the country, states that it was Sung by Harry Ernest of the Quaker City Quartette, With the Al. G. Field Greater Minstrels, has a photograph of probably Harry Ernest, shows the publisher at three other addresses and lists three agents, and the price is 50¢ - 2/. p. [2] blank. m. on pp. 3–5. p.n. 6003-3. Back cover adv. *Down.. - You're..* JF (autographed by the composer). The above is the same as the edition deposited at LC on Jan. 28, 1904, except that the latter refers to Walter S. Brower as the plugger; however, it is well established that the song was introduced by the Quaker City Quartette.[2]

Armstrong had originally composed the melody in 1896, calling it *My Old New England Home*; Gerard's lyric was originally entitled *Sweet Rosalie*—but there was no publication under either title. The revised title was suggested by a billboard advertisement of the Italian opera singer, Adelina Patti. The composer and lyricist had been introduced to each other by James J. Walker, then a lyricist, and later Mayor of New York City. The success of this close-harmony barbershop quartet song has been attributed to its fine echo—the chorus repeating the solo part. Armstrong was born in Somerville, Mass., in 1879, became a composer and musician, and died in New York City in 1951.[2] Gerard was born in New York City in 1876. A composer, lyricist, postal clerk, he died in New York City in 1948.[3]

Sweet and Low

Sweet and low, sweet and low, wind of the west-ern sea____

m. J. Barnby. w. Alfred Tennyson. The poem was published in Tennyson's *The Princess* (3rd ed., London, 1850), p. 51, dedicated to Henry Lushington. BM. The poem is not in the first two editions of this work; BM.

A copy of the music and words was deposited at BM on Feb. 12, 1863, by Foster & King, 16 Hanover Street, Regent Stt. [*sic*], London. First edition: p. [1] has a dedication to Henry Leslie, states that *Sweet and Low* is a Four Part Song, the price is 1/6, the arrangement is for Treble, Mezzo

---

[1] Copyright records; LC. Also, according to these records, an edition had been deposited on Nov. 17, 1903, "without title pages."

[2] Obituary of the composer, *New York Herald Tribune*, March 1, 1951; Spaeth, p. 335; Geller, p. 228; and signed statement by the composer on the front cover of the copy described in the text above (illustrated in Fuld, *American*, p. [48]).

[3] *ASCAP*, p. 177.

Soprano, Tenor, Bass and Piano, but a note states that although the piano-forte part may be useful at practice, it must not be played during performance, and the p.n. is 632. m. on pp. [1]–3. p. [4] blank. BM(CDC).

Tennyson, a poet laureate, was born in 1809 in Somersby, Lincolnshire, and died in 1892 in Aldworth. Joseph Barnby was born in York in 1838, became an organist, composer and conductor, and died in London in 1896.[1]

Sweet Genevieve

O Gen-e-vieve, sweet Gen-e-vieve, the days may come, the days may go

m. Henry Tucker. w. George Cooper. Copyrighted May 26, 1869,[1] by Wm. A. Pond & Co., 547 & 865 Broadway, New York, N.Y. Probable first edition: Engraved. Front cover has a dedication to John C. Meacham, the price is 3, five agents are listed and there is a border design. p. [2] blank. m. on pp. 3–5. No plate number. Back cover blank. LC and JF.

Tucker, a composer, was born in 1826 in New York State and died in 1882 in Brooklyn, N.Y.[2] Cooper was born in 1838, became a songwriter and wrote lyrics for Stephen C. Foster and others, and died in New York City in 1927.[3]

Sweet Rosie O'Grady

Sweet Ro - sie O' - Gra - dy

mw. Maude Nugent. Copyrighted July 25, 1896,[1] by Jos. W. Stern & Co., 45 East 20th St., New York, N.Y. First edition: Front cover has a photograph of Annie Hart, and is brown and white. p. [2] blank. m. on pp. 3–5. p. 3 adv. *No.*. p. 4 adv. *Kathleen.* p. 5 adv. *My.*. p. [6] adv. *Parlor.*. p. [7]

[1] *Grove's*, vol. 1, p. 441.

[1] Copyright records; LC.

[2] W. G. Waller Goodworth, *Musicians of All Times* (London, 1907), p. 149; UCH.

[3] MCO, Oct. 6, 1927, p. 30.

[1] Copyright records; LC.

adv. *My.. - Kathleen.* Back cover adv. *Mother.. - You're..* LC(CDC).

Unable to have the song published or sung, Maude Nugent introduced it herself from the stage of Tony Pastor's, New York City. In 1946 she sued Twentieth Century-Fox Motion Picture Company for $12,500,000, alleging that it had unlawfully used the title of her song as the title of its movie; she lost her case.[2] Nugent was born in Brooklyn in 1877, became an actress and composer, married William Jerome, and died in New York City in 1958.[3]

Sweet Sue—Just You

Ev - 'ry   star   a - bove_____   knows the   one   I   love

m. Victor Young. w. Will J. Harris. Published April 10, 1928,[1] by Shapiro, Bernstein & Co. Inc., Cor. Broadway and 47th Street, New York, N.Y. Possible first edition: Front cover has drawings of sweet Sue against a background of tree leaves, and is blue, red and white. p. [2] adv. *Grand..* m. on pp. 3–5. Center fold adv. *Gem..* p. 4 adv. *Jake..* p. 5 adv. *Ferera..* Back cover adv. *Just.. - You..* All the songs advertised in this edition were published before April 10, 1928. No photograph of Sue Carol (who helped popularize the song) on the front cover, and no reference on p. 5 to a dance arrangement which was published April 24, 1928. JF.

Brief biographic information regarding Young appears above under *Around the World.* Harris, a lyricist, was born in New York City in 1900 and died in Chicago in 1967.[2]

The Sweetest Story Ever Told

Tell   me,   do   you   love   me?   Tell me soft - ly, sweet - ly, as   of   old!

[2] Emurian, *Songs,* p. 30.
[3] Obituary, *The New York Times,* June 4, 1958.

[1] Copyright records; LC.
[2] *ASCAP,* p. 219, and ASCAP files.

mw. R. M. Stults. Copyrighted Dec. 19, 1892,[1] by Oliver Ditson Company, 453–463 Washington Street, Boston. First edition: Front cover says that the song was written for and sung by Miss Myra Mirella, mentions two other songs by the author, gives a London address for the publisher and lists four agents. p. [2] blank. m. on pp. (3) [sic]–5. Back cover adv. I Wish.. - The Miller's.. There is no drawing of a man courting a lady on the front cover. LC(CDC).

The song is frequently known by the subtitle on later editions, Tell Me, Do You Love Me; the subtitle does not appear on the first edition described above. Stults, was born in Hightstown, N.J., in 1861, became a composer of many types of music and died in 1923.[2]

The Sweetheart of Sigma Chi

The girl of my dreams is the sweet - est girl of all the girls I know

m. F. Dudleigh Vernor. w. Byron D. Stokes. Published Feb. 19, 1912,[1] by Richard E. Vernor Publishing Company, Albion, Mich. First edition: Front cover has a drawing of a girl in a hat, and is light blue, gold and white. p. [2] blank. m. on pp. 3–5. Back cover blank. LC(CDC).

The Historical Society of the State of Michigan has placed a plaque on the Old South Hall at Albion College, Albion, Mich., which states that the two authors, then freshmen at the College, wrote the song in this Hall in the spring of 1911. The lyricist points out that the song was not intended to be about a girl. It was a love song to a fraternity, written for the 25th reunion of Albion College's Sigma Chi chapter.[2] Vernor was born in 1892 in Detroit, did not graduate from Albion College, became the organist at the Metropolitan Methodist Church in Detroit and died in that city in 1974.[3] Stokes was born in 1886 in Jackson, Mich., went into the advertising business in Pasadena, Cal., and died in 1974.[3]

[1] Copyright records; LC.
[2] ASCAP, p. 490.

[1] Copyright records; LC.
[2] Independent Star-News (Pasadena, Cal.), Feb. 13, 1966, p. 1; Pasadena Public Library, Pasadena, Cal.
[3] Information from the authors. ASCAP, p. 514. Obituary of F. Dudleigh Vernor, The New York Daily News, April 25, 1974.

Sweethearts

Sweet-hearts make   love   their   ver - y   own

m. Victor Herbert. w. Robert B. Smith. Published March 22, 1913,[1] by G. Schirmer, New York, N.Y. First edition: Front cover is blue, black and white, lists five titles, the Vocal Score and Entr'acte from the comic opera *Sweethearts*, and mentions Boston and London agents. m. on pp. 2–5. p.n. 24206 c. Back cover adv. *Serenade - In..* LC(CDC).

The comic opera *Sweethearts* opened in Baltimore on March 24, 1913. On April 2, 1913,[1] a piano-vocal score of the comic opera was published with a multicolored front cover at $2.00; LC(CDC). The opera opened in New York City on Sept. 8, 1913.

Sweethearts was the song involved in the test case which the United States Supreme Court decided in 1917 upholding the right of the owner of a copyrighted song to prevent its unauthorized public performance for profit.[2] Brief biographic information regarding Herbert appears above under *Ah! Sweet Mystery of Life.* Smith, a librettist and lyricist, was born in Chicago in 1875 and died in New York City in 1951.[3]

Swing Low, Sweet Chariot

Swing low,   sweet   char - i - ot,—   com - in' for to car - ry me   home

This Negro spiritual first appeared in print in *Jubilee Songs*, as sung by the Jubilee Singers, of Fisk University (Nashville, Tenn.), copyrighted March 11, 1872,[1] and published in New York, N.Y., at p. 6. There is no mention of "Complete" or "New Edition." LC(CDC), NYPL and JF.

[1] Copyright records; LC.
[2] Waters, *Herbert*, chap. 18. ASCAP was founded in 1914 with Herbert as Vice-President, and its subsequent importance is based directly on this decision.
[3] *ASCAP*, p. 468.

[1] Copyright records; LC.

'S Wonderful

'Swon - der - ful! _____   'Smar - vel - ous!

© 1927 New World Music Corp. Copyright renewed. Used by permission.

m. George Gershwin. w. Ira Gershwin. Published Oct. 26, 1927,[1] by New World Music Corporation, New York, N.Y. First edition: Front cover gives the name of the musical comedy as *Smarty*, mentions Fred and Adele Astaire and Robert Benchley among others, lists five titles, refers to Harms Inc. and is red, black and white. p. [2] blank. m. on pp. [2]–5 (actually 3–6). p.n. 56-4. p. [7] adv. *Rhapsody..* and *Concerto..* Back cover adv. *That.. - So..* LC(CDC) and JF.

The song is sometimes mistakenly sung "*It's* wonderful. *It's* marvelous."[2] The name of the musical comedy was subsequently changed to *Funny Face*, and under the new title it opened in New York City on Nov. 22, 1927. Brief biographic information regarding the Gershwins appears above under *I Got Rhythm*.

Sylphs' Ballet—The Damnation of Faust

m. Hector Berlioz. *La Damnation de Faust*, op. 24, in which the *Ballet des Sylphes* appears, was published about April 2, 1854,[1] for orchestral score, orchestral parts and piano-vocal score by S. Richault, Boulevart [*sic*] Poissonnière 26 au 1ᵉʳ, Paris. First edition of the orchestral score: Frontispiece of Faust being pushed down into Hell by devils with forks. Portrait dated Londres, 1851, in some copies. Title page gives the price of the orchestral score as 60 Fr., also lists the orchestral parts, choral parts and piano-vocal score (and no others) and mentions Cramer et Beale, London, and Fr. Hofmeister, Leipzig. vb. Cast and Index. vb. Vorwort and Avant-Propos, pp. 1–4. Text, pp. [5]–32. m. on pp. 1–410, the *Ballet* on p. 169. French and

---

[1] Copyright records; LC.
[2] Gershwin, p. 251.

[1] *FM*, April 2, 1854, p. 116, the orchestral score "à paraître." Entered for Dépôt Légal, Archives, on May 4, 1854 (orchestral score?). Hopkinson, *Berlioz*, p. 115. The music of the *Sylphs' Ballet* did not appear in Berlioz's earlier *Huit Scènes de Faust*, oeuvre 1 (1829); copies as indicated in Hopkinson, *Berlioz*, p. 13.

German text. p.n. 11,605 (with minor modifications). BN, COP, CH and JF*.

No first edition of the orchestral parts, with p.n. 11,606 and a price of 60 francs, has been found. A first printing of the piano-vocal score, with p.n. 11,605 [sic], is at BN and BM.

Saint-Saëns amusingly used the melody of the *Sylphs' Ballet* for the "Elephant" in his *Le Carnaval des Animaux*. *La Damnation de Faust* was performed in Paris Dec. 6, 1846. Berlioz was born in La Côte St. André, near Grenoble, in 1803 and died in Paris in 1869.

Sylvia

Syl-via's hair is   like the night, touched with glanc - ing   star - ry beams

Copyright 1914 by G. Schirmer, Inc. By permission.

m. Oley Speaks. w. Clinton Scollard. Published July 21, 1914,[1] by G. Schirmer, 3 East 43d Street, New York, N.Y. Possible first edition: Folio size. Front cover is entitled "Two Songs by Oley Speaks," lists *Eternity* (in two keys) and *Sylvia* (in three keys, this being Low in E flat), has the price of 50 cents, shows the publisher also at London and a Boston agent, and is purple, black and white. p. [2] blank. m. on pp. 3–5. p.n. 24974c. Back cover adv. Her.. (published June 18, 1914). JF.

The poem *Sylvia* is believed to have been first printed in the "Sunday Times, Nov. 24, 1912,"[2] a clipping of which is at HA. The newspaper and date are so indicated in pencil on the clipping, but the identity of the newspaper has not been ascertained. It is neither *The New York Times* nor *The Sunday Times* (London). Brief biographic information regarding Speaks appears above under *On the Road to Mandalay*. Scollard was born in Clinton, N.Y., in 1860, became a poet and professor of English literature and died in Kent, Conn., in 1932.[3]

[1] Copyright records; LC.
[2] Letter from HA.
[3] *Dict. Am. Biog.*, vol. 16, p. 485.

Symphonie Classique—Prokofiev

m. Sergei Prokofiev. The *Symphonie Classique* was published in 1925 for orchestral score by A. Gutheil, Moscow.[1] Probable first edition: Front cover in gray and black is in two columns, one in Russian and the other in French, states the opus number 25, mentions that the publisher is at four other cities, refers to Breitkopf & Härtel in two cities, gives a Paris address and contains a legal claim. Instrumentation. No title page. m. on pp. [1]–96. p.n. RMV 419. Folio. Inside and outside of back cover blank. BM* and JF (with metronome indications in the hand of Prokofiev).† No early printing of the orchestral parts has been found.

The piano arrangement by the composer was published by Édition Russe de Musique, Berlin and other cities, in 1931;[1] LC and JF. The *Symphony*, the composer's first, was completed in 1917 and was performed in Petrograd on March 21, 1918. Brief biographic information regarding Prokofiev appears above under *The Love of Three Oranges—March*.

Symphonie Fantastique—Berlioz

m. Hector Berlioz. *Episode de la Vie d'un Artiste, Grande Symphonie Fantastique* was published in a piano arrangement by Franz Liszt in 1834[1] by Maurice Schlesinger, 97 Rue Richelieu, Paris. First edition: Title page shows the opus number erroneously as 4me, and the price as 20 f, and has a stamped facsimile signature of Liszt. vb. Half title. vb. m. on pp. 1–22. Half title. vb. m. on pp. 23–37. vb. Half title. m. on pp. 38–53. vb. Half title. m. on pp. 54–63. vb. Half title. m. on pp. 64–89. vb. No plate number. Engraved. Folio. BN.

---

[1] Nestyev, p. 506. Prokofiev, *Autobiography*, p. 296. The piano arrangement states "XXXI" on page 26.

---

[1] Hopkinson, *Berlioz*, 36D, p. 76.

Cecil Hopkinson, London, believes that the Advance Edition of the orchestral score, with the erroneous performance date of Dec. 5, 1836, on the title page, was never actually published;[2] BN. The *Symphony* was performed on Dec. 5, 1830, in Paris.

Episode de la Vie d'un Artiste, Symphonie Fantastique was published soon after June 15, 1845,[3] for orchestral score and parts by Maurice Schlesinger, 97 Rue Richelieu, Paris. First edition of the orchestral score: Title page has a dedication to Emperor Nicolas Ier of Russia, the opus number is 14, the price of the orchestral score and parts is 40 f. each, the [engraver] is A. Lafont, and there is reference to a Berlin affiliate. vb. Program in French in two pages. m. on pp. 1–127. p.n. 4208. p. [128] blank. Engraved. Folio.

Nicholas Temperley, Urbana, Ill., notes that, in the first edition of the orchestral score, on page 1, 10th stave (1st violins), there are four notes under the first slur; and on page 67, there is no footnote commencing "Ou Tuba."[4] BRB, RCM and Richard Macnutt, Tunbridge Wells, Kent, England. These points are in addition to those noted in Hopkinson, *Berlioz*, 36B, p. 75. Berlioz's corrections of these and other errors appear in his hand in a copy at BN with a later title page.

In addition, the F notes in the third and fourth bars of the first announcement of the "idée fixe," quoted above, are not tied on page 8 of the first and early editions of the orchestral score; the tie is lacking for both the flute and the first violins.

The foregoing four paragraphs are confirmed by Nicholas Temperley in *Hector Berlioz, New Edition of the Complete Works* (Kassel, 1967–), vol. 16 (edited by Temperley), p. 172. The Advance Edition is there identified as P1 (late 1844 or early 1845), and the first edition as P2(i) (May 4, 1845).

A first edition of the orchestral parts, engraved and with plate number 4052, is at Société des Concerts du Conservatoire (Orchestre de Paris), and is identified in the above work, page 173, as PO1 (1844–1845).

Over one hundred years before LSD, Berlioz composed the first musical "trip"; it resulted from the taking of opium by the central figure in the *Symphony*. Brief biographic information regarding Berlioz appears above under *Sylphs' Ballet*.

---

[2] Hopkinson, *Berlioz*, 36A, p. 75.

[3] Hopkinson, *Berlioz*, 36B, p. 75. "Pour paraître incessament," in *RGM*, May 4, 1845, p. 144, without prices. Müller-Reuter, p. 200, states that the orchestral score appeared in Aug., 1845, and the orchestral parts in Oct., 1845.

[4] Letter from Nicholas Temperley to the author.

Symphony no. 1—Beethoven

m. Ludwig van Beethoven. Published under the title *Grande Simphonie* in orchestral parts in Dec., 1801,[1] by Hofmeister & Comp., Vienna. First edition: Engraved. The title page sets forth the instrumentation, has a dedication to Baron van Swieten, mentions that the Oeuvre is XXI, states the copublisher is au Bureau de Musique, Leipzig, and says No. 64. The plate number on the 17 orchestral parts is also 64. LC* and JF. The orchestral score was published in Jan.–Feb., 1809, by Cianchettini & Sperati, London.

The *Symphony* was performed in Vienna on April 2, 1800. Brief biographic information regarding Beethoven appears above under his *Concerto for Piano no. 5.*

Symphony no. 1—Brahms

m. Johannes Brahms. *Symphonie* (C moll), op. 68, was published about Oct. 31, 1877,[1] for orchestral score and parts by N. Simrock, Berlin. First edition of the orchestral score: Front cover is black and gray and has the price of 30 Mk. vb. Title page has no price, lists four agents, including Stanley Lucas, Weber & Co., London, and mentions the year 1877. **(See Plate IV.)** Statement regarding performance rights. m. on pp. 3–100, engraved. p.n. 7957. p. 26 reads "Poco sostenuto." Back cover missing. GM (lacks front cover) and JF.

No printing of the orchestral parts with engraved music pages has been found; early lithographed printings, with p.n. 7958, are at GM and CI. The arrangement for piano four hands, published the same month,[1]

[1] Kinsky-Halm, p. 52. Kinsky-Halm's description of the first edition, however, contains two errors: The opening words on the title page are "Grande Simphonie pour 2 Violons," not "Grande Simphonie pour Violons"; and "No. 64" appears in the lower left-hand corner of the title page of the first edition.

[1] On Oct. 31, 1877, Fritz Simrock wrote Brahms he was sending Brahms a specially bound orchestral score; *Brahms-Simrock*, p. 111. "November" per Deutsch, *Brahms*, p. 256. Hofmeister *Monatsbericht*, Nov., 1877, p. 318. Hofmann, *Brahms*, p. 147.

has p.n. 7959. The *Symphony* was completed in 1876 and performed Nov. 4, 1876, in Karlsruhe. Brief biographic information regarding Brahms appears above under his *Concerto for Piano no. 1.*

Symphony no. 1—Mahler

m. Gustav Mahler. The *Symphonie no. 1* in D dur was published in orchestral score about Feb., 1899,[1] by Josef Weinberger, 8 Kohlmarkt, Vienna. Probable first edition: Folio. Front cover is light and dark blue with a design border, lists the Partitur (orchestral score) at 30 Mk. and 18 Fl., and a piano arrangement without prices, has legal notices, mentions Leipzig and Paris agents and states that the printer is Jos. Eberle & Co., Vienna VII. vb. Title page is same as front cover, except in blue and white. vb. m. on pp. 3–171. No plate number. p. [172], and inside and outside of back cover, blank. BPL, HU, LC, NYPS (copy stamped "Gustav Mahler, Wien") and JF. Interestingly, each of the above copies has a clearly visible erasure on both the front cover and the title page directly below "Partitur"—it is not known what was erased. The arrangement for piano four hands was published at about the same time.[2] A set of the orchestral parts, of uncertain date, without covers or indication of publisher, with plate number 7, is at NYPS.

The *Symphony* was completed in 1888 and performed on Nov. 20, 1889, in Budapest. Mahler was born in 1860 in Kalischt, Bohemia, and died in 1911 in Vienna.

Symphony no. 2—Brahms

m. Johannes Brahms. The *Zweite Symphonie* (D dur) was published on

1 Hofmeister *Monatsbericht*, Feb., 1899, p. 43.
2 *Id.*, Jan., 1899, p. 12.

Nov. 1, 1878,[1] for orchestral score, and about the same time for orchestral parts, by N. Simrock, Berlin. First edition of orchestral score: Front cover is tan and black. vb. Title page mentions the opus number 73, has no price, sets forth legal claims, lists agents in eight cities, mentions the year 1878 and states that the lithographer was C. G. Röder, Leipzig. Verso contains further legal claims and plate numbers 7957, 8019 and 8028. m. on pp. 3–71. p.n. 8028. p. [72] blank. Engraved throughout. Folio. BM, HU, LC and JF.

No copy of the first edition of the orchestral parts, which are also engraved, with plate number 8029 has been found; an early edition is at CI.

Brahms jokingly suggested that the published score should have a black border because of the dirgelike quality of the *Symphony*.[2] The *Symphony* was composed in the summer of 1877 and performed on Dec. 30, 1877, in Vienna. Brief biographic information regarding Brahms appears above under his *Concerto for Piano no. 1*.

Symphony no. 2—Sibelius

m. Jean Sibelius. *Symphonie no. 2*, D dur, was published probably in late Sept., 1903,[1] for orchestral score and parts by Breitkopf & Härtel, Leipzig. The following first edition of the orchestral score was deposited at LC on Oct. 8, 1903: Front cover refers to the publisher's Partitur-Bibliothek and is dark and light blue. vb. Title page has a dedication to Axel Carpelan, lists the orchestral score at M. 20 and 24 orchestral parts at 90 Pf. each, shows the publisher also at Brussels, London and New York, mentions as a copublisher NYA Musikhandel (Fazer & Westerlund), Helsinki, claims a 1903 copyright and says Part. B. 1784. Orch. B. 1610/12. No opus number. vb. m. on pp. 3–145. p.n. Part. B. 1784. p. 3 says: Revised by Fr. W. Höhne; Jean Sibelius 1902; and printed in Leipzig. pp. [146] and [147] blank. Back cover adv. *Björneborgarnes.. - (Carelia..) Stämmor*. LC(CDC). The number of orchestral parts listed was later changed to 25; UL.

---

[1] According to the entry at Stationers' Hall on Jan. 20, 1879. Deutsch, *Brahms*, p. 257, says Aug., 1878. Hofmeister *Monatsbericht*, Dec., 1878, p. [374], stating that the price of the orchestral score was 30 Mk. and of the orchestral parts 36 Mk. Hofmann, *Brahms*, p. 157.

[2] Letter to Elisabeth von Herzogenberg, Dec. 29, 1877; *Johannes Brahms im Briefwechsel mit Heinrich und Elisabet von Herzogenberg* (Berlin, 1912), p. 12. NYPL.

[1] A copy was deposited at LC on Oct. 8, 1903. Hofmeister *Monatsbericht*, Oct., 1903, p. 513.

Possible first printings of the orchestral parts, with number Orch. B. 1610/12, are at CI and FLP. The *Symphony* was performed March 8, 1902, in Helsinki. Brief biographic information regarding Sibelius appears above under *Finlandia*.

Symphony no. 3—Beethoven

m. Ludwig van Beethoven. *Sinfonia Eroica*, op. 55, no III delle Sinfonie, was published for 18 orchestral parts about Oct. 19, 1806,[1] by Contor delle arti e d'Industria, 582 Hohenmarkt, Vienna. First edition: Front cover of the Violin I part, in Italian, sets forth the instruments, states it was composed to celebrate the memory of a great Man, has a dedication to the Prince of Lobkowitz, p.n. 512, and price of f. (blank). Verso has a note in Italian. m. on pp. 2–17; measures 151 and 152 (measures 6 and 5 before the end of the exposition) in the first movement are repeated. p.n. 512. Engraved. GM.

The orchestral score of the *Symphony* was published March–April, 1809, by Cianchettini & Sperati, London; BMI*. The work was composed in 1803, privately performed at the Viennese palace of the dedicatee in Dec., 1804, and publicly performed in Vienna on April 7, 1805. The story of Beethoven's dedicating the *Symphony* to Bonaparte, and then striking out the dedication in a rage at the news of Bonaparte's accepting the title "Emperor of the French" is well known. Brief biographic information regarding Beethoven appears above under *Concerto for Piano no. 5*.

Symphony no. 3—Brahms

m. Johannes Brahms. The *Dritte Symphonie* (F dur) was published in May, 1884,[1] for orchestral score and parts by N. Simrock, Berlin. First

---

[1] Stated to have been advertised that day in *Weiner Zeitung*, Kinsky-Halm, p. 128; and Anderson, *Beethoven*, p. 116. Hofmann, *Brahms*, p. 191.

[1]Hofmann, *Brahms*, p. 191. Deutsch, *Brahms*, p. 259. Hofmeister *Monatsbericht*, June, 1884, p. 146. On Nov. 8, 1883, Brahms ordered string parts to be engraved at his expense; no copies are known. The arrangement for two pianos was published in April, 1884; BM(CDC).

edition of orchestral score: Title page mentions the opus number 90, has no price, sets forth legal claims, mentions the year 1884 and states that the lithographer was C. G. Röder, Leipzig. vb. Foreword by N. Simrock. vb. m. on pp. 5–109. p.n. 8454. p. [110] blank. Engraved throughout. Folio. BM (Hirsch M. 803 [3]) and GM, "Aus dem Nachlass von Johannes Brahms." Rare.

No copy of the first edition of the orchestral parts, which are also engraved, with plate number 8455, has been found; an early edition is at CI. The *Symphony* was composed in 1882–1883 and performed on Dec. 2, 1883, in Vienna. Brief biographic information regarding Brahms appears above under his *Concerto for Piano no. 1.*

Symphony no. 4—Brahms

m. Johannes Brahms. *Vierte Symphonie* (E moll), op. 98, was published in Oct., 1886.[1] for orchestral score and parts by N. Simrock, Berlin. First edition of the orchestral score: Front cover is lithographed and has the price of 30 Mk. vb. Title page has no price and mentions the year 1886. Statement regarding performance rights, engraved. m. on pp. 4–113, engraved. p.n. 8686. GM, "Aus dem Nachlass von Johannes Brahms," and JF.

No printing of the orchestral parts with engraved music pages has been found; early lithographed printings, with p.n. 8618, are at GM and CI. The arrangement for two pianos, four hands, with p.ns. 8667 and 8668, had been published May 20, 1886;[2] BR* and HU. The *Symphony* was composed in 1884–1885 and performed Oct. 25, 1885, in Meiningen. Brief biographic information regarding Brahms appears above under his *Concerto for Piano no. 1.*

Symphony no. 4 (Italian)—Mendelssohn

m. Felix Mendelssohn Bartholdy. *Symphonie no. 4* was published in March,

---

[1] Deutsch, *Brahms*, p. 261. Hofmeister *Monatsbericht*, Nov., 1886, p. 404. Hofmann, *Brahms*, p. 209.

[2] According to the entry at Stationers' Hall on July 8, 1886.

1851,[1] for orchestral score and parts by Breitkopf & Härtel, Leipzig. Probable first edition of orchestral score: Title page mentions the opus number 90 and no. 19 of posthumous works, makes a legal claim, refers to a London agent, gives the price as 4 Thlr. 15 Ngr. and mentions the plate number 8347. vb. m. on pp. 1–193. p. [194] blank. Engraved throughout. Large octavo. BM (copyright copy deposited Feb. 9, 1852, with covers), NYPS, ONB and JF.

Probable first edition of orchestral parts: Title page is the same as that of the orchestral score except that the price is 5 Thlr. and the plate number is 8336. Engraved throughout. GM, LC*, NYPS and JF. The *Symphony* was completed March 13, 1833, in Berlin and performed on May 13, 1833, in that city. Brief biographic information regarding Mendelssohn appears above under his *Concerto for Violin*.

Symphony no. 4—Tchaikovsky

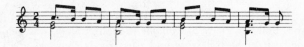

m. P. Tchaikovsky. The *Quatrième Symphonie*, op. 36, was published in 1878[1] for orchestral score by P. Jurgenson, Moscow. Possible first edition: Front cover in French gives the title as *Symphonie no. 4*, is yellow and black, states Edition Jurgenson, mentions J. Jurgenson, St. Petersburg, and G. Sennewald, Warsaw, and gives the price of the orchestral score at 9 Rb., and that of the arrangement for piano four hands at 5 Rb. vb. Title page in French, states Edition P. Jurgenson, has a dedication "A mon meilleur ami" [N. F. von Meck], and otherwise has the same information as the front cover. vb. m. on pp. 3–225. p.n. 3376. p. [226] blank. Inside of back cover is blank. Outside of back cover adv. works of various composers, including Tchaikovsky up to *Jeanne d'Arc* (1879). BN, BPL*, GL*, BM*, COP* and JF*.

A possible first edition of the orchestral parts is at NYPS and JF*; it is the same as the orchestral score described above except that F. Mackar has been added as the Paris agent, the price is 15 Rb., two French prices have been added, and the plate number is 3377. The arrangement for piano four hands has p.n. 3378[2] and a price of 5 Rb. The D. Rahter, Leipzig, edition of the orchestral score, printed by Jurgenson, Moscow, and with

---

[1] Müller-Reuter, p. 72. Hofmeister *Monatsbericht*, April, 1851, p. [58].

[1] Dombayev, p. 40.
[2] Jurgenson *Catalog*, Moscow, 1889, p. 193; NYPL.

Jurgenson's p.n. 3376, was published about March, 1880;[3] MH. The *Symphony* was completed Jan. 7, 1878 (N.S.), and performed Feb. 22, 1878 (N.S.), in Moscow. Brief biographic information regarding Tchaikovsky appears above under *Chant sans Paroles.*

Symphony no. 5—Beethoven

m. Ludwig van Beethoven. The *Sinfonie,* "No. 5 des Sinfonies," oeuv. 67, was published in April, 1809,[1] for 21 orchestral parts by Breitkopf & Härtel, Leipzig. First edition: Front cover of the Violino Imo part states the instrumentation, has a dedication to the Prince of Lobkowitz, Duke of Raudnitz, and the Count of Rasumoffsky, and gives the price as 4 Rthlr. 12 gr. Engraved. p.n. 1329. The first 100 copies printed have the opening bars:[2]

(See Plate IV.) BM (only known copy; looked for, because of the manuscript, and found by Kinsky in Hirsch's collection). The opening bars were soon changed at Beethoven's directions as set forth at the very beginning of this discussion; JF.

The orchestral score was published in March, 1826, by the same concern with p.n. 4302; GM and BM. The *Symphony* was composed 1804–1808 and performed on Dec. 22, 1808, in Vienna. Brief biographic information regarding Beethoven appears above under his *Concerto for Piano no. 5.*

[3] Hofmeister *Monatsbericht,* March, 1880, p. 111.

[1] Kinsky-Halm, p. 157. Anderson, *Beethoven,* p. 188; Beethoven's receipt for payment for the *Symphony,* dated Sept. 14, 1808, is at p. 1427. *AMZ Int-Bl,* April, 1809, col. [30].

[2] Paul Hirsch, "A Discrepancy in Beethoven," in *Music and Letters,* London, July, 1938, p. 265; *ULS,* p. 1839. Two letters by Beethoven mention changes in the orchestral parts: letter 204, dated March 28, [1809], and letter 228, dated Nov. 2, 1809. (Anderson, *op. cit.,* pp. 220 and 246.) Emily Anderson was not certain which of these two letters refers to the change mentioned above.

Symphony no. 5—Dvořák

m. Anton Dvořák. The *Aus der Neuen Welt "Z Nového Světa" Symphonie*
(no. 5, E moll), op. 95, was published at the beginning of 1894[1] for orchestral score and parts by N. Simrock,[2] Berlin. Probable first edition of the
orchestral score: Hard front cover in gray and black gives the price of the
orchestral score at MK 30, of the parts at MK 36 and of certain individual
parts at MK 3, and has an 1894 copyright date. Title page has no price
information and does not refer to the other arrangements, but has the 1894
copyright date. vb. Statement in German and English regarding performance rights. m. on pp. 4–79. p. [80] blank. p.n. 10139. GM, "Aus dem
Nachlass von Johannes Brahms,"[3] and JF. The *Symphony* is frequently
known now as no. 9.

Possible first printings of the orchestral parts, with p.n. 10140, are at
CI, FLP, PBA, UI and the publisher. The *Symphony* "From the New
World" was composed Jan. 10–May 24, 1893, in New York City and per-
formed in Carnegie Hall, New York City, on Dec. 15, 1893. The above
Largo is also known as *Goin' Home*, the words of which by William Arms
Fisher were published in 1922. Brief biographic information regarding
Dvořák appears above under *Humoreske*.

Symphony no. 5—Shostakovitch

m. D. Shostakovitch. The *Cinquième Symphonie*, op. 47, was published
for orchestral score between Jan. 24, 1939, and March 19, 1939,[1] by
Editions de Musique de L'URSS, Moscow and Leningrad. First edition:

---

[1] Šourek, Series III, vol. 3, p. [xi]. Hofmeister *Monatsbericht*, Sept., 1894, p. 362.
[2] G.m.b.H. was added to the publisher's name after the death of Fritz Simrock in
1901.
[3] Brahms probably corrected the proofs; Šourek, *op. cit.*, Editors' Notes (no page
number).

---

[1] Jan. 24, 1939, is the latest date mentioned on p. [166] as part of the Soviet
publishing procedure. The composer inscribed LPL's copy of the published work on
March 19, 1939. *AML*, April–June 1939, p. 28. E. Sadovnikov, *D. D. Shostakovitch*
(Moscow, 1965), p. 61; BM, LC and JF.

Hard front cover is in gray and gold. Title page is in Russian and French and mentions the year 1939. Orchestra composition and Index. m. on pp. 3–165. p.n. 16313. Page [166] has information regarding Soviet publishing procedure, the latest date being Jan. 24, 1939. The outside of the back cover has the price of 20 rubles. LPL (inscribed by the composer, March 19, 1939), LUC and JF. Orchestral parts of the *Symphony* with plate number 30680, without covers, are in the Hire Library of Boosey & Hawkes Music Publishers Ltd., London.

The *Symphony* was composed from April 18–Sept. 20, 1937, and performed Nov. 27, 1937, in Leningrad. Dmitri Shostakovitch was born in St. Petersburg in 1906 and died in Moscow in 1975.

Symphony no. 5—Tchaikovsky

m. P. Tchaikovsky. *Symphonie no. 5*, op. 64, was published for orchestral score and parts in late 1888[1] by P. Jurgenson, Moscow. Possible first edition of the orchestral score: Title page is in French, states Edition Jurgenson no. 13991, has a dedication to Monsieur Theodore Ave-Lallement, Hamburg, mentions F. Mackar, Paris, D. Rahter, Hamburg, J. Jurgenson, St. Petersburg, and G. Sennewald, Warsaw, and lists the orchestral score at 8 Rb. 32 frs., the orchestral parts at 17 Rb. 68 fr., and the arrangement for piano four hands without price; the colors are black and white within a green frame. vb. m. on pp. 3–211. p.n. 13991. p. [212] blank. GL, BM (copy purchased Oct. 20, 1896) and COP. No copy has been found with covers.

A possible first printing of the orchestral parts with p.n. 13992,[2] is at TM. The D. Rahter, Hamburg, editions of the orchestral score and parts were published about July, 1889;[3] the orchestral score was printed by Jurgenson, Moscow, and has Jurgenson's p.n.—HMA, HU, LML and NYPL. The *Symphony* was completed Aug. 26, 1888, and performed Nov. 17, 1888, in St. Petersburg. Brief biographic information regarding Tchaikovsky appears above under *Chant sans Paroles*.

[1] Dombayev, p. 42.

[2] Jurgenson *Catalogue*, Moscow, 1889, p. 196; NYPL.

[3] Hofmeister *Monatsbericht*, July, 1889, p. 259.

Symphony no. 6—Beethoven

m. Ludwig van Beethoven. The *Sinfonie Pastorale* was published in orchestral parts in May, 1809,[1] by Breitkopf & Härtel, Leipzig. First edition: The title page gives the instrumentation, has a dedication to the Duc de Raudnitz and the Comte de Rasumoffsky, makes a legal claim, states that this is Symphony no. 6, mentions the price is 4 Rth. 12 gr. and states that the Oeuv. is 68. Twenty orchestral parts. p.n. 1337. Engraved. GM, ONB and JF.

The orchestral score was published in May, 1826, by the same concern; ONB. The *Symphony* was completed in June, 1808, in Vienna and performed on Dec. 22, 1808, in Vienna. Brief biographic information regarding Beethoven appears above under *Concerto for Piano no. 5.*

Symphony no. 6—Tchaikovsky

m. P. Tchaikovsky. *Symphonie no. 6 (Pathétique)*, op. 74, was published about March, 1894,[1] by P. Jurgenson, Moscow, for orchestral score, orchestral parts and piano four hands. Possible first edition of the orchestral score: Front cover in Russian is green and gray, has the title *6-ая Симфонія*, says no. 19097, has the dedication mentioned below, does not state "Pathétique," lists the orchestral score at 9 p. (rubles), the parts at 20 p. and the arrangement for piano four hands at 5 p. vb. Title page in French has a dedication to Mr. W. Davidow, mentions "(Pathétique)," refers to J. Jurgenson, St. Petersburg, G. Sennewald, Warsaw, Mackar & Noël, Paris, and R. Forberg, Leipzig, and mentions the arrangements and prices as on the front cover. vb. m. on pp. 3–227. p.n. 19097 4665. p. [228] and inside of back cover blank. Outside of back cover adv. a Catalogue of

[1] Kinsky-Halm, p. 161. *AMZ*, April 12, 1809, p. 435.

[1] The Jurgenson edition was presumably published at about the same time as the Forberg edition mentioned later in the text. Dombayev, p. 42.

Jurgenson's works, none of which is known to be later than this *Symphony*. Short title on spine. BN and GL*.

A possible first edition of the orchestral parts, the front cover of which is the same as the title page of the orchestral score described above, with p.n. 19098, is at JF* (only known copy). The composer's arrangement for piano four hands has p.n. 19099. The Rob. Forberg, Leipzig, editions of the orchestral score (at HMA, HU and NEC) and parts were published about March, 1894.[2] The *Symphony* was completed Aug. 31, 1893, and performed Oct. 28, 1893, in St. Petersburg, nine days before the composer's death. Brief biographic information regarding Tchaikovsky appears above under *Chant sans Paroles*.

Symphony no. 7—Beethoven

m. Ludwig van Beethoven. The *Siebente Grosse Sinfonie* in A dur was published in orchestral score and parts in Nov., 1816,[1] by S. A. Steiner und Comp., Vienna. Orchestral score: Half title page; vb. Title page states that this is the 92nd work, has the plate number 2560, makes a legal claim, the price is blank and mentions agents in 14 cities and also in k.k. oester. Provinzen. vb. Dedication to Moritz Reichsgrafen von Fries. Three blank pages. m. on pp. 2–224. Title page and dedication page engraved; music pages lithographed. Quarto.

"Distasteful ... disastrous ... such a defective imperfect version of a work composed by me has never appeared. ..." So Beethoven characterized, in Nov., 1816, the first edition of this work in a letter to the publisher.[2] A copy of such an edition of the orchestral score is probably at JF (lacking the title page and dedication page, but a regular printing, not a proof). There are at least 25 errors on the first music page, page 2; for example, in the opening A major chord, oboes are to play a D, rather than a C sharp! There are at least nine errors on page 3 (for example, there is no "dim:" marking for the Viole in the 4th bar and there is no "dol:"

[2] Hofmeister *Monatsbericht*, March, 1894, p. 99.

[1] Kinsky-Halm, p. 256. *AMZ*, Nov. 27, 1816, p. 817.

[2] Anderson, *Beethoven*, letter no. 675, p. 615. See Alan Tyson, "Beethoven in Steiner's Shop" in *Music Review*, London, May, 1962, p. [119]; BM, LC and NYPL. Dr. Alan Tyson, London, has been helpful in connection with this title.

marking for the Fagotti in the 6th bar). There are many other errors on succeeding pages. In a later printing, the oboe and some other errors on pages 2 and 3 have been corrected but, for example, the Viole error on page 3 continues; copies at BM, BSM and AVH. In a still later printing, the Viole error on page 3 has also been corrected; copies at NYPL and JF. The Diabelli proof, referred to in Kinsky-Halm, p. 259, now at DS, is the second mentioned printing with further corrections indicated.

A similar situation exists with respect to the orchestral parts. In general, the title page gives the orchestration, has the plate number 2561 and is otherwise the same as the title page of the orchestral score. vb. Dedication. vb. Advertisement. Seventeen orchestral parts. Engraved throughout. Folio. BM, LC and ONB*. However, in a possible first edition, for example, in the Violoncelli primi part, page 5, 11th stave on page, last bar (bar 32 of the second or slow movement), there is no sharp sign before the first note of the bar, whereas in a later printing, the sharp sign has been inserted. Both printings at BM. The *Symphony* was composed in 1811–1812 and performed on Dec. 8, 1813, in Vienna. Brief biographic information regarding Beethoven appears above under *Concerto for Piano no. 5.*

Symphony no. 7—Bruckner

m. Anton Bruckner. The *Siebente Symphonie* (E dur) was published in orchestral score and parts about Dec., 1885,[1] by Albert J. Gutmann, Vienna. Possible first edition of orchestral score. Title page states Verlag Gutmann, gives the price of the orchestral score as 30 Mk. and 18 Fl., lists the orchestral parts and piano four hands, makes legal claims, lists agents in Leipzig, New York, Christiania and London, has an 1885 copyright claim and states that the lithographer is Engelmann & Mühlberg, Leipzig. vb. Dedication to King Ludwig II of Bavaria. vb. m. on pp. 3–97. On p. 45, at bar 177 of the second movement, at "W," there is a direction to the Cymbal to "ausklingen lassen," or die away.[2] p.n. 576. p. [98] blank. Folio. Lithographed. BM, BPL (including blue and black front cover), LC (including yellow and black covers) and JF. A variant, possibly later, is the same

---

[1] Hofmeister *Monatsbericht*, Dec., 1885, p. [350]. The arrangement for piano four hands is listed the same month, p. 358.

[2] Bruckner's original version of the *Symphony* did not have this direction; the original version was published in 1944; NYPL.

as the above except that the verso of the dedication page has a legal claim in three languages dated 1885; ONB.

A possible first edition of the orchestral parts, but without covers, with plate number 578 is at NYPS. The *Symphony* was completed on Sept. 5, 1883, and performed in Leipzig on Dec. 30, 1884. Bruckner was born in Ansfelden, Austria, in 1824 and died in Vienna in 1896.

Symphony no. 9—Beethoven

Freu-de schö-ner   Göt-ter-fun-ken,   Toch-ter aus E - ly - si-um

m. Ludwig van Beethoven. The *Sinfonie* mit Schluss-Chor über Schillers Ode "An die Freude," 125tes Werk, was published the end of Aug., 1826,[1] for orchestral score and parts by B. Schotts Söhne, Mainz and Paris. First edition of the orchestral score: Front cover, in French, is gray and black and states Sinfonie en Ré mineur, Oeuvre 125, Partition. vb. Title page, in German, mentions that the *Symphony* is for large orchestra, four solo and four choral parts, dedicated to the King of Prussia, Friedrich Wilhelm III with his coat of arms, and mentions A. Schott, Antwerp. vb. Subscribers' list on two pages. m. on pp. 1–226, engraved. The word "frech" appears instead of "streng" in the first bar of p. 207. p.n. 2322. pp. [227], [228], and the inside and outside of the back cover blank. GM and JF. No price and no metronome marks.

In the first edition of the 26 orchestral and four solo parts, the single leaf title is the same as the title page of the orchestral score; vb. Front cover of the first violin part, in French, recites the composition of the orchestra and gives a street address of the Paris branch. Some of the parts also have brief titles. Engraved. p.n. 2321. GM.† The *Symphony* was composed between 1822–1824 and performed May 7, 1824, in Vienna; at this performance, it is said that, because of his deafness, Beethoven had to be turned around to see the applause. Brief biographic information regarding Beethoven appears above under *Concerto for Piano no. 5*.

Schiller's *An die Freude* was first published in 1787[2] in his periodical *Thalia* (Leipzig), vol. I, part 2, p. [1]; *ULS*, p. 2762. However, as Dr. Halm wrote the author, the *Thalia* version of the poem contains variants which show that Beethoven used another print of the poem. Johann Christoph Friedrich von Schiller was born at Marbach, Württemberg, in 1759 and died in Weimar in 1805.

---

[1] Kinsky-Halm, p. 371.

[2] Karl Goedeke, *Grundriss zur Geschichte der Deutschen Dichtung* (Dresden, 1893), vol. 5, p. 175; NYPL and YU.

Symphony no. 40 (K 550)—Mozart

m. W. A. Mozart. The *Sinfonie* à grand orchestre, oeuvre 45me (K 550), was published in 1794[1] for 11 orchestral parts by J. André, Offenbach sur le Mein. First edition: Front cover has no. 685 and the price of f. 2.24 Xr. Engraved. There are no clarinet parts. RCM and JF*.

The orchestral score was published about 1808–1810 by Cianchettini & Sperati, London; BMI. The *Symphony* was completed in Vienna July 25, 1788. Brief biographic information regarding Mozart appears above under *Eine Kleine Nachtmusik*.

Symphony no. 94 (Surprise)—Haydn

m. Joseph Haydn. Orchestral parts of this *Symphony* were printed by a number of publishers at about the same time—after its first performance at Mr. Salomon's Concert at London on March 23, 1792—and priority and authenticity are difficult to establish.[1] Hoboken considers the first edition to have been published by J. André, Offenbach s/M, under the title *Sinfonie* à Grand Orchestre, Oeuvre 80me, with p.n. 857 and price F. 2, 24 Kr.; no mention of "Livre" or "911." AVH and JF*. However, this edition, published not later than the fall of 1795, is considered by Robbins Landon as a secondary print. Also considered by Robbins Landon as of doubtful authenticity is an edition of orchestral parts published by Artaria et Comp., Vienna, about June 13, 1795,[2] under the title *Grand Simphonie* à plusieurs instruments, no. [21], with p.n. 544; SA.

Authentic editions of various arrangements were printed in England in connection with Mr. Salomon's Concert. One such edition, published 1795–1796, and to be had of [Mr. Salomon] at the Hanover Square Rooms, London, is entitled no. [1, 2, 3] of *Haydn's Grand Symphonies* Composed for Mr. Salomon's Concerts, and is for two violins, a German flute, a tenor,

---

[1] Köchel, p. 622.

[1] See, generally, Robbins Landon, p. 748, and *Supplement*, p. 58, and Hoboken, p. 183.

[2] Announced in *Wiener Zeitung* of that date; ONB.

a violoncello and piano, with a front cover for three symphonies, nos. 1, 2 and 3 (of which this is no. 3); *BUC*, p. 459 (GU*, MIT, RAM and SM). Another, referring to Mr. Salomon's Concert, published by Corri, Dussek & Co., [London] and Edinburgh (watermarked 1795 or 1796), is for violin, violoncello and piano; Hoboken, vol. II, pp. 185 and 197.

Robbins Landon believes the most important edition to have been published in orchestral parts by Salomon privately about 1797 and then by Monzani & Cimador, London, ca. 1800–1805, for a larger orchestra, but no copy of either printing has been found.[3] There were a number of other editions and arrangements issued at about the same time by various publishers in several countries.[1]

The orchestral score of the *Symphony* was published in Dec., 1808, by Breitkopf & Härtel, Leipzig, under the title *Sinfonie de Joseph Haydn*, *Partition*, no. 6; ONB. The *Symphony* was composed in London in 1791. Brief biographic information regarding Haydn appears above under *Emperor's Hymn*.

Symphony no. 101 (Clock)—Haydn

m. Joseph Haydn. A number of publishers printed orchestral parts of this *Symphony* at about the same time—after its first performance at Mr. Salomon's Concert at London on March 3, 1794—and priority and authenticity are difficult to establish.[1] Robbins Landon believes that an authentic print of the orchestral parts was first published privately about 1797–1799 by Salomon. In this possible first edition, the title is no. [11] of *Haydn's Grand Symphonies* Composed for Mr. Salomon's Concerts for a Full Band, the price is [7.6], and the imprint is London, Printed for the Proprietor, Mr. Salomon, and to be had at Monzani and Cimador's Music Shop, no. 2 Pallmall. (See Plate V.) p.n. 1369. AVH. Robbins Landon believes that this edition was turned over to Monzani & Cimador about

---

[3] The plates for the private edition may have been made by J. André, Offenbach s/M; see *Symphony no. 101 (Clock)*, below. RM. 26. a. 12(7), at BM, may be an incomplete copy but it lacks a title page.

---

[1] See, generally, Robbins Landon, p. 771, and *Supplement*, p. 54; and Hoboken, p. 210.

The only entry at Stationers' Hall that could be found for any of Haydn's symphonies printed for Mr. Salomon was on Oct. 2, 1797, when the arrangement for piano, violin and violoncello, nos. 7–12, was entered.

1800–1805.[2]

The plates used for the preceding Salomon edition were the same as those used by J. André, Offenbach s/M, in 1799, entitled *Grande Sinfonie*, Oeuvre 95, Livre 2, with p.n. 1369 and price f. 3. AVH, ONB and JF. Hoboken considers this André printing the first edition. This author is unable to establish priority. Robbins Landon considers another possibly authentic print of the orchestral parts to have been published by Artaria et Comp., Vienna, in 1799, probably in the autumn, under the title *Grand Simphonie à plusieurs instruments*, no. [27], with p.n. 839; HWM*.

The *Symphony* was published for piano, violin and violoncello about 1796–1797 with the imprint, Printed for Mr. Salomon and to be had of him at the Hanover Square Rooms, London. There are two variants of this edition, priority unknown, both entitled *Haydn's Celebrated Symphonies;* in one, at KC* and NYPL*, there is an individual front cover for no. [11], this *Symphony*. In the other variant, at GU*, there is a collective title front cover for nos. 7, 8, 9, 10, 11, 12.

The *Symphony* was published about 1795–1796 with the same imprint for two violins, a German flute, a tenor, a violoncello and piano under the title no. [10, 11, 12] of *Haydn's Grand Symphonies; BUC*, p. 459 (RAM and SM).

The orchestral score was published in 1808 by Breitkopf & Härtel, Leipzig, under the title *Sinfonie de Joseph Haydn*, Partition, no. 4; ONB. The *Symphony* was composed in London in 1794. Brief biographic information regarding Haydn appears above under *Emperor's Hymn*.

Symphony in D Minor—Franck

m. César Franck. This *Symphonie pour Orchestre* was published for orchestral score near the end of 1889[1] by J. Hamelle, 22 Boulevard Malesherbes, Paris. Possible first edition: Front cover is gray and black and identical with the title page. vb. Title page has a dedication to Henri Duparc, lists the arrangement for piano four hands by the composer at Fr. 10, the orchestral score at 25 Fr., and the orchestral parts without price, and p.ns.

---

[2] RM. 26. a. 12(7), at BM, may be an incomplete copy but it lacks a title page.

[1] The publisher advises that the orchestral score was delivered to the printer Aug. 28, 1889, and that the printing was probably completed about three months thereafter.

3019 and 3059. vb. m. on pp. 1–151, engraved. p.n. 3059. p. [152] and inside and outside of back cover blank. BM (copy purchased July 7, 1897) and JF. A variant, probably later, states at the bottom of the front cover and title page: La copie des parties est interdite . . . ; IU.

No engraved edition of the orchestral parts, apparently published after the orchestral score, has been found; lithographed editions, with p.n. 3059, are at CI, FLP and RAM. The arrangement for piano four hands, with the same title page as that of the orchestral score, with p.n. 3019 on the engraved music pages, is at BN. The *Symphony* was composed in 1886–1888 and performed in Paris Feb. 17, 1889. Franck was born in Liège in 1822 and died in Paris in 1890.

Symphony "Jupiter" (K 551)—Mozart

m. W. A. Mozart. The *Grande Sinfonie* à plusieurs instruments, oeuvre 38me (K 551, and sometimes known as no. 41), was published in 1793[1] for 14 orchestral parts by Jean André, Offenbach sur le Mein. First edition: Front cover has the price of f. 2.24 Xr. p.n. 622. Engraved. RCM and JF*.

The orchestral score was published about 1808–1810 by Cianchettini & Sperati, London. The *Symphony* was completed in Vienna Aug. 10, 1788. Brief biographic information regarding Mozart appears above under *Eine Kleine Nachtmusik*.

Symphony (Unfinished)—Schubert

m. Franz Schubert. *Zwei Sätze* der unvollendeten *Sinfonie* [no. 8], in H moll, were published in orchestral score and parts Dec., 1866,[1] by C. A. Spina, Vienna. Probable first edition of the orchestral score: Title page mentions that the two movements of the unfinished *Symphony* are a Nachgelassenes

---

[1] Köchel, p. 623.

[1] Deutsch, *Schubert*, no. 759, p. 456. Hofmeister *Monatsbericht*, Dec., 1867 [*sic*] p. 194. *Signale*, Nov. 2, 1866, p. 791, "to appear in middle December."

(posthumous) Werk, the p.n. is 19,138,[2] the prices Fl. 4.74 kr. Ö.W./R.3, and the year 1867. (See Plate V.) vb. m. on pp. 3–103. p. 3 states Componirt 1822. Music pages engraved. p. [104] blank. ONB, NYPL and JF.

Possible first edition of the orchestral parts: the title is the same as above, three additional arrangements are listed, the orchestral parts at fl. 5.90 Nkr./R. 3.20 Ngr., and for piano and for piano four hands without prices. p.n. 19,165. Engraved. 19 parts. ONB. The two movements were composed in 1822 but were not performed until Dec. 17, 1865, in Vienna. Brief biographic information regarding Schubert appears above under his *Ave Maria*.

Take Me Out to the Ball-Game

m. Albert von Tilzer. w. Jack Norworth. Copyrighted May 2, 1908,[1] by The York Music Co., Albert von Tilzer, Mgr., 40 West 28th St., New York, N.Y. The copyright copy deposited at LC is a professional edition. Possible first regular edition: Front cover has a drawing of a baseball, a photograph of Sadie Jansell and is gray, blue and white. p. [2] adv. *Story*.. m. on pp. 3–5. p. 3 has a dedication to J. A. Sternad. No plate number. Back cover adv. *Smarty* and *Dolly*.. All the songs advertised in this edition were copyrighted on or before May 2, 1908. JF (autographed by the composer).

Jack Norworth's original poem is at the Baseball Hall of Fame, Cooperstown, N.Y.; it is said that he had never seen a major league ball game until after he had written it.[2] Brief biographic information regarding Von Tilzer and Norworth appears above under *Put Your Arms Around Me, Honey* and *Shine On, Harvest Moon*.

Tales from the Vienna Woods

m. Johann Strauss. *Geschichten aus dem Wienerwald*, op. 325, was pub-

---

[2] 1866, per Deutsch, *Plate Numbers*, p. 12, in spite of the year in the title page and Hofmeister.

[1] Copyright records; LC.

[2] Emurian, *Songs*, p. 134.

lished for piano by June 25, 1868, by C. A. Spina, Vienna.[1] Probable first edition: Front cover has drawings of four scenes from the Vienna woods, has a dedication to Prince Constantin zu Hohenlohe-Schillingsfürst, mentions London, Milan and St. Petersburg agents and gives the prices as Fl. 1.5 Nkr./20 Ngr.; no reference to the arrangement for piano four hands, or plate number on the front cover. vb. m. on pp. 3–14, engraved. p.n. 21600. Back cover missing. JF (copy inscribed and dated July 31, 1868, by the composer). This edition is earlier than the edition with prices of 80 Nkr./15 Ngr. (as stated in Hofmeister), which has the plate number on the front cover, renumbers the music pages to pp. 2–13 (omitting the b'ank verso of the title page frequently in first editions) and, most important, has much weaker engraving. SB (M 4508/c) and JF. The arrangement for piano four hands was published about April, 1869.[2]

The orchestral parts of the *Walzer* were published about April, 1869, by the same concern;[3] an early engraved edition, with p.n. 21640, but mentioning op. 351 (about Aug., 1871), is at LLD. The *Waltz* was performed June 19, 1868, in Vienna by Strauss's orchestra. Brief biographic information regarding the composer appears above under *Artist's Life*.

Tango, España—Albéniz

m. I. Albéniz. A copy of *España*, op. 165, in which *Tango* in D, no. 2, for piano, appears, was deposited at LC on Dec. 22, 1890,[1] by Pitt & Hatzfeld, London W., and H. B. Stevens & Co., Boston. Probable first edition: Front cover has a Spanish scene, states that it was printed by C. G. Röder, Leipzig, and is brown and tan. vb. The title page has a subtitle, *Six Album Leaves* for Pianoforte, lists six pieces at 2/ each and complete 4/, and is red and white. vb. m. on pp. 3–29, *Tango* on p. 7. p.n. P.H. 331. Dedicated to Arthur Chappell, Esq. 1890 copyright claim by H. B. Stevens & Co. pp. [30] and [31] blank. Back cover adv. *Albums.*. LC(CDC). Schott & Co., Ltd., London, has written this author that it was not the original publisher of this work, having purchased the rights from H. B. Stevens & Co. Max Eschig, Paris, has written this author it published this work in 1927.

---

[1] *Abendblatt des "Wanderer,"* nr. 174, Vienna, June 25, 1868.†
[2] Hofmeister *Monatsbericht*, April, 1869, p. 67.
[3] *Id.*, p. [62].
[1] Copyright records; LC.

Copies of *España* in leading Spanish libraries are English or French, not Spanish, editions. Isaac Albéniz was born in Camprodón, Catalonia, in 1860 and died in Cambó les Bains, Pyrenees, in 1909.[2]

Taps

The composition of *Taps* is generally ascribed to Gen. Daniel Butterfield in July, 1862, while in command of a brigade in the Army of the Potomac in Confederate territory, on the banks of the James River in Va.[1] He is said to have suggested to his bugler and aide-de-camp, Oliver Willcox Norton, more soothing music for *Extinguish Lights,* and the latter was the first to play *Taps* that month. The bugle call was not called *Taps* until many years later; no sensible explanation of the new title has been given.

The first known printing of *Taps* is in Emory Upton, *Infantry Tactics* (New York, N.Y., 1874), copyrighted March 14, 1874,[2] under the title *Extinguish Lights,* p. 403;[3] NYPL. Gen. Butterfield was born in Utica, N.Y., in 1831, rose to the rank of Major General and died in 1901.[4]

Ta-Ra-Ra Boom-Der-É

Ta - ra - ra   boom-der-é   ta - ra - ra   boom-der-é

[2] *Grove's,* vol. 1, p. 88.

[1] *Army Times,* Washington, Dec. 4, 1954, p. 26; LC. Editorial, *The New York Times,* July 5, 1962, p. 24. The article in *Army Times* states that Butterfield made claim of authorship in a letter to the editor of *Century Magazine,* New York, N.Y., Aug. 31, 1898, *ULS,* p. 635, but this is evidently an erroneous citation. In any event, the claim was substantiated by the bugler, Oliver Willcox Norton, in his *Two Bugle Calls* (n.p., n.d.), p. 6, reprinted in *Army Letters* (Chicago, 1903), p. 327; both at NYPL.

[2] Copyright records; LC.

[3] Neither *Taps* nor *Extinguish Lights* is in a great many other official manuals of *Infantry Tactics, Artillery Tactics* or *Cavalry Tactics*—Northern or Confederate—published up to 1873 examined by this writer. The author of the article in *The New York Times,* March 11, 1962, sec. 10, p. 9, later admitted that her statement that the call was made official by the end of the Civil War was "just an assumption." White, p. 265, says that *Taps* has some slight resemblance to *Les Refrains des Compagnies;* however, no call by this name has been found in this country or in France.

[4] *NIL,* vol. 4, p. 224.

mw. Henry J. Sayers. Copyrighted Sept. 10, 1891,[1] by Willis Woodward & Co., 842 & 844 Broadway, New York, N.Y. First edition: Front cover refers to the Minstrel Farce Comedy, *Tuxedo*, has a dedication to Miss Hattie F. Townley, Washington, D.C., and is black and white. p. [2] blank. m. on pp. 3–5. p.n. 964. Back cover blank. No arrangements listed on the front cover. LC(CDC). The same copy was deposited at BM on Oct. 5, 1891. This edition precedes a number of other editions deposited subsequently at LC and BM by other publishers.[2]

Sayers wrote the song after having visited Babe Connors' notorious St. Louis cabaret, but the song was not successful in this country until after Lottie Collins had introduced it in England.[3] Sayers was born in Toronto, Canada, in 1854, became an Army bandmaster and manager of minstrel shows, and died in New York City in 1932.[4]

Judge Robert P. Patterson later held that the music and words of the chorus were not original, but the first two verses were.[5] The exact descriptions of the earlier appearances of the music do not appear in the decision or in available files relating to the case, but possible sources which are indicated in the files are: *Deutschlands Liederschatz*, published by Alfred Michow, Berlin, containing a song entitled *Storchlied*; a booklet by Von R. Forster, published by Strauss, Berlin, containing a composition entitled *Tarara Bumtara*, but without music; and a collection of Tyrolean songs for zither and voice, title unknown, dated 1809, published in Tyrol, Austria, with music entitled *Ta rada Boom di e*. Unfortunately, none of these earlier sources has been found.[6]

Curiously, about Jan., 1891,[7] there was published a song containing the phrase "Tsching-ta-ta-ra! Bumm-ta-ta-ra!" These words appear in a song entitled *Tschingtatara!* with words and music by Karl Maxstadt and published by Franz Dietrich, 13 Brühl, Leipzig. JF. The music and remaining words are entirely different from those in *Ta-Ra-Ra Boom-Der-É*.

---

[1] Copyright records; LC.

[2] The earliest English editions are by Francis, Day & Hunter, London, deposited at BM on May 7, 1892, and by Charles Sheard & Co., London, deposited on June 16, 1892. An 1893 French edition by "H. Tonk" (Honky Tonk??), a "Chanson Américaine," is at BN. An undated French edition of *Ta-ra-ra- Boum-der-é*, published by F. Wittert, Paris, refers to the melody as a "Polka Américaine"; JF.

[3] Spaeth, p. 258.

[4] Obituary, *New York Herald Tribune*, Feb. 21, 1932.

[5] *Henry J. Sayers* vs. *Sigmund Spaeth et al.*, United States District Court, Southern District of New York, E 49-336, Feb. 23, 1932.

[6] *Deutschlands Liederschatz*, vol. 1, published by Alfred Michow, m.b.H., 4 Am Karlsbad, Berlin W 35, without date, but dated 1907 in pen and ink, is at LC. P. 17 contains the words of *Storchlied*, but they bear no relation to the words of *Ta-Ra-Ra Boom-Der-É*. A complete run of this work has not been located.

[7] Hofmeister *Monatsbericht*, Jan., 1891, p. 26; HU.

Tea for Two

Pic‑ture you up‑on my knee, just tea for two and two for tea

m. Vincent Youmans. w. Irving Caesar. Published June 10, 1924,[1] by Harms Incorporated, New York, N.Y. First edition: Front cover is orange, purple and white, refers to the musical comedy *No No Nanette*, and lists nine titles. m. on pp. 2–5. p.n. 7076-4. Back cover adv. *Memory.*. LC(CDC).

Tea for Two is said to have been the result of a threat by the producer of *No No Nanette* that, if Youmans did not provide better music for the show than originally submitted, the producer would call upon George Gershwin.[2] *No No Nanette* opened in Detroit in April, 1924, then played in Chicago and London before opening in New York City on Sept. 16, 1925. The piano-vocal score of *No No Nanette* was published by Chappell & Co. Ltd., London, at 8/ on May 14, 1925;[1] LC(CDC) and JF. Brief biographic information regarding Youmans and Caesar appears above under *Carioca* and *Sometimes I'm Happy*.

There Is a Tavern in the Town

There is a tav‑ern in the town (in the town)

The first known printing of this song is in William H. Hills, *Students' Songs*, 3rd edition, copyrighted May 14, 1883,[1] Cambridge, Mass., p. 8, LC(CDC) and JF. The song is not in the 1st or 1880 edition at HU, or in the 2nd or 1881 edition at LC.

It is occasionally said[2] that the song is Cornish and sung by miners

[1] Copyright records; LC.

[2] "Voice of Broadway" in *New York Journal American*, Aug. 18, 1949, p. 13; NYPL.

[1] Copyright records; LC.

[2] E.g., S. Baring-Gould and H. Fleetwood Sheppard, *A Garland of Country Song* (London, 1895), p. vi; NYPL.

from Cornwall, in southwest England, the opening words being "There is an ale-house in our town," possibly under the title *The Brisk Young Miners.* However, the earliest known English printing of the song is in the 1st or 1891 edition of the *Scottish Students' Song Book* (Glasgow and London), p. 164; NLS.

A letter written May 27, 1850, says "Tell her to wait . . . and not let my leaving *grieve her.*" As the words are partly underscored in the original, the author may be thinking of the refrain of *There Is a Tavern in the Town,* "Do not let the parting grieve thee." Letter from John T. Weaver, New London, Conn., to S. A. M. Moore, Pomeroy, Ohio, on his way around the Horn to California on the Ship *Zoe,* quoted in *Manuscripts* (New York, N.Y., Fall, 1969), pp. 262 and 267, at LC.

There's a Long Long Trail

There's a   long, long trail a - wind - ing   in - to the   land of   my dreams

m. Zo Elliott. w. Stoddard King. Published Feb. 18, 1914,[1] by West & Co., 24 Rathbone Place, Oxford Street, London W. The following edition, deposited at BM on Dec. 19, 1914 [*sic*], may be the first regular edition: Front cover has a drawing of a man walking a long trail, a 1914 copyright claim, the price of 1/6 and is silver gray, black and white. p. [2] blank. m. on pp. 1–3 (actually 3–5). There is a 1913 copyright claim on p. 1. p.n. 159. Back cover blank. No other keys or arrangements mentioned. BM(CDC).

Elliott, while at college in the United States and reading of Napoleon's retreat from Moscow, composed the melody for a fraternity banquet and suggested the title,[1] but King's words describe a trail to home and romance. Elliott could not find a publisher in this country, subsequently entered Trinity College, Cambridge, and sold the song to the English publisher mentioned above. It became a favorite of the British troops during World War I, and a manuscript copy of the song is among the relics of the war in the Musée de l'Armée at the Hôtel des Invalides in Paris.

[1] Copyright records; LC. Zo Elliott, "It's Not My Song Any More" in *The American Legion Monthly,* New York, N.Y., Sept., 1926, p. 24; *ULS,* p. 175. The song was published in Dec., 1913, according to Zo Elliott, "There's a Long, Long Trail A-Winding" in *Etude,* Feb., 1940, p. 79. The song may have first been published in a professional edition. See, also, Clark, p. 11, and "The Story of 'A Long, Long, Trail'" in *MCO,* May 16, 1918, p. 14.

Alonzo Elliott was born in 1891 in Manchester, N.H., became a composer and died in 1964 in Wallingford, Conn.[2] King, a lyricist, was born in Jackson, Wis., in 1889, and died in Spokane, Wash., in 1933.[3]

There's No Business Like Show Business

There's no bus - 'ness like show bus - 'ness

Copyright 1946 Irving Berlin. Used by permission of Irving Berlin Music Corporation.

mw. Irving Berlin. Published April 12, 1946,[1] by Irving Berlin Music Company, 1650 Broadway, New York 19, N.Y. First edition: Front cover has drawings of scenes from the show, mentions that Rodgers and Hammerstein are the producers, refers to the musical show *Annie Get Your Gun* with Ethel Merman, lists 15 titles and is red, black and white. p. [2] blank. m. on pp. 3–7. Back cover adv. *They.. - Doin'..* LC(CDC) and JF.

The song has become the unofficial anthem of the Theater.[2] *Annie Get Your Gun* opened in New York City on May 16, 1946, but the piano-vocal score was not published until after the show had opened in London on June 7, 1947. The copy of the piano-vocal score deposited at BM on Nov. 14, 1947, by Irving Berlin, Ltd., London, probably a first edition, has a price of 10/ and the p.n. of the back cover is I. B. 55; BM(CDC) and JF (signed by Irving Berlin). Brief biographic information regarding Berlin appears above under *Alexander's Ragtime Band.†*

They Didn't Believe Me

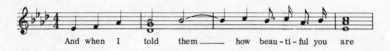

And when I told them —— how beau - ti - ful you are

© 1914 by T. B. Harms Company. Copyright renewed. By consent.

m. Jerome D. Kern. w. Herbert Reynolds. Published Aug. 19, 1914,[1] by T. B. Harms and Francis, Day & Hunter, New York, N.Y. Probable first edi-

---

[2] *ASCAP*, p. 143. Obituary, *The New York Times*, June 26, 1964.

[3] *ASCAP*, p. 276.

---

[1] Copyright records; LC.

[2] See, generally, Irving Berlin, "There's No Business," in *New York Herald Tribune*, Dec. 17, 1954, p. 23.

---

[1] Copyright records; LC.

tion: Front cover has photographs of Donald Brian, Julia Sanderson and
Joseph Cawthorn (in that order), mentions the show *The Girl from Utah*,
lists seven titles and is pink, orange and blue. m. on pp. 2–5. p.n. 5050-4.
Back cover adv. *Valse.*. (published March 9, 1914). JF. The above edition is
the same, to the extent possible, as the other contemporary, regular edition,
copyright deposit copies at LC from the show. The front cover illustrated
on p. 5 of *The Jerome Kern Song Book* (New York, N.Y., 1955), at NYPL,
is of a later edition.

This song was Jerome Kern's first big hit; as in the case of his other
early music, he included the middle initial in his name. *The Girl from Utah*
opened in New York City on Aug. 24, 1914; Kern's music was not in the
1913 London production of the same name. Brief biographic information
regarding Kern appears above under *All the Things You Are*. Herbert
Reynolds is a pseudonym of M. E. Rourke, a lyricist, who was born in
Manchester, England, in 1867 and died in New York City in 1933.[2]

A Thousand and One Nights

m. Johann Strauss. *Tausend und Eine Nacht*, op. 346, was published for
piano, piano four hands and orchestral parts about Aug., 1871,[1] by C. A.
Spina, Vienna. Probable first edition of the piano arrangement: p.n. C. S.
22,249 (C. S. for C. A. Spina) and the music pages are engraved; the front
cover mentions the operetta *Indigo*, has the price of 80 Nkr./ 15 Ngr., lists
the arrangement for piano four hands, refers to a "Petersburg" agent and is
brown and white. p. [2] blank. m. on pp. 3–11. Back cover blank. JF (only
known copy). In July, 1872, C. A. Spina was succeeded by Friedrich
Schreiber, and the *Walzer* was republished for piano with p.n. F. S. 22,249;
AW and JF.

Probable first edition of the arrangement for piano four hands: Front
cover is the same as that first described above, the price of this arrangement being fl. 1. 32/ 25 Ngr.; the music is engraved on pp. 2–19; the p.n.
is C. S. 22,220; and the back cover is blank. ONB*, SS and JF.

---

[2] *ASCAP*, p. 424.

[1] Hofmeister *Monatsbericht*, Aug., 1871, pp. 159, 170 and 164. *Weinmann*, Strauss,
p. 99. Several arrangements for other instruments were published at about the same
time. For example, parts of the melody of this *Waltz* are in *Potpourri no. 1* and *no. 2*
with p.ns. 22130 and 22166, dates unknown; variant editions, priority unknown, are at
ONB and SB. Hofmeister *Annual*, 1871, p. 181—not in Hofmeister *Monatsbericht* for
that year; NYPL.

An early edition of the orchestral parts, with p.n. C. S. 22,254 but not engraved, is at WP*.

Indigo und die Vierzig Räuber, Strauss's first operetta, was performed Feb. 10, 1871, in Vienna. A piano-vocal score of the operetta was published by C. A. Spina about Nov., 1871,[2] with p.ns. 22,131-22,154 and music pages engraved and with this waltz at pp. 41, 47, 51, 53, 182 and 183; SUH. Brief biographic information regarding Strauss appears above under *Artist's Life.*

Three Blind Mice

Three blind mice, three blind mice, see how they run, see how they run!

Three Blind Mice is believed to be the **earliest printed secular** song which is still extremely well known. The music and words were published about Oct. 12, 1609,[1] in *Deuteromelia: or The Second part of Musicks melodie, or melodius musicke. Of Pleasant Rondelaies; K.H. mirth, or Freemens songs. And such delightfull Catches . . . London, Thomas Adams. Three Blinde Mice,* a Round or Catch of 3 voices, is on p. 13. In some copies there is a preface To The Reader signed by T. R. (Thomas Ravenscroft). *RISM,* p. 425; *BUC,* p. 870; FO, HU and JF. (**See Plate VIII.**)

Three Little Maids from School—The Mikado

Three lit - tle maids from school are we, pert as a school-girl well can be

m. Arthur Sullivan. w. W. S. Gilbert. The piano-vocal score of *The Mikado,* in which *Three Little Maids from School* appears, was published April 20, 1885,[1] by Chappell & Co., 50 New Bond Street, London W. Probable first edition: Front cover is blue and gray. Verso adv. *Patience.* Title page mentions the subtitle *The Town of Titipu,* states that the arrangement for

[2] Hofmeister *Monatsbericht,* Nov., 1871, p. 256; NYPL.

[1] *Deuteromelia* was entered at Stationers' Hall on that day.

[1] According to the entry at Stationers' Hall on May 18, 1885, and copyright records at LC. *ILN,* April 25, 1885, p. 434 ("Now Ready"). Entered for copyright in Ottawa on May 9, 1885; *Canadian Copyright,* p. 19.

pianoforte was by George Lowell Tracy (of Boston, U.S.A.[2]), lists the piano-vocal score at 5s. unbound and 7s. 6d. bound, the pianoforte score and the libretto, has an 1885 copyright claim, and **Stoddart & Co.,**[3] Philadelphia, is the American agent. **(See Plate V.)** Cast. Contents. m. on pp. [4]–152. The *Trio* is on p. 56. No plate number on title page or elsewhere. The printer on p. 152 is Henderson, Rait, & Spalding, 3 & 5 Marylebone Lane, Oxford Street, London W. Inside of back cover adv. *Princess.*. Outside of back cover adv. *The Mikado*. BM*, RA and JF*.

The sheet music of *Three Little Maids* was also published about the same time;† a possible first printing was deposited at BM on June 30, 1885. Front cover is black and white, states that the song was sung by Miss Braham, Miss Jessie Bond & Miss Sybil Grey, mentions that the song was extracted from G. L. Tracy's vocal score, the price is 4/, and the publisher is also shown at 15 Poultry. m. on pp. 2–7. p.n. 18040. Back cover adv. *Mother - Sybil*. BM(CDC).

The orchestral score of *The Mikado* was published perhaps as early as 1893[4] by Bosworth & Co., Leipzig. Probable first edition: Front cover in German is gray and black. vb. No title page. m. on pp. 3–335, a lithographing of a handwritten score. No plate number. English text. No date. The publisher's name does not appear. BM, LC, RA, John Wolfson, New York City, and JF (probably Sullivan's copy). However, the orchestral parts of *The Mikado* have not been published.

The Mikado was performed in London on March 14, 1885. Brief biographic information regarding Sullivan and Gilbert appears above under *Bow, Bow, Ye Lower Middle Classes*.

[2] An American arranger was selected with the (unsuccessful) hope of obtaining American copyright protection. *The Mikado (Carte* vs. *Duff)*, 25 Fed. 183 (Circuit Court, New York, N.Y., Sept. 16, 1885); NYPL. George W. Hilton, "'The Mikado' American Copyright, 1885," in *The Gilbert & Sullivan Journal*, London, May, 1963, p. 167; NYPL.

[3] Cecil Hopkinson, London, has noted a presentation Stoddart edition dated "20.4.1885." The second edition, with William A. Pond & Co. as the American agent, a copy of which was deposited June 30, 1885, at BM, adds p.n. 18056 at the bottom of the title page, adds many arrangements to the list of music from *The Mikado* on the outside of the back cover and corrects the misprint on the back cover of the first edition, "Heart's," to read "Hearts Do Not Break." A copy of the Pond edition with covers is at RA.

The pianoforte score was copyrighted in the United States on June 10, 1885; it and other arrangements were deposited at BM on June 30, 1885.

[4] The late Carroll Wilson's notes, at RA, say that 75 copies were published in Jan., 1893. The year is given as 1898 in Arthur Lawrence, *Sir Arthur Sullivan* (Chicago), Bibliography by Wilfrid Bendall, p. 331, NYPL; while the title of this book is dated 1900, it was entered for copyright at the Library of Congress on Sept. 29, 1899, and two copies were received by the Library of Congress on Dec. 4, 1899. The year is given as 1900 by William C. Smith in Sullivan-Flower, p. 279; this was perhaps based on the announcement of the publication in Hofmeister *Monatsbericht*, Oct., 1900, p. 557, at 80 Mk.

Three O'Clock in the Morning

It's   three   o' - clock in   the   morn - ing

m. Julian Robledo. w. Dorothy Terriss. *Three O'Clock in the Morning (Las Tres de la Mañana)* was published for piano without words in 1919 by Jack Wilton, Musicpublisher [*sic*], New Orleans. Probable first edition: Front cover has the titles as indicated above, with the subtitles "Valtz Hesitation (Vals de las Campanas)," a drawing of a church steeple and is blue and white. m. on pp. [2] and [3]. The bottom of p. [2] states "Copyright 1919 by Jack Wilton, New Orleans," but no record of such copyright can be found at LC. Back cover blank. No words. Folio. JF. The song, still without words, was published about Sept., 1920,[1] with a 1920 copyright claim by West's Ltd., London (photostat at B. Feldman & Co. Ltd., London, and later edition at JF), and about Oct., 1920,[2] by C. M. Roehr, Berlin (JF).

The situation with respect to the piano-vocal edition is not certain. The copyright copies deposited June 3, 1921,[3] at both LC and BM are professional editions, with a copyright claim of 1921 by West's Ltd., London, but printed by Leo. Feist, Inc., New York, N.Y., with p.n. 4801-3. Possible first regular edition of piano-vocal arrangement: The song (with words) was published with a show cover of *Greenwich Village Follies 1921* (opened in New York City Aug. 31, 1921) in green, brown and white, listing 14 titles, by Leo. Feist Inc., Feist Bldg., New York, N.Y. p. [2] blank. m. on pp. 3–5. p.n. 4801-3. 1921 copyright claim. Back cover adv. mostly *Mon.. - Peggy..* (both copyrighted in 1921) and with p.n. H.C. 22. JF. The first regular edition may also have been published by West's Ltd., 12 Moor St., Charing Cross Road, London W.1. Front cover has a drawing of a couple dancing while 3 o'clock shows on Big Ben, the price is 2/, Leo Feist, Inc., is the New York City agent, there are agents in Paris and The Hague, and the colors are black, gray and white. p. [2] blank. m. on pp. [3]–5. p.n. 2984. The copyright claim is for 1922. p. [6] adv. *Lazy.. - Arena.* p. [7] adv. *Almond.. - Cock..* Back cover adv. *When..* BM (copyright copy deposited Jan. 27, 1922).

Robledo, a composer, was born in 1887 in Avila, Spain, and died in

[1] *MO*, Sept., 1920, p. 920.
[2] Hofmeister *Monatsbericht*, Oct., 1920, p. 159.
[3] Published the day before; copyright records, LC.

1940 in Buenos Aires, Argentina.[4] Dorothy Terriss is a pseudonym of Dolly Morse, a lyricist, who was born in 1890 in Brooklyn, N.Y., and died in 1953 in New York City.[5]

Tiger Rag

Where's that ti - ger! Where's that ti - ger!
Hold

© Copyright 1917 (renewed) Leo Feist, Inc., New York, N.Y. Used by permission.

Published Sept. 8, 1917,[1] by Leo. Feist Inc., New York, N.Y. The copyright copy deposited at LC is probably a professional edition.[2] Possible first regular edition: Folio. No words. The collective title front cover is entitled "Latest Jazz Numbers Composed and Played by The Original Dixieland Jazz Band," has a photograph of the Band, lists 12 numbers at .60 of which *Tiger Rag*, One-Step, is the sixth, mentions a London agent, and is orange, black and white.[3] p. [2] blank. m. on pp. 3–5, the music credited to "D.J. La Rocca, the original Dixieland Jazz Band." p.n. 3688–3. pp. [6] and [7] blank. Back cover adv. *Amerinda* (copyrighted in 1916). Some of the numbers listed on the front cover were published as late as mid-1918. JF.

Neither the music nor the words of the "Hold That Tiger" chorus is in the above sheet music edition, but the chorus was in the original playing, serving as the third chorus. The music of the "Hold That Tiger" chorus, without words, is in the first recording of the piece by the Original Dixieland Jazz Band on Aeolian-Vocalion record no. 1206, released in Sept., 1917,[4,5] at JF, and also in the second recording by the same band on Victor record no. 18472, released March 28, 1918,[6] at NYPL and JF.

---

[4] Information from SACEM.

[5] *ASCAP*, p. 361, and ASCAP records.

[1] Copyright records; LC.

[2] Front cover is illustrated in Elliott Shapiro, "Ragtime, U.S.A.," in *Notes*, June, 1951, p. 469.

[3] Front cover is illustrated in Fuld, *American*, p. [49].

[4] H. O. Brunn, *The Story of the Original Dixieland Jazz Band* (Baton Rouge, La., 1960), p. 97; NYPL. Also, letter from H. O. Brunn, Snyder, N.Y.

[5] The record is listed in *The Aeolian-Vocalion Records*, New York, N.Y., Bulletin 5 (1918), no page number; LC. A Notice of Use of *Tiger Rag* for phonographic records was filed by the copyright owner on March 9, 1918. The name of the record company is not indicated in such a Notice. No Notice of Intention to Use *Tiger Rag* for a phonographic record was filed by any record company in 1917 or 1918. Copyright records; LC.

[6] Information from RCA Victor Listing Department, New York, N.Y.

Orchestral parts of *Tiger Rag*, with music credited to the Original Dixieland Jazz Band and "Vocal Chorus" by Harry de Costa, were published by Leo. Feist Inc. on Feb. 19, 1932,[1] but as no copy of the first edition has been found, it is not certain that the music or words of the "Hold That Tiger" chorus were included. A revised version of the sheet music of *Tiger Rag* was published on March 10, 1932.[1] Possible first edition: Front cover is green and white, refers to Vocal and Piano Solo without prices, and gives entire credit to D. J. La Rocca of the Original Dixieland Jazz Band. Music on pages 2–5, with credits on page 2 of the words to Harry de Costa and of the music solely to Original Dixieland Jazz Band. p.n. 6587–4. The music and words of the "Where's That Tiger" chorus are on page 3. Back cover adv. *Legion Airs* (published Sept. 16, 1932[1]). Leo. Feist Inc. is shown on page 2 at 56 Cooper Square, and on the back cover at 60 Cooper Square, New York, N.Y. Page 2 also refers to a Canadian affiliate. BR and JF.

There has been major dispute as to the authorship of the various parts of *Tiger Rag*.[7] Jelly Roll Morton is one claimant. Jack Carey and Ernest "Punch" Miller are also said to be the composers of the "Hold That Tiger" chorus. D. J. La Rocca, whose name appears on the first printing of the sheet music, has consistently claimed to be the composer of the entire piece. The first part is also claimed to have been based on an old French Marseilles quadrille. The entire piece is also said to have been Negro or Creole in origin. Current printings credit authorship solely to the Original Dixieland Jazz Band.

Another uncertainty is whether the word "Tiger" in the title refers to the animal or derives from barrelhouse lingo to the lowest hand a man could draw in a poker game.[7]

Till Eulenspiegel's Merry Pranks—Richard Strauss

[7] See footnote 4, above; Alan Lomax, *Mister Jelly Roll* (New York, N.Y., 1950), pp. 66 and 68, at NYPL; Samuel B. Charters, *Jazz New Orleans 1885–1963* (rev. ed., New York, N.Y., 1963), pp. 24 and 86, at NYPL; and Obituary of La Rocca, *The New York Times*, Feb. 23, 1961. Thornton Haggert, Arlington, Va., has been helpful regarding this paragraph.

m. Richard Strauss. *Till Eulenspiegels Lustige Streiche*, op. 28, was published for orchestral score and parts in Sept., 1895,[1] by Jos. Aibl, Munich. Probable first edition of the orchestral score: Front cover is black and green with the same text as the title page. vb. Title page has a dedication to Dr. Arthur Seidl, states "Nach alter Schelmenweise—in Rondeauform," lists these two arrangements with their p.ns. 2832 and 2833 at Mk. 25 each plus p.n. 2835 for an unspecified arrangement and has an 1895 copyright. Orchestral instrumentation. m. on pp. 3–60. p.n. 2832. Inside of back cover blank. Outside of back cover adv. works of Strauss from op. 2 to op. 29 (op. 29 also published in 1894–1895). BSM and JF.

A set of the orchestral parts was deposited at LC on Oct. 16, 1895. First edition: Front cover and back cover are the same as those described above. p.n. 2833, stamped. 1895 copyright claim. LC(CDC). The work was completed May 6, 1895, and performed Nov. 5, 1895, in Cologne. Brief biographic information regarding Strauss appears above under *Don Juan*.

Till We Meet Again

Smile   the   while   you   kiss   me   sad   a - dieu

m. Richard A. Whiting. w. Raymond B. Egan. Published Aug. 30, 1918,[1] by Jerome H. Remick & Co., Detroit and New York. Possible first edition: Folio size. Front cover has a drawing of a soldier and a girl in the moonlight and is blue, black and white. m. on pp. 2–3. p.n. 597-2. World War I patriotic appeals at the bottom of pp. 2–3 and at the top of the back cover. Back cover adv. *Smiles* and many other songs (*A Little.. - Wondrous..*) and has p.n. 4332 8. This copy is dated in ink on the front cover "10-30-18." JF.

This song had one of the highest sheet music sales in history. Whiting was born in Peoria, Ill., in 1891, became a composer and died in Beverly Hills, Cal., in 1938.[2] Egan, a lyricist, was born in Ontario, Canada, in 1890 and died in Connecticut in 1952.[2]

[1] Mueller von Asow, p. 156. Müller-Reuter, p. 608. Hofmeister *Monatsbericht*, Dec., 1895, p. 515.

[1] Copyright records; LC.
[2] *ASCAP*, pp. 536 and 140, and ASCAP records.

Time on My Hands

Time on   my hands,___   you in   my arms

© Copyright 1930 (renewed) Miller Music Corporation and Vincent Youmans, Inc., New York, N.Y. Used by permission.

m. Vincent Youmans. w. Harold Adamson and Mack Gordon. Published Dec. 10, 1930,[1] by Vincent Youmans, Inc., 67 West 44th Street, New York, N.Y. First edition: Front cover is silver and blue, refers to the Ziegfeld Production *Smiles*, with Marilyn Miller and Fred and Adele Astaire, and lists two titles. m. on pp. 2–5. Back cover adv. *Say*.. LC(CDC) and JF.

Marilyn Miller reportedly refused to sing this fine song in *Smiles*,[2] which opened in New York City on Nov. 18, 1930, and which ran only 63 performances. Brief biographic information regarding Youmans and Adamson appears above under *Carioca* and *Around the World*. Gordon was born in Warsaw, Poland, in 1904, came to this country as a youth and became a lyricist and actor, and died in New York City in 1959.[3]

'Tis the Last Rose of Summer

'Tis   the last rose   of___sum-mer, left___bloom - ing a - lone

The melody of *'Tis the Last Rose of Summer* is thought by some to derive from *The Young Mans* [*sic*] *Dream*, the two earliest known printings of which were in *Cooke's Selection of Twenty One Favorite Original Airs* (Never before Printed), published by B. Cooke, Dublin, ca. 1793–1798,[1] p. 9 (BM), and in Edward Bunting, *A General Collection of the Ancient Irish Music*, published by Preston & Son, 97 Strand, London, in 1796, p. 10 (BUC, p. 142).[2] In the title in the latter collection, there is an apostrophe in the word "Man's."

[1] Copyright records; LC.

[2] Green, p. 134.

[3] Obituary, *The New York Times*, March 1, 1959.

---

[1] According to Humphries-Smith, p. 114; ca. 1795, according to *BUC*, p. 213; and ca. 1793, according to Donal O'Sullivan, Dublin.

[2] This is the date given in *BUC*, p. 142. The next entry in *BUC* mentions an edition published by Hime, Dublin, about 1798; also at JF. The work was entered at Stationers' Hall on Oct. 13, 1797, unfortunately without indication of publisher.

Moore himself attributes the melody[3] of *'Tis the Last Rose of Summer* to *The Groves of Blarney*, the first known appearance of which was in *A Collection of Old Established Irish Slow & Quick Tunes*, Book 1, published by S. Holden, Dublin, in 1806,[4] p. 18; BM. It has also been said that *The Groves of Blarney* is a burlesque imitation of *Castle Hyde*, sometimes called *Sweet Castle Hyde*;[5] however, no printing of either of the latter two titles has been found before 1806.

In any event, Thomas Moore frankly stated that he altered the melody of *The Groves of Blarney*,[6] and, of course, the words of *'Tis the Last Rose of Summer* are entirely original with him. The music and words of *'Tis the Last Rose of Summer* were first published in Dec., 1813,[7] in the 5th Number (the first number of the third volume) of *A Selection of Irish Melodies* by J. Power, 34 Strand, London, and W. Power, 4 Westmorland Street, Dublin, p. 15. In the first edition of this number, there is an erratum note on the advertisement leaf, an engraved footnote on p. 3, and two printed footnotes on p. 5; and the printed text and the engraved text of the first verse of the first poem are not identical in wording.[8] JF. The separate sheet music of *The Last Rose of Summer* was probably published by the London firm soon after; JF (copy watermarked 1811). The song was greatly popularized by its interpolation in 1847 in Flotow's *Martha* as a "Volkslied"; JF. Brief biographic information regarding Moore appears above under *Believe Me If All Those Endearing Young Charms*.

To a Wild Rose

m. Edward MacDowell. *Woodland Sketches*, op. 51, for piano, in which *To a Wild Rose* appears, was copyrighted in a regular edition on Dec. 23,

---

[3] On p. 14 of the 5th Number of *A Selection of Irish Melodies*, described in the text.

[4] This is the date given by Chinnéide, p. 122. Dated 1804? by BM. Fitz-Gerald, p. 150, states that a Richard Jones obtained copies of *The Groves of Blarney* in Cork in the summer of 1800, but this information has not been confirmed. The copies may have been in manuscript. *The Groves of Blarney* is generally attributed to Alfred Milliken.

[5] See, generally, Elson, *Modern Music*, p. 455, and *O'Neill's Music*, p. 40.

[6] Chinnéide, p. 122. Bunting complained bitterly of the change; O'Neill, *Irish Folk*, p. 242.

[7] 1813 is the date generally given (Muir, 13th unnumbered page, and Chinnéide, p. 122); the advertisement leaf is dated Dec., 1813.

[8] Muir, 13th unnumbered page.

1896,[1] by P. L. Jung, New York, N.Y. Possible first regular edition: Title page lists 10 compositions of which *To a Wild Rose* is no. 1, the price is $1.25, and Breitkopf & Härtel are shown as Agents. vb. m. on pp. 3–28, *To a Wild Rose* on p. 3. p.n. P.L.J. 403 a–k. pp. [29] and [30] blank. pp. [31] and [32] adv. *Compositions*, no. 1–no. 32. LC and JF. This edition is believed to precede another edition published by P. L. Jung with music on pp. 6–47, at LC, as this edition is similar in pagination and arrangement to the 1899 edition published by Schmidt.

A De Luxe edition of *Woodland Sketches* was published by P. L. Jung on Dutch handmade paper, limited to 110 copies. The music pages are engraved but lack pagination. LC. There is a copy inscribed by the composer to P[hilip] H[ale], dated Dec. 25, 1896, at NEC, so the De Luxe edition was probably published at about the same time as the regular edition.[1] MacDowell was born in New York City in 1861 and died there in 1908.

Tonight—West Side Story

To - night, to - night, won't be just an - y night

m. Leonard Bernstein. w. Stephen Sondheim and Leonard Bernstein. Published Aug. 27, 1957,[1] by G. Schirmer, Inc., and Chappell & Co., Inc., 3 East 43rd Street, New York, N.Y. First edition: Front cover has a photograph of a couple running on a New York City sidewalk, mentions the musical, *West Side Story*, lists eight titles, the price is 60¢ and the colors are pink, black and white. p. [2] blank. m. on pp. 3–5. p.n. 44282 c. The copyright is in the name of the authors. Back cover adv. *The Donkey..* and *Will..* LC(CDC) and JF (autographed by the composer).

West Side Story opened in New York City on Sept. 26, 1957. The piano-vocal score of the musical was published Feb. 19, 1959,[1] at $9.00 with the same imprint and with music on pp. 3–200; LC(CDC) and JF. Bernstein was born in Lawrence, Mass., in 1918, and resides in New York City. Sondheim was born in New York City in 1930 and resides there.[2]

[1] O. G. Sonneck, *Catalogue of First Editions of Edward MacDowell* (Washington, 1917), p. 38; LC.

[1] Copyright records; LC.
[2] *International Celebrity Register*, U.S. edition (New York, N.Y., 1959), p. 710; NYPL.

Too-Ra-Loo-Ra-Loo-Ral, That's an Irish Lullaby

Too - ra-loo - ra-loo-ral,_____ too - ra-loo - ra - li

© 1913 M. Witmark & Sons. Copyright renewed. Used by permission.

mw. J. R. Shannon. Published July 14, 1913,[1] by M. Witmark & Sons, New York, N.Y. The copyright copy deposited at LC is a professional edition. Possible first regular edition: Front cover has a photograph of Chauncey Olcott, refers to the production *Shameen Dhu*, lists five titles, shows the publisher at five other cities and is brown, green and white. p. [2] adv. *Mother.. - I..* (the songs advertised on this page were published in 1910–1912). m. on pp. 3–5. p.n. 13094-3. Back cover adv. *The Artistic..* JF.

Shameen Dhu opened in New York City on Feb. 2, 1914. James Royce Shannon was born in Adrian, Mich., in 1881, became a composer, lyricist, actor and theater executive, and died in Pontiac, Mich., in 1946.[2]

Toreador Song—Carmen

To-ré - a-dor, en gar - de! To-ré - a-dor!__ To - ré - a-dor!

m. Georges Bizet. w. H. Meilhac and L. Halévy. The piano-vocal score of *Carmen*, in which the *Chanson du Toréador* appears, was published by mid-March, 1875,[1] by Choudens Père et Fils, 265 Rue St. Honoré, près l'Assomption, Paris. First edition: Title page is the standard Choudens title page of this period with its drawing of three women on an ornamental frame; there is a dedication to Jules Pasdeloup, the Opéra Comique is in 4 acts and based on the story by Prosper Mérimée; and the piano arrangement is by the composer. **(See Plate V.)** vb. Cast and Index. vb. m. on pp. 1–351, the *Toreador Song* on p. 131. p.n. A.C. 3082. p. [352] blank. BN(CDC), JMM and JF. Scene no. 2 in Act I, *Attention! chut!*, deleted in

[1] Copyright records; LC.

[2] *ASCAP*, p. 449.

[1] *CNO*, Feb., 1875, p. 19. *Le Ménestrel*, March 14, 1875, "vient de paraître." Entered for Dépôt Légal on March 18, 1875; Archives.

later editions, is included; other points are noted in H. Baron, *Catalogue 71* (London [1965]), no. 191, at JF. While the p.n. is that of the predecessor publisher, A. Choudens, no title page has been found with this imprint. A possible first printing of the sheet music edition of the *Chanson du Toréador*, no. 7, issued at about the same time,[2] has plate number A.C. 3113 and the same imprint as that of the piano-vocal score; JF.

Orchestral parts of the opera, published by Choudens Père et Fils, with plate number A.C.3276, lithographed, possibly their first printing, with covers, are at CI.

The orchestral score of *Carmen* was printed in 1877[3] with the same imprint as that of the piano-vocal score. First edition: Folio, two volumes. First volume: Title page is the same as that of the piano-vocal score, merely substituting Partition Orchestre for Partition Chant et Piano. vb. Cast and Index. vb. m. on pp. 1–330, the *Toreador Song* at p. 219. p.n. A. C. 3795. Second volume: Same title page and introductory pages. m. on pp. 331–579. p. [580] blank. BN. The orchestral score was later published in the Edition Peters.

The *Habanera* in *Carmen* was based upon Sebastian Yradier's *El Areglito*, and a footnote in the first edition of the piano-vocal score of *Carmen* states at p. 49 "Imitée d'une chanson espagnole, propriété des Editeurs du Ménestrel." *El Areglito* had been included as no. 3 in Yradier's *Fleurs d'Espagne* published in 1864 by Heugel & Cie., au Ménestrel, Paris. WNH and JF. See *La Paloma*, above.

Carmen was performed March 3, 1875, in Paris. The publisher is still using the original plate number for its piano-vocal scores now being sold by it! Bizet was born in Paris in 1838 and died in Bougival, near Paris, on June 3, 1875, three months after the first performance of *Carmen*. Brief biographic information regarding Meilhac appears above under *Le Rêve*. Ludovic Halévy, also a dramatist, was born in Paris in 1834 and died in 1908.[4]

Torna a Surriento!

Ma nun me   las - sà,   nun dar-me stu tur - mien - to!

m. E. de Curtis. w. G. B. de Curtis. *Torna a Surriento!* is believed to have

---

[2] *CNO*, Feb., 1875, p. 19.

[3] So given in several dealers' catalogues and reasonable from the viewpoint of the plate number.

[4] *NIL*, vol. 15, p. 356, and vol. 10, p. 588.

been first published shortly before Sept. 30, 1904,[1] in a booklet of songs entitled *Piedigrotta-Garibaldi; Album Ricordo,* compiled by Luigi Conforti, the publisher of which was Premiato Stabilimento Tipografico Bideri, 17 Via. S. Pietro a Majella, Naples. Probable first edition: Front cover in many colors has a drawing of two girls in a garden, mentions the year 1904 and states that the price is Lire Due, but after Sept. 30, L. Cinque. *Torna a Surriento!* is one of the songs included, on two unnumbered pages. SCR. Bideri deposited the sheet music edition of the song with the Prefect of Naples on Dec. 13, 1904;[2] later sheet music editions have a dedication to Comm. Guglielmo Tramontano; DTP, SS and JF. †

Ernesto de Curtis, a pianist and composer, was born in Naples in 1875 and died there in 1937.[3] His brother, Giovanni Battista or Giambattista, a poet and painter, was born in Naples in 1860 and died there in 1926.[3]

Toyland

Toy - land! Toy - land! Lit - tle girl and boy - land

m. Victor Herbert. w. Glen MacDonough. Copyrighted May 13, 1903,[1] in a professional edition at LC by M. Witmark & Sons, New York, N.Y. Copyrighted Oct. 16, 1903,[1] in a regular edition by the same publisher. First regular edition: Front cover has drawings of toys, refers to the Stupendous Extravaganza as produced at the Grand Opera House, Chicago, *Babes in Toyland,* lists 20 titles, the publisher is shown at three other cities, there are two foreign agents, and the colors are orange, white, black and gray. p. [2] blank. m. on pp. 3–5. p.n. 5442-3. pp. [6] and [7] blank. Back cover adv. *Fleurette - Under..* LC(CDC) and JF.

Babes in Toyland opened in Chicago on June 17, 1903, and in New York City on Oct. 13, 1903. The piano-vocal score was copyrighted Aug. 22, 1903.[1] First edition: Front cover is similar to that described above, the prices are $2.00 and 6/, and the music is on pp. 5–145. LC(CDC) and JF. Brief biographic information regarding Herbert appears above under *Ah! Sweet Mystery of Life.* MacDonough, a librettist and lyricist, was born in Brooklyn, N.Y., in 1870, and died in Stamford, Conn., in 1924.[2]

---

[1] Bideri advises that the song was first published in 1904. *DUM,* p. 419, however, gives the year (composition? publication?) as 1902.

[2] Copyright records; UDP.

[3] *DR,* p. 377.

[1] Copyright records; LC.

[2] *ASCAP,* p. 321.

Tramp! Tramp! Tramp!

Tramp, tramp, tramp, the boys are march - ing,   cheer   up, com-rades, they will come

mw. Geo. F. Root.† Copyrighted as sheet music on Jan. 5, 1865,[1] by Root & Cady, 95 Clark Street, Chicago. First edition of the sheet music edition: Front cover is engraved, has a subtitle, *The Prisoners* [sic] *Hope*, there are vignettes of Civil War scenes and songs, and the price is 3. p. [2] blank. m. on pp. 3–5. p.n. 420–3. Back cover blank. No copyright notice on the front cover or elsewhere. LC(CDC). It is possible that the copyright deposit copy, with the engraved front cover, is a proof or specimen copy, and that similar copies were not sold as no other such copy has been found. A similar copy, but with a lithographed front cover having an 1864 [sic] copyright notice, with p. [2] adv. Cabinet Organs and with the back cover adv. *Musical..*, is at JF.

George Frederick Root was born at Sheffield, Mass., in 1820, became a composer and publisher, and died at Bailey's Island, Me., in 1895.[2]

Träumerei

m. Robert Schumann. *Kinderscenen* (*Children's Scenes*) Leichte Stücke for the piano, op. 15, in which *Träumerei* (*Dreams*) appears as no. 7, was published in Sept., 1839,[1] by Breitkopf & Härtel, Leipzig. Probable first edition: the front cover has the price of **20 Gr.**, a border design and p.n. 6016, and is black and white. (**See Plate VI.**) vb. m. on pp. 3–20, engraved and with a blue border. *Träumerei* is no. 7 on p. 11. BSM, SH and JF.

Kinderscenen was composed in April, 1838. Brief biographic information regarding Schumann appears above under *Carnaval*.

[1] Copyright records; LC.

[2] George F. Root, *The Story of a Musical Life* (Cincinnati, 1891), p. 137; NYPL.‡ *Grove's*, vol. 7, p. 226.

[1] Dörffel, p. 4. However, he gives the price as 25 Gr., which is at variance with the printed edition described above and with the contemporaneous notice in Hofmeister *Monatsbericht*, Sept., 1839, p. 119. No copy has been found with the price of 25 Gr. Hofmann, *Schumann*, p. 41.

Trees

m. Oscar Rasbach. w. Joyce Kilmer. Published March 18, 1922,[1] by G. Schirmer Music Stores, Inc., Los Angeles. First edition: Front cover has a drawing of trees, states that it is sung by Cecil Fanning, the price is 60 Cents and the colors are black and white. m. on pp. [2]–[3]. Dedication on p. [2] to Mrs. L. L. Krebs. Back cover blank. Only one key (D) on front cover. LC(CDC) and JF.

The old oak tree that is said to have inspired Joyce Kilmer's poem was at Ryder's Lane and Route 1, New Brunswick, N.J.[2] The poem was first printed in the magazine *Poetry*, Chicago, Aug., 1913, p. 160, *ULS*, p. 2225; thereafter, in *Anthology of Magazine Verse for 1913*, edited by William Stanley Braithwaite (Cambridge, 1913; Introduction dated Dec., 1913), p. 7, NYPL; and then in Joyce Kilmer, *Trees and Other Poems* (New York, N.Y., 1914), without "Printed in the United States of America" on the verso of the title page, p. 19, NYPL Rare Book Room.

Rasbach, a composer and educator, was born in Dayton, Ky., in 1888 and lives in San Marino, Cal.[3] Kilmer, a poet and journalist, was born in New Brunswick, N.J., in 1886 and died in 1918 as an Army sergeant in France during World War I.[2]

Triumphal March—Aida

m. G. Verdi. Notwithstanding the availability of important information not described by Hopkinson in his Verdi bibliography and the correction of important errors[1] by him, and the subsequent discovery of two hitherto

---

[1] Copyright records; LC.

[2] *The New York Times*, June 22, 1961, p. 20; July 5, 1961, p. 67; Aug. 18, 1963, sec. 1, p. 71; and Sept. 19, 1963, p. 19.

[3] *ASCAP*, p. 399.

[1] Errors in Hopkinson, *Verdi*, relating to the priority of the first edition of *Aida* are: The earliest advertisements for the three candidates are not in 1879, but in 1871–1872, as indicated in the text. The Rome Conservatory copy of the octavo piano-vocal score has the plate number. On page 150 of his work, eighth line of text, "1892" should be "1872." Hopkinson 62A(c), of which I am shown as the only owner, has the later, longer ballet, and should be deleted; the copy is thus 62B(c). The 1879 advertisements mentioned under 62A and 62B probably relate to the later editions with the longer ballet, 62B and 62B(c).

Hopkinson describes the score with plate numbers 42486–42502 as "folio"; however, since the Ricordi title pages refer to this score as "quarto," the Ricordi term is used here.

unknown important scores, the priority of the earliest piano-vocal scores of *Aida* published by Ricordi, Milan, is a mystery.

Each of the candidates below is believed to have the same music and text, including specifically the original, shorter ballet at the beginning of the second act; in the later Ricordi editions, the longer ballet is on a repeated page, e.g., page 116 (1–7).

The candidates are: (1a) An engraved large quarto piano-vocal score with plate numbers 42486–42502, listed with these plate numbers in the *Ricordi Catalogue Supplement*, Oct., 1871–Feb., 1872, p. 4; LC. The engraving of the first piece began Feb. 4, 1871, and the engraving of the three last pieces began Jan. 20, 1872, according to the Ricordi *Libroni*. 293 pages. Title page refers to an octavo piano-vocal score (which one?), and other arrangements, all with prices, this score at 50, but there is no reference at the bottom of the title page to "Parigi—Escudier." No libretto. The engraver's initial at the bottom of pages 3–10 is "m," the original engraver indicated in the Ricordi *Libroni*. Front cover in many colors shows the final scene of the opera in two levels. vb. Inside and outside of back cover blank. Copy at Roger V. Clements, London. This copy was not known to Hopkinson.

(1b) Same as (1a) above except there is a reference at the bottom of the title page to "Parigi—Escudier" and the engraver's initial at the bottom of pages 3–10 is "c." This edition is probably later than (1a) above. BM, NLS, SCR and JF. Hopkinson, *Verdi*, 62A(b) (listing two other copies).

(2a) A large octavo piano-vocal score with plate number 42602 throughout. One copy unknown to Hopkinson is engraved; University of California, Berkeley, Cal.[2] The engraver's initial at the bottom of page 17 is "a." Unfortunately, the Ricordi *Libroni* do not state the name of the original engraver of page 17.

(2b) Same as (2a) above except all other known copies of this octavo edition are lithographed, and at least the copies at BM, SCR and JF have the initial "m" at the bottom of page 17.[†]

(3) A lithographed large octavo piano-vocal score without plate number, possibly a photograph of the preceding score, as it has the same title page and number of pages. The *Ricordi Catalogue Supplement*, Oct., 1871–Feb., 1872, p. 4, referred to in (1a) above, also lists an octavo piano-vocal score without plate number, and this may be the score referred to.[3] Libretto. Not mentioned in the Ricordi *Libroni*. Only one known copy—at BM (RM. 10. d. 6.). Hopkinson, *Verdi*, 62A.[‡]

---

[2] Hopkinson, unfortunately, did not inquire into the wealth of Verdi editions in American libraries.

[3] Although no plate number was listed, the *Ricordi Catalogue Supplement* may also refer to the octavo score with the plate number.

Turkey in the Straw (Zip Coon)

Zip Coon, as *Turkey in the Straw* was originally known, was published about 1834 in five editions, priority uncertain: (a) copyrighted March 29, 1834[1]—this edition has an 1834 copyright claim by Endicott & Swett on the front cover below a full-page drawing of Zip Coon, an 1834 copyright claim by Thos. Birch, New York, N.Y., the publisher, on p. [2], the music pages have the music and words in white against a blue background, and seven stanzas—"A famous comic song, as sung by all the celebrated comic singers," LC (CDC dated May 17, 1834?); (b) an edition similar to (a), but with the front cover blank, and the music pages in black and white, JF; (c) published by J. L. Hewitt & Co., 137 Broadway, New York, N.Y. (1830–1835)[2]—front cover has a three-quarter-page drawing of Zip Coon and mentions the singer, G. W. Dixon, and there are seven stanzas, JF; (d) published by Firth & Hall, 1 Franklin Sq., New York, N.Y. (1832–1847)[2]—front cover has a drawing of a Negro couple and mentions Geo. W. Dixon, and there are nine stanzas, LC and JF; and (e) published by G. Willig, Junr., Baltimore (1829–1867)[2]—front cover has a drawing of a Negro couple and mentions Mr. Dixon, and there are nine stanzas, LC and JF. In each of the above, the music is on pp. [2]–[3]; the back cover is blank; and none is engraved.

Both George Washington Dixon on the one hand, and Bob Farrell and George Nichols on the other hand, claimed the authorship of *Zip Coon*, a dispute not yet resolved.[3]

The melody apparently acquired the name *Turkey in the Straw* in a strange way. On July 12, 1861,[1] there was copyrighted a song by Dan Bryant entitled *Turkey in de Straw*. The music and words of the song were new, but at the end there was included the "Old melody" without words. The song was published by H. B. Dodworth, 6 Astor Place, New York, N.Y. LC (CDC).

The following Irish, Scottish and English titles have been urged as precedents for *Zip Coon*; none seems a clear precedent, and may have been

---

[1] Copyright records; LC. The March 29, 1834, date makes unlikely the accuracy of the frequent statement that the song was introduced by Bob Farrell on Aug. 11, 1834.

[2] Dates are as indicated by Dichter-Shapiro.

[3] Carl Wittke, *Tambo and Bones, A History of the American Minstrel Stage* (Durham, N.C., 1930), pp. 16 and 33; NYPL.

found in print only subsequent to 1834: (1) the Irish *Glasgow Hornpipe;*[4] (2) the Irish *The Post Office;*[5] (3) the Scottish *Lady Shaftsbury's Reel;*[6] (4) the English *Haymaker's Dance;*[7] (5) the Irish *Rose Tree in Full Bearing;*[8] (6) the Morris dance tune known in England and Scotland, *Old Mother Oxford;*[9] (7) the Irish *Kinnegad Slashers;*[10] and (8) the English *The Jolly Miller.*[11]

12th Street Rag

m. Euday L. Bowman. Published Aug. 31, 1914,[1] by Euday L. Bowman, Fort Worth, Texas. Probable first edition: Front cover has a drawing of people ragging in 12th Street and is brown and white.[2] m. on pp. 2–5. 1914 copyright notice at bottom of p. 2. Back cover blank. LC(CDC).†

12th Street Rag was recorded in an early jazz record, Columbia A 2298, by Earl Fuller's Rector Novelty Orchestra, released about Sept., 1917;[3] record at JF. Bowman, a composer and lyricist, was born in Fort Worth, Texas, in 1887 and died in New York City in 1949.[4]

---

[4] Letter from Hans Nathan. This hornpipe is in *O'Neill's Music,* p. 306.

[5] Also, per Hans Nathan. This hornpipe is in *O'Neill's Music,* p. 298.

[6] Also, per Hans Nathan. This is said to be in Elias Howe, *The Caledonian Collection* (Boston, 1860), but no copy of this collection has been found. *Lady Shaftsbury's Strathspey* is in Niel Gow's *Third Collection of Strathspeys and Reels* (Edinburgh, 1792), p. 15; *BUC,* p. 392.

[7] Per Downes-Siegmeister, p. 147. The dance is in Rutherford's *Country Dances* (London, ca. 1800); EFDSS.

[8] Also, per Downes-Siegmeister, p. 147. The tune is also known as *The Old Rose Tree,* and is in George Pullen Jackson, *Spiritual Folk Songs of Early America* (Locust Valley, N.Y., 1953), p. 118, under the title *Rose Tree;* NYPL.

[9] The tune is in Cecil J. Sharp and Herbert C. Macilwaine, *The Morris Book* (London, 1919), part II, p. 25; NYPL.

[10] O'Neill, *Waifs,* p. 135. The tune was published in *O'Farrell's Pocket Companion for the Irish or Union Pipes* (London, ca. 1795), part 3, p. 31; *BUC,* p. 741, and NLI.

[11] Josiah H. Combs, *Folk-Songs of the Southern United States* (Austin, Texas, and London, 1967), p. 93; NYPL. *The Jolly Miller* is quoted in Chappell, vol. II, p. 668, and bears no similarity.

---

[1] Copyright records; LC. A history of the song is recounted in *Shapiro, Bernstein & Co. Inc. vs. Jerry Vogel Music Co., Inc.,* 115 Fed. Supp. 754 (Southern District, N.Y., 1953); NYPL.

[2] Front cover is illustrated in Elliott Shapiro, "Ragtime, U.S.A.," in *Notes,* June, 1951, p. 470.

[3] *Columbia Records* [Catalogue] (New York, N.Y.), Sept., 1917, p. 11; NYPL.

[4] *ASCAP,* p. 49.

Twinkle, Twinkle, Little Star—(ABCDEFG; Baa, Baa, Black Sheep; Schnitzelbank)

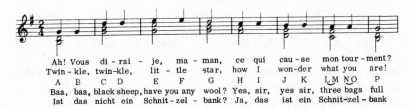

Ah! Vous	di - rai -	je,	ma - man,	ce	qui	cau - se	mon tour - ment?
Twin - kle,	twin-kle,	lit - tle	star,	how	I	won-der	what you	are!
A	B	C D	E	F	G H I	J K	L M N O	P
Baa, baa,	black sheep,	have you any	wool?	Yes, sir,	yes sir,	three bags	full
Ist	das nicht ein	Schnit - zel -	bank?	Ja,	das	ist ein	Schnit-zel - bank

This melody was first known as *Ah! Vous Dirai-Je, Maman,* the music of which appeared (without words) in 1761[1] in *Les Amusements d'une Heure et Demy* by Mr. Bouin (Paris), p. 1; BN. The words and music appear in a manuscript entitled *Recueil de Chansons* about 1765 under the title *Le Faux Pas,* p. 43; BN (Vm7 3640). The earliest known printing of the words and music of the song is in vol. two of *Recueil de Romances* by M.D.L. (De Lusse) published in Brussels in 1774, p. 75, under the title *La Confidence— Naive.* BN and JF. The words and music also appear in sheet music under the title *Les Amours, de Silvandre* (Paris, 1780?); BM. Mozart wrote 12 variations on the melody for piano in 1778 while in Paris, which were published in 1785 by Christoph Torricella, Vienna, under the title *Airs Variée [sic]* (Köchel 265).[2] And Beethoven also improvised on the theme in his second public concert in Prague in 1798.[2A]

The melody soon became associated with other words in this country as *Mark My Alford* which was included in Carr's *The Gentleman's Amusement,* published in Philadelphia in 1794–1796, p. 53 (Sonneck-Upton, p. 157, and JF); and in Carr's *Four Songs from an Unidentified Collection,* published in New York, N.Y., about 1795 under the title *The Delights of Wedded Love* (Sonneck-Upton, p. 403).

[1] Per Simone Wallon, "Romances et Vaudevilles Français dans les Variations pour Piano et pour Piano et Violon de Mozart" in *Bericht über den Internationalen Musikwissenschaftlichen Kongress—Wien Mozartjahr 1956* (Graz, 1958), p. [666]; BN. *Mercure de France,* Feb., 1762, p. 154. Although the title page of *Les Amusements* says "Avec Privilege du Roy," no royal privilege can be found.

Weckerlin wrote that he had found this melody as early as 1740 (J. B. Weckerlin, *Chansons Populaires du Pays de France* [Paris, 1903], vol. II, p. 36), BN; but Wallon disputes this.

In the 4th edition of *La Clé du Caveau* (Paris, ca. 1848), p. 245, there is a note that the melody is attributed to Campra and to Rameau; NYPL. No substantiation has been found for this statement. See, also, *Mitteilungen der Internationalen Stiftung Mozarteum,* Salzburg, June, 1959, p. [1]; JF.

[2] Köchel, p. 320. Deutsch-Oldman, *Mozart-Drucke,* p. 141.

[2A] H. C. Robbins Landon, *Beethoven* (New York, N.Y., 1970), p. 104, quoting Johann Wenzel Tomaschek.

The song came to be sung as *A B C D E F G* under the title *The School-master* which was copyrighted by C [*sic*] Bradlee, Boston, Feb. 4, 1834.[3] In the copyright deposit copy, the publisher's street address is Washington Street (without a street number, and without a front cover); LC (CDC) and JF.

The words, *Bah, Bah, a Black Sheep* appeared in print about 1744 in *Tommy Thumb's Pretty Song Book* (London?), vol. 2, p. 29;[3A] BM. The words and the above music were printed in A. H. Rosewig, (*Illustrated National*) *Nursery Songs and Games*, copyrighted Oct. 25, 1879,[3] by W. F. Shaw [Philadelphia], p. [9]; LC(CDC) and JF.

The words of *Twinkle, Twinkle, Little Star* were written by Jane Taylor and published in 1806 under the title *The Star* in her *Rhymes for the Nursery* (London, 1806), p. 10; BM. She was born in London in 1783, became a poetess, and died in Ongar, Essex, in 1824.[4]

The above music and words of *Twinkle, Twinkle, Little Star* were probably first printed together in *The Singing Master* [volume] No. III, *First Class Tune-Book* (London, 1838), Second Edition, p. [100]; NC[4A] and JF.

The words of *Ist das Nicht ein Schnitzelbank?*, a pointing game also known as *Hobelbank*, are indicated in a "Flugblatt" or pamphlet published about 1830 entitled *Vier Neue Lieder* (n.p.), no. 3, as "Das ist Klein und Das ist Gross," at Badische Landesbibliothek, Karlsruhe, Germany (50/A 1432), and in Ludwig Erk, *Neue Sammlung Deutscher Volkslieder* (Berlin, 1845), vol. I, part 3, nos. 45 and 46, each as "Ein Lied beim Pfänderspiel" ("A Song of a Forfeiture Game"), at FR. A "Schnitzelbank" or "Hobelbank" is a carpenter's bench. The music accompanying these words varies, but frequently is similar to the music quoted above.[5] A large chart of the *Schnitzelbank* pointing game, with music, words and pictures for pointing, published in 1935 in the Pennsylvania Dutch area, is at JF.

---

[3] Copyright records; LC.

[3A] Opie, p. 88. The other references cited by Opie either lack music or contain a different melody.

[4] *Dict. Nat. Biog.*, vol. 19, p. 420. Opie, p. 397.

[4A] Diana R. Tillson, New Canaan, Conn., called this printing to the attention of the author. *Twinkle, Twinkle, Little Star* was not included in the first edition of *The Singing Master* published in 1836 in which the preface was signed by W. E. Hickson; BM.

[5] Deutsches Volksliedarchiv, Freiburg, Germany, advised the author of the references in the above paragraph. See, also, "Das Lied von der Hobelbank" in *Zeitschrift für Volkskunder*, 1931, Neue Folge, vol. III (Berlin and Leipzig, 1932), p. 178; FR and NYPL.

Two Guitars

Двѣ Гитары За Стѣной (*Two Guitars Behind the Wall*), a Russian gypsy song, was first published about 1912 by two different Russian publishers, priority uncertain. In one, which states it won the 1911 Rome Grand Prize, the publisher is S. Ya. Yambor, Moscow, the no. is 558, the price 10 k, there is a photograph of a Russian Cossack on the front cover, the music is on pp. 2–3, and the back cover advertises nos. to 545. PUS. The text of the song as published by Yambor is a folklore variant of a poem by Apollon A. Grigoriyev, *Tzyganskaya Vengerka* (*Hungarian Gypsy*), which poem had been published for the first time in the periodical *Syn Otechestva* (*Son of Fatherland*), St. Petersburg, in 1857, nos. 44–49.[1]

The other Russian edition of the song was published about 1912 by Evterpa, St. Petersburg. Front cover has a photograph of a man with a guitar, the no. is 37, and the price is 10 k. m. on pp. 2–3. Back cover lists 40 songs. SSL.

The familiar pizzicato music was not part of the original *Two Guitars* as published in Russia, but rather an improvisation on *Two Guitars* which Harry Horlick used as the "theme song" for his A & P Gypsy Ensemble on the Atlantic & Pacific radio hour from 1922 to 1937. Horlick advises that this improvisation, and the balance of the improvisation, had been composed by Shasha Makarov, a Russian Czarist officer refugee, and himself while they were in Russia.[2] However, the improvisations were not published or copyrighted until Dec. 9, 1925,[3] when they were copyrighted under the title *Two Guitars* for orchestral score and the following day for piano, the publisher being Carl Fischer, Inc., Cooper Square, New York, N.Y. The plate number of the orchestral score is 23760-22 and the price $1.50. Front cover of the piano sheet music has drawings of two guitars and Russian gypsies, a photograph of Harry Horlick who is stated as the composer, mentions the publisher's Boston and Chicago addresses, and is brown and tan. m. on pp. 2–5. p.n. CC23761-4; Sheet Music Edition P.1512. Back cover adv *Motion..* Both at LC(CDC). Horlick was born in 1898 near Kiev, met Makarow in Tiflis in 1917 or 1918, came to the United States in 1921 and resides in New York City.

[1] Information from PUS.
[2] Information from Harry Horlick, New York City.
[3] Copyright records; LC.

Un Bel Dì—Madama Butterfly

Un bel dì, ve - dre - mo   le - var - si un fil di   fu - mo

m. Giacomo Puccini. w. L. Illica and G. Giacosa. The piano-vocal score of *Madama Butterfly*, in which *Un Bel Dì* (*One Fine Day*) appears, was deposited Feb. 6, 1904, with the Prefect of Milan, and two days later[1] at the Library of Congress, by G. Ricordi & C., Milan; latter copy has Jan., 1904, pressed on title page by seal of the publisher. First edition: Hard front cover is red, gray and black. Half-title page. Drawing of orange blossoms. Dedication to La Regina Elena. vb. Photograph of the composer. vb. Title page mentions John L. Long and David Belasco, lists the piano-vocal score at Fr. 15—Mk. 12, and the piano score at Fr. 10—Mk. 8, shows the publisher also at Rome, Naples, Palermo, Paris, London and Leipzig, and has a 1904 copyright claim. Copyright statements. Cast. Ars et Labor symbol, without words. Index. Drawing of butterflies. m. on pp. 1–403, *Un Bel Dì* on p. 214. p.n. 110000. p. [404] blank. Back cover has Ars et Labor symbol and words. LC(CDC, collation varies slightly—music pages engraved, not a commercial copy), SCR(17 B 15), BM* (date stamped April 22, 1904— collation varies slightly) and JF.†

Madama Butterfly was produced at Milan on Feb. 17, 1904, but withdrawn after one performance to enable Puccini to make drastic revisions for a new production at Brescia on May 28, 1904. The piano-vocal score was similarly revised, the next printing being designated "Nuova Edizione" and the music is on pp. 1–399. LC (copyright copy deposited May 9, 1904 —music pages engraved, not a commercial copy).

An early printing of the sheet music of *Un Bel Dì*, Solo di Butterfly, was published about Feb. 15, 1904,[2] with p.n. 110011; JF.

The copyright copy of the orchestral score of the opera was deposited at S. Cecilia, Rome, on July 3, 1907, and at the Library of Congress on July 5, 1907, by G. Ricordi & Co., Milan. First edition: Folio. Hard front cover is black and gray; while the composer is mentioned, the lyricists are not; there is a 1907 copyright claim; and the publisher is also shown at the cities mentioned in the piano-vocal score, plus Buenos Aires. No title page. m. on pp. 1–368, engraved. This aria is in vol. 2, p. 178. p.n. 111378. SCR

---

[1] Copyright records; UDP and LC. *MM*, Feb. 15, 1904, inside of back cover. See, generally, Hopkinson, *Puccini*, p. 24.

[2] *MM*, Feb. 15, 1904, p. 129.

and LC (both CDC), CI and JMM.[3] Engraved orchestral parts, designated "New edition," with plate number 111379, with a 1907 copyright claim, with covers, are at CI and MET*. Brief biographic information regarding the composer and lyricists appears above under *Musetta's Waltz*.

Valentine

Elle   a - vait   de   tout pe - tits pe - tons

© 1925 Francis Salabert. Copyright renewed. Used by permission.

m. H. Christiné. w. Albert Willemetz. Published Dec. 31, 1925,[1] by Éditions Francis Salabert, 35 Bd. des Capucines, 107 Avenue Victor-Hugo, Paris. Possible first edition: Folio. Front cover in red, white and blue, has a drawing of a woman with a very large head, a photograph of Maurice Chevalier, refers to the Revue *Paris Qui Chante*, the price is 4 fr., and the publisher is shown also at New York City. m. on pp. 2–3. p.n. 3787. Back cover adv. *Bouche.. - Avec..* BN(copyright copy deposited March 30, 1926). The orchestral parts with p.n. 3859 were deposited the same day, and the piano arrangement with p.n. 3924, June 2, 1926; both at BN (CDC).

Brief biographic information regarding Christiné and Willemetz appears above under *Petite Tonkinoise* and *Mon Homme*.

Valse Bleue

m. Alfred Margis. The earliest known copy of *Valse Bleue* was deposited at BM on May 17, 1900, by William Salabert, 106 bis Boulevard Péreire, Place Péreire, Paris, with the notation at the top of the front cover "11ᵉ Mille." The front cover is blue and white, has a drawing of a girl and a boy in a garden, refers to the Répertoire des Bals de l'Opéra et des Concerts du Jardin d'Acclimatation, has a dedication to Mademoiselle Jeanne Debruyère, lists six arrangements, this being for piano at 6 f., and mentions that Chappell & Co., Ltd., London, is the English agent. m. on pp. 2–7. p.n. W.S. 119. Back cover adv. *L'Ange.. - Valse..* BM(CDC).

Margis was born in 1874 in Colombes, Seine, France, became a com-

---

[3] The orchestral score was published in octavo in 1920 with p.n. 118378.

[1] Copyright records; LC.

poser, and died in 1913.[1]

Valse Triste—Sibelius

m. Jean Sibelius. *Valse Triste* appears to have been published first for piano by Helsingfors Nya Musikhandel (K. G. Fazer), Helsinki, and the following probable first edition was deposited June 24, 1904,[1] at LC: Front cover is a collective title front cover headed Jean Sibelius Kompositionen, has a photograph of the composer, lists many of his compositions, the first of which is *Andantino* (*Valse Triste* is listed for piano at 1.60) and the last of which is *Valse Triste* for orchestral score and parts without prices, Breitkopf & Härtel is shown at four cities, two Scandinavian publishers are mentioned and the colors are brown and white; no opus number. m. on pp. 2–7. p. 2 states that the music is from Arvid Järnefelt's Drama *Kuolema*. p.n. H.N.M. 401. Copyrighted 1904 by Breitkopf & Härtel and printed by it. Back cover adv. *Musikalier..* LC(CDC) and JF. Breitkopf & Härtel did not publish the piano arrangement until Aug., 1906;[2] an early edition with p.n. 2224 is at NYPL. The arrangement for piano four hands with p.n. 2273 was deposited June 29, 1907,[1] by the same publisher at LC.

A probable first printing of the orchestral score of *Valse Triste* was deposited Nov. 3, 1904,[1,3] by Breitkopf & Härtel, Leipzig, at LC: Front cover in blue and green refers to the publisher's Partitur-Bibliothek and mentions the Helsinki agent. vb. Title page mentions A. Järnefelt's Drama, *Kuolema*, lists three arrangements, the orchestral score at Mk. 3, the 10 orchestral parts at 30 Pf. each and the piano arrangement at Mk. 1. 60, the publisher is also shown at Brussels, London and New York, the Helsinki agent is mentioned, there is a 1904 copyright by the publisher, and the p.ns. are Part. B. 1853, Orch. B. 1704 and H.N.M. 401; no opus number. m. on pp. 2–11. p.n. Part. B. 1853. pp. [12] and [13] blank. Back cover adv. *Musikalier..* LC(CDC). Early printings of the orchestral parts published by Breitkopf & Härtel at about the same time[2] with p.n. Orch. B. 1704

[1] Letter from SACEM.

[1] Copyright records; LC. Hofmeister *Monatsbericht*, June, 1904, p. 311. Breitkopf & Härtel *Musik-Verlagsbericht*, Leipzig, 1904, p. 42, lists the Finnish edition of the piano arrangement; NYPL.

[2] Letter from Breitkopf & Härtel, Leipzig.

[3] Breitkopf & Härtel *Mitteilungen*, Leipzig, Jan., 1905, p. 3171, states that the orchestral score was published Nov.–Dec., 1904; NYPL.

are at CI, FLP and JF. As far as can be determined, Helsingfors Nya Musikhandel (K. G. Fazer), Helsinki, did not publish the orchestral score or parts
at this time.

This work was composed 1903. Brief biographic information regarding
Sibelius appears above under *Finlandia*.

The Very Thought of You

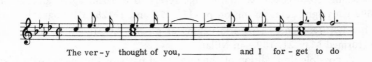

The ver - y   thought of you, _____   and I   for - get   to do

mw. Ray Noble. Published April 16, 1934,[1] by Campbell, Connelly & Co.,
Ltd., 11 Denmark Street, London W. C. 2. The copyright copies deposited
that day at BM and thereafter at LC are professional editions. Possible first
regular edition: Front cover has a photograph of Bertini and refers to his
band, the price is 6d, and the colors are black and white. m. on pp. 2–3.
p.n. 839. Back cover adv. *Rollin'.. - Aloma*. All the songs advertised were
published by June 14, 1934. BBC. Brief biographic information regarding
the composer appears above under *Goodnight Sweetheart*.

Vesti la Giubba—Pagliacci

Ri - di   Pa - gliac - cio,   sul tuo   a - mo-re in - fran - to!

mw. R. Leoncavallo. Copies of the piano-vocal score of *Pagliacci*, in which
Vesti la Giubba (*Put on the Motley*) appears, were deposited June 1, 1892,[1]
with the Prefect of Milan by Edoardo Sonzogno, Milan. The following
edition, of which copies were deposited Nov. 17, 1892, at S. Cecilia, Rome,
and the following day at the Library of Congress,[2] is probably the first edition: Front cover has a drawing of a clown and is red, black and brown.
Verso and next two pages blank. Half-title page. vb. Title page refers to a

---

[1] Copyright records; LC.

[1] Copyright records; UDP.
[2] Copyright records; LC.

Berlin agent and has an 1892 copyright date. Additional copyright statements. Dedication to the memory of the composer's parents. vb. Cast and
Index. vb. m. on pp. 1–204, *Vesti la Giubba* on p. 128. p.n. E. 654 S. Next
two pages and inside of back cover blank. Outside of back cover has the
price: L. 12. SCR (CDC-101. D. 22), LC (CDC), BM (purchased July 13,
1893) and JF.

The orchestral score of *Pagliacci* was deposited Nov. 18, 1892, with
the Library of Congress by the same publisher.[2] Probable first edition: Folio.
Makeshift front cover. vb. Title page refers to a Berlin agent and has an
1892 copyright date. vb. m. on pp. [1]–278 and 1–128, a lithographing of
a handwritten score. This aria begins at p. 270. LC(CDC). *Pagliacci* was
performed May 21, 1892, in Milan.

A possible first edition of the orchestral parts of the opera, with plate
number E.644 S., lithographed, without a copyright claim on each part,
and with covers, may also have been published in 1892; CI and MET*.

Vesti la Giubba, sung by Enrico Caruso and recorded on Feb. 1, 1904,[3]
was the first classical record to sell a million copies. Victor record 81032,
at NYPL and JF. Ruggiero Leoncavallo was born in Naples in 1858 and
died at Montecatini, near Florence, in 1919.

La Vie en Rose

Quand il me prend dans ses bras, il me par-le tout bas, je vois la vie en ro-se

© 1947 Éditions Arpège Musicales. © 1950 Harms, Inc. Used by permission.

m. Louiguy. w. Edith Piaf. Published Aug. 4, 1946, by Arpège Éditions
Musicales, Paris IVᵉ, according to a letter from Paul Beuscher, the present
publisher. The publication date was Jan. 2, 1947, according to the copyright
records at LC. A professional edition was deposited Sept. 11, 1947, at LC
with a 1946 copyright claim, the publisher's street address is 3 Rue du Pas
de la Mule, the p.n. is E.A. 100 and the printer is Michel Dillard, Paris. A
professional edition with a later address (25 Boulevard Beaumarchais) was
deposited at BN on Oct. 20, 1950. No regular edition has been found with
the publisher at the earlier address. Possible first regular edition: The publisher on the front cover is Éditions Arpège, the address on p. [2] is 25 Bd.
Beaumarchais, Paris (4ᵉ), and the printer is Michel Dillard, Paris. Front
cover has photographs of Edith Piaf and Marianne Michel, and is red and

---

[3] Information from RCA Victor Listing Department, New York, N.Y.

white. m. on pp. [2]–[3], with a 1946 copyright claim. p.n. E.A. 100. Back cover adv. *Tous les Succès en Vogue* [no. 1] and no. 2 (dates of publication not known). JF. The song was subsequently published by Paul Beuscher-Arpège.

Louiguy is a pseudonym of Luis Guglielmi, a composer, who was born in 1916 in Barcelona and lives in Paris under the French name Louis Guillaume.[1] Edith Piaf is a pseudonym of Edith Giovanna Gassion, a chanteuse also known as Môme Piaf, who was born in 1915 in Paris and died in France in 1963.[2]

Vienna Dreams—Wien, Du Stadt Meiner Träume

Wien, Wien nur du al - lein

mw. Rudolf Sieczyński. *Wien, Du Stadt Meiner Träume* was published April–May, 1914,[1] by Adolf Robitschek, 14 Graben, Vienna I, and 16 Salomonstr., Leipzig. Possible first edition: Front cover has a drawing of Vienna by night, mentions that the song is a Wienerlied and the composer's op. 1, lists five arrangements of which this, the piano-vocal edition, is M. 1. 50, and the colors are blue, tan and white. p. [2] adv. works by Ascher. m. on pp. 3–5. p.n. 5031. Dedication to Frau Lisl Breycha. Back cover adv. works by Ehrich. Included is an extra leaf with words and music for singer and p.n. 5031a; verso adv. Henriquez.. - Wagner.. All advertised works were published by June, 1914. SB, LC (copyright copy deposited Oct. 31, 1914) and JF. The melody was set to English lyrics by Irving Caesar in 1923 under the title *Someone Will Make You Smile* from the show *Poppy*. *Vienna Dreams* is the name of the more commonly known 1937 version with English lyrics also by Irving Caesar. †

Sieczyński was born in Vienna in 1879, became a composer and lyricist and died in Vienna in 1952.[2]

---

[1] Information from SACEM and ASCAP.
[2] *The New York Times*, Jan. 22, 1961, magazine sec., p. 9. Obituary, *The New York Times*, Oct. 12, 1963.

[1] Hofmeister *Monatsbericht*, April, 1914, p. 97. May 15, 1914, according to copyright records at LC.
[2] *MA*, June, 1952, p. 28.

Vienna Girls

m. C. M. Ziehrer. *Weaner Mad'ln*, op. 388, was published on Nov. 4, 1887,[1] for piano by Ludwig Doblinger (Bernhard Herzmansky), 10 Dorotheergasse, Vienna I. Probable first edition: Front cover has a drawing of three girls being looked at by two men, lists four arrangements, this for piano at 90 Kr./Mk. 1. 80 Pf., but the other three without prices, mentions a Leipzig agent and is dark green and white. m. on pp. 2–9. p.n. 570. Back cover adv. dance music, Ziehrer's up to op. 371. SB and JF.

A possible first edition of the orchestral parts, published on Dec. 12, 1887,[1] with plate number 572, without front cover, is at JF. The first performance was on Oct. 30, 1887.[1] Carl Michael Ziehrer, a composer and band leader, was born in Vienna in 1843 and died there in 1922.[2]

Vienna Life

m. Johann Strauss. *Wiener Blut*, Walzer, op. 354, was published for piano about July, 1873,[1] by C. A. Spina's Nachfolger (Friedrich Schreiber), Vienna. Probable first edition: Front cover has eight drawings of Viennese scenes, an incorrect p.n. 22,459 (corrected in later editions to 22,959), the prices are 80 Nkr./15 Ngr., there is reference to a Petersburg agent and the colors are brown and white. vb. m. on pp. 3–11, engraved. p.n. C. S. 22,959. Back cover blank. No reference on the front cover to other arrangements, and no reference at the bottom of p. 3 to F. Hahn. JF. An identical edition, but mentioning F. Hahn (whose name appears in other later editions), is at SB and JF. An edition published by Friedrich Schreiber (vormals C. A. Spina) with a dedication to Christian IX, King of Denmark, listing three arrangements and a different black and white front cover, and also mentioning F. Hahn, seems later; JF.

[1] Max Schönherr, *Carl Michael Ziehrer* (Vienna, 1974), pp. 326–327; NYPL. Hofmeister *Monatsbericht*, Dec., 1887, pp. 583 (piano), and March, 1888, p. 92 (orchestra).

[2] *Riemann*, p. 967.

[1] Hofmeister *Monatsbericht*, July, 1873, p. 199. Weinmann, *Strauss*, p. 100, says Aug., 1873.

The orchestral parts of *Wiener Blut* were published about Oct., 1873;[2] an engraved set with p.n. C.S. 23,109 but lacking covers and imprint is at KH*. The operetta *Wiener Blut* was assembled many years later by Adolf Müller the younger with Strauss's permission, using various Strauss dances, and was first performed on Oct. 25, 1899. Brief biographic information regarding the composer appears above under *Artist's Life.*

Vilikens and His Dinah—(Sweet Betsey from Pike)

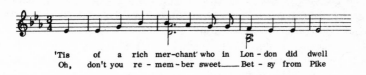

'Tis   of   a   rich mer–chant' who   in   Lon - don   did   dwell
Oh,   don't you   re - mem - ber sweet___ Bet - sy from Pike

The first known printing of this song was on Nov. 11, 1853,[1] by Campbell, Ransford & Co., 53 New Bond St., London, under the title *Vilikens and His Dinah.* Possible first edition: Front cover has a drawing of F. Robson who, it is stated, sings the song in the musical farce of *The Wandering Minstrel* and is tan, black and white.[2] p. [2] blank. m. on pp. [1]–4 (actually [3]–6). p.n. 583. Additional words on page [7]. Back cover blank. JF.

Other known early editions were published by: (a) J. Layzell, 14 Hand Court, High Holborn, London, deposited at BM June 12, 1854, with the first word of the title spelled "Villikens," at BM(CDC); (b) B. Williams, 11 Paternoster Row, London (ca. 1847–1868),[3] the first word of the title on p. 2 spelled "Villikins," at JF; (c) G. H. Davidson, Peter's Hill, Doctors' Commons, London (ca. 1847–1860),[3] the first word of the title on the first music page spelled "Willikind," the last page referring (tongue-in-cheek) to the "original Chaldean MSS. In the British Museum," three variants at JF; (d) Horace Waters, 333 Broadway, New York, N.Y., copyrighted Aug. 26, 1854,[4] at LC and JF; (e) C. Sheard, Musical Bouquet Office, 192 High Holborn, London, deposited at BM on Oct. 2, 1855—also at ML and JF; (f) in Sam Cowell, *New Universal Illustrated Pocket Songster* (London, n.d.), words only at p. 12, deposited Feb. 12,

---

[2] Hofmeister *Monatsbericht*, Oct., 1873, p. 303; LC.

[1] According to the entry at Stationers' Hall on Nov. 15, 1853.

[2] The particular copy is trimmed; on the basis of the "7th edition," at JF, there was probably a price of 2/ at the bottom of the front cover.

[3] Dates are per Humphries-Smith.

[4] Copyright records: LC.

1856, at BM; (g) in Sam Cowell, *The Comic Vocalist* (Glasgow, ca. 1861), words only at p. 13, ML; (h) in Sam Cowell, *120 Comic Songs*, ca. 1850, no copy of which has been located;[5] (i) by Miller and Beacham, Baltimore, with p.n. 2756, late 1854–1855, at LL; and (j) by J. E. Boswell, Baltimore, without p.n. and difficult to date, at LL.

Considerable secondary literature exists about this song, pointing out that it had two forms, a tragic ballad, *William and Diana*, and the comic parody *Vilikens and His Dinah*,[6] although no substantiating evidence is shown. In one case it was said that the former was printed by James Catnach in broadside—presumably, words only—but no copy has been located. In any event, no printing of *William and Diana* has been found prior to those described above.

Stephen C. Foster wrote satirical words to this melody during the 1856 Presidential campaign, entitled *The Great Baby Show; or, The Abolition Show*, which were published in the Sept. 26, 1856, issue of the *Pittsburgh Post*; microfilm at Carnegie Library of Pittsburgh.[7]

The first known printing of *Sweet Betsey from Pike* was in *Put's Golden Songster* (San Francisco, 1858), copyrighted Aug. 23, 1858,[4] which has the complete words, without music, but specified to the "Air, *Villikins and His Dinah*," p. 50; NYPL and JF. As the copyright is in the name of John A. Stone and the introduction by the "Author" indicates that the words are original, it is believed that John A. Stone is the author of the new words. Stone had crossed the plains from Pike County, Mo., in 1849–1850, and had a small group of singers, the Sierra Nevada Rangers, which toured the mining camps. He died in 1864 and is buried in Greenwood, Neb.[8]

La Violetera

Lle-ve-lo̱us-te se-ño - ri - to —— no va-le más que̱un re-al ——

[5] Cited in A. G. Gilchrist, "Three Folk-Ballads and Tunes from Scarce Printed Sources," in *JFSS*, 1929, p. 146.

[6] Prof. G. L. Kittredge in *JAF*, 1916, p. 190; Belden, p. 147; and *JAF*, 1922, p. 419. The suggestion that a John Parry may have composed this song seems unlikely. This author also sees no real similarity between the melody of the song, *Peggie is over Ye Sie*, quoted in William Dauney, *Ancient Scotish* [*sic*] *Melodies*, based upon the Skene Manuscript (Edinburgh, 1838), p. 217, at NYPL, and the melody of *Vilikens and His Dinah*.

[7] The reference to *Villikins and His Dinah*, in Fuld, *Foster*, p. 13, under *Hurrah for the Bigler Boys*, should be to *De Camptown Races*.

[8] Louise Pound, *Nebraska Folklore* (Lincoln, Neb., 1959), p. 176; NYPL.

m. José Padilla. w. Eduardo Montesinos. The copyright copy of *La Violetera*, deposited in 1918[1] as no. 64,374 at the Biblioteca Nacional, Madrid, lacks covers. m. on pp. 1–4 (actually 3–6). p.n. 20409. Dedication to Doctor Batalla. 1918 copyright notice. The publisher, Union Musical Española, is shown on p. 1 at four cities. BNM. Possible first complete edition: In addition to the foregoing, the front cover mentions that the song is the creation of Raquel Meller, has a photograph presumably of her, gives the publisher's Madrid address as 34 Carrera de San Jerónimo and refers to five branch offices, has the price of Ptas. 2.50 and is violet, brown and white. pp. [2] and [7] blank. Back cover adv. Alonso - Villar. JF. An edition published 1925 or later[2] with the publisher at 26 Carrera de San Jerónimo is at MBM. The earlier Spanish edition is believed to precede the French edition published by Editions Francis Salabert, as the latter acknowledges it was published by arrangement with Union Musical Española; JF.

Brief biographic information regarding Padilla appears above under *El Relicario*. Eduardo Montesinos López was born in Seville, Spain, in 1868, and died in 1929.[3]

Vissi d'Arte—Tosca

Vis - si   d'ar - te,   vis - si   d'a - mo - re

m. Giacomo Puccini. w. V. Sardou, L. Illica and G. Giacosa. Copyright copies of the piano-vocal score of *Tosca* were deposited on Nov. 28, 1899, with the Prefect of Milan (this copy so dated now at S. Cecilia Library, Rome), and on the following day at the Library of Congress, Washington, D.C., by G. Ricordi & C., Milan.[1] First edition: Half-title page. Next two pages blank. Photograph of composer. Title page states that the piano arrangement is by Carlo Carignani, gives the price as 15 Fr., contains an 1899 copyright notice and says that it is printed in Italy; no reference to date of first performance. Verso has legal notices. Cast. vb. Index. Verso has publisher's emblem. m. on pp. 1–310; *Vissi d'Arte* is on p. 222. p.n. 103050.

---

[1] Copyright records; RG.

[2] See *El Relicario*, above, footnote 1.

[3] Information from PAU and SGAE.

[1] Hopkinson, *Puccini*, p. 20. Copyright records; UDP. *GMM*, Dec. 21, 1899, p. 6.† The piano score of the opera was published Dec. 21, 1899, according to copyright records, UDP.

LC (covers in gray and black; music pages engraved; hand-sealed on title page Nov., 1899); SCR (hand-sealed Nov., 1899); and JF (covers in gold, blue and white; music pages lithographed; hand-sealed Jan., 1890). It is almost certain that commercial copies were not engraved. An early printing of the sheet music of this aria, entitled *Preghiera di Tosca, Vissi d'Arte, Vissi d'Amore,* has plate number 103314;† JF.

Probable first edition of orchestral score: No front cover, title page or preliminary pages. Folio. Engraved. States copyrighted 1899 by G. Ricordi & Co. m. on pp. 1–300, *Vissi d'Arte* at p. 218. p.n. 103378. CI, JMM and JF.‡ A generally similar lithographed edition mentioning a New York branch of the publisher was issued in 1911 or later; JMM.[2]

The engraving of the orchestral and choral parts commenced, according to the Ricordi *Libroni,* on Sept. 13, 1899, with plate numbers 103053–103059; possible first printings, engraved and with covers, are at the Bayerische Staatsoper, Munich. *Tosca* was performed in Rome on Jan. 14, 1900. Brief biographic information regarding Puccini, Illica and Giacosa appears above under *Musetta's Waltz.* Victorien Sardou, a French dramatist, was born in Paris in 1831 and died there in 1908.

Vive la Compagnie

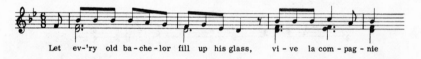

Let ev-'ry old ba-che-lor fill up his glass, vi-ve la com-pag-nie

The words and/or music of this French-titled song have been found published in Germany, England and the United States—but not in France![1] The earliest known printing of a substantial portion of the words is in an 1818 edition of *Neues Liederbuch für Frohe Gesellschaften* (2nd ed., Nurnberg, 1818), p. 35, in the refrain of a song the first line of which is *Ich Nehm' Mein Gläschen in die Hand;* FR. The first edition of this book has not been located.

The first printing of the music, together with much of the words, was in 1838 in two companion volumes, one with the music, *Vollständiges Melodienbuch oder Vollständige Sammlung der Melodien,* and the other with the words, *Allgemeines Deutsches Liederbuch oder Vollständige Sammlung der Bekannten und Beliebten Deutschen Lieder und Volksgesänge,* both by Guido Reinhold, and published in Leipzig, 1838. The title of the song is again *Ich Nehm' Mein Gläschen in die Hand,* and is on p.

---

[2] See page 68, *supra.* The orchestral score was published in octavo in 1924 with p.n. 119160.

[1] "Cette chanson ne nous est pas connue." Simone Wallon, BN.

85 of the former and p. 130 of the latter. Both at FR.

The melody unquestionably bears a considerable similarity to the English *Lincolnshire Poacher* which was published in 1840 in William Chappell, *A Collection of National English Airs* (London, 1840), vol. 1, p. 32; NYPL. It has been said that the *Lincolnshire Poacher* was printed at York about 1776 under the title *Lincolnshire*,[2] but no such edition has been found. The melody is also known as *The Gallant Poacher*.[3] The melody also bears a similarity to [*Young*] *Bucks A-Hunting Go*, sung in Cheshire and Shropshire, England, between 1820–1830, and quoted in Frank Kidson, *Traditional Tunes* (Oxford, 1891), p. 143; NYPL.[4]

Vive la Compagnie in its presently known form was copyrighted April 19, 1844,[5] by F. D. Benteen, 137 Baltimore St., Baltimore. Probable first edition: Front cover refers to the Maryland Cadet's [*sic*] Glee Club and the price is 25 Cts. p. [2] blank. m. on pp. 3–5. p.n. 326. Back cover blank. Engraved. JF.

Voices of Spring

m. Johann Strauss. *Frühlingsstimmen*, op. 410, was published March 9, 1883,[1] for piano by Aug. Cranz, Hamburg. Possible first edition: Front cover has a drawing of a spring scene in the country, one of the two birds is sitting on the "W" in "Walzer," the colors are brown and white, words are stated to be by Richard Genée, four arrangements are listed but only the piano arrangement has a price, namely Fl. 1.20 Kr./ Mk. 2, and Brussels and Vienna agents are listed followed by drawings of medals. p. [2] blank. m. on pp. 3–11. p.n. C. 25854. Back cover adv. waltzes and marches of various composers, Johann Strauss up to op. 410. SB and JF. Another possible first edition has a slightly different front cover; for instance, one of the two birds is sitting on a branch almost an inch above the "W" in "Walzer" and there are no drawings of medals on the front

---

[2] Robert Bell, *Ancient Poems, Ballads and Songs* (London, 1857), p. 216; LC.

[3] Baring-Gould, vol. III, p. 28. See, also, Chappell, p. 732, and *JFSS*, 1901, p. 118.

[4] Harold Barlow, New York City, advised the author of this similarity.

[5] Copyright records; LC.

[1] According to the entry at Stationers' Hall on June 1, 1883. Hofmeister *Monatsbericht*, May, 1883 p. 95. Weinmann, p. 108, gives the month as May, no doubt on the basis of the Hofmeister listing.

cover. There is a French title, *Rêves de Printemps*, on p. 3. The back cover adv. *Myrthenblüthen.. - Schön..*, all published 1883 or earlier. JF. The orchestral parts were published at about the same time[2] at Mk. 8.80. A possible first edition with p.n. 25865 and advertising works of Johann Strauss up to op. 410 is at SB. This composition was composed as a coloratura waltz song for the soprano Bianca Bianchi (Bertha Schwarz), who apparently first sang it at the Theater an der Wien on March 1, 1883, however, the piano-vocal arrangement was not published until about May, 1883.[3] Brief biographic information regarding Strauss appears above under *Artist's Life.*

Die Wacht am Rhein

Es braust ein Ruf, wie Don-ner-hall, wie Schwert-ge-klirr und Wo-gen-prall

m. Carl Wilhelm. w. Max Schneckenburger. The words of *Die Wacht am Rhein* were written in the last week of Nov., 1840, as a patriotic poem when the left bank of the Rhine River seemed threatened by the French, and at the poet's request were set to since discarded music by J. Mendel of Berne the following week.[1] The words and this music were published in Dec., 1840, under the title *Die Wacht am Rhein* by J. F. J. Daly, Berne, Chur and Leipzig, on three lithographed pages; while the composer's name appears, the poet's name is abbreviated. No copy has been found.

The common music of *Die Wacht am Rhein*, together with the words, were first published about Nov., 1854,[2] in the 9th vol. of Wilhelm Greef, *Männerlieder, alte und neue, für Freunde des mehrstimmigen Männergesanges* (Essen, 1854), p. 3; LS.

The song became particularly famous during the Franco-Prussian War of 1870–1871 and the composer was awarded an annual pension for it. Wilhelm was born in Schmelkalden in 1815, became a conductor and died in Schmelkalden in 1873.[3] Schneckenburger was born in Thalheim, Württemberg, in 1819, became a businessman and died in 1849.[1]

[2] Hofmeister *Monatsbericht*, May, 1883, p. 81.

[3] Information from Andrew Lamb, Littlehampton, West Sussex, England. Weinmann, p. 108.

[1] Georg Scherer and Franz Lippersheide, *Die Wacht am Rhein* (Berlin, 1871), p. 14; LC.

[2] Hofmeister *Monatsbericht*, Nov., 1854, p. 652; BM.

[3] *Grove's*, vol. 9, p. 296.

Wait for the Wagon

Wait   for   the   wag - on,   wait   for   the   wag - on

The music and words in the earliest printing of *Wait for the Wagon* are considerable variants from the traditional song. This edition was published by Wm. T. Mayo, 5 Camp St., New Orleans; the music is attributed to Wiesenthal and the words to a Lady. There is an 1850 copyright notice although the copy was not deposited until Jan. 14, 1851. pp. [1] and [4] blank. m. on pp. [2] and [3]. Engraved. LC(CDC).

The next two printings have the traditional music and words and describe the song as an "Ethiopian Song." The first, copyrighted May 24, 1851,[1] was published by F. D. Benteen, Baltimore, arranged by Geo. P. Knauff, the price is 25 cts., there is a New Orleans agent, p. [2] is blank, the music is on pp. 3–5, the p.n. is 2169, the back cover is blank, and all pages are engraved. LC (not CDC) and JF. The second, copyrighted Sept. 13, 1851,[1] was published by James E. Boswell, Baltimore, and arranged by W. Loftin Hargrave; JF.

Describing the song as "for the South West," an edition published by Peters, Webb & Co., Louisville, Ky., has a different melody and an 1851 copyright notice. JF. Another edition describes the song as a "Song of the Western Emigrant" and was published by Balmer & Weber, St. Louis; this edition has both a different melody and different words and an 1851 copyright notice. JF. There is no entry in the copyright records now at LC for the former, and copyright records are not available for Missouri for 1851.

Of three known English editions, one describes the song as a "popular Yankee Song" (published by B. Williams, London, ca. 1847–1869);[2] another states it is a Popular Melody sung by Christy's Minstrels (published by A. W. Hammond, London, late Jullien & Co., after ca. 1858);[2] and the third was published by C. Sheard, London, after 1855[2]—all at JF.

Illustrating a Studebaker Wagon, an attractive edition of *Wait for the Wagon!* was published in 1884 with the compliments of The Studebaker Bros. Manufacturing Co., South Bend, Ind. (later, the automobile manufacturing company). JF.

---

[1] Copyright records; LC.
[2] Dates are per Humphries-Smith.

It seems likely from the above that *Wait for the Wagon* had an Ethiopian or minstrel origin. It has been suggested that R. Bishop Buckley, an Englishman born about 1810 who came to the United States and organized Buckley's Minstrels in 1843, was the composer of the music of the song. Buckley died in Quincy, Mass., in 1867.[3]

Wait 'till the Sun Shines, Nellie

m. Harry von Tilzer. w. Andrew B. Sterling. Copyrighted March 31, 1905,[1] by Harry von Tilzer Music Publishing Co., 37 W. 28th St., New York, N.Y. Copyright deposit copy at LC is a professional edition. Possible first regular edition: Front cover has a drawing of a couple holding hands, photographs of the composer and Master Willie Tilden, shows the publisher also at Chicago, "Frisco" and London, and is blue, pink and white. p. [2] adv. *Just..* m. on pp. 3–5. Back cover adv. *Down..* Both advertised songs were copyrighted by Jan. 3, 1905. JF.

The title was suggested to von Tilzer when he overheard a honeymooner consoling his wife because rain had prevented their excursion to Coney Island, New York.[2] Brief biographic information regarding the composer appears above under *I Want a Girl*. Sterling, a lyricist, was born in New York City in 1874 and died in Stamford, Conn., in 1955.[3]

Waltz, op. 39, no. 15—Brahms

---

[3] Reddall, p. 390.

[1] Copyright records; LC. See, generally, Geller, p. 187.

[2] "Voice of Broadway" in *New York Journal American*, Aug. 18, 1949, p. 13; NYPL.

[3] Obituary, *New York Herald Tribune*, Aug. 12, 1955.

m. Johannes Brahms. *Walzer für das Pianoforte zu vier Händen*, op. 39, was published about the first week of Sept., 1866,[1] by J. Rieter-Biedermann, Leipzig and Winterthur. Three variants have been found, priority unknown, one of which may be the first edition. In all, the title page has a dedication to Dr. Eduard Hanslick, the price is 1 Thlr. 15 Ngr., the pages are not engraved, and there is a brown border. m. on pp. 2–33, *Waltz* no. 15 on p. 30. p.n. 470. p. [34] blank. In one variant, at GM, the title page shows agents at Amsterdam, Vienna, London and Paris; and there is a reference to Röder at the bottom of p. 2; there is also a green and black front cover. In the second variant, at SB, the title page shows agents at Toulouse and Milan and there is no reference to Röder. The third variant, at JF, shows an agent at Toulouse and there is no reference to Röder.

The *Waltzes* were composed in 1865. Brief biographic information regarding Brahms appears above under his *Concerto for Piano no. 1*.

Waltz, op. 34, no. 2—Chopin

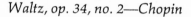

m. Fréd. Chopin. No. 2 of *Trois Valses Brillantes* for piano, op. 34, probably was published in four different editions within a few days of each other, or even possibly on the same day, namely, Dec. 1, 1838. An *Album des Pianistes*, containing this *Waltz*, published by Maurice Schlesinger, 97 Rue de Richelieu, Paris, was advertised Nov. 15, 1838, to appear Dec. 1, 1838.[1] AT and Robert F. Commagère, Los Angeles. Chopin was annoyed by the inclusion of his *Waltzes* in this *Album*.[2]

The French sheet music edition of this *Waltz* was deposited Jan., 1839,[3] at the Conservatoire, Paris. First edition: Front cover has a dedication to Madame la Baronne E. d'Ivry, the price is 6 f., and there are Leipzig and London agents. m. on pp. 2–9. p.n. 2716. Back cover blank.

[1] *Brahms Briefwechsel*, pp. 131–132. Deutsch, *Brahms*, p. 139. *Leipziger Allgemeine Musikalische Zeitung*, Sept. 12, 1866, p. 37; NYPL. Hofmeister *Monatsbericht*, Nov., 1866, p. 165. Hofmann, *Brahms*, p. 83, preferring the first variant.

[1] *RGM*, p. 472, and again Nov. 25, 1838, p. 480. Brown, p. 115, is misleading in indicating that the publication was to take place on Nov. 15, 1838. The *Album* was reviewed in the Dec. 23, 1838, issue, p. 521. See, in general, *Chopin Works*, vol. IX, p. 123.

[2] Brown, p. 116.

[3] *RGM*, Jan. 6, 1839, p. 8.

Engraved. COP(CDC) and JF (also has front wrapper in black and rose).

The English sheet music edition was entered at Stationers' Hall on Dec. 1, 1838, by Wessel & Co., Frith Street,[4] Soho Square, London. Possible first edition: the *Waltzes* are described as "Grandes" Valses, the edition is no. (96, in ink) of Le Pianiste Moderne, the price is 3/, the address of the publisher is 67 Frith Street, Soho Square, and there is a reference to the Paris and Leipzig agents. vb. Page B advertises a Catalogue of the publisher, his address on this page being the earlier address of 6 Frith Street. m. on pp. 2–9, the dedicatee's middle initial being "G." p. 9 also mentions the publisher's earlier address and Chopin's *Mazurkas*. p.n. 2281. Back cover blank. Engraved (except page B). JF.

The German sheet music edition was published about Dec., 1838,[5] by Breitkopf & Härtel, Leipzig. Probable first edition: Front cover has the price of **14 Gr.** and refers to the Paris and London agents. vb. m. on pp. 3–9. p.n. 6033. Back cover blank. Engraved. AVH. The *Waltz* was composed in 1831. Brief biographic information regarding Chopin appears above under his *Etude.*

Waltz, op. 64, no. 1—Chopin

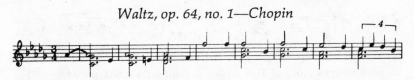

m. Fréd. Chopin. No. 1 of *3 Valses*, op. 64, for piano was published shortly after Oct. 17, 1847,[1] by Brandus et Cie., Maison Mce. Schlesinger Successeurs, 97 Rue Richelieu, Paris. Possible first edition: Front cover has a dedication to Madame la Comtesse Delphine Potocka, the price is 5 f., and there is reference to Breitkopf & Härtel, Leipzig, and Jullien et Cie., London. Next two pages blank. m. on pp. 2–5 (actually 4–7). p.n. 4743 (1). Back cover blank. Engraved. COP(CDC), BN and JF.†

The *Trois Valses* as a set were published about Nov. 3, 1847,[2] by

---

[4] Unfortunately, the entry at Stationers' Hall gives no street number.

[5] Hofmeister *Monatsbericht*, Dec., 1838, p. 182. "Nächstens Erschienen" ("To appear very soon"); AMZ, Nov. 21, 1838, p. 792.

---

[1] RGM, Oct. 17, 1847, p. 344, saying the *Waltzes* will appear immediately. They were, however, not entered for Dépôt Légal, at Archives, until Feb. 12, 1848, and the copyright deposit copy at COP, Acp 2720(1), is Feb., 1848; same edition, COP Acp 2708(1)—1848 9bre (November). See, in general, *Chopin Works*, vol. IX, p. 125.

[2] AMZ, Nov. 3, 1847, p. 765, with prices. Hofmeister *Monatsbericht*, Dec., 1847, p. 194. Brown, p. 160, also gives Nov., 1847. Niecks, vol. II, p. 356, states Sept., 1847, without indicating his authority, perhaps AMZ, Sept. 8, 1847, p. 623, announcing publication but without prices.

Breitkopf & Härtel, Leipzig. Curiously, there were two completely different printings; either may be the first edition, as it has been impossible for this author to establish priority. In both, the front cover gives the price as 1 Thlr. and mentions the Paris agent; vb; half-title page; m. on pp. 4–19, no. 1 on p. 4; p.n. 7721; engraved throughout; and back cover blank. There are a number of textual and musical differences between the two editions: for example, in one, at ONB and JF, the last line of the front cover refers to registration in the Archives of the Union; in the other,[2A] at JF, the last line of the front cover is "7721." The separate German printing of the first *Waltz* has plate number 7715 but was apparently first published about Aug., 1849;[3] AVH and JF.

While Jullien et Cie., London, is mentioned in the Brandus edition described above, no publication of the *Waltz* by Jullien & Co. has been found, and it is probable that there was none.[4] An edition by Cramer & Beale, London, was published about April 29, 1848,[5] at AT, and an edition published by Wessel & Co., London, was deposited at BM on Sept. 20, 1848. This *Waltz*, known as the *Minute Waltz*, was composed in 1846–1847. Brief biographic information regarding Chopin appears above under his *Etude*.

Waltz of the Flowers—Nutcracker Ballet

m. P. Tchaikovsky. Щелкунчикъ, or *Casse-Noisette*, op. 71, in which the above Вальсъ Цвѣтовъ, or *Valse des Fleurs* or *Waltz of the Flowers*, appears, was published in orchestral score about July, 1892,[1] by P. Jurgenson, Moscow. Probable first edition of the orchestral score of the entire

---

[2A] Discovered by Richard Macnutt, Tunbridge Wells, Kent, England.

[3] Hofmeister *Monatsbericht*, Aug., 1849, p. 86; not in Hofmeister *Monatsbericht* before then. Not in *AMZ*, 1847–8 (*AMZ* was not published in 1849); the piano four-hand arrangement of the separate *Waltzes* was advertised in *AMZ*, Aug. 30, 1848, p. 575.

[4] Brown, pp. 158 and 160.

[5] *MW*, April 29, 1848, p. 288.

---

[1] Dombayev, p. 10, says, merely, 1892. Hofmeister *Monatsbericht*, July, 1892, p. 243 lists the Rahter, Hamburg, orchestral score of the *Suite*. The German edition was printed by P. Jurgenson in Moscow; HU and NYPL. As stated in the text above, the *Ballet* and *Suite* were published by Jurgenson at about the same time. Early Rahter printings of the *Suite* are at CI and FLP.

Ballet: Front cover in Russian is red and tan. vb. Two blank pages. Title page in French, black and white and lists five arrangements, this at 150 Rbl. and 600 frs. (the others being score and parts of the overture, a piano arrangement and a simplified piano arrangement, the latter two without French prices); agents are J. Jurgenson in St. Petersburg, G. Sennewald in Warsaw, W. Goltz & Co. in Riga, **Mackar & Noël** in Paris and D. Rahter in Leipzig. vb. m. on pp. 3–511, the *Waltz* commencing at p. 385. p.ns. 17668–17688 xv. Two blank pages. Inside and outside of back cover blank. KT and SSL. Copies at LC, LPL and MC are identical except they lack blank pages and back cover. No early printing of the orchestral parts of the *Ballet* has been found. An early piano arrangement, with p.n. 17669, is at BM.

The *Nutcracker* was completed April 4, 1892, and performed as a ballet on Dec. 18, 1892, in St. Petersburg. While the *Suite* from the *Ballet* is said to have been completed Feb. 21, 1892, and was performed on March 19, 1892, in St. Petersburg, a letter from Tchaikovsky to Jurgenson and the reply indicate that the *Ballet* and the *Suite* were published at about the same time.[2]

Probable first edition of Jurgenson's orchestral score of the *Сюита*, or *Suite*, from the *Ballet:* Front cover is in Russian in light and dark blue. vb. Title page in French, blue and white and lists only this score at 6 Rbl. and the orchestral parts at 10 Rbl. The opus number is 71a. The agents are the same as for the entire *Ballet*. vb. m. on pp. 3–119. p.n. 17668 (same as orchestral score of the *Ballet!*). p. [120] and inside of back cover blank. Outside of back cover lists the composer's *Oeuvres*, including four volumes of his complete works.[3] SSL, and without covers at COL. The probable first edition of the orchestral parts of the *Suite* has the same title page as above and p.n. 17671; COP (lacks covers).

A possible first printing of the *Valse des Fleurs* for piano, with a front cover in Russian and French and listing numbers from the *Ballet*, has p.n. 17795; JF. The literary basis of the *Ballet* was E. T. A. Hoffmann's children's story of *The Nutcracker and the Mouse King* of which Alexander Dumas had made a French version. Brief biographic information regarding Tchaikovsky appears above under his *Chant sans Paroles*.

[2] Dombayev, p. 42; П. И. Чайковский, *Переписка с П. И. Юргенсоном* (Moscow, 1952), vol. 2, nos. 369 and 373 (O.S.); SSL.

[3] SSL advises that Jurgenson began to publish the complete works of Tchaikovsky before the latter died in 1893.

Waltz, A Waltz Dream—Oscar Straus

m. Oscar Straus. w. Felix Dörmann and Leopold Jacobson. The sheet music edition of *Walzerträume* Walzer for piano was published March 1, 1907,[1] by Ludwig Doblinger, Leipzig and Vienna. An early printing refers to the operetta *Ein Walzertraum*, based on Hans Müller's *Buch der Abenteuer*, has a drawing of a girl playing the violin, is red, black and white, lists 13 arrangements of the *Waltz*, this at K 2.40/M 2, has a 1907 copyright and refers to a Riga agent. p. [2] blank. m. on pp. 3–13. p.n. 3591. Back cover adv. many selections from the operetta. JF. The sheet music edition of the same melody as the song, *Walzertraum—Leise, Ganz Leise*, was probably published at about the same time.[2] An early printing has the same front cover as that mentioned above except listing 10 arrangements of the song, this at K 1.80/ M 1.50, and eight titles from the operetta. Text on p. [2]. m. on pp. 3–7. p.n. 3589. Back cover adv. many selections from the operetta. JF.

The piano score of the operetta with underlying text was published April 11, 1907.[1,3] Possible first edition: Front cover is two shades of green. vb. Title page is brown and white, mentions Felix Bloch Erben and Dr. O. F. Eirich, has a photograph of, presumably, Mitzi Zwerenz and Fritz Werner,[4] lists two arrangements, this at K. 6/ M. 5, has a 1907 copyright claim and shows the same imprint as that described above. Cast and index. m. on pp. 3–81, the *Walzerduett* on p. 31. p.n. 3629. p. [82] and inside and outside of back cover blank. JF.

The piano-vocal score of the operetta was published April 30, 1907.[1,5] First edition: Front cover is purple and light green. vb. Title page is the same as that of the piano score, the price of the piano-vocal score being K. 12/ M. 10. Cast and index. m. on pp. 3–131, the *Walzerduett* on p. 46. p.n. 3653. p. [132] and inside and outside of back cover blank. LC (copyright copy deposited May 31, 1907), ONB and JF.

Ein Walzertraum was performed March 2, 1907, in Vienna. Brief biographic information regarding the composer and Jacobson appears above under *Komm, Komm! Held Meiner Träume*. Felix Dörmann is a pseudonym of Felix Biedermann, a librettist, who was born in Vienna in 1876 and died there in 1928.[6]

---

[1] Information from publisher. Hofmeister *Monatsbericht*, March, 1907, p. 129.
[2] *Id.*, p. 147.
[3] Hofmeister *Monatsbericht*, April, 1907, p. 195.
[4] See Grun, photograph opposite p. 65.
[5] Hofmeister *Monatsbericht*, May, 1907, p. 279.
[6] *GB*, vol. 5, p. 49.

Waltz, Coppélia—Delibes

m. Léo Delibes. The piano score of *Coppélia* was published about June 26, 1870,[1] by E. Heu, 10 Rue de la Chaussée d'Antin, Paris. First edition: Title page mentions the Théâtre Impérial de l'Opéra, gives the alternative title to the ballet, *La Fille aux Yeux d'Émail*, states that the ballet is by Ch. Nuitter and Saint-Léon, has a drawing of a scene from the ballet in green, black and white, gives the price as 10 f., makes legal claims and states that the printer is Michelet, Paris. vb. Cast, with p.n. 1845. vb. m. on pp. 1–152, the *Valse* on p. 8. BN(CDC) and JF. An early printing of the *Valse-Entr'acte* in sheet music form for piano by Louis Gregh, Paris, with p.n. E. H. [E. Heu] 1858, is at JF.

Surprisingly, the orchestral score of *Coppélia* has not been published.[2] An 1882 printing of the orchestral parts of the *Entr'acte & Valse* by Louis Gregh et Cie., Paris, is at BN(CDC). An early printing of the orchestral parts of *Coppélia* with plate number H. 9368, some printed and some a lithographing of a manuscript, folio, without covers is at Heugel et Cie., Paris. The ballet was performed on May 25, 1870, in Paris. Brief biographic information regarding Delibes appears above under *Bell Song*.

Waltz, The Count of Luxemburg—Lehár

m. Franz Lehár. w. A. M. Willner and Rob. Bodansky. The piano-vocal score of *Der Graf von Luxemburg* in which the *Waltz, Bist Du's Lachendes Glück* appears, was published Sept. 17, 1909,[1] by W. Karczag & C. Wallner, 8 Magdalenenstrasse, Vienna VI. First edition: Front cover is tan and black and has no drawing. vb. Title page is the same as the front cover except in

---

[1] *RGM*, June 26, 1870, p. 208. *BF*, July 9, 1870, p. 329.

[2] Information from Jean-Marie Martin, Hollognes-aux-Pierres, Belgium, and letter from present publisher, Heugel et Cie., Paris.

---

[1] Copyright records; LC. Hofmeister *Monatsbericht*, Dec., 1909, p. 372.

black and white, lists no prices, has a Leipzig address for the publisher, shows that the copyright is in the name of Breitkopf & Härtel, New York, N.Y., and mentions Russian and French agents. Cast and index. m. on pp. 3–165, the *Waltz* on p. 53. p. [166] blank. p.n. 361. Back cover missing. LC (copyright copy deposited Oct. 7, 1909).

The operetta opened in Vienna on Nov. 12, 1909, and the sheet music edition of *Bist Du's Lachendes Glück*, with words and music, was published four days thereafter;[2] a possible first edition with the copyright in the name of Breitkopf & Härtel, New York, N.Y., and with p.n. 389, is at JF. The *Waltz* for piano only under the title *Luxemburg-Walzer* has p.ns. 372 and 437; JF. The piano score of the operetta has p.n. 427; LC (copyright copy published Dec. 31, 1909,[2] and deposited Feb. 18, 1910).

The orchestral score of the *Walzer-Intermezzo* was published Oct. 3, 1911,[3] at the prices of K6 M5 with p.n. 756; LC (copyright copy deposited Jan. 31, 1912) and SB ("Aus dem Archiv Franz Lehárs," according to the card catalogue).

Brief biographic information regarding Lehár appears above under *Gold and Silver Waltz*. Willner was born in 1859, became a lyricist and librettist, and died in 1929 in Venice.[4] Bodansky was born in Vienna in 1879, became a lyricist and librettist, and died in Vienna in 1923.[4]

Waltzes, Der Rosenkavalier—Richard Strauss

m. Richard Strauss. The piano-vocal score of *Der Rosenkavalier*, op. 59, was first published separately by acts, the first act on Oct. 1, 1910, the second act on Oct. 25, 1910, and the third act on Dec. 9, 1910,[1] by Adolph Fürstner, 18 Rue Vignon, Paris 9, and 34A Victoriastrasse, Berlin W. 10. First edition: Front cover is rose and black. vb. Title page is the same as the front cover but in black and white, gives the French translation of the title, *Le Chevalier à la Rose*, mentions that the libretto is by Hugo von Hofmannsthal, the copyright year is 1910 on both the title page and p. 5,

---

[2] Copyright records; LC. The sheet music edition and the piano score are in Hofmeister *Monatsbericht*, March, 1910, pp. 64 and 72.

[3] Copyright records; LC. The orchestral parts were published the same day. *Ibid.*

[4] Information from AKM.

[1] Copyright records; LC. Archives. Mueller von Asow, pp. 467 and 468, says merely 1910.

and the prices are 24 M. and 30 Fr. vb. Cast. vb. m. on pp. 5–442. p.n. 5903. German text only. No dedication. The printer is Buttner-Thierry, Paris. The above *Waltz* is at p. 284. BN (copyright copies, the three acts entered for Dépôt Légal on Oct. 14 and 28, and Dec. 10, 1910), LC (copyright copies deposited Oct. 29, Nov. 18 and Dec. 23, 1910) and JMM.

This 1910 French piano-vocal edition was also published as a whole; JMM and JF (copies identical to that described above except the front cover is black and tan). All German editions examined so far have a 1911 copyright date[2] on either or both of the title page or p. 5; NC, UI, SS, WU and JF. It is not known why the French edition was selected for copyright deposit and prior publication. Mueller von Asow, p. 468, confirms that the first publication was made in Paris.

The orchestral score of *Der Rosenkavalier* was published in Paris Dec. 16, 1910.[1] First edition: Folio. Separate green and black covers for each act (separate covers probably only for copyright copies). vb. Title page is similar to that described above except that there is a dedication to the Pschorr family in Munich and there are no prices. The copyright year is 1910. There are 168 pages in the first act, 165 pages in the second act (the above *Waltz* at p. 154) and 190 pages in the third act. p.n. 5900. BN (copyright copies, the first act entered for Dépôt Légal on Nov. 19, 1910, and the last two acts on Dec. 17, 1910) and LC (copyright copy deposited Jan. 9, 1911), in each case the first act dated in ink Nov. 15, 1910, and the latter two acts dated Dec. 16, 1910. The printer is Chaimbaud & Cie., Paris.

A French edition of the orchestral score published as a whole has not been found and may not have been issued. However, a German edition printed by C. G. Röder, Paris, and Chaimbaud & Cie., Paris, was published by Adolph Fürstner, Berlin-Paris, with two 1910 copyright notices, on the title page without city and on p. 5 mentioning Paris. The pagination is consistent with the copies described in the preceding paragraph. Copy at JMM (copy no. 36). The title page—entirely in German—is illustrated in *Hans Schneider Catalogue 81* (Tutzing, Munich, n.d.), no. 689; JF.

A possible first printing of the orchestral parts of the opera with plate number A 5901 F, lithographed and folio, but without covers, is at MET.

The opening bars of the above *Waltz* bear a considerable resemblance to the opening bars of the first Waltz in Josef Strauss, *Geheime Anziehungskräfte (Dynamiden)*, op. 173, published for piano in 1865[3] by C. A. Spina, Vienna, with engraved music pages and p.n. 18,520. ONB and JF.

Der Rosenkavalier was completed Sept. 26, 1910, and performed Jan. 26, 1911, in Dresden. Brief biographic information regarding Strauss ap-

---

[2] The German edition is listed in Hofmeister *Monatsbericht*, Feb., 1911, p. 46.
[3] Hofmeister *Annual*, 1865, p. 109.

pears above under *Don Juan*. Hugo von Hofmannsthal, a writer, was born in 1874 in Vienna and died in 1929 in Rodaun, Austria.[4]

Waltzing Matilda

Waltz-ing Ma-til - da waltz - ing Ma-til - da you'll come a waltz-ing Ma - til - da with me

Copyright 1936 by Allan & Co., Prop. Ltd., Melbourne, Australia. Copyright 1941 by Carl Fischer, Inc., New York. By permission.

There is considerable controversy as to the origin and authorship of both the music and the words of *Waltzing Matilda*. The first printing of the possible source of this melody, *Thou Bonny Wood of Craigie Lee*, was about 1818[1] in *Miniature Museum of Scotch Songs*, Edinburgh, vol. 2, p. 256; NLS. The song is also known as *Craigielea*. The music is generally attributed to James Barr (although his name does not appear in this printing), and the words of *Craigielea* were by Robert Tannahill.

According to one version, in 1894 *Craigielea* was played as a march at a racing carnival in Warrnambool, Australia, and heard by Christina Macpherson.[2] The next year she played it for A. B. Paterson and the same day her husband told Paterson the story of an Australian swagman; that night Paterson is said to have written a poem to fit the tune.

A more recent study claims that a Harry Nathan composed the music as an entirely original composition;[3] his manuscript is at MLS. The same study also believes that the words were originally an Australian folk or bush ballad and were merely polished by Paterson. Nathan's manuscript ascribes the words to Paterson.

In any event, the song became well known and was published in 1903[2] under the title *Waltzing Matilda* by Inglis and Co., 60 & 62 York Street, Sydney. Probable first edition: The words are credited to A. B. Paterson, and the music is stated to have been "arranged" by Marie Cowan (in later editions she is stated to be the composer). Front cover is black

---

[4] *MGG*, vol. 6, p. 566.

[1] Marion P. Linton, at NLS, found this earliest printing of the music. The year 1818 appears at the end of the first volume. See, also, Stenhouse, p. [293].

[2] Sidney May, *The Story of "Waltzing Matilda"* (Brisbane, 1955); NYPL. Front cover of the first edition is illustrated between pp. 72 and 73. The authorship of Paterson and Cowan has been established in an Australian court, *Sydney Daily Telegraph*, March 14, 1959, p. 3; JF.

[3] Oscar Mendelsohn, *A Waltz with Matilda* (Melbourne, 1966); Harold Barlow, New York City.

and white, has a drawing of a few flowers, mentions that the price is 1/6 nett, says that the song was "printed and published" for the proprietors and mentions a Brisbane office.[4] m. on pp. [2]–[3]. Back cover adv. teas. MLS. Allan & Co. Pty. Ltd., the present Australian publisher, has written this author that the original publisher was in the tea business, and that the printing described above was "merely for private circulation to Mr. and Mrs. Cowan's friends." The quoted phrase is hardly credible as the front cover states: "Price 1/6 nett." Allan & Co. has further written this author that the publisher issued advertising folders and the song was used for advertising.

A "matilda" is not a girl, but a knapsack which "waltzes" or bounces as it is carried by a poor walking Australian worker or "swagman." In 1911 the song was published in *The Australasian Students' Song Book* (Melbourne et al.), p. 172, at MLS; and Allan & Co. further wrote this author that "after the outbreak of war in 1914 . . . copies were distributed among military camps"; the song became a particularly great favorite during World War II, and has become Australia's national anthem. It is in C or ⁴⁄₄, not ³⁄₄, time.

Barr was born in Scotland in 1779, became a weaver and music teacher and died as a farmer in Canada in 1860.[5] Andrew Barton ("Banjo") Paterson was born in Narrambla, Molong, New South Wales, Australia, in 1864, had a varied career and died in Sydney, Australia, in 1941; his nickname relates to his interest in horses, not to music.[6] Marie Cowan was the wife of W. Cowan, the manager of Inglis and Co., the original publisher; she died in 1919. Nathan was born in Sydney in 1866, was an organist and choirmaster and died in Brisbane in 1906.[8]

Warsaw Concerto

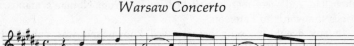

© 1942 by Keith Prowse & Co. Ltd. Published in USA and Canada by Chappell & Co. Inc. By consent.

[4] James Inglis & Co. was at 60 and 62 York Street, Sydney, and at 161 Adelaide Street, Brisbane, from 1902 to 1910 according to city directories. The lithographers, Turner & Henderson, are also listed in Sydney directories for the same period. Letter from MLS.

[5] Information from NLS.

[6] Before its revival during World War II, *Waltzing Matilda* as a poem was printed in A. B. Paterson, *Saltbush Bill, J.P.* (Sydney, 1917), p. 23; CNL.

m. Richard Addinsell. The *Theme from the Warsaw Concerto* was published for piano on Jan. 30, 1942,[1] by Keith Prowse & Co. Ltd., London W.1. First edition: Front cover is blue and white, lists three arrangements, the price of this arrangement being 2/6, and states from the film *Dangerous Moonlight*. m. on pp. 2–7. Dedication on p. 2 to J.N.B. p.n. 6239. The bottom of p. 7 says "Iffley 1941," presumably the place and year of composition. Back cover has monogram (K P). BM (copyright copy deposited April 23, 1942—also includes the *Theme* for violin and piano, the second of the three arrangements); piano arrangement also at JF.

The orchestral parts of the *Theme* were deposited at BM on May 7, 1942. First edition: Three arrangements are listed, the price of this being 3/6, there is reference to the film and the p.n. is 6242. BM(CDC).

The complete *Warsaw Concerto* was published for piano May 6, 1942.[1] First edition: Front cover is red and white. vb. Title page refers to the film, lists four arrangements, the price of this being 7/6, mentions that three arrangements of the complete *Concerto* are available for hire only, and has the dedication to J. N. B. m. on pp. 2–15. p.n. 6253. pp. [16] and [17] blank. Back cover has monogram (K P). BM (copyright copy deposited June 19, 1942) and LC (copyright copy deposited June 29, 1942). The orchestral score and parts of the complete *Concerto* have been available for hire, but have not been published.

The movie *Dangerous Moonlight* was renamed *Suicide Squadron* in the United States. Addinsell was born in Oxford in 1904, became a composer and resides in England.[2]

The Washington Post March

m. John Philip Sousa. Copyrighted Aug. 14, 1889,[1] for band parts by Harry Coleman, Philadelphia, Pa. Two variant single parts by this publisher, both with publisher's number 187 and one with an 1889 copyright claim, are at UIB; priority unknown. Copyrighted Sept. 23, 1889,[1] for piano. First edition of the piano arrangement: Front cover has a photograph of part of the first page of the newspaper *The Washington Post* for June 16, 1889, somehow stamped Philadelphia, Aug. 28, 3 PM, 1889, has a dedication to Frank Hatton and Beriah Wilkins and is silver, blue, black and

[1] Copyright records; LC.

[2] Gammond-Clayton, p. 3.

[1] Copyright records; LC.

white. p. [2] blank. m. on pp. 1–3 (actually 3–5). 1889 copyright claim. The street address of the publisher is 228 N. 9th St. Back cover adv. *Gladiator..* - *Odaliska..* No advertisements at the bottom of inside pages. LC(CDC). A brief biography of Sousa appears above under *El Capitan*.

Water Music—Handel

m. G. F. Handel. Portions of *The Celebrated Water Musick* in seven parts, including the above 13th movement, were published for orchestral parts about 1733 by I. Walsh, London.[1] First edition: Title page refers to Bass Violin, and the plates used were uncracked. p.n. 489. NLS and WCS.

The complete *Water Music* was published on Feb. 26, 1743,[2] for harpsichord under the title *Handel's Celebrated Water Musick Compleat* by I. Walsh, London.[1] First edition: Two blank pages after the title page. m. on pp. 2–27. p. [28] blank. No plate number. The two Geminiani *Minuets* are paginated 20–27 at the top of the pages. BM, WCS and JF. The *Water Music* was composed for, and played at, one or more royal water parties on the River Thames in or about 1717 while Handel was in England. Brief biographic information regarding the composer appears above under *Hallelujah Chorus*.

Waves of the Danube

m. I. Ivanovici. Published in 1880 under the title *Valurile Dunări* for piano by Const. Gebauer, Bucharest, Rumania.[1] First edition: Front cover has a drawing of waves of the Danube, states that it is dedicated to Bnei Emma Gebauer (the publisher's wife) and says that it is a "valsu." The music appears on seven pages. (Incomplete description.) Collection of Viorel

---

[1] Smith, *Handel*, p. 255. William C. Smith, "The Earliest Editions of the Water Music," in *Concerning Handel* (London, 1948), p. 269; NYPL.

[2] "This Day is publish'd"; *The London Daily Post, and General Advertiser*, Feb. 26, 1743, p. [2], at BM.

---

[1] The author is indebted to the Biblioteca Centrală de Stat, Bucharest, for its assistance in obtaining the above information.

Cosma, a Rumanian musicologist[2] (photocopy of front cover at JF).

The waltz became widely known and published under various translated titles, including *Donauwellen, Flots du Danube* and *Danube Waves*. In 1946 words by Al Jolson and Saul Chaplin were set to the music under the title *Anniversary Song*, for the motion picture *The Jolson Story*. Ion Ivanovici was born in 1845 in Banatul, Rumania, became a popular Rumanian composer and died in Bucharest in 1902.

'Way Down Yonder in New Orleans

'Way down yon - der in   New Or - leans__   in the land__ of dream-y scenes

mw. Creamer & Layton. Published July 6, 1922,[1] by Shapiro, Bernstein & Co. Inc., Cor. Broadway and 47th Street, New York, N.Y. First edition: Front cover has a drawing of a girl on a spice bottle, refers to the musical *Spice of 1922*, lists seven titles and is orange, blue, gray and white. m. on pp. 2–5. "Strut, Miss Lizzie/ 'Spice of 1922' " appears at the top of p. 2. Back cover adv. On.. - Ohio.. LC(CDC) and JF. *Spice of 1922* opened in New York City on the above date of publication.

Henry Creamer was born in Richmond, Va., in 1879 and died in New York City in 1930.[2] Turner Layton was born in 1894 in Washington, D.C., became a music hall artist and resides in London.[3]

We Shall Overcome

The music and words of *We Shall Overcome*, the unofficial Negro freedom anthem which was given prominent recognition by President Johnson,[1] are derived from a number of sources.

The simple melody of the first four bars of *We Shall Overcome* is al-

---

[2] The history of *Valurile Dunǎri*, and a biography of the composer, are in Viorel Cosma, *Maiorul I. Ivanovici* (Bucharest, 1958). JF.

---

[1] Copyright records; LC.

[2] Obituary, *Variety*, Oct. 22, 1930.

[3] Information from Layton.

---

[1] On March 15, 1965, before Congress in a nationally televised address. *The New York Times*, March 16, 1965, p. 1.

most identical with that of the hymn whose opening words are "O Sanctissima."

O   San - ctis - si - ma

The origin of the hymn is uncertain, but its first known printing[2] was,
curiously, in the United States in May, 1794, in R. Shaw, *The Gentleman's
Amusement* (Philadelphia, New York and Baltimore), p. 25, under the title
Prayer of the Sicilian Mariners; Sonneck-Upton, pp. 157 and 341, and JF.
It was published in London in 1795 with English text, a paraphrase of
Psalm 19, *God the Heav'ns Aloud Proclaim* in the late Rev. James Merrick
and the Rev. William Dechair Tattersall, *Improved Psalmody,* vol. I, p. 48,
to "Sicilian Hymn"; NYPL. The text and tune of *O Sanctissima* were
recorded by the German poet Johann Gottfried von Herder, probably during his Italian trip of 1788–1789, but were not published by him until the
collected edition of his works in 1807, *Stimmen der Völker in Liedern*
(Tubingen), vol. 8, p. 175, where it is referred to as a Sicilian mariners'
song and also as an Italian folksong; BSM. The *Sicilian Mariner's Hymn*
was also published in sheet music by various publishers commencing about
1795; *BUC,* p. 6.[3] Beethoven made a setting of *O Sanctissima* in 1814–1815;
Kinsky-Halm, p. 655. The melody also accompanied other texts under various titles: *Dismissal, Lord Dismiss Us with Thy Blessing, Saviour Like a
Shepherd Lead Us,* and *O Du Fröhliche.* There is no Italian record of the
song, and it may have been an air from an obscure Neapolitan opera of the
eighteenth century. It has also been conjectured to be as old as the sixteenth century, at least as to the words.[4]

The words of *We Shall Overcome* seem to have had their source in an
original hymn by C. Albert Tindley, entitled *I'll Overcome Some Day,*
included in *New Songs of the Gospel* by the Reverend C. A. Tindley and
the Reverend A. R. Shockly, which was published Dec. 22, 1900,[5] by
Hall-Mack Co., 1020 Arch St., Philadelphia; LC(CDC-M 2198.M) and JF.
This hymn is no. 27, is indicated to be an original hymn, and includes the
words: "If in my heart I do not yield, I'll overcome some day." Tindley's
music is not similar to that of *We Shall Overcome.* There are several
editions of this book: while all say Jan., 1901, on the verso of the title page,

---

[2] *The Hymnal 1940 Companion* (2nd ed., revised, New York, N.Y., 1951), p. 166;
UTS.

[3] But the ca. 1785 year given in *BUC,* p. 6, for the Thos. Preston edition should
be ca. 1798–   , according to Humphries-Smith, p. 264.

[4] *The New Yorker,* March 27, 1965, p. 37. *America,* New York, N.Y., Nov. 2, 1963,
p. 531; NYPL.

[5] Copyright records; LC.

the first edition has only 94 hymns with music (plus 24 without music) and is not referred to as the "Sunday School Edition" (other editions at LC and UTS). This hymn was reprinted in at least one Baptist hymnal, *Baptist Standard Hymnal,* edited by Mrs. A. M. Townsend (Nashville, Tenn., 1924), p. 346; LC(CDC) and Harold Barlow, New York City. No biographic information has been found regarding Tindley.

The first printed confirmation of the wedding of the above introductory music and the above title is in the Negro gospel song *I'll Overcome Someday.* published May 1, 1945,[5] by Martin & Morris Music Studio, Chicago. The sheet music states that the original words were by Atron Twigg, and the revised lyrics and music by Kenneth Morris. The opening music and words of this song are similar to those of *We Shall Overcome:*

Copyright 1945 by Atron Twigg and Kenneth Morris. Published by Martin & Morris Music Studio, Chicago. By permission.

In an early edition, the size is octavo, the front cover has a photograph of Kenneth Morris and the Martin & Morris Gospel Singers, the price is 15 cents, the publisher's address is 4315 Indiana Avenue, Chicago 15, Ill. (the address in 1945),[6] the music is on pages 2–3, the copyright is in the name of Twigg and Morris, and the back cover advertises later gospel songs. LC and JF. Morris was born in New York City in 1918, is a gospel singer and lives in Chicago.[7]

Roberta Martin of Chicago claims to be the author of the essential part of the music of the Negro civil rights song. On May 3, 1945,[5] Martin's Studio of Music published another gospel song, *I'll Be Like Him Someday*, crediting Roberta Martin's pseudonym, Faye E. Brown, as the author of the music and words. *The music of the last twelve bars* of this song appears to be the source of the comparable part of *We Shall Overcome*, the last few bars being:

Copyright 1945 by Faye E. Brown. Published by Martins Studio of Music, Chicago. By permission.

[6] Information from CPL.
[7] Information from author.

In addition, the closing words of the first stanza of the Verse are "I'll overcome someday," thereby linking the music and the title. Possible first edition of *I'll Be Like Him Someday:* there are no front or back covers, the
music and words are printed on one side of one unnumbered page, the song
is designated "A Martin Song," there is no price, the publisher's address
is 69 East 43rd St., Chicago, and the copyright is in the name of Faye E.
Brown. vb. LC (copyright copy deposited Dec. 3, 1951) and JF. Roberta
Evelyn Martin was born in Helena, Ark., in 1912, is a gospel singer
and lives in Chicago. In a telephone interview with this writer, she claimed
that her song was entirely original. She stated she is a good friend of
Kenneth Morris, mentioned in the preceding paragraph, but that she is not
the Martin referred to in the preceding paragraph.

The Negro church song *I'll Be All Right Someday* is mentioned
vaguely in one article[4]—no printed confirmation of such a song has been
found, but these are the closing words in the fourth stanza of the Verse of
I'll Be Like Him Someday, referred to in the preceding paragraph.

With this background *We Shall Overcome* has developed, first, as a
labor song, and then as the unofficial hymn of the Negro civil rights movement. In spite of the means of publicity available in the middle of the
twentieth century, many important facts relating to the oral development
of both the music and the words of the song are unknown. It appears that
a CIO Food and Tobacco Workers' strike occurred in Oct., 1945, in
Charleston, S.C., and it is said that strikers there first sang the song with
the plural pronoun: "*We* will overcome." Two of the pickets attended a
labor workshop at the Highlander Folk School, Monteagle, Tenn., and
Zilphia Horton, the wife of the founder of the school, heard the song and
taught it to others; Guy Carawan, a white folk singer who has been at the
scene of civil rights protests in the South, has a tape of Zilphia Horton
singing the song before her death in 1957. Pete Seeger sang the song in the
North, changing "We will overcome" to "We shall overcome." Frank
Hamilton, another folk singer, added to the momentum.

We Will Overcome was one of the *Eight New Songs for Labor,* re-
corded by Joe Glazer and the Elm City Four and released by the CIO
Department of Education and Research in June 1950, according to Glazer;
record at George T. Guernsey, Washington. The song was included in
Songs of Work and Freedom, edited by Edith Fowke and Joe Glazer
(Chicago, 1960), p. 33; NYPL and JF. *We Shall Overcome* was included in
Charlton Heston Reads "Out of Egypt," with the Robert D. Cormier
Chorale, Vanguard record no. 9061, released Nov., 1959,[8] at JF, and the
song was copyrighted as an unpublished composition in connection there-
with on Dec. 14, 1959.[5] It was similarly copyrighted as an unpublished

[8] Information from the record company.

composition by Ludlow Music, Inc., on Oct. 27, 1960.[5] It was included in *Sing Out!*, New York, N.Y., April–May, 1961, p. 19; LC. The song was reproduced in the form of a musician's "lead sheet" on July 23, 1963, in *The New York Times*, p. 21, and similarly in *Saturday Review*, New York, N.Y., Sept. 28, 1963, p. 66, at LC.

In a current version, *We Shall Overcome* was published Oct. 7, 1963,[5] by Ludlow Music, Inc., New York, N.Y. First edition: Front cover is blue and white, states the song is dedicated by the writers to The Freedom Movement and that the new words and music adaptation are by Zilphia Horton, Frank Hamilton, Guy Carawan and Pete Seeger; the price is 75¢. m. on pp. 2–3. Back cover has a design. LC(CDC) and JF. Royalties derived from this composition are being contributed to The Freedom Movement under the trusteeship of the writers.

We shall o - ver come____   We shall o - ver come some   day

The song *We Shall Overcome* was on the dying lips of Mrs. Viola Gregg Liuzzo, the civil rights worker who was murdered in Alabama on March 25, 1965.[9]

The song was also sung on April 1, 1965, on the gallows of a prison in Johannesburg, South Africa, by John Harris just before he was hanged; *We Shall Overcome* has subsequently been almost entirely suppressed in South Africa.[10]

Lift Ev'ry Voice and Sing, the official song of the N.A.A.C.P., with words by James Weldon Johnson and music by J. Rosamond Johnson, was copyrighted by Jos. W. Stern & Co., New York, N.Y., on Oct. 19, 1900;[5] LC(CDC).

We Three Kings of Orient

We three kings of   O - ri - ent are,   bear - ing gifts, we   tra - verse a - far

---

[9] *The New York Times*, May 5, 1965, p. 33.
[10] *Id.*, July 31, 1965, p. 7.

mw. John H. Hopkins, Jr. This carol written for Christmas, 1857, was probably published in December, 1863, in John H. Hopkins, Jr., *Carols, Hymns and Songs* (New York, N.Y.), p. 12, under the title "Three Kings of Orient." BM*, BR, UTS and Washington Cathedral, Washington, D.C. Though the book does not mention 1863 or make a copyright claim, and there is no copyright entry in that year,[1] a handwritten note in the copy at UTS states that the book was published in December, 1863; the copy at BM was purchased on April 6, 1865.

The preface of the first edition of the book states that any one of the pieces may be procured separately. However, the earliest known separate printing of this carol was copyrighted on Sept. 25, 1865,[1] under the title "Three Kings of Orient, A Christmas Carol," by Hurd & Houghton, 401 Broadway, New York, N.Y., in a handsome multicolored, thin quarto, cloth booklet. BPL, HU, LC, NYPL and Washington Cathedral, Washington, D.C.

Hopkins, a clergyman, journalist and author, was born in Pittsburgh in 1820 and died in Hudson, N.Y., in 1891.[2]

The Wearin' o' the Green

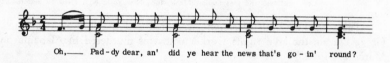

Oh,___ Pad-dy dear, an' did ye hear the news that's go-in' round?

Several writers[1] have referred to an Irish broadsheet of *The Wearin' o' the Green* and said it was published in 1798, but it is not clear whether any writer has seen the broadsheet; it has not been located, photographed or described. It presumably lacks music. None of the writers who quote the words states that the words quoted by the writer were obtained from the broadsheet.

A booklet containing the words of five songs was published in Dundalk (east coast of Ireland) and is dated 1802. One of the songs is *Green on My Cape*, described as "a favourite new Song." The song tells the story

---

[1] Copyright records; LC. The publisher, Church Book Depositary, 762 Broadway, is not in New York City directories 1863–66; NYPL. Later editions of the book do not state the date of the first edition.

[2] Louise E. Koier, "Vermont's Father Christmas" in *News and Notes*, Vermont *Historical Society*, Montpelier, Vt., Dec., 1953, p. [25]; Herringsham's *National Library of American Biography* (Chicago, 1914), vol. III, p. 210; and Rev. Charles F. Sweet, *A Champion of the Cross* (New York, N.Y., 1894). All at NYPL.

---

[1] Anne G. Gilchrist, "The Tulip," in *Southern Folklore Quarterly*, Jacksonville, Fla., June, 1945, p. 119, ULS, p. 2648; Sparling, pp. 8, 368 and 372; Moffat, *Minstrelsy of Ireland*, p. 56; and Fitz-Gerald, p. 382.

of an Irish hero who had to leave his country because he "wore Green upon my Cape" and "they hang men and women for wearing the green." RIA (12.B^1.12). An undated, but later, broadside, also without music, tells the same story under the title *The Wearing of the Green*. RIA (RR 66.H.17).

Many sources have been given for the music and/or words of *The Wearin' o' the Green*. One, the music in *The Tulip*, in James Oswald's *Airs for the Spring* (London, 1747),[2] *BUC*, p. 747, seems to this writer to have no real similarity to the music of *The Wearin' o' the Green*. Two others are: *I Met with Napper Tandy* and *I Met with Buonaparte*. No early printing has been found of the music or words of either of the latter two, and no early printing of the music has been found of *The Green upon the Cape*, mentioned above. A song entitled *The Suit of Green*, with entirely different music and substantially different words, appears in Colm O Lochlainn, *Irish Street Ballads* (Dublin, 1939), p. 48; the original song could not be dated by the editor—p. ix. RIA and NYPL.

Another writer says that the melody derives from the first song in *A Compleat Tutor for the Guittar*, printed for I. Oswald, London, about 1760;[3] BM - *BUC*, p. 1025. However, this reference is a mistake. The same writer also refers to the ballads *From the Man Whom I Love* and *Balance a Straw*. The former has not been located; the latter[4] bears no resemblance to the melody of *The Wearin' o' the Green*. Yet another writer claims that *The Wearin' o' the Green* was originally an (unnamed) English melody.[5] Interestingly, the melody has been said to be Irish, English and Scottish in origin.[6]

In any event, the modern history of the song begins on Oct. 4, 1838, with the first provable reference to the song in the *Army and Navy Chronicle* (Washington, D.C.), p. 215, where an original poem *Benny Havens, O!* appears to the "Air—'Wearing of the Green.'" No music is included. *ULS*, p. 328. A note states that Benny Havens was the proprietor of a "restaurant" in the vicinity of the United States Military Academy, at West Point, N.Y. (Sheet music containing the poem and the common melody was copyrighted on Aug. 29, 1855,[7] under the title *Benny Havens,*

---

[2] Gilchrist, footnote 1, above, gives the exact date as Oct. 23, 1747. Compare this meticulosity with the complete absence of detail as to the 1798 broadsheet.

[3] Wm. H. Grattan Flood, "The Wearing of the Green" in *Ireland's Own*, Dublin, April 25, 1906, p. 10; NLI.

[4] In *Rutherford's Compleat Collection of 200 of the Most Celebrated Country Dances* (London, ca. 1756), vol. 2, p. 14; *BUC*, p. 909.

[5] S. Baring-Gould and H. Fleetwood Sheppard, *A Garland of Country Song* (London, 1895), p. viii; NYPL.

[6] Irish: Grattan Flood. English: Baring-Gould. Scottish: Gilchrist.

[7] Copyright records; LC.

Oh! by J. Sage & Sons, 209 Main St., Buffalo; LC(CDC).)

The first known printing of the melody of the song is in *The Spirit of the Nation* . . . Ballads and Songs by the Writers of "The Nation" with original and ancient music (Dublin, 1845). On p. 216 is *Up! For the Green* —"Air, *The Wearing of the Green*"; the common melody—new words.[8] BM and NYPL.

On Sept. 26, 1864,[9] the drama *Arrah na Pogue* played in Manchester, England, and included in the drama was the song *Wearin' o' the Green.* The date of publication of the song is not known, but the following copy was deposited at BM on Oct. 5, 1865, by Chappell & Co., 50 New Bond Street, London. Front cover is green and white, states that the song was "written to an old melody by Dion Boucicault," is sung by him in *Arrah na Pogue* and harmonized by Charles Hall and the price is 2/6. p. [2] blank. m. on pp. 1–5 (actually 3–7). p.n. 12968. Back cover adv. *Vocal..* BM(CDC); also at JF. A similar and possibly earlier copy with a blank back cover is at JF. The words for this revival were newly written by Boucicault, but are in part similar to those in the 1802 booklet mentioned in the second paragraph. These English editions are not engraved.

That the copy at the British Museum may not have been promptly deposited is indicated by the fact that two American editions were copyrighted prior to the English deposit although *Arrah na Pogue* played for the first time in the United States in New York City on July 12, 1865.[10] *Up with the Green* (*Up "For" the Green,* on p. [2]) *or the Wearing of the Green* was copyrighted Aug. 3, 1865,[7] by John J. Daly, New York, N.Y.; LC (CDC). *Wearing of the Green* was copyrighted Aug. 7, 1865,[7] by H. B. Dodworth, New York, N.Y.; JF. In an edition claimed to have been copyrighted in 1865 by Chas. W. A. Trumpler, Philadelphia, the song is referred to as the "favorite Irish song," at JF; no such copyright appears in the copyright records at LC. These American editions are engraved.

During the Fenian period in the middle of the nineteenth century, it is said that it was a crime in Great Britain to sing or whistle *The Wearin' o' the Green.*[11]

---

[8] The *Nation* was published as a newspaper in Dublin commencing 1842; it included no music, and a search for the years 1842–1845 fails to reveal any printing of the words of this song. Letter from NLI. In 1844 *The Spirit of the Nation* was published in Boston without music; BPL. Neither *Up! For the Green* nor *The Wearing of the Green* is included.

[9] Nicoll, vol. V, p. 268. *Arrah na Pogue* means *Exchange of Kisses.*

[10] Odell, vol. VII, p. 647.

[11] However, The Law Society Services Limited, London, and The Incorporated Law Society of Ireland, Dublin, wrote the author that no such penal law is known.

Wedding March-Lohengrin—Wagner

Treu - lich ge-führt   zie - het da - hin
Here comes the bride   all dressed in white

mw. Richard Wagner. The piano-vocal score of *Lohengrin* in which the *Wedding March* appears was published about Dec. 10, 1851,[1] by Breitkopf & Härtel, Leipzig. Probable first edition: Title page has the price of 8 Thaler. vb. Cast and Index. vb. Text on pp. [1]–10. m. on pp. 3–237, the *Brautchor*, or *Bridal Chorus*, on p. 174. p.n. 8411. p. [238] blank. Music, and cast and index, pages engraved. GM and JF.

There are four early editions of the orchestral score of *Lohengrin*. The earliest was a presentation edition limited to six copies, five of which were sent by Breitkopf & Härtel to Wagner on Aug. 11, 1852,[2] the receipt of which was referred to in a letter from Wagner to Theodore Uhlig dated Aug. 23, 1852, and the sixth to Liszt; three of Wagner's were subsequently presented by him to Robert Franz, Theodore Uhlig and Röckel.[3] Robert Franz's copy has been located: Green and black stiff cardboard covers. The title page contains Wagner's signed inscription to Franz, there is no price, and the publisher's imprint (Breitkopf & Härtel, Leipzig) is in script. vb. Dedication to Franz Liszt, in script. vb. Next two pages contain a letter from Wagner to Liszt, dated Zurich, May, 1852, in script. Cast and index. vb. m. on pp. 1–395, a lithographing of a manuscript. On page 1, the word "Langsam" at both the top and bottom of the page has the "L" in script with a loop at the top. No plate number. The *Brautchor* is on p. 275. Folio. Carnegie-Mellon University, Pittsburgh.

---

[1] Breitkopf & Härtel wrote Wagner on that date that it had received the first few copies from the binder and was sending copies to Wagner, Liszt, Uhlig and Brendel; Altmann, vol. I, p. 36. Hofmeister *Monatsbericht*, Jan., 1852, p. 19 (advertisement). *Id.*, Feb., 1852, p. 35. The publisher accepted the rights to *Lohengrin* in 1851 in payment of the balance of a debt Wagner owed it for a concert grand piano. Klein, pp. 26–27.

[2] Altmann, vol. I, p. 53—letter dated Aug. 13, 1852. Oskar von Hase, *Breitkopf & Härtel* (Leipzig, 1919), p. 243; NYPL. The printing of the orchestral score commenced in Jan., 1852; Altmann, vol. I, p. 40.

[3] *Correspondence of Wagner and Liszt* (New York, N.Y., 1897), vol. 1, p. 222, letter dated Sept. 12, 1852; NYPL. Wagner's acknowledgment to Breitkopf & Härtel of receipt of the copies is dated Sept. 29, 1852; Altmann, vol. I, p. 53.

The first regular edition of the orchestral score, published about Aug., 1852,[4] is the same as the presentation copy except there is, of course, no signed inscription, and the title page shows the price of 20 Thaler. (See Plate VI.) The publisher's imprint, the dedication page and the letter are in script, and page 1 is the same as in the presentation edition. ONB, BM (Hirsch II, 933), COP and JF (the last copy with green and black stiff cardboard covers). This edition was limited to 60 copies.[4]

The second regular edition of the orchestral score was completely reprinted. While the price is still 20 Thaler, the publisher's imprint and other words are now in **block letters**. The dedication page and the letter to Liszt are also in block letters, and the "L" in the word "Langsam" on the first page of the Vorspiel is straight and lacks a loop at the top. The collation is the same as the preceding edition, but the lithographing is of a different music manuscript.[5] BM (R.M. 13.b.8) and NYPL (Drexel 5015). In the third regular edition, the price is 36 Thaler and there is a p.n. 13100 (1873) at the bottom of the title page.† BSM, NYPL (*MSI +) and JMM. In subsequent editions of the orchestral score the price is 108 or 120 Marks.

Engraved orchestral parts of *Lohengrin* with plate number 16069 (1882–1883), but without covers, possibly their first printing, are at MET.

This and the Mendelssohn *Wedding March* were linked together at the royal wedding in 1858 of Princess Victoria of England and Prince Frederick William of Prussia, thus establishing a tradition still with us.[6] *Lohengrin* was completed the end of March, 1848, and performed Aug. 28, 1850, in Weimar under Liszt.[7] Brief biographic information regarding Wagner appears above under *The Flying Dutchman—Overture*.

---

[4] Letter from Breitkopf & Härtel to Wagner dated Aug. 13, 1852; Altmann, vol. I, p. 53. Ernest Newman, *The Life of Richard Wagner* (New York, N.Y., 1933), vol. 2, p. 301; NYPL.‡

[5] For example, in the first regular edition, on p. 9, the word "Trompeten" is partly in the 5th bar and partly in the 6th bar. In the second regular edition, the word is entirely in the 5th bar. §

[6] Jessica M. Kerr, "English Wedding Music," in *MT*, Jan., 1965, p. 53. ‖

[7] The earliest printing of any part of *Lohengrin* was in Franz Liszt, *Lohengrin et Tannhäuser de Richard Wagner* (Leipzig, 1851) listed in Hofmeister *Monatsbericht*, Nov., 1851, p. 226—the Supplement of which contains a few excerpts from the opera (but not the *Wedding March*); LC and JF. The piano score of the opera was published about July, 1853; Hofmeister *Monatsbericht* of that month, p. 361. The earliest separate printing of the *Wedding March* under the title *Brautlied—Treulich Geführt* for soprano was published about Feb., 1854; Hofmeister *Monatsbericht* of that month, p. 505. The only mention of the orchestral score of the opera in any Hofmeister is in his *Handbuch*, 1868–1873; p. 514.

Wedding March–
A Midsummer Night's Dream—Mendelssohn

m. Felix Mendelssohn Bartholdy. The piano-vocal score of *Ein Sommer-nachtstraum* (*A Midsummer Night's Dream*), op. 61, was published by May 1, 1844,[1] by Breitkopf & Härtel, Leipzig, the piano arrangement being for four hands. Probable first edition: Front cover is tan and black. vb. Title page mentions Shakespeare, has a dedication to Heinrich Conrad Schleinitz, states that the piano arrangement is by the composer, refers to three foreign agents and gives the price as 5 Thlr. m. on pp. [2]–115, the *Hochzeitmarsch* on p. 90. p.n. 7040. p. [116] blank. Engraved. Oblong. JF. The J. J. Ewer & Co., London, edition of this score was deposited June 5, 1844,[2] at BM. The *Hochzeitmarsch* was published separately by Breit-kopf & Härtel for piano about Nov., 1844,[3] and for piano four hands about Feb., 1845;[4] copies of each at JF. Similar separate editions published by J. J. Ewer & Co.[2] are at JF. The German piano score of *Ein Sommernachts-traum* was published June–July, 1845;[5] ONB.

The orchestral score of *Ein Sommernachtstraum* was published about July, 1848,[6] by Breitkopf & Härtel, Leipzig. Probable first edition: Title page is similar to that described above, the price being 10 Thlr. (**See Plate VI.**) vb. m. on pp. 3–177, engraved, the *Hochzeitmarsch* on p. 137. p.n. 7774. p. [178] blank. GM and JF. A probable first printing of the orches-tral parts, engraved and with plate number 7852, probably published the following month, is at BOD.[6]

This and the Wagner *Wedding March* were linked together at the royal wedding in 1858 of Princess Victoria of England and Prince Frederick William of Prussia, thus founding a tradition still with us.[7] The work was composed in 1842 and performed Oct. 14, 1843, in Potsdam. Brief biographic information regarding Mendelssohn appears above under his *Concerto for Violin.*

[1] *AMZ*, May 1, 1844, p. 511. Hofmeister *Monatsbericht*, May, 1844, p. 77. Müller-Reuter, p. 112, states Sept., 1844.

[2] *MW*, June 27, 1844, p. 218, also listing the separate printing of the *Hochzeit-marsch* for piano four hands.

[3] Hofmeister *Monatsbericht*, Nov., 1844, p. 165.

[4] *Id.*, Feb., 1845, p. 20.

[5] *Id.*, July, 1845, p. 102.

[6] *Id.*, July, 1848, p. 111. Müller-Reuter, p. 112, states June, 1848. The latter also gives Aug., 1848, as the publication date of the orchestral parts.

[7] Jessica M. Kerr, "English Wedding Music," in *MT*, Jan., 1965, p. 53.

We're Called "Gondolieri"—The Gondoliers

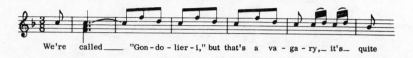

We're   called_____   "Gon-do-lier-i," but that's   a   va-ga-ry,__ it's__   quite

m. Arthur Sullivan. w. W. S. Gilbert. The piano-vocal score of *The Gondoliers; or, The King of Barataria,* in which *We're Called "Gondolieri"* appears, was published about Feb. 17, 1890,[1] by Chappell & Co., 50 New Bond Street, London. First edition: Front cover is light and dark blue. Verso adv. *The Yeomen..* Title page lists four arrangements, the vocal score complete at 5s. 0d. and bound at 7s. 6d., mentions that the arrangement for pianoforte is by J. H. Wadsworth (of Boston, U.S.A.),[2] has an 1890 copyright claim, refers to a Cincinnati agent and has a Caution. Verso mentions the printers, Henderson and Spaulding, 3 & 5 Marylebone Lane. Cast. Index. m. on pp. [V]–XII and 1–185, this song at p. 19. p.n. 18844. p. [186] adv. *The Martyr..* and *Trial..* p. [187] adv. *Patience.* p. [188] adv. *You.. - The Lady..* The inside of the back cover adv. *The Mikado.* The outside of the back cover adv. *The Gondoliers.* BM (copyright copy deposited June 24, 1890—lacks pages [187] and [188]), RA (copy dated Feb. 17, 1890) and JF (copy dated Feb., 1890).

No separate sheet music edition of *We're Called "Gondolieri"* was published† at the time. The piano score of *The Gondoliers* has p.n. 18845; BM(CDC). *The Gondoliers* was presented Dec. 7, 1889, at London. Brief biographic information regarding the authors appears above under *Bow, Bow, Ye Lower Middle Classes.*

Westminster Chimes

[1] *ILN*, Feb. 22, 1890, p. 251 ("Just published"). The piano-vocal score and the piano score entered for copyright as to title at LC on Dec. 6, 1889, but copies were not deposited until Feb. 19, 1890, and Feb. 18, 1890, respectively. According to an entry at Stationers' Hall on July 1, 1892, the date of publication of the piano-vocal score was Dec. 7, 1889, at the Savoy Theatre, London (confusing the date of first performance?). The publisher gives the date as Feb., 1890, for the piano-vocal score. As noted in the text, a copy dated Feb. 17, 1890, is at RA.

[2] An attempt to obtain American copyright protection. See *Three Little Maids from School,* footnote 2.

Westminster Chimes, also known as *Westminster Quarters* or *Cambridge Quarters,* was composed in 1793–1794 for St. Mary's Church (the Great), Cambridge, England, in all probability by William Crotch. In 1859–1860 the *Chimes* were copied for Big Ben at the Houses of Parliament, and it was after this that they became known as the *Westminster Chimes.*

No printed musical notation of the *Chimes* is known until about April 9, 1867, on which date a sheet music edition of *The Westminster Chimes Polka* for piano, composed by Duncan S. Miller, was deposited at BM, published for the Author by B. F. Grist, 40 Charlotte St. Fitzroy Sq., London W. Probable first edition: Front cover is black and white, states that the piece was composed for the Poland Street Temperance Hand Bell Ringers and gives the price as 3/. vb. m. on pp. 1–5 (really 3–7). Back cover blank. BM(CDC). A similar copy, with multicolored front cover at 4/, was also published for the Author by Wm. Tweedie, 337 Strand, London W.C.; this publisher was at this address from before 1859 to at least 1875;[1] JF. The music was also included in J. J. Raven, *The Church Bells of Cambridgeshire* (Lowestoft, 1869), in leaf between pp. 62–63, together with an account of its origin;[2] BM and LC. In general, earlier books on chimes and bell-ringing had merely set forth the numbers of the chimes and the order in which they were rung, without any indication of the musical notes of the particular chimes, which varied greatly in different sets of bells.[2A]

The opening four notes of the *Chimes* are the same as a phrase of four notes in the fifth and sixth bars of the opening symphony of Handel's *I Know That My Redeemer Liveth* in his *Messiah,* and it is possible that Crotch knowingly used and expanded this phrase. Crotch was born in Green's Lane, Norwich, in 1775, was a child prodigy organist, serving at Great St. Mary's Church in Cambridge from about 1786–1788, continued as a composer and organist, and died in Taunton in 1847.[3]

What Is This Thing Called Love?

What   is   this   thing_____   called   love?

---

[1] *London Post Office Directories;* BM.

[2] See, also, J. J. Raven, *The Bells of England* (London, 1906), p. 265; NYPL.

[2A] For some of the information herein the author is indebted to the authority on chimes and bell-ringing, Ernest Morris, Leicester, England.

[3] *Grove's,* vol. 2, p. 544.

mw. Cole Porter. Published March 25, 1929,[1] by Chappell & Co. Ltd., 50 New Bond Street, London W. 1. First edition: Front cover refers to Charles B. Cochran's 1929 Revue *Wake Up and Dream!*, listing seven titles, the title at the top of the front cover lacks a question mark, the publisher is also shown at Sydney, there is a New York City copublisher, and the colors are red, white and blue. m. on pp. 2–5. p.n. 30015. The copyright is in the name of Harms Inc. p. [6] adv. *This..* p. [7] adv. *I..* Back cover adv. *Japansy - Baby's..* BM (copyright copy deposited April 11, 1929) and JF.

Wake Up and Dream! opened in London on March 27, 1929, and in New York on Dec. 30, 1929. *What Is This Thing Called Love?* is said to have been inspired by the rhythm of a native dance Porter saw at Marrakech on one of his many travels.[2] Brief biographic information regarding the composer appears above under *Begin the Beguine.*

What's New Pussycat?

© Copyright 1965 United Artists Music Co., Inc. Used by permission.

m. Burt Bacharach. w. Hal David. Published July 14, 1965,[1] by United Artists Music Co., Inc., 729 Seventh Avenue, New York 19, N.Y. First edition: Front cover has a drawing of a pussycat in front of the nine stars in the movie, *What's New Pussycat?*, the price is 75¢ and the colors are purple, black and white. p. [2] blank. m. on pp. 3–5. No plate number. Back cover adv. *Goldfinger - The Love..* LC(CDC) and JF.

The movie, *What's New Pussycat?*, was copyrighted June 22, 1965,[1] and released in June, 1965. Bacharach, a composer, was born in Kansas City, Mo., in 1928 and lives in Beverly Hills, Cal.[2] David, a lyricist, was born in New York City in 1921.[2]

---

[1] Copyright records; LC.
[2] Margaret Case Harriman, *Take Them Up Tenderly* (New York, N.Y., 1944), p. 146; NYPL.

---

[1] Copyright records; LC.
[2] *ASCAP* (1966 edition, New York, N.Y.), pp. 26 and 155.

When I, Good Friends, Was Called to the Bar—
Trial by Jury

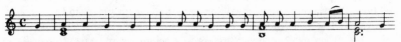

When I, good friends, was called to the bar, I'd an ap - pe-tite fresh and_ heart - y

m. Arthur Sullivan. w. W. S. Gilbert. The piano-vocal score of *Trial by Jury*, in which *When I, Good Friends, Was Called to the Bar* appears, was published about May 8, 1875,[1] by Chappell & Co., 50 New Bond Street, London W. First edition: Front cover, in tan and black, **mentions Sullivan, but not Gilbert!** vb. Title page mentions both names. Cast. Text on pp [iii]–vi. m. on pp. [3]–53, *The Judge's Song* on p. 18. No plate number. p. [54] and inside of back cover blank. Outside of back cover adv. *Chappell's Musical Magazine* to no. 110 (112 in second edition). The printer on p. 53 is Henderson, Rait & Fenton, 69 Marylebone Lane, Oxford Street, London W. BM* (copyright copy deposited June 9, 1875), RA and JF.

The sheet music edition of *The Judge's Song* was published about May 22, 1875.[2] First edition: Front cover is black and white, refers to *Trial by Jury*, has no drawing of the Judge and the price is 4/. pp. [2] and [3] blank. m. on pp. 2–7 (actually 4–9). p.n. 15992. Back cover adv. *Chappell's.*. BM (copyright copy deposited June 9, 1875). The edition with the drawing of Fred Sullivan, the composer's brother, as the Judge was deposited at BM on April 3, 1876. *Trial by Jury* was performed in London on March 25, 1875. Brief biographic information regarding the authors appears above under *Bow, Bow, Ye Lower Middle Classes.*

When I'm Not Near the Girl I Love—Finian's Rainbow

Oh my heart is beat - ing wild - ly___

[1] *ILN*, May 8, 1875, p. 444, removing the "Ready in a few days" in the previous advertisement. The copyright copy of the piano-vocal score was deposited at BM on June 9, 1875. Entered at Stationers' Hall on June 5, 1905 [*sic*]! The date of publication is not given in the entry—only the date of first performance.

[2] *ILN*, May 22, 1875, p. 492; *MW*, June 5, 1875, p. 386.

m. Burton Lane. w. E. Y. Harburg. Published Dec. 19, 1946,[1] by Crawford Music Corporation, RKO Building, Rockefeller Center, New York, N.Y. The copyright copy deposited at the Library of Congress is a professional edition. Possible first regular edition: Front cover, in green and black, has drawings of scenes from the musical *Finian's Rainbow* and lists six titles; no price. m. on pp. 2–7. Page 2 refers to a selling agent. p.n. 1462–6. Back cover adv. *Oklahoma—People*.. All the titles listed and advertised were published before Dec. 19, 1946. JF.

The piano-vocal score of *Finian's Rainbow* was published Dec. 31, 1947,[1] by Chappell & Co. Ltd., 50 New Bond Street, London W.1, with a price of 10/. BM(CDC), LC(CDC) and NYPL. The musical opened in New York City on Jan. 10, 1947. Lane, a composer, was born in New York City in 1912, and lives in Beverly Hills, Cal.[2] Brief biographic information regarding Harburg appears above under *April in Paris*.

When Irish Eyes Are Smiling

When   I - rish   eyes   are   smil - ing

© 1912 M. Witmark & Sons. Copyright renewed. Pub. by arr. with Ross Jungnickel Inc. Used by permission.

m. Ernest R. Ball. w. Chauncey Olcott and Geo. Graff, Jr. Published Aug. 12, 1912,[1] by M. Witmark & Sons, New York, N.Y.; the copyright deposit copy at LC is a professional edition. Possible first regular edition: Front cover has a photograph of Chauncey Olcott, refers to his new production *The Isle o' Dreams*, lists six titles, shows the publisher at five additional cities and is red, green and white. p. [2] adv. *Mother*.. m. on pp. [3]–[5]. p.n. 5772; 12687-3 (only the latter on the professional CDC). p. [6] adv. *Who*.. p. [7] adv. *I*.. Back cover adv. *Note. - Music*.. All the advertised music was published by Oct. 21, 1912. SS. *The Isle o' Dreams* opened in New York City on Jan. 27, 1913.

---

[1] Copyright records; LC.
[2] *ASCAP*, p. 290.

---

[1] Copyright records, at LC, which refer to *The Isle o' Dreams*.

Graff had never been to Ireland prior to writing the words. Brief biographic information regarding Ball and Olcott appears above under *A Little Bit of Heaven* and *Mother Machree*. Graff, a lyricist and business executive, was born in New York City in 1886 and died in Stroudsburg, Pa., in 1973.[2]

When Johnny Comes Marching Home

When   John-ny comes march-ing home   a-gain, hur - rah,——   hur - rah

By a curious coincidence, the melody of *When Johnny Comes Marching Home* was probably published a few months earlier under the title *Johnny Fill Up the Bowl*. About July, 1863,[1] the latter was published by John J. Daly, 419 Grand St., New York, N.Y. Probable first edition: Front cover has the collective title "Daly's New Collection of Comic and Sentimental Songs & Ballads," *Johnny Fill Up the Bowl* being the second of 48 titles listed (the last title in the second column being *See the Dawn from Heaven*); no price. m. on pp. 2—3. p.n. 167. Engraved. Back cover blank. JF. A number of American broadsides of *Johnny Fill Up the Bowl* are described in Edwin Wolf 2nd, *American Song Sheets, Slip Ballads and Poetical Broadsides 1850–1870* (Philadelphia, 1963), nos. 1139 *et seq.*; NYPL. Most of the broadsides are not dated, some are parody versions and many are by reprint publishers.

It has been claimed that *Johnny Fill Up the Bowl* (or *Cup*) is Irish,[2]

---

[2] *ASCAP*, p. 193, and obituary, *The New York Times*, Jan. 26, 1973.

[1] The sheet music has an 1863 copyright claim, but, strangely, there is no entry of an 1863 copyright deposit in the copyright records at LC. The plate number 167 indicates publication about July 1, 1863. Following are the plate numbers and the copyright dates for this publisher of four songs by Stephen C. Foster, as stated in Whittlesey-Sonneck, *Foster:*

Title:	Plate Number:	Copyright Date
Happy Hours at Home	156	Nov. 22, 1862
Lena Our Loved One Is Gone	**166**	**June 27, 1863**
Kissing in the Dark	176	Aug. 8, 1863
Sitting by My Own Cabin Door	184	April 20, 1864

[2] *O'Neill's Music*, p. 82, and O'Neill, *Waifs*, p. 44.

although there is no indication of this on the above sheet music. Another claimed Irish antecedent for *When Johnny Comes Marching Home* is *Johnny, I Hardly Knew Ye*, a song said to date from the beginning of the nineteenth century when Irish regiments were raised for the East India Service.[3] The only known early printing of the music and words of *Johnny, I Hardly Knew You* is in sheet music with this title, "written and composed" by J. B. Geoghegan, deposited at the British Museum on Feb. 20; 1867;[4] the melody bears no relation to the melody of *When Johnny Comes Marching Home*. However, the music and words of *Johnny, I Hardly Knew Ye!* appear in Herbert Hughes, *Irish Country Songs* (London, 1935), vol. 3, p. 38 (at NLI and NYPL), where the melody is the same as that of *When Johnny Comes Marching Home*. An interesting attempt to trace the history of the song is in the second unnumbered page of the Preface. Nonetheless, Donal O'Sullivan, the Irish authority, has written the Library of Congress that he does not consider the melody of *When Johnny Comes Marching Home* as Irish in origin.

When Johnny Comes Marching Home, with music and words credited to Louis Lambert, was copyrighted Sept. 26, 1863, by Henry Tolman & Co., 291 Washington St., Boston. First edition: Front cover has a dedication to the Army & Navy of the Uinon [*sic*], states that the music was "introduced and performed by Gilmore's Band," and the price is 3. p. [2] blank. m. on pp. 3–5. p.n. 3604. p. 5 also adv. *Laura.. - Once..* Engraved. There is no reference on the front cover to the *Soldier's Return March*. LC (CDC) and JF. Louis Lambert is a pseudonym for Patrick Gilmore, who was born in Ballygar, Galway County, Ireland, in 1829, came to Boston in 1847, became a famous bandmaster and died in 1892 in St. Louis.[5]

In addition to its possible (a) Irish antecedents, the music has also been variously described as being in origin: (b) Negro,[6] (c) Scottish,[7] and

[3] Sparling, p. 369.

[4] Andrew Lamb, Littlehampton, West Sussex, England, called the author's attention to this printing.

[5] Spaeth, p. 154. *American War Songs*, p. 119. Silber, p. 174. *Band Encyclopedia*, edited by Kenneth Berger (Evansville, Ind., 1960), p. 97; LC.

[6] Allegedly by Gilmore himself; Downes-Siegmeister, p. 189.

[7] Kidson, *Minstrelsy of England*, p. 103, stating it derives from *John Anderson, My Jo*, which was published in vol. III of *The Scots Musical Museum* in 1790 (See *The Campbells Are Coming*, footnote 1, above), if not earlier. To this observer, the connection between the two melodies is only slight.

(d) English.[8] In any event, no printing of music of any of these three latter origins which this author believes to be substantially similar to that of *When Johnny Comes Marching Home*, has been found prior to 1863.

When the Saints Go Marching In

Oh when the Saints, oh when the Saints, oh when the Saints go march-ing in

The written history of this Negro spiritual commences with the deposit, on June 17, 1896,[1] of the title *When the Saints Are Marching In* by J. M. Black, Williamsport, Pa.; no copy of this separate publication, the copyright copy of which was deposited on July 3, 1896,[1] has been found. However, a few days later, on July 6, 1896,[1] *Songs of the Soul No. 2, for Use in Sunday Evening Congregations, Revivals* . . . (Cincinnati et al.), edited by James M. Black, was copyrighted; on page 59 appears *When the Saints Are Marching In*; BE and UTS. The music and words are quite similar to those in the present form and, in particular, include the famous "echo." J. M. Black is credited with the music, and Katharine E. Purvis is credited with the words; the extent of their contributions is not known.

Black's version was soon included in *Sacred Songs No. 1 . . . for Use in Gospel Meetings* . . . (New York, N.Y.), edited by Ira D. Sankey et al., copyrighted Oct. 21, 1896,[1] no. 114; LC(CDC) and JF. On April 15, 1897,[1] the title *When the Saints Are Marching In* was entered for copyright by Rev. R. Alonzo Scott, Fayetteville, N.C., but no copyright copy was deposited and no copy has been found.

The melody and words of this Negro spiritual were also suggested in the composition, *When the Saints March In for Crowning*, by Harriet E. Jones and James D. Vaughan and included as no. 49 in *The Silver Trumpet for Revivals, Sunday-Schools, Conventions* . . . , edited and published by James D. Vaughan, Lawrenceburg, Tenn., and copyrighted Jan. 3, 1908;[1] LC(CDC received March 14, 1908—no. 49, alone, copyrighted and de-

---

[8] Donal O'Sullivan, in the letter mentioned in text above, sees a resemblance to *There Were Three Ravens* in *Melismata*, by T. R. (London, 1611), no. 2, at LC; this observer sees no substantial resemblance. When *When Johnny Comes Marching Home* was published about the late 1860's by Hopwood & Crew, 42 New Bond Street, London W., at JF, as sung by G. W. Moore of the Christy's Minstrels, there was no claim on the sheet music that the melody was English.

[1] Copyright records; LC. The author is heavily indebted to Harold Barlow, New York City, for information regarding this title.

posited March 5, 1908, LC[CDC]). As this song is one that has a separate copyright notice on its own page, some claim of originality was being made thereto.

This song may have developed in the Bahama Islands. It was heard in Nassau in 1917.[2] *When All the Saints Come Marching In* was recorded in mid-November, 1923, by the [Elkins-Payne] Paramount Jubilee Singers on Paramount record 12073-A, without credits as to authorship; NYPL.[2A] *When All the Saints Come Marching In* by Thomas Dorsey (not the orchestra leader) was published on Oct. 23, 1924,[1] by Chicago Music Pub. Co., Chicago, Ill. No copy has been found. In a telephone interview, Mr. Dorsey told the author that this song was not original with him.

The song in its present form was included in a book of native songs of Treasure Island in the Bahama Islands, *The Island Song Book*, collected by John and Evelyn McCutcheon, and privately printed in Chicago on Jan. 15, 1927;[3] the music and words are at p. 9 under the title *When the Saints Go Marching Home*. NYPL and JF. The next known printing is under the title *When the Saints Go Marching In*, in Edward Boatner, *Spirituals Triumphant—Old and New* (Nashville, Tenn., 1927), no. 33. LC (copyright copy deposited Dec. 27, 1927).

The song was included as a Negro spiritual in *The Green Pastures*, which opened in New York City on Feb. 26, 1930, under the title *When de Saints Come Marchin' In*.[4] There is a widespread but unsubstantiated rumor that the spiritual was played in New Orleans about 1900 at funerals —slowly, to the cemetery—and quickly, from the cemetery.[5]

It has been said that the song is a jazzed-up version of *Old Time Religion* and *Old Ship of Zion*;[6] this author disagrees. However, the song does have a general structural similarity to an earlier song by J. M. Black, *When the Roll Is Called Up Yonder*; this was separately copyrighted on Jan. 6, 1893,[1] and included in Chas. H. Gabriel, *Salvation Songs*, Cincinnati, Ohio, and New York, N.Y., no. 88, copyrighted on Mar. 25, 1895[1]; both at LC(CDC).

---

[2] On the honeymoon of Mr. and Mrs. John McCutcheon. Letter from Mrs. McCutcheon, Lake Forest, Ill.

[2A] Robert M. W. Dixon and John Godrich, *Blues & Gospel Records 1902–1942* (Harrow, Middlesex, England, 1963), p. 189; BM and NYPL.

[3] The date appears in the book opposite the title page.

[4] Included in *The Green Pastures Spirituals*, arranged by Hall Johnson (New York, N.Y., 1930), p. 4. NYPL.

[5] Informal advice from William Lichtenwanger, LC, the late Sigmund Spaeth and others.

[6] Lomax, *North America*, p. 449. The first spiritual was published at least as early as 1867 in *Slave Songs of the United States* (New York, N.Y.), p. 18, LC, and the second spiritual was published at least as early as 1872 in *Jubilee Songs*, Complete Edition (New York, N.Y.), p. 35, JF.

When You and I Were Young, Maggie

I wan-dered to-day to the hill, Mag-gie, to watch the scene be - low

m. J. A. Butterfield. w. George W. Johnson. Copyrighted May 19, 1866,[1] by the composer and published by J. A. Butterfield & Co., 75 East Market St., Indianapolis. First edition: Front cover has an inscription to Mrs. S. L. Atwell and the price of 3. p. [2] blank. m. on pp. [3]–[5]. Back cover blank. LC(CDC) and JF. Butterfield later published in Chicago.

The poem had previously appeared in George Washington Johnson, *Maple Leaves* (Hamilton, U.C. [Upper Canada], 1864), p. 164, under the title *When You and I Were Young*; BR and HU. The poem was written to the poet's sweetheart, Maggie Clark, who died the following year.

James Austin Butterfield was born in England in 1837, came to this country in 1856, became a composer, conductor and publisher, and died in 1891.[2] Johnson was born in 1839 at Binbrook, Upper Canada, became a newspaper editor in Detroit and a professor of languages and mathematics at the University of Toronto, and died at Pasadena, Cal., in 1917.[3]

When You Were Sweet Sixteen

I love you as I nev - er lov'd be - fore,— since first I met you on the vil-lage green;—

mw. James Thornton. Copyrighted Oct. 31, 1898,[1] by M. Witmark & Sons, New York, N.Y. First edition: Front cover has a dedication to Mr. & Mrs. Alphonze Comey and photographs of Bonnie Thornton and Lillie Leslie, refers to five arrangements and is purple, pink and white. p. [2] adv. *Marvelous..* m. on pp. [3]–[5]. p.n. 2158. p. [3] adv. *Fortune..* p. [4] adv. *Just..* p. [5] adv. *Because..* p. [6] adv. *Dream..* p. [7] adv. *Witmark..* Back cover adv. *Queen.. - Tempest.* LC(CDC).

There is a curious copyright entry on Jan. 29, 1895,[1] of the same song

---

[1] Copyright records; LC.

[2] NYPL Music Division Clipping and Biography Files.

[3] William S. Wallace, *The Dictionary of Canadian Biography* (Toronto, 1926), p. 201; and *Toronto Globe and Mail*, June 22, 1953, p. 21. Both at UT.

[1] Copyright records; LC.

by the same composer published by T. B. Harms & Co., New York, N.Y.,
copyright number 6763, but neither T. B. Harms & Co. nor M. Witmark &
Sons knows anything about any earlier publication, and no such copy has
been found.[2] Thornton was born in Liverpool, England, in 1861, became a
composer, lyricist and actor and died in Astoria, N.Y., in 1938.[3]

When You Wore a Tulip and I Wore a Big Red Rose

When   you wore   a   tu - lip   a sweet yel - low   tu - lip

© Copyright 1914 (renewed) Leo Feist, Inc., New York, N.Y. Used by permission.

m. Percy Wenrich. w. Jack Mahoney. Published July 13, 1914,[1] by Leo.
Feist, Inc., Feist Building, New York, N.Y. The copyright copy deposited at
LC is a professional edition with music on pp. 3–5. Possible first edition:
Front cover has a drawing of two girls in tulips, a photograph of a lady in
a white dress, and is orange, blue, green and white. p. [2] adv. *When..* m.
on pp. 3–5. p.n. 3143-3. Back cover adv. *You're.. - The Game..* All the
foregoing advertised songs which were published were copyrighted by
July 27, 1914. JF.

Brief biographic information regarding Wenrich appears above under
Put on Your Old Grey Bonnet. Mahoney was born in Buffalo in 1882, became a lyricist and died in New York City in 1945.[2]

When You're Away

When   you're   a - way,   dear

© 1914 M. Witmark & Sons. Copyright renewed. Used by permission.

m. Victor Herbert. w. Henry Blossom. Published Sept. 25, 1914,[1] by M.
Witmark & Sons, New York, N.Y. First edition: Front cover has a drawing

---

[2] Spaeth, p. 256, adds further confusion unless "Stern-Marks" should have read
"T. B. Harms & Co."

[3] *ASCAP*, p. 500.

[1] Copyright records; LC.

[2] *ASCAP*, p. 331.

[1] Copyright records; LC.

of roses, mentions the Musical Farcical Comedy *The Only Girl*, lists 14 titles, shows the publisher also at Chicago and London, and is light blue, red and white. m. on pp. 2–5. p.n. 13392-4. Back cover adv. *Artistic..* and gives the publisher's New York address as 10 Witmark Building. LC(CDC). There is no photograph or drawing of a person on the front cover which is entirely different from that of later editions.

The Only Girl opened in New York City on Nov. 2, 1914. The piano-vocal score was published Nov. 23, 1914,[1] at $2.00 with an orange, black, gray and white front cover having a photograph of [Adele Rowland?] and music on pp. 8–96. LC(CDC) and JF. Brief biographic information regarding Herbert and Blossom appears above under *Ah! Sweet Mystery of Life* and *Kiss Me Again.*

The Whiffenpoof Song

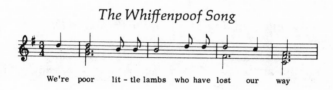

We're poor lit-tle lambs who have lost our way

© Copyright 1936 (renewed) Miller Music Corporation, New York, N.Y. Used by permission.

The first known printing of this song[1] is in the 1918 edition of *The New Yale Song-Book*, published July 2, 1918,[2] by G. Schirmer, New York and Boston. *Whiffenpoof Song* appears on p. 118 without mention of composer, lyricist or special copyright notice. The copyright deposit copy at LC has a paper binding; also at JF. In 1936 the song, with very few changes, was published in sheet music by Miller Music Corporation, New York, N.Y., with music and words credited to Meade Minnigerode, George S. Pomeroy and Tod B. Galloway, revision by Rudy Vallee, and the credits on the current sheet music so read.

A Yale investigator[3] claims that most of the melody of this Yale song was composed by a Harvard man, Guy H. Scull, before entering Harvard, about 1893–1894, to accompany the words of Kipling's poem, *Gentlemen-Rankers.* In 1909 a choral group at Yale called themselves "The Whiffenpoofs" after the imaginary Whiffenpoof fish mentioned by Joseph Cawthorne in Victor Herbert's *Little Nemo*, which opened in New York City on Oct. 20, 1908. In 1909 Minnigerode and Pomeroy wrote new words to Kipling's poem, while retaining some of the original words, and Galloway

[1] The best history of the song and of The Whiffenpoofs is in James M. Howard, "The Whiffenpoofs: 'Gentlemen Songsters Off on a Spree'" in *Yale Alumni Magazine*, New Haven, March, 1959, p. 8; YU. This article mentions Scull's role in the history of the song.

[2] Copyright records; LC.

[3] Letter from Carl B. Spitzer, Yale '99, in *Yale Alumni Magazine*, New Haven, Oct., 1950, p. 4; YU.

adapted the music. The song was popularized in 1935 by Rudy Vallee, a Yale graduate but not a member of The Whiffenpoofs, who turned over his royalties from the song to Yale until the latter made uncomplimentary remarks about him.[4]

Minnigerode was born in 1887 in London of American parents, graduated from Yale College in 1910, became an author and lives in Essex, Conn.[5] Pomeroy was born in 1888 in Wernersville, Pa., graduated from Yale College in 1910, and is retired and lives in Wyomissing, Pa.[5] Galloway was born in Columbus, Ohio, in 1863, graduated from Amherst College in 1885, became a judge and composer and died in Columbus in 1935.[6] Scull was born in Boston in 1876, graduated from Harvard College in 1898, became a journalist and died in New York City in 1920.[7]

While Strolling Through the Park One Day

While stroll-ing through the park one day all in the mer-ry month of May

mw. Ed. Haley. Copyrighted under the title *The Fountain in the Park* on May 21, 1884,[1] by Willis Woodward & Co., 842 & 844 Broadway, New York, N.Y., as piano-vocal sheet music and as a Schottische. First edition of the piano-vocal sheet music: Front cover is a collective title cover, listing four titles of which this is the first; the heading is "Popular Music," and this song is described as a Song & Dance by Healy [*sic*] at 40 (cents). p. [2] blank. m. on pp. 3–5, engraved, with a dedication to Mr. Robt. A. Keiser. No p.n. Back cover adv. *New.*. LC(CDC). The Schottische arrangement, listed second on the front cover, is essentially the same. LC(CDC) and JF. *The Fountain in the Park* with a separate front cover having photographs of the Du Rell Twin Brothers was apparently published later. Jean King, St. Petersburg, Fla., received the copy from the late Elliott Shapiro.

No biographic information is available regarding an Ed. Haley or Healy. Elliott Shapiro thought the name was a pseudonym of Robert A. Keiser, also known as Robert A. King.[2] This seems unlikely: Keiser-King, in the

[4] Jack Stone, "The Whiffenpoof Story," in *The American Weekly*, New York, N.Y., April 17, 1949, p. 12. NYPL Music Division Clipping File under Minnigerode.

[5] Information from the author.

[6] *ASCAP*, p. 172.

[7] Information from HU.

[1] Copyright records; LC.

[2] Spaeth, p. 233.

music business, did not renew the copyright; his daughter, Jean King, never heard her father make the claim, nor did anyone else, as far as is known; and it would be highly unusual for the user of a pseudonym to dedicate the song to his true name.

Whispering

Whis - per - ing   while you   cud - dle   near   me

© Copyright 1920 (renewed) Miller Music Corporation, New York, N.Y. Used by permission.

m. John Schonberger. w. Malvin Schonberger. Published July 22, 1920,[1] by Sherman, Clay & Co., San Francisco. First edition: Quarto. Front cover has a drawing of a couple, states "Standard," and is gray, pink, purple and white. p. [2] adv. *Louisiana*. m. on pp. [3]–5. p.n. 169 3 20. Back cover adv. *Planning*. LC(CDC) and JF.

John Schonberger was born in Philadelphia in 1892, became a composer and violinist and lives in North Hollywood, Cal.[2] According to John Schonberger, the lyrics were not written by Malvin Schonberger (about whom no biographical information has been found), but rather by Richard Coburn, a lyricist and singer, who was born under the name of Frank D. de Long, in Ipswich, Mass., in 1886, and who died in Los Angeles in 1952.[3] Current sheet music editions credit the music and words of the song to John Schonberger, Richard Coburn and Vincent Rose; the latter, a composer and director, was born in Palermo, Italy, in 1880, and died in Rockville Center, N.Y., in 1944.[4]

The Whistler and His Dog

m. Arthur Pryor. Copyrighted July 26, 1905,[1] for band parts by Carl Fischer, 6–10 Fourth Ave., New York, N.Y. First edition: The band

[1] Copyright records; LC.

[2] *ASCAP*, p. 441.

[3] *ASCAP*, p. 90 (confirming the authorship). Obituary, *The New York Times*, Oct. 31, 1952.

[4] *ASCAP*, p. 421 (confirming the authorship).

[1] Copyright records; LC.

arrangement is no. 1253. p.n. 9988 8 1/2. LC(CDC) and JF. The sheet
music edition for piano was copyrighted Aug. 30, 1905.[1] First edition:
Front cover has a drawing of a whistling boy and his dog standing (not
sitting, as in later editions), and is red, green and white. m. on pp. 2–5.
p.n. 10020-4. Back cover adv. On.. - For.. No advertisements on pp. 2–5.
LC(CDC) and JF.

Pryor was born in St. Joseph, Mo., in 1870, became a bandmaster
and composer, and died in West Long Branch, N.J., in 1942.[2]

White Christmas

I'm   dream-ing of   a   white   Christ-mas

Copyright 1942 Irving Berlin. Used by permission of Irving Berlin Music Corporation.

mw. Irving Berlin. Published May 6, 1942,[1] by Irving Berlin, Inc., 799
Seventh Ave., New York, N.Y. The copyright copy deposited at LC is a
professional edition. There are at least seven possible first regular editions,
each with a front cover having photographs of scenes from the movie
Holiday Inn, listing nine titles, in red, white and blue, and with music on
pp. 2–4, but with varying p. [5] and back cover. One of these editions,
advertising only songs published 1941 or earlier, has advertisements on p.
[5] *Marie.. - The Song..* and back cover advertisements, *This.. - America..*
A seventh variant lacks the war bond emblem present on the other six.
All variants at JF (one autographed by the composer).

It has been said that *White Christmas* is probably the most valuable
music copyright in the world—recently estimated at over $1,000,000.[2] To
Dec. 31, 1962, 40,449,535 recordings and 5,587,259 copies of sheet music
and other arrangements of the song had been sold. Bing Crosby's recording
of the song has been said to have had the greatest sales of any recording
of a single song by a particular singer.[3] *Holiday Inn*, starring Bing Crosby
and Fred Astaire, was copyrighted June 12, 1942, and released June 15,
1942, and centered on the principal American holidays, with a song for
each holiday. *White Christmas* was awarded the "Oscar" for the best
movie song in 1942 by the Academy of Motion Picture Arts and Sciences.
The composer has admitted that he was fooled by the success of *White*

---

[2] *ASCAP*, p. 396.

[1] Copyright records; LC.

[2] *Variety*, Dec. 18, 1963, p. 1.

[3] 23,000,000 through 1965. An original Decca record 18429 A in six-record album
A–306 at LC and JF. Album listed in *Decca Catalog* (n.p.), Oct., 1942, p. [5]; not in the
Decca Catalog for July, 1942; both *Catalogs* at NYPL.

Christmas,[4] caused, in part, perhaps by a "musical escapism" during the war. Brief biographic information regarding Berlin appears above under *Alexander's Ragtime Band.* †

Who?

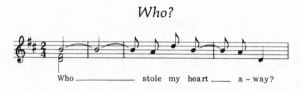

Who —————— stole my heart ——— a - way?

© 1925 by T. B. Harms Company. Copyright renewed. By consent.

m. Jerome Kern. w. Otto Harbach and Oscar Hammerstein 2nd. Published Sept. 19, 1925,[1] by T. B. Harms Company, New York, N.Y. First edition: Front cover has a drawing of a girl and flowers, refers to the musical comedy *Sunny,* with Marilyn Miller, listing two titles, and is green, orange and white. m. on pp. 2–5. p.n. 276–4. Back cover adv. *June..* LC(CDC) and JF.

Sunny opened in New York City on Sept. 7, 1925. The piano-vocal score was published Aug. 1, 1934,[1] by Chappell & Co., Ltd., London, at 8/; LC(CDC). Brief biographic information regarding Kern, Harbach and Hammerstein appears above under *All the Things You Are* and *The Desert Song.*

Why Was I Born?

Why was I born?——— Why am I liv - ing?

© 1929 by T. B. Harms Company. Copyright renewed. By consent.

m. Jerome Kern. w. Oscar Hammerstein 2nd. Published Sept. 4, 1929,[1] by T. B. Harms Company, New York, N.Y. First edition: Front cover has a drawing of a gentleman watching a lady dancing, refers to the musical play *Sweet Adeline,* lists four titles, and is red, black and white. m. on pp. 2–5. p.n. 317-4. Back cover adv. *Don't.. - Here..,* the address of the publisher being 62 W. 45th St., New York, N.Y. LC(CDC) and JF.

---

[4] *New York World-Telegram and Sun,* Nov. 6, 1954, magazine sec., p. 10; copy at publisher.

[1] Copyright records; LC.

[1] Copyright records; LC.

Sweet Adeline opened in New York City on Sept. 2, 1929. No piano-vocal score has been published. Brief biographic information regarding Kern and Hammerstein appears above under *All the Things You Are*.

Wiegenlied—Brahms

Gu - ten A - bend, gut' Nacht,   mit __ Ro - sen   be - dacht __

m. Johannes Brahms. w. Anonymous. *Fünf Lieder*, op. 49, for voice and piano, in which *Wiegenlied* (*Lullaby*) is no. 4, was published Oct.–Dec. 15, 1868,[1] by Simrock'schen Musikhandlung [i.e., Fritz Simrock], 18 Jäger-strasse, Berlin. Probable first edition: Title page is headed *Lieder und Gesänge*, lists Gesänge and Lieder from Brahms's opp. 46, 47, 48 and 49, including the title, poet and first line of each number and has a green frame. The "poet" for this song is "Aus Simrock's Kinderbuch." m. on pp. 2–15, lithographed. *Wiegenlied*, dedicated to B.F.[2] in Vienna, is on p. 11, with one verse; in the 14th complete bar, the last note in the bass to the word "Morgen" is B flat.[3] No price on title page. p.n. 323. p. [16] blank. BM (dated April 10, 1869), GM (aus Brahms Nachlass) and JF (with green and black covers; price of 25 Sgr. on front cover).

Three Brahms authorities concur that the foregoing is the first printing,[4] the plate number indicating a Berlin plate number,[4A] even though the music pages are lithographed. They believe that a similar edition with engraved music pages and plate number 6982, indicating a Bonn plate number[4A] where Fritz Simrock's father also published, is later; BSM (4° Mus. pr. 10626).

[1] The entry at Stationers' Hall on March 22, 1869, gives Dec. 15, 1868, Berlin, as the date and place of publication, and the publisher is Simrock'schen Musikhandlung. Deutsch, *Brahms*, p. 141, gives the date as Oct., 1868. Hofmeister *Monatsbericht*, Dec., 1868, p. 218.

[2] Bertha Faber. *Wiegenlied* was composed for one of the Fabers' children (Florence May, *The Life of Johannes Brahms*, London, 1905, vol. 2, p. 428, and Richard Specht, *Johannes Brahms*, London, 1930, p. 109; both at NYPL).

[3] Should be E flat; *Brahms Sämtliche Werke* (Leipzig [1928]), vol. 24, p. iv, at NYPL.

[4] Deutsch, *Brahms*, p. 141. Hofmann, *Brahms*, p. 103. Dr. Siegfried Kross, Bonn, in a letter to the author.

[4A] Deutsch, *Plate Numbers*, p. 26.

If an engraved copy with plate number 323 is found, this would be the first printing. In later editions, there is a second verse of words by Georg Scherer; such a copy, with plate number 323 and lithographed music pages, is at GM.

The words of the *Wiegenlied* were probably first published in *Kinder-lieder* (Heidelberg, 1808), Anhang zum Wunderhorn, p. 68; LC. The latter is *Des Knaben Wunderhorn*, by L. Achim v. Arnim and Clemens Brentano, published in Heidelberg and Frankfurt in 1806–8; BM.

Brahms's original[5] melody of "Wiegenlied" was superimposed on an accompaniment[6] which was an Austrian Ländler, a folk song in the form of a slow waltz. The melody of the accompaniment, with new words by Alexander Baumann, had been published in 1843–1844[7] as no. 1 of part 2 of *Gebirgs-Blĕameln* (*Mountain Flowers*) under the title *S'is Anderscht* (*It's Different*), with the opening words, "Du Moanst Wol" ("You mean well"), the publisher being Ant. Diabelli und Comp., Vienna, and the p.n. 7839. Baumann's new words were said to be in Austrian dialect to national melodies. BSM.

Wiegenlied was composed by Brahms in July, 1868. He later suggested to his publisher that there should be a special edition in a minor key for naughty children! Brief biographic information regarding Brahms appears under his *Concerto for Piano no. 1*.

Will You Remember (Sweetheart)

Sweet - heart, sweet - heart, sweet - heart

m. Sigmund Romberg. w. Rida Johnson Young. Published Aug. 16, 1917,[1] by G. Schirmer, New York and Boston. First edition: Front cover has a drawing of a girl under trees, refers to the play with music *Maytime*, listing 10 titles, and is green, black and white. p. [2] blank. m. on pp. 3–6. p.n. 27755. p. [7] blank. Back cover adv. *You're.. - Boola..*, and gives the

---

[5] Although see *Die Rheinisch-bergischen Melodien bei Zuccalmaglio und Brahms* in Dr. Karl Meisen, *Quellen und Studien zur Volkskunde*, Band 1 (Bad Godesberg, 1953), pp. 106 and 168; FR.

[6] Max Kalbeck, *Johannes Brahms* (Berlin, 1912), vol. 1, part 2, p. 367 ("the vocal part adds a freely invented counterpoint"); BSM.

[7] Deutsch, *Plate Numbers*, p. 11.

---

[1] Copyright records; LC.

New York address as 3 East 43d St. LC(CDC) and JF. In later editions, "(Sweetheart)" is added after "Will You Remember" on the top and bottom of the front cover and on the top of p. 3.

Maytime opened in New York City on Aug. 16, 1917, and the piano-vocal score was published on Sept. 25, 1917.[1] First edition: Front cover is green, yellow and white, the price is $2.50, the music is on pp. 1–77, and the p.n. is 27863. LC(CDC). Brief biographic information regarding Romberg and Young appears above under *Deep in My Heart, Dear* and *Ah! Sweet Mystery of Life.*

William Tell-Overture—Rossini

m. G. Rossini. The piano-vocal score of *Guillaume Tell* was published about Sept. 19, 1829,[1] by E. Troupenas, 3 Rue de Menars, Paris. Probable first edition: the title page mentions the Répertoire des Opéras Français in an ornamental frame containing names of nine composers, and refers to the librettists, Jouy and Hypolite Bis; the address of the publisher is the earlier address. vb. Cast and index. vb. m. on pp. 1–396. p.n. 329. Engraved. Folio. In this probable first edition, the price on the title page is "60f." and Hedwige's recitative on page 364 ends with "Hedwige tombe à vos genoux" (as in the autograph score). BM, COP (L 2218), JMM and JF. In the next edition, the price is "40f."[2] and the recitative ends with "Sur mon époux tu veilleras." COP (X 737) and JMM.

The *Overture* to the opera may have been published a few days earlier,

---

[1] The author is grateful to Prof. Philip Gossett, Chicago, for information regarding this title. See Gossett, p. 456, and dissertation on the *Operas of Rossini* at PUL.

BF, Sept. 19, 1829, at 60 fr., p. 640. The Schott, Mainz, edition of the piano-vocal score, claiming it is an "Original-Auflage," is in Hofmeister *Monatsbericht*, Nov.–Dec., 1829, p. 98, with German and French words, HD; copies of score at AT and ONB. This author believes the French edition preceded the German edition: the French edition was advertised several months earlier; the opera was performed in Paris months before its first German performance in Frankfurt on March 24, 1830; and the French edition has French text only, whereas the German edition has both French and German text.

[2] The title page of the 40 franc edition is illustrated in John Grand-Carteret, "Les titres illustrés et l'image au service de la musique" in *Rivista Musicale Italiana* (Turin, 1902), p. [559], at p. 625; NYPL.

about Sept. 12, 1829,[3] for piano with accompaniment for violin, although
the address of the publisher, E. Troupenas, is a later address, 23 Rue St.
Marc, Paris.[3A] The piano part has plate number 329 and the violin part
plate number 332. BN.

The orchestral score of *Guillaume Tell* was published probably in
1829[4] by E. Troupenas, 23 Rue St. Marc, Paris. Probable first edition: Title
page states "Dédié au Roi" (either Charles X who abdicated Aug. 2, 1830,
or Louis Philippe I who succeeded him on Aug. 9, 1830—perhaps inten-
tionally ambiguous in the turbulent France of 1830), states that the opera
was first performed on Aug. 3, 1829 (in Paris), has the price of **180 f.**, and
refers to London and Mainz-Antwerp agents; the address of publisher is
the later one. vb. Cast and index. vb. m. on pp. 1–837. p.n. 347 throughout
all the pages. Engraved. p. [838] blank. ONB, JMM and JF.

The earliest known orchestral parts of the opera were published by
Ricordi, Milan. The engraving of the string parts commenced on Sept. 15,
1864, with plate numbers 36411–36414.†

Guillaume Tell was composed in 1829 and requires about four and
one-half hours for a complete performance. Brief biographic information
regarding Rossini appears above under *The Barber of Seville—Overture*.
Victor Joseph Étienne de Jouy, a librettist and writer, was born at Jouy,
near Versailles, in 1764, and died in Saint-Germain-en-Laye in 1846.[5]
Hippolyte Louis Florent Bis was born at Douai, France, in 1789, became a
librettist and author, and died in Paris in 1855.[6]

Wine, Woman and Song

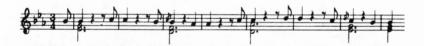

m. Johann Strauss. *Wein, Weib und Gesang*, op. 333, was published for
piano about Aug., 1869,[1] by C. A. Spina, Vienna. Probable first edition:

---

[3] *BF*, Sept. 12, 1829, p. 623. A piano arrangement at 4 Fr. by this publisher was
listed in Hofmeister *Monatsbericht*, Sept.–Oct., 1829, p. 78, HD, and also by Schott,
Mainz, and Arteria, Vienna. No copies have been found.

[3A] Hopkinson, *Parisian*, p. 116.

[4] Gossett, p. 456. Radiciotti, vol. 3, p. 244, mentions no date either for this edition or
for the Ratti e C., Rome, edition, with p.n. 565, copies of which are at BM and JMM.

[5] *Larousse XX*, vol. 4, p. 200.

[6] *GE*, vol. 6, p. 924.

[1] Hofmeister *Monatsbericht*, Aug., 1869, p. 143.

Oblong. Front cover has a drawing of a seated couple in the **center** of the page, a dedication to Johann Herbeck, mentions that the text (not, however, included in this edition) is by J. Weil, the title is followed by an exclamation mark, the front cover lists three arrangements but only this one has a price, namely, 80 Nkr., 15 Ngr., refers to three agents and is brown and white. vb. m. on pp. 3–11, engraved. p.n. C. S. 21,731. Back cover blank. SB and JF. Later editions have a completely different front cover with the couple seated to the left of the page. An early edition of the arrangement for piano four hands, also published at about the same time,[2] with p.n. C.S. 21,778, is at SB. The arrangement for piano and male chorus was also published at about the same time with p.n. C.S. 21,740.[3]

The orchestral parts of *Wein, Weib und Gesang* were also published about Aug., 1869.[4] An incomplete first edition, engraved and with p.n. C.S. 21,748, is at SB. The *Walzer* were first performed Feb. 2, 1869.

It has been said that Richard Wagner, upon hearing Anton Seidl conduct the music, was so moved by it that he seized the baton from Seidl's hand and conducted the remainder of the work himself.[5]

Brief biographic information regarding Strauss appears above under *Artist's Life.*

Wintergreen for President—Of Thee I Sing

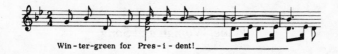

Win-ter-green for Pres-i-dent!

m. George Gershwin. w. Ira Gershwin. The piano-vocal score of *Of Thee I Sing* in which *Wintergreen for President* was first printed, was published April 13, 1932,[1] by New World Music Corporation, New York, N.Y. First edition: Front cover has a drawing of the Capitol, Washington, D.C., and is red, black and white. vb. Title page states that the book is by George S. Kaufman and Morrie Ryskind, has the price of $5.00 and mentions that Harms, Inc. is the sole selling agent. vb. Cast. vb. Synopsis. vb. Musical

---

[2] *Id.*, p. 138.

[3] Weinmann, *Strauss*, p. 98. Hofmeister, footnote 1, above, p. 145.

[4] Hofmeister, footnote 1, above, p. [134].

[5] Ewen, *Lighter Classics*, p. 296.

---

[1] Copyright records; LC.

Program. Copyright credits. m. on pp. 5–198, this song at p. 14. p.n. 107-
198. pp. [199] and [200] and inside and outside of back cover blank.
LC(CDC; lacks blank pp. [199] and [200]) and JF. *Of Thee I Sing* opened
in New York City on Dec. 26, 1931.

The first musical comedy to be awarded the Pulitzer Prize, *Of Thee
I Sing* derived its title from the third line of the first stanza of *America*.[2]
Brief biographic information regarding the Gershwins appears above under
I Got Rhythm.

Wi' a Hundred Pipers

Wi' a hun-dred pi-pers an'   a', an' a', wi' a hun-dred pi-pers an'   a', an' a'

m. Possibly either Lady Caroline Nairne or Elizabeth Rainforth. w. Possibly Lady Caroline Nairne. According to Alfred Moffat, the song was first
published about 1851 under the title *The Hundred Pipers* by Wood & Co.,[1]
12 Waterloo Place, Edinburgh. Probable first edition: Front cover refers to
the song as The Celebrated Jacobite Song from Mss. Lays of Strathearne,
arranged and sung by Miss Rainforth, there is a many-colored drawing of
Bonnie Prince Charlie entering Carlisle preceded by 100 pipers, the
price is 2/-, the publisher is also shown at Glasgow and Aberdeen, and
there are two London agents.[2] p. [2] blank. m. on pp. 1–5 (actually 3–7).
p. "1" states that the Symphonies & Accompaniments are by Elizabeth
Rainforth. p. "1" also tells the story of Charles Edward entering Carlisle preceded by 100 pipers, and after 2,000 Highlanders crossed the stream with
water up to their shoulders, "the pipers struck up, and they danced reels
until they were dry again." Back cover blank. No mention anywhere of
Lady Caroline Nairne. JF.

The song is included in Caroline, Baroness Nairne, *Lays from Strat-
hearn*, New Edition, published by R. Addison & Co., 210 Regent Street,
London, and Paterson & Sons, 27 George Street, Edinburgh, and 152
Buchanan Street, Glasgow, p. 97, under the title *The Hundred Pipers* (without mention of Rainforth or special mention of Nairne); the date of this

---

[2] See generally, Gershwin, p. 336, and Bernstein, p. 171.

[1] Moffat, *Minstrelsy of Scotland*, p. 272, who gives the year as about 1852, but,
as indicated in footnote 2, below, the latest year could be 1851. Grieg, *Scots*, vol. IV,
pp. vii and 72.

[2] The dates of the publisher and agents, per Humphries-Smith, are 1848–1851.

issue of the New Edition is about 1851–1857;[3] NLS and HU. The song did not appear in the first printing of this work about 1846.[4] A copy of the song published under the title *The Hundred Pipers* (without mention of Nairne or Rainforth) by Paterson & Sons, Edinburgh and Glasgow, was deposited at BM on Nov. 27, 1861.

It has also been said that the song was a true Jacobite song,[5] and again that the melody was an ancient Scottish "catch" merely adapted by Lady Nairne.[6] The first part of the melody bears a distinct resemblance to the first part of *The Lee Rigg*,[7] published about 1758 in (James) Oswald, *The Caledonian Pocket Companion* (London), vol. VIII, p. 20 (*BUC*, p. 747), and in a more similar version in 1787 in James Johnson, *The Scots Musical Museum* (Edinburgh), vol. I, p. 50 (*BUC*, p. 557, and JF).

Caroline Oliphant was born in 1776 at Gask, Perthshire, Scotland, the daughter of a distinguished family of Jacobites, married Major Nairne, wrote a great deal of verse, and died in 1845 at Gask.[8] Miss Rainforth was born in London in 1814, became a soprano vocalist, resided in Edinburgh about 1851, and died in Redland, Bristol, in 1877.[1]

With a Song in My Heart

With a song in my heart,——— I be-hold your a - dor - a - ble face

m. Richard Rodgers. w. Lorenz Hart. Published March 14, 1929,[1] by Harms Incorporated, New York, N.Y. First edition: Front cover has a drawing of oranges and flowers, mentions the New Musical Farce *Spring Is Here*, listing six titles, and is orange, green and white. p. [2] adv. *Watching..* and *Who's..* m. on pp. 2–5 (actually 3–6). p.n. 8338-4. p. [7] adv. *Say..* and *I..* Back cover adv. *In.. - Right..* LC(CDC) and JF.

[3] Humphries-Smith.

[4] Moffat, footnote 1, above. Letter from dealer offering a copy of first printing of this work. *Brit. Mus. Biog.*, p. 130. Rogers, vol. 1, p. 193. Allibone, vol. 2, p. 1397.

[5] Nettel, p. 136. Flood, *Bagpipe*, p. 143.

[6] *Gem Selection—Scottish Songs* (Dundee, ca. 1940), p. xi; JF.

[7] Not to be confused with *Old Lee Rig*, in Neil Gow, *A Second Collection of Strathspey Reels* (Edinburgh [1788]), *BUC*, p. 392, and JF.

[8] *Dict. Nat. Biog.*, vol. 14, p. 23.

[1] Copyright records; LC.

Spring Is Here opened in New York City on March 11, 1929; the piano-vocal score has not been published. Brief biographic information regarding Rodgers and Hart appears above under *If I Loved You* and *Lover*.

The Worms Crawl In (The Hearse Song)

The worms crawl in, the worms crawl out

This melody is known in a number of variants and by many titles: *The Worms Crawl In*; *The Hearse Song*; *Did You Ever Think As the Hearse Rolls by?*; *Rogues' March*; *Army Duff*; *The Elephant Walk*; *Oh, Marguerite!*; *The Bums' March*; and *A Hundred Years from Now*.[1]

It is possible that the song had a military origin, as it has been frequently associated with various aspects of the soldier's life. One authority believes it was known to British soldiers at the time of the Crimean War, 1854–1856.[2] The melody may have derived from the American march played when a punished soldier had his head shaved and was drummed out of camp. Certainly, a generally similar melody in the major, without words, appears under the title *Rogues' March* in Edward Arthur Dolph, *"Sound Off!"* (New York, N.Y., 1929), p. 72; LC(CDC) and JF. While no earlier printing of the *Rogues' March* has been found, the tune appears under this title in several early undated American musical manuscript books, e.g., "Enoch Peirce's Book, Newburyport," circa 1800, at page 113; Irving Lowens, Baltimore.†

A somewhat closer approximation to the above-quoted melody, but in the major and without words, was under the title *Army Duff* in *A Musical Switch*, Humoresque, adapted and arranged by Kenneth J. Alford for military band parts, a set of which was deposited at BM on April 20, 1921, by Hawkes and Son, Denman Street, Piccadilly Circus, London W.1. *A Musical Switch* is a medley of 44 familiar tunes, *Army Duff* appearing on p. 6 of the piano-conductor score. According to a letter to the author from an ex-British Army musician, W. D. Trigg, Toronto, the word "duff" means a sticky, heavy pudding; thus the connection with a slow, heavy tune. Almost the same melody, also in the major and without words, appears as *The Elephant Walk*, arranged for children and published in 1948 by J. J. Robbins & Sons, Inc., New York, N.Y.; JF. A similar melody, in the

---

[1] Harold Barlow, New York City, has been most helpful in connection with this song.

[2] Spaeth, p. 130.

major, with the opening words, *Oh, Marguerite!*, appears in Botkin, p. 796.

As *The Worms Crawl In*, the song seems to have become popular during World War I—as the hearse rolled by on the battlefield, one soldier told another what would happen if one were killed during battle and later buried underground: in the third stanza or so, the worms crawl in, the worms crawl out, they crawl all over, etc., etc. Its first known printing in this form, in the minor and with words, was in Annetta Eldridge and Ruth E. Richardson, *Stunt Songs for Social Sings* (Denver, Col., and Franklin, Ohio), p. 25, under the title *Hearse Song*; this booklet was first published Nov. 14, 1923, with 48 pages;[3] LC(CDC). It was printed in the minor with words, with slight variations, in Sandburg in 1927, p. 444. It was printed in the major with words, and with further slight variations, in Dick and Beth Best, *Song Fest* (New York, N.Y., 1948), p. 61; LC(CDC).

Wunderbar—Kiss Me Kate

Wun - der - bar,⎯⎯⎯⎯ wun - der - bar!

mw. Cole Porter. Published Nov. 29, 1948,[1] by Buxton Hill Music Corporation [New York, N.Y.] The copyright copy deposited at LC is a professional edition. Probable first regular edition: Front cover refers to the musical comedy *Kiss Me Kate*, lists four titles, and is purple, red and white. p. [2] adv. *Warsaw*.. m. on pp. 3–7. p.n. 1604-5. The copyright is in the name of Cole Porter; T. B. Harms Company, RKO Building, Rockefeller Center, New York, N.Y., is the sole selling agent. Back cover adv. *Ace*.. - *You*.. All advertised compositions were published prior to 1948. JF.

Kiss Me Kate opened in New York City on Dec. 30, 1948, and was the composer's favorite of his shows.[2] The piano-vocal score was published June 28, 1951,[1] by Chappell & Co., Ltd., 50 New Bond St., London W. 2, at 12/6 and with the back cover advertising *So*.. - *Always*.. LC(CDC) and JF. Brief biographic information regarding Porter appears above under *Begin the Beguine*.

---

[3] Copyright records; LC.

---

[1] Copyright records; LC.
[2] *The New York Times*, June 8, 1962, p. 36.

Yankee Doodle

Yan - kee Doo - dle went to town up - on a lit - tle po - ny

A book is waiting to be written regarding *Yankee Doodle*, and all that can be said here is to summarize its most important written history, refer to some excellent scattered articles which otherwise may escape notice, and mention newly discovered information.

While one authority[1] believes that the earliest words of *Yankee Doodle* were written shortly after the capture of Louisburg, on Cape Breton Island, Canada, on June 17, 1745, the written history of the song begins April 6–13, 1767,[2] when the libretto of *The Disappointment: or, The Force of Credulity*, a new American comic opera by Andrew Barton, was published in New York City; included in the libretto as "Air IV 'Yankee Doodle'" on p. 22, is one verse of words, mentioning at the end: "Exit, singing the chorus, yankee doodle, etc." No music is included. Sonneck-Upton, p. 109.

The song must thus have been well-known in the colonies in the 1760's. In the balance of the eighteenth century there were a great many American references to the song, and printings of poems to the melody, in newspapers (one authority says dozens, perhaps hundreds of these), theater libretti, broadsides and elsewhere; these desperately need to be assembled and studied.[3] †

The earliest datable foreign printed reference to *Yankee Doodle* is in Joel Collier, *Musical Travels through England* (London, 1774), a satire on Dr. Burney's travels on the continent; LC, PUL, YU and JF.‡ The next datable foreign reference is in the Nov. 21, 1776, issue of *The Bath Chronicle.* §

Almost no secular music was printed in the colonies until about five years after the conclusion of the Revolutionary War in 1783, whereas huge amounts of secular music were printed in Great Britain during this period. Thus, it is to be expected that the first printing of the music of *Yankee Doodle* would not be American.

[1] S. Foster Damon, *Yankee Doodle* [Providence], Oct., 1959, p. 11; BR.

[2] *Pennsylvania Chronicle*, Philadelphia, April 20–27, 1767, p. 56; LCP.

[3] Some of these are mentioned in the standard authority, Sonneck, *Report*, pp. 79–156; Damon, footnote 1, above; Washington Chauncey Ford, *Broadsides, Ballads Etc. Printed in Massachusetts 1639–1800* ([Boston], 1922), nos. 1940–1941 and 3417–3420, NYPL; and John Bach McMaster, *History of the People of the United States* (New York, N.Y., 1885), vol. 2, pp. 379 *et seq.*, NYPL. Others are at NYPL Rare Book Room. ‖

The earliest printing of the music of *Yankee Doodle* may have been in the first issue of [Volume First of] *A Selection of Scotch, English, Irish and Foreign Airs*, printed by James Aird, Glasgow, in Aug., 1782, at p. 36 under the title *Yanky Doodle*, without words. In the first edition, the words "Volume First" do not appear on the title page;[4] NLS. The earliest printing of the music may also have been in sheet music entitled *Yankee Doodle* published by "Sk:" (Thomas Skillern, London), with words. One authority believes that this sheet music was published between the battles of Lexington and Bunker Hill, April 19–June 17, 1775;[1] however, the song is not included in Skillern's *Catalogue* issued in 1782, at BM. In none of the copies found, at BPL, BR and WNH, is there a dated watermark.

The earliest known printing of the music in America is either in *The Federal Overture*, published by B. Carr's Musical Repositorys, Philadelphia and New York, and J. Carr, Baltimore, about Nov. 24, 1794,[5] in which *Yankee Doodle* appears on p. 6 without words, at NYPL, or in a newly discovered sheet of music entitled *General Waynes* [sic] *New March, Stoney Point & Yanky doodle*, also without words, with the identical imprint, at JF. In Aug., 1796, the same publishers issued variations for the piano of *Yankee Doodle*, "An Original American Air"; Sonneck-Upton, p. 480, and JF.[6] †

The earliest known printing of the common words of *Yankee Doodle* relating to "pony, feather and macaroni" is in James Orchard Halliwell, *The Nursery Rhymes of England* (London, 1842), p. 82; NYPL.

Most of the authorities now conclude that the song is American in origin.[7]

---

[4] Information from NLS. The second issue of the first volume mentions both the first volume and the second volume (which appeared three weeks later); the third issue mentions volume 3 (which appeared in 1788). Copies of all three issues of the first volume are at NLS. Glen, pp. x and xi. Neither Aird's *Selection* nor Skillern's *Yankee Doodle* was entered at Stationers' Hall. Aird's first volume also includes two "Virginian" pieces, *Old Plantation Girls* and *Sam Jones*, and one "Negroe" piece, *Pompey Ran Away*.

[5] Sonneck-Upton, p. 139, referring to an advertisement in the *American Daily Advertiser*, Philadelphia, of that date, p. 2; PHS.

[6] Lewis A. Maverick makes some unusual suggestions, not convincing to this observer, in "Yankee Doodle," in *The American Neptune*, Salem, Mass., April, 1962, p. [106]; NYPL.

[7] The melody is called the American "National Air" in a sheet of music published, according to Wolfe, p. 442, no. 4530, in the United States, 1807–11, entitled *A Musical Coalition* "wherein the prevailing [sic] Discords between America, France & England, are Harmoniously adjusted, or a Humorous Combination of their National Airs" by Dr. G. K. Jackson. *Ça Ira* is arranged for a French Zauber Flote, *Yanke* [sic] *Doodle* for an American Martial Band and *God Save the King* for an English Man of Wars Drum Beating. NYPL and JF. There are no words, imprint or watermark. The compo-

The Yellow Rose of Texas

There's a yel - low rose in Tex - as   that   I am going to see

mw. J. K. Copyrighted Sept. 2, 1858,[1] by Firth, Pond & Co., 547 Broadway, New York, N.Y. First edition: Front cover states that the song & chorus were composed and arranged expressly for Charles H. Brown by J. K., the price is 2½ and the copublisher is Charles H. Brown, Jackson, Tenn. m. on pp. 2–5. p.n. 4449. Back cover blank. Engraved. No reference on the front cover to Piano and Guitar. LC(CDC).

The identity of J. K. is unknown. †

Yes Sir! That's My Baby

Yes   sir,   that's my ba - by,   no   sir,   don't mean "may-be"

m. Walter Donaldson. w. Gus Kahn. Published April 27, 1925,[1] by Irving Berlin, Inc., 1607 Broadway, New York, N.Y. Possible first edition: Front cover has a drawing of a "baby" and a photograph of Lieut. Frankel, and is orange, black and white; no price. m. on pp. 2–5. No plate number. Back cover adv. *Ukulele Lady* (published March 11, 1925). JF.

Brief biographic information regarding Donaldson appears above under *My Blue Heaven*, and regarding Kahn under *Carioca*.

sition was not entered at Stationers' Hall or copyrighted in the United States. Jackson emigrated from England to America in 1796. H. Earle Johnson, *Musical Interludes in Boston 1795–1830* (New York, N.Y., 1943), p. [201]; NYPL.

See, also, Frank Kidson, "Some Guesses About Yankee Doodle," in *MQ*, Jan., 1917, p. 98; Opie, p. 439; and Dichter-Shapiro, p. 17.

[1] Copyright records; LC.

[1] Copyright records; LC.

Yes! We Have No Bananas

Yes!   We have no   ba - na - nas

mw. Frank Silver and Irving Cohn. Published March 23, 1923,[1] by Skidmore Music Co. Inc., 218 West 47th Street, New York, N.Y., the copyright deposit copy at LC being a professional edition with only two stanzas. Possible first regular edition: Front cover has a drawing of a fruit vendor, is orange, black and white, and refers to Shapiro, Bernstein & Co. as selling agents. p. [2] has eight extra choruses, stanza no. 3 referring to "From fine cemeteries." m. on pp. 3–5. Back cover adv. 'Way.. - Red.. (all advertised songs published by Jan. 18, 1923). LC (M 1630.2) and JF. A variant is identical (including the same advertised songs) except that stanza no. 3 refers to "COO-cum-bers and cherries"; JF. Priority of the two variants is not known.

The words of the title are said to have been uttered by a Long Island Greek fruit peddler.[2] Sigmund Spaeth has devised a clever, analytical text to the melody of this song.[3] Silver, a composer and lyricist, was born in Boston in 1896 and died in Brooklyn in 1960.[4] Cohn, also known as Irving Conn, was born in London in 1898, became a composer and lyricist in America and died in Fort Lee, N.J., in 1961.[4]

Yodel Call

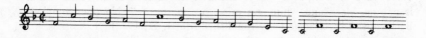

The above excerpts from the earliest known yodel call are in *Bicinia Gallica, Latina, Germanica*, published by Georg Rhaw in Württemberg in 1545.[1] In vol. 1, no. LXXXIIII, is the music of *Der Appenzeller Kureyen*

---

[1] Copyright records; LC.

[2] Obituary of Frank Silver, *The New York Times*, June 15, 1960. Wickes, p. 25.

[3] Spaeth, p. 437.

[4] *ASCAP*, pp. 458 and 93, and ASCAP files.

---

[1] The author is indebted to Paul-Émile Schazmann, SL, for this information. The earliest known collection of yodel calls is in *Acht Schweizer-Kühreihen*, edited by Sigmund von Wagner (Bern, 1806); SL. See A. Hyatt King, "Mountains, Music, and Musicans," in *MQ*, Oct., 1945, p. 395.

(*The Call of a Cowherd from Appenzell*, now a Canton in northeast Switzerland). *RISM*, p. 150.

You Made Me Love You (I Didn't Want To Do It)

You made me love you, I   did-n't want to do it, I   did-n't want to do it

m. James V. Monaco. w. Joe McCarthy. Published April 30, 1913,[1] in a professional edition; LC(CDC). The following edition, published May 5, 1913,[1] by Broadway Music Corporation, 145 West 45th Street, New York, N.Y., is the first regular edition: Front cover refers to Al Jolson and the Winter Garden production *The Honeymoon Express*, has the price of 5, and is black and white. m. on pp. 2–5. No plate number. Back cover adv. *I Have..* Front cover has no drawing or photograph of a crying girl. LC(CDC). *The Honeymoon Express* opened in New York City on Feb. 6, 1913.

Monaco was born in Genoa, Italy, in 1885, came to America at the age of six, became a pianist and composer, and died in Beverly Hills, Cal., in 1945.[2] McCarthy, a lyricist, was born in Somerville, Mass., in 1885 and died in New York City in 1943.[3]

You're a Grand Old Flag

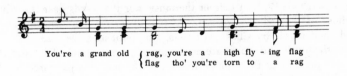

You're a grand old { rag, you're a   high fly - ing flag
                     { flag tho' you're torn to   a   rag

mw. Geo. M. Cohan. Copyrighted Jan. 19, 1906,[1] by F. A. Mills, 48 West 29th St., New York, N.Y. First edition: The title is *You're a Grand Old Rag*. Front cover has a photograph of the composer in a revolutionary military uniform, refers to the musical play *George Washington Jr.*, and is red,

---

[1] Copyright records; LC.
[2] Burton, p. 208. *ASCAP*, p. 354.
[3] *ASCAP*, p. 318.

---

[1] Copyright records; LC.

white and blue. p. [2] adv. *We'll.. - Watch..* m. on pp. [3]–[6]. p. [7] adv. *Nothin'.. - Good-Bye..* Back cover adv. *Geo..* LC(CDC) and JF.

The last word of the title was soon changed to "Flag" because of protest that the original word, "Rag," was disrespectful to the American flag; *You're a Grand Old Flag* was copyrighted June 2, 1906.[1]

"You're a Grand Old Bag" is another variant used in a complimentary birthday card; card at JF. *George Washington Jr.* opened in New York City on Lincoln's Birthday, 1906! Brief biographic information regarding the composer appears above under *Give My Regards to Broadway*.

You're in the Army Now

You're in the ar - my now,_____ you're not be-hind the plow

The familiar words set to a different melody were published under the title *We're in the Army Now* on Aug. 27, 1917,[1] by Tell Taylor, Chicago and New York, with the words credited to Tell Taylor and Ole Olsen and the music credited to Isham Jones. A photostat of the copyright deposit copy at LC, in the possession of Isham Jones, shows the front cover to have a drawing of soldiers, states that the song is Sung by Every Soldier in the United States, music on pp. 2–3; folio. A copy meeting this description has a blue and white front cover, and the back cover adv. *There's.. - I..* (all advertised songs published before Aug. 27, 1917). JF.

I'm in the Army, with music and words by Victor Ormond, was published Oct. 1, 1917,[1] but neither the music nor the words bear resemblance to those of the well-known song; LC(CDC). *I'm in the Army Now*, with music and words by Chas. A. Bayha, was published Dec. 28, 1917,[1] but again, the music and words are not commonly known; LC(CDC) and JF.

No printing of the familiar melody of the bugle corps march has been found before its inclusion in 1929 in Edward Arthur Dolph, *"Sound Off!"* (New York, N.Y., 1929), p. 12; LC(CDC) and JF. The common words are also included in this work which was published April 26, 1929.[1]

[1] Copyright records; LC.

Yours Is My Heart Alone—Lehár

Dein	ist	mein	gan-zes	Herz!	Wo	du	nicht	bist,	kann	ich	nicht	sein
Yours	is	my	heart a - lone	and	with-out			you	life	holds	no	charm

m. Franz Lehár. w. Ludwig Herzer and Fritz Löhner. The melody of *Dein Ist Mein Ganzes Herz* (*Yours Is My Heart Alone*) was originally set to two sets of other words, both sets included in Lehár's operetta *Die Gelbe Jacke* (*The Yellow Jacket*), which was performed on Feb. 13, 1923, in Vienna. The piano-vocal score of *Die Gelbe Jacke* was published April 10, 1923,[1] by W. Karczag, 36/38 Nürnbergerstr., Leipzig, and 6 Linke Wienzeile, Vienna VI. Possible first edition: Front cover has a drawing of a Chinese scene with a bridge and lanterns and is yellow and light and dark blue. vb. Title page states that the words are by Victor Léon and lists the piano score and piano-vocal scores without prices. Cast and index. m. on pp. 3–124, this melody on p. 120 to the words, "Duft lag in Deinem Wort." p.n. 1571. Inside of back cover blank. Outside of back cover mentions Waldheim. ONB and JF. The piano score, presumably published about the same time, with a different yellow, gold, red and black front cover having a drawing of a seated Chinese lady, has the identical title page and p.n. 1572, but with this melody on p. 91 to entirely different words, "Lebt in der Seele uns." ONB and JF. Neither *Duft Lag in Deinem Wort* nor *Lebt in der Seele Uns* was separately published or listed on sheet music from the operetta; EW and JF. Brief biographic information regarding Léon appears above under *Merry Widow*.

The operetta *Das Land des Lächelns* (*The Land of Smiles*) was performed in Berlin on Oct. 10, 1929, and *Dein Ist Mein Ganzes Herz* became its featured song. Possible first edition of the piano-vocal score published that month:[2] Front cover has a drawing of a Chinese scene with a bridge and lanterns and is yellow and light and dark blue (basically the same as that of the piano-vocal score of *Die Gelbe Jacke*). vb. Next page blank. Photograph of the composer. Title page mentions only the piano-vocal score, the imprint being W. Karczag, 36/38 Nürnbergerstrasse, Leipzig,

---

[1] Copyright records; LC.

[2] Information from present publisher. Dec. 28, 1929, per copyright records at LC. Hofmeister *Monatsbericht*, Feb., 1930, p. 40.

and 6 Linke Wienzeile, Vienna VI. Cast and index. m. on pp. 3–95, this song at p. 56 with a dedication: "Mein lieber Richard [Tauber]! Hier hast du *dein Tauber-Lied!!* Bad Ischl, 17/8, 1929. Dein Franz." p.n. 1571 (same as that of *Die Gelbe Jacke!*). p. [96] and inside of back cover blank. Outside of back cover mentions Waldheim.. JF (inscribed by the composer on the title page). The piano score, probably published the same month,[3] has a different yellow, gold, red and black front cover having a drawing of a seated Chinese lady (basically the same as that of the piano score of *Die Gelbe Jacke*) and p.n. 1572; ONB. The sheet music of *Dein Ist Mein Ganzes Herz* may also have been published the same month;[4] a possible first edition with an "operetta cover" and p.n. 1933 is at JF.

The English words were written by Harry B. Smith in 1930. Brief biographic information regarding Lehár appears above under *Gold and Silver Waltz*. Herzer, a librettist and lyricist, was born in Vienna in 1872 and died in St. Gall, Switzerland, in 1939.[5] Löhner, also a librettist and lyricist, was born in Wildenschwert, Bohemia, in 1883, and died in the Auschwitz concentration camp in 1942.[5]

Zampa-Overture—Hérold

m. F. Hérold. The *Overture* probably first appeared in the orchestral score. of *Zampa ou La Fiancée de Marbre* published by J. Meissonnier, 22 Rue Dauphine, Paris, probably sometime after its performance in Paris on May 3, 1831, although no evidence as to date of publication has been found.[1] Probable first edition: Title page states that the words are by Mr. Mélesville, has a dedication to Louis Philippe and lists only the orchestral score and orchestral parts, each at 125 f. vb. Cast and index. vb. m. on pp. 1–419. p.n. 538. p. [420] blank. Engraved. French text. NC, ONB* and JMM. The above edition is earlier than an edition which is identical except that the

---

[3] Hofmeister *Monatsbericht*, Feb., 1930, p. 40.

[4] Published in Oct., 1929, according to the present publisher. Hofmeister *Monatsbericht*, Feb., 1930, p. 40.

[5] Information from AKM.

[1] Separate numbers from the opera published by Meissonnier, but not the *Overture*, in sheet music form were listed in *BF*, May 21, 1831, p. 311. The *Overture* for piano was published in 1831 by P. Mechetti, Vienna, with p.n. 2108, at SB, and also perhaps by Tobias Haslinger, Vienna, with p.n. 5970, at ONB. Deutsch, *Plate Numbers*, pp. 17 and 24.

prices are 150 f.; BM and NYPL. A probable first edition of the orchestral parts of *Zampa*, engraved, with plate number 539, without covers, is at MAP.

The piano-vocal score of the opera by this publisher has p.n. 711 and is therefore presumably later; the edition at 50 fr. is earlier than the one at 30 fr. (copies of both at JMM).† The Mainz, Schott, piano-vocal score was published about May–June, 1832.[2] Two editions are known, priority uncertain: one, with the price of 12 Fl. 36 kr. / 7 Rthlr., is at BSM; the other, with the price of 12 Fl. 36 kr., is at JF.

Louis Joseph Ferdinand Hérold was born in Paris in 1791 and died at Les Ternes in 1833. Mélesville was a pseudonym adopted by Anne-Honoré-Joseph Duveyrier, a dramatic author, who was born in Paris in 1787 and died at Marly-le-Roi in 1865.[3]

Zwei Herzen im Dreivierteltakt

Zwei   Her - zen   im   Drei - vier - tel - takt

m. Robert Stolz. w. W. Reisch and A. Robinson. A booklet of songs from the movie *Zwei Herzen im Dreivierteltakt*, including the title song, was published March 1, 1930,[1] by Alrobi Musikverlag G.m.b.H., 34 Rankestr., Berlin W. 50. First edition of the booklet: Front cover has a drawing of two hearts and cherubs, mentions the movie, lists four songs of which the title song, a Walzerlied, is first, and is pink, light green and white. m. on pp. 2–9, this song, op. 548, on p. 2. p.n. 197a-d. Back cover adv. *Die Zwei..* LC(copyright copy deposited May 10, 1930) and JF. The world premiere of the movie was on March 13, 1930, in Berlin, the movie being copyrighted in the United States on March 13, 1930.

Because of the success of the movie, an operetta entitled *Der Verlorene Walzer*, based on the film, was produced in Zurich on Sept. 30, 1933, including the song *Zwei Herzen im Dreivierteltakt*. The title in English is *Two Hearts in Three-Quarter Time*. Stolz was born in Graz in 1880, became

---

[2] Hofmeister *Monatsbericht*, May–June, 1832, p. 44; HD.

[3] *DGB*, p. 1864.

[1] Copyright records; LC. Hofmeister *Monatsbericht*, April, 1930, p. 103, which also lists the separate song.

a conductor and composer, lived in Vienna and died in West Berlin in 1875.[2] Walter Reisch, a film-writer and lyricist, was born in Vienna in 1903 and lives in Los Angeles.[3] A. L. Robinson, also a lyricist and publisher was born in Vienna in 1900 and lives in West Germany.[3]

[2] Gustav Holm, *Im ¾ Takt durch Die Welt* (Linz and Pittsburgh, 1948); NYPL. Obituary, *The New York Times*, June 28, 1975.

[3] Information from AKM.

SUPPLEMENT

See the Note to the Dover Edition, page viii

Page 5

† Simultaneous publication of a work in several different countries was frequently intended in the early and middle nineteenth century—for example, many works by Chopin and Mendelssohn in England, France and Germany. One reason for this effort was the fear at that time that copyright in one country might be lost by prior publication in another country. (See, e.g., Tyson, p. 144.)

Not considered a "publication" is a manuscript copy such as was made by a professional copyist of a work by Bach, Mozart or others in the second half of the eighteenth century prior to the availability of engraved or printed copies of the particular work. (The Breitkopf firm issued a number of important catalogs of music available in manuscript copies beginning in 1761. See also, e.g., Schneider, p. 99, and Otto Erich Deutsch, *Mozart, A Documentary Biography*, Stanford, Cal., 1966, pp. 226 *et seq.*; NYPL.)

Page 9

† Priority of edition can be established in some Ricordi publications by the change of the engraver's letter appearing next to the plate number. The name of the original engraver is in the Ricordi *Libroni,* and it is easy to match the name of an engraver with his letter. Since plates were frequently replaced, it is helpful to know the letter on the original plate.

Page 10

† For example, a British copyright law adopted on Aug. 10, 1882, required the title page to have a notice to the effect that the right of public representation or performance is reserved. (45 & 46 Vict. c. 40; BM.)

‡ There were apparently occasional instances in which the first edition was printed primarily from a flat process, but at about the same time a few copies were printed from engraved plates, probably for presentation or copyright deposit. (See, for example, the piano-vocal score of *Parsifal.*)

Page 12

† "After 1837/38," is given erroneously and without substantiation by Krummel, pp. 108 and 190. It is contradicted by *AMZ,* as stated above, by the Hofmeister *Monatsbericht* and by music published during the period.

Page 13

† Curiously, these important C.M. and W.W. designations are not mentioned as dating tools in Krummel.

Page 20

† There are also folio volumes entitled "Régistre du Dépôt des Oeuvres de Musique" containing handwritten lists of receipt of Dépôt Légal music from March 14, 1812, to date in the Music Department of the Bibliothèque Nationale, Paris (no library number). (See Joel Sachs, "Authentic English and French Editions of J. N. Hummel," in *Journal of the American Musicological Society*, Ithaca, N.Y., Summer, 1972, p. 219; LC.)

Page 21

† C. A. Spina, a music publisher in Vienna, maintained an "Ablieferungsbuch" (Delivery Book) of musical compositions from Jan. 8, 1858, to Aug. 13, 1867. This book contains receipts of copies of musical publications by the Imperial Minister of the Interior, the Library of the Police, the Director of the Police, the State Attorney, the Royal Library and the Vienna University Library; SB (JA 159.610). It is not known what law required these deliveries or where the delivered copies are now.

Page 22

† A libretto published by G. Ricordi in 1843 (Donizetti's *Don Pasquale*; at JF) refers to a Sovrana Convenzione published by Government Notification N. 26699-3107 on Aug. 25, 1840, but no copy of this sovereign convention has been located.

‡ Pacini's *Il Corsaro*, apparently published by Lib. delle Belle Arti, Roma, at Patric Schmid, London, refers on the title page to a copyright law dated Sept. 23, 1826. This law refers to a "license to . . . publish . . . provided . . . the usual number of copies [are] presented to us"; law at Archivio di Stato di Roma, copy at JF. I have not been able to locate the record of licenses or the copies presented.

Page 24

† The title of the foreign work was to be entered at, and one copy delivered to, Stationers' Hall within a time to be fixed by Order in Council which might vary from country to country. Since the foreign country had to have reciprocal legislation, the 1838 Act was in the nature of an "enabling" law, authorizing the Government from time to time to implement the Act as to a foreign country when the conditions in that foreign country were satisfied. The 1838 Act was replaced by the similar but stronger Act of 1844 (7 & 8 Vict. c. 12; BM), which was in turn amended from time to time.

On Aug. 27, 1846, an implementing Order in Council was issued extending British copyright protection to musical works published in Prussia, and on Sept. 26, 1846, similar protection was extended to works published in Saxony, where the important music publishing city of Leipzig was located. (*The London Gazette*, 1846, pp. 3142 and 3478; BM.) The musical work had to be registered at, and a copy delivered to, Stationers' Hall within one year after the first performance in the particular foreign country.

On Nov. 3, 1851, and Jan. 8, 1852, a similar Convention was signed with the French government. (*The London Gazette*, 1852, p. 125, setting forth the elaborate Convention in full; BM.) The title had to be registered, and a copy deposited, within three months after first performance. Similar treaties were signed by Order in Council in 1865 with Italy and at other times with certain other countries, but not with Austria, Russia or the United States. (Copinger, *Copyright*, p. 578.)

It is not known when the first foreign musical work was copyrighted in England, but on Feb. 9, 1852, a copyright deposit copy of the orchestral score of Mendelssohn's *Symphony no. 4*, published by Breitkopf & Härtel, Leipzig, was received by the British Museum.

Eighteen hundred and fifty-four was the first year that the report of the British Museum copyright office specifically referred to the International Copyright Act, there being a total of 327 music publications received in that year by International Copyright. In 1855, 3,669 foreign music publications were received by the British Museum by International Copyright.

This International Copyright procedure provided a wonderful way for the British Museum to receive first and early editions free of charge, and at the same time to be useful to the international music community!

Pages 34-60

† The following abbreviations, for references added to the Dover edition, supplement the List of Abbreviations, pages 34–60.

Gossett	Philip Gossett, "Catalogo delle Opere," in Luigi Rognoni, *Gioacchino Rossini* (rev. ed., Turin, 1977); NYPL.
Hoboken Bach	*Katalog Sammlung Anthony van Hoboken* . . . vol. I: *Johann Sebastian Bach*, edited by Thomas Leibnitz (Tutzing, West Germany, 1982); ONB.
Hoboken Beethoven	*Katalog Sammlung Anthony van Hoboken* . . . vol. II: *Ludwig van Beethoven*, edited by Karin Breitner and Thomas Leibnitz (Tutzing, West Germany, 1983); ONB.
Hofmann, *Brahms*	Kurt Hofmann, *Die Erstdrucke der Werke von Johannes Brahms* (Tutzing, West Germany, 1975); LC.
Hofmann, *Schumann*	Kurt Hofmann, *Die Erstdrucke der Werke von Robert Schumann* (Tutzing, West Germany, 1979); LC.
Hopkinson, *Berlioz*, 2nd edition	Cecil Hopkinson, *A Bibliography of the Musical and Literary Works of Hector Berlioz*, 2nd ed., edited by Richard Macnutt (Tunbridge Wells, Kent, England, 1980); NYPL.
Hopkinson, *Verdi*	Cecil Hopkinson, *A Bibliography of the Works of Giuseppe Verdi, 1813–1901* (New York, N.Y., 1973 and 1978); LC. All references are to volume II.
ILN	*The Illustrated London News* (London, 1842—)
Johann Strauss Gesamtausgabe	*Johann Strauss (Sohn) Gesamtausgabe* (Vienna, 1974); BOD.

Klein   Horst F. G. Klein, *Erstdrucke der Musikalischen Werke von Richard Wagner* (Tutzing, West Germany, 1983); BM.

Krummel   *Guide for Dating Early Published Music*, compiled by D. W. Krummel (Hackensack, N.J., 1974); LC.

Lesure   François Lesure, *Catalogue de l'Oeuvre de Claude Debussy* (Geneva, 1977); BN.

Ricordi *Libroni*   The manuscript catalogues of the Ricordi music publishing house, Milan, arranged by plate number, 1808—; original at G. Ricordi & C., Milan—microfilm of most years at the American Institute for Verdi Studies, New York University, New York, N.Y.

Schott *Auslieferungslager*   The Warehouse Delivery book of the B. Schott's Söhne music publishing house, arranged by plate number; B. Schott's Söhne, Mainz. This book records the date of printing or publication, and the number of copies printed, of both the first edition and subsequent reissues.

Page 68

† Before the withdrawal of the Austrians from Milan in 1859, the double-eagle emblem of the Austrian Empire frequently appears in the middle of Ricordi's imprint, and the phrase I. R. Stabilimento ("Imperiale Regio"—or "Imperial Royal"—Establishment) precedes Ricordi. After the unification of Italy in 1861, the cross emblem of the Italian House of Savoy replaced the Austrian imperial emblem and the phrase R. Stabilimento replaced I. R. Stabilimento. During the uncertain political situation between 1859 and 1861, the following occurs with Verdi's *Un Ballo in Maschera*: (a) in the advance printing of at least one of the separate pieces, the Austrian imperial emblem and "I. R." are present; (b) in the early arias in the piano-vocal score, there is a blank space in the middle of Ricordi's imprint and nothing precedes Stabilimento!; and (c) in the later arias in this score, the House of Savoy emblem has been inserted in the blank space and an "R." has been inserted before Stabilimento; all at JF.

Page 69

† Thomas F. Heck, "Ricordi Plate Numbers in the Earlier 19th Century: A Chronological Survey," in *Current Musicology*, New York, N.Y., no. 10, 1970, p. 117; NYPL.

‡ According to the Ricordi *Catalogo in Ordine Numerico* (*Catalogo 3 delle Opere Pubblicate* ... *Tito di Gio. Ricordi*, Milan, n.d.; at G. Ricordi & C., Milan—microfilm at the American Institute for Verdi Studies, New York University, New York, N.Y.), these numbers were generally assigned, but only a few pieces of actual printed music with plate numbers between about 55,000 and about 93,000 have been seen by the author or by others interested in this subject. This block of plate numbers was assigned to the Lucca catalog, which had been recently purchased.

Page 70

† The *Libroni* are arranged by plate number in numerical order. They occasionally indicate an intended publication date, but usually show the date a work was assigned to an engraver. This latter date is usually close to the corner date frequently engraved on music published by Ricordi in the early 1850's. The name of the engraver is also usually shown, and it is easy to match the name of an engraver with his letter next to the plate number on the music. Since plates were frequently replaced, it is helpful to know the letter on the original plate, and thereby establish priority. The *Libroni* are at G. Ricordi & C., Milan, and a microfilm of most years is at the American Institute for Verdi Studies, New York University, New York, N.Y.

Page 88

† The first printing of the orchestral score of the opera may have been a lithographing of a score in a handwriting that may have been the composer's. No printer is shown. Folio. 735 pages. German text. Copy offered in Hans Schneider *Catalog 252* (Tutzing, West Germany, 1981), no. 84; copy of *Catalog* at JF.

Page 103

† Other separate numbers were published by Jan. 30, 1853; *GMM*, Jan. 30, 1853, p. 146, and subsequent issues. However, the first mention of the *Coro di Zingari* is the *Ricordi Catalogue Supplement*, Milan, May–July, 1853, p. 23, which states that this number will be published in Aug., 1853; NYPL. The copies of this number in the piano-vocal scores noted in the text are dated June 9, 1853. The engraving of this number commenced June 13, 1853; the "da pubblicarsi" (for publication) date, and the date of receipt at the Office of Public Order, was August 6, 1853; Ricordi *Libroni*.

‡ The date of the first printing of the orchestral score of the opera is unknown. Since there is no plate number, the Ricordi *Libroni* furnish no information in this regard. BM, LC, NYPL, JMM and JF have G. Ricordi e C.'s folio orchestral score, without plate number, a lithographing of a handwritten score. m. on pp. 1–675, this *Chorus* at p. 145. BM dates this as circa 1880, LC "considerably after" 1853, and NYPL as after 1888. (See, also, Kinsky, *Opern*, p. 386.) Hopkinson and Chusid err in their descriptions of the earliest orchestral score. There is no known copy of the orchestral score of this opera either with 595 pages or published by R. Stabilimento Tito di Gio. Ricordi e Francesco Lucca, Milan. Hopkinson, *Verdi*, 54C, and Chusid, p. 162.

Engraved orchestral parts of the opera, with plate numbers 21297 et al., without covers, are at MET. The plate numbers would ordinarily indicate a date of 1849, but such year is not possible; the Ricordi *Libroni* unfortunately are not helpful as to date. As the imprint is G. Ricordi, the year is not later than 1853, and these are probably the first edition.

Verdi was born at Le Roncole, Italy, in 1813, and died in Milan in 1901. Cammarano, a poet and librettist, was born in Naples in 1801 and died there in 1852, i.e., before the production of *Il Trovatore*. (Baker, p. 245.)

Page 117

† Obituary, *Union Advertiser*, Oct. 18, 1867; Rochester Public Library, Rochester, N.Y. Charles Eugene Claghorn, Riverside, Conn., advised the author of this obituary.

Page 118

† An edition with a title page in French was also published by this publisher; Répertoire International des Sources Musicales, *Einzeldrucke vor 1800* (Kassel, 1971), B 500. However, the edition with a German title page was probably earlier because it was the one mentioned in contemporary references *(AMZ Int-B1,* nos. VIII and XIII, May and Sept., 1801), and because, on the copies seen by the author, the inking on the edition with the German title page is darker, and there is a handsome engraved plate which seems to be lacking in the copies with a title page in French.

‡ Manuscript copies of the entire work were soon available for purchase. (Schneider, p. 99.) In 1782 Mozart arranged several of the fugues for chamber-music combinations (Köchel 404a and 405). And in 1783 Beethoven played the *Well-Tempered Clavier* at the age of thirteen in a famous performance. (Carl Friedrich Cramer, *Magazin der Musik,* Hamburg, 1783, p. 394, a report from Bonn dated March, 2, 1783, mistakenly giving Beethoven's age as eleven; NYPL.)

Page 119

† *Méditation* was performed in Paris on April 10, 1853. (James Harding, *Gounod,* New York, N.Y., 1973, p. 80; NYPL.)

Page 123

† Ricordi, Milan, published the song with plate number 32496, apparently also in 1860; JF*.

Page 124

† An orchestral score without indication of publisher was listed in Scribner *Catalogue 133* (New York, N.Y., [1946]), no. 125; *Catalogue* at The Grolier Club, New York, N.Y. However, the purchaser of the orchestral score has advised the author as to the publisher's address and plate number 346, which indicate the score was published by A La Lyre Moderne; see text, p. 125.

‡ Rossini's *L'Equivoco Stravagante* was performed in Bologna on Oct. 29, 1811. The above *Overture* was included in the Ricordi piano-vocal score of the opera. This score with plate number 22971 was first published about 1851; proof copy at Albi Rosenthal, London. No separate printing of the *Overture* from this opera has been found. However, Prof. Gossett believes that Rossini had essentially nothing to do with the Ricordi publication of his complete works in piano-vocal score about 1850; that the corrections in the proof copy are not in the hand of Rossini; that the *Overture* was not originally composed for this opera; that contemporary manuscript copies of this opera do not contain this *Overture;* and that for both stylistic and bibliographic reasons, this *Overture* was not associated with the original production of this opera.

Page 132

† *Glory! Glory! Hallelujah! Or, Children of the Union* is included in the copy at NYPL of the New Edition of L. O. Emerson, *The Golden Wreath* (Boston), p. 79, which mentions the copyright year of 1857. However, the copyright deposit copies of the New Edition at LC do not contain this song and have an entirely different index page; moreover, the copy at NYPL contains several Civil War songs and was obviously published during the Civil War.

‡ It has been said that the "John Brown" words were written at Fort Warren about a Scot soldier, John Brown, in the 2nd Battalion of the 12th Mass. Volunteer Infantry, the Webster Regiment. James Beale, *A Famous War Song* (Philadelphia, n.d.); BPL. As the author was a member of this regiment, the above explanation may well be true. The author also says, without authority, that the melody had been originally written in the late 1850's by a Philadelphia musician as a "chantez" for a fire-company in Charleston, S.C., for use on a proposed excursion, with the opening words "Say, bummers, will you meet us?" The author proceeds to say the Methodists then changed the opening words to "Say, brothers, will you meet us?"

The *Cambridge History of American Literature—Later National Literature* (Cambridge, 1931), Part III, vol. 4, p. 496, at NYPL, states that *Say Brothers Will You Meet Us* appeared in Henry Ward Beecher, *Plymouth Collection of Hymns and Tunes* [New York, N.Y.] in 1852. This seems erroneous. An extensive search has located no copy of the *Plymouth Collection* earlier than 1855, and this hymn is not included in editions of the *Plymouth Collection* until at least after 1858. Plymouth Church, Brooklyn, N.Y., LC, NYPL and UTS.

Page 148

† It was first performed in orchestral form on March 10, 1867, in Vienna.

‡ See, also, Irving Berlin's comment under *There's No Business Like Show Business*.

Page 154

† *The British Grenadiers March* appears in a manuscript book of Giles Gibbs, Jr., a Connecticut fifer, 1777–1780; The Connecticut Historical Society, Hartford, Conn.

Page 156

† W. W. Graves, *History of Neosho County* (St. Paul, Kan., 1951), vol. 2, p. 631; Chanute Public Library, Chanute, Kan. Eugene Claghorn, Riverside, Conn., discovered this information.

‡ Apparently, Sousa had made a band arrangement in 1918 which he used at a Liberty Loan concert in New York City that year.

Page 168

† A variant, with Gluck's signed initial "G," was probably published about the same time, with some text on the title page absent (including the second reference to 1764); Hopkinson, *Gluck*, 30A(a).

Page 171

† *The New Grove Dictionary of Music and Musicians*, edited by Stanley Sadie (London, 1980), vol. 8, p. 296. Charles Looker, New York City, was helpful in connection with this paragraph.

Page 177

† It should be pointed out that the Atlantic Ocean seaboard loomed large to the United States in the 1840's, whereas Britain is surrounded by the English Channel, the North Sea and the Irish Sea.

Page 185

† *Beethoven Beiträge*, p. 217. There is no known contemporary advertisement of the *Concerto for Violin*. The advertisement of the *Concerto* arranged for Piano, in the *Wiener Zeitung*, Aug. 10, 1808, p. 4112, at ONB, has the price of 7 florins.

‡ The piano arrangement is listed in the same issues of *AMZ* and Hofmeister *Monatsbericht*. Nigel Simeone, London, was helpful in connection with this title.

Page 189

† Letter from PRS, and Peter Gammond, *Music Hall Songbook* (Newton Abbot, Devonshire, England, 1975), p. 16; NYPL.

Page 191

† The Ricordi *Libroni* show, for the number of pages, 370 crossed out and replaced with 345, seeming to confirm that the original number of pages had been 370. Curiously, the commencing of the engraving date is stated to be July 10, 1876. The *Libroni* also state that the commencing of the engraving date for the *Danza* arranged for piano four hands was May 3, 1876.

‡ Since there is no plate number, there is no information about this orchestral score in the Ricordi *Libroni*.

§ The date Aug. 10, 1895, as the commencement of engraving, appears for this piece in the Ricordi *Libroni*, as well as for the orchestral parts of the *Danza* with the next higher plate number.

Page 196

† The first two notes of the chorus, and the accompanying "text," are identical to those in *Dinah*, with music by Henry I. Marshall and words by Stanley Murphey, and published by Jerome H. Remick & Co., New York, N.Y., and Detroit, in 1913. JF.

Page 198

† In all three printings the words are the traditional words.

‡ Many other broadsides, mostly or entirely by reprint publishers, a few with the traditional words, mostly not dated and some without mention of publisher, are described in Edwin Wolf 2nd, *American Song Sheets, Slip Ballads and Poetical Broadsides 1850–1870* (Philadelphia, 1963), nos. 482 *et seq.*; NYPL. In addition, generally similar undated broadsides with traditional words, entitled *Dixie's Land*, are at Wayde Chrismer, Bel Air, Md. (publisher is B. Leverett Emerson, 112 Washington Street, Boston), and at JF (H. De Marsan, 38 & 60 Chatham Street, New York, N.Y.); and with other words entitled *Dixey's Land*, at NYPL (H. De Marsan, as above), and *O, Lovely Dixie's Land*, at Wayde Chrismer, as above (no publisher, but stating Baltimore, April, 1861).

Page 214

† Haydn was a Croatian by birth and it has been suggested that the melody of the *Emperor's Hymn* was derived from a Croatian folk song, *Stal Se Jesem*. (*Grove's*, 3rd ed., vol. V, p. 32, footnote 8.) It has also been suggested that the melody should be traced back to the Church. (*Id.*)

A reproduction of the described edition was made in 1923 by Drei Masken Verlag, Munich, with a separate explanatory cover. JF. The reproduction is on thinner paper than the original, and the inking is less clear than on the original.

Page 221

† The above may have been special engraved pre-publication copies for copyright deposit as the printing or publication date in the Schott *Auslieferungslager* is Feb. 28, 1894, when 600 copies were printed.

‡ The Schott *Auslieferungslager* is confusing as to dates of printing or publication of the orchestral score and orchestral parts.

Page 239

† The price is 6/, there is a reference to Stationers' Hall and a mention of Troupenas and Breitkopf & Härtel. The publisher is Wessel & Co., 67 Frith St., corner Soho Square, London. vb. m. on pp. 1–19 (really 3–21). p.n. 3549. Engraved. Back cover adv. Page A and states No. 6 [*sic*] Frith St. BM.

Page 248

† Royalties from *God Bless America* to 1978 have totaled $673,939, all to the benefit of the Boy Scouts and Girl Scouts.

Page 249

† At one point Shakespeare wrote, "God rest you, merry sir" (*As You Like It*, Act V, Scene i, line 58); at another point, "Rest you happy!" (*Antony and Cleopatra*, Act I, Scene i, line 72). (See, also, Harold C. Schonberg, "God Rest You, Wandering Comma," in *The New York Times*, Dec. 26, 1971, sec. 2, p. 17.)

Page 251

† There are two issues: in what is probably the earlier, page [vi] has an incorrect plural heading "Recommendations." and is poorly set, at BPL, BR, LC (2), UCH and JF; in the other, the page has a correct singular heading and is well set, at AAS, NYPL and JF; there are other minor differences.

Page 253

† The Aria is included as a Sarabande in *Anna Magdalena Bach's Notebook*, 1725, which, however, was not published until the nineteenth century. (*Das Notenbuch der Anna Magdalena aus dem Jahre 1725*, in *Bach Gesellschaft* [vol. 43 (1)], p. 39.) Brief biographic information regarding Bach appears above under *Air for the G String*.

Page 262

† The earliest advertisement in the *Illustrated London News* was in the Nov. 27, 1880, issue, at page 528, where the piano-vocal score was announced as "Now Ready."

Page 263

† On the other hand, there are connections between Sanderson and this song.

James Sanderson was engaged at the Surrey Theatre, London, as composer and musical director for many years, and *The Lady of the Lake* was presented at this theater on Sept. 24, 1810. (*Grove's*, vol. 7, p. 400. *London Times*, Sept. 24, 1810, p. 2; there is no mention of Sanderson as the composer, merely a statement that there is "entirely new music.") More importantly, when *The Lady of the Lake* was presented in Philadelphia on Jan. 1, 1812, the advertisement stated that "The Music is by the celebrated Sanderson [no first name given] and Dr. Clarke of Cambridge, and M. Pellesierre." (*General Advertiser*, Philadelphia, Jan. 1, 1812, p. 3; NYPL.) Robert E. Knox, Jr., Denton, Tex., has been helpful in connection with the information in this paragraph. However, his statement that the celebrated *Hail to the Chief* first appeared in 1810 is erroneous; this different melody was by Carr. (Robert E. Knox, Jr., *The Lady of the Lake*, Anson, Tex., 1978, p. 9; LC. Wolfe, no. 1579.)

Page 264

† A manuscript of the music and words of *Hail to the Chief* from about the same period appears in a copybook, presumably American, containing keyboard music and songs; FLP, Music Division, uncataloged manuscript, no place, no date, [40 pages], 11¾″ × 9½″, at page [16].

‡ Lester S. Levy, Pikesville, Md., advised the author of this reference. See, generally, Glenn D. Kittler, *Hail to the Chief!* (Philadelphia and New York, 1965), p. 58; LC.

Page 266

† After considering all the variant copies and difficult points, the author has concluded that *Messiah* was probably first issued in parts. In such case, the newly discovered copy at the Royal Academy of Music, London, with a title page and separate index page to each part and with a blank page at the end of the first part and a blank page at the beginning of the second part, presently has the best claim to being considered the earliest known printing of the complete *Messiah*. (James J. Fuld, "The First Complete Printing of Handel's 'Messiah,'" in *Music and Letters*, London, Oct., 1974, p. 454.)

No early printing of the orchestral parts of the *Messiah* was known to William C. Smith. (Letter from William C. Smith, Chislehurst, Kent, England.) A Violino Primo part, with a title page reading in full "Messiah, An Oratorio, Composed in the Year, 1741, by G. F. Handel," without imprint or watermark but similar to the Arnold Edition of Handel's works (1787–1797), engraved and without plate number, is at Albi Rosenthal, London. A similar part, and two other parts, with an 1817 watermark, are at BM.

Page 268

† The words of *Happy Birthday to You* were probably written by Patty Hill about 1893 as variant words to be sung on a child's birthday at the demonstration kindergarten, of which Patty Hill was the Principal, run by the Louisville, Ky., Kindergarten Training School. The teachers in training, and the children, apparently spread the song.

‡ Margot Gayle, "The Birthday Song," in *The American Family*, New York, N.Y., Jan., 1950, p. 10; NYPL.

Page 282

† *Strand Musical Magazine*, London, 1895, p. 13, NYPL, and supported by entry in index of Registrar General, London. Andrew Lamb, Littlehampton, West Sussex, England, furnished this information. Parker, 13th ed., p. 1434, states that Bucalossi died at the age of eighty-six.

Page 293

† A booklet of "Vocal Parts" of *Carousel* (consisting of a reproduction of a copyist's manuscript of the melody line and words) for the private use of singers and chorus, probably printed prior to rehearsal for the original production, is at JF.

Page 300

† A privately printed edition, described as "Author's Property," was published by Hutchings & Romer, with a facsimile signature of the composer with her single name on the front cover and plate number 107a; copy at Andrew Lamb, Littlehampton, West Sussex, England. In the regularly published sheet music edition described on pages 299–300, the facsimile signature is of the composer with her married name.

Page 313

† The melody of the original chorus was different from the above presently familiar chorus. (Richard Jackson, NYPL, called this to the attention of the author.) The earliest known printing of the familiar chorus was in *Students' Songs*, published and arranged by Harvard Students, and copyrighted June 9, 1880 (copyright records; LC), by S. P. Clarke [Boston], p. 6, and there is a comma after "Jingle"; HU.

Page 317

† Katherine K. Scott, "Lena Guilbert Ford," in *Chemung County Historical Journal*, Elmira, N.Y., March, 1965, p. 1343; NYPL. Eugene Claghorn, Riverside, Conn., advised the author of this article.

Page 319

† The edition with French text states that the song was dedicated to and inspired by K-K-K Katy Richardson; JF (autographed by the composer).

Page 321

† See A. Z. Idelsohn, *Jewish Music* (New York, N.Y., 1929), pp. 154, 157 and 160; NYPL.

Page 324

† Gerhard Herz, "The Performance History of Bach's *B Minor Mass*," in *American Choral Review*, New York, N.Y., Jan., 1973, pp. 7 and 14; NYPL.

Page 332

† *Who's Who in the Theatre* (6th ed., London, 1930), p. 106, NYPL, and supported by entry in index of Registrar General, London. Andrew Lamb, Littlehampton, West Sussex, England, furnished this information.

Page 336

† The "lady" may have been Lady John Scott, as suggested on pages 336–337. (However, no reference to the song is made in the best biography of Lady John Scott—*Thirty Songs by Lady John Scott,* Edinburgh, 1910, at LC and JF.) The above sheet music seems to be the early printing mentioned in one or two secondary sources. (Moffat, *Minstrelsy of Scotland,* p. 34. Ford, p. 280.) However, the second source states that the early printing was under the title *By Yon Bonnie Banks.* A third source states an early printing was under the title *Bonnie Banks of Loch Lomond.* (W. Christie, *Traditional Ballad Airs,* Edinburgh, 1876, vol. I, pp. 278 and 295; JF.) No copy has been found of an early printing under either of these latter two titles, nor was there an entry at Stationers' Hall.

Page 337

† The actual London Bridge that was built in 1831, the last in a line of London Bridges dating back to the Roman conquest, was sold in 1968, dismantled block by block, and reassembled in Lake Havasu City, Ariz., as a tourist attraction. (*The New York Times,* May 23, 1971, sec. 10, p. 1.)

Page 338

† This song was originally written for *Zip, Goes a Million,* an uncompleted musical adaptation of *Brewster's Millions.* (P. G. Wodehouse and Guy Bolton, *Bring on the Girls!,* New York, N.Y., 1953, p. 152; NYPL.)

Page 344

† A Klavier-Direktionsstimme score, with plate number 8849, was published probably in late 1928 for rental only. Copy at Theodore Presser Company, Philadelphia. An orchestral score was not published at the time; the miniature orchestral score published in the 1970's states at Supplement, page ix, that this was the first printing of the orchestral score but also mentions "remaining printed orchestral parts," which, however, have not been located.

Page 346

† The important opening phrase of the song is similar to, and may have been derived from, the opening phrase of the Trio in *General Chaffee's March,* by James O. Brockenshire, and copyrighted April 29, 1899, for band parts by Harry Coleman, Philadelphia; LC(CDC) and U.S. Military Academy, West Point, N.Y. Brockenshire, a U.S. Army bandmaster, was born in Cornwall, England, and died in Everett, Wash., in 1938. (Information from Robert Hoe, Jr., Poughkeepsie, N.Y., a nephew of Brockenshire.)

Page 347

† This edition was probably a small advance first edition since a copy with the correct title "The Man I Love" at the top of the front cover, and otherwise identical, was received at LC for copyright deposit on Dec. 2, 1924; also at JF.

Page 351

† David Shulman, New York City, called this publication to the attention of the author.

Page 371

† Another copy, without Zulehner's signatures, was offered in Richard Macnutt's *Quarto 12* (Tunbridge Wells, Kent, England, 1975), no. 51.

‡ Including, curiously, Mozart!

§ The fifth variant is the same as the fourth, with two prices but with two blank pages after the title page; Dr. Eric Offenbacher, Seattle, Wash.

‖ Manuscript copies of the piano-vocal score of the opera were advertised in the *Wiener Zeitung*, May 24, 1788; ONB.

AMZ Int-Bl, July, 1801.

¶ With green and black covers for each volume, in French stating "Oeuvres de Mozart. Don Juan . . . No. 2 des Partitions."

Page 375

† Published in Emanuel Aguilar and D. A. DeSola, *The Ancient Melodies of the Liturgy of the Spanish and Portuguese Jews* (London, 1857), sec. 42, p. 39—NYPL; at p. 17, it is said that each melody in the collection is at least 150 years old. (Information from Carl Alpert, Haifa. Mr. Alpert also writes that it has been claimed that Henry Busato or Russotto, a Sephardic Jew, or the Rev. Mr. Perlzweig from his contacts with the Sephardic Congregation in London, adapted *Hatikva* from *Hillel*.)

Page 378

† No printing of the "Mulberry Bush" words to the traditional music is known, however, before Oct. 25, 1879 (copyright records; LC), when they were published in A. H. Rosewig, *(Illustrated National) Nursery Songs and Games*, by W. F. Shaw [Philadelphia], p. [37], under the title *Here We Go 'Round the Mulberry Bush*; LC(CDC) and JF.

Alice, Tweedledum and Tweedledee sang and danced *Here We Go Round the Mulberry Bush* in Lewis Carroll, *Through the Looking-Glass* (1871), chap. IV.

Page 379

† But the earliest discovered parts, engraved, with an 1898 copyright claim and stating Nuova Edizione, folio, with plate number 99005, with covers and referring to the same cities as in the orchestral score, are at Bayerische Staatsoper, Munich.

Page 391

† Alex Haley, *Roots* (Garden City , N.Y., 1976), p. 227, refers to women singing "No-body Knows de Troubles I'se Seed" in 1767. A letter from the author to Mr. Haley requesting the basis for this statement was not answered.

Page 400

† The reason for the reference to the "Bohemian" is not known; Bohemia as a possible source of the folk song is noted in Erk-Böhme, vol. II, p. 751, which refers to *Neun*

Variationen über das Böhmische Volkslied (probably music only) published in 1804 by C. F. Barth, Jun., Breslau. However, the Czechoslovakia Academy of Sciences Institute of Theory and History of Art, Prague, wrote the author it believed this song originated in Vienna and merely traveled through Bohemia.

Page 404

† The Ricordi *Libroni* state the engraving commenced Aug. 21, 1899, and add that this publication is in joint ownership with Bideri.

‡ The present Italian publisher of the song, Bideri, Naples, contends there was a third co-author, Maestro Alfredo Mazzucchi, who died on Feb. 10, 1972 (copy of letter at JF); this is contrary to contemporary evidence.

Page 412

† The "first edition" copy auctioned by Charles Hamilton, New York City, on Sept. 14, 1978, had the later red, black and white front cover showing persons walking up a gangplank.

Page 417

† However, one reader of this book wrote he had heard this song played for dancing almost nightly in Moscow, Kiev and Leningrad in 1968 to great applause mostly by Russians, many of them young; and Duke Ellington and his orchestra played this piece in Leningrad to wild ovation on Sept. 13, 1971. (*The New York Times*, Sept. 14, 1971, p. 49.)

Page 418

† The Moscow censor's approval dated March 7, 1884, and the permission of the publisher A. Büttner, appear on page 2. Back cover adv. 94 titles. PUS* and SSL. Words are included without indication of authorship. A similar copy not referring to the permission of Büttner and with 151 titles on the back cover is at JF. It is possible that Büttner never published the piece but merely consented to Gutheil's doing so, and the latter edition may have been published before such permission was received.

A copy of the first printing of the *Hommage-Valse*, op. 21, by Florian Hermann has not been located; it presumably preceded the above printings of *Otchi Tchorniya*. A "Nouvelle Edition" published by D. Rahter, Hamburg, and A. Büttner, St. Petersburg, for piano, without words, published about 1890, is at SSL. A similar "Nouvelle Edition," published by A. Gutheil, Moscow, is at LLM and SSL. Nothing is known about Hermann other than that Pazdírek mentions many words by him, including *Hommage-Valse*; vol. XII, p. 415, no. 21.

Page 420

† A variant is the same as the foregoing edition except that the front cover names the publisher as Anastasio García. Page [2] and the back cover are blank. JF. It is not known which of the two variants is the earlier.

Page 428

† The orchestral score sets forth the first version of the opera. The manuscript

notations on, for example, pages 1 and 17 of copies of this edition are probably in Wagner's handwriting. The score had been completed earlier, and on June 5, 1845, Wagner sent a copy of the score to Carl Gaillard in Berlin, stating that publication of the score would follow the first performance of the opera. (Letter from Wagner to Gaillard of that date. *Musikalisches Wochenblatt*, Leipzig, 1877, p. 411; NYPL. Gaillard's advance copy does not have the manuscript additions; Musikantiquariat Hans Schneider *Katalog Nr. 192*, Tutzing, West Germany, 1974, no. 199, *Katalog* at JF.)

Page 438

† The plate number is 119 with no higher number except 120 for the piano solo pages. The *Polovtsian Dances and Chorus* are at p. 197. JF (formerly JMM). The front cover, lacking in this copy, would probably show the price of the piano-vocal score at M. 30/R. 15. The *Polovtsian Dances* were also published separately at about the same time (copyright records; LC) for orchestral score at M. 12/R. 6, and for orchestral parts at M. 24/R. 12; no copies have been found.

Page 439

† The front cover of the first printing of the regular trade edition lists the two *Quick Marches* separately and together, a total of 14 arrangements with prices; nothing engraved. JF (copy inscribed by Elgar to A. J. Jaeger).

Page 440

† Diana R. Tillson, New Canaan, Conn., called this printing to the attention of the author. Curiously, the song was omitted in the second printing of *The Golden Wreath*, in 1857; NYPL.

Page 441

† It has been suggested that the song was probably of erotic origin. (See Eric Partridge, *A Dictionary of Slang and Unconventional English*, 7th ed., New York, N.Y., 1970, p. 649; NYPL.) The song, or at least the words, have been attributed to W. R. Mandale in the nineteenth century (*The Oxford Dictionary of Quotations*, 2nd ed., Oxford, 1953, p. 328); however, no substantiation of this has been found.

Page 445

† A copy inscribed and dated by Debussy "Oct. 1895" was illustrated in Libraire C. Coulet & A. Faure, *Catalogue* (Paris, 1972), no. 1374 (*Catalogue* at JF). Lesure, p. 86. Letter from successor publisher. Vallas, p. lviii.

Page 446

† Lithographed copies of the first edition, with all errors, are at BM (CDC, deposited June 30, 1882—H. 637. l.), PML (copy inscribed by Wagner to Liszt) and JF. An engraved copy has all the errors, the plate number 23406 is not on the title page but on the cast page, and there are two blank pages before the music pages. Copy at Arioso, Paris. The foregoing corrects Klein, pp. 54-55.

‡ Five copies were printed on Japan paper; copy no. 4 at BM (Hirsch II, 941). Klein, pp. 52–53.

§ The Schott *Auslieferungslager* states that 200 copies were printed or published on Oct. 6, 1882, and 50 more on Dec. 1, 1882.

‖ The Schott *Auslieferungslager* states that the printing or publication began Dec. 10, 1883, and was completed Dec. 20, 1883.

Page 449

† BM (copy no. "22," CDC deposited Dec. 16, 1868, H. 636.d.), ONB (no. "56") and JF (no. "74"). Klein, p. 33, errs in stating that p. (A) and p. (B) are on separate leaves and that the verso of each is blank; such a copy is no. "99," at BM (Hirsch II, 937).

‡ *Signale*, April 24, 1868, p. 494. The Schott *Auslieferungslager* is confusing as to dates of printing or publication of the piano-vocal score, orchestral score and orchestral parts.

Page 453

† Some help as to dating the separate pieces may be in the Ricordi *Libroni* which, as to *Rigoletto*, give "da pubblicarsi" (for publication) dates. While these are probably prospective target dates, rather than actual dates, the "da pubblicarsi" dates are generally similar to advertised dates. Thus no. 1, which has the corner date of May 25, 1852, also has a "da pubblicarsi" date of May 25, 1852. No. 10, which has the April 4, 1852, corner date, also has a "da pubblicarsi" date of May 25, 1852. These publication dates are confirmed in the advertisements mentioned in the footnotes on page 452. While a corner date is usually the date engraving begins, in some instances in *Rigoletto* the corner date seems to be the date of intended publication.

The first regular edition of the piano-vocal score, which may have been published at about the same time as the above "Advance" edition, is similar to the foregoing except that the title page has a vignette, lacks a red border and refers also to the piano score and score for piano four hands. There is an index, with the cast on the verso. p.ns. 23071–23090, complete. m. on pp. 5–231, with double pagination, complete. p. [232] blank. All arias are included. The engraver's initial on some pages with plate number 23079 is K. It is possible that in the earliest copies there are 14 corner dates ranging up to April 4, 1852. Hopkinson, *Verdi*, 53A(a). Sant' Agata, Italy (special copy with the vignette printed in colors), BM, ESM, LC, NLS and JF. Other copies of the regular edition have one or two additional corner dates of May 25, 1852; this corner date is the same as in the "Advance" edition, and the number or numbers with this date also were to be published on May 25, 1852. Thus, these copies were probably published at about the same time as the copies with 14 corner dates. IU (one additional corner date—this variant not in Hopkinson). Hopkinson, *Verdi*, 53A(b) (two additional corner dates).

The preparation of the orchestral score of *Rigoletto* commenced Jan. 8, 1895. (Ricordi *Libroni*.) Probable first edition: Folio. Publisher is G. Ricordi & C., Milan, Rome, Naples, Palermo and London. Front cover is gray and black. No title page. m. on pp. 1–580, a lithographing of a handwritten score. The *Quartetto* is on p. 453. p.n. 98189. Chusid, p. 140. Hopkinson, *Verdi*, 53B. LC (copy received Jan. 26, 1904), BOP, CI, NYPL, JMM, RAM and JF.

Engraved orchestral parts of the opera, with plate numbers 21240 et al. and 21310 et al., some oblong and some upright, are at MET, ML and JF*. The plate numbers would ordinarily indicate a date of 1849, but such year is not possible; the Ricordi *Libroni* unfortunately are not helpful as to date. G. or Giovanni Ricordi appears at the bottom of the pages, indicating a year not later than 1853, and these are probably the first edition.

Rigoletto was produced March 11, 1851, in Venice. Brief biographic information regarding Verdi and Piave appears above under *Anvil Chorus* and *Drinking Song*.

Page 455

† The engraving of the work commenced in June, 1820, according to the Ricordi *Libroni*. See, also, Albi Rosenthal, "Paganini's Caprices: An Intriguing Copy of the First Edition," in *Nicolò Paganini e il suo Tempo*, Genoa, 1982 (Verona, 1984), p. 235; BM.

Page 461

† A copy marked "Première épreuve" (first proof) has an autographed dedication by the composer to Danbé, the conductor of the first performance, dated March 1, 1886, and many corrections by the composer; m. on pp. 1–415. JMM.

Page 462

† The earliest located copy was in the Nov. 16, 1895, issue of the Paris magazine *L'Illustration*, in the Supplément Musical, p. 177; BM, BN, *ULS*, p. 1264, and JF. The next separate edition of *Rêverie* was published in 1904 by E. Fromont, Paris, with plate number 1403; JF.

Page 463

† Piano rolls of the *Rhapsody in Blue*, performed by Gershwin, were released in May, 1925 (Part II) [*sic*], and Jan., 1927 (Part I), on Duo-Art 68787 and 70947 (Robert Kimball and Alfred Simon, *The Gershwins*, New York, N.Y., 1973, p. 290; LC and NYPL); JF. At the launching of the first American–Soviet Union joint manned space effort in July, 1975, Soviet radio played the *Rhapsody in Blue*.

Page 464

† BM (CDC, deposited Jan. 6, 1866—H. 637. i.), NYPL and JF. Klein, p. 53, states the music begins on p. 3; he does not locate such a copy nor state why such a copy is earlier than the copy described above.

‡ There is something puzzling about the verso of the title page either having, or not having, a legal notice. In the first edition of each *Ring* orchestral score, this page is supposed to be blank. Klein, *passim*. Yet, *Die Walküre* orchestral scores were first published on Sept. 1, 1874, and an unnumbered copy *with* the legal notice was entered at Stationers' Hall on Sept. 25, 1874, and deposited in the British Museum on Oct. 8, 1874. Early *Das Rheingold* orchestral scores, published in 1873, do not have the notice, but copy no. 51 was published Sept. 7, 1875, and does have the notice (at JF).

Yet thereafter, *Siegfried* and *Götterdämmerung* orchestral scores were published on Dec. 30, 1875, and June 28, 1876, and the early copies of each again lack the notice.

It seems probable that, irrespective of date, at least in the case of *Die Walküre*, some early copies had, and some early copies did not have, the legal notice on the verso of the title page.

The absence of a rubber-stamped number on an early copy may mean either that there never was a number, or that there had originally been a number but it was trimmed away when the copy was bound.

§ The Schott *Auslieferungslager* states that 400 copies were printed or published on April 16, 1863.

‖ The Schott *Auslieferungslager* states that 100 copies were printed or published on July 29, 1865.

Signale, Sept. 1, 1874, p. 652. The Schott *Auslieferungslager* states that 75 copies were published on Sept. 10, 1874, and the next edition of 25 copies was on Sept. 4, 1876.

Page 465

† The Schott *Auslieferungslager* states that the parts for the strings were printed or published Nov. 12, 1885, but it is not clear when the other parts were printed or published.

‡ A presentation copy, inscribed by Wagner, has engraved music pages—copy at Bruno Lussato, Paris; this is apparently the edition described by Klein, pp. 46–47.

§ A few copies had engraved pages; Hans Schneider *Catalog 276* (Tutzing, West Germany, 1984), no. 220. Klein, pp. 50–51.

‖ These are the dates given in Kinsky, *Opern*, p. 385. The orchestral score of *Das Rheingold* was entered at Stationers' Hall on July 2, 1873, with a June 4, 1873, publication date; Hofmeister *Monatsbericht*, July, 1873, p. 208; the Schott *Auslieferungslager* states that 50 copies were printed or published on March 20, 1873. The orchestral score of *Siegfried* was entered at Stationers' Hall on Feb. 7, 1878 [*sic*], with a Feb. 1, 1878 [*sic*], publication date; Hofmeister *Annual*, 1876, p. 287—not in Hofmeister *Monatsbericht* in 1876; the Schott *Auslieferungslager* states that 112 copies were printed or published on Dec. 30, 1875. The orchestral score of *Götterdämmerung* does not seem to have been entered at Stationers' Hall; Hofmeister *Monatsbericht*, Sept., 1876, p. 198; the Schott *Auslieferungslager* states that 50 copies were printed or published on June 28, 1876.

The Schott *Auslieferungslager* shows that 100 copies were printed or published on March 4, 1861; 50 copies on March 10, 1861; and 50 copies on March 24, 1861. It is not known which edition was printed or published on which date. Wagner complained to Schott on March 8, 1861, that the title page was too elaborate and had nothing to do with the opera; Altmann, vol. II, p. 18. John Deathridge, Cambridge, furnished this information.

¶ However, the publication date was April 15, 1871, according to the entry at Stationers' Hall on Sept. 14, 1871. Hofmeister *Monatsbericht*, Oct., 1871, p. 232.

†† The first date mentioned in the Schott *Auslieferungslager* is April 24, 1875, on which date 600 copies were printed or published.

Page 466

† The Schott *Auslieferungslager* states that the parts for the strings of the three operas were printed or published commencing in Jan., 1891, but it is not clear when the other parts were printed or published.

‡ According to the entry of the orchestral score at Stationers' Hall on Feb. 7, 1878, Müller-Reuter, p. 472 (Feb., 1878). Hofmeister *Monatsbericht*, Feb., 1878, p. 31. Kastner, p. 104, says 1877, but this date is incorrect as Wagner, on Jan. 5, 1878, acknowledged receipt from Schott of corrections of the orchestral score and parts—Strecker, p. 219. The Schott *Auslieferungslager* states that 200 copies of the orchestral score were printed or published on Feb. 4, 1878, and 150 copies of at least some of the orchestral parts were printed or published on the same day.

The copy illustrated in Klein, p. 152, has a later Paris address and is not the first edition.

Page 481

† "New Edition" may mean a "new publisher" (succeeding Shteding) or an edition for piano (from the original edition for choir).

Page 490

† Walter Huston said he would play the villainous Peter Stuyvesant in *Knickerbocker Holiday* only if he could have one love song with the young girl, and *September Song* was written by Weill and Anderson as a result. (Alfred S. Shivers, *The Life of Maxwell Anderson*, New York, N.Y., 1983, p. 174; NYPL.) The words of a second chorus for Huston to sing at the curtain call were published for the first time in 1983. (Joshua Logan, review of *The Life of Maxwell Anderson* by Alfred S. Shivers, in *The New York Times*, Sept. 11, 1983, sec. 7, p. 45.)

Page 492

† See, also, the original 1946 New York edition of Deutsch, *Schubert*, no. 957, p. 470.

Page 514

† *Old Joe* was also included about the same time in a broadside, with words only, by Walker, Printer, Durham, with the number 3 but without date; at JF.

Page 524

† Dmitri Shostakovitch and Aram Khatchaturian were among a number of composers who were directed during World War II to compose a Soviet Union national anthem to pre-written words. A Soviet Union anthem was deemed necessary to replace the French communist *L'Internationale*. Shostakovitch and Khatchaturian were first directed to submit separate entries and, later, a joint entry, an assignment they disliked and believed unsound because of their different musical styles. Stalin actively participated in the consideration of the various entries, and when Shostakovitch and Khatchaturian were summoned to meet him, they were searched! However, the Alexandrov entry was ultimately selected. The pre-written words, which praised Stalin, were changed after his death. (*Testimony: The Memoirs of Dmitri Shostakovich*, edited by Solomon Volkov, New York, N.Y., 1979, p. 256.)

Page 526

† The above edition in parts, with Pianoforte I on the left-hand side and Pianoforte II on the right-hand side, was objected to by Brahms by letter to Simrock dated Novem-

ber 10, 1873, and, according to Hofmann, *Brahms*, p. 121, was thereafter withdrawn from sale. An edition in score for two pianos (with Pianoforte I directly above Pianoforte II) was, according to Hofmann, then published, still in November, 1873, the front cover having the single title *Variationen über ein Thema von Joseph Haydn*, the same opus number, price and imprint as above, and the year 1873. m. on pp. 2–29. p. [30] blank. p.n. 7397. Folio. Not engraved. This edition referring at the bottom of page 2 to "Röder'schen" (copies at NYPL and JF) had been unknown to Hofmann and has been acknowledged by him in a letter to this author to be earlier than the edition, described by him in his book, without such reference.

‡ *Signale*, Nov., 1873, no. 4 of 6 issues in that month, contains an advertisement that the arrangement for two pianos has just appeared at 1½ Thlr. No copy has been found with the price in Thalers.

§ *Signale*, Jan., 1874, no. 3 of 7 issues in that month, contains an advertisement that the orchestral score and parts will appear in a week at 3 Thlr. and 6 Thlr. respectively. No copy has been found of either with the price in Thalers.

Page 530

† *BUC*, p. 959, and JF (copy presented by Smith to his wife). Smith was born in Gloucester, England, in 1750, was a composer of secular and sacred music, and died in London in 1836.

Page 532

† It has been usually believed that the above Carr printing was the first time that the melody (in the key of C) has an F sharp as the third note in the second full bar. In all prior printings of this melody, the note was F natural. However, in an undated American music manuscript, circa 1800, "Enoch Peirce's Book, Newburyport," at page 114, this melody under the title *Adams & Liberty* has the F sharp; Irving Lowens, Baltimore. Fuld-Davidson, p. 80.

Page 539

† The story of Porgy originated from an article in the Charleston, S.C., *The News and Courrier* about a real-life Negro cripple, Samuel Smalls, who had a goat and cart and whose life was full of passion, hate and despair. Samuel Smalls was born about 1889 on James Island, near Charleston, S.C., without legs. After spending most of his life in Charleston, including several skirmishes with the police there, he returned to James Island, where he died in 1924. His mother and sister were interviewed in the 1950's and also the woman who had loved him and whom he married shortly before he died. His grave has also been found on James Island. DuBose Heyward, "Introduction," p. xi, to Dorothy and DuBose Heyward, *Porgy*, a play (Garden City, N.Y., 1928); NYPL and JF. The "Introduction" did not appear in the first printing of the play in 1927, at NYPL, or in the printing of the novel (on which the play was based) in 1925, at NYPL and JF. Bryan Collier, "Porgy's Mother Still Lives in Charleston," in *The News and Courrier*, Charleston, S.C., March 11, 1951, and Dorothy Heyward, "Anyone Here Know Porgy?" in the same newspaper, July 26, 1959, p. 6-C; Charleston County Library, Charleston, S.C.

No orchestral score of the opera has been published; Gershwin's manuscript orchestral score is at LC.

Page 549

† Prokofiev, *Autobiography*, and Nestyev state the publisher of the first edition is Russian Music Publisher. The above edition states at the bottom of page [1] "Russicher Musikverlag"; Gutheil was taken over in 1914 by S. and N. Koussevitzky (who are named on the front cover of the above edition) using the trade name, in German, Russicher Musikverlag.

Page 563

† The first edition of the four choral parts is engraved and has plate number 360; *Hoboken Beethoven*, no. 505.

Page 569

† Cited in *Johann Strauss Gesamtausgabe*, Ser. 1, vol. 20 (Vienna, 1971), p. 378. Weinmann, *Strauss*, p. 96. Hofmeister *Monatsbericht*, Oct., 1868, p. 173.

Page 574

† After seeing Cole Porter's show *Can-Can*, Berlin wrote Porter a complimentary letter, closing with "to paraphrase an old bar-room ballad, 'anything I can do, you can do better.' " (Robert Kimball, *Cole*, New York, N.Y., 1971, p. 234; NYPL.) The quoted reference, of course, is to Berlin's song *Anything You Can Do, I Can Do Better* included in *Annie Get Your Gun*. (See, also, Brahms's comment about the *Blue Danube*.)

Page 577

† ILN, April 25, 1885, p. 434 ("Now Ready").

Page 587

† The song is said to owe its origin in September, 1902, to the desire of the Mayor of Sorrento for a new post office. The Prime Minister of Italy was staying in Sorrento in a hotel owned by the Mayor, who asked the Prime Minister for a new post office. To remind the Prime Minister, the Mayor asked the de Curtis brothers to write a song, which was sung at the railroad station when the Prime Minister left for Rome. The Prime Minister remembered, and Sorrento received a new post office. (Sleeve note to RCA Record Album NL 33072. Noted by Andrew Lamb, Littlehampton, West Sussex, England.)

Page 588

† Probably first published shortly before Jan. 1, 1865, in an "Extra . . . New Year's, 1865" issue of the Root & Cady monthly magazine, *The Song Messenger of the North-west*, Chicago, pp. [2]-[3]. LC. No copyright notice in the magazine, and no record of copyright at LC. The publication was probably before the New Year as subsequent copyright notices on sheet music state the year of publication as "1864."

‡ Root tells of the New Year's extra at pages 140-141. The statement in David Ewen, *American Popular Songs* (New York, N.Y., 1966), p. 408, that the song was published in the 1863 Christmas issue of *The Song Messenger* is erroneous.

Page 590

† The engraving of this octavo edition began Sept. 29, 1871, according to the Ricordi *Libroni*, which also state "Alla Procura di Stato" (to the State Attorney) on Feb. 9, 1872 (proof copy? final? when was State approval, if needed, received?). Copies were received by the British Museum on April 17, 1872 (copyright deposit copy), and by the S. Cecilia Conservatory, Rome, on April 20, 1872. Also, at the other locations mentioned in Hopkinson *Verdi*, 62(A)a, and at JF, a total of 10 copies. I–IV and 289 music pages. Title page mentions no price (which is unusual) and does not refer to the quarto score. The BM copy (E. 190. d.) is on poor quality paper and has been trimmed, but the sizes of the music portion of the page are the same as in the score without plate number described in the next paragraph. Libretto, except at BM.

‡ Facts relating to all the candidates mentioned on page 590, which, however, do not specify which candidate is referred to, are: By Feb. 11, 1872, three days after the first performance in Milan, the first edition was announced as completely sold (*GMM*, Feb. 11, 1872, p. 43). The second edition, after several false promises, was to be completed by the second fortnight in April, 1872. (*GMM*, March 31, 1872, p. 103). On April 13, 1872, a copyright copy of the piano-vocal score was deposited with the Prefect of Milan. Which score is referred to in each of the preceding three sentences is not known.

If the first edition was sold by Feb. 11, 1872, this would not allow much time for the last pieces of the quarto scores to be engraved, as the engraving of the last pieces began on Jan. 20, 1872. If the octavo score with the plate number was taken to the Procura di Stato on Feb. 9, 1872, and sale could commence only thereafter, this also does not allow much time for an edition to be sold; and why a delay of two months to deposit with Rome and London libraries, and perhaps with the Prefect of Milan?

This leaves the octavo score without plate number, of which there is only one known copy and about which there is almost no information, favorable or unfavorable. The existence of an engraved octavo copy may mean that all lithographed octavo copies, including the one without plate number, were published after the engraved octavo copy. Moreover, the score without plate number is the only Ricordi piano-vocal score this author has ever seen without a plate number; what is the reason for this?

So, the mystery continues. (No help as to relative priority is furnished by the engravers' names in the Ricordi *Libroni* or initials in the scores except as between (1a) and (1b). While names and initials are known with respect to the quarto scores, no names are in the *Libroni* with respect to the octavo score with plate number, and no information is given with respect to the octavo score without plate number.) The earliest French piano-vocal score, published by Léon Escudier, Paris, was advertised on March 21, 1872; BN(CDC). Hopkinson, *Verdi*, 62A(d). An early Ricordi piano score with p.ns. 42486–42526 is at ONB. The separate sheet music *Triumphal March*, published about the same time as the first piano-vocal score, was published by Ricordi under the title *Gran Finale Secondo—Inno, Marcia Trionfale e Danze*, with p.n. 42495, at 7 Fr. It is listed in the *Ricordi Catalogue Supplement* mentioned above. The engraving commenced Jan. 20, 1872. (Hopkinson did not consider Ricordi's separate pieces from this opera.)

The engraving of the Ricordi string orchestral parts of the opera commenced Aug. 8, 1871, with plate numbers 42480–42483 according to the Ricordi *Libroni*. Engraved parts are at MET, but they show the publisher as G. Ricordi & C., presumably 1898—because of the imprint.

The preparation of the Ricordi orchestral score of the opera commenced Sept. 24,

1894, with plate number 97825 according to the Ricordi *Libroni*. The earliest score is a folio lithographing of a manuscript, with music on pages 1–662. No title page. The *Triumphal March* is at p. 259. BM, LC, NYPL, JMM and JF. Hopkinson, *Verdi*, (62C), and Chusid, p. 11, err in their descriptions of the earliest orchestral score; there is no known copy of the Ricordi orchestral score of this opera without plate number.

The score of *Aida* was completed by Verdi by the autumn of 1870, but the Franco-Prussian War delayed the first performance, in Cairo, until Dec. 24, 1871, as the sets were prepared in Paris. A. Ghislanzoni was the librettist. Brief biographic information regarding Verdi appears above under *Anvil Chorus*.

Page 592

† The edition with a rubber-stamped copyright notice, or no copyright notice, was copyrighted Jan. 2, 1915, and the music differs considerably from the music in the first printing; LC(CDC) and JF. (Thornton Hagert, Washington, D.C., called this information to the attention of the author.)

Page 596

† A De Luxe copy of the above edition, not mentioned in Hopkinson, *Puccini*, with thick paper and a colored sunken portrait on the front cover, was formerly at Hermann Baron, London; its present location is unknown. Priority as between this De Luxe copy and the trade edition mentioned in the preceding paragraph is not known, but the trade edition was probably published first.

Page 601

† It has been stated that the song was first published by Emil Maxa in Vienna on May 31, 1913, on the basis of an announcement in the *Fremdenblatt* of the same date. (Max Schönherr, *Carl Michael Ziehrer*, Vienna, 1974, pp. 468 and 685, at NYPL, and letter from Schönherr to the author.) No Maxa printing has been found. The Maxa printing is not mentioned in the 1913 or 1914 Hofmeister publications (it is said because Maxa was not a member of the publishers' association) or in the United States copyright records (for which such membership was not necessary). The statement appears to be contradicted by the composer's claim that he could find no publisher for the song until Robitschek. (Rudolf Sieczyński, *Wienerlied, Wiener Wein, Wiener Sprache*, Vienna, 1947, p. 81; NYPL.)

Page 605

† The Ricordi *Libroni* state the engraving commenced July 12, 1899.

Page 606

† The engraving of this aria commenced Jan. 3, 1900.

‡ (With gray and black cardboard covers for each act.) The Ricordi *Libroni* state the engraving commenced Feb. 14, 1900.

Page 612

† This *Waltz* also appeared between Dec. 19, 1847, and Jan. 2, 1848 (*RGM*, Dec. 19, 1847, p. 416, "sous presse"; *id.*, Jan. 2, 1848, p. 6, "Les étrennes . . . sont à leur dis-

position"), in *Album de Piano de la Gazette Musicale 1848* par Chopin . . . Wolff, p. 2, published by the same concern; AT.

Page 632

† The lithographed music manuscript is the same as in the second regular edition.

‡ See Hunt, "Music in the Rosenbloom Collection of Hunt Library at Carnegie-Mellon University," in *Notes*, March, 1977, p. 553. Klein, pp. 24-25.

§ Hunt, *id.*, at page 555 reports that Hopkinson's notes indicated that this edition had been printed in July, 1852. However, it subsequently appeared that the notes were not in Hopkinson's handwriting, the notes contained other errors, no substantiation for the July, 1852, date was given, and in any event Hunt rejected this date both at pages 556-557 and in later letters to this author and to *Notes*, Dec., 1979, p. 506.

‖ No early printing of the words "Here comes the bride all dressed in white" has been found.

Page 634

† *ILN* advertised *The Gondoliers* from Feb. 22, 1890, to June 30, 1890, without mentioning this separate sheet music edition.

Page 649

† Berlin's special "transposing" piano, on which he composed *White Christmas* and other songs, is at the Smithsonian Institution, Washington, D.C.

Page 653

† According to the Ricordi *Libroni*. Such engraved oblong parts, without imprint or covers, are at MAP.

Page 657

† A possible antecedent is *Rally on the Battalion* in Silas Casey, *Infantry Tactics* (New York, N.Y., 1862), p. 272; LC. Another possible antecedent is *Rally on the Reverse* in Emory Upton, *A New System of Infantry Tactics* (New York, N.Y., 1867), p. 344; LC.

Page 659

† At least 18 manuscript versions of the melody of *Yankee Doodle* have been found in eighteenth-century American music manuscripts in libraries and private collections, but never with words. This is curious. Fuld-Davidson, *passim*. The only known eighteenth-century manuscript of the words of *Yankee Doodle* is in a manuscript book of poems bearing a date of 1779, at JF, but without the melody. *Id.*, p. 45. There is also a curious American manuscript version of *Yankee Doodle* under the title "Thehos Gendar" written by Giles Gibbs, Jr., for the fife in 1777-1780. This title has not been traced. (The title is at page 14r of a manuscript at The Connecticut Historical Society, Hartford, Conn. Kate Van Winkle Keller, Coventry, Conn., has studied the title. The manuscript is dated 1777 and Gibbs died in 1780. J. A. Leo Lemay — "The American Origins of 'Yankee Doodle,' " in *The William and Mary Quarterly*, Williamsburg, Va., 1976, p. 462, footnote 3, at NYPL—and others believe the title, which

is not Gaelic, Irish, Scottish or Welsh, may merely be a phonetic spelling of, for example, "The Horse Grenadiers." The title may also refer to "The House Gander," kept as a house pet in Scotland.)

‡ On page 37, under the heading of Carlisle, appears this paragraph in its entirety:

> As I walked down to the river side, I remarked a boy, who was humming the tune of *Yanky Doodle;* and as I knew this to be an extremely popular air in some parts of *America,* I conjectured that this part of *England* was originally peopled from that continent.

This reference to *Yankee Doodle* does not appear in any of the standard authorities. (Joel Collier was probably a pseudonym of John Laurens Bicknell the elder. The work is sometimes mistakenly attributed to George Veal. See Percy A. Scholes, *The Great Dr. Burney,* London, 1948, vol. I, p. 272, and Roger Lonsdale, *Dr. Charles Burney,* Oxford, 1965, p. 153, both at NYPL. In the second edition of the work, published in 1775, the paragraph quoted above appears under the heading of Worcester, at page 89; BM, NYPL and YU. *Notes,* Dec., 1978, p. 454.) It is interesting that the earliest foreign reference to *Yankee Doodle* indicates that it originated in America.

§ Where the words of "A New Song . . . To the Tune of Yankey Doodle" were included as having been received from "a gentleman, just arrived from Newfoundland, the . . . verses written at Quebec soon after the late siege thereof," pp. [5] and [6]. BML.

‖ See, also, Lemay, *id.,* p. 435.

Page 660

† A British manuscript by Charles Dibdin of the music of *Yankee Doodle,* with parody words commencing "I Sing Ulysses," probably dated 1780 is at the British Museum; Add. 30954, No. 27, f. 133b. (*Catalogue of Manuscript Music in the British Museum,* London, 1908, vol. II, pp. 376–377, which also says the song comes from *Reasonable Animals.* The latter was produced in London on March 1, 1780; *Grove's,* vol. 2, pp. 687–688. The song was included in *The Musical Tour of Mr. Dibdin,* Sheffield, 1788, between pp. 342–343; BM and JF.)

While the music was probably performed for American patriotic purposes at a relatively early date, no patriotic words are known to have been written to the music until the naval war with France in 1798, when words commencing "Columbians all the present hour" were written and published. Dichter-Shapiro, p. 25.

Page 661

† Without any real substantiation, there is a legend that Emily Morgan, the unwilling black mistress of Mexican President Antonio López de Santa Anna at the Battle of San Jacinto in 1836, inspired *The Yellow Rose of Texas.* (See Martha Anne Turner, *The Yellow Rose of Texas,* El Paso, Tex., 1971; LC.)

Page 667

† A copy with the price of 60 fr. is listed in Burnett & Simeone Ltd. *Catalogue 9* (London, 1983), no. 87, with early state of plates—*Catalogue* at JF.

INDEX

A

À la Bien-Aimée, 421
Abbreviations, 34
ABCDEFG, 593
Abdulla Bulbul Ameer, 84
Abide with Me, 85
Ach, Mein Lieber Augustin, 399
Ach! So Fromm, 87
Adams, A. Emmett, 141
Adams, Frank R., 290
Adams, Sarah F., 387
Adams, Stephen, 386
Adamson, Harold, 110, 582
Addinsell, Richard, 621
Adeste Fideles, 86
Advertisements, 30
After the Ball, 87
Ager, Milton, 268
Ah! So Pure—Martha, 87
Ah! Sweet Mystery of Life, 88
Ah! Vous Dirai-je, Maman, 593
A-hunting We Will Go!, 282
Aida, 589
Ain't Gonna Rain, 307
Ain't Misbehavin', 89
Air for the G String—Bach, 90
Akst, Harry, 196
Albéniz, I., Tango, 569
Album für die Jugend, 269
Aldighieri, G., 123
Alexander's Ragtime Band, 91
Alexandrov, A. V., 524
Alford, Kenneth J., 175
Alfred: A Masque, 477
Alfvén, Hugo, Midsommarvaka, 368
All People That on Earth Do Dwell, 409
All the Things You Are, 92
All Through the Night, 92
Allen, Euphemia, 170
Almira, 324
Almost Like Being in Love, 93
Aloha Oe, 93
Alouette, 95
Alte und Neue Volks-Lieder, 406
Always, 96
Amateur's Song Book, The, 413
America, 251, 655
America the Beautiful, 96
American Patrol, 97
Amor an Bord, 297
Amor Brujo, El, 466

Amour des Trois Oranges, L', 340
Amour-Toujours-L'Amour, L', 97
Amusements d'une Heure et Demy, Les, 593
An den Frühling, 98
An der Schönen, Blauen Donau, 147
An die Freude, 563
Anacreontic Song, The, 529
Anchors Aweigh, 99
And the Monkey Wrapped Its Tail Around the Flagpole, 387
Andalucia, 100
Andantino in D Flat, 100
Anderson, Maxwell, 490
Annie Get Your Gun, 574
Annie Laurie, 101
Annie Lisle, 102
Anniversary Song, 623
Anvil Chorus, 102
Anything Goes, 287
Apache Dance, 104
A.P.D.R., 8
Apprenti Sorcier, L', 522
April in Paris, 105
April in Portugal, 105
April Showers, 106
Ar Hyd Y Nos, 92
Araby's Daughter, 413
Aragonaise, Le Cid, 106
Arditi, L., 123
Areglito, El, 586
Arizona Home, An, 274
Arkansas Traveler, 107
Arlen, Harold, 418, 537
Arlésienne, L', 109
Armide, 109
Armstrong, Henry W., 541
Army and Navy Chronicle, 629
Army Duff, 657
Army Goes Rolling Along, The, 157
Arndt, Felix, 393
Arne, Thomas Augustine, 477
Around the World, 110
Arrangement, 33, 35
Artist's Life, 110
As the Saints Go Marching In, 641
As Thousands Cheer, 210
As Time Goes By, 111
Asaf, George, 419
ASCAP, 546
Asleep in the Deep, 112
Assembly, 112

695

Aston, William, 299
At a Georgia Campmeeting, 112
At Dawning, 113
Athalia, 447
Atisket, Atasket, 113
Atlantic Monthly, The, 133
Atteridge, Harold R., 154
Au Clair de la Lune, 114
Aufforderung zum Tanze, 304
Auld Lang Syne, 115, 179
Aura Lea, 117
Aureliano in Palmira, 124
Auswahl der Beliebtesten Märsche, 454
Ave Maria—Bach-Gounod, 117
Ave Maria—Schubert, 120
Avec Privilège du Roi, 8
Aveu, L', 501
Away in a Manger, 120
Away We Go!, 405
Ay-Ay-Ay, 121, 172
Ayer, Nat. D., 407

B

B Minor Mass, Bach, 322
Baa, Baa, Black Sheep, 593
Babes in Toyland, 587
Bacchanale, 122
Bach, Johann Sebastian
    Air for the G String, 90
    B Minor Mass, 322
    Bourrée (Gavotte), 151
    Goldberg Variations, 252
    St. Matthew Passion, 171
    Well-Tempered Clavier, 118
Bacharach, Burt, 636
Bacio, Il, 122
Bagley, E. E., 387
Baker, Dr. Theodore, 442
Balfe, M. W., The Bohemian Girl, 286
Ball, Ernest R., 334, 377, 638
Ballad Book, A, 101
Ballet des Sylphes—Berlioz, 547
Balm of Gilead, 272
Baltimore Patriot, 531
Band Played On, The, 123
Band Wagon, The, 191
Barber of Seville, The—Overture, 124
Barbier, Jules Paul, 128, 215, 509
Barbiere di Siviglia, Il, 124
Barcarolle, Tales of Hoffmann, 127
Baring-Gould, Rev. Sabine, 416
Barkai, 375
Barnacle Bill the Sailor, 128
Barnard, Charlotte Alington, 178
Barnby, J., 542
Barr, James, 619
Bartered Bride, The—Overture, 129
Bártfay Emlék, 281
Bartók, Béla, Concerto for Orchestra, 179
Basin Street Blues, 131
Bates, Katharine Lee, 96
Bath Chronicle, The, 659
Battle Hymn of the Republic, 131
Bayes, Nora (Mrs. Jack Norworth), 497
Bayly, Thomas Haynes, 338

Bear Went over the Mountain, The, 231
Beatles, The, 367
Beautiful Dreamer, 135
Beautiful Ohio, 135
Beer Barrel Polka, 136
Beethoven, Ludwig van
    Concerto for Piano no. 5, 183
    Concerto for Violin, 184
    Fidelio, 326
    Für Elise, 241
    Leonore Overture no. 3, 326
    Minuet in G, 370
    Missa Solemnis, 187
    Moonlight Sonata, 376
    Quartet, op. 59, 450
    Sonata Pathétique, 517
    Symphony no. 1, 551
    Symphony no. 3, 554
    Symphony no. 5, 557
    Symphony no. 6, 406, 560
    Symphony no. 7, 561
    Symphony no. 9, 563
Beggar's Opera, The, 344
Beggar's Wedding, The, 468
Begin the Beguine, 137
Bei Mir Bist Du Schön, 137
Belasco, F., 313
Belasco, Lionel, 478
Believe Me If All Those Endearing Young
    Charms, 138
Bell Bottom Trousers, 139
Bell Song, Lakmé, 140
Bells of St. Mary's, The, 141
Benny Havens, Oh!, 629
Benson, Arthur Christopher, 439
Berceuse—Firebird, 142
Berceuse—Jocelyn, 143
Berlin, Irving, 91, 96, 210, 248, 401, 447, 458,
    486, 574, 648
Berlioz, Hector
    Damnation of Faust, The, 455, 547
    Symphonie Fantastique, 549
Bernauer, Rudolf, 321
Berne Convention, 24
Bernstein, Leonard, 495, 584
Bessel, V., & Co., 63
Best Things in Life Are Free, The, 144
Bicinia Gallica, Latina, Germanica, 662
Bicycle Built for Two, A, 188
Biedermann, Felix, 615
Bielsky, V. I., 227, 283
Bill, Kern, 412
Bill Bailey, Won't You Please Come Home?, 145,
    235
Bill You Done Me Wrong, 234
Bingham, C. Clifton, 342
Bingo, 272
Biographic Information, 79
Birch, Harry, 460
Birth of the Blues, The, 146
Bis, Hippolyte Louis Florent, 653
Bishop, Henry R., 275
Bitter Sweet, 295
Bizet, Georges
    Arlésienne, L', 109
    Carmen, 585

Blackbirds of 1928, 285
Blake, Eubie, 297
Blake, James W., 499
Bland, James A., 164, 399
Blihmele, 360
Bloom, Sol, 276
Blossom, Henry, 318, 644
Blow the Man Down, 146
Blue Danube, 147
Blue Tail Fly, The, 312
Boccherini, Luigi, Minuet, 370
Bock, Jerry, 224
Bodansky, Rob., 616
Body and Soul, 148
Bohème, La, 378
Bohemian Girl, The, 286
Bolero, Ravel, 149
Bolten-Bäckers, 246
Bond, Carrie Jacobs-, 289, 425
Bonny, Bonny Banks o' the Lomond, The, 336
Book of Instruction for the Field-Trumpet and
  Drum, The, 489
Booke of New Lessons for the Cithern & Gittern,
  259
Boola, 150
Borel-Clerc, Ch., 358
Born to Dance, 310
Borodin, Alexander
  Paraphrases, 170
  Prince Igor, 437
Boston Melodeon, The, 413
Bote & Bock, 64
Bottoms Up!, 139
Bourgeois, Louis, 409
Bourrée, Bach, 151
Bow, Bow, Ye Lower Middle Classes, 151
Bowery, The, 152
Bowman, Euday L., 592
Braham, Philip, 332
Brahms, Johannes
  Concerto for Piano no. 1, 181
  Hungarian Dance no. 5, 280
  Symphony no. 1, 551
  Symphony no. 2, 552
  Symphony no. 3, 554
  Symphony no. 4, 555
  Variations, Haydn, St. Anthony Chorale, 526
  Waltzes, op. 39, 611
  Wiegenlied, 650
Brammer, Julius, 431
Brandl, Johann, 414
Brandy and Water, 272
Brecht, Bert., 343
Brennan, J. Keirn, 334
Bridal Chorus—Lohengrin, 631
Bride Cuts the Cake, The, 224
Bridge on the River Kwai, The, 175
Brigadoon, 93
Bring Back My Bonnie to Me, 381
Britannia, the Pride of the Ocean, 176
British Grenadiers, The, 153
British Museum receipt indicators, 6
Brooks, Harry, 89
Brooks, Rev. Dr. Phillips, 402
Brooks, Shelton, 193, 512
Brown, Lew, 144, 146

Brown, Seymour, 407
Bruckner, Anton, Symphony no. 7, 562
Bryan, Alfred, 424
Bryan, Vincent, 299
Bryant's Power of Music, 197
Bucalossi, Procida, 282
Buck, Richard Henry, 317
Bucket, The, 413
Buckley, R. Bishop, 610
Buda, Budapest, 15
Bullard, Frederic Field, 536
Bums' March, The, 657
Bunn, Alfred, 286
Burkhard, Paul, 403
Burnett, Ernie, 384
Burns, Robert, 115, 179, 228
Bury Me Not on the Lone Prairie, 397
Butterfield, Gen. Daniel, 570
Butterfield, J. A., 643
By the Beautiful Sea, 154
By the Light of the Silvery Moon, 155
By the Waters of Minnetonka, 155
By Yon Bonnie Banks, 336

C

Cadman, Charles Wakefield, 113
Caesar, Irving, 166, 515, 541, 572
Caissons Go Rolling Along, The, 156
Caledonian Country Dances, 157
Caledonian Pocket Companion, The, 157
California Here I Come, 157
Callahan, J. Will, 507
Callirhoë, 487
Calypso Songs of the West Indies, 478
Calzabigi, Raniero de, 168
Cambridge Quarters, 634
Cammarano, Salvadore, 102, 493
Campbell, Jimmy, 256, 498
Campbells Are Coming, The, 157
Camptown Races, De, 158
Can Can, Offenbach, 159, 541
Canciones Mexicanas, 188
Cannon, Hughie, 145, 234
Capitan, El, 160
Capoul, Victor, 143
Capricci, Paganini, 455
Capriccio Espagnol, 161
Caprice Viennois, 162
Capua, Edoardo di, 404
Capurro, G., 404
Careless Love, 162
Carioca, 163
Carmen, 585
Carmichael, Hoagy, 528
Carmina Collegensia, 102, 355
Carmina Princetonia, 309
Carmina Yalensia, 209, 255, 516
Carnaval, Schumann, 164
Carnaval des Animaux, Le, 160, 540, 548
Carols for Christmas-Tide, 254
Carols, Hymns and Songs, 628
Carousel, 292
Carré, Michel, 215, 509
Carroll, Harry, 154
Carry Me Back to Old Virginny, 164
Carry Me Back to the Lone Prairie, 396

Caryll, Ivan, 380
Casey Jones, 165
Casse-Noisette, 613
Casson, Margaret, 317
Castellvi, José Na. García, 458
Cat and the Fiddle, The, 496
Caucasian Sketches, 166
Cavalleria Rusticana, 301
Cavanass, J. M., 155
CDC, 38
Celebrated Chop Waltz, The, 170
Chabrier, Emmanuel, 216
Chaminade, Cécile, 486
Chanson, Chansonette, Friml, 166
Chansons et Rondes Enfantines, 539
Chansons, Vaudevilles et Ariettes Choisis par
    Duchemin, 231
Chant de Guerre pour l'Armée du Rhin, 354
Chant sans Paroles—Tchaikovsky, 167
Chants et Chansons Populaires de la France, 114
Chants Revolutionnaires, 303
Chappell & Co., 64
Charles, Jacques, 376
Charleston, 168
Chávez, Carlos, 188
Che Farò Senza Euridice, 168
Cheek to Cheek, 210
Chicken Reel, 169
Children's Corner, 253
Choclo, El, 169
Chocolate Soldier, The, 321
Choice Collection of 200 Favourite Country
    Dances, A, 158
Choir, The, 251
Chopin, Fred., Bibliographic information, 64
    Etudes, op. 10, 219
    Fantaisie-Impromptu, 222
    Funeral March, 238
    Grande Valse Brillante, 257
    Nocturnes, op. 9, 392
    Polonaise, op. 53, 435
    Polonaise Militaire, op. 40, 436
    Preludes, op. 28, 443
    Sonate, op. 35, 238
    Waltzes, op. 34, 611
    Waltzes, op. 64, 612
Chopsticks, 170
Chorale, Erkenne Mich, Mein Hüter, Bach, 171
Choson Kale Mazel Tov, 359
Christian Register, 308
Christiania, 16
Christiné, H., 427, 597
Christmas Carols and Hymns for School and
    Choir, 308
Church Chorals and Choir Studies, 308
Church Porch, The, 402
Church Times, 416
Cid, Le, 106
Cielito Lindo, 121, 172
Cinquantaine, La, 172
Ciribiribin, 173
Clair de Lune, 174
Clari, 275
Claribel, 177
Clavier Ubung, 252
Clé du Caveau, La, 114, 237

Clementine, 174
Clerc, Ch. Borel, 358
C.M., 13
Cobb, Will D., 488
Coburn, Richard, 647
Cohan, George M., 245, 357, 419, 663
Cohn, Irving, 662
Coimbra É uma Lição de Amor, Fado, 105
Coin des Enfants, 253
Colcord, Lincoln, 346
Cole's Selection of Favourite Cotillions, 205
Collection of Russian Folksongs, A, 520
Collective title front cover, 39
College Hornpipe, 484
Colonel Bogey, 175
Columbia, the Gem of the Ocean, 176
Columbia the Land of the Brave, 177
Come Back to Erin, 177
Come, Friends, Who Plough the Sea, 262
Come to the Fair, 178
Comin' Thro' the Rye, 178
Commersbuch, 356
Concerto for Orchestra—Bartók, 179
Concerto for Piano no. 5—Beethoven, 183
Concerto for Piano no. 1—Brahms, 181
Concerto for Piano—Grieg, 180
Concerto for Piano no. 1—Liszt, 181
Concerto for Piano no. 2—Rachmaninoff, 183
Concerto for Piano no. 1—Tchaikovsky, 182
Concerto for Violin—Beethoven, 184
Concerto for Violin—Mendelssohn, 185
Concise System of Instructions and Regulations,
    A, 461
Concise System of Instruction for the Volunteer
    Cavalry of the United States, A, 112, 226
Congregationalist, 96
Conn, Irving, 662
Connecticut Yankee, A, 383
Connelly, Reg, 256, 498
Conrad, Con, 350
Contes d'Hoffmann, Les, 127
Coochi-Coochi, 276
Cook's Selection of Twenty One Favorite Origi-
    nal Airs, 582
Cooper, George, 543
Coppélia, 616
Copyright deposit copy, 38
Copyright Laws, 16
Coq d'Or, 283
Coro di Zingari, 103
Coronation March, Meyerbeer, 186
Coronation Ode, 439
Cortéz, Quirino Mendoza y, 172
Cory, Adela Florence, 316
Costa, Carl, 330
Coteletten Polka, The, 170
Cotton Club Parade, 537
Cottrau, T., 485
Count of Luxemburg, The, 616
Countess Maritza, 431
Country Gardens, 187
Cowan, Marie, 619
Coward, Noël, 293, 295, 472, 512
Cowboy Songs, 244
Creamer, Henry, 623
Creation, The, 271

Credo, Missa Solemnis, 187
Crémieux, Hector, 160
Crockett, Effie I., 469
Crotch, William, 634
Cucaracha, La, 188
Cuckoo, The, 317
Cummings, Dr. W. H., 270
Currencies and Prices, 10
Currier and Ives, 108, 413
Curtis, E. de, 586
Curtis, G. B. de, 586
Cushing, Catherine Chisholm, 98
Cygne, Le, 540
Czibulka, Alphons, 537

D

Da Ponte, Lorenzo, 353, 372
Dacre, Harry, 188
Dainty Songs for Little Lads and Lasses, for Use
    in the Kindergarten, 121
Daisy Bell, 188
Daly, Joseph M., 169
Damnation of Faust, The, 455, 547
Dance of the Belly, 276
Dance of the Corregidor, 189
Dance of the Hours, 190
Dance of the Midway, 276
Dancing in the Dark, 191
Dancing Master, The, 259
Danks, H. P., 501
Danny Boy, 337
Danse Macabre, 192
Danube Waves, 622
Dark Eyes, 417
Darktown Strutters' Ball, The, 192
David, Hal, 636
Davies, David Ivor, 317
Davis, Benny, 350
De Calzabigi, Raniero de, 168
De Camptown Races, 158
De Curtis, E., 586
De Curtis, G. B., 586
De Falla, Manuel
    El Amor Brujo, 466
    The Three-Cornered Hat, 189
De Jouy, Victor Joseph Étienne, 653
De Koven, Reginald, 403
De Lau Lusignan, J., 218
De Lemaire, Ferdinand, 122
De Leuven, Adolphe, Count Ribbing, 457
De Lisle, Claude Rouget, 354
De Lisle, Leconte, 213
De Long, Frank D., 647
De Lulli, Arthur, 170
De Sylva, B. G., 106, 144, 146, 157, 293, 318,
    338
Debussy, Claude
    Clair de Lune, 174
    Golliwogg's Cake Walk, 253
    Prélude à l'Après-Midi d'un Faune, 445
    Rêverie, 462
Deck the Hall with Boughs of Holly, 193
Deep in My Heart, Dear, 194
Deep in the Heart of Texas, 194
Deep River, 195

Defence of Fort M'Henry, 530
Degeyter, Pierre, 303
Dein Ist Mein Ganzes Herz, 665
Deitcher's Dog, Der, 406
Delibes, Léo
    Coppélia, 616
    Lakmé, 140
    Sylvia, 430
Denza, L., 240
Dépôt Légal, 20, 39
Descriptions of First Appearances in Print, 29
Desert Song, The, 195
Determining the Date of a Particular Copy, 5
Determining When, and by Whom, a Musical
    Work Was First Published, 3
Deuteromelia, 576
Deutsche Companie, Die, 209
Deutschland über Alles, 214
Di Capua, Edoardo, 404
Dichter und Bauer, 433
Did You Ever See a Lassie?, 399
Did You Ever Think As the Hearse Rolls By?,
    657
Dietz, Howard, 191
Dillon, Will, 290
Dinah, 196
Dinicu, Grigoras, 277
Disappointment, The, 659
Dissoluto Punito, Il, 371
Dixie, 196
Dixon, Mort, 298
Dober, Conrad K., 350
Don Giovanni—Mozart, 371
Don Juan—Richard Strauss, 200
Donaldson, Walter, 380, 382, 661
Donauwellen, 622
Donizetti, G., Lucia di Lammermoor, 493
Donkey Serenade, The, 167
Donnelly, Dorothy, 194
Don't Sit Under the Apple Tree with Anyone
    Else but Me, 338
Doodah, 159
Dörmann, Felix, 615
Dos Canciones Mexicanas, 217
Double pagination, 40
Douglas, William, 101
Dove, The, 421
Down by the Old Mill Stream, 200
Down by the River Lived a Maiden, 174
Down in Alabam, 408
Down in the Valley, 201
Drdla, Franz, 523
Dreigroschenoper, Die, 343
Dresser, Paul, 382
Drigo, Richard, 490
Drink It Down, Drink It Down, 272
Drink to Me Only with Thine Eyes, 202
Drinking Song, La Traviata, 203
Drunken Sailor, 205
Du Alter Stefansthurm, 414
Du, Du Liegst Mir im Herzen, 207
Du Lieber Augustin, 399
Du und Du, 207
Dukas, Paul—The Sorcerer's Apprentice, 522
Duke, Vernon, 105
Dunderbeck, 515

Dutch Company, The, 209
Duveyrier, Anne-Honoré-Joseph, 667
Dvořák, Antonín
  Humoreske, 280
  Slavonic Dances, op. 46, 504
  Slavonic Dances, op. 72, 505
  Songs My Mother Taught Me, 521
  Symphony no. 5, 558

E

Eardley-Wilmot, D., 335
Earl, Mary, 135
East Is Red, The, 209
East Side, West Side, 500
Eastburn, 334
Easter Parade, 210
Eberhart, Nelle Richmond, 113
Edinburgh Musical Miscellany, The, 468
Edwards, Gus, 155, 299, 488
Egan, Raymond B., 581
1812 Overture, 210
Eileen Aroon, 468
Eili, Eili, 211
Einzug der Gladiatoren, 245
Eisenhower, President, 301
Elegant Extracts for the Guittar, 398
Élégie—Massenet, 212
Elephant Walk, The, 657
Elgar, Edward
  Pomp and Circumstance, 438
  Salut d'Amour, 484
Elisabetta, 124
Eliscu, Edward, 163, 258
Ellington, Duke, 522
Elliott, James William, 502
Elliott, Zo, 573
El-Registan, Gabriel, 524
Emerson, Ida, 272
Emmett, Daniel Decatur, 197
Emperor Quartet, Haydn, 214
Emperor's Hymn, Haydn, 213
Enesco, Georges, Rumanian Rhapsody, 479
Engraved edition, 10
Entr'acte-Gavotte—Mignon, 215
Entry of the Gladiators, 245
Eppel, John Valentine, 373
Érinnyes, Les, 212
Erkenne Mich, Mein Hüter, 171
Erlkönig, 216
España, Albéniz, 569
España, Chabrier, 216
Esquisses Caucasiennes, 166
Essay on the Church Plain Chant, An, 86
Estrellita, 217
Estudiantina, 218
Etudes, op. 10—Chopin, 219
Eugen Onegin, 220
Evans, George, 300
Evening Office of the Church, in Latin and Eng-
  lish, The, 86
Evening Prayer, 221
Exercise Song Book, The, 378
Eyes of Texas, The, 309
Eyton, Frank, 148

F

Fair Harvard, 138
Falla, Manuel de
  El Amor Brujo, 466
  The Three-Cornered Hat, 189
Fallersleben, Hoffmann von, 214
Fantaisie-Impromptu, Chopin, 222
Far Above Cayuga's Waters, 102
Farewell Ladies, 255
Farmer in the Dell, The, 224
Fauré, Gabriel, Requiem, 459
Faust, 509
Fazer, K. G., 70
Fellowship Hymns, 96
Fenstad, E. A., 346
Ferrão, Raúl, 105
Fest-Gesang für Männerchor, 270
Fibich, Zdenko, 432
Fiddler on the Roof, 224
Fidelio, 326
Fields, Dorothy, 285
Finden, Amy Woodforde-, 316
Finian's Rainbow, 637
Finlandia, 225
Firebird, The, 142
First Call, 226
First edition, 31
First Noel, The, 226
Fisher, Fred, 424
Fledermaus, Die, 207
Fleurs d'Espagne, 586
Fliegende Holländer, Der, 229
Flight of the Bumble Bee, The, 227
Florin, 13
Flotow, F. von, 87
Flow Gently Sweet Afton, 228
Flying Dutchman, The—Overture, 229
Flying Trapeze, The, 230
Folk-Song Research, 28
For He's a Jolly Good Fellow, 231
For Me and My Gal, 233
Forberg, Robert, 66
Ford, Lena Guilbert, 316
Fortune Teller, The, 261
Forty-Five Minutes from Broadway, 357
Fosdick, William W., 117
Foster, Stephen C., 28, 135, 158, 311, 358,
  384, 404, 407, 408
Fountain in the Park, The, 646
Four Indian Love Lyrics, 316
Franck, César, Symphony in D Minor, 566
Frankie and Johnny, 146, 233
Franklin Square Song Collection, The, 193, 476
Freire, Osman Perez, 121
Freischütz, Der—Overture, 235
French, Percy, 84
Frère Jacques, 237
Friedman, Leo, 327
Friedrich, W., 87
Friml, Rudolf, 98, 167, 301, 520
Fröhlichter Landmann, 269
Frühlingsstimmen, 607
Fučik, Julius, 245
Fugue for Tinhorns, 226
Funeral March, Chopin, 238
Funeral March of a Marionette, 239

Funiculì—Funiculà, 240
Funny Face, 547
Für Elise, 241
Furber, Douglas, 141, 332

G

Gabriel-Marie, 172
Gade, Jacob, 311
Gade & Warny-Musikforlag, 71
Gaîté (Gaieté) Parisienne, La, 160
Galhardo, José, 105
Gallet, Louis, 213
Galloway, Tod B., 645
Games and Songs of American Children, 224
Garden of Kama and Other Love Lyrics, The, 316
Gassion, Edith Giovanna, 601
Gaudeamus Igitur, 241
Gaunt, Percy, 152
Gavotte, Bach, 151
Gavotte—Mignon, 215
Gay Divorce, 388
Gayaneh, 482
Geheime Anziehungskräfte, 618
Geibel, Adam, 317
Gelbe Jacke, Die, 665
General Collection of the Ancient Irish Music, A, 582
Genetz, Emil, 225
Genevan Psalter, 409
Geneviève de Brabant, 350
Gently Down the Stream, 475
George White's Scandals, 146
Gerard, Richard H., 541
Gershwin, George, 288, 347, 463, 513, 538, 539, 541, 547, 654
Gershwin, Ira, 288, 347, 513, 538, 547, 654
Geschichten aus dem Wienerwald, 568
Get Out of the Wilderness, 408
Giacosa, Giuseppe, 379, 596, 605
Gilbert, W. S., 64, 151, 262, 296, 576, 634, 637
Gille, Philippe, 140, 460
Gilman, Rev. Samuel, 139
Gilmore, Patrick, 640
Gin a Body Meet a Body, 178
Gioconda, La, 190
Gipsy Love Song, 260
Girl Crazy, 288
Girl I Left Behind Me, The, 242
Git Along Little Dogies, 244
Give My Regards to Broadway, 245
Gladiators' Entry, The, 245
Glinka, M. I., Ruslan and Ludmila, 479
Glory Hallelujah, 131
Glow-Worm, 246
Gluck, C. W. von
    Armide, 110
    Orpheus and Euridice, 168
Glühwürmchen Idyll, 246
Go Down, Moses, 247
God Bless America, 248
God Rest You Merry, Gentlemen, 249
God Save the Czar!, 480
God Save the King, 249

Godard, Benjamin, 143
Goethe, Johann Wolfgang von, 216, 395
Goetz, E. Ray, 233
Goin' Home, Dvořák, 558
Gold and Silver Waltz, 252
Goldberg Variations, 252
Golden Wedding Anniversary, 173
Golliwogg's Cake Walk, 253
Golondrina, La, 253
Gondinet, Edmond, 140
Gondoliers, The, 343, 634
Gooch, William, 460
Good King Wenceslas, 254
Good Morning to All, 267
Good News, 144
Goodnight, Irene, 305
Goodnight Ladies, 255, 355, 514
Goodnight Sweetheart, 256
Gordon, Mack, 582
Gospel Magazine, The, 469
Gott, Erhalte den Kaiser!, 213
Götterdämmerung, 463
Gould, Rev. Sabine Baring-, 416
Gounod, Charles
    Ave Maria, 117
    Faust, 509
    Funeral March of a Marionette, 239
Graf von Luxemburg, Der, 616
Graff, Geo., Jr., 638
Gräfin Mariza, 431
Graham, Roger, 284
Grand Canyon Suite, 257
Grande Valse Brillante, 257
Grant, Rupert, 478
Great Day!, 258
Green, John W., 148
Greensleeves, 259
Grey, Clifford, 264, 515
Grieg, Edvard
    An den Frühling, 98
    Bibliographic information, 65
    Concerto for Piano, 180
    Ich Liebe Dich, 291
    Lyrische Stücke, op. 54, 347
    Lyrische Stückchen, op. 43, 98
    March of the Dwarfs, 347
    Norwegian Dances, 393
    Peer Gynt, 423
Grofé, Ferde, 257, 373
Groschen, 12
Grosse Passionsmusik nach dem Evangelium Matthaei, 171
Gruber, Edmund L., 156
Gruber, Franz, 500
Grünwald, Alfred, 431
Guglielmi, Luis, 601
Guillaume Tell, 652
Gusyev, Victor, 360
Guys and Dolls, 226, 260
Gwine To Run All Night, 158
Gypsy Love Song, 260
Gypsy Songs—Dvořák, 521

H

Haas, Ferdinand, 482
Habanera, Carmen, 586

Hadjidakis, Manos, 388
Hail! Hail! The Gang's All Here, 261
Hail to the Chief, 263
Hale, Sarah J., 355
Halévy, L., 585
Haley, Ed., 646
Hall, Wendell W., 307
Hallelujah Chorus—Messiah, 265
Hallelujah!, Youmans, 264
Hammerstein, Oscar, 2nd, 92, 195, 292, 301,
    310, 325, 342, 390, 405, 412, 494, 511,
    523, 649 (2)
Hampton and Its Students, 392
Handefull of Pleasant Delites, A, 259
Handel, G. F.
    Largo, Xerxes, 324
    Lascia Ch'io Pianga, Rinaldo, 324
    Messiah, 265
    Water Music, 622
Handy, W. C., 527
Hansel and Gretel, 221
Happy Birthday to You, 266
Happy Day, 279
Happy Days Are Here Again, 268
Happy Farmer, 268
Harbach, Otto, 195, 301, 496, 508, 649
Harburg, E. Y., 105, 418, 638
Harfe, Die, 359
Hark! The Herald Angels Sing, 269
Harmonia Anglicana, 250
Harnick, Sheldon, 224
Harris, Charles K., 87
Harris, Will J., 544
Harrison, Annie Fortescue, 299
Hart, Lorenz, 341, 383, 656
Harvest Hymns, 267
Haschka, Lorenz Leopold, 214
Hastings, Thomas, 470
Hatikva, 374
Hawthorne, Alice, 333
Hayden, Joe, 278
Haydn, Joseph
    Creation, The, 271
    Emperor's Hymn, 213
    Quartet, op. 76, 213
    Schöpfung, Die, 271
    St. Anthony Chorale, 525
    Symphony no. 94 (Surprise), 564
    Symphony no. 101 (Clock), 565
He Done Me Wrong, 234
Hearse Song, The, 657
Heavens Are Telling the Glory of God, The, 271
Heifetz, Jascha, 277
Hello, Ma Baby, 272
Helsingfors Nya Musikhandel, 70
Henderson, Rait & Fenton (Spalding), 65
Henderson, Ray, 144, 146
Herbert, Victor, 88, 260, 318 (2), 382, 546, 587,
    644
Here We Go Round the Mulberry Bush, 378
Here's to ——— and ———, 272
Hérold, F., Zampa Overture, 666
Hershey, June, 194
Herzer, Ludwig, 665
He's a Jolly Good Fellow, 231
He's Got the Whole World in His Hand, 273

Hey, Diddle Diddle, 502
Heyduk, Adolf, 521
Heyman, Edward, 148
Heyward, DuBose, 539
Higley, Dr. Brewster M., 273
Hill, Lady Arthur, 299
Hill, Mildred J., 267
Hill, Patty S., 267
Hindoo Song, 518
Hinky Dinky Parlez-Vous, 344
Hirsh, A. M., 150
Hit the Deck, 264, 515
Hjertets Melodier, 291
H.M.S. Pinafore, 296
Hoch Soll Er Leben, 273
Hochzeit des Figaro, Die, 352
Hochzeitsmarsch—Mendelssohn, 633
Hoffmann, August Heinrich, 215
Hofmannsthal, Hugo von, 617
Hofmeister Monatsbericht, 45
Hohe Messe in H-Moll, Die, 322
Hold That Tiger, 579
Holiday Inn, 648
Home on the Range, 273
Home! Sweet Home!, 274
Hoodah, 159
Hooker, Brian, 520
Hoola Boola, La, 150
Hoolah! Hoolah!, 276
Hootchy Kootchy Dance, 276
Hope, Laurence, 316
Hopkins John H., Jr., 628
Hora Staccato, 277
Horlick, Harry, 595
Hot Time in the Old Town, A, 278
Hough, Will M., 290
Hovey, Richard, 536
How Dry I Am, 279
Howard, Joseph E., 272, 290
Howe, Julia Ward, 134
Hoyt, Charles H., 152
Humoreske, 280
Humperdinck, E., Hansel and Gretel, 221
Humpty Dumpty, 502
Hundred Pipers, The, 655
Hundred Years from Now, A, 657
Hungarian Dance no. 5—Brahms (Kéler), 280
Hungarian Rhapsody no. 2—Liszt, 281
Hungarian Rhapsody no. 15—Liszt, 455
Hunt Theme, 282
Hupfeld, Herman, 111
Hymn of the Soviet Union, 524
Hymn to the Sun, 282
Hymnal for Use of the English Church, A, 86
Hymns Ancient and Modern, 85
Hymns and Anthems, 387
Hymns and Sacred Poems, 269

I

I Ain't Got Nobody, 284
I Can't Give You Anything but Love (Baby), 285
I Could Have Danced All Night, 286
I Dreamt That I Dwelt in Marble Halls, 286
I Get a Kick out of You, 287
I Got Rhythm, 287

I Like Coffee, I Like Tea, 288
I Love Coffee, I Love Tea, 288
I Love Little Pussy, 502
I Love You Truly, 289
I Want a Girl Just Like the Girl That Married Dear Old Dad, 289
I Wonder Who's Kissing Her Now, 290
Ibsen, H., 423
Ich Liebe Dich—Grieg, 291
Ida Sweet as Apple Cider, 292
Idzikovski, 66
If a Body Meet a Body, 179
If I Loved You, 292
If I Were on the Stage, 318
If You Knew Susie like I Know Susie, 293
I'll Follow My Secret Heart, 293
I'll Give to You a Paper of Pins, 294
I'll Overcome Some Day, 624
I'll See You Again, 294
I'll See You in My Dreams, 295
I'll Take You Home Again, Kathleen, 296
Illica, Luigi, 379, 596, 605
Illustrated National Nursery Songs and Games, 114, 337, 378, 594
Illustration, L', 462
I'm Always Chasing Rainbows, 223
I'm Called Little Buttercup, 296
I'm in the Army, 664
I'm Just Wild About Harry, 297
I'm Looking Over a Four Leaf Clover, 298
Imber, Naphtali Herz, 375
Immortalia, 128
Imprint, 45
In a Persian Market, 298
In an Eighteenth Century Drawing Room, 517
In My Merry Oldsmobile, 299
In Old Town To-night, 278
In the Bright Mohawk Valley, 457
In the Gloaming, 299
In the Good Old Summertime, 300
Indian Love Call, 301
Intermezzo—Cavalleria Rusticana, 301
Internationale, L', 303
Introduction et Rondo Capriccioso, 303
Invitation to the Dance, 304
Iohansen, A., 71
Iolanthe, 151
Ippolitov-Ivanov, M., *Caucasian Sketches,* 166
Irene (Goodnight, Irene), 305
Irish Washerwoman, 306, 489
Island Song Book, The, 642
It Ain't Gonna Rain No Mo', 307
It Came upon the Midnight Clear, 308
Itisket, Itasket, 114
It's a Long, Long Way to Tipperary, 308
It's Always Fair Weather, 536
It's Wonderful, 547
Ivan Skivitsky Skivar, 84
Ivanov, M. Ippolitov-, *Caucasion Sketches,* 166
Ivanovici, I., 622
I've Been Working on the Railroad (The Eyes of Texas), 309
I've Got Rhythm, 287
I've Got You Under My Skin, 310
I've Told Ev'ry Little Star, 310

J

Jack and Jill, 502
Jacobs, J., 137
Jacobs-Bond, Carrie, 289, 425
Jacobson, Leopold, 321, 615
Jacques-Charles, 376
Jarabe Tapatio, 366
Jealousy, 311
Jeanie with the Light Brown Hair, 311
Jenny's Baubie, 400
Jessel, Léon, 421
Jim Crack Corn, 312
Jingle Bells, 313
Jocelyn, 143
Johansen, A., 71
John Brown, 131
John Brown Had a Little Injun, 205
John Brown's Baby Has a Cold upon His Chest, 131
Johnny Fill Up the Bowl, 639
Johnny Get Your Gun, 313, 419
Johnson, George W., 643
Johnson, Jimmy, 168
Jolson, Al, 157
Jonas, Isham, 295
Jonson, Ben, 202
Journal of American Folklore, 163, 201, 273, 305, 416, 497
Jouy, Victor Joseph Étienne de, 653
Joy to the World, 314
Juanita, 325
Jubilee, Porter, 137
Jubilee Songs, 247, 391, 546, 642
Judge, Jack, 308
Jurgenson, P. I., 66
Juvenile Miscellany, 355
Južno-Slovjenske Narodne Popievke, 348

K

Kahn, Gus, 163, 295, 382, 661
Kaiser-Walzer, 314
Kálmán, Emmerich, 431
Kamennoi-Ostrow, 315
Kashmiri Song, 315
Keep the Home Fires Burning, 316
Keiser, Robert A., 646
Kéler, Béla, 281
Kelley, Daniel E., 273
Kentucky Babe, 317
Keppell, Lady Caroline, 468
Kern, Jerome, 92, 310, 325, 338, 412, 496, 508, 574, 649 (2)
Kerry Dance, The, 317
Ketèlbey, Albert W., 298
Kethe, William, 410
Key, Francis Scott, 275, 530
Khatchaturian, A., *Saber Dance,* 482
Kiallmark, G., 413
Kilmer, Joyce, 589
Kind, Johann Friedrich, 237
Kinderlieder, 651
Kinderscenen, 588
King and I, The, 494
King, Irving, 498
King, Robert A. (Keiser), 135, 646
King, Stoddard, 573

Kipling, Rudyard, 415
Kiss in the Dark, A, 318
Kiss Me Again, 318
Kiss Me Kate, 658
K., J., 661
K-K-K-Katy, 319
Kleine Hafenorgel, Die, 331
Kleine Nachtmusik, Eine, 320
Knaben Wunderhorn, Des, 651
Knickerbocker Holiday, 490
Knipper, Lev, 360
Knock a Man Down, 146
Koehler, Ted, 537
Kol Nidre, 320
Komm, Komm! Held Meiner Träume, 321
Komm Zigány!, 431
Koven, Reginald de, 403
Kreisler, Fritz
    Caprice Viennois, 162
    Liebesfreud, 327
    Liebesleid, 327
    Viennese Popular Song, 414
Kreuzer, 13
Kristiania, 16
Künstler-Leben, 111
Kutchy Kutchy, 276
Kyrie—B Minor Mass, 322

L

Lacome, P., 218
Lady, Be Good!, 347
Lady Fair, 195
Lady of the Lake, The, 120, 263
Lakmé, 140
Lamb, A. J., 112
Lambert, Louis, 640
Land des Lächelns, Das, 665
Land of Hope and Glory, 439
Land of Smiles, The, 665
Lane, Burton, 638
Largo—Dvořák, 558
Largo—Handel, 324
Lascia Ch'io Pianga, 324
Lascombe, Georges, 426
Last Rose of Summer, The, 582
Last Time I Saw Paris, The, 325
Lateiner, Joseph, 359
Lauriger Horatius, 355
Lawlor, Chas. B., 499
Layton, Turner, 623
Lecuona, Ernesto, 100, 499
Lehár, Franz, 252, 364, 616, 665
Leichte Cavallerie, 330
Leighton Bros., 535
Leip, Hans, 331
Lemaire, Ferdinand, 122
Lemare, Edwin H., 100
Leningrad, 16
Lennon, John, 367
Lenoir, Jean, 422
Léon, Victor, 364
Leonard, Eddie, 292
Leoncavallo, R., Pagliacci, 599
Leonore Overture no. 3, 326
Lerner, Alan Jay, 93, 286
Leslie, Edgar, 233

Let Me Call You Sweetheart, 327
Let My People Go, 247
Leuven, Adolphe de, Count Ribbing, 457
Levee Song, 309
Lewis, Sam M., 196
Leybourne, George, 230
Liebesfreud, 327
Liebesleid, 327
Liebestod, 328
Liebestraum, 329
Lied der Deutschen, Das, 214
Lieder für Freunde der Geselligen Freude, 242
Lieder ohne Worte—Mendelssohn, 525
Lieurance, Thurlow, 155
Light, Ben, 384
Light Cavalry—Overture, 329
Lili Marleen, 331
Liliuokalani, 93
Lilli Marlene, 331
Limehouse Blues, 332
Lincke, Paul, 246
Lincoln, President, 312, 333
Lisle, Claude Rouget de, 354
Lisle, Leconte de, 213
Listen to the Mocking Bird, 333
Liszt, Franz
    Concerto for Piano no. 1, 181
    Hungarian Rhapsody no. 2, 281
    Liebestraum (O Lieb), 329
    Préludes, Les, 446
Litoria! Litoria!, 412
Little Annie Rooney, 333
Little Bit of Heaven, Shure They Call It Ireland,
    A, 334
Little Bo-Beep, 502
Little Brown Jug, 334
Little Children's Book: for Schools and Families,
    120
Little Grey Home in the West, 335
Little Jack Horner, 502
Little Star, 218
Livre tournois, 12
Loch Lomond, 336
Loesser, Frank, 260, 441
Loewe, Frederick, 93, 286
Logan, Frederic Knight, 373
Lohengrin, 631
Löhner, Fritz, 665
Löhr, Hermann, 335
London Bridge, 337
Londonderry Air, 337
Lone Prairie, The, 396
Lonesome Tunes, 416
Long, Frank D. de, 647
Long, Long Ago!, 338
Look for the Silver Lining, 338
Lord's Prayer, The, 339
Lost Chord, The, 339
Lou Tambourin, 109
Louiguy, 600
Love Me Tender, 117
Love of Three Oranges, The, 340
Loveless Love, 163
Lover, 341
Lover, Come Back to Me!, 342
Lover, Samuel, 243

Love's Old Sweet Song, 342
Lucia di Lammermoor, 493
Lullaby—Brahms, 650
Lulli, Arthur de, 170
Lusignan, J. de Lau, 218
Lustige Witwe, Die, 364
Lustigen Weiber von Windsor, Die, 365
Lvov, Alexei, 480
Lyrische Stücke, op. 54—Grieg, 347
Lyrische Stückchen, op. 43—Grieg, 98
Lyte, Henry Francis, 85

M

Má Vlast, 374
MacDonough, Glen, 587
MacDowell, Edward, 583
Mack, Cecil, 168
Mack the Knife, 343
Madama Butterfly, 596
Madden, Ed, 155
Mademoiselle from Armentières, 344
Mademoiselle Modiste, 319
Mahler, Gustav, Symphony no. 1, 552
Mahoney, Jack, 644
Maine Stein Song, 346, 536
Malagueña, 100
Malbrouk, 231
Mallet, David, 477
Malotte, Albert Hay, 339
Man I Love, The, 346
Man in the Moon, The, 249
Man on the Flying Trapeze, The, 230
Manisero, El, 422
Männerlieder, 608
Manon, 460
Maple Leaves, 643
March of the Dwarfs, 347
March of the Kings, 109
Marche du Sacre, Le, 186
Marche Funèbre—Chopin, 238
Marche Funèbre d'une Marionnette, 239
Marche Militaire—Schubert, 348
Marche Slave, 348
Marching Through Georgia, 349
Mardi Gras, 373
Margie, 350
Margis, Alfred, 597
Marie, Gabriel, 172
Marines' Hymn, The, 350
Marionettes—Poldini, 441
Mark, 12
Marks, Godfrey, 483
Marks, Johnny, 476
Marlbourouck, 231
Marriage of Figaro—Overture, The, 352
Marseillaise, La, 354, 534
Martha, 87
Martin, Easthope, 178
Martin, Roberta, 625
Mary Had a Little Lamb, 256, 354
Maryland, My Maryland, 355
Mary's a Grand Old Name, 357
Mascagni, Pietro, Cavalleria Rusticana, 301
Mason, Lowell, 314, 387
Mass in B Minor—Bach, 322
Massa's in de Cold Ground, 358

Massenet, Jules
  Cid, Le, 107
  Élégie, 212
  Manon, 460
  Méditation—Thaïs, 361
Mattchiche, La, 358
Maxixe, La, 359
Maybrick, Michael, 386
Mays, Cad. L., 278
Maytime, 651
Mazel Tov, 359
McCarthy, Joe, 663
McCartney, Paul, 367
McCree, Junie, 450
McHugh, Jimmy, 285
McLellan, C. M. S., 380
McPherson, Richard C., 168
Me and Juliet, 390
Meacham, F. W., 97
Meadowlands, 360
Meany, Stephen Joseph, 176
Méditation sur Ier Prélude de Piano de S. Bach, 119
Méditation—Thaïs, 361
Meilhac, Henri, 460, 585
Meistersinger von Nürnberg, Die, 449
Melancholy, 384
Mélesville, 667
Mélodie in F—Rubinstein, 362
Melodien zum Mildheimischen Liederbuche, 355
Melodies of Various Nations, 275
Men of Harlech, 363
Menasci, G., 302
Mendelssohn, Felix
  Concerto for Violin, 185
  Hark! The Herald Angels Sing (Fest-Gesang), 269
  Midsummer Night's Dream, A, 633
  Priests' March—Athalia, 447
  Songs without Words, 525
  Symphony no. 4 (Italian), 555
  Wedding March, 633
Merrily We Roll Along, 256
Merry Muses of Caledonia, The, 179
Merry Widow Waltz, 364
Merry Wives of Windsor, The—Overture, 365
Messe Solennelle, 187
Messiah, Handel, 265, 314, 635
Metz, Theo., 278
Mexican Hat Dance, 366
Meyer, George W., 233
Meyer, Joseph, 157, 293
Meyerbeer, G., Le Prophète, 186
Michelle, 367
Midsommarvaka, 368
Midsummer Night's Dream, A, 633
Midsummer Vigil, 368
Mighty Lak' a Rose, 368
Mignon, 215
Mihalkov, Sergei, 524
Mikado, The, 576
Milburn, Richard, 333
Miles, Alfred H., 99
Millions d' Arlequin, Les, 490
Mills, Kerry (F.A.), 113
Minatò, Nicola, 324

Minnigerode, Meade, 645
Minstrel-Boy, The, 369
Minuet—Boccherini, 370
Minuet—Paderewski, 372
Minuet—Don Giovanni, 371
Minuet in G—Beethoven, 370
Miss Lucy Long, 312
Missa Solemnis, 187
Mississippi, 372
Missouri Waltz, The, 373
Mlle. Modiste, 319
Modern Psalmist, The, 314
Mogulesco, Sigmund, 359
Mohr, Joseph, 500
Moldau, 374
Molloy, J. L., 317, 342
Molly Put the Kettle On, 400
Moment Musicale—Schubert, 375
Mon Homme, 376
Monaco, James V., 663
Monk, William Henry, 85
Monkey Wrapped Its Tail Around the Flagpole,
    The, 387
Monkey's Wedding, 205
Montesinos, Eduardo Montesinos, 605
Montrose, Percy, 174
Moonlight and Roses, 100
Moonlight Sonata, 376
Moore, Thomas, 138, 243, 369, 583
More Than You Know, 259
Moritat von Mackie Messer, 343
Morse, Dolly, 579
Mosenthal, Hermann Salomon von, 366
Moszkowski, Moritz, 491
Mother Goose's Melody, 469
Mother Machree, 377
Motherless Child, 514
Moya, 519
Mozart, W. A.
    Don Giovanni, 371
    Kleine Nachtmusik, Eine, 320
    Marriage of Figaro, 352
    Serenade (K 525), 320
    Sonata (Rondo alla Turca) (K 331), 516
    Sonata in C Major (K 545), 517
    Symphony "Jupiter" (K 551), 567
    Symphony no. 40 (K 550), 564
Mulberry Bush, 378
Munguia, Enrique, 172
Munson, Eddie, 292
Murphy, Stanley, 449
Musetta's Waltz, 378
Music Box Revue, 486
Music in the Air, 310
Music in the Judgment of Paris, The, 477
Musical and Poetical Relics of the Welsh Bards,
    92, 193, 363
Musical Excerpts, 71
Musical Switch, A, 657
Musical Times, The, 417
Musical Visitor, 296
Mussorgsky, Modeste
    A Night on the Bald Mountain, 389
    Pictures at an Exhibition, 427
My Beautiful Lady, 380
My Blue Heaven, 380

My Bonnie Lies over the Ocean, 381
My Buddy, 381
My Country! 'Tis of Thee, 251
My Darling Clementine, 174
My Dream Girl, 382
My Fair Lady, 286
My Gal Sal, 382
My Heart Stood Still, 383
My Hero, 321
My Lodging Is on the Cold Ground, 138
My Ma Gave Me a Nickel, 359
My Man, 376
My Melancholy Baby, 384
My Old Kentucky Home, 384
My Wild Irish Rose, 385
Mysterioso Pizzicato, 385

N

Nairne, Lady Caroline, 655
Names of Cities, 15
Nancy Dawson, 378
Nancy Lee, 386
Narcissus, 386
Nathan, Harry, 619
National Emblem March, 387
National Nursery Rhymes and Nursery Songs,
    502
National Union Catalogue, 25
Naughty Marietta, 88
Neale, The Rev. J. M., 254
Nearer, My God, to Thee, 387
Nederlandtsche Gedenck-Clanck, 442
Negro Folk Songs as Sung by Lead Belly, 306
Neue Briefe Beethovens, 241
Neues Liederbuch für Frohe Gesellschaften, 606
Neugroschen, 12
Neukreuzer, 13
Never on Sunday, 388
Nevin, Ethelbert, 368, 386, 473
New Moon, The, 342
New Orleans Sunday Delta, 356
New Yale Song-Book, The, 645
Newton, Eddie, 165
Nicolai, Otto, The Merry Wives of Windsor, 365
Night and Day, 388
Night on the Bald Mountain, A, 389
No No Nanette, 572
No Other Love, 390
Noble, Ray, 256, 599
Nobody Knows de Trouble I've Seen, 391
Nocturne, op. 9, no. 2—Chopin, 392
Nola, 393
Nolan, Michael, 333
None but the Lonely Heart, 394
Norton, Caroline Elizabeth Sarah, 325
Norton, Geo. A., 384
Norwegian Dance—Grieg, 393
Norworth, Jack, 497, 568
Norworth, Nora Bayes, 497
Nôs Galan, 193
Notice of intention to use, 579
Notice of use, 579
Novello, Ivor, 316
Nozze di Figaro, Le, 352
Nugent, Maude, 543
Nur Wer die Sehnsucht Kennt, 394

Nursery Rhymes of England, The, 288, 660
Nursery Songs and Games, 114, 337, 378, 594
Nutcracker Ballet, 613

O

O Beautiful for Spacious Skies, 96
O, Bury Me Not on the Lone Prairie, 396
Oh! Dear, What Can the Matter Be?, 398
Oh dem Golden Slippers, 399
O Du Lieber Augustin, 399
Oh, Give Me a Home Where the Buffalo Roam, 274
O Happy Day, 279
Oh, How I Hate to Get Up in the Morning, 401
Oh Johnny, Oh Johnny, Oh, 401
Oh, Kay!, 513
Oh, Lady! Lady!!, 412
O! Let My People Go, 247
O Lieb—Liszt, 329
O Little Town of Bethlehem!, 402
Oh, Marguerite!, 657
O Mein Papa, 403
Oh My Darling Clementine, 174
Oh, Promise Me!, 403
'O Sole Mio!, 404
Oh! Susanna, 404
O Tannenbaum, O Tannenbaum!, 355
Oh They Don't Wear Pants in the Southern Part of France, 276
Oh, What a Beautiful Mornin', 405
Oh Where, Oh Where Has My Little Dog Gone, 406
Oh, You Beautiful Doll, 407
Oberon—Overture, 395
Of Thee I Sing, 654
Offenbach, J.
    Apache Dance (Le Papillon and Le Roi Carotte), 104
    Can Can (Orphée aux Enfers), 159
    Marines' Hymn (Geneviève de Brabant), 350
    Tales of Hoffmann, 127
O'Hara, Geoffrey, 319
Oiseau de Feu, L', 142
Oklahoma!, 405
Ol' Man River, 412
Olcott, Chauncey, 377, 385, 638
Old Black Joe, 407
Old Clown's "W-H-O-A January" Songster, The, 232
Old Folks at Home, 407
Old Grey Mare, The, 408
Old Hundred, 409
Old Joe, 513
Old MacDonald Had a Farm, 410
Old Man River, 412
Old Oaken Bucket, The, 413
Old Plantation Hymns, 496, 514
Old Refrain, The, 414
Old Scots Songs, 179
Old Time Religion, 642
Oliphant, Caroline, 656
Oliveros, Armando Millan, 458
Olman, Abe, 402
On Board the "Rocket," 146
On the Road to Mandalay, 415
On the Trail—Grofé, 257

On the Trail of Negro Folk-Songs, 498
On Top of Old Smoky, 416
On Your Toes, 503
One Alone, 195
One Fine Day, 596
One Horse Open Sleigh, 313
100 Comic Songs, 440
Only Girl, The, 645
Onward, Christian Soldiers, 416
"Opie" Two-Step, 346
Orange Blossoms, 318
Orchestral Parts, 72
Orchestral Suite no. 3—Bach, 90
Orfeo ed Euridice, 168
Orlob, Harold, 290
Orphée aux Enfers, 159
Orpheus and Euridice, 168
Orpheus in the Underworld, 159
Orred, Meta, 299
Oslo, 16
Otchi Tchorniya, 417
Our Monthly Casket, 132
Over the Rainbow, 418
Over the Waves, 509
Over There, 418
Overture, in D—Bach, 90
Owen Wister Out West, 244

P

Pack Up Your Troubles in Your Old Kit-Bag, 419
Paderewski, I., Minuet, 372
Padilla, José, 458, 605
Paganini, Nicolo, 24 Capricci, 455
Pagliacci, 599
Palmer, John F., 123
Paloma, La, 420
Pammelia, 489
Pan-Ein Lustiges Liederbuch für Gymnasiasten, 273
Panella, Frank, 409
Paper of Pins, 294
Papillon, Le, 104
Papillons d' Amour, 421
Parade of the Wooden Soldiers, The, 421
Paraphrases, 170
Parish Choir, 96
Parish, Mitchell, 528
Parlez-Moi d'Amour, 422
Parsifal, 445
Pas des Echarpes, 486
Paterson, A. B., 619
Patineurs, Les, 503
Payne, John Howard, 275
Peanut Vendor, The, 422
Peer Gynt, 423
Peg o' My Heart, 424
Perfect Day, A, 425
Pest, 15
Pestalozza, A., 173
Peter and the Wolf, 425
Peters, C. F., 65
Petite Tonkinoise, 426
Petrie, H. W., 112
Petrie Collection of the Ancient Music of Ireland, The, 337
Petrograd, 16

Peyton, Dave, 284
Phonograph Records, 29, 193, 280, 331, 462,
    528, 579, 592, 623, 642
Piae Cantiones Ecclesiasticae et Scholasticae, 254
Piaf, Edith, 600
Piave, Francesco Maria, 204, 452
Pictures at an Exhibition, 427
Piedigrotta-Garibaldi, 587
Pierpont, J., 313
Pierre et le Loup, 425
Pilgrims' Chorus, 428
Pirates of Penzance, The, 261
Pizzicati—Sylvia, 430
Planché, James Robinson, 396
Plate number, 53
Play Gypsies-Dance Gypsies, 431
p.n., 53
Pocket Book for the German Flute or Violin, 243
Pocket Song Book for the Use of the Students
    and Graduates of McGill College, A, 95
Poëm, Fibich, 432
Poet and Peasant—Overture, 433
Poldini, Ed., 441
Polka—Schwanda, 434
Polly Put the Kettle On, 399
Polly-Wolly-Doodle, 434
Polo, 359
Polonaise, op. 53—Chopin, 435
Polonaise Militaire, op. 40—Chopin, 436
Polovtsian Dances, 437
Pomeroy, George S., 645
Pomp and Circumstance, 438
Ponce, M. M., 217
Ponchielli, Amilcare, La Gioconda, 190
Ponte, Lorenzo Da, 353, 372
Pop Goes the Weasel, 440
Popular Rhymes, Fireside Stories, and Amuse-
    ments of Scotland, 378
Porgy and Bess, 539
Porter, Cole, 137, 287, 310, 388, 636, 658
Portuguese Hymn, 86
Postal Districts, 15
Pottier, Eugène, 303
Poulton, George R., 117
Poupée Valsante, 441
Powell, Felix, 419
Powell, George Henry, 419
Praise the Lord and Pass the Ammunition!!, 441
Prayer of Thanksgiving, 442
Preislied—Wagner, 448
Prélude à l'Après-Midi d'un Faune, 444
Prelude in C Sharp Minor—Rachmaninoff, 444
Prelude—Parsifal, 445
Preludes, op. 28—Chopin, 443
Préludes, Les—Liszt, 446
President Eisenhower, 301
President Franklin D. Roosevelt, 268
President Lincoln, 312, 333
President Truman, 297, 373
Presley, Elvis, 117
Pretty Girl Is Like a Melody, A, 447
Prices, 10
Priests' March—Mendelssohn, 447
Prince Igor, 437
Princess, The—Tennyson, 542
Private Lives, 512

Prize Song—Wagner, 448
Proctor, Adelaide A., 340
Prodaná Nevěsta, 129
Professional edition, 53
Prokofiev, S.
    The Love of Three Oranges, 340
    Peter and the Wolf, 425
    Symphonie Classique, 549
Prophète, Le, 186
Pryor, Arthur, 647
Pseaumes de David, 410
Puccini, Giacomo
    Bohème, La, 379
    Madama Butterfly, 596
    Tosca, 605
Pulitzer Prize, 654
Pussy-Cat, 502
Put on Your Old Grey Bonnet, 449
Put Your Arms Around Me, Honey, 450
Put's Golden Songster, 604

Q

Quaker's Opera, The, 187
Quando Me'n Vo', 378
Quartet, op. 59—Beethoven, 450
Quartet, op. 76—Haydn, 214
Quartet, op. 11—Tchaikovsky, 451
Quartet—Rigoletto, 452
Quintet, op. 163—Schubert, 453
Quintet, op. 44—Schumann, 454

R

Rachmaninoff, Sergei
    Concerto for Piano no. 2, 183
    Prelude in C Sharp Minor, 444
    Rapsodie on a Theme of Paganini, 456
Rahter, 66
Rainforth, Elizabeth, 655
Rakoczy March, 454
Rambling Wreck from Georgia Tech, 515
Randall, James Ryder, 356
Rapsodie on a Theme of Paganini, 455
Rasbach, Oscar, 589
Ravel, Maurice, Bolero, 149
Raymond—Overture, 456
Razaf, Andy, 89
Recueil de Rondes avec Jeux et de Petites Chan-
    sons, 238
Red River Valley, The, 457
Red, White & Blue, The, 176
Redner, L. H., 402
Reichsthaler, 12
Reisch, W., 667
Relicario, El, 458
Rellstab, Ludwig, 492
Remember, 458
Remick Folio of Moving Picture Music, 385
Requiem—Fauré, 459
Reuben and Rachel, 460
Rêve, Le—Manon, 460
Reveille, 461
Rêverie—Debussy, 462
Rexford, Eben E., 501
Reynolds, Herbert, 574
Rhapsodie Hongroise—Liszt, 281
Rhapsody in Blue, 462

Rhapsody on a Theme of Paganini, 455
Rhein Nixen, Die, 127
Rheingold, Das, 463
Ribbing, Count, 457
Ricketts, Frederick J., 175
Ricordi, 67
Ride of the Valkyries, The, 463
Riese, F. W., 87
Rigoletto, 452
Rimbault, Edward F., 279
Rimsky-Korsakov, N.
  Capriccio Espagnol, 161
  Coq d'Or, 283
  Flight of the Bumble Bee, The, 227
  Sadko, 518
  Scheherazade, 487
Rinaldo, 325
Ring des Nibelungen, Der, 465
Ritual Fire Dance, 466
Roberta, 508
Roberts, Lee S., 507
Robin, Leo, 264
Robin Adair, 468
Robin des Bois, 236
Robin Hood, 403
Robinson, A., 667
Robinson, J. Russel, 350
Robledo, Julian, 578
Rock-a-Bye Baby, 468
Rock of Ages, 469
Röder, C. G., 70
Rodgers, Richard, 292, 341, 383, 390, 405, 494,
  503, 511, 523, 656
Rodriguez Moisés Simons, 422
Rogers, Robert Cameron, 473
Rogues' March, 657
Roi Carotte, Le, 104
Romance, op. 44—Rubinstein, 470
Romance, op. 24—Sibelius, 471
Romberg, Sigmund, 194, 195, 342, 651
Romeo and Juliette—Tchaikovsky, 471
Rondo alla Turca (K 331)—Mozart, 516
Room With a View, A, 472
Roosevelt, Franklin D., President, 268
Root, Geo. F., 588
Rosamunde Ballet, 473
Rosary, The, 473
Rosas, Juventino, 509
Rose, Ed., 402
Rose, Vincent, 647
Rose, William, 258
Rose-Marie, 301
Rosen aus dem Süden, 474
Rosenfeld, M. H., 313
Rosenkavalier, Der, 617
Roses from the South, 474
Roses of Picardy, 475
Rosier, Joseph Bernard, 457
Rossi, Giacomo, 324
Rossini, G.
  Aureliano in Palmira, 124
  Barber of Seville, The, 124
  Elisabetta, 124
  William Tell, 652
Rouget de Lisle, Claude, 354
Rourke, M. E., 574

Row, Row, Row Your Boat, 475
Roxburghe Collection, 249
Royal Privileges, 8
Royalties, 178
Rubinstein, Anton
  Kamennoi-Ostrow, 315
  Mélodie in F, 362
  Romance, op. 44, no. 1, 470
  Soirées à St. Petersbourg, 470
Rudolph the Red-Nosed Reindeer, 476
Rule Britannia, 477
Rum and Coca-Cola, 477
Rumanian Rhapsody, op. 11, no. 1—Enesco, 479
Ruslan and Ludmila—Overture, 479
Russian Czarist National Anthem, 480

S

Sabbath Hymn and Tune Book, The, 387
Saber Dance, 482
Sabina, Karel, 130
Sacramento, 158
Sadko, 518
Sailing, 483
Sailor's Hornpipe, The, 484
Sailors' Songs, or "Chanties," 206
Saint-Saëns, Camille
  Carnaval des Animaux, Le, 160, 540, 548
  Danse Macabre, 192
  Introduction et Rondo Capriccioso, 303
  Samson and Delilah, 122
  Swan, The, 540
Sally, 338
Salut d'Amour, 484
Sammlung von Johann Christian Günthers, 242
Samson and Delilah, 122
Sanderson, James, 263
Sandler, Jacob, 211
Santa Lucia, 485
Sardou, V., 605
Saunders, Joe, 230
Say, Brothers, Will You Meet Us?, 131
Say It with Music, 486
Sayers, Henry J., 571
Scarf Dance—Chaminade, 486
Scheherazade, 487
Schiller, Friedrich von, 563
Schneckenburger, Max, 608
Schnitzelbank, 593
Schön Rosmarin, 328
Schonberger, John, 647
Schonberger, Malvin, 647
School-Days, 488
Schöpfung, Die, 271
Schubert, Franz
  Ave Maria, 120
  Erlkönig, 216
  Marche Militaire, 348
  Moment Musicale, 375
  Quintet, op. 163, 453
  Rosamunde Ballet, 473
  Serenade, Schwanengesang, 491
  Symphony (Unfinished), 567
Schultze, Norbert, 331
Schumann, Robert
  Album für die Jugend, 269
  Carnaval, 164

Happy Farmer, 269
Kinderscenen, 588
Quintet, op. 44, 454
Träumerei, 588
Schütt, Edouard, 421
Schwanda, 434
Schwanengesang—Schubert, 491
Schwartz, Arthur, 191
Scollard, Clinton, 548
Scotch Bagpipe Melody, 306, 489
Scots Musical Museum, The, 115, 116, 158, 228
Scots Observer, The, 415
Scots Poems, 115
Scott,. Clement, 403
Scott, Lady John, 101, 336
Scott, Walter, 120, 263
Scottish Students' Song Book, The, 84
Scotto, Vincent, 426
Scull, Guy H., 645
Sears, Edmund H., 308
Sechs Variationen über das Volkslied: Ei du
   Mein Lieber Augustin, 399
Secunda, Sholom, 137
See-Saw, Margery Daw, 502
Seibert, T. Lawrence, 165
Select Collection of Original Scottish Airs, A,
   116
Selected Songs Sung at Harvard College, 209
Selection of Irish Melodies, A, 138, 243, 369,
   583
Selection of Scotch, English, Irish and Foreign
   Airs, A, 660
Selection of Titles, 60
Semper Fidelis, 489
Sennewald, G., 66
September Song, 490
Serenade—Drigo, 490
Serenade—Moszkowski, 491
Serenade—Eine Kleine Nachtmusik, 320
Serenade (K 525)—Mozart, 322
Serenade—Toselli, 493
Serenade-Schwanengesang, 491
Serradell, Narciso, 254
Sextet—Lucia di Lammermoor, 493
Shakespeare, 259, 365, 410, 471
Shall We Dance?, 494
Shannon, J. R., 585
Shave and a Haircut, Bay Rum, 495
She Didn't Say "Yes," 496
She'll Be Comin' Round the Mountain, 496
Shields, Ren, 300, 535
Shine On, Harvest Moon, 497
Short'nin Bread, 497
Shostakovitch, D., Symphony no. 5, 558
Show cover, 56
Show Me the Way to Go Home, 498
Showboat, 412
Sibelius, Jean
   Bibliographic information, 70
   Finlandia, 225
   Romance, op. 24, no. 9, 471
   Symphony no. 2, 553
   Valse Triste, 598
Siboney, 499
Sidewalks of New York, The, 499

Sieben Gesänge aus Walter Scott's Fräulein vom
   See, 120
Sieczyński, Rudolf, 601
Siegfried, 463
Siegfried Idyll, 466
Sierra, G. Martinez, 190, 466
Silbergroschen, 12
Silent movies, 385
Silent Night, 500
Silver, Frank, 662
Silver Threads Among the Gold, 501
Silvers, Louis, 106
Silvestre, Armand, 143
Simons, Moisés, 422
Simple Aveu, 501
Simrock, N., 13, 71
Sinclair, John Lang, 309
Sing a Song of Sixpence, 502
Sissle, Noble, 297
Size of paper, 9
Skaters, The, 503
Škoda Lásky, 136
Slaughter on Tenth Avenue, 503
Slave Songs of the United States, 391
Slavonic Dances, op. 46—Dvořák, 504
Slavonic Dances, op. 72—Dvořák, 505
Sleeping Beauty Waltz, 505
Smetana, B.
   Bartered Bride, The, 129
   Moldau (Má Vlast), 374
Smile and Show Your Dimple, 210
Smiles: song, 507; musical play, 582
Smith, Harry B., 260
Smith, John Stafford, 529
Smith, Robert B., 546
Smith, Samuel Francis, 251
Smith, Wilmot M., 102
Smoke Gets in Your Eyes, 508
Sobre las Olas, 509
Soirées à St. Petersbourg, 470
Soldiers' Chorus—Faust, 509
Sombrero de Tres Picos, El, 189
Some Ancient Christmas Carols with the Tunes,
   227
Some Enchanted Evening, 510
Some o' Dese Days, 511
Some of These Days, 511
Someday I'll Find You, 512
Someone to Watch over Me, 513
Someone's in the Kitchen with Dinah, 256, 513
Sometimes I Feel Like a Motherless Child, 514
Sometimes I'm Happy, 515
Sommernachtstraum, Ein, 633
Son of a Gambolier, 515
Son of a Gun, 515
Sonata in A Major (K 331)—Mozart, 516
Sonata in C Major (K 545)—Mozart, 517
Sonate, op. 35—Chopin, 238
Sonate Pathétique—Beethoven, 517
Sondheim, Stephen, 584
Song of India, 518
Song of Songs, The, 519
Song of the Vagabonds, 520
Song of the Volga Boatmen, 520
Song Stories for the Kindergarten, 267
Song Without Words—Tchaikovsky, 167

Songs My Mother Taught Me, 521
Songs of New China, 209
Songs of the Soul No. 2, 641
Songs without Words—Mendelssohn, 525
Sophisticated Lady, 522
Sorcerer's Apprentice, The, 522
Sorella, La, 359
Sound of Music, 523
"Sound Off!," 657, 664
Sour, Robert, 148
Sousa, John Philip, 156, 160, 489, 535, 621
South Pacific, 510
Souvenir—Drdla, 523
Souvenir de Hapsal, 167
Soviet Union National Anthem, 524
Speak to Me of Love, 422
Speaks, Oley, 415, 548
Special Message to Music Librarians, 72
Spilman, J. E., 228
Spirit of the Nation, The, 630
Spiritual Songs for Social Worship, 470
Spirituals Triumphant—Old and New, 273, 642
Spottiswoode, Alicia Anne, 101
Spring Is Here, 656
Spring Song—Mendelssohn, 524
St. Anthony Chorale, 525
St. Louis Blues, 527
St. Matthew Passion—Bach, 171
St. Petersburg, 16
Stanton, Frank L., 368
Star Dust, 528
Star Spangled Banner, The, 529
Stars and Stripes Forever!, The, 535
Stationers' Hall, 18
Steamboat Bill, 535
Stein, Leo, 364
Stein Song, A, 346, 536
Stephanie-Gavotte, 536
Sterbini, Cesare, 127
Sterling, Andrew B., 610
Sterneholde, Thomas, 410
Stille Nacht, 500
Stokes, Byron D., 545
Stolz, Robert, 667
Stone, John A., 604
Stormy Weather, 537
Story of the Jubilee Singers, The, 195
Stranger in Paradise, 438
Straus, Oscar, 321, 615
Strauss, Johann
    Artist's Life (Künstler-Leben), 111
    Blue Danube, 147
    Fledermaus, Die, 207
    Kaiser-Walzer, 314
    Roses from the South, 474
    Tales from the Vienna Woods (Geschichten
        aus dem Wienerwald), 568
    Thousand and One Nights, A, 575
    Vienna Life (Wiener Blut), 602
    Voices of Spring (Frühlingsstimmen), 607
    Wine, Woman and Song, 653
Strauss, Josef, 618
Strauss, Richard
    Don Juan, 200
    Rosenkavalier, Der, 617
    Till Eulenspiegel's Merry Pranks, 580

Stravinsky, Igor, The Firebird, 142
Streets of Cairo, The, 276
Strike Up the Band!, 347, 538
Student Prince, The, 194
Studentenlieder, 242
Students' Songs, 381, 435, 572
Stults, R. M., 545
Stunt Songs for Social Sings, 134, 658
Suite Bergamasque, 174
Sullivan, Arthur
    Bibliographic information, 64
    Gondoliers, The, 634
    H.M.S. Pinafore, 296
    Iolanthe, 151
    Lost Chord, The, 339
    Mikado, The, 576
    Onward, Christian Soldiers, 416
    Pirates of Penzance, The, 262
    Trial by Jury, 637
Summertime—Porgy and Bess, 538
Sunny, 649
Suppé, Franz von
    Light Cavalry Overture, 330
    Poet and Peasant Overture, 433
Sur le Pont d'Avignon, 539
Swan, The—Saint-Saëns, 540
Swander, Don, 194
Swanee, 541
Swanee River, 407
Sweet Adeline: song, 541; musical play, 649
Sweet and Low, 542
Sweet Betsey from Pike, 603
Sweet Genevieve, 543
Sweet Rosie O'Grady, 543
Sweet Sue—Just You, 544
Sweetest Story Ever Told, The, 544
Sweetheart—Romberg, 651
Sweetheart of Sigma Chi, The, 545
Sweethearts—Herbert, 546
Swift, James Frederick, 483
Swing Low, Sweet Chariot, 546
'S Wonderful, 547
Sword Dance—Khatchaturian, 482
Sylphs' Ballet—The Damnation of Faust, 541,
    547
Sylva, B. G. de, 106, 144, 146, 157, 293, 318,
    338
Sylvia—Delibes, 430
Sylvia—Speaks, 548
Symphonie Classique—Prokofiev, 549
Symphonie Fantastique—Berlioz, 549
Symphony in D Minor—Franck, 566
Symphony no. 1—Beethoven, 551
Symphony no. 3—Beethoven, 554
Symphony no. 5—Beethoven, 557
Symphony no. 6—Beethoven, 406, 560
Symphony no. 7—Beethoven, 561
Symphony no. 9—Beethoven, 563
Symphony no. 1—Brahms, 551
Symphony no. 2—Brahms, 552
Symphony no. 3—Brahms, 554
Symphony no. 4—Brahms, 555
Symphony no. 7—Bruckner, 562
Symphony no. 5—Dvořák, 558
Symphony no. 94 (Surprise)—Haydn, 564
Symphony no. 101 (Clock)—Haydn, 565

Symphony no. 4—Knipper, 360
Symphony no. 1—Mahler, 552
Symphony no. 4 (Italian)—Mendelssohn, 555
Symphony no. 40 (K 550)—Mozart, 564
Symphony "Jupiter" (K 551)—Mozart, 567
Symphony no. 5—Shostakovitch, 558
Symphony no. 2—Sibelius, 553
Symphony no. 4—Tchaikovsky, 556
Symphony no. 5—Tchaikovsky, 559
Symphony no. 6—Tchaikovsky, 560
Symphony (Unfinished)—Schubert, 567

T

Tableaux d'une Exposition, 427
Take Me Out to the Ball-Game, 568
Tale of Tsar Saltan, The, 227
Tales from the Vienna Woods, 568
Tales of Hoffmann, The, 127
Tambourin Chinois, 162
Tango (dance), 169
Tango, España, 569
Tannhäuser, 428
Tantivy! Tantivy! Tantivy!, 282
Tapfere Soldat, Der, 321
Taps, 570
Ta-Ra-Ra Boom-Der-É, 570
Targioni-Tozzetti, G., 302
Taschen-Liederbuch, Das, 207
Tausend und Eine Nacht, 575
Tavern in the Town, 572
Taylor, Helen, 178
Taylor, Jane, 594
Taylor, Tell, 200
Tchaikovsky, P.
    Bibliographic information, 71
    Chant sans Paroles, 167
    Concerto for Piano no. 1, 182
    1812 Overture, 210
    Eugen Onegin, 220
    Marche Slave, 348
    Nur Wer die Sehnsucht Kennt, 394
    Nutcracker Ballet, 613
    Quartet, op. 11, 451
    Romeo and Juliette, 471
    Sleeping Beauty Ballet, 505
    Symphony no. 4, 556
    Symphony no. 5, 559
    Symphony no. 6, 560
Tea for Two, 572
Tell Me, Do You Love Me, 545
Ten Little Injuns, 205
Tennyson, Alfred, 542
Terriss, Dorothy, 578
Thaïs, 361
Thaler, 12
There Is a Tavern in the Town, 572
There's a Long Long Trail, 573
There's a Monkey in the Grass, 112
There's No Business Like Show Business, 574
Thesaurus Musicus, 250
They Didn't Believe Me, 574
They Don't Wear Pants in the Southern Part of
    France, 276
Third Collection of Strathspey Reels, A, 306
Thomas, Ambroise
    Mignon, 215

Raymond Overture, 456
Thomé, Francis, 501
Thompson, H. S., 102, 174
Thompson, James, 477
Thornton, James, 643
Thousand and One Nights, A, 575
Three Blind Mice, 576
Three-Cornered Hat, The, 189
Three Kings of Orient, 628
Three Little Maids from School, 576
Three More Songs of the Fair, 178
Three O'Clock in the Morning, 578
Threepenny Opera, The, 343
Three's a Crowd, 148
Tiger Rag, 579
Tilken, Félix, 380
Till Eulenspiegel's Merry Pranks, 580
'Till the Boys Come Home, 316
Till We Meet Again, 581
Tilzer, Albert von, 450, 568
Tilzer, Harry von, 290, 610
Timbre Fiscal, 8
Time on My Hands, 582
Tindley, C. Albert, 624
Tiochet, Carlo, 173
'Tis the Last Rose of Summer, 582
To a Wild Rose, 583
Tomlinson, Ralph, 529
Tommy Thumb's Pretty Song Book, 337, 502,
    594
Tommy's Tunes, 201, 412
Tonight—West Side Story, 584
Too-Ra-Loo-Ra-Loo-Ral, That's an Irish Lullaby,
    585
Toplady, Augustus, 469
Toreador Song, 585
Torna a Surriento!, 586
Tosca, 605
Toselli, Enrico, 492
Toyland, 587
Tozzetti, G. Targioni, 302
Tramp! Tramp! Tramp!, 588
Träumerei, 588
Traviata, La, 203
Tre Sonate per il Violino solo senza Basso, 151
Trees, 589
Trial by Jury, 637
Tristan und Isolde, 328
Triumphal March—Aida, 589
Trovatore, Il, 102
Truman, President, 297, 373
Tucker, Henry, 543
Tung Fang Hung, 209
Turco, G., 240
Turkey in the Straw, 591
12th Street Rag, 592
Twice 55 Community Songs, 232
Twinkle, Twinkle, Little Star, 593
Two Guitars, 595
Two Hearts in Three-Quarter Time, 667

U

Un Bel Dì, 596
Ungarische Tänze—Brahms, 281
Union Harp and Revival Chorister, The, 132

Union Musical Española, 71
Universal Magazine, The, 378
University of Texas Community Song Book, The, 309
U.S. Field Artillery March, 156

V

Vagabond King, The, 520
Valentine, 597
Valse Bleue, 597
Valse des Fleurs, 613
Valse des Rayons, 104
Valse Triste, 598
Valurile Dunări, 622
Vaucaire, Maurice, 519
vb. (verso blank), 59
Vejvoda, Jaromír, 136
Verdi, Giuseppe
  Aida, 589
  Rigoletto, 452
  Traviata, La, 204
  Trovatore, Il, 102
Verein Deutscher Musikalienhändler, 21
Vernor, F. Dudleigh, 545
Verso blank, 59
Very Thought of You, The, 599
Very Warm for May, 92
Vesti la Giubba, 599
Vicar of Bray, The, 187
Vicars, Harold, 519
Victory at Sea, 390
Victory Calypsoes, 478
Vie en Rose, La, 600
Vienna Dreams, 601
Vienna Girls, 602
Vienna Life, 602
Viennese Popular Song, 414
Vier Ächte Tyroler-Lieder, 500
Vier Lieder—S. T. Friedland, 375
Vilikens and His Dinah, 603
Villard, 426
Villoldo, A. G., 169
Violetera, La, 604
Vissi d'Arte, 605
Vive la Compagnie, 606
Vltava, 374
Vocal Magazine, The, 529
Vocal Melodies of Scotland, 101
Vocal Music: or the Songster's Companion, 138
Voices of Spring, 607
Vollständiger Jahrgang von Terzett-und Chorgesängen der Synagoge in München, 321
Vollständiges Melodienbuch, 606
Von Fallersleben, Hoffmann, 214
Von Hofmannsthal, Hugo, 617
Von Mosenthal, Hermann Salomon, 366
Von Suppé, F.
  Light Cavalry Overture, 330
  Poet and Peasant Overture, 433
Von Tilzer, Albert, 450, 568
Von Tilzer, Harry, 290, 610
Von Weber, Carl Maria, 236, 304, 395

W

Wacht am Rhein, Die, 608
Wade, John Francis, 86
Wagner, Richard
  Fliegende Holländer, Der, 229
  Götterdämmerung, 463
  Lohengrin, 631
  Meistersinger von Nürnberg, Die, 449
  Parsifal, 445
  Rheingold, Das, 463
  Siegfried (and Siegfried Idyll), 463
  Tannhäuser, 428
  Tristan und Isolde, 328
  Walküre, Die, 463
Wagner y Levien, A., 71
Wait for the Wagon, 609
Wait 'till the Sun Shines, Nellie, 610
Waldteufel, Emile, 217, 218, 503
Walküre, Die, 463
Waller, Thomas, 89
Waltz—Coppélia, 616
Waltz—The Count of Luxemburg, 616
Waltz, op. 39—Brahms, 610
Waltz, op. 34—Chopin, 611
Waltz, op. 64—Chopin, 612
Waltz Dream, A, 615
Waltz of the Flowers, 613
Waltzes—Der Rosenkavalier, 617
Waltzing Matilda, 619
Walzertraum, Ein, 615
Ward, Mrs. Amy, 316
Ward, Charles B., 123
Ward, Samuel A., 96
Warfield, Charles, 284
Warny & Co., 71
Warsaw Concerto, 620
Washington Post March, The, 621
Watch on the Rhine, 608
Water Music, 622
Water Scenes, 386
Watermarks, 14
Watts, Isaac, 314
Waves of the Danube, 622
Way Down upon de Swanee Ribber, 408
'Way Down Yonder in New Orleans, 623
We Gather Together, 442
We Shall Overcome, 623
We Three Kings of Orient, 627
We Won't Go Home till Morning!, 231
Weaner Mad'ln, 602
Wearin' o' the Green, The, 628
Weatherly, Frederick E., 337, 386, 475
Weber, Carl Maria von
  Freischütz, Der, 236
  Invitation to the Dance, 304
  Oberon, 395
Wedding March—A Midsummer Night's Dream, 633
Wedding March—Lohengrin, 631
Weeks, Archibald C., 102
Weill, Kurt, 201, 343, 490
Wein, Weib und Gesang, 653
Weinberger, Jaromír, 434
Weisenbuch zu den Volksliedern für Volkschulen, 356

Well-Known Music by Women Composers, 61
Well-Known Music from Smaller Countries, 61
Well-Tempered Clavier, 118
Wende, E., & Co., 66
Wenrich, Percy, 450, 644
We're Called "Gondolieri," 634
We're in the Army Now, 664
Wesley, Charles, 269
Wesleyan Sacred Harp, The, 279
West Side Story, 495, 584
Westendorf, Thomas P., 296
Westminster Chimes, 634
Wette, Adelheid, 221
What Is This Thing Called Love?, 635
What Shall We Do with a Drunken Sailor?, 206
What's New Pussycat?, 636
When a Merry Maiden Marries, 343
When I, Good Friends, Was Called to the Bar,
    637
When I'm Not Near the Girl I Love, 637
When Irish Eyes Are Smiling, 638
When Johnny Comes Marching Home, 639
When the Saints Go Marching In, 641
When You and I Were Young, Maggie, 643
When You Were Sweet Sixteen, 643
When You Wore a Tulip and I Wore a Big Red
    Rose, 644
When You're Away, 644
Whiffenpoof Song, The, 645
While Strolling Through the Park One Day, 646
Whispering, 647
Whistler and His Dog, The, 647
White Christmas, 648
Whiting, George, 380
Whiting, Richard A., 581
Whitson, Beth Slater, 327
Who?, 649
Whoopee Ti Yi Yo, 244
Why Was I Born?, 649
Wi' a Hundred Pipers, 655
Wide Dispersal of Music Publishing in the United
    States, 62
Wiegenlied, 650
Wien, Du Stadt Meiner Träume, 601
Wiener Blut, 602
Wilhelm, Carl, 608
Wilhelmj, A., 90
Will You Remember, 651
Willemetz, Albert, 376, 597
William Tell—Overture, 652
Williams, Frank, 511
Williams, Harry, 308
Williams, Spencer, 131, 284
Williams, Thomas E., 176
Willis, Richard Storrs, 308
Willner, A. M., 616
Wilmot, D. Eardley, 335
Wind in the Clearing, The, 473
Wine, Woman and Song, 653

Winner, Joseph Eastburn, 335
Winner, Septimus, 333
Wintergreen for President, 654
Wit and Mirth, 411
With a Hundred Pipers, 655
With a Song in My Heart, 656
Without a Song, 259
Wizard of Oz, The, 418
Wohltemperirte Clavier, Das, 117
Wonders in the Sun, 411
Wood, Haydn, 475
Woodforde-Finden, Amy, 316
Woodland Sketches, 583
Woods, Harry, 298
Woodworth, Samuel, 413
Work, Henry Clay, 349
Worms Crawl In, The, 657
Wunderbar, 658
W.W., 13

X

Xerxes, 324

Y

Yale Boola, 150
Yale Songs, 435
Yankee Doodle, 659
Ye A.E.F. Hymnal, 344
Yellen, Jack, 268
Yellow Rose of Texas, The, 661
Yes Sir! That's My Baby, 661
Yes! We Have No Bananas, 662
Yodel Call, 662
You Forgot to Remember, 458
You Made Me Love You, 663
Youmans, Vincent, 163, 258, 264, 515, 572, 582
Young, David, 284
Young, Joe, 196
Young, Rida Johnson, 88, 377, 382, 651
Young, Victor, 110, 544
You're a Grand Old Flag, 663
You're in the Army Now, 664
You're My Baby, 234
Yours Is My Heart Alone, 665
Yradier, Sebastian, 420, 586
Yvain, Maurice, 376

Z

Zampa—Overture, 666
Zeman, Vašek, 136
Zhukovský, W. A., 480
Ziegfeld Follies, 155, 447
Ziehrer, C. M., 602
Zigeunermelodien—Dvořák, 521
Zimmerman, Charles A., 99
Zip Coon, 591
Zu Lauterbach, 406
Zwei Herzen im Dreivierteltakt, 667